Naval Warfare 1919–1945

This is an excellent book, and one that I would recommend to all students of the Inter-War and Second World War era.

Andrew Lambert, *King's College, London*

Naval Warfare 1919–1945 is a comprehensive history of the war at sea from the end of the Great War to the end of World War II. Showing the bewildering nature and complexity of the war facing those charged with fighting it around the world, this book ranges far and wide: sweeping across all naval theatres and those powers performing major, as well as minor, roles within them.

Armed with the latest material from an extensive set of sources, Dr. Murfett has written an absorbing as well as comprehensive reference work that is not afraid to re-examine the naval past in a stimulating way, or to take issue with those aspects of it that deserve closer attention. He demonstrates that superior equipment and the best intelligence, ominous power and systematic planning, vast finance and suitable training are often simply not enough in themselves to guarantee the successful outcome of a particular encounter at sea. Sometimes the narrow difference between victory and defeat hinges on those infinite variables: the individual's performance under acute pressure and sheer luck.

Naval Warfare 1919–1945 is an analytical and interpretive study that examines why things happened when they did. This vividly written volume is an accessible as well as fascinating read both for students and for interested members of the general public.

Malcolm Murfett is a Fellow of the Royal Historical Society and the author of a number of works on naval themes, including *Fool-proof Relations: The Search for Anglo-American Naval Cooperation in the Chamberlain Years, 1937–40* (1985), *Hostage on the Yangtze: Britain, China and the Amethyst Crisis of 1949* (1991) and the co-written *Between Two Oceans: A Military History of Singapore from First Settlement to Final British Withdrawal.* He is also the editor of *The First Sea Lords* (1999).

Naval Warfare 1919–1945

An operational history of the volatile war at sea

Malcolm Murfett

Routledge
Taylor & Francis Group

LONDON AND NEW YORK

First published in paperback 2013
First published 2009
by Routledge
2 Park Square, Milton Park, Abingdon, Oxon OX14 4RN

Simultaneously published in the USA and Canada
by Routledge
711 Third Avenue, New York, NY 10017

Routledge is an imprint of the Taylor & Francis Group, an informa business

© 2009, 2013 Malcolm Murfett

Typeset in Baskerville by Taylor & Francis Books

All rights reserved. No part of this book may be reprinted or reproduced or utilised in any form or by any electronic, mechanical, or other means, now known or hereafter invented, including photocopying and recording, or in any information storage or retrieval system, without permission in writing from the publishers.

British Library Cataloguing in Publication Data
A catalogue record for this book is available from the British Library

Library of Congress Cataloging in Publication Data
Naval warfare 1919–1945 : an operational history of the volatile war at sea / Malcolm H. Murfett.
  p. cm.
 Includes bibliographical references and index.
 1. World War, 1939-1945–Naval operations. 2. Naval art and science–History–20th century. I. Title.
 D770.M87 2008
 359'.0309041–dc22
                                    2008015244

ISBN13: 978-0-415-45804-7 (hbk)
ISBN13: 978-0-415-64008-4 (pbk)
ISBN13: 978-0-203-88998-5 (ebk)

Printed and bound in Great Britain by
TJ International Ltd, Padstow, Cornwall

To the memory of my beloved Dad and Mum who taught me many wonderful things – the most priceless of which was love

Contents

Abbreviations	viii
List of maps	xii
Preface	xiii
Acknowledgements	xvi
1 Neither one thing nor the other (1919–39)	1
2 The opening gambit (1939)	49
3 Much more than a phoney war (1940)	66
4 Uncompromising hostilities (January–November 1941)	100
5 From Pearl Harbor to Madagascar (December 1941–May 1942)	135
6 Stalling the juggernaut in the early summer of 1942	176
7 From defence to attack in the autumn of 1942	223
8 A change in momentum (January–August 1943)	257
9 Striking back (September–December 1943)	291
10 Seizing the initiative (January–August 1944)	324
11 Tightening the grip (September–December 1944)	369
12 Stranglehold (1945)	418
Conclusion: Rising to the challenge of fighting the war at sea	461
Maps	511
Appendix I: Allied convoy statistics (1939–45)	530
Appendix II: Units of measurement – Conversion equivalents	534
Glossary	535
Select bibliography	548
Index	590

Abbreviations

A.A.	Anti-Aircraft
ABC-1	American, British and Canadian Staff Talks (March 1941)
ABDACOM	American, British, Dutch, and Australian Command
ABDAFLOAT	Naval C-in-C of ABDACOM
ANCXF	Allied Naval Commander Expeditionary Force
ASDIC	Acronym for Allied Submarine Detection Investigation Committee
ASV	Air to Surface Vessel Radar
ASW	Anti-Submarine Warfare
BAD	British Admiralty Delegation (Washington, DC)
BdU	Befehlshaber der Unterseeboote – Commander-in-Chief of U-boats
BEF	British Expeditionary Force
BEIF	British East Indies Fleet
BLT	Battalion Landing Team
BPF	British Pacific Fleet
CAGS	Chief of the Army General Staff (Japan)
CCS	Combined Chiefs of Staff (Anglo-American)
CCOS	Abbreviation sometimes used for CCS
C-in-C	Commander-in-Chief
CINCPAC	Commander-in-Chief Pacific
CNGS	Chief of the Navy General Staff (Japan)
CNO	Chief of Naval Operations (US)
COMINCH	Commander-in-Chief (USN)
COMINT	Communications Intelligence
COMSOWESPAC	Commander, South West Pacific Area
COS	Chiefs of Staff
CU	Curacao–UK and after CU9 New York–UK convoy tanker series
DCNS	Deputy Chief of Naval Staff
DF	Direction Finding
DNI	Director, Office of Naval Intelligence
DO	Dornier

DRC	Defence Requirements Sub-Committee
DSO	Distinguished Service Order
DUKW	1942 designed utility, all wheel drive, vehicle with two rear driving axles used for amphibious operations
EASTOMP	Eastern Ocean Meeting Point (off the coast of Ireland)
EIF	East Indies Fleet
ENIGMA	German cipher machine used for the encrypting of secret messages
FAA	Fleet Air Arm
FAT	Federapparat–German search pattern running torpedo
FDO	Fighter Direction Officer
FDR	Franklin Delano Roosevelt
F.d.U.	Führer der Unterseeboote (Flag Officer/Commander of U-boats)
Fl K	Fliegerkorps–German Air Corps
FRUPac	Fleet Radio Unit, Pacific (also known as Station HYPO)
FuMO	Funkmessortungsgerät (radar detection equipment)
FW	Focke-Wulf
GC&CS	Government Code and Cypher School
GNAT	German Naval Acoustic Torpedo–also known as a T5
GUF	Oran or Naples–USA (fast) convoy series
HF/DF	High Frequency Direction Finding (also known colloquially as Huff-Duff)
HG	Homeward bound from Gibraltar (1939–42) convoy series
HMS	His Majesty's Ship
HX	Halifax–UK (later New York–UK) convoy series
IGHQ	Imperial General Headquarters (Daihon'ei)
IJA	Imperial Japanese Army
IJN	Imperial Japanese Navy (**Nihon** Nippon Tei Koku Kaigun)
JCS	Joint Chiefs of Staff (US)
JICPOA	Joint Intelligence Center Pacific Ocean Area
JPS	Joint Planning Staff (UK)
KG	Kampfgeschwader or bombing group
KMF	UK–Mediterranean (fast) convoy series from November 1942
KMS	UK–Mediterranean (slow) convoy series from November 1942
KMT	Kuomintang–Chinese Nationalist government led by Marshal Chiang Kai-shek
K-Verband	Kleinkampfverband or small battle unit
KX	UK–Gibraltar convoy series from October 1942
LCI	Landing Craft Infantry
LCT	Landing Craft Tank
LSD	Landing Ship Dock
LSI	Landing Ship Infantry

LST	Landing Ship Tank
MAD	Magnetic Anomaly Detector
MAS	Motoscafo Anti Sommergibile–fast Italian MTBs which had originally been designed as submarine-chasers
Me	Messerschmitt
MGB	Motor Gun Boat
MKF	Mediterranean–UK (fast) from November 1942
MKS	Mediterranean–UK (slow) from November 1942
MMS	Motorized Minesweeper
MTB	Motor Torpedo Boat
MOMP	Mid-Ocean Meeting Point
NID	Naval Intelligence Division (Admiralty)
nm	Nautical Mile
OA	Thames/Methil to Liverpool and onward into Atlantic convoy series
OB	Liverpool outward into Atlantic convoy series
ObdM	Oberbefehlshaber der Marine (Supreme C-in-C of the Navy)
OG	Outward from UK to Gibraltar
OIC	Operational Intelligence Centre (Admiralty)
OKM	Oberkommando der Marine (Supreme Naval Command)
OKW	Oberkommando der Wehrmacht (Supreme Armed Forces Command)
ON	Northward bound convoy series from the UK–Norway (1939–40) and USA/Canada from 1941
ONS	Slow northward bound convoy series
OPINTEL	Operational Intelligence
OS	Southward convoy series from the UK to Freetown, Sierra Leone from 1941
PLA	People's Liberation Army – the military arm of the Chinese Communists led by Mao Tse-tung
POW	Prisoner-of-War
RAF	Royal Air Force
RAI	Regia Aeronautica Italiana (Royal Italian Airforce)
RAN	Royal Australian Navy
RCN	Royal Canadian Navy
RCT	Regimental Combat Team
RDF	Radio Direction Finding (original British term for radar)
RE	Range Estimation
RFP	Radio Finger Printing
RMI	Regia Marina Italiana – Royal Italian Navy
RN	Royal Navy
RNZN	Royal New Zealand Navy
RU	Convoy series from Reykjavik to Loch Ewe and later Belfast
SAC	Supreme Allied Commander

SC	Sydney, Cape Breton (later Halifax or New York)–UK convoy series
SCAEF	Supreme Commander Allied Expeditionary Force
SHAEF	Supreme Headquarters Allied Expeditionary Force
SIGINT	Signals Intelligence
SL	Freetown, Sierra Leone to UK convoy series
SLC	Siluro Lento Corso (also known as Maiali – slow human submersible chariots)
SONAR	SOund Navigation And Ranging – the detection of underwater objects by sound waves (an American version of ASDIC).
TBS	Talk Between Ships
TF	Task Force
TG	Task Group
TINA	Means of identifying an individual radio code operator
UC	UK–New York convoy tanker series
UDT	Underwater Demolition Team
UGF	USA–Gibraltar (later Naples) convoy series from November 1942
UGS	USA–Gibraltar, later Port Said convoy series from November 1942–May 1945
UR	Loch Ewe (later Belfast) – Reykjavik convoy series
USAAF	United States Army Air Force
USN	United States Navy
USSR	Union of Soviet Socialist Republics (Soviet Union)
VCNS	Vice Chief of Naval Staff
VHF	Very High Frequency
VLR	Very Long Range
WESTOMP	Western Ocean Meeting Point (off the Atlantic coast of Canada)
W/T	Wireless Telegraphy
WWII	World War Two
XK	Gibraltar–UK convoy series
Y	Radio Intelligence

List of maps

1.	Adriatic Sea	511
2.	Aegean Sea	512
3.	Barents Sea	513
4.	Black Sea	514
5.	Central and South America	515
6.	Central and South Pacific	516
7.	Japan and the Ryukyu Islands	517
8.	Mediterranean	518
9.	Midway Island	519
10.	New Guinea	520
11.	Normandy and the French Channel coast to the Belgian border	521
12.	North Atlantic	522
13.	North Pacific	523
14.	North Sea	524
15.	Norway	525
16.	Philippines	526
17.	Solomon Islands	527
18.	South Pacific	528
19.	West Atlantic	529

Preface

Beginning in what was supposedly a time of peace, *Naval Warfare 1919–1945* demonstrates that the 1920s and 1930s were rarely that quiescent or immune from naval issues and conflict before the war at sea was officially resumed in September 1939. In those twenty years, each of the naval powers conducted a searching examination of their record from the last war and set about applying some of those hard-learnt lessons in their future planning and development for the next one. While implementing some of these reforms undoubtedly served them well when they were obliged to fight once again, it didn't mean that their preparations were foolproof or that they were protected from the imponderability of warfare, as would be shown time and again in World War II. Dynamic, unpredictable and multifaceted, the war at sea continued to pose innumerable challenges to all those engaged in it.

It also poses all kinds of challenges to those who seek to write about it. Naval history is both vivid and compelling and deserves to be written in a lively, lucid and informative way based on the latest and most up-to-date research. My aim was to write a single-volume operational history of naval warfare from 1919 to 1945 in this manner and make it accessible to a wide audience. I hope I have achieved that aim and that those who consult this book will agree that it is a valuable addition to the existing literature on the war at sea.

There are, of course, some caveats. While I admire the painstaking skill and the unbridled enthusiasm of military historians and accomplished naval experts, I cannot expect them to be content with an abbreviated account of whatever it is that they know intimately well and in the finest detail. Clearly, this book was neither written for them nor those revisionist scholars who often view any kind of narrative history with the deepest suspicion if not active disdain. Needless to say, it won't stop these individuals from complaining about my views or approach, but as a very wise Australian professor once told me if one goes into print one must be prepared for anything!

Having spent much of my early to mid-career encamped in archival depositories around the world, I won't quarrel with the thesis that primary-source-based research is of crucial importance. Moreover, I freely concede that scholarly contributions to our understanding of the past can be based upon a substantial paper trail that has been left by individuals previously employed within the various departments of state and/or service and defence ministries. Even so, I do not delude myself that on all occasions the unvarnished truth will only finally emerge through exclusive use of primary documentation. Life isn't quite that beguilingly simple.

So if *Naval Warfare 1919–1945* wasn't intended for either the anti-Marder clique of naval historians or the ranks of the hard-bitten naval professionals, who was it written for? It's quite simple; from the very outset I had the general reader in mind. I saw my main task as assisting those uninitiated, but discerning, individuals who were both curious and anxious to learn about what happened at sea during these harrowing years of conflict. As a starting point, therefore, this book doesn't presume much, if any, pre-existing knowledge of the subject material and seeks instead to explain the pitfalls and successes of fighting the naval war in what I trust is an accessible way and one not driven by dogma and polemical discourse, or littered by too many mysterious acronyms and expert catchphrases. As a result, I believe this volume may be dipped into for a host of factual information on who did what to whom and when; explored profitably as a guide to all kinds of naval campaigns that were conducted in these years; or read simply as a chronicle of an often imponderable war fought out on the oceans, seas, and rivers of the world between 1919 and 1945.

Although works of synthesis are usually frowned upon in some circles, I thought it the only logical approach to take given the wide canvas on which I aimed to draw in depicting these events. My approach, therefore, was to opt for a modern, secondary-source-based narrative that would tap the research findings published in a host of scholarly books and articles over the past fifteen years. In analysing the vicissitudes of the naval war, I have attempted to mould the latest scholarship and my own views together in a balanced manner so as to present an intriguing and fascinating story in what I hope is an engaging and credible way. While no book can claim to be the definitive work on the naval war, I have taken great pains to try and present an authentic picture of the war as it unfolded around the world. Even so, the discordant statistical and factual evidence that exists on so many subjects ensures that the conclusions I have reached and the figures I have quoted in the text will differ on occasion (sometimes radically) from already published works in the field. Where major disagreements do occur on the issues touched upon in this text, however, I have recommended a list of alternative sources in the endnotes for readers to consult if they so desire.

Anthony Eden once remarked that there are no chapters in foreign policy but only chapters in books written about foreign policy issues. He may not have got many things right at the end of his career, but he was on the ball as far as this assertion was concerned. His observation is as applicable to war as it is to foreign policy. War is a very complex undertaking at the best of times and it is complicated still further by action taking place in several different theatres hundreds or, in some cases, thousands of miles apart at precisely the same time. A sense of ordered, discreet sequence is often missing as crises arise and develop simultaneously across the world testing the patience of even the most stoical of naval and military commanders as they do so. I wanted this study to illustrate this dramatic situation and the kind of strategic, tactical and logistic problems confronting the leaders – both military and political – as the war they waged ebbed and flowed over the years but rarely in a routine way. Chronological, as distinct from being thematic or theatre-driven, this study of naval warfare is not seen from the perspective of a single combatant or a group of powers – instead it tries to adopt a non-partisan approach in which naval performance is judged purely on its own merits and is not influenced by other external political factors or ideals.

Naval Warfare 1919–1945 is certainly not a hagiographical account of naval warfare or those engaged in it. I am not in thrall to the world of the services. Indeed many servicemen may feel I have been unduly harsh about military command and the business of warfare. Nonetheless, I hope a sense of balance has been struck between the genuine admiration I have for the skill and heroism exhibited by those caught up in the war at sea and the sheer horror and sadness I feel about the descent into war and the emotional, mental and physical cost that warfare invariably brings to those engaged in it or to their loved ones back home.

In conclusion, I should like to express my grateful thanks to my book reviewers who have urged my publisher to put this volume into paperback and at a price the general reader can afford and am delighted that my editors at Routledge have seen fit to take their advice. I'm also greatly encouraged by the enthusiastic response of those readers who have read the manuscript and enjoyed it and can only hope that many more will do so in future.

Acknowledgements

When it comes to research, my debt to Professor Jürgen Rohwer is immense. His *Chronology of the War at Sea 1939–1945: The Naval History of World War Two* (London: Chatham Publishing, 2005) is a meticulous work of scholarship distilled from more than half a century of research enterprise. It was Professor Rohwer's work that provided me with a bedrock of data on the war and inspired me to adopt the methodology I did for my own operational history.

I also owe debts to all those whose work I have read in conventional published form or in bytes downloaded from the Internet: even though I may not agree with their interpretation of an incident, battle or campaign, their work has helped to make me far better informed on many subjects than had been the case previously.

I am also immensely grateful to Professor Jeremy Black for encouraging me to write a history of twentieth-century naval warfare for his Warfare and History series. Although it took a decade to come to fruition and morphed into a much longer and more concentrated study of what happened at sea during the Second World War, my gratitude to Jeremy for issuing the initial challenge to me remains genuine. As a result of accepting his invitation to write this book, I have found myself working closely with a number of superb editors at Routledge. Some have come and gone over the years but Vicky Peters, Eve Setch and latterly Michael Strang have all proved to be professionals of the highest class. It has been a privilege to work closely with them and their production team.

As I have been researching and writing this book, my family and friends have also stepped in repeatedly to offer me massive amounts of assistance in myriad ways. I have benefited from their critical input as well as their incredible generosity. Parts of this book have been formed and revised in various locations around the world. My gratitude extends to Charlie and Liz Barker at Radley College; Grant Baird off the beaten track in California; David and Awen Campbell in Langley; Professor Bill and Dr. Jane Chia in Greenwich; Janet Chisholm in London; Janey and Jeremy Cook in Hampton; Professor Peter and Iréna Dennis in Canberra; Gill Doherty in Newbury; Mike and Jo Emery in Wrea; Professor Grant Goodman in Lawrence, Kansas; Professor John and Berit Hattendorf in Newport, RI; Drs Caroline and Ben Henry in Long Eaton; Dr. Jack and Vivian Humphrey in Long Beach, California; Ernst Kaltner in Abtenau;

Helga, Helmut and Monika Kaltner in Salzburg; Drs. Terry and Cath O'Sullivan and Professor Michael Toolan and Julianne Statham in Birmingham; Eddy and Janet Phipps in Cheltenham; Professor David Ralston and Catherine Hunt in Sarasota, Florida; Dr. Srilata Ravi in Perth; Dr. Nicholas Rodger in Acton; Rick and Paula Silverman in Steamboat Springs, Colorado; Professor Geoffrey Till in Watchfield; Stephanie and Ian Williams in Balham; Frank and Catherine Willsdon in Sydney; Mike and Abby Wilson in the Weald of Kent; Stephanie and Howard Witt on the Wiltshire Downs; Michael and Stephanie Woodward in Abingdon; Allen and Cherry Yhearm in Mells; and Dr Hubert and Francesca Zawadzki in Abingdon. Professor John Young and Haniel Riviere-Allen from the Department of History, University of Nottingham, also got into the act by arranging for me to spend my sabbatical year 2004–05 attached to that fine institution. I appreciated their support in what was a truly splendid year spent in the East Midlands.

In addition, Dr. Dan Crosswell and Professor Brian Farrell, my departmental colleagues at the National University of Singapore (NUS), could always be relied upon as founts of knowledge on military-related matters. I didn't always agree with their trenchant views on military affairs, but their advice was always worth listening to and often deserved to be acted upon. I have also benefited from my close friendship with Professor Peter Dennis who has become a kind of scholarly mentor to me. I have known and worked under Peter's leadership at the Australian Defence Force Academy (ADFA) in Canberra and have no hesitation in saying that he led by example and it's an example worth following. Peter offered to help read the proofs of this book for me. What more need be said about his generosity?

NUS is also extremely fortunate to have Tim Yap at the head of the Information section of its Central Library. He is a superb librarian with a deep and abiding fascination for all things historical, especially military affairs. Nothing is too much trouble for Tim. He goes to great lengths to track down obscure sources and discovered various gems while doing so that I have used profitably subsequently. Tim is the Singaporean equivalent of Christopher Dawkins, the military specialist librarian at ADFA and a librarian of great talent and resourcefulness. I'm also immensely grateful to Alison Pratt, Olga Wronecki and Imelda Winn for the help they gave me while I was revising my manuscript at the Joint Services Command and Staff College Library in the Defence Academy at Watchfield, Oxfordshire. I have also been extremely fortunate to have a resource-rich research base in Singapore. Led initially by Barbara Quek, the chief librarian of the Singapore Armed Forces Training Institute's Military Institute Library in Upper Jurong, and her successors Mary Ho and Kym Loo, most ably supported by the indomitable pair of Julaiha and Ratha, SAFTI MI has been an excellent and congenial place in which to do my work. Apart from being consistently helpful and considerate to me, all of the staff have gone out of their way to make me welcome in a library which is one of the best kept secrets in Singapore. Nothing seemingly is too much trouble for them. They really are an admirable team.

In London my research attachment at LSE IDEAS has provided me with an excellent academic base and the unstinting support of Professor Odd Arne Westad and Tiha Franulovic, as well as that of Professor Michael Rainesborough at KCL and Roderick Suddaby at the Imperial War Museum, has been much appreciated.

I am also deeply indebted to my old friend and former colleague, Dr. John W. (Jack) Humphrey, a wonderful cartographer from Diversa Consulting in Long Beach, California, for the superb quality of the maps he has drawn for each of the maritime regions of the world mentioned in the text. In eschewing the complex tracking charts of individual ships or battlefleets that adorn many of the naval histories of the past, Jack's maps are intended as spatial guides that will help orientate the reader to the action being described in the book. I think they do this task wonderfully.

My thanks must also be extended to Professor Albert Lau, the head of my department, who encouraged me to run a public outreach programme in 2006–07 in which I was able to try out some of my ideas about naval warfare on a fascinating cross section of people drawn from all walks of life in Singapore. In other words, it was just the type of audience that *Naval Warfare 1919–1945* has been geared to. I was delighted with the reception my work received at the hands of these very talented people. Ever supportive from the time he joined the Department of History and a constant feature throughout the lecture series, Professor Merle Ricklefs continues to inspire me both as a scholar and a shrewd observer of the academic scene. I really appreciate his judicious counsel on a wide range of matters.

Once again, the Lee Foundation came to my aid as it has done consistently over the past dozen years and funded a substantial amount of my research. I can't thank Mr. Lee Seng Gee enough for his generosity to me. I hope he will feel that *Naval Warfare 1919–1945* has been worth the investment his Foundation has made in it.

My greatest debt of gratitude, however, is justifiably reserved for my wife Ulrike and our four wonderful children: Marianne, Caroline, Nicolas and Stephanie, none of whom can remember a time when I wasn't working on this volume in some capacity or another. They are the rarest of all joyous gifts and they continue to light up my life on a daily basis. Words simply cannot express my love for every one of them.

Despite all the help I have received from so many quarters in completing this study, however, I willingly acknowledge that I am solely responsible for any mistakes of omission or commission that may be found in this piece of work.

Oberalm, Salzburgland,
12 July 2012

1 Neither one thing nor the other (1919–39)

Such was the grotesque nature and cost of the Great War in both human and economic terms that it soon became referred to as 'the war to end all wars'.[1] Alas, it didn't prove to be so. Whatever pious hopes may have been expressed for peace in the months after the armistice had been arranged in November 1918 they amounted to little more than well intentioned wishful thinking. As a utopian concept, the renunciation of war was to have a brief renaissance in Europe before faltering and being abandoned in the years of acute economic, political and social upheaval that followed the Wall Street Crash in 1929 and the onset of the Great Depression at the outset of the 1930s.[2] Thereafter the world began lurching from one international crisis to the next with alarming frequency. Before the end of the decade the 'lamps' of peace that had gone out once before in July 1914 were extinguished yet again in Europe as the continent was dragged into another tumultuous war by the forces of craven personal ambition and belligerent national expansionism.[3]

A little over twenty years before Hitler was to open his blitzkrieg (lightning war) offensive against Poland and usher in the Second World War on 1 September 1939, the major naval powers had emerged from the 1914–18 conflict in some disarray. So much had not gone according to plan. Some cherished notions had fallen well short of expectations.[4] Instead of being the final arbiter of the war at sea, the capital ship had not exercised the decisive influence on these encounters that so many naval experts had confidently predicted beforehand it would have done.[5] Controversy has stalked the issue ever since. Were the British capital ships let down by poor equipment or inferior tactics or by inadequate training and dangerous practices? While it is customary to blame problems in range-finding, gun-laying and fire control for undermining their gunnery potential especially over long distances, the jury remains defiantly out on whether the usual suspects – the Admiralty and its use of the Dreyer Tables in preference to Pollen's Argo system – were really so inept.[6] To add to the general frustration of those on board the capital ship, even when its gunnery problems were corrected and hits were made on enemy vessels, their shells would often malfunction and fail to explode on impact. Again, in defiance of confident predictions to the contrary, a final definitive set piece battle between the capital ship fleets of the various adversaries had not been waged amidst the dying embers of the war.

Instead, contradictorily, the numerically weaker enemy combatants had preferred to retain their principal naval assets as a 'fleet-in-being' by keeping them in their bases as a latent threat rather than risking them in some final epic *Götterdämmerung* on the high seas that could well have totally eliminated them.[7]

While the battleship and battlecruiser had clearly failed to live up to their pre-war hype, the submarine, on the other hand, had comfortably exceeded expectations. Coping with the menace of the U-boat and its withering attack on mercantile trade was to tax the British Admiralty to the hilt. What made its leaders so culpable was that they possessed the means of effectively tackling or neutralising the threat posed by the submersible if only they had adopted it sooner than they did. Convoy had a long history of success when operating under hostile conditions. It was designed for the practice of defending mercantile supplies and war matériel, but it was blatantly ignored by the Admiralty for specious reasons for far too long and at great cost to the Allied war effort. Instead of merely being a defensive tool, the convoy was far more proactive than it was given credit for. As destroyer escorts improved their anti-submarine warfare (ASW) methods so convoy losses fell to below 1% in 1918 while the toll on their would-be U-boat predators increased to over 7%.[8]

It was precisely this 'blind spot' mentality amongst a number of senior naval officers in the Admiralty that ensured that non-optimal use was made of the priceless signals intelligence that flooded into Room 40 during the war.[9] It was also present in the attitude of those within the Senior Service who tended to denigrate the importance and potential of the submarine in the immediate post-war world. Despite its performance in the Great War, or perhaps because of it, the submarine had acquired a reputation for such unscrupulous and devious conduct that a school of opinion developed within Royal Navy circles that looked to ban these vessels in future. Other powers, most notably the French, found this curious British reluctance to embrace the submarine as a key vessel in any future naval struggle as being thoroughly unworldly and peculiarly short-sighted given the problems caused by the U-boats in the recent war.[10]

There was much, therefore, for the leading naval powers to absorb and reflect upon in the early days of peace. Would they heed the lessons of the First World War and be better prepared in future if the collective yearning for peace was once again replaced by a nation striving for war? What changes would be made to both strategic and tactical doctrine so as to position naval powers to their best advantage for future operations at sea? Would there be sufficient time to critically test these ideas and theories through rigorous war gaming and naval manoeuvres so as to ensure their viability in time of war?[11] What role, for instance, might be played by the aeroplane in any future conflict conducted at sea?[12] To what purposes might radio and radar be used on board ship?[13] Would sufficient finance, research and training be devoted to improving a ship's capacity to strike an enemy more often than not, regardless of weather, sea, and rapidly changing battle conditions? What of weapons technology and improvements in warship design and construction? Would sufficient investment be made in the field of cryptology to improve cipher security and, if so, would sufficient attention be also paid to cryptanalysis in a bid to penetrate the communication systems of foreign powers?[14] While any naval staff worth its salt would be forced to consider these questions to improve their combat readiness, solving them would take an immense amount of money. Would governments be prepared to devote the sums necessary to improve their navies when there would be other military claimants seeking a larger share of the service estimates? Could the services expect to receive vast subventions when across Europe most of the continental powers desperately needed time for reconstruction and redevelopment work and required the financial resources to pay for them?[15]

Unfortunately, just when a period of calm retrospection and sober accountancy was urgently needed to tackle these momentous tasks, the world braced itself once more for the prospect of yet another naval race. Both the United States Navy (USN) and the Imperial Japanese Navy (IJN) seemed poised to embark on new warship construction programmes in the months after the armistice.[16] They could both see a number of strategic and commercial advantages accruing to those who possessed substantial fleets and felt, not unreasonably, that they had the economic clout to afford them. Despite not being able to afford the necessary expenditure to match this construction effort, the leading European powers with naval positions to protect nonetheless felt this twin riposte could not go unanswered and they also began to plan ambitious programmes of their own. Fortunately the world was saved from this collective madness by the American decision to take the lead in active disarmament at the time of the Washington Conference in November 1921.[17] Secretary of State Charles Evans Hughes' decision to take the initiative and lay down an audaciously comprehensive schedule of scrapping took all the naval powers by surprise. Not for the first time an enlightened decision was greeted with angst and much soul searching from those who felt that some nefarious design or sinister purpose lay behind this desire to cut the fleets of the various leading naval powers so appreciably. Weathering the predictable storm of protest, the Americans – who wished to remove possible sources of friction between the victorious Allied and Associated Powers – calmly and firmly insisted upon their plan of naval limitation and the rest of the invited delegates were left to ponder on what this unprecedented scale of disarmament meant for each of them.[18]

Of the three treaties to emerge from the Washington Conference, the Five Power Naval Limitation Agreement enshrined the principle of parity between the capital ship force levels of the Americans and the British and established a fixed ratio between their fleets and those of the Japanese, French and Italians on the basis of a 5:5:3:1.75:1.75 proportion. In other words, as the Americans and the British were to be awarded fifteen capital ships each, the IJN would be allowed to build up to nine and the French and Italians five each. Although the non-American delegates expressed harsh words over the final allocation, the principle of disarmament was grudgingly accepted by all concerned.[19] While dealing an unprecedented quantitative blow to the Royal Navy, in particular – by surgically removing a vast amount of old naval clutter that had been accumulated by the Admiralty over the course of time – it proved to be a real qualitative stimulus for those signatory powers that now sought to build a set of modern and powerful capital ship units to replace those that were technically inferior to the new behemoths.[20] Complaints about the details of this agreement persisted, however, not least from leading figures in the USN who felt that the parity they had desired and regarded as their due for some time past was still compromised for years to come by the fact that the British had been allowed to retain a higher total tonnage figure for their capital ships than the Americans had been given. Anglophobia was never far from the surface of many of the leading USN personnel at this time and the suspicion that the British had used their wiles to get away with something at the expense of the USN rankled with many American naval officers.[21]

Over the course of the next few years there would be many more sources of disagreement that would conspire to bedevil Anglo-American relations. Almost all would stem from the reluctance of the British Admiralty to embrace anything that was seen as undermining the Royal Navy's once privileged position on the high seas. In British eyes, Hughes' startling coup at Washington over the numbers and ratio of capital ships and aircraft carriers must not be repeated in future by accepting similarly punitive agreements over the future of their fleet of cruisers. Setting their faces against such an eventuality on the basis that the United Kingdom was the only island nation to have a worldwide empire and that cruisers were the most appropriate vessels to defend the maritime trade routes between the colonies and the mother country, the British resolutely defended their position in various international forums for the rest of the decade and frustrated those who saw no validity in their special pleading.[22]

Notwithstanding what was offered to the British at Washington to win their approval for this agreement, the Japanese gained by far the most important concession. As part of a package deal that would not only place a cap on future Japanese building programmes but also see the forced abrogation of the Anglo-Japanese Alliance, the Americans were prepared to provide a level of security for the Japanese in the Western Pacific that was as dramatic as it was ill-conceived. In essence, the Japanese were to be given a decisive measure of monopoly control in the waters of the region by an agreement to prohibit the construction and/or maintenance of any first class naval base closer to Japanese shores than Singapore for the British and Pearl Harbor for the Americans.[23] By offering such an undertaking, the Americans revealed the intensity of their dislike for the Anglo-Japanese Alliance and their intention to scrap this nineteen-year-old diplomatic arrangement by any means at their disposal. Whatever the Americans thought about the alliance, cancelling it was a bitter pill for both the British and the Japanese governments to swallow and the more so because it had been administered by the Americans on grounds that were far from convincing. If the US authorities could be believed, the existence of the alliance was deemed to be fundamentally against the Harding administration's trading interests in the Far East and particularly in China. Since the US saw the entire Pacific as lying within its own sphere of influence, the prospect of an Anglo-Japanese axis contending for power and penetration in the region was unwelcome. Whereas US officials felt thoroughly justified in being cautious and were wont to cite the alliance as a potential threat to peace, neither the British nor the Japanese thought this reason was anything more than a spurious attempt by the Americans to kill a diplomatic accord that didn't include them.[24] Even so the fact that the British succumbed to American pressure and forced the unwilling Japanese to abrogate their strategic alliance was not taken kindly in Tokyo and the reverberations of this momentous decision were to be felt for many years to come both at home and abroad. Apart from anything else, it certainly did nothing to strengthen the hands of the Japanese government or assist those seeking a democratic future in the country. Moreover, it may also be seen as one of those major turning points in the United Kingdom's fortunes after the war, not least because it managed to convert an admittedly difficult ally into a potential enemy with a disturbing agenda that it would reveal incrementally and ominously to the non-Japanese world over the course of the following two decades.[25] That neither the Four Power nor Nine Power Treaties, which rounded out the Washington system, proved to be anything other than calamitous for those of the signatory powers with interests in the Pacific Ocean should surprise few people. Both diplomatic arrangements had been devised with one thing in mind – the elimination of the Anglo-Japanese Alliance. That they replaced it with a much less effective system of supposedly interlocking relationships was one of the least satisfactory aspects of American diplomacy in the inter-war period, if not the century as a whole.[26]

In the aftermath of the Washington Conference as the signatory powers learnt to cope with the various aspects of the new system bequeathed to them, the post-war European world entered an ugly phase in which anger and suspicion were never very far from the surface. Those nations defeated in the Great War, Germany, Austria-Hungary, Bulgaria and Turkey, had been left in no doubt as to where they stood in the new continental power structure and what their former enemies thought of them. As usual, the victors had turned on the vanquished. Harsh and even punitive terms had been levied against them in the peace treaties that had been drawn up by the victors at Versailles, St. Germain, Trianon and at Sèvres during the course of 1919–20. From the outset the Allied and Associated Powers were absolutely determined to exact the maximum reparations from the Central Powers for starting the war in the first place. Subjectivity reigned and emotion, alas, was given its due reward at the expense of seeking a just settlement.[27] Inevitably, therefore, no sense of shared responsibility for the outbreak of that war was forthcoming. Instead the victors applied the old principle that winning was all that mattered. Apart from the financial obligations that were applied to the defeated nations, the severe restrictions that were placed on their military force structures meant that erstwhile global or regional naval powers were deliberately reduced in status to little more than localised self-defence forces. Refusing to contemplate such a fate, the Reichsmarine pre-empted the Versailles settlement by ordering its officers to take decisive action and scuttle the German High Seas Fleet in the Orkney base of Scapa Flow. With this single act of defiance, the problem of what to do about the bulk of this major international naval force had been effectively resolved. Even so, the orchestrated German resistance left a simmering sense of resentment among those who had hoped to benefit from the post-war redistribution of the former Imperial German Navy.[28]

In the case of Russia, however, the extraordinary events of 1917–20 had left it an international and ideological outcast detested by all those powers that now felt threatened by its very existence. After surviving two revolutions – one to eliminate its Tsarist past and the other to establish a communist dictatorship – a civil war (in which its counter-revolutionary enemies had been aided fitfully and unconvincingly by some of its former wartime allies) and a territorial dispute against its old adversary Poland that had degenerated into an impassioned war of fluctuating fortunes, Russia's Marxist-Leninist leaders could not be easily written off by their detractors.[29] What they might do in the future with the military power at their disposal was, of course, a vital consideration for all non-communist states. There was no easy or definitive answer to this seminal question. While the Red Army had proved itself surprisingly durable in the wake of the Bolshevik revolution, the resurrection of Russian naval power in the future could neither be guaranteed nor dismissed out of hand by Western governments. Unlike the Central Powers, the Russians were not arraigned before the victorious powers and as such, the latter found themselves unable to impose any quantitative or qualitative restrictions on either arm of the Russian military services. Apart from preventing Russia from joining the League of Nations and refusing to establish diplomatic relations with this new pariah state, the British and the French, in particular, were left fervently hoping that the Soviet economy was in such poor shape that it could not immediately sustain a major naval rebuilding programme and therefore would be unable to pose a significant threat to their own fleets for years to come. Their wish was to be granted.[30]

As the Americans withdrew self-consciously from the affairs of Europe into a form of isolationism – refusing to ratify the Versailles Treaty and rejecting membership of the League of Nations, the brainchild of their president Woodrow Wilson – the other members of the victorious alliance were left to get on with things as best they could. That they did not demonstrate an unerring touch in dealing with the outstanding issues of the day – albeit diplomatic, defence, economic or foreign policy issues – is hardly surprising. United on very little, driven by individual national agendas that left a reservoir of mutual suspicion and forced by a Republican-led Congress to assume leadership of the League in the absence of the world's strongest power, the governments in London and Paris found themselves very exposed on a range of issues, not least in dealing with the question of what to do about two of their old foes: Turkey and Germany. Both were to pose considerable problems for the governments in London and Paris where neither issue was handled with assurance or diplomatic skill by the leading politicians who all too frequently tended to behave with bellicosity and aggressive intent. David Lloyd George may have been a fine war leader, but his handling of the Greek–Turkish imbroglio in 1919–22 was hopelessly biased in favour of the former and callowly unrealistic in respect of the latter, especially once Mustapha Kemal emerged on the scene to lead the Turkish nationalist forces. Lloyd George and his coalition government continued to play with fire until the Chanak crisis led to his ousting from power in October 1922.[31] War between Britain and Turkey had come close on several occasions and the Mediterranean Fleet had played a prominent role throughout, often exercising restraint on the belligerent forces or tackling the consequences when indiscretions from either side arose to complicate matters or create the circumstances that bred humanitarian tragedies, such as the Smyrna fire of September 1922.[32]

When it came to dealing with Germany, the French invariably led the way. Uncomfortable with what they saw as the practical shortcomings of collective security, the French continued to seek more effective safeguards against a German renaissance in the future. For this reason, if for no other, they were loath to accommodate any perceived German wavering on their financial obligations to the international community. Embroiled in their own domestic political struggles, the British were ignored as an unedifying combination of German intransigence, French exasperation and Belgian complicity was responsible for the lamentable occupation of the Ruhr in January 1923 and the concomitant meteoric descent into hyperinflation that did so much to assist the early rise to national prominence of Adolf Hitler.[33]

Given the unstable situation in Europe and a somewhat rudderless League, it was fortunate that international crises were rare at this time. Those that did occur were essentially small-scale disputes that could be resolved without imposing a great strain on the members of the League or exposing the fragility of collective security.[34] Moreover, once the French and the Belgians were able to extricate themselves from Germany and sanity began to prevail in Anglo-French–German relations with the rise of Briand, Chamberlain and Stresemann and the signing of the Locarno agreement, Europe began to settle down to enjoy a period of relative tranquillity.[35]

Elsewhere, however, the same calm did not always prevail. In the case of China, for example, the allure that the former Middle Kingdom had historically exerted upon foreign states and driven their much sought after economic penetration of the country, had intensified after the ending of the Great War. China's military weakness, which it had suffered throughout the nineteenth century, proved to be an irresistible magnet for those foreign powers seeking a sphere of influence in the most populous place on earth and aware of the massive market potential that could be exploited if only they could establish more than a mere foothold in the country. After wringing a series of concessions from the hapless Chinese at various times over the past eighty years – the much vilified 'Unequal Treaties' – the international community wished to protect these interests and if possible expand upon them. For this purpose an international flotilla was formed consisting of American, British, French and Japanese gunboats whose prime task was to ply Chinese coastal and inland waters and thereby ensure that their interests and possessions were not subject to encroachment by hostile forces whether foreign or local. Such foreign interventionism sat uneasily, however, with a raised national consciousness and increasing xenophobia – both by-products of the May Fourth Movement of 1919.[36] As national authority broke down in the face of a merciless civil war, the fledgling republic was left at the mercy of extremists on all sides of the political divide. Despite being beset by many debilitating challenges in the turbulent post-revolutionary period, a new tougher China emerged, one in which military weakness was fast becoming consigned to the past. Warlordism with its emphasis on the coupling of military and regional political power ensured that indigenous Chinese militia forces were better armed and also quite prepared to use their weapons to confront any of their enemies either local or foreign. If this was not sufficient reason for caution on behalf of foreign powers, the political cauldron in China boiled over in 1926 with the first of Chiang Kai-shek's Northern Expeditions to unify the country under his nationalist Kuomintang forces. In a very real sense, therefore, the stage was set for an explosive encounter and it was not long in coming.[37]

Although the Wanhsien Incident of August–September 1926 was to prove to be the most dramatic, contentious and costly episode in which a foreign naval power was pitted against local Chinese forces, the sad fact is that it was far from being the first occasion when such a clash had occurred in a riverine environment. Both parties were to blame for this very unfortunate state of affairs: the international powers for mounting an indiscreet and disdainful naval presence in China which succeeded in inflaming local passions, and the local warlords and their henchmen for the practice of routinely commandeering foreign merchant vessels for transporting their troops and material from one place to another and for indulging in random and indiscriminate firing upon foreign steamers as they passed up or down river. Apart from the loss of life on both sides arising out of the rescue bid mounted by British gunboats on the Yangtze, the Wanhsien Incident is important because its unsatisfactory resolution managed to greatly intensify the state of anti-foreignism in China.[38] More clashes arose and the foreign powers responded by redeploying a number of major warships from other stations to Chinese waters to deal with the menace posed by their local adversaries. By January 1927, for instance, the British alone had an aircraft carrier, eight cruisers, nine destroyers, twelve submarines, four sloops, two minesweepers and fifteen river gunboats amongst other vessels in Chinese waters. In addition, the Americans, French and Japanese likewise increased their naval contingents in Chinese waters, though none of them maintained a force that was as impressive quantitatively or qualitatively as that of the British.[39]

Regardless of its problems in China, the UK continued to see the Far East and Australasia as being vitally important to its long-term economic recovery. For this reason once the Washington Conference had conferred on the Japanese a substantial degree of autonomy in the Western Pacific, the British scrambled to find a suitable site to establish a first class naval base for the region. Facing a dearth of alternative choices, the British became convinced that they needed to upgrade their port facilities in Singapore so that it would become a major repair and maintenance facility in their Asia-Pacific theatre of operations. Unfortunately, the financial outlay for a base such as this was so prohibitive that the Baldwin government in London could not possibly afford the most comprehensive scheme and was forced to compromise on a number of crucial items that left the Sembawang naval base in the Strait of Johor something of a hostage to fortune if Malaya was ever to fall to some superior enemy force. Political considerations also intruded: building work on the base was suspended by Ramsay MacDonald's short-lived Labour government in January 1924, only to be resumed under its Conservative successor later in the year and then subject to delay once more as MacDonald returned to 10 Downing Street in October 1929. MacDonald's pacifism and general disinclination to pursue military options close to home, let alone far afield, left the conservative naval establishment in Admiralty House seething and reluctant to embrace any further disarmament scheme that would be prejudicial to its world-wide interests.[40]

This naturally fed latent Anglophobia as was evident in the surly reaction of the American naval establishment to all things British. US Navy Department officials continued to nurse a grudge against their British counterparts for a range of alleged misdemeanours. This attitude found a receptive audience in Defense and State Department circles and expressed itself in a firm American preference for absenting themselves from European affairs for the balance of the Harding administration and the early phase of Calvin Coolidge's time in the White House. While the politicians rejected internationalism in favour of dealing with their domestic agenda, their military experts were engaged in a conscious test of will at home over the forging of future US defence policy. Solving that difficult equation took a number of years and a huge psychological toll on those intimately involved in these matters.[41] Under sustained pressure from the Army for its introspective ways, the Navy Department was also subject to the beginnings of a movement to advance the cause of the aeroplane at the expense of the capital ship. No one made more noise on this heretical subject than 'Billy' Mitchell. His sterling advocacy of the combat merits of the aircraft *vis-à-vis* the battleship and the successful trials that were held against old vessels of that type – *Indiana*, *Ostfriesland* and *Alabama* – in 1920–21 to prove his point, did much to put the US Navy Department on the defensive for years to come.[42]

If it was any comfort to the Americans, the same type of contentious argument over the emerging role of the aircraft *vis-à-vis* the enduring legacy of the battleship was being waged with characteristic vigour (and arguably even greater vehemence) across the Atlantic where the Admiralty and the Air Ministry were engaged in an on-going battle for supremacy as far as defence spending was concerned. Did the aircraft make the battleship redundant as its supporters, inspired by the views of the military theorist Giulio Douhet, claimed it would? Sir Hugh Trenchard, chief of the air staff in the 1920s and the first marshal of the Royal Air Force, certainly believed that the balance of advantage now lay with the bomber rather than the capital ship. A combative individual at the best of times, he proved to be a doughty opponent to all those within the Senior Service who wished to exercise independent control over the fledgling Fleet Air Arm.[43]

Under attack by the other services, the general wellbeing of both the USN and the Royal Navy was not improved by taking part in the acrimonious sessions that so disfigured the Geneva Conference in June–August 1927. Naval disarmament became an increasingly fraught affair with the British delegates ill-disposed to accepting any blanket extension of the Washington system that would cover cruisers as well as lesser classes of naval vessel. By stoutly resisting American pressure for a reduction of its cruiser strength to fifty and holding out for a minimum force level of seventy in the face of much vocal opposition from the representatives of the US Navy Department, the Board of Admiralty uniquely demonstrated its capacity for inflexibility on those matters impinging on its own interests and revealed tellingly the very modest lengths it was prepared to go in order to preserve Anglo-American naval relations at this time. That cooperation between London and Washington now sank to a new low surprised few of those who had been at Geneva. As the two naval establishments recoiled from one another, the individuals who were deeply antagonistic and inherently suspicious of the other side in this cross-Atlantic divide came into their own with depressingly negative effects on policy formation for at least eighteen months.[44]

Although none of the naval powers had been enthusiastic about the imposition of forced disarmament of their stocks of capital ships under the Washington treaty system, all had naturally sought to make the best of the situation and still find means of providing the ideal balanced fleet for themselves. One way of doing so was to build up those classes of warship that hadn't been expressly disallowed at Washington, namely, the cruiser and destroyer. After all, both types of warship could perform a number of indispensable tasks for the fleet. Cruisers were fast, well armed, armoured to a degree (whether reasonably or adequately is a moot point), and long on endurance. They could, therefore, continue to fulfil their usual long-range reconnaissance or 'scouting' role, and be used to protect their own shipping or raid enemy commerce, take part in any ship-to-shore bombardment of enemy positions, and serve as an integral offensive/defensive unit along with a task force of capital ships (and increasingly with carriers in the years to come).[45] Over the years destroyers had basically developed into a more sophisticated and far heavier type of fast torpedo boat, but one that was much smaller and more vulnerable than the cruiser. As they were much cheaper and faster to build, they had become consequently more plentiful than any other type of warship by the end of the 1914–18 war. Their prime role as protective escorts for the battlefleet had been enlarged in wartime to encompass convoy protection and offensive anti-submarine warfare (ASW).[46]

Although the USN had begun laying down the first four vessels of the much criticised Omaha class of light cruiser (i.e. those using no larger than 6-inch [155mm] guns for their main armament) even before the Washington Conference had begun, American cruiser development in the 1920s and early 1930s largely concentrated on the building up of the heavy type of cruiser (those that used nothing less than 8-inch [203mm] guns for their heavy armament) as a means of producing a viable range of what Norman Friedman has described as a 'junior capital ship'.[47] All four classes of heavy cruiser laid down in stages from 1926 to 1934 were designed to achieve speeds in excess of 32 knots, but their armour protection against anything larger than a 5-inch (127mm) shell (the sort that a destroyer would fire) was much less convincing.[48] Although the British tackled the thorny problem of a ten-year naval building holiday for capital ships in much the same way as their American counterparts, none of the five classes of heavy cruiser which the Royal Navy developed in the mid-to-late 1920s could quite reach the speed of the USN types described above.[49] As a result of the London Naval Treaty of 1930 and the restrictions it imposed on heavy cruisers, the British used the 1930s to develop their light cruiser classes laying down eight new classes of this type of vessel before the war broke out in September 1939.[50]

Poignantly and rather gallingly for both the General Board in the US and the Admiralty in the UK, the Japanese – the third ranked naval power – managed to eclipse both. Experimenting with different types of hull, better armour protection both underwater and in the areas around previously vulnerable areas such as the bridge, and by steadily improving their 4-shaft geared turbines and boilers to create vastly increased shaft horse power and speed, the eight classes of Japanese cruiser developed during the interwar period raised the bar in terms of cruiser design. While the Japanese undoubtedly led the way in cruiser development, the Navy General Staff's insistence on building as much firepower into these ships as possible made many of them dangerously unstable.[51]

Of the various design teams from the subordinate powers that were pressed into action around the globe, arguably none managed to produce a range of vessels under the treaty limits with more flair and panache than the Italians. Encouraged by the fascist dictatorship that Mussolini had erected after becoming prime minister in October 1922, the Italian Navy needed no second bidding to create something of a stir in the Mediterranean.[52] Apart from the appearance of their ambitious 10,000-ton cruisers – *Trento* and *Trieste* – in 1927, units of the new light 'condottieri' type Giussano class (5,110 tons) were achieving sea trial speeds of roughly 40 knots by 1930 without sacrificing armaments to do so. Their new destroyers were soon going even faster, even though they were notoriously poor sea keepers and rolled viciously in bad weather.[53] Speed was, of course, an extremely useful asset for any vessel to have at her disposal, but better protection for her crew was imperative if she was to be combative as well as swift and be able to make any lasting impression on those that she would be employed against. In this respect the Japanese were in a class of their own. While they could not compete for basic speed with the Italians, the Japanese Fubuki class – incorporating new features, such as gas-proof gun-houses instead of open shields for the guns and multiple tubes – could claim to be among the safest and most efficient destroyers afloat.[54]

At the capital ship end of the spectrum, American interest in the future role of the aeroplane was also taken several steps further by the conversion of the fleet collier *Jupiter* into the first of its flat tops *Langley* (12,700 tons) in 1922 and by redesigning the battlecruisers *Lexington* and *Saratoga* (37,681 tons) to make them into the first of the USN's fleet carriers when they were commissioned at the end of 1927. It was claimed for several years that they did not breach the 35,000 ton rule laid down by the Washington Treaty for carriers, but it is clear that they did. Funds were also set aside for the construction of a new Ranger class of aircraft carrier (14,575 tons) that could carry 76 aircraft (thirteen more than the Lexington class) and could reach speeds of 29.9 knots at her sea trials in 1933. Despite being the first of the American carriers to be designed as such from the outset, *Ranger* was not a great success. Her captain would later testify in 1939 that she sometimes pitched so violently in heavy seas that all flying operations would have to be suspended from her decks.[55]

Despite the Admiralty's love of the dreadnought battleships in its midst, it had laid down the largest carrier fleet in the world by the time the war came to an end, ranging from *Pegasus* at 3,300 tons (deep load) to that of *Eagle* (26,800 tons) when operational. Within a decade most had become rather antiquated and *Vindictive* (12,095 tons) had already been converted back into a Hawkins class heavy cruiser. Beginning in 1922 with *Furious* (22,450 tons) which was designed originally as a light battlecruiser, the British converted both *Courageous* and *Glorious*, both of which had both been launched in 1916 as light battlecruisers, into fleet carriers. They operated on similar tonnages to *Furious*, but each was able to carry a dozen more aircraft than she did by the time they emerged from reconstruction in 1928 and 1930 respectively.[56]

Like the other two principal naval powers, the first three Japanese carriers were converted from other forms of naval vessel: *Hōshō* had originally been a naval oiler before being converted into a light carrier; *Akagi* had begun life as a 41,200 ton battlecruiser and *Kaga* had been designed as a 39,000 ton battleship. Only the light carrier *Ryūjō* which was laid down in 1929 was supposed to have been a carrier from the outset. In a bid to ensure that she could carry more aircraft, a second hangar was added in the mid-1930s but this caused real stability problems.[57]

Perhaps the most ominous development of the lot, however, came from the Germans who returned to the world of naval building in 1929 by unveiling an armoured ship known as the *Preussen* (renamed *Deutschland*) – a cross between a small battleship and battlecruiser – and the forerunner of the class of pocket battleship (described as *Panzerschiff*) that would circumvent the restrictions on maximum tonnage and gun calibre imposed by the Treaty of Versailles and become such a feature of German naval construction in the 1930s. What disturbed the British most about this type of ship was that it looked to be designed as a high speed, long endurance and heavily-armed merchant raider, and one that was in a class of its own in terms of these combinations of quality assets. Of the existing fleets, only the three British battlecruisers (*Hood*, *Renown* and *Repulse*) were a match for these pocket battleships. As the naval powers didn't know what to expect from the Germans in future, the French decided to lay down their Dunkerque class of battleship in 1932 which was based on, but not as heavy as, the British Nelson class that had been laid down in 1922. Once launched in 1935–36 both *Dunkerque* and *Strasbourg* were capable of reaching speeds of over 30 knots during their 8-hour power trials.[58]

Whatever emotions were raised in western European capitals by the re-emergence onto the world stage of the German Navy in 1929, they were utterly eclipsed by those generated by the disastrous stock market crash on Wall Street in October of that same year. As countries around the world reeled from the effects of the first 'Black Thursday' and panic set in as fortunes and profits disappeared in a welter of falling prices and stocks and shares indices, a huge blow was administered to both the capitalist and democratic systems upon which twin edifices a number of regimes now rested. It is difficult not to see 1929 as a decisive turning point in the political fortunes of the world ushering in a collapse of international economic institutions and financial arrangements, businesses – ranging from the vibrant to the staid – and personal credit lines and the lifestyles that went with them. Political parties that had won their way into power through the ballot box now found the experience of being in power distinctly uncomfortable. Those that managed to hold onto power did so at great cost to themselves and were seen, perhaps unfairly, by many of their constituents both at the time and subsequently as being weak and incompetent. Few democratic regimes lasted beyond their next major electoral test before being unceremoniously replaced by their political opponents.[59]

While fatal harm was being done to some political careers by the ominous descent into what became known as the 'Great Depression', others took off meteorically – none more so than that of Adolf Hitler. His dire warnings about the so-called 'November Criminals', the iniquities of the Versailles settlement and the savaging of German pride on the altar of Allied expediency now began to find common cause with a nation that succumbed once more to soaring unemployment and rampant inflation. It made little difference that the Social Democrats and their coalition partners in Berlin were not directly responsible for the calamity that now befell the German nation. The fact was they were the ones in power and this meant that they were held to be accountable to the people for the grievous misfortunes that the latter were experiencing at this time. Just what this meant in practice could be glimpsed from the results of the Reichstag elections of June 1930 when the National Socialist German Workers Party that Hitler led emerged as the most dynamic political movement in the country.[60]

As pressures mounted on governments around the world, the old Washington Treaty powers met once more in an effort to carry forward the disarmament message that the original meeting in 1921–22 had proclaimed so shrilly. After the misunderstandings and mistrust generated by the failed talks at Geneva in 1927, the British government – under the stewardship of Ramsay MacDonald once more – was particularly determined to take naval disarmament to another level and improve the unsatisfactory state of Anglo-American relations at the same time. Naturally, the Admiralty feared the consequences of this political interference, but was powerless to stop the prime minister and his pacifist tendencies from inflicting further cuts on the Senior Service.[61] MacDonald was not alone in seeking restraint and international understanding. Indeed it had been the key to the advocacy of the Kellogg–Briand Pact and its sublime, if always idealistic, intention of outlawing war – a document signed with much fanfare by more than sixty nations in August 1928 and then promptly ignored by a number of the signatory powers.[62]

By the time the naval delegates gathered in London to begin this disarmament revival, therefore, the signs of international instability were becoming obvious to all. In Japan, the frail experiment with Taisho democracy had been dispensed with as militarism resurfaced in a number of guises – virtually all of them inimical to moderation. In fascist Italy Mussolini, emboldened by the recent understanding reached with the Vatican, was proving to be considerably more astute in power and far less easy to outmanoeuvre than his many foreign detractors had imagined he would be.[63] In France politicians continued to rise and fall in the rather heady fashion of the Third Republic, but a growing sense of apprehension was detectable not least because of the death in early October 1929 of Gustav Stresemann – the sturdy German nationalist figure who had done so much to transform Franco-German relations in the previous six years – first as chancellor and then as foreign minister. Thereafter French foreign policy assumed an ultra defensive mode symbolised in the erection of the Maginot Line of fortifications that was to be constructed at phenomenal expense along the Franco-German border.[64]

Although the London Naval Conference could not be described as an unqualified success, it was less dramatically controversial than the Hughes-dominated assembly of 1921–22. Spurred on by Macdonald, the British delegates were prepared to accept the previously untenable American demand for an upper limit of fifty cruisers and a maximum displacement limit of 339,000 tons. This spirit of constructive co-operation was matched on the American side by their willingness to select the Anglophile Captain Veazie Pratt as the technical leader of the USN delegation. Inspired by Pratt's positivism, the Americans worked closely with their Royal Navy counterparts to bury a good deal of the animosity that had so disfigured this cross-Atlantic relationship throughout the past decade. As a result, agreements were forthcoming on a range of matters. Under the arrangements for capital ships, the Americans, British and Japanese all agreed not to build any more before 1937, while the French and Italians, who could both have built a 35,000-ton vessel in 1927 and 1929 but had chosen not to do so in either year, indicated that they would exercise their option to build these vessels before 1937 and proceeded to do so. In examining the case for the development of aircraft carriers, the 5:5:3:1.75:1.75 principle was re-endorsed and submarine equality with the USN and RN was permitted for the IJN, though not without some qualms expressed in private by representatives of the two leading naval powers. American fondness for the destroyer was recognised and the USN's lead in this class of warship was duly protected.[65]

Whatever agreements had been forged in London, however, began to look a good deal less permanent only a short while later as the spectre of an uncompromising nationalism stalked the globe. It was bad enough that Hitler's rise to prominence in Germany was not stalled by his presumptuous electoral duel with the incumbent Paul von Hindenburg for the presidency of the republic in March and April 1932, underlining the notion that Europe had not heard the last of him or his party, but even this undesirable prospect had been upstaged several months before by the machinations of the Japanese military in East Asia. Eyeing territorial acquisitions in Manchuria and China and realising that the only way they were going to get them was by force, infantry troops of the Imperial Japanese Army staged the Mukden incident on 18 September 1931 and used the ensuing disorder as a pretext for a full scale invasion and eventual annexation of Manchuria. China's appeal to the League of Nations hardly inconvenienced the by now exultant Japanese military, and the government in Tokyo knew better than to try to restrain its troops in the field let alone yield the territorial and economic gains made by them following the outbreak of the Manchurian war. Not content with bringing Manchuria under their control, the Japanese swiftly turned their attention to the Chinese mainland that beckoned invitingly as a key economic cog in a new colonial empire ruled from Tokyo. Unrestrained Japanese enthusiasm for the spoils of war soon caught up with them, however, and the belligerent behaviour of their troops in Shanghai in January 1932 and their warships subsequently was to bring them into confrontation with the Western Powers who jealously guarded their own interests in the International Settlement and had no wish to see them infringed upon or lost entirely to the Japanese. As a result, additional naval units were brought in by both the Americans and the British at the beginning of February to reinforce their existing presence in the city and act as a deterrent to those who might otherwise have been tempted to trample on their national interests. Although heightened naval activity in local waters did nothing to cool the xenophobia of the Chinese, it may have been a sufficient indication to the Japanese that they would have to tread more warily in future where foreign powers were concerned. Nonetheless, the aggressive intent of their forces both in Manchuria and China and the government's failure to restrain them, demonstrated convincingly that moderation was a commodity in rather short supply in Japanese political and military circles at this time.[66]

In setting the first real challenge to the League of Nations, the Japanese were, of course, to expose the political bankruptcy of the organisation and the fragility of the concept of collective security. Neither failing surprised the French who had never been comfortable with the League's ability to resolve international crises or to impose its will upon errant states. Even before the Lytton Commission had begun gathering information on the background to the dispute and seven months before rendering its judgement, the Japanese had shown where they stood on the issue by bringing into existence a new Manchurian republic that would henceforth be known as Manchukuo. While taking great pains to couch its report in non-inflammatory language, the Lytton Commission still managed to infuriate the Japanese by finding them guilty of several breaches of the League Covenant and the Kellogg–Briand Pact. In the months following the publication of the Lytton Commission's report in October 1932, the world was treated to a variety of unseemly diplomatic schemes intended to circumvent the necessity for taking direct action against the aggressor Japan and providing some form of restitution for its victim China. It is sobering to note that the leading members of the League were often in the vanguard of this movement and therefore did much to undermine the credibility of the institution to which they were supposedly committed.[67]

At precisely the same time as the Lytton Commission was conducting its ponderously thorough investigation in East Asia, the League of Nations Disarmament Conference began its own painfully frustrating proceedings in Geneva. Whatever hopes for world peace may have been pinned on the successful outcome of this international gathering at the outset were dispelled almost immediately by the unhelpful behaviour of some of the delegations who were in no mood to placate their traditional foes or assist even those of their recent allies who were striving for goals different from their own.[68]

If these were not sufficient causes for disquiet, lurking in the background was yet another menace to world peace, namely, Adolf Hitler. His Nazi Party, buoyant that their leader's presidential bid had netted more than thirteen million votes in April 1932, drew on this reservoir of support again in the Reichstag elections of June and polled slightly in excess of that figure nationally. From a low point of 12 seats at the 1928 elections, the Nazis had been transformed from a small provincial outfit to the largest party in the entire parliament with 230 seats at their disposal. Although they were to lose more than thirty seats in the new elections held in November 1932, they remained the largest party overall and their brooding presence on the German political scene was such that they could no longer be ignored as merely a lunatic fringe element either by their domestic opponents or by foreign governments.[69]

By the end of 1932, therefore, the stage seemed set for a new and more unpredictable phase in international relations and one that was mirrored in the British government's decision to abandon the underlying principle of its foreign and defence policy that it had maintained after 1919, namely, that of the ten-year no-war rule. Although not officially interred by the cabinet until March 1933, MacDonald's National government had come to the conclusion well before the end of the previous year that such a comforting analysis could no longer be sustained. It was a correct assumption to make as the events of the following months would confirm.[70]

Those pessimists who felt that 1933 was destined to become a momentous year in international relations soon found plenty of evidence to support their theory. January had not even passed before the Austrian-born, ex-corporal Hitler was reluctantly installed by Feldmarschall Hindenburg as the German chancellor. Whatever else might lie in store for Germany, his elevation to power appeared to spell an abrupt end to the spirit of European co-operation and harmony that had existed from the time of the Locarno agreements. Foreign governments read the warning signs and altered tack immediately becoming more defensive in nature and more inclined to the concept of re-armament than that of disarmament.[71]

A significant culture of change arose in the United States too, but less out of a knee-jerk reaction to events in Europe than the fact that less than five weeks after Hitler's elevation to power, Franklin Delano Roosevelt was inaugurated as the thirty-second president of the United States on 3 March 1933. Although to supporters of the Republican Party this was looked upon as a quintessential disaster in its own right, Roosevelt's entry into the White House was initially, at least, to have far more importance domestically than internationally. Consumed with a burning commitment to tackling the scourge of mass unemployment at home, Roosevelt had little time or enthusiasm for making sweeping gestures on the foreign stage.[72]

As a result, the democracies were left bereft of the type of strong, balanced and cohesive leadership or support that the United States might have provided in better economic times than these. Instead the members of the League continued to look to the British and the French for guidance precisely at a time when they were incapable of performing this sort of role. Confirmation that democracy had assumed a somewhat jaded appearance and that a new age of unrestrained excesses had dawned came in the most dramatic way possible in March, with Japan's withdrawal from the League of Nations and the implementation in the same month of a series of draconian internal security measures introduced in Germany by the Nazis in the wake of the Reichstag Fire. To make matters worse, a sense of futility now masked the wearisome sessions of the Disarmament Conference in Geneva, where progress had stalled amid mutual acrimony and insouciant manoeuvring from some of the leading European delegates. This unsatisfactory state of affairs worsened still further in October 1933 when Germany, viewing the League as an anachronistic and irrelevant institution that had long passed its sell by date, promptly left it and the ill-fated Disarmament Conference, while reminding those who wished to listen that it rejected the *diktat* of Versailles and considered itself no longer bound by any treaty restrictions on the size and shape of its armed forces. This latest rebuff naturally did nothing to bolster the confidence of the other League members and finally put paid to any thoughts that an exhaustive system of disarmament measures could be agreed upon and implemented worldwide. Whatever one feels about Germany's hedonistic diplomacy at this time, the fact is that the League had performed inadequately in the Manchurian crisis and looked woefully incapable of settling anything other than the most minor of skirmishes. Collective decision-making had proved just as burdensome and time consuming to orchestrate as its detractors had imagined it would be, while the prospect of enforcing its decisions upon any power of more than modest proportions looked more remote in 1933 than it had done since the League had been formally proposed in 1919.[73]

Far from being discomforted by the enormity of these international developments, the leading naval authorities wasted little time on sentimental schadenfreude preferring instead to warn their political masters of the dangers of being caught unprepared for trouble should it arise in the near future. While the American and Japanese naval establishments put in hand large replacement construction programmes to bring their navies up to the limits set by the London Treaty, the British government continued, quite properly, to agonise over the financial propriety of increasing defence spending at a time of great economic austerity.[74] As it did so supporters of the Royal Navy were left to bewail the perilous state of the United Kingdom's preparedness for war and the inadequacy of the Senior Service *vis-à-vis* its potential rivals on the high seas. In particular, the ever-controversial topic of the number of cruisers available to the Admiralty received the usual hand wringing attention from naval enthusiasts anxious to torpedo the restrictions imposed upon this class of warship by the Washington and London treaties.[75]

Faced with a world that was growing ever more dangerous and belligerent leaders who seemed to have shrugged off restraint for immoderation, the Baldwin and Roosevelt administrations and their military advisors had already been forced to respond. Both had laid down new classes of aircraft carrier allowed to them under the terms of the London Naval Treaty – the Americans settled on a modern design (Yorktown class) that embodied the knowledge they had gained from operating their earlier carriers. They initially laid down two ships in this class (*Yorktown* and *Enterprise*) in May and July 1934 respectively and would add a third five years later (*Hornet*). All exceeded 20,000 tons standard displacement, were capable of achieving a top speed exceeding 33 knots and each carried 96 aircraft. They were to be the prototype of the substantially heavier, better armed, protected, and only slightly slower ships of the Essex class that were to do so much to win the war in the Pacific from 1943 onwards. For their part, the British settled on their first carrier (*Ark Royal*) that had not started life as something else. When it was laid down in September 1935 it displaced over 2,200 tons more at deep load than the *Yorktown*, but carried only 60 aircraft and was on average 1.5 knots slower than the American carrier.[76]

It was just as well they did respond, for the Japanese had stolen a march on them not only with their latest carrier designs but also, and more significantly, with the carrier aircraft they developed during the course of the 1930s. Behind this determined thrust to improve naval aviation and make it into a national asset was Rear-Admiral Isoroku Yamamoto – a naval officer who was destined to carve an incredible niche for himself in the annals of the IJN at Pearl Harbor in December 1941 and throughout the Pacific in the months thereafter. Yamamoto, chief of the Naval Aviation Department in 1935–36, was insistent that complacency must be guarded against and that the IJN must constantly strive to improve the performance of all aircraft types. Feedback from Japanese pilots in their campaigns over China helped to improve design features and increase performance. In this way the Mitsubishi A6M 'Zeke' (more popularly known as the 'Zero') emerged in 1940 as the IJN's carrier fighter of choice, combining high speed (332mph [534kph]) and great range (1,000 miles [1,609 km]), while the Nakajima B5N 'Kate' became the best torpedo bomber available to any of the naval powers, and the Aichi D3A 'Val' dive bomber was as good as any equivalent aircraft manufactured either by the Americans (Douglas SBD Dauntless) or by the Germans (Junkers Ju-87 'Stuka') and well ahead of anything the British had manufactured.[77]

This kind of technical success was seen in the growth of Japanese carriers during the 1930s too where they easily surpassed the British both in terms of qualitative and quantitative development and matched anything emanating from the US shipyards. Once it became clear that the Japanese wouldn't remain signatories to the London Naval Treaty, *Sōryu* (19,800 tons deep load) was re-designed to become a fast carrier when she was launched in late 1935 with a hull and propulsion system that could provide her with a masterful 34.5 knots, reflecting her original cruiser-carrier hybridity. Learning from their unsettling experience with the *Sōryu*, the Japanese improved the stability of her slightly larger successor the *Hiryu* by modifying and strengthening her hull, forecastle and beam by the time she was launched in November 1937. Once the London Treaty was officially dead, the Navy General Staff sought to design and build a much heavier class of carrier that would contain all the best virtues of the existing carriers without sacrificing stability and could be used on offensive missions in conjunction with the superbattleships *Yamato* and *Musashi*. It was looking for the same aircraft complement as on the reconstructed *Akagi* and *Kaga* (roughly 90), a similar speed to the *Hiryu* (34.3 knots) and an ability to cruise over 10,000nm (18,520km) at 18 knots. It basically got what it wanted – a fast carrier that packed a considerable offensive punch – when the two impressive fleet carriers the *Shōkaku* and *Zuikaku* were completed in August–September 1941. They were in a class of their own until the Americans brought their Essex class into service in 1943–44.[78]

Although few of the lesser naval powers wished to embark on a new naval race, they knew only too well that they could not afford to be left trailing in the wake of those who had no qualms about using government money in this way. French pessimism for the future, so emblematically associated with the building of the Maginot Line, might also be advanced in part for their government's decision to lay down the battleship *Dunkerque* in 1932 and her sister ship *Strasbourg* in November 1934. These moves, though defensively inclined and in accordance with their specific rights under the Washington Treaty, were nonetheless capable of being misinterpreted by others and unwittingly stimulated a new wave of capital ship construction around the world. A crisis in central Europe did not help matters either. After the botched coup against the legitimate Austrian government by forces striving for union with Germany and the callous murder of the chancellor Engelburt Dollfuss in August 1934, however, Mussolini not only mobilised four troop divisions and sent them to the Brenner Pass to demonstrate to Hitler that the Italians were opposed to any take-over of their neighbouring state, but the Fascist Grand Council also approved the laying down of the *Littorio* and *Vittorio Veneto* in October 1934. This news had the effect of propelling the French to seek permission from their government to build two 35,000-ton battleships (the *Richelieu* and the *Jean Bart*) to match the latest Italian vessels and the Germans to build two ostensibly 26,000-ton battleships (*Scharnhorst* and *Gneisenau*) to rival those of the Dunkerque class.[79]

It was not what the German naval industry had built or was building that caused such misgivings in the corridors of power in Whitehall but rather what they might build in the future. It was the long term potential of the Kriegsmarine that the British politicians were anxious to thwart if they could. Suspecting as much, Hitler offered the British government a secret deal in the spring of 1935, which would peg the German capital ship fleet to 35% of that of the Royal Navy.[80] This restriction did not, however, apply to submarines that had done so much to strangle British trade in the First World War. Nonetheless, the view of the British government seemed to be that something was better than nothing and that the Anglo-German Naval Agreement of June 1935 provided a wonderful opportunity to improve their bilateral relationship and yet exercise restraint upon their North Sea rivals at the same time. Moreover, if the agreement held, it would save the British exchequer a vast amount of money that would otherwise have to go into building an entirely new standard of naval strength.[81]

Unfortunately, the negative side of conducting this secret diplomacy was that it was likely to undermine the recently signed Stresa Front between France, Italy and the United Kingdom that had been designed as an anti-German association of states. By concluding the Anglo-German Naval Agreement in such a clandestine manner, however, the British government seems to have tacitly concluded that forging a direct naval agreement with its main potential adversary represented a far better option for keeping Germany at bay than through the emergence of an unstable ring of deterrence involving the unpredictable and volatile Italians and the highly idiosyncratic French. Therefore when the announcement of the naval agreement brought forth the anticipated cries of betrayal from their Stresa partners, the British tried unconvincingly to suggest that such protests were exaggerated and that nothing had been done to harm the interests of the other powers in the Front. Neither the French nor the Italians needed to be paranoid to feel that the British had connived with the Germans to gain their own selfish ends and that this perfidious behaviour had shown them in a very unattractive light. Not surprisingly, the Stresa Front never recovered from this self-inflicted diplomatic blow.[82]

Believing themselves released from even the most tenuous of agreements to behave – given the latest British example of surreptitious double dealing – the Italians did not take long to show just how belligerent they could be if the mood took them. In October 1935 the border dispute in the Horn of Africa that had been simmering between the Abyssinians and themselves since the previous December broke out into a full-scale colonial war. That this latest act of aggression was to wreak further havoc on the credibility of the League of Nations came as no surprise to those who had followed the lamentable performance of the world body in dealing with the Manchurian crisis. Appalled by the scale and ferocity of the attack that was launched on an independent state and fellow member of the League, the British and French were once more pitched reluctantly into leading the chorus of institutional disapproval against a state that they would have much preferred not to have alienated. Alas, in the words of the cliché, the die had already been cast and quiescence would have sent the wrong message to those of a totalitarian persuasion who needed little passive encouragement to be disruptive or inflammatory.[83]

British ambivalence on this subject was suitably demonstrated by the Admiralty's reinforcement of the Mediterranean Fleet even before Mussolini had launched his military operation against the hapless Abyssinians. If this move had been intended to deter the Italians from embarking upon this colonial adventure, it utterly failed in its objective. If, however, it was designed to serve notice on the Italians that the United Kingdom had interests to protect in the Mediterranean and North Africa and would not hesitate to do so, the initiative could be said to have worked since the feared assaults upon Gibraltar, Malta and the Suez Canal did not take place. While Mussolini entertained wild notions of sinking the Mediterranean Fleet in a surprise attack, his naval commanders were less given to exuberant over-confidence. For a time, therefore, restraint succeeded.[84]

On the wider stage and true to form, the League took its time to move on the Abyssinian crisis and even when it did make some forward momentum the rate of progress was glacial. While deploring the Italian invasion, the League did little constructively to seek redress for the Abyssinians. Instead a craven form of realpolitik reared its ugly head in the form of a grotesque plan devised in December 1935 by Sir Samuel Hoare, the British foreign secretary, and Pierre Laval, the French foreign minister, to reward Italy's calculated aggression with a considerable swathe of territory at Abyssinia's expense. Fortunately, when news of this outrageously unfair document reached the ears of the press the response was one of instantaneous condemnation and both Hoare and Laval were forced to resign their ministerial offices in disgrace. Although the Hoare–Laval Pact was dead that did not mean the League was ready to take on the Italians in earnest. Indeed even when Italy's guilt in provoking the crisis had been clearly established and faced by robust intransigence from the authorities in Rome, the League still opted for the most ineffective type of sanctions, ignoring a ban on scrap metal and oil supplies that would have done much more to disrupt and inconvenience the Italian war effort.[85]

As the League continued to move cautiously forward, groping for a way to resolve the issue without driving the Italians any further into the camp of its enemies, the British and French naval authorities sought to avoid being dragged into a war in the Mediterranean. This was perfectly understandable given the lack of readiness for war that existed in both of these countries in 1936. Although re-armament was now very much in vogue, there was a considerable time lag between the government approving the expenditure for new construction and the naval authorities actually having the finished warship at their disposal. Capital ships took, for instance, upwards of four years to become operational and they were still very much the yardstick by which a navy's fighting strength was judged. Faster and more robust than the older battleships and battlecruisers that they replaced, these latest vessels were also set to carry a much heavier weight of armament and be far more expensive to construct than those that had gone before. Acutely aware of this and being anxious to set some form of upper limit to rein in the expense and yet still remain competitive on the high seas, the American, British and French naval authorities had tried vainly for months to persuade the Japanese to agree to a new naval treaty to replace the Washington and London treaties when they expired on 31 March 1936. Driven by a restless quest for national honour, the Japanese Navy General Staff set its implacable face against any continuance of naval inferiority towards either the

Americans or the British. By mid-January 1936, convinced that some common upper limit would not be acceptable to the other delegations, the Japanese withdrew sullenly from the last concerted effort to limit the growth of navies before the onset of the Second World War.[86]

Left to themselves the Americans, British and French delegations moved away from the contentious area of compulsory restriction and signed a five-year qualitative agreement instead. Under the terms of the new London Naval Treaty agreed between them in March 1936, the three signatory powers voluntarily agreed to exchange information on all forms of new construction and neither build nor acquire any capital ship exceeding 35,000 tons and not arm them with anything larger than 16-inch (406mm) diameter guns. In a similar manner guidelines were established for the other main classes of naval vessels: aircraft carriers were not to displace more than 23,000 tons or carry more than 6.1-inch (155mm) ordnance; light surface vessels (a category that was used to describe those cruisers, destroyers and all surface ships other than auxiliaries and minor warships of more than 100 tons and less than 10,000 tons mounting guns not exceeding 8 inches) were to be limited to an upper limit of 8,000 tons and carry nothing more than 8-inch (203mm) guns; while submarines were to be limited to a maximum displacement of 2,000 tons and have nothing larger than 5.1-inch (110mm) armament. A so-called escalator clause was added that allowed the signatories under certain circumstances to build cruisers up to a maximum 10,000 ton limit. An age limit was also placed on each class of warship – the understanding being that capital ships would be withdrawn from the fleet once they had reached 26 years, aircraft carriers would not exceed 20 years, light surface vessels (depending upon their particular categorisation and construction date) would not be older than between 16–20 years and submarines would be below 13 years of age.[87]

Respect for international agreements – still evident in the Anglo-American building plans – was not something the German government offered across the board however. After bluntly announcing a marked expansion of the Wehrmacht and the existence of an air force in March 1935, in defiance of the military restrictions of the Treaty of Versailles, the German government took another startling initiative once again a year later.[88] Just over three weeks before the 1936 London Naval Treaty was signed, Hitler boldly sent a relatively small number of German troops and police to reoccupy the Rhineland in contravention of both the Versailles and Locarno treaties. In so doing, the German Führer had issued yet another deft challenge to the leading European powers. Although acknowledging that the symbolic and strategic significance of the military reoccupation could not be denied, neither the British nor French governments felt strong enough to contest it in anything other than a rhetorical fashion. By reacting in this way, of course, both governments showed an appeasing nature that Hitler would exploit unerringly for the next three years.[89]

As one crisis evaporated so the next took its place in 1936. Shortly after the Italo-Abyssinian war had come to an inglorious end and the European continent was beginning to come to terms with the German reoccupation of the

Rhineland, a dramatic civil war broke out in Spain in mid-July pitching the Republican government and its supporters against their assorted right wing rivals whose armed forces were commanded by General Francisco Franco. Apart from disrupting Spanish exports of mineral ores, the civil war threatened to destabilise international relations in the Mediterranean once more and pose problems for seafaring nations along the Atlantic seaboard both of Europe and West Africa. This was not an exaggerated fear. Spain's territorial dominance at the narrow western end of the Mediterranean, its sovereignty over the Canary Islands and the colonial enclaves it retained off the coast of Guinea meant that it possessed a latent potential as a choke point for all forms of seaborne trade. Therefore, if Spain became an enemy of the European democracies, the international outlook for all of them would deteriorate markedly. Despite not wishing to alienate either side in the constitutional dispute and vowing to stay out of what they saw as an internal affair, both the British and French governments were powerless to prevent other states and even volunteers from their own countries from aiding one or other of the combatants in this desperate ideological struggle for ascendancy in the Iberian peninsula. Although their pragmatic policy of containment achieved some early illusionary success with the formation of a Non-Intervention Committee in early September, ultimately the desire to leave well alone fell on deaf ears.[90]

Germany's attitude to the leftist Spanish government, which had been predictably hostile from the outset, had worsened still further in August after an explosive incident near Cadiz involving the German steamer *Kamerun* and a cruiser and submarine belonging to the Republican Navy. Apart from issuing a strongly worded protest, the Germans immediately rewrote the rules of engagement for their vessels in Spanish waters permitting them to respond robustly to all future unjustified acts of force. While this action sufficed for the time being, a marked shift in emphasis and tempo soon emerged with the signing on 21 October 1936 of a secret protocol between Germany and Italy covering the use of military force in the war in Spain and Mussolini's dramatic public announcement of the existence of the Rome–Berlin Axis on 1 November.[91] Whatever else it might presage, this quasi-diplomatic partnership between the Italian and German governments created a new and disturbing constellation of power in central and southern Europe and set the seal on the provision of joint military assistance to Franco's falangist troops – a policy that was contrary to the stated aims of the Non-Intervention Committee and one that was sure to pose considerable problems for any naval enforcement of these principles in the Mediterranean in the weeks and months to come.[92]

As the world began to take stock of the serious implications arising from the forging of this sinister compact, the German and Japanese governments added to the general confusion by calmly announcing the existence of the Anti-Comintern Pact. Although it was seen initially as a purely ideological device to demonstrate their mutual antipathy for communism, the prospect of some future form of dual alliance between these two increasingly militaristic states was not calculated to make the leaders of the European democracies sleep easier in their beds.[93]

Anxious as ever to avoid being caught between a menacing proliferation of hostile forces and seeking some means of reducing their international liabilities, the British, in particular, lost little time in identifying the Italians as being the weakest link in this growing fascist chain and tailored their foreign policy accordingly. For his part, despite being increasingly contemptuous of the British race and wildly dismissive of the Royal Navy, Mussolini, for a mix of personal and pragmatic motives, still indulged those who thought he was the key to the totalitarian dilemma faced by the democracies on the continent. As a result, the concerted diplomatic offensive launched by Baldwin's government in the late autumn of 1936 culminated in the signing on 2 January 1937 of the rather unfortunately named 'Gentlemen's Agreement' between the British and Italian governments. Limited in scope and designed to remove the Mediterranean as a potential source of friction in Anglo-Italian relations, the 'Gentlemen's Agreement' soon fell into disrepair and became about as singularly ineffective as the Non-Intervention Committee was in preventing foreign states from supplying direct military assistance to the belligerents in the Spanish Civil War.[94]

Matters were scarcely any better on the Anglo-German naval front, but the German Naval War Staff (Seekriegsleitung) and a number of other leading shore-based officers, such as Conrad Albrecht, the head of the Baltic Station, and Otto Schulze, his counterpart at the North Sea Station, were generally pessimistic about the Kriegsmarine's prospects of survival if war should break out with the British and anxious to avoid such a prospect if at all possible. Unfortunately, while the time for restraint had not completely passed, war with the Royal Navy could no longer be ruled out and must be prepared for. It was in this mood that the Anglo-German Naval Agreement was renewed on 17 July 1937.[95]

While the emergence of a North Sea threat was hardly ideal for either party to this agreement, the Spanish Civil War was of more pressing immediacy and reclaimed much of the attention in European diplomatic and military circles. Whatever momentum had been with the Nationalist forces in the early stages of the war was temporarily stalled by the spirited Republican victory at Guadalajara in mid-March 1937. This military setback infuriated Mussolini who, having typically underrated the abilities of his opponents' forces and over-estimated those of his own troops, had been confidently predicting the imminent fall of Madrid before the news reached him of the upset at Guadalajara. While this defeat was definitely a blow to fascist pride, it provided a much-needed boost to the Republican government's forces and the international assortment of leftist supporters who had rallied to its cause. Mussolini's agitated response to this news was predictably to send more troops to Spain and vow to crush all of his enemies wherever they may lurk in the peninsula and elsewhere. His action, and the anti-British tone of the Italian press, did not say much for either the effectiveness or longevity of the 'Gentlemen's Agreement' – a situation not lost on Anthony Eden, the British foreign secretary, whose personal antipathy for Il Duce was well known in cabinet circles by this time.[96]

Too much can be made of an isolated campaign victory, however, and before long the Nationalist forces had retaken the initiative with their concentrated attack on the Basque Republic. Once this new theatre of operations had opened on 31 March and the Nationalists had announced a blockade of Republican ports on the Cantabrian coast on 6 April, units of both the Royal Navy and the French Navy were drawn into providing protection for those of its merchant ships that were either supplying food to Bilbao or ferrying refugees away from the scene of the fighting in the Basque Country.[97] In response to this upsurge in fighting, the Non-Intervention Committee inaugurated a naval patrol of ports and frontiers, which failed comprehensively when put to the test. Under pressure on the ground, the Republicans fought back by bombing the German pocket battleship *Deutschland* near the island of Ibiza on 29 May, causing substantial casualties among the crew and bringing forth a sustained retaliatory bombardment of the town of Almeria at virtually point blank range by a German cruiser and four destroyers a couple of days later.[98] In this uncompromisingly ruthless way the Germans served an ominous warning to the Republicans to steer clear of attacking their warships in future or face the consequences.[99]

It was a message that the Republican high command could not fail to notice or to act upon. Indalecio Prieto, the socialist minister of defence, was personally disinclined to submit meekly to this act of force majeure, but his inflammatory call for the Republican air force to open a sustained bombing campaign against all German warships was overruled by no less a figure than Stalin who did not wish to provoke Hitler needlessly at this time. As a result, there were no subsequent efforts to bomb German warships, but according to the authorities in Berlin a Spanish government submarine did make four unsuccessful attempts to torpedo the German cruiser *Leipzig* some three weeks later. This served as a sufficient pretext for the Germans to withdraw their naval units from the Non-Intervention Committee's already discredited patrol scheme leaving the Italians to play an increasingly obvious double game in which their predatory instincts triumphed over their supposed protectoral duties. In the summer months, using both submarines and bombers based in Majorca, the Italians began to wage a war of attrition against all mercantile shipping engaged in trading with those ports still in Republican hands. In August 1937 alone this aggressive campaign managed to sink eight British and eighteen neutral merchant vessels or roughly 200,000 deadweight tons of shipping. These maritime attacks on trade could not simply be ignored and all the governments on the receiving end of these punitive attacks demanded action of some kind to prevent this scale of destruction in the future.[100]

Unfortunately, Eden's preference for taking a forceful diplomatic line with the Italians conflicted with and became subordinate to Prime Minister Chamberlain's desire to woo Mussolini and undermine the Rome–Berlin Axis. Unwilling to estrange the fascists, the limp British response merely encouraged the Italian submarine fleet to even more brazen acts of defiance. On 31 August, for instance, *Iride* unsuccessfully attempted to torpedo the Royal Navy destroyer *Havock*, but on the following day the British tanker *Woodford* was not as fortunate. Even these acts of naval piracy failed to convince Chamberlain that his appeasement of Mussolini ought to be jettisoned and it was left to Yvon Delbos, the

French foreign minister, to try to arrest this increasingly unacceptable situation in the Mediterranean by calling for a naval conference to be convened on the subject at Nyon in early September. Although both the Italians and the Germans declined to attend, Delbos and Eden pressed ahead with a swiftly agreed strategy for dealing with the submarine menace. In essence this meant that their warships reserved the right to attack and sink any unidentified submarines in those areas where merchant ships had been attacked. This uncharacteristically tough response from the democracies achieved a modicum of success as submarine attacks in the Mediterranean ceased for several months before flaring up again in the following January.[101]

On this occasion the problem stemmed from a self-congratulatory decision of the Nyon signatories to modify the naval patrol system they had implemented after the conference agreement on 14 September because it had been working so well. Immediately the strength of these patrols was reduced, submarine attacks and piratical incidents began taking place once more. Merchant vessels belonging to American, British, Dutch, French and Panamanian owners were either torpedoed or intercepted in a hectic twenty-day period beginning on 11 January 1938, culminating on 31 January when an unidentified submarine without warning attacked and sank the British ship *Endymion* bound for Cartagena with a cargo of coal. Ten lives were lost in this latest act of callous terrorism on the high seas, including the Swedish non-intervention observer on board.[102] Apart from strengthening the naval patrols once more, Eden now sought approval from his French and Italian ministerial contemporaries for the implementation of far more punitive rules of engagement for their warships in the Mediterranean. According to the British proposal, warships on patrol should be allowed to attack any submerged submarine found in their zones of responsibility. When another British ship the *Alcira* was attacked and sunk by two seaplanes off the coast of Barcelona on 4 February, Eden's patience with Franco reached its lowest ebb yet. Threats of retaliatory action by the British and French, however, served to curtail the submarine menace for the rest of the year but did little to restrain the Nationalist surface fleet and air force from continuing to interfere with ships that were engaged in trading with the Republican authorities much to the consternation of ship owners and governments alike. Occasionally, however, the Nationalists didn't get it all their own way. At midnight on 5–6 March the Nationalist fleet was proceeding past Cartagena without any German or Italian escorts when it came under a surprise attack from two Republican cruisers and three of their destroyers. Using their torpedoes to deadly effect, the Republican destroyers hit and blew up the cruiser *Baleares* before stealing away undetected from the scene of their triumph.[103]

While the Spanish Civil War stole the headlines in Europe during 1937, the situation in Asia was dominated by the non-declared Sino-Japanese War, which began with a small incident at the Marco Polo Bridge situated not far from Peking on the evening of 7 July and developed progressively into one of the most ferocious and pitiless struggles of the entire twentieth century. Using a slight pretext for the opening of hostilities, much as they had done over the Mukden

Incident, the Japanese set out to conquer the Chinese mainland and establish control over all forms of coastal and riverine traffic in Chinese waters. By the middle of August they had opened a major air, land and sea offensive against Shanghai and had begun bombing the city of Nanking some two hundred kilometres up the Yangtze River. Shortly afterwards the Japanese announced that they intended to impose a naval blockade of the entire Chinese coastline from Sanhaikwan on the Manchurian border to Swatow in the south. According to the IJN, all Chinese ships would be subject to its restrictions and while foreign vessels were not to be targeted for action, the Japanese reserved the right to verify the identity of every vessel sailing in the disputed area.[104]

News that the Japanese invasion was spreading was particularly unwelcome to the international community in China. It placed the principal actors in something of a dilemma since none of those with significant trading interests to protect on the mainland wished to see the Japanese gain at their expense and yet the overwhelming majority remained equally anxious to avoid offending them if they still could. Not all subscribed to this ethos, however. Indeed, of all those powers still heavily involved in China, the British were by far the most capricious. Unconvinced by the merits of Chamberlain's European appeasement policy and unwilling to accept the notion of 'imperial overstretch', Eden, at the Foreign Office, was ready to strike out on his own elsewhere. Seeing distinct advantages accruing to the United Kingdom if it was able to forge a new dynamic relationship with the Americans in the Far East, he spent an increasing amount of time during the autumn and early winter of 1937–38 trying to persuade the Roosevelt administration that the two governments should work together to contain the burgeoning strength of the Japanese military in China and the Pacific. In striving to make the 'Singapore Strategy' a viable concept rather than a hostage to fortune by linking it to close Anglo-American naval co-operation, Eden sought to show the totalitarian states that the democracies were not going to be pushed around and were capable of standing up for themselves. Convincing the Americans to abandon their neutrality legislation and adopt a forward policy in the Western Pacific, however, was always likely to prove difficult, if not impossible, to orchestrate. Despite individual incidents of bravado and concerted acts of violence from the Japanese, President Roosevelt stopped short of abandoning congressional isolationism and embracing interventionism much to Eden's chagrin. In the end, therefore, the British foreign secretary's extravagant gestures came to naught and his anti-appeasement policy became yet another 'what might have been' of history.[105]

As war engulfed both Spain and China in 1937, a new wave of competitive naval building was set in motion around the world. Despite the experience of the First World War, all seven of the principal naval powers remained obsessed with the power of the capital ship and were committed to laying down ever more powerful units in their building programmes. In the UK the case for a new standard of naval strength had been forcefully made by the Admiralty and the Defence Requirements Sub-Committee of the Cabinet from 1935 onwards but resisted with even greater vigour by the Treasury who had ensured that the

Royal Navy wouldn't get all the items on its wish list. Nonetheless, it would get to build the King George V class of battleship – a somewhat heavier, faster class of five warships than the Nelson class that had preceded them in 1927.[106] These five modern ships could reach a top speed of 28 knots when operational at over 42,000 tons, but the decision to carry ten 14-inch (355mm) guns as their main armament (rather than 15-inch or 16-inch) meant that their offensive potential was less than three existing battleship classes (Queen Elizabeth, Royal Sovereign and Nelson) as well as the Hood class of battlecruiser that pre-dated the Washington Conference![107] Approval was also given for the laying down in 1937 of three ships of the Illustrious class of fleet carrier.[108] These were unique because they each had a fully armoured hangar – the first of its kind in the world. When operational in 1940–41 these carriers displaced a little over 29,000 tons, but for all of their protection they only carried 33 aircraft – an obvious shortcoming unless these carriers were going to be used by the Admiralty on missions where they could be accompanied by strong numbers of land-based aircraft. In order to increase her aircraft complement, a fourth ship (*Indomitable*) was built to different specifications but roughly similar displacement. By yielding some of her armour, a second hangar could be built and a larger flight deck could be created to accommodate the extra dozen planes that the only ship of this new class of fleet carrier was able to take with her on operational duty.[109]

Across the Atlantic the Americans, who were still working to the restrictions of the London Naval Treaty, used the allowance left over after the laying down of the first two ships of their Yorktown class to create their new carrier *Wasp*. At 14,700 tons, she was basically a modified and slightly improved *Ranger* with an increased cruising range of 12,500km at 15 knots, a top speed of 29.5 knots, and an aircraft capability of 76.[110] As far as the conventional capital ship was concerned, the General Board had been thinking of developing a new battleship since 1928. After drawing up no less than seventy-seven designs for this new class, with major changes demanded in displacement and armament to reflect what was going on in new construction elsewhere, the keel of the *North Carolina* was finally laid on 27 October 1937. Bristling with a total of fifty-seven pieces of ordnance, including a main battery of nine 16-inch (406mm) guns, *North Carolina* and her sister ship *Washington* were each given substantial armoured protection so that they could absorb significant punishment if they found themselves caught up in a long-range duel with enemy battleships. This caused a weight problem that was only partly alleviated by welding roughly 30% of the ship and riveting the rest of it. When at deep load the two ships of this class displaced over 44,300 tons and their 4-shaft General Electric turbines were capable of producing 115,000 shaft horse power (shp) and a top speed of 27.5 knots. Although *North Carolina* was eventually commissioned on 9 April 1941, she encountered severe vibration while on her trials and it took until 10 June 1942 to begin her tour of duty in the Pacific theatre.[111]

Although the signatories to the latest London Naval Treaty had reached substantial agreement on the qualitative shape of navies in the years to come, only time would tell whether or not the other four major naval powers would fall into line with them. Indeed it soon became clear in this new era of competitive naval building that the Japanese were intent on establishing a class of battleship that would greatly exceed the 35,000 ton limit agreed to at London in March 1936. They were to be as good as their word with the development of the two super-battleships *Yamato* and *Musashi* which were laid down in late 1937 and early 1938 respectively, both of which eventually exceeded their design specifications displacing a prodigious 71,659 tons when operational at deep load.[112] While the Germans, Italians and Soviets were clearly committed to new capital ship building programmes, it was hoped initially that none might breach the treaty limit, even though all would be wary of the position adopted by their potential rivals on these matters.[113] This hope soon died. Both ships of the new Bismarck class of battleship (*Bismarck* and *Tirpitz*) exceeded 41,000 tons standard displacement and 50,000 tons when at deep load. When the Italians launched two of the four ships of the Littorio class (*Littorio* and *Vittorio Veneto*) in the summer of 1937 and laid down their two sister ships (*Impero* and *Roma*) in the following year all were just a little shy of 41,000 tons. Not to be outdone, the Soviets designed the three ships of the Sovyetskiy Soyuz class from 1938 onwards to be 59,150 tons each, but once the Second World War broke out none of them were completed.[114]

Not all were oblivious to the lessons of recent history, however, as was evident in the concentration on submarine development in both the Italian and Soviet navies and the installation of heavy anti-aircraft armament on escort vessels and some destroyers in the Royal Navy. Providing the financial outlay for naval rearmament was, of course, one thing, but ensuring efficiency in building the new ships was quite another. In this respect, the French had much to learn from their Italian neighbours. While shipyard delays were relatively commonplace in France, the Italians managed to deliver new vessels with commendable ingenuity and dispatch.[115]

Although the British government and its military advisors were still apt to see Italy – the latest nation to leave the League of Nations – as the weakest link in the newly expanded Anti-Comintern Pact, few doubted that it remained a disruptive influence in the Iberian peninsula and posed an actual, as distinct from potential, threat to the commercial interests of those democratic states that were using the Mediterranean trade routes. In an effort to take them out of the strategic equation in the early months of 1938, therefore, Prime Minister Chamberlain was prepared to play on the vanity of Mussolini and his fascist ministers by offering to establish a new diplomatic accord with them that would include, controversially, the granting of de jure recognition of their conquest of Abyssinia. While this latest initiative caused ructions in British political circles and did precious little to minimise the external threat posed by the Italians in Europe, both Chamberlain and the British Chiefs of Staff felt that the risk was worth taking, particularly in the light of the forced union of Austria and Germany in the Anschluss of 12 March 1938. Since Mussolini had lent his tacit support to Hitler's annexation of Austria, the rationale for this policy of appeasement – presumably a type of insurance policy – seems a trifle odd to say the least. Nonetheless, the new Anglo-Italian pact of friendship was signed in April

1938 and became a by-word for futility within a few weeks as Mussolini eagerly played host to his Axis partner Hitler in May and unveiled a repressive racial policy, with which the Nazis could readily identify, a mere couple of months later.[116]

By the late summer of 1938, the German nationalist policy of *lebensraum* – the much sought after 'living space' for the new Germanic Empire – had brought Europe to the brink of war. As politicians and the service chiefs braced themselves for what looked like an inevitable clash between Germany and Czechoslovakia over the fate of the border region of the Sudetenland, the continent was rescued from war at virtually the last minute by the egregious settlement reached at the diplomatic gathering in Munich of Hitler, Mussolini, Chamberlain and Edouard Daladier, the French prime minister, in the early hours of 30 September.[117] Although war was barely averted on this occasion, it did not take long for the euphoria to wear off and disillusionment to set in. Within a few weeks intelligence reports from Germany indicated that Hitler was furious that he had been prevented from crushing the Czechs and that he was ready to repudiate the Munich Settlement when the time was right.[118] Appeasement had not, therefore, changed any entrenched attitudes and it had merely bought a few months' grace before the next act in the drama was set in motion. After an all too familiar pattern of an orchestrated press campaign laced with diplomatic threats and intimidation, the Czech President Hacha was eventually forced, under the baleful influence of the Nazis, to sign away his country's independence on 15 March 1939. This act demonstrated to the world at large that Germany simply was not content with its territorial acquisitions and would now seek to take issue with the government in Warsaw over the existence of the highly controversial Polish Corridor – another legacy of the much-vilified Treaty of Versailles – the stain of which Hitler had pledged to remove.[119]

Hitler had already spoken to the leading members of his General Staff on this theme sixteen months before. At this meeting in the Reich Chancellery in Berlin on 5 November 1937 he sketched out three possible military scenarios that could arise from a future reorientation of German foreign policy towards territorial expansion at the expense of the non-Aryan nations in Eastern Europe. Hitler had accurately predicted that the Nazi creed of *lebensraum* might only be finally obtained by military threats or actual territorial conquest. He returned to the same theme once again in conversation with Admiral Dr. Erich Raeder, the C-in-C of the Kriegsmarine, in late May 1938.[120] By then he seems to have convinced himself that a future military confrontation with the British and the French was likely within a few years and that the pace of German re-armament would have to be quickened to reflect this probability. Raeder was instructed to increase the rate of battleship and U-boat construction so that the Germans would be able to take advantage of any war that might break out with the democracies in three to four years' time. Time was evidently not on Raeder's side. He was later to claim in his memoirs that he viewed the prospect of war with the Royal Navy before 1944 at the earliest as being 'completely unrealistic'.[121] Nonetheless, the unsettled nature of European affairs was to prove to be the inspiration for the cherished *Ziel Plan* (Target Plan) for naval construction that Raeder and the German Naval High Command (Oberkommando der Marine [OKM]) devised in late 1938. Their goal was to build up the Kriegsmarine into an astonishingly powerful naval force exceeding 1 million tons of surface warships spearheaded by seventeen massive capital ships and with an accompanying U-boat fleet of approximately 200,000 tons.[122] Any premature disclosure of the existence of the Z Plan would, of course, prove to be the kiss of death for the Anglo-German Naval Agreement, but that was already in terminal decline and didn't survive long after the Czech coup of March 1939. Hitler chose to administer the coup de grâce to both the Naval Agreement and the Non-Aggression Pact with Poland on the same day (28 April) that he gave one of his most impassioned speeches to the Reichstag, ridiculing Roosevelt and his request for an agreement on peace and disarmament. This looked like an ominous development from the outset and it didn't disappoint those who judged it to be so.[123]

In providing guarantees of assistance to Poland, Romania and Greece, the British and French governments published an intentional warning to the German government to respect the territorial sovereignty of the Polish state or face the consequences. In other words, there could no second Munich conference to settle the problem of the Polish Corridor. Despite the steely conviction shown belatedly by the democracies in confronting totalitarian excess in Europe, the news of Franco's victory at Madrid at the end of March and Mussolini's cynical attack on Albania in April suggested that the military tide was flowing strongly in favour of fascism on the continent and that appeasement as a political concept had utterly failed to make the world a safer place to live in or to discourage violent and aggressive political leaders from intimidating their weaker national or foreign opponents. When the Pact of Steel was announced in May linking Germany and Italy in an offensive and defensive military treaty, the signal for war over Poland looked to have been hoisted.[124]

If war was to break out, the main naval protagonists were in a far from secure position in 1939. Despite the utopian nature of the Z Plan, the reality was that the ten-year gestation period had hardly begun. Raeder's Z Plan had been overtaken by events and was now the stuff of fiction and wishful thinking. With the spectre of war fast approaching, Raeder was now forced to revise his priorities when it came to new construction. Battleships and U-boats were to be given top billing, followed by heavy cruisers and only then by aircraft carriers and light cruisers.[125]

In the case of the Royal Navy the re-armament programme had also oscillated from one level to the next in the 1930s, lurching from that which the Treasury felt the UK could barely afford (the so-called DRC Fleet) to that which the Admiralty wished to have (the New Standard of Naval Strength) before settling for a modified new standard which was a compromise between the two. Quite apart from its new building programme, the Admiralty was forced to modernise some of its ageing capital ship fleet. This meant that three of the fifteen capital ships, the battleships *Queen Elizabeth* and *Valiant*, and the battlecruiser *Renown*, were being modernised and were out of action from 1937 until the summer of 1939. Of the rest of the fleet two other battleships, *Malaya* and *Royal Oak*, were only partly modernised and four of the Royal Sovereign class (*Ramillies*, *Revenge*, *Resolution* and *Royal Sovereign*) were long past their best and verging on the obsolescent, if not actually meeting that description.[126]

As Hitler's territorial intentions became transparent in the weeks that followed, the combination of the French government's dithering and the Chamberlain administration's brooding suspicion of communism was sufficient to prevent a wide-ranging military alliance being fashioned between the democratic governments of Paris and London and that of Stalin's totalitarian regime in Moscow.[127] Into the diplomatic void left by the inept handling of this issue by the hesitant democracies strode a pragmatic Hitler intent on seizing his chance to divide his enemies and keep them weaker than they otherwise would have been had they been able to devise an effective military treaty between them. Unpredictably shrewd, Hitler encouraged Joachim von Ribbentrop, his foreign minister, to make overtures to the Soviet Union for the avoidance of hostilities between Berlin and Moscow and the formation of a non-aggression pact between them that would give both parties significant advantages in Europe. It made little political or ideological sense since Hitler's visceral hatred for communism was well known and documented as was Stalin's for National Socialism. Furthermore, it contradicted both the spirit and letter of the Anti-Comintern Pact which he had forged with both Japan and Italy. Despite its inconsistency, the Nazi–Soviet Pact, unveiled to the incredulous world on 23 August 1939, did allow Hitler crucial breathing space to further his ambitions in Western and Central Europe without having to worry about any intervention from the USSR in the war against Poland that the Führer was determined to start within a few days. This was a priceless opportunity that would ensure Poland's swift defeat and leave the Western democracies more vulnerable than ever. In order to gain these advantages Hitler was prepared to allow the Soviet Union a free hand in the eastern part of Poland, throughout the Baltic States and in Finland as well. Hitler was wont to see this settlement as a temporary expedient – a loan that would be repaid with interest later on. It didn't mean that he became a lover of communism or an admirer of Stalin. Neither did it mean that his cherished concept of *lebensraum* would end on the banks of the River Vistula. For once Hitler was content to play a waiting game.[128]

If he thought his Soviet coup would overawe the Western democracies and deter them from extending more than platitudinous support for the Poles he was to be profoundly mistaken. Within days a renewal of the Anglo-French guarantee to Poland quashed that idea. He was soon to suffer another setback when his blustering and unreliable Axis partner, Mussolini, denied the mediatory role he craved, slithered away from active involvement in the coming war in favour of adopting a policy of non-belligerency favoured by the court and his senior ministers. It smacked of inglorious self-preservation and lacked the spirit of heroic virtue that the fascists supposedly tapped into. Hitler's contempt for the King of Italy and all those who had undermined Mussolini's position was heartfelt: 'The Italians are behaving just as they did in 1914.'[129]

In the last days of peace the naval forces on both sides of the Channel and North Sea began to ready themselves for future conflict. Spearheading the British offensive effort against the Kriegsmarine would be the Royal Navy's Home Fleet which was based at Scapa Flow in the Orkney Islands. It contained the aircraft carrier *Ark Royal*, the five battleships *Nelson*, *Ramillies*, *Rodney*, *Royal Oak* and *Royal Sovereign*, and the two battlecruisers *Hood* and *Repulse*, along with the heavy cruiser *Norfolk*, fourteen light cruisers, the anti-aircraft (A.A.) cruiser *Calcutta*, seventeen destroyers and twenty-one submarines. Apart from its other carrier, *Furious*, which was based at Rosyth, the Home Fleet would soon welcome back the battlecruiser *Renown*, which was coming to the end of her latest refit by the end of September. In the Humber Force, operating off the Lincolnshire port of Grimsby, were another two light cruisers and eight 'J' class destroyers; while the Channel Force based at Portland contained the carriers *Courageous* and *Hermes*, two more battleships *Resolution* and *Revenge*, a couple of light cruisers, along with the A.A. cruiser *Cairo* and nine 'A' class destroyers. Around the southern coast extending from Dover in the east to Milford Haven in Pembrokeshire in the west were scattered over fifty more destroyers. These figures did not take into account the warships which the Admiralty had deployed elsewhere to look after British interests further afield.[130]

Apart from whatever the British could muster in their own waters, the French could also rely upon a capital ship fleet that was fairly potent in its own right. As a result of a series of Anglo-French staff talks that had been held in various stages over the past three years, *la Marine française* (the French Navy) knew exactly what was expected of it and where it would be deployed. While the bulk of its fleet would be deployed in the Mediterranean, it was committed to providing a raiding force that would assist in the protection of Allied convoys in the Western Approaches and defend British trade in the Bay of Biscay as well. In order to do this it had two of its modern battleships (*Dunkerque* and *Strasbourg*) based at Brest along with the sole aircraft carrier *Béarn*, its seaplane tender *Commandante Teste*, three light cruisers and eight super-destroyers. In addition, Brest was home to two older and less powerful battleships (*Courbet* and *Paris*), four super-destroyers (a variant that made them virtually light cruisers), twelve regular fleet destroyers, a dozen submarines and a handful of other lighter craft. Two fine modern battleships *Jean Bart* and *Richelieu*, each of 35,000 tons and boasting eight 15-inch (381mm) guns, were also under construction in the Atlantic dockyards of St. Nazaire and Brest respectively. Once they were completed in 1940 the French were confident that they would be a real handful for any power seeking to challenge them. Further along the coast Dunkirk played host to the French command centre for the English Channel and North Sea. This was served by its four submarines and a mix of lighter surface vessels ranging from sloops and torpedo boats to sub-chasers and a minelayer and three naval air squadrons. In the Mediterranean at the Algerian naval complex of Oran and Mers-el-Kebir there were a further three modernised battleships (*Bretagne*, *Lorraine* and *Provence*) and nine fleet destroyers, while at Toulon another six heavy cruisers and nine super-destroyers were under the orders of the French chief of naval operations, Admiral François Darlan. Under the Mediterranean command of Admiral Jean Pierre Esteva and scattered around the ports of Bizerte, Casablanca, Oran and Toulon were another three light cruisers, ten super-destroyers, five fleet destroyers, a seaplane carrier, forty-five submarines, thirteen naval air squadrons and a handful of sloops, torpedo boats and sundry other craft.[131]

Facing this formidable defensive line, Großadmiral (Grand Admiral) Raeder, at the head of the Kriegsmarine, could only muster a total of two fast battleships (*Scharnhorst* and *Gneisenau*), two obsolescent battleships (*Schlesien* and *Schleswig-Holstein*), the three pocket battleships *Deutschland*, *Admiral Graf Spee* and *Admiral Scheer*, three heavy cruisers (*Blücher*, *Hipper*, together with the *Prinz Eugen*, which was nearing completion), five light cruisers, seventeen destroyers and a total of fifty-seven U-boats.[132] Owing to the lack of submarine construction in the years immediately preceding the war, however, Kapitän Zur See (Captain) and Führer der U-boote (Flag Officer of the U-boat arm) Karl Dönitz initially had only twenty-two ocean-going U-boats at his immediate disposal on 1 September 1939.[133] What they lacked in ocean-going vessels the Germans sought to make up for by commissioning thirty 250-ton (Type II) submarines which could be used in coastal waters in and around the North Sea and the Baltic. Eighteen of these squat craft (known euphemistically as ducks) were ready by 1 September.[134] While neither Raeder nor Dönitz were optimistic about the coming struggle, both acknowledged that they would use their limited resources to wage war against British commerce and the vital sea communications upon which this trade was based.[135] As Correlli Barnett points out, however, numbers are not everything and may on occasion prove to be deceptive. What looked like an unequal contest on paper did not turn out that way in practice.[136]

Sensing that the forthcoming attack on Poland might well lead to war with both Britain and France, the German Seekriegsleitung (Naval War Staff) had already dispatched five of these U-boats from Kiel and nine more from Wilhelmshaven on 19 August with orders to take up position in the North Atlantic and await further orders. Over the next few days four more U-boats were sent forth on the same mission. By 1 September Dönitz had deployed seventeen of his smaller Type II U-boats in the North Sea, had ten Type VII and six Type VIIB vessels in a grid system in the Atlantic and all five of his Type IX models lurking in Spanish waters. What remained of his serviceable submarine fleet was either keeping station in the waters of the Heligoland Bight or in the Baltic. Getting the U-boat fleet out to sea was a sensible precaution given the likelihood that the Royal Navy would impose a close blockade of German ports and naval bases if war broke out in the aftermath of the attack on Poland.[137] This growing probability had convinced Raeder that other German warships, such as the pocket battleships *Admiral Graf Spee* and *Deutschland*, should be readied for action and they were deployed accordingly in the third week of August – the former to Pernambuco in the South Atlantic and the latter to a position south of Greenland. As the countdown to the attack on Poland proceeded, all German merchant vessels had been informed by wireless telegraphy on 27 August to try and get home, or to ports of friendly or neutral states, by the end of the month.[138]

While the Germans were putting their naval and mercantile craft on notice that a dramatic change in international relations was likely to take place within a matter of days, the British had also begun responding to the accelerating German–Polish crisis in mid-to-late August. As the last days of peace ebbed away, so preparations for a future war at sea were mounted by RAF Coastal Command, British merchant shipping became subject to Admiralty control and units of the Home Fleet were ordered to assume a patrol of the seas between Iceland and Norway in order to search for any German merchant vessels that might be trying to reach their home ports before the balloon went up and the European world was plunged into war again.[139]

Notes

1 Both Niall Ferguson, *The pity of war* (London: Allen Lane, The Penguin Press, 1998), pp.290–303, 339–66, 436–39, 448–57, and Paul Kennedy, *The rise and fall of the great powers* (New York: Vintage Books, 1989), pp.256–74, explore the costs of that war. For contrasting personal experiences of it, see Paul Fussell, *The Great War and modern memory* (Oxford: OUP, 2000), and Martin Stephen, *The price of pity: poetry, history and myth in the Great War* (London: Leo Cooper, 1996).

2 Sally Marks, *The ebbing of European ascendancy. An international history of the world, 1914–1945* (Oxford: OUP, 2002); Zara Steiner, *The lights that failed: European international history, 1919–1933* (Oxford: OUP, 2005).

3 Zara Steiner, 'The war, the peace and the international state system', in Jay Winter, Geoffrey Parker and Mary R. Habeck (eds), *The Great War and the twentieth century* (New Haven, Conn: Yale University Press, 2000), pp.263–98; Kennedy, *Rise and fall of the great powers*, pp.275–343.

4 Despite evidence to the contrary, old doctrinal attachments withstood the challenge of World War I for some time to come. Professor Herwig encapsulates this situation perfectly by observing: 'Mahan remained the prophet and *The Influence of Sea Power upon History* the Bible'. Holger H. Herwig, 'Innovation ignored: the submarine problem – Germany, Britain, and the United States, 1919–39', in Williamson Murray and Allan R. Millett (eds), *Military innovation in the interwar period* (Cambridge: CUP, 1998), pp.227–64.

5 Arguably the most effective of the British first sea lords in the inter-war period, Lord Chatfield was not persuaded that the day of the capital ship was over. Writing in his autobiography in 1947, he referred to it as the queen on the chessboard. In his opinion, once the queen was lost the game was over. By 1947, of course, the capital ship classification had widened to include the aircraft carrier. *It might happen again, Vol.2, The navy and defence* (London: Heinemann, 1947), pp.100–101. Proponents of air power such as the Italian military theorist General Giulio Douhet were not convinced. He thought that the fate of future naval wars would be determined by aircraft rather than capital ships. Brian R. Sullivan, 'Italian naval power and the Washington Disarmament Conference of 1921–22', in Erik Goldstein and John Maurer (eds), *The Washington Conference, 1921–22: naval rivalry, East Asian stability and the road to Pearl Harbor* (London: Frank Cass, 1994), pp.220–48; Paul Kennedy, *The rise and fall of British naval mastery* (London: Penguin Books, 2004), pp.281–82; Lawrence Sondhaus, *Navies of Europe: 1815–2002* (London: Longman, 2002), p.208.

6 John Brooks, *Dreadnought gunnery and the Battle of Jutland: the question of fire control* (Abingdon, Oxon: Routledge, 2006).

7 Paul G. Halpern, *A naval history of World War I* (Annapolis, Md: NIP, 1994); Robert K. Massie, *Castles of steel: Britain, Germany, and the winning of the Great War at sea* (New York: Random House, 2003).
8 Apart from its reluctance to employ convoy because of its overtly defensive nature, the Admiralty felt it didn't have sufficient escort vessels to defend the vast number of merchant ships that were constantly underway to and from British waters. It was a tragic mistake that would cost millions of tons of shipping before convoy was belatedly adopted in 1917. Ferguson, *The pity of war*, pp.282–83; Halpern, *Naval history of World War I*, pp.69–70, 75–76, 78, 82, 84, 86–88, 90, 95, 204, 207–8, 343–44, 351–57, 360–65, 369, 372, 375–76, 378–80, 385, 392–98, 400, 405–6, 417–21, 426–27, 431–32, 435–40; Richard Hough, *The Great War at sea 1914–1918* (Oxford: OUP, 1983), pp.306–9, 314; Massie, *Castles of steel*, pp.728–33, 737–40, 747.
9 Patrick Beesly, *Room 40: British naval intelligence 1914–18* (London: Hamish Hamilton, 1982); John Ferris, 'The road to Bletchley Park: the British experience with signals intelligence, 1892–1945', *Intelligence and National Security*, Vol.17, No.1 (2002): 61–62.
10 Admiral Sir Arthur 'Tug' Wilson, a former first sea lord, was typical of those who considered the submarine as being 'underhand, unfair and damned un-English'. Wilson was joined in his condemnation of and loathing for the submarine by two of the leading British delegates to the Washington Conference: Admiral Sir David Beatty, the first sea lord and chief of naval staff, and Lord Lee, the first lord of the Admiralty. Patrick Beesly, *Room 40: British naval intelligence 1914–18* (London: Hamish Hamilton, 1982), p.87; Sondhaus, *Navies of Europe*, p.207; Malcolm H. Murfett, 'Look back in anger: The Western Powers and the Washington Conference of 1921–22', in B.J.C. McKercher (ed.), *Arms limitation and disarmament: Restraints in war, 1899–1939* (Westport, Conn: Praeger, 1992), pp.96–98. For an examination of the contribution made by the submarine to the British war effort, see Edwyn Gray, *A damned un-English weapon: the story of British submarine warfare 1914–18* (London: Seeley, Service & Co., 1971). For what the powers did with this knowledge, see Herwig, 'Innovation ignored: the submarine problem', in Murray and Millett (eds), *Military innovation in the interwar period*, pp.227–64; David Henry, 'British submarine policy, 1918–39', in Bryan Ranft (ed.), *Technical change and British naval policy 1860–1939* (London: Hodder & Stoughton, 1977), pp.80–107.
11 Christopher M. Bell, *The Royal Navy, seapower and strategy between the wars* (Stanford, Ca: Stanford University Press, 2000); Edward S. Miller, *War plan ORANGE* (Annapolis, Md: NIP, 1991); Joseph Moretz, *The Royal Navy and the capital ship in the interwar period: an operational perspective* (London: Frank Cass, 2002), pp.1–31; Malcolm H. Murfett, '"Are we ready?" The development of American and British naval strategy, 1922–39', in John B. Hattendorf and Robert S. Jordan (eds), *Maritime strategy and the balance of power: Britain and America in the twentieth century* (Basingstoke, Hants: Macmillan, 1989), pp.214–42; Jürgen Rohwer and Mikhail S. Monakov, *Stalin's ocean-going fleet: Soviet naval strategy and shipbuilding programmes 1935–1953* (London: Frank Cass, 2001), pp.3–109; James J. Sadkovich, *The Italian Navy in World War II* (Westport, Conn: Greenwood Press, 1994), pp.1–44; Jon Tetsuro Sumida, '"The best laid plans": the development of British battle-fleet tactics, 1919–42', *The International History Review*, Vol.XIV, No.4 (1992): 681–700; Milan Vego, 'On major naval operations', *Naval War College Review*, Vol.60, No.2 (2007): 94–126; Baer, *One hundred years of sea power*, pp.83, 89, 97, 106, 111, 136, 143; David C. Evans and Mark R. Peattie, *Kaigun: strategy, tactics, and technology in the Imperial Japanese Navy, 1887–1941* (Annapolis, Md: NIP, 1997), pp.201–23, 238–98, 353–90, 411–86, 492–517.
12 Douglas V. Smith, *Carrier battles: command decision in harm's way* (Annapolis, Md: NIP, 2006), pp.7–38; Evans and Peattie, *Kaigun*, pp.299–352.
13 Alan Beyerchen, 'From radio to radar: interwar military adaptation to technological change in Germany, the United Kingdom, and the United States', in Murray and Millett (eds), *Military innovation in the interwar period*, pp.265–99; J.F. Coales, 'The

origins and development of radar in the Royal Navy, 1935–45, with particular reference to decimetric gunnery equipments'; J.S. Shayler, 'Royal Navy metric warning radar, 1935–45'; C.A. Cochrane, 'Development of naval warning and tactical radar operating in the 10-cm band, 1940–45', in F.A. Kingsley (ed.), *The development of radar equipments for the Royal Navy, 1935–45* (Basingstoke, Hants: Macmillan, 1995), pp.5–66, 133–83, 185–275.

14 Studies on British cryptology in the inter-war period are well served by the prolific John Ferris. See his *Intelligence and strategy: selected essays* (Abingdon: Routledge, 2005), pp.138–80; and his articles 'Whitehall's black chamber: British cryptology and the Government Code and Cypher School, 1919–29', *Intelligence and National Security*, Vol.2, No.1 (1987): 54–91, and 'The road to Bletchley Park': 53–84. Arguably the best and most comprehensive study of the science elsewhere still remains that of David Kahn, *The codebreakers: the comprehensive history of secret communication from ancient times to the internet* (New York: Scribner, 1996), pp.266–97, 351–512, 561–671. For individual studies, see Anthony Adamthwaite, 'French military intelligence and the coming of war 1935–39', in Christopher Andrew and Jeremy Noakes (eds), *Intelligence and international relations 1900–1945* (Exeter: Exeter University Publications, 1987), pp.191–208; J.W.M. Chapman, 'Japanese intelligence, 1918–45: a suitable case for treatment', in ibid., pp.145–89; J.W.M. Chapman, 'No final solution: a survey of cryptanalytical capabilities of German military agencies, 1926–35', *Intelligence and National Security*, Vol.1 No.1 (1986): 13–47; Edward Drea, 'Reading each other's mail: Japanese communication intelligence 1920–41', *The Journal of Military History*, Vol.55 No.2. (1991): 185–205; Ken Kotani, 'Could Japan read Allied signal traffic? Japanese codebreaking and the advance into French Indo-China, September 1940', *Intelligence and National Security*, Vol.20, No.2 (2005): 304–20; Victor Madeira, '"Because I don't trust him, we are friends": signals intelligence and the reluctant Anglo-Soviet embrace, 1919–24', *Intelligence and National Security*, Vol.19, No.1 (2004): 29–51; Frank B. Rowlett, *The story of Magic: memoirs of an American cryptologic pioneer* (Laguna Hills, Ca: Aegean Park Press, 1998); Jean Stengers, 'Enigma, the French, the Poles and the British, 1931–40', in Christopher Andrew and David Dilks (eds), *The missing dimension* (Basingstoke: Macmillan, 1985), pp.126–37.

15 For a fascinating discussion on the limits to spending in the post-war world and in particular the cost-growth of both battleships and aircraft carriers as well as the cost-effectiveness of the submarine, see Philip Pugh, *The cost of seapower: the influence of money on naval affairs from 1815 to the present day* (London: Conway Maritime Press, 1986), pp.6–31, 46–59, 152–97, 224–49. See also Paul Kennedy, *The realities behind diplomacy: background influences on British external policy, 1865–1980* (London: George Allen & Unwin, 1981), pp.145–51; Ferguson, *The pity of war*, pp.322–38; 395–432.

16 Roger Dingman, *Power in the Pacific: the origins of naval arms limitation* (Chicago: University of Chicago Press, 1976), pp.122–35, 178–95; Josephus Daniels, *The Wilson era, Vol. I: years of peace 1910–1917* (Chapel Hill, N.C.: University of North Carolina Press, 1946), pp.326–29; George W. Baer, *One hundred years of sea power* (Stanford, Ca: Stanford University Press, 1994), pp.59–63.

17 Robert W. Love, Jr., *History of the U.S. Navy: 1775–1941*(Harrisburg, Pa: Stackpole Books, 1992), pp.524–40; Murfett, 'Look back in anger', pp.83–103; Sondhaus, *Navies of Europe*, pp.204–12.

18 Thomas H. Buckley, 'The Icarus factor: the American pursuit of myth in naval arms control, 1921–36'; Joel Blatt, 'France and the Washington Conference'; and Brian R. Sullivan, 'Italian naval power and the Washington Disarmament Conference of 1921–22', in Goldstein and Maurer (eds), *The Washington Conference*, pp.124–46, 192–219; 220–48; Baer, *One hundred years*, pp.83–103.

19 Evans and Peattie, *Kaigun*, pp.191–98.

20 Although Hughes had proposed a ten-year naval building holiday in respect to capital ships, the British were allowed to build two new battleships (*Nelson* and *Rodney*)

in 1922 though both had to conform to the 35,000 tons standard for battleships laid down by the Washington Treaty. Both battleships were launched in 1925 and were completed in August and November 1927 respectively. They displaced 41,250 tons at extra deep load. Their two-shaft geared turbines and eight Admiralty three-drum boilers could generate 45,000 shaft horse power and a top speed of 23 knots. Although their main armament of nine 16-inch (406mm) guns caused problems initially, they were improved over time. Under the terms of the Washington agreement, the Admiralty had to scrap four of its older battleships (*Ajax, Centurion, King George V, Thunderer*) to make way for the new arrivals. All the naval powers were allowed to modernise their existing fleets of older vessels providing they didn't exceed the treaty quotas. Murfett, 'Look back in anger', pp.83–103; Alan Raven and John Roberts, *British battleships of World War Two: the development and technical history of the Royal Navy's battleships and battlecruisers from 1911 to 1946* (London: Arms and Armour Press, 1976), pp.107–45; Robert Gardiner (ed.), *Conway's all the world's fighting ships 1922–1946* (London: Conway Maritime Press, 1980), pp.2–4, 7–9, 14, 86–92, 167–69, 171–73, 218–20, 222, 255–57, 259–60, 280–84; Jordan, *Warships after Washington*, pp.74–107.

21 Robert W. Love, Jr. (ed.), *The Chiefs of Naval Operations* (Annapolis, Md: NIP, 1980), pp.28–31, 39–40, 44–45, 71–85; Murfett, 'Are we ready?', pp.214–42; John Ferris, '"It is our business in the Navy to command the seas": the last decade of British maritime supremacy, 1919–29', in Greg Kennedy and Keith Neilson (eds), *Far-flung lines: essays on imperial defence in honour of Donald Mackenzie Schurman* (London: Frank Cass, 1996), pp.124–70.

22 Ibid.; B.J.C. McKercher, 'The politics of naval arms limitation in Britain in the 1920s', in Goldstein and Maurer (eds), *The Washington Conference, 1921–22*, pp.35–59; Philip T. Rosen, 'The treaty navy, 1919–37', in Kenneth J. Hagan (ed.), *In peace and war: interpretation of American naval history, 1775–1978* (Westport, Conn: Greenwood Press, 1978), pp.221–36.

23 Evans and Peattie, *Kaigun*, pp.199–237; Keith Neilson, '"Unbroken thread": Japan, maritime power and British imperial defence, 1920–32', in Greg Kennedy (ed.), *British naval strategy east of Suez 1900–2000* (Abingdon, Oxon: Frank Cass, 2005), pp 62–89.

24 Murfett, 'Look back in anger', pp.84–88, 92–93; Sadao Asada, 'From Washington to London: the Imperial Japanese Navy and the politics of naval limitation, 1921–30', in Goldstein and Maurer (eds), *The Washington Conference, 1921–22*, pp.147–91.

25 Murfett, 'Reflections on an enduring theme: the "Singapore strategy" at sixty', in Brian Farrell and Sandy Hunter (eds), *Sixty years on: the fall of Singapore revisited* (Singapore: Eastern Universities Press, 2002), pp.9, 25; Greg Kennedy, 'The Royal Navy and imperial defence, 1919–56', in Greg Kennedy (ed.), *Imperial defence: the old world order 1856–1956* (Abingdon, Oxon: Routledge, 2008), pp.133–51.

26 Warren Cohen, 'American leaders and East Asia, 1931–38', in Akira Iriye and Warren Cohen (eds), *American, Chinese, and Japanese perspectives on wartime Asia 1931–1949* (Wilmington, Del: SR Books, 1990), pp.1–27; Dorothy Borg and Shumpei Okamoto (eds), *Pearl Harbor as history: Japanese-American relations 1931–1941* (New York: Columbia University Press, 1973), pp.25–52, 81–126, 197–223, 225–59.

27 Margaret Lamb and Nicholas Tarling, *From Versailles to Pearl Harbor: the origins of the Second World War in Europe and Asia* (Basingstoke: Palgrave, 2001), pp.21–70.

28 Dan Van der Vat, *The grand scuttle: the sinking of the German fleet at Scapa Flow in 1919* (Edinburgh: Birlinn, 2007); Holger H. Herwig, *'Luxury' fleet: the Imperial German Navy 1888–1918* (London: George Allen & Unwin, 1980), pp.253–57; Stephen Roskill, *Naval policy between the wars, vol. I 1919–1929* (London: Collins, 1968), pp.92–96.

29 Allied naval intervention in the Russian Civil War covered several theatres of operations (Northern Russia, the Baltic, the Black Sea and Caspian Sea and also fitfully in the Far East) with a range of substantial forces in the period 1918–20. It began during the last months of the war in a bid to safeguard the military supplies

the Western Powers had provided for their Russian allies before the revolution had broken out and the Bolshevik rulers had decided to withdraw from the war. Thereafter, the intervention became a politico-military tool to assist the White counter-revolutionary forces in their vain bid to defeat the Bolsheviks. In what became a doleful story of overall failure for the Allies and the Whites and a resounding triumph for Trotsky and the Red Army, the naval aspects of this struggle deserve close scrutiny. While the Allied statesmen and their shore-based advisors far removed from the action often engaged in wishful thinking and paralysing indecision, those charged with the responsibility of putting their often oracular and confusing policies into action performed with considerable courage and resourcefulness. One need look no further than the role played by the smaller naval units, such as the shallow draught minesweepers that undertook a host of operations on the River Dvina and the coastal motor boats that recorded some remarkable coups in the Baltic. Of the latter, undoubtedly the most compelling was the sinking of the Russian light cruiser *Oleg* by CMB-4 on 16–17 June 1919 and the marauding attack in Kronstadt harbour on 17–18 August 1919 involving eight of these vessels in which the dreadnought (*Petropavlovsk*) and the old armoured cruiser (*Pamiat Azova*) were sunk and the pre-dreadnought *Andrei Pervozanny* was seriously damaged. See Michael Kettle, *Churchill and the Archangel fiasco: November 1918–July 1919* (London: Routledge, 1992), pp.38, 42, 101, 161, 168, 172–76, 178, 203–4, 232, 280–85, 295–96, 299–305, 334, 341, 346–48, 350–52, 355–57, 359–60, 363, 418, 446, 453–54, 461, 469–73, 475–82, 485–89, 495–96, 499, 501–3, 515–17, 520, 532–35, 541; Evan Mawdsley, *The Russian Civil War* (Boston, Mass: Allen & Unwin, 1987), pp.127–31, 143–44, 153–54, 156, 158–59, 166–68, 196, 198–200, 208, 214–15, 223–24, 227–28, 232, 239, 264, 266–67; Roskill, *Naval policy between the wars. Vol.I: 1919–1929* (London: Collins, 1968), pp.131–80.

30 Gunnar Åselius, *The rise and fall of the Soviet Navy in the Baltic, 1921–1941* (London: Frank Cass, 2005); Sergei G. Gorshkov, *Red star rising at sea* (Annapolis, Md: NIP, 1974), pp.60–75; Donald W. Mitchell, *A history of Russian and Soviet sea power* (London: André Deutsch, 1974), pp.355–76; Rohwer and Monakov, *Stalin's ocean-going fleet*, pp.6–109; J.N. Westwood, *Russian naval construction 1905–45* (Basingstoke: Macmillan, 1994), pp.126–228; Sondhaus, *Navies of Europe*, p.211.

31 For an interesting counterpoint to the usual interpretation of the Chanak crisis, see J. R. Ferris, 'Far too dangerous a gamble? Britain, intelligence and policy during the Chanak crisis, September–October 1922', *Diplomacy and Statecraft*, Vol.14, No.3 (2003): 139–84; and his 'Intelligence and diplomatic signalling during crises: the British experiences of 1877–78, 1922 and 1938', in Len Scott and R. Gerald Hughes, *Intelligence, crises and security: prospects and retrospects* (Abingdon, Oxon: Routledge, 2008), pp.29–33, 41.

32 Kenneth O. Morgan, *Consensus and disunity: the Lloyd George coalition government, 1918–1922* (Oxford: Clarendon Press, 1979), pp.141, 303, 318–36, 342, 346, 352–53, 355, 367; Roskill, *Naval policy, I*, pp.181–203; Geoffrey Till, 'Retrenchment, rethinking, revival, 1919–39', in J.R. Hill (ed.), *The Oxford illustrated history of the Royal Navy* (Oxford: OUP, 1995), pp.329–31; Eric Grove, *The Royal Navy since 1815: a new short history* (Basingstoke, Hants: Palgrave Macmillan, 2005), pp.152–54.

33 Mary Fulbrook, *History of Germany 1918–2000: the divided nation* (Oxford: Blackwell, 2002), pp.27–31; Ian Kershaw, *Hitler 1889–1936: hubris* (London: Allen Lane, The Penguin Press, 1998), pp.191–219.

34 Collective security was the ultimate principle of deterrence that would be invoked by the League against aggressive states who showed no sign of moderating their unacceptable behaviour towards their victims.

35 John Robert Ferris, *The evolution of British strategic policy, 1919–26* (Basingstoke, Hants: Macmillan, 1989), pp.142–89; Martin Gilbert, *A history of the twentieth century. Volume one: 1900–1933* (New York: William Morrow & Co., 1997), pp.686–88, 695–96, 743,

753–54, 769, 789, 823, 825; Jon Jacobson, *Locarno diplomacy: Germany and the West, 1925–1929* (Princeton, NJ: Princeton University Press, 1972); Donald Kagan and Frederick W. Kagan, *While America sleeps: self delusion, military weakness, and the threat to peace today* (New York: St. Martin's Press, 2000), pp.160–93; Sally Marks, *The illusion of peace: international relations in Europe, 1918–1933* (New York: St. Martin's Press, 1976), pp.60–107.
36 Gilbert, *A history of the twentieth century*, pp.712–14; Immanuel C.Y. Hsü, *The rise of modern China* 5th Edition (New York: OUP, 1995), pp.493–513; Peter Zarrow, *China in war and revolution, 1895–1949* (London: Routledge, 2005), pp.83–94, 145–69.
37 Hsü, *The rise of modern China*, pp.514–39; Zarrow, *China in war and revolution*, pp.230–47.
38 Arnold J. Toynbee (ed.), *Survey of international affairs 1926* (London: OUP, 1928), pp.306–20; Kemp Tolley, *Yangtze patrol: the U.S. Navy in China* (Annapolis, Md: NIP, 1971); pp.139–45; www.hmsfalcon.com/Wanhsien/Wangxian.htm.
39 Tolley, *Yangtze patrol*, pp.81–147, 177–78, 180–84, 206–7, 213, 220–22, 232; Toynbee (ed.), *Survey of international affairs 1926*, pp.316–17; R. Blake Dunnavent, *Brown water warfare: The U.S. Navy in riverine warfare and the emergence of a tactical doctrine, 1775–1970* (Gainesville, Fla: University Press of Florida, 2003), pp.103–9.
40 Carolyn J. Kitching, *Britain and the problem of international disarmament 1919–1934* (London: Routledge, 1999), pp.33–37, 115–35; Malcolm H. Murfett, 'Living in the past: a critical re-examination of the Singapore naval strategy, 1918–41', *War and Society*, Vol.xi, No.i (May 1993): 73–103.
41 Murfett, 'Are we ready?' pp.214–22.
42 Roger Burlingame, *General Billy Mitchell: champion of air defense* (Westport, Conn: Greenwood Press, 1978), pp.1–12, 121–24; Burke Davis, *The Billy Mitchell affair* (New York: Random House, 1967), pp.68–69, 72–74, 80, 88, 100–112, 116, 119, 121–28, 201, 235. Also contrast the opinion set out in Roskill, *Naval policy*, I, pp.247–48, with that of Baer, *One hundred years of sea power*, p.107.
43 Moretz, *The Royal Navy and the capital ship*, pp.46–64; Geoffrey Till, *Airpower and the Royal Navy, 1914–1945: a historical survey* (London: Jane's Publishing Co., 1979), pp.29–55 and his 'Air power and the battleship in the 1920s', in Ranft (ed.), *Technical change and British naval policy*, pp.108–22; Edward Warner, 'Douhet, Mitchell, Seversky: theories of air warfare', in Edward M. Earle (ed.) and with collaboration of Gordon A. Craig and Felix Gilbert, *Makers of modern strategy: military thought from Machiavelli to Hitler* (Princeton, NJ: Princeton University Press, 1971), pp.485–503.
44 Norman H. Gibbs, 'The naval conferences of the inter war years: a study of Anglo-American relations', *Naval War College Review*, 30 (1977): 50–63; Richard W. Fanning, 'The Coolidge conference of 1927: disarmament in disarray'; Marc Epstein, 'The historians and the Geneva naval conference', in McKercher, *Arms limitation and disarmament*, pp.105–27, 129–48; Christopher Hall, *Britain, America and arms control, 1921–37* (New York: St. Martin's Press, 1987), pp.36–54.
45 Technically the distinction between heavy and light cruisers was officially established by the London Naval Treaty of 1930. Light cruisers were those whose main armament could not exceed 6.1 inches (155mm). Gun calibre was the only consideration in this typology between classes of cruiser and had nothing to do with a cruiser's displacement tonnage. For example, the standard displacement of the US light cruisers, such as the Brooklyn (9,767 tons), Wichita (10,589 tons) and Cleveland (11,744 tons) classes was actually heavier than the heavy cruisers of the Pensacola (9,097 tons) and Northampton (9,006 tons) classes. There were instances of this in the ranks of the Royal Navy and the IJN too. See Gardiner (ed.), *Conway's all the world's fighting ships*, pp.26–36, 112–24, 186–92. Amongst the best of the books devoted to the cruisers of the leading naval powers of this period one should consult Norman Friedman, *U.S. cruisers: an illustrated design history* (London: Arms and Armour Press, 1985); Eric Lacroix and Linton Wells II, *Japanese cruisers of the Pacific War* (Annapolis, Md: NIP, 1997); Alan Raven and John Roberts, *British cruisers of World*

War Two (Annapolis, Md: NIP, 1980); and M.J. Whitley, *German cruisers of World War Two* (Annapolis, Md: NIP, 1987). For easy access to this subject, see Anthony Preston, *Cruisers: an illustrated history 1880–1980* (London: Arms and Armour Press, 1980).

46 Fleet destroyers grew heavier as the interwar period progressed. While the British 'A' and 'B' classes that were launched in 1929–30 were typically of 1,360 standard displacement tons, the 'J' and 'K' classes launched in 1938–39 were supposedly 1,690 tons but actually rose to 1,773 tons. When the Tribal class fleet destroyers were launched in 1937 they were designed as being 1,854 tons but actually reached 1,959 tons. When the Royal Navy launched the Hunt class of destroyer escorts in 1939–40 they were significantly smaller, being 1,000 tons standard displacement and only 1,450 at deep load. Gardiner (ed.), *Conway's all the world's fighting ships*, pp.37–46; Jordan, *Warships after Washington*, pp.262–85. Apart from the classic tomes on the subject by Norman Friedman – *U.S. destroyers: an illustrated design history* (Annapolis, Md: NIP, 2004) and *British destroyers and frigates: the Second World War and after* (London: Chatham Publishing, 2006) – a useful additional source on the role of destroyers over the years may be gauged from consulting Eric W. Osborne, *Destroyers: an illustrated history of their impact* (Santa Barbara, Ca: ABC-Clio, 2005), pp.69–115.

47 One of the singular advantages of the 6-inch gun was its higher rate of fire than the 8-inch gun that formed the main armament of the heavy cruiser. Friedman, *U.S. cruisers*, pp.111–16.

48 All ten vessels of the Omaha class came to be regarded as fast ships that were too lightly constructed and over armed to be of stellar use under all circumstances. Ultimately, the Brooklyn class (nine vessels) would be developed in the mid-to-late 1930s and the Cleveland class (twenty-nine vessels) in the 1940s as significant improvements on the earlier model. Another class of light cruiser (Atlanta) was developed in the early 1940s. Apart from being the smallest of its type with only 5-inch (127mm) guns, the eleven ships of this class were thought to be over-rated. In the mid to late 1920s the USN built both the Pensacola and Northampton classes of heavy cruiser (two and six vessels respectively) and followed it up with the Portland (two) and New Orleans (seven) in the early 1930s. They were to commission another class of heavy cruiser (Wichita) in February 1939. It was seen as a heavier version of the Brooklyn class and the forerunner of the Baltimore class that was laid down during the war. Only two warships of the Alaska class using 12-inch (305mm) calibre guns as their main armament were ever commissioned (*Alaska* in July 1944 and *Guam* in September 1944). Gardiner (ed.), *Conway's all the world's fighting ships*, pp.112–22.

49 Fifteen heavy cruisers were laid down by the British in the period 1924–28. Of this total the Kent class supplied seven, London provided four, Norfolk two and there was only a solitary one each from both the York and Exeter classes. Wartime losses amounted to two from the Kent class (*Canberra* and *Cornwall*), one from the Norfolk class (*Dorsetshire*) and both *York* and *Exeter* succumbed too. Ibid., pp.26–29.

50 Leander was the first of the classes to be laid down in 1931–33, followed by Perth (1933), Arethusa (1933–35), Southampton (1934–35), Gloucester (1936), Edinburgh (1936), Dido (1937–39) and Fiji (1938–39). Ibid., pp.30–34.

51 Five classes of heavy cruiser were completed by the Japanese before 1939. Each class had something different to offer. Furutaka (with a flush deck), Aoba (the first to use a catapult), Myokō (a triple hull and an arched bulkhead to improve underwater protection), Takao (greater bridge protection) and Tone (five aircraft). Of the light cruisers, the four ships of the Sendai class, by concentrating on engine development and boiler configuration, could reach speeds of 35.2 knots, more than 2 knots faster than anything the Americans could produce during the interwar period. Only one Yūbari was ever completed, but she could reach 35.5 knots. Nonetheless, she is best remembered for her side armour which was fitted internally and at a slightly inclined angle. It was an experiment that would be repeated in the later classes of heavy

cruiser. Of all the light cruisers, however, the four ships of the Mogami class inspired envy if not fear in the hearts of the British. Their engines could develop a thrust of 152,000 shaft horse power and a speed of 37 knots. This made them about 4.5 knots faster than the Leander class that had been completed only 2–4 years before them. Ibid., pp.186–90; Evans and Peattie, *Kaigun*, pp.223–45.

52 B.R. Sullivan, 'A fleet in being: the rise and fall of Italian seapower, 1861–1943', *The International History Review*, Vol.X, No.1 (1988):106–24.

53 Oscar Parkes and Francis McMurtrie (eds), *Jane's fighting ships 1927* (London: Sampson, Low, Marston & Co, 1927), pp.5–6. *Alvise Cadamosto* (subsequently renamed *Alvise Da Mosto*), for example, was logged at 44 knots at the beginning of her trials in 1931 and was known to touch 45 knots for short periods of time. See Oscar Parkes (ed.), *Jane's fighting ships 1931* (London: Sampson Low, Marston & Co., 1931), p.vi; Gardiner (ed.), *Conway's all the world's fighting ships*, p.299.

54 Evans and Peattie, *Kaigun*, pp.223–32; Oscar Parkes and Francis McMurtrie (eds), *Jane's fighting ships 1929* (London: Sampson Low, Marston & Co., 1929), p.6; Gardiner (ed.), *Conway's all the world's fighting ships*, p.193.

55 Gardiner, *Conway's all the world's fighting ships*, pp.100–103; Thomas Hone, Norman Friedman and Mark D. Mandeles, *American and British aircraft carrier development, 1919–1941* (Annapolis, Md: NIP, 1999), pp.30–57, 81–82.

56 Hone, Friedman and Mandeles, *American and British aircraft carrier development*, pp.87–92; Geoffrey Till, 'Adopting the aircraft carrier: the British, American and Japanese case studies', in Murray and Millett (eds), *Military innovation in the interwar period*, pp.191–226; Gardiner (ed.), *Conway's all the world's fighting ships*, pp.10, 17–18.

57 Andrew Field, *Royal Navy strategy in the Far East 1919–1939: planning for war against Japan* (London: Frank Cass, 2004), pp.183–212; Gardiner (ed.), *Conway's all the world's fighting ships*, pp.179–80.

58 Under the terms of the Treaty of Versailles (1919) Germany had been forbidden to build any warships exceeding 10,000 tons. All three ships of the Deutschland class (*Deutschland, Admiral Scheer* and *Admiral Graf Spee*) comfortably exceeded that limit being 11,700 tons standard displacement and up to 16,200 tons when operational and at deep load capacity. Parkes and McMurtrie (eds), *Jane's fighting ships 1929*, p.5; Erich Gröner, *German warships 1815–1945. Vol. One: major surface vessels* (Annapolis, Md: NIP, 1990), pp.60–61; Gardiner (ed.), *Conway's all the world's fighting ships*, pp.227–28, 259–60; Sondhaus, *Navies of Europe*, pp.209–10.

59 J.A.S. Grenville, *The Collins history of the world in the twentieth century* (London: HarperCollins, 1994), pp.161–78; D.C.Watt, Frank Spencer and Neville Brown, *A history of the world in the twentieth century* (London: Hodder & Stoughton, 1967), pp.430–63.

60 Fulbrook, *History of Germany*, pp.44–49; Klaus P. Fischer, *Nazi Germany: a new history* (New York: Continuum 1995), pp.211–29; Kershaw, *Hitler: hubris*, pp.315–46.

61 G.A.H. Gordon, *British seapower and procurement between the wars: a reappraisal of rearmament* (Basingstoke: Macmillan Press in association with King's College, London, 1988), pp.69–75; Ferris, 'It is our business in the Navy to command the seas', pp.146–62.

62 Robert H. Ferrell, *Peace in their time: the origins of the Kellogg–Briand Pact* (New York: Norton, 1969); Steiner, *The lights that failed*, pp.572–73.

63 Denis Mack Smith, *Mussolini* (London: Phoenix Giants, 1994), pp.159–69.

64 J.E. Kaufmann and H.W. Kaufmann, *Fortress France: the Maginot Line and French defenses in World War II* (Westport, Conn: Praeger Security International, 2006), pp.1–118; William L. Shirer, *The collapse of the Third Republic: an inquiry into the fall of France in 1940* (London: William Heinemann/Secker & Warburg, 1970), pp.150–78; Martin Thomas, *Britain, France and appeasement: Anglo-French relations in the Popular Front era* (Oxford: Berg, 1996), pp.13–24.

65 Gregory C. Kennedy, 'The 1930 London Naval Conference and Anglo-American maritime strength, 1927–30', in McKercher, *Arms limitation and disarmament*, pp.149–71;

Hall, *Britain, America and arms control*, pp.88–115; Gerald E. Wheeler, *Admiral William Veazie Pratt, U.S. Navy* (Washington, D.C.: Department of the Navy, 1974), pp.281–314.
66 W.G. Beasley, *The rise of modern Japan: political, economic and social change since 1850* (London: Weidenfeld & Nicolson, 1995), pp.159–75; David Bergamini, *Japan's imperial conspiracy: how Emperor Hirohito led Japan into war against the West* (London: Heinemann, 1971), pp.379–542; Yoshihisa Tak Matsusaka, *The making of Japanese Manchuria, 1904–1932* (Cambridge, Mass: Harvard University Press, 2001), pp.349–87.
67 Steiner, *The lights that failed*, pp.707–51; Bergamini, *Japan's imperial conspiracy*, pp.489–542. See also Christopher Thorne, *The limits of foreign policy: the West, the League, and the Far Eastern crisis of 1931–33* (New York: Putnam, 1973).
68 Steiner, *The lights that failed*, pp.755–96; Richard Lamb, *The drift to war 1922–1939* (London: W.H. Allen, 1989), pp.69–89; Kitching, *Britain and the problem of international disarmament*, pp.136–80.
69 Fischer, *Nazi Germany*, pp.230–58; Fulbrook, *History of Germany*, pp.49–54; Grenville, *Collins history of the world*, pp.192–204.
70 Gordon, *British seapower and procurement*, pp.105–8; Murfett, *Fool-proof relations*, p.4; Jon T. Sumida, 'British naval procurement and technological change 1919–39', in Phillips P. O'Brien (ed.), *Technology and naval combat in the twentieth century and beyond* (London: Frank Cass, 2002), pp.128–48.
71 Gordon, *British seapower and procurement*, pp.109–27, 142–51; Grenville, *Collins history of the world*, pp.214–24; Keith Neilson, 'The Defence Requirements Sub-Committee, British strategic foreign policy, Neville Chamberlain and the path to appeasement', *English Historical Review, Vol.118, No.477* (2003): 651–84.
72 Robert Dallek, *Franklin D. Roosevelt and American foreign policy, 1932–1945* (Oxford: OUP, 1995), pp.23–97.
73 Fischer, *Nazi Germany*, pp.404–5; Hall, *Britain, America and arms control*, pp.116–42; Kershaw, *Hitler: hubris*, pp.490–94, 548, 554; B.J.C. McKercher, 'Of horns and teeth: the Preparatory Commission and the World Disarmament Conference, 1926–34', in McKercher, *Arms limitation and disarmament*, pp.173–201.
74 Keith Neilson, 'The Defence Requirements Sub-Committee, British strategic foreign policy, Neville Chamberlain and the path to appeasement', pp.651–84; Kennedy, *Rise and fall of British naval mastery*, pp.283–88.
75 Much was made of the fact that the Mogami class of cruiser (8,500 tons) would carry 15 × 6.1-inch guns – an armament that would reduce the five ships of the latest British Leander class (laid down from 1930 to 1933) to impotence. Evans and Peattie, *Kaigun*, pp.233–45; Oscar Parkes (ed.), *Janes's fighting ships 1933* (London: Sampson Low, Marston & Co., 1933), p.vi.
76 Gardiner (ed.), *Conway's all the world's fighting ships*, pp.18–19, 102–3; Kennedy, *Rise and fall of British naval mastery*, p.208.
77 Yamamoto also encouraged the development of land-based medium and long range bombers to assist the IJN in its future mission overseas. Mitsubishi produced two types, the G3M 'Nell' and its successor the G4M 'Betty', that were capable of going 2,300 miles (3,701km), climbing to over 9,100 metres (29,900 feet) fast and travelling at 230mph (370kph) with a payload that could be either a 800-kilo bomb or a torpedo. Evans and Peattie, *Kaigun*, pp.304–14; Hone, Friedman, and Mandeles, *American and British aircraft carrier development*, pp.106–32.
78 Actually both ships of the Shokaku class displaced 32,105 tons at deep load and could make a top speed of 34.2 knots. Each carried a total of 84 aircraft (including 12 reserves). Evans and Peattie, *Kaigun*, pp.314–24; Gardiner (ed.), *Conway's all the world's fighting ships*, pp.179–83.
79 Both *Gneisenau* and *Scharnhorst* weighed in at 34,841 tons standard displacement and 38,900 tons deep load rather than the 26,500 tons standard displacement and 35,500 tons deep load of the Dunkerque class vessels they were built to rival. Gardiner (ed.), *Conway's all the world's fighting ships*, pp.225, 289–90; H. James Burgwyn, *Italian foreign*

policy in the interwar period 1918–1940 (Westport, Conn.: Praeger, 1997), pp.87–112; Sondhaus, *Navies of Europe*, pp.212–16.

80 Joseph A. Maiolo, *The Royal Navy and Nazi Germany, 1933–39: a study in appeasement and the origins of the Second World War* (New York: St. Martin's Press, 1998), pp.11–37; Reynolds M. Salerno, 'Multilateral strategy and diplomacy: the Anglo-German Naval Agreement and the Mediterranean crisis, 1935–36', *Journal of Strategic Studies*, Vol.17 No.2 (1994): 39–78.

81 There was more than an element of symbolism in the fact that the Reichsmarine was renamed the Kriegsmarine (literally the War Navy) by Hitler in May 1935. By doing so, the Führer provided a clue that the German naval arm was being built up with scarcely peaceful intentions in mind. As part of the Anglo-German Naval Agreement, the Kreigsmarine was allowed to build up to five heavy cruisers each of 10,000 tons, but these were scaled back by the London Naval Treaty to three heavy and two light cruisers. When the five ships of the Hipper class were eventually launched two were of 14,050 tons (*Admiral Hipper* and *Blücher*) while the other three (*Prinz Eugen, Seydlitz* and *Lützow*) displaced 16,974 tons. Of these three, only *Prinz Eugen* was eventually commissioned. *Seydlitz* was converted into being a carrier in 1942–43, but Hitler withdrew her funding before she could be finished. She was towed to Königsberg in 1943 and scuttled in April 1945. *Lützow* was sold to the USSR in early 1940 and was renamed *Petropavlovsk*. She became a floating battery during the siege of Leningrad, was hit repeatedly by German shells and was beached. She was refloated in September 1942 and served again as a floating battery from 1943 under her new name *Tallin*. Ibid., pp.38–62; Norman H. Gibbs, *Grand Strategy. Vol.I. Rearmament policy* (London: HMSO, 1976), pp.155–70; Hall, *Britain, America and arms control*, pp.171–92; Kershaw, *Hitler: hubris*, pp.556–58.

82 Reynolds M. Salerno, *Vital crossroads: Mediterranean origins of the Second World War, 1935–1940* (Ithaca, NY: Cornell University Press, 2002), pp.10–12, 14–15, 55, 124; Burgwyn, *Italian foreign policy*, pp.112–30; Fischer, *Nazi Germany*, pp.409–10; Gaines Post, Jr., *Dilemmas of appeasement: British deterrence and defense, 1934–1937* (Ithaca, NY: Cornell University Press, 1993), pp.40, 83–86, 102–3, 106, 125, 153, 201, 208.

83 Kagan and Kagan, *While America sleeps*, pp.194–210; Mack Smith, *Mussolini*, pp.188–203; Post, Jr., *Dilemmas of appeasement*, pp.81–115.

84 Robert Mallett, *The Italian Navy and fascist expansionism, 1935–1940* (London: Frank Cass, 1998), pp.21–37; Arthur J. Marder, *From the Dardanelles to Oran: studies of the Royal Navy in war and peace 1915–1940* (London: OUP, 1974), pp.64–104; Mack Smith, *Mussolini*, pp.195–96, 208.

85 Gibbs, *Grand strategy*, *I*, pp.187–226; Burgwyn, *Italian foreign policy*, pp.118, 125–27, 133–35; Post, Jr., *Dilemmas of appeasement*, pp.116–54; Salerno, *Vital crossroads*, pp.11–15, 17, 19–20, 43, 53, 55, 60, 65, 80, 94, 96, 122, 129, 178, 188, 200, 213, 215, 219.

86 Meredith W. Berg, 'Protecting national interests by treaty: the second London Naval Conference, 1934–36', in McKercher, *Arms limitation and disarmament*, pp.203–27; Hall, *Britain, America and arms control*, pp.143–70; Evans and Peattie, *Kaigun*, pp.293–98.

87 Baer, *One hundred years*, pp.119–45; Berg, 'Protecting national interests', pp.203–27; John Major, 'The navy plans for war, 1937–41', in Hagan (ed.), *In peace and war*, pp.237–62.

88 In March 1935 the boastful Hermann Göring, whom Hitler had made responsible for the growth of the Luftwaffe, typically exaggerated its size. Fact merged with fiction and the result was pure theatre. Kershaw, *Hitler: hubris*, pp.549–52; Max Domerus (ed.), *Hitler's speeches and proclamations 1932–1945. Vol.Two: 1935–1938* (Wouconda, Ill: Bolchazy-Carducci Publishers, 1992), pp.650–56; Gibbs, *Grand strategy*, *I*, pp.133–85.

89 Gibbs, *Grand strategy*, *I*, pp.227–72; Kagan and Kagan, *While America sleeps*, pp.210–16; Post, Jr., *Dilemmas of appeasement*, pp.157–244; Thomas, *Britain, France and appeasement*, pp.25–53.

90 Germany sent its Condor Legion consisting of four fighter bombers, four fighters, one reconnaissance and two seaplane squadrons, together with ground staff, a number

of heavy anti-aircraft batteries and radio units. Walter Görlitz, *History of the German General Staff 1657–1945* (New York: Praeger, 1954), p.305. Italy sent 50,000 troops, tanks and heavy guns by the spring of 1937. Burgwyn, *Italian foreign policy*, p.158.
91 Burgwyn, *Italian foreign policy*, pp.130–55; Mack Smith, *Mussolini*, pp.207–8; Kershaw, *Hitler 1936–1945: nemesis* (New York: W.W. Norton, 2000), pp.26, 98; Mallett, *Italian Navy and fascist expansionism*, pp.63–65.
92 Mallett, *Italian Navy and fascist expansionism*, pp.50, 54, 62, 103, 192; Salerno, *Vital crossroads*, pp.16–20, 22–23, 53, 81–82, 104, 116, 216, 219; Sondhaus, *Navies of Europe*, pp.216–19.
93 James Morley (ed.), *Deterrent diplomacy: Japan, Germany, and the USSR 1935–1940* (New York: Columbia University Press, 1976), pp.9–39; Tajima Nobuo, 'The Berlin–Tokyo Axis reconsidered: from the Anti-Comintern Pact to the plot to assassinate Stalin', in Christian W. Spang and Rolf-Harald Wippich (eds), *Japanese–German relations, 1895–1945: war, diplomacy and public opinion* (Abingdon: Oxon: Routledge, 2006), pp.161–79; Arthur Stam, *The diplomacy of the new order: the foreign policy of Japan, Germany and Italy: 1931–1945* (Soesterberg, Netherlands: Uitgeverij Aspekt, 2003), pp.16–22.
94 Gerald Howson, *Arms for Spain: the untold story of the Spanish Civil War* (London: John Murray, 1998), pp.130–45, 260–303; Burgwyn, *Italian foreign policy*, pp.152–62; Gibbs, *Grand strategy, I*, pp.380–86; Mack Smith, *Mussolini*, pp.209–10; Post, Jr., *Dilemmas of appeasement*, pp.248, 263–64, 271–73, 293.
95 Charles S. Thomas, *The German Navy in the Nazi era* (London: Unwin Hyman, 1990), pp.166–71.
96 Burgwyn, *Italian foreign policy*, pp.158–60; Gibbs, *Grand strategy, I*, pp.386–89; Post, Jr., *Dilemmas of appeasement*, pp.248, 258, 262–64, 272–73, 276, 289–90, 300, 338.
97 James Cable, *The Royal Navy and the siege of Bilbao* (Cambridge: CUP, 1979).
98 Hugh Thomas, *The Spanish Civil War* (New York: Harper & Row, 1961), pp.440–41; R.A.C. Parker, *Chamberlain and appeasement: British policy and the coming of the Second World War* (New York: St. Martin's Press, 1993), pp.80–92; Martin Thomas, *Britain, France and appeasement*, pp.89–114.
99 Erich Raeder, *My life* (Annapolis, Md: US Naval Institute, 1960), pp.220–29; Ian Kershaw, *Hitler: nemesis*, pp.43–44.
100 Thomas, *Spanish Civil War*, pp.441–42, 457, 467–68, 475–78; Beevor, *The battle for Spain*, pp.289–90; David Dutton, *Anthony Eden: a life and reputation* (London: Arnold, 1997), pp.75–76; *Keesing's contemporary archives*, 20, 23 June 1937, pp.2626, 2633.
101 Peter Gretton, 'The Nyon Conference – the naval aspect', *The English Historical Review*, Vol.90, No.354 (1975):103–12; Dutton, *Anthony Eden*, pp.90–91; Thomas, *Spanish Civil War*, pp.475–78; Reynolds M. Salerno, 'Italy's pirate submarine campaign of 1937', in Gregory C. Kennedy and Keith Neilson (eds), *Incidents and international relations: people, power, and personalities* (Westport, Conn: Praeger, 2002), pp.159–78.
102 Thomas, *Spanish Civil War*, p.513.
103 Ibid., pp.513, 518; Sondhaus, *Navies of Europe*, p.217; James S. Corum, 'The Spanish Civil War: lessons learned and not learned by the Great Powers', in Black (ed.), *The Second World War, Vol.VI*, pp.341–62; Beevor, *The battle for Spain*, p.323.
104 Murfett, *Fool-proof relations*, pp.41–61; John Paton Davies, Jr., *Dragon by the tail: American, British, Japanese, and Russian encounters with China and one another* (New York: W.W. Norton, 1972), pp.184–209; Kennedy, *Rise and fall of British naval mastery*, pp.290–93; Tolley, *Yangtze patrol*, pp.239–53.
105 Murfett, *Fool-proof relations*, pp.62–161; Malcolm H. Murfett, 'A keystone of imperial defence or a millstone around Britain's neck? Singapore 1919–41', in Malcolm H. Murfett, John N. Miksic, Brian P. Farrell and Chiang Ming Shun, *Between two oceans: a military history of Singapore from first settlement to final British withdrawal* (Singapore: OUP, 1999), pp.145–74; Greg Kennedy, *Anglo-American strategic relations and the Far East, 1933–1939* (London: Frank Cass, 2002), pp.15–50, 211–61; and his 'What worth the Americans? The British strategic foreign policy-making elite's view of American

maritime power in the Far East, 1933–41', in Kennedy (ed.), *British naval strategy east of Suez*, pp.90–117.
106 Apart from the *King George V*, her sister ships were the *Prince of Wales*, *Duke of York*, *Anson* and *Howe*. All were laid down in 1937, launched in 1939–40 and completed in stages between December 1940 (*King George V*) and August 1942 (*Howe*). Gardiner (ed.), *Conway's all the world's fighting ships*, p.15; Murfett, *Fool-proof relations*, pp.4–12.
107 While *Nelson*'s nine 16-inch guns could deliver a broadside of 21,375 pounds of shell, *King George V* with her ten 14-inch guns could only fire one of 15,900 pounds. As Joseph Moretz points out, significantly reducing the offensive potential of this latest class of battleship *vis-à-vis* those battleships with a set of either 15-inch or 16-inch heavy guns was one of the most controversial design aspects of the inter-war period. Moretz, *Royal Navy and the capital ship*, pp.72–112.
108 All three ships of this class were laid down in April–June 1937 and were completed in stages in May 1940 (*Illustrious*), November 1940 (*Formidable*) and finally May 1941 (*Victorious*).
109 Gardiner (ed.), *Conway's all the world's fighting ships*, pp.15, 19–20; Hone, Friedman and Mandeles, *American and British aircraft carrier development*, p.92.
110 *Wasp* would be the last new US carrier class to be laid down before the European war began. *Hornet*, the third and last ship of the Yorktown class, would be laid down in late September 1939 and commissioned in October 1941. *Essex* and the class that took their name from her, would be the next fleet carrier to be laid down in April 1941. She was commissioned on New Year's Eve 1942, displacing 34,881 tons at deep load. Her engines were capable of raising 150,000 shaft horse power (shp) and a top speed of 32.7 knots. Fifteen other carriers of the Essex class would ultimately be commissioned before the end of the Pacific war. Gardiner (ed.), *Conway's all the world's fighting ships*, pp.102–5; Geoffrey Till, 'Adopting the aircraft carrier: the British, American and Japanese case studies', in Murray and Millett (eds), *Military innovation in the interwar period*, pp.191–226; Gardiner (ed.), *Conway's all the world's fighting ships*, pp.102–5.
111 Armoured protection of the citadel – the armoured decks and side armour belt – of the North Carolina class was supposedly designed to give immunity against the 1,500 pound (680 kg) shells that might be fired by a 14-inch (356mm) gun, such as that used by the Japanese Kongō class of converted battleships, at distances between 19,000–29,000 yards (17.37km–26.52km). Immunity against the fall of one of the 3,230 pound (1,465 kg) shells likely to be delivered by the 18.1-inch (460mm) guns of the ships of the Yamato class would be correspondingly less. William H. Garzke, Jr. and Robert O. Dulin, Jr., *Battleships: United States battleships, 1935–1992* (Annapolis, Md: NIP, 1995), pp.27–69.
112 Evans and Peattie, *Kaigun*, pp.370–83.
113 Arnold J. Toynbee (ed.), *Survey of international affairs 1936* (London: OUP, 1937), pp.49–116; Sondhaus, *Navies of Europe*, pp.216–22.
114 Although *Impero* was launched in November 1939, she was never completed, unlike her sister ships *Littorio* (May 1940), *Roma* (June 1940) and *Vittorio Veneto* (July 1937). Gardiner (ed.), *Conway's all the world's fighting ships*, pp.178, 224, 289–90, 325; Mallett, *Italian Navy and fascist expansionism*, pp.68–80; Tobias R. Philbin III, *The lure of Neptune: German–Soviet naval collaboration and ambitions, 1919–1941* (Columbia, SC: University of South Carolina Press, 1994), pp.23–37.
115 Sadkovich, *The Italian Navy in World War II*, pp.1–35; Sondhaus, *Navies of Europe*, pp.217–22; Gardner (ed.), *Conway's all the world's fighting ships*, pp.289–305.
116 Gibbs, *Grand strategy, I*, pp.386–93; Mack Smith, *Mussolini*, pp.213–45; Mallett, *Italian Navy and fascist expansionism*, pp.111–21; Salerno, *Vital crossroads*, pp.49–51, 56, 58–59, 62, 65, 77, 82–83, 117, 123, 214, 216–17.
117 After the naval reservists had been called up and the fleet had been mobilised on 28 September by the First Lord of the Admiralty Alfred Duff Cooper, the Munich

Settlement ensured the reservists could be allowed to return home within a few days and the fleet was demobilised on 25 October. Gordon, *British seapower and procurement*, p.271; Parker, *Chamberlain and appeasement*, pp.156–81.
118 Alan Bullock, *Hitler: a study in tyranny* (Harmondsworth, Middlesex: Penguin Books, 1971), pp.471–73; Kershaw, *Hitler: nemesis*, pp.122–23.
119 Niall Ferguson, *The war of the world: history's age of hatred* (London: Allen Lane, 2006), pp.312–44; Bullock, *Hitler*, pp.482–89; Kershaw, *Hitler: nemesis*, pp.163–75.
120 Keith W. Bird, *Erich Raeder: Admiral of the Third Reich* (Annapolis, Md: NIP, 2006).
121 Raeder, *My life*, pp.266–70; Thomas, *German Navy in the Nazi era*, pp.173–79.
122 Clay Blair, Jr., *Hitler's U-boat war. Vol. I: the hunters 1939–1942* (New York: Random House, 1996), pp.45–49.
123 Kershaw, *Hitler: nemesis*, pp.189–90; Thomas, *German Navy in the Nazi era*, pp.179–82.
124 Mack Smith, *Mussolini*, pp.228–37; Fischer, *Nazi Germany*, pp.432, 435–36; Maiolo, *Royal Navy and Nazi Germany*, pp.176–85; Mallett, *Italian Navy and fascist expansionism*, pp.141–59; Salerno, *Vital crossroads*, pp.60–61, 79–80, 105–6, 123–27, 131, 145–46, 214, 216–17.
125 *Fuehrer conferences on naval affairs 1939–1945* (London: Chatham Publishing, 2005), p.33; Holger H. Herwig, 'The failure of German sea power, 1914–45: Mahan, Tirpitz and Raeder reconsidered', *The International History Review*, Vol.X, No.1 (Feb.1988): 68–105; Eberhard Rössler, *The U-boat: the evolution and technical history of German submarines* (London: Arms and Armour Press, 1981), pp.114–19; Blair, Jr., *Hitler's U-boat war: hunters*, pp.45–49; Maiolo, *Royal Navy and Nazi Germany*, pp.163–72.
126 George Peden, *British rearmament and the Treasury: 1932–1939* (Edinburgh: Scottish Academic Press, 1979), pp.106–17, 128–34, 160–67; Murfett, *Fool-proof relations*, pp.5–11.
127 John Erickson, *The Soviet high command: a military–political history 1918–1941* (Boulder, Col: Westview Press, 1984), pp.522–32; Parker, *Chamberlain and appeasement*, pp.216–45, 318–19; Geoffrey Roberts, 'The alliance that failed: Moscow and the triple alliance negotiations, 1939', in Jeremy Black (ed.), *The Second World War: Vol.VI, Causes and background* (Aldershot, Hants: Ashgate, 2007), pp.197–228.
128 For the most comprehensive treatment of the background to and effects of this extraordinary agreement see Anthony Read and David Fisher, *The deadly embrace: Hitler, Stalin and the Nazi–Soviet Pact 1939–1941* (London: Michael Joseph, 1988); Geoffrey Roberts, *The Soviet Union and the origins of the Second World War: Russo-German relations and the road to war, 1933–1941* (Basingstoke, Hants: Macmillan, 1995), pp.62–150. For a more succinct appraisal of the origins of the pact see Michael Bloch, *Ribbentrop* (London: Bantam Books, 1992), pp.230–50; Kershaw, *Hitler: nemesis*, pp.194–97, 204–5, 210–11. For its naval dimensions, see Philbin, *Lure of Neptune*, pp.41–77.
129 Bullock, *Hitler*, p.535; Kershaw, *Hitler: nemesis*, pp.214–16, 219, 222; Mallett, *Italian Navy and fascist expansionism*, pp.166–73; Salerno, *Vital crossroads*, pp.131–36, 143–47.
130 Jürgen Rohwer and Stephen Roskill differ on the number of destroyers that were on the various stations around the British coast. Correlli Barnett follows Roskill in this respect, while James Levy fails to address the question. Correlli Barnett, *Engage the enemy more closely: the Royal Navy in the Second World War* (London: W.W. Norton, 1991), p.62; James P. Levy, *The Royal Navy's Home Fleet in World War II* (Basingstoke: Palgrave Macmillan, 2003), pp.19–34; Jürgen Rohwer, *Chronology of the war at sea 1939–1945: The naval history of World War Two* (London: Chatham Publishing, 2005), p.1; Stephen W. Roskill, *The war at sea 1939–1945. Vol.I* (London: HMSO, 1954), pp.583–87.
131 Gibbs, *Grand strategy*, *I*, pp.607–88; Paul Auphan and Jacques Mordal, *The French Navy in World War II* (Westport, Conn: Greenwood Press, 1976), pp.21–24, 389–90; E.H. Jenkins, *A history of the French Navy* (London: MacDonald & Jane's, 1973), pp.317–18.

48 Neither one thing nor the other

132 Ten of these vessels were training boats and unsuitable for combat purposes. Eight more were undergoing operational trials at the outbreak of war. Jak P. Mallmann Showell, *The German Navy in World War Two: a reference guide to the Kriegsmarine, 1935–1945* (London: Arms and Armour Press, 1979), p.63.

133 Dönitz had a total of twenty-seven ocean-going U-boats at his disposal in late August 1939, but two were experimental craft (*U25* and *U26*) and three others were not combat-ready at this time. At the outset of the campaign, he was able to deploy the experimental Type-1A in British coastal waters and ten Type-VII, six Type-VIIB and five Type-IX in North Atlantic and Spanish waters. Blair, *Hitler's U-boat war: hunters*, pp.54–55.

134 Type IA was an experimental large U-boat of 750 deadweight tons; Type II (and subsequently IIB and IIC) were small at 250 tons; Type VII and VIIB were classified as medium size at 500 tons; Type IX was considered large at 750 tons. Once they became operational, however, their war load increased their tonnage in some cases quite significantly, as can be seen from the following figures: Type IA's displacement rose to 826 tons; Type II (to 254 tons); Type IIB (to 280 tons); Type IIC (to 291 tons); Type VII (to 626 tons); Type VIIB (to 753 tons); and Type IX (to 1,032 tons). Ibid., pp.39–47, 53–64, 701–2.

135 At the outset of the war Raeder wanted Dönitz, as Führer der U-boote, based in the U-boat command headquarters West on the outskirts of Wilhelmshaven rather than in Berlin. As the war progressed he was to move his HQ first to Paris after the fall of France and then in the autumn of 1940 to a chateau at Kerneval overlooking the Atlantic close to the U-boat base at Lorient. After the Allied raid on St. Nazaire in March 1942, however, Hitler compelled Dönitz to return to Paris. He took over a modern apartment block on the Avenue Maréchal Maunoury on 29 March 1942. Peter Padfield, *Dönitz: the last führer* (London: Victor Gollancz, 1984), pp.187, 222–23, 245–46.

136 Barnett, *Engage the enemy*, pp.61–64.

137 Peter Padfield, *War beneath the sea: submarine conflict during World War II* (New York: John Wiley, 1996), p.54; *Fuehrer conferences*, p.36; Rohwer, *Chronology*, pp.1–2.

138 Rohwer, *Chronology*, p.1.

139 In truth, RAF Coastal Command was in no real state to fight any such war against an enemy submarine force that would draw it right out into the North Atlantic in its attack on Allied trade and shipping. At the outset of the war Coastal Command only had seventeen squadrons of aircraft that were operational. Most of these aircraft were already obsolete, while those that weren't needed to be equipped with LRASV radar sets. Before it could begin to fulfil adequately its role of defending the vital trade routes to and from the British Isles, Coastal Command urgently required far more long-range aircraft. John Buckley, *The RAF and trade defence 1919–1945: constant endeavour* (Keele, Staffs: Ryburn Publishing, 1995), pp.116, 209, 211; Barnett, *Engage the enemy*, p.55.

2 The opening gambit (1939)

By late August 1939 Hitler's determination to obliterate Poland's independence even at the risk of a general European war was not in question. There would be no 1939 version of the Munich conference to deny him the satisfaction of seeing Poland disappear before his eyes. Appeasement was dead. Hitler had to face up to the fact that if his forces moved against Poland, the British, French and Dominion governments were likely to declare war on Germany. Nonetheless, armed with the pact that had just been negotiated with the Soviets, he was prepared to run this risk.[1]

Once the German Führer had given his approval for the commencement of *Fall Weiss* (literally *Case White*) which began with a blitzkrieg offensive across the Polish border shortly before dawn (0445 hours) on 1 September, the governments in London and Paris were confronted with a stark choice: either to invoke or ignore their territorial guarantee to the beleaguered state. It took them a little over forty-eight hours to do the decent thing and go to war with Nazi Germany. Ironically, their fateful decision didn't help the Poles who were left alone to try vainly to stem the tide of the invasion. They did their courageous best, but it was a quite hopeless task against a formidable enemy. At sea at least their force of five submarines defied the German surface fleet in the Baltic and kept laying mines until they ran out of supplies on 11 September. Thereafter three of them sought internment in Swedish waters and the other two (*Orzel* and *Wilk*) succeeded in the far more hazardous undertaking of trying to get through to British waters. Although their submarines escaped destruction, the same could not be said of the modest Polish surface fleet, the remaining units of which were either summarily destroyed or rendered inoperable by German air and naval forces in the first days of the campaign.[2]

As Prime Minister Neville Chamberlain went on radio to inform the British people that a state of war existed between Britain and Germany as of 11.00am GMT on 3 September, a message was sent out to the British fleet from Admiralty House in Whitehall. It simply stated: 'TOTAL GERMANY repetition TOTAL GERMANY.'[3] In his insatiable quest for Poland, therefore, Hitler had brought Germany into a premature collision with its old European adversaries, the British and the French, several years before his Kriegsmarine was ready to tackle them on at least a comparable footing. While First Sea Lord Admiral Sir Dudley Pound possessed a fleet with a significant numerical advantage over his German counterpart Großadmiral Dr. Erich Raeder at the outbreak of conflict in the West, he didn't need reminding that there was little room for complacency, particularly if the crisis in the Far East worsened to the point of war with Japan. At least the Germans were on their own – neither of their partners in the now moribund Anti-Comintern Pact (Italy and Japan) was going to be an active combatant at the outset of the war, even though the two powers could hardly claim to be neutral. Of course, much the same could be said of the Americans too – but what the Soviets would do in this new diplomatic world of theirs was anyone's guess at least for the time being.[4]

As the conflict at sea widened beyond the Baltic, other casualties were soon in evidence. Only a few hours after both France and the United Kingdom had declared war on Germany on 3 September, the German U-boat *U30* set the tone for the struggle ahead by torpedoing and sinking the British passenger liner SS *Athenia* in the Western Approaches of the North Atlantic with the loss of at least 112 passengers and crew – a high proportion of whom were women and children.[5] Apologists for Fritz-Julius Lemp, the captain of the *U30*, might have pretended it was a case of mistaken identity, but it soon became obvious to Karl Dönitz and the rest of the German Naval War Staff that it was a deliberate act of aggression against an unarmed ship. Naturally, they preferred to pretend otherwise and Lemp, though subsequently severely reprimanded for an excess of zeal, retained his sea-going command.[6] Unrestricted submarine warfare of this kind was not in Germany's best interests at this stage. It was bound to alienate the neutral and non-combatant states – the most powerful of which was the USA. Since Hitler had no wish to complicate the existing picture by drawing any of these powers into war, the rules of naval engagement would have to be spelt out so as to prevent other would-be Lemp-type figures from carrying out acts at sea that would be detrimental to Germany's best interests.[7]

Erich Raeder, like Dönitz and others in the naval arm, had little doubt that conducting a campaign of unrestricted warfare against their confirmed enemies at sea actually made good strategic and economic sense.[8] An unstinting war on trade was vital in their view to undermine the British military position and force Chamberlain's government to withdraw from the war. Anything less and they feared that the Royal Navy would begin to exert its own influence through the establishment of a close blockade in German waters designed to prevent trade of all kinds from getting through and especially the importation of essential war matériel. This activity had intensified after 6 September once a British cruiser patrol had been established with some success in northern waters between the Faeroes and Iceland.[9] Even before the British commenced mining operations in both the North Sea and the Straits of Dover on 9–11 September, advance units of the British Expeditionary Force (BEF) had been ferried across the English Channel from Portsmouth to the French port of Cherbourg a day after war had broken out. A more substantial troop convoy left Southampton for the same destination a few days later. Ensuring protection against submarine attacks was a justifiable concern for the Admiralty because the Germans would have loved to wreak havoc with these troopships if they could.[10]

If the last war was any guide, providing a convoy for all types of cargo substantially reduced the chances of interference by U-boats, whereas ships sailing alone without any escorting vessels to protect them literally took their life in their hands every time they sailed forth. U-boat commanders preyed upon lone vessels and particularly those that steered a straight course without practising any zigzag manoeuvres to make torpedoing them more difficult.[11] As a result, convoys plying the east-to-west trans-Atlantic routes were formed in a variety of British ports from as early as 7 September and a corresponding set began to be used in American waters for the west-to-east run just over a week later. Convoys would ultimately be divided into two types: the fast convoys, such as the HX series, which would proceed initially from Halifax, Nova Scotia (and subsequently in 1942 from New York) to the British Isles and the OB series (renamed the ON series in July 1941) that would run in the opposite direction from ports dotted around the Irish coast to North American waters, with all ships able to maintain (in theory at least) average speeds between 8.08 and 9.24 knots over the 1940–45 period; and slow convoys, designated with the suffix S which were expected to be capable of maintaining an average speed of 7.0–7.5 knots on their routes.[12] At the same time the USN implemented a series of extensive neutrality patrols along the east coast from Halifax, Nova Scotia in the north to the tropical waters off Kingston, Jamaica in the south. While destroyers provided the backbone of most of these patrols, a few cruisers were gainfully deployed off Cape Hatteras, North Carolina and amongst the Caribbean islands.[13] Throughout the war the principle of convoy worked. Major U-boat successes would come in those seas where for some reason a convoy system had not been established – throughout the Caribbean in 1942, for example – or in those parts of the mid-Atlantic which were beyond the range of the Very Long Range (VLR) aircraft that were otherwise available to help in identifying and destroying them. They were also particularly effective in British coastal waters and especially along the Eastern seaboard of the United States where convoys remained absent for far too long before arrangements were put in hand to cut down on the German carnage in May 1942.[14]

Although Poland's fate was sealed when the Soviet Union attacked it from the east on 17 September, the British and French governments did not revert to type and seek the peace option that Hitler had hoped they would. Sensing that appeasement was thoroughly dead in London if not in Paris, Raeder quickly seized his opportunity and persuaded the Führer to ease some of the restrictions he had imposed on the Kriegsmarine at the outset of hostilities.[15] If appeasement couldn't be relied upon to force the Allies to come to their senses, the Germans sought to get them to recognise a fait accompli when it stared them in the face by attacking their ships wherever they could. Although their effectiveness may have been nullified to a considerable extent when they were pitched against well-defended convoys, U-boats were still able to eliminate 1,904 ships (representing 9,235,113 gross registered tons) belonging to Allied or neutral powers in the first three years of the war. Such a trail of destruction handsomely repaid the investment made in the U-boat fleet by the Kriegsmarine.[16]

While Dönitz sought to employ groups of U-boats (wolf packs) against convoys in an effort to overwhelm their escorts by conducting a series of well coordinated attacks against them (*Rudeltaktik*), Raeder looked to his capital ships to blow them and the merchant ships they were protecting out of the water. If his naval signals intelligence service the Beobachtungs-Dienst (B-Dienst) could unravel the basic British naval cipher – and it often could – he hoped to be in a position to deploy both U-boats and surface craft to interdict the convoys and savage them.[17] Few in the Admiralty doubted the capacity of the German capital ships to destroy any convoy they fell upon and Churchill, restored at the outset of the war as first lord, was more anxious than most to ensure that these big gun surface ships should be hounded from the oceans of the world before they could do real damage to the British cause in the war. As a result, therefore, whenever the cryptanalysts at Bletchley Park – the Government Code and Cipher School (GC&CS) – could crack any of the German Naval Enigma codes and provide information concerning the movements of these capital ships, Churchill responded by forming groups of warships often backed by aerial assistance to hunt them down. His recurring nightmare was that these armed raiders would break out into the Atlantic and cause havoc on the convoy routes destroying much needed Allied supplies of war materiel. He was determined to prevent this from happening and never wavered from expending much time, effort and money on eliminating this threat whenever and wherever it was formed.[18]

In these early days of the war the difficulty of detection, let alone destruction, of the submarine was experienced by both the surface fleets of the Royal Navy and its German counterpart. Unfortunately for the Admiralty, its confident prediction that Asdic could be relied upon to detect the underwater prowler and neutralise its threat soon proved to be unfounded. Asdic may have been good in ideal circumstances, such as calm seas and not extravagant depths, but its severe technical flaws – both in its limited range and blind spot potential – meant that those vessels equipped with this device would continue to face frustration in trying to find, let alone eliminate, the submarine predator.[19] Only time would reveal the true extent of the problem, but in the meantime the Admiralty, taking its cue from Churchill, sought to grasp the initiative from the U-boats by hunting them down in specially assembled and Asdic-equipped task forces. Much misapplied effort had gone into this pursuit during the First World War, but its lack of success on that occasion did not faze the first lord at all. Once again the new version of the old initiative did not reap the rich rewards that its zealous promoter was looking for and was rapidly abandoned in the light of bitter experience. Three days after the fleet carrier *Ark Royal* had fortuitously survived a torpedo attack from *U39* off the west coast of Scotland on 14 September, another carrier *Courageous*, working with two destroyers well out to sea off the southwest coast of Ireland, was not so fortunate. She was sunk by *U29* at a range of less than 3,000 yards (2743m) with the loss of 514 hands. It was a case of the biter being bitten and Churchill didn't need any more evidence to suspend the practice: carriers were far too precious to waste in this way.[20]

Ark Royal's charmed life persisted when she and other units of the Home Fleet were attacked by Junkers-88 and Heinkel 111 bombers as they were going to the aid of the crippled submarine *Spearfish* in the North Sea on 26 September. Apart from it being the first case of an aerial attack on a fleet at sea, this action also saw the first successful use of radar on board the British battleship *Rodney* and the light cruiser *Sheffield* to give early warning of an approaching enemy air strike. Although the Luftwaffe had achieved neither total surprise nor success in this venture they had come perilously close to doing so; registering a near miss against the carrier and hitting the *Hood* with a bomb that had actually bounced off the battlecruiser and fallen harmlessly into the sea.[21] These initial failures appeared to offer hope for those both on shore and at sea who still clung to the outmoded belief in the primacy of the capital ship over anything that took to the skies. As someone who had consistently supported the Fleet Air Arm in the past, Churchill was far more astute. Despite being the political head of the 'Senior Service', he was only too well aware that once sufficient financial and industrial resources were channelled into the building of aircraft, the results were likely to demonstrate that air power would grow in importance and become a key element in the war at sea.[22]

While these high profile incidents helped to shape naval policy on both sides of the North Sea, the Germans wasted no time in beginning mining operations both in what could be termed their home waters – where the establishment of an integrated system of contact mine barrages known as the 'Westwall' was devised to protect their major naval bases – and in British coastal waters and particularly outside harbour entrances on the east coast where the intention was to cause as much damage and disruption to sea traffic as possible.[23] For their part the British put most of their own effort into mining the Strait of Dover in order to make it a no-go area for U-boats much as it had been when Sir Roger Keyes had introduced a split level mine barrage in these same waters in 1917.[24]

Despite the initial successes the U-boats were able to claim in their war on trade – and these were not insignificant in themselves – the results would have been even more dramatic if they had not suffered from repeated equipment failures. Torpedoes could not be entirely relied upon to run at the requisite depth and even if they did, too many didn't explode on impact or did so prematurely. It was deeply frustrating for the U-boat captains. They could manoeuvre their way into position to both close the range and get a clear uninterrupted shot at an enemy ship, fire their torpedoes and still not register a hit on the targeted vessel. It wasn't complacency that held up improvements in these areas of concern, for the recurring problems of depth keeping and unreliable detonators were addressed by German naval engineers from early on in the campaign. Much to Dönitz's agitation, developmental research programmes geared to rectifying torpedo problems were unable to provide a more effective alternative for many months to come. Even so, the stealth of the U-boat, the degree of success it was already achieving in sinking merchant shipping, and the relative difficulty that the Allies had in finding and destroying them were all key advantages that were not lost on the OKM or on Hitler. U-boat construction became a matter of the highest priority as could be seen in the cancellation of six battleships, three battlecruisers, an aircraft carrier, four light cruisers and twelve destroyers before the end of September and the freeing up of resources in the naval dockyards so that sixteen small coastal submarines (Type IID) and fifty-five ocean-going U-boats could be built in their stead. By the end of October another sixty of the larger workhorses destined for operations in the Atlantic would be ordered as well.[25]

Whatever Raeder and his contemporaries from the old naval school might have thought about the merits of the surface fleet, the overall utility of the U-boat could hardly be denied. Despite being much slower and less powerful than any of the main types of surface warships, the submersible in the hands of an expert was still capable of being used with flair. Gunther Prien's dashing act of impertinence in penetrating the vulnerable main base of the Home Fleet at Scapa Flow in *U47* and sinking the battleship *Royal Oak* in the early hours of 15 October proved this beyond all doubt. To add salt to the Admiralty's wound, Prien had then escaped unharmed through the same porous defences.[26] His heroic exploits won him instant acclaim, added immeasurably to a cause that Hitler increasingly identified with, secured a further promotion for Dönitz, and underlined the wisdom of investing in such a relatively small, cheap and easily built craft.[27]

October was not a good month for the Allies. Quite apart from Prien's stunning escapade at Scapa and the steady drip of mercantile victims succumbing to U-boat attacks along the trade routes, two of the German pocket battleships – the *Admiral Graf Spee* and the *Deutschland* – were out on the loose in the vastness of the Atlantic and threatening to create mayhem wherever they went. Churchill and the Admiralty wasted little time in forming hunting groups to tackle both menaces, but neither naval force remotely succeeded in homing in on their quarry or preventing them from doing what they wanted with whoever they pleased. While the *Deutschland*'s foray promised far more than it actually achieved, the same could not be said for the *Graf Spee*. Here was a commerce raider worthy of the name. Under her wily captain Hans Langsdorff, the *Graf Spee* adopted the classic technique of hitting and running and was highly effective in both phases of the game. Langsdorff revelled in his elusiveness and unpredictability. In order to achieve the element of surprise that he enjoyed so much, he was willing to cover vast tracts of the ocean, backtracking when necessary and lying low for long spells to refuel as well, so as to throw his pursuers off the scent. While he understood that his primary task was to destroy as much mercantile shipping as he could, he was under strict instructions not to get into a firestorm with heavier units of the Royal Navy that were vainly searching for him. If there was any danger of such a set-piece battle taking place, Langsdorff was supposed to employ 'cut and run' tactics, leaving the scene as quickly as he could so as to ensure that his ship could live to fight another day. These orders became chafing for a dashing man of adventure such as himself. Inspired by his own success, Langsdorff felt his ship had the firepower, speed and manoeuvrability to cope with anything the Allies might throw at him. A mixture of hubris and overconfidence has undermined many warriors in the past and Langsdorff was the latest to fall victim to it a few weeks later in the South Atlantic.[28]

As the Allies cast around in growing agitation and frustration for either of the pocket battleships, the Germans stirred the mix by sending two of their battleships *Scharnhorst* and *Gneisenau* out into the Faroes–Iceland passage of the North Atlantic in late November to meddle with the Northern Patrol and complicate the search for the *Graf Spee*. They did both. *Scharnhorst* swiftly dispatched the auxiliary cruiser *Rawalpindi* in a hail of gunfire on 23 November and lured the Home Fleet into another vexatious search that was only finally abandoned several days later long after the 'two sisters' had used a spell of atrocious weather to make good their escape back into the North Sea and had regained the safety of their home base of Wilhelmshaven.[29]

While the struggle at sea was expanding on the eastern side of the Atlantic, the neutral or non-belligerent nations on its western rim were anxious to preserve themselves from the rigours of it in their own waters. Meeting in Panama City in early October, a conference of Pan-American states agreed on establishing a Security Zone around their shorelines (with certain exceptions being made for Canada and the European colonies) that would extend 300nm (556km) out to sea and exclude all belligerent naval vessels from entering these waters. This measure was lukewarmly accepted by the British and in particular by Churchill who saw it primarily as a means of excluding U-boats from American waters. In his mind the essential element was enforcement procedure. If the zone was patrolled by units of the USN, there was little to worry about. If it was policed by what he termed a 'weak neutral', however, the British would have much more to say on the matter as the zone could easily be exploited by the Germans.[30] Whether the Germans would respect this zone in any case – given the extreme difficulty that the Americans would have in policing it adequately – was, of course, the crucial question. Only time would tell. Meanwhile neither Churchill nor the British government were particularly sanguine about the revisions of the latest US Neutrality Act which came into force on 4 November 1939, since the new law would make it unlawful for US ships and citizens to enter any designated war zones worldwide. Nonetheless, their objections were ameliorated to some extent by the so-called 'cash-and-carry' provisions of the legislation which were clearly designed to assist the Allies by allowing them to send their ships into US waters in order to collect American supplies that the British government and its Allies had purchased from the Roosevelt administration. All was well while the Allies had the financial resources to pay for their supplies, but this was unlikely to last indefinitely. Whatever the economic strength of the Allies may have been – it was weak and would get much weaker still – the 'cash and carry' provision was blatantly anti-neutral and had been designed to aid only one side in the war. This much was obvious to the non-interventionist opponents of President Roosevelt (FDR) and made them inchoate in anger at their inability to do anything about it.[31]

Shortly thereafter the 'Phoney War' ended as far as the Soviet Union was concerned. Its Baltic Fleet, which had seized the major naval bases of the Baltic

States during October, now turned its guns on neighbouring Finland on the spurious grounds that Leningrad was vulnerable to a military thrust from the Nordic state! A Finnish refusal to yield territorial sovereignty to the USSR in the Gulf of Finland and denials that it was ever intending to launch such an attack on Russia's old imperial city carried no weight with Stalin and the military leadership in the Kremlin. They wanted a compliant Finland and it was a price that Hitler was initially prepared to pay in order to obtain the Nazi–Soviet Pact. Although the hopelessly outmatched Finnish Navy could hardly be expected to put up much of a contest with the Red Banner Fleet once the 'Winter War' had begun on 30 November, the same could not be said of the Finnish resistance struggle on land where innovative use was made of the Arctic conditions to keep the Red Army at bay until peace was finally declared on 13 March 1940.[32]

While the Allies might have cast a doleful eye on Soviet naval ambitions in the Baltic and in the Barents Sea, their attention was still firmly fixed on tackling the menace posed by Germany's commerce raiders. Although *Deutschland* had escaped back to Germany and been renamed *Lützow*, the *Graf Spee* was still thought to be hiding somewhere in the South Atlantic or the Indian Ocean and the vast Allied naval dragnet – consisting of no less than five aircraft carriers, four battleships, a battlecruiser, twenty cruisers, nine destroyers, a sloop and a submarine – was no closer to finding and destroying her at the end of November than it had been at the beginning of the month. Spread as they were across two oceans, the various Allied hunting groups desperately needed any shred of evidence that could help to pinpoint where Langsdorff and his pocket battleship might be or give them a semblance of a clue as to where he might strike next. A breakthrough was finally made when reports came in of attacks by an enemy warship on the Blue Star liner *Doric Star* and the British freighter *Tairoa* on 2–3 December in the South Atlantic between St. Helena and Cape Town. Both ships were sunk in these exchanges but not before they had sent out distress calls indicating that they were under attack from a large enemy warship. This looked like the handiwork of the *Graf Spee* and a hunting group was sent off to check on whether she was still at large off the west coast of southern Africa. What these reports did was to scotch any rumours that the *Graf Spee* had somehow managed to evade all of the search groups that were out looking for her and had left the region to return to her German base.[33]

One of these groups – the depleted cruiser Force G under the command of Commodore Henry Harwood – was monitoring developments all the way down the South American coastline from Brazil to the Falkland Islands. In early December 1939 Harwood had only the heavy cruiser *Exeter* and the two light cruisers *Achilles* and *Ajax* at his disposal. His other heavy cruiser *Cumberland* was being repaired in Port Stanley. Knowing that he couldn't afford to engage the *Graf Spee* on a one-to-one basis, Harwood decided to consolidate his group 150nm (278km) off the coast of Uruguay at 0700 hours on 12 December and wait to see whether Langsdorff would be attracted to the busy mercantile shipping routes extending north from the Argentinean capital Buenos Aires to the Brazilian coastline. It was an inspired decision.[34]

After making good his escape from African waters, Langsdorff was intent on crossing the South Atlantic so that he could raid exactly the same trade routes that Harwood had identified. It was an option he liked even before he recovered some documents thrown overboard from the cargo ship *Streonshahl* which he had attacked and sunk on 7 December. These papers indicated that a convoy of four ships with few escorts worthy of the name was due to sail from the Uruguayan port of Montevideo on 10 December. In his eyes, it was too good an opportunity to miss even though he knew from the intelligence reports he had been receiving from the B-Dienst roughly where the Allied hunting groups were in their pursuit of him.[35]

As the *Graf Spee* ploughed her way through the waters of the South Atlantic, Harwood was busy thrashing out the battle tactics he wanted his three captains to orchestrate should they come across the German raider. In essence his ships would be split into two divisions so that ideally his two light cruisers could engage the *Graf Spee* from one wing of the pocket battleship, while his heavy cruiser *Exeter* would weigh in from the other wing. These tactics made very good sense since Langsdorff would be unable to concentrate all of his fire in one direction and it might give Force G the chance of hitting her and causing some damage, possibly slowing her down and forcing her to use up a good deal of her ammunition into the bargain. If Harwood's cruisers couldn't finish her off on their own, they might make her more vulnerable and set her up for destruction at the hands of one of the other Allied hunting groups that were scouring the Atlantic for the armed raider. His tactics would come to naught, however, if the *Graf Spee*'s 60cm *Seetakt* radar alerted her to Force G's presence before the Allied warships could spot her on the horizon. In that case Langsdorff could choose to avoid an engagement with a numerically superior set of enemy warships (as his standing orders indicated) or risk doing battle with them. If he chose the latter option he would have to determine quickly what these blips on the radar screen actually represented. If they were three modest warships, he could use his superior armament to keep out of their range while using his big guns to pound them into submission, picking them off one by one. If any of them was a fast, heavy ship, however, his tactics were likely to be profoundly different. Such a ship would pose the gravest threat to the *Graf Spee* and would have to be dealt with first of all. In this case he would expect to rely upon his own ship's excellent range finding and fire control to account for the heaviest enemy warship in the group. Once he had either disabled or destroyed the heavy ship, Langsdorff could then attempt to take on the rest of the group and seek to defeat them in detail.[36]

At 0500 hours on 13 December – some twenty-two hours after Force G had rendez-voused well out to sea off the mouth of the River Plate – the *Seetakt* radar set aboard the *Graf Spee* performed admirably once again detecting three ships sailing southwest of her. Ignoring his standing orders not to engage even an inferior set of enemy warships, a confident Langsdorff opted to close the ships and see what type they were. Even when his lookout crew spotted one large warship and two smaller ones (type unknown) sailing as a group at a distance of

17nm (31.5km) less than an hour later, he was inclined to think that they might be a light cruiser and two destroyers possibly out on convoy duty. Despite the fact that his radar hadn't picked up a trace of any convoy formation in the vicinity, Langsdorff changed course at 0600 hours and increased his speed to 24 knots in a deliberate move to close the three warships and engage them in gunfire with his superior armament. Fourteen minutes later a lookout on Harwood's light cruiser *Ajax* spotted a smudge of smoke on the horizon and *Exeter* was instructed to go and investigate what type of vessel had left this sign of her presence in the area. Within a couple of minutes Harwood received word from Captain Bell of the *Exeter* indicating that it was likely to be a pocket battleship.[37]

By this time Langsdorff had also discovered the nature of Force G. It was a good deal more formidable than he had previously imagined, but since he couldn't outrun the much faster cruisers, there was little he could do but to engage them at distance and hope he could knock them out before they had a chance to respond with concentrated fire or get close enough to his ship to use their torpedoes against the *Graf Spee*. As *Exeter* swiftly executed a turn to the westward and reached top speed once Bell realised who was in the offing, Langsdorff swung his own ship to port and unfurled his 6 × 280mm (11-inch) guns in an effort to pick off the heavy cruiser at a distance of 18,700 yards (17.1km), while training his secondary armament of 8 × 150mm (5.9-inch) guns on the two light cruisers on his other wing. Opening fire at 0618 hours, the gun crews of the *Graf Spee* swiftly found their range and within five minutes had begun straddling *Exeter* with only their third salvo of High Explosive shells. Although a number of casualties and some structural damage were sustained on board *Exeter*, her plight could have been far worse had all of the German shells actually exploded on impact. As it was, those that did in the early exchanges took out her 'B' turret, made a mess of the bridge and primary conning position and penetrated the forward part of the deck in a number of places. Just when it seemed that she might well have succumbed totally if the *Graf Spee* had continued her assault on her, Langsdorff broke off the engagement at 0630 hours and concentrated his full attention on the two light cruisers who had already shown considerable enthusiasm for the fight. Harwood's tactical ploy of dividing his force into two polarised fronts had indeed been sufficient to give Langsdorff pause for thought, not least because of the hits his own ship had been taking and the fact that the British light cruisers posed a torpedo threat as they churned closer to his warship. Weaving their way out of trouble with masterly precision, both *Achilles* and *Ajax* proved to be far more difficult to hit than Langsdorff would have hoped. Worse was to follow for him almost immediately when the pugnacious *Exeter*, momentarily freed from sustaining constant punishment at the hands of the *Graf Spee*, fired off the first salvo of torpedoes from her starboard tubes at the pocket battleship at 0632 hours. Langsdorff now found himself rapidly getting into an unenviable position. With the light cruisers only 13,000 yards (11.9km) away and spoiling for a fight on one wing and *Exeter* refusing to play dead on the other, Langsdorff reacted by making a 150° turn away to port in a bid to avoid the torpedoes and put some distance between him and the light cruisers. As he did so, he resumed his shelling of the heavy cruiser knocking out her 'A' turret, setting off a major fire amidships and driving a hole in the front part of the ship. Despite listing 7°, *Exeter* was not finished yet and with her speed remarkably unimpaired, Bell was able to turn his vessel so that she could fire her port side torpedoes at the *Graf Spee*. Langsdorff was forced to alter course yet again – this time 120° away from his enemies – but without having the speed to outrun them, he was left with few alternatives other than to try to destroy *Exeter* before coping with *Achilles* and *Ajax*.[38]

Sensing that his adversary was about to do just that, Harwood decided to intervene by turning westward and shortening the distance between his light cruisers and the *Graf Spee*. Once Langsdorff made yet another turn to port (0716 hours) so that he could bring his guns to bear on *Exeter*, Harwood ordered *Ajax* to turn to starboard so that his own guns could resume firing at the pocket battleship. After one of these shells had hit the *Graf Spee* amidships, Langsdorff was forced to turn once again to starboard to try to silence the impertinent light cruisers once and for all. Thereafter the duel continued with Langsdorff directing a withering amount of fire at *Ajax* – some of which struck home knocking out her after turrets – but Harwood's ship survived and was not cajoled into silence. In the jostling for position that continued apace, *Ajax* responded by turning to starboard once again and firing a volley of four torpedoes at the *Graf Spee* from a distance of 9,000 yards (8.23km). Langsdorff combed their tracks and avoided them with ease, responding with his own spread of torpedoes all of which received the same fate. At 0730 hours *Exeter*'s guns at last fell silent. Although she was something of a floating wreck by this time and had lost sixty-one dead and twenty-three wounded in these exchanges, she had at least survived the pummelling the pocket battleship had given her. Ten minutes later Harwood, believing that *Ajax* had already used 80% of her 6-inch (152mm) AP shells, ordered his light cruisers to stop firing and turned east to put some extra distance between them and the westward fleeing *Graf Spee*. Learning that his ship had already expended 60% of her ammunition on this redoubtable trio of enemy ships, and having taken twenty assorted hits from them – some of which needed urgent attention before a homeward passage could be contemplated – Langsdorff opted not to continue pressing home the attack but struck west towards the estuary of the River Plate and the neutral port of Montevideo making smoke and firing her guns as she did so.[39]

Thereafter Harwood's light cruisers, operating without the benefit of radar, were forced to shadow the *Graf Spee* as she made for the Uruguayan coast throughout the daylight hours. For the most part they were able to stay out of harm's way, but they were soon alone in their quest to do so as *Exeter*'s plight got worse as the morning wore on and Harwood was left with little alternative but to order her south to Port Stanley in the early afternoon for major repairs. As *Exeter* bore away and laboured south towards the Falklands, Harwood's other heavy cruiser *Cumberland* was proceeding north in the opposite direction on the long slog to join Force G. Whether she would arrive in time was an open question for much, if not everything, now depended upon what Langsdorff might decide to do in the next few hours. If he opted to enter the estuary of the River Plate as a ploy or feint to throw Harwood off the scent before stealing away northward again under cover of darkness, Force G would be hard pressed to counter the manoeuvre. If he decided to enter the harbour at Montevideo in order to make some running repairs to the *Graf Spee*, the critical factor would be the time he would have to spend in port to repair the damage inflicted upon her by the British ships. Obviously the more serious the damage his ship had sustained, the longer he would need to stay in port to remedy the problem and the greater the difficulty he would have in escaping from the River Plate.

Knowing from the reports of his damage control parties that her oil purification plant had been ruined and the hole in her bows needed patching up before any sustained attempt was made to cross the Atlantic and return to German waters, Langsdorff suspected that he would need at least a fortnight in port to make good these defects. Even if the Uruguayan president Alfredo Baldomir could be persuaded to interpret his nation's neutral status in a novel way so as to grant him such a respite, Langsdorff realised that the British would use the interval to bring up a host of naval reinforcements that would be waiting offshore for him once he emerged from the harbour once again. Entering the port of Montevideo at 2350 hours on 13 December, therefore, Langsdorff left himself with only two options: one was to remain there indefinitely – interned for the duration of the war – the other was to leave port after his ship had been patched up and fight his way out probably against overwhelming odds. Neither option looked particularly desirable, but he was soon left with yet a third that was easily the worst of them all. Assailed diplomatically on all sides, President Baldomir chose ultimately to grant the *Graf Spee* only a 72-hour stay in Uruguayan waters. As this wasn't nearly long enough for her to be made seaworthy again, what would Langsdorff do to resolve his dilemma?[40]

Matters were simplified somewhat by the diplomatic exchanges that took place over the next three days and by the fact that neither Hitler nor Raeder wished to see their pocket battleship permanently marooned in Uruguayan or Argentinean waters. Langsdorff was no fool. He recognised that he was in a trap of his own making. While he was prepared to pay the ultimate price for committing that cardinal error, he saw no earthly reason why others who were not responsible for making this mistake, namely, his ship's company and their prisoners, should be forced to do the same.[41] After deciding that the Allies should not have the satisfaction of sinking or capturing the *Graf Spee*, Langsdorff made meticulous preparations to ensure that his officers and men would have the final word in deciding the fate of their own boat. In a final defiant gesture, the pocket battleship that had caused the Allies so much agitation sailed out from Montevideo harbour in the early evening of 17 December with a skeleton crew on board. While four miles offshore, those aboard left her for the last time and at 2200 hours the scuttling charges they had laid now did their work and she was blown apart. Accepting the ultimate blame for the loss of his own ship, Kapitän zur See Hans Langsdorff committed suicide in Buenos Aires two days later by shooting himself in the temple with his own revolver. When told of

Langsdorff death, Hitler is cruelly reputed to have observed: 'He should have sunk the *Exeter*.'[42]

While much of the Admiralty's attention had been taken up with the chase of the *Graf Spee* in the months of November and December, the OKM had used the opportunity to engage in offensive minelaying operations using some of its U-boats, destroyers and even seaplanes in a wide swathe of the North Sea. These mining activities claimed twenty-two merchant victims at a cost of 37,075 tons in December alone. Sometimes the ships engaged upon these mining operations also chanced upon other Allied ships and could resort to the use of conventional methods to try and dispose of them too.[43] Most of the U-boats in British coastal waters were not engaged in mining activities but in mounting regular patrols designed to ensnare as many enemy ships of all types as possible. Twenty ships at a cost of 34,948 tons were to succumb to these missions in December 1939.[44]

It is not an exaggeration to state that during the early months of the war British results in these fields paled in comparison to the German effort, being neither as dramatic nor as numerous as their enemy counterparts. It took until 20 November before the British submarine crews were able to register their first success of the war when *Sturgeon* sank the patrol vessel *V209* in the Heligoland Bight. Occasional sorties in this region did eventually yield more fruit, but *Salmon*'s fine feat of sinking *U36* on 4 December and her torpedoing of both the light cruisers *Leipzig* and *Nürnberg* on 13 December was distinctly unusual and earned lavish praise, the DSO and promotion to commander for her captain Edward Bickford.[45]

Nonetheless, the one area that brought quiet satisfaction to the Allies was the astounding success of their on-going convoy operations. Only three vessels had been lost out of 431 ships that had sailed in twenty-two convoys from Halifax, Nova Scotia to ports in the UK from September to December 1939 (a loss rate of 0.70%). Three more had been lost in the fourteen convoys that had brought 473 ships from Gibraltar to the UK (0.63%), and two out of 302 ships had been sunk from twenty-one convoys that had made the passage from Sierra Leone to the UK (0.66%). Of the 131 outward bound convoys from the UK, only eight had been lost out of 2,516 ships sailing on those routes (0.32%). This phenomenal rate of success proved beyond all reasonable doubt how effective convoy was and made Dönitz even more determined to disrupt the process if the attack on trade was to succeed.[46]

As the year reached its end, however, a noticeable new trend was emerging – the use of aircraft to prosecute the naval war – whether by conducting reconnaissance flights, aerial mining, bombing operations against seaplane and fleet bases, or intentional seek and destroy missions directed against warships underway at sea. Clearly coordination between the two arms of the military was becoming an increasingly utilised feature of the overall war scene. As yet, though, whatever these aerial operations may have been touted as achieving, the simple fact was that after three months of war they had not proved to be wildly successful affairs and if one was to assess their impact on the war on a strictly cost–benefit basis they had shown a substantial deficit.[47]

Notes

1 Kershaw, *Hitler: nemesis*, pp.211–24, 228–30.
2 Three of the Polish destroyers avoided the immediate carnage by setting off for the UK on 30 August (Operation *Pekin*). All three arrived safely and were immediately modified for use in Atlantic waters. Of the five Polish submarines, three sought internment in Swedish waters between 17–25 September, while *Wilk* and *Orzel* escaped and made their way to the UK reaching Rosyth on 20 September and 14 October respectively. Rohwer, *Chronology*, pp.1–4; Gardiner (ed.), *Conway's all the world's fighting ships*, pp.347–50.
3 Barnett, *Engage the enemy more closely*, p.55.
4 Sondhaus, *Navies of Europe*, pp.220–22.
5 Peter Padfield puts the number of fatalities as 118 out of a total complement of 1,418 passengers and crew. Jürgen Rohwer gives the figure of fatalities as being 112. Padfield, *War beneath the sea*, pp.1–7; Rohwer, *Chronology*, p.2.
6 Lemp, the C.O. of the *U30*, didn't survive the war. It was claimed that he had mistaken the *Athenia* for either a troopship or a naval auxiliary (armed merchant cruiser). Padfield shows fairly conclusively that this excuse was almost certainly a lie and that Lemp must have known or had a fairly good idea that the vessel he was firing upon without warning was a passenger ship. Admiral Godt, the chief of staff to Dönitz, confirmed that Lemp had disobeyed orders and had been carried away by the excitement of the moment. Padfield, *Dönitz*, pp.191–94; *Fuehrer conferences on naval affairs*, p.39
7 Dönitz issued a reminder to his U-boat crews that the Prize Regulations remained in force. By these he meant that while enemy merchant vessels could indeed be stopped and searched while on passage, the intercepted vessel could not be sunk until the passengers and crew of the ship had been off-loaded into lifeboats. Blair, Jr., *Hitler's U-boat war: hunters*, pp.66–69; Karl Doenitz, *Memoirs: Ten years and twenty days* (New York: Da Capo Press, 1997), pp.57–58; *Fuehrer conferences on naval affairs*, pp.39–40.
8 Peter Padfield, 'Grand Admiral Karl Dönitz', in Howarth (ed.), *Men of war*, pp.177–206.
9 By 28 September 1939, the Northern Patrol, under the command of Vice-Admiral Sir Max Horton, had stopped 108 merchant ships and had ordered twenty-eight of them into the port of Kirkwall in the Orkney Islands. Levy, *Royal Navy's Home Fleet*, pp.xvi, 25, 41, 44–45, 86, 160; Barnett, *Engage the enemy*, pp.67–68; Lance E. Davis and Stanley L. Engerman, *Naval blockades in peace and war: an economic history since 1750* (Cambridge: CUP, 2006), pp.239–320; Rohwer, *Chronology*, p.3.
10 Rohwer, *Chronology*, pp.3–4.
11 In the first recorded attack on a convoy (OB.4) on 16 September, the steamer *Aviemore* (4,060 tons) was sunk by *U31*. Ibid., p.4; Blair, Jr., *Hitler's U-boat war: hunters*, p.89; Padfield, *War beneath the sea*, p.57.
12 Ships that could reach average speeds of 15 knots were classified as independents and were often allowed to sail alone since it was thought they could outrun any U-boat bent upon their destruction. In November 1940 the qualification for independent sailings was reduced to 13 knots. SC convoys were added in August 1940 running from Sydney, Cape Breton to ports in the UK. These convoys tended to be slower on average than the HX ones ranging from 6.67 knots in 1940 to 7.64 knots in 1945. Arnold Hague, *The Allied convoy system 1939–1945: its organization, defence and operation* (Annapolis, Md: NIP, 2000), pp.23–28.
13 Ships on the West African route were assembled in convoys off Freetown, Sierra Leone beginning on 14 September. They were given the convoy code SL. Fast convoys would be designated SLF and slow ones SLS. Convoys going in the opposite direction from Liverpool to Freetown were established in 1941 as OS. Hague, *Allied convoy system*, pp.109–14; Rohwer, *Chronology*, p.4.
14 Blair, Jr., *Hitler's U-boat war: hunters*, pp.88–91.

15 On 23 September permission was granted for German ships to fire on merchant vessels using W/T (wireless/telegraphy) and in early October the rules were revised to allow them to fire on any camouflaged ship they found both in British waters and in the Bay of Biscay and to destroy any armed Allied merchant vessel they confronted wherever that may be. These rules were hardened in mid-October and by the end of the month any passengers ships caught travelling in a convoy could be seen as being an appropriate target. For their part, the Admiralty instructed those commanding merchant shipping to be prepared to ram any U-boat they met on passage. Blair, Jr., *Hitler's U-boat war: hunters*, pp.95–96; Padfield, *Dönitz*, pp.197–98; Rohwer, *Chronology*, pp.5, 7.

16 Any doubts on this score would be cleared up by consulting the table of Allied and neutral shipping and tonnage lost to German and Italian submarines in the first three years of the war drawn up by Clay Blair and based on earlier work by V.E. Tarrant. It reveals the total of losses as being 147 ships (509,321 tons) from 3 September – 31 December 1939; 520 ships (2,462,867 tons) in 1940; 457 ships (2,298,714 tons) in 1941; and 780 ships (3,964,211 tons) from 1 January–31 August 1942. Blair, Jr., *Hitler's U-boat war: hunters*, p.771.

17 John Ferris has noted that the Government Code and Cypher School (GC&CS) and the military intelligence services remained badly integrated in the first two years of the war and that miscalculations on the extent of radio use in war had been a feature of the inter-war period. As a result of these and other shortages, such as Typex cipher machines, the British cryptographic system creaked at the joints before 1942. John Ferris, 'The British "enigma": Britain, signals security and cipher machines, 1906–53', in John Robert Ferris, *Intelligence and strategy: selected essays* (London: Routledge, 2005), pp.138–80; Ferris, 'The road to Bletchley Park', 53–84. For a study of the B-Dienst, see Jak P. Mallmann Showell, *German naval code breakers* (Annapolis, Md: NIP, 2003).

18 Martin Gilbert (ed.), *The Churchill war papers, Vol.I: At the Admiralty. September1939 – May 1940* (London: Heinemann, 1993), pp.183, 197, 199, 212, 217, 246, 273–75, 280, 288, 299, 315, 329, 421–23, 426, 429, 435–36, 439, 441, 452, 454, 459, 491, 506–9, 519–20, 528–29, 549–50, 700–703, 988, 1021, 1097–98.

19 Padfield notes that even at its maximum range of 2,500 yards (2.3km), Asdic was well short of the range of even a World War I torpedo. In operational situations, however, its average range fell to 1,300 yards (1.2km) making the problem of detection even more acute. While these were serious shortcomings, the Asdic equipment also proved wanting in detecting submerged submarines at distances of less than 200 yards (185m). Padfield, *War beneath the sea*, pp.23–24; Terry Hughes and John Costello, *The battle of the Atlantic* (New York: The Dial Press/John Wade, 1977), pp.31–34.

20 Blair, *Hitler's U-boat war: hunters*, pp.87–91; Padfield, *War beneath the sea*, pp.56–58.

21 Barnett, *Engage the enemy*, pp.69–70; Edwin P.Hoyt, *The life and death of HMS Hood* (London: Barker, 1977), pp.40–41.

22 Gilbert (ed.), *Churchill war papers, I*, pp.101, 156, 175, 188–89, 252–53, 511, 660–61, 669, 743.

23 Starting on 3 September the Germans established the 'Westwall', stretching from the Frisian Islands (off the Dutch–German border) north to the Jutland coast of Denmark. Rohwer, *Chronology*, pp.6–10.

24 After initially sowing 3,000 mines in the Strait of Dover from 11–15 September, the British returned to build up the new defensive anti-U-boat barrage. By late October the split level system, bristling with nearly 7,000 mines set at shallow and much deeper depths, was operational and claiming its first victims. Ibid., p.5; Barnett, *Engage the enemy*, pp, 90–92.

25 Jak P. Mallmann Showell, *The German Navy in World War Two: a reference guide to the Kriegsmarine, 1935–1945* (London: Arms and Armour Press, 1979), pp.28–31; Hughes and Costello, *Battle of the Atlantic*, pp.30, 49; Rohwer, *Chronology*, pp.4, 6, 8.

26 H.J. Weaver, *Nightmare at Scapa Flow: the truth about the sinking of H.M.S. Royal Oak* (Peppard Common, Oxon: Crescelles, 1980); Gerard S. Snyder, *The Royal Oak disaster*

64 *The opening gambit*

(London: Kimber, 1976); Blair, *Hitler's U-boat war: hunters*, pp.104–9; *Fuehrer conferences on naval affairs*, pp.48–51.
27 Dönitz having been promoted to Konteradmiral (Rear-Admiral) on 1 October, now became Befelshaber der U-boote (C-in-C of the U-boat arm or BdU for short). Prien, for his part, received the Knight's Cross from Hitler personally in recognition of his startling initiative. Blair, *Hitler's U-boat war: hunters*, pp.104–9; Dan van der Vat, 'Günther Prien', in Howarth (ed.), *Men of war*, pp.394–404; Padfield, *War beneath the sea*, pp.60–64.
28 Intelligence was hard to come by for the Admiralty's Operational Intelligence Centre (OIC) in the early months of the war. Photographic reconnaissance remained sporadic and lacking the means to keep track of what was going on in the major German naval bases meant that ships could move in and out of port unknown to the British authorities. Patrick Beesly, *Very special intelligence: the story of the Admiralty's Operational Intelligence Centre in World War II* (London: Sphere, 1980), pp.52–59; David Brown, 'Admiral John Godfrey', in Howarth (ed.), *Men of war*, pp.531–40; Stephen, *Sea battles in close-up*, p.15; Barnett, *Engage the enemy*, pp.81–82.
29 Barnett, *Engage the enemy*, pp.73–78.
30 Gilbert, *Churchill war papers. Vol.1*, pp.211–12.
31 Dallek, *Franklin Roosevelt and American foreign policy*, pp.200–232; Justus D. Doenecke, *Storm on the horizon: the challenge to American intervention, 1939–1941* (Lanham, MD: Rowman & Littlefield, 2000), pp.51, 59–68, 119–20.
32 Rohwer, *Chronology*, p.10; H.M. Tillotson, *Finland at peace and war 1918–1993* (Norwich: Michael Russell, 1993), pp.121–75; Carl Van Dyke, *The Soviet invasion of Finland, 1939–40* (London: Frank Cass, 1997).
33 Louis Brown, *A radar history of World War II: technical and military imperatives* (Bristol: Institute of Physics Publishing, 1999), pp.76, 105; Eric Grove, *Price of disobedience: the battle of the River Plate reconsidered* (Stroud, Glos: Sutton, 2000), pp.49–52.
34 Barnett, *Engage the enemy*, p.83; Grove, *Price of disobedience*, pp.52–54; Grant Howard, *The Navy in New Zealand: an illustrated history* (London: Janes, 1981), pp.44–56.
35 Grove, *Price of disobedience*, pp.43–44; Hughes, *Battle of the Atlantic*, p.51.
36 Barnett, *Engage the enemy*, p.83; Stephen, *Sea battles in close-up*, pp.16–18.
37 Ibid.; Grove, *Price of disobedience*, p.64.
38 Stephen, *Sea battles in close-up*, pp.18–20.
39 In a single sentence Stephen summed up the mess that the *Exeter* was in: 'Her casualties were 61 men killed and 23 wounded, she was unable to shoot, had more holes in her than a sieve, and her mainmast was held up by little more than faith and defiance of the laws of gravity.' Ibid., pp.20–24.
40 Apart from *Cumberland* which was scheduled to rejoin the newly promoted and knighted Rear-Admiral Sir Henry Harwood and Force G in the late evening of 14 December, the aircraft carrier *Ark Royal*, the battlecruiser *Renown*, the two heavy cruisers *Dorsetshire* and *Shropshire*, and the light cruiser *Neptune* had all been ordered to the estuary of the River Plate and were due to arrive in stages from 17–23 December. Stephen, *Sea battles in close-up*, pp.25–27; Nathan Miller, *War at sea* (New York: Scribner, 1965), pp.45–50.
41 In addition to the figures already cited for *Exeter* (see endnote 39 above) the other casualty figures for the ships involved in the Battle of the River Plate were as follows: *Achilles*: 4 dead; *Ajax*: 7 dead, 5 wounded; *Graf Spee*: 36 dead, 60 wounded. Rohwer, *Chronology*, p.11.
42 Stephen, *Sea battles in close-up*, pp.25–28; Grove, *Price of disobedience*, pp.116–39; *Fuehrer conferences on naval affairs*, pp.67–69, 72.
43 In this way the German destroyer *Erich Giese*, after minelaying duties off Cromer on the Norfolk coast, torpedoed but didn't sink the British destroyer *Jersey* on 7 December, and *U30* did the same to the British battleship *Barham* on 28 December. Hughes and Costello, *Battle of the Atlantic*, pp.49–50; Rohwer, *Chronology*, pp.11–12.

44 In his regular meetings with Hitler during the autumn of 1939, Raeder had repeatedly raised the benefits for the Germans of waging all-out economic warfare against the UK. Dönitz approved of the intensification of this campaign and wanted to see the Prize Regulations completely abandoned. In a message to his U-boat crews in November 1939, he left them in no doubt where he stood on the issue of humane principles of war: 'Rescue no one and take no one with you. ... we must be hard in this war.' Padfield, *War beneath the sea*, p.65; *Fuehrer conferences on naval affairs*, pp.46, 51–62, 70–73; Rohwer, *Chronology*, pp.10–12.
45 Rohwer, *Chronology*, pp.9–11; Padfield, *War beneath the sea*, pp.73–75.
46 See Appendix I.
47 RAF Bomber Command had got into the act early on in the war and had begun making a series of sorties against some of the principal German capital ships in the Heligoland Bight. Unfortunately, these missions often proved to be conspicuously unsuccessful. *Admiral Scheer*, one of Germany's three pocket battleships, was struck three times by five Blenheims from No.110 Squadron in the very first mission in the Schilling Roads on 4 September but all three bombs failed to explode on impact. A number of other missions were launched against German ships and naval bases over the course of the next three months with very disappointing results. Too often the British bombers either failed to spot their targets or missed them with their bombs. See entries for 4, 29 September, 7–9 October, 3, 12, 14 and 18 December 1939 in Ibid., pp.3, 5–6, 9–12.

3   Much more than a phoney war (1940)

Collective morale within the Royal Navy – having improved with Winston Churchill back at the helm as the tireless political head of the Admiralty and in the wake of the scuttling of the *Admiral Graf Spee* – began to suffer something of a decline as the New Year unfolded, ushering in the coldest winter in forty years and bringing with it repeated successes for the Germans in their mining and U-boat offensives around British shores. Of the two, mining operations could have been even more deadly had the OKW been truly convinced that aerial mine-laying might pose a decisive threat to the Royal Navy and had Hermann Göring, as the head of the Luftwaffe, sanctioned the release of sufficient aircraft to sow their stock of 22,000 magnetic mines in busy waterways around the British coast. Offensive mining operations were indeed mounted in many of the river estuaries on both the east and west coasts of Britain – the Thames, the Tyne and the Humber being especially favoured by German aircraft, torpedo boats and minelaying submarines – but the steady toll of small merchant ships or trawlers and even the occasional warship, such as the destroyer *Grenville*, which strayed into their path could have been far greater than it was.[1]

This was not the only piece of luck the British experienced. In November 1939 the Germans had inadvertently dropped a couple of magnetic mines onto the mud flats at Shoeburyness in the Thames estuary. These were recovered and defused by explosive experts and the information was used as a basis for providing an effective series of counter-measures against this type of mine in the years to come. In their outstanding book *The Battle of the Atlantic*, Terry Hughes and John Costello put it succinctly:

> Their courageous efforts contributed to the development of the highly effective 'LL' electrical sweep and a system for 'degaussing' a ship's magnetism by passing a current through cables wrapped around its hull. Small vessels were degaussed at special stations where their magnetism was 'wiped', allowing them to pass over the mines.[2]

There is little doubt that minelaying, given its true potential, ought to have been exploited more fully by the Germans. Apart from the material damage that minelaying did on a regular basis, the sobering reality for the Allies was that these enemy activities spoke eloquently of the German ability to sortie in British waters – a feature that cannot have gone down unnoticed by those inhabiting the Admiralty buildings in Whitehall.[3]

If the Allies had dodged the proverbial bullet as far as mining was concerned, indisputable evidence existed to prove that the U-boats were becoming more ruthlessly effective in their wisely chosen operational areas in both the North Sea and North Atlantic. In a five-week spell, 6 January–10 February, for example, sixteen U-boats on patrol in the North Sea dispatched the destroyer *Exmouth* along with nineteen merchant ships (67,831 tons) for the loss of only one of their number (*U15*). A marker was being put down by Dönitz's crews. It was also evident in the North Atlantic where six U-boats engaged in individual operations spread over almost a month (15 January–13 February) managed to inflict twenty-four losses on Allied merchant shipping at the cost of 92,800 tons for the loss of two U-boats.[4] While most of the ships that perished in these engagements were small merchant freighters, the cumulative effect of the loss of both the vessels themselves and their cargoes was far more significant. It would only get worse in time as new, faster and more robust U-boats became available and were able to remain operationally on station for longer periods; existing commanders became even more experienced and guileful in their art of selecting their victims and positioning their own craft to ensure a higher likelihood of success when engaging them; and improvements in torpedo design and explosive impact meant that fewer defects marred the operational performance of the entire destructive package.[5]

Being aware of the danger posed by submarine warfare and being able to do anything effective against it, however, was to be a persistent problem for the Admiralty and one that would test its ingenuity to the fullest extent over the course of the next four years. It would not be an exaggeration to say that for much of that time, the U-boat arm of the Kreigsmarine retained the upper hand. While a properly escorted convoy remained a vital key to neutralising the effectiveness of the individual U-boat, the growing experimentation with groups of U-boats working together (wolf packs) and the success that began to accompany these collaborative efforts, was a worrying trend for those on the Allied side who saw that the war on trade was a potentially crippling factor. Detection of a single U-boat, let alone a pack of them working together, remained a frustratingly elusive science that would haunt the Allies until 1944. Mastering the threat would require improved signals intelligence, the development of more sophisticated sonar equipment, aerial cooperation, and changes to the operational principles of convoy, not least in re-routing them away from danger but also in escorting the ships into port rather than merely to the edge of British territorial waters or those of their allies or trading partners. There were too many easy 'kills' in these early years of the war. Ships sailing alone in local waters – either after the convoy they had been in had dispersed or before they had even reached the convoy assembly point – proved to be a rich source of commerce for the U-boats to prey on and they did not resist this kind of temptation. Although the Admiralty could point to the lack of destroyers to help explain the reason for this vulnerability, the suspicion exists that in a strictly cost–benefit analysis, the task of providing escort cover for convoys from port-to-port would be prohibitively high. Establishing assembly points on both outward and inward legs of the journey made obvious logistical sense because the ships would be coming from and going to different ports. Whether the convoy assembly points were well chosen, however, is a matter of debate.[6]

Although they often took the initiative, not all of the German naval thrusts were rapier-like in their precision or as destructive or disruptive as the OKM hoped that they would be. Success could never be guaranteed in advance regardless of the size or composition of the force undertaking an operation – a fact aptly demonstrated in mid-February by an unsuccessful sortie (*Fall Nordmark*) mounted by the fleet commander Admiral Wilhelm Marschall with a mix of capital ships (*Gneisenau* and *Scharnhorst*) and other surface warships, plus the inevitable U-boat component, against convoy traffic on the northern route to Scandinavia. Sometimes the inexplicable happened and fate turned confident expectation into a disastrous mêlée as was the case with *Fall Wikinger* in which six German destroyers sent to savage a group of British trawlers in the Dogger Bank region of the North Sea ended up by being bombed by a group of He-111 aircraft from their own side. While 'friendly fire' may have accounted for both the *Leberecht Maass* and *Max Schultz,* it is quite possible that they may have also strayed unsuspectingly into an un-swept mine channel and run over a new mine barrage recently laid by the British. Whatever the disputed circumstances, both of these new fleet destroyers were lost with most of their officers and crew.[7]

It would be wrong, however, to give the impression that Allied success at sea was either minimal or entirely dependent upon German mistakes. Sheer weight of numbers and intelligence yields meant that some of their search and destroy operations were greeted with success. British warships were particularly effective in interdicting enemy merchant vessels and freighters that were intent on evading them as they sought to find their way home. A few did get through, but a significant number were apprehended. Faced by imminent seizure, most opted to scuttle themselves in one last defiant gesture to the enemy. As a graphic example of this trend, only one of six merchant vessels that tried to break out of Vigo on 10 February ever reached Kiel.[8]

A more immediate cause for elation in mid-February – and one that was to be a headline making news story around the world – was provided by the dashing exploits of Captain Philip Vian in the destroyer *Cossack*. Ever since the *Admiral Graf Spee* had come to grief, the Allies had been looking for her supply and prison ship, the *Altmark*. After learning that the tanker had been spotted in Norwegian waters, Vian completely disregarded the tenets of the International Law of the Sea, Norwegian territorial sovereignty and all diplomatic niceties by entering Jössingfjorden, boarding the prison ship and releasing from her hold 303 former crew members of ships previously sunk by the *Admiral Graf Spee*.[9] It was a brief but euphoric note and one that Churchill revelled in for it showed the kind of John Bull spirit that he personally typified and so admired in others. Vian was to become a personal favourite of Churchill's as the war progressed and his naval career advanced – the two things not being entirely mutually exclusive.[10]

While there was to be no corresponding propaganda boost for any of the naval combatants in March, the dreariness of the month and its weather was soon forgotten by the animated excitement of a major campaign – the Norwegian adventure. It would be one that the Germans would look back upon with great satisfaction: their strategical awareness and the logistical and tactical efficiency they brought to *Fall Weserübung (Case Weser Exercise)* being such as to humble the Allies who were out-thought and outmanoeuvred by their single-minded opponents.[11] On this occasion, Norway would not be a triumph of British naval arms, let alone a blueprint for future combined arms operations.[12]

Chamberlain's Cabinet had been grappling for months with the problem of what to do about the Swedish iron ore supplies bound for Germany that in winter – when the Gulf of Bothnia was frozen – would be transported by rail to Narvik, the Norwegian port well within the Arctic Circle, and then shipped down the west coast to Germany. While the Allies were only too well aware that some 40% of the total supplies of iron ore for the German steel industry and the military establishment it served came from these Swedish sources, the constant problem had been finding an appropriate means of choking them off. From the outset Churchill had been for mining the Norwegian Leads – the inner sea passage between the outer islands and the western coastline – which was the route taken by the freighters carrying these iron ore supplies.[13] Over the winter of 1939–40 Chamberlain's government in London procrastinated, not wishing to drive the Norwegians into the arms of the Germans by totally disregarding their territorial integrity and taking direct action in the manner advocated by the abrasive Churchill. Various military operations were mooted (often by the irrepressible first lord) and appreciations drawn up for consideration by the Chiefs of Staff (COS), but for all the time spent on planning and the importance of the cause, something always got in the way of their acceptance by the government. When the Finnish government finally signed its peace treaty with the Soviet Union on 13 March 1940, the latest of these would-be Allied operations – an initial attack on Narvik – was jettisoned.[14]

While the British showed commendable democratic restraint and futile military resolve, the Germans were not inconvenienced by either consideration. Hitler and the OKM did not need reminding that these iron ore supplies had to be guaranteed if their military objectives were going to be gained in the short to medium term. Planning to take both Norway and Denmark out of the strategic equation began seriously towards the end of January 1940 and was given added urgency by Vian's dramatic boarding of the *Altmark* in Norwegian waters three weeks later. Raeder and Hitler were not alone in seeing this incident as a revealing demonstration of the British willingness to acquire Norway by whatever means it might take in the future. Pre-empting the British, therefore, became a matter of the highest importance and General Nikolaus von Falkenhorst was assigned by Hitler to command the operation and report directly to the Führer personally. It made sense to begin this operation sooner rather than later.[15]

As the rival combatants continued to eye the same prize seemingly oblivious to one another's plans, Churchill finally convinced his Cabinet colleagues that to do nothing was to invite an eventual aggressive response on the part of the enemy. In the apparent absence of any definitive intelligence – what had been received was considered by the Admiralty to be circumstantial at best – Churchill persuaded the Supreme War Council on 28 March to give its permission for the launching of Operation *Wilfred* – the mining of three different areas in the Norwegian Leads – on 5 April.[16] He was well aware that *Wilfred* was merely a metaphorical sprat to catch a larger mackerel and that it could never really be a stand-alone operation. Once the Germans retaliated, as they must do under the circumstances, the Cabinet was prepared to send troops to occupy the southern port of Stavanger, while others would make landfall up the west coast at Bergen, Trondheim and Narvik in the far north of the country. Once again, however, a lack of urgency cloaked British efforts as the Cabinet delayed the start of the operation by three days. Correlli Barnett, echoing the views of Professor Harry Hinsley, was right to question whether this virtual state of ignorance about German planning accurately reflected the accumulation of raw intelligence data by the British military authorities at this time. Clearly, the evaluation of intelligence and the coordination of the various groups charged with this task both within the Admiralty and in the wider military community once again left much to be desired. It seemed that the British had failed to heed the lesson of the last war in preparing to wage this one.[17]

A couple of days after the ships of the British minelaying contingent and their covering group under Vice-Admiral Sir Jock Whitworth had left port on 5 April, and even before they had begun to lay any mines in Norwegian waters, a substantial German invasion fleet put to sea on 7 April. It was divided into eleven groups – six being designated to seize Norwegian ports ranging from the capital Oslo in the southeast to Narvik in the far north, and five which were required to apply the same tactics to a set of selected Danish ports scattered around their three principal islands.[18] Assembled for this purpose, the main elements of the invasion force consisted of four battleships of varying vintage and potency: *Scharnhorst*, and *Gneisenau*, representing the modern face of the fleet; and *Schleswig Holstein* and *Schlesien*, an archaic duo whose deployment was designed for purely limited ends. Supporting this mix of capital ships on the mission were the three heavy cruisers *Admiral Hipper*, *Blücher* and *Lützow*; four light cruisers; and a host of other warships.[19]

At the Admiralty the Operational Intelligence Centre interpreted the initial evidence it had received from 'Ultra' sources as a calculated move on the part of the Germans to send their capital ships out into the North Atlantic on a commerce raiding expedition.[20] As such, the enemy's invasion force moved north in almost total secrecy, while the British Home Fleet was busy making preparations (including disembarking troops from its cruisers) to intercept the German heavy ships in the North Sea before they could break out into the Atlantic. Beginning on the afternoon of 7 April and extending through to the morning of the next day the Admiralty had begun ordering the units of a substantial Allied surface fleet north from their bases at Rosyth and Scapa Flow to the Shetlands–Norway Passage and recalled others from convoy duty to assist them. By midday on 8 April Sir Charles Forbes, the stolid C-in-C Home Fleet, had the two battleships *Rodney* and *Valiant*, the battlecruiser *Repulse*, the three heavy cruisers *Berwick*, *Devonshire* and *York*, eight light cruisers, and thirty destroyers at his disposal for the task in hand. Unfortunately, it was the wrong task.[21]

Unaware of the precise nature, let alone the sheer scale, of the German operation, but sensing the need for speed, Vice-Admiral Sir Max Horton, Flag Officer Submarines, wasted no time on 7 April in ordering all his operational submarines out into the North Sea to take up a range of positions in the Kattegat, Skagerrak and around the Norwegian coastline in an effort to intercept any German attempt to interfere with Operation *Wilfred*. By 9 April he had seventeen British, three French and a solitary Polish submarine on station.[22]

As the weather deteriorated in the North Sea, the British continued to remain ignorant of the true state of play. They were not to remain in this state for long. In the teeth of what had turned out to be a fierce gale on the morning of 8 April, the destroyer *Glowworm*, which had become detached from Whitworth's covering force off Bodø while searching for a rating who had been swept overboard, discovered rather more than she had bargained for when she ran into scattered units of the German invasion fleet en route for Narvik. Lieutenant-Commander Gerard Roope, the *Glowworm*'s courageous captain, tackled in turn the destroyers *Hans Lüdemann* and *Bernd von Arnim* before being confronted by the heavy cruiser *Admiral Hipper* who loomed out of the storm to come to the aid of her compatriots in arms. Overmatched as he was, Roope's brave decision to ram the *Hipper* cost him and many of his crew their lives, but his gallantry was such as to win him a posthumous Victoria Cross. His brief signal reporting action with an unidentified warship was sufficient to arouse the anticipation of all those at sea. Forbes immediately dispatched the battlecruiser *Repulse*, the light cruiser *Penelope* and four destroyers from his own group and ordered them to make their way forward to join Whitworth's covering force consisting of the battlecruiser *Renown* and his three remaining destroyers further up the Norwegian coast.[23]

It is clear, however, from the orders issued by the Admiralty in the immediate aftermath of the *Glowworm*'s report, that neither Pound nor Churchill suspected at the time that the Germans were intent on invading Norway, let alone Denmark. By insisting that the four minelaying destroyers and their accompanying destroyer escorts withdraw from Vestfjorden – the tricky entrance to Narvik – to the relative safety provided by Whitworth's covering force further southward, the Admiralty managed to do both the unfathomable and the unjustifiable. Instead of being mined to try to prevent the German invasion force from landing at Narvik, the perilous navigable waters of the Vestfjorden were not made any more inhospitable than they normally were – an omission that was to bring much relief to the ten German fleet destroyers with their elite consignment of 2,000 mountain troops that were intent on taking the port at its head later that same day. In describing these orders, Eric Grove dolefully remarks: 'This was another disastrous piece of back-seat driving by the Admiralty where Churchill's emotional and mercurial enthusiasm combined with First Sea Lord Sir Dudley Pound's centralising professional style to cause much unnecessary trials for the fleet at sea.'[24]

Within three hours of the *Glowworm*'s fiery demise on the mid-morning of 8 April, the Polish submarine *Orzel* had sunk the troopship *Rio de Janeiro* off Kristiansand and in so doing provided positive proof that a major northern invasion by the enemy was definitely underway. A stunned Admiralty alerted Forbes and his commanders of what, they assumed, was afoot. Although the Home Fleet at Forbes' disposal was quantitatively impressive and its ships and men fought bravely and did their best with what few opportunities came their way, the fact remained that the bulk of the fleet was not deployed in such a way as to prevent the German invasion fleet from putting its troops ashore at any of the various landing areas that had been designated for them along the length of the Norwegian coastline. Whatever opposition that was mounted initially came from the Norwegian defenders, particularly in the Drøbak Narrows in the Oslofjorden, where the coastal artillery rained down shells and sent torpedoes into the newly built, heavy cruiser *Blücher*, sinking her with a loss of 320 sailors and soldiers, and damaging the pocket battleship *Lützow* (the former *Deutschland*). Even this setback didn't stop the Germans from landing an infantry division in the area around Oslo, or receiving assistance from a squad of paratroopers who had been flown in specially to seize the city's airport.[25] Elsewhere sporadic and heroic defence proved to be no match for the power of the German destroyers who swiftly dispensed retribution for any defiant gestures on the part of the Norwegians.

By the evening of 9 April, therefore, the Germans had much to celebrate for *Weserübung* had largely gone according to plan and especially in the swift occupation of Denmark. On the Allied side, defeat loomed. A combination of intelligence failures and the issuing of a series of contradictory and strategically unsound Admiralty orders could be blamed for doing much of the damage to their cause in the early stages of the Norwegian campaign. Thereafter Forbes' task was to minimise the scale of this damage by sealing off the escape routes of those German ships that had been involved in this operation and by eliminating as many of them as possible. A determined counter-attack was vital and air power would soon prove to be the key ingredient in implementing such a strategy, but Forbes' regrettable decision to leave port without the fleet carrier *Furious* left him initially bereft of such a striking force.[26]

Further north Captain Bernard Warburton-Lee in command of the 2nd Destroyer Flotilla had reached the conclusion in the late afternoon of 9 April that something needed to be done about the situation in Narvik where the port already appeared to be in German hands. While the Admiralty left the decision about whether or not to attack the German force up to him, the issue was hardly in doubt. A bold, dynamic figure who believed in action and who wished to take some retribution of his own for what had happened in Norway, Warburton-Lee planned a bold surgical strike at the enemy force in Ofotfjorden as dawn broke on 10 April in a bid to catch the unsuspecting Germans by surprise and create as much damage as he could before withdrawing.[27] According to his Norwegian sources of information, which in the end proved to be utterly unreliable, the enemy had six destroyers and a U-boat in the harbour. Undeterred by these reports, or by his own suspicion that the Germans may have mined the entrance channel into the port, the fact was that he was not about to engage a marginally superior force at all but one that was substantially superior to his own since it contained a total of ten destroyers and three U-boats. Unaware of the extent of the problem his five destroyers would be confronting in the morning, Warburton-Lee placed his faith in the element of duplicity and surprise.[28]

That surprise didn't last long. Once a volley of torpedoes and shells had struck home against both enemy merchant vessels and five German 1936-type destroyers riding at anchor in these confined waters, Narvik was quickly transformed into a scene of utter chaos and confusion.[29] Apart from the merchant ships that succumbed in this action, *Anton Schmitt* blew up, *Wilhelm Heidkamp* lost her stern, *Hans Lüdemann* wrecked her steering gear, *Hermann Künne* was damaged by the explosive demise of her compatriot, and *Diether von Roeder* was basically immobilised. While the Germans did what they could to get at the British destroyers, their torpedoes malfunctioned and the smoke screen laid down by *Havock* hindered their efforts to hit back at the impertinent enemy as they were retreating from the scene of devastation within the harbour. At this point with visibility extremely poor, Warburton-Lee called off his destroyers and, regrouping outside the harbour, discussed what to do with his staff.[30]

As the British were discussing what further action to take, the Flotilla Adjutant on *Hans Ludemann* issued an alarm call to the other five German destroyers in the vicinity: *Georg Thiele* which was located with *Bernd von Arnim* off Ballangen to the west of Narvik and *Wolfgang Zenker*, *Erich Giese* and *Erich Koellner* which were off to the northeast in Herjangsfjorden.[31] They responded immediately and set off to repel the danger. Before they could reach the harbour, however, the British had resumed their re-entry run to the same arena in line-ahead formation at 20 knots. It was 0544 hours. Visibility was still murky but *Hostile*, at the end of the line, went closer inshore to see whether she could penetrate the gloom. She was soon to receive a 127mm shell on her forecastle to suggest that the defenders might have the best of the conditions. As the British ships drew away from the mêlée, they discovered a trio of German reinforcements coming down Herjangsfjorden some 7,000 yards (6.4km) away. Warburton-Lee, believing he was confronting at least one cruiser, decided to withdraw his warships at high speed, laying down a dense smokescreen as they did so. He reported the sighting to the Admiralty at 0551 hours. As the British force sped off westwards at 30 knots, they were suddenly confronted by two more destroyers coming from the opposite direction in squally weather and poor visibility.[32]

It didn't take long for Warburton-Lee to discover that the two ships belonged to the enemy. Before he could manoeuvre his ship to port to enable all his guns to bear on *Georg Thiele* and *Bernd von Arnim*, the enemy ships had a priceless opportunity to take advantage of the situation at a distance of 4,000 yards (3.7km). They did so. *Thiele*'s accuracy was such that after straddling *Hardy*, she began hitting her at will. At 0555 hours Warburton-Lee issued a final signal to the rest of his captains that they should keep on engaging the enemy, but shortly afterwards he and many others on his ship perished as two shells burst on the bridge and in the wheelhouse, destroyed the forward guns, but otherwise left the destroyer's engines and hydraulic systems untouched. Another hit – this time wrecking the boiler – finished off the engines and left the surviving officers and crew with little alternative than to beach the *Hardy*.[33]

Over the course of the next ten minutes of hectic short range shelling, *Hunter*, *Hotspur* and *Thiele* were all hit, the former probably by a torpedo which stopped her dead in the water and turned her into a blazing wreck. Though not in the same condition as her unfortunate sister ship, *Hotspur* was far from sound. Two shells had caused such severe damage to her own hydraulic and telegraph system that she was incapable of avoiding ploughing into the stalled *Hunter* at a sickening 30 knots. Involuntarily locked together as they were, both British destroyers looked to be destined for the bottom of the fjord as their enemies would be expected to close in for the kill. In a crisis such as this with little real prospect of escape, Commander Layman and the crew of the *Hotspur* came to the fore. Using a combination of courage, skill and initiative, they performed their various tasks with great aplomb. Once the order to put *Hotspur*'s engines to full astern got through to Engineer Officer Osborne and his men, the destroyer was able to drive herself free from the doomed *Hunter*. It now needed a feat of engineering class to secure her safety. Using processes that Osborne had developed earlier to allow salt water to be used in the ship's boilers without ill effect, *Hotspur* made sufficient progress to keep her 5,000 yards (4.6km) from the three enemy destroyers (*Zenker*, *Giese* and *Koellner*) coming belatedly from the direction of Narvik. Once she had been spotted by *Hostile* and *Havock* some 2nm (3.7km) behind them, *Hotspur* was swiftly re-united with the two surviving members of the flotilla and they escorted her down Vestfjorden to safety at Skjeldfjorden in the Lofoten Islands later that afternoon.[34]

Fregattenkapitän Erich Bey, in overall command of the German flotilla on *Zenker*, decided not to give chase or slug it out with the retreating Allied destroyers or any reinforcements that the British might have sent to their aid. Instead he returned to pick up *Hunter*'s survivors and take them back to Narvik where he rejoined his battered flotilla. His situation, already chronic, would soon be made worse by the spectacular demise of his armament ship *Rauenfels* at the hands of *Havock* and *Hostile* when they met her shortly before 0700 hours coming up the Vestfjorden in the opposite direction.[35]

After hitherto enjoying far better news from the Norwegian campaign than the Admiralty had been used to receiving, the head of Marinegruppenkommando West (Naval Group West) based at Wilhelmshaven, Admiral Alfred Saalwächter, was distinctly unimpressed by the reports he began receiving about the First Battle of Narvik. He was also mystified by Bey's somewhat fatalistic reluctance to take active steps to extricate his ships from the mess in which they now found themselves. An abortive escape run made by *Zenker* and *Giese* during the evening of 10 April, forestalled by the presence of British destroyer patrols in the Vestfjorden, did nothing to inspire Bey or to improve the mood in Wilhelmshaven. This mood soured still further with the news that a second supply ship, *Alster*, bound for Narvik had been captured by the British and taken to Skjeldfjorden, and it would have darkened even more had Naval Group West known the fate of the third supply ship, the tanker *Kattegat*, which had already been sunk by the resilient Norwegians. Already desperate, Bey's plight worsened still further on the evening of 11 April when two of his few remaining fit destroyers managed to run aground as they were seeking to navigate their way to their night anchorages, causing extensive damage to *Koellner* and a bent port propeller to *Zenker*. His luck was out and it would not improve.[36]

After extensive units of the Home Fleet had spent a fruitless couple of days vainly searching for the German heavy ships off the west coast of Norway, the Admiralty decided that it could vent its frustration on the enemy naval contingent holed up at Narvik. Whitworth's force was duly strengthened with the addition of the battleship *Warspite* and a plan of action was agreed upon for the following day.[37] This secret soon leaked out through B-Dienst's reading of the Royal Navy's signals traffic and led Group West to warn Bey at 0838 hours on Saturday 13 April of what lay in store for him and his men later that same afternoon. Rejecting the possibility of scuttling his ships, Bey decided to defend them to the last and to try and inflict as much punishment on the enemy warships as possible.[38]

It would be a vain hope as those imponderable companions in arms – luck, fate and equipment failures – conspired to ensure that the Germans weren't able to take the chances they were given to inflict a series of crushing blows on Whitworth's expanded force. By late Saturday afternoon, therefore, what was left of the entire German destroyer flotilla had all succumbed to either enemy firepower or their own scuttling charges. While the Germans had been routed as a result of these two encounters on 10 and 13 April, the British had emerged pretty battle-scarred themselves; losing *Hardy* and *Hunter*, while suffering extensive damage to one of their light cruisers, three Tribals, and another H class destroyer in the process.[39] It could have been a lot worse since *Warspite*, in particular, had borne something of a charmed life throughout and could have been torpedoed on several occasions. While the British could at least repair their damaged warships and get them back into action, there was nothing that the Germans could do to revive the fortunes of the destroyers that had been wiped out at Narvik. Losing ten out of a grand total of twenty-two fleet destroyers – several of which were non-operational – was a terrific blow to the Kriegsmarine and would, as Eric Grove suggests, help to compromise their operations in the Channel and undermine Hitler's invasion plan for the United Kingdom (*Fall Seelöwe*).[40] Judged by the standards set at Narvik, the rest of the mopping up operation was nothing like as successful. Many of the German heavy ships involved in *Weserübung*, by using the poor weather to their advantage and with W/T intelligence to guide them, managed to evade both the surface units and most of the submarines of the Home Fleet as well as the Fleet Air Arm on their way home.[41]

While the German ships left Norwegian waters as fast as they could, the Allies now began their own ill-starred northern invasion. Stung by the German invasion, they had dispatched a troop convoy (NP.1) from the Clyde and Scapa Flow on 11–12 April and landed forces at Namsos north of Trondheim and at Harstad on Andfjorden in the Lofoten Islands to the north of Narvik. Hastily cobbled together, the focus of the entire operation kept changing as Churchill moved from supporting one objective (the capture of Narvik – Operation *Rupert*) to a dual goal (Narvik with a diversionary attack on Trondheim – Operation *Maurice*) which was designed to confuse and stretch the German defensive troops between the two targets. He settled finally for a direct seaborne assault on Trondheim (Operation *Hammer*) seen by the first lord at least as key to the overall military campaign in Norway. *Hammer* was by far the most hazardous mission of the lot given the virtually enclosed nature of the fjord at Trondheim, coupled with the fact that the Luftwaffe would be certain to contest such a landing. Churchill didn't give up easily on his strategic whims, however, and he was still toying with *Hammer* when the Allies began landing the 148th Infantry Brigade at Andalsnes (Operation *Sickle*) roughly some 160km southwest of Trondheim. Fortunately, Churchill's reckless enthusiasm for the *Hammer* adventure was ultimately not shared by the COS who turned it down as an operational plan on 19 April. Thereafter Pound, who shared some of his political chief's strategic views, sought a compromise solution in which both 'Mauriceforce' and 'Sickleforce' could be used to capture Trondheim. Unfortunately, the troops that had been landed had not been adequately prepared and lacked essential supplies for the task in hand. These shortcomings were bad enough, but matters were made much worse by a blurring of command responsibility. Again the fault lies at Churchill's door and that of the Military Coordination Committee for choosing the type of individuals they did and then in not encouraging them to coordinate their activities before the campaign began in earnest. 'Murphy's Law' was seen to work once more – what could go wrong, did so. It did not take long for problems to surface between the fiery old Admiral, Lord Cork and Orrery, the naval C-in-C of the Norwegian campaign, and his opposite number – the far more cautious army commander Major General P.J. Mackesy. Their differences in temperament and ideas were such as to make any concept of joint planning seem like an ironic tragicomedy. As a case study of just what not to do in combined arms operations, the Norwegian campaign was a classic of its kind.[42] Theory became swiftly detached from practical reality – not least because in the exposed wastes of Norway the Luftwaffe had established total aerial superiority and was already in a dominant position to disrupt the strategic plans of the Allies from the outset.[43]

Things could have been much worse for the Allies if the U-boats that had been sent north by Dönitz to create maximum disruption in the wake of *Weserübung* had been able to exact this kind of mayhem. Instead, the U-boats found themselves quite unable to perform up to expectations. Deployed with the latest G7e electric torpedoes that were equipped with what turned out to be a faulty magnetic firing pistol, the U-boats suffered the indignity of one equipment failure after another as their much heralded torpedoes either found their way to their intended targets only to fail to detonate on impact, or were unable to keep to the requisite depth setting so that they missed their targets altogether. A third variant – a premature explosion caused by a faulty fuse – just added to the collective exasperation of all concerned. Günther Prien, who had already become one of the finest U-boat aces by this stage of the war, expressed the collective exasperation of his fellow submariners when he likened using the flawed torpedoes 'to having to fight with a dummy rifle'.[44] Prien was not exaggerating and neither was Dönitz whose caustic anger was vented on those responsible for delivering such a 'useless weapon' into the hands of his U-boat crews.[45] German dismay at the technical deficiencies of both the G7a compressed air torpedoes and the later G7e electric torpedoes would remain a constant feature until 1942 when the design flaws that had made them so harmless were finally rectified. One doesn't have to be a counter-factual enthusiast to recognise the harm that could have been done to the Allied cause if the U-boats had been supplied with an effective torpedo not only during these early operations in Norwegian waters but also in the formative years of what would later become known as the Battle of the Atlantic.[46]

By the end of April 1940, the Allied campaign in Norway was in dire straits. Wave after wave of bombers had continued to hit the Allied positions in Andalsnes and what was left of Namsos, forcing the evacuation of both 'Sickleforce' and 'Mauriceforce' from these towns in stages from 30 April to 3 May. Despite a blanket of fog that cloaked its embarkation efforts, the success of the Allied naval forces in lifting off over 10,000 troops from the crowded quaysides in Andalsnes, Molde and Namsos and bringing them home for the loss of only two destroyers and a sloop in the teeth of everything that the Luftwaffe could throw at them deserves greater praise than it usually receives.[47]

Although the Allies continued to build up their troop levels in the Narvik area in order to prevent any resumption of the Swedish iron ore supply route to Germany, they were destined not to remain there for long. Once a new war front had opened with the German blitzkrieg attack (*Fall Gelb*) against France and the Low Countries on 10 May, the Allied position in Norway was cruelly exposed. Within a fortnight the Allied Supreme Command, recognising the futility of maintaining troops there when grave danger lurked much closer to home, ordered a total evacuation of the remaining Allied forces from Norway.[48]

Before this could be arranged, a far larger withdrawal operation had to be mounted elsewhere. By 21 May the spearhead of the German military offensive in north-western France had reached the English Channel near to the port of Abbéville, closing an armoured noose around the men of the British Expeditionary Force (BEF) who found themselves trapped in a narrow salient between the French port of Boulogne and Ostende on the Belgian coast with no prospect of escape except by sea. Vice-Admiral Sir Bertram Ramsay, the hard-bitten flag officer on the Dover station, was handed the Herculean task of organising this evacuation by the Admiralty and a more inspired choice could hardly have been made.[49] His inspirational performance in this role was matched by the heroism of those who took orders from him over the course of the next fortnight as an armada of boats ranging from the large to the ridiculously small was assembled and conveyed across the Channel to pick up the survivors of the Wehrmacht's attack on the West.[50]

Typical of the entire enterprise, the evacuation began on a stirring note with Anglo-French sorties at both Boulogne and Calais which helped to delay the German advance and enabled the rest of the BEF to retreat to the final Allied defensive perimeter line at Dunkirk (Dunkerque). With disaster looming for the BEF, Hitler controversially called a temporary halt to the German advance when the vanguard of his Panzer divisions was less than twenty kilometres away from the Allied troops. Taking the initiative from the armoured corps and handing it to the Luftwaffe was a colossal mistake and provided the British with an unlikely way out of the military mess they were in.[51]

Captain William G. Tennant, Ramsay's man on the spot in France, knew that evacuating the BEF would be a race against time. Apart from using their shallow draught vessels for lifting troops off the sandy beaches to the south and north of the town, the Allies had to get as many destroyers and other larger vessels as possible into the outer basin of the harbour to rescue the maximum number of troops in the least amount of time. In this he was aided by the individualistic nature of the Dunkirk port. It had two wooden breakwaters (moles) that jutted out into the open sea for nearly a mile (1.61km). These had been constructed to provide a more sheltered anchorage in peacetime for all the ships using the harbour and its docks. Although the West Mole leading from the burning oil terminal was obscured by smoke and flames and could not be used as a berthing stage, the East Mole stretching from the town out to sea didn't suffer from these disadvantages. While not being designed for this purpose, it could still be used by the larger ships at Tennant's disposal (destroyers, personnel carriers and hospital ships) as a temporary quayside if skill and ingenuity were applied to the task in hand and if the entire enterprise was graced with more than its fair share of fine weather and good luck. Unfortunately, a tricky embarkation was the least of the Admiralty's worries since a successful homeward passage across the English Channel in the face of determined German shore-based artillery, dive-bombers and prowling U-boats could hardly be said to be a foregone conclusion.[52] Maybe it was too much to expect but, staggeringly (some would say miraculously), all the essential ingredients for a successful evacuation held over the course of the following eight days to afford the Allies a rare psychological victory in the midst of a substantial military defeat.

Operation *Dynamo* was finally given Admiralty approval at 1900 hours on 26 May and was launched on the following day with only a fairly limited expectation of success.[53] It began modestly and far from efficiently and achieved a commensurate level of success – a mere 7,669 evacuees being plucked off the sandy beaches on 27 May. While it was better than nothing, there was general agreement that there were grounds for improvement. Apart from anything else, more and larger ships were required and greater coordination was needed at every stage of the evacuation process. As space on board the evacuation vessels was at an absolute premium, it was accepted from the outset that all the supplies of the BEF would have to be left behind to free up room for the carrying of more troops back across the Channel. Despite the frenzied efforts of enemy dive-bombers, MTBs and U-boats to disrupt the rescue mission, the numbers of BEF troops getting away from the chaos of Dunkirk ballooned over the next few days from 17,804 on 28 May to 47,310 on the following day.[54] Although the prospect of high attritional losses and damage had been anticipated beforehand, the effect of the mayhem caused by the Germans as they redoubled their efforts to bring *Dynamo* to a soggy end still left the Admiralty reeling. Ramsay was hard pressed to persuade an initially reluctant Pound to continue authorising the use of their most modern destroyers for this operation. After 53,823 troops got away from the East Mole and the northern beaches on day four (30 May), the record haul of 68,014 evacuees was reached on the following day. On the anniversary of the 'Glorious First of June' 64,429 troops somehow managed to embark successfully on the vessels sent in for them even though they had to do so under a hail of bombs and strafing, and through the swirling smoke and shrieking din that accompanied an almost incessant series of air attacks. It was a tough day with such significant losses for the Allies that the Admiralty and Ramsay agreed on the need to suspend daylight operations. By then it was clear to the leading members of Ramsay's entourage that the game was nearly up; the German Panzers were closing in on the Allied defensive perimeter around Dunkirk and it wouldn't be long before the beaches themselves would come within enemy artillery range.

Before the ring finally closed around Dunkirk, however, a vast assortment of small craft joined their larger brethren in negotiating the Channel crossing during the late afternoon and early evening of 2 and 3 June in order to resume the evacuation exercise in heroic defiance of everything that the Germans could throw at them.[55] Only six hours after the last of the 848 ships involved in *Dynamo*, HMS *Shikari*, pushed off from the East Mole at 0340 hours on 4 June the town of Dunkirk finally fell to forward units of the 18th German Army trapping 40,000 French soldiers within the breached perimeter. Amazingly, the surviving members of the BEF, along with a host of French troops together numbering 338,226, had been spirited away from the town and its beaches in eight days of evacuation. This was the upside of *Dynamo*; the downside was the total loss of seventy-two ships, including the flotilla leader *Keith* and eight destroyers, and virtually all the equipment, supplies and stores of the BEF. This scale of loss was significant in its own right, but the overall logistical impact was worsened by the fact that many more vessels were damaged than had actually been sunk and the worst affected ones would have to be withdrawn from active service until their repairs had been completed.[56]

As a propaganda tool, however, *Dynamo* could still be trumpeted by the Allied leadership not only as an outstanding operational feat carried out under extreme duress, but also as a miraculous delivery staged literally at the last moment and from under the noses of the enemy. One senses that many on the Allied side found the idea that chance and coincidence alone were at work in this operation as being far too preposterous to contemplate. For those with faith, therefore, the successful nature of this entire episode was interpreted as a clear sign of God's active intervention against Nazi Germany. For Winston Churchill, who had replaced Neville Chamberlain as British prime minister on 10 May, *Dynamo* was a psychological boost – the feel good factor was immense – and the safe return of so many troops who could be re-employed in the Allied cause again in the future was also crucially important. But the ex-first lord would need no reminding that the Allies were militarily worse off in early June than they had been when he had taken over at 10 Downing Street less than a month before. Moreover, the military retreats were not over for as one evacuation came to an end another – the withdrawal from the Allied naval base at Harstad in the Lofoten Islands – began.

Before this latest evacuation could be set in motion, however, the Allies attacked Narvik by air, land and sea during the night of 27–28 May. Designed to drive the enemy from the port and convince them that the Allies were determined to remain in northern Norway for the foreseeable future, the operation had two other aims – those of sabotaging its railway infrastructure and port facilities to prevent the immediate resumption of iron ore shipments to Germany, while providing cover for the main event which was the embarkation and withdrawal of some 24,500 Allied troops from the Narvik region. While it succeeded to some extent in achieving its more concrete aims, the operation did not bluff the Germans for long. If anything, the capture of Narvik attracted their attention and made them determined to undermine the isolated Allied position in the area. So by a coincidental quirk of fate, on the very same day that the Allies began their final Norwegian evacuation from Harstad (Operation *Alphabet*), Wilhelm Marschall steamed out of Kiel on 4 June with the *Gneisenau, Scharnhorst, Admiral Hipper* and four destroyers intent on raiding the very same base (*Fall Juno*). As the Germans steamed northwards they became acutely aware from both signals analysis and aerial reconnaissance reports that instead of building up their forces in the north, the Allies were actually in the process of withdrawing them. This played into Marschall's hands as did Admiral Forbes' constant pre-occupation with preventing any German heavy ships from breaking out into the North Atlantic. Acting on the Q-ship *Prunella*'s report on 5 June that indicated two unidentified vessels were making for the Iceland–Faeroes Passage, Forbes suspected that it might be Marschall's two battleships intent on indulging themselves on the convoy traffic they would find in the broader reaches of the ocean.[57] Determined to thwart any such plan, Forbes weakened his covering forces in the North Sea by sending off both of his battlecruisers, a couple of light cruisers and five destroyers with Jock Whitworth to investigate. Unfortunately, unbeknown to him the two German battleships that he was so apprehensive of would soon be in Norwegian waters and homing in on the two Allied troop and supply convoys that had left Harstad on 7 June bound for Scapa Flow. Unless something extraordinary happened, carnage would almost certainly result from such a meeting.[58]

Fall Juno began promisingly – an empty troop transport, a tanker and a trawler were all effortlessly sunk by the German task force during the morning of 8 June. Encouraged by these early successes, Marschall ordered the *Hipper* and his four destroyers into Trondheim harbour to take on fuel as he took the battleships *Gneisenau* and *Scharnhorst* on ahead to hunt for the real prizes. While not finding either of the convoys, the two battleships – with their 80cm *Seetakt* radar sets operating to good effect – chanced upon a most unlikely bonus: the carrier *Glorious*, loaded with a squadron of Gladiators and Hurricanes from Bardufoss, accompanied by the destroyers *Acasta* and *Ardent* as her only escorts, was steaming south at 17 knots in serene weather conditions and maximum visibility, totally oblivious to the enemy's presence in their vicinity. No aerial reconnaissance was being carried out, none of the ships had radar and no lookout was posted up in the crow's nest. Maintaining such lax operating standards was unforgivable and reckless in the extreme, but the captain of the *Glorious*, Guy D'Oyly-Hughes, was by this stage emotionally overwrought and perhaps even mentally unbalanced. He was certainly not the man to cope with Marschall's battleships and his orders throughout lacked both inspiration and merit. Once some smoke had been spotted by a lookout on the *Scharnhorst* at 1546 hours and a mast had become visible at 44,000 yards (40.2km) a quarter of an hour later, the hunt was on. Sadly, D'Oyly-Hughes made an easy quarry for the Germans. He seemed totally out of his depth. Inexplicably, no SOS was broadcast for twenty minutes and even when it was the message went out on a discontinued frequency. Worse still he didn't immediately order his ships to turn away to the southeast to put some distance between them and the enemy. It didn't take long for his ineptitude to have tragic consequences. Six minutes after opening hostilities at 1632 hours, one of *Scharnhorst*'s 279mm (11-inch) shells fired at a range of 26,400 yards (24.1km) ploughed its way through the carrier's flight deck and exploded in her upper hangar engulfing the entire area in flames and eliminating any possibility of getting her aircraft aloft. Inexcusably, *Glorious* forged on for another nine minutes before belatedly turning away. It was the last of a number of crass errors her temperamental captain made that afternoon. Only nine minutes later a shell from *Gneisenau* struck the bridge of the carrier killing him instantly. While *Glorious* was wreathed in smoke for several minutes thereafter, the battleships turned their attention to *Ardent* and brought her under fire. Although she fought bravely, it was an unequal struggle and by 1722 hours she was no more. By then *Glorious* was also in a terminal state having been hit a couple of minutes before by a shell from *Gneisenau* which had plunged down and exploded in her centre engine room with devastating effect. It would take another fifty minutes before she sank. In the meantime *Acasta* courageously took up the challenge. Engaging the enemy with everything at her disposal, the lone British destroyer even managed to torpedo the *Scharnhorst*, punching a substantial hole (fourteen metres long by six metres high) in her starboard side, forcing her to take on about 2,500 tons of water, putting her after-turret (Caesar) out of action, and killing forty-eight German sailors in the process. Listing 5° and with her stern down by almost a metre, *Scharnhorst* had to cut her overall speed to 20 knots. Although under sustained attack, *Acasta* kept pounding away at her and even managed to strike the battleship's B turret (Bruno) with one final defiant blow before sinking about ten minutes later at 1820 hours.[59]

Despite his emphatic victory on this occasion, the severity of *Scharnhorst*'s damage came as a blow to Marschall. It left him with little option other than to abandon his pursuit of the Allied convoys temporarily and return to Trondheim where the battleship could be temporarily patched up before she undertook the journey back to Kiel for a full scale repair job.[60] By the time *Gneisenau* re-emerged with the *Hipper* to resume the convoy chase on 10 June, the vulnerable troop transports had long gone. Many thousands of servicemen had cause, therefore, to thank everyone aboard *Acasta* for their heroic performance in the face of superior firepower. Sadly, only one of her crew of 160 lived to tell the tale. He joined two others from *Ardent* and forty-three from *Glorious* to survive these encounters. Alas, 1,515 other Allied servicemen, did not.[61]

There is, if anything, an even sadder coda to this story. Suspicion continues to exist that the heavy cruiser *Devonshire*, on her way back from Tromsö after rescuing the Norwegian royal family, government ministers and the country's gold reserves, picked up a garbled distress call from *Glorious* in the late afternoon of 8 June at a distance of only 70nm (129.6km). It is alleged that this message from the W/T room was passed to her commanding officer Vice-Admiral Sir John Cunningham who not only steadfastly refused to respond to the SOS call but may have actually doctored the ship's log to strike any evidence from it that such a call had been received in the first place. Whatever the real truth of this story is, we know that *Devonshire* never broke radio silence to report the SOS call and an unknown number of servicemen who survived the sinking of their ships eventually perished before they could be rescued.[62] What makes this scale of loss even more horrendous is that the entire episode was completely unnecessary. *Glorious* should never have been released from Lord Cork's fleet or given so little protection on her homeward journey, and, to compound matters still further, the volcanic and unbalanced D'Oyly-Hughes should never have been allowed to exercise command over anything at this stage, let alone one of the Royal Navy's few invaluable carriers.[63]

It was a wretched end to a Norwegian campaign that had revealed real weaknesses in the Allied command structure at all levels; distressingly poor appointments had been made; strategic and tactical decision making had been faulty, inconsistent and slow; the enemy had often been underestimated; combined arms operations had rarely been effective; and optimum use had not been made of intelligence sources. Any of these errors would have been bad enough on their own, but taken together they posed problems that the Allies could not solve. It is sobering to think that it could have been far worse but for *Acasta*'s spirited intervention in the late afternoon of 8 June. Even with a decent corps of cruiser escorts, the troop and supply convoys from Harstad would not have been favoured to survive intact if the two German battleships – let alone Marschall's entire *Juno* fleet – had caught up with them on their homeward passage to Scapa Flow.

By winning this stuttering campaign, the Germans had secured both their iron ore supplies and a range of Norwegian ports for their operations in the North Sea, but these assets had come at the cost of having their modern destroyer fleet ripped apart and losing a third of their cruisers. Neither Hitler nor Raeder were impressed by Marschall's handling of the fleet and he paid the penalty for their disapproval by being brusquely shunted aside as Flottenchef (fleet commander) shortly afterwards. His replacement Admiral Günther Lütjens – a supposedly more incisive figure – enjoyed no better luck in these waters as the *Gneisenau* joined her sister ship *Scharnhorst* on the sidelines for an extended period after being torpedoed in the bows by the submarine *Clyde* on 20 June.[64]

Churchill's luck wasn't too good either at this time. France was already stumbling towards defeat when the Italians joined the war on the side of the Axis on 10 June.[65] Although four of its six battleships were not immediately operational, the Regia Marina Italiana (Royal Italian Navy) still had seven heavy cruisers, fourteen light cruisers, sixty-one destroyers, 144 torpedo boats and 117 submarines at its disposal from the outset. As such, its deployment in the Mediterranean and the Aegean was bound to complicate the Allied war effort in these seas and through its active presence in the Red Sea and Indian Ocean potentially compromise the safe operation of the Suez Canal as well.[66] Dudley Pound and his trusted VCNS Tom Phillips certainly believed that with the French Navy apparently out of the equation, the Italians could make things very uncomfortable for the British in the Mediterranean. While they were in favour of withdrawing the fleet from Alexandria, neither Churchill nor his combative C-in-C Mediterranean, Admiral Sir Andrew Browne Cunningham, would hear of it. Churchill's fervent support for an active presence in the Mediterranean was crucial in convincing the COS to endorse the decision to retain the Alexandria base for the time being. This left Cunningham with a fleet that was certainly capable of holding its own in the Eastern Mediterranean, but whose scattered units looked acutely vulnerable at both Malta and Gibraltar without substantial French support and with the Spanish dictator General Franco weighing up the option of abandoning neutrality in favour of joining the Axis Powers as Hitler and Mussolini fervently wished he would.[67]

Once the Reynaud cabinet fell in mid-June, the British government's concern about the eventual fate of the French Navy grew perceptibly as Marshal Pétain – the veteran hero of Verdun – emerged to press the case for an immediate armistice and the formation of an administration that would be prepared to collaborate with the Nazis. In the days leading up to the signing of the armistice at Compiègne on 22 June, the French Navy had opted to move their larger warships from their metropolitan ports to those in colonial Africa.[68] While it was considered essential that these vital warships should not be employed by either the Germans or their Vichy French partners in support of the Axis, the Admiralty had first to arrange for another set of evacuations to bring back 191,870 Allied troops from a total of nine ports dotted along the Channel and Biscay coasts by the time France exited from the war on 25 June.[69]

Whilst their former Allies were engaged in withdrawing from the war, the attitude of the British hardened considerably and by the end of the month they had begun assembling Force H under Vice-Admiral Sir James Somerville at Gibraltar.[70] Flying his flag in the aging battlecruiser *Hood*, Somerville had a decidedly mixed force of old and limited battleships (*Resolution* and *Valiant*), a modern carrier (*Ark Royal*), two cruisers (*Arethusa* and *Enterprise*) and fifteen destroyers at his disposal. Force H desperately needed time to train together before it went out on any operational sorties, but that was a luxury it would not receive. Somerville's operational brief (Operation *Catapult*) looked disarmingly simple and direct: he was to deal with the French warships that had gathered at the Algerian naval base of Mers-el-Kebir and its adjacent port of Oran. Ideally, Somerville ought to persuade the proud and irascible French naval commander, Admiral Marcel Gensoul, to recognise a case of force majeure and comply with the terms of a British ultimatum drawn up in order to take the French fleet out of the wartime equation. If he chose to ignore the ultimatum, however, Somerville was meant to disable or destroy these vessels so that they would not fall into the hands of the Germans and be used against the Royal Navy at any stage in the war. Although Admiral Jean-François Darlan, the C-in-C of the French Navy, had assured the British before the armistice had been signed that none of his fleet would ever be transferred to the Germans, the Admiralty – who considered him to be an Anglophobe – frankly didn't believe him. When news emerged that he had been appointed minister of marine in Pétain's Vichy government on 27 June, this distrust deepened. Already appalled at the post-armistice arrangements for dealing with the French fleet, the British (and in particular Churchill) didn't trust either the Vichy regime or the Axis Powers to keep their word on the permanent demobilisation of these warships.[71]

Somerville reluctantly anchored Force H off Mers-el-Kebir in the early hours of 3 July. He found *Catapult* distasteful in the extreme and his undistinguished performance over the next few hours fully reflected this fact. Before the unpalatable Churchillian ultimatum had been delivered to Gensoul at 0935 hours, the British had already seized those French warships that had been in the British ports of Dundee, Falmouth, Plymouth and Portsmouth (Operation *Grasp*).[72] News of this treachery further poisoned the already strained atmosphere in Oran and gave Gensoul and his superiors at *la Marine française* even more reason to distrust the British. After stalling for time and with the latest and apparently final deadline looming, Gensoul finally rejected the British terms. A little while later at 1755 hours the *Hood*, *Resolution* and *Valiant* opened fire. It was the last thing that Somerville had wanted to happen and yet now there was nothing else that he could do. In the chaos and confusion that followed the older battleship *Bretagne* was blown up with the loss of 977 of her crew, two other battleships, the modern *Dunkerque* and the older *Provence*, were badly damaged and beached (with another 210 officers and crew dead on the flagship alone), the destroyer *Mogador* lost her stern (another forty-two dead) as a result of a direct shell hit and the aircraft depot ship *Commandante Teste* was set on fire.[73] Amazingly, perhaps, the modern battleship *Strasbourg* and five large destroyers all made it through the thick pall of smoke and out of the harbour avoiding Force H as they did so. Somerville was slow to believe that any vessel could have escaped from the mêlée inside the Algerian harbour and only began to track down the coast in search of these ships at 1830 hours after receiving two aerial reconnaissance reports confirming the fact that they were out on the loose.[74] Despite giving chase, Force H missed its quarry; even a torpedo attack by six Swordfish from the British carrier didn't disable the *Strasbourg* and she disappeared into the night along with her destroyer escort and eventually reached the safety of Toulon harbour on the evening of 4 July. Somerville admitted afterwards that this had not been his finest hour in command and it wasn't. London was not amused and Vichy was incandescent with rage – breaking off diplomatic relations with the British with immediate effect. French anger and resentment was further inflamed when aircraft from the *Ark Royal* launched a torpedo attack on the *Dunkerque* on 6 July, destroying the auxiliary ship *Terre Neuve* lying alongside her at Mers-el-Kebir. As the *Terre Neuve*'s cargo of depth charges exploded, they ripped open the side of the battleship and led to the loss of another 150 French sailors.[75]

Fortunately, Cunningham was in a better position and had a more malleable individual in Admiral René Godfroy to effect the demobilisation of the French fleet at Alexandria. He was also given more time to bring about this desirable outcome. Notwithstanding his good personal relations with his French compatriot, however, the effect of *Catapult* had vastly complicated the situation. In the end, Cunningham, listened to the advice of his chief of staff, Rear-Admiral Algernon Willis, and asked his officers to make a direct appeal to the men under Godfroy's command by sending a series of signals and arranging visits to individual ships, explaining the gravity of the situation in person and appealing to their erstwhile allies to avoid a battle that would pit them against overwhelming odds and cause unnecessary loss of life. It was an extraordinarily unconventional gesture, aided and abetted by the French naval liaison officer with the Mediterranean Fleet, Capitaine Philippe Auboyneau. Nevertheless, it succeeded. Godfroy's captains and their crews put pressure on the French commander on 5 July to bow to Cunningham's demands for demilitarisation and on 7 July a formal agreement was worked out between the two commanders to this effect.[76]

On the same day the Admiralty ordered the carrier *Hermes* and the heavy cruisers *Australia* and *Devonshire* to impose an ultimatum on the French fleet in port at Dakar on the most westerly tip of the African continent. This ultimatum was designed to ensure that the yet-to-be-completed battleship *Richelieu* would not become a factor in the war. After being refused entry into the harbour to deliver the ultimatum, the British were forced to improvise. During the night of 7–8 July, a fast launch from the *Hermes* was dispatched with depth charges to do the job that the ultimatum was designed to arrange. Evading the boom at the entrance to the harbour and entering the inner basin swiftly and stealthily, the launch dropped her depth charges under the stern of the *Richelieu* and withdrew unharmed. For some reason the depth charges failed to explode, so a wave of carrier-based Swordfish bombers were sent in to torpedo the battleship. Only a solitary torpedo from the six aircraft employed in the attack scored a hit on the

Richelieu, but it was sufficient to wreck the propeller shaft and cause flooding in three of her compartments – damage that would take nearly a year to repair.[77]

It was with unalloyed relief that both Cunningham and Somerville put their recent confrontations with the French behind them and sought to take the fight to their real enemy – the Italians – in the Mediterranean during the next few weeks. An initial 105-minute engagement between the two fleets took place off the southeast coast of Calabria during the afternoon of 9 July. Although indecisive, the Battle of Punta Stilo demonstrated that Admiral Inigo Campioni's capital ships were fast and were well supported by light forces that had 'outnumbered, outgunned and outranged' Cunningham's own cruisers.[78] When the numerical advantage enjoyed by the Italians in all types of aircraft was also factored in, Cunningham's Mediterranean Fleet looked decidedly shorthanded and desperately in need of a modern carrier if it was do something more than merely hold its own in these waters. Churchill wanted much more than a mere stalemate in the Mediterranean and was prepared to support the call for reinforcements to be sent to Alexandria so that the fight could be taken to the Regia Marina. His enthusiasm for doing so was heightened by the action off Cape Spada (Crete) on 19 July and in the Gulf of Bumbah (off Tobruk) on the following day when a mixture of Allied warships and carrier aircraft got much the better of the Italians. What these three encounters in July revealed was an underlying inconsistency in the performance levels of the Italian Navy. While it could be good on occasion, it could also be demonstrably lame on others. It was a mercurial condition that afflicted the other services too, and left both friends and enemies alike wondering just what to expect from the Italians in the war.[79]

Although it was tempting for those in Whitehall to dismiss the bombastic Mussolini as a preposterous poseur and his military as more of a liability than an asset to the Axis cause, the fact was that both were still perfectly capable of complicating the strategic picture for the British and they demonstrated this art to perfection by invading British Somaliland at the beginning of August. Once again the British were forced to retreat and conduct the latest of their series of evacuations – a small scale affair from Berbera to Aden – within a few days.[80] Success in one theatre was quickly followed by failure in another. Throughout the war Italian combined arms operations routinely promised more than they actually delivered. Too often the degree of liaison between the services or the level of competence of any one of them left much to be desired. Above all, however, the failure of the Italian military to make the most of its geographical position was to be a recurring and galling theme for the fascist leadership. An early example of what was to come was shown in late August when an important Allied reinforcement convoy (Operation *Hats*) sailed through the heart of the Mediterranean to join Cunningham's Fleet at Alexandria defying and evading aerial reconnaissance, submarine patrols and an Italian Fleet bristling with five battleships, thirteen cruisers and thirty-nine destroyers that had been deployed to detect and destroy it.[81]

While the news from the naval side of the Mediterranean and Middle Eastern theatre was mixed for all the combatants, the Germans were clearly in the ascendant in more northerly latitudes. Benefiting from a combination of good signals intelligence, distinct operational advantages now that they were largely based in French and Norwegian waters, and an improvement in tactics, Dönitz's U-boat crews enjoyed a hugely destructive month (7 August–8 September) and referred to it as a 'happy time' (*glückliche Zeit*). It wouldn't be their last.[82] As long as Allied ASW (Anti-Submarine Warfare) remained fairly primitive, the U-boat was likely to escape detection and destruction more often than not. It would take many months for developments in centimetric radar, direction finding and range estimation to bring about improvements in detection methods even if the signals intelligence (SIGINT) coups emanating from the GC&CS cryptanalysts at Bletchley Park told the Admiralty where to start looking for them.[83] As with the process of detection, the methods of destruction were fairly basic and essentially came down to either depth-charging or ramming, before mortars like the 'Hedgehog' were introduced in early 1942 and the aerial 'Leigh Light' came into operation a few months later to illuminate U-boats running on the surface and lead to a greater chance of successfully destroying them through aerial bombing.[84]

Hitler's intensification of the war against the United Kingdom both at sea and in the air during the late summer and early autumn of 1940 underlined the nature of the titanic struggle that beset Churchill's government at this time. Alone in Europe, it remained acutely vulnerable. If the RAF lost the Battle of Britain, for example, an invasion was bound to follow. It didn't, but the result was in doubt for several weeks. As this drama was being played out in the skies above the Channel and over the Home Counties, the grim toll at sea mounted. Already bad enough, it could have been even worse if the Germans had possessed a larger force of operational U-boats at this time.[85] Dönitz certainly believed that a great opportunity was being missed to wreak such untold damage upon the Allied cause that the entire complexion of the war may well have been changed in favour of the Axis Powers. His frustration was not eased by the addition of twenty-six Italian submarines to his command over the next few months. Their operational performance was unimpressive in absolute terms and if viewed relative to their German allies rather pathetic.[86] He sensed that they were too pampered in their well-appointed boats and didn't possess the killer instinct that his own hard-bitten crews had. As a result, he deployed them well to the west of his own U-boats in the hope that they wouldn't get in the way of those whom he could trust.[87]

Fortunately for the British, all was not gloom and despair. If any further evidence was required that Roosevelt's administration in Washington had abandoned any pretence at neutrality and actively embraced a very partial non-belligerency in favour of the British Commonwealth, it was provided by the signing of an Executive Order on 2 September that exchanged fifty over-age destroyers for the long-term lease by the US Navy of several bases in the Caribbean, along with others in the Bahamas, Bermuda and Newfoundland. Although the American destroyers were awkward and uncomfortable to operate, rolled up to 70° in swells, were slow and prone to malfunctioning, their transfer was still more than just a symbolic gesture. Once in working order, some of them would help to supplement the Royal Navy's hard-pressed destroyer strength and were slated for use on the vital convoy escort routes in the North Atlantic. Their defects were such, however, that the Americans were seen by the British as getting by far the better part of the deal since the bases that the US inherited in this exchange could at least be made operational with the minimum of delay. That could not be said of these old, poorly designed and constructed 'four stackers'. Most needed several months of intense work to become fully serviceable. Some never made it.[88]

Although the Allies had accepted the principle of convoy from the outset of this war – unlike their reluctance to embrace it in the early stages of the Great War – one sensed that their politicians (even those with some experience of naval business who should have known better) still regarded them as being inherently vulnerable and hostages to fortune. In some sense, of course, they were, but until aerial surveillance, information gathering and code breaking vastly improved, the fact was that many convoys (even the slowest moving ones) still often managed to escape detection from a variety of hostile craft – aircraft, surface ships and submarines – deployed against them. This was understandable in the vastness of the oceans since without some indication as to the routing of these ships and much more plentiful resources devoted to the task, the enemy was often casting around searching for the proverbial needle in a haystack. What was far more surprising and frustrating for the pursuers, however, was that even in relatively confined waters convoys often got through and not just because they were protected by their destroyer screens and other escorts. Both sides of this coin were seen in September. Early in the month the Italians somehow managed to miss a convoy on its way from Aden to Suez even though a combination of destroyers, submarines and torpedo boats were arrayed against it, and they drew another blank when looking for a convoy of twenty-three ships in the Red Sea on 19–21 September. On both occasions the convoy had been spotted from the air and directions had been given to the search and destroy vessels. For their part the British could hardly gloat about the incompetence of the Italians when the Vichy regime was able to run 540 convoys (containing 1,750 ships) through the Straits of Gibraltar in both directions over the course of the next twenty-six months.[89]

Churchill's anguish about the failure to cut off these or any other enemy ships from entering or exiting the western end of the Mediterranean at will was to become a marked feature of this period. His ire was particularly roused by the high speed passage of three light cruisers and three large destroyers through the Straits of Gibraltar on 11 September en-route for Libreville in Gabon – a French West African colony that had already gone over to Charles de Gaulle's Free French forces. Apart from eluding what was left of Force H at Gibraltar and then again at Casablanca, the Vichy ships swept imperiously into Dakar on 15 September undetected by John Cunningham's 1st Cruiser Squadron and the carrier, *Ark Royal*, who were out looking for them. Furious that these warships had not been intercepted, both Churchill and Pound cast around for a scapegoat and found one in Admiral Sir Dudley North, the Flag Officer on the North

Atlantic station, based in Gibraltar. Accused of lacking initiative in an emergency, North was harshly relieved of his command. As Barnett suggests, however, the blame for this combined failure could just as easily have been laid at the Admiralty's door or that of 10 Downing Street.[90]

Churchill's temper was sorely tested by another fiasco off Dakar (Operation *Menace*) later in the same month. An ill-judged encounter that had been planned on the mistaken assumption that the authorities in Dakar would renounce the Vichy regime in order to enthusiastically welcome de Gaulle and his Free French forces, *Menace* went badly awry almost from the beginning. Having already had the light cruiser *Fiji* torpedoed before the troop convoy had even cleared the Hebrides, a large force of Allied warships and three Free French sloops arrived off Dakar on 23 September to discover that neither the port nor the warships assembled within it were interested in embracing the Free French cause.[91] *Menace* proved to be a grossly misnamed operation. It was finally called off on 25 September when the battleship *Resolution* was put out of action for a year after sustaining massive torpedo damage from the sole remaining Vichy submarine (*Bévéziers*) operating in Senegalese waters. Although the Vichy naval authorities had lost two of its own submarines and a large destroyer in foiling this attack on its territory, the British had suffered proportionately more. Apart from the damage done to the *Resolution*, the other battleship *Barham* had also been hit, though not seriously, a cruiser and two destroyers had been damaged, and nineteen aircraft from *Ark Royal* had been destroyed.[92]

If the news was depressing at sea for the Allies, there was some relief as the war in the air at least showed distinct signs of promise. Hitler and the German High Command (OKW) had made a number of critical strategic mistakes in prosecuting the Battle of Britain.[93] These shortcomings had allowed the RAF a breathing space that it had used profitably to check the massive assault by Göring's Luftwaffe and deny it the opportunity of achieving aerial superiority over the Channel.[94] Aware that he could not afford to risk launching *Fall Seelöwe* (*Case Sea Lion*) without establishing this requisite aerial dominance, Hitler reached an initial decision on 17 September to postpone, but not cancel, the cross-Channel invasion. In the end, however, it was merely a semantic difference, as this postponement became nothing less than a preliminary cancellation of the entire operation.[95] Thereafter while the huge invasion fleet the Germans had assembled in an arc of ports from Le Havre to Antwerp languished for months on end, the Luftwaffe continued to wage an all-out bombing offensive against the major British cities and ports in a bid to destroy their infrastructure and civilian morale. Despite the material damage caused by the 'Blitz', the prevention of the invasion was yet another compelling defensive effort in what was already proving to be a war in which heroic defiance had been turned into notable psychological successes. Churchill had been right in August to extol the virtues of the RAF and to describe the performance of its aircrews as representing a signal epoch in the history of the British people.[96]

Even so, there was no time for the British to bask in their success on this front because the daily bulletins from the North Atlantic suggested that the German war on trade was being won convincingly by Dönitz and his U-boat fleet. In addition to the carnage they wreaked on merchant shipping sailing alone, their use of well-coordinated wolf-pack tactics (*Rudeltaktik*) threatened to decimate even the most heavily-defended convoys as SC.7 and HX.79 both found to their cost on 17–20 October. Losing 70% of the ships from the former and 24.5% of the latter was sobering news for the Admiralty and made it imperative for the Allies to find some way of evading these marauding groups of U-boats in future.[97]

Further proof that the Axis Powers were prepared to widen the war even more came with the signing of the Tripartite Pact linking them with Japan in late September and reports of a meeting held between Hitler and the Spanish Caudillo Francisco Franco at Hendaye in the Pyrenees on 23 October.[98] Mussolini had struck both before and after these diplomatic initiatives had been arranged. His reckless enthusiasm for the Axis war effort had been shown firstly in a cross-border attack launched by his 10th Army on Egypt in mid-September and then by an invasion of Greece from across the Albanian border in late October.[99] While his military forces didn't cover themselves in glory in either of these two new theatres, the Regia Marina – now boasting six battleships – was not doing much more than engaging in mining operations, escorting convoys and skirmishing unsuccessfully with Cunningham's Mediterranean Fleet.[100] Worse was to follow for Il Duce and his fleet before November was out. During the night of 11–12 November, two waves of Swordfish aircraft from the carrier *Illustrious* had the temerity to attack the Italian Fleet as it lay at anchor in harbour at Taranto, crippling three of its battleships while slightly damaging a heavy cruiser and a destroyer into the bargain.[101] Everyone on the British side was delighted with the results of Operation *Judgment*, since it appeared to have eased the Allied naval position in the Central Mediterranean, by reducing the risks to their convoy traffic and boosting morale in their own ranks, while complicating the Italian strategic situation and deflating the enemy. Cunningham summed up the cost–benefit analysis of the entire operation perfectly by stating: 'As an example of "economy of force" it is probably unsurpassed.'[102] He was not prone to exaggeration and his enthusiasm for taking the fight to the Italians was infectious.

Somerville needed little encouragement in this respect and the next chance to do battle with Admiral Inigo Campioni, the Italian Fleet Commander, fell to him off the southern tip of Sardinia (Cape Teulada) on 27 November. Unlike *Judgment*, the engagement (Operation *Collar*) was a limited and inconclusive affair and was broken off by Campioni before the battle fleets had a chance of getting to grips with one another. Campioni's tactical withdrawal in the face of what he thought was a superior force was the last straw for an enraged Mussolini who linked his caution with pusillanimity (a quaintly Churchillian interpretation of the word) and looked for a dramatic change of fortune for the Regia Marina in the weeks to come. It was hoped in Italian circles that this would result from a fundamental reorganisation of both the naval establishment, with Admiral Arturo Riccardi replacing Admiral Domenico Cavagnari as under secretary of state and head of the Supermarina and the fleet itself, with Admiral Angelo

Iachino becoming fleet commander at the expense of Campioni.[103] If December was anything to go by, however, it looked like a case of wishful thinking since Cunningham's aircraft attacked Italian airfields on Rhodes, his battleships bombarded the Albanian port of Valona and Allied convoys continued to bring in supplies and reinforcements for Malta.[104]

Although the year ended on an indisputably upbeat note for the Allied naval forces in the Mediterranean, the same could not be said of their fortunes elsewhere. Apart from the killing sprees of the U-boats in the North and Central Atlantic from which there appeared to be no early respite, and the existence of disguised armed raiders who preyed on unsuspecting merchant vessels around the globe, the likelihood was that heavier units of the German surface fleet would be sent out on raids to disrupt convoys, savage vessels sailing alone and tie up large concentrations of Allied warships that would be drafted in to try to hunt them down.[105] Some evidence of this trend was already unmistakable in the activities of *Admiral Scheer* off Newfoundland in the early part of November and in the South Atlantic a month later and in the less successful sortie undertaken by *Admiral Hipper* in the North Atlantic in December. More worrying still was the plan made by those ubiquitous sisters *Gneisenau* and *Scharnhorst* to break out into the North Atlantic at the end of the year – an attempt foiled by storm damage in the North Sea rather than by constructive action from the British.[106] Solutions for these very real problems were not easy to come by. When added to the German penchant for aerial mining and bombing of British ports and estuaries, the members of the Commonwealth were confronted with some very stiff challenges as they said goodbye to the old year and ushered in 1941.[107]

Notes

1 While the Germans mostly used contact mines at this stage, they did possess a far more effective variety – the magnetic mine – that was both deadly and not easily detectable. This type of mine was activated by the electro-magnetic effect that occurred when an unsuspecting vessel passed over such a mine lying on the seabed. In this case the ship's own magnetic field would trigger the detonating mechanism of the mine. In fairly shallow waters, these explosions were often catastrophic. Sown in an estuary of a large river, such as the Thames, therefore, the magnetic mine could cause major disruption. Rohwer, *Chronology*, p.13. Correlli Barnett notes that contact mines accounted for seventy-nine merchant ships (262,697 tons) in the first four months of the war. Barnett, *Engage the enemy*, p.90.

2 Hughes and Costello, *Battle of the Atlantic*, p.50.

3 Mining operations conducted off the coasts of East Anglia and Tyneside on 10–11 January by two groups of German destroyers subsequently claimed another four victims (11,406 tons). These raids increased the hazards to be encountered in British coastal waters by all types of craft and underlined the need for the Allies to sweep their coastal areas thoroughly. Even so, accidents could always happen particularly if the German sorties were undetected. Rohwer, *Chronology*, p.13.

4 Blair, Jr., *Hitler's U-boat war: hunters*, pp.135–45; Rohwer, *Chronology*, pp.13–14.

5 John Terraine, *Business in great waters: the U-boat wars 1916–1945* (London: Leo Cooper, 1989), pp.255–74; Geoffrey P. Jones, *U-boat aces* (Bristol: Cerberus, 2004);

V.E. Tarrant, *The U-boat offensive 1914–1945* (London: Arms and Armour, 1989), pp.81–96.
6 Further losses to U-boat activity in the North Sea alone in a little over a month (25 February–29 March 1940) underlined the gravity of the problem. Nine U-boats operating in this area claimed nineteen victims (44,812 tons) at the cost of two U-boats. Rohwer, *Chronology*, p.16; Hague, *Allied convoy system*, pp.23–75, 107–8. For the impact of the U-boat in the period 1941–44, see Tarrant, *U-boat offensive*, pp.97–132; Terraine, *Business in great waters*, pp.275–652.
7 What seems to be clear is that a He-111 torpedo bomber of Fliegercorps X hit the *Leberecht Maass* with three bombs. What isn't so clear is whether the same aircraft hit the *Max Schultz* as well. There is a suspicion that it may have done so. Rohwer, *Chronology*, p.15; Paul Kemp, *Friend or foe: friendly fire at sea 1939–1945* (London: Leo Cooper, 1995), pp.40–46.
8 Of the six ships that left Vigo on 10 February, *Wangoni* was the only vessel to make it through safely to a German port. Three were intercepted and taken to British ports; one was scuttled east of Iceland and one foundered in northern Norway. Moreover, the fate of other would-be blockade runners (*Hannover, Heidelberg, La Coruña, Mimi Horn, Seattle, Troja, Uruguay, Wakama* and *Wolfsburg*) in different parts of the Western and North Atlantic in the six weeks up to the end of March 1940 is eloquent testimony to the fact that the Allies got it right some of the time. Rohwer, *Chronology*, pp.15–16.
9 Richard Wiggan, *Hunt the Altmark* (London: Robert Hale, 1982), pp.118–55; Miller, *War at sea*, pp.51–52; Barnett, *Engage the enemy*, pp.101–2.
10 Stephen Howarth, 'Admiral of the Fleet Sir Philip Vian', in Howarth (ed.), *Men of war*, pp.491–505.
11 Jack Adams, *The doomed expedition: the Norwegian campaign of 1940* (London: Leo Cooper, 1989); Adam Claasen, 'Germany's expeditionary operation: the invasion of Norway, 1940', in Peter Dennis and Jeffrey Grey (eds), *Battles near and far: a century of operational deployment* (Canberra: Army History Unit, Department of Defence, 2005), pp.141–62; Vincent O'Hara, *The German fleet at war, 1939–1945* (Annapolis, Md: NIP, 2004), pp.15–59; Patrick Salmon (ed.), *Britain and Norway in the Second World War* (London: HMSO, 1995), pp.1–36; Till, *Air power and the Royal Navy*, pp.11–28; Wesley K.Wark, 'Beyond intelligence: the study of British strategy and the Norway campaign, 1940', in Michael G. Fry (ed.), *Power, personalities and policies: essays in honour of Donald Cameron Watt* (London: Frank Cass, 1992), pp.233–57.
12 Some military terms occasionally undergo definitional changes over time. Combined operations is a case in point. While these days the term may refer to military operations in which the services of two or more allied nations participate, the term was used during World War II to cover those operations where two or more services of a particular nation were either fully integrated or were obliged to cooperate with one another to achieve a common aim. To add to the potential confusion, a Combined Operations Command was formed in the UK in 1940 to plan and execute small scale amphibious operations. Supported by Churchill but bedeviled by inter-service suspicion, it struggled to launch any substantive raids before the Dieppe fiasco and was kept on a short leash thereafter. In order to avoid confusion, therefore, this work will refer to inter-service arrangements of a single nation as combined arms operations. It will also take the concept of joint operations to be those where the services of more than one allied nation cooperated under their separate commanders to seek a common military objective.
13 Gilbert (ed.), *Churchill war papers*, *I*, pp.522–25, 790, 824–27, 843, 878–80.
14 Ibid., pp.878–80, 902, 920–21; Barnett, *Engage the enemy*, pp.97–102; *Fuehrer conferences*, pp.83–87.
15 Hitler designated 7 April as the date that *Fall Weserübung* would commence. This was postponed by 48 hours so that the task force could avoid some of the ice floes en route. Barnett, *Engage the enemy*, p.103; *Fuehrer conferences*, p.90.

16 These three areas were off Bodø at the entrance to the Vestfjorden in the north; Bud, south west of Kristiansund, along the central part of the west coast; and Stadlandet, a little further to the south west and not far from the port of Alesund. Gilbert (ed.), *Churchill war papers, I*, pp.780, 926, 929–31, 934. 942–43, 948, 966, 971–72, 977–78, 986.
17 F.H. Hinsley, E.E. Thomas, C.F.G. Ransom and R.C. Knight (eds), *British intelligence in the Second World War. Vol.One: Its influence on strategy and operations* (London: HMSO, 1979), pp.127–43; Maurice Freedman, *Unravelling Enigma: winning the code war at Station X* (London: Leo Cooper, 2000), pp.12–14; Hugh Sebag-Montefiore, *Enigma: the battle for the code* (London: Phoenix, 2001), pp.78–88; Barnett, *Engage the enemy*, p.106.
18 Apart from the two Norwegian ports mentioned, the others in sequence from north to south were Trondheim, Bergen, Egersund, Kristiansand South and Arendal. Apart from Esbjerg and Thyboren on Jutland, the other Danish ports were located on the other main islands of Fyn and Sjalland (Copenhagen, Middelfart, Nyborg and Korsør).
19 Apart from the leading warships, fourteen destroyers, an equal number of U-boats, and a host of other vessels ranging from a dozen S-boats, and six torpedo boats to a glut of minesweepers, tankers, trawlers and much else were in attendance to support the cutting edge of the invasion fleet. Seventeen additional U-boats were also assigned to areas such as the Pentland Firth, as well as the Orkney and Shetland Isles. Rohwer, *Chronology*, p.18.
20 'Ultra' was the codename given to the top secret information derived from the breaking of enemy enciphered signals traffic by the cryptanalysts of the Government Code and Cypher School (GC&CS) at Bletchley Park. It would ultimately become the name that was used by the Allies for all information obtained from the breaking of enemy codes and ciphers.
21 Ibid.; Gilbert, *Churchill war papers, I*, pp.977–78.
22 This force would be supplemented by five more British submarines – three of which were minelaying types. Horton's submarines had given a good account of themselves and they would continue to do so over the course of the next three weeks. Although they were to lose three of their submarines during the course of these operations, the group were far more effective than their German counterparts on this occasion. *Truant* managed to torpedo the light cruiser *Karlsruhe* and leave her in such a state that she had to be finished off by the German torpedo boat *Greif*, while a torpedo from *Spearfish* so badly damaged the pocket battleship *Lützow* that it would keep her out of action for a full year. In addition to the transport she sank, *Orzel* did the same to another ship of 5,261 tons; *Sunfish* sank three ships (12,034 tons), as did *Snapper*, with two of her victims being minesweepers. *Trident* weighed in with the destruction of a tanker and another ship of 8,036 tons. *Triton* destroyed two more ships and a patrol vessel for an accumulated figure of 9,221 tons; while *Sealion, Seawolf, Sterlet* and *Triad* all registered one victim each for a total haul of 11,479 tons. Rohwer, *Chronology*, pp.18–19.
23 Vincent P. O'Hara, *The German fleet at war, 1939–1945* (Annapolis, Md: NIP, 2011), pp.17–18. Haarr, *German invasion of Norway*, pp.90–97. Apart from Forbes's four destroyers (*Bedouin, Eskimo, Kimberley* and *Punjabi*), his remaining three units (*Greyhound, Hero* and *Hyperion*) would be supplemented by the addition of *Hostile* on the following day.
24 Eric Grove, *Sea battles in close-up: World War 2. Volume Two* (Shepperton, Surrey: Ian Allan, 1993), p.10; Peter Kemp, 'Admiral of the Fleet Sir Dudley Pound', in Howarth (ed.), *Men of war*, pp.17–41.
25 Haarr, *German invasion of Norway*, pp.97–99; David Brown, 'Norway 1940: the balance of interference', in Salmon (ed.), *Britain and Norway in the Second World War*, pp.26–32.
26 Once it became clear that a German invasion was underway in Norwegian waters, the Admiralty ordered *Furious* and the battleship *Warspite* north to join Forbes and the rest of the Home Fleet. They rendezvoused with them on 10 April. Rohwer, *Chronology*, p.19; Barnett, *Engage the enemy*, pp.109, 113–14.

27 Before Warburton-Lee entered Ofotfjorden in the early hours of 10 April, the 2nd Destroyer Flotilla had been reinforced by *Hostile* back from service elsewhere.
28 Grove, *Sea battles in close-up*, 2, p.10.
29 1936-type fleet destroyers were faster, heavier and improved versions of the 1934A type. All six ships of this class were launched between August 1937 and September 1938. They each displaced 3,415 tons at deep load and could reach a top speed of 40 knots. Gardiner (ed.), *Conway's all the world's fighting ships*, p.233.
30 Haarr, *German invasion of Norway*, pp.317–74; Grove, *Sea battles in close-up*, 2, pp.16–18.
31 *Georg Thiele* was the only 1934-type fleet destroyer involved in this action, the other four ships being the slightly improved 1934A-type destroyers: *Bernd von Arnim, Wolfgang Zenker, Erich Giese* and *Erich Koellner*. The 1934-type destroyers formed the basis for successive classes of German destroyers. Launched in the latter part of 1935, the four individual units of this class were commissioned in early 1937. They displaced 3,156 tons at deep load and could achieve a top speed of 38.2 knots from 70,000shp. The 1934A-type destroyers had a slightly different configuration and were 6 feet (1.83m) longer than the original model, but generated the same power and matched, but didn't exceed, the top speed of the earlier version. Gardiner (ed.), *Conway's all the world's fighting ships*, pp.232–33.
32 Grove, *Sea battles in close-up*, 2, p.18; O'Hara, *German fleet at war*, p.36.
33 Grove, *Sea battles in close-up*, 2, p.18; O'Hara, *German fleet at war*, pp.31–40.
34 Grove, *Sea battles in close-up*, 2, p.20; O'Hara, *German fleet at war*, pp.38–39.
35 Grove, *Sea battles in close up*, II, pp.13–22; Captain Peter Dickens, *Narvik: Battles in the fjords* (London: Ian Allan, 1974), pp.13–96.
36 Dickens, *Narvik*, pp.103–6.
37 Codenamed *DW* it was devised by Forbes's Staff Officer (Operations) Commander Cecil Hughes-Hallett on 12 April 1940. Grove, *Sea battles in close up*, II, pp.23–25.
38 Dickens, *Narvik*, pp.112–17; Beesly, *Very special intelligence*, pp.59–60, 67–68.
39 *Penelope*, the light cruiser, which had been sent to assist the trio of British destroyers in Vestfjorden, managed to run aground during the night of 11 April and had to be towed away for repairs. Along with the three Tribal destroyers *Cossack, Eskimo* and *Punjabi*, the H-class destroyer *Hotspur* also suffered damage in the Narvik encounters. Rohwer, *Chronology*, p.19.
40 Dickens, *Narvik*, pp.151–59; Grove, *Sea battles in close-up*, II, pp.22–35; Miller, *War at sea*, pp.57–77.
41 Barnett, *Engage the enemy*, p.117; Miller, *War at sea*, p.66.
42 Barnett, *Engage the enemy*, pp.119–39.
43 As Barnett indicates, by early May the Luftwaffe could rely upon 710 aircraft that were able to operate from Norwegian airfields. Barnett, *Engage the enemy*, pp.122–25, 129–38; Adam R.A. Claasen, *Hitler's northern war: the Luftwaffe's ill-fated campaign, 1940–1945* (Lawrence, Ks: University Press of Kansas, 2001), pp.62–140.
44 Hughes and Costello, *Battle of the Atlantic*, p.67.
45 Torpedo defects were encountered by each of the following thirteen U-boats on station in Norwegian waters at this time: *U8, U9, U25, U34, U37, U38, U46, U47, U48, U51, U56, U58* and *U65*. Blair, *Hitler's U-boat war: hunters*, pp.145–57; Doenitz, *Memoirs*, pp.84–99; Padfield, *Dönitz*, pp.211–12; Rohwer, *Chronology*, pp.18–21.
46 Rössler, *The U-boat*, p.143; Mallmann Showell, *German Navy in World War Two*, pp.28–31.
47 Miller, *War at sea*, pp.71–73; Rohwer, *Chronology*, pp.21–22.
48 W.J.R. Gardner (ed.), *The evacuation from Dunkirk: 'Operation Dynamo'* (London: Frank Cass, 2000); Barnett, *Engage the enemy*, pp.140–67; Auphan and Mordell, *French Navy in World War II*, pp.68–82.
49 Brian Farrell, 'Ramsay, Sir Bertram Home', in Brian Harrison (ed.), *Oxford dictionary of national biography*. Vol.45 (Oxford: OUP, 2004), pp.918–23; W.J.R. Gardner, 'Admiral Sir Bertram Ramsay', in Howarth (ed.), *Men of war*, pp.349–62.

50 David Jefferson, *Coastal forces at war: Royal Navy 'little ships' in World War 2* (Sparkford, Somerset: Patrick Stephens, 1996), pp.84–107; Miller, *War at sea*, pp.79–91.
51 Much has been made of Hitler's decision to halt the motororised divisions outside Dunkirk. Kershaw asserts that Hitler wasn't offering the British a novel means of escaping his armoured noose. Instead he was swayed by the military arguments presented by Gerd von Rundstedt, the Commander of Army Group A, who believed the tanks should not be wasted on the British rearguard, but should be retained for more pressing assignments in the south. A couple of days later Hitler, sensing his original decision had been misguided, reversed his decision and sent in his tanks to try and stem the flow of the British evacuation from the beaches of Dunkirk. By then it was too late. Operation *Dynamo* was in full swing and the Luftwaffe failed to perform up to Göring's boastful expectations. Bullock, *Hitler*, pp.585–86; Kershaw, *Hitler: nemesis*, pp.295–97.
52 For more on the three routes that were used, see Barnett, *Engage the enemy*, pp.150–51.
53 Barnett writes of a figure of 45,000 men to be evacuated over two days. Ibid., p.141.
54 Rohwer, *Chronology*, pp.24–25.
55 Jefferson, *Coastal forces at war*, pp.84–107; Peter Scott, *The battle of the narrow seas: a history of the light coastal forces in the Channel and North Sea, 1939–1945* (London: White Lion Publishers, 1974), pp.16–19.
56 Rohwer, *Chronology*, p.25; Barnett, *Engage the enemy*, pp.140–67; Christopher Hibbert, 'Operation Dynamo', in Liddell Hart (ed.), *History of the Second World War*, pp.34–46.
57 Q-ships were disguised merchant vessels that carried hidden guns and other weaponry that could be used against unsuspecting enemy shipping. They had been used in the First World War without ever being very successful, and were only used sparingly by the Admiralty in the Atlantic in 1939–41. Although the Americans tried using them as bait for U-boats in 1942–43, the experiment was generally unsuccessful. Kenneth M. Beyer, *Q-ships versus U-boats: America's secret project* (Annapolis, Md: NIP, 1999).
58 Rohwer, *Chronology*, p.25.
59 Haarr, *German invasion of Norway*, pp.318–66; O'Hara, *German fleet at war*, pp.54–59.
60 *Fuehrer conferences*, pp.107–9.
61 Vernon W. Howland, 'The loss of HMS *Glorious*: an analysis of the action', www.warship.org/no11994.htm; James Levy, 'The inglorious end of the *Glorious*: the release of the findings of the Board of Enquiry into the loss of HMS *Glorious*', *The Mariner's Mirror*, Vol.86, No.3 (Aug. 2000): 302–9; Barnett, *Engage the enemy*, pp.134–38.
62 Neither *Acasta* nor *Ardent* put out any distress calls and those that *Glorious* may have made did not register with the Admiralty. As a result, no search and rescue mission was sent off to pick up the survivors in the hours immediately after the sinking of the three ships. Malcolm H. Murfett, 'Cunningham, Sir John Henry Dacres', in Harrison (ed.), *Oxford dictionary of national biography. Vol.14*, pp.691–93; O'Hara, *German fleet at war*, pp.54–59 and especially note 23, pp.280–81.
63 D'Oyly-Hughes was a decorated submariner, but had little operational experience in charge of a carrier. Vindictive in the extreme, he was anxious to get back to Scapa Flow in order to begin courts martial proceedings against his subordinate – the former officer in charge of carrier operations on *Glorious* – with whom he had clashed repeatedly in the past and who had been offloaded in the Orkneys before the converted carrier had proceeded to Norway. Levy, *The Royal Navy's Home Fleet*, pp.50–67.
64 Forbes's tenure at sea was relatively short-lived. On 2 December 1940 he was quietly replaced as C-in-C Home Fleet by Admiral Sir John Tovey (whose promotion owed much to Admiral Sir Andrew B. Cunningham's support and Churchill's desire for change). Forbes was shuffled off to become a somewhat hapless figure as C-in-C Plymouth, a position from which he was not rescued. Ibid., pp.68–78; Rohwer, *Chronology*, p.27; Graham Rhys-Jones, *The loss of the Bismarck: an avoidable disaster* (Annapolis, Md: NIP, 1999), pp.33–34, 37, 39, 45.

65 Mallett, *Italian Navy and fascist expansionism*, pp.174–85.
66 Figures for the deployment of the Regia Marina Italiana (RMI or Royal Italian Navy) differ according to the sources one consults. See Ibid., pp.197–204; Gardiner (ed.), *Conway's all the world's fighting ships*, pp.280–317; James J. Sadkovich, *The Italian Navy in World War II* (Westport, Conn: Greenwood Press, 1994), pp.1–55; Rohwer, *Chronology*, p.27; Roskill, *The war at sea, I*, pp.593–97.
67 ABC had an aircraft carrier, four battleships, nine light cruisers, twenty-one destroyers (with four more deployed in the Red Sea) and six submarines at his immediate disposal at Alexandria. In addition, he had another carrier, a battleship, a light cruiser and nine destroyers based at Gibraltar and a solitary destroyer and six submarines at Malta. Michael Simpson (ed.), *The Cunningham papers. Vol.I: the Mediterranean Fleet, 1939–1942* (Aldershot: Ashgate for the Navy Records Society, 1999), pp.55, 69–74, 77; Paul Preston, *The politics of revenge: fascism and the military in twentieth-century Spain* (London: Routledge, 1995), pp.51–84; Martin Gilbert (ed.), *The Churchill war papers. Vol.II. Never surrender. May 1940–December 1940* (New York: W.W. Norton, 1995), pp.482, 524–25; Barnett, *Engage the enemy*, pp.211–13.
68 *Richelieu*, a battleship nearing completion at Brest, left for Dakar accompanied by two destroyers (*Fougueux* and *Frondeur*) on 18 June, and arrived safely in the Senegalese capital five days later. After an abortive attempt to make for Casablanca was foiled, *Richelieu* returned to Dakar and was joined there by four auxiliary cruisers (*El Djezair, El Kantara, El Mansour* and *Ville d'Oran*) and two more destroyers (*Epervier* and *Milan*) from the same Channel port of Brest. *Jean Bart*, another unfinished battleship, was towed out of St. Nazaire and together with two new destroyers (*Le Hardi* and *Mameluk*) reached the Moroccan port of Casablanca on 22 June. Rohwer, *Chronology*, p.29. For a brief but useful survey of what happened to the French Navy see Claude Huan, 'The French Navy in World War II', in James J. Sadkovich (ed.), *Reevaluating major naval combatants of World War II* (Westport, Conn: Greenwood Press, 1990), pp.79–97.
69 Evacuation of the remaining elements of the BEF (the British 51st and 52nd Divisions and 'Norman Force') along with the 1st Canadian Division, RAF personnel and additional Allied troops took place from the Channel ports of Brest (32,584), Cherbourg (30,630), Le Havre (11059), St. Malo (21,474) and St. Valéry-en-Caux (3,321) in a series of forays (Operation *Cycle*). Other evacuations (Operation *Ariel*) were organised for those withdrawing from the ports of St. Nazaire and Nantes (57,235) on the Atlantic coast. These operations were completed by 18 June. Additional evacuations of another 19,000 Allied troops (mostly Polish soldiers) took place from the southern Pyrenean ports of Bayonne and St. Jean-de-Luz before a ceasefire was finally arranged on 25 June 1940. A largely civilian evacuation from the Channel Islands took place on 30 June – 1 July and 26,656 people were brought back safely across the Channel to the British coast. Barnett, *Engage the enemy*, p.163; Rohwer, *Chronology*, pp.28–30.
70 David Brown, 'Admiral of the Fleet Sir James Somerville', in Howarth (ed.), *Men of war*, pp.455–73.
71 Under the terms of the armistice, all French warships both in metropolitan and overseas ports were to sail to certain designated French ports where they would be demobilised and disarmed under German or Italian supervision. Auphan and Mordal, *French Navy in World War II*, pp.83–95, 104–21; Barnett, *Engage the enemy*, pp.171–81.
72 David Brown, *Road to Oran: Anglo-French naval relations, September 1939–July 1940* (London: Frank Cass, 2004); Warren Tute, *The deadly stroke* (London: Collins, 1973); Auphan and Mordal, *French Navy in World War II*, pp.122–39; Jenkins, *History of French Navy*, pp.322–26.
73 On 3 July the British submarines *Pandora* and *Proteus* lying off the coast of Algeria were ordered to attack any French ship leaving the port of Algiers and Oran. While

Pandora sank the colonial sloop *Rigault de Genouilly*, *Proteus* missed the chance of dealing with the *Commandante Teste*. Rohwer, *Chronology*, p.31.

74 Somerville didn't realise at the time that Gensoul had given orders to open the boom barrage across the harbour entrance to allow his warships to leave port once they were under fire. Somerville had neither foreseen this response nor had planned to counter it in advance. This helps to explain his slow response to their escape. He was lucky that his negligence on this occasion was not held against him. Other naval officers would not be so fortunate later in the war. Ibid.

75 Ibid., p.32.

76 This arrangement covered the battleship *Lorraine*, the three heavy cruisers *Duquesne*, *Suffren* and *Tourville*, the light cruiser *Duguay Trouin*, the three destroyers *Basque*, *Le Fortuné* and *Forbin*, and the submarine *Protée*. Ibid.; Martin Stephen, *The fighting admirals*, pp.68–71; Simpson (ed.), *The Cunningham papers*, *I*, pp.56–58, 86–97.

77 In response to Operation *Catapult*, the Vichy government had ordered the operational arm of their naval forces based in Dakar to leave port and attack any British ships found sailing off the West African coast. On 5 July they did just that by seizing three steamers and three Danish ships sailing under the British flag. Rohwer, *Chronology*, p.31; Auphan and Mordal, *French Navy in World War II*, pp.136–39.

78 Cunningham to Admiralty, 16 July 1940, in Simpson (ed.), *The Cunningham papers*, *I*, p.115; G. Hermon Gill, *Royal Australian Navy 1939–1942* (Sydney: Collins in association with the Australian War Memorial, 1985), pp.172–80.

79 Cunningham to Admiralty, 21 September 1940 in Simpson (ed.), *The Cunningham papers*, *I*; Pound to Cunningham, 24 July 1940, in ibid., pp.118–20; Sadkovich, *Italian Navy in World War II*, pp.63–66; Rohwer, *Chronology*, p.33.

80 On 17–18 August, 6,585 troops and civilians were evacuated. Rohwer, *Chronology*, p.36.

81 Gilbert (ed.), *Churchill war papers*, *II*, pp.661, 664, 727, 785, 791, 820.

82 Of the new bases that were swiftly pressed into service in the summer of 1940, Lorient, located on the southern coast of Brittany, proved to be a wonderful base for U-boat activities in the Atlantic. It also became Dönitz's U-boat command headquarters. After the galling experience of the Norwegian campaign, the U-boats enjoyed a series of 'happy times' from June 1940 onwards with peaks of carnage lasting throughout the rest of the year. Blair, Jr., *Hitler's U-boat war: hunters*, pp.166–217; Jean Kessler, 'U-boat bases in the Bay of Biscay', in Howarth and Law (eds), *The Battle of the Atlantic 1939–1945*, pp.252–65; Jak P. Mallmann Showell, *Hitler's U-boat bases* (Stroud, Glos: Sutton, 2002); Gordon Williamson, *U-boat bases and bunkers 1941–45* (Oxford: Osprey, 2003); Padfield, *Dönitz*, pp.222–23.

83 According to an excellent article by David Syrett, the Royal Navy had a chain of eighteen D/F (Direction Finding) stations in the UK (up from five in 1939) and a similar number in Canada and South Africa by the spring of 1942. At the outset of the war D/F stations existed in Gibraltar, Jamaica, Malta, Sierra Leone and Singapore. By the end of the war the system of Allied D/F stations was vast and circled the globe. David Syrett, 'The infrastructure of communications intelligence: the Allied D/F network and the Battle of the Atlantic', *Intelligence and National Security*, Vol.17, No.3 (Autumn 2002): 163–72. For interesting developments on Range Estimation (RE) and Radio Finger Printing (RFP) techniques, see Timothy Wilford, 'Watching the North Pacific: British and Commonwealth intelligence before Pearl Harbor', *Intelligence and National Security*, Vol.17, No.4 (Winter 2002): 131–64.

84 Padfield, *War beneath the seas*, p.286; Barnett, *Engage the enemy*, pp.256–59.

85 According to Barnett, only twenty-eight of these U-boats were operational in July 1940. Blair indicates that after the recent losses of *U26*, *U102* and *U122*, Dönitz only had four ocean-going U-boats for Atlantic duty. Of these both Fritz-Julius Lemp in *U30* and Otto Salmann in *U52* reported that their vessels were suffering from major engine problems. This left Wilhelm Rollmann in *U34* and Otto Kretschmer in *U99*

to sail forth from Lorient in the last week of July. Barnett, *Engage the enemy*, p.187; Blair, Jr., *Hitler's U-boat war: hunters*, pp.172–73, 712.
86 Blair indicates that a total of 32 Italian submarines were deployed to Bordeaux between 4 September 1940 and 20 February 1943. Of this total, 16 were lost while on operational duty (50%). According to the table he sets out in Appendix 8, the Italian submarines sank 106 ships (564,473 tons) in the seventeen months they were attached to Dönitz's command. Blair, Jr. *Hitler's U-boat war: hunters*, pp.739–40.
87 For the composition and activities of *Betasom* (Italian Submarine Command) established in Bordeaux on 1 September under Rear-Admiral Angelo Parona's leadership, see ibid.; Rohwer, *Chronology*, pp.34, 37–38, 42, 44, 46, 50; Hughes and Costello, *Battle of the Atlantic*, p.102; Milner, *Battle of the Atlantic*, pp.42, 48–49.
88 Gilbert, *Churchill war papers, II*, pp.771–72, 842, 1044, 1163, 1193–94, 1199, 1229, 1233, 1269, 1296–97, 1311–12; Patrick Abbazia, *Mr. Roosevelt's Navy: The private war of the U.S. Atlantic Fleet, 1939–1942* (Annapolis, Md: NIP, 1975), pp.91–107; Miller, *War at sea*, pp.105–6; Barnett, *Engage the enemy*, pp.183–84.
89 Rohwer, *Chronology*, pp.39–41.
90 Barnett, *Engage the enemy*, pp.236–38; Charlotte and Denis Plimmer, *A matter of expediency: the jettison of Admiral Sir Dudley North* (London: Quartet Books, 1978).
91 Operation *Menace* was led by Sir John Cunningham and involved two battleships (*Barham, Resolution*), a carrier (*Ark Royal*), three heavy cruisers (*Australia, Cumberland, Devonshire*), a light cruiser (*Delhi*), ten destroyers, five sloops, six troop transports, five freighters, a tanker and an armed tug. Arthur Marder, *Operation Menace: the Dakar expedition and the Dudley North affair* (London: OUP, 1976); John Williams, *The guns of Dakar: September 1940* (London: Heinemann, 1976); Gill, *Royal Australian Navy 1939–1942*, pp.215–21; Rohwer, *Chronology*, p.42.
92 Barnett, *Engage the enemy*, pp.204–5; Gilbert (ed.), *Churchill war papers, II*, pp.659–60, 698–99, 710–11, 730–31, 817, 820–22, 831, 843, 861–62, 866–70, 893. This wasn't the end of it either as the Vichy regime hit back by sending in waves of their own aircraft from Morocco to drop 105 tons of bombs on Gibraltar on both 24 and 25 September. Slight damage was caused but it was the gesture that counted. Rohwer, *Chronology*, pp.38, 40, 42.
93 Failure to press home the attacks on the chain of radar stations around the British coast (known as 'Chain Home') and the decision to divert attacks from RAF bases to centres of urban population in the major cities were undoubtedly the gravest mistakes made by the Luftwaffe in the aftermath of *Adler Tag* (*Eagle Day*) or the opening of the Battle of Britain on 8 August 1940. Brown, *Radar history*, pp.49–64, 97–99.
94 A vast number of books and articles have been devoted to the Battle of Britain. Some of the very best and most illuminating of these studies are the following: T.C. G. James (ed.), *The battle of Britain* (London: Frank Cass, 2000); Francis Mason, *Battle over Britain: a history of the German air assaults on Great Britain, 1917–18 and July–December 1940, and of the development of Britain's air defences between the wars* (London: McWhirter Twins Ltd., 1969), pp.121–488; Williamson Murray, *Strategy for defeat. The Luftwaffe 1933–1945* (Maxwell Air Force Base, Al.: Air University Press, 1983), pp.39–56; John Ray, *The battle of Britain: new perspectives behind the scenes of the great air war* (London: Arms and Armour, 1994); John Terraine, *The right of the line: the Royal Air Force in the European War 1939–45* (London: Hodder & Stoughton, 1985), pp.185–222.
95 Hitler's invasion fleet comprised 155 transports, 1277 barges and lighters, 471 tugs and 1161motor boats. In raids on these ports, the RAF had destroyed a total of fifty-one barges, nine steamers and a solitary tug by mid-September 1940. Rohwer, *Chronology*, p.41; *Fuehrer conferences*, pp.138–40.
96 In his speech to the House of Commons on 20 August 1940, Churchill had declared: 'Never in the field of human conflict was so much owed by so many to so few.' David Cannadine (ed.), *Blood, toil, tears and sweat* (London: Cassell, 1997), pp.179–92.

97 Blair, Jr., *Hitler's U-boat war: hunters*, pp.194–202; Milner, *Battle of the Atlantic*, pp.43–46; Donald P. Steury, 'The character of the German naval offensive: October 1940-June 1941', in Runyan and Copes, *To die gallantly*, pp.75–94; Rohwer, *Chronology*, pp.40–42, 44.
98 Preston, *The politics of revenge*, pp.51–84.
99 Mack Smith, *Mussolini*, pp.255–61.
100 Sadkovich, *Italian Navy in World War II*, pp.90–95.
101 Three significant torpedo hits were made on the modern battleship *Littorio* and one each on *Caio Duilio* and *Conte di Cavour* – the latter sinking where she stood. She was subsequently salvaged but her days of roaming the Mediterranean and Adriatic were over. *Littorio*'s damage was sufficient to put her out of action for four months, while *Caio Duilio* sustained a blow that kept her from operational duty for six months. Both the heavy cruiser *Trento* and the destroyer *Libeccio* escaped with slight damage as the hits made on them did not explode. Thereafter Taranto was abandoned as the main naval base. Remnants of the fleet initially retired to Naples, but after another couple of air raids on that port on 14 December 1940 and 8–9 January 1941, the heavier units were transferred out of harm's way to La Spezia, a port on the Ligurian Sea. Rohwer, *Chronology*, pp.47, 52, 55. See also David Wragg, *Carrier combat* (Stroud, Glos: Sutton Publishing, 1997), pp.32–39; Allan Beckman, 'Taranto: catalyst of the Pearl Harbor attack', *Military Review*, *Vol.LXXI, No.11* (Nov.1991): 73–78.
102 Simpson, (ed.), *The Cunningham papers, I*, 'Fleet Air Arm operations against Taranto on 11 November 1940', 16 Jan.1941, pp.178–80; David Hamer, *Bombers versus battleships* (Annapolis, Md: NIP, 1998), pp.67–75; David Wragg, *Swordfish: the story of the Taranto raid* (London: Weidenfeld & Nicolson, 2003).
103 Rohwer, *Chronology*, p.51; Sadkovich, *Italian Navy in World War II*, pp.95–100.
104 Simpson, (ed.), *Cunningham papers*, I, pp.212–16. Rohwer, *Chronology*, pp.51–52.
105 According to Wesley Olson, by the end of 1940 the six German raiders in existence at that time had managed to sink or capture fifty-four merchant vessels (366,644 tons). Wesley Olson, *Bitter victory: the death of HMAS Sydney* (Annapolis, Md: NIP, 2000), pp.135–40. See also Paul Schmalenbach, *German raiders: a history of auxiliary cruisers of the German Navy 1895–1945* (Cambridge: Patrick Stephens, 1977); Rohwer, *Chronology*, pp.48–49, 51.
106 Mallmann Showell, *German Navy in World War Two*, pp.119–22; Rohwer, *Chronology*, pp.52–53; Levy, *The Royal Navy's Home Fleet*, pp.77–78; Brown, *Radar history*, p.122.
107 Aerial mining concentrated on the estuaries of the Clyde, Humber, Mersey, Severn, Thames and Tyne. 'The Blitz' continued against London and other important ports and industrial centres, such as Birmingham, Bristol, Coventry, Glasgow, Liverpool, Manchester, Newcastle, Southampton and Wolverhampton. See John Ray, *The night blitz 1940–1941* (London: Arms and Armour, 1996).

4 Uncompromising hostilities (January–November 1941)

Whatever one may have thought of the multi-faceted nature of the naval war up to this point, it was destined to get far more onerous and complicated as 1941 proceeded. What had been essentially a limited Western hemisphere-based war in 1940, in which the British Commonwealth (along with their Free French allies) had been pitched against the Axis combination of Germany and Italy, widened dramatically and became a truly global affair by the end of 1941 as the Soviet Union, the Japanese and the United States were all sucked into the military vortex.

Although the British had survived the very real challenges of the old year, 1941 had hardly begun before further problems were encountered. On 10 January the carrier *Illustrious*, a vital component of the Mediterranean Fleet, was found on escort duty west of Malta by a host of German Ju-87 dive-bombers and in a ten-minute ordeal was hit six times and suffered three near-misses. While she and the battleship *Warspite*, which was also hit but not seriously, lived to fight another day, the damage the carrier had sustained in this and further attacks made on her in Valletta harbour over the course of the next few days was such as to keep her out of action for the rest of the year.[1] At least she could be repaired. This was not the case with the light cruiser *Southampton*, another victim of a well-coordinated dive-bombing attack that swept down out of the sun and achieved total surprise on the following day. *Southampton* was a total loss. Cunningham judiciously described the outcome as a 'setback'.[2] It was, not least because it underlined just what damage aircraft could do to warships if they caught them unprepared. Moreover, the damage to *Illustrious* would keep the Mediterranean Fleet critically short of airpower for two months until the carrier *Formidable* was able to join up with Cunningham's force in March.[3]

Aircraft were also poised to assist the Axis cause in carrying out the war on trade in the North Atlantic. Dönitz had acquired a group of FW 200 Condor long-range reconnaissance aircraft for use in combined arms operations with his U-boats. In theory, once the Condors had spotted a convoy (or any ships sailing independently), they could either supply the coordinates to those U-boats operating in the sector so that they could intercept them or they could carry out bombing raids on the ships themselves. These planes were to bring an added threat dimension to the Battle of the Atlantic.[4] In a six week period (7 January–18 February) a total of twelve U-boats and three Italian submarines working with the Condors located and destroyed forty-six merchant ships (264,964 tons) in the area west of the North Channel and Ireland.[5]

Although the steady loss of vessels to the underwater menace was worrisome to the Admiralty, the merits of convoy were still there for all to see. Since the start of the war convoy success rates had remained incredibly impressive with only 316 losses out of 22,126 ships being convoyed to and from the UK – a miserly loss rate of 1.43%.[6] Even so, there was no room for complacency since not all merchant shipping could be convoyed from port to port. Apart from anything else, there just weren't the number of escort vessels in existence to cater to that need, and independent sailings, therefore, could not be avoided, particularly in those areas that were neither close to convoy assembly points nor on existing convoy routes.[7]

Despite the U-boat peril it confronted on a daily basis, the Admiralty was, if anything, even more anxious about the threat posed to Allied traffic by the Kriegsmarine's heavy surface ships. If any of these broke out into the North Atlantic they could create havoc with even the best-defended convoys. Therefore, they could not be left alone to carry out their marauding activities on the high seas and intelligence reports of an imminent sailing or news of a sighting of one these ships underway was enough to put the Admiralty into high gear, deploying its best vessels in a bid to snuff out the threat before untold damage was done to Allied shipping interests.

Early February saw not one, but three, armed raiders leaving port on cruises of destruction. *Admiral Hipper*, a heavy cruiser, left Brest for her second Atlantic foray on the first day of the month and only a couple of days later the even more formidable battleship duo of *Gneisenau* and *Scharnhorst* successfully passed through the Denmark Strait undetected by the British. Although the Admiralty had been able to prevent an earlier excursion of theirs in late January thanks to timely intelligence reports, the sobering fact was that without this type of assistance, or a large dose of good fortune, it was virtually impossible to stop these ships from leaving their home waters and reaching the North Sea. Even if Admiral Tovey, the new C-in-C, Home Fleet, kept all elements of his force constantly on patrol in the North Sea, there was no guarantee that these enemy warships would be spotted while on passage to and from their home bases. Once news reached London that an armed raider had either left port and was making for the Atlantic, or was already engaging in a killing spree on the high seas, the Admiralty went into overdrive and with good reason. Just to underline the gravity of the situation, *Admiral Hipper* appeared off the southern Portuguese coast on 11 February and within a day had sunk a straggler from one convoy (HG.53), and battered the unescorted convoy (SLS.64) by destroying seven of its twenty-one ships (32,806 tons) and severely damaging three others in no more than thirty minutes of action.[8]

A few days after *Admiral Hipper* had returned unscathed to the port of Brest, *Gneisenau* and *Scharnhorst* took up the action some 500nm (926km) east of Newfoundland. Five merchant ships (25,784 tons) were summarily destroyed on this one occasion, but it would be merely a precursor to more ruthless raiding in the central North Atlantic on 15–16 March, when the two battleships between them sank thirteen ships (61,773 tons) and captured three tankers (20,139 tons) from what had started life as a convoy but had broken up en route to the United States.[9] These incidents underlined two vitally important lessons: one, that armed raiders really meant business and there was no realistic alternative for the Royal Navy but to deploy a significant number of its own warships to chase and harry them into making a mistake; two, that the scattering of a convoy, whether planned or not, and/or the sailing of ships in an unescorted convoy were both open invitations for disasters to occur and ought to be avoided at all cost. While the Admiralty already knew the first lesson, it would have done well to have fully absorbed the second. Once again, however, the net around the German battleships was not closed swiftly enough and they evaded the group of British warships that had been redeployed to hunt them down. By the time that they had returned to Brest, *Admiral Hipper* was on her way safely to Kiel and the pocket battleship *Admiral Scheer*, returning after a long and fruitful voyage in the Indian Ocean, was only days away from reaching the same destination.[10]

Even though these ships had not been apprehended on the high seas, the fact that *Gneisenau* and *Scharnhorst* had taken refuge in Brest rather than a German port meant that the British government could now attempt to choke off all avenues of their escape and attempt to destroy them in detail from the air. Trying to corner an armed raider was very much like playing a game of chess – anticipating one's opponent's moves and moving one's own pieces to surround the king and put it in checkmate. By slipping undetected into the admittedly heavily fortified port of Brest to evade the naval dragnet that was out to ensnare them, the German battleships looked to have made a tactical mistake of immense proportions. Unless they left the Atlantic port before the British realised that they were there, their chances of taking much further part in the war seemed slim. Once British aerial reconnaissance had established that they were at Brest on 28 March, the game seemed to be up.[11] Hemmed in initially by a large armada of British vessels offshore that basically sealed off the entrance to the harbour, the two battleships were soon subjected to a concerted bombing campaign that would last on and off for more than ten months. It seems quite extraordinary that they survived this aerial barrage and the dashing manner in which they were to demonstrate their powers of recuperation in February 1942 was to be mortifying for both the Admiralty and the Air Ministry as well as cruelly embarrassing for the British government that had devoted so much time and effort in a vain bid to destroy these capital ships.[12]

While the British were wrestling with the problems of armed raiders in the Atlantic and Indian oceans, they also found themselves having to confront a far more formidable opponent than their erstwhile enemies, the Italians, in both the Mediterranean and North African operational theatres. On 11 January Hitler signed a directive that committed all three services to an enhanced role in this vital region in a bid to prop up Mussolini's forces in both Albania and Libya. Apart from retaining its base in Sicily for the Luftwaffe's Fliegerkorps X from where it could increase its attacks on Allied shipping using the Mediterranean, Hitler required the Kriegsmarine to provide the means by which substantial military supplies could be transferred to the forces needing them, and approved the formation of a regiment that was later to become the legendary Afrika Korps, the German armoured defence force for Libya, which was desperately needed to regain the initiative in the war in the desert.[13]

Although the strategic picture was decidedly mixed, the British were comforted by the fact that the Italians had over-extended themselves everywhere and had even become vulnerable in their old colonial outposts in the Horn of Africa.[14] In southeast Europe, however, the British could find little comfort in the strategic situation. By 1 March the Hungarian, Romanian and Bulgarian governments had all joined the Axis Powers. Yugoslavia looked increasingly vulnerable and the military outlook for Albania and Greece had been completely transformed by the introduction of German troops into this theatre in December 1940. These fresh troops had served to rescue their Italian partners from yet another military embarrassment, stopping the headlong retreat across the Albanian border and regaining the initiative.[15] By early March the warning signs of an impending Axis victory in the Aegean were unmistakeable unless more British troops could be redeployed from the North African front to stiffen Greek resistance. Although Churchill felt the risks were worth taking, the business of transferring 58,000 troops from Libya and Egypt to Greece (Operation *Lustre*) was going to pose huge logistic problems to Cunningham and the Mediterranean Fleet.[16] Of far greater overall significance, however, was the possibility that Churchill's strategic gamble might not pay off and that these troops would not be enough to stop the rot in the Aegean, while their absence from the North African theatre could actually imperil the Allied position there.[17] Judged from Cunningham's perspective, the loss of any of his warships on passage to and from Greece was always going to make it much harder to accomplish his primary task of keeping the route through the Mediterranean open and Malta safe. He remained highly sceptical about the Greek adventure – a fact that did not endear him to Churchill and helped make their relationship even edgier than it already was. Although twenty-five ships (115,026 tons) were lost in the month-long operation (mostly after unloading both their troops and supplies), Cunningham was relieved to have got away with only these losses.[18]

Fortunately for him, the Italian submarines assigned to the task of disrupting the Allied redeployment were quite unable to make any impact on the troop movements and there was minimal disruption of the convoys while on passage. This can't have pleased those in the Italian Naval Operational Command Centre (Supermarina). Admiral Riccardi, the Italian Chief of Naval Staff, and other leading members of the RMI, such as Admirals Campioni and Iachino, were particularly anxious to deliver a knock-out blow to Cunningham's Mediterranean Fleet. There is more than a suspicion that they entertained and even cherished the thought of bringing about some form of massive set piece battle in which the British could be put to the sword in the Mediterranean – a type of new style Jutland with a different result from the original encounter in the North Sea. These ideas were all very well in theory, but the reality of the situation was what counted in Berlin and Wilhelmshaven.[19] Appreciating that something needed to be done to improve its standing in the eyes of its Axis partner, Supermarina strove to orchestrate a plan (codename *Gaudo*) that would succeed in restoring some pride to the Italian Navy. One effective way of doing that would be to intercept and destroy a couple of lightly screened Allied convoys scheduled for late March: AG.9 en route from Alexandria to Piraeus and GA.9 going in the opposite direction. As John Winton suggests, it was an excellent plan which might well have succeeded had it not been discovered in advance.[20]

Its secrecy was compromised to some extent by the Italians themselves. Their rather understandable eagerness in checking repeatedly on the location of the Mediterranean Fleet through increased surveillance patrols of both Alexandria and the convoy routes south of Crete in the days leading up to the launching of *Gaudo* certainly alerted Cunningham and his staff to the likelihood of some imminent action in the Eastern Mediterranean. These suspicions were confirmed by the latest 'Ultra' intercepts provided for the Admiralty by the members of Hut 6 (working on the Luftwaffe's 'Light Blue' code) and Dilly Knox and Mavis Lever (who concentrated on the RMI's 'Alfa' code) at Bletchley Park. This signals intelligence suggested that German exasperation at the Italian failure to deal effectively with the Allied convoys to Piraeus and Suda Bay was such that the Supermarina intended to send its main surface fleet south of Crete in search of the troop transports and supply ships that had so far eluded its submarine arm and that 28 March was scheduled as D-Day for this operation.[21]

Forewarned of Admiral Iachino's intended operational sortie off Crete, but not the composition of the force that would be undertaking it, the Admiralty swiftly re-routed and then recalled its two merchant convoys. If the Italians were spoiling for a fight, so was Cunningham. Risks had to be accepted in such a situation, but the prospect of doing real harm to the Italian Fleet was too good an opportunity for him to miss. He sought to make the most of his advantages by sending Vice-Admiral Sir Henry Pridham-Wippell's Force B (four light cruisers and four destroyers) out from Pireaus to act as live bait for Iachino's warships in the waters off Crete and lure them unwittingly into the steely embrace of Cunningham's Force A (the carrier *Formidable*, three battleships and nine destroyers) coming up from the southeast. If this could be done successfully, Cunningham felt his warships could then set about the enemy with some gusto.[22]

On the same day (27 March) that Pridham-Wippell's Force B left port to get into its pre-arranged position south of Crete to begin trailing its cape for Iachino's fleet to follow, the very ships it was hoping to attract rendezvoused south of the Straits of Messina and moved off south-eastwards towards Crete – and the convoy routes to and from Greece that lay further to the south. Although the RMI had no carriers to rely upon, the force that gathered in Sicilian waters was still quite impressive. Apart from his flagship the battleship *Vittorio Veneto* and four destroyers that had come from Naples, Iachino had gathered a fleet of six heavy cruisers, two light cruisers and nine other destroyers from their bases at Taranto, Brindisi and Messina. It was a fleet that could have done an awful lot of damage to any Allied convoy it came across, but it lacked constant air cover and reconnaissance support. In the absence of a carrier, however, Supermarina had fully expected to have at its disposal the planes of Fliegercorps X operating from their base in Sicily – so the aerial deficiency was not regarded as being critical at this stage.[23]

Whatever the Fliegerkorps might have done for the Italians, the fact remained that Cunningham was far better served by aerial reconnaissance than his opponents. At lunchtime on 27 March, an RAF flying boat based on Crete reported that three Italian heavy cruisers of the Trento class and a destroyer were at sea and heading towards the island. This report confirmed the accuracy of the earlier signals intelligence and convinced Cunningham that action was in the offing. Despite his aggressive instincts, he didn't want to reveal his hand too soon lest the enemy fleet break off the operation and return to its home bases. Wishing to deceive Italian agents in Alexandria about his intentions to leave port and go out for a showdown with Iachino's warships, Cunningham behaved ashore as if hoisting anchor was about the last thing on his mind on the evening of 27 March. What Michael Simpson describes as an 'elaborate charade' seemed to work perfectly.[24] Force A left Alexandria after dark undetected by spies and sped towards its pre-arranged meeting with Force B south of Crete later in the morning of 28 March.

Over the course of the next thirty hours a fleet action that had promised so much for the Italians turned into another grievous defeat every bit as bad as the earlier Taranto débâcle, if not worse. Whether the Battle of Matapan deserves the ringing epithet of 'a naval Caporetto' given to it by the Italian critic Gianni Rocca is arguable, but what is clear is that it was a tragedy and one that had been largely, and sadly, self inflicted. While aircraft and radar both had a critical role in assisting the British cause on 28 March, the stunning victory that would come his way after nightfall was gifted to Cunningham by his adversary Iachino. Aware from a lunchtime air raid that the *Gaudo* operation had already lost its surprise element, Iachino had opted for a safety-first policy by turning westward in a bid to put his ships beyond the range of what he assumed had been purely shore-based RAF units. Once the *Vittorio Veneto* had been hit and holed in the stern during a torpedo attack in the mid-afternoon, he could do no more than abandon the operation and – after sterling work by his damage control party – make course for home at the best possible speed. As the Italian Fleet limped westward it was spotted by one of *Warspite*'s reconnaissance planes and targeted again at dusk by both carrier and land-based aircraft. As luck would have it in trying to finish off the battleship an Albacore 5A, the last carrier plane to make an attack, succeeded in totally immobilizing the heavy cruiser *Pola* at 1946 hours.[25] As she remained dead in the water, the rest of the fleet retired from the scene as hastily as possible. After exchanging a series of messages about the plight of the *Pola* and her crew with Carlo Cattaneo, one of his divisional commanders, Iachino made a gross tactical error at 2018 hours in sending back two other Zara class heavy cruisers and four destroyers to go to the aid of the crippled warship. While Iachino's humanity cannot be faulted for trying to rescue her officers and men, the return of Cattaneo's entire group to retrieve the *Pola* by towing her to safety when he knew by this time that the Mediterranean Fleet was at sea is simply unfathomable. One can only imagine he thought the British ships weren't close enough to be an active threat during the hours of darkness and that by morning he would have arranged sufficient air cover for Cattaneo's entire group that Cunningham wouldn't dare to intervene. It was an egregious error. Iachino may have thought that the British wouldn't risk engaging in any night fighting, but if he did he didn't know his opposite number. Cunningham was determined not to let the battleship get away and was prepared to bring the enemy fleet to action in the dark if need be, even though his ships had not practised night fighting for some months and the skills necessary to become good at it still remained rudimentary at best.[26]

In the end, of course, the night action that took place didn't involve Iachino's entire fleet, but just Cattaneo's division of it. They had the wretched luck to return to the stricken *Pola* just when Cunningham arrived at the same spot with Force A. Martin Stephen describes the scene graphically: 'With flashless cordite and radar the British were sighted men in a world of the blind.'[27] At what amounted to point blank range the result was never in doubt. *Fiume* and *Zara* were soon rendered into smoking hulks by the broadside they received. In a little over four minutes the Zara class of heavy cruiser had, for all practical purposes, ceased to exist. As Cunningham described it later it was 'more like murder than anything else'.[28] Removing his battlefleet from what Barnett describes perfectly as a 'chaotic mêlée', Cunningham left his own destroyers to deal with their Italian equivalents. During the course of the evening, two of the four enemy destroyers were sunk (*Alfieri* and *Carducci*) while *Oriani* was damaged but managed to escape along with the unscathed *Gioberti*.[29]

It was a magnificent victory for Cunningham, but it might have turned out even better had he not sent a sloppily phrased signal to the rest of his ships shortly after putting the heavy cruisers out of action that seemed to imply that all those not engaged in dealing with the enemy should withdraw to the northeast. While the ambiguous message was not intended for his light cruiser squadron, Pridham-Wippell didn't realise that at the time. He broke off his pursuit of the *Vittorio Veneto* and withdrew to the northeast to conform with his C-in-C's apparent orders. By the time that Cunningham had become aware of what had happened, Iachino's flagship and her accompanying warships had escaped to live and fight another day.[30] That was more than could be said for Vice-Admiral Cattaneo and 2,302 officers and men of the Regia Marina who perished in these engagements.[31] Correlli Barnett calls it 'the Royal Navy's greatest victory in a fleet encounter since Trafalgar'.[32] Is it churlish to suggest that it could have been even greater? It might well have been but for the ambiguously worded signal Cunningham had sent while basking in the glow of his battlefleet's destructive blitz against Cattaneo's heavy cruisers. Michael Simpson, the editor of Cunningham's papers, draws another valid conclusion about the Battle of Cape Matapan, namely, that the C-in-C would have been far better served had he had two carriers rather than only one with him on this operation. Extra aircraft would have given him far more systematic reconnaissance and firepower than was available to him from only having *Formidable* and some of the land-based RAF torpedo-bombers at his disposal.[33]

One thing that all the leading naval analysts who have reviewed the action off Cape Matapan agree upon is that this crushing defeat for the Regia Marina was as much psychological as it was material. It dealt a real blow to the esteem in which the Italian fleet was held and made the Supermarina far more cautious than it otherwise might have been.[34] This attitude of restraint was further reinforced by yet another rout its forces suffered at the hands of the British only a few days later in the Red Sea, in what became an ultimately fruitless Italian quest both to attack Port Sudan as well as to retain their base of Massawa on the coast of Eritrea. In the face of a sustained land and aerial offensive launched by the enemy which closed in on the port on 6 April and captured it two days later, the Italians would lose six seaworthy destroyers, a torpedo boat, five MAS (fast motor torpedo boats) and nineteen of their merchant vessels, while six German ships, including the passenger ship *Colombo*, suffered the same fate. Somehow the degree of hopelessness into which the Italian naval cause had sunk was typified by the scuttling of the vast majority of these craft by their own crews at a total cost of 151,760 tons.[35]

There was little time for the British to savour this latest *dénouement* for the fascist authorities in Rome before their revelry was disturbed by a most ominous chain of events that occurred in the Balkans. Following a coup in Belgrade, the pro-German government in Yugoslavia had been turned out of office on 27 March. Apart from jeopardising the entire Italian military campaign in the region (already badly awry), it also raised the spectre of some form of Balkan League being established in the future that might have strong British backing. So far so good for the British, but neither scenario remotely appealed to Hitler who was now obliged to deal with this new and largely unforeseen twist in the Balkan drama at a time when he wished to devote his full attention to the plans that were being drawn up for his eventual campaign against the Soviet Union. On 6 April German ground forces, backed by a strong Luftwaffe presence, attacked Yugoslavia and Greece and made quick headway against both. Eleven days later Yugoslavia's brief flurry of independence came to an end and what was left of its scattered and modest fleet was thereafter taken over by the Italians during the course of the next week.[36]

Even before the British War Cabinet was forced to respond to the German advance in the Balkans, units of the Mediterranean Fleet were on hand to react to yet another strategic retreat. This time the British Eighth Army was withdrawing from Cyrenaica (with the solitary exception of the troops that were besieged in the fortress at Tobruk) and retreating towards the Egyptian border in the face of a sustained offensive launched by General Erwin Rommel's Afrika Korps which had already crushed the 2nd Armoured Division along the way.[37] There was little solace for the British troops in North Africa or their naval forces in either the Mediterranean or the Aegean at this time. Their 10th Submarine Flotilla based at Malta had been unable to staunch the flow of supply convoys that were getting through to Rommel, partly because they operated without up-to-date signals intelligence; partly because the submarines used were slow and antiquated, technically inadequate and poorly armed; and partly because they were commanded by relatively inexperienced officers. They would improve but it would take time to do so.[38] What few isolated successes came the way of their surface forces, such as the 'Skirmish off Sfax' on 16 April, when the four destroyers of Captain Philip Mack's Force K wiped out an entire eight ship convoy, or Cunningham's bombardment of Tripoli on 20–21 April, didn't mask the overall reality of Axis dominance in the region.[39]

Proof of this indisputable fact emerged within the next twenty-four hours. By then General Wavell had been given permission to begin making preparations for extracting his troops from the disintegrating Allied position in Greece and returning them to the Egyptian front where they were desperately needed to shore up their shaky situation in North Africa. It was not a moment too soon because on 21 April Greek forces surrendered to Feldmarschall (Field Marshal) Wilhelm List.[40] It now became vital for the Mediterranean Fleet to respond swiftly to this latest setback and so Pridham-Wippell left Alexandria on 24 April to launch Operation *Demon* with a large evacuation force that had been collected together for the purpose spearheaded by six light cruisers and twenty destroyers. Their destination was the coastal area between Athens and Korinth and the island of Peloponnesus where the majority of the 50,672 Allied servicemen were waiting to be rescued from a variety of open beaches and other landing areas along its southern and eastern coasts. Although the Luftwaffe managed to sink four transports and two destroyers of the evacuation force, another 'miracle of deliverance' was orchestrated under intense pressure. In five days of frenetic activity, these vital Allied troops were recovered from an assortment of locations and brought to relative safety. Invaluable experience gained from both the Norwegian and Dunkirk evacuations had once more been put to good use, this time in the Aegean. Again, the Germans might reasonably have been expected to do more to thwart this withdrawal than they did, but their success in all other phases of their operation was marked. By 27 April they had seized Athens and had completed their occupation of the Greek mainland by the end of the month.[41] It would not be the end of the affair. A far worse situation lay in wait for the British only three weeks later in the battle for control of the island of Crete.

Fortunately for the authorities in London not all the news was bad. Indeed for a time their spirits were lifted by a number of coups made against Dönitz's U-boat fleet beginning in early March with the loss of one of his greatest underwater aces, the coolly aloof but brilliant Günther Prien, the so-called 'Bull of Scapa Flow'. In the midst of a torrential rainstorm during the night of 7–8 March, *U47*, seeking to attack the ships of convoy OB.293, had been detected by one or more of the destroyer escorts that were fitted with a Type 286M air–surface search radar set. Prien was forced to dive and remain at great depth for five hours as the destroyers sought to discover his whereabouts and depth-charge him out of existence. He survived only for *U47* to resurface close to the destroyer *Wolverine* which first tried to ram her and then in company with destroyer escort *Verity* depth-charged the diving U-boat with devastating results.[42] Within a few days of Prien's death, two more of Dönitz's aces from the Lorient base – Joachim Schepke and Otto Kretschmer – had also been lost to the war in a single evening's work. In a group operation of five U-boats against the homeward bound convoy HX.112, with its rich bounty of forty-one ships, Schepke was the first to go. He was killed instantly as *U100* became another early radar casualty, detected in the first instance by the destroyer *Vanoc* on the night of 16–17 March and then rammed decisively by her. A short while later Kretschmer's own ship, *U99*, was also spotted by radar installed on the destroyer *Walker* and forced to the surface by being depth-charged. Kretschmer, known throughout the service as the 'Tonnage King', and the majority of his crew were taken prisoner before their craft sank too.[43]

It demonstrated that improved radar would definitely assist the British in fighting the U-boat scourge and help to redress some of the advantages that the unseen predator had hitherto held over the surface ships that they had been stalking. Nonetheless, the limitations of the 286M radar sets were such that it wasn't until the 10cm Type 271 microwave radiation sets were installed throughout the service that the Royal Navy would have a far more sophisticated and effective means to find, let alone destroy, Dönitz's fleet of U-boats.[44] While the British waited for better radar sets and detection equipment to come on stream, the Admiralty sought to compete with the U-boats by other means. One such possibility was in receiving timelier intelligence gained from reading German signal traffic. This information was vital since it would enable the Admiralty to re-route convoys away from the lines of U-boats that were strung out across the ocean to interdict the convoys. Before this could be done effectively, the Bletchley Park cryptanalysts needed some help in trying to unravel the key for the daily settings of the Enigma M-3 machines that were used by the U-boats to encode their messages. Top of their wish list, of course, was the possibility, however remote, that a U-boat might be captured at some stage in the war and that a boarding party primed for the purpose might seize her highly confidential codebooks before her crew could destroy them. It was a hope that was shared fervently by both the Naval Intelligence Division (NID) and Operational Intelligence Centre (OIC) of the Admiralty and schemes for bringing this unlikely scenario about were hatched and shared with the leading officers on convoy escort duty.[45] Boarding parties were to be formed in advance and those assigned to this task were trained for the purpose. It was understood that nothing should be left to chance since precious minutes saved might make all the difference between capturing some invaluable papers and just missing the opportunity. Despite the long odds against this situation ever occurring, the more German ships – both surface and submarine – there were on the oceans of the world, the shorter the odds became that an accident or a delayed sinking might afford an eager and resourceful boarding party the kind of chance and the time necessary to gather these crucial documents. This point was underscored on 4 March in a commando raid (Operation *Claymore*) on four ports in the Lofoten

Islands. In the process of destroying their fishery installations, the five Allied destroyers and two assault ships surprised and sank ten merchant and fishery vessels as well as the German armed patrol boat, *Krebs*. Before the *Krebs* sank, however, it yielded several vital pieces of information to the alert group of three seamen led by the signals expert Lieutenant Sir Marshall Warmington from the destroyer *Somali* who took the initiative personally to board the vessel even though his captain had been lukewarm to the plan and reluctant to embrace it. Such are the ironies of life. An unplanned and spontaneous initiative ended up in this small-scale boarding party finding a treasure trove of documents that revealed, amongst other things, the grid system and its accompanying naval chart devised by the Germans for indicating a ship's location (thus dispensing with the need for latitude and longitude bearings). Better still, Warmington also retrieved two discs that he guessed were designed for use with a cypher machine (even though he was blissfully unaware of the existence of Enigma), together with the key table of settings that the Enigma machines had been using in February 1941 to cover all ships in *Heimische Gewässer* (Home Waters).[46] These glittering prizes – for such they were – enabled the mathematical genius Alan Turing and his group of naval cryptanalysts in Hut 8 at Bletchley Park to make some sense of what the Germans were doing even though it didn't mean that all past signals that had been intercepted could now be read.[47]

Progress in this respect, however, was aided by two wonderful operational coups in early May that brought absolutely invaluable information to the Allied code breakers. One of the signals analysts installed in Hut 4 at Bletchley Park, Harry Hinsley, had suggested to his superiors that if a British warship was able to locate and capture any of the trawlers being used by the Germans to report on the weather at sea in isolated parts of the North Atlantic, they might yet secure a working Naval Enigma cipher machine along with its codebooks and other documentation. Hinsley even identified the trawler *München* – which he estimated would be on patrol north of Iceland for at least two months – as being the likeliest target for such a specific operation. Approval for Operation *EB* was swiftly given. *Somali* spotted her on 7 May and opened fire at a range of 3nm (5.6km). She soon reduced the weather ship into a hapless state. In the time it took Warmington and his boarding party to climb aboard the trawler, however, her crew had thrown their Enigma machine and the codebooks for May overboard in a weighted sack. What they did not have time to destroy, however, were the documents that revealed the inner and outer settings the Enigma machine would be using for the entire month of June. These were duly seized and sent back to Scapa Flow in *Nestor*, one of the fastest destroyers in the fleet. They eventually arrived at Bletchley Park three days later.[48]

Even before these top-secret papers had made it onto Turing's desk on 10 May, an even bigger haul had been made in another area of the North Atlantic. It came in the form of a priceless Naval Enigma machine belonging to Fritz-Julius Lemp's *U110*. Lemp's boat, one of a group formed to attack the large outward-bound convoy OB.318, tracked the convoy until just before lunchtime on 9 May when the merchant vessels were at a point roughly 300nm (556km) southwest of Greenland. Running short on fuel, Lemp decided to attack and torpedoed three ships but in the process betrayed his presence to the 3rd Escort Group. His fourth torpedo misfired for some reason and caused real stability problems on *U110*. While Lemp's attention was fully occupied in trying to regain control of his boat, the corvette *Aubretia* steamed towards the spot at which a contact had been made by her hydrophones. *U110* dived, but *Aubretia* would not be denied. Her depth charges found their mark and caused such damage that Lemp's boat rose to the surface. He ordered everyone to leave *U110* before she sank. As Lemp and his crew emerged at the top of the conning tower they were greeted with a volley of shells from *Bulldog* and *Broadway*, the leading destroyers from the 3rd Escort Group, who had joined *Aubretia* in closing in on the stricken U-boat. In an effort to try and save themselves, the crew members abandoned ship by leaping into what was an already raging sea.[49]

A raiding party from the *Bulldog* clambered onto *U110* and found a wealth of material scattered throughout the boat that took them ninety minutes to extract. In the telegraph office the Enigma machine remained screwed to the table. It was quickly dismantled and passed along the human chain formed in the boat and brought up-top ready for transfer to *Bulldog*. When the Admiralty received word of this coup, the whole incident became instantly cloaked in the utmost secrecy. From then onwards, it became known as Operation *Primrose*. Its significance was underscored by a personal signal from the first sea lord to Baker-Cresswell, the captain of the *Bulldog*, which simply read: 'Hearty congratulations. The petals of your flower are of rare beauty.'[50] Although an effort was made to tow *U110* back to Iceland, it failed and she sank somewhat fortuitously well out of sight of land since, without any evidence to the contrary, it became far easier to prevent Dönitz and the German authorities from guessing that the Enigma secret had been compromised in this way. As Hugh Sebag-Montefiore asserts, however, *Primrose* was not going to be the revolutionary find that the Admiralty hierarchy believed at the time it was. A monthly change to the Naval Enigma bigram tables meant that unless the Royal Navy could capture the latest settings for July 1941, Turing and his fellow cryptanalysts would not be able to read these signals.[51]

While Dönitz may have lost some of his best submariners, deplored the abilities of the Italian submarine crews that had been bequeathed to him, and questioned the overall efficacy of working closely with the long range Condor reconnaissance aircraft that he had inherited, the forces at his disposal had still managed to sink more than half a million tons of enemy shipping (92 ships) in May alone. This was a truly horrendous attrition rate and one that simply couldn't be sustained by the British for long.[52]

Despite the U-boat toll in the Atlantic, the Allies were still able to negotiate their way through the Mediterranean in both directions with convoys of badly needed war matériel. In a sense, success came to be measured in what had been saved rather than that which had been lost on these missions.[53] This was most tellingly seen in the dangerous supply runs to Tobruk. These replenishment operations began under cover of darkness in May 1941 and remained in existence despite the intensity of the attacks made upon the Australian and British destroyers and sloops engaged upon the Tobruk run until the fortress was finally relieved on 8 December 1941.[54]

May proved to be a remarkable month. Before it was over the British Commonwealth and the Axis Powers would have further cause for both elation and despair.[55] While encouraged by the deeds of the U-boat arm in carrying out its war on trade, there were still too many convoys getting through to their intended destinations for Erich Raeder to be entirely satisfied that Dönitz's vessels held the only key to unlocking this particular puzzle. In his opinion, it was high time the German surface fleet grasped some of the spoils of war by launching a series of raids on the convoys that were plying the Atlantic route. This was the background to *Fall Rheinübung* (*Case Rhine Exercise*) which had been subject to several postponements but finally got underway when the 50,900-ton battleship *Bismarck*, with the German Fleet Commander Admiral Günther Lütjens aboard, finally left the Baltic port of Gotenhafen (Gdynia) along with the heavy cruiser *Prinz Eugen*, on the night of 18–19 May.[56]

British intelligence soon learned from a Scandinavian tip-off that an operation involving two of Raeder's heavy ships was underway and the Admiralty responded predictably by devoting a mass of its most potent warships in a determined bid to try to track them down. Over the course of the next week no less than two carriers (*Victorious* and *Ark Royal*), three battleships (*King George V*, *Prince of Wales* and *Rodney*), three battlecruisers (*Hood*, *Renown* and *Repulse*), four heavy cruisers, nine light cruisers, twenty-five destroyers and a number of flying boats and trawlers were deployed on this task.[57] That such a vast naval dragnet should have eventually ensnared one of the enemy ships is hardly surprising given the advantages that Admiral Sir John Tovey, the C-in-C Home Fleet, possessed and the mistakes made by B-Dienst and Lütjens at critical phases of the operation. Nonetheless, while the British were able to rely upon the quality of their radar even in the foulest weather and derive important contributions from aerial reconnaissance and torpedo bombing which ended up in disabling her on the evening of 26 May, these positives had to be offset against the negatives that emerged from this clash with the *Bismarck*. Chief amongst these was the sobering fact that it had taken only five minutes for the guns of the German battle squadron to turn Vice-Admiral Holland's flagship, the battlecruiser *Hood*, into an incandescent wreck just after dawn on 24 May; 1,418 officers and crew died on that ship. Only three men survived. Poorly designed and inadequately protected where it mattered most against plunging fire, the *Hood* was a behemoth that was fatally flawed. Size alone doesn't count if real weaknesses are evident and can be exploited by one's opponents.[58] Quite apart from her feeble deck protection, the degree of protection given to the storage of her eight torpedoes was simply insufficient. But the battlecruiser's vulnerabilities didn't end there, for the ship's company had developed the highly dangerous practice of storing ammunition outside of magazines designed for their use so as to relay the shells to the gun crews faster and improve their rate of fire. There is an eerie sense of déjà vu in this story and others have had little difficulty in pointing out the distressing similarity with the catastrophe that had engulfed Beatty's battlecruisers at Jutland twenty-five years before. Had the Admiralty learnt from this earlier disaster? Judged from the *Hood*'s catastrophic demise the answer was apparently not. Graham Rhys-Jones summed it up succinctly when he wrote: 'The origins of the disaster are to be found in institutional weakness rather than in command error.'[59]

It took another seventy-six hours to dispose of the *Bismarck* and for that to happen luck as well as skill had a role to play. Although she had received seven hits, the *Prince of Wales* had struck Lütjens' flagship three times in their brief engagement on the morning of 24 May. One of these shells had exploded against her torpedo bulkhead, damaged one of her turbo generators, flooded the forward port boiler room and fractured a fuel line. Thereafter the German battleship left a telltale oil slick in her wake.[60] It ought to have been a vital clue for the Allied hunting groups in the days to come, but indelible mark or not, the trail for the *Bismarck* went cold on more than one occasion until Lütjens unwittingly gave his position away by not observing radio silence and communicating at length with Admiral Saalwächter's Group West HQ.[61] Some of the other aspects of the chase were less satisfactory from an Allied point of view. Apart from anything else, the *Prinz Eugen* escaped undamaged; DF bearings on the *Bismarck* were wrongly calibrated and conveyed to Tovey on 25 May by the Admiralty resulting in diversions that cost him about 100nm, hours of misapplied effort and a wastage of fuel that he could ill afford.[62] On the following day a case of 'friendly fire' occurred with eleven of fourteen Swordfish aircraft from the *Ark Royal* attacking the light cruiser *Sheffield* assuming she was the enemy battleship. That such a mistake should have happened says far more about the air crews' wishful thinking than the quality of their eyesight![63] Then finally on the morning of 27 May two battleships (*King George V* and *Rodney*) and two heavy cruisers (*Devonshire* and *Norfolk*) pumped 2,878 rounds into an already disabled *Bismarck* and still didn't manage to sink her. It finally took three more torpedoes from a third heavy cruiser (*Dorsetshire*) and the efforts of her own scuttling party to finish her off.[64]

Tovey was not even present to see the *dénouement*. Worried about his shortage of fuel and certain that his adversary could not survive, the C-in-C had ordered a ceasefire fifteen minutes before the end and had turned for home with the other warships in his force. His decision to depart the scene without finishing the job brought a strange and controversial ending to what had been an extraordinary operation. What should have been his finest hour instead became something of an anti-climax for him and his men. It was also to wound him in the eyes of Churchill and Pound, both of whom were obsessed with sinking the *Bismarck* and didn't appreciate his unwillingness to be on hand when she finally went down.[65]

There is little doubt that the Admiralty needed a victory to celebrate because at exactly the same time as the hunt for the *Bismarck* was taking place in the North Atlantic, defeat was very much on the cards for the British in the Eastern Mediterranean. Greece and Yugoslavia had already fallen to the Germans and it was obvious that their next military target was the island of Crete, lying to the southeast of the Greek mainland and due south of the Kyklades. At 8,336 sq. km, Crete is the largest Greek island and the fifth largest in the entire Mediterranean. By capturing this island, the Germans would make life far more difficult for Cunningham's Mediterranean Fleet by denying it the use of Suda Bay, imperilling the Allied convoy route through the Eastern Mediterranean and increasing the vulnerability of Alexandria as the home base for that fleet. It would also have vital strategic value for the German military forces by securing their flank before their planned offensive against the Soviet Union in June and prevent the island's airbases from being used by the RAF for long-range bombing attacks on the Romanian oilfields. Uninterrupted supplies from these oilfields were deemed essential for *Barbarossa* to succeed. Once again the men and women of Bletchley Park came to the aid of the British government by providing detailed intelligence from intercepted and deciphered German cables. On this occasion, 'Ultra' provided early warning of the type and strength of the German airborne and amphibious attack on the island that was about to occur. It was excellent intelligence material but the Allied forces on Crete were simply not provided with the airpower necessary to withstand the determined nature of this assault.[66]

After several days of softening up the air defences on the island, *Fall Merkur* (*Case Mercury*) began at 0800 hours on 20 May with massive air strikes on the still functioning airfield at Maleme and the destruction of the miniscule Allied air force gathered there. This was followed by the parachute drops that disgorged 13,000 troops west of the airfield and elsewhere in the Canea (Chania), Heraklion (Iraklion) and Retimo (Rethimnon) sectors. Armed with the knowledge of what the Germans were planning, the Allied defenders were in place to try and prevent them from gaining their initial objectives. This was one case, however, where unimpeachable evidence about the enemy's plans was not sufficient to prevent them from attaining their objective. Air power was the decisive factor in winning the battle for Crete. While the Mediterranean Fleet did everything it could, under very trying circumstances, to prevent any amphibious invasion from taking place, the enemy was still able to augment its force on Crete by using paratroopers and those who had been flown in on heavy transport aircraft. All the while the Germans held the airbases and the means to boost their numbers of men and materiel; therefore, the Allied troops, without air cover to afford any relief from the relentless bombing of their own positions, faced a mounting problem that in the end they couldn't resist. They would have been in a far worse plight had it not been for Cunningham's four groups of warships who showed remarkable resilience in enduring often torrid bombing and strafing attacks from the Luftwaffe. Day after day they continued to comb the waters to interdict and eliminate enemy forces coming by sea. Enemy motor sailing flotillas were decisively engaged and troop convoys were routinely demolished, airfields at Maleme and Scarpanto (Karpathos) were shelled and Allied troops and supplies were brought in, but the Luftwaffe swarmed everywhere in numbers and so even with the courage, determination and expert shiphandling skills shown by the Mediterranean Fleet units, the toll on them was severe.[67]

By 27 May Wavell, the C-in-C Middle East, considered the battle for Crete was lost and he persuaded Churchill and the COS that it was absolutely vital for them to arrange an early evacuation of the 22,000 Allied servicemen on the island. Approval was swiftly given, but an improvised evacuation largely from an open shingle beach at Cora Sfakion (Sphakia), a small fishing village on the southern coast of the island, made under intense fire called for qualities of bravery and endurance that were remarkable. Danger lurked everywhere. Organising an evacuation was one thing, negotiating a safe return passage to Alexandria some 360nm (667km) away was quite another as the Luftwaffe hounded the ships of the withdrawal force mercilessly. On 1 June Cunningham reluctantly accepted the fact that the military position on Crete was such that any further attempt at evacuation might end tragically for all concerned. He had already continued the operation a day longer than the authorities in London had thought was possible.[68]

Looking back at the intense nature of the Cretan campaign, Cunningham was at pains to point out that the Mediterranean Fleet had not only prevented a seaborne invasion from taking place, but his ships and men had also evacuated roughly 17,000 troops from the island in the face of a hostile enemy air force that had flown hundreds of sorties against them in support of *Merkur* throughout the latter half of May. Apart from the 1,828 naval officers and men under his command who had lost their lives in this ordeal, he had also been permanently deprived of two modern light cruisers, one AA cruiser and six destroyers – all sunk while on operational duty.[69] In addition, two of his battleships (his erstwhile flagship *Warspite* and *Barham*), the carrier *Formidable*, two light cruisers (*Dido* and *Orion*) and two destroyers (*Kelvin* and *Nubian*) had been so seriously damaged that they would need to be sent overseas for repair. Of the rest of his battered ensemble, three more cruisers and six destroyers would be laid up under repair for several weeks in Alexandria.[70] This left him two battleships (*Queen Elizabeth* and the slightly damaged *Valiant*), three cruisers (two of which *Ajax* and *Coventry* needed some repairs) and seventeen destroyers to face the Italian fleet, and try to cope with the Luftwaffe and any U-boats that Dönitz might be inclined to send to the Eastern Mediterranean to prey on the convoy routes and generally make a nuisance of themselves at a time of great privation for the British.[71] Cunningham's obvious pride in the overall performance of both ships and men in the service of the Fleet is evident in his cable of 14 September 1941:

> It is not easy to convey how heavy was the strain that men and ships sustained. ... They had started the evacuation already over-tired and they had to carry it through under conditions of savage air attack such as had only recently caused grievous losses in the fleet. ... More than once I felt the stage had been reached where no more could be asked of officers and men, physically and mentally exhausted by their efforts and by the events of these fateful weeks. It is perhaps even now not realised how nearly the breaking

point was reached, but that these men struggled through is the measure of their achievement and I trust that it will not lightly be forgotten.[72]

These two simultaneous incidents in late May had perfectly demonstrated the highs and lows of the naval war. There was no time for Churchill's government to savour a solitary triumph in the North Atlantic with the destruction of the *Bismarck* when defeat stared it in the face in the Aegean.

Realising it was in for a long drawn out conflict, the Admiralty was determined to hit the enemy where it could and one obvious target was to do something about disrupting the German supply chain around the globe. In a bid to reduce the number of armed raiders and auxiliary cruisers in existence, the OIC decided that a purge should be made of the merchant ships that supplied them with their fuel and supplies. If they were eliminated, then the auxiliaries and Raeder's big surface ships would be unable to roam the seas at large for weeks at a time. Working with 'Ultra' decrypts from Bletchley Park, thirteen enemy ships – blockade runners, weather ships, tankers and patrol vessels – were identified and destroyed in a month-long spell from late May onwards.[73] It was a promising start but no more than that.[74] It certainly didn't cripple the supply chain or ensure that commerce raiding by Raeder's heavy ships was stifled, a point demonstrated by the abortive sortie of the *Lützow* in mid-June. On this occasion it wasn't the supply chain that let her down before she could break out into the Atlantic. Instead the heavy cruiser and her five destroyer escorts were spotted late at night by an aircraft from Coastal Command off the southern coast of Norway on 12 June. Torpedoed by one of the squadron of Bristol Beaufort bombers sent out to find her, the *Lützow* returned to the Baltic and an unscheduled date with a berth in the dry dock at Kiel where she would remain being repaired until January 1942.[75]

While the OKM was being frustrated in its efforts to keep the British off balance in the North Sea and the Atlantic, elsewhere the focus of activity had turned to the battle for Syria. This pitched Anglo-Gaullist forces against an entrenched Vichy French colonial presence in one of their two Mandated territories in the Levant (the other one being Lebanon). Hostile to the British from the outset, the Vichy authorities in Damascus were amenable to the idea of providing airfield facilities to the Germans. Cunningham was concerned that unless something was done to arrest this development, the Luftwaffe would be in an ideal position to attack his fleet base at Alexandria, as well as his other bases in the Red Sea and the shipping that passed through the Suez Canal in both directions. Naval operations began on 6 June with Cunningham's fleet units establishing a blockade of both Syrian and Lebanese waters and bombarding the coastal road to lend support to the Allied land offensive. Although subject to persistent air offensive and periodic attacks by two to three fast, well armed and expertly handled destroyer leaders from Beirut, which forced some withdrawals from the blockading force, the measure still proved very effective and in combination with the Allied ground campaign eventually forced the Vichy French colonial authorities to sue for peace. An armistice was drawn up and signed rather poignantly on Bastille Day (14 July). This led to the withdrawal of all Vichy French naval forces from Beirut to Bizerte and Toulon. Of far greater significance for the theatre as a whole, the Allied victory in Syria prevented the Luftwaffe from gaining a foothold in the country where it could have posed a real threat to Cunningham's lines of communications and vital oil supplies that were lying in Iraq.[76] When coupled to the successful launching on 10 June of Operation *Chronometer*, the capture of Assab (the last Italian naval base in the Red Sea) and an Allied submarine offensive throughout the Mediterranean in June that netted twenty vessels, Cunningham had some reason to be satisfied with the results of these concerted efforts to combat the Axis presence throughout his Mediterranean command even though the enemy continued to take a toll of his destroyers and sloops on their nightly supply run to Mersa Matruh and Tobruk.[77]

Hitherto the discussion of the naval war has been largely focused upon the Anglo-German-Italian confrontation. It was destined to become far more complicated as the war soon widened to pull in more combatants. Even before the signal event of the month took place – the launching of the massed invasion of the Soviet Union by the Germans (*Fall Barbarossa*) on 22 June – the Americans had agreed to an extension of the area in which their warships operated in the Central North Atlantic from 30° to 26° West. This meant that from 14 June the units of their Atlantic Fleet would continue to go out on patrol duties with one another, but they would now be able to sortie almost to the west coast of Iceland while doing so.[78] This type of activity had been made much easier as a result of the opening on 7 April of the US naval base in Bermuda – a direct consequence of the earlier 'Destroyers for Bases Deal' arranged between the Churchill and Roosevelt administrations and a confirmation of the main principle – the defeat of the Axis forces in the Atlantic and European theatres – that had been unanimously agreed upon at the joint American, British and Canadian staff talks (ABC-1) which had ended on 27 March.[79] In a sense this was all part of a much larger commitment on the part of the US government to assist the Allied war effort. Nothing exemplified this more than Congressional approval of the Lend-Lease Act that Roosevelt had duly signed into law on 11 March 1941.[80] This measure – worth initially $7 billion – allowed the Americans to furnish the British with critically needed war supplies, providing they carried them in their own vessels, and permitted them to bring their damaged warships into US Navy yards for repair. Once the Central Atlantic Neutrality Patrol had been established in April, Roosevelt negotiated a deal with the Danish Minister in Washington, allowing the Americans to assume a de facto protectorate over Greenland and permitting them to construct bases there for the defence of the Western hemisphere. Permission was also given for the redeployment of three battleships, four cruisers and thirteen destroyers from their bases in San Diego and Pearl Harbor to the Atlantic over the course of the next couple of months.[81] While Roosevelt's partiality for the Allied cause had been obvious from the outset of the war, further evidence of his intentions was given on 6 June when the US Navy was instructed to seize a total of sixty-five ships belonging to foreign powers that had either been detained or laid up in American ports. They were subsequently transferred to Allied control for the duration of the war to help make up for the shortfall in merchant vessels suffered by them as a result of the prolonged war against trade engaged in by the enemy.[82]

As American material support of the Allied cause increased so the sense that the fortunes of war might be beginning to turn against the Axis gained ground in London. It was ratcheted up a further notch when Hitler opened another vast new war front by driving into Soviet territory on 22 June bringing his pragmatic, but ideologically bankrupt, pact with the USSR to a violent end. Indications of what was about to take place had filtered through to the Soviet High Command and somewhat belatedly Admiral N.G. Kuznetsov, the People's Commissar for the Soviet Navy, issued a Grade 2 Alert for his subordinate fleet commanders on 19 June and the critical Grade 1 Alert just before midnight (2337 hours) two days later.[83] Kuznetsov warned his officers to exercise extreme caution and avoid any actions that might inflame tensions and lead to any military retaliation from the German naval forces in the vicinity. In truth, the request for caution and restraint, while commendable, was also quite immaterial, as the German naval forces were intent on preparing for war and had been mining various channels throughout the Baltic and Gulf of Finland for several days. Within minutes of the official start of the invasion at 0300 hours on 22 June, a couple of German S-boats (Schnellboote) quickly made their presence felt with the sinking of the Latvian steamer, *Gaisma*.[84]

At the time of the invasion the Soviet Navy was divided into four fleets, across two continents and many time zones.[85] After languishing for many years with largely obsolescent forces at its disposal, efforts had been made in the late 1930s to improve this arm of the services and many heavy fleet units were in the shipyards at various stages of completion when *Barbarossa* pitched the USSR rudely into war. Although it did not have either the cachet or the money of the Red Army, was deficient in many technical aspects like radar and sonar, and had too many vessels of dubious quality and vintage amongst its active contingent, the Red Navy had a resilience about it that would stand it in good stead over the next few years.[86] Unlike the Red Banner Fleet in the Baltic which was busying itself with minelaying activities and trying to counter an increasing German presence in these waters, the Black Sea Fleet was in a position of total dominance at the outset. It wouldn't last thanks to extensive aerial mining by the Luftwaffe and the activities of a variety of U-boats, S-boats, midget submarines and torpedo boats that the Germans and Italians had either sent down the Danube or freighted in a semi-constructed fashion on trains and re-assembled at the Romanian naval base of Constanza.[87]

While the Germans were locked in their expanding war with the USSR on the Eastern Front, the struggle for supremacy in the Mediterranean and North African theatre never slackened. Cunningham's resources were stretched very thin in constantly resupplying Malta and Tobruk to ensure their continued survival. Both were deemed to be crucial for the Allied war effort and both took a huge logistic effort to keep them fortified and out of Axis hands.[88] Part of the key to their retention was increasing the number of aircraft available on Malta to vie with those German and Italian fighter-bombers that were regularly sent to pummel the territory and make life as uncomfortable as possible for anyone living there. Cunningham believed it was crucial for the future of the Mediterranean Fleet as well as the continuation of merchant shipping using the Suez Canal that enemy aircraft should be prevented from establishing an ascendancy over Malta, thereby making it into an untenable military and naval base for the Allies. Vice-Admiral Somerville and Force H, operating out of Gibraltar, became the designated agent for handling a raft of carrier operations that brought much needed Hurricanes to the waters of the Balearic Islands and flew them off to Malta where they boosted the Allied air defences of the island.[89] Somerville's warships also continued to prove their worth by regularly escorting troop and supply convoys through the Western Mediterranean in both directions – a fact that underlined once again the vital importance attached to retaining Gibraltar for the Allied cause. By getting more troops and supplies into the garrison and having more aircraft to contest the skies over the island, it was clear that the Maltese situation was better by the end of July 1941 than it had been at any time since the Italians had joined the war in June 1940.[90]

A somewhat unlikely tale of success in the Mediterranean theatre was matched by an unaccustomed avoidance of disaster in another! In the North Atlantic mid-summer had brought a blip in the U-boat war. At last Dönitz and his U-boat crews were beginning to experience something of a barren time of it on the high seas.[91] 'Ultra' had been the key to this change of fortune, of course, but the evidence that something was awry in the intelligence world did not seem to register with either Dönitz or the OKM. This demonstrates a degree of hubris on their part since they placed far too much confidence in the sophisticated nature of their Engima encryption machine and couldn't bring themselves to believe that the Allies might have overcome the phenomenal odds that were set against anyone cracking their system. This type of complacency was significantly missing at Bletchley Park where the cryptanalysts knew only too well that the window they had opened onto the world of German signals intelligence could close at any minute unless they continued to keep pace with the monthly changes that were made to the Enigma settings.[92] Harry Hinsley, whose hunch about seizing the German 'weather' ship *München* had proved so successful in providing a rich cache of intelligence material in the recent past, targeted another – the trawler *Lauenburg* – in late June. Operation *EC* was conducted with clinical efficiency. DF equipment aboard the tribal destroyer *Bedouin* picked up a signal from the quarry to the north of Jan Mayen Island and the British task force homed in on the location. A few shells and a boarding party did the trick and a mass of written material was swiftly bagged before the trawler was sunk. Amongst the papers were instructions for plug connections and inner settings that would enable Turing and his team to work out the wheel order and ring settings for the Naval Enigma machine for July.[93]

While there was good reason for modest Allied satisfaction at these recent developments in the overall nature of the war at sea – a feeling underscored by the American occupation of Iceland that took place in the early weeks of July and the US Atlantic Fleet's assumption of responsibilities for its overall defence later in the same month – elsewhere the new phase of the conflict in the east was more troubling.[94] Early successes both on land and at sea, backed up by massive aerial support, suggested that the Germans had not only caught the Soviets napping but were also poised to exploit their opportunity to unravel the Soviet defences decisively in the coming weeks of their eastern campaign. On one of the two northern fronts, the Soviets soon found themselves recoiling under the weight of the German offensive in the Baltic and being forced to evacuate their naval forces from both Riga and Dünamünde, on the southern coast of the Gulf of Riga (Latvia), and send them northeast to the Estonian capital of Tallinn (Reval). This war front was a dour encounter from the outset, with both sides engaging in extensive mining operations in what were confined and relatively shallow waters. So complex and densely laid were the mines in some of the German-Finnish barrages, such as the *Allirahu*, *Apolda*, *Juminda* and *Valkjärvi*, for example, that these areas just had to be avoided unless one wished to court disaster. For their part, the Soviets laid the majority of their mines throughout the Gulf of Finland and off the west coast of Estonia in a largely defensive gesture aimed at delaying, rather than preventing, the German offensive that was directed against their naval base at Tallinn.[95]

Further north in the Arctic, the first two German U-boats (*U81* and *U652*) began to make their presence felt off the Kola coast in early-to-mid July. At the same time a flotilla of five German destroyers reached the forward air and naval base of Kirkenes in a Norwegian fjord of the Barents Sea not far from the Petsamo region of north-western Russia. Their arrival to join the gunnery training ship *Bremse* and other German ships in what was shaping up to be an important German base in the north prompted the Allies to mount a significant carrier-led operation against both Kirkenes and land targets in the Petsamo region. Fortified with both *Furious* and *Victorious*, aided and abetted by two heavy cruisers and four destroyers, the Allied force did little damage but lost a total of twelve torpedo-bombers and three fighter aircraft in their foiled attempt to disrupt the German build up.[96]

Frustrated in the northern latitudes, the Allies found some relief from the growing level of support forthcoming from the supposedly non-belligerent (if not non-neutral) United States in the war. In the latest move in this direction on 1 August, a de facto embargo on both the sale and export of oil and aviation fuel to Japan came into force. This was not really what Roosevelt may have intended at the outset, if Robert Dallek is to be believed, but the implementation of a freezing order on Japanese assets and restrictions on the sale of fuel and aviation spirit caused major concern in military and government circles in Tokyo and did nothing to arrest the movement towards a showdown in the Pacific.[97] Further grist to the mill was added by news reports of the clandestine meeting, code-named Operation *Riviera*, which had taken place in Argentia Bay, Newfoundland on 9–12 August between President Roosevelt in the heavy cruiser *Augusta* and the irrepressible Churchill on board the new battleship *Prince of Wales*. Although the discussions were to result in an agreement on the so-called Atlantic

Charter – setting out the general principles that ought to underpin civilisation in the post-war world – the fact that the talks took place at all was more important than their actual results. Despite the vague and flowery nature of the Atlantic communiqué, *Riviera* did nothing to still the fears of the Japanese that moves were being coordinated by the leaders of an Allied combine for future use against them.[98]

Shortly afterwards the Allies began supplying the Soviets with their first batch of Hurricane fighters and sending war supplies by experimental convoy from Iceland for use by the Red Army in the defensive perimeter of Murmansk and further east to the port of Archangel. Later in September these regular convoys either used the original route from Hvalfjordur to Archangel or one that linked Scapa Flow with the same White Sea naval base. This war matériel was vital for their troops fighting in the Arctic, but on their other war fronts the Soviets were giving ground to the relentless German invader.[99]

In the Black Sea – the one area in which the Soviets had a superior naval advantage over the Axis forces – the deteriorating military position in the Ukraine forced them to evacuate their naval base at Nikolayev in mid-August. This was a huge blow as all the vessels being built at the Marti South shipyard – the 45,000-ton battleship *Sovetskaya Ukraina*, the light cruiser *Ordzhonikidze*, the flotilla leaders *Perekop* and *Ochakov*, two destroyers, three submarines and two gunboats – had to be blown up to prevent them from being finished and used by the Kriegsmarine against them. In the Kommunar 61 North shipyard the same thing happened to the 35,240-ton battlecruiser *Sevastopol*, the 11,300-ton cruiser *Sverdlov* and four destroyers. Those vessels that had been fitted out and were capable of being towed away – a couple of light cruisers and flotilla leaders, three destroyers, five submarines and a solitary ice-breaker – were escorted south to relative safety in the Crimea by eight Soviet destroyers.[100] A few days later the city of Kherson fell to the Germans putting even greater pressure on the Ukrainian port of Odessa. A full-scale evacuation of all their military forces and as much of their supplies as possible could not be long delayed and was resorted to reluctantly from early October onwards. After using three convoys in order to evacuate the 157th Rifle Division to the Crimea on 3–5 October, another 35,000 troops were embarked successfully in one night alone (15–16 October) and taken out of Odessa on eleven transports, two minelayers, a couple of survey ships and a host of minor vessels, accompanied by a motley selection of cruisers, destroyers, patrol ships, minesweepers, tugs and other smaller craft. Despite the attentions of the Luftwaffe, only one transport was sunk en route to Sevastopol.[101] By the end of the month, however, with German victories on the Perekop Isthmus, Sevastopol was in the process of being cut off and put under siege. While the Soviet Military Council approved the reinforcement of the Crimean base, the battleship *Parizhskaya Kommuna* and the cruiser *Molotov* made good their escape to ports on the Caucasian coast.[102]

Evacuations, even successful ones, are hardly a promising sign of the times. Things weren't going any better for the Soviets in the Baltic either judging from the withdrawal of the Baltic Fleet and what was left of X Rifle Corps from

Tallinn on 28 August. Along with four convoys, the main, covering and rearguard forces moved off in a vast armada of 159 ships towards the eastern base of Kronstadt in the Gulf of Finland. On their way both the *Juminda* mine barrage and the Luftwaffe took a heavy and indiscriminate toll of them. Forty-one vessels (including nineteen transports) were sunk or run aground while on passage and seven more vessels, including the flotilla leader *Minsk*, were heavily damaged.[103] Within six weeks the Germans had largely mopped up the resistance to them in the offshore islands of the Gulf of Riga and were advancing on a variety of fronts. Throughout the autumn Soviet troops were on the retreat in the Baltic and needed all the support they could get from their naval arm. Detachments of the Baltic Fleet were, for instance, deployed to provide artillery support for their ground troops in and around Leningrad, Krasnoe Selo and Peterhof, but did so at considerable cost to themselves. Other Soviet ships were engaged in supplying their shrinking outposts at Hangö in southern Finland, but these missions would soon turn into a series of evacuations before the harsh winter would intervene to slow the pace at which they were succumbing to the German invasion.[104]

Short of the requisite air power to take the fight to the enemy in the Mediterranean theatre, Cunningham had been forced to mark time. As a man of action, he was irked by the necessity for his fleet to remain in a rather subdued and passive state. Reinforcing and relieving Tobruk and resupplying Malta was laborious, unglamorous and dangerous work even though it needed to be done, and great effort was expended on keeping these two bases from falling into the hands of the enemy.[105] While these tasks remained an ordeal, better news for Cunningham had come from a breakthrough made by the Bletchley Park cryptanalysts in understanding how the Hagelin C38m encryption machine worked. As a result, they had been able to crack the Italian naval cipher for the first time in early June 1941. Thereafter, critical 'Ultra' intelligence was supplied to the nerve centre of Mediterranean Command in Alexandria on a whole range of matters, not least the timing and location of Italian convoys to Tripoli. Armed with this information, Captain G.W.G. 'Shrimp' Simpson's submarines based at Malta began to get amongst the Italian troopships and supply vessels and cause some damage. By the end of August six of his underwater fleet had made their presence felt throughout the Central Mediterranean with some initial 'kills' and greater success was to come their way in the following weeks.[106]

Nonetheless, it was far from plain sailing in the Central Mediterranean even if the Allies could read Italian signals traffic. Running convoys like Operation *Halberd* from Gibraltar to Malta in late September with nine transports (81,000 tons of equipment and supplies) involved the deployment of no less than three Allied battleships, a carrier, five light cruisers, eighteen destroyers and nine submarines as escort vessels and additionally brought Cunningham and the rest of his Mediterranean Fleet out of Alexandria in an effort to fool the Italians into thinking the convoy was bound for the Eastern rather than Central Mediterranean.[107] Cunningham's counterpart as C-in-C of the RMI, Angelo Iachino, had not been expecting a convoy run to Malta when he learnt that British warships from Gibraltar were at sea on 25 September. He and the Supermarina were inclined to think that the British were engaged on an act of revenge for a raid on the Bay of Gibraltar by several *Maiali* (slow human torpedoes) several nights before in which a tanker and two other vessels had been sunk. Accordingly, those parts of Iachino's fleet that weren't laid up or lacking fuel were sent to Asinara on the north coast of Sardinia so that they could guard the port of La Maddalena, or intercept any force that might be seeking to attack any of the ports or shipping on the Ligurian coast. A combination of persistent poor weather and low cloud and inadequate and inaccurate aerial reconnaissance information frustrated both Iachino and the Supermarina's efforts to interfere with the *Halberd* operation over the course of the next two days. While the Allies certainly had more reason for satisfaction than their enemies in getting eight of the nine transports into Malta, they had still lost the services of the battleship *Nelson* for six months (bomb damage) in doing so. *Halberd* had proved to be yet another case of what might have been for the Axis Powers. They could curse the poor weather and the intelligence fed to them, but it had been yet another lame effort by Iachino's ships with the only damage done to the convoy by Royal Italian Air Force (RAI) planes.[108]

More than ever convinced that the Axis Powers ought to pose more of a threat to the Allied position in the Mediterranean than they did, Hitler made an offer to supply up to twenty U-boats to Mussolini in late August so that they could be used to disrupt and preferably stem the nightly destroyer replenishment of the besieged fortress of Tobruk. If these sailings could be savaged or stopped, Tobruk would undoubtedly fall. If that happened, the psychological blow to the Eighth Army and the boost for Rommel's Afrika Korps was likely to be immense. With this in mind the *Goeben* group of six U-boats were sent through the Straits of Gibraltar in late September and early October to operate against these nightly sailings from Alexandria. Despite the fact that these craft only accounted for three lighters, two small transports and a gunboat in the whole of October, the Germans sensed that with more U-boats at their disposal the Allied supply run would become an even more tortuous undertaking than it already was.[109]

Before the Germans could do anything about making the situation more complicated for the defenders of Tobruk, however, they and their Italian Axis brethren found themselves ironically at the end of a deteriorating supply chain of their own. Churchill, whose strategic interventions in the war had enjoyed mixed fortunes hitherto, was not always wide of the mark. As early as August 1941 he had begun prompting Dudley Pound to base a small but fast strike force at Malta to intercept Rommel's supplies at sea. This idea was taken up by the Admiralty and resulted in the formation of Force K on 21 October under the command of Captain William Agnew. Apart from his own light cruiser *Aurora*, 'Bill' Agnew had with him a sister ship from the Arethusa class *Penelope*, and two new L class destroyers, *Lance* and *Lively*. In addition, they had the key advantage of 'Ultra' and aerial reconnaissance from three Wellingtons to help them in their quest for enemy convoys. Force K soon struck it rich. Alerted initially by 'Ultra' decrypts to the sailing of the *Beta* supply convoy from Naples to Tripoli, Agnew received precise information about its strength and location from a reconnaissance flight in the early afternoon of 8 November. Making good use of his ships' radar capability and in wonderfully clear conditions, he first located the convoy visually at 0039 hours on 9 November some 135nm (250km) east of the Sicilian port of Siracusa (Syracuse). It was about 8nm (14.8km) away making nine knots in two columns about 0.5nm (approximately 900m) apart, surrounded by six fleet destroyers oblivious to the danger, with two heavy cruisers *Trento* and *Trieste* and four more destroyers covering the entire convoy and escorts some 3nm (5.6km) astern of the convoy and on its starboard wing.[110] Agnew quickly sized up the situation and in turning immediately to port was able to use the moonlight to frame the enemy ships in a silhouette that the radar-controlled guns of his light cruisers scarcely needed. In a matter of forty-two minutes Force K sank all seven supply ships (39,787 tons) and their cargoes (32,170 tons of matériel, fuel and ammunition, as well as 389 vehicles), sank one of the fleet destroyers and damaged two others. Sloppy Italian defence measures and inadequate decision making combined to unwittingly assist Agnew's cause and imperil their own. Force K returned to a triumphant reception at the Grand Harbour in Valetta at 1305 hours on 9 November. Agnew's performance was duly recognised with the instant conferment of a CB (Companion of the Order of the Bath). Just to add insult to injury, *Upholder* torpedoed the destroyer *Libeccio* while she was engaged in rescuing survivors from the debacle. After being put under tow, she broke up and sank in quick order. Therefore, by whatever standards one employs, this was an extraordinarily successful venture for the Allies and an extremely maudlin one for the Italians. Mussolini was not amused and scapegoats were quickly found for the entire affair, with both Bruno Brivonesi on the *Trieste* and Ugo Bisciani on the lead destroyer *Maestrale* being relieved of their commands.[111]

News of *Beta*'s destruction came hard on the heels of the relief of the Cyprus garrison by the fast minelayer *Abdiel* and a flotilla of Allied destroyers which managed to transport 14,000 troops safely to and from Alexandria between 2 and 8 November.[112] Prolonged success was not something that blessed the naval activities of either side in the Mediterranean, however, as *U81* demonstrated on 13 November when she torpedoed the carrier *Ark Royal* on her way back to Gibraltar. This success, and that of *U331* in spectacularly sinking the battleship *Barham* north of Bardia later in the month, convinced the Kriegsmarine to send eighteen more U-boats into the Mediterranean in December to shore up the security of its supply chain to Tripoli and put some additional pressure on Allied convoy traffic.[113]

In this very fluid situation, the ebb and flow of success and failure at sea was also tested on land when, on 18 November, the 8th Army launched a massive counter-attack, codenamed Operation *Crusader* designed to relieve the fortress of Tobruk and re-establish the Allied presence in Libya. This operation was to become a battle of attrition that fully exposed the weakness of both sets of forces before the Allied objective was finally realised when the Eighth Army re-established a land link to the previously besieged fortress on 8 December. This meant that Cunningham was no longer faced with the necessity of resupplying the fortress by sea. As a measure of what had been involved in this nightly operation, 32,667 troops and 33,946 tons of supplies had been taken to Tobruk from the time that the siege of the fortress had begun on 12 April, and units of the Mediterranean Fleet had returned to Alexandria carrying 34,115 troops, 7,516 wounded personnel and 7,097 prisoners of war.[114] Although he had fretted about the supply missions and the effect the nightly ordeal was having on his ships and crew, it is difficult not to see the overall military return as a high, but invaluable, one in line with the heroic defiance of those Allied troops within the fortress itself who had held up Rommel's advance and given time for the Eighth Army to recover its poise.[115]

To Churchill's circle in London the war in early December 1941 could hardly fail to have been seen as an extraordinary mosaic of both light and shade. There were plenty of optimistic signs and one didn't have to look far to see them. Roosevelt's expanded version of the Monroe Doctrine, involving a 'shoot on sight' order issued in September against all Axis shipping caught within those seas deemed vital to the defence of the continental United States, was obviously a case in point; particularly as the president had distorted an incident between an American destroyer *Greer* and a U-boat on 4 September in order to establish the rationale for this more aggressive attitude![116] Another encouraging sign had been the willingness of the US Navy to assume greater responsibility from September onwards for escorting HX convoys between Newfoundland and Iceland and ON convoys going in the opposite direction. Above all, however, the growing presidential steadfastness in the war effort was shown by a change in the Neutrality Law that he had advocated and which had been passed somewhat unenthusiastically by Congress in November, allowing American merchant ships to be armed and to sail anywhere including even entry into a designated war zone.[117]

An altogether gloomier picture, however, was offered by the situation in East Asia where the Japanese and the Allies appeared to be on a collision course. Roosevelt's administration, supported by the other Allied governments, had responded to the seizing of Camranh Bay on 24 July 1941 and the airfields in the southern part of Vietnam shortly thereafter by freezing all Japanese assets in their possession. War was definitely in the offing. Churchill returned from his mid-August meeting with President Roosevelt in Argentia Bay, Newfoundland convinced that unless the regime in Tokyo under Prince Konoye saw sense and brought the military's southern advance to a rapid halt, the US would be drawn into the war.[118] It was apparent by the middle of October when the War Minister General Hideki Tōjō replaced Konoye as Prime Minister that there would be no such restraint on the part of the Japanese. If anything, a mixture of intransigence and belligerence seemed to define their foreign policy at this time. American decrypts of intercepted Japanese diplomatic signals traffic (known by the name 'Magic') to Ambassador Nomura in Washington in the following weeks made it very apparent that unless Tōjō's military government was given satisfaction by the Americans on the outstanding issues dividing them, relations would descend into chaos. Although nothing more specific was spelt out for Nomura, the veiled warning was interpreted in a sinister way by both the Roosevelt and Churchill governments.[119]

For this reason in late October the Admiralty had created a special unit, Force G, consisting of the new but not yet worked up battleship *Prince of Wales*, the old battlecruiser *Repulse*, the carrier *Indomitable*, and four destroyers of mixed vintage, speed and effectiveness. While Force G was supposed to be deployed as a 'flying squadron' in Singaporean waters, it lost its fast carrier when *Indomitable* ran aground off Kingston, Jamaica on 3 November.[120] A pale imitation of the once much vaunted 'Singapore Strategy', the weakened Force G was supposed to be a deterrent. Would it prove to be so in practice? It didn't take long for the world to find out.[121]

Notes

1. David Wragg, *Carrier combat* (Stroud, Glos: Sutton Publishing, 1997), pp.40–44; Jack Greene and Alessandro Massignani, *The naval war in the Mediterranean 1940–1943* (London: Chatham Publishing, 1998), pp.133–35.
2. Cunningham to Pound, 18 Jan.1941, in Simpson (ed.), *The Cunningham papers, I*, p.262; Greene and Massignani, *Naval war in the Mediterranean*, pp.133–35.
3. This deployment was delayed by the successful German mining offensive against the Suez Canal in mid-February. These attacks had closed it for several days, causing shipping delays and preventing *Formidable* from joining the Mediterranean Fleet until March 1941. Rohwer, *Chronology*, p.59.
4. For a useful study detailing the role of the Focke-Wulf Condor in World War II, see Kenneth Poolman, *Scourge of the Atlantic: Focke-Wulf Condor* (London: Macdonald & Jane's, 1978).
5. Aircraft operating in the same stretch of ocean claimed the loss of eighteen more ships (66,563 tons) and damaged several more. Rohwer, *Chronology*, pp.55, 57.
6. Throughout 1940 18,404 ships had been convoyed along the North Atlantic, Gibraltar and Sierra Leone routes with only 300 being lost – a loss ratio of 1.63%. 1941's figures fell away somewhat: 13,051 ships convoyed with losses at 405 – a loss ratio of 3.10%. See Appendix I.
7. Arnold Hague, *The Allied convoy system 1939–1945: its organization, defence and operation* (Annapolis, Md: NIP, 2000), pp.18–28, 35–36, 45–50.
8. HG convoys plied the route from Home Waters to Gibraltar and SLS were slow convoys running from Freetown, Sierra Leone to the UK. Bernard Edwards, *Beware raiders! German surface raiders in the Second World War* (Barnsley: Leo Cooper, 2001), pp.124–50; Levy, *The Royal Navy's Home Fleet*, pp.79–81; Rohwer, *Chronology*, pp.58–59.
9. In fact, overall the two battleships had accounted for twenty-two merchant vessels at a cost of 115,622 tons. Rohwer, *Chronology*, pp.60, 63; Richard Garrett, *Scharnhorst and Gneisenau: the elusive sisters* (Newton Abbot, Devon: David & Charles, 1978), pp.58–72.
10. *Admiral Scheer*'s toll of Allied shipping stood at seventeen vessels of 113,233 tons. Rohwer, *Chronology*, pp.64–65.
11. Ibid., p.64; Garrett, *Scharnhorst and Gneisenau*, pp.68–85.
12. While their forced detention in Brest tied up a considerable amount of British shipping, the fact that three effective commerce raiders couldn't engage in belligerent activities on any of the trade routes was also a waste of resources. In the end the cost–benefit analysis of this situation remains murky.
13. Hitler's action was timely since Italian military weakness was not confined to the Adriatic and the Aegean but extended to North Africa as well – a point that was proved emphatically when both Tobruk was captured on 22 January and then Benghazi fell to Allied troops in early February 1941. *Fuehrer conferences*, pp.169–73; Rohwer, *Chronology*, p.55.

14 Rohwer, *Chronology*, pp.56, 59; John Connell, 'Wavell's 30,000', in Basil Liddell Hart (ed.), *History of the Second World War* (London: Phoebus Publishing, 1980), pp.88–107.
15 James J. Sadkovich, 'The Italo-Greek War in context: Italian priorities and Axis diplomacy', in Jeremy Black (ed.), *The Second World War, Vol.I. The German War 1939–1942* (Aldershot, Hants: Ashgate, 2007), pp.281–306.
16 Simpson (ed.), *Cunningham papers, I*, pp.296–302, 305, 308, 327–33, 354, 396, 399, 412.
17 Sheila Lawlor, *Churchill and the politics of war, 1940–1941* (Cambridge: CUP, 1995), pp.165–259.
18 Simpson (ed.), *Cunningham papers, I*, pp.233–37; Gill, *Royal Australian Navy 1939–1942*, pp.304–7.
19 Italian resentment against the British was fanned by attacks made by ships of Force H under the command of Vice-Admiral Somerville (the carrier *Ark Royal*, the battleship *Malaya*, the battlecruiser *Renown* and the light cruiser *Sheffield*) which bombarded Genoa and caused extensive damage to the city port with 273 rounds of 15-inch (381mm) shells, 782 of 6-inch (152mm) and 400 of 4.5-inch (114mm) on 9 February. *Ark Royal* and four destroyers added insult to injury by carrying out a raid subsequently on Livorno and her planes mined the harbour entrance to the naval base of La Spezia. All escaped and returned safely to Gibraltar on 11 February. Rohwer, *Chronology*, p.58; Dannreuther, *Somerville's Force H*, pp.72–78.
20 *Gaudo* was the Italian name for Gavdo, an island south of Crete. John Winton, *Cunningham* (London: John Murray, 1998), pp.135–38; Rohwer, *Chronology*, pp.65–66.
21 Greene and Massignani, *Naval war in the Mediterranean*, pp.145–47; Sebag-Montefiore, *Enigma*, pp.121–27.
22 Rohwer, *Chronology*, p.66.
23 Green and Massignani, *Naval war in the Mediterranean*, pp.148–60; Sadkovich, *Italian Navy in World War II*, pp.125–34; Marc de Angelis, 'Operation 'Gaudo' and the Battle of Matapan', accessed at www.regiamarina.net/battles/matapan/part2_us.htm (15 March 2006).
24 Simpson (ed.), *Cunningham papers, I*, p.237.
25 Sub-lieutenant G.P.C. Williams and his two-man crew aboard the Albacore 5A ran out of fuel on their return journey from making the successful attack on the *Pola*. They were forced to ditch the plane in the sea. All three men survived. Williams was subsequently awarded the DSC (Distinguished Service Cross). www.rathbonemuseum.com/GB/FAA/GPCWilliams.html (accessed 15 March 2006).
26 O'Hara, *Struggle for the middle sea*, pp.91–98; Marc Antonio Bragadin, *The Italian Navy in World War II* (Annapolis, Md: US NIP, 1957), pp.85–98.
27 Stephen, *The fighting admirals*, p.96.
28 Simpson (ed.), *Cunningham Papers, I*, p.239.
29 Barnett, *Engage the enemy*, pp.344–45; Gill, *Royal Australian Navy 1939–1942*, pp.308–17; Winton, *Cunningham*, pp.161–75.
30 Stephen, *Sea battles in close-up, 2*, pp.48–69.
31 Exact numbers of losses at Matapan remain disputed. While Sadkovich contends that 2,300 men died during the course of the battle, Commander Marc Antonio Bragadin suggests the figure is about 3,000. For their part, Greene and Massignani put the total of Italian losses at 2,303 and 1,411 prisoners-of-war. Rohwer concurs with the latter on the number of Italian dead. Bragadin, *The Italian Navy in World War II*, p.96; Greene and Massignani, *Naval war in the Mediterranean*, p.159; Rohwer, *Chronology*, p.66; Sadkovich, *Italian Navy in World War II*, p.131.
32 Barnett, *Engage the enemy*, pp.344–45. Sadkovich begs to differ, seeing it as merely 'a temporary setback'. His well-documented enthusiasm for the Italian cause is such that he finds himself in agreement with Nino Arena, Raymond De Belot, Bragadin and Angelo Iachino in disputing the comprehensiveness of the British naval victory at Matapan. This leads him to assert: 'In fact, the British victory was not as complete

nor as significant as it seemed at the time.' Warming to his task, Sadkovich goes on to claim that the British had made a number of mistakes and had also been very lucky in these engagements. His argument has some merit but is hardly conclusive. Sadkovich, *Italian Navy in World War II*, pp.131–33.

33 Simpson (ed.), *Cunningham papers, I*, p.239; L. Johnman and H. Murphy, '"The first fleet victory since Trafalgar": the battle of Cape Matapan and signals intelligence, March 1941', *The Mariner's Mirror, Vol.91, No.3* (Aug.2005): 436–53; Jon Robb-Webb, 'Sea control in narrow waters: the battles of Taranto and Matapan', in Ian Speller (ed.), *The Royal Navy and maritime power in the twentieth century* (London: Frank Cass, 2005), pp.33–49.

34 Brian R. Sullivan, 'A fleet in being: the rise and fall of Italian sea power, 1861–1943', *The International History Review, Vol.X, No.1* (Feb.1988): 106–24.

35 Marc Antonio Bragadin, *The Italian Navy in World War II* (Annapolis, Md: US NIP, 1957), pp.73–77; Gill, *Royal Australian Navy 1939–1942*, pp.370–74; Rohwer, *Chronology*, pp.66–67.

36 Yugoslavia's fleet consisted of a training cruiser, four destroyers, four submarines, six torpedo boats, ten MTBs, eight minesweepers, six minelayers and an aircraft depot ship. They remained initially in harbour at Cattaro, Sibenik and Split. In the face of sustained Italian air attacks some of these vessels were damaged. Rather than endure these aerial assaults, the submarine *Nebojša* and two MTBs opted to make a dash for freedom down the Adriatic and reached Suda Bay between 22–24 April. Another dramatic gesture was offered by the officers of the destroyer *Zagreb* who blew her up in protest over the surrender on 17 April. Rohwer, *Chronology*, p.67; Murray, *Strategy for defeat*, pp.74–76.

37 Brian Padair Farrell, *The Basis and making of British grand strategy, 1940–43: Was there a plan? Book I* (Lewiston N.Y.: The Edward Mellen Press, 1998), p.120

38 Jim Allaway, *Hero of the Upholder: the story of Lieutenant Commander M.D.Wanklyn VC, DSO*** (Shrewsbury: Airlife, 1991), pp.93–109; Padfield, *War beneath the sea*, pp.131–49.

39 Greene and Massignani, *Naval war in the Mediterranean*, pp.161–64; Sadkovich, *Italian Navy in World War II*, pp.139–41; Winton, *Cunningham*, p.177; Rohwer, *Chronology*, p.69; Simpson (ed.), *Cunningham papers, I*, pp.239–40, 341–51; Winton, *Cunningham*, pp.177–80.

40 Rohwer, *Chronology*, p.69.

41 Simpson (ed.), *Cunningham papers, I*, pp.243–44, 370–97, 399, 424; Barnett, *Engage the enemy*, pp.346–50; Gill, *Royal Australian Navy 1939–1942*, pp.317–35; Rohwer, *Chronology*, p.70.

42 OB convoys were outward bound from Liverpool for North America. Padfield, *War beneath the sea*, pp.109–12; Hughes and Costello, *Battle of the Atlantic*, p.135.

43 Blair, Jr., *Hitler's U-boat war: hunters*, pp.248–58; Bodo Herzog, 'Admiral Otto Kretschmer', in Howarth (ed.), *Men of war*, pp.383–93; Padfield, *War beneath the sea*, pp.113–15; David Jordan, *Wolfpack: the U-boat war and the Allied counter-attack 1939–1945* (Staplehurst, Kent: Spellmount, 2002), pp.73–77; Vause, *Wolf*, pp.90–91.

44 Early versions of the 286M radar sets came equipped with a fixed antennae. This meant that the ship would have to change direction to alter the point of the radar beam. Even then the 286M radar was only capable of detecting a surfaced submarine at a range of no more than 1km. Type-271 radar sets had a range of between 10–25nm (18.5–46.3km). Brown, *Radar history*, pp.335–37; Alfred Price, *Aircraft versus submarine in two world wars* (Barnsley: Pen & Sword Aviation, 2004), pp.54–60, 69, 81–82, 86, 88, 111–12, 126, 149, 156, 160, 166, 169–71, 180, 203–4, 206, 214, 216. www.navweaps.com/Weapons/WNBR_Radar.htm (accessed 27 Nov. 2007); www.vectorsite.net/ttwiz_01.html (accessed 27 Nov. 2007).

45 David Brown, 'Admiral John Godfrey', in Howarth (ed.), *Men of war*, pp.531–40.

46 Hugh Sebag-Montefiore, *Enigma: the battle for the code* (London: Phoenix, 2001), pp.132–36.

47 A visit to the site of the Bletchley Park complex near Milton Keynes in Buckinghamshire is recommended for all those with an interest in this subject and a little time to spare. Guided tours of the site and many of its buildings are particularly recommended. For further information see the website www.bletchleypark.org.uk. See also John Ferris, 'The road to Bletchley Park: the British experience with signals intelligence, 1892–1945', *Intelligence and National Security*, Vol.17, No.1 (Spring 2002): 53–84; F.H. Hinsley and Alan Stripp (eds), *Codebreakers: the inside story of Bletchley Park* (Oxford: OUP, 1993); Stephen Budiansky, *Battle of wits: the complete story of codebreaking in World War II* (New York: The Free Press, 2000); Michael Smith, *Station X: the codebreakers of Bletchley Park* (London: Channel 4 Books, 1998).
48 Sebag-Montefiore, *Enigma*, pp.138–48.
49 Although thirty-two men of the *U110* survived, Lemp did not. His death meant that yet another one of his U-boat aces had been lost to Dönitz.
50 Sebag-Montefiore, *Enigma*, p.162.
51 Ibid., pp.149–65; Jak. P. Mallmann Showell, *Enigma U-boats: breaking the code* (Shepperton, Surrey: Ian Allen Publishing, 2000), pp.64–79; Blair, *Hitler's U-boat war: hunters*, pp.277–85.
52 Rohwer, *Chronology*, pp.70, 73. Despite these losses, however, Milner is inclined to see May 1941 as a point at which the British 'grip on the Atlantic war' began to solidify. He outlines his reasons for reaching this conclusion in his *Battle of the Atlantic*, pp.63–68.
53 In Operation *Tiger* three convoys were escorted by units of the Mediterranean Fleet through the Mediterranean (5–12 May). One went eastbound to Alexandria and two were westbound for Malta and Gibraltar. They eventually arrived at their intended destinations with the loss of the transport *Empire Song* and damage to not only *New Zealand Star* but also the destroyer *Fortune* from the 8th Destroyer Flotilla. In terms of war materiel, 57 out of 295 tanks and 10 out of 53 Hurricane fighter aircraft were lost during this operation. Rohwer, *Chronology*, p.72; Winton, *Cunningham*, pp.190–92.
54 Simpson (ed.), *Cunningham papers*, *I*, pp.236, 241, 245, 251, 259, 261, 263–64, 266, 269, 271–72, 275, 277–79, 281–84, 287–89, 293–94, 299, 329–36, 352, 355, 357, 360, 362, 365, 368, 370, 395–404, 406, 419, 421, 451, 454, 456–57, 474, 476, 481–82, 485–88, 490, 494, 502, 504, 508–9, 511, 515, 518, 520–22, 531–33, 542, 544, 547–48, 555, 558–59, 572, 574–75, 578, 585–86; Eric Grove, 'The Royal Australian Navy in the Mediterranean in World War II', in David Stevens (ed.), *The Royal Australian Navy in World War II* (St. Leonards, NSW: Allen & Unwin, 1996), pp.74–76.
55 A momentary fillip to the Allied cause was occasioned by the news of the destruction in the Indian Ocean on 8 May of *Schiff 33 Pinguin*, one of the most successful auxiliary cruisers of the war. She had been credited with sinking or capturing a total of thirty-two boats (154,619 tons) in her infamous career and had run amuck through the whaling fleet in the South Atlantic. She was finally caught by the heavy cruiser *Cornwall* and sunk in an artillery duel off the Seychelles. Rohwer, *Chronology*, pp.72–73; Schmalenbach, *German raiders: a history of auxiliary cruisers*, p.115; August Karl Muggenthaler, *German raiders of World War II* (Englewood Cliffs, N.J.: Prentice-Hall, Inc., 1977), pp.94–120, 162–67.
56 David J. Bercuson and Holger H. Herwig, *Bismarck: the story behind the destruction of the pride of Hitler's navy* (London: Pimlico, 2003), pp.47–65; Bird, *Erich Raeder*, pp.177–82.
57 *Fuehrer conferences*, pp.200–218; Bercuson and Herwig, *Bismarck*, pp.94–96, 98–101, 121–53; Beesly, *Very special intelligence*, pp.108–26; Stephen, *Sea battles in close-up*, pp.70–98.
58 Bercuson and Herwig, *Bismarck*, pp.137–59; O'Hara, *German fleet at war*, pp.76–86; Stephen, *Sea battles in close-up*, pp.73–80; see also Andrew Norman, *HMS Hood: Pride of the Royal Navy* (Staplehurst, Kent: Spellmount, 2001), pp.51–152; Hoyt, *Life and death of HMS Hood*, pp.111–42.
59 Rhys-Jones, *The loss of the Bismarck*, p.122.
60 Ibid., pp.125–26, 132–33, 140–41; Bercuson and Herwig, *Bismarck*, pp.159–65.

61 Radio communications with the mainland had been fraught with difficulty from the outset and led to Lütjens's long signal of 25 May in which he repeated four of the messages he had sent the previous evening. This signal allowed the British the opportunity of finally getting an accurate fix on *Bismarck*'s actual position. Timothy P. Mulligan, '*Bismarck*: not ready for action', *Naval History, Vol.15, No.1* (Feb. 2001): 20–26; Bercuson and Herwig, *Bismarck*, p.236; Brown, *Radar history*, pp.126–27.

62 Rhys-Jones, *The loss of the Bismarck*, pp.164–69, 235–40; Stephen, *Sea battles in close-up*, pp.84–87.

63 Barnett, *Engage the enemy*, p.307; Brown, *Radar history*, pp.126–27; Stephen, *Sea battles in close-up*, pp.89–91.

64 Barnett, *Engage the enemy*, pp.278–315; O'Hara, *German fleet at war*, pp.90–95; Rhys-Jones, *The loss of the Bismarck*, pp.194–208; Stephen, *Sea battles in close-up*, pp.92–98; Hamer, *Bombers versus battleships*, pp.91–101; Rohwer, *Chronology*, p.76.

65 Barnett, *Engage the enemy*, pp.314–15; Levy, *The Royal Navy's Home Fleet*, pp.83–106; Stephen, *The fighting admirals*, pp.105–12; Rhys Jones, *The loss of the Bismarck*, pp.211–33.

66 Sources on the Cretan campaign are plentiful. Three of the most readable on the campaign as a whole are Antony Beevor, *Crete: the battle and the resistance* (London: John Murray, 1991); Callum MacDonald, *The lost battle: Crete 1941* (London: Macmillan, 1993) and Tony Simpson, *Operation Mercury: the battle for Crete, 1941* (London: Hodder & Stoughton, 1981). For the influence of air power in this invasion, see Peter D. Antill, *Crete 1941: Germany's lightning airborne assault* (Oxford: Osprey, 2005) and Hamer, *Bombers versus battleships*, pp.76–90. Naval aspects are dealt with persuasively by Simpson (ed.), *Cunningham papers, I*, pp.244–50, 313, 332, 351, 356, 367, 369–70, 390, 405–6, 408–46, 449–51, 454, 458, 460, 468, 470, 475, 478–80, 487; Greene and Massignani, *Naval war in the Mediterranean*, pp.161–73; Grove, *Sea battles in close-up, II*, pp.36–52.

67 Gill, *Royal Australian Navy 1939–1942*, pp.336–62.

68 Simpson (ed.), *Cunningham papers, I*, pp.436–46.

69 A further 183 were wounded and another 300 were taken prisoner. www.navy.mil.nz/mzn/article (accessed 17 March 2006).

70 War diary, 2 June, 'State of the Fleet', in Simpson (ed.), *The Cunningham Papers, I*, p.475.

71 Allied losses during the battle for Crete stood at 15,743 (excluding the numbers for the Royal Navy which totalled 2,011) while the German losses were 6,580 dead, missing or wounded and 30 aircraft shot down. Rohwer, *Chronology*, p.75.

72 'Cunningham's Dispatch on the Evacuation of Crete', 14 Sept. 1941, in Simpson (ed.), *Cunningham papers, I*, p.439.

73 Four were blockade runners (*Alstertor, Babitonga, Elbe* and *Lech*), two were weather observation ships (*August Wriest* and *Hinrich Freese*), six were tankers (*Belchen, Egerland, Esso Hamburg, Friedrich Breme, Gedania* and *Lothringen*) and *Gonzenheim* was a patrol ship. Sebag-Montefiore, *Enigma*, pp.179–80; Rohwer, *Chronology*, pp.77–78.

74 Notwithstanding these measures, German auxiliary cruisers remained a real threat to all unsuspecting Allied and neutral shipping, as can be seen from the controversial engagement between the Australian light cruiser HMAS *Sydney* and *Schiff 41/Kormoran* on 19 December 1941 off the west coast of Australia. Both ships perished after a mysterious gun battle between them – the *Sydney* sinking with the loss of her entire crew of 645. For 66 years the actual site of both wrecks defied many private and publicly funded efforts to find them, but finally perseverance was rewarded with an announcement by Kevin Rudd, the Australian premier, in March 2008 that both ships have been found some 12nm away from one another. Both sites will become official war graves, but one suspects that the controversies about just what happened on that fatal day will persist for many years to come. *The Australian*, 17 March 2008. For an illuminating review of the controversies spawned by this battle in the Indian Ocean, see Peter Dennis, 'The unknown and the unknowable: the loss

of HMAS *Sydney*', in Malcolm H. Murfett (ed.), *The imponderables of war* (forthcoming 2009); Gill, *Royal Australian Navy 1939–1942*, pp.446–60.
75 Buckley, *RAF and trade defence*, p.201; Rohwer, *Chronology*, p.78.
76 For their part, two squadrons of the Fleet Air Arm (815 Sqdn and 829 Sqdn) operating out of Nicosia in Cyprus returned the favour by sinking both a flotilla leader that was being employed as an ammunition transport (*Chevalier Paul*) and the supply ship, *St. Didier*, on 16 June and 4 July respectively. In addition, the submarine *Souffleur* was sunk by the British submarine *Parthian* in the Bay of Djounieh on 25 June. Simpson (ed.), *Cunningham papers*, *I*, pp.449–50, 453, 474–77, 479, 482–87, 489–95, 498–99, 502; Gill, *Royal Australian Navy 1939–1942*, pp.377–83; Rohwer, *Chronology*, p.78.
77 *Auckland* and *Waterhen* were sunk off Bardia on 24 and 29 June respectively and *Defender* suffered the same fate off Sidi Barani on 11 July. Rohwer, *Chronology*, p.79.
78 Thomas A. Bailey and Paul B. Ryan, *Hitler vs Roosevelt: the undeclared naval war* (New York: The Free Press, 1979), pp.135–36, 148–49, 156–58; Rohwer, *Chronology*, p.79.
79 On 7 April the newly acquired naval base at Bermuda was put into commission by the US Navy. On the following day Task Group TG.7.3, led by the carrier *Ranger* and supported by the heavy cruisers *Tuscaloosa* and *Wichita* and a couple of destroyers, began operating the Central Atlantic Neutrality Patrol. From 18 April the USN was not only permitted to extend its patrols up to 30° West but also began running its Caribbean Patrol. Farrell, *The basis and making of British Grand Strategy*, *I*, pp.129–36; Rohwer, *Chronology*, pp.68–69.
80 The Senate approved the bill by 60 votes to 31 and the House by 317 – 71. Dallek, *Franklin Roosevelt and American foreign policy*, pp.260–61.
81 Beginning on 1 June, the US Coast Guard operated a South Greenland Patrol with four of their ships covering the routes between Cape Brewster, Cape Farewell and Upernivik. Rohwer, *Chronology*, p.77.
82 Dallek, *Franklin Roosevelt and American foreign policy*, pp.260–61.
83 Rohwer and Monakov, *Stalin's ocean-going fleet*, pp.144–45.
84 These fast MTBs were capable of achieving 39 knots in shallow coastal waters. *S-59* and *S-60* combined to sink the *Gaisma* (3077 tons). Rohwer, *Chronology*, p.80.
85 The Red Navy was divided into the Red Banner Fleet, based in the Baltic under the command of Vice-Admiral Tributs; the Black Sea Fleet, based at Sevastopol in the Crimea under the command of Vice-Admiral Oktyabrskiy; the small-scale Northern Fleet, based at Murmansk on the White Sea under the command of Vice-Admiral Golovko; and the Pacific Fleet, based at Vladivostok under Vice-Admiral Yumashev. Rohwer, *Chronology*, pp.80–81.
86 V.I. Achkasov and N.B. Pavlovich, *Soviet naval operations in the Great Patriotic War 1941–45* (Annapolis, Md: NIP, 1981), pp.24–28, 45–46, 48–51; Friedrich Ruge, *The Soviets as naval opponents 1941–1945* (Cambridge: Patrick Stephens, 1979), pp.11–24, 63–77, 135–48; O'Hara, *German fleet at war*, pp.97–101; Rohwer and Monakov, *Stalin's ocean-going fleet*, pp 58–143.
87 Miller, *War at sea*, pp.179–83; Ruge, *The Soviets as naval opponents*, pp.63–77; Rohwer, *Chronology*, p.80.
88 Many excellent studies of the role performed by Allied forces in keeping Malta from falling into the hands of the Axis forces have been published. Amongst the best and most recent are: Douglas Austin, *Malta and British strategic policy, 1925–43* (London: Frank Cass, 2004); Tim Clayton and Phil Craig, *The end of the beginning: from the siege of Malta to the Allied victory at El Alamein* (New York: Free Press, 2003); Tony Spooner, *Supreme gallantry: Malta's role in the Allied victory, 1939–1945* (London: John Murray, 1996); and Richard Woodman, *Malta convoys 1940–1943* (London: John Murray, 2003). Supplying Tobruk is not served so well in the literature, but the long-running effort may be studied profitably in works devoted to the on-going Mediterranean and North African campaigns. A part of the naval story can be found in Chester Wilmot, *Tobruk 1941* (Ringwood, Vic: Penguin Books, 1993), pp.8–9, 16, 19, 67, 115, 155–57,

251, 255–56, 267–70, 282, 284–85, 288–89. For information on the role of Allied aircraft in the 1941 campaign, see Brian Cull with Don Minterne, *Hurricanes over Tobruk: the pivotal role of the Hurricane in the defence of Tobruk, January–June 1941* (London: Grub Street, 1999).

89 Operations *Splice* (19–22 May), *Rocket* (5–7 June), *Tracer* (13–15 June), *Railway* (26 June–1 July) and *Substance* (21–27 July) helped to boost the Allied air defences over Malta. Rohwer, *Chronology*, pp.75, 78–79, 83.

90 Ibid., p.88; Simpson, *Cunningham Papers, I*, pp.497–98.

91 Frustrated by the lack of success of his 'West' group of U-boats, Dönitz resorted in late June to a scattering of them in a much looser formation over the central North Atlantic. This didn't reap much in the way of rewards either as twenty-two U-boats managed only to sink eleven ships (57,215 tons) for the loss of two U-boats (*U556* and *U651*) and the Italian submarine *Glauco* in the period 20–29 June. Their luck didn't improve over the next seventeen days in the Central Atlantic as thirteen U-boats managed only five kills in the run-up to 15 July. Rohwer, *Chronology*, pp.79–80, 84.

92 Sebag-Montefiore, *Enigma*, pp.180–83. For a contrary opinion on what he calls 'Ultra's 'ubiquitous criticality', see W.J.R. Gardner, *Decoding history: the battle of the Atlantic and Ultra* (Basingstoke: Macmillan, 1999) pp.217–18.

93 Turing had already invented an electro-magnetic machine, the 'Bombe', which when operated in conjunction with a 'Crib' (a piece of guessed plain language text that exactly matched a corresponding piece of cipher text), could determine the individual wheel settings and plugboard socket connections that were being used by the Germans on a daily basis. He went on to develop an indicator system, known as the 'Banburismus', that with the correct 'bigram' (a combination of two letters) tables would enable the Bletchley Park cryptanalysts to do their stuff and read the German messages without much of a delay. These inventions were strokes of genius and kept the Allies ahead in the intelligence game. Sebag-Montefiore, *Enigma*, pp.62–63, 79–81, 87–88, 135, 138–48, 166–72, 367–68, 375–88.

94 Rohwer, *Chronology*, pp.84, 87.

95 In one celebrated case on 9 July, three German minelayers sank after running onto a mine barrage that the Germans had asked the Swedes to lay off the island of Öland on their behalf! Rohwer, *War at sea 1939–1945*, pp.70–74; Achkasov and Pavlovich, *Soviet naval operations*, pp.56–65.

96 Rohwer, *Chronology*, pp.85, 87–88; Chris Mann and Christer Jorgensen, *Hitler's Arctic war: the German campaign in Norway, Finland and the USSR 1940–1945* (New York: St. Martin's Press, 2003).

97 Dallek, *Franklin Roosevelt and American foreign policy*, pp.274–75; Waldo Heinrichs, *Threshold of war: Franklin D.Roosevelt and American entry into World War II* (Oxford: OUP, 1988), pp.118–79; Akira Iriye, *The origins of the Second World War in Asia and the Pacific* (London: Longman, 1987), pp.108–9, 146–59; Norman A. Graebner, 'Hoover, Roosevelt, and the Japanese', in Borg and Okamoto (eds), *Pearl Harbor as history*, pp.47–52.

98 Warren Kimball, *Forged in war: Roosevelt, Churchill and the Second World War* (New York: William Morrow & Co., 1997), pp.97–103; Joseph P. Lash, *Roosevelt and Churchill 1939–1941: the partnership that saved the West* (London: André Deutsch, 1977), pp.16–17, 332, 383, 386, 391–412, 445; Farrell, *Basis and making of British Grand Strategy, I*, pp.180–81.

99 An exhaustive treatment of this subject is given by Richard Woodman, *The Arctic convoys 1941–1945* (London: John Murray, 1994). A more succinct account of the early years of the Arctic convoy run can be found in Levy, *The Royal Navy's Home Fleet*, pp.109–33.

100 Rohwer, *Chronology*, pp.92–93.

101 As this force withdrew, the Soviets left a memento of their stay by laying a mine barrage south of the city at Ilyichevka that would claim three Axis steamers and two

Romanian MTBs over the course of the next couple of months. Achkasov and Pavlovich, *Soviet naval operations*, pp.70–76; Rohwer, *Chronology*, pp.94, 100, 104–5, 108.
102 Rohwer, *Chronology*, pp.111; Ruge, *Soviets as naval opponents*, pp.63–77.
103 Three German minelayers laid out the first phase of the Juminda mine barrage (D.10-D.30) with 673 EMC mines and 636 explosive floats in stages from 8 to 26 August 1941 and a couple of Finnish minelayers added the F.18-F.22 barrages with 696 mines and 100 explosive floats during the same time period. A combination of the Juminda mine barrage and Luftwaffe patrols began making their presence felt from the outset. On 14–15 August, for example, the Luftwaffe had attacked a convoy from the Estonian base and sunk the motor ship, *Sibir*, with 2,500 wounded soldiers on board. A day later another convoy going from Suursaari to Tallinn suffered losses trying to pass through the Juminda mine barrage, while on 24–25 August a destroyer, three minesweepers and five transports were lost to either mines or air attacks. Rohwer, *Chronology*, pp.91–92, 95–96.
104 Several evacuation missions to the Finnish port would be arranged from Kronstadt during the month of November. In this way 14,442 men were withdrawn from Hangö along with some of their war matériel. Achkasov and Pavlovich, *Soviet naval operations*, pp.24–25, 65–70; Rohwer, *Chronology*, p.102, 111–12, 114–16, 118–20; Ruge, *Soviets as naval opponents*, pp.22–24.
105 Rohwer, *Chronology*, pp.92, 99, 108,112; Simpson (ed.), *Cunningham papers, I*, pp.451, 454, 456–57, 474, 476, 481–82, 485–88, 490, 494, 502, 504, 508–9, 511, 515, 518, 520–22, 531–33, 542, 544, 547–48, 555, 558–59, 572, 574–75, 578, 585–86.
106 Simpson had a number of submarine aces of his own in the Mediterranean. Leading the pack was the quiet, unruffled Scot, David Wanklyn in the *Upholder*, but both Lt. Cdrs. E.P. Tomkinson in a sister ship *Urge* and R.D. Cayley in *Utmost* were submariners of the highest calibre. Allaway, *Hero of the Upholder*, pp.93–129; John Wingate, *The fighting tenth: the tenth submarine flotilla and the siege of Malta* (London: Leo Cooper, 1991); Rohwer, *Chronology*, pp.94, 99–101; Padfield, *War beneath the sea*, pp.131–49, 167–70, 172, 177–78, 225–27, 260, 263, 271–72, 353, 414, 471; Sebag-Montefiore, *Enigma*, pp.211–12.
107 Simpson (ed.), *Cunningham papers, I*, pp.454, 511; Rohwer, *Chronology*, pp.88, 103–4.
108 Ibid.; Sadkovich, *Italian Navy in World War II*, pp.179–82; Greene and Massignani, *Naval war in the Mediterranean*, pp.174–91.
109 Rohwer, *Chronology*, pp.100–101; Padfield, *Dönitz*, pp.232–33; *Fuehrer conferences*, pp.222–29.
110 Vince O'Hara, 'The Duisburg [sic] (Beta) Convoy Battle: November 9th, 1941' at www.regiamarina.net/engagements/duisburg/duisburg_us.htm (accessed 19 March 2006).
111 *Contrammiraglio* Brivonesi who had been in overall command of *Beta* would be given a reprieve later in the war. O'Hara, *Struggle for the middle sea*, pp.143–47; Grove, *Sea battles in close-up, 2*, pp.56–63; Allaway, *Hero of the Upholder*, pp.131–33.
112 Rohwer, *Chronology*, p.112.
113 *Ark Royal* had been operating with Force H out of Gibraltar and along with the carrier, *Argus*, had brought thirty-seven Hurricane fighters into the Western Mediterranean so that they could fly off to Malta (Operation *Perpetual*). She was returning to Gibraltar on 13 November when she was torpedoed and, although under tow, she sank within 25nm (46km) of Gibraltar. *Barham*, along with other heavy units from the Mediterranean Fleet, was out in support of Force K looking to interdict an Italian convoy north of Bardia. She was hit by three torpedoes from *U331* on 25 November and sank within five minutes. Ibid., pp.114, 118; Greene and Massignani, *Naval war in the Mediterranean*, pp.193, 196–97.
114 Counting the cost of the eight-month operation, Cunningham had seen two of his destroyers, a minelaying cruiser, three sloops, seven submarine-chasers and minesweepers, a gunboat, seven supply ships and six A-lighters sunk and had temporarily

134 Uncompromising hostilities

lost the services through war damage of a further seven destroyers, a sloop, eleven submarine-chasers and minesweepers, three gunboats, a troop transport, three A-lighters, a schooner and six other merchant vessels. Rohwer, *Chronology*, pp.116, 122; Simpson (ed.), *Cunningham Papers*, *I*, pp.482, 485–88, 494, 496, 500–504, 507–18, 520–21, 527, 531–34, 537, 539–42, 547–54, 557–59, 578–80; Winton, *Cunningham*, pp.234–36.

115 Cunningham's biographer, Michael Simpson, does not agree and implies that his hero didn't either! 'Cunningham seems to have been rueing his springtime promise to succour Tobruk; it was hardly a cost-effective operation.' Simpson (ed.), *Cunningham Papers*, *I*, p.451. Barnett implies he agrees with Cunningham's view of this Tobruk 'milk run' as a running sore. Barnett, *Engage the Enemy*, p.371.

116 Dallek, *Franklin Roosevelt and American foreign policy*, pp.287–89; Love, Jr., *History of the U.S. Navy*, pp.646–47.

117 Dallek, *Franklin Roosevelt and American foreign policy*, pp.290–92; Milner, *Battle of the Atlantic*, pp.71–81.

118 James Lord Neidpath, *The Singapore naval base and the defence of Britain's eastern empire, 1919–1941* (Oxford: Clarendon Press, 1981), pp.179–82.

119 Antony Best, *British intelligence and the Japanese challenge in Asia, 1914–1941* (Basingstoke: Palgrave Macmillan, 2002), pp.160–87; Donald M. Goldstein and Katherine V. Dillon (eds.), *The Pacific War papers: Japanese documents of World War II* (Washington, D.C.: Potomac Books, 2004), pp.136–221; Jonathan G. Uttley, *Going to war with Japan 1937–1941* (Knoxville, Tenn: The University of Tennessee Press, 1985), pp.138–82; Heinrichs, *Threshold of war*, pp.180–214; Iriye, *The origins of the Second World War*, pp.168–86; Hosoya Chihiro, 'The role of Japan's foreign ministry and its embassy in Washington, 1940–41', in Borg and Okamoto (eds), *Pearl Harbor as history*, pp.157–64.

120 Malcolm H. Murfett, 'Living in the past: a critical re-examination of the Singapore naval strategy, 1918–41', *War and Society*, Vol.11, No.1, (May 1993): 73–103. For an alternative view see Ian Cowman, *Dominion or Decline: Anglo-American naval relations in the Pacific, 1937–1941* (Oxford: Berg, 1996).

121 Antony Best, '"This probably over-valued military power": British intelligence and Whitehall's perception of Japan, 1939–41', in *Intelligence and National Security*, Vol.12, No.3 (July 1997): 67–94.

5 From Pearl Harbor to Madagascar (December 1941–May 1942)

By the time a carrier-less Force G had reached the Sembawang naval base in Singapore and received an enthusiastic welcome from the civilian population on 2 December, the crisis in East Asia was only days from exploding into war. Some of the Japanese military forces who were slated to launch that war were already on the move. A submarine flotilla was nearing Oahu and a large strike force, spearheaded by six carriers with 423 aircraft on board, was six days out of Hittokappu Bay, observing complete radio silence and bound for the eastern Pacific under the command of Vice-Admiral Chuichi Nagumo.[1] On the same day (4 December) that acting-Admiral Sir Tom Phillips left his fledgling Eastern Fleet behind and flew to Manila to confer with Admiral Thomas Hart, the C-in-C of the US Asiatic Fleet, an enemy troop convoy with 26,640 infantrymen on board eighteen transports left Hainan for their southern Thai and northern Malayan landing sites. By the afternoon of the following day the Southern Expeditionary Fleet with seven more transports had weighed anchor and set out from Saigon to join the convoy south of Cape Camao on 6 December. Before a shell was even fired in the Pacific War, therefore, the Japanese had seven carriers, four battleships, twelve heavy cruisers, five light cruisers, forty-five destroyers and thirteen submarines underway at sea – all of which were moving into place to strike at Allied interests at the appropriate time.[2]

Oblivious to all these deployments, Phillips instructed Captain W.G. Tennant to leave the Strait of Johor and take the battlecruiser *Repulse* down through the Indonesian archipelago on a sortie to Port Darwin not only to 'show the flag' to the Australians in the Northern Territory but also as a means of encouraging the government in Canberra to release a cruiser to supplement the newly formed Eastern Fleet in the 'near north'. Well before Tennant had reached his destination, however, ominous news filtered through from aerial reconnaissance indicating that three convoys of Japanese transports, totalling thirty-eight ships in all and flanked by strong naval escorts, had been spotted off the southern coast of French Indo-China steaming in the direction of the Gulf of Siam. At this news, Phillips ordered Tennant to return to Singapore with all haste. Lacking the *Repulse* and with his own flagship having her boilers overhauled, Phillips found himself in the thoroughly uncomfortable position of being unable to do anything immediately to investigate, let alone disrupt, these naval movements going on well to the north of him. Unfortunately for the Allies, the seasonal bad weather had come to the aid of the Japanese. Heavy monsoon rains and low cloud combined to keep Allied reconnaissance aircraft from getting an up-to-date fix on these Japanese activities in Thai waters. And even when one of the RAF Catalina flying boats threatened to rediscover the whereabouts of the invasion fleet at lunchtime on 7 December, Japanese fighter planes shot it down before it could relay any vital information about the location of the task force. Consequently, the Allies did not know that the convoy had divided at midday on that day with the majority of the troop transports and their escorts going south towards the beaches at Songkhla (Singora), Patani and Khota Bharu, with the remainder scattered along the Isthmus of Kra at Prachaup, Chumphon, and Surat Thani, with three transports and a frigate going to Nakhon.[3]

Sixteen hours later at precisely 0755 hours (local time in Hawaii) on 7 December (0155 hours on 8 December in Singapore), the Pacific and the wider world was turned upside down by the first wave of Japanese carrier aircraft that attacked the American military installations on the island of Oahu; in particular the three army air bases at Bellows Field, Hickham Field and Wheeler Field; the marine base at Ewa; and the naval air stations on Ford Island and at Kaneohe, destroying 188 aircraft in all and damaging another 159. Such was the mauling that only forty-seven American aircraft got away unscathed from these attacks on their airfields. At the same time part of the carrier force attacked the anchorage of the US capital ships, the so-called 'Battleship Row', at the naval base in Pearl Harbor. When they had finished the *Arizona, California, Nevada, Oklahoma* and *West Virginia* had all been sunk along with the minelayer *Oglala* and the target ship *Utah*; while the battleships *Maryland, Pennsylvania* and *Tennessee* had all been fortunate to escape with relatively light damage from the successive wave of attacks. Three light cruisers, three destroyers, a flying boat tender and a repair ship suffered more extensive damage, but at least they remained repairable.[4]

As H.P. Willmott was to comment in his excellent book, *Empires in the balance*, perhaps the most surprising aspect of this unexpected attack was that the Japanese did not do more damage to the vulnerable Pacific Fleet on this occasion than they did. After all, two heavy cruisers, three light cruisers, twenty-four destroyers, four destroyer-minelayers, eight fast minesweepers, five submarines and a host of auxiliary ships that lay at anchor in the roads, or had been tied up along the quays, or had actually been in dry dock at Pearl Harbor that morning, escaped undamaged. Part of the reason lies in the startling eclipse of the Japanese submarine threat. All five midget submarines assigned to the task were thwarted in their efforts to wreak havoc with these unsuspecting and tempting targets. Four of them were sunk either entering the anchorage or inside it and the last one was captured before she could do any damage. It was to be a massive blow to the Japanese submarine arm both in terms of its own self-confidence and of the trust reposed in it by the naval high command. While the Japanese aircrews cannot be faulted for not getting the two carriers *Lexington* and *Enterprise*, seven cruisers, fifteen destroyers and five submarines that were at sea, they might have wrecked more ships had they not been so fixated upon dealing with those on 'Battleship Row'. Moreover, in the two waves of attacks they had not attempted to smash the oil storage tanks and fuel lines, repair yards, supply sheds and other shore installations at the base whose wholesale destruction would have severely compromised the US Navy's ability to wage war in the Pacific at least in the short to medium term. A third strike was thus critically necessary in order to rectify some of these shortcomings, but Vice-Admiral Nagumo, the officer commanding the 1st Naval Air Fleet, never consented to such a mopping up operation. This was clearly a crucial strategic blunder and said a great deal about the man himself. Rather as Jellicoe had felt about the crushing effects that losing his battlefleet would have for the British war effort at the time of Jutland, Nagumo was well aware that he might similarly lose the war that his aircraft had started if he was to suffer losses to his carrier fleet while executing an unplanned manoeuvre. This degree of responsibility made him far more wary and conservative and much less likely to take any uncharted initiative of his own.[5]

Disappointed that none of the carriers were in port, Nagumo saw little reason to imperil his own mission by remaining in the area any longer than he needed to. He didn't wish to become the target for any air or submarine attacks that the Americans might have been able to launch against his carrier fleet and, having lost twenty-nine of his own planes in the earlier strikes, he didn't wish to add to that number by taking any further gratuitous risks over Oahu. Such a defensive attitude – a 'let us keep what we have' mentality – effectively ruled out the option of launching another air strike because that would mean waiting around for several hours before the planes setting out on this unplanned mission could be safely recovered and his carrier fleet could beat a hasty retreat. It was indeed fortunate for the Americans that Nagumo was not a bolder or more experienced practitioner when it came to handling his carrier fleet. A less conservative, or more flexibly imaginative, commander might have been tempted to give full rein to his airmen and opted for yet another strike at the naval base where 4.5 million barrels of oil had been stockpiled and which now lay vulnerable to aerial attack by either the Japanese 'Kate' or 'Val' bombers at Nagumo's disposal. If these oil stocks and other essential shore facilities could have been wrecked, the attacks on Pearl Harbor and Oahu would have turned what was already an audacious success into an even more horrific rout. As it was, 2,403 Americans died in Hawaii that morning and another 1,178 lay wounded after the two-hour ordeal.[6]

Addressing Congress on the following day, Roosevelt was to describe the assault upon Pearl Harbor as a day that would live in infamy and called upon the legislative body to allow him to issue a formal declaration of war against Japan. After receiving almost unanimous support for such a declaration, the President still demurred from requesting a similar stance against the other Axis nations. He did so believing emphatically that the American public was not yet ready to endorse such an extension of the conflict. While this represented a personal dilemma for him since he had the highest disdain for both the leaders of Nazi Germany and Fascist Italy, his discomfort on this score did not last long.

On 11 December, these two other members of the Tripartite Pact joined their Japanese ally by gratuitously declaring war on the United States.[7] In this wilfully extravagant gesture both Hitler and Mussolini had solved Roosevelt's problem for him, much to the relief of the President and his friend, the 'Former Naval Person', in London who slept soundly for once, convinced that the tide of the war had now irreversibly turned in the Allies' favour. His words reflect this perfectly:

> So we had won after all! Yes, after Dunkirk; after the fall of France; after the horrible episode of Oran: after the threat of invasion. ... after seventeen months of lonely fighting and nineteen months of my responsibility in dire stress. We had won the war. England would live; Britain would live; the Commonwealth of Nations and the empire would live.[8]

Despite believing that Hitler and Mussolini's fate would be sealed and confidently predicting that the Japanese would be ground to powder, the British Prime Minister was soon to discover that the Showa nation would not be destroyed so lightly.

Shortly after the first wave of air strikes against Hawaii, Japanese bombs began to fall on the city of Singapore. Thereafter, news quickly filtered through that Japanese troops were landing along the southern coast of Thailand and the northeastern shore of Kelantan in Malaya. In addition, reports spoke of a wave of aerial attacks taking place on the American air bases at Clark Field and Iba Field on the island of Luzon and against the city of Davao on the southern island of Mindanao in the Philippines. These stories would soon be added to by the landing of an assault group on the Bataan peninsula across the bay from the Philippines capital of Manila. It was clear that the Japanese had embarked upon their legendary *nanshin* or southern expedition.[9]

Bereft of any Admiralty instructions to the contrary, Tom Phillips was left to ponder what to do for the best. His fleet anchorage at Singapore was obviously not a safe haven any longer, but a retreat to Australia, Ceylon or the Dutch East Indies was still feasible if he wished to keep his fleet-in-being status alive. Deskbound for many years and not accustomed to operational command at sea, Phillips still chose not to take the safe option. Instead he decided that it was incumbent upon him and his Eastern Fleet to try to do something to disrupt the Japanese landings off Khota Bharu. He appears to have reached the not unreasonable assumption that if his capital ships could get in amongst the troop transports and their close escorts, they could cause carnage. If this happened it would surely help to delay the Japanese offensive and buy the Allies time to get more ships, aircraft and guns to their forces in Malaya. Quite how long Phillips expected the Japanese to take in landing their troops along the Thai and Malayan coasts is unclear, but he must have banked upon the northeasterly monsoon inhibiting their amphibious operations with its heavy squalls and rough seas. Unfortunately, the vital adjunct to any search and destroy mission – airpower – was unlikely to be available to him in significant strength for the duration of his mission or be there to protect him if things went badly askew. For this reason, it was essential that the presence of the renamed Force Z (the capital ships *Prince of Wales* and *Repulse* and the four destroyers, the modern and fast *Electra* and *Express* and the old and slow *Tenedos* and *Vampire*) should remain undetected by either enemy aircraft or submarines on its journey up the east coast to the invasion beaches at Songkhla or further south at Khota Bharu. Even if Phillips's luck held on this score and Force Z wasn't observed on its outward passage, he still needed to arrive in Thai waters before the Japanese invasion fleet had disgorged all of its troops and supplies; otherwise his bold gesture of 'sailing to the sound of the guns' would have been all for naught. What luck there might have been only took a few hours to desert him. Force Z was initially spotted through the periscope of submarine *I-65* at 1345 hours on 9 December, about 100 miles north of the Anamba Islands. Phillips remained oblivious to this fact for nearly four hours more, but that ignorance was rudely dispelled at 1740 hours when three Japanese seaplanes hove into view, remaining in sight but out of artillery range on the horizon, shadowing every move of his ships until dusk fell. Phillips knew that his gamble had failed and that any chance Force Z might once have had of being able to carry out a decisive blow against the Japanese transports at either of the invasion spots had vanished. All there was left for him to do was to extricate his ships and men from the predicament they found themselves in. It wouldn't be easy. It was obvious that an enemy aerial dragnet would be cast out for him. Once under cover of darkness, Phillips made two alterations to his course and then reluctantly turned for home at 2015 hours. Approaching midnight he received a signal from Singapore in which his chief of staff reported that a landing by Japanese troops was taking place at Kuantan, a town to the south of Force Z on the coast of Pahang and less than 200nm (370km) from his naval base at Sembawang. Unwilling to compromise on the need for radio silence, Phillips didn't ask Rear-Admiral Palliser for confirmation that the report was accurate but, figuring that it made logical sense for the Japanese to try to establish a bridgehead there, he altered course to investigate the incident. Phillips didn't signal Palliser to request any fighter cover and the latter didn't send any. When Force Z finally reached the waters off Kuantan at 0800 hours on 10 December, it rapidly became obvious to one and all that the sleepy town was not the site of a Japanese invasion. For some unaccountable reason, however, Phillips did not quit the scene immediately but wasted more than two hours scouring the seas of the coastline checking for what was a non-existent invasion fleet. It was to prove to be a fatal error of judgement. His ships were still engaged on this futile exercise when a Japanese reconnaissance plane finally spotted them at 1015 hours.[10]

At this point Phillips had nothing to lose by breaking radio silence and requesting Palliser to send all available aircraft to protect Force Z as it sped home, since the Japanese now knew exactly where his ships were and they would be bound to spare nothing in trying to eliminate them. Stunningly, however, no such request was ever transmitted from the *Prince of Wales*. Decades later the seminal question of why Phillips continued to maintain radio silence at this stage remains unanswered. Whether the Brewster Buffaloes that could have been sent from Singapore would have made any material difference to the eventual outcome is, of course, purely speculative, but the fact that they weren't covering Force Z on its homeward passage is little short of amazing.[11] Less than an hour later, at 1113 hours to be precise, the sky above the two British capital ships was filled with a swarm of Japanese high-level Mitsubishi 'Nell' medium bombers. These softened up the big ships for the successive wave of 'Betty' medium bombers to do the rest. Despite quite exceptional sea handling by Captain Tennant, the *Repulse* finally succumbed to this brilliantly orchestrated aerial assault at 1233 hours, followed by the *Prince of Wales* at 1320 hours. Ironically, the lumbering old Brewster Buffaloes that Tennant had finally called for by emergency signal arrived too late to do anything but become poignant witnesses to the end of an era. They watched helplessly as Phillips's flagship sank beneath the waves of the South China Sea taking the acting-Admiral and Captain Leach, the captain of the *Prince of Wales*, down with her. In all 840 officers and men from these two capital ships lost their lives that December lunchtime.[12]

In sinking these vessels as decisively as they did, the Japanese pilots from the 22nd Naval Air Flotilla had graphically revealed the fact that time had caught up with both the battleship and the battlecruiser. Their day had passed. This action had proved it demonstratively. It had taken half a century to overturn the persistent belief fostered in naval circles from the days of Alfred Thayer Mahan that the battleship was the supreme fighting machine at sea, but in a little over two hours on that bright tropical day in December 1941 the myth – for such it now was – had been emphatically debunked.[13]

As Churchill digested the sombre news from Singapore that the backbone of the Eastern Fleet had been broken at the cost of a few enemy aircraft, more signals were received in Allied capitals over the next few days underlining the daring scope of the Japanese advance throughout the Pacific and East and Southeast Asia and the lack of any substantial Allied naval presence to prevent it. Further attacks and landings had been made at scattered points throughout the Philippines, Guam had fallen and the International Settlement in Shanghai had been occupied by Japanese troops. As the days passed so the pressure on the Allies grew more intense. By Christmas Day they had lost Wake Island, Hong Kong and parts of the oil-rich island of Borneo. Worse still from Whitehall's perspective, the fate of the entire Malayan peninsula and the once supposedly impregnable fortress of Singapore were being increasingly called into question by the uncontested passage of troop transports from Camranh Bay filled with men of the 5th Infantry Division and General Tomoyuki Yamashita's 25th Army bound for landfall at Songkhla and all points south of the Thai port.[14]

By this time Churchill and a British delegation of service chiefs, both uniformed and political, were in Washington to meet and discuss future war strategy with their American hosts at the Arcadia Conference. Somewhat uncoordinated as they were, these meetings, as Brian Farrell indicates, may be seen as being the starting point of the 'rolling seminar' that would become a far more sophisticated feature of Anglo-American war planning from then onwards. Churchill's keen desire to work closely with Roosevelt was evident from the outset, although it may be fair to state that the same level of enthusiasm was missing from the joint meetings of their respective staffs. Whereas Churchill sought to develop an ever more intimate partnership of trust and personal friendship with the president, the rest of his delegation were more guarded and wary of their opposite numbers – a feeling reciprocated by those in the Roosevelt administration. This did not mean an element of distrust, let alone hostility, existed between the staffs, but the personal magnetism of their chiefs for one another was simply not there at the outset. Nonetheless, while the British delegation was receiving a reaffirmed commitment to an Anglo-American strategy that sought to wear down the Germans first in Europe, the notion that the Japanese advance in both the Pacific and Southeast Asian theatres would somehow be held without devoting huge resources to the task proved to be about as vague as it was unlikely in the last weeks of 1941 and in the first quarter of 1942.[15]

Although the success of the Japanese amphibious operations and the progress of their invasion forces may have caused genuine surprise and gloom in both Washington and London, the war at sea in the other theatres did not miss a beat over the Christmas season. Allied ingenuity in converting the captured German merchant vessel *Hannover* into a light carrier was put to the test with convoy HG.76 in mid-December.[16] In vastly improving the convoy escort screen by taking the fight to the enemy in a convincing manner, downing reconnaissance aircraft and driving off U-boats, the re-named *Audacity* ushered in a new era of the light escort carrier. While her performance certainly showed the value of having such a vessel, her own career was cut short by *U751* which put three torpedoes into her on the shortest night of the year.[17]

Further north the Allies enjoyed mixed success in their small-scale amphibious raids on the Lofoten Islands (*Anklet* and *Archery*). While they were unable to achieve their primary objective of cutting the link between these outlying islands and the Norwegian mainland, their exploits against the three German trawlers *Geier*, *Föhn* and *Donner* resulted in the seizure of a vital cache of intelligence material including two complete Enigma cipher machines and several additional wheels for them, important codebooks and complete sets of current bigram tables. This coup would enable the cryptanalysts at Bletchley Park to penetrate the *Heimisch* (Home Waters) Naval Enigma net used by the Germans for communicating with their surface ships as well as their U-boat fleet that was stationed in the Arctic and read their messages from this time forward for the duration of the war.[18]

As the year came to an end, there was, for once, slightly better news to report from Soviet operations in the Black Sea. Although the city of Sevastopol was still under siege it received badly needed reinforcements from Soviet ports in the Caucasus during the period 19–27 December when 14,100 men were landed at the naval base in a shuttle service operated by two cruisers and four destroyers who used the opportunity to shell German forces and advance positions around the city. A vast armada of Soviet shipping collected from Gorshkov's Azov Flotilla, supplemented by naval units from bases in and around the Kerch peninsula, were used to bring over 30,000 troops and their supplies to confront the German 46th Infantry Division in the on-going battle for the Crimea from 26 December onwards. Overseeing this entire operation were three cruisers, two flotilla leaders and six destroyers. All of the Soviet cruisers were hit repeatedly while they were on duty in the roads off the port city of Feodosiya, but being hardy creatures that were built to last, all survived. Confronted by this significant build up in Soviet forces, the German 46th Infantry Division was forced to beat a retreat westward and stop its attack on Sevastopol.[19]

In the Mediterranean–North African theatre, the operational world was every bit as intense as – and arguably even more inconsistent than – elsewhere. Isolated successes enjoyed by both sides were welcomed but calamity was never far away. December demonstrated this perfectly. In the Eastern Mediterranean the Allied submarine force experienced both highs and lows, sinking several vessels, missing even more and losing *Perseus* into the bargain. Further west around the North African coastline the Allies were more consistently successful, a fact that was due in no small measure to the existence of 'Ultra' intelligence decrypts which provided crucial information on the whereabouts of Italian convoys. Commander G.H. Stokes, on his way from Gibraltar to Alexandria in the Tribal class destroyer *Sikh*, accompanied by three other Allied destroyers – *Maori*, *Legion* and the Dutch built *Isaac Sweers* – demonstrated what could be done with this information when his force intercepted the two Italian light cruisers *Albercio da Barbiano* and *Amberto di Guissano* and a small torpedo boat off Cape Bon in the early hours of 13 December. Both of these fast Condottieri-type cruisers were being used as petrol transports for the Axis forces in Libya, but neither of them was capable of withstanding a well-placed Mark IX torpedo, let alone a spread of them and both of them succumbed in short order.[20]

It was not the only Italian operational mishap in these waters at this time. Further 'Ultra' intelligence revealed that a much larger operation from the Italian mainland to Libya was planned and underway. Codenamed M.41, it involved moving eight troop transports in three convoys across the Mediterranean to Benghazi. So important was it seen as being, that virtually the entire Italian Fleet was on hand to ensure its success. *Upright*, a member of Simpson's 10th Submarine Flotilla, struck an initial blow against the convoy in the early hours of 13 December by torpedoing two of its motor vessels while they were still in the Gulf of Taranto. It was not a good augury and the news wouldn't get any better because on the following morning another U-class submarine *Urge* would succeed in torpedoing (but not sinking) the battleship *Vittorio Veneto* off the Straits of Messina. Despite Supermarina cancelling the operation, the Italians' misery continued as two more of their steamers collided with one another, forcing them both to limp home for repairs. *U557*, lurking near to the entrance of the Alexandria Channel just before midnight on 14–15 December, provided the only ray of light for the Axis cause from this entire operation by sinking *Galatea*, one of Force B's light cruisers, with three torpedo strikes as she was returning to base after completing her truncated deployment against M.41. Even this fillip proved momentary since *U-557* was rammed (presumably accidentally) and sunk by the Italian torpedo boat *Orione* only a day later.[21]

While M.41's abandonment had been sensible in the light of what had already taken place, Supermarina was committed to running its convoys through to Libya and had planned another attempt to convoy the four undamaged vessels of M.41 from Taranto to Benghazi beginning on 16 December. What the Italians didn't know was that their operation would actually coincide with one being mounted by the Allies which would involve ushering the fast transport *Breconshire* through the Eastern Mediterranean with much needed supplies for Malta. Only a few hours after the loss of *Galatea*, therefore, Rear-Admiral Vian left Alexandria at the head of Force B (two light cruisers, an A.A. cruiser and eight destroyers) to begin the first stage of the operation. His task was to escort *Breconshire* from Alexandria to a pre-arranged rendezvous at sea on 17 December with Captain Agnew's Force K and Stokes's four destroyers from Malta. According to the original plan, Force K would then escort the transport back to Malta, while Stokes's destroyer detachment would return with Force B to Alexandria.[22]

A couple of hours before Force K and Commander Stokes's destroyer division left Malta at 1800 hours on 16 December, a vast new convoy operation (M.42) had begun from Taranto. Three undamaged Italian motor vessels resumed their interrupted journey to Libya with an escort of six destroyers. It was quickly followed by a second convoy with the German freighter *Ankara* accompanied by a destroyer and torpedo boat. Determined that on this occasion these supply ships would get through, Supermarina had deployed the battleship *Duilio*, three light cruisers and three destroyers as a close supporting force and had Admiral Iachino in command of three more battleships, *Cesare*, *Doria* and *Littorio*, two heavy cruisers and ten more destroyers as a distant covering force. As these two sets of forces moved towards one another during the following day the stage was set for an extraordinary and unplanned encounter in the Gulf of Sirte (Sidra) in which the Italians would unknowingly find themselves interdicting a combined British force that was far weaker than itself. Here was an opportunity for Iachino and his admirals to avenge the Italian defeats at Matapan and Taranto by wrecking Force B and giving Force K and Stokes's destroyer division their comeuppance. What became known as the first Battle of Sirte was, in fairness, more a tale of what might have been than what was. As the two enemy forces became aware of one another's existence during the late afternoon on 17 December, some long range shelling took place as darkness fell. Although some skirmishing did occur during the night of 17–18 December, both sides wished to avoid doing anything to compromise the safety of their own convoys and so the engagements petered out. This rather tepid approach by Iachino, when he had the distinct advantage both of aerial support and heavier units at his disposal, confirms a defensive characteristic – an aversion to risk – that while not undermining the Axis position in the Mediterranean would not enhance it either. For once Vian was also prepared to adopt a conservative rather than bold strategy and after nightfall departed east with Force B and the four destroyers he had inherited from Malta. Not all were disposed to take the line of least resistance, however, and once he had discharged his duty of taking *Breconshire* into Malta at

1500 hours on 18 December, Agnew steamed back with an enlarged Force K towards the coast of Libya with the intention of mutilating either of the Italian convoys if he could find them. In searching for them in the waters off Tripoli, all three of his light cruisers (*Aurora*, *Neptune* and *Penelope*) and one of his four destroyers (*Kandahar*) ran into an Italian mine barrage and came off much the worse for wear. *Neptune* hit four mines and promptly sank with the loss of approximately 550 men; *Kandahar*, which had gone to her aid, was disabled aft when she hit another mine and was eventually scuttled by her crew on the following day; *Aurora*, Agnew's own ship, suffered extensive damage, and *Penelope*, though the least affected, was pockmarked with bomb splinters. In this way the battered Force K limped back to Malta, demonstrating that sometimes in war fortune does not favour the brave.[23]

Worse was to follow. In opening the boom to allow Vian's ships to re-enter the harbour at Alexandria on the night of 18–19 December, the authorities unwittingly exposed the Mediterranean Fleet to yet further misery. Three Italian *Maiali* chariots with their two-man crews were released from the submarine *Scirè* which had been operating off the entrance to the eastern harbour and they used this opportunity to move stealthily into the inner harbour and place limpet mines under the Norwegian oil tanker *Sagona* and more critically under the battleships *Queen Elizabeth* and *Valiant*. Although one of the human torpedo crews was spotted and arrested at 0325 hours adjacent to the bow buoy of the *Valiant* and a general warning was issued to the ships in the anchorage, the interrogation of the two-man crew had yielded nothing by the time an explosion occurred under the stern of the *Sagona* at 0547 hours, wrecking her shafts and rudder and sending her to the bottom of the harbour while damaging the bow of the destroyer *Jervis*. Nineteen minutes later another mighty explosion took place, this time under 'A' turret of *Valiant* flooding her forward compartments. It preceded by four minutes another of the same under the boiler rooms of *Queen Elizabeth*. Both ships joined *Sagona* on the shallow floor of the harbour. Cunningham, who had been catapulted into the air by the whiplash effect of his flagship, was a witness to the virtual extinction of his Mediterranean Fleet.[24]

1941 ended, therefore, on an utterly dispiriting note for Mediterranean Command. Throughout the Mediterranean from the Straits of Gibraltar to the Suez Canal, the Allies found themselves seriously weakened and unable to adopt the kind of dominant naval control in the theatre that they would have liked to have exercised. It would take many more months for Cunningham's most powerful ships to be patched up and made ready for service once again. As early reinforcements were not in the offing, he could not even begin to seek to do much more than make the best of a gruelling situation. While his destroyers sought to combat the growing presence of German U-boats off both the Egyptian and Libyan coasts and help the Eighth Army's ground offensive along the coastal route in Cyrenaica, his submarines were doing what they could to carry out their own attacks on enemy trade. While the news of the evacuation of Benghazi by Axis troops on 23 December was welcome to the C-in-C, it did nothing materially to assist his own cause. After all, Rommel was not routed and North Africa was far from won.[25]

In the Pacific theatre dramatic change became the order of the day. As a direct consequence of the humiliation suffered by the Americans on that fateful day in early December, the hierarchy of the US Navy was quite ruthlessly overhauled. Admiral Chester W. Nimitz was selected by President Roosevelt and Secretary Frank Knox, the Secretary of the Navy, to replace Admiral Husband E. Kimmel as Commander-in-Chief Pacific (CINCPAC).[26] Despite feeling sorry for his friend who had paid the price for what had happened on his watch at Pearl Harbor, Nimitz felt up to the gigantic task that lay before him. A day before he took over command at Pearl Harbor on New Year's Eve, another momentous appointment had gone into effect thousands of miles away in Washington, DC, that would reverberate in Allied naval circles in the months and years to come. On 30 December Admiral Ernest J. King had assumed the role of C-in-C US Fleet (COMINCH) and would acquire the additional role of Chief of Naval Operations (CNO) less than three months later. As Nimitz's superior officer, King was a ruthless and uncompromising driving force, a man who had no time for mediocrity or a laissez-faire attitude to work. In Nimitz he had a more personable, but equally talented and grimly determined subordinate. Both of these men shared a similar work ethic, a passion for their country and a fierce longing to exact a punishing retribution for the embarrassing and sickening defeat the US had sustained at the hands of the Japanese at Pearl Harbor. They were not afraid to take risks and to shake up the naval establishment in the interests of winning the war. This shared attitude would galvanise the USN in the future and make it into a reflection of its two leading officers – one that the Axis Powers in Europe and the Pacific would find were shrewd and obdurate opponents with a will to win that could not be easily extinguished.[27]

As the New Year began the international scene looked broodingly sombre. Axis forces were rampaging forward on several fronts and compelling evidence was mounting that having caught the Allies off guard they were now in a dominant position to exploit this situation. Worse from an Allied perspective, it seemed that distressingly little could be done by their governments in London, Moscow and Washington to arrest this momentum in the near future. Nowhere was this more evident than along the Black Sea coastline and in the bitter fighting that engulfed the Crimea. This ought to have been one area in which the Soviets were dominant. There was no other naval presence of a comparable size in this theatre, the Romanians and Bulgarians hardly inspired fear within Red Navy circles, and the main Soviet naval base for the entire Black Sea region lay at Sevastopol on the southwestern side of the peninsula. Axis penetration took place on land rather than at sea, however, as the German 11th Army continued to put the Ukrainian city and naval base to the test for months to come. Under siege, Sevastopol was deemed by the Soviets as being too important to lose. They would go to any lengths to reinforce it and so the vital process of their warships bringing in fresh men and supplies while evacuating the wounded and bombarding German positions – a variation of the Tobruk shuttle run – continued under intense and deadly conditions. It didn't help that one of the 180mm gun cruisers engaged on these runs, *Krasnyy Kavkaz*, was set upon by six Ju-87s on 4 January and put out of action for ten months.[28]

In the Mediterranean the loss of so many of Cunningham's heavy ships in the latter weeks of 1941 was felt almost immediately. Largely confined to Alexandria, what was left of the surface fleet under his command was unable to do as much as he would have liked in the early weeks and months of the year to dent or disrupt the Axis convoys that served Tripoli from several ports on the Italian peninsula. An increasing number of supply ships for Rommel's forces had begun making their way on this north–south line and reaching their destination in North Africa largely unscathed. Stuck in Alexandria Cunningham knew he could do little about it other than fume about his lack of air cover and the naval impotency that it guaranteed. For months to come the task of disrupting these supply convoys was going to reside with the submarine fleet. His surface forces in Malta, which had done so much in conjunction with Simpson's submarines to disrupt this traffic in the past, found themselves and their port facilities the target of a sustained aerial bombardment by the Luftwaffe from the outset of the year onwards, while a succession of Italian torpedo boats conducted a mining offensive outside the harbour at Valletta and in the waters off the island.[29] Both ploys were designed, of course, to take Malta out of the strategic equation as far as the Germans and their Axis partners were concerned. They were not to succeed in this objective, but it wasn't for the want of trying. Despite the battering it took from the enemy's attentions, the island was regularly replenished with food and war supplies as well as critical air cover. Alexandria was largely responsible for the bulk of these supplies, but the two carriers of Force H at Gibraltar took the credit for bringing the Spitfire fighter planes to a point south of the Balearic Islands where they had the range to fly off to Malta under their own power. Staggeringly, perhaps, neither the German U-boats nor the Italian submarine or surface fleets appeared capable of discovering where the carriers were when they were out on these missions or of doing anything about them even if they did know their location. This is all the more remarkable considering that if either of the two carriers involved in these operations had been put out of action for any length of time the consequences for Malta would have been dire indeed. As it was, most of the Spitfires were transshipped safely to their point of departure and then flown off across the central Mediterranean to their Maltese destination.[30]

While the Allied heroics in investing Malta contributed to a stalling of the Axis momentum in both the Mediterranean and North Africa, by far the most decisive theatre of war lay in the Far East where the Japanese began the year in an extraordinarily robust fashion. Their successes throughout the Pacific and Southeast Asia were built on the backs of a series of successful amphibious operations and the lack of any credible Allied opposition, whether by land, air or sea, to their breathtakingly ambitious plan of simultaneous territorial conquest across several time zones and many hundreds of kilometres. Although the Allied ABDA (American, British, Dutch and Australian) Command was formed under General Wavell in the Dutch East Indies on 3 January, it began its short life on the defensive and never knew anything different before it was formally disbanded a couple of months later.[31] Not content with merely consolidating their Malayan and Philippine campaigns, the Japanese audaciously took the fight to the Allied enemy throughout the Dutch East Indian archipelago in January 1942. An invasion fleet supported by the 23rd Naval Air Flotilla appeared off Tarakan, the blazing port and oil terminal on the east coast of the island of Borneo, during the night of 10–11 January, and a few hours later another amphibious force made successful landfall at the northern tip of the Celebes (Sulawesi) where in the face of slight resistance the towns of Manado and Kema on either side of the peninsula were swiftly taken without much fuss.[32] It was to be a sign of the times.

An expansion of the Japanese presence in this region was heralded barely three days later when another of their invasion fleets steamed off from Guam, accumulated additional forces from Truk and homed in on the port of Rabaul on the island of New Britain in the Bismarck Archipelago. They were followed by yet another group that left Truk on 20 January for the main port of Kavieng on the island of New Ireland, lying to the northwest of Rabaul in the same archipelago. Softening up the defences at Rabaul began with heavy aerial bombardment from their carrier aircraft on 20 January and troops were put ashore during the night of 22–23 January. Within 48 hours the assault troops had seized their main objectives, initial preparations for establishing air bases on the two islands could be put in hand, and the invasion fleet was nearing Truk on its return journey.

There was a chilling efficiency to this steady encroachment of Japanese power across the Southwest Pacific. Using their newly acquired bases in the Celebes and Borneo, the Japanese sought to expand their strategic hold over the coastal areas of these islands by targeting specific ports that inevitably served as the leading provincial towns of their distant region. In this respect, the Eastern Force (under Rear-Admiral Kyuji Kubo) that had covered the Manado landings now turned its attention towards Kendari, a port on the southeastern coast of the Celebes which was taken on 24 January.[33] Rear-Admiral Sueto Hirose, at the head of the Central Force that had taken Tarakan, repeated the pattern by arriving at the oil rich port of Balikpapan roughly 400nm (741km) to the south after nightfall on 23–24 January. Resistance on this occasion came initially from the lone Dutch submarine *K-XVIII* and subsequently from four Allied destroyers deployed for the purpose of disrupting the invasion. In a hit-and-run operation which succeeded in drawing off the entire Japanese destroyer force, *K-XVIII* left the way open for the Allied destroyers to deal a savage blow to the invasion by picking off the Japanese transports as they waited offshore for the invasion to begin. Despite firing forty-eight torpedoes at short distance and in good visibility, only three transports and one fast assault boat were sunk and a couple of other vessels were damaged before the Allied destroyers had to withdraw. Once again torpedo failures had reduced the lethality of the weapon. What could have been a major disruption to the invasion was rendered manageable and once the Japanese destroyer force had returned to provide essential cover, the landing of the troops began in the morning and they swiftly occupied the port and town of Balikpapan on 24 January. Reinforcements began arriving within a couple of days and the airfield had become home to the 23rd Naval Air Flotilla by 28 January.[34]

A further cast of the strategic net was made by the Japanese in the direction of Ambon (Amboina), an island lying in the Moluccan (Maluku) chain in the Banda Sea, east of the Celebes and southwest of New Guinea. Selected as the site for another crucial air base that would enable the Japanese to control the eastern part of the Dutch East Indies, Ambon was attacked in a classic pincer movement on 31 January. It took a couple of days for the invasion forces from north and south to meet up and overcome their stubborn Dutch and Australian opponents, but by 2 February Ambon was secure.[35]

Elsewhere the Japanese conquest of the Asia-Pacific was moving along in a hectic and seemingly unstoppable way. Complementing their amphibious operations, they also enjoyed some belated submarine successes throughout the theatre, including the torpedoing of the US carrier *Saratoga*, which had been operating with Task Force (TF) 14 southeast of Pearl Harbor on 11 January, and the sinking of the sole escort tanker *Neches* belonging to TF11 twelve days later – a casualty that forced TF11 to abandon its planned raid on Wake Island.[36] As their land forces moved to exert an increasing measure of control over the Malayan peninsula, the Philippines and the parts of the Dutch East Indies, an increasing surface fleet presence was steadily being built up throughout the region with the transfer of two carriers (*Hiryu* and *Soryu*), two battleships (*Haruna* and *Kongō*), three heavy cruisers (*Atago*, *Maya*, and *Takao*), a heavy seaplane cruiser (*Tone*) and eight destroyers from the Pescadores and Kure to their new base at Palau, while another four destroyers moved south from Hong Kong to Davao. In addition, the Western Force based at Camranh Bay and consisting of the small carrier *Ryūjō*, the five heavy cruisers *Chōkai*, *Kumano*, *Mikuma*, *Mogami* and *Suzuya*, three light cruisers and thirteen destroyers was on hand in the South China Sea to cover supplementary invasion fleets that were being sent to bolster existing operations, such as the Malayan campaign, as they entered their final stages.[37]

As more troops poured into the ports of Songkhla, Patani and Kuantan in late January there was little that the Allies could do to prevent the Japanese from consolidating their hold over the peninsula. Brave efforts to use what aircraft and warships were left to them to try and destroy the two transports that were approaching Endau on 26 January ended up by losing thirteen out of sixty-eight planes and one of the two destroyers that were deployed for this task. Within days the Allies were faced with what only two months before had been a previously unthinkable proposition – a general retreat south to the supposed island fortress of Singapore.[38]

Vice-Admiral Sir Geoffrey Layton, the C-in-C, Eastern Fleet (the successor to Tom Phillips who had perished in the *Prince of Wales* off Kuantan on 10 December), had already moved his headquarters staff to Batavia (Jakarta) on 5 January, two days before General Wavell assumed command of ABDACOM in the same city.

Layton was merely following Admiralty orders. He had been instructed by the Admiralty on 20 December to withdraw his ships from Singapore at his discretion and send them into the Indian Ocean and away therefore from the attentions of the Japanese air force. Wavell's arrival in Batavia could not have been more inauspicious coinciding as it did with the disastrous loss of the 11th Indian Division at Slim River in Perak, and the overall situation that he inherited continued to deteriorate from then onwards. Unable to do anything to advance the Allied case or retard the Japanese push down the peninsula, Layton's remaining warships were gathered into a convoy escort force under the command of Commodore Collins on 20 January.[39] China Force, as it was called, consisted of three light cruisers, six destroyers and two sloops and it was their mission to ply the route between Java and Singapore with supplies for the swelling numbers of troops on the latter. Wavell spelt out the order for a general retreat on 27 January, the day after the Endau engagement had ended with the sinking of *Thanet*, one of Layton's precious few destroyers, and the withdrawal was completed on 31 January. In this perilous environment a few units of China Force continued to escort ships through the Riau Archipelago into the Singapore Roads and only subsequently to carry civilian evacuees off the island in the opposite direction. By far the majority of Collins's ships were reassigned to convoy duty between Colombo and the Sunda Strait, or were deployed for special missions such as escorting Dutch troop transports through the Bangka Strait to the island of Sumatra.[40]

Before the final curtain fell on the drama being played out in Singapore, however, the Japanese had already signalled their intention of getting to grips with their next victims by bombing Surabaya in East Java for the first time on 3 February, and bringing troops from Kendari to land near Makassar, on the southwest coast of the Celebes, a few days later (8–9 February).[41] That same evening the first of the Japanese troops came ashore in Singapore. As they were doing so, the advance units of yet another Japanese armada set out from Camranh Bay for the area around Palembang on the southeastern coast of Sumatra. In the days that followed the humanitarian mission of getting as many women and children away from Singapore assumed precedence in Allied circles. More and more ships of all types and sizes were belatedly devoted to the task, but sadly and ironically as these boats took to the water many of them would set off southwards into the path of the on-coming enemy fleet of Vice-Admiral Jisaburo Ozawa bringing with him the Western Force whose carrier, *Ryūjō*, would be used to telling effect against these merchant vessels on 13 February.[42] While Admiral Thomas C. Hart, the American commander of ABDAFLOAT, could not do anything about the fate of Singapore, he was determined to try and thwart the opening of the Sumatran campaign. In this he had ample backing from the Dutch naval officers on his staff – all of whom were absolutely determined to keep the Japanese from making landfall if it could possibly be avoided. Quickly assembling an Allied Striking Force, Hart put a mixed force of five cruisers and ten destroyers under Rear-Admiral Karel Doorman's command charging him with the responsibility of disrupting the invasion by every means at his disposal. Attacked by carrier aircraft from *Ryūjō* throughout 14 February, Doorman, who has been described by Ronald Spector as a man of 'excessive caution and conservatism', promptly withdrew from the scene leaving ABDACOM with the only option of sending in their aircraft to do the job that Doorman's surface force was meant to do.[43] Although attacks by a combination of Allied bombers and fighters did sink one Japanese transport and delayed the invasion by a few hours, they were powerless to prevent the enemy from making two parachute drops behind their lines to the north and east of Palembang. A total of 460 paratroopers wrested control of the airfield that served the city and seized the refinery and oil fields at Pladjoe as well. This was merely a foretaste of what was to come once the rest of the invasion fleet joined its advance detachment off Muntok on the eastern side of the Bangka Strait and moved in on Palembang. As a result, the city had to be evacuated by the Allies on 16 February.[44]

A day before, the supposedly impregnable island fortress of Singapore had finally fallen to General Yamashita's 25th Army, the latest high profile casualty of a sweeping Japanese offensive that amazingly had carried all before it up to this point and still did not appear to be running out of steam. This much could be seen in the offensives they had planned for Bali and Timor within the next week and the preparatory work for an invasion of Java that would begin a mere ten days after Singapore fell.[45] It was breathtaking stuff. Psychologically and militarily the Japanese had the Allies on the run and they were making the most of it. Whether everyone involved was living on adrenalin or merely exploiting existing Allied weaknesses, the result was the same: an unprecedented land grab, the speed and scope of which almost defied imagination. It didn't stop there. Bali was next on the invasion agenda (19 February), while a psychological point was made with a bombing raid later that same morning by 152 carrier aircraft on Port Darwin in the Australian Northern Territory.[46] By wrecking so many transports in Australian waters, the Japanese had made it much more difficult for Vice-Admiral Conrad Helfrich, the newly-designated Dutch commander of ABDAFLOAT, to bring in reinforcements to help the defenders of Dutch and Portuguese Timor on the following day (20 February) once they found themselves confronting a substantial invasion of their territory in two places: at Koepang (Kupang) in the west and Dili in the northeast. Within four days the island was in Japanese hands.[47]

A prickly character at the best of times, Helfrich hated to yield any territory to the Japanese and after failing to prevent the loss of Bali, he was absolutely determined to hold on to Java come what may.[48] It was logical that this most populous island in the Dutch East Indies would be their next invasion target so there was little time for him to absorb the lessons of the recent past before confronting this new and far graver crisis. If the Japanese truly meant business and devoted significant forces to the invasion, ABDAFLOAT did not possess the warships necessary to deny them. Helfrich could only hope to use his forces to get in amongst the transports and sink as many of them as possible. This might only delay the inevitable, but if considerable casualties were suffered by the invasion forces it might cause the Japanese to rethink their strategy. It was to be a vain hope.

Responding to staggered submarine reports that indicated the enemy had two large invasion forces underway, one from the Anamba Islands to the northwest and the other from Balikpapan in Borneo, Helfrich redeployed his naval forces beefing up those at Surabaya in East Java and calling for reinforcements for his squadron at Tangjok Priok, the port for Batavia. Once the Japanese learnt of these moves from their own aerial reconnaissance, they promptly postponed their invasion plans by forty-eight hours and retired to a safe distance from the island. Rather than sit on the defensive, Helfrich decided to take the initiative and sent his most powerful ships out of Batavia and Surabaya on 26–27 February to engage the invasion forces. Neither of these naval sorties was successful as the Allied ships could not locate any of the enemy forces, let alone engage them productively. Air missions by both sides also drew a blank, but this stalemate was not to last for long. Doorman, having returned empty-handed from his first mission, had barely made port at midday on 27 February when a new reconnaissance report was received that sent him back out to sea from Surabaya once more in the direction of Bawean Island in the Java Sea. He had five cruisers and nine destroyers with him, more than enough to make mincemeat out of the troop transports belonging to the Eastern Force had they been able to surprise them, but aerial reconnaissance was a feature that both sides enjoyed and so the Japanese transports were diverted westwards while its covering force of four cruisers and fourteen destroyers moved at high speed to engage Doorman's forces. Two of the Japanese heavy cruisers *Haguro* and *Nachi* opened fire at a distance of 26km just after 1600 hours and a hit was registered on the heavy cruiser *Exeter*, which exploded in her boiler room with devastating results, knocking her out of the line but not sinking her. Her sudden crippling was a loss that Doorman could ill afford. As *Exeter* slowed down and turned away, confusion reigned since the three cruisers immediately following her, *Houston, Java* and *Perth*, all turned away too. This said much about the lack of communication in this mixed command, a woeful situation deriving, of course, from the failure to establish a signal code common to all. After the shelling, destroyers from both wings of the Japanese forces launched a fusillade of 'Long Lance' torpedoes – some 120 in all – at the Allied ships. Fortuitously only one of them found its way to a target, but it was sufficient to sink the Dutch destroyer *Kortenaer*. Appreciating that the *Exeter* was now a liability, Doorman sent her east towards Surabaya, accompanied by the destroyer *Witte de With* in the hope that she would live to fight another day. Thereafter, he sought to recover what little initiative was left to him. In the van of his dwindling force were only three destroyers: *Electra, Encounter* and *Jupiter*. These were needed to attack the leading Japanese warships in order to divert their attention from pursuing the stricken *Exeter*. Attack they did, but amidst the smoke and confusion, both sides sustained losses. *Electra* perished and the Japanese destroyer *Asagumo* was shelled and put out of action.[49]

After more failures on both sides to cause any more damage and concerned about the prospect of being drawn onto Dutch mine barrages in the gloom of the late afternoon, Rear-Admiral Takeo Takagi opted to withdraw the 5th

Cruiser Squadron from the encounter. This proved to be a wise move since another one of Doorman's destroyers (*Jupiter*) was lost later in the afternoon to an explosion that was likely to have come from one of these very mines. Persistent to the end, Doorman was determined to continue searching for the missing Japanese troop transports even though some of his own ships were running short of fuel. In the end, shorn of his four US destroyers which were making their back to Soerabaya to refuel and with *Encounter* assigned to picking up survivors from *Kortenaer*, he went north in his flagship *De Ruyter* once more with only three other cruisers to try to evade the escorts and get in amongst the troop convoy. He would not be so fortunate. Japanese skill and technique at night fighting was improving all of the time and Takagi's cruisers, *Haguro* and *Nachi*, demonstrated their talent in this respect by torpedoing and sinking both *De Ruyter* and *Java* at a range of over 8,000 yards (7.3km) before the night was out. Doorman went down with his flagship but not before ordering his two remaining cruisers (*Houston* and *Perth*) to break off the action and escape southwest to Batavia while they still could. In removing what was left of the Allied naval perimeter force, the Japanese invasion fleet (Eastern Force) resumed its journey to the Javanese coast and began disembarking its troops in the evening of 28 February at Kragan about 100nm (185km) west of Soerabaya. Although Allied air raids damaged the Japanese light cruiser *Kinu* and struck a solitary transport, the landings continued. On the following day (1 March) as a coda to the Battle of the Java Sea, the ailing *Exeter*, accompanied by the destroyers *Encounter* and *Pope*, prevented by the fall of Bali from going south to join the other Allied units under Helfrich's command at Tjilatjap, were making their laborious way south of Borneo towards the Sunda Strait when they found themselves surrounded by two groups of Japanese warships which they had wished to avoid. It was no contest. *Exeter* and *Encounter* were soon sunk by a combination of shelling and torpedo hits and the *Pope*, though more elusive initially, was later located and immobilised by six dive-bombers from the *Ryūjō* and finished off by shells from *Myokō* and *Ashigara*.[50]

If this was closure for East Java, the battle would soon be joined in the waters off the western half of the island where the Japanese had an even stronger invasion fleet than that which had eclipsed Doorman's force in the Java Sea. Even before any landings took place in the west, the Allies lost the potential capacity to maul at least part of the invasion force when the US aircraft depot ship *Langley* was sunk along with her cargo of fighter planes in the Indian Ocean on 27 February. Just to complicate the picture for the Allied defenders, the Japanese Western Force was divided the next day into three unequal groups. A group of ten transports were ushered into the Sunda Strait by the light cruiser *Yuru* and four destroyers and began landing troops at Anjer Lok (Anyer-Lor) during the night of 28 February–1 March. Another group of troopships, roughly the same size and escorted by the light cruiser *Sendai* and three destroyers, went east to land troops near Semarang on the northern coast of central Java, while the main bulk of the invasion force homed in on Banten Bay in the northwest part of the island which it reached during the evening of 28 February. While the troops were being disembarked under the watchful gaze of the destroyer *Fubuki*, the Allied heavy cruiser *Houston* and light cruiser *Perth* suddenly emerged out of the dark just after midnight to surprise everyone. By the time that they had both been sunk, they had left a calling card of their own. At the end of an admittedly confusing series of engagements, two transports (*Horai Maru* and *Sakura Maru*) had been sunk, and three destroyers and a minesweeper had been damaged. Whether the two Allied warships had inflicted all of this pain upon the enemy or whether some of it was self-induced is impossible to tell, but it left the Japanese smarting from the encounter and so they fell upon the Dutch destroyer *Evertsen* with alacrity when she unwittingly sailed right into their path a few hours later. It did not take long for her to be ablaze and by the time she beached herself in the Sunda Strait she had become a total wreck.[51]

In the hours that followed the calamitous loss of the Battle of Java Sea, some of the Allied warships that had been based at Batavia were able to escape through the Sunda Strait to Colombo, but those that were ordered out of Tjilatjap by Helfrich were not always so fortunate and many perished at the hands of the enemy. A host of merchant vessels that couldn't escape from Soerabaya and Tjilatjap for whatever reason were scuttled before the Allies finally took their leave of these naval bases on 3–5 March. Resistance on the populous island of Java itself (Willmott estimates it to have been home to 41 million people in 1942) did not last much longer for a slew of reasons that need not detain us in this study and so on 9 March in almost indecent haste 60,000 Allied troops capitulated to the Japanese invaders.[52]

Even before the collapse of the Dutch East Indies, the writing had been on the wall for the Philippines. President Roosevelt had recognised this on 23 February when he had ordered General Douglas MacArthur, the C-in-C of US forces on the island archipelago, to leave for Australia so as to assume command of Allied forces in that theatre.[53] What was true for the Philippines was true too for the rest of Southeast Asia. Was any place on land or sea in this region or that of the Southwest Pacific immune from Japanese influence and control? In March 1942 it didn't look like it. When one looks at the scale, spread and momentum of the Japanese victories in the three months from Pearl Harbor, the sheer extent of their successes still almost defies belief more than seven decades later. There was no slackening of pace, no resting on their laurels; territories taken were not, in Churchill's terminology, to be used as sofas but as springboards to other desirable pieces of real estate. Was there any obvious point beyond which the Japanese would not go? In the spring of 1942 if there was it wasn't obvious to the onlooker. Burma, Ceylon and the Indian sub-continent beckoned to the northwest, New Guinea and Australia to the southeast. Had the Japanese learnt the lessons of imperial overstretch from the British? Would wiser heads prevail? We know the answers in the twenty-first century, but back in the spring of 1942 the Japanese appeared to be rewriting the manual on how to acquire imperial possessions through military means.

While the war had speeded up in the Asia-Pacific, the other theatres had not been exactly quiet either. From the start of the year a number of concerted steps were taken by the American, British and Canadian naval authorities in order to divide the workload between them along the North Atlantic convoy route.[54] As part of these administrative arrangements, agreement was forged on the system of who escorted what along the Great Circle route between North America and the British Isles.[55] In addition, the Admiralty had discarded their Naval Cypher No.2 (which B-Dienst had little difficulty in reading) and replaced it on New Year's Day with the more sophisticated Naval Cypher No.4 in the hope that increasing the number of circuits in the cipher to sixteen and the code to twenty-six would make it more secure. It succeeded in this goal but it didn't make the cipher impossible to crack.[56] Despite these sensible precautions taken against U-boats in the North Atlantic, much work needed to be done elsewhere. In his excellent study *Battle of the Atlantic,* Marc Milner makes the very telling point that 1942 was to be an appalling year for shipping losses worldwide. Citing statistics that show that the Allies had lost an average of 2.1 million tons of shipping per year up to the end of 1941, he reveals that their merchant shipping losses alone went up astronomically to 7.2 million tons in the 1942 calendar year. In his assessment, U-boats claimed the credit for sinking 6.1 million tons of this alarming total.[57]

A contributory factor in this new and productive phase of Axis submarine warfare had begun off the east coast of the United States in early January 1942 with the arrival of five German Type IX U-boats to conduct what Dönitz hoped would be a very successful mission against a mass of soft un-convoyed shipping. One suspects that *Fall Paukenschlag* (*Case Drumbeat*) may have exceeded even his most optimistic assessments. For too many weeks the Germans were able to devour easy victims – ships sailing alone either intent on domestic coastal trade or on reaching a convoy assembly point – seemingly oblivious to the real danger that lurked under American waters. It was as if the Pan-American Security Zone remained in existence and that the Kriegsmarine would not dare take on the US in its own waters. If the Americans still believed in the sanctity of their exclusion zone, they ought to have been quickly disabused of this notion. Over a six-month period in waters stretching from Cape Hatteras (North Carolina) to Newfoundland the successive waves of U-boats involved in the *Paukenschlag* offensive sank somewhere between 220–30 vessels of roughly 1.25 million tons and torpedoed or damaged a further twenty-nine at a cost of over 200,000 tons.[58] These figures do not take account of the losses and damage inflicted on commercial traffic in and around the Caribbean or in the waters of the Gulf of Mexico. If these were added too, the figures would be even more horrendous.[59]

In the Far North another ominous development for the Allied cause was afoot. German intentions to disrupt and destroy the Soviet supply chain that had been forged between Iceland, Scapa Flow, Archangel and Murmansk had been clear since mid-January when for the first time a specially-dedicated group of three U-boats (*Ulan*) had begun to operate together against the Arctic convoys. In order to break through the destroyer screen surrounding the supply vessels on these routes, the German U-boats began to employ coordinated tactics (*Rudeltaktik*) with attacks being mounted simultaneously on both enemy ships and escorts to create maximum havoc within the convoy. Some of these attacks would merely be diversionary ploys to detach the Allied warships and enable other U-boats from their group, or the heavy surface ships that were now being based in Norwegian waters, to exploit the situation. Both Dönitz and Raeder realised, however, that having the right tactics to employ against these convoys was one thing, but finding their intended victims on the high seas in often foul conditions was quite another. Information for both sides was, therefore, absolutely priceless. If the Germans could locate these convoys they stood a great chance of staunching the flow of these vital supplies to Northern Russia, either by sinking the ships carrying them or by making these sailings so dangerous for the Allies that they might end up in suspending them. This was not to be a pious hope as the catastrophic failures of PQ.17 and PQ.18 would reveal later in the year when intelligence blackouts occurred and the Bletchley Park cryptanalysts weren't able to read the German *Heimische Gewasser* (Home Waters) Naval Enigma code for several days at a time.[60]

A timely demonstration of the limits that bad weather in these latitudes placed on intelligence and the toll it took on the ships and crews of the convoys was shown in March 1942. Gale force winds and tempestuous squalls could last for days at a time in these Arctic regions. Monstrous waves, freezing conditions and low visibility were all significant threats on this route round the Northern Cape (*Nordkapp*). When they came together – as they often did in winter – they possessed the force necessary to wreck even the best-defended of convoys. Ships would be scattered by heavy storms. It was tremendously difficult in raging seas to keep on station and as part of a coordinated whole. PQ.13, with nineteen ships and an escort of eight vessels led by the light cruiser *Trinidad*, was a victim of one such storm that remained intense for three days (24–27 March). Ships fell out of line, labouring in heavy swells, and as a result became independent entities and were all the more vulnerable because of it. Once the storms had petered out and these ships had been detected by aerial surveillance, they became cannon fodder for the patrolling U-boats, and the destroyers and aircraft that were sent specially to deal with them.[61] One does not need to be very prescient to sense that these Arctic convoys were distinctly vulnerable and often arduous, nerve-racking experiences for those employed on them.[62]

Three of the heavy units that Hitler wanted to use in Norway to put an end to this Arctic supply system had been languishing in the French port of Brest for the latter part of 1941. Unlike Raeder, whose desire to preserve their integrity was uppermost in his mind, the Führer was no longer prepared to retain the two battleships (*Scharnhorst* and *Gneisenau*) and the heavy cruiser (*Prinz Eugen*) as a miniature fleet-in-being and felt that the risk should be taken to bring them out of their enforced idleness and back into the war effort once more. For this to happen, of course, the three ships would have to first of all break out of the stranglehold the Allies had applied to all shipping in the port and make their way along the English Channel, through the Straits of Dover and out into the North Sea. While Raeder worried about their ability to run the gauntlet of forces that the Allies would throw at them, Hitler was determined that the effort be made since their survival in Brest was simply not helping the Axis war effort. It mattered little to him that the Allies had continued to expend much time, effort and material resources in trying to sink the ships or at the very least keeping them detained in harbour rather than at liberty on the high seas. As a result, Hitler ordered Raeder on 12 January to take active steps to bring the ships back into circulation.[63]

In the event *Fall Cerberus* (the operational name given to the 'Channel dash') would prove to be a triumph for the Germans and a severe embarrassment for the British. Not only did the three heavy ships, in company with six destroyers, move off undetected from Brest at 2245 hours on the night of 11 February, their group, swollen by the addition of five torpedo boats from Le Havre, was not located by shore-based radar for a further twelve hours until they had reached the area of Le Touquet roughly an hour's steaming time from Cap Gris Nez and the narrowest part of the Dover Straits.[64] An additional five well-armed E-boats joined the group from Cap Gris Nez and another four torpedo boats joined in from Dunkirk as the German force moved at pace (20 knots and above) through the Straits with air cover provided by units from Air Fleet 3 whose commanding officer, Feldmarschall Sperrle, had made a total of 176 fighters and heavy bombers available for this operation. This meant that at any time throughout the mission a minimum of sixteen aircraft were in the air above the German ships affording them some protection from whatever fighter and bomber resources the Allies might be able to scramble to pit against them and the naval squadron they were ushering through these narrow waters. As Correlli Barnett witheringly points out, whatever British counter-measures were applied – whether shelling from coastal batteries at the extent of their range, equipment failures on the part of the Dover and Ramsgate-based MTBs or suicidal attacks by slow, lumbering Swordfish aircraft – the results were always the same, failure. Barnett is unsparing in his criticism of the material inadequacies, although not the bravery of those who did not spare themselves in trying to overcome these deficiencies and combat the enemy.[65]

While the German ships forged ahead hugging the Belgian and Dutch coastline as they did so, the RAF put more than six hundred aircraft in the sky over the southern part of the North Sea in an effort to find and destroy them. Pathetically few of them ever found the ships and those that did rarely did much damage to them. It is a telling indictment of the state of British defences at this time that only one patrol ship was sunk (*V1302*) and two torpedo boats (*T13* and *Jaguar*) were damaged as a result of all this aerial activity and that the only serious inconvenience to one of the capital ships was when *Scharnhorst* struck a mine off the entrance to the River Scheldt at 1432 hours. Even this was overcome within seventeen minutes and without further penalty. There is a savage irony in the fact that five elderly destroyers based at Harwich should succeed where most of their aerial brethren had failed by getting a radar fix on the German squadron once it was underway again. Another brave effort launched by the destroyers in the fading light of the late afternoon was, however, easily beaten off by the guns of the battleships at some cost to the venerable British craft. After swatting away this latest interference, the Germans swept on serenely until both of their battleships struck mines in the waters off the West Frisian Islands. Fortunately for them, the damage was not sufficient to prevent *Gneisenau* and *Prinz Eugen* from reaching Brunsbuttel in the estuary of the Elbe at 0700 hours of 13 February and a limping *Scharnhorst*, with her port engine dead and shipping a thousand tons of seawater, eventually put into Wilhelmshaven in the Jade estuary later that same morning.[66]

Although the British press had a field day in bemoaning the loss of pride that had resulted from Vizeadmiral Ciliax and his heavy ships making a triumphant dash through the Channel to the safety of their home waters, Raeder sagely wrote at the time: 'We have won a tactical victory and suffered a strategic defeat.'[67] By quitting Brest after nearly eleven months the Germans had finally released the British from their long-standing vigil off the French Atlantic coast where they had maintained a perpetual presence to prevent the German fleet-in-being from being re-activated. These ships could now be redeployed to other duties. It would also save Bomber Command from indulging in more fruitless operations against shipping in the port. Moreover, Hitler's wish of transferring these big ships to Norwegian waters so that they could feed off the Arctic convoys would be thwarted too. *Prinz Eugen* duly reached Trondheim only to be torpedoed on 23 February. She returned to Germany for repairs and spent the rest of the war in the Baltic. *Gneisenau* never went to Norway at all because she was badly damaged in an RAF bombing raid on Kiel harbour on 26–27 February. She was sent to Gotenhafen (Gdynia) for extensive rebuilding but the funding dried up and she never went to sea again. *Scharnhorst* spent months under repair and was only transferred to Norway in March 1943.[68] Even so, *Fall Cerberus* had not just given the British a much needed lesson in humility, it had also exposed real limitations in inter-service coordination, as well as the shockingly inadequate and unreliable resources that both Vice-Admiral Sir Bertram Ramsay, in his capacity as head of Dover Command, and Vice-Admiral Sir George d'Oyly Lyon, as C-in-C Nore, had found themselves working with in defending British shores. Perhaps the most sobering lesson learnt from this grave embarrassment, however, was just how much the Allies had come to rely upon 'Ultra' to give them forewarning of German plans and dispositions. Without receiving this crucial information, their counter-measures had proved to be inadequate when they had been put to the test. This underlined, once again, the vital necessity for the brilliant, if eccentric, teams inhabiting the huts of Bletchley Park to crack the Enigma codes with the minimum of delay. This lesson would be learnt in a number of tragic ways before the year was over.[69]

Even when enemy signals could be read, disseminated and acted upon, the struggle at sea was still intense. Malta was a case in point. It needed regular deliveries of both fuel and supplies from Gibraltar and/or Alexandria or else its defence capability would have been severely undermined. Despite losing two out of the three transports that had been involved in the last supply operation (MF.5) from Alexandria in mid-February, Cunningham was required to mount the latest convoy operation in the Eastern Mediterranean in mid-March 1942.[70]

This was always likely to be a tough assignment to pull off successfully and so it proved. Once the Italian naval authorities learnt from two of their submarines that the four Allied transports and the seven escort vessels of convoy MW.10 were at sea, they gathered a fleet from Taranto and Messina to interdict it. Although Admiral Iachino had the battleship *Littorio*, three cruisers, ten destroyers and six submarines (three of which were German U-boats) under his command, these warships were unable to do any damage to the supply ships.[71] Once again they were thwarted by a detachment of the Mediterranean Fleet. On this occasion, it wasn't Cunningham in command but Vice-Admiral Sir Philip Vian. He spearheaded Force B, the convoy's covering force, consisting of three light cruisers and four destroyers, and it was his prudent decision making and his captains' expert ship-handling skills in heavy seas that frustrated the Italian fleet yet again. Detecting the Italian ships just after 1400 hours on 22 March, Vian laid a smokescreen and ordered the transports and their escorts to go south so as to put as much distance between themselves and the Italian surface fleet as possible, while he and Force B turned north and took the fight to the enemy. His captains were up to the task. They skilfully dodged in and out of the smokescreen and attacked the enemy cruisers at the limit of their range. It was too much for the Italians on this occasion and after about an hour of these exchanges, they turned away and retreated from the action.[72]

Although the weather was rapidly deteriorating, Iachino's flagship, *Littorio*, along with his group of warships from Taranto, emerged through the squalls at 1618 hours to threaten the convoy once more from the north. Again Vian proved up to the task. More dense smoke was laid and 'hit-and-run' tactics were employed to arrest the attention of the Italians and prevent them from pressing home an attack on the supply convoy and its escorts which, though attacked by roughly 150 Axis aircraft, didn't receive a single hit on 22 March. Vian's warships did more than merely delay or distract the Italians; they managed to hurt them too. In this respect he and his captains were helped by the bad weather and rough seas which combined to affect the gunnery of Iachino's bigger ships, while providing their own destroyers with the opportunity of pressing home a torpedo attack on their adversaries from a distance of 6,000 yards (5,486 metres). What could have been a rout, given the superior firepower of the Italian force, was turned into a spirited battle from which the Allies emerged with great credit. Five of the British ships were hit in these exchanges, two of them quite seriously – *Havock* in her boiler room and *Kingston* in her engine room – both of whom lost power and speed as a consequence of this damage. Two officers and six ratings died onboard *Havock* and thirteen ratings succumbed on *Kingston*. Vian's own flagship, *Cleopatra*, was not spared either. A 150mm (5.9-inch) shell struck the bridge early in the action killing fifteen officers and men and knocking out the radio on a temporary basis. Fortunately, the cruiser did not suffer any devastating loss either in manoeuvrability or in speed from this calamity and she was able to take a full part in the action as the weather and visibility deteriorated and the sea got rougher still. Although the light cruiser *Euryalus* and the destroyer *Lively* received some slight structural damage in the shelling, mostly from flying splinters, they too continued to harry the Italians as and when they could. In the frenetic mêlée that took place over two hours and forty minutes that spring afternoon in what became known as the Second Battle of Sirte, the British managed to hit the *Littorio* twice and set her on fire, and claimed to have damaged two of Iachino's cruisers, one seriously. Whether Cunningham's War Diary entry was strictly factual or a little hyperbolic, the damage was enough to convince the Italian commander to break off the action at 1858 hours as the last rays of light began to fade away.[73]

As his adversary turned away northwards, Vian could redeploy his forces confident that Iachino's surface forces were no longer in a position to molest the convoy. As such, he was absolutely determined that MW.10 must press on towards Malta in the hope that it might get there before the enemy bombers returned on the following morning. This was to be a forlorn hope given the prolonged diversion of the convoy and its escorts from their original course that afternoon. They were now too far away from Malta to reach the safety of Valetta during the hours of darkness. This meant that they would have to complete their ordeal in daylight when Axis aircraft would be on hand to try to exact some retribution for what had elapsed on the high seas the previous day. Aware of this situation, Vian opted to disperse the convoy with each of the transports being escorted on the final leg of their journey to Malta by at least one of the six Hunt class destroyer escorts that had been sent out in advance of the convoy to do an anti-submarine sweep of the route. He deliberately broke up the convoy in the vain hope that enemy aircraft would have greater difficulty in locating and dealing with smaller units of ships than an entire convoy group. After saving the convoy from the menace of the enemy surface fleet, Vian returned to Alexandria and a hero's reception at midday on 24 March. Convoy MW.10 and its escorts would not be so fortunate.[74]

Although aerial attacks had been expected, the intensity and accuracy of them on the morning of 23 March wrought havoc with the convoy. Of the four transports, two (*Clan Campbell* and *Breconshire*) never even reached the Grand Harbour at Valetta, while the other two (*Pampas* and *Talador*) reached port only to be bombed for three days and sunk on 26 March. As a result, only 5,000 tons of supplies were put ashore out of the total of 25,900 tons that the four supply ships had originally brought with them from Alexandria. It wasn't a great return on the investment of time, energy and courage displayed in this operation. Unfortunately, the mayhem didn't end there as the Allies also lost the Hunt-class destroyer escort *Southwold* to a mine on 24 March, and the Maltese-based fleet destroyer *Legion*, already seriously damaged by an earlier bomb hit, finally sank when she was hit by yet another bomb as she came alongside in the Grand Harbour two days later. A seventh victim, the submarine *P-39*, was also split amidships and had to be beached after a near-miss on 26 March.[75]

This operation was to be the last major sortie that was conducted under Cunningham's leadership in the Mediterranean. His time as C-in-C ended at the end of the month when he hauled down his flag and returned to London to take up an appointment as the head of the British Naval Staff Mission in Washington,

D.C. Depressing though it was, he left the Mediterranean Fleet at its most forlorn and weakest state in a generation. Assessing the situation in this theatre, Cunningham claimed that the high cost of sustaining Malta had been, and continued to be, worth the huge effort put into it since the island's dogged resistance forced the Axis air forces to expend a vast amount of time and resources into trying to crush it and while they were intent on doing that they couldn't be re-deploying these resources in another theatre of operations, such as North Africa, where they might have tilted the balance of advantage to the side of the Axis. In short, the beneficial effects of maintaining the Allied hold on Malta were still considered by him and other leading figures in the British government and military to be disproportionately greater than the high costs involved in ensuring its survival. Nonetheless, Cunningham realised only too well that with Axis aerial dominance at its peak at this time, the moment had arrived to withdraw the last remaining surface units from the island and send them east to operate from Alexandria. This left the RAF with the task of trying to regain the initiative in the Central Mediterranean.[76] Nearly two decades later Khrushchev was to claim that West Berlin was 'a bone stuck in his throat'.[77] Malta, aptly described by Correlli Barnett as 'the Verdun of Maritime War', was to prove to be something of the same impediment for Rommel.[78]

While the naval war in the Western Hemisphere remained a dour struggle for supremacy, the situation in the Far East continued to favour the Axis forces. After the fall of Rangoon on 8 March, the Japanese steadily increased their presence in the Andaman Sea region by acquiring the sites for naval bases at Phuket, Mergui and Port Blair as the month proceeded.[79] Possession of these strategic ports in Thai, Burmese and Andaman waters gave them the opportunity of developing an external protective screen for their expanding Southeast Asian empire by investing them with sufficient resources to make it far more difficult for the Allies to try to re-establish themselves as a naval power in this part of the world.

Sir James Somerville, who had formerly been in charge of Force H at Gibraltar, was the naval officer charged with the responsibility of bringing about that resurgence in Allied fortunes when he assumed the role of C-in-C, Eastern Fleet, on 27 March. He was to be given a swift baptism of fire by the Japanese. In many respects the Japanese raid on Ceylon and their show of force throughout the Bay of Bengal in the early days of April were designed to show just what they might be capable of if they decided to move into the area systematically in the months to come. What the Admiralty couldn't determine at this stage was whether the Japanese raid was a foretaste of trials to come or merely a spectacular foray that was meant to underline the real qualitative difference in naval power between the enemy and the forces at Somerville's disposal. Either way, it was a reality check that they could not ignore. Professor Willmott has pointed out that many of the vessels in the Eastern Fleet had either become obsolescent, such as four of the five battleships (the venerable 'Four Rs'), or were comparatively inferior to their Japanese equivalents, notably the fleet carriers and their planes. Nonetheless, the very fact that the Allies had managed to assemble a force that contained eight capital ships (three carriers and five battleships), seven cruisers, sixteen destroyers and seven submarines so soon after the loss of Singapore and Malaya, was impressive in itself and showed that they intended to defend the Indian subcontinent as resolutely as possible. Unfortunately, as Willmott indicates, and the raid into the Indian Ocean was to prove conclusively, the Eastern Fleet was simply not equipped at this stage to prevent the IJN from going where it liked and doing what it wanted if it moved in force.[80]

Somerville was to become a reluctant witness to the veracity of this statement over the course of the next fortnight. While what happened to his forces was bad enough, it could have been a lot worse had the Japanese caught the Eastern Fleet unawares in harbour at either Colombo or Trincomalee. They didn't because he had received intelligence reports on 29 March indicating that the Japanese 1st Carrier Fleet was poised to strike at these Ceylonese bases within a few days. Somerville took the warning seriously. After dividing his ships into a fast group (Force A) which he commanded and an older and more vulnerable collection of vessels which he gave to Vice-Admiral Willis (Force B), the Eastern Fleet left port and steamed south in a bid to locate the enemy. While Somerville realised he couldn't afford to meet the full extent of Nagumo's forces on the open sea if he wished to preserve even the semblance of a fleet-in-being, pride alone meant that he couldn't just beat a headlong retreat from Ceylonese waters without being prepared to attack some of the forward units of the advancing enemy fleet, particularly under cover of darkness, if he could find them. Try as he might, he was unable to locate the enemy over the next few days. Lacking any further intelligence reports, Somerville reached the erroneous conclusion that Nagumo may have decided to abort the attack. This initial mistake was then compounded by two more he made: detaching the light carrier *Hermes* and sending her back to Trincomalee for repairs and ordering one of her three escorts, the heavy cruiser *Dorsetshire*, to return to Colombo to complete the refit she had had to abandon in late March. Neither decision made much sense at a time when so much was still uncertain. As these ships went north, the now weakened Force A and B retired further to the southwest on 2 April so that they could take on additional supplies from the secret British base at Addu Atoll. While the Eastern Fleet replenished itself at the most southerly island of the Maldives chain on Easter Saturday (4 April), the Malaya Force, under the command of Vice-Admiral Jisaburo Ozawa, had reached the Andaman Islands and was now poised to cross the Bay of Bengal and do as much damage as it could to Allied shipping interests along the busy Indian coastline. Given the fact that Ozawa had the carrier *Ryūjō*, five heavy cruisers, a light cruiser and four destroyers with him, it seemed as if the old proverbial sledgehammer was about to be wielded to crack a very weak and vulnerable nut. It would be no contest. Excessive force was to be pitted against undefended mercantile craft and in this collision only one result was possible.[81]

As the British braced themselves for bad news in the Indian Ocean, Nagumo's force was finally reported by a Catalina flying-boat during the afternoon of 4 April. This news prompted Somerville to leave Addu Atoll shortly after midnight and return northeast towards Colombo. Willis followed him a few hours later. By the time Force B had left port, the 1st Carrier Fleet, while still some 300nm (556 km) southeast of Colombo, had launched fifty-three high level bombers, thirty-eight dive-bombers and thirty-six fighters to attack the Ceylonese capital and deal with any aerial opposition that would be sent up against them. In the aerial mêlée that followed, nineteen Allied planes were lost out of the forty-eight that got airborne that morning. While the Japanese lost seven of their own aircraft in the raid, the attack was pressed home with vigour against the port's facilities causing extensive damage to the infrastructure of the naval base and sinking the auxiliary cruiser *Hector* and the destroyer *Tenedos* that had remained in the harbour. Worse was to follow in the early afternoon of that Easter Sunday when a Japanese reconnaissance plane spotted the two heavy cruisers *Cornwall* and *Dorsetshire* steaming away from Colombo at high speed in an attempt to rejoin Somerville and the rest of Force A who were still over 200nm (370 km) away to the southward but closing with them. Fifty-three dive-bombers took off from Nagumo's carriers to deal with the two Allied cruisers and in a furious series of attacks soon smashed them to bits. It was clearly Nagumo's day, but it could have been an even better one for the Japanese commander had he insisted on more extensive reconnaissance sweeps and been able to locate the rest of Somerville's warships. He didn't and so Force A remained undetected and lived to fight another day. After their exertions on Easter Sunday, Nagumo steered his carrier fleet away from Ceylon to the east for a couple of days before changing course and returning to attack the Allied base at Trincomalee on the northeastern shore of Ceylon on 9 April. By this time Somerville and Willis were back in Addu Atoll and a non-factor in what was about to ensue. All that they could do was to wait and hope that it wouldn't be a case of Colombo revisited. It was. Committing roughly the same number of aircraft as in the earlier attack on the capital, Nagumo flew off ninety-one high-level bombers and dive-bombers and thirty-eight fighter aircraft to attack Trincomalee. A mix of only thirty-two Blenheim, Fulmar and Hurricane aircraft took to the skies to defend the subordinate Allied naval base on the island and eighteen of them were shot down. While the raid recorded some structural damage to the naval base, the attack on the warships and other vessels that were caught out at sea was far more dramatic. After locating the light carrier *Hermes* along with the destroyer *Vampire*, the corvette *Hollyhock* and two tankers south of Trincomalee, Nagumo sent eighty more dive-bombers to deal with them. They did. All five ships were sunk; *Hermes* being the only British carrier to be sunk by aircraft during the Second World War. Their job done, Nagumo's Carrier Fleet turned away from Ceylon and made passage for the Strait of Malacca, reaching it safely on 12–13 April some three days after Ozawa's fleet had returned from its short and explosive foray against the merchant shipping that it found plying the east coast of India from Puri in the state of Orissa southwards. Quite apart from the warships the twin-pronged Japanese naval raid had destroyed, and the damage done by carrier aircraft to shore-based facilities, twenty-three merchant vessels (112,312 tons) had also been sunk by these surface forces in a matter of only a few days. Five

Japanese submarines, operating off the west coast of India, had also taken part by dispatching another 32,404 tons of mercantile shipping. As a result, this one Japanese raid had inflicted damage of a most remarkable kind on Allied economic interests and its military position in the subcontinent and the entire Bay of Bengal.[82]

It was a very sobering experience for those at Admiralty House in Whitehall and especially galling for Somerville whose first thirteen days in command had seen the Eastern Fleet depleted by the loss of a light carrier, two heavy cruisers, an auxiliary cruiser, two destroyers and a corvette. Worse still, he had been forced by this dual operation to abandon his former Ceylonese base and withdraw in the first instance to Bombay and subsequently right across the Indian Ocean to Kilindini harbour at Mombasa in southern Kenya. This was to be Somerville's base until the end of July 1942, when he returned with the Eastern Fleet to Colombo.[83]

While the Admiralty was absorbing the news about its current weakness in the Indian Ocean, disturbing news from other Allied operational theatres did not lift the gloom. A gallant Commando raid in the Bay of Biscay designed to blow up the massive St. Nazaire dockyard gates and render the naval base unserviceable had ended in grisly failure on the night of 27–28 March, and an intensified Axis bombing offensive against Malta finally forced what was left of the 10th Submarine Flotilla to quit their battered anchorages at Lazaretto Creek in mid-April.[84]

Extensive German bombing operations were not, of course, solely confined to the Central Mediterranean. Much further north the leading warships of the Soviet Navy's Red Banner Fleet, which remained in port at Leningrad while waiting for the winter ice shelf to melt, were the subject of a great deal of attention too.[85] German air attacks were also directed against the naval bases at Novorossisk and Tuapse on the Black Sea, both of which were used by Soviet warships for running supplies and reinforcements into the beleaguered city of Sevastopol and for bringing out the wounded defenders. These critical supply missions kept the base from succumbing to the Germans and made the Crimean port the Red Navy's Tobruk. Despite the efforts put into these raids, none of them seriously inconvenienced the supply chain, as can be gauged from the fact that three more of these missions were still run to Sevastopol from these ports during the next week and that one of the destroyers that had been damaged in the initial raid, *Nezamozhnik*, had been patched up sufficiently so that she could carry out a solo mission to the Crimea on 15 April.[86]

Clearly, the message that ought to have got through to the military leadership of all sides by this time was that even the best aircraft alone – impressive machines though they were – couldn't win every phase of the war at sea. This, of course, was exactly what the naval establishments of the world had been saying for years, but the quantitative argument remained a compelling factor for the use of aircraft in most situations where they could be deployed feasibly. In essence, aircraft were far more plentiful and vastly exceeded the number of leading warships that could be brought to bear operationally for a range of crucial tasks that needed to be undertaken in war. Apart from the substantial savings that could be made in their construction, maintenance and running costs, they could be built, worked up and deployed operationally in less time than all but the most basic of water-borne craft. When taken together all of these factors were persuasive arguments for using aircraft whenever they could be despite their indifferent strike rate under all but the most favourable of conditions.

Although the results of deploying FW Condor surveillance aircraft and submarines together in the Western Approaches had fallen off in the latter part of 1941 as 'Ultra' kept the Allies aware of enemy dispositions in these waters, the Germans sensed correctly that it might still be a winning combination in the Arctic, where they could use aircraft, heavy surface ships, and U-boats along the hazardous Polar route used by the Allied convoys in sailing to and from Murmansk and Archangel. Each time the Allies ran these supply missions the odds against them succeeding grew larger as the Germans put more effort and resources into the task of choking off this supply link.[87] Even those convoys that didn't lose a significant proportion of their supply ships on these Arctic runs, such as PQ.15 and QP.11 (26 April–12 May), for example, did not escape scot-free.[88]

Another sign of the times was discernible a few days later in a distant theatre of war. Although the Japanese were still in the process of mopping up the islands in the Philippine archipelago, having taken both Cebu and Panay and making their first forays into Mindanao before the end of April, the relentless tide of their military successes was beginning to peter out. While there would still be more conquests for them in the Philippines and South Pacific theatres over the next few weeks, the war would no longer be as one-sided as it had been since their attack on Pearl Harbor in early December.[89]

Once the Anglo-American Combined Chiefs of Staff (CCOS) had decided on 24 March 1942 to award the US with prime strategic responsibility for reclaiming the Pacific from the Japanese, a formidable and yet potentially combustible military partnership was formed between Admirals King and Nimitz, representing the USN, and General MacArthur, the sole but decidedly vocal Army representative, who was to be made the Supreme Commander for the Southwest Pacific area (COMSOWESPAC). Although Nimitz in his capacity as CINCPAC had responsibility for the rest of the Pacific, MacArthur's seniority was still sufficient to pose all kinds of weighty logistic and communication problems for his naval counterpart in the months and years to come. A cantankerous individual at the best of times, MacArthur was not greatly enamoured with the Navy or its ways of doing business. Regardless of that uncompromising fact, Nimitz was a man of principle and dogged self-assurance and no less committed to overall victory than his illustrious service colleague was. Far more prudent and diplomatic, however, he used his skill and resourcefulness to circumvent problems with the charismatic and forceful general. While he knew that MacArthur was used to having his own way in the Army, Nimitz wasn't prepared to become merely a doormat for him or anyone else to walk all over. Even so, his diplomacy would be sorely tested at times in the future as the strategic plans for rolling back the Japanese throughout the Pacific became subject to all kinds of special pleading from the restless spirit in the southwest part of that ocean.[90]

Although the early weeks in their new positions had not been happy ones, a small sign that the tide of war was beginning to ebb slightly was registered even before the Battle of the Coral Sea in early May confirmed this impression and the momentous battle for Midway a month later proved it dramatically. In staging a highly symbolic daylight-bombing raid on Tokyo and Yokohama, Kobe and Nagoya on 18 April, the US military brought the war home to the Japanese mainland and its people for the first time since Pearl Harbor.[91] It didn't matter that the material damage caused by the Doolittle Raid was minor, the fact that the Americans had the means and the guile to outwit their opponents in the way that they had was sufficient in itself to deliver a psychological riposte to the Tojo leadership that would last long after the bomb damage had been swept away. Japanese pride had been hurt by this single demonstration of American power projection. A psychological message out of all proportion to the number of bombs dropped on these four cities had been delivered by Lieutenant-Colonel James Doolittle and his force of sixteen B-25B Mitchell twin-engined bombers that morning in April 1942. It would not be lost on Admiral Isoroku Yamamoto.[92] He had never been convinced that Pearl Harbor had been as decisive an event as his other military colleagues had hoped or believed that it had been. He realised that a United States with a carrier fleet intact was a perpetual danger to Japan. Unless and until that fleet was destroyed the war would not be won.[93] This doctrine was to be tested in the Coral Sea and later proved demonstrably at Midway. For the moment, however, the audacity of the Doolittle Raid brought cheer to the American public and to the wider Allied world. It was the stuff of a heroic comic strip with Doolittle and his intrepid men defying the odds, flying off from the *Hornet* while still 668nm (1,237 km) away from Tokyo, knowing that they could not be recovered by the carrier; executing their mission by reaching their targets and catching the Japanese almost completely by surprise, before setting off for enemy-occupied China without sufficient fuel left to make anything other than a forced landing once they were over dry land. It was a stirring and hazardous mission and one that would cost the lives of four of the Americans and countless Chinese peasants who led the rest of the flight crew to safety through the Japanese lines.[94]

Elsewhere in the long-running war waged between the submarine and its foes, the news was mixed. For the Allies the loss of one of their greatest aces, David Wanklyn, V.C., of the *Upholder*, was a huge blow. After a rather fumbling start, he had grown into his role and to such an extent that his boat had become the most successful British submarine of the war in the Mediterranean until *Upholder* and her entire crew perished at the hands of the Italian torpedo boat *Pegaso* on their twenty-fourth mission on 14 April. Wanklyn had been one of those commanders who had developed a gut instinct for where the action really was and a knack for finding it wherever he was sent. He would be sorely missed.[95] Coincidentally on the very same day that the British ace was lost, another blow was struck against the submarine when the corvette *Vetch*, on convoy escort duty in the North Atlantic, became the first vessel to pick up the 'ping' of a U-boat at a distance of 7km on her 10cm Type-271 radar set and used this device to home in on *U252* with the sloop *Stork* sinking the U-boat with a combination of gunfire and depth charges.[96] This technological success came hard on the heels of yet another significant advance when a convoy escort carrying a HF/DF (High Frequency/Direction Finding) radio succeeded in locating the U-boat (*U587*) in the same ocean on 27 March and orchestrating her destruction by four destroyers thereafter.[97] Both the use of radar and the 'Huff-Duff' radio sets were promising signs for the future, but even though they had achieved an initial success it would take a long time before this equipment would become standard issue on surface warships. Although a tentative breakthrough was therefore being made in the fight against the underwater predator, too much could be read into these isolated successes; in truth, much more still had to be done before the submarine could be said to be under control.[98]

A more concerted move aimed at reducing the impact of the U-boat came, however, with the establishment of the first rota of eleven escort groups for both fast (HX) and slow (SC) Allied convoys making the North Atlantic crossing from WESTOMP (Western Ocean Meeting Point) off the Canadian east coast to EASTOMP (Eastern Ocean Meeting Point) off the west coast of Ireland and for the return journey that they would make with the ON and ONS convoys.[99] This was another small, but important, organisational step on the road to containing the menacing threat posed by Dönitz's force. Nonetheless, the Allies would not begin to stifle the effectiveness of the U-boats until they could do something to close the substantial 'air gap' of roughly 1,200 miles that existed on these Atlantic crossings between those areas where aerial surveillance and support was provided and where it was lacking. It was precisely in this 'air gap' in the mid-Atlantic south of Greenland that Dönitz was instructing his commanders to congregate so that they could reap a wonderful harvest untroubled by the spectre of aerial detection or assault. He was also much encouraged by the development of the first Type 14 U-boat tanker (*U459*) and the operational success of this '*Milchkuh*'(milk cow) some 500nm (926km) off the coast of Bermuda.[100] U-boat tankers provided a relatively unobtrusive way of refuelling and replenishing the vessels assigned to them. As more of these tankers were put into service, therefore, they would help to lengthen the time that individual U-boats could remain on station and be a threat to Allied shipping. Enough damage was being done by them in any case, as was evident in the news that emerged from the Western Atlantic in May and June where fourteen U-boats working mostly independently managed to sink a total of eighty-six ships (411,425 tons) and damage eight others in the waters between the Bahamas and the Greater Antilles, off Cuba and around the Yucatan peninsula (24 April–30 June) and four other U-boats continued the killing spree in the Caribbean throughout both May and June and early July sinking another forty-five vessels (214,217 tons). It was simply wholesale slaughter and would remain so until a convoy system was introduced in these waters.[101] It was only after the Americans had finally established a convoy route (NK) from the Hampton Roads (Virginia) to Key West (Florida) on 14 May and one in the opposite direction (KN) a day later, and arranged for the first of the feeder convoys to leave Boston for Halifax, Nova Scotia (BX) on 19 May that the attrition rate was cut along the eastern seaboard of the United States.[102]

Away from the ongoing contest between the submarine and those seeking to blunt its cutting edge, the Allies decided to undertake a little unfinished business of their own in African waters with the operation (*Ironclad*) to invade and capture the island of Madagascar from the Vichy French authorities in early May. Designed to remove both a modest aerial and naval threat to Allied shipping interests along the eastern coast of the African continent, success in this venture was seen as providing a timely psychological boost for the men of the Eastern Fleet who were still reeling somewhat after the recent Japanese excursion into the Indian Ocean. Before any of the troops and supplies gathered for this operation could be landed safely in the Baie du Courrier at the northern tip of the island, however, carrier aircraft pounded the Vichy airfields and ports on 5 May sinking both the auxiliary cruiser *Bougainville* and the submarine *Bévéziers* in the process. Although the Allied troops got ashore from their transports and landing craft without encountering any resistance, the Vichy French troops and the guns of their gunboat *D'Entrecasteaux* fought resolutely over the next few hours to restrict the bridgehead. It was only after the landing of a force of Marine Commandos that this resistance was finally overcome, enemy installations were captured, the gunboat was beached, and victory was ultimately secured on 8 May. A welcome fillip though the victory in Madagascar was to the Allied cause in the Indian Ocean, the Axis Powers would return to these waters repeatedly in the course of the next two years to do what submarines did best – sink anything that moved if it even vaguely belonged to the enemy![103]

Of far greater significance for the future course of the naval war, however, was the collision that took place at exactly the same time in the Coral Sea pitching the previously rampant IJN against a chastened but resolute American opponent bent on revenge.

Notes

1 Kiyoshi Ikeda, 'Vice Admiral Chuichi Nagumo', in Howarth (ed.), *Men of war*, pp.263–77; Rohwer, *Chronology*, pp.116, 118–20; Paul S. Dull, *A battle history of the Imperial Japanese Navy 1941–1945* (Cambridge: Patrick Stephens, 1978), pp.3–20.
2 H.P.Willmott, with Haruo Tohmatsu and W. Spencer Johnson, *Pearl Harbor* (London: Cassell, 2001); Rohwer, *Chronology*, p.121; Evans and Peattie, *Kaigun*, pp.471–86.
3 Malcolm H. Murfett, 'Phillips, Sir Tom Spencer Vaughan', in Harrison (ed.), *Oxford Dictionary of National Biography*, Vol.44, pp.150–54; Martin Middlebrook and P. Mahoney, *The sinking of the Prince of Wales and the Repulse: the end of the battleship era* (Barnsley: Leo Cooper, 2004), pp.74–111; Dull, *A battle history of the IJN*, pp.35–41; Arthur Nicholson, *Hostages to fortune: Winston Churchill and the loss of the Prince of Wales and Repulse* (Stroud: Sutton Publishing, 2005).
4 A vast publishing industry has been generated by the attacks on Pearl Harbor. Even accounting for the terrorist attacks of 9:11, no attack on the United States has

generated such rancour and controversy as the events of that early morning in Oahu in December 1941. Apart from the classics such as Samuel Eliot Morison, *History of United States naval operations in World War II. Vol.III: The rising sun in the Pacific 1931–April 1942* (Boston: Little, Brown & Co: 1965), pp.48–146; and Gordon W. Prange, *At dawn we slept* (New York: McGraw Hill, 1981), the following are a sample of some of the excellent accounts that have been written in recent years on various aspects of this tragic episode: Charles R. Anderson, *Days of lightning, years of scorn: Walter C. Short and the attack on Pearl Harbor* (Annapolis, Md: NIP, 2005); Fred Borch and Daniel Martinez, *Kimmel, Short, and Pearl Harbor: the final report revealed* (Annapolis, Md: NIP, 2005); Burl Burlingame, *Advance Force Pearl Harbor* (Annapolis, Md: NIP, 1992); Michael Gannon, *Pearl Harbor betrayed: the true story of a man and a nation under attack* (New York: Henry Holt, 2001); William Bruce Johnson, *The Pacific campaign in World War II* (London: Routledge, 2006), pp.44–90; John Prados, *Combined fleet decoded: the secret history of American intelligence and the Japanese navy in World War II* (New York: Random House, 1995), pp.118–97; H.P. Willmott, *Empires in the balance: Japanese and Allied Pacific strategies to April 1942* (Annapolis, Md.: NIP, 1982), pp.130–42.

5 Willmott, *Pearl Harbor*, pp.74–141; Hamer, *Bombers versus battleships*, pp.102–17.

6 A most persuasive, practical counter-argument to the possibility of a third strike is given by Professor Willmott in his latest book on the battle. Contrast this assessment with the conventional view on Nagumo offered by Prange, *et al.* Willmott, *Pearl Harbor*, pp.142–57; Prange, *At dawn we slept*, pp.541–50; Gannon, *Pearl Harbor betrayal*, pp.261–63.

7 Dallek, *Franklin Roosevelt and American foreign policy*, pp.311–13; Kershaw, *Hitler: nemesis*, pp.442–49; Mack Smith, *Mussolini*, p.273.

8 Winston S. Churchill, *The Second World War, Vol. III. The grand alliance* (London: Penguin Books, 1985), p.539.

9 Malcolm H. Murfett, John N. Miksic, Brian P. Farrell and Chiang Ming Shun, *Between two oceans: A military history of Singapore from first settlement to final British withdrawal* (Singapore: Marshall Cavendish Academic, 2004), pp.218–306; Dull, *A battle history of the IJN*, pp.21–34; Rohwer, *Chronology*, p.122.

10 Middlebrook and Mahoney, *The sinking of the Prince of Wales and Repulse*, pp.7–170; Murfett, 'Phillips, Sir Tom', in Harrison (ed.), *Oxford Dictionary of National Biography*, 44, pp.150–54.

11 One of the Brewster Buffalo pilots, Flight Lieutenant Tim Vigors, certainly believed that had they been keeping a standing patrol over the fleet they could have kept shadowing aircraft away and that even if the Japanese learnt of the exact position of the two capital ships, their torpedo bombers had no fighter escorts and were heavily laden. In his opinion, six Buffaloes 'could have wrought merry hell with them and certainly prevented a lot of the torpedo strikes'. Middlebrook and Mahoney, *The sinking of the Prince of Wales and Repulse*, pp.257–58.

12 Malcolm H. Murfett, 'Reflections on an enduring theme: the "Singapore strategy" at sixty', in Brian Farrell and Sandy Hunter (eds), *Sixty years on: the fall of Singapore revisited* (Singapore: Eastern Universities Press, 2002), pp.3–28; Hamer, *Bombers versus battleships*, pp.118–36; Stephen, *Sea battles in close-up*, pp.99–114; David Ian Hall, 'Looking skyward from below the waves: Admiral Tom Phillips and the loss of the *Prince of Wales* and the *Repulse*', in Greg Kennedy (ed.), *British naval strategy east of Suez, 1900–2000: influences and actions* (London: Frank Cass, 2000), pp.118–27.

13 Middlebrook and Mahoney, *The sinking of the Prince of Wales and Repulse*, pp.171–314.

14 Willmott, *Empires in the balance*, pp.175–254; Brian P. Farrell, *The defence and fall of Singapore 1940–1942* (Stroud, Glos: Tempus, 2005); Roman Bose, *Secrets of the battlebox: the history and role of Britain's Command HQ in the Malayan campaign* (Singapore: Marshall Cavendish Editions, 2005); Rohwer, *Chronology*, pp.123, 125–26.

15 Farrell, *Basis and making of British grand strategy, I*, pp.217–52; Grace Person Hayes, *The history of the Joint Chiefs of Staff in World War II: the war against Japan* (Annapolis, Md: NIP, 1982), pp.36–60.

16 HG.76 with thirty-two ships and escorted by four sloops, nine corvettes, two Hunt class destroyers, one ex-USN destroyer and the escort carrier *Audacity* left Gibraltar for the UK on 14 December and took ten days to reach safety in home waters. During that time it was constantly hounded by up to twelve U-boats and supporting FW 200s. The convoy lost three ships on passage to home waters as well as the escort destroyer *Stanley* and *Audacity*. It was as clear to Dönitz as it was to the Admiralty, however, that the escort carrier's presence had been crucial in taking the fight to the *Seeräuber* wolf pack which lost five U-boats, had at least two FW 200s shot down and perhaps as many as three others damaged by her Martlet fighters. Jan G. Heitmann, 'The front line: convoy HG76 – the offence'; and A.B. Sainsbury, 'The front line: convoy HG76 – the defence', in Howarth and Law (eds), *The Battle of the Atlantic 1939–1945*, pp.490–507, 508–15.

17 Kenneth Poolman, *The sea hunters: escort carriers v. U-boats, 1941–1945* (London: Arms and Armour, 1982); Barnett, *Engage the enemy*, pp.275–77; Milner, *Battle of the Atlantic*, pp.85–87; Rohwer, *Chronology*, p.126; Gardiner (ed.), *Conway's all the world's fighting ships*, p.23.

18 Sebag-Montefiore, *Enigma*, pp.219–29; Rohwer, *Chronology*, p.128.

19 Achkasov and Pavlovich, *Soviet naval operations*, pp.106–16; Rohwer, *Chronology*, pp.128–29; Ruge, *Soviets as naval opponents*, pp.68–77.

20 Commander G.H. Stokes, like Bill Agnew before him, was awarded the CB for his ships' feat off Cape Bon. Grove, *Sea battles in close-up*, 2, pp.70–72; Rohwer, *Chronology*, p.120.

21 *Galatea* sank in only three minutes. Gardiner (ed.), *Conway's all the world's fighting ships*, p.31; Miller, *U-boats*, pp.188–89; Grove, *Sea battles in close-up*, 2, p.72; Rohwer, *Chronology*, pp.124–25.

22 Grove, *Sea battles in close-up*, 2, pp.72–74; Rohwer, *Chronology*, p.125.

23 Ibid.; Greene and Massignani, *Naval war in the Mediterranean*, pp.200–202; Sadkovich, *Italian Navy in World War II*, pp.212–18.

24 Simpson (ed.), *Cunningham papers I*, pp.458–62, 551–59; Barnett, *Engage the enemy*, pp.376–77; Winton, *Cunningham*, pp.248–50.

25 Simpson (ed.), *Cunningham papers*, *I*, pp.457–63, 532–61; Rohwer, *Chronology*, pp.125, 127–28.

26 E.B. Potter, 'Fleet Admiral Chester William Nimitz', in Howarth (ed.), *Men of war*, pp.129–57.

27 King would succeed Admiral Harold R. Stark as Chief of Naval Operations (CNO) on 12 March 1942. He held this appointment in tandem with his role as COMINCH. Ernest J. King and Walter M. Whitehill, *Fleet Admiral King: a naval record* (New York: W.W. Norton, 1952), pp.349–59; Robert W. Love, Jr., 'Fleet Admiral Ernest J. King', in Howarth (ed.), *Men of war*, pp.75–107; E.B. Potter, *Nimitz* (Annapolis, Md: NIP, 1976), pp.1–47.

28 Rohwer, *Chronology*, p.131; Ruge, *Soviets as naval opponents*, p.69.

29 Michael Simpson indicates the damage that Malta's strike force had inflicted upon their adversaries in the second half of 1941 by pointing out that the enemy's monthly losses of supplies ran from 40 to 80% of those dispatched. This superb accomplishment was achieved by fewer than 100 strike aircraft, a flotilla of submarines and Force K, which had on average a mere two cruisers and two destroyers at its disposal. Simpson (ed.), *Cunningham Papers*, *I*, p.469.

30 Rohwer, *Chronology*, pp.133, 136, 138, 143, 149, 152–53, 158–59, 163, 166, 171, 173–74, 179, 181, 186–87, 189, 207, 213; Benady, *The Royal Navy at Gibraltar*, pp.194–95.

31 For an insight into the vexed problems of the ABDACOM and the struggles that it faced, see Gill, *Royal Australian Navy 1939–1942*, pp.513–649. It could be said that the title of Professor Spector's chapter 'The short, unhappy life of ABDACOM' was entirely apposite for this beleaguered institution. Ronald Spector, *Eagle against the sun:*

the American war with Japan (New York, The Free Press, 1985), pp.123–41; Farrell, Basis and making of British grand strategy, I, pp.225–26, 237–46, 257–58.
32 Rohwer, Chronology, pp.133–34; Willmott, Empires in the balance, pp.283–84, 286–90.
33 Rohwer, Chronology, pp.135–37.
34 Willmott, Empires in the balance, pp.289–92.
35 One Japanese minesweeper was lost and two more were damaged in bringing the invasion troops ashore on Ambon (Amboina). Ibid., pp.284–85, 289–93; Rohwer, Chronology, p.139.
36 Saratoga, which had only recently arrived on station from the west coast of the US, was put out of action for several months. USN's attempt to relieve Wake Island in December 1941 has remained a matter of controversy ever since and sullied the names of those deemed responsible for its failure. Gregory J.W. Urwin, Facing fearful odds: the siege of Wake Island (Lincoln, Neb: University of Nebraska Press, 1997), pp.407–30, 441–43, 516–22; Padfield, War beneath the sea, p.251; Rohwer, Chronology, pp.134, 138.
37 Rohwer, Chronology, pp.134–35.
38 Ibid.; Farrell, Defence and fall of Singapore, pp.293–313; Willmott, Empires in the balance, pp.310–35.
39 Gill, Royal Australian Navy 1939–1942, pp.517–21.
40 Along with the ships that moved from Singapore on 5 January, the Far Eastern Combined Bureau units left their Kranji base. While some of the 'Y' wireless interception units were assigned to ABDACOM on Java, the signals intelligence (SIGINT) group was sent in the first instance to the Indian Ocean naval headquarters at Colombo and later in April to Kilindini on the East African coast. Richard J. Aldrich, Intelligence and the war against Japan: Britain, America and the politics of secret service (Cambridge: CUP, 2000), p.236; Brian P. Farrell, 'Sir Geoffrey Layton', in Harrison (ed.), Oxford Dictionary of National Biography, Vol.32, pp.931–33; Farrell, Defence and fall of Singapore, pp.170–71, 283; Rohwer, Chronology, p.137.
41 An Allied force of four cruisers and seven destroyers sent by ABDACOM to the Makassar Strait was located and attacked by 37 bombers en route to Surabaya on 4 February with the result that two of the American cruisers (Marblehead and Houston) were badly damaged by hits and near misses. Rohwer, Chronology, p.140.
42 Two large tankers (Manvantara and Merula), a steamer (Subador) and many other smaller vessels were sunk and two transports (Anglo-Indian and Empire Star) and a tanker (Seirstad) were badly damaged by carrier aircraft from the Ryūjō, and the submarine I-55 also got into the act by sinking an ammunition transport (Derrymore) on the same day (13 February). Rohwer, Chronology, p.142.
43 Spector, Eagle against the sun, p.132
44 Rohwer, Chronology, p.142; Willmott, Empires in the balance, pp.297–302.
45 Willmott, Empires in the balance, pp.336–65; John Costello, The Pacific War (London: Collins, 1981), pp.160–202.
46 This raid claimed a host of victims. Apart from the US destroyer Peary, seven large transports and four smaller vessels were also sunk and damage was inflicted upon the Australian sloop HMAS Swan, an American aircraft tender and six large transports. Rohwer, Chronology, p.144.
47 Willmott, Empires in the balance, pp.302–9; Rohwer, Chronology, pp.141–42, 144–45; Spector, Eagle against the sun, pp.129–34.
48 In the confusing encounter that took place late at night on 19 February and in the early hours of 20 February two Allied naval forces under Doorman's command and consisting of the three light cruisers De Ruyter, Java and Tromp and eight destroyers intercepted a number of Japanese ships in the Bandoeng Strait which were withdrawing after offloading their troops on Bali. While hits were made on both sides, the action is probably best remembered for the poor execution of the Allied attacks. In the unsatisfactory mêlée that took place in the dark a Dutch destroyer Piet Hein

was sunk, the cruiser *Tromp* was badly damaged as was the US destroyer *Stewart*. For their part, the Japanese had a transport and two destroyers damaged (the *Michishio* seriously). In reviewing the action, Willmott is unsparing in his criticism of the failure of the Allied force to use its dominant position to better advantage. He has a point. Willmott, *Empires in the balance*, pp.307–8; Rohwer, *Chronology*, p.144.

49 A minor dispute exists over which of the Allied ships shelled *Asagumo*. Willmott and Costello believe it was *Electra;* Rohwer contends it was the light cruiser *Perth*; while Van Oosten and Grove are inclined to think the damage was caused by a destroyer with *Witte de With* being a prime candidate. Willmott, *Empires in the balance*, pp.349–50; Costello, *The Pacific War*, pp.202–10; Rohwer, *Chronology*, pp.147–48; Grove, *Sea battles in close-up, II*, pp.75–97; F.C. Van Oosten, *The battle of the Java Sea* (Annapolis, Md: NIP, 1976), p.51.

50 Willmott, *Empires in the balance*, pp.352–55; Rohwer, *Chronology*, p.148; Grove, *Sea battles in close-up, II*, pp.96–97.

51 Ibid., W.G. Winslow, *The ghost that died at Sunda Strait* (Annapolis, Md: NIP, 1984), pp.112–44.

52 Rohwer, *Chronology*, pp.148–49; Willmott, *Empires in the balance*, p.362.

53 MacArthur was allowed to delay his departure for a few days, but after more prodding from Washington in early March he finally left the Philippines and arrived in Australia on 17 March. D. Clayton James, *The years of MacArthur. Vol.II: 1941–1945* (Boston: Houghton Mifflin, 1975), pp.96–107; Willmott, *Empires in the balance*, pp.386–87.

54 Several excellent in-depth surveys of the extensive role played by the Royal Canadian Navy in the North Atlantic convoy system have been published over the past two decades. Apart from W.A.B. Douglas, Roger Sarty and Michael Whitby, *No higher purpose: the official history of the Royal Canadian Navy in the Second World War, 1939–1943. Vol.II, part 1* (St. Catherine's, Ont: Vanwell Publishing, 2002); see also the companion volumes written by Mark Milner, *North Atlantic run: the Royal Canadian Navy and the battle for the convoys* (Annapolis, Md: NIP, 1986) and *The U-boat hunters: the Royal Canadian Navy and the offensive against Germany's submarines* (Annapolis, Md: NIP, 1994); Roger Sarty, *The maritime defence of Canada* (Toronto: Canadian Institute of Strategic Studies, 1996); Brian Tennyson and Roger Sarty, *Guardian of the Gulf: Sydney, Cape Breton and the Atlantic wars* (Toronto: University of Toronto Press, 2000).

55 Under the terms of the Allied convoy agreement, fourteen USN and RCN task units were established and given responsibility to take HX and SC convoys from the WESTOMP (Western Ocean Meeting Point) to MOMP (Mid Ocean Meeting Point) where they would be taken over by any one of eight British escort groups for the passage to EASTOMP (East Ocean Meeting Point). In return the British would escort ON and ONS convoys from EASTOMP to MOMP, where they would be handed over to the American and Canadian groups who would proceed with them to WESTOMP. A further set of Canadian Western Local Escort Groups would escort all shipping in both directions between the Nova Scotian ports of Halifax and Sydney and WESTOMP. Rohwer, *Chronology*, pp.131–32; Milner, *North Atlantic run*, pp.90–95.

56 Sharing of intelligence between the Royal Navy and the USN was not all it could be in these years. In June 1941 the Americans had refused to allow the Admiralty to have any of the ECM Mark II enciphered teleprinter machines on the grounds that an existing agreement between the US Army and USN precluded their use unless they were operated by US officers. Unfortunately, production of the outstanding British secure cipher machine, the Mk.II Typex, was very slow and there were never sufficient numbers of these very complicated machines in Admiralty hands to equip all the ships of the Royal Navy for many months to come. As a result, the British were forced to introduce the Naval Cypher No.3 for supposedly secure communications with their allies and for organising convoys on the North Atlantic route.

German penetration of this new cipher began to yield fruit by December 1942 and in the following six months about 80% of all communications using this code (known as 'Frankfurt' to the Germans) were read by the B-Dienst operatives. Rohwer, *Chronology*, pp.79, 131; Ralph Erskine, 'The Admiralty and cipher machines during the Second World War: not so stupid after all', *The Journal of Intelligence History*, Vol.2 (Winter 2002): 49–68.

57 Milner, *Battle of the Atlantic*, p.85. In his magisterial two-volume work on the U-boat war, Blair confirms this tonnage figure as 6,149,473. Blair, Jr., *Hitler's U-boat war: hunters*, p.770, and Clay Blair, Jr., *Hitler's U-boat war: the hunted: 1942–1945* (New York, Random House, 1998), p.820.

58 Milner, *Battle of the Atlantic*, pp.83–104; Padfield, *Dönitz*, pp.236–47, 287–88; Hughes and Costello, *Battle of the Atlantic*, pp.190–207; Rohwer, *Chronology*, pp.134–35, 138, 142–43, 150, 152, 154, 158, 162, 169, 173. For an in-depth study of the U-boat campaign against the Americas from December 1941–August 1942, see Blair, Jr., *Hitler's U-boat war: hunters*, pp.431–700. For a gripping narrative of the same campaign, see Michael Gannon, *Operation drumbeat: the dramatic story of Germany's first U-boat attacks along the American coast in World War II* (New York: Harper Perennial, 1991).

59 Clay Blair Jr. indicates that Allied tanker losses in American waters in 1942 alone amounted to 142 ships and 1,073,283 tons. As he points out, tanker losses to Axis submarines in all waters in 1942 (213 ships and 1,667,505 tons) were such as to exceed the number of new tankers that had been built and were coming into service in the same period (92 tankers and 925,000 tons) by 121 ships and nearly three-quarters of a million tons. In the period from the beginning of the war in September 1939 to 31 December 1942, the Allied tanker fleet lost about 10% of its total. It would make up for this by a quite spectacular building programme in 1943. Blair, Jr., *Hitler's U-boat war: hunters*, pp.764–70.

60 In 1942 the German cryptologists began referring to the *Heimisch* code system as *Hydra*. At Bletchley Park it was known as *Dolphin*. Sebag-Montefiore, *Enigma*, pp.219–29.

61 Five freighters and one anti-submarine whaler from the convoy were sunk in this way, while the *Trinidad* and one of the destroyer escorts (*Eclipse*) were both heavily damaged in these exchanges. In the case of the *Trinidad* it was self-inflicted since she was hit by one of her own torpedoes! Losses were not confined solely to the Allies, however, as the Germans lost two of their U-boats and a destroyer to Allied reinforcements sent from Murmansk. Rohwer, *Chronology*, p.153; O'Hara, *German fleet at war*, pp.130–34; Woodman, *Arctic convoys 1941–1945*, pp.83–101; Schofield, *Arctic convoys*, pp.28–32.

62 Paul Kemp, *Convoy! Drama in Arctic waters* (London: Arms and Armour, 1993), pp.27–28; Rohwer, *Chronology*, p.134.

63 *Fuehrer conferences*, pp.255–64; Michael H. Coles, 'The Channel dash', in Robert Cowley (ed.), *No end save victory: perspectives on World War II* (New York: G.P. Putnam's Sons, 2001), pp.175–90.

64 Brown, *Radar history*, pp.224–28; Jefferson, *Coastal forces*, pp.121–25.

65 Lieutenant-Commander Esmonde, who led the attack of the six unprotected *Swordfish* torpedo planes on the German force, was posthumously awarded the Victoria Cross for gallantry, having pressed ahead with his attack in the face of the fiercest anti-aircraft fire. All six Swordfish were shot down in the attack. Barnett, *Engage the enemy*, pp.450–55; Hamer, *Bombers versus battleships*, pp.137–49; O'Hara, *German fleet at war*, pp.112–18.

66 Barnett, *Engage the enemy*, pp.444–55; Stephen, *Sea battles in close-up*, pp.115–36; John Deane Potter, *Fiasco: the break-out of the German battleships* (London: Heinemann, 1970); Garrett, *Scharnhorst and Gneisenau*, pp.86–118.

67 Stephen, *Sea battles in close-up*, p.134; F.H. Hinsley et al., *British intelligence in the Second World War. Vol.Two* (London: HMSO, 1981), pp.179–88.

68 Ibid.; Garrett, *Scharnhorst and Gneisenau*, pp.119–28.

69 Although radar had not been used by either side to any real effect in the 'Channel Dash', there could be little doubt that if operated properly it could be a tremendous asset to whichever side possessed the most advanced and durable of its many forms. One such use was in directing anti-aircraft (A.A.) fire by shore batteries against incoming flights. When photographic evidence confirmed the presence of a Würzburg radar facility that had been established by the Germans in an isolated house on a cliff-top at Bruneval on the Atlantic coast near Le Havre, R.V. Jones, the deputy director of Intelligence Research, persuaded Churchill and Mountbatten, the chief of Combined Operations Command, to carry out a Commando raid (Operation *Biting*) on the premises in order to steal some of its vital components. Parachuted in rather than brought ashore on the night of 27 February 1942, the Commandos executed a brilliant coup and returned home with vital parts of the Würzburg 50cm radar set for close study by Allied electronic engineers. Brown, *Radar history*, pp.229–31. For a full length treatment of this dramatic operation, see George Reid Millar, *The Bruneval Raid: stealing Hitler's radar* (London: Cassell's Military Paperbacks, 2002).
70 Simpson (ed.), *Cunningham papers, I*, pp.573–75, 585; Rohwer, *Chronology*, pp.143.
71 In a bid to ensure that the convoy route to Tobruk was clear of enemy submarines, seven Hunt class destroyer escorts left Alexandria ahead of convoy MW.10. *Heythrop* was torpedoed by *U652* off Salum (off the coast of northwest Egypt) at 1100 hours on 20 March four hours after convoy MW.10 had left port to begin its journey westward. Although taken in tow by *Eridge*, *Heythrop* was badly holed, took on too much water and sank at 1600 hours. Simpson (ed.), *Cunningham papers, I*, pp.584–85; Rohwer, *Chronology*, pp.152–53; Grove, *Sea battles in close-up, II*, pp.98–104.
72 Simpson (ed.), *Cunningham papers, I*, pp.460, 463–65, 585–92; Grove, *Sea battles in close-up, II*, pp.98–115.
73 According to Sadkovich, a solitary 120mm shell struck against the rear gangplank of the Italian battleship at precisely the same time as a muzzle flash from the *Littorio*'s own guns set alight fuel in her seaplane (the Ro.43). As a result of the smoke and flames that rose from the battleship immediately thereafter, the British could be excused for thinking that they had seriously damaged the *Littorio*. Sadkovich, *Italian Navy in World War II*, pp.244–45; Simpson, *Cunningham papers, I*, p.586; Greene and Massignani, *Naval war in the Mediterranean*, pp.216–22.
74 Vian was knighted for his role in this action. Barnett, *Engage the enemy*, p.502.
75 Simpson, *Cunningham papers, I*, pp.587–92; Sadkovich, *Italian Navy in World War II*, pp.242–46, 248, 285; Barnett, *Engage the enemy*, pp.496–503; Rohwer, *Chronology*, p.153.
76 It sought to do this with the faster, more manoeuvrable Spitfire rather than the lumbering Hurricane as the fighter aircraft of choice on Malta. Simpson (ed.), *Cunningham papers, I*, pp.465–72; Barnett, *Engage the enemy*, p.503; Rohwer, *Chronology*, pp.159, 163.
77 *Time*, 16 June 1961.
78 When King George VI bestowed the George Cross upon the island for its valiant endurance throughout the Second World War, the award was richly deserved. This award was announced by the Governor of Malta on 15 April 1942. Barnett, *Engage the enemy*, pp.491–526; Padfield, *War beneath beneath the sea*, p.226; Laddie Lucas, *Malta: the thorn in Rommel's side* (London: Stanley Paul, 1992), p.112.
79 Willmott, *Empires in the balance*, pp.422–24.
80 Ibid., pp.439–46; G. Hermon Gill, *Royal Australian Navy 1942–1945* (Sydney: Collins in association with the Australian War Memorial, 1985), pp.15–23.
81 Kiyoshi Ikeda, 'Vice Admiral Jisaburo Ozawa', in Howarth (ed.), *Men of war*, pp.278–92; Rohwer, *Chronology*, pp.154–55.
82 Ibid.; Hamer, *Bombers versus battleships*, pp.150–64.
83 While the British had been focusing on the raids carried out by Nagumo and Ozawa, the Japanese had also been pouring troops into Burma in an effort to shore

up their position in the capital city of Rangoon and extend their hold over the rest of the country. Forty-six transports carried the 18th Infantry Division from Singapore to Rangoon where they arrived safely on 7 April. Rohwer, *Chronology*, pp.155, 184; Willmott, *Empires in the balance*, p.445.

84 For sources on the St. Nazaire raid, see James G. Dorrian, *Storming St. Nazaire: the gripping story of the dock-busting raid March 1942* (London: Leo Cooper, 1998); John Laffin, *Raiders: great exploits of the Second World War* (Stroud, Glos: Sutton Publishing, 1999), pp.100–12; Jefferson, *Coastal forces*, pp.126–30; O'Hara, *German fleet at war*, pp.120–24; Scott, *Battle of the narrow seas*, pp.43–61. As for Malta, German bombers flew a record number of daylight and night-time sorties against the island in April (4,082 and 256 respectively). Barnett, *Engage the enemy*, pp.491–526; Rohwer, *Chronology*, p.156.

85 In the operations against Leningrad in April alone (*Fall Eisstoss* and *Fall Götz von Berlichingen*) the Germans flew 596 sorties against various targets in the city and during the same period Air Fleet 1 flew a total of 9,047 sorties in support of Army Group North. In flying all of these sorties, the Germans lost twenty-nine aircraft. While the raids hit the battleship *Oktyabrskaya Revolutsiya* four times and the cruiser *Maksim Gorkiy* seven times and seriously damaged the 180mm gun cruisers *Kirov* and *Petropavlovsk* and the destroyer *Silny*, the results were not as spectacular as the Germans would have hoped for. Rohwer, *Chronology*, p.157.

86 Ibid., p.158.

87 Woodman, *Arctic convoys 1941–1945*, pp.102–15; Schofield, *Arctic convoys*, pp.32–33.

88 Apart from the light cruiser *Edinburgh*, the Tribal destroyer *Punjabi*, the Polish submarine *P551/Jastrzab* (a victim of 'friendly fire') and four freighters were sunk and the battleships *King George V* and *Washington*, three destroyers (*Amazon*, *Foresight* and *Forester*) and a freighter were damaged. O'Hara, *German fleet at war*, pp.134–41; Woodman, *Arctic convoys 1941–1945*, pp.116–43; Schofield, *Arctic convoys*, pp.34–40; Rohwer, *Chronology*, pp.161–62.

89 H.P. Willmott, *The war with Japan: the period of balance. May 1942–October 1943* (Wilmington, Del: SR Books, 2002); Rohwer, *Chronology*, pp.159, 163.

90 Hayes, *History of the Joint Chiefs of Staff in World War II*, pp.96–103; Potter, *Nimitz*, pp.1–47.

91 Carroll V. Glines, *The Doolittle raid: America's daring first strike against Japan* (West Chester, Pa: Schiffer Military History, 1991); Ronald J. Drez, *Twenty-five yards of war: the extraordinary courage of ordinary men in World War II* (New York: Hyperion, 2001), pp.1–26.

92 Stephen Howarth, 'Admiral of the Fleet Isoroku Yamamoto', in Howarth (ed.), *Men of war*, pp.108–28.

93 Hiroyuki Agawa, *The reluctant admiral: Yamamoto and the Imperial Navy* (Tokyo: Kodansha International, 1982), pp.298–300; Edward Behr, *Hirohito: behind the myth* (New York: Vintage Books, 1990), pp.263–64; Gordon W. Prange, Donald M. Goldstein and Katherine V.Dillon, *Miracle at Midway* (New York: McGraw-Hill, 1982), pp.24–27; Donald M. Goldstein and Katherine V.Dillon (eds), *Fading victory: the diary of Admiral Matome Ugaki 1941–1945* (Pittsburgh, Pa: University of Pittsburgh Press, 1991), pp.98, 111–13

94 Prados, *Combined Fleet decoded*, pp.285–90, 293–94; Willmott, *Empires in the balance*, pp.447–50, 459–60; Edward P. Stafford, *The big E: the story of the USS Enterprise* (Annapolis, Md: NIP, 2002), pp.74–82; Edwin P. Hoyt, *Tojo against the world* (Lanham, Md: Scarborough House, 1993), pp.94–96, 98–99, 103, 109, 184, 214, 221.

95 Allaway, *Hero of the Upholder*, pp.163–74; Padfield, *War beneath the sea*, pp.225–27; Bernard Ireland, *The war in the Mediterranean 1940–1943* (London: Arms and Armour, 1993), p.122.

96 According to Bernard Lovell, however, the first U-boat to be detected by 10-centimetre radar on board a ship had been *U433* which had been found and subsequently sunk near Gibraltar by the corvette *Marigold* on 16 November 1941. Bernard Lovell,

Echoes of war: the story of H2S radar (Bristol: Adam Hilger, 1991), p.53; Rohwer, *Chronology*, pp.113, 159.
97 Rohwer, *Chronology*, p.155.
98 Huff-Duff was adapted from Robert Watson-Watt's device for gathering exact information on lightning strikes from across a range of frequencies. Instead of using an extensive band of frequencies for the pooling of this information, the revised HF/DF method sought messages being relayed on a single frequency. It was especially accurate on a low frequency and over short distances where there was less interference from atmospheric distortions. U-boats assembled in wolf packs were often engaged in relaying short messages to one another in order to coordinate their activities and HF/DF was excellent in detecting the existence of this type of message and pinpointing its exact location. When handled expertly, this device would become a boon to the convoy escort groups. Brown, *Radar history*, p.345. See also Kathleen Broome Williams, *Secret weapon: U.S. high frequency direction finding in the battle of the Atlantic* (Annapolis, Md: NIP, 1996).
99 Rohwer, *Chronology*, p.160.
100 Milner, *Battle of the Atlantic*, p.93.
101 Rohwer, *Chronology*, pp.161–62, 164, 167–69.
102 Ibid., pp.165–66; Milner, *Battle of the Atlantic*, pp.94–95; Doenitz, *Memoirs*, pp.221–24.
103 Rohwer, *Chronology*, p.161; Auphan and Mordal, *French Navy in World War II*, pp.203–6.

6 Stalling the juggernaut in the early summer of 1942

After the humiliation of the Doolittle Raid, the Japanese military high command wished to repay the insult by hitting the Americans where it would hurt most. Yamamoto, the architect of the Pearl Harbor attack, planned to bring this about by luring the US carrier fleet unsuspectingly into action before overwhelming it with a massive combination of firepower in which his own carrier planes, supported by both a significant number of capital ships and some of his submarine units, would participate. This was to be yet another of his stealthily and meticulously planned operations in which surprise was to be a key element. On this occasion, Yamamoto figured that if the Japanese went ashore on the two small US islands of Midway in the Central Pacific, some 1,135nm (2,102 km) northwest of Pearl Harbor, the Americans would not be able to help themselves.[1] They would be drawn to it like a moth to a flame.[2]

If Midway was to become the irresistible magnet to the US Navy in the near future, there were others in the Japanese naval command who felt that they could put some of their fleet to good use in the interim period by extending the degree and area of control that it was already exercising in Southeast Asia. Various options presented themselves, but after the successful foray into the Indian Ocean in early April, the Japanese looked for tempting targets that were not far from the Central Pacific where the fleet would be needed in early June for the forthcoming invasion of Midway. One of those possibilities was to do something to hinder Australia's continuing participation in the war effort. A full-scale invasion of Australia was ruled out because it would interfere with the planning that was being made for the Midway adventure, but an attack on the Allied naval base at Port Moresby, the largest port on the southeast coast of New Guinea, offered an inviting possibility. New Guinea was a sprawling and largely undeveloped island that lay wedged between Australia, the Solomon Islands and the Bismarck Archipelago. Taking Port Moresby out of the Allied strategic equation would therefore give the Japanese an active presence in the Coral Sea as well as help to jeopardise the smooth functioning of the supply chain across the South Pacific linking the Australian war effort with that of the Americans. As Martin Stephen and Eric Grove point out, however, the Japanese were almost addicted to complex plans and the important addendum to the Port Moresby operation (*MO*) would be an invasion of the Louisiade Archipelago and the islands of Santa Isabel and Tulagi in the southern Solomon group in order to establish advance air bases there that could be used in the ongoing battle for control over the entire Solomon chain.[3]

Support for these plans came through the confident, but ultimately mistaken, belief that the US Navy had only one carrier at its disposal close enough to intervene once the multifaceted operation had begun. While faulty intelligence may have afflicted the Japanese, the Americans enjoyed the singular advantage of having cracked the *Purple* diplomatic code used by the Imperial Japanese government to contact its embassies around the world and they could also read some of the other less demanding codes that were used for carrying routine administrative business. Their efforts to crack the most important of the codes used by the IJN, however, had been fraught with difficulties. *KO* – the code used for communication between flag officers and for communication at the highest levels between Admiral Yamamoto of the Combined Fleet and Admiral Nagano, the Chief of the Naval General Staff, in Tokyo – was phenomenally complex and the Americans never succeeded in breaking it. Fortunately for the Allies the Japanese themselves also found *KO* so difficult to operate that they finally abandoned it in favour of a less demanding code that wouldn't be so troublesome and error strewn to use. American cryptanalysts had far more success penetrating the mysteries of the *D* (better known as *JN25*) and later *RO* codes that were used to carry a fair amount of the IJN's operational traffic. Their work on the *JN25* code yielded significant fruit in April 1942 allowing them to read up to 20% of the signals traffic sent using this cipher.[4] From their analysis of the signals traffic and the messages that they could read, the Americans knew that an operation involving several carriers was being planned for the Southwest Pacific even though they did not know specifically which targets were going to be attacked. Even so, this intelligence windfall was sufficient for them to make an intelligent guess that the Japanese plan was likely to include an assault on Port Moresby. This presented Admiral Nimitz, CINCPAC, with his first opportunity to strike back against the Japanese since the attack on Pearl Harbor and he was determined not to let the chance slip. Orders were dispatched for the veteran fleet carrier *Lexington* and the modern, more manoeuvrable *Yorktown* (with a total combined complement of 143 aircraft), seven heavy cruisers, a light cruiser, thirteen destroyers, eleven submarines and two tankers to assemble west of Espiritu Santu (southeast of the Solomons) on 1 May under the overall command of Vice-Admiral Frank J. Fletcher.[5]

While the Americans orchestrated their plans to disrupt Operation *MO*, Vice-Admiral Shigeyoshi Inouye, the Japanese commander based in Rabaul, was given the two fleet carriers *Shokaku* and *Zuikaku*, the light carrier *Shōhō* (with a total of 174 aircraft and an additional twenty-four in reserve), six heavy cruisers, and a variety of other warships and support craft to complete the multiple tasks set for him by his superiors. He divided his surface forces into six distinct groups and dispatched them southward towards the four key objectives of the Louisiade Archipelago, Port Moresby, Santa Isabel and Tulagi.[6] Landings were made initially by some of the 3rd Kure Special Landing Force on Tulagi during 3 May.

News of this invasion caught the Allies completely by surprise and in a state of disarray. Refuelling difficulties had led to the carrier *Lexington* and her group (TF 11) being detached from the *Yorktown* and her group (TF 17). Moreover, Rear-Admiral J. Crace, at the head of the supporting TF 44, was still some hours away from rendezvousing with either group. Despite facing an extensive band of bad weather stretching due south from the Solomons, and learning from intelligence intercepts that a substantial invasion force was also on its way to Port Moresby, Fletcher controversially decided to mount a series of air strikes against Tulagi before doing anything else. *Yorktown* and TF 17 steamed north for several hours in filthy weather to reach a point about 100nm (185km) from Guadalcanal before Fletcher released his planes to make their attack on the enemy invasion fleet in the waters off Tulagi and to strike at the troops that had been put ashore on the island. By the time that the first of his three waves of carrier planes had reached the island after daybreak on 4 May, all the elite Japanese troops had been landed and most of the ships that had brought them there had been withdrawn from the landing sites. *Yorktown*'s planes bombed what they could find, but the results were modest and definitely not worth the great expenditure of fuel and bombs devoted to the enterprise or the risk Fletcher had taken in detaching TF 17 from the other Allied task forces in order to put his carrier planes within reach of Tulagi.[7] He was fortunate that Rear-Admiral Aritomo Gotō's Covering Force, including *Shōhō*, was too far away to interfere with TF 17 and that Vice-Admiral Takeo Takagi's Carrier Striking Force, with its two large carriers, was refuelling at this time or else his dubious initiative could have ended up in bringing swift and massive retribution from the Japanese.[8]

Once this unsatisfactory diversion was over, Fletcher sped south again to join the rest of the Allied task force that had congregated some 300nm (556km) south of Guadalcanal early on the morning of 5 May. After being refuelled at sea by their two tankers, the ships of TF 17 and TF 44 entered the Coral Sea at 1930 hours and headed northwest towards the Jomard Passage, which Fletcher believed would be the route used by the invasion fleet bound for Port Moresby. Next day (6 May) was an especially frustrating one for both the combined Allied Task Force (now officially unveiled as TF 17) and their Japanese adversaries. A combination of bad weather and poor visibility managed to keep both sets of carrier forces from discovering the presence of one another even though at times the enemies were only as little as 70nm (130km) apart. As one of his tankers, *Neosho*, was low on fuel and had done its job, Fletcher decided to send her and the fleet destroyer, *Sims*, southward out of harm's way. Unfortunately, this deployment sent the two ships into a veritable hornet's nest from which there would be no escape on the following day.[9]

When dawn broke on 7 May Rear-Admiral Chuichi Hara, in command of the Japanese Carrier Striking Force, prevailed upon Takagi, his superior officer, to cruise south once more and renew aerial surveillance sweeps of the Coral Sea. At 0730 hours a report came in from one of the pilots that caused much commotion on the decks and in the hangars of *Shokaku* and *Zuikaku*, since it claimed to have discovered an enemy carrier accompanied by a heavy cruiser. Hara assumed the report was correct and sent off seventy-eight planes to bomb the life out of what were actually the *Neosho* and the *Sims*. By an extraordinary coincidence at exactly the same time as the Japanese carrier planes took off for their appointment with the Allied tanker and destroyer, Crace's force of three cruisers and three destroyers that Fletcher had earlier sent towards the Jomard Passage was spotted by another reconnaissance plane and their position was passed on to Inouye at Rabaul. As Crace braced himself for a hostile assault by Japanese shore-based aircraft, he had to endure a fairly torrid encounter with a force of the USAAF's B-26s who mistook him for the Port Moresby Invasion Force and attempted to obliterate both him and his ships. Only great ship handling by Crace and his other captains averted a disaster from occurring. As it was, his flagship, the HMAS heavy cruiser *Australia*, was straddled and the heavy cruiser *Chicago* and the destroyer *Perkins* received near-misses from what was poignantly referred to as 'friendly fire'.[10] While Crace was living on his wits, Inouye ordered the invasion fleet to reverse course until the Allied ships had been forcefully put out of commission.

While this was going on to the northwest of him, Fletcher's task force was moving due north towards the Louisiade Archipelago. Aerial reconnaissance gave him a fix on Rear-Admiral Kuninori Marumo's Support Force some 235nm (435km) to the northwest of him at 0815 hours. Unfortunately, Marumo's ships (the two old light cruisers *Tatsuta* and *Tenryū*, an aircraft depot ship and three gunboats) were mistakenly reported as two carriers and four cruisers! Fletcher erroneously assumed, therefore, that he had found Takagi's Carrier Striking Force and busied himself with preparations for a major strike against it using ninety-three carrier planes from both the *Lexington* and the *Yorktown* to swarm down upon them. At 0830 hours, however, a Japanese reconnaissance plane also sighted Fletcher's TF 17. Thereafter the race was on to see which of the two sides could exploit the opportunity the most. Within two hours, however, Fletcher received the discomforting news that far from finding *Shokaku* and the *Zuikaku*, his planes were homing in on a much less distinguished quarry. But luck was with Fletcher, as it had been on several occasions in the recent past, and quite by accident the pilot in the leading Dauntless dive bomber, already off course, managed to stumble across Gotō's Covering Force off Misima Island at 1022 hours. He quickly spread the word of his discovery. Once the US carrier planes had gathered over the target area they attacked the light carrier *Shōhō* in three waves. Unable to launch many of her planes because they were refuelling, *Shōhō* could only hope for a miracle of deliverance. It was not to come. Five planes were blown off her deck in the first wave of low-level attacks and subsequent ones riddled her with thirteen bombs and seven torpedoes to wipe her out by 1135 hours. As the Americans celebrated the sinking of the first enemy carrier for the loss of only three of their own planes, news came in that the Japanese had exacted a measure of revenge by bombing and disabling the *Neosho* and breaking the back of the *Sims* before she sank in short order shortly after midday.[11]

After taking stock of the situation, Takagi sent fifteen of his 'Kate' torpedo-bombers and twelve 'Val' dive-bombers aloft at 1630 hours in a renewed bid to find the enemy's task force. Fletcher for once exercised caution and restraint and allowed another tropical squall to cloak his presence. It did so most effectively. Takagi's experienced pilots couldn't spot the ships of TF 17 and were returning empty-handed from their mission when they were picked up on the *Yorktown*'s radar screen at 1800 hours. Fletcher instantly scrambled his Wildcat fighter planes and in the ensuing dogfight seven 'Kates' and one 'Val' were downed for the loss of three Wildcats. About an hour later in an almost comical aftermath to this mission three of the Japanese planes, with neither radar nor homing beacons to assist them, found the *Yorktown* in the gloom and mistakenly identified her as one of their own and attempted to land on her before they were driven off by A. A. fire. Thereafter the night closed in and both forces steaming in opposite directions waited for the dawn of a new day before trying anything else.[12]

Few doubted that battle would be joined between the two forces once daylight returned. Seven 'Kates' were sent off southward to look for the American carriers at 0600 hours on 8 May and the Americans, being more uncertain as to the whereabouts of the Japanese, committed eighteen Dauntlesses to a 360-degree search at 0625 hours. Although the Japanese aircraft had taken to the skies earlier than the Americans, each side was to discover the existence of the other's fleet at almost exactly the same time. At 0820 hours the Americans issued their first sighting report of the Carrier Striking Force, but within two minutes one of the Japanese 'Kates' was to report the location of TF 17 – so neither side was able to gain an initial advantage over the other. Although the American sighting report had been somewhat garbled and a subsequent one was both incomplete and inaccurate, the Americans readied eighty-five planes for launch from the *Lexington* and *Yorktown* and eventually cleared them for take-off at 0907 hours. They had an eight-minute start on the sixty-nine Japanese aircraft committed to the attack from the *Shokaku* and *Zuikaku*.[13]

Hara's decision to divide his forces into two separate squadrons rather than keep them concentrated in one group meant that when the American dive bombers fortuitously spotted both groups for the first time at 1030 hours they were already 8nm (15km) apart. Thereafter yet another spell of poor weather was to put in a decisive appearance, as the distance between the two squadrons grew ever larger. By the time that the 'Devastator' torpedo bombers joined their dive-bombing brethren and began the first wave of attacks at 1057 hours, a sudden rain squall and a bank of thick clouds had managed to envelop the *Zuikaku* and her two recently acquired heavy cruiser escorts, *Furutaka* and *Kinugasa*, hiding them from their foes. Unfortunately for the *Shokaku* and her minders, the heavy cruisers *Haguro* and *Myokō*, there was a gap in the weather front and they lay exposed to aerial scrutiny. While the 'Devastators' from the *Yorktown* operating with deficient torpedoes failed to make any impression on the Japanese squadron, the Dauntless dive-bombers, and Lieutenant John Powers in particular, found the target. Powers perished in the attempt, but his 1,000-pound (454-kilo) bomb released at an altitude of only 200 feet (61 metres) smashed into the starboard side of the *Shokaku* in the anchor windlass room close to her bow and started a massive aviation gas fire that looked actually worse than it was. Despite all the attention she was receiving from the Americans, *Shokaku* still managed to evade most of the punishment that was being meted out to her. *Lexington*'s planes which had gathered over the scene later than the *Yorktown*'s had no greater success. After both waves of attacks were over the *Shokaku*, though hit a total of three times and receiving numerous other near-misses, was still very much in existence. Nonetheless, because her arrester gear had been damaged, she couldn't use her flight deck either to launch planes or to allow them to land on her. Unable to perform as a carrier any longer, she was ordered by Hara to transfer the bulk of her remaining aircraft to the *Zuikaku*, after which *Shokaku* left the scene at 1300 hours accompanied by her two heavy cruisers and two destroyer escorts for the island of Truk in Micronesia and onward to the naval repair base at Kure on the main Japanese island of Honshū. Although the *Shokaku* had not been dramatically sunk, the Americans had still forced her to retire from operational duty for several months, a point of great significance both at Midway and in the weeks thereafter when the existence of such a modern carrier and a host of her experienced pilots lost in the Battle of the Coral Sea would have been vital to the Japanese cause.[14]

At least *Shokaku* structurally survived the battle more or less in one piece. *Lexington* did not. She was in trouble from the time that two 'Kate' bombers breached her defences and torpedoes struck her port side almost simultaneously at 1120 hours. Within five minutes she was struck again as a 120-pound (54-kilo) bomb from one of the 'Val' dive-bombers struck her on the port bow igniting an ammunition box and burning some crew members alive and a second 500-pound (227-kilo) bomb smashed home close to her funnel resulting in even more casualties, as well as putting four pairs of guns out of action, and causing some minor flooding and damage to three of her boiler rooms and berthing spaces. Another bomb's near miss had weakened some of her hull plates and inflicted yet more casualties on board the carrier. At the end of these skirmishes, with her siren jammed on and emitting a hysterical screech, the *Lexington* had developed a 7° list to port. Despite the blows she had taken, the 43,055-ton carrier seemed capable of withstanding the punishment she had received. What wasn't appreciated at the time, however, was that some of the aviation fuel lines had been ruptured in absorbing these attacks and a dangerous accumulation of highly volatile and inflammable fumes had begun to seep throughout the bowels of the ship. A random spark from a motor generator did the rest. A massive and crippling explosion shook the *Lexington* from stem to stern at 1247 hours. It was the beginning of the end for her. Although she was capable of making 25 knots and her planes were still being recovered and flown off for another two and a half hours, the fires on board the carrier steadily grew worse and in the end became uncontrollable so that by 1630 hours she lay dead in the water. At 1707 hours the order was given to abandon ship and 2,735 officers and crew were expeditiously evacuated before her store of torpedoes blew up at 1830 hours and she was finally put out of her misery by the five torpedoes put into her by the destroyer *Phelps* at 1952 hours.[15]

Yorktown did not suffer the same fate as her older partner had done. Lighter at 25,500-tons and with a turning circle of 1,000 yards (914 metres) as distinct from the 1,650 yards (1509 metres) required by the *Lexington*, the *Yorktown* managed, by good ship-handling, to avoid all the torpedoes that were aimed at her and to be hit by only one 500-pound bomb which ploughed through three decks before exploding in a fiery ball on the fourth killing thirty-seven crew members and injuring thirty-three others as it did so. Damage control parties quickly extinguished the fire that had been started and flying operations were never seriously interrupted thereafter. As a result, the carrier was on hand to receive nineteen planes from the stricken *Lexington* before being ordered by Admiral Nimitz at Pearl Harbor to leave the Coral Sea. Before she did so, two cruisers and three destroyers were deployed to organise the evacuation of *Lexington*'s officers and crew once the call for them to abandon ship had been made in the late afternoon.[16]

This action brought the Battle of the Coral Sea to an end. It was the first occasion when a battle at sea was fought entirely by aircraft and without a warship on both sides either catching a glimpse of, let alone firing at, an enemy vessel. As a result of these aerial jousts, a total of ninety-two Japanese planes and sixty-six American carrier aircraft were destroyed. While claims from both sides of even greater destruction proved ultimately to be unfounded, the losses of such a large number of experienced aircrew were more than enough to hamper the activities of the *Zuikaku* and ensure that she was not present at Midway in June. In deciding to postpone the planned invasion of Port Moresby intended for 10 May until 3 July, and to call upon Takagi's Carrier Striking Force to withdraw from the area, Vice-Admiral Inouye failed to exploit the favourable situation that his pilots had gained for him at such great cost to themselves. His reluctance to pursue the Americans at sea or to put his invasion force in harm's way from land-based enemy aircraft was such as to convince many military historians that this whole series of encounters must be regarded as a tactical defeat and yet a strategic victory for the Americans. Such a juxtaposition of results seems odd until one looks beyond the Coral Sea to the forces engaged in and the decisive nature of the Battle for Midway that Admiral Yamamoto had set his heart upon and which could not be long delayed.[17]

There was to be a most inconclusive naval coda to Operation *MO* when Yamamoto, despairing of Inouye's caution, overruled his subordinate's orders at midnight on 8 May, forcing Takagi's ships to reverse course yet again and steam deeper into the Coral Sea on what proved to be a fruitless thirty-six-hour quest to catch and annihilate what was left of the Allied fleet. Had these orders been issued at lunchtime that day rather than at midnight the Battle of the Coral Sea might well have ended in the most crushing of defeats for the Allied and American cause. As it was, however, the Japanese did not press home their advantage quickly enough to catch and destroy their enemy. On 10 May Yamamoto, realising that his quarry had evaded him, made the decision to abandon Takagi's mission and bring his ships back to Rabaul.[18] Operation *MO* was therefore a rather unsatisfactory affair for both sides. While both of the protagonists gained something from the experience, each lost heavily too. Although the results judged from a purely quantitative perspective suggest a modest Japanese victory, it was far from being an emphatic one. Moreover, from a psychological point of view, it could be said to have been a blow to their self-esteem. After all, this was the first occasion when they were denied a major territorial objective – in this case Port Moresby – which they had set themselves. Whether it was sensible for them to have set themselves this objective in the first place is, of course, a moot point. One suspects that they went for Port Moresby much in the way that George Mallory explained his desire to conquer Everest in the 1920s: 'Because it is there.'[19] Port Moresby might have been there but it was no territorial or strategic Everest. It would have been useful to have – particularly in assisting in the final conquest of the Solomons and for new sorties they might wish to make further into the South Pacific – but it was not vital to the Japanese cause at this time. It could have been mopped up once Operation *MI* at Midway was over. Nonetheless, the Japanese adopted *MO* when they did because they confidently assumed that they would succeed in the venture and that they would not suffer the substantial casualties in both human and material resources that they eventually did. So overconfidence in themselves and an underestimation of their enemy may have gone hand in hand to thwart them.

The month of May also brought more news of a troubling nature for the Allies from three distinct European locations. As the Soviet position on the Kerch Peninsula crumbled under a determined assault from the German 11th Army, the siege of Sevastopol was intensified and the task of re-supplying the city and naval base from beyond the Crimea became an even more arduous one for the Soviet Navy.[20] There was to be no respite from the Arctic either as reports were received that one of Raeder's heavy ships, the *Admiral Scheer*, was to be transferred to Narvik and she would be joined there in the middle of the month by the heavy cruiser *Lützow* – a replacement for the damaged *Prinz Eugen*. These deployments would pose a grave threat to the supply convoys that sailed through these hazardous waters en route to or from Murmansk and Archangel.[21] Ominous in the Black Sea, threatening in the Arctic Circle, the situation wasn't any more reassuring in the Mediterranean where a series of Ju-88 attacks on 11 May managed to sink three more of the Mediterranean Fleet's already depleted force of destroyers. These losses complicated the role of the Mediterranean Fleet still further, restricting its ability to fulfil the range of tasks assigned to it and making it into even more of a local rather than regional force.[22]

Important though these conflicts were in Europe, the campaign in the Pacific was about to enter a critical phase. Yamamoto was convinced that the war could not be won in this theatre unless the US carrier fleet was decimated in a fleet action. His plan to bring this scenario about (Operation *MI*) was immensely detailed and logistically convoluted – a complex and sophisticated kind of *Schlieffen Plan* at sea. Unfortunately for the Japanese IGHQ, *MI* shared some of the original German plan's limitations in that it failed to provide much or any leeway for human error and unpredictability once the operation was underway – a serious shortcoming that would come back to haunt Yamamoto as *MI* unfolded. While the comparison may be pushed too far, there is little doubt that in hindsight *MI* would have been far more suitable as a rigorous theoretical exercise rather than implemented as the operational imperative on which the fate of the IJN would rest. Once again, however, the margin between success and failure over Midway was narrow. It could have gone the other way. Defeat could have been turned into victory and vice versa had some of the classic variables, such as luck and the human dimension, behaved differently. Disaster was neither pre-ordained for the Japanese, nor was a stunning victory guaranteed for the Americans.[23]

What has often been referred to as a diversionary feint into the Aleutians – Operation *AL* – was in fact anything but the crucial operational precursor to the launching of *MI* and its ultimate success that many historians have claimed it to be. On the contrary, as Parshall and Tully indicate, the plan was foisted upon Yamamoto and was meant to be launched concurrently with the attack on Midway. Rather than drawing off a substantial proportion of the USN from Pearl Harbor, Parshall and Tully claim that it was nothing more than an 'expedient landgrab' and that Yamamoto was far from convinced that news of it would lure the Pacific Fleet northwards rather than westwards.[24] What Yamamoto didn't know was that the American cryptanalysts at Station HYPO (later known as Fleet Radio Unit, Pacific: FRUPac) on Oahu in Hawaii were having some success in cracking part of the Japanese naval code JN25b and that Commander Joseph Rochefort was therefore in a position to figure out in advance what Yamamoto was planning to do and the approximate size and composition of the forces that he would be devoting to the cause.[25] Rochefort duly informed Nimitz that the main focus of enemy activity in the Pacific would soon be focussed upon Midway. This priceless information allowed Nimitz time and opportunity to prepare an appropriate and timely response to *MI*, while largely ignoring the attack on Dutch Harbor and the actual occupation of the islands of Adak, Attu and Kiska in the Aleutian chain (*AL*).[26]

Yamamoto was blissfully unaware that the secrecy of the Japanese plans had been compromised when Rear-Admiral Kakuji Kakuta took the carriers *Jun'yō* and *Ryūjō*, the heavy cruisers *Maya* and *Takao*, three destroyers and a tanker out of Ominato harbour in Hokkaido on 25 May and set forth on their northern sortie to attack Dutch Harbor. As they embarked on their limited quest, reconnaissance of the Aleutian Islands by the craft of the 1st Submarine Flotilla was actually taking place. This revealed that Kakuta's targets were as vulnerable as the Japanese naval planning staff had imagined that they were. At this stage, therefore, the signs looked propitious for both *AL* and *MI* so Vice-Admiral Chuichi Nagumo was encouraged to leave Hashirajima Bay on the Inland Sea a day later and set out for the attack on Midway. He took with him the four carriers *Akagi*, *Hiryū*, *Kaga* and *Sōryū*, mustering a total of 72 dive-bombers, 81 torpedo-bombers, 72 fighters and some reserves between them, the two battleships *Haruna* and *Kirishima*, the two heavy cruisers *Chikuma* and *Tone*, the light cruiser, *Nagara*, twelve destroyers and five tankers. This fleet was obviously the cutting edge of *MI*.[27] It was expected to stay well to the north of Midway and use its planes to soften up the defences of the two small US islands before turning to engage whatever carrier strength the Americans sent against them.[28]

Following Kakuta's lead, Rear-Admiral Sentaro Omori and Captain Takeji Ohno left Ominato a couple of days later with two relatively lightweight forces and a total of 2,450 troops earmarked for the invasion of Attu, Adak and Kiska. Both groups were covered by another modest set of escorting warships under the command of Vice-Admiral Boshiro Hosogaya on his flagship the heavy cruiser *Nachi*. On the same day (27 May), three distinct escort groups – a destroyer flotilla under Rear-Admiral Raizo Tanaka; a seaplane force led by Rear-Admiral Ruitaro Fujita; and a minesweeping unit led by Captain Miyamoto – shepherded the occupation fleet of twelve transports, three fast assault boats, a solitary tanker and 5,000 troops out of Saipan in the Marianas on their northeastern run to Midway. As these ships cleared harbour so Rear-Admiral Takeo Kurita set out from Guam to cover the entire group with four heavy cruisers, two more destroyers, and a tanker.[29]

Although the Japanese had already committed an impressive armada of vessels to *MI* and *AL*, there was far more to come. Vice-Admiral Nobutake Kondo oversaw the next phase of the Midway operation when he left Hashirajima Bay on 28 May with the light carrier *Zuihō*, supported by two battleships, five cruisers and eight destroyers. Admiral Yamamoto himself followed with the training carrier *Hōshō*; three more battleships in the shape of *Mutsu*, *Nagato* and the massive *Yamato*; the seaplane carrier *Chiyoda*, which was assuming the role as a midget submarine mother ship; a light cruiser; nine destroyers; and two tankers. To round off matters Vice-Admiral Shira Takasu set out from the Inland Sea for the Aleutians on 28 May taking with him four more battleships, two light cruisers, twelve destroyers and two tankers as he went. In total, therefore, the Japanese had committed virtually their entire fleet to these two interlinked operations. It was a huge risk for them to take. Would it be worth it?[30]

To meet this formidable challenge, Nimitz selected Rear-Admiral Raymond A. Spruance to lead Task Force 16 in the absence of the hospitalised Vice-Admiral William 'Bull' Halsey and invited Rear-Admiral Frank 'Black Shoe' Fletcher to return as head of Task Force 17 to finish the job he had started in the Coral Sea. By virtue of being the senior admiral, Fletcher was placed in overall and tactical command of the operation even though Spruance had the stronger carrier task force with him.[31] On the same day that Yamashita and Kondo left Japan to steam to their pre-assigned positions northwest of Midway (28 May), Spruance left Pearl Harbor for a position to the northeast of the same island – Point Luck – taking his two carriers, *Enterprise* and *Hornet*, five heavy cruisers, the A.A. cruiser *Atlanta*, eleven destroyers and two tankers with him as he cleared the island of Oahu and moved out into the Central Pacific. A couple of days later Fletcher followed bringing with him the battered carrier *Yorktown*, amazingly restored in record time by the repair crews in Hawaii, two heavy cruisers and six destroyers.[32]

Paradoxically, the focus of all this firepower, Midway, was a disappointingly small landfall a mere six miles (9.7km) in diameter. In itself it was nothing, but its sovereignty and geographical position gave Midway its importance and led to it becoming unarguably the most crucial test of strength between the Americans and the Japanese of the entire war. After the Battle of the Coral Sea and armed with accurate intelligence of the Japanese battle plans, Midway had been reinforced by the Americans in recent weeks. Apart from having more than 3,000 troops to defend it against an amphibious invasion, Midway's main strategic importance lay in its triangular airstrip which was home to a mixed assortment of 110 aircraft ranging from B-17 Flying Fortresses to Catalina flying boats. While most of these aircraft were hardly state-of-the-art planes, they were a useful supplement to the carrier planes that Fletcher and Spruance were bringing from Pearl Harbor. Although the Japanese had a decided numerical and qualitative advantage in terms of warships and possessed the better planes and torpedoes (and some critics would say the better pilots too), the Americans did have two vital assets – radar and the windfall of SIGINT – that gave them the ability to detect the Japanese when they least expected it. This was to prove to be a priceless combination that more than made up for their other hardware and technical deficiencies.[33]

Apart from the Aleutian operation (*AL*), which the Americans had known all about in advance, Yamamoto had hoped to wreck part of the US Navy's response to the invasion of Midway by establishing the first of a series of three lines of Japanese submarines between Oahu and Midway from 30 May onwards. Even if these submarines didn't sink any of the American vessels that were being sent to counter the Japanese attack, they would be expected to provide early warning of the size, composition and location of the warships that Nimitz had dispatched to the Central Pacific. Unfortunately, for Yamamoto they were not even to provide the most basic of assistance. All were established too late – even the first one was set up well after the Americans had cleared Oahu. By the time the fourteen submarines slated for the second and third patrol lines had arrived in place on 4 June, the battle for Midway had already begun. Although Rear-Admiral Charles Lockwood had the American submarines deployed in time for the operation, they too became bystanders in what became a major engagement at sea.[34]

In avoiding the submarine trap that was being prepared for them and steering a wide berth from those islands that the Japanese sought to use as flying boat operation centres, such as French Frigate Shoal and Lisianski Island, the two American task forces rendezvoused unbeknown to the Japanese forces at Point Luck some 325nm (602km) northeast from Midway on 2 June. While they had circumvented the best laid enemy plans, the Americans were not in a position to benefit substantially from these advantages since neither the reinforcements (the two battleships *Colorado* and *Maryland*, and three destroyers) sent from San Francisco on 31 May, nor the carrier *Saratoga*, which was only ready to leave San Diego on 1 June, reached the Central Pacific in time to become engaged in the battle for Midway. Nonetheless, the Americans knew the Japanese carrier fleet was on its way and had a decent idea as to the general direction that the strike force was likely to be coming from. They had time on their hands and could afford to wait for the enemy warships to come to them.[35]

Next day, 3 June, Operation *AL*, the oft-described diversionary hors d'oeuvre to *MI*, went into high gear with an attack by Kakuta's forces on Dutch Harbor.

Anticipating this ploy, Nimitz steadfastly refused to take the bait offered him by the Japanese C-in-C relying instead upon Rear-Admiral Robert Theobald's reinforced Task Force 8, consisting of the two heavy cruisers *Indianapolis* and *Louisville*, three light cruisers and fourteen destroyers, formed south of Kodiak Island to cope with the threat to the Aleutians. As such, Kakuta's two carriers *Jun'yō* and *Ryūjō* would have been far more useful to the Japanese cause if they had been deployed in the Central Pacific rather than up in the Aleutian chain where their presence only caused disquiet to the local population and actually did nothing to improve their chances of victory much further south where the real action was going to take place.[36]

Even before the Japanese had begun to show their flag aggressively in Aleutian waters, an initial sighting of the Japanese minesweeping group was made by an American Catalina flying boat operating out of Midway at 0904 hours on 3 June. Another Catalina soon discovered Tanaka's main invasion fleet when it was still 600nm (1,111km) from Midway and shadowed it for some time thereafter. Yamamoto could not fail to know that the essential element of the Midway operation – surprise – had been lost even before *MI* had begun in earnest. Although some might have seen it as an unlucky coincidence that the first reconnaissance aircraft had appeared over the vanguard of his invasion fleet, the second Catalina's presence and her dogged stalking of the fleet shortly thereafter could not be explained away. Clearly, the Americans would be receiving detailed messages as to the size, location and course of Tanaka's fleet from either the first or the second Catalina or from both. Worse still, his own signals intelligence alerted Yamamoto to the likelihood that a group of Lockwood's submarines would be lying in wait for Tanaka's transports and landing craft in the Central Pacific.[37] As none of these unwelcome developments had appeared in his cherished *MI* plan beforehand, contingencies for dealing with them would have to be improvised on the spot – not one of the great strengths of the Japanese military mindset. Whatever Yamamoto decided to do, however, it was obvious that Midway was destined not to be another Pearl Harbor. Despite the fact that his cover had been irretrievably blown, Yamamoto still pressed on with the operation. Whether this was a courageous or foolhardy act, or something in between, the decision reveals him as a self-assured man of action and one who presumably felt, in the last analysis, that the risks of proceeding were justifiable. This degree of self confidence on an issue as momentous as the immediate future of the IJN, and possibly even the fate of the entire Pacific war, is amazing and must have stemmed in large part from the huge advantages he possessed in fleet size and composition over those of his American opponents, regardless of whether they were deployed to meet him or not.

Tanaka's invasion fleet was attacked for the first time from a height of between 8,000–12,000 feet (2,438–3,658 metres) by nine B-17 bombers from Midway in the late afternoon (somewhere between 1623–40 hours) on 3 June. No hits were recorded on any of the Japanese vessels even though several claims were made subsequently by the US Army pilots that a range of important warships had been struck. Shortly after midnight, four Catalina flying boats, equipped with torpedoes, attacked the force once again but only succeeded in hitting the tanker *Akebono Maru* in the bow without disabling her or reducing the speed of the convoy which continued towards its objective at 19 knots. Reports of these engagements underlined both the invaluable nature and accuracy of the intelligence reports Fletcher and Spruance had been receiving about Japanese intentions in the recent past. It enabled them to identify Tanaka's forces as merely the operational spearhead and predict that the real striking force of the Japanese fleet would lie behind the invasion forces. It was with this in mind that Fletcher signalled his intention of steaming to intercept the Japanese carriers. It now became a question of who would find one another first.[38]

According to the *MI* plan, once Nagumo's force came within striking range of Midway, he would send in wave after wave of carrier-based bombers to soften up the island's defences before turning to intercept the American carriers that were expected to be sent against them. Beginning at about 0430 hours on 4 June, therefore, 108 aircraft (72 bombers and 36 fighters) took off from the decks of Nagumo's four carriers (*Akagi*, *Hiryū*, *Kaga* and *Sōryū*), in a bid to wreck both the aerial and ground defences of the two islands. Although a Catalina reconnaissance plane piloted by Howard Ady was the first to report the presence of Japanese carriers at 0534 hours, and another Catalina plane with William Chase at the controls stumbled across a host of enemy aircraft heading in Fletcher's direction at 0540, US forces radar on Midway only picked up the incoming Japanese formations at a distance of 93 miles (150km) some thirteen minutes later. While the Americans scrambled to get their own planes airborne before the enemy bombers appeared over the island's runways and airbase within the course of the next hour, Fletcher, some 240nm (445km) to the north of Midway, only knew the exact position of these warships – some 200nm (370km) west-southwest of his own flagship *Yorktown* at 0603. Unwilling to delay a moment longer than necessary, Fletcher opted to divide his forces and sent Spruance off with his two carriers, *Enterprise* and *Hornet*, to attack Nagumo's ships, while he sought to recover all ten of his reconnaissance aircraft before setting off in swift pursuit of his deputy. Spruance would be joined in this venture by a mixed force of American bombers that had hurriedly taken off from Midway before the swarm of Japanese 'Kates' and 'Vals' hove into view. Twenty ageing fighter aircraft and seven fixed-wing Wildcat fighters were left behind in the skies above Midway in order to cope with the incoming attack. They were not a match for the Japanese 'Zeros' and by the end of the raid only three survived.[39]

Despite their success in this aspect of the operation, the rest of the attack was anti-climactic for the Japanese. They lost fourteen of their own carrier planes – mostly to ground based A.A. fire – while failing to destroy either the key primary targets – the American bombers – or the secondary ones – the vital defence installations of these two small strips of US territory.[40] In a report to Nagumo from the sky above Midway, the flight leader, Lieutenant Jōichi Tomonaga, indicated that while some destruction of the airfield's base facilities had indeed taken place, the scale of the damage had not been sufficient to rule out its immediate use by American aircraft if the need presented itself. Tomonaga therefore urged Nagumo to send in a second wave of bombers to finish the job properly.[41] This was not the news that Nagumo wished to hear. He had already chosen controversially to have a second wave of aircraft sitting on his flight decks primed for launching against enemy carriers if they were detected by his reconnaissance planes, but none of them were equipped with the right type of bomb for attacking ground-based targets on Midway. As he agonised about what to do for the best – whether to rearm his bombers to have another go at Midway or to leave them just in case the American carriers were spotted – the first ten of the Midway-based torpedo-bombers planes appeared from over the horizon at 0705 hours and commenced their bombing raids of his warships. Although no hits were recorded and the Americans lost seven of their aircraft to a combination of lethal fighter protection and punishing A.A. fire, the bombing raid had convinced the prudent Nagumo that Tomonaga's wish should be fulfilled. Midway would have to be bombed to eliminate this kind of attack in future. At 0715 hours he ordered the 'Kates' on the carriers *Akagi* and *Kaga* to offload their torpedoes and be rearmed with heavy bombs suitable for a second strike on the runway, fuel tanks and other ground facilities on Midway.[42] They had barely started on this time consuming and laborious task when Nagumo received a most disconcerting message from one of his seaplanes whose reconnaissance mission had been initially delayed by a malfunctioning catapult on board the heavy cruiser *Tone*. Searching belatedly in the eastern sector, the 'Jake' reported at 0728 hours that he had spotted ten enemy surface ships some 240nm (445km) from Midway, proceeding at more than 20 knots on a course and bearing that brought them very much into the reckoning and particularly if any of those vessels were carriers. Without more specific information at his disposal, however, Nagumo wavered not really knowing what to do for the best. If the American force contained carriers, he would have to attack them before they found him. If it didn't he would have sufficient time to send off his planes on a second mission to Midway, while recovering those from the first strike and rearming them with torpedoes to engage the surface fleet that was closing on his Carrier Fleet. It was a matter of timing.[43] As he waited anxiously for the 'Jake' to identify the nature of that enemy force, Nagumo ordered those of his torpedo-bombers that had not been rearmed to attack the American ships regardless of whether they contained carriers or not. Before he could send them off, however, sixteen Dauntless dive-bombers emerged from Midway to complicate the picture. Although none of their bombs hit the target, the *Hiryū* especially had to manoeuvre wildly to avoid a number of near misses. Once more the reprisals were savage with the 'Zeros' and A.A. fire accounting for ten of the American planes. Nagumo had hardly recovered from this closer call when a wave of fifteen B-17s began their high-level bombing operations. Again no hits were recorded even though they managed to drop 108 bombs in the process. After what must have seemed like an eternity, the lone 'Jake' finally radioed a report at 0809 hours that the ten warships he had spotted earlier were made up of five cruisers and five destroyers. A palpable sense of relief must have been felt by those in Nagumo's circle. It wasn't to last. A final wave of eleven lumbering Vindicator dive-bombers from

Midway homed in on his ships, but once again the aircrews retained the unenviable record of futility achieved by the rest of their colleagues in failing to hit the target with any of their weapons.[44]

While all of this frenetic activity was going on another disquieting development took place with the sudden emergence on the scene of the American submarine *Nautilus*. She managed to fire a torpedo at the battleship *Kirishima* before diving to avoid the depth charging that greeted her insolent appearance. Having absorbed the shock of this latest encounter, Nagumo was soon to receive another surprise of far more sinister import. At 0820 hours the 'Jake' reported once more from the eastern sector, with the following dire message: 'The enemy is accompanied by what appears to be a carrier.'[45] This was precisely the news he had not wished to receive, even if it did clear up one issue – the abandonment of any plan to strike Midway a second time. Unfortunately, his new dilemma was in deciding whether to send off those torpedo-bombers that had not been rearmed to attack the sole carrier or to stand them down and clear his decks to recover the planes that were just about to return from the first Midway strike. If he went with the former choice, as his deputy, Rear-Admiral Tamon Yamaguchi, urged him to do, the torpedo-bombers would have no fighter cover as those 'Zeros' which had accompanied the force to Midway and the rest which had remained behind both needed refuelling before they could set out on another mission. Furthermore, even if he did choose to follow Yamaguchi's advice, he did not have sufficient time to fly off his torpedo-bombers and only then recover all of his returning Midway planes since many of them were critically short of fuel and couldn't stay airborne while the torpedo-bombers were being launched. If he chose that option, many of the returning planes would have to make do with a watery landing. Being unwilling to sacrifice both pilots and planes, Nagumo reluctantly decided shortly after 0830 hours to recover the planes from the attack on Midway before scheduling a force of thirty-six dive-bombers and fifty-four torpedo-bombers accompanied by twelve Zero fighters to attack the American carrier at 1030 hours. It was to be a fateful decision that would return to haunt him within a couple of hours. By 0918 hours all of the planes that were to return from Midway had completed the trip and were back on the carrier decks once more. At that point Nagumo changed course to north-northwest and began closing with the American force.[46]

If the Battle of Midway exposes the shortcomings of Yamamoto's strategic planning and Nagumo's tactical acumen, which it does, it also reflects huge credit on Spruance's admirable foresight, initiative and decisiveness under conditions of extreme pressure. Spruance was also lucky, but the old expression of 'fortune favours the brave' applies here too. While it might stretch credibility to talk of individuals making their own luck, it is fair enough to say that some people have a knack for using what luck comes their way. Spruance certainly did that at Midway.[47] Hearing the news that enemy aircraft had attacked the air base on the island, he calculated that if he flew off his own planes at their maximum range his pilots might reach the Japanese carriers shortly after they had recovered the Midway strike force and while they were rearming and refuelling them for further operations. It was a bold and risky move. He ordered both of his own carriers, *Enterprise* and *Hornet*, to begin launching their planes at 0702 hours. It took more than thirty minutes for the fifty-seven planes from the former and sixty from the latter to get airborne. A frantic and somewhat uncoordinated launch, combined with the cloudy weather conditions and the distance to the target, ensured that two distinct groups of planes from each carrier were underway, independent of one another and in some cases regrettably unescorted. It was a recipe for carnage. When the four separate air groups reached Nagumo's estimated position they found an empty sea. *Hornet*'s group of thirty-five Dauntless dive-bombers and ten Wildcat fighters opted to turn towards Midway and missed their quarry altogether. Her fifteen 'Devastator' torpedo-bombers saw telltale signs of smoke on the northern horizon at 0930 hours and found the Carrier Fleet and more significantly the 'Zero' fighters who simply swarmed all over them destroying the entire squadron in short order. Only one 'Devastator' got close enough to a carrier to release her torpedo before she crashed into the sea and even that missed.[48] *Enterprise*'s fourteen 'Devastators' were a little more fortunate. Seven of them perished before they could attack the *Hiryū* and three more fell victim to enemy fire once they had released their torpedoes, but surprisingly perhaps four managed to return safely to their own carrier. Once again, however, none of their torpedoes struck home. At this point in the proceedings, the *Yorktown*'s complement of seventeen dive-bombers, twelve torpedo-bombers and six Wildcat fighters finally arrived on the scene to take up the challenge. They had only begun their journey from the third American carrier at 0838 hours and had done well to reach the enemy so quickly. Unfortunately, what ought to have been a closely coordinated attack turned out to be a disjointed affair with the torpedo-bombers and fighters losing contact with the dive-bombers in the clouds above them. In the mêlée that followed, further mayhem resulted with only five torpedo-bombers launching their torpedoes and none of them obtaining a hit on any of Nagumo's ships. Three more were cut down and only two of the eighteen aircraft made it back to rejoin the *Yorktown*. So far, therefore, the various attacks on the Japanese carriers had yielded nothing and cost plenty. It was, however, about to change.[49]

Although in gaining height the *Yorktown*'s dive-bombers had lost contact with the rest of their carrier's aircrews, they did manage to find the only other set of planes still over the target – the thirty-two dive-bombers from *Enterprise*. They had wasted some time in finding the carriers and had only succeeded in doing so through the unwitting help of the destroyer *Arashi* which was spotted while on her way back to rejoin the fleet after abandoning the attempt to sink the errant submarine *Nautilus*. Despite the fact that four of *Yorktown*'s planes had already shed their bomb loads, there was still a host of American planes that could wreak a fearful toll on the three carriers *Akagi*, *Kaga* and *Sōryū* that were lying beneath them if only they could drop their large 1,000 pound (454-kilo) bombs anywhere on the flight decks, and preferably on or between the fully-loaded aircraft waiting to be launched. Whether the theory could be applied in practice was going to be the crucial thing. In the event, the fact that the Japanese 'Zero' fighters had abandoned their normal operational position high above the carriers in order to swoop down and cope with the latest low level torpedo-bombing assault by the *Yorktown*'s pilots was to be extremely significant. This left the way open for the Americans to exploit the situation and they did so almost unerringly.[50]

According to the conventional accounts of the action, it was just after 1020 hours – less than ten minutes before the carriers would supposedly start launching their planes for the attack on the American fleet – when the first of the *Enterprise*'s dive-bombers attacked *Kaga*. Parshall and Tully are scornful of the idea (often depicted as incontrovertible fact) that the Japanese were so close to flying off their carrier aircraft from the decks of the *Kidō Butai*. They claim it is a myth – castigating it as 'A Fallacious Five Minutes' – because the Japanese were simply in no practical position to do so at this time.[51] After three misses, four large bombs struck home, the first of which exploded in an inferno amongst the 'Kates' on the starboard quarter of the deck, two more smashed into the deck near the carrier's island wrecking the bridge and a fourth landed in the middle of the flight deck before carving its way like the other bombs before it through to the hangars below. *Kaga* became almost an instant blazing wreck. *Akagi* was not spared either. Two bombs exploded near to the flagship, but a solitary hit from Lieutenant Richard Best's dive-bomber was sufficient to turn Nagumo's flagship into yet another exploding furnace. His 1,000-pound bomb drove through the flight deck and exploded in a huge ball of flame in the upper hangar amongst the carrier bomber planes that were parked there. Although badly damaged, *Akagi* was far from dead in the water. In fact, she was making battle speed 3 at 1040 hours when she spotted a lone American plane off her starboard bow. In heeling the carrier over to starboard and opening up with her A.A. guns, the flagship survived this latest attack. In doing so, however, the steering failed – the rudder jamming at 30° to starboard. Within a few minutes the situation was complicated still further by a fire breaking out on the flight deck which in turn spread to a 'Zero' parked by the bridge. As a result of the acrid smoke that arose from the resulting inferno, the command centre became uninhabitable. *Akagi*'s days as the flagship of the First Mobile Striking Force (*Kidō Butai*) were at an end.[52] While *Kaga* and *Akagi* were bearing the brunt of the *Enterprise*'s Dauntlesses, the dive-bombers from the *Yorktown* concentrated primarily on *Sōryū* and at 1026 hours the first of three bombs smashed into the starboard bow of the ship by the No.1 A.A. gun and obliterated the forward bulkhead and everything around it. A second bomb had carved its way through the middle of the flight deck and penetrated deep into the lower hangar before exploding venomously rupturing boiler steam pipes as it did so. A third struck the flight deck aft igniting in a ball of flame and thereafter engulfing everything from the command centre to the stern. By 1030 hours this whirlwind of destruction had signalled the active end of *Sōryū*'s existence. Like the other two carriers, she did not sink immediately but hung around as a smoking ruin for several more hours before sliding beneath the waves at 1913 hours taking 718 crew members with her as she did so.[53]

As a result of her earlier manoeuvring when she had been the focus of the Midway-based bombing attacks, *Hiryū* had found herself some distance from the three other Japanese carriers when the American pilots from *Enterprise* and *Yorktown* had delivered their knockout blows between 1024 and 1030 hours. Undiscovered by the enemy on this occasion, she was able to begin launching the first wave of her eighteen 'Val' dive-bombers and six 'Zeros' at 1054 hours. Retribution was clearly in order and they were helped in their quest for it by discreetly following some of the Dauntlesses as they made their way home to the *Yorktown*. Radar, however, helped to even up the score by allowing the Americans to pick up the incoming Japanese strike at a distance of 40nm (74km) and prepare a fighter reception for them 20nm from Fletcher's flagship. For once the 'Zeros' were caught unawares and five of them were either lost or damaged in aerial jousting with the *Yorktown*'s fighters and ten of the 'Vals' were similarly disposed of, while one more was downed by A.A. fire from a cruiser. Despite these losses, seven Japanese dive-bombers survived and three of them soon established hits on the US carrier immediately disabling her. One bomb struck the starboard side of the flight deck and set the hangar below on fire, another cut through the port side of the *Yorktown* and ploughed its way into the base of the uptakes to the funnel, and a third hit the carrier forward with sufficient force to reach down to the fourth deck and set fire to a compartment alongside a magazine.[54] By 1211 hours *Yorktown* was ablaze and it soon became clear that her days as a flagship were over. Fletcher recognised that doleful fact by transferring to the heavy cruiser *Astoria* at 1324 hours while giving Spruance authority to handle all future air sorties. Although his old flagship would have to be towed back to Pearl Harbor, she was nothing but a doughty old fighter with a crew that were immensely resourceful. *Yorktown* soon proved that she was far from being down and out. At 1437 hours her crew had four of her boilers working and steam was raised to give her at least 19 knots. It was not to last. *Hiryū*'s pilots had not finished with her yet. At 1330 hours a second wave of ten 'Kate' torpedo-bombers and another six 'Zeros' were launched from the only remaining carrier in Nagumo's fleet. They homed in on *Yorktown* believing she was either the *Enterprise* or the *Hornet* since she was a member of the same class of carrier, was making steady progress, didn't appear to be in any kind of distress, no fires were visible, and she had planes on her flight deck. It must have been inconceivable to the pilots that this could have been the same vessel that had been hit earlier. Despite losing half of their 'Kates' and 'Zeros' in making their second attack on the *Yorktown*, four of the bombers evaded the combat air patrol and penetrated the additional A.A. protective screen thrown up by Spruance around the damaged carrier to deliver two crippling torpedo thrusts that struck home on her port side from a distance of only 500 yards (457 metres) at 1442 hours. Fatally wounded, *Yorktown* lost all power and took on an immediate list of 17° that proceeded to get worse as the minutes ticked by. Thirteen minutes after the first torpedo tore into the carrier her captain gave the order to abandon ship. Despite her condition, she remained defiantly afloat for more than two-and-a-half days and might even have survived to regain port had she and the destroyer *Hammann* accompanying her not been found by the Japanese submarine *I-168* and torpedoed at 1331 hours on 6 June. Even then the *Yorktown* only finally perished at 0458 hours on 7 June.[55]

Spruance was well aware that *Hiryū* had escaped the mauling that had been administered to the other three Japanese carriers by his pilots in their earlier raid on Nagumo's fleet and was absolutely determined to eliminate her in a similar manner as soon as he could discover where she was. One of his reconnaissance planes provided that information at 1445 hours – *Hiryū* had been spotted 110nm (204km) northwest of the floating wreck of *Yorktown*. Spruance wasted little time in sending off forty-one dive-bombers to deal with her. They left at 1530 hours and went without fighter escort – there being too few of them to spare for this operation – but *Hiryū*, with only six 'Zeros' left at her disposal, was not going to be in a position to exploit that weakness so the risk turned out to be fully justifiable. Spruance was prepared to lose some of his planes on this mission, but bargained on enough getting through to repay *Hiryū* for what she had done to *Yorktown* earlier that afternoon. His calculations proved right yet again. At 1703 hours the first of four large bombs rained down on the Japanese carrier tearing back her forward deck as if it were a can of sardines, while the other three penetrated deep into the bowels of the ship before exploding leaving a trail of destruction that could not be overcome. She was yet another write-off. Burning fiercely, she still refused to sink and for a time was capable of making 28 knots. In the end, however, her fires became uncontrollable and she finally came to a standstill at 2123 hours with a 15° list to port. She was finally scuttled by a torpedo from the Japanese destroyer *Makigumo* at 0510 hours on the following day. Even then she remained afloat and only finally disappeared under the waves about four hours later. Her former flagship *Akagi* also remained afloat until she was finally put out of her misery by a broadside of torpedoes fired without enthusiasm from four Japanese destroyers. She succumbed a few minutes later at 0520 hours on 5 June.[56]

Once the news was received that the last Japanese fleet carrier had been conclusively dealt with, Spruance did not wait around in the gathering dusk to ride his luck any further but began to withdraw eastwards towards Midway. It was a prudent and judicious move putting his two carriers out of harm's way. At this stage the surface fleets of Kondo in the southwest, Kakuta and Takasu in the far north and Yamamoto in the northwest were all too far away to pose an active threat to the Americans as long as they left the scene of their triumph without inordinate delay and at a reasonable speed using darkness to cover their course and bearing. Yamamoto was so unimpressed by Nagumo's tortured performance, his lack of conviction and increasingly supine attitude that he relieved him of command at 2255 hours, giving the task of hounding the American carriers and bringing them to heel to Kondo.[57] While the latter may have had a lot more spirit than his predecessor in that role, he didn't enjoy any better luck. While he was more than willing to do his duty, the task of chasing after a fast retreating enemy who would be able to deploy its planes against his surface fleet shorn of any fighter protection was not an ideal commission for Kondo. Within a few hours, however, his task was made far simpler when Yamamoto cast aside his earlier bravado and opted at 0255 hours to call off the Midway invasion.[58]

That was not the end of the matter because Kurita's force of four heavy cruisers, whose original task was to provide close support for the landings on Midway, now came into play. Until Yamamoto's call to abandon the invasion was sent out, Kurita's cruiser division was intent on reaching and bombarding Midway as soon as dawn broke on 5 June. This mission was similarly abandoned at 0230 hours when the Japanese force was less than 50nm (93km) from Midway. In turning away from their objective Kurita's ships then inadvertently and unknowingly put themselves on a high speed collision course with the American submarine *Tambor* that was patrolling the seas off Midway. A lookout on the *Kumano* spotted the enemy submarine ahead and to port of the flagship which quickly sounded the alarm and ordered sudden evasive action by executing an emergency turn to port. At this speed and without prior warning, confusion and chaos were never very far away. Although the first three cruisers were far from flawless in their coordinated movements they still somehow managed to avoid one another. This was not the case with the last heavy cruiser in the line. *Mogami* did not spot the signal or *Mikuma*'s sudden change of direction and collided with her at full speed but at an oblique angle. Neither ship sank as a result of this collision even though *Mogami*'s prow was 40 feet (12.2 metres) shorter than it had been before it had rammed into her sister ship. Later that day American B-17 bombers from Midway tried to dispatch both warships but failed to hit them and it was left to Spruance's carrier planes to sink the *Mikuma*. Somehow the *Mogami* survived the renewed battering, remarkably increased her speed to 20 knots and made it back eventually to Truk with as many as 800 holes in her port side. Her survival was astonishing and is a glowing tribute to those engaged in the damage control operations on board ship.[59]

Although Spruance was not able to find the rest of the Japanese fleet which was withdrawing from the Central Pacific, he had overseen the most important and successful air raids of the entire war. All four of Nagumo's carriers and a heavy cruiser had been destroyed for the loss of the venerable *Yorktown* and a solitary destroyer. While both sides had lost a host of planes, the death of so many experienced pilots would cost the Japanese especially dear. Air frames could be relatively easily replaced; skilled pilots with a wealth of combat experience were a totally different proposition. By throwing caution to the wind and gambling on an inspired hunch, Spruance achieved a scale of victory at Midway that was as unprecedented as it was unlikely, given that his past record had suggested that he was far more at home behind a desk on dry land than demonstrating flair, dash and spontaneity on the high seas. Highly regarded as a staff officer, his operational judgement and handling of his carriers throughout the mission had been uncanny.[60] Yamamoto, on the other hand, author of Operation *MI*, without playing an active role in the carrier battles or being present even to fire a gun in anger in any of the engagements, was undoubtedly the big loser in this seminal clash in the Central Pacific. His aura of invincibility, built up by the attack on Pearl Harbor and the subsequent heady conquests in the Asia-Pacific over the course of the next five months, had been shredded by the reverse at Midway. If the engagement in the Coral Sea had been less than a resounding success, it had still been considered by the military dictatorship in Tokyo as a victory. Midway could not be so favourably interpreted. Yamamoto's plan had resulted in four of his own capital ships being ruthlessly eliminated with the loss of 2,181 of their officers and crew, while at least 253 and perhaps as many as 332 planes had gone the same way, and worse still, its eleven prized battleships had not featured in any way either at Midway or in the Coral Sea encounter.[61] These were all disquieting things for the naval command to ponder over, for if naval battles were to be decided in future by airpower and not by massive guns, the scale of the IJN's defeat at Midway was even more crushing than it may have first appeared. Even a best case scenario made morbid reading for the Japanese. Instead of seeing the US Navy vanquished, it was the IJN that had received a massive blow to its own self-esteem that undermined its ability to do as it liked in the Pacific and elsewhere. Somehow a landing on Attu and Kiska in the Aleutians was a pathetically small return for what had been lost further south.[62]

If the Allies sensed that they may have turned a significant corner in the Pacific War with the comprehensive defeat of the Japanese at Midway, they had little time to celebrate the fact before ominous news of the Axis Powers' ability to hurt them elsewhere was received. June 1942 became the most deadly and productive month of the entire war for Dönitz's U-boat fleet: 136 ships being sunk at the cost of 637,000 tons. Although Anti-Submarine Warfare (ASW) techniques were poised to become more sophisticated and effective over the next few months, they could not come fast enough for the Admiralty as it sought to prevent this daily carnage upon the high seas. Moreover, the Germans had already begun taking counter-measures against the ASW tactics being employed against them. One of the most effective was the radar receiver R600A known by the nickname 'Metox'. This device which operated across a wavelength band from 0.9 – 3.8 metres picked up the pulse repetition of airborne radar at far greater distance than the enemy patrol plane would be able to detect those submarines fitted with the 'Metox' device.[63]

Another highly disturbing feature of the war that could not be ignored in Whitehall at this time was the growing aerial, surface and submarine threat to the Arctic convoys – one that was especially grave in the almost continuous daylight found in these northerly latitudes during the summer months. Determined to staunch the flow of war supplies to the Soviets or eliminate them completely, the Germans had steadily built up their military presence in northern Norway and had already disrupted several sailings over the past few months.[64] This problem would have been far worse had it not been for the intelligence coups of the Bletchley Park cryptanalysts in determining where the enemy naval threat lay. In this way the Admiralty had been able to route their convoys away from enemy concentrations and in situations where the threat was perceived to be an acute one had either suspended sailings altogether or ordered ships that were already underway to return to port. 'Ultra' could do nothing against aerial reconnaissance and torpedo bombing, however, as convoy PQ.16 had discovered in late May when it avoided the U-boats lying in wait for it and still lost over 75,000 tons of shipping and cargo to attacks from the Luftwaffe.[65] It was a warning sign that life was becoming ever more difficult on these Arctic runs and that the Germans were becoming steadily more selective about which convoys to attack and which they could safely leave alone. Nothing demonstrated this preferential treatment more acutely than what the Germans were about to do to PQ.17.[66]

There are a few names in history that go down in the collective memory for the glory, infamy or tragedy associated with them. PQ.17 is on that list and it's not hard to see why it should be. This ill-starred convoy began its tortuous journey from Reykjavik in late June with forty ships, but three of them were soon forced to return to Icelandic ports for repairs after either running aground or being damaged by ice. It was not a good augury for the entire venture. Worse was to follow. Bletchley Park was experiencing one of its periodic intelligence blackouts when the ability to decipher enemy signals traffic was temporarily compromised by changes made by the Germans to their Enigma wheel settings. This led to frustrating delays in reading these messages and ensured that vital information covered in them simply could not be given to the Admiralty in a timely fashion.[67] As luck would have it, just at the time when the British were experiencing difficulties in this field and were unable to provide information on the German plans for interdicting either PQ.17 or QP.13, the Soviet convoy coming in the opposite direction, the B-Dienst, was at its predictive best. It was able to provide the Germans with the exact location on 1 July of PQ.17, the one convoy that they wished to attack and dismember. This information was corroborated by sightings of the convoy during the morning of 1 July by two of the U-boats (*U255* and *U408*) lying in wait for it 60nm (111km) east of Jan Mayen Island. Two other U-boats (*U334* and *U456*) soon joined them while six others formed the *Eisteufel* group further to the east. Here was a golden opportunity for a series of coordinated attacks on the convoy providing the U-boats could circumvent the twenty-one escort vessels and elude the grasp of the four heavy cruisers and three destroyers that formed the close covering forces of PQ.17.[68] A number of probing attacks were carried out on the convoy throughout 2 July by both U-boats and by seven He-115s without material success, but Commodore Dowding, in command of PQ.17, was left in little doubt that tougher tests lay ahead now that the enemy knew where his ships were and he didn't need to be a clairvoyant to imagine the kind of reception they would be receiving from the Luftwaffe's dive-bombing squadrons based in northern Norway in the days to come. What Dowding didn't know at the time was that Raeder's big ships were also about to join the hunting party. During the afternoon of 2 July Force I, under Admiral Otto Schniewind, consisting of the battleship *Tirpitz*, the heavy cruiser *Admiral Hipper*, four destroyers and two torpedo boats had left Trondheim for Altenfjorden which was to be the base for *Fall Rösselsprung* (*Case Knight's Move*). Next day Force II under Vizeadmiral Oskar Kummetz, comprising the two pocket battleships *Lützow* and *Admiral Scheer*, accompanied by six destroyers, left

Narvik for the same Norwegian destination to join the other surface ships for a major attack on PQ.17 and its estimated cargo value of $700 million. All did not go to plan, however, as *Lützow* and three destroyers from Force I managed to go aground in Grimsöystraumen utterly compromising their participation in the forthcoming operation. Raeder, already under pressure to show his doubting Führer that there was still a place for the capital ship in naval warfare, must have been apoplectic at this turn of events. Matters did not improve during the day as the weather closed in and hid the convoy from the prying eyes of reconnaissance aircraft and sabotaged the efforts of six of the U-boats to maintain contact with it.[69]

On the Allied side ominous news was received from their own reconnaissance aircraft that some of the German heavy ships had been spotted steaming northwards. This could only mean one thing – that they were planning a sortie against PQ.17. If such an operation was on the cards, what could the Admiralty do to protect the convoy? It could reinforce its escort, add more ships to the close covering force, and alert its own submarines and those of its Soviet ally to the potential threat, but if the Germans really meant business and came out intending to cut a swathe amongst both escorts and freighters, only the arrival of the distant covering force under Admiral Tovey might be able to save the convoy from massive destruction. Notwithstanding this possibility, the acute dilemma facing Admiral Sir Dudley Pound, the First Sea Lord, was that even if Tovey's force did prove to be a deterrent to Schniewind's ships, it could not fail to exert a powerful magnetic attraction to the U-boats and the Luftwaffe who would go all out to destroy elements of it. Although he would have loved to get his hands on these heavy German ships, it was not in his nature to send his own capital ships into harm's way if he could help it. In essence, therefore, if Tovey's force did not prove to be a distant deterrent, it was unlikely to become a close escort agency.[70]

American Independence Day was not celebrated in Admiralty House in 1942. It proved to be a sombre day that began badly and became foul. A successful torpedo attack on the convoy by a lone He-115 registered the first hits of the operation on the steamer *Christopher Newport* critically disabling her. Other attacks, both by a squadron of dive-bombers and by several U-boats, were beaten off during the day until another swarm of twenty-five torpedo-bombers showed up in the evening to harass the convoy. In this latest raid a freighter was sunk, another was damaged and finished off later by a U-boat and a Soviet tanker was torpedoed for the loss of three He-111 aircraft.[71] Pound became more agitated as the day proceeded. He sensed that all of these attacks appeared to prefigure an all-out assault on PQ.17 in which the *Tirpitz* would take part. Lacking the Bletchley Park decrypts necessary to prove conclusively that the heavy surface ships had already been committed, but aware of what they intended to do, Pound panicked and decided on his own initiative that they must have sortied. Once he had reached that hasty conclusion, he looked to preserve as many of his ships as possible by withdrawing the destroyer escorts and the close covering cruiser force and ordering the convoy, which would now be defenceless, to disperse. He followed that order with another one thirteen minutes later in which he insisted that the convoy was to scatter, believing that to do so offered the individual ships the best chance they had of surviving such an attack by the surface fleet.[72] It was a grotesque and fatal error of judgement. Captain Jack Broome, in command of the destroyer escort force, could scarcely believe his eyes when he read the orders sent at 2123 hours. In a signal to Dowding, he exclaimed: 'What part of the bloody War Plan is this[?].' He reluctantly set course for Iceland and left PQ.17's commander in little doubt that he thought the order was a fundamental mistake: 'Sorry to leave you like this. Goodbye and good luck. It looks like a bloody business.'[73] It was. Pound's decision to abandon the convoy principle in this case and order his cargo freighters to steam on ahead independently into the jaws of the enemy forces has been criticised ever since and rightly so. It was to be a death sentence for many of them that were now cast adrift on their own.[74]

Ironically, the heavy surface ships that he was so fearful of were to play no part in the destruction of the convoy. They had remained in port and only sortied on 5 July when aerial reconnaissance sightings and U-boat reports confirmed that the Allied cruisers had been pulled back and PQ.17 had broken up into individual units that were sailing alone. Although *Tirpitz*, *Admiral Scheer*, *Admiral Hipper*, seven destroyers and a couple of torpedo boats did put to sea they were soon challenged off Ingöy by a Soviet submarine which fired a torpedo at Schniewind's flagship. Although it missed, it was not the introduction to *Rösselsprung* that the Germans appreciated. They had more cause for concern later that day when reports from an RAF Catalina flying-boat and the British submarine *Unshaken* were intercepted giving the precise location of Schniewind's surface fleet. This unwelcome news prompted Raeder to call off the operational sortie and order his warships to return to base. Once again, the safety-first option had been taken. Ships had been preserved, danger avoided and no risks had been taken. Schniewind's ships remained more a potential predatory force than an actual one. Was this enough to impress the Führer with the versatility of the capital ship and convince him that it still had an important role to play in the naval war, or was it more likely to reinforce his opinion that its time had passed? Raeder and his heavy ships got the benefit of the doubt on this occasion because the operational aim of destroying PQ.17 was achieved (though not by them), but he wouldn't be given endless opportunities to show their mettle in future. Merely remaining a fleet-in-being would not always be a sufficient reason to retain them; they would need to perform at sea if they were to be judged worthy of receiving the substantial funds devoted to their upkeep.[75]

While Raeder's day of reckoning was deferred for several more months, Pound's tragic blunder was to have far more immediate and dire consequences for the forces under his command. Throughout 5 July a virtual ceaseless series of aerial attacks took place over the now broken and widely dispersed convoy. In most cases, individual ships, as well as those sailing in small groups, were without even the most basic sort of A.A. protection. Their intense vulnerability was swiftly exposed as the day proceeded. Before it was over, five freighters and a rescue ship had been sunk and three other steamers and a tanker had been seriously damaged. None survived. Two were sunk later in the day by *U334* and *U703*, while the abandoned tanker *Aldersdale* was finally sent to the bottom by *U457* on 7 July and the wreck of the steamer *Paulus Potter* by *U255* on 13 July. Apart from finishing off the scraps left by the Luftwaffe, the U-boats also had the luxury of indulging their own taste for destruction: on 5 July *U88* sank two more freighters, and *U456* and *U703* sank one apiece. Another excruciating round of bombing on the following day took out one more tanker and a steamer and U-boats accounted for two more transport vessels on that day and yet another steamer on 8 July.[76]

Despite the murderous assaults on them, some of the survivors of PQ.17, including Dowding, managed to reach the Matochkin Strait over the course of the next couple of days. After acquiring the services of two Soviet destroyers, Dowding reformed the convoy escort on 8 July using his two A.A. ships (*Palomares* and *Pozarica*), and a mix of corvettes, minesweepers, trawlers and rescue ships to shepherd five steamers south along the west coast of Novaya Zemlya towards the entrance of the White Sea. When the slowest members of the convoy got there on 10 July, however, two more steamers were lost to a combination of bomb damage and U-boat torpedoes before the rest of the convoy finally reached the safety of Archangel. Learning that five more stragglers from his original convoy had reached and anchored by the ice barrier in the Matochkin Strait, having camouflaged their superstructures with white paint in order to blend in with their Arctic surroundings, Dowding left Archangel on 16 July taking three corvettes and a Soviet destroyer with him to try and get them. Gaining an additional steamer that had been sheltering elsewhere, he returned to the Soviet port with the entire group on 24 July. Bringing up the rear, the steamer *Winston Salem* survived a beaching and became the last ship of PQ.17 to make it to port on 28 July. She at least had been spared. Seventeen freighters, four steamers, two tankers and a rescue ship representing a total of 142,695 tons from her convoy had not been so fortunate. Apart from the loss of the ships and 120 merchant seamen, their cargo of 210 aircraft, 430 Sherman tanks, 3,350 vehicles and 99,316 tons of other war supplies was also lost on this most punishing convoy run of the entire war.[77]

In whatever way the Admiralty might have wished to depict this tragic episode, the bottom line was that a series of false steps had been taken by Pound principally based on little or no verifiable information, much confusion and great anxiety. Once made, Pound's pride and obduracy ensured that the mistaken orders he had issued would not be rescinded. In this way, an old and ailing man's hubris helped to turn PQ.17 into an unmitigated disaster. It did nothing for relations amongst the members of the Grand Alliance. Twenty-two of the ships in the convoy had been American; the Soviets had lost material that could have equipped a force of 50,000 troops; and when strong leadership was needed, the head of the British Admiralty had failed to supply it. Confidence in the Admiralty to run the naval war in the European theatres, therefore, did not run too deep in either Washington or Moscow. After PQ.17 the question that was being posed in other Allied centres was could the British Admiralty be trusted to use the naval resources at its disposal wisely? Allied solidarity on this issue was decidedly only lukewarm.[78]

It didn't help that Tobruk had finally fallen to the Afrika Korps only a fortnight before on 20 June. Although it wasn't the Admiralty's fault and blame for the loss of the beleaguered fortress in Cyrenaica couldn't be laid at its door, the overall effect was still a negative one. Paradoxically enough, the Mediterranean was one theatre in which Admiralty direction had not been lacking and the Royal Navy, in particular, had maintained a consistently high level of performance in supplying both Tobruk as well as the garrison in Malta in the face of everything that the enemy had thrown at them by day and especially at night. Since the Mediterranean Fleet at Alexandria had been whittled down by enemy action during the winter months of 1941–42, it had used its limited stock of destroyers for the nightly forays to Tobruk, while Force H based at Gibraltar had come into its own as the principal supply source for British forces in the Central Mediterranean. As the pressure mounted on Malta, Force H made frequent operational runs into the Mediterranean south of the Balearic Islands in order to fly Spitfire planes to the British redoubt.[79] Fighter protection was a crucial aspect in reducing the sheer scale of the aerial threat to Malta. In knocking a host of enemy bombers out of the sky before they had the chance to drop their bomb loads on Malta, the Spitfires were more than earning their keep. It is a given that good intelligence is a key asset in disrupting enemy operations. Knowing where the enemy was going to be and having the wherewithal to do something about it were obviously not one and the same thing, but without the basic information on its location and strength, much fruitless time could be spent on hunting down a potential quarry. Even so, it remains a mystery why more Axis submarines were not devoted to the task of patrolling south of the Balearics in the hope of ensnaring a carrier on one of its short, sharp Spitfire sorties.[80]

Despite their ineptness in staunching the flow of fighter aircraft getting to Malta in the first instance, the Axis forces could become far more resolute when the spirit took them. They demonstrated this capacity by mounting considerable resistance to the simultaneous pincer-like convoy operations, *Harpoon* and *Vigorous*, launched in aid of Malta from Gibraltar and Alexandria in mid-June.[81] Unfortunately, their determination to destroy the Allied convoys was not matched by their results. In the event, none of the twenty-eight submarines devoted to the cause even registered a hit on any of the Allied ships, and the surface fleet only managed to sink a single Allied destroyer and damage another one throughout the entire operation. It was hardly a stirring epic, not least because the low loss/damage operational yield they achieved was matched exactly by the much smaller force of German MTBs, who operated solely against the eastern convoy, and even exceeded by a newly-laid minefield that trapped and finished off a destroyer and damaged two other destroyers, as well as a minesweeper and a freighter. It was left to *U205* to fire the only torpedo in anger, sinking the light cruiser *Hermione* as she did so at the end of the operation. Aircraft had a far greater impact. A combination of German dive-bombers (Ju-87s and Ju-88s) and Italian torpedo-bombers (Savoia S79s) showed the fleet just what it meant to turn potential menace into actual destruction by inflicting substantial material damage upon the two convoys.[82]

Despite the fact that Allied aircraft based on Malta torpedoed the battleship *Littorio* as well as the heavy cruiser *Trento* on 15 June (the latter being sunk by the British submarine *Umbra* later that same day), the fact remained that neither *Harpoon* nor *Vigorous* were great adverts for Allied convoy operations. After all, of the twenty supply ships that set off from both ends of the Mediterranean on 12 June, 50% of them either ended up sunk (seven) or damaged (three) in transit. Although Iachino's Battle Fleet had arrived late and was largely anonymous throughout these operations, the Allied covering force had not shown any greater zeal and had opted for discretion over valour and self preservation over the risk of destruction by turning off to the west on 14 June once the going got rough.[83]

In the Black Sea the struggle for Sevastopol was always tough. Replenishment of supplies – both human and material – was brought in by both Soviet surface and submarine fleets right up to the eve of a massive attack made by the German 11th Army on the fortress on 8 June. Thereafter, von Manstein's forces, aided by von Richthofen's air corps and an MTB flotilla, combined to make these journeys even more hazardous than before. Nonetheless, the Soviet Black Sea Fleet, under the command of Vice-Admiral F.S. Oktyabrskiy, was committed to maintaining these relief operations and evacuating wounded personnel from the Crimean base regardless of the high danger and cost involved. Over the course of the next three weeks before the Soviet High Command finally gave the order to evacuate the fortress on 30 June, the courage and resourcefulness of Oktyabrskiy's officers and men in the face of what ought to have been overwhelming odds were such as to limit the extent of these losses to only three destroyers and two transports. It was a quite extraordinary achievement in the midst of great adversity. Unfortunately, the defiance exhibited in delaying the evacuation order until all was lost ended up in consigning a large body of Soviet troops to death and imprisonment as only the smallest of Oktyabrskiy's ships and his submarines could manoeuvre their way into the harbour to collect those waiting to be shipped out of the city.[84]

Success in the Crimea was obviously not going to be enough for the Germans. They sought to wipe out Soviet ground forces in an incremental fashion wherever they could be found and they were determined to hound Oktyabrskiy's warships from one coastal base to another in the most methodical fashion. Their statement of intent was delivered as early as 2 July with a Luftwaffe attack on the naval base at Novorossisk. Thereafter, the pace never slackened. During August the city's fortunes began to be tied ever more closely with the eventual fate of the Taman Peninsula lying to the north on the Sea of Azov. If the Romanian air and ground forces succeeded in their attack on the Soviet defences on the River Don, Novorossisk's future would look bleak indeed. Learning from their earlier mistake with Sevastopol, the Soviets began ferrying several thousand men and hundreds of tons of supplies from Novorossisk much further south to the Georgian city of Batumi. It is as well they did because the Romanian Cavalry Corps broke through to reach the Black Sea coastal town of Anapa on 31 August. Once there the Axis forces were given the green light to launch a massive amphibious operation (*Fall Blücher*) of the Taman Peninsula in a bid to wipe out Soviet resistance on the peninsula and open the sea route to the Crimea. Under the watchful gaze of the 3rd Motorised Minesweeping Flotilla and the active support of the Luftwaffe, the Germans used a host of assorted ferries, landing and assault craft to land their 46th Infantry Division on both the western and northern coasts of the Taman Peninsula on 2 September. Unable to prevent this invasion from occurring, Rear-Admiral Sergei Gorshkov, commanding the Azov Flotilla, did the next best thing – saving as many of the Soviet 47th Army and remaining naval personnel on the peninsula as he could by removing them from the south coast to Novorossisk over the course of three turbulent days of withdrawal operations.[85] Gorshkov's success in bringing the survivors of the Taman rout to the naval base was something of a double-edged sword, however, as it brought in extra troops at a time when the resources at Novorossisk were already stretched to breaking point in trying to resist the attack on the city by the German V Army Corps. By 9 September the harbour had been seized and many of the Soviet forces that had been driven out of the city by the intensity of the German attack were forced to make their way by sea to Gelendzhik to help form the next defence line.[86]

Despite having to give ground grudgingly in the Caucasus and Black Sea, the Soviets were unwilling to remain always on the back foot. They were particularly keen to make an impression in the northerly latitudes and saw in their Finnish adversary an opponent whose relative weakness they could exploit profitably. They ought to have known better. It was only a matter of a couple of years since they had thoroughly underestimated the doughty Finns in the Winter War and had struggled to subdue them on that occasion despite the gross disparity in power between them. This time was no different. Finland remained an enterprising and industrious enemy that was quite capable of surprising the Soviets if they tried taking them for granted. Apart from their willing assistance to their German ally when it came to laying mines in the Gulf of Finland, and particularly in the Suursaari region, the Scandinavians were quite capable of expelling foreign invaders from their own land as they proved after the Soviets had mounted an amphibious operation using up to thirty vessels to land eighty troops initially on the island of Someri in the Gulf of Finland on 7 July. Within a couple of days and despite landing reinforcements, the Soviets had been rapidly defeated on land and suffered the loss of six torpedo cutters and a gunboat to a largely Finnish combined arms operations offensive at sea. While the so-called Continuation War proved a compelling national cause for the Finns, it remained an irritating sideshow to the Soviets. While they had every intention of undermining Finnish resistance when they could, it was not as high on their list of priorities as was the desire to do some significant damage to the German war machine.[87]

One way of doing that was to get their submarines through the dense mine barrages barring their way to the Baltic so that they could begin to take a toll of German mercantile shipping in what had hitherto been a protected area. These mine barrages had been laid out by both the Germans and the Finns from the early days of the war and had grown more formidable over time as more mines, protection floats and explosive floats were added to the combustible mix. As a result, it would require considerable skill and some luck to get through each of these obstacles both on the outward as well as the homeward bound journeys.[88]

While the Axis forces had enjoyed the better of the early summer months in the various European theatres of the naval war, the same could not be said of the Pacific campaign. Although Midway had not broken the back of the IJN, it had sustained a heavy blow. Even to the most rabid nationalist in the Japanese military-politico elite, the loss of four fleet carriers simply couldn't be passed off as a matter of little consequence and as a result the invasions that had been planned for Fiji and Samoa were cancelled in favour of consolidating the territorial gains they already had. While Yamamoto still had a significant weapon at his disposal, he was unwilling to expose it to another major confrontation with the American carrier fleet for the time being.[89] Although his views were respected within the IGHQ, it did not mean that Tokyo was prepared to adopt a purely defensive mentality in the Southwest Pacific. On the contrary, the Japanese military leadership was determined that their forces should resume their operations against Port Moresby and Papua New Guinea which they had started earlier in the year as a means of fracturing the supply route between Hawaii and Australia. In addition, they were also keen on building a series of strategic air bases on the Solomon Islands to the southeast of Rabaul in the Bismarck Archipelago where they had established an important forward naval base for the region.[90]

A start was made on capturing these two strategic targets in early July with the convoying of two construction battalions to Guadalcanal to begin building what the Japanese hoped would be a new regional airbase on the island. Yamamoto was far less enthusiastic about the Papuan adventure and was simply not prepared to launch a full scale frontal assault on Port Moresby any longer. All he would do was approve the use of a couple of his light cruisers, a few destroyers and other subsidiary forces on convoy protection duty in late July as a series of troop transports set out from Rabaul and landed near the town of Buna on the northeast coast of Papua. Once safely ashore, the troops and men of the South Sea Detachment of the IJA commanded by General Tomitaro Horii were required to hike overland crossing the mountainous Owen Stanley Range by using the Kokoda Trail before finally mounting an attack on Port Moresby on the southern coast of the island from the landward side. Once again theory and practice would be at variance with one another.[91]

For their part, the Americans emerged from the Coral Sea and Midway engagements with a heightened sense of optimism. From the outset of the war, it had been the Japanese who had been the ones taking the initiative, setting the agenda by choosing the ground where they would attack and having the planning and logistical support to assist their troops achieve most of their objectives. By contrast, the Americans and their Commonwealth Allies had been forced onto the defensive for the first five months of that campaign, only occasionally being able to counter-attack and rarely from a position of strength. After the exchanges in the Coral Sea and at Midway, however, that phase of the war was destined to change. In order to prepare for this emerging role, the US Pacific Fleet was divided into seven distinct task forces, four of which were to be based ultimately at Pearl Harbor (TF1, TF11, TF16 and TF17), with the others in San Diego (TF18), the Aleutians (TF8), and Australian and New Zealand waters (TF44).[92]

Although Midway in particular was a welcome boost for the US military, it did not mean that the two services thought alike on the way forward in the war. Indeed, far from it. In much the same way that there was little love lost between the IJA and IJN, a similar hostility and rancour bedevilled relations between the US Army and the US Navy. Part of this was due to the institutional culture and historical rifts that traditionally divided the two services, but much had to do with the personalities who drove both service institutions. In Admiral Ernest J. King, COMINCH and CNO, the USN had someone who would not take a backward step on anything, let alone strategic matters, even though his opposite number General George C. Marshall was seen to be a favourite of President Roosevelt. Moreover, King was not thrilled about the concept of combined arms operations and didn't trust the prima donna whom Roosevelt had installed as COMSOWESPAC – General Douglas MacArthur. This was particularly germane at this time since MacArthur was anxious to leave his Australian abode and return to the Philippines at the head of a marauding force that would roll up the Japanese from the Southwest Pacific. Despite their profound differences on some things, King, Marshall and MacArthur were all agreed that the Pacific theatre could not just be consigned to the back burner as the Allies devoted their full attention to the defeat of the Axis Powers in Europe.[93]

MacArthur wasted no time in proposing that the focus of US attention in the South Pacific should be a consolidated effort to seize the eastern half of New Guinea and use it as a springboard for capturing Rabaul at the northern tip of New Britain. He claimed he could secure Rabaul within three weeks. It looked, and was, a patently absurd notion. King disliked MacArthur intensely, distrusted his strategic grasp of the military situation and had no intention of seeing him and the Army assume command of an offensive that he strongly disagreed with. In a bid to foil MacArthur's plan and secure ownership of it for the Navy and Nimitz as CINCPAC, King made a proposal to Marshall on 25 June that in essence became the plan that the Joint Chiefs of Staff endorsed and President Roosevelt finally approved in mid-July. It called for a three-stage operation in which the Santa Cruz Islands, Tulagi and 'adjacent positions' (Guadalcanal) would be tackled first in early August under the command of Nimitz (Operation *Watchtower*), followed later by action under MacArthur's command against other targets in both the Solomons and eastern New Guinea, with an attack on Rabaul and 'adjacent positions' in New Britain and New Ireland relegated to the final phase of the operational plan that was initially called *Pestilence*.[94]

As MacArthur fumed at being sidestepped by his naval colleagues and planned an amphibious assault on eastern New Guinea a few days after the opening of *Watchtower*, the Japanese beat him to the punch by landing the first of a series of troop convoys at Basabua in eastern New Guinea on 21 July. Japanese reinforcements were disembarked twice more before the end of the month, but increasing Allied Air Force operations against Japanese shipping in the Solomon Sea did enough to force the abandonment of a further enemy convoy that had been arranged for 31 July.[95] While it became abundantly clear to General Horii and his men on the Kokoda Trail that more troop convoys would be needed to assist those already ashore to finish the job assigned to them, the nature of the Pacific War was about to change profoundly and Japanese plans for resuming a forward policy in the region were soon to be grievously disrupted.[96]

In a bid to ensure that the *Watchtower* offensive would be discharged successfully, King and Nimitz opted to employ the irascible, hard driven and rather mean-spirited Rear-Admiral Richmond Kelly Turner as the man responsible for getting the US troops and their equipment ashore in the first stage of this amphibious operation. Although he couldn't claim to have much experience in these matters, it proved to be an inspired appointment.[97] Strangely enough his lack of experience didn't seem to matter because he grew into the role and became a quite astounding success – something which he had never been ashore – assuming almost legendary status as the man who could deliver under the roughest conditions and in virtually all circumstances. What he lacked in operational experience, he made up for in intuitive skill. Turner had no doubts that air power would become a critical resource in the South Pacific and saw the construction and maintenance of an airfield on Guadalcanal as a vital asset for the Americans to have since this would help to safeguard their strategic interests in the region.[98]

Operation *Watchtower* was to be almost as significant in amphibious operations as Midway had been as a carrier battle. If the Japanese could be rooted out of this important island in the Solomons chain, the Americans and their allies would inherit a significant strategic foothold in the Southwest Pacific with a crucial air base, Henderson Airfield, that once fully operational could be used for missions designed to bolster their own war effort and undermine that of their enemies. Denying Guadalcanal – and by extension the entire Solomons archipelago – to the Japanese would be a huge boost for the Allies in the Pacific theatre and would put a severe dent in Japanese plans for consolidating their hold over the South Pacific. It was a matter of speculation as to how the Japanese would respond to being put on the back foot for once. It didn't take long to find out. Retreat might have been in their military lexicon, but Japanese commanders rarely resorted to it and never willingly. By the same token they may have believed that the Allies would not have the stomach for such a dour and bloody struggle, so one suspects that the intensity of the fight for Guadalcanal over the course of the next five months surprised both sides.[99]

Watchtower began with the dispatch of the South Pacific Amphibious Force (TF62) from Fiji on 31 July. It was made up of a large convoy (TG62.1) of twenty-three troop and supply transports, escorted and protected by four groups of warships. Cover for this entire convoy was provided by an accumulation of warships drawn from within the Pacific Fleet and spearheaded by three carriers and a battleship, and supported by thirty other warships and five fleet tankers. Overall command of this operation was given to Vice-Admiral Robert Ghormley in Noumea (New Caledonia). Fortunately for him, bad weather discreetly hid the entire ensemble from the eyes of Japanese reconnaissance aircraft and submarines along their route until 6 August, preventing attacks on the transports and not slowing the pace of the advancing armada. Early the next morning (7 August) after an opening series of attacks by carrier aircraft from the *Enterprise*, *Saratoga* and *Wasp*, and a furious artillery assault from the cruisers and destroyers of the Fire Support Groups, the South Pacific Amphibious Force put ashore the bulk of the 1st Marine Division from fifteen transports on the northern coast of Guadalcanal and the rest of the reinforced division from the other eight transports on Tulagi. Of the two landing sites, the latter was the more fiercely contested as bridgeheads were being established on both spots.[100]

In response to these unwelcome developments, Vice-Admiral Gunichi Mikawa's 8th Fleet left Rabaul for Guadalcanal. His warships – five heavy and two light cruisers and a single destroyer – reached Guadalcanal unharmed even though they had been spotted at the outset of their journey by the US submarine *S38* and again when much closer to their destination by Australian reconnaissance aircraft.[101] Communication errors may be blamed for not making more of these sightings, but the failure to carry out a proper surveillance of the narrow funnelled passage (popularly known as 'The Slot') that flowed between the islands of Choiseul and Santa Isabel on the eastern side of the strait and New Georgia on the western side was both lax and negligent. These fundamental errors, born of complacency and mistaken assumptions, were soon to have grave consequences. Shortly after midnight on 8–9 August all eight Japanese warships having successfully negotiated 'The Slot' in squally weather now eased their way past two American radar-equipped destroyers (*Blue* and *Ralph Talbot*) set up on a picket line 20nm (37km) apart to the northwest of Guadalcanal to provide early warning of any approaching enemy force. Neither destroyer discovered their presence. Radar had not come to the Allies' aid when they needed it most.[102] There would be no early warning of impending disaster. Making the most of their surprise, Mikawa's fleet soon showed their skill at night-fighting. Using a mixture of torpedo strikes and accurate gunfire, assisted by the illuminated flares dropped by float planes which doubled as aerial shell spotters, the Japanese fleet took both the southern and northern halves of Crutchley's covering force by storm, destroying four heavy cruisers (*Astoria*, *Canberra*, *Quincy* and *Vincennes*) in the process and damaging the heavy cruiser *Chicago* and two destroyers, *Patterson* and *Ralph Talbot*, before they left the scene of their triumph relatively unscathed.[103]

Mikawa had achieved a notable triumph, but it could have been even more dramatic and comprehensive had he pressed on to attack and destroy Turner's transports, as Yamamoto had originally wanted him to. But having shown boldness and imagination in attacking Crutchley's warships, Mikawa now chose caution over adventure and opted to make use of the remaining hours of darkness to cover his escape from the area rather than to waste any more time in carrying out a search and destroy mission in the waters off Guadalcanal and Tulagi for the vulnerable and undefended transports when it would almost certainly leave his fleet exposed to aerial attack from Fletcher's carrier planes at first light. Yamamoto would be exasperated by this controversial decision because the express purpose of Mikawa's mission had been to destroy the enemy transports and thereby strand the American forces on Guadalcanal without immediate possibilities of reinforcement. In a metaphorical sense, therefore, the celebratory glass raised to toast Mikawa's success was seen to be either half full or half empty depending on where one stood on his decision making.

Once again one of the infinite variables – personal decision making – had come into play in war. Instead of persevering with his mission, Mikawa may have chosen to withdraw from the waters off Savo Island when he did so believing his fleet had already secured a considerable bonus to the Japanese cause and one that more than made up for not eliminating the transports in the Lunga Roads. He also appears to have thought that the preservation of his own fleet was more important than putting his ships at risk from Allied retaliation once dawn broke. Whatever the rationale, it is difficult not to see this as a wasted opportunity to inflict even more damage to the Allied cause than was actually achieved in the early hours of 9 August and the more so because Fletcher's carriers were no longer in the vicinity! He had withdrawn them the previous evening – twelve hours earlier than planned – primarily because he wished to avoid any torpedo attack being launched against them during the hours of darkness. Fletcher's caution may have been understandable to those on board the carriers, but it left Turner's transports without any air cover whatsoever. It was hardly surprising that the volcanic Turner became acutely angry at what he saw as an act of desertion. Fletcher's withdrawal has remained a point of controversy ever since.[104]

On the Allied side there was no celebratory glass in evidence and no problem of ambiguity when it came to interpreting the action at Savo Island. In fact, it is difficult to imagine a more diabolical start to any major campaign than that registered by the dismemberment of the Allied naval forces by Mikawa's fleet on this occasion.[105] Best summed up as a mixture of shocking incompetence, glaring overconfidence and inadequate watchkeeping, their defeat became the subject of an official inquiry even though the US Navy was not inclined to publicise the extent of its losses either at the time or for months later.[106] Being economical with the truth is, alas, often a casualty of war, and refusing to learn the lessons of failure is about as reprehensible. Mikawa's action at Savo Island ought to have dispelled some of the mistaken notions about Japanese weakness and inferiority in military matters that were popularly held by many serving officers and men within the US Navy, but these images stubbornly persisted. Kelly Turner knew the warning signs. He thought that racial stereotyping had lulled the Americans into 'a fatal lethargy of mind which induced a confidence without readiness, and a routine acceptance of outworn peacetime standards of conduct'.[107] Needing no more convincing proof that the enemy was a formidable foe and shocked by the losses suffered by his Support Force, Turner felt obliged to withdraw from the waters off Guadalcanal and leave the Marine Corps to it. As Richard Frank wryly observes, it would take 'some more hard blows to Navy pride around Guadalcanal' to shake off the complacency that Turner had alluded to.[108]

Mikawa's success, though welcome to the Japanese military authorities, was insufficient in itself. Guadalcanal could not be limply forsaken. Instead, Japanese troops on the island would now need to be reinforced and replenished in order to resist the American challenge which was already being bolstered by supplies brought in by fast transports. As a gesture of intent Yamamoto moved part of the Combined Fleet from the Inland Sea to Truk and took the 2nd and 3rd Fleets with him. Other ambitious plans for conquests would have to be put on hold until the fate of Guadalcanal was decided. It was a case of the future being judged to be 'right here and right now'.[109]

Once fourteen Japanese submarines had been deployed off the Solomons and Kondo and Nagumo's forces had duly arrived in these waters from Truk, the operation to land 1,500 troops on Guadalcanal proceeded on the night of 23–24 August. As with most Japanese plans that bore the imprint of Yamamoto on them, Operation *KA* was not straightforward. It involved several different elements and various stratagems. Rear-Admiral Raizo Tanaka's task was the least elaborate and involved softening up the opposition by shelling their positions and trying to put Henderson Airfield (now home to thirty-one Marine Corps fighter planes) out of action before manoeuvring his seven troop transports ashore.[110] Rear-Admiral Chuichi Hara's force (the light carrier *Ryūjō*, the heavy cruiser *Tone*, and two destroyers) was to be the diversionary hare that was meant to draw the American carrier force into the path of Kondo and Nagumo's avenging fleets east of the Solomons. This, at least, was the bare bones of the plan.[111] Once off the drawing board, it soon changed in unexpected ways. To begin with Hara's force was found on 24 August, as was called for in the blueprint, but *Saratoga*'s planes were not expected to bomb and torpedo the *Ryujo* into oblivion and damage the *Tone* and the seaplane carrier *Chitose* into the bargain in the way they did. Although Hara's role was brutally extinguished in this way, the Americans did not have it all their own way. Yamamoto would still get his chance to hurt the enemy carrier forces. Once Japanese reconnaissance had established where all three were, carrier planes from the *Shokaku* and *Zuikaku* eluded the fighter cover above them and their accompanying forces and registered three hits on the *Enterprise* forcing her to return to Pearl Harbor to be patched up. More reciprocal treatment was dished out by both sides over the course of the next few hours as a group of five Japanese destroyers spent a fruitless night in shelling Henderson Airfield, only to witness planes from that still functional airbase next morning sink the fast transport *Kinryu Maru*, the destroyer *Mutsuki*, and damage Tanaka's flagship, the light cruiser *Jintsu*, for good measure.[112] Although the *KA* operation (Battle of the Eastern Solomons) was abandoned at this point without any decisive victory being recorded by either side, it would not prevent both of them from striving to land troops on Guadalcanal to bolster their own positions on what would become known to the US Marine Corps as 'Starvation Island'. It would stay that way to the bitter end.[113]

It was apparent from the outset that this was to be a gruelling, high cost campaign for both sides and massive efforts were made from the outset to try and thwart the enemy's supply line operations. In the case of the Japanese military a mixture of submarine patrols and aerial surveillance was resorted to in an effort to detect American reinforcements in time for them to be destroyed before they reached Guadalcanal. Judged by their recent performances, however, things could only get better for the Japanese submarine arm. Its efforts in the Solomons campaign up to this point had been gravely disappointing and indeed something of a redundancy. Despite their inadequacy so far, Vice-Admiral Teruhisa Komatsu still had ten submarines in place in the waters off the Solomons in late August. A constant tinkerer and unwittingly the source of much of the submarine arm's woes in the recent past, he redesignated the picket lines he had originally established and then redrew them again at the end of the month and created a new line that was to run southeast of Guadalcanal specifically between the islands of San Cristobal and the Santa Cruz group. Komatsu's efforts finally began to pay off on 31 August. At dawn on that day to the east of San Cristobal and along the new picket line he had established, *Saratoga* became his first carrier victim when she was torpedoed at a distance of 3,800 yards (3,475m) by Minoru Yokota in the *I-26*. One of her six torpedoes struck home amidships on the starboard side of the carrier causing sufficient damage to the old campaigner to necessitate her making an unscheduled trip firstly to Tonga for patching up with cement filler and then on to Pearl Harbor for more thoroughgoing repairs.[114]

It would not be long before there was further rejoicing in Truk and elsewhere and with good reason. After *I-11* had attacked but missed the flagship of TF 18, the carrier *Hornet*, on 6 September, and *I-31* had got into the act by shelling the island of Graciosa two days later, *I-19* and the other eight submarines on the picket line took up the challenge of interfering with the American supply train. After learning that a new carrier group had been spotted 200nm (370km) southeast of San Cristobal Island on the afternoon of 13 September they waited to see if the enemy would continue to bear down on them. At 1350 hours on 15 September *I-19* was in the centre of Komatsu's picket line roughly 140nm (259km) southeast of San Cristobal when she caught sight of the carrier group at a distance of about 8nm (14.8 km). Takakazu Kinashi manoeuvered his way towards the warships and aided by their own changes of course the gap between them fell to a point where he had a wonderful opportunity to do some damage to the closest carrier *Wasp*. At 1445 hours Kinashi fired six Type 95 torpedoes at her some 1,000 yards (914m) distant. Three of these torpedoes struck home on the starboard side of the carrier with such devastating effect that her planes were tossed around like corks, fire engulfed the forward part of the ship at various levels and a series of huge explosions swiftly rent the air shortly after 1500 hours leaving her effectively dead in the water and listing badly. She was abandoned at

1520 hours and eventually torpedoed by the destroyer *Lansdowne* at 2100 hours. Kinashi's other three torpedoes went on to run into another carrier group a further 12nm (22km) away. One struck the modern battleship *North Carolina* causing sufficient damage to put her out of action for two months; another hammered into the destroyer *O'Brien* weakening her to such an extent that on her way back to the US on 19 October she broke apart and sank. Only one of Kinashi's spread of six torpedoes didn't actually find a target. It was an extraordinary attack and underlined the quality of the Japanese torpedoes. Was this an augury of what was to come in the waters around the Solomons or was it a case of beginner's luck? Only time would tell.[115]

While the opening moves for ultimate control of Guadalcanal and the entire Solomons group were being made in the South Pacific, the Japanese made an effort to wrest the southeastern peninsula of Papua New Guinea from the grip of the Allied forces by orchestrating a three-stage amphibious invasion of Goodenough Island and Milne Bay in late August. Although over 3,200 troops of the Kure and Sasebo Special Landing Forces were involved in the invasion, they were unable to break out of their beachhead as the battle hardened American and Australian ground troops and fierce aerial bombing and strafing put them on the defensive. Lacking sufficient troops and resources to do the job assigned to them and sustaining considerable casualties from a relentless series of attacks upon them, the battered remnants of the Japanese invasion force were swiftly withdrawn in early September before they were totally wiped out.[116]

A growing sense that the fortunes of war were shifting was also encouraged by an improvement in the Allied position in the Indian Ocean as could be seen in the return from exile of the Eastern Fleet to Colombo at the end of July, and the sharp reduction in mercantile losses to Japanese submarine activity in the weeks thereafter. While some of this improvement in the trade war was down to pure luck rather than the result of calculated design on the part of the Allied naval and mercantile authorities, the feeling grew that the momentum built up by the all-conquering Japanese in the recent past appeared at last to be slowing down.[117] This attitude was encouraged still further by the mounting of two highly successful amphibious operations in the following month (*Stream* and *Jane*) in which the 29th Infantry Brigade was ferried to the Vichy French-held island of Madagascar and assisted in the capture of its capital Tananarive on 23 September. Although the fall of Madagascar certainly had flag-waving potential for the Allies, it also meant that there was one less refuge for Axis ships to use while out on operational sorties in the Indian Ocean.[118]

These successes were needed as the war in the European theatres remained as debilitating as ever. Upbeat after their recent mauling of the convoy system in the Arctic, the Germans continued to flex their muscles in August using the pocket-battleship *Admiral Scheer* on a fortnight's mission to barnstorm her way along the Siberian supply route that linked the White Sea ports with those in the Barents Sea and Kara Sea causing as much damage as she could. Although *Fall Wunderland* may have been only moderately successful, by staging it in the first place the Germans were making a statement that their capital ships were not about to be mothballed in Norwegian ports and were capable of being used decisively against convoys operating along any route in the Arctic and those ports, such as Dikson Island, serving that trade.[119]

By the time that the *Admiral Scheer* returned to Narvik on 30 August, the Allies were counting the cost of a failed experiment much further south in the English Channel. Operation *Jubilee* was always going to be controversial since it amounted to something more than just a cross-Channel 'smash and grab' raid on the French port of Dieppe.[120] In essence, it was an example of war gaming at its most irresponsible. In brief, the plan called for the ferrying of more than six thousand infantry troops and a strong contingent of tanks across the Channel in order to make landfall on both sides of the town. Both groups were to be given robust aerial support to assist them in taking control of Dieppe and allow them to hold the port for up to twenty-four hours before they staged a complete withdrawal once again. In this way, it was thought that the Allies would get to probe the strength of enemy defences and gain relevant, practical experience that would be useful in planning far larger amphibious invasions in the future. Reminiscent of the hijack strategy employed by Mussolini's fascists against a number of northern Italian towns in 1922 and yet far more complicated to orchestrate, *Jubilee* looked utterly out of place in the context of the war in August 1942. Instead of being played out in a staff college classroom where no material damage could be done, the plan became a grim operational reality to the 4th and 6th Brigades of the 2nd Canadian Division and the 3rd and 4th Royal Navy Commandos who were to count the heavy cost of participating in it against a substantially stronger, more cohesive enemy than the ramshackle government forces confronted by Il Duce's compatriots two decades before. In all 252 vessels were involved in mounting this untimely operation on 19 August. Things started to go badly awry even before the troops got ashore. It was certainly not in the script that the eastern landing party and its escort group would find themselves interdicting a German convoy in the dark, thereby blowing their cover, nor that the landing ships would be scattered in the mêlée that followed. As we have observed before, however, the unexpected does tend to happen to even the best laid plans and *Jubilee* was some way short of that ideal. Stout German resistance from the 302nd Infantry Division, effective coastal artillery and trusty fighter-bombers took a severe toll on those troops and tanks that got ashore and the Allied aircraft and naval vessels supporting them. By midday, judging the cause to be irretrievably lost, the order to evacuate was given and the Allies set about the doleful business of withdrawing their troops from the shoreline of the town. There was to be no miraculous Dunkirk-type escape this time. Amidst the frenzy and disarray that attended the hasty withdrawal, the Germans didn't waste their opportunity to inflict further punishment on the Allies and teach them a stark military lesson in not underestimating the enemy or the difficulty of successfully enacting any further cross-Channel enterprise in the future. As Hitler discovered to his chagrin in 1940 the relatively narrow stretch of sea between France and England looked a deceptively easy barrier to overcome, but using it as a major invasion route was quite another thing altogether. *Jubilee* was misnamed; there was little to celebrate if you were on the Allied side. Trying to take Dieppe cost the lives of 1,179 of their troops and led to another 2,190 being taken prisoner. A destroyer and thirty-three miscellaneous ships, including a number of landing craft, were sunk; three more destroyers sustained varying degrees of damage, while 106 aircraft and thirty tanks were written off.[121] Although poorly conceived and a harsh lesson to bear especially for the Canadians who bore the brunt of the German counter-attack, the Allies did nonetheless learn from this debacle, not least in giving much more thought to the potentialities of radar when it came to planning any subsequent amphibious operations than they had done on this disastrous occasion. Directly as a consequence of what had happened at Dieppe, the Allies became far more wary of committing themselves to any cross-Channel incursions in future and waited until June 1944 to open what the Soviets would see as a legitimate Second Front on the beaches of Normandy.[122]

Notes

1. Midway was a tiny Pacific atoll consisting of two islands Sand and Eastern which were hemmed in by a coral reef. Sand was the larger of the two small islands and contained most of the infrastructure of the naval base including a modern seaplane facility which could accommodate a group of PBY Catalina flying boats that would be used to patrol the seas off Midway. Eastern had three landing strips which were used as a US airbase. Jonathan Parshall and Anthony Tully, *Shattered sword: the untold story of the battle of Midway* (Washington, DC: Potomac Books, 2005), p.33.
2. Ibid., pp.33–38; Prange, *et al.*, *Miracle at Midway*, pp.21–23, 26, 28–30; Stephen, *Sea battles in close-up*, pp.137–78; John B. Lundstrom, *The first South Pacific campaign: Pacific Fleet strategy, December 1941 – June 1942* (Annapolis, Md: Naval Institute Press, 1976), pp.42–46.
3. Stephen, *Sea battles in close-up*, pp.137–38.
4. Michael Smith, *The emperor's codes: the breaking of Japan's secret ciphers* (New York: Arcade Publishing, 2007), pp.118–35, 137.
5. H.P. Willmott, *The barrier and the javelin: Japanese and Allied Pacific strategies February to June 1942* (Annapolis, Md: Naval Institute Press, 1983), pp.171–200; Prados, *Combined Fleet decoded*, pp.300–312.
6. Stephen, *Sea battles in close-up*, pp.138–39.
7. Three American aircraft out of the 99 used were lost in the three waves of attacks against what was left of the invasion fleet at Tulagi. These attacks stretched throughout the morning and into the early afternoon of 4 May. All they ended up in sinking was a solitary destroyer-transport and three minesweepers, while damaging four other vessels. Stephen, *Sea battles in close-up*, p.141; John B. Lundstrom, 'Frank Jack Fletcher got a bum rap. Part One', *Naval History*, Vol.6, No.2 (1992): 22–27; Smith, *Carrier battles*, pp.54–59.
8. For an excellent in-depth study of the Coral Sea engagement see Willmott, *Barrier and the javelin*, pp.203–87. A far briefer version by the same author is also available: H.P. Willmott, *The war with Japan: the period of balance. May 1942–October 1943* (Wilmington, Del: SR Books, 2002), pp.37–51. See also Gill, *Royal Australian Navy 1942–1945*, pp.25–57; John B. Lundstrom, *The first team: Pacific naval air combat from Pearl Harbor to Midway* (Annapolis, Md: NIP, 2005), pp.157–305. A succinct account of the aerial action can be found in Hamer, *Bombers versus battleships*, pp.165–84; Smith, *Carrier battles*, pp.39–82.

9 John B. Lundstrom, *Black shoe carrier admiral: Frank Jack Fletcher at Coral Sea, Midway, and Guadalcanal* (Annapolis, Md: NIP, 2006); Stephen D. Regan, *In bitter tempest: the biography of Admiral Frank Jack Fletcher* (Ames, Iowa: Iowa State University Press, 1994), pp.133–48.
10 Robert J. Cressman, *The Official Chronology of the US Navy in World War II* (Annapolis, Md: Naval Institute Press, 2000), p.92; Gill, *Royal Australian Navy 1942–1945*, pp.48–52.
11 Stephen, *Sea battles in close-up*, pp.145–49; Gill, *Royal Australian Navy 1942–1945*, pp.41–47.
12 Stephen, *Sea battles in close-up*, pp.145–50.
13 Of the sixty-nine Japanese aircraft that were flown off from the *Shokaku* and *Zuikaku*, thirty-three were 'Val' dive bombers, eighteen were 'Kate' torpedo bombers and eighteen were 'Zeke' fighter aircraft. Ibid., p.150.
14 One hundred and eight members of the *Shokaku*'s crew died as a result of these bomb hits and forty others were injured, while the Americans lost eleven aircraft (four from *Yorktown* and seven from *Lexington*) in the course of making these attacks. Willmott, *Barrier and the javelin*, pp.261–63.
15 Two hundred and sixteen crew members died on board the *Lexington* on this fateful day. Stephen, *Sea battles in close-up*, pp.151–55.
16 Thirty-six aircraft could not be flown off the *Lexington* and were doomed to sink with her. Ibid., pp.155–58; Willmott, *Barrier and the javelin*, p.286; A.A. Hoehling, *The Lexington goes down: a fighting carrier's last hours in the Coral Sea* (Mechanicsburg, Pa: Stackpole Books, 1993).
17 Stephen, *Sea battles in close-up*, pp.156–57; Cressman, *Official chronology of US Navy*, p.93.
18 Willmott, *Barrier and the javelin*, pp.277–78.
19 Walt Unsworth, *Everest* (London: Allen Lane, 1981), p.100.
20 Achkasov and Pavlovich, *Soviet naval operations*, pp.76–79; Ruge, *Soviets as naval opponents*, pp.77–81.
21 As an example of how fraught these passages could be, the harrowing experience of the light cruiser *Trinidad* may be cited. She had survived a torpedoing on her way out to Murmansk on 29 March only to succumb to a fatal dive-bombing attack on her return journey on 14 May. Ablaze and terminally damaged, *Trinidad* was finally put out of her misery by the Allied destroyer *Matchless* on 15 May. Mark Llewellyn Evans, *Great World War II battles in the Arctic* (Westport, Conn: Greenwood Press, 1999), p.69; Rohwer, *Chronology*, pp.164–66.
22 Four destroyers had left Alexandria on 11 May intent on attacking enemy convoys running into Benghazi. They were spotted south of Crete and attacked by fourteen Ju-88s from their base at Heraklion. *Lively* was the first to be sunk and in a second wave of attacks later in the day both *Jackal* and *Kipling* also succumbed. Rohwer, *Chronology*, p.165.
23 For a lively analysis of the operational rationale for Japanese war planning at this time see Willmott, *Barrier and the javelin*, pp.81–120.
24 Parshall and Tully, *Shattered sword*, pp.43–48.
25 Roger Pineau, 'Captain Joseph John Rochefort', in Howarth (ed.), *Men of war*, pp.541–50.
26 Smith, *The emperor's codes*, pp.132–44; Ronald Lewin, *The American magic: codes, ciphers and the defeat of Japan* (New York: Farrar Straus Giroux, 1982), pp.81–111; Potter, *Nimitz*, pp.78–90; Prados, *Combined Fleet decoded*, pp.314, 319, 323, 331–33; Spector, *Eagle against the sun*, pp.449–50; Willmott, *Barrier and the javelin*, pp.298–99, 304.
27 Known by the Japanese term *Dai-ichi Kidō Butai*, the First Mobile Striking Force had been carrying all before it in the first six months of the war. This ensured that Vice-Admiral Nagumo, though unappreciated by Yamamoto, was still basically untouchable at this time. Yamamoto's relations with Nagumo and those who supported him were poor and had been from the time of the Washington Conference onwards. Nagumo and the so-called Fleet Faction had bitterly opposed the disarmament

treaty, whereas Yamamoto had been an active supporter of it. Parshall and Tully, *Shattered sword*, pp.13–15, 22–27; Agawa, *The reluctant admiral*, pp.45, 130, 238–39, 253–54, 264–66, 308–9.

28 Many excellent accounts exist of the Battle of Midway. Any of the following sources may be consulted with advantage: Hugh Bicheno, *Midway* (London: Cassell Military, 2001); Mitsuo Fuchida and Masatake Okumiya, *Midway: the battle that doomed Japan: the Japanese Navy's story* (Annapolis, Md: Naval Institute Press, 1992); Jack Greene, *The Midway campaign, December 7, 1941 – June 6 1942* (Conshohocken, Pa: Combined Books, 1995); Philip D.Grove, *Midway* (London: Brassey's, 2004); Hamer, *Bombers versus battleships*, pp.185–203; Victor Davis Hanson, *Courage and culture: landmark battles in the rise of Western power* (New York: Anchor, 2002), pp.334–88; Alvin Kernan, *The unknown battle of Midway: the destruction of the American torpedo squadrons* (New Haven, Conn: Yale University Press, 2005); Ariel Levite, *Intelligence and strategic surprises* (New York: Columbia University Press, 1987), pp.95–134; Walter Lord, *Incredible victory* (Short Hills, N.J.: Burford Books, 1997); Parshall and Tully, *Shattered sword*; Potter, *Nimitz*, pp.91–107; Prange, *et al.*, *Miracle at Midway*; Regan, *In bitter tempest*, pp.149–78; Lisle A. Rose, *The ship that held the line: The USS Hornet and the first year of the Pacific War* (Annapolis, Md: NIP, 1995), pp.97–155; Smith, *Carriers in combat*, pp.83–150; Craig L. Symonds, *Decision at sea: five naval battles that shaped American history* (Oxford: OUP, 2005), pp.201–62; Thomas Wildenberg, 'Midway: sheer luck or better doctrine', *Naval War College Review*, Vol.58, No.1 (Winter 2005): 121–35. Much of the following account is, however, drawn from Parshall and Tully, *Shattered sword*; Prange, *et al.*, *Miracle at Midway*; Stephen, *Sea battles in close up*, pp.159–78; and Willmott, *Barrier and the javelin*, pp.291–510.

29 Rohwer, *Chronology*, pp.168–69.

30 Ibid.; Hamer, *Bombers versus battleships*, pp.185–203, p.159–65.

31 In practice this wasn't the contradiction that it seemed since the current doctrine for carrier operations was that once in combat the carrier groups would manoeuvre independently. As such, it was agreed beforehand that Spruance, as commander of TF16 with its two fleet carriers *Enterprise* and *Hornet*, would be responsible for the offensive action to be taken against the Japanese fleet, while Fletcher, on the patched up *Yorktown*, would be responsible for maintaining the combat air patrol as well as the search planes to be used in the operation. Thomas B. Buell, *The quiet warrior: a biography of Admiral Raymond A. Spruance* (Boston: Little, Brown & Co., 1974), p.129; John F. Wukovits, 'Raymond A. Spruance', in Howarth (ed.), *Men of war*, pp.158–76.

32 *Yorktown* was repaired by 1,400 men working around the clock. They did so sufficiently to enable her to go back out to sea in three days. Stephen, *Sea battles in close-up*, p165; Frank A. Driskill and Dede W. Casad, *Admiral of the hills: Chester W. Nimitz* (Austin, Tx: Eakin Press, 1983), pp.156–58; Buell, *The quiet warrior*, pp.119–28.

33 This total comprised nineteen B-17 'Flying Fortress' bombers, four B-26 'Marauder' bombers, six TBF Avenger torpedo bombers, eleven SB2U 'Vindicator' scout bombers, sixteen SBD-2 Dauntless scout bombers, twenty F2A-3 'Buffalo Brewster' fighters, seven F4F-3 Wildcat fighters, thirty-two PBY-5 Catalina flying boats and five PBY-5A Catalina flying boats. Prange, *et al.*, *Miracle at Midway*, p.435.

34 Rohwer, *Chronology*, p.169; Carl Boyd and Akihiko Yoshida, *The Japanese submarine force and World War II* (Annapolis, Md: NIP, 1996), p.79–84; Prange *et al.*, *Miracle at Midway*, pp.30–32.

35 Gill, *Royal Australian Navy 1942–1945*, pp.80–88; Stephen, *Sea battles in close-up*, p.166.

36 Theobald's dispositions in the Aleutians were highly questionable and derived largely from his disbelief that the Japanese would bother with such unimportant slabs of rock as Adak, Attu and Kiska. He thought they were bound to go instead for Dutch Harbor. Potter, *Nimitz*, p.88; Willmott, *Barrier and the javelin*, pp.354–59; Cressman, *Official chronology of US Navy*, p.100, Prange *et al.*, *Miracle at Midway*, pp.155–59.

37 Stephen, *Sea battles in close-up*, p.166.

38 Timings differ slightly depending upon the source one consults, ranging from 1623 hours in the case of Parshall and Tully, *Shattered sword*, p.106, to 1640 cited by Prange, *et al.*, *Miracle at Midway*, p.172. Stephen, *Sea battles in close up*, p.166, opts for 1624 hours.
39 Of the three survivors one was a 'Brewster Buffalo' and the other two were Wildcat fighters, one of which couldn't retract its undercarriage. Willmott, *Barrier and the javelin*, p.380.
40 Seven were lost in combat, four were ditched in the sea and three were found to be inoperable once they had returned to their carriers. Ibid., pp.377–78.
41 Prange, *Miracle at Midway*, pp.199–206.
42 Parshall and Tully, *Shattered sword*, pp.149–57.
43 Ibid., pp.159–64.
44 Ibid., pp.170–83; Willmott, *Barrier and the javelin*, pp.382–92; Stephen, *Sea battles in close-up*, pp.167–69.
45 Parshall and Tully, *Shattered sword*, p.183; Willmott, *Barrier and the javelin*, p.392.
46 Willmott, *Barrier and the javelin*, pp.392–99.
47 Buell, *The quiet warrior*, pp.129–50.
48 Controversy continues to stalk the destruction of Lt.-Cdr. John C. Waldron's VT-8 – the fifteen torpedo bombers from *Hornet* on the morning of 4 June. No one emerges from historical scrutiny without some of the blame attached to them for the annihilation of what was popularly known as Torpedo Eight. Mitscher, Ring and Waldron have all been subject to varying degrees of criticism in recent years and deservedly so for a number of mistakes they made that day that led to this scale of disaster. Did these aviators die in vain? Perhaps not. At the very least they prevented the Japanese carriers from embarking upon their counter-offensives earlier than they would have done otherwise. See Kernan, *Unknown battle of Midway*, pp.76–144; Parshall and Tully, *Shattered sword*, pp.xxii, 173–74, 206–7, 209, 211, 213, 216–17, 271–75, 432; Clark G. Reynolds, 'Admiral Marc A. Mitscher', in Howarth (ed.), *Men of war*, pp.244–62; Rose, *The ship that held the line*, pp.125–32, 136–37, 142–46, 149–54.
49 Stephen, *Sea battles in close-up*, pp.167–71; Willmott, *Barrier and the javelin*, pp.405–9.
50 Stephen, *Sea battles in close-up*, p.171.
51 Parshall and Tully, *Shattered sword*, pp.229–31.
52 Much against his will, Nagumo was finally prevailed upon to leave the bridge and transfer his flag to the light cruiser *Nagara*. Ibid., pp.232–36, 239–43, 256–61.
53 Parshall and Tully assert that *Sōryū* was scuttled by the destroyer *Isokaze* with three torpedoes at 1913 hours. *Kaga* was scuttled by two torpedoes fired at it by the Japanese destroyer *Hagikaze*. She finally sank at 1925 hours on 4 June. Ibid., pp.236–39, 333–39; Prange *et al.*, *Miracle at Midway*, pp.307–12; Stephen, *Sea battles in close-up*, pp.171–73.
54 Parshall and Tully, *Shattered sword*, pp.262–63; 288–99.
55 Ibid., pp.308–18, 372–75; Prange *et al.*, *Miracle at Midway*, pp.440–45; Stephen, *Sea battles in close-up.*, pp.173–76; Boyd and Yoshida, *Japanese submarine force*, pp.83–86.
56 Parshall and Tully, *Shattered sword*, pp.323–29, 333, 339–41, 349–53; Stephen, *Sea battles in close-up*, p.174.
57 Parshall and Tully, *Shattered sword*, pp.341–43.
58 Ibid., pp.342–45; Stephen, *Sea battles in close-up*, p.175.
59 Parshall and Tully, *Shattered sword*, pp 345–49, 362–63, 366–72, 375–82; Rohwer, *Chronology*, p.171.
60 For a non-aviator and a man who had never commanded a carrier before, taking over Halsey's Task Force was not an easy assignment for Spruance. Halsey had strongly supported his candidacy, but he had to convince the 'Bull's' staff that he was the man for the job. He did so by performing admirably in a calm and methodical way. Nimitz was also impressed. He is alleged to have said twenty years after Midway that 'it was a great day for the navy when Halsey had to go into hospital'.

Willmott, *Barrier and the javelin*, p.339; Michael Bess, *Choices under fire: moral dimensions of World War II* (New York: Alfred A. Knopf, 2006), pp.136–65.
61 Exact figures for aircraft lost in the Battle of Midway are still in dispute. According to Rohwer, the figure was 253, but Prange *et al.*, citing Fuchida and Okumiya and E.B. Potter, puts the figure at 332. Their respective figures for losses of American aircraft in the battle are 150 (Rohwer) and 147 (Prange *et al.*). Prange *et al.*, *Miracle at Midway*, p.396; Rohwer, *Chronology*, p.171.
62 According to the tables presented by Parshall and Tully, 110 aircrew from the carrier aircraft of the *Kidō Butai* also perished at Midway. Whether this figure is included in the overall total of 2,181 officers and crew lost on board these four carriers is not certain. Parshall and Tully, *Shattered sword*, p.476; Stephen, *Sea battles in close-up*, pp.176–77; Willmott, *Barrier and the javelin*, pp.513–23.
63 Brown, *Radar history*, p.338; Milner, *Battle of the Atlantic*, p.107.
64 For the Luftwaffe's contribution to this northern campaign see Claasen, *Hitler's northern war*, pp.194–220.
65 Woodman, *Arctic convoys 1941–1945*, pp.144–84; Schofield, *Arctic convoys*, pp.41–54; Rohwer, *Chronology*, p.167.
66 *Fuehrer conferences*, pp.284–88; Theodore Taylor, *Battle in the Arctic seas: the story of convoy PQ17* (New York: Thomas Crowell, 1976).
67 F.H. Hinsley, *et al.*, *British intelligence in the Second World War: its influence on strategy and operations. Vol.2* (London: HMSO, 1981), pp.213–14; Sebag-Montefiore, *Enigma*, pp.199–214.
68 Woodman, *Arctic convoys 1941–1945*, pp.185–257; Schofield, *Arctic convoys*, pp.55–65; Rohwer, *Chronology*, pp.175–76.
69 Rohwer, *Chronology*, p.176. Hughes and Costello, *Battle of the Atlantic*, pp.213–14.
70 Tovey's covering force was spearheaded by the two battleships *Duke of York* and *Washington* and had the carrier *Victorious*, supported by the heavy cruiser *Cumberland*, the light cruiser *Nigeria* and ultimately fourteen destroyers in attendance. Schofield, *Arctic convoys*, pp.41–65.
71 Claasen, *Hitler's northern war*, pp.210–19; Captain Jack Broome, *Convoy is to scatter* (London: William Kimber, 1972), pp 146–67; Woodman, *Arctic convoys 1941–1945*, pp.204–12.
72 Sebag-Montefiore, *Enigma*, pp.202–9; Levy, *The Royal Navy's Home Fleet in World War II*, pp.120–25; Hinsley, *British intelligence*, 1, pp.214–23; Patrick Beesly, 'Convoy PQ 17: a study of intelligence and decision-making', in Michael I. Handel (ed.), *Intelligence and military operations* (London: Frank Cass, 1990), pp.292–322.
73 Broome, *Convoy is to scatter*, pp.188–92; Woodman, *Arctic convoys 1941–1945*, pp.213–57; Hughes and Costello, *Battle of the Atlantic*, pp.213–14.
74 Barnett, *Engage the enemy*, pp.714–22; Robin Brodhurst, 'Admiral Sir Dudley Pound (1939–43)', in Malcolm H. Murfett (ed.), *The First Sea Lords* (Westport, Conn: Praeger, 1995), pp.185–200; Brian P. Farrell, 'Admiral Sir Dudley Pound', in Harrison (ed.), *Oxford Dictionary of National Biography*, Vol.45, pp.54–58.
75 Robert P. Kissel, 'PQ-17: convoy or bait?' *Command*, Vol.31 (Nov/Dec 1994): 84–91; *Fuehrer conferences*, pp.288–89.
76 Rohwer, *Chronology*, pp.175–76; Woodman, *Arctic convoys 1941–1945*, pp.220–57.
77 Although Convoy QP.13 was not subject to the same intense harassment that PQ.17 was to endure over the next few days, it too had a fraught journey to its final destination. In the dense fog and mist that covered the Denmark Strait on 5 July, five steamers and a minesweeper all perished by running onto an Allied minefield. Rohwer, *Chronology*, p.176; Schofield, *Arctic convoys*, pp.55–65.
78 Barnett, *Engage the enemy*, pp.710–22.
79 Eighty were flown off in three carrier forays during 18 May – 9 June with only four being lost to enemy action en route. Any doubts on the value of these carrier runs would be more than adequately resolved by consulting the sources devoted to the

aerial defence of Malta. See, in particular, Christopher Shores and Brian Cull with Nicola Malizia, *Malta: the Hurricane years 1940–41* (London: Grub Street, 1987) and *Malta: the Spitfire year 1942* (London: Grub Street, 1991). See also Gill, *Royal Australian Navy 1942–1945*, pp.89–99.

80 Part of the reason may lie in the lack of radar aboard the vessels of the RMI. Italian radar development had been stalled in the late 1930s and was only revived after the Battle of Matapan had proved fairly conclusively that the enemy possessed radar and that the Italians needed to develop their own capability in this technical area if they were to combat the Allied menace. A radar set of doubtful capability was duly installed on the battleship *Littorio* by the close of 1941 and its performance may have done little to advance the technological cause. Ultimately, both the delay in developing its own radar system and the lack of its own carrier planes would hamstring the Italian Navy's performance in the war. Brown, *A radar history of World War II*, pp.205–15.

81 Such was the size and importance of these two convoys that the Axis Powers deployed two battleships, three heavy cruisers, four light cruisers, eighteen destroyers and six German MTBs along with twenty-two Italian submarines and six U-boats in a vain bid to wreck them. Richard Woodman, *Malta convoys 1940–1943* (London: John Murray, 2003), pp.317–68; Greene and Massignani, *Naval war in the Mediterranean*, pp.232–41; Admiralty Historical Section, *The Royal Navy and the Mediterranean convoys*, pp.55–79.

82 German planes sank two destroyers, four freighters and a tanker, and secured bomb hits on a cruiser, a corvette and two freighters, while the Italian Savoias sank a freighter and damaged a cruiser. Their tally would have almost certainly been much higher still but for the determined A.A. fire of the convoys' close escort groups. Rohwer, *Chronology*, pp.173–74.

83 Ibid.; Greene and Massignani, *Naval war in the Mediterranean*, pp.232–41; Sadkovich, *Italian Navy in World War II*, pp.256–65.

84 Rohwer, *Chronology*, p.172, 176–77; Achkasov and Pavlovich, *Soviet naval operations*, pp.79–81; Ruge, *Soviets as naval opponents*, pp.79–82.

85 It was a fraught and deadly evacuation. Lt-Cdr. Christiansen, commanding the 1st S-Boat Flotilla, demonstrated this perfectly by sinking nineteen vessels of the Soviet evacuation fleet over the course of three nights for the self-induced loss of *S-27*, accidentally sunk by one of her own torpedoes! Rohwer, *Chronology*, pp.177, 181–82, 184–85, 188–90, 192–94.

86 Ibid., p.193; Achkasov and Pavlovich, *Soviet naval operations*, pp.156–61, 188; Ruge, *Soviets as naval opponents*, pp.81–86.

87 Rohwer, *Chronology*, pp.178–79; Ruge, *Soviets as naval opponents*, pp.24–27. Achkasov and Pavlovich erroneously give the date for the failed invasion of Sommers Island (Someri) as 8–10 June, see *Soviet naval operations*, pp.230–34.

88 Aided by torpedo cutters, patrol boats and supported by units of the naval air force, five of their submarines had finally broken through the *Seeigel* mine barrage in the Gulf of Finland by mid-June, only to lose one of them (*M-95*) on a mine east of Suursaari on 13 June. In the weeks thereafter further attempts were made to get successive waves of submarines through these obstacles so that their operational scope could be extended and more German ships could be attacked and their trade disrupted. Finnish and German submarine-chasers were employed to bring additional menace to what was already a complicated undertaking. Achkasov and Pavlovich, *Soviet naval operations*, pp.233–39; Rohwer, *Chronology*, p.172.

89 Spread across the Pacific, the IJN was reorganised on 14 July and contained a total of six fleet carriers (*Hiyo, Jun'yō, Ryūjō, Shōkaku, Zuihō, Zuikaku*); two escort carriers (*Taiyo, Unyo*); three seaplane carriers (*Chitose, Chiyoda, Nisshin*); ten battleships (*Fusō, Haruna, Hiei, Kirishima, Kongō, Musashi, Mutsu, Nagato, Yamashiro, Yamato*); fifteen heavy cruisers (*Aoba, Atago, Chikuma, Chōkai, Furutaka, Haguro, Kako, Kinugasa, Kumano, Maya, Myōkō, Nachi, Takao, Suzuya, Tone*); fourteen light cruisers (*Abukuma, Jintsu, Kashima,*

Katori, Kiso, Kitakami, Nagara, Oi, Sendai, Tama, Tatsuta, Tenryū, Yūbari, Yura); three auxiliary cruisers; sixty-eight destroyers; and forty-eight submarines. Rohwer, *Chronology*, pp.180–81.
90 A battalion of the South Sea Detachment of the IJA had been landed in Salamaua and a naval unit had landed at Lae on the Huon Gulf of New Guinea on 8 March. Later in the month Japanese troops were ferried to Buka, Kessa and finally to Shortland in the northern Solomons and throughout April elements of the IJA had secured a number of other towns in the western and central parts of New Guinea, including Manus Island, Sarmi and Hollandia. Shortland had been converted into a seaplane base by 28 April and Tulagi in the Solomons group was occupied on 3 May as the potential site for another airfield. Shortly afterwards, Guadalcanal was identified by the Yokohama Air Group (18 May) as having considerable potential as a regional airbase. Given the loss of his carriers, the necessity for establishing aerial dominance in the region took on added significance for Yamamoto. Willmott, *War with Japan*, pp.103–5.
91 Ibid.
92 TF1, under Vice-Admiral William Pye, contained seven old battleships (*Colorado, Idaho, Maryland, Mississippi, New Mexico, Pennsylvania, Tennessee*) and between eight and ten destroyers; TF11, under Rear-Admiral Fitch, was to have the carrier *Saratoga*, three cruisers (*Astoria, Minneapolis, New Orleans*) and seven destroyers; Rear-Admiral Frank Fletcher took over TF16, with the carrier, *Enterprise*, the A.A. cruiser *Atlanta*, two additional cruisers (*Chester, Portland*) and seven destroyers; while TF17, with the carrier *Hornet*, four cruisers (*Northampton, Pensacola, Salt Lake City, San Diego*) and seven destroyers, became the responsibility of Rear-Admiral Marc Mitscher. Of the other groups TF8, commanded by Rear-Admiral Robert Theobald, had five cruisers (*Honolulu, Indianapolis, Louisville, Nashville, St. Louis*) and five destroyers in its ranks; TF18, commanded by Rear-Admiral Noyes, had the carrier *Wasp*, the new battleship *North Carolina*, the heavy cruisers *Quincy* and *Vincennes* and two other cruisers (*San Francisco, San Juan*) and eight destroyers in its ranks; and TF44, under the command of Rear-Admiral Crutchley from the Royal Navy, had with him a total of four cruisers (*Australia, Canberra, Chicago, Hobart*) and nine destroyers. Rohwer, *Chronology*, p.172.
93 Clayton James, *Years of MacArthur: 1941–45*, pp.184–202; Thomas B. Buell, *Master of sea power: a biography of Admiral Ernest J. King* (Boston: Little, Brown & Co., 1980), pp.214–17.
94 In order to facilitate these command arrangements, the boundary of Nimitz's area of responsibility in the South Pacific was moved 1° West to include the islands of Florida, Guadalcanal, Malaita, the Russells, San Cristobal and Tulagi. Willmott, *War with Japan*, pp.90–99; Ernest J. King and Walter M. Whitehill, *Fleet Admiral King: a naval record* (New York: W.W. Norton, 1952), pp.381–89.
95 MacArthur had much to say about the Allied Air Forces and its commander Lt. General George Brett, but little of it was good. Brett was replaced on 14 July by General George Kenney – a man who revamped the air strategy and its leading personnel. MacArthur approved his plans for attacking Japanese aerial domination of the region until the Allies 'owned the air over New Guinea'. Kenney was subsequently put in charge of the newly formed Fifth Air Force on 5 September. MacArthur and Kenney admired one another greatly and worked wonderfully well together. Clayton James, *Years of MacArthur: 1941–45*, pp.192–202.
96 Willmott, *War with Japan*, pp.104–8, 113–15.
97 Paolo E. Coletta, 'Admiral Richmond K. Turner', in Howarth (ed.), *Men of war*, pp.363–79.
98 George Carroll Dyer, *The amphibians came to conquer: the story of Admiral Richmond Kelly Turner. Vol.I* (Washington, D.C.: Department of the Navy, 1972), pp.229–353, 403–34; Johnson, *The Pacific campaign in World War II*, pp.136–316. For a less sympathetic treatment of Turner, see William H. Bartsch, 'Operation Dovetail: bungled

Guadalcanal rehearsal, July 1942', *The Journal of Military History*, Vol.66, No.2 (April 2002): 443–76.

99 There is a wealth of literature on the struggle for Guadalcanal. Apart from the sources already cited in this work that bear on it, one may profitably consult the following volumes for insights on the campaign: Richard B. Frank, *Guadalcanal* (New York: Random House, 1990); Eric Hammel, *Guadalcanal: the carrier battles. Carrier operations in the Solomons August–October, 1942* (New York: Crown Publishers, 1987) and *Guadalcanal: starvation island* (Pacifica, Ca: Pacifica Press, 1995); Edwin P. Hoyt, *Guadalcanal* (New York: Stein & Day, 1982).

100 Rohwer, *Chronology*, pp.183, 185; Prados, *Combined Fleet decoded*, pp.355–96; Schom, *Eagle and the rising sun*, pp.311–456; Spector, *Eagle against the sun*, pp.184–87, 190–214.

101 Mikawa's flagship *Chōkai* led the other four heavy cruisers *Aoba*, *Kako*, *Kinugasa* and *Furutaka*, the light cruisers *Tenryū* and *Yūbari*, and the solitary destroyer *Yūnagi* in a single line-ahead formation that stretched over two nautical miles.

102 Writing of this failure of American radar to detect enemy craft at close quarters, Louis Brown states that it was caused by a combination of 'poor equipment performance, inadequate training and the confusion for meter-wave sets caused by the presence of nearby land'. Brown, *Radar history*, p.251.

103 William Bruce Johnson, *The Pacific campaign in World War II: from Pearl Harbor to Guadalcanal* (London: Routledge, 2006), pp.177–96; Vincent P. O'Hara, *The U.S. Navy against the Axis: surface combat, 1941–1945* (Annapolis, Md: NIP, 2007), pp.67–81; Bruce Loxton with Chris Coulthard-Clark, *The shame of Savo* (Annapolis, Md: NIP, 1994); Dennis and Peggy Warner with Sadao Seno, *Disaster in the Pacific: new light on the Battle of Savo Island* (Annapolis, Md: NIP, 1992); Dyer, *The amphibians came to conquer*, pp.355–402.

104 Fletcher's reputation, which had already taken a few knocks after the failure to relieve Wake Island in the Central Pacific in December 1941 and after a somewhat lacklustre performance in the Battle of the Coral Sea, suffered greatly as a result of his withdrawal of the three carriers at Guadalcanal. John B. Lundstrom doesn't believe it's a fair assessment and provides a sterling defence of one of Nimitz's friends in his 'Frank Jack Fletcher got a bum rap. Part two Guadalcanal', *Naval History*, Vol.6, no.3 (Fall 1992): 22–28; Smith agrees wholeheartedly with Lundstrom and is utterly scathing about the performance of Kelly Turner, see his *Carrier battles*, pp.161–64, 176–79; Brown, *Radar history*, pp.250–52; Dull, *Battle history of the IJN*, pp.184–94; Frank, *Guadalcanal*, pp.104–23; Johnson, *Pacific campaign in World War II*, pp.177–96.

105 Although the heavy cruisers *Chōkai* and *Kinugasa* were slightly damaged in the Battle of Savo Island, Mikawa was to lose *Kako*, another of his heavy cruisers, to three torpedoes from the US submarine *S44* off Kavieng on 10 August. Frank, *Guadalcanal*, pp.116–17; Regan, *In bitter tempest*, pp.195–211.

106 Left in tactical command of the Support Force when Rear-Admiral Crutchley went to meet Rear-Admiral Turner for a conference in the Lunga Roads during the evening of 8 August, Captain Howard Bode had fallen asleep in his cabin of the heavy cruiser *Chicago* and was not on active duty when Mikawa's warships began the action after midnight. In the official inquiry that followed he was censured for his dilatory behaviour on the night in question (8–9 August). He subsequently committed suicide. Frank, *Guadalcanal*, pp.120–23; Gill, *Royal Australian Navy 1942–1945*, pp.131–55.

107 Frank, *Guadalcanal*, p.123.

108 Ibid.; Pfennigwerth, *Missing pieces*, pp.81–90.

109 If so, a more grisly start could hardly be imagined since all 916 men of the Ichiki Detachment having been landed by six destroyers to the east of the Marine division's bridgehead on Guadalcanal during the night of 18–19 August were killed in attacks on it subsequently. Frank, *Guadalcanal*, pp.124–58; Rohwer, *Chronology*, p.187.

110 A vital role in the defence of Henderson Field was played by the relatively small number of pilots from the US Army, Marine Corps and Navy who formed the so-called Cactus Air Force and were based at this crucial air base on Guadalcanal. Their story is told graphically in Thomas G. Miller, Jr., *The Cactus Air Force: the story of the handful of fliers who saved Guadalcanal* (New York: Harper & Row, 1969); Johnson, *The Pacific campaign*, pp.227–32.

111 Dull, *Battle history of the IJN*, pp.197–207; Frank, *Guadalcanal*, pp.159–93; Hammel, *Guadalcanal: the carrier battles*, pp.92–235.

112 Smith, *Carrier battles*, pp.64–73.

113 Four B-17s from the 11th Heavy Bombardment Group at Espiritu Santo got into the act on the morning of 25 August when they found the destroyer *Mutsuki* picking up survivors from the sinking transport *Kinryu Maru* some 40nm north of Santa Isabel. They swiftly bombed and sank the destroyer. This brought the action to a close. Eric Hammel, *Carrier clash: the invasion of Guadalcanal and the Battle of the Eastern Solomons: August 1942* (Pacifica, Ca: Pacifica Press, 1997); Frank, *Guadalcanal*, pp.194–217; Rohwer, *Chronology*, pp.190–91; Stafford, *Big E*, pp.137–69.

114 Only twelve crew members were injured by the torpedoing. Despite the fact that most accounts suggest that Admiral Frank Fletcher's head wound forced him to return with his carrier, Harry Smith, his flag lieutenant, cannot remember him having any head wound, much less a serious one. Admiral King was not enamoured of Fletcher (or his caution) and saw little place for a man of his talents in the upper echelons of his service, and even Nimitz, who liked and respected him, put him on shore leave to allow him to rest and recuperate after a hectic year in command. Frank, *Guadalcanal*, pp.203–5; Lundstrom, 'Frank Jack Fletcher got a bum rap. Part two': 22–28; Regan, *In bitter tempest*, pp.212–23; Boyd and Yoshida, *Japanese submarine force*, p.98.

115 Aboard the *Wasp*, 173 officers and crew died and 400 were injured. She lost all forty-five aircraft that were on the carrier at the time of the attack and one of those that were airborne. *Hornet* became the temporary home for the remaining twenty-five that had been on patrol. Frank, *Guadalcanal*, pp.247–51; Hammel, *Guadalcanal: the carrier battles*, pp.239–80; Boyd and Yoshida, *Japanese submarine force*, p.99; Dull, *Battle history of the IJN*, p.214; Garzke, Jr. and Dulin, Jr., *Battleships*, pp.35–39; Rohwer, *Chronology*, pp.193–95.

116 Peter Brune, *The spell broken: exploding the myth of Japanese invincibility* (London: Allen & Unwin, 1997), pp.1–146; Clive Baker and Greg Knight, *Milne Bay 1942: the story of 'Milne-Force'*. Fourth edition (Loftus, NSW: Australian Military History Publications, 2000); David Wilson, *The decisive factor: 75 and 76 Squadrons – Port Moresby and Milne Bay 1942* (Melbourne, Vic: Banner Books, 1991), pp.77–195; Gill, *Royal Australian Navy 1942–1945*, pp.114, 116, 120, 128, 134, 156–57, 165–67, 172–76, 181–83, 224–25; Clayton James, *Years of MacArthur: 1941–1945*, pp.206–9; Rohwer, *Chronology*, p.191; Dull, *Battle history of the IJN*, pp.176–78.

117 An interesting contrast can easily be made by looking at the figures for the period 30 May – 26 July in which four Japanese submarines and two auxiliary cruisers sank a total of twenty-five ships (120,119 tons) and comparing them with both the six-week cruise which five submarines undertook from 15 August which sank only five ships (28,540 tons) and the three-week cruise of three submarines immediately thereafter in which five vessels (14,679 tons) were sunk. In what could be seen as the good old days, midget submarines from *I-16* and *I-20* even managed to get in amongst the Allied naval forces in Diego Suarez and torpedo the old battleship, *Ramillies*, on 31 May. Rohwer, *Chronology*, pp.169–70, 189, 198; Agawa, *The reluctant admiral*, pp.323–28; Hoyt, *Yamamoto*, pp.173–78.

118 Vichy French resistance continued until the last of their troops surrendered finally at Ihosy on 5 November. Gill, *Royal Australian Navy 1942–1945*, pp.187–90; Rohwer, *Chronology*, pp.184, 195.

119 Achkasov and Pavlovich, *Soviet naval operations*, pp.300–303; Ruge, *Soviets as naval opponents*, pp.148–49; *Fuehrer conferences*, pp.291–92.

120 Mountbatten's role in promoting and implementing *Jubilee* (a replacement for Operation *Rutter*) is highly controversial. Combined Operations Command which he headed had not been the stellar success that either he or his mentor Churchill had wished. It remains a moot point whether the Dieppe raid was officially sanctioned or whether Mountbatten circumvented COS and War Cabinet approval. See Peter J. Henshaw, 'The British Chiefs of Staff Committee and the preparation of the Dieppe raid, March–August 1942: did Mountbatten really evade the committee's authority?' *War in History*, Vol.1, No.2 (1994): 197–214; Brian L. Villa, *Unauthorized action: Mountbatten and the Dieppe Raid* (Toronto: OUP, 1989); Philip Zeigler, *Mountbatten: the official biography* (London: Collins, 1985), pp.185–97, 200, 204, 207, 523, 657–58; Barry Hunt and Donald Schurman, 'Prelude to Dieppe: thoughts on Combined Operations policy in the "raiding period" 1940–42', in Gerald Jordan (ed.), *Naval warfare in the twentieth century* (London: Croom Helm, 1977), pp.186–209; Robin Neillands, *The Dieppe raid: the story of the disastrous 1942 expedition* (London: Aurum Press, 2006).

121 German losses were 311 dead or missing and forty-eight aircraft destroyed. Rohwer, *Chronology*, p.190; Jefferson, *Coastal forces*, pp.130–31; Miller, *War at sea*, pp.313–14; Scott, *Battle of the narrow seas*, pp.92–108.

122 For additional full length treatments of this emotive subject see Ronald Atkin, *Dieppe 1942: the Jubilee disaster* (London: Macmillan, 1980); John Campbell, *Dieppe revisited: a documentary investigation* (London: Frank Cass, 1993); Villa, *Unauthorized action*.

7 From defence to attack in the autumn of 1942

Messages from other theatres of the war were not always so readily understood or acted upon as that occasioned by the egregious Dieppe raid. In the Western Atlantic and particularly in the Caribbean and Gulf of Mexico, for instance, the Allies either failed to appreciate or chose to ignore the degree to which the U-boat was carving up mercantile trade in those seas. In many cases it came down to a simple question of priorities. Much of the local and regional mercantile trade – especially in perishable items – would continue to be carried independently by cargo ships in these waters until more warships were made available for escort duty and the authorities could begin to organise convoy facilities to protect the steamers and small craft engaged in this trade. Crudely put, unless these cargoes were important internationally, or to the war effort specifically, they would remain on a relatively low rung of importance in Admiralty thinking. All the while the trade was carried on in an unprotected way, a relatively small number of U-boats feasted upon it with relish. In a seven-month spell from 3 June onwards, for example, Dönitz committed a total of forty-six U-boats and an Italian submarine – often in groups of three or four at a time – to the Caribbean and Gulf of Mexico sinking at least 185 ships (926,153 tons) for the loss of only five of his U-boats. This scale of devastation could not be tolerated for long and a 'through' convoy system already resorted to on the East Coast of the US in mid-May had to be extended further into the West Atlantic as the summer of 1942 reached its peak. Once again the convoy system worked its magic reducing the number of easy kills for Dönitz's craft, but there were still hunting grounds, such as off the southeast coast of Trinidad and off the West African coast in the Central Atlantic, where the U-boat could perform to his overall satisfaction.[1]

In those areas deemed critical to the war effort, however, such as the North Atlantic, the dour struggle to contain the U-boat went on apace. Although the mid-Atlantic 'air gap' persisted well into 1943 – affording the Germans greater opportunities to strike at even the best equipped convoys – the provision of improved and more plentiful radar devices on board both ship and aircraft escorts, along with the development and introduction of other devices, such as Magnetic Anomaly Detectors (MAD) and sono-buoys, helped to pinpoint the lurking predators with much greater accuracy than ever before. While better detection aids were vitally important, finding means to deal with the U-boats once they had been discovered, other than avoiding them, was crucial too. Scientists and engineers were primed for the task and responded with a series of weapons, such as the 'Hedgehog' (a contact-fused 65 pound [29.5 kilo] mortar bomb that was thrown in a pattern up to 230 yards [210m] ahead of a destroyer escort), the 'Retro-bomb' (which was fired backwards from a MAD-equipped plane), and 'Fido' (the air-launched acoustic homing torpedo), that began to do the trick.[2] These advances helped to balance what had formerly been a grossly uneven contest. They could not come quickly enough for the Allies as a string of great ocean liners, such as the *Queen Elizabeth* and the *Queen Mary*, and other large passenger ships began transporting ever more American troops to the British Isles from early August onwards as part of Operation *Bolero* – part of the US build up in Europe. If the U-boats could get amongst these troop convoys massive damage could be done to the Allied cause. Although destroying troop transports would be a bonus, attacks against trade and the destruction of supplies of war materiel still remained the primary focus of Dönitz's campaign. Convoys of all types were therefore still tracked, harassed and attacked by groups of U-boats, but there was usually not the slaughter of old unless something untoward happened as it did to Convoy ON.127 in early to mid-September when all the radar equipment failed on board its escort ships (EG C.4) with the result that the destroyer *Ottawa* and seven merchant ships perished and four tankers were torpedoed but not sunk by the newly-formed *Vorwärts* group.[3]

While Dönitz was alert to the fact that Allied shipbuilding resources were being devoted to producing ever increasing numbers of 'Liberty Ships' and other cargo vessels to try to replace those steamers that his U-boats had sunk since the outset of hostilities, even he failed to appreciate just how immense American industrial resources were and what could be produced from their yards. He suspected that the US was unlikely to build more than 5 million tons of replacement craft in 1942 – a shortfall of 3.2 million tons on what he and his experts thought the American might be capable of building if they fully exerted themselves. Even though he admitted that the Allies might be able to lift their potential output to 10.4 million tons in 1943, Dönitz trusted that these figures for new construction would not be reached and that even if they were his U-boats could still keep pace with them by continuing to sink 700,000 tons of Allied shipping a month as they were already doing in 1942. As Hughes and Costello indicate, however, there was a major flaw in his assumptions:

> The United States alone was building ships faster than the Germans were sinking them by the late summer of 1942. In the autumn of that year there was a net gain for the first time of over 700,000 tons in Anglo-American tonnage and this was repeated in the next quarter. In the first quarter of 1943 it was doubled to nearly 1 ½ m. tons and the balance of new construction over losses never fell below 2 m. tons throughout 1944.[4]

Regardless of his arithmetical flaws, Dönitz acknowledged that if his U-boats were to make the sort of impact he believed they must in order to break the back of the Allies and win the war for his Führer, sharp inroads would have to be made in the enemy's overall shipping total rather than just their stock of replacement vessels. It wasn't just a question of having more U-boats to spare for the task at hand, he needed them to be faster, quieter, and to remain underwater for longer periods of time. He remained convinced that the answer lay in the pioneering work of Professor Hellmuth Walter, whose designs for a new range of U-boats incorporating the use of hydrogen peroxide turbine units inspired him as much as the promised speed of up to 30 knots satisfied Hitler when his approval was sought to develop these new vessels on 28 September 1942.[5]

Hitler's support for this new construction programme followed further U-boat successes against the Arctic convoy system. After the earlier disaster that had befallen PQ.17 in July, the Allies had resisted sending another convoy on the northern route until September. When they did finally consent to resume the supply chain with PQ.18, their concern was evident in the size of the forty-eight assorted warships that were sent to protect the thirty-nine cargo-laden freighters that formed the heart of the convoy.[6] Under these circumstances, the cost of maintaining the convoy route to Archangel and Murmansk was bound to become a matter of lively debate even if all the freighters made it to port unscathed. They didn't and the issue became as much a political as a military wedge in Anglo-Soviet relations thereafter. From the time that the convoy was first spotted on 12 September, PQ.18 was on dangerous ground. As before, a combination of Luftwaffe squadrons and a group of U-boats did the damage over the course of the next few days. A freighter, a steamer and a tanker all fell victim to a series of U-boat attacks and a mix of dive and torpedo-bombers demolished nine freighters and a Soviet steamer belonging to the convoy. Without *Avenger*'s carrier planes, a blanket of persistent bad weather, and a high number of torpedo failures, the toll might well have been a good deal heavier than it was. For once, though, the Allies were not the only ones to suffer. Three of the German U-boats perished at the hands of the close support group's destroyers and twenty-two of their aircraft were downed for the loss of four Allied Hurricanes.[7] Nonetheless, an attritional rate of 28% – though a good deal better than its unfortunate predecessor's 65% – was high for any convoy and especially so because of the amount of protection it had been afforded on its passage to the Kola Inlet.[8] Whether it was too high became a matter of interpretation and the focus of much animated discussion in Admiralty circles in Whitehall. While the Soviets insisted that these convoys must be maintained – warning the British that they would consider any cancellation of them as an article of bad faith – their case was undermined to some extent by the fate of QP.14 which set off from Archangel bound for Iceland with fifteen cargo ships and thirteen escorts on 13 September. Seven U-boats were deployed to deal with this new convoy and in a series of attacks lasting from 20 to 22 September, four Allied freighters, a minesweeper and a destroyer from the close support group that had previously been assigned to PQ.18 were all sunk. Unless this was a one-off episode, it looked as though the Germans were now prepared to try and stifle this leg of the convoy route in addition to the PQ series and the

Admiralty sensed that the time had come to enlist Churchill's support for a moratorium on these sailings for the time being.[9]

At the same time that the drama surrounding PQ.18 was being played out in the Arctic, a singularly unfortunate chain of events was taking place in the South Atlantic. Human errors of judgement that end up in costing lives are always to be regretted whether they occur in peace or wartime, and the *Laconia* affair was one such tragedy that could have been avoided but sadly wasn't for all the wrong motives. It began some 500nm (926km) northeast of Ascension Island with the torpedoing late at night (2200 hours) of a large Allied transport by the Type IX U-boat *U156* on 12 September. Kapitänleutnant Werner Hartenstein, *U156*'s much decorated commander, had not bargained on the former White Star liner *Laconia* (19,695 tons) carrying in addition to her crew of 136 a group of eighty women and children, 428 British and Polish troops and some 1,800 Italian POWs at the time of her sinking. Once *U156* had surfaced after the attack, Hartenstein was greeted by a quite unforgettable sight of well over two thousand people bobbing around in the water struggling for survival. After informing his superiors in Hamburg, he began picking up as many survivors as possible, stashing them wherever room could be found for them both above and below deck, and helping to cram even more into *Laconia*'s few usable lifeboats. Helpful though this was, there were still hundreds of others who were clinging to life in the sea and so Hartenstein used his W/T to broadcast in plain language an appeal for help in rescuing these survivors from both friend and foe alike. All sides scrambled to help: Dönitz sent two U-boats (*U506* and *U507*) as well as an Italian submarine (*Cappellini*) to the scene; the Vichy French agreed to send some vessels from their ports in Senegal and Dahomey; and the British dispatched their auxiliary cruiser *Corinthian* and merchant ship *Empire Haven* from Takoradi, but did so with a request for air support from the American base on Ascension Island just in case the German promise not to attack them did not amount to much. After being on the surface for more than two and a half days, *U156* was joined on 15 September by the other U-boats that Dönitz had sent to assist in the rescue attempt. All four submarines with Red Cross flags festooned all over their gun decks and their hulls lined with survivors then began the slow process of towing the serviceable lifeboats to a rendezvous with the Vichy French ships that were coming from the West African coast. On the following day Lieutenant James Harden piloting a US B-24 Liberator bomber from the USAAF 343rd Bombardment Squadron was on his way from Ascension Island to Africa when he chanced upon this strange procession far below him and radioed back to base on Ascension Island informing the American authorities of what seemed to be afoot. It fell to Captain Robert Richardson III, the senior officer on duty that morning, to make the fatal decision of whether to help or hinder the rescue attempt. Richardson decided that U-boats were fair game wherever and whenever they were spotted, regardless of whether they were flying Red Cross flags or not, and ordered Harden to attack the submarines while they remained sitting ducks on the surface and before they had a chance to dive out of sight. It was the wrong move and had tragic consequences. Harden failed to plant a bomb on any of the four submarines, but in straddling *U156* he did manage to drop one bomb that landed amongst the lifeboats. Amazed by this turn of events, Hartenstein cast off the remaining lifeboats and promptly submerged, cascading all those survivors that had been living on his hull for several days into the water. In the end, 1,083 managed to survive the entire ordeal, the majority of them being picked up some hours later by three Vichy French warships and taken back to port in West Africa. Although all four U-boats escaped Harden's bombing and depth charging, Dönitz was so incensed by this example of squalid opportunism on the part of the Allies that he issued the fateful *Laconia* orders on 17 September. These would be used four years later to convict him of war crimes at the Nuremberg Trials. His orders were quite explicit and indicated that in future no U-boat commanders would trouble themselves attempting to rescue any survivors from enemy vessels other than those drawn from the ranks of captain or chief engineer who were needed for purposes of interrogation. His *Laconia* orders exposed a deep vein of ruthlessness in Dönitz, but Richardson's crass error of judgement in the first place in seeking to take advantage of the situation was surely no better.[10]

In the Mediterranean Dönitz's main source of aggravation centred on the lamentable performance of the Italian military services in failing to eliminate Malta from the war. It was a feeling shared by many of his compatriots who saw the island's continued existence as an Allied redoubt – in what even the Supermarina acknowledged ought to have been an exclusively Italian domain – as a glaring example of Italian military incompetence.[11] While carriers, submarines and fast minelayers were pressed into service in order to assist the island's defence, they remained no more than short term expedients resorted to in the absence of large supply convoys.[12] If the Allies were serious about holding onto the island, therefore, they would have to organise something more substantial than a few willing, but limited capacity, submarines to keep the forces and people on Malta going.[13] Acknowledging this and the risks linked to it, the Allies set about establishing a large supply convoy in early August. Operation *Pedestal*, with thirteen transports and a tanker at its heart, was essentially two missions in one. A force of Spitfires would be flown off to Malta by the carrier *Furious* while three other carriers (*Eagle, Indomitable* and *Victorious*), would be expected to provide fighter protection for the rest of the convoy and its strong warship escorts on their route into Malta. *Pedestal*'s aims would not be easy to accomplish. For a start, the Allied convoy was expected and the Supermarina, stung by German criticism and its own record of inadequacy, was more determined than ever to take a prominent role in destroying as much of it as possible. In the hope of trapping the convoy, the Italians set out three submarine lairs. In the gap between Algiers and the Balearics they deployed five of their own submarines and two U-boats; another eleven of their own submarines were deployed in a line from the north of Tunisia to Cape Bon, and one more submarine was stationed to the west of Malta. Their surface forces, consisting of six cruisers and eleven destroyers, would be held in reserve and only committed if the convoy broke through and threatened to reach Malta.[14]

Pedestal really got underway when the supply convoy passed through the Strait of Gibraltar on 10 August with its escort of four light cruisers and eleven destroyers, along with the strong covering force of the four carriers mentioned above, the two battleships *Nelson* and *Rodney*, three more light cruisers and another fourteen destroyers. Before *Furious* had even reached her target area south of the Balearics and flown off thirty-seven Spitfires to Malta on 11 August, she and the other carriers were unsuccessfully attacked by the Italian submarine, *Uarsciek*. It was left to *U73* to show the other members of her group how to settle scores with the enemy when she fired four torpedoes into the *Eagle* sinking her and drowning 260 of her crew. This was an early and profound setback for the Allies, one on which they had not bargained beforehand. *Furious*, her job done, wasted no time in setting course for Gibraltar. On her way home accompanied by five destroyers she was attacked by the Italian submarine *Dagabur* – another from the group formed south of the Balearics. In her efforts to take out a second carrier, the submarine was surprised, rammed and sunk by *Wolverine*, one of the five destroyer escorts given to *Furious*. *Giada*, from the same group, fared a little better: although bombed and damaged by a Sunderland flying-boat she was not a total write off. Dive-bomber and torpedo-bomber attacks on the main *Pedestal* convoy for Malta intensified as the day continued; 199 German and Italian planes were committed to a series of punishing attacks that came in waves that lasted from early morning until midnight on 12–13 August. After two Italian Re 2001 fighter-bombers had found and struck the carrier *Victorious* with armour-piercing bombs that failed to live up to their manufacturers' hype by rebounding from her flight deck, a smothering group of Ju-87s had more luck in one of the afternoon sessions by wading in with three massive blows on the carrier *Indomitable* knocking out her air operations capability altogether. Interspersed with this frequent aerial activity came a probing series of submarine raids which, though effectively neutralised early in the day by the destroyer screen, began to get through during the evening as tiredness told and the requisite protective vigilance was not quite what it had been earlier in the day. By midnight these persistent attacks by Axis air and sea forces had inflicted considerable punishment on the Allied convoy. Two transports and one destroyer had been sunk; three cruisers, three transports and a tanker had all been torpedoed; and another destroyer had been badly damaged in a ramming incident with the Italian submarine *Cobalto*.[15]

It would not get any better on the following day as a number of Italian motor torpedo boats (MAS) took up the early challenge by mounting fifteen attacks in a four-hour period that netted the light cruiser *Manchester* and four transports (sunk), while another, *Rochester Castle*, despite also being bombed, eventually reached Malta later that same day. Along with the MAS boats came more aircraft in a virtually ceaseless series of raids that took out two more transports and damaged two others and a tanker. Eventually, only four transports and the sole tanker *Ohio* from the supply convoy of fourteen vessels were ushered into Maltese waters. A survival rate of only 35.7% for the supply side of the convoy meant that *Pedestal* had nearly been as costly in percentage terms as that of the infamous PQ.17. What was more worrying was that this convoy, unlike its Arctic comparison, had stuck together as much as it could under the circumstances and not been told to scatter by the Admiralty. Moreover, it had lost these transports and seen its principal escorts decimated without any intervention from the Italian surface fleet whatsoever. Held in reserve, it hadn't ventured out because of a lack of suitable air cover. So what was already a bad result might have been much worse. What this operation showed only too clearly was just how dangerous a stretch of sea the Mediterranean could be for the Allies if the Axis forces got their act together and were able to work with one another effectively. If they could exploit the singular advantages they held, such as occupation of the littoral shoreline for much of the length and breadth of the Mediterranean, the Allies would be hard put to resist them. Despite these problems, however, the Mediterranean could not be abandoned. An Allied presence there was essential for the North African theatre, and for exposing what Churchill was apt to call the soft underbelly of the Axis.[16] As such, the Allied high command was prepared to live with the inconvenience and the losses in order to maintain their presence there. *Pedestal* had barely ended when the next Spitfire supply operation, *Baritone*, was launched on 16 August.[17]

Taking heart from the spirited example set by Malta in defying all that the Axis had thrown at it, the Allies decided to take the fight to their enemies by launching a small-scale amphibious raid on Tobruk in conjunction with a simultaneous Commando raid to be engineered from the landward side. Codenamed *Agreement*, this audacious gung-ho exercise, cast in the spirit of Operation *Jubilee*, began with the departure of two destroyers (*Sikh* and *Zulu*) and 350 Marines from Alexandria on 13 September. Out at sea they met the A.A. cruiser *Coventry*, supported by the Hunt class 5th Destroyer Flotilla, eighteen MTBs and three launches containing another 150 troops. As they approached Tobruk during the following night (13–14 September), the RAF carried out a series of very heavy air raids on the fortress and the surrounding area. It wasn't enough to soften up the enemy defences, as could be painfully seen when the Marines tried to land the next morning. From the outset a chill tone was set by the Axis Powers. *Sikh* was singled out by a German coastal battery and swiftly sunk before she could cause any embarrassment to the defenders of the fortress. Warming to their task, the gunners took out another two motor launches as well. While the shore batteries were giving a good account of themselves, two squadrons of German and Italian bombers added to the chaos by homing in on *Coventry*, *Zulu* and three MTBs, sinking them all. A lone MTB ushered in by the boats of the 6th Motorised Minesweeping Flotilla made it to shore with 117 men, many of whom were swiftly rounded up along with the bedraggled survivors from the ships that had been sunk offshore. A total of 576 Allied personnel were made POWs by this latest strategic flourish that others would be quick to condemn as yet another bit of costly madcap nonsense that was not thought through sufficiently in advance before it was embarked upon. Tobruk was definitely a prize worth having, but to prise it out of the grip of the Axis troops would take more than the token forces devoted to it in Operation *Agreement*.[18]

While *Agreement* may be considered an exercise in flamboyance, the work of Allied submarines in the Mediterranean remained low key but resourceful. Over the course of the late summer and early autumn, they upped the tempo of their work in the central and eastern sectors of the Mediterranean and profited at the expense of their Italian rivals by disrupting Axis convoys, sinking escorted transports, as well as ships sailing independently, laying their own mine barrages, and supplying quantities of aviation fuel, ammunition and torpedoes on what were called their 'Magic Carpet' forays to Malta. Their sterling efforts were rewarded with steady rather than irresistible successes, but these were such as to more than justify their deployment in these waters.[19]

While Roosevelt and Churchill were still committed to a 'Germany First' strategy, the US had shown in the attack on Guadalcanal (*Watchtower*) and in the extensive measures it was prepared to take to seize control of this island in the following weeks that the vicious war against the Japanese in the Pacific had a real dynamism of its own.[20] If this was the subordinate operational theatre, it lacked none of the intensity and drama of the primary one as the naval battle off Cape Esperance, the ferocious struggle for control of Henderson Field, and the carrier battle near the Santa Cruz Islands were to prove before the month of October was out.[21] By this stage Guadalcanal had become a costly litmus test that was revealing the true state of the war in the South Pacific. If the Americans could continue reinforcing and resupplying their troops on the island, make safe their hold over Henderson Field, and force the Japanese to withdraw from Guadalcanal, the whole course of the Pacific war might begin to change. Midway had blunted some of the IJN's cutting edge, but victory at Guadalcanal would thwart Japanese designs and expansionism in the region and expose the fringes of their power in the South Pacific. It would also provide a new advance base of military operations for the US and its Allies to begin implementing their strategic design of taking the fight to the enemy and recovering some of the territories lost to the Japanese in the early months of the war. Guadalcanal would not be won by the fainthearted. It would prove to be a wretched killing slog on land, in the air and at sea from first to last. In the end final victory on Guadalcanal would come to the side that could invest the most resources and best absorb the high costs of the campaign.[22]

As the weeks went by, resupplying the troops ashore with both men and equipment became a vital ingredient in the unremitting struggle being played out in the Solomons. While the Americans set themselves the task of disrupting the enemy's nightly 'Tokyo Express' run from Rabaul and Shortland to landfall on Guadalcanal, the Japanese were equally as determined to eliminate its US equivalent from assisting in these replenishment exercises.[23] Their task was made more complicated by the fact that the Japanese submarines struggled to make any kind of impact after their short glorious burst of activity in early to mid-September.[24]

Despite the presence of Japanese submarines in the waters off Guadalcanal, convoys of ships laden with American troops from their bases at Noumea and Espiritu Santo were still making landfall on Tulagi and around Lunga Point.

One such convoy left Noumea on 9 October under Kelly Turner's command with 3,000 troops from the 164th Infantry Regiment on board two transports and eight auxiliary personnel destroyers (fast transports) accompanied by a typical destroyer escort. Covering them were three distinct groups of American warships containing the carrier *Hornet*, the battleship *Washington*, ten cruisers and sixteen destroyers, lurking south of Guadalcanal, east of Malaita and near Rennell Island. Just as the Americans sought to bring in more troops and equipment to bolster their position on Guadalcanal, the Japanese did likewise – pre-empting their opponents on this occasion by convoying 728 soldiers from the 2nd Infantry Division, along with much needed heavy artillery and tanks, into their selected anchorage at Tassafaronga on 11 October, a full two days before the Americans safely disembarked their fast transports at Lunga Point. While the American convoy was still at sea, Rear-Admiral Aritomo Gotō's Covering Force, consisting of three heavy cruisers (*Aoba*, *Furutaka*, *Kinugasa*) and two destroyers, was located by US reconnaissance planes on 11 October. It fell to Rear-Admiral Norman Scott and TF 64 patrolling in the vicinity of Rennell Island to exploit the situation. Aided by his onboard radar, Scott manoeuvred his way just before midnight (11/12 October) into the classic textbook position of 'Crossing the enemy's T' so that he was able to bring all of his guns to bear on the exposed line ahead formation of Gotō's Covering Force. Blazing away, Scott's gunners were soon rewarded with the wrecking of a heavy cruiser and a destroyer (*Furutaka* and *Fubuki* respectively) and the shelling of Gotō's flagship, the heavy cruiser *Aoba*, as well as his other destroyer (*Hatsuyuki*). Although they killed Gotō in these exchanges and landed telling blows on four of his five warships, they paid for doing so with the loss of the destroyer *Duncan* and varying degrees of damage to two of their four cruisers (*Boise* and *Salt Lake City*) and a destroyer (*Farenholt*). It was not, therefore, the unqualified success that theoretically it ought to have been; Gotō's ships had performed better at night fighting than expected and the Americans, with the advantage of surprise and numbers, had certainly not vanquished their opponents. Dive-bombers from Henderson Field did increase the yield by sinking two Japanese destroyers as they withdrew from Tassafaronga on 12 October, but the pattern of few easy victories had been set by this battle off Cape Esperance and would continue in this vein.[25]

Such was the importance given to the struggle for ascendancy on Guadalcanal that the Japanese planned an all-out effort by land, sea, and air to gain control of Henderson Field on 21 October in order to eliminate the aerial threat to their position on the island and throughout the Solomons chain posed by the American aircraft operating from that base. Vice-Admirals Kondo and Nagumo were dispatched from Truk on 11 October with their two fleets and a formidable cast of nine capital ships (five carriers and four battleships), eight heavy cruisers, two light cruisers, twenty-eight destroyers, six submarines, three freighters and four tankers to settle the matter once and for all.[26] Even before this impressive concentration of firepower had reached the waters off Ndeni on 14 October, two battleships (*Haruna* and *Kongō*) under Takeo Kurita's command had spent the previous night battering Henderson Field with 918 rounds of 356mm

(14-inch) shells, roughly 300 of which were primed with High Explosive fuses. Of ninety aircraft on the ground at this prized air base all but one were either destroyed (forty-eight) or damaged (forty-one). Another savage arterial bombardment took place on the following night (14–15 October) with Gunichi Mikawa's two heavy cruisers (*Chōkai* and *Kinugasa*) firing 752 rounds of 203mm (8-inch) shells at the same target, and the dose was repeated once more during the night of 15–16 October when Rear-Admirals Omori and Tanaka brought two heavy cruisers (*Maya* and *Myokō*) to pound the airfield with nearly 1,500 rounds of 203mm shells. Henderson Field somehow absorbed the punishment it received and was not rendered inoperable. While these ferocious onslaughts had been going on in the waters off Guadalcanal, eleven Japanese destroyers had been able to escort six of their transports through to Tassafaronga under cover of darkness on 14–15 October and safely disgorge the 4,500 troops they had on board belonging to the 2nd and 38th Infantry Divisions. Thereafter, destroyers from both sides were involved in nightly runs to Guadalcanal bringing in much needed supplies for their troops and providing them with the means to continue the fight for possession and control of Henderson Field.[27]

Amphibious operations are rarely easy when invasions are fiercely contested, but once ashore the logistical problem of keeping the men and their equipment together in preparation for a major push against a stubbornly held target like the air base proved to be far more difficult than anticipated. Attacks on the US Marines guarding the perimeter of Henderson Field continued, but the attackers did not possess sufficient firepower on the ground to enable the Japanese troops to capture the base. What was meant to have fallen into Japanese hands by 21 October still remained beyond their control three days later. Premature but welcome news that its defences had finally been breached during the night of 24–25 October provided the Combined Fleet with the opportunity to capitalise on this apparent success by dealing with the reconstituted American task force (TF 64) that had been repeatedly spotted by Japanese reconnaissance planes over the past few days. While Kondo and Nagumo aimed to overwhelm Scott's warships, Rear-Admiral Tamotsu Takama set out from Shortland with another cruiser (*Yuru*), a destroyer leader (*Akizuki*) and seven destroyers to engage in the first recorded daylight bombardment of Lunga Point. *Yuru* never got to shell the enemy disembarkation point. She was found by enemy dive-bombers from Henderson Field on 25 October and hit repeatedly forcing Takama to abandon her later that same day. Nonetheless, the plan, suffused with Japanese overconfidence and an underestimation of their American foe, had said it all. Success had been rather taken for granted and was based on the assumption that once (not if) the Americans had lost Henderson Field their hold on Guadalcanal would be loosened and their aerial threat would be severely diminished.[28]

While Takama disconcertingly found that there was surprising life in the old dog yet, the rest of the Combined Fleet, out hunting for the oft-sighted TF 64, were soon to discover rather more than they bargained for as well. It was catching. While the Americans knew about the existence of Abe's Vanguard Group (the battleships *Hiei* and *Kirishima*; the three heavy cruisers *Chikuma*,

Suzuya and *Tone*; a light cruiser; and seven destroyers) thanks to a report logged by a shore-based Catalina flying-boat on 23 October, they did not learn of Nagumo's Striking Force carriers steaming malevolently behind them until two days later. By this time (25 October) they too had a combined task force at sea. TF 61 and TF 17 had joined up 273nm (506km) northeast of Espiritu Santo the day before. As a group it contained two carriers, a battleship, three heavy cruisers, three light cruisers and thirteen destroyers – more than adequate to deal with Abe's Vanguard Group, but definitely not sufficient to cope with all of the elements of the Combined Fleet unless it did so on a 'hit-and-run' basis. If they were drawn into a full scale engagement with the Japanese, Rear-Admirals Thomas C. Kinkaid and George Murray (the commanders of TF 61 and TF 17 respectively) would need the battleship *Washington*, the heavy cruiser *San Francisco*, the pair of light cruisers and six destroyers belonging to Willis Lee's TF 64 with them to make a decent fight of it. Even then they would still be outnumbered by the Japanese in every department other than in light cruisers. Leaving Takama's ships out of the calculation, the Japanese had double the number of carriers (four) and battleships (four) that their opponents possessed, they also led in heavy cruisers (eight to four), and in destroyers (twenty-five to nineteen). Only in light cruisers (two to five) did they lag behind the Americans. No wonder the Japanese were confident. They rarely failed to commit substantial forces to their operations regardless of what the Americans sent to sea. This meant that sometimes a mismatch occurred and an opportunity presented itself to overwhelm their opponents. Here close to the Santa Cruz Islands was just such an opportunity.[29]

After some skirmishing on 25 October, the carrier battle began in earnest on the following day. A reconnaissance plane belonging to the *Tone* from the Vanguard Group set the scene by locating the two US carriers (*Enterprise* and *Hornet*) early in the morning. As a result, 109 planes from Nagumo's three carriers flew off to attack them in two waves of sixty-five and forty-four and the *Jun'yō*, some distance in the rear, supplied twenty-nine more planes a little while later. While the Japanese were preparing their response, sixteen dive-bombers from the *Enterprise* rediscovered the Vanguard Group and the Striking Force and promptly set about attacking the carriers. They struck the *Zuihō*'s flight deck knocking her out of the forthcoming battle but not sinking her. Once this news was reported, another seventy-three planes were readied for action from the *Enterprise* and the *Hornet*. Those from the *Hornet*'s first group set course for the carriers and managed three massive hits on the *Shōkaku*, forcing Nagumo to move his flag yet again, and *Hornet*'s second group teamed up with those from the *Enterprise* to take on the ships in the Vanguard Group recording five powerful strikes on the *Chikuma* before wheeling away to return from whence they came, or so they thought. When they returned from their mission, however, they found the *Hornet* unable to receive them. Although her fighter cover had done sterling service in knocking out many of the incoming dive and torpedo-bombers, enough had got through to hit the *Hornet* nine times (four bombs, three torpedoes and two planes). Not surprisingly, given this sort of rough treatment, she had become a floating wreck. That she remained afloat for many hours more and defied further tremendous punishment is testament to her design and obduracy.[30] Once they had eliminated her as a practical threat, the Japanese carrier planes turned their attention to the *Enterprise* and managed two hits and a near miss on her, and recorded hits on the battleship *South Dakota*, the heavy cruiser *Portland*, the light cruiser *San Juan* and the two destroyers *Hughes* and *Smith*, for good measure. While all this was going on the Japanese submarine *I-21* also joined in the act by sinking the US destroyer *Porter*. As the Americans beat a strategic retreat to the southeast, the Japanese made moves to chase them down during the evening with their heavy ships. These efforts were unsuccessful partly because of the distances involved, partly because the carriers weren't with them – they had retired northward for the night – and partly because they were short of fuel. Although this battle is regarded as a tactical victory for the Japanese, it wasn't quite as comprehensive as that sounds. Altogether the Americans had lost a carrier and a destroyer. Their other carrier was damaged but still operational, as were one of their battleships, two of their heavy cruisers and two of their destroyers. All, admittedly, would need some dockyard attention. On the other side, two of the Japanese carriers had been rendered inoperable and one received a near-miss, a heavy cruiser had been badly damaged, while a battleship and a destroyer had also received a near-miss. They too would need extensive repairs. In addition, they had lost a large number of shore-based and carrier planes into the bargain. When all of these factors are taken into account, the Battle of Santa Cruz cannot be judged to be anything more than a narrow and increasingly hollow victory for the IJN. Contrary to earlier reports, Henderson Field had not fallen to Japanese ground troops and remained resolutely in American hands. Despite the pounding it had received, the landing strip was still, somewhat amazingly, operational and new American planes were being flown in to replace those that had been destroyed by the Japanese in the recent past. In terms of outcome, the Battle of Santa Cruz neither meant that the American presence on Guadalcanal was shakier than it had been before it began nor were the Japanese any closer to securing the all-important air base on the island. Guadalcanal's fate was not settled. Extensive supply and reinforcement operations would have to continue and the physical, emotional and materiel drain on both sides would go on for weeks more.[31]

While the struggle in the South Pacific was no nearer resolution, the same could not be said for the North African theatre. Here progress was about to be made. Despite the setbacks that had attended some of their initiatives in the Mediterranean, the Allies were about to stage their most successful ones to date with the launching of the Eighth Army's major offensive against Rommel's Afrika Korps on the El Alamein front in Cyrenaica on 23 October. Bernard Montgomery's *Lightfoot* and *Supercharge* offensives were a vital prelude to the massive Allied invasion of French North Africa (Operation *Torch*) which was designed to assist in clearing the Axis forces from this entire theatre of operations and lead on to the attack on Sicily and Italy – the supposedly soft underbelly of the enemy – in the following year. Quite apart from profoundly changing the military situation in North Africa, the ramifications of the Eighth Army's attacks in the east and the *Torch* landings in the west and the consequences that flowed from them both were to have an enormous impact on the Mediterranean, vastly altering the entire complexion of the naval struggle throughout its length and breadth and turning it from something of a supporting act to the main event in the Western hemisphere. Unlike some of the half-baked efforts that had been tried in the past, Montgomery's forces had been methodically built up to provide him with a real opportunity to do serious damage to Rommel's Panzerarmee.[32] Despite their marked superiority in terms of numbers of men, tanks and guns committed to the assault, the Eighth Army's progress during the first week of the campaign was certainly not as rapid as either London or Washington had desired. While the 'Desert Rats' slogged their way forward in Cyrenaica, reports of a substantial build up of Allied naval vessels at Gibraltar convinced the Axis Powers that an invasion was about to be staged, but they could only guess where it might be launched since they did not possess definite knowledge about its location gained from signals intelligence. Believing Sicily might be the target, the Axis forces on the island were rapidly increased and efforts to wipe out Malta as a military factor were redoubled. As the battered Allied fortress became the focus of an even more intensive bombing assault than usual, the need to keep it supplied and defended took on huge importance. As a result, Force H continued its Spitfire missions to south of the Balearics, while the fast minelayer *Welshman* and four submarines were engaged in running supply missions to the island proper. On 4 November, however, came the news of a breakthrough for the Eighth Army at El Alamein, preceding that of a crushing victory over the retreating Afrika Korps a couple of days later. Churchill was ecstatic, proclaiming it 'one of the greatest victories ever won by the British Empire in the field'.[33] Was it an augury of brighter things to come? Would *Torch*, which had been debated long and somewhat acrimoniously in Allied military circles over the summer, and was due to begin in earnest in 8 November, prove to be another stellar example of Allied cooperation and military prowess as *Lightfoot* and *Supercharge* had been?

Unfortunately, as an invasion plan *Torch* represented a compromise on the part of the Anglo-American authorities and like most compromises satisfied neither party wholly. For *Torch* to be fully successful, the Allies would have to overrun Tunisia before the Germans did. If Tunisia fell, the success of El Alamein could be built upon swiftly. If the Germans flooded new troops and armoured units into Tunisia to bolster Rommel's Panzerarmee Afrika, however, the Eighth Army would have a much harder slog on their hands to clear them out of North Africa. This is why the British, in particular, wanted to have landings east of Algiers. American concern over the U-boat threat to the Straits of Gibraltar and the safety of their troop and supply transports, however, eventually won the day and led to them taking responsibility for the landings in the west. So after a summer spent arguing about the main objective of the *Torch* offensive and the respective merits of how best to achieve it, the Allies opted for a tri-pronged assault in French North Africa that would begin simultaneously on 8 November.[34]

In the west Rear-Admiral H. Kent Hewitt (USN) was put in command of a massive invasion fleet in which the cutting edge covering forces led by the fleet carrier *Ranger* and supported by fifty-six leading warships outnumbered the twenty-nine transports and three tankers they brought with them.[35] Hewitt steered his imposing task force – carrying Major-General George C. Patton and his 34,305 troops, 54 medium tanks and 198 light tanks – to a number of landing sites along the Atlantic coast of Morocco between Safi and Mehedia. Once the troops from the 2nd US Armoured Division, as well as the US 3rd and 9th Infantry Divisions were safely ashore, their task would be to set about capturing the port city of Casablanca from the Vichy French authorities and removing it as a refuge for Axis warships and submarines. If the Allies could capture or destroy the unfinished battleship *Jean Bart* and any other vessels lying in harbour at this time so much the better.[36] Several hundred kilometres to the east in the Mediterranean, a second invasion group, led by the British Commodore Thomas Troubridge in the headquarters ship *Largs*, was charged with the task of putting Major-General Fredenhall and his 39,000 men from the 1st US Infantry Division and the US Armoured Division ashore in the vicinity of the city of Oran and the Vichy naval base at Mers-el-Kebir, scene of the infamous naval action of 3 July 1940.[37] As at Casablanca some unfinished naval business remained to be conducted in addition to the seizure of Oran from the Vichy French administration. It was very clear that the British, in particular, were anxious to eliminate, disable, or acquire as many Vichy French vessels as possible in these attacks to ensure that they wouldn't fall into the hands of the Germans and be used against them in future. A third naval juggernaut commanded by Rear-Admiral Harold Burrough (RN) on the headquarters ship *Bulolo* shepherded seventeen landing ships and sixteen supply transports containing 33,000 troops drawn from the 1st US Armoured Division, the 9th and 34th US Infantry Divisions, and the 78th British Infantry Division to their designated landing sites further east around the metropolitan port city of Algiers and headquarters of Admiral Jean François Darlan, C-in-Chief of the Vichy French Navy.[38] Closely supervising these activities was Force O which contained the carrier *Argus*, the escort carrier *Avenger*, three light cruisers and five destroyers. Should this assembled firepower not be sufficient to subdue their opponents, the two Mediterranean-based task forces could rely upon another seven capital ships, three light cruisers and seventeen destroyers belonging to Force H to assist them in their endeavours. *Torch* was never likely to go easily. Stout resistance was put up by forces loyal to the Vichy French authorities in all three major port cities targeted by the Allies. A series of valiant attacks were mounted on the Western Task Force off Casablanca by both warships and submarines but none of these efforts succeeded in preventing the landings from going ahead. Most of those engaged in these assaults perished in their attempts to get in amongst the Allied heavy ships. Of the Vichy ships at Casablanca, the light cruiser *Primauguet*, two flotilla leaders, four destroyers and eight submarines were either destroyed, beached or scuttled. Despite being shelled, bombed and severely damaged, *Jean Bart*, the focus of much of Churchill's ire and anxiety, was not broken apart. In and around Oran two Allied sloops failed to breach the harbour's defences and were sunk by a combination of coastal artillery and Vichy warships. These were isolated successes. Most of the time, the defenders lost heavily.[39]

Axis efforts to counter whatever the Allies were planning relied initially upon the number of craft that Dönitz could deploy in the Western Mediterranean. Working on reports of large concentrations of vessels in the Gibraltar area, he ordered as many U-boats as he could spare from his Mediterranean forces (twelve) and seven newly arrived from the Atlantic to take up duty west of a perpendicular line drawn from the Balearics to Algiers on 5 November. To the east of that line twenty-one Italian submarines were positioned ready for action. In theory, if and when the Allies decided to build on their success in the desert, Dönitz and his crews would be waiting for them. What they didn't expect was that *Torch* would begin as three widely dispersed and yet simultaneous invasions of the Moroccan and Algerian coastlines and that the main thrust would not be directly against the Axis Powers as such, but against the Vichy French regime in North Africa. Once the *Torch* landings began to take place, Dönitz sensed his chance and wasted no time in recalling from their stations in the North Atlantic twenty-five of his U-boats that had sufficient fuel to make the journey to the western entrance of the Mediterranean at top speed. This meant that he had a total of sixty-five submarines in position to do significant damage to the Allied supply chain in the opening fortnight of their offensive in Morocco and Algeria. In the event, the groups east of Gibraltar formed before the *Torch* landings had even begun had managed to sink two destroyers, six transports and a minesweeper, while torpedoing four more transports (beaching one of them) as well as a sloop for the loss of five U-boats and one Italian submarine. Clay Blair describes their overall performance as 'pitiful'.[40] Of the two groups that were formed after the tripartite invasion had been launched, the *Schlagetot* boats and the *Westwall* group may have sunk eleven ships (119,000 tons) and damaged five others, but they did not put a large dent in the Allied supply operation.[41] Worst of all from Dönitz's perspective, he was to lose three U-boats from his Atlantic force and have another thirteen suffer battle damage to varying degrees of severity in pursuing what was manifestly a lost cause. Much improved convoy protection and the obsolescent nature of his Type VII and IX U-boats and their malfunctioning equipment had combined to stifle the threat of Dönitz's underwater arm on this occasion. New boats and more sophisticated equipment were needed if it wasn't to face a bleak future.[42]

Although the amphibious part of the *Torch* operation had largely gone to plan – the landings had been successfully carried out and the Allies had an immediate foothold in North Africa – its scale had neither induced the Vichy French authorities to renounce their deal with Nazi Germany and cross sides in the war, nor had it led to a ready acceptance of Allied aims in Tunisia. It was clear before *Torch* began that if Montgomery and the Eighth Army were going to be able to exploit their victory over Rommel at El Alamein they needed to secure Tunisia immediately. As *Torch* did not achieve that desired goal, it cannot be judged to be an unqualified success. Nonetheless, it was extremely unsettling for the Axis Powers. Anglo-American forces were now in North Africa and needed to be bogged down there for months to come. Since the only way that would be possible was for the Germans to plug the gap between their enemies now ensconced in the west and Montgomery's forces moving slowly from the east, they made immediate moves to enter Tunisia. Although the Allies ought to have done something to disrupt or prevent that from happening, their forces in Malta were not really in a position to attack supply convoys in a convincing manner until after Operation *Stone Age* – a convoy of four merchant ships laden with supplies and escorted by three cruisers and ten destroyers – had reached the island on 20 November. This operation has been depicted as providing the final relief of Malta after such a horrendously long and dour struggle for its survival.[43]

Such a claim can be advanced on the ground that the Axis forces were now far more concerned about the situation in Tunisia than the island of Malta. In their thinking Malta could be dealt with later. Tunisia was the more pressing target. It needed huge numbers of soldiers and supplies immediately if the Allied pincer movement along the North African littoral was to be resisted. In a bid to protect the supply convoys that would be making these essential journeys from Trapani to Tunis, the Italians used a total of 1,170 mines in a series of flanking mine barrages between Bizerte on the northern coast of Tunisia across the Sicilian Channel to Capo San Vito at the tip of the northwest coast of Sicily from 29 November onwards.[44] Although an occasional profitable sortie was resorted to by some of the Mediterranean Fleet against the Italian convoys, including some rather desultory minelaying, the Allies reserved most of their surface ships for protecting their own supply traffic and building up their forces in North Africa rather than raiding the enemy's efforts to do the same.[45]

Another by-product of *Torch* was the momentous decision of Hitler's government to dispense with some of the formalities of its uneven relationship with the Vichy French. In instructing the II S.S. Armoured Corps to take over the city of Toulon in the south of France, home of the major naval base of the Vichy French forces, the Germans showed a callous disregard for the sensitivities of their erstwhle ally. In their eyes, however, *Fall Lila* made sense on two strategic levels: one that they would now be in a position to offer port facilities for their own reinforced submarine fleet in the Western Mediterranean; and two, they could nip in the bud any temptation that some elements within the Vichy authorities might be entertaining to forsake Pétain and the Axis for an accommodation with De Gaulle and the Free French forces. *Fall Lila* was extremely controversial and demonstrated that relations between the Axis forces and their fellow travellers had fallen a long way from their once giddy heights. From the Vichy French perspective the German move was considered an immense betrayal and posed a very considerable dilemma for Admiral Jean de Laborde, the C-in-C of the Vichy French Navy, about the nature of his response. While it was obvious that the Germans would not allow the Vichy French fleet to join forces with the Free French, let alone become part of a revived Mediterranean Fleet, was there any guarantee that they would allow these ships to be disabled and not use them for their own purposes in future? Laborde obviously didn't think so. When *Fall Lila* was implemented on 27 November, he defiantly ordered his officers and men to scuttle the entire fleet of French warships that was anchored in the harbour at Toulon.[46]

It was the most dramatic gesture possible revealing the bankruptcy of trust in the relationship between the Vichy French and the Germans at this time. Laborde's controversial decision may have removed a source of temptation for the Axis Powers, but it didn't materially help the Allies either since they wouldn't be able to benefit from acquiring these warships and using them against their enemies in the future. Nonetheless, there was a sense of relief in Admiralty circles that the guessing game over whether the French fleet could be used against them had now been irrevocably solved. Laborde's decision also cleared the decks for further German action against Vichy French interests elsewhere. On 8 December, for instance, a German battle group took control of the Tunisian port of Bizerte, seizing the coastal batteries and a destroyer, nine submarines, three torpedo boats, two sloops and a minelayer belonging to the Vichy French authorities that were anchored in the harbour. Whatever animosity Admiral Darlan, the High Commissioner for French North and West Africa, might have felt towards the Allies for their past misdemeanours, the complete disregard for Vichy sensitivities exhibited by the Germans since *Torch* began gave credence to the cynical retort that 'with friends like those, who needs enemies'?[47] Although Dönitz and his U-boat fleet had not played a significant role in contesting the *Torch* landings, they were still doing enormous harm to the Allied war effort elsewhere. As could be seen in the Atlantic theatres, he adroitly handled the boats he had at his disposal forming, dissolving and fusing patrol groups together for effective convoy penetration. In the North Atlantic not all of these patrol lines reaped massive rewards and those that didn't were soon moved on or broken up.[48]

Although it took time for a patrol group to work well together, Dönitz was more impressed by quantitative gains than purely qualitative finesse exhibited by those under his charge. For him the bottom line was always tonnage sunk.[49] There were not extra points to be gained for technical flourish unless that was allied to vessels destroyed. It was deadly, but it was not sport. Much to Dönitz's satisfaction, in an early winter in which the foulest weather for fifty years ensured that the fiercest gales blew more often than not, the Axis submarines accounted for fifty-nine ships on the North Atlantic run in November–December 1942.[50] His relief at the renaissance of his U-boat forces and the renewed mayhem they were causing worldwide was understandable, but not everything was positive. As Blair points out tellingly: only three out of 627 loaded Allied ships sailing in eastbound convoys from the US were destroyed in this period and forty-three out of eighty-four of his boats out on patrol recorded no sinkings at all.[51]

Determined that the Allies should do something to tackle the scourge of the U-boats, Churchill established the Anti-U-boat Warfare Committee to counter their menace. Composed of the COS, the ministers of both production and transport and the prime minister's chief scientific advisor, Lord Cherwell, this body met for the first time on 4 November. Despite agreeing on the need to close the 'mid-Atlantic air gap', the committee members struggled to find the most appropriate means of doing so. They did not need reminding that it was essential that the range of the VLR aircraft they currently possessed be increased so as to wipe out the 'black hole' in mid-ocean that Dönitz's U-boat crews exploited so mercilessly. Yet having sufficient numbers of such aircraft was going to be a problem that could only be resolved at the highest levels of government. While Bomber Command and Coastal Command argued about who should get the new and improved versions of the VLR Mark III Liberator aircraft – the former wanting it for the bombing of industrial targets in Germany and the latter for closing the 'air gap' – weeks went by with the problem unresolved. Despite Churchill's personal appeal to Roosevelt for the issuing of thirty Liberators equipped with centimetric radar for use over the Atlantic, the Americans had few of these planes and their kit to spare and none that could be transferred immediately. As a result, the U-boats continued to plunder the mercantile traffic that they found in the wilds of the mid-Atlantic for the first few months of 1943. Disappointed on this score, the Admiralty at least made a concerted attempt to take the fight to the U-boats with its appointment of Admiral Sir Max Horton, a former submariner, as C-in-C Western Approaches on 19 November. Horton would be an inspired choice to orchestrate the anti-U-boat war. Someone with a deep appreciation of what was involved, Horton was the classic poacher turned gamekeeper and his tenure in command at Derby House in Liverpool became synonymous with the defeat of Dönitz's U-boat fleet.[52]

Horton's task of stifling and then eliminating the U-boat peril was immense and the scale of it was seen at the end of 1942, for quite apart from plundering the American route as they did, Dönitz's crews were also enjoying themselves at the Allies' expense in other areas of the Atlantic. While the returns were modest around the Gulf of St. Lawrence and off the Belle Isle and Cabot Straits, the area southeast of Trinidad continued to remain a favourite haunt of theirs as many ships were still allowed to sail independently in these waters without even the most rudimentary convoy protection.[53] Down in the South Atlantic the Brazilian coast offered another rich source of plunder. Nonetheless, the real 'Happy Time' was being experienced off the coast of South Africa. Here Dönitz had formed the *Eisbär* group of four U-boats and they plundered the coastal trade to such an extent that in a five-week sortie from 7 October they sank twenty-seven ships at a total cost of 175,616 tons. It was mayhem.[54] Dönitz could hardly contain himself because it was obvious that this degree of material loss could not be sustained indefinitely by the Allies, particularly since in these areas of the West, Central and South Atlantic the U-boats that were inflicting this punishment were rarely in danger of being attacked themselves. While by no means all of this destruction was directly war-related, the impact on local, regional and world trade resulting from the loss of these vessels and cargoes was enormous.[55]

Although it is a cliché to talk of the ebb and flow of war, the disconcerting fact is that when applied to certain periods it has a ring of truth to it. Success and failure were being experienced by both sides in the war by the close of 1942. Italy discovered this to its cost in December. A founding member of the Rome–Berlin Axis, the Italians had reason to remember the last month of the year as it represented the start of a campaign by the Allies to knock them out of the war. On 4 December the US 9th Air Fleet delivered its first instalment of a bombing programme that would increase exponentially in the New Year. On this occasion, the bombers sought to deal with the Italian warships anchored at Naples. Unusually a fair amount of damage was caused by this air raid. *Attendolo*, a light cruiser, was sunk and two others were damaged along with four destroyers. It could have been far worse, but the three battleships *Littorio*, *Roma* and *Vittorio Veneto* escaped harm. Nonetheless, the warning signs were there and the Italians wasted little time in moving their capital ships north to the safety of the Ligurian coastal port of La Spezia. At the same time the two heavy cruisers *Gorizia* and *Trieste* were moved out of immediate harm's way from the Sicilian port of Messina and transferred to the northern tip of Sardinia at La Maddalena.[56] While this took the heavy ships out of the reach of the Allied bombers, there was no such safety zone at sea for either side. While Allied submarines appeared off Naples and Sardinia as well as in Tunisian waters to engage Italian convoy traffic with some success, courageous Italian frogmen from Mario Arillo's crew in the submarine *Ambra* got some of their own back by guiding their torpedoes to hit and severely damage four Allied freighters (20,266 tons) in Algiers harbour on 12 December. It was a flamboyant and stirring episode that did something to repair the rather battered reputation of the Italian submarine service.[57]

Further to the east in the Black Sea the Soviet Red Army and its naval counterpart were also in the process of rebuilding their reputations. After spending much of the year yielding ground to the Germans, as well as being subject to periodic harassment by the Bulgarians and Romanians too, the Soviet forces used the autumn to establish a strong base at Tuapse investing it with troops and supplies drawn from Batumi, Poti and Sokhumi. Clearly, a new phase on this Caucasian war front was imminent. It began with a sortie made by the Soviet Squadron under Vice-Admiral L.A. Vladimirskiy along the Bulgarian and Romanian coastline at the end of November. To be fair the outcome was disappointing, but the fact that it was undertaken at all spoke volumes for a growing self-belief in Soviet military circles – symptomatic of the fact that the German juggernaut had been stalled around Stalingrad and the nightmare of the past eighteen months had begun to recede. Other sorties along the same coastline, against Yalta in the Crimea, and off the Bosporus in December, also yielded little in terms of material damage but gave ominous notice to the Balkan members of the Axis that the tide of war might just be turning.[58]

While the Soviets sensed progress in the south, their momentum was stalled by the challenging climatic conditions that prevailed for months at a time further north. In the Baltic, North Sea and the Arctic, for instance, the severity of the weather from November to March is often such that naval operations have to be suspended or cancelled altogether for days or weeks at a time. Ice had formed in the Baltic by mid-November 1942 and forced the Soviet submarines to curtail their operations and return through the mine barrages set up in the Gulf of Finland to Lavansaari for the duration of the winter. Since these barrages had habitually claimed a number of victims when the submarines attempted to break through them in the past, the procedure was anything but normal. On this occasion none of the six remaining submarines perished, but they needed a host of minesweepers, patrol craft and torpedo cutters – along with aerial support for surveillance and attack purposes – to get through the obstructions unscathed. In the Arctic wastes, the ice shelf was a permanent fixture and in parts of the Barents Sea required ice-breakers to smash their way through the pack ice even at the best of times. In the furthest reaches of the North Sea, the Polar coast and the White Sea, the winter months posed the harshest physical test for both ships and seamen alike. Negotiating bitterly cold, often mountainous, seas in virtually perpetual darkness with tons of ice forming an unwelcome and dangerously heavy sheath on the superstructure of their vessels was an uncomfortable and perilous task.[59]

It was made even more unpredictable for the Allies by the latent threat posed to them by those units of Dönitz's U-boats, Raeder's heavy surface warships and Göring's Luftwaffe, that were expressly deployed in Norway to sever the Soviet supply link. After the PQ disasters of July and September and with the pressing needs of the *Torch* offensive to be met, the COS had opted not to keep the convoy traffic flowing northwards during the autumn. Nonetheless, Churchill, in particular, recognised the dangers of alienating Stalin and the Soviets and the necessity of keeping them from making a separate peace with Nazi Germany on the best terms possible. This fear had expressed itself in several declarations of intent and vague promises to establish a 'Second Front' by members of both the Churchill and Roosevelt administrations in the past. If the Combined Chiefs of Staff (CCOS) thought that Stalin would be appeased by the *Torch* landings in North Africa they were sadly mistaken; the Soviet dictator did not regard these invasions of French North Africa as being the promised 'Second Front' as they were not expected to draw off large numbers of the German Army from their gruelling campaigns in Russia or lead to regiments going south in order to support the sagging fortunes of the Vichy regime or the Panzerarmee Afrika. Instead, he urged the resumption of the Arctic convoys to bring much-needed war supplies to the Red Army.[60]

Churchill had some sympathy for Stalin's viewpoint. He had become closely associated with an operational scheme (*Jupiter*) which he had been advocating for months past. Essentially it was a re-run of what Stalin had proposed the British should do shortly after the surprise Blitzkrieg attack had been unleashed upon the Soviet Union by Germany (*Fall Barbarossa*) in June 1941. Back then the proposal to land a significant number of Allied troops in northern Norway had been greeted by Churchill with disdainful incredulity. Now the situation was different and Churchill warmed to the idea of securing the convoy route (and appeasing Stalin) by capturing the naval bases at Altenfjorden, Narvik and Trondheim, as well as the Luftwaffe bases in the north of the country and then rolling up the rest of the Axis forces before them in a concerted sweep southwards. Churchill's scheme was not one that found too many enthusiastic supporters on either side of the Atlantic within the CCOS or its British counterpart, the COS. Although *Jupiter* remained a glint in his eye, Churchill was willing to resume the Arctic convoys as a show of faith, if nothing else, to his brooding and mistrustful ally, Marshal Stalin, who had never wanted them suspended in the first place.[61]

Admiralty concerns about their validity were mitigated by the almost perpetual darkness of the northern winter since this natural phenomenon, and the inevitable poor visibility resulting from bad weather, might be expected to cloak the passage of the supply convoys from the watching German forces. Stalin had already insisted on thirteen freighters sailing independently from Reykjavik to Murmansk and Archangel on 29 October. They had made the journey with 200nm (370km) between each of them and six had been lost to a combination of bombs and torpedoes – a loss rate of 46% – convincing proof, if one needed it, that the Arctic route remained a hazardous undertaking regardless of how it was managed. These results did nothing to deter Stalin. After all, seven freighters had got through with their supplies and to that extent the Red Army was better off than if this journey hadn't been made. Eight days after the last of the independent freighters reached port, the convoy, QP.15, left the Kola Inlet with twenty-eight ships and thirteen Soviet escorts for Iceland. It steadily accumulated additional Allied warships as it made its way westward into the teeth of some very heavy weather. By 20 November the gale force winds had whipped up such a storm that the convoy remained that in name only; ships fell out of line and were left to fend for themselves as the escorts battled for their own survival; in the case of the Soviet destroyer *Sokrushitelny* the effort was in vain since it broke apart and sank. Her Soviet counterpart, *Baku*, fared slightly better only losing parts of her superstructure in the prolonged storm but not foundering completely. Horrendous though the weather was, it did contain a positive: hiding the convoy from the Germans and allowing the ships to get through to their final destination. QP.15's success provided further 'ammunition' for those, like Stalin and Churchill, who saw good reason in maintaining the supply run.[62]

As a result, a new convoy, JW.51A, set out from Loch Ewe on the northwest coast of Scotland with sixteen freighters and 100,000 tons of cargo bound for Murmansk on 15 December. Escorted at the outset by a couple of destroyers, corvettes and trawlers together with a lone minesweeper, the convoy was reinforced by five more destroyers before it reached the really dangerous area inside the Arctic Circle. Once more the convoy slipped past the enemy surveillance unnoticed and reached Murmansk on Christmas Day. Jubilation at a job well done was quickly tempered by the fact that they were spotted by aerial reconnaissance in the Kola Inlet and swiftly attacked, losing five of their number to a combination of bombs and mines.[63]

A week after JW.51A had departed, the next convoy, JW.51B, left the Highland port of Loch Ewe with fourteen freighters and the usual mixed escort screen and a range of warships offering both close and more distant cover.[64] This was exactly the type of convoy that Raeder's heavy ships were meant to savage. *Lützow* (the former pocket battleship – now designated a heavy cruiser) had joined the other heavy cruiser *Admiral Hipper* at Altenfjorden in the Finnmark region of northern Norway just prior to Christmas. Although *Fall Regenbogen (Case Rainbow)* was not originally designed with *Lützow* in mind, it made sense for her to join the operation in a bid to destroy all vestiges of convoy JW.51B and reinforce the impression that the Germans wished to relay to London, namely, that the Arctic convoys were too costly for the Allies to run even in winter. As a result, the two heavy cruisers left port together at 1745 hours on 30 December accompanied by six destroyers. Under the operational command of Vizeadmiral Oskar Kummetz on board the *Admiral Hipper*, the plan was hardly the stuff of Yamamoto complexity and ought to have worked far better than it did. Simply put, the *Hipper*, accompanied by the three destroyers *Friedrich Eckholdt, Richard Beitzen* and *Z29*, was to plough on ahead of Kapitän zur See Rudolf Stange in command of the *Lützow* and his three destroyers *Theodor Riedel, Z30* and *Z31* during the night to open up a gap between the heavy cruisers of 75–85nm (139–57km) by first light on 31 December. In between the two heavy cruisers the destroyers were to be deployed some 15nm (28 km) apart from one another. This would widen the convoy search area and provide some opportunities for the destroyers to cause some confusion once the convoy had been sighted. In theory at least it was expected that Kummetz, working on information first supplied by German aerial reconnaissance and then subsequently derived from tracking reports from *U354*, would be the first to intercept the unsuspecting convoy. According to the plan, the *Hipper* and her destroyers were to engage the Allied destroyer escorts and lure them away from the convoy they were guarding. If this phase went according to plan, it was thought quite reasonably that the unprotected freighters would flee in the opposite direction – in other words to the south and straight into the arms of the *Lützow* and her destroyers. In this way the *Hipper* and the northern group of destroyers would eliminate the convoy escorts while the *Lützow* and her group would fall on the rest of the convoy and reap another PQ.17 whirlwind.[65] That at least was the theory. In practice the operation turned out to be something quite different. Far from being a belated, but glorious, opportunity to show Hitler that the surface fleet still possessed value and hitting power, *Fall Regenbogen* was to demonstrate to the Führer just what Raeder's heavy ships had lost.

In far from ideal conditions with a heavy swell running and sea sickness rampant amongst all the crews of the German vessels, *Hipper* first glimpsed some elements of an already partly scattered convoy at 0718 hours on New Year's Eve and sent the destroyer *Friedrich Eckholdt* to confirm that these ghostly silhouettes were indeed from the convoy. Kummetz now waited for dawn to break but even when it did the visibility was poor and a grey murkiness disguised the ships of both sides. While Kummetz and Stange seemed to be neutralised to some extent by the inclement weather conditions and the latter especially behaved with excessive caution throughout, Captain Robert Sherbrooke in the destroyer *Onslow* showed tactical acumen and considerable bravery in combating the far superior enemy force pitted against him once he realised that they and not some

Russian vessels were in the offing. Sherbrooke only received confirmation that he was about to confront a German force when the *Friedrich Eckholdt* opened fire on the British destroyer *Obdurate* from about 8,000 yards (7,315m) at 0929 hours. He wasted little time in signalling the destroyers *Obdurate*, *Obedient* and *Orwell* to join the *Onslow* and gave orders for the only other destroyer *Achates* and the remaining vessels of his convoy screen to close with the freighters and lay a smokescreen to try and hide their retreat to the southeast. As *Achates* began to make smoke so the *Hipper* hove into view and opened fire on her. Splintered by a near-miss and with her power lines ruptured, the ageing destroyer slowed to 15 knots. At precisely the same time that Kummetz had concentrated his guns upon *Achates* (0941 hours), Sherbrooke had opened fire on the *Hipper* from about 9,000 yards (8,229m). Sherbrooke realised he had no chance in an artillery duel with the far heavier weight of shot available to Kummetz's flagship, but he hoped by steering directly at her and then hauling away he might give the impression that he was firing torpedoes at the heavy cruiser. If his ploy worked, of course, Kummetz would turn away to avoid being hit. Sherbrooke's only realistic chance was to simulate this type of torpedo attack more than once in a bid to keep the enemy on edge and stall for time until Force R (the light cruisers *Jamaica* and *Sheffield* some 50nm [93km] distant) came to his and the other vessels' rescue. Unfortunately, help was anything from one to four hours away. If the Allied force was to survive for that long and not be crippled in the meantime it would take much initiative, fine shiphandling and raw courage from Sherbrooke and the others captains of his destroyer flotilla. They were up to the task but they needed a slice of luck too and this arrived in the shape of a series of snowy squalls that would temporarily obscure the protagonists from one another. After at least thirty-five minutes of feinting and weaving to good effect and shortly after ordering two of his lightly-armed destroyers (*Obdurate* and *Obedient*) to rejoin the convoy to give it added protection, *Onslow* was finally hit with telling effect by *Admiral Hipper* at approximately 1016 hours.[66] Holed, on fire, without the use of either her 'A' or 'B' guns and with forty of her crew either dead or wounded, *Onslow* was in no shape to continue the action. Sherbrooke who had continued to direct operations on the bridge didn't escape punishment either. Badly injured by flying splinters and having lost the sight of one eye from the flying metal shards, he nonetheless remained at his post, issued orders to lay a smokescreen and only afterwards passed over command to Commander Kinloch on the *Obedient* before taking his burning vessel out of the line of fire. In putting paid to *Onslow* (but not sinking her), Kummetz's gun crews had used 48 × 8-inch (203mm) and 72 × 4.1-inch (104mm) shells to strike her only three times.[67]

Orwell now stood in her path but before Kummetz could do anything on this score, the weather intervened once more blanketing the British destroyer from the sight of the German heavy cruiser. Instead of waiting for the snowstorm to lift, Kummetz decided on a turn to the northeast. This route took him away from the *Orwell* and the convoy itself now lying some 12nm (22km) distant, but put him on track to meet the minesweeper *Bramble*. She was quickly rendered into a smoking hulk by a total of 51 × 8-inch (203mm) and 38 × 4.1-inch

(104mm) shells that began to rain down on her from shortly after 1036 hours onward. It was no contest, but why Kummetz devoted so much time and attention to destroying *Bramble* is not clear. She would be finally put out of her misery by the two German destroyers *Friedrich Eckholdt* and *Richard Beitzen*, but precious time had been lost in destroying a vessel that posed no real threat to the operation as a whole or to the heavy cruisers in particular. If Kummetz can be faulted for this error, Stange's entire performance in the *Lützow* was unsatisfactory. Coming up from the south he and his three destroyers had not sought any action whatsoever. They had crossed the path of the convoy and had reached a point by 1050 hours only 2–3nm (3.7–5.5km) ahead of the freighters. There was nothing in their way and mass slaughter appeared on the cards. Amazingly, Stange failed to respond to this enviable situation. Citing poor visibility, he decided to wait for the weather system to blow itself out and for better conditions to present themselves before taking decisive action. It was an extraordinary blunder. Grossadmiral Raeder would long have cause to regret Stange's aversion to risk-taking and his appointment to the *Lützow*.[68]

Even if Stange didn't recognise the Allied vessels, they had little trouble in determining the *Lützow*'s identity. Gathering all the British destroyers around the *Obedient* and displaying none of the restraint of his far more powerful adversary, Kinloch decided that action was called for. Before he could launch any attack, however, the picture became more complicated as Kummetz brought the *Hipper* back into contention. At 1115 hours she announced her return by opening up once more on the *Achates* with deadly effect. After pulverising the small destroyer, the German heavy cruiser next turned her attention to the *Obedient* and quickly straddled her knocking out Kinloch's wireless as she did so. Command shifted for the second time in a little more than an hour and was passed on this occasion to Lieutenant-Commander Sclater on board the *Obdurate*. Once again the tactics would be the same – a torpedo feint to force the *Admiral Hipper* to turn away. It succeeded as before and at 1130 hours the heavy cruiser did just that to comb the tracks of any torpedoes sent her way. Within a minute Force R finally made an appearance and began to make its presence felt as the first shells from the light cruisers *Jamaica* and *Sheffield* began to fall around Kummetz's flagship. Despite frantic manoeuvring, the *Hipper* was hit by one of *Sheffield*'s 6-inch (152mm) shells that penetrated her starboard hull beneath her armoured belt some 11 feet (3.35m) below the waterline, causing extensive flooding and knocking out two of her boiler rooms and reducing her power temporarily to 15 knots. Two more shells struck home within the next six minutes: one passing through her hull on the starboard side without exploding and the other detonating inside the aircraft hangar and starting a blazing fire. These were unwelcome and surprising developments, but none were critical and need not have caused the abandonment of the entire operation. After all, neither *Jamaica* nor *Sheffield* was actually a match for the two heavy cruisers if they had coordinated their activities better. What Kummetz didn't know, of course, was whether there were any other Allied ships that would enter the fray and tip the balance of advantage to the other side. He remained very mindful of the advice which Admiral Klüber (Flag Officer, Northern Waters) had given him shortly after he had sailed on the previous evening. 'Contrary to operational order regarding contact with the enemy. ... use caution against enemy of equal strength because it is undesirable for the cruisers to take any great risks.'[69] Klüber's original message, coincidentally repeated in condensed form just at this crucial juncture in the battle, would weigh on Kummetz's mind and dictate his actions subsequently. At 1137 hours he signalled his other ships to break off their action with the Allied vessels and to turn away to the west. As they did so, both the *Friedrich Eckholdt* and *Richard Beitzen* unsuspectingly found themselves on a collision course with the two British light cruisers a mere 2nm away (3.7km). *Sheffield* sank the former in a blaze of gunfire but *Jamaica* somehow managed to miss the latter. A minute before *Sheffield* opened up on the German destroyer (1143 hours), Stange at last got *Lützow* into the act by opening fire on one of the freighters (*Calobre*) in the convoy. As the British destroyers congregated to meet this latest threat, they laid a dense smokescreen to obscure the emergency turn to the southwest that the convoy made in an effort to put some distance between the freighters and the German surface vessels. It worked. Kummetz reinforced the order to withdraw back towards Altenfjorden at 1149 hours before darkness fell and Stange complied in a rather languid and desultory way that had marked his entire approach to the naval action throughout. As a result, he failed to make further inroads into the convoy and though the *Lützow* would inflict some splinter damage on *Obdurate* at midday, the Battle of the Barents Sea was largely over. There might yet have been a successful resolution of the affair for the Germans after midday as Rear-Admiral Burnett in the *Sheffield* in grey, misty conditions suddenly stumbled upon the two heavy cruisers and *Lützow*'s destroyers once more at 1223 hours. A lucky man at the best of times, Burnett was once more fortunate as Stange couldn't recognise *Sheffield*'s shape or identity in the prevailing gloom. An awkward interlude of six minutes followed in which both ships challenged one another by flashlight, but Burnett brought that episode to an end by firing upon the *Lützow* and straddling her at 1229 hours from a distance of about 8nm (15km). Stange replied a minute later but the *Lützow*'s first shells fell short. Shortly afterwards, Kummetz reappeared once more to join in the shelling at 1234 hours. Her gunners were more accurate and Burnett found his ship being straddled almost immediately. It didn't take him long to decide that this was an unenviable position to be in and at 1236 hours he retired swiftly to the northwest and out of range. Neither Stange nor Kummetz followed and *Sheffield* and *Jamaica* were spared destruction as was convoy JW.51B which had been the objective of *Fall Regenbogen* in the first place. In this unsatisfactory way, the Battle of the Barents Sea ended for the Germans. It was hardly a ringing endorsement of what the surface fleet could do for their war effort at sea and would scarcely impress the Führer whose patience with Raeder's heavy ships was wearing intolerably thin by the end of 1942. Once again the line between success and failure was very thin. *Fall Regenbogen* could have been a classic triumph for the beleaguered surface fleet, but it ended up in exposing it to ridicule and incurring the Führer's undying contempt.[70]

There was to be more bad news for the Axis Powers from the South Pacific as the Japanese continued to expend immense efforts in a fruitless bid to clear the Americans off the island of Guadalcanal. Although they had 'won' some of the naval exchanges of the past three months, these successes had never been decisive enough to prevent reinforcements and supplies getting through to the American troops on the ground. Henderson Field defiantly remained in the hands of the US Marines and was seen as emblematic of what had been a very torrid campaign. It was obvious to both sides that the key to eventual success on this island, if not for the entire Solomons chain, was going to be the continuing ability to land troops and supplies on Guadalcanal and for them to be prepared to battle it out in hand-to-hand fighting until one or the other secured a decisive victory against their resolute opponents. To that end both sides prepared to bring in thousands more troops throughout November and much of December and sent substantial covering forces to protect them. In doing so they unwittingly presented themselves with yet further chances to gain the elusive victory that both needed to secure a dominant position in this sapping encounter. One such naval encounter between the two sides took place some hours after the forces of Kelly Turner and Daniel Callaghan had arrived at Lunga Point on the morning of 12 November with another 6,000 American troops to bolster the US position on the island.[71] Their orderly disembarkation was disrupted by an air raid from Rabaul that caused some damage to a couple of Callaghan's covering force and by the news relayed from reconnaissance planes that Japanese capital ships were in the area and advancing upon them. As Turner's transports temporarily withdrew from their landing sites, accompanied by a shield of three destroyers and a couple of minesweepers, Callaghan's modified task force of five cruisers and eight destroyers (TG.67.4) steamed north to try to get between Savo Island and Lunga Point to be in a position to ambush Vice-Admiral Hiroshi Abe's force of two battleships (*Hiei* and *Kirishima*), the light cruiser *Nagara*, and eleven destroyers before they could do any damage to American forces either at sea or on the ground at Guadalcanal. Abe and Callaghan's warships met at close quarters during the night of 12–13 November and in the fusillade of shells and torpedoes that were exchanged between them massive damage was done to TG.67.4. Within minutes the American task force was without both its commanding officer, Callaghan, and his deputy, Norman Scott, both of whom had been killed in the opening exchanges on board their flagships. In the resulting mêlée, the Americans not only lost Scott's light cruiser *Atlanta*, as well as four destroyers, but also suffered extensive damage to both of their heavy cruisers (*Portland*, and *San Francisco*), their light cruiser *Juneau*, and two more of their destroyers. It was a rout. Only the light cruiser *Helena* and the destroyers *Fletcher* and *O'Bannon* survived intact. Although Abe's warships had displayed their prowess at night fighting and won this battle unmistakably, they did not emerge unscathed from this ferocious encounter. There is little doubt that the eventual loss of the battleship *Hiei*, after sustaining massive punishment, together with two of her destroyer escorts, did take some of the gloss off their undoubted success.[72]

TG.67.4's costly action had also prevented Abe from shelling Henderson Field which had been his original intention before Callaghan's task force had intercepted him that night. Abe's brief had been to put the American air base finally out of action. If it was made inoperable, it would have allowed Raizo Tanaka to bring his eleven troop transports with the rest of the 38th Infantry Division from the island of Bougainville to Guadalcanal on the following night (13–14 November) and disembark them without aerial interference from Henderson Field. Without Abe's bombardment, however, those assumptions obviously did not hold. As such, the entire operation was delayed by twenty-four hours. It would prove to be a very costly postponement. Despite everything that Rear-Admiral Shoji Nishimura's two heavy cruisers (*Maya* and *Suzuya*) threw at it during the following night, Henderson Field remained defiantly operational. Its aircraft proved that on the morning of 14 November by attacking the rest of Nishimura's force (the light cruiser *Tenryū* and four destroyers) and the units of Gunichi Mikawa's 8th Fleet (the two heavy cruisers *Chōkai* and *Kinugasa*, the light cruiser *Isuzu* and two destroyers) which had been acting as a covering force for the previous evening's bombardment. Along with carrier aircraft from the *Enterprise*, the Americans swiftly got their own back on the Japanese for the destruction of TG.67.4. After waves of attacks, hits and near-misses, the heavy cruiser *Kinugasa* was sunk, while two others (*Chōkai* and *Maya*) and the light cruiser *Isuzu*, along with one of Nishimura's destroyers, were damaged to the extent that they could not go to Tanaka's assistance as he brought his transports down 'The Slot' to their landing sites on Guadalcanal later that day. More punishment was meted out to the Japanese when carrier aircraft from the *Enterprise*, along with planes from both Henderson Field and Espiritu Santo, found these troop transports. Six were sunk and one was damaged in a series of savage attacks that killed 400 troops and left another 5,000 to be rescued and put ashore by their destroyer escorts. Tanaka stoically pressed on with only four transports left and got his troops ashore on the northwest of the island during the hours of darkness (14–15 November). It was just as well because more air attacks followed the next day and all the empty transports were hit and sunk.[73]

As Tanaka was disembarking his troops, Kondo's 2nd Fleet – comprising the battleship *Kirishima*, the heavy cruisers *Atago* and *Takao*, two escort cruisers and their eight destroyers – were trying to do what Abe and Nishimura's forces were supposed to have done the previous two evenings and eliminate Henderson Field. Once again, the night time operation was thwarted. On this occasion the perpetrators were the two battleships *South Dakota* and *Washington* and four destroyers belonging to Rear-Admiral Willis Lee's TF 64 which Vice-Admiral William 'Bull' Halsey, the recently appointed C-in-C South Pacific, had sent the previous day from their holding position south of Guadalcanal to go to Turner's aid after the loss of Callaghan, Scott and their ships.[74] Once again, the night-fighting skills of the Japanese wreaked havoc with the American ships when they confronted one another in Iron Bottom Sound off the northeast coast of Guadalcanal. Three of Lee's destroyers were swiftly dispatched by a mixture of shells and torpedoes and the other one, *Gwin*, was damaged. His leading battleship (*South Dakota*) lost her radar and shortly thereafter the ability to avoid the concentrated fire of her heaviest opponents. Despite being battered, she was still able to defend herself as the destroyer *Ayanami* found out the hard way when she tried to torpedo her. While all of this was going on, Lee's other battleship (*Washington*) remained unseen and unaffected. Captain G.B. Davis, expertly using his radar, brought her to within 8,000 metres of the *Kirishima* and sank her in a seven-minute bout of shelling. Kondo, on his flagship *Atago*, had no option but to abandon his mission and withdraw taking the rest of his fleet with him. Henderson Field's extraordinary durability was set to continue.[75]

Once again lacking the 'decisive' battle that would determine the long-term future of Guadalcanal, both sides resorted to doing what they had been doing for months past – bringing in supplies for their own troops under cover of darkness and attacking those of their enemy. This was exactly what took place off Tassafaronga on the night of 30 November–1 December when Tanaka with a force of eight destroyers laden with supplies for their forces onshore was surprised by Rear-Admiral Carleton Wright's task force TF 67 which had been sent expressly from Espiritu Santo to overwhelm them. Blessed with the advantage of surprise and far superior force, 'Bosco' Wright, with four heavy cruisers, a light cruiser and six destroyers, certainly had the force to vanquish Tanaka's supply train and should have done so. After a solid start to doing just that – with the destroyer *Takanami* so badly damaged that she had to be abandoned later – the night action went desperately awry for TF 67. Tanaka proved to be a resolute and wily opponent. Splitting his force in two he ordered four of his remaining destroyers to press on to Guadalcanal and once offshore to pitch their supply canisters overboard for the incoming tide to bring them to the Japanese soldiers on shore. With the rest of his flotilla he led a heroic torpedo attack on Wright's far larger force and turned what could easily have been a suicide mission into a singular triumph. It was an impressive feat of arms; just the type of scenario – with destroyers punching above their weight – that Jellicoe had been so anxious to avoid back in the Great War and for which he had been roundly criticised both at the time and subsequently. On this occasion, all four of Wright's heavy cruisers received disabling hits: *Northampton*, to the extent that she sank; *New Orleans*, so badly that she lost her bow; *Minneapolis* and *Pensacola*, such that they were forced to limp away from the engagement.[76]

Halsey, the author of the planned raid, was not best pleased at its outcome. Thereafter, he tended to use motor torpedo boats (MTBs) and submarines to disrupt these supply operations. Both sides had learnt the lesson of the night action at Tassafaronga: heavier ships were more of a liability than an asset in these situations. For their part, the Japanese persevered with their destroyer and submarine missions to bring in supplies to counter the Americans. Tanaka was on hand once again during the night of 3–4 December in a mission which saw 1,500 canisters tossed overboard from seven destroyers off Cape Esperance, but the vagaries of the weather exposed the imprecision of the whole exercise when the tide bore only 310 of them to shore where they could be picked up by Japanese troops. A lack of success on this occasion did not inhibit Tanaka from repeatedly resorting to the exercise throughout the first part of December with varying degrees of success.[77]

December became a critical month for the Japanese war effort in the Southwest Pacific. There was a growing sense that the surprisingly obdurate Allies were not going to be pushed off Guadalcanal any time soon and that rather than putting in a huge effort to try to eliminate Henderson Field, the Japanese might be better served by constructing an alternative air base at Munda on the south coast of the largest island in the New Georgia chain lying roughly 200nm (370km) northwest of the prized air base on Guadalcanal. To this effect Tanaka was employed for the rest of the month in carrying out six transport missions from Rabaul and Shortland. At the same time, unwelcome news of the landing of three battalions of Allied troops at Oro Bay, near Buna in New Guinea, meant that this setback to their plans for making the whole of New Guinea their own would have to be resisted. In the light of this latest reverse and the overall situation in the Southwest Pacific, therefore, Yamamoto and the military leadership in Tokyo recognised the need to recast their strategic focus in the region so that their forces, rather than the enemy, were able to set the agenda and play to their strengths in future military operations. Guadalcanal no longer fitted into that schema and would have to be jettisoned. So, after expending huge efforts in a vain bid to resist the Allied invasion of the island, the Japanese government decided quite unsentimentally to turn its back on Guadalcanal. On New Year's Eve Imperial Headquarters reached the crucial decision to stage a tactical withdrawal from the island in the New Year in order to shore up their defences elsewhere. By so doing, Tojo's government had turned a significant page in the chronicle of the Pacific war.[78]

Notes

1 An illustration of this fact can be seen in the exploits of five U-boats in this area from 1 September to 25 October (*U175*, *U512*, *U514*, *U515*, *U516*) which sank thirty-one ships (147,438 tons) for the loss of one of their number (*U512*). Rohwer, *Chronology*, pp.171, 176, 179, 182, 184, 187–89, 191–93, 196, 199, 202, 218; *Fuehrer conferences*, pp.280–84, 290–91, 294–95.
2 Milner, *Battle of the Atlantic*, pp.108–9; Padfield, *War beneath the sea*, pp.286, 367, 400.
3 A sharp contrast can be made with the little success of the *Lohs* and *Pfeil* groups in their relatively unproductive pursuit of convoy *SC.100* on 6–25 September. Clay Blair, *Hitler's U-boat war: the hunted, 1942–1945* (New York: Random House, 1998), pp.31–35; Rohwer, *Chronology*, pp.192, 194; Hughes and Costello, *Battle of the Atlantic*, p.226; Milner, *Battle of the Atlantic*, pp.121–22.
4 Hughes and Costello, *Battle of the Atlantic*, p.218; Joel R. Davidson, *The unsinkable fleet: the politics of U.S. Navy expansion in World War II* (Annapolis, Md: NIP, 1996), pp.54–69; 94–118; 160–81; *Fuehrer conferences*, pp.280–83.
5 Development of this radical new type of propulsion unit was far from routine and production delays bedevilled the Type XVII and XVIII. *Fuehrer conferences*, p.296; Hughes and Costello, *Battle of the Atlantic*, pp.221, 284–86, 295.
6 In addition to the thirty-nine freighters in PQ.18 were three tankers, a similar number of minesweepers and a rescue ship. Rohwer, *Chronology*, p.195.
7 *U88* was destroyed by the destroyer *Onslow*'s depth charges on 12 September; *U589* perished in a similar manner at the hands of the destroyer *Faulkner* on 14 September;

and two days later *U457* was destroyed by depth charges from the destroyer *Impulsive*. Blair, *Hitler's U-boat war: hunted*, pp.20–21; Woodman, *Arctic convoys 1941–1945*, pp.258–83; Schofield, *Arctic convoys*, pp.66–77; Evans, *Great World War II battles*, pp.85–98; Peter C. Smith, *Arctic victory; the story of convoy PQ18* (London: William Kimber, 1975); Wragg, *Carrier combat*, pp.66–75; Rohwer, *Chronology*, pp.193–96.

8 It should be noted that four Soviet destroyers also came out of port to join in escorting the rest of the convoy into port. Blair, *Hitler's U-boat war: hunted*, pp.18–22.

9 Woodman, *Arctic convoys 1941–1945*, pp.284–95; Martin Gilbert, *Winston S. Churchill. Vol.VII. Road to victory 1941–1945* (Boston: Houghton Mifflin, 1986), pp.232–33; Rohwer, *Chronology*, pp.195–97.

10 Padfield, *War beneath the sea*, pp.294–300; Doenitz, *Memoirs*, pp.255–64; Hughes and Costello, *Battle of the Atlantic*, pp.218–19; Léonce Peillard, *U-boats to the rescue: the Laconia incident* (London: Coronet, 1976); Rohwer, *Chronology*, p.195.

11 Successful carrier operations continued with *Pinpoint* in mid-July, with the carrier *Eagle* reaching her objective south of the Balearics before flying another thirty-one Spitfires to Malta. Neither of the two Italian submarines, *Emo* and *Otario*, assigned to prevent this from occurring, managed to catch sight of Force H at all. Less than a week later on the next Allied operational sortie, the appropriately named *Insect*, two more Italian submarines, *Dandolo* and *Platino*, were dispatched to deal with *Eagle* when she revisited the same area once again. On this occasion, *Dandolo* actually spotted the carrier and fired four torpedoes in her direction on 20 July. None struck *Eagle* or any of the seven warships accompanying her. They steamed blithely on and flew a further twenty-eight fighter planes to Malta before returning safely to Gibraltar on 22 July. *Platino*, characteristically, never caught a glimpse of her or any of the other vessels from Force H that were engaged on what had become by now a routine supply mission. Woodman, *Malta convoys*, pp.369–72; Benady, *The Royal Navy at Gibraltar*, pp.195–217; Rohwer, *Chronology*, p.181.

12 Rohwer, *Chronology*, pp.177, 179, 181, 189, 199, 207, 212.

13 Both the Italians and the Germans wanted to be rid of this aggravating Allied enclave in their midst: the former to regain a little self-respect and stake out their claim to making the Central Mediterranean a no-go area for Allied surface vessels; the latter to ensure that the resources currently devoted to smashing Maltese resistance could be profitably redeployed elsewhere, such as in North Africa, where they were badly needed. Mussolini had led the calls for Malta's capture in early 1942 and Operation *C3* (known to the Germans as *Fall Herkules*) had been devised to bring this about. Although both Raeder and Kesselring had joined in the chorus for the invasion of Malta in March, Rommel's plans for the conquest of Libya and then Egypt had managed to win over Hitler, and the Afrika Korps' success at Gazala and Tobruk in June 1942 had led to the Maltese operation being lowered in priority and successively postponed as the year proceeded until the entire plan became totally redundant after Rommel's reverse at El Alamein in October. Greene and Massignani, *Naval war in the Mediterranean*, pp.223–31; *Fuehrer conferences*, pp.261, 266–67, 277–79, 284–85, 288, 292, 298; Sadkovich, *Italian Navy in World War II*, pp.272–84.

14 Supermarina held back the two heavy cruisers *Gorizia* and *Trieste*, as well as the light cruisers *Attendolo*, *Bolzano*, *Eugenio di Savoia* and *Montecuccoli*, along with eleven destroyers until 13 August, but in the end they were never brought up to take part in the action because of a lack of suitable air cover. Ibid., pp.186–87; O'Hara, *Struggle for the middle sea*, pp.183–86; Woodman, *Malta convoys*, pp.372–454; Greene and Masignani, *Naval war in the Mediterranean*, pp.242–63; Hamer, *Bombers versus battleships*, pp.204–20; Sadkovich, *Italian Navy in World War II*, pp.285–301.

15 A total of 122 aircraft (86 Ju-88s, 29 Ju-87s, 7 He-111s) were used by the Luftwaffe on 12 August and the Italians committed a total of 77 (47 S-79s, 20 S-84s, 8 G-42s, 2 Re-2001s) to these attacks. Rohwer, *Chronology*, pp.186–87; Peter C. Smith, *Pedestal:*

the *Malta convoy of August 1942* (London: Crécy Books, 1994); Wragg, *Carrier combat*, pp.60–65.
16 Gilbert, *Churchill, VII*, pp.233, 242, 253, 258–59.
17 Another thirty-two fighter aircraft were loaded on board *Furious* and taken south of the Balearics to fly to Malta. All but three of them arrived safely. Woodman, *Malta convoys*, pp.372–454; Rohwer, *Chronology*, p.189.
18 Peter C. Smith, *Massacre at Tobruk: the story of Operation Agreement* (London: William Kimber, 1987); Rohwer, *Chronology*, p.196.
19 Rohwer, *Chronology*, pp.188–89, 192, 195, 199, 201, 204; Greene and Massignani, *Naval war in the Mediterranean*, pp.264–71.
20 Gilbert, *Churchill, VII*, pp.23–44.
21 Gill, *Royal Australian Navy 1942–1945*, pp.226–31.
22 Hammel, *Guadalcanal: the carrier battles*, pp.283–331.
23 Jack D. Coombe, *Derailing the Tokyo Express: the naval battles for the Solomon Islands that sealed Japan's fate* (Harrisburg, Pa: Stackpole Books, 1991).
24 While *I-4* had managed to torpedo a transport (*Alhena*) off Lunga Point on 29 September, the rest had not been so lucky. By early October the operational group had shrunk to four with the loss of *I-22* (sunk) and *I-5* (damaged). Rohwer, *Chronology*, pp.197–98; Boyd and Yoshida, *Japanese submarine force*, p.101.
25 Charles Cook, *The battle of Cape Esperance; encounter at Guadalcanal* (Annapolis, Md: NIP, 1992); Dull, *Battle history of IJN*, pp.209–21; Frank, *Guadalcanal*, pp.292–312; Rohwer, *Chronology*, p.201.
26 This force was depleted when one of the carriers *Hiyo* developed engine trouble and returned to Truk on 22 October escorted by two destroyers. Rohwer, *Chronology*, p.201; Frank, *Guadalcanal*, pp.313–67.
27 Dull, *Battle history of the IJN*, pp.223–27; Frank, *Guadalcanal*, pp.313–36; Rohwer, *Chronology*, pp.201–2.
28 Frank, *Guadalcanal*, pp.337–67.
29 Ibid., pp.368–403; Hammel, *Guadalcanal: the carrier battles*, pp.335–478; Dull, *Battle history of the IJN*, pp.227–35; Hamer, *Bombers versus battleships*, pp.221–36; Stafford, *Big E*, pp.170–211.
30 Two American destroyers, *Anderson* and *Mustin*, were ordered to sink her in the evening. *Anderson* hit her with six more torpedoes and *Mustin* with three and they expended 430 rounds of 5-inch (127mm) shells on her without sinking *Hornet*. In the end it was left to two Japanese destroyers, *Akigumo* and *Makigumo*, to do what the rest hadn't been able to do and apply the *coup de grâce* with more torpedoes before she sank out of sight. *Hornet* would be the last heavy carrier that the USN would lose in battle. Lisle, *The ship that held the line*, pp.219–70; Rohwer, *Chronology*, p.205.
31 Frank, *Guadalcanal*, pp.368–403; Dull, *Battle history of the IJN*, pp.227–35; Gill, *Royal Australian Navy 1942–1945*, pp 229–31; Rohwer, *Chronology*, pp.205–6.
32 In Farrell's excellent study on Grand Strategy, he indicates the nature of the military imbalance between the two corresponding sets of forces. Erwin Rommel had 50,000 men, 250 tanks and 68 × 88mm guns on his side, while Montgomery could field the same number of divisions (11) but with 195,000 men, over 1,000 tanks and 1,400 guns. O'Hara, *Struggle for the middle sea*, pp.187–96; Farrell, *Basis and making of British grand strategy, 1*, p.412; Major-General Sir Francis de Guingand, 'Alamein: the tide turns', in Liddell Hart (ed.), *History of the Second World War*, pp.232–40.
33 Chief of the Imperial General Staff General Alanbrooke observed that this was the only occasion he could remember when Churchill praised the Army during a War Cabinet meeting. Farrell, *Basis and making of British grand strategy, I*, p.413.
34 Ibid., pp.413–19; Sir Basil Liddell Hart, 'Operation Torch', in Liddell Hart (ed.), *History of the Second World War*, pp.260–77; Kevin Smith, *Conflict over convoys: Anglo-American logistics diplomacy in the Second World War* (Cambridge: CUP, 1996); Wragg, *Carrier combat*, pp.120–24.

254 *From defence to attack*

35 Apart from his fleet carrier *Ranger*, Hewitt had the services of four escort carriers (*Chenango, Sangamon, Santee, Suwanee*), three battleships (*Massachusetts, New York, Texas*), three heavy cruisers (*Augusta, Tuscaloosa, Wichita*), four light cruisers (*Brooklyn, Cleveland, Philadelphia, Savannah*), thirty-eight destroyers and four submarines. Thaddeus V. Tuleja, 'Admiral H. Kent Hewitt', in Howarth (ed.), *Men of war*, pp.313–30; Rohwer, *Chronology*, p.209.

36 Norman Gelb, *Desperate venture: the story of Operation Torch, the Allied invasion of North Africa* (New York: W.W. Morrow, 1992), pp.166–238; O'Hara, *The U.S. Navy against the Axis*, pp.138–50; R.T. Thomas, *Britain and Vichy: the dilemma of Anglo-French relations 1940–42* (London: Macmillan, 1979), pp.138–82.

37 Two escort carriers (*Biter, Dasher*), the A.A. cruiser *Delhi*, two light cruisers *Aurora* and *Jamaica*, thirteen destroyers, two submarines and thirty-seven other ships were on hand to protect the nineteen landing ships and twenty-eight supply transports under Troubridge's command. Rohwer, *Chronology*, p.209; Tomblin, *With utmost spirit*, pp.55–79.

38 Burrough was supported by a force of eight destroyers, three submarines, three A.A. ships, the monitor *Roberts* and thirty-two other escort vessels (corvettes, launches, minesweepers, sloops and trawlers) in bringing the Eastern Task to Algiers. Ibid.

39 At Oran the Vichy French lost a flotilla leader, three destroyers, six submarines, a minesweeper and a number of smaller vessels that got in the way were all sunk on this first day of the operation. A similar attempt to force their way into the harbour of Algiers by two Allied destroyers also ended in failure with the *Broke* living up to her name and only the *Malcolm* escaping. Ibid.; Auphan and Mordal, *French Navy in World War II*, pp.219–37; Greene and Massignani, *Naval war in the Mediterranean*, pp.272–80; Blair, *Hitler's U-boat war: hunted*, pp.90–95.

40 Blair, *Hitler's U-boat war: hunted*, p.102.

41 Among the Allied ships sunk with huge loss of life was the 13,000-ton escort carrier *Avenger* on 15 November. She was torpedoed by the Type IXC U155. *Avenger*'s loss was not disclosed by the Admiralty at the time. Ibid., p.112.

42 It has to be admitted that the twenty-seven Allied submarines that were deployed to assist with the *Torch* offensive in the Mediterranean only achieved fairly modest results and lacked a decisive impact. Despite making numerous attacks on enemy convoys over the course of a four-week deployment, only thirteen ships, including a submarine and, alas, a hospital ship, were sunk along with three much small vessels, and a destroyer was torpedoed. Ibid., pp.106–15; Rohwer, *Chronology*, pp.208–12; *Fuehrer conferences*, pp.298–302.

43 Ibid., p.213; Greg Kennedy, 'Sea denial, interdiction and diplomacy: the Royal Navy and the role of Malta, 1939–43', in Speller (ed.), *Royal Navy and maritime power*, pp.50–66.

44 At this point the Sicilian Channel is roughly 200km (108nm) wide.

45 Force Q (three cruisers and two destroyers) did have some success on 1–2 December sinking all four ships in the Italian convoy H along with a destroyer escort, while damaging another destroyer and a torpedo boat. Its success still didn't lead to an all out blitz on this traffic. Rohwer, *Chronology*, pp.215–16.

46 At a stroke this eliminated three battleships (*Dunkerque, Provence* and *Strasbourg*), four heavy cruisers (*Algérie, Colbert, Dupleix* and *Foch*), three light cruisers, an aircraft depot ship, thirty destroyers, three torpedo boats, sixteen submarines, eleven gunboats and a collection of other smaller vessels. Ibid., p.215; Thomas, *Britain and Vichy*, pp.171–82; *Fuehrer conferences*, p. 302; Auphan and Mordal, *French Navy in World War II*, pp.238–71.

47 Darlan was not long for this world. He was murdered at his office in Algiers on Christmas Eve by a young fanatic, Fernand Bonnier de la Chapelle, who acted alone but may have been encouraged to do so by other shadowy forces ranging from the Allies and Free French to the Germans. Anthony Verrier, *Assassination in Algiers: Churchill, Roosevelt, de Gaulle and the murder of Admiral Darlan* (London: Macmillan, 1990); Auphan and Mordal, *French Navy in World War II*, pp.276–77; Gelb, *Desperate venture*, pp.278–80.

48 There was no room for sentimentality in these decisions as the *Büffel, Drachen, Draufgänger, Luchs, Natter, Panther* and *Wotan* groups soon discovered in the last three months of 1942. Blair, *Hitler's U-boat war: hunted*, pp.117–35; Rohwer, *Chronology*, pp.199, 208, 214–15, 218.
49 In November 1942 alone, Axis submarines sank 119 merchant ships (729,160 tons). Of this total twenty-nine were destroyed on the North Atlantic run. Blair, *Hitler's U-boat wars: hunted*, p.120.
50 Some patrol lines, such as the *Puma, Veilchen, Streitaxt, Kreuzotter, Raufbold, Spitz* and *Ungestüm* groups, did exactly what Dönitz was seeking. Each of them waded into convoys with telling effect. His satisfaction with what his boats could do even against escorts equipped with the latest HF/DF direction-finding apparatus was particularly evident in the work of the *Spitz* and *Ungestüm* groups (ten and nine-U-boats respectively) which he brought together after Christmas to track and deal with convoy ONS.154 (forty-five ships). Repeated attacks by members of both groups in the last five days of the year led to the *Spitz* group accounting for nine ships of 44,785 tons and *Ungestüm* sinking a further six ships of 30,809 tons. Rohwer, *Chronology*, p.220.
51 Blair, *Hitler's U-boat wars: hunted*, pp.134–35; Doenitz, *Memoirs*, pp.272–98.
52 Michael Wilson, 'Admiral Sir Max Horton', in Howarth (ed.), *Men of war*, pp.428–40; Hughes and Costello, *Battle of the Atlantic*, pp.229–32; Blair, *Hitler's U-boat war: hunted*, pp.120, 122.
53 Blair, *Hitler's U-boat war: hunted*, pp.135–48; Rohwer, *Chronology*, p.199.
54 So attractive were the possibilities in this region that Dönitz sent three Type IX-D2 boats to the same area at the start of November. In six weeks they managed to sink another twenty-five vessels (134,730 tons). Further north along the West African coast from the Gulf of Guinea north to the Cape Verde Islands six more U-boats helped themselves to thirteen ships (62,413 tons) over a five-week period from mid-November. Rohwer, *Chronology*, pp.200, 208, 213,
55 According to Dönitz, in December 1942 he had a daily average of ninety-eight U-boats in the Atlantic of which at any given moment thirty-nine would be operational and fifty-nine on passage either to or from their operational area. Doenitz, *Memoirs*, p.315.
56 Rohwer, *Chronology*, p.217; James J. Sadkovich, 'Re-evaluating who won the Italo-British naval conflict, 1940–42', in Black (ed.), *The Second World War, I*, pp.307–23.
57 Rohwer, *Chronology*, p.218; Greene and Massignani, *Naval war in the Mediterranean*, p.277.
58 Achkasov and Pavlovich, *Soviet naval operations*, pp.266–69; Rohwer, *Chronology*, pp.215–16, 218–20; Ruge, *Soviets as naval opponents*, pp.87–89, 93–94.
59 Jürgen Rohwer and Mikhail S. Monakov, *Stalin's ocean-going fleet: Soviet naval strategy and shipbuilding programmes 1935–1953* (London: Frank Cass, 2001), p.168; Achkasov and Pavlovich, *Soviet naval operations*, pp.320–21; Ruge, *Soviets as naval opponents*, pp.24–33, 148–50, 152, 161–62; Rohwer, *Chronology*, p.209.
60 For works on the Second Front see Mark A. Stoler, *The politics of the Second Front: American military planning and diplomacy in coalition warfare, 1941–1943* (Westport, Conn: Greenwood Press, 1977); Trumbull Higgins, *Winston Churchill and the Second Front, 1940–1943* (Westport, Conn: Greenwood Press, 1974); George Bruce, *Second Front now! The road to D-day* (London: MacDonald & Jane's, 1979).
61 Farrell, *Basis and making of British grand strategy, I*, pp.297–343, 417–22; Gilbert, *Churchill, VII*, pp.231–33, 236, 265, 284; Stephen, *Sea battles in close-up*, pp.179–80.
62 Woodman, *Arctic convoys 1941–1945*, pp.296–309; Schofield, *Arctic convoys*, pp.79–80; Rohwer, *Chronology*, pp.213–14.
63 Rohwer, *Chronology*, p.219; Schofield, *Arctic convoys*, pp.81–82; Woodman, *Arctic convoys 1941–1945*, pp 311–12.
64 Convoy JW.51B was responsible for transporting 12,650 tons of aviation spirit, thirty-three bomber aircraft, eighty-seven fighter aircraft, 11,500 tons of fuel oil, 202 tanks, 2,046 vehicles and 54,321 tons of other supplies to Murmansk. Woodman, *Arctic*

convoys 1941–1945, pp.312–30; Stephen, *Sea battles in close-up*, pp.181–97; Schofield, *Arctic convoys*, pp.82–94; Whitley, *German capital ships of World War II*, pp. 189–93.
65 Ibid.; Frank Pearce, *Running the gauntlet: the battles for the Barents Sea* (London: Fontana, 1989), pp.199–217; Michael Pearson, *Red sky in the morning: the Battle of the Barents Sea* (Shrewsbury: Airlife, 2002); Dudley Pope, *73 north: the Battle of the Barents Sea* (London: Secker & Warburg, 1988); O'Hara, *German fleet at war*, pp.141–50.
66 O'Hara indicates it was 1016 hours, while Pearson puts the time at 1018 hours and Stephens at around 1020. O'Hara, *German fleet at war*, p.146; Pearson, *Red sky in the morning*, p.64; Stephen, *Sea battles in close-up*, p.187.
67 Sherbrooke was to receive the Victoria Cross for his gallantry on this occasion. O'Hara, *German fleet at war*, p.146.
68 Ibid., p.147.
69 Mark Llewellyn Evans, *Great World War II battles in the Arctic* (Westport, Conn: Greenwood, 1999), p.103.
70 Ibid., pp.99–109; Pearson, *Red sky in the morning*, pp.72–106; O'Hara, *German fleet at war*, pp.141–50; Stephen, *Sea battles in close-up*, pp.179–97.
71 Gill, *Royal Australian Navy 1942–1945*, pp.231–36; Jack S. Harker, *Well done Leander* (Auckland, NZ: Collins, 1971), pp.265–72.
72 James W. Grace, *The naval battle of Guadalcanal: night action 13 November 1942* (Annapolis, Md: NIP, 1999); Frank, *Guadalcanal*, pp.428–61; Dull, *Battle history of the IJN*, pp.237–42; O'Hara, *U.S. Navy against the Axis*, pp.99–116; Rohwer, *Chronology*, pp.210–11;
73 Frank, *Guadalcanal*, pp.462–92; Dull, *Battle history of the IJN*, pp.242–49; Rohwer, *Chronology*, p.211.
74 Halsey had succeeded Vice-Admiral Robert Ghormley as C-in-C South Pacific (COMSOPAC) on 18 October. Johnson, *Pacific campaign in World War II*, pp.258–64; James A. Merrill, 'Fleet Admiral William F. Halsey Jr', in Howarth (ed.), *Men of war*, pp.229–43; O'Hara, *U.S. Navy against the Axis*, pp.95, 118–28.
75 Rohwer, *Chronology*, p.211; Frank, *Guadalcanal*, pp.462–92; Dull, *Battle history of the IJN*, pp.242–49.
76 Dull, *Battle history of the IJN*, pp.253–58; Frank, *Guadalcanal*, pp.493–518; O'Hara, *U.S. Navy against the Axis*, pp.130–37; Gill, *Royal Australian Navy 1942–45*, pp.247–48; Harker, *Well done Leander*, pp.273–80; Rohwer, *Chronology*, p.216.
77 Further efforts to throw canisters of supplies overboard were made on 7–8 and 11–12 December. Frank, *Guadalcanal*, pp.519–27; Rohwer, *Chronology*, pp.217–19; Wukovits, *Admiral 'Bull' Halsey*, pp.122–23.
78 Frank, *Guadalcanal*, pp.534–39; Rohwer, *Chronology*, pp.218–19, 221.

8 A change in momentum (January–August 1943)

When Roosevelt, Churchill and their military staffs met at Casablanca for a war planning conference (*Symbol*) in mid-January 1943 they did so believing that a dramatic change had recently taken place in the fortunes of those involved in the global struggle for supremacy. It was not hard to detect that the operational momentum in virtually every theatre of the war had begun swinging from what had been an assertive Axis presence – and in many a dominant position – to one that had the Allies beginning to dictate the pace of the encounters, taking the bold initiatives, or responding far more adequately to Axis interventions than they had been able to do in the past. It was a strange and comforting reality and it led them to think of a time when the Axis threat would not just be contained but actually beaten. At sea and in amphibious operations either ongoing or recently concluded, the sense that the Allies were in the ascendancy could hardly be denied. Their resurgence was one thing, but victory was still a long way off. None of the principal enemy combatants had yet been forced out of the war and enormous problems thrown up by their continued participation in this unremittingly dour conflict still had to be overcome. Casablanca was no more than an opportunity, therefore, for both the American and British leaders and their planning staffs to revise their grand strategy for the year ahead preserving the 'Europe First' principle, but not at the risk of ignoring the war in the Pacific; agreeing upon a concerted campaign to beat the U-boats in 1943 in order to safeguard their supply chain; allowing the invasion of Sicily to take place after the conquest of Tunisia and before the launching of any 'Second Front' invasion of northern France; and planning for the re-conquest of Burma as a step on the road to the relief of the Chinese. It was apparent to everyone present that all of these plans to wear down their enemies were going to take time to mature. As such, Casablanca represented a compromise between what the American and the British service chiefs wanted. Each gained some, but by no means all, of what they wanted out of the eleven-day conference. A general outline was set for the year and an ultimate goal – the unconditional surrender of Germany – but few, if any, present at this gathering were under any illusions about the enormity of the task still before them. Peace was, therefore, unlikely to return to the world any time soon.[1]

As Casablanca had shown, the British remained wedded to knocking the weakest link out of the Axis chain and committed to a furtherance of the campaign in the Mediterranean to bring this about. Unfortunately, the Eighth Army's success at El Alamein in November 1942 had not led on to the immediate seizure of Tunisia and the sweeping away of Rommel's Panzerarmee from North Africa. It was clear to all concerned that no attack on any part of Italy could be countenanced until Rommel had been finally defeated and if Bernard Montgomery was to be believed that operation couldn't even begin in earnest until he had consolidated his own forces in their Libyan redoubt. While Montgomery took stock of the situation and gathered his reinforcements, Rommel made a series of strategic retreats westward to avoid encirclement and defeat and looked to fall back upon an improved military position in Tunisia itself. Ultimate defeat was never really in doubt given the *Torch* landings on 8 November, but Rommel's main task was to try to stall the Allied advance for as long as possible. In this way, the Allies would have to delay their invasion of Europe until later in the year – and the later that took place the better it would be from an Axis perspective – as the weather could be relied upon to deteriorate during the autumn and early winter making the whole undertaking much more problematic than it would be if it were undertaken during the height of summer.[2]

As a result, both sides sought to reinforce their positions and disrupt the supply effort for the enemy. Axis attacks on Allied shipping in Algerian waters by a mixed combination of submarines, MTBs and Ju-87s continued in January with the destruction of ten vessels and the damaging of nine more, for the loss of an Italian submarine and a solitary U-boat. For their part, the Allies began the year with an adventurous Latin flourish – sending in a team of specialists on two-man submersibles ('Chariots') to penetrate the harbour at Palermo and attach limpet mines to some of the Italian ships anchored there. It would be fair to admit that only modest, rather than stunning, success greeted these daring activities.[3] A far more effective response at jolting the Italian psyche was administered by Force K and the British submarines from Malta which hounded the Italian convoys that were still sailing defiantly to and from Tripoli with supplies for Rommel's retreating forces. Over the course of a fortnight they combined to sink a total of over thirty vessels on this route ranging from steamers and minesweepers to sailing vessels and submarines before Tripoli was finally evacuated on 23 January.[4] Thereafter, a collection of forty-eight Italian destroyers, torpedo boats and corvettes were employed in escorting convoys of retreating Panzerarmee troops from Zuara (Zuwārah) and bringing reserve troops to Tunis and Bizerte, as well as evacuating the wounded and the POWs to the island of Marettimo off the coast of Sicily. While their assistance undoubtedly helped the Axis cause, they were unable to stop the Allies from engaging in a continued wave of destruction against this shipping.[5]

Within the ambit of the 'Europe First' commitment, the discussions at Casablanca had focused upon the urgent necessity to get to grips with Dönitz's fleet of U-boats and begin winning the war in the Atlantic. It was a very pressing matter since he could count upon a force of 212 operational U-boats by the start of the year.[6] These were matters of the gravest importance since imported supplies were seen as determining the ultimate success and longevity of the Allied campaign in Europe. Even before Churchill and the COS had left for Casablanca, the Anti U-Boat Committee had painted a dreary picture of continuing high losses on the Atlantic route and the necessity for preserving as much shipping as possible by substantially reducing the number of sailings to the Middle East and India.[7] They had reached this doleful conclusion largely on the basis that the 'mid-Atlantic air gap' still needed to be bridged by committing more Very Long Range (VLR) aircraft to this area and the number of convoy escorts needed to be enhanced. As Marc Milner indicates, the research conducted by Dr P.M.S. Blackett confirmed that 64% of all previous losses could have been avoided if convoys had received air support through this unprotected area of the Atlantic. All the while no air cover existed in this mid-ocean 'gap', therefore, all convoys – whether fast or slow – were liable to receive rough treatment at the hands of the groups of U-boats that Dönitz was able to deploy in lines throughout this area. Blackett's research also suggested that convoys themselves could afford to be larger in number – they didn't need to be restricted to an average of thirty to forty vessels and could be twice that size – as long as the number of ships in each escort group was increased from routinely six to a total of nine ships and providing these warships were individually better equipped to detect and then tackle the U-boat menace.[8]

Things would not have been so dire had the Allies been able to read the German Naval Enigma on a consistent basis. They couldn't and hadn't been able to for much of 1942. Blackouts of intelligence were the bane of those working in the Admiralty's Operational Intelligence Centre. Without being able to read the messages being exchanged between Dönitz's Headquarters and his U-boats on patrol, the OIC was unable to route the convoys away from the waiting lines of enemy predators. This intelligence blackout had begun when the Germans had introduced a new wheel and reflector to their Enigma cipher machine. They called the new improved code 'Triton', but, as Hugh Sebag-Montefiore muses, the Bletchley Park cryptanalysts had their own term for it – 'Shark' – a term that ruefully acknowledged 'the blood spilled as a result of its use'.[9] 'Triton' ('Shark') was only used by the Atlantic U-boats. All other surface vessels and the U-boats that were assigned to the Arctic route continued to use the less sophisticated, but regularly modified 'Heimisch' code that the Bletchley Park cryptanalysts could read for a mere fraction of the time that the code remained relevant. Their difficulties were compounded by the fact that the Germans changed the inner wheel settings on their Enigma encryption machine on a forty-eight hour basis to ensure the secrecy of their communications. They were not helped by the dearth of sufficient decryption machines which the Bletchley Park cryptanalysts needed to test out the masses of potential combinations that each new setting created before discovering those that gave them access to the coded messages. Unfortunately, the installation of a new and far more difficult code would have been quite bad enough for the Allies, but it coincided with a breakthrough made by the B-Dienst in cracking the 'Naval Cypher Number 3', which was the code used by the American, British and Canadian navies to communicate with each other in the Atlantic. By reading what passed between the Allied escort vessels, Dönitz and his staff could determine which routes the convoys were taking especially through the vital part of the mid-ocean 'air gap' where the U-boats lurked in profusion. This priceless information had been put to very good use throughout much of 1942 at great cost to Allied merchant shipping. Now that the Allies had begun to hit back at the Axis with the *Torch* invasion of North Africa and plans were afoot for further attacks on Italy in the months to come and a cross-Channel attack on Germany, if not in 1943 certainly in 1944, the operational build up (*Bolero*) could not afford to be compromised by wholesale losses on the passage across the Atlantic. Although 'Triton' remained shark-like for much of 1942, resisting all the efforts to break it and consuming vast amounts of valuable time and a high level of frustration in the process, the capture of vital documents, including the latest version of the weather report codebook, recovered from on board the sinking *U559* between Port Said and Haifa on 30 October 1942, helped the cryptanalysts enormously. Using the information contained in this 'new' codebook, the Bletchley Park cryptanalysts were able finally to break into 'Triton'. Once a new version of the weather report codebook was introduced on 10 March 1943, however, access to 'Triton's' secrets were once again denied to the Allies. This time, however, the period of the intelligence blackout was only nine days in duration.[10]

If the Allies required any spur to their discussions at Casablanca about the pressing need to quell the U-boat menace, news from the Central Atlantic merely days before the conference began in Morocco re-affirmed the urgency of the problem in the most graphic terms possible. A convoy (TM1) consisting of nine tankers and four escort vessels (a solitary destroyer and three corvettes) bringing much needed fuel for the Allied forces in North Africa was located by *U514* while northeast of Trinidad. She managed to inflict a heavy torpedo hit on one of the tankers and passed on the report of the convoy's progress to U-boat command headquarters which ordered an expanded *Delphin* group of ten U-boats to intercept the convoy west of the Azores. It did so on 8 January and over the course of the next four days managed to sink another six of the tankers with only two of the original nine eventually making it safely into port at Gibraltar on 14 January. Apart from the loss of 100,000 tons of fuel, 56,453 tons of shipping went down in this operation – the attritional rate of 77.7% being far higher than normal. What made this loss more difficult to accept was that the OIC's order to reroute TM1 around the known *Delphin* group had been ignored by the escort leader. It was a very costly mistake to have made smacking of both arrogance and complacency. TM1's loss was, of course, Dönitz's gain. This triumphant demonstration of just how much damage the wolf packs could do to the Allied cause if they were taken for granted illustrated two things above all. One, that the U-boat menace was from being contained regardless of whether the Allies could read 'Triton' or not; and two, it reconfirmed the opinion shared by both Hitler and Dönitz that the U-boat rather than the capital ship was by far the most effective instrument available to them in the naval war.[11] Actually, the heady success against TM1 was to prove rather deceptive as Clay Blair points out unmistakably in his magisterial work on the U-boat war.[12]

American insistence at Casablanca on taking the initiative against the U-boats and not merely adopting a defensive stance against them – a forthright attitude most associated with the combative Admiral Ernest J. King – was implemented as the year proceeded. Bomber Command even began the process before the Allied staff meetings got underway with the first of a series of strikes against the Atlantic U-boat bases at Brest, La Pallice, Lorient and St. Nazaire. Despite the weight of numbers – by mid-February 1943, for example, 2,000 bombers had concentrated their sorties solely on Lorient – the results were woefully ineffective. Reinforced concrete shelters for the U-boats did not cave in even when bombs hit them and so individual vessels of Dönitz's fleet could return from their operational tours and be refuelled and replenished without concern over their safety while doing so. Over the months to come British and American planes pounded these bases and other enemy-held ports unmercifully, devoting phenomenal efforts in an increasingly vain and costly effort to disrupt either new U-boat construction or the essential repair and modification work that was being carried out on existing craft in the very ports that were being blitzed so regularly. It may be fair to state that Allied bombing of these bases did not actually advance the cause against the U-boat and certainly wasn't worth the effort devoted to them.[13]

Although the abrasive King could do nothing about the renewed Allied commitment to the 'Europe First' strategy at Casablanca, he proposed that at least 25% of the overall war effort should be given to the Pacific theatre. He sensed that the Americans had firmly wrested the initiative from the Japanese in the Southwest Pacific, but acknowledged that they had been able to do so partly because Chiang Kai-shek's forces were tying down a large body of elite IJA troops in China, preventing the bulk of them from being shifted to those areas of the expanded Japanese empire where they were desperately needed and could have made a vital contribution to the Imperial cause.[14]

A barometer of growing American success in this theatre was shown in the rather 'easy' kills their submarines were making throughout the Pacific. For months past they had been quietly and methodically removing Japanese merchant shipping from these waters and, most gallingly for the Imperial authorities in Tokyo, from their own coastal areas as well.[15] For its part, the Japanese submarine arm had been withering away during 1942, weakened by losses on poorly planned transportation duties in the Southwest Pacific and by their general ineffectiveness in policing the waters off Guadalcanal. Although a few Japanese submarines wandered elsewhere to both European and American waters, their performances were far from eye-catching. By the start of 1943, therefore, the 'silent service' had become that in more ways than one.[16]

Regaining a foothold in the Aleutians, as a weak American force did in occupying Amchitka on 12 January, merely served to underline the fact that the Allies were steadily chipping away at the wartime acquisitions of the Japanese.[17] From the Imperial Japanese perspective this was a worrying trend and the more so because they appeared powerless to prevent it from happening. Nothing illustrated this more clearly than the evacuation from Guadalcanal. Acknowledgement of their failure to regain control of this island in the Solomons chain was a bitter pill for the Imperial authorities in Tokyo to swallow and they took no comfort in making the strategic decision to withdraw from it even though to do so made much military sense. Tojo and his military advisors didn't need reminding that wars are rarely won by withdrawals – even when successfully staged – and there was little solace in comparing this evacuation with that of the Allied 'miracle' at Dunkirk. Japanese stoicism would be called upon to make up for this latest setback and the decision reached on New Year's Eve was duly ratified and passed along the line to the subordinate commanders on 4 January. In the month that passed between opting for withdrawal and actually beginning the process of bringing it about, both the 2nd and 4th destroyer flotillas were actively involved in running a number of supply missions by night from Rabaul to Cape Esperance with air cover from their planes based at the Munda and Vila airfields on New Georgia. Known as the 'Tokyo Express', these operations were designed to keep the Japanese forces in the field going until they could be withdrawn. On three of these occasions, the Americans sought to ambush them – deploying cruisers, destroyers, patrol boats and a range of both high-level bombers and dive bombers in an effort to dry up the Japanese supplies and to eliminate their air support. Six of the twenty-five Japanese destroyers employed on these night-time runs were damaged in these exchanges, but not sufficiently for them to abort their missions. American pressure on the Japanese intensified as January continued with the transfer of the 'Cactus Striking Force' – a group of four destroyers – to Tulagi. From their new forward base they began shelling the Japanese positions on Guadalcanal and assisting in sorties against Munda and Vila too as the Americans turned the screw even more on their exhausted enemy.[18]

When Japanese surface vessels were not employed on these risky assignments, submarines filled in for them. On one such occasion the *I-1* was caught and rammed by two New Zealand corvettes (*Kiwi* and *Moa*) at Kamimbo Bay on 29 January. This was not a routine piece of destruction as a number of highly classified codebooks and other documents were recovered from the submarine after she had been driven ashore and deserted by her crew. While the codebooks had a relatively short shelf-life, obtaining complete sets of old codes and fleet vocabularies would prove to be very useful to the Allied cryptanalysts, providing them with further clues about how best to penetrate the latest intricate mysteries of the Japanese naval code and give their troops some foreknowledge of what lay in store for them.[19]

Allied success in gaining entry into Japanese SIGINT could never be taken for granted and before April 1943 access into the highest level IJA codes remained only partial. This meant that the Japanese capacity to strike with deadly effect against Allied positions would still be keenly felt on many occasions in the months to come. Even as they were about to relinquish what remained of their own position on Guadalcanal, the Japanese still managed to deliver a sharp reminder of what their torpedo-bombers could do to those opposed to them by hitting three US cruisers in one attack on 29 January and sinking the heavy cruiser *Chicago* and torpedoing a destroyer in a second raid on the following day. It was a defiant gesture but it was no more than that. What became known as the Battle of Rennell Island failed to change the reality of the overall situation.[20] As the Americans consolidated their hold on Guadalcanal, the evacuation of Japanese troops from Cape Esperance (Operation *KE*) began on 1 February. Three waves of Japanese destroyers (numbering sixty in all) took the remaining 11,706 troops off the island over the course of the next week for the loss of a destroyer, and damage to six others (four seriously). Japanese involvement on Guadalcanal was at an end. American delight at this victory did not obscure the glaring fact that it had taken them six months of massive effort to wrest control over what was, after all, a single island in the Solomon chain. If Guadalcanal was going to be a typical of other such military redoubts in future, the Americans (and their allies) were in for the long haul. Rolling up the Japanese Empire would be no easy task and was bound to be extremely costly in both human and material terms.[21]

Allied relief in the Pacific was more than matched by the extraordinary and harrowing scenes played out in the Caucasus where the recently promoted Feldmarschall Friedrich Paulus earned Hitler's undying wrath by finally surrendering what remained of the German 6th Army (91,000 troops) in the first instance to an obscure Red Army lieutenant in the ruins of Stalingrad on 31 January. Being forced into an evacuation at Guadalcanal was an unsavoury experience for the Axis, but it didn't have remotely the same impact on the Second World War as that generated by the unconditional defeat of the famed Wehrmacht in the city bearing Stalin's name and upon which Hitler had striven so hard and lost so much in a vain attempt to impose his will. Germany's ultimate defeat in the war has been traced to this ill-judged campaign and its juddering collapse by countless military experts ever since. It was one of those seminal points in a conflict from which there appears to be no return to supremacy for one power and no limit to the optimism of its adversary. Stalingrad became a legendary turning point and, unlike Trevelyan's caustic view of the 1848 Revolutions, it was one in which history did take a substantial turn.[22]

Another changing of the guard took place on the same day in Berlin with the promotion of Dönitz to the rank of Grossadmiral (Grand Admiral) and his appointment as C-in-C of the Kriegsmarine in place of Erich Raeder. Dönitz and the U-boat fleet inspired confidence in Hitler whereas Raeder and his lingering commitment to the heavy surface fleet did not. After being on the receiving end of a ninety-minute tirade from the Führer on 6 January about the abject nature of the capital ship fleet's performance in Norwegian waters, Raeder had decided that the time had come to clear his desk and go into a subdued retirement leaving the fortunes of his beloved Kriegsmarine in the hands of his worthy successor.[23] Although Dönitz's appointment was to take effect on 31 January, the date was not a propitious one given what was to happen later that same day at Paulus's command post in the ruins of the Univermag department store in Stalingrad. Dönitz was not known for his superstition or the lack of self-confidence, however, so the day he achieved command of the naval arm was not sullied by any negative thoughts of what might actually be a spoilt inheritance. Instead the sheer relief that he now exercised largely unfettered personal control over German naval operations was the dominant emotion. He could now implement his plan for squeezing the Allied supply lines even harder than before by flooding the 'mid-Atlantic air gap' in both the North and Central Atlantic with groups of U-boats to attack those convoys identified for them by the successful intelligence operations of B-Dienst. There was no time to lose if the Axis were to derail the Allied build up in the United Kingdom and prevent them from forging ahead with their plan to invade the European continent at some time in the not too distant future. Starting immediately and stretching over the next few months, Dönitz and his team set to work on realising his vision of a rampant U-boat offensive that would unhinge the Anglo-American grand strategic design elaborated at Casablanca.[24]

They were to take some encouragement from the news that the first of these new large wolf packs – *Pfeil* – formed initially of thirteen U-boats (later expanded to twenty) to attack the sixty-one ships of SC.118, had managed to sink ten vessels (55,320 tons) from the convoy in the course of five days of incessant attacks even though they had lost three U-boats and had three more heavily damaged in the process.[25] On this basis the attrition rate for both sides was far from ideal. Even so, for every group like the *Hartherz*, *Haudegen* or *Neptun* that came up short, there would be one pack like the *Knappen* that would strike it rich. In a six-day spell (20–26 February) what started off with four U-boats and expanded to twenty as it became engaged with the forty-nine ships of ON.166, the *Knappen* cut a vast swathe amongst the vessels of the convoy sinking fourteen of its ships at a cost of 95,699 tons, losing three of its U-boats in the process.[26] It was this type of statistical return that encouraged Dönitz to proceed with his plan for providing almost saturation coverage of the most vulnerable expanse of sea that the Allied convoys had to negotiate as they made their way across the Atlantic.[27]

He was to do so in March in quite spectacular style. Learning of the existence of SC.121 early in the month from German radio intercepts, Dönitz drew U-boats from three existing groups and formed two new patrol lines with seventeen U-boats in the *Westmark* group and nine in the *Ostmark*. These U-boats converged on the fifty-nine ships of the convoy sinking twelve of them (55,661 tons) without losing a U-boat in so doing. Foul weather with Gale Force 10 winds had played into the hands of the Germans: helping initially to break up the convoy and make the independent stragglers far easier prey for the U-boats, while damaging much of the radar and W/T equipment of the escort group and consequently undermining their ability to detect the presence of the individual members of what became a marauding wolf pack.[28] Things proceeded to get much better for Dönitz from 16 to 20 March as Bletchley Park struggled to break down the latest changes to 'Triton' at a time when B-Dienst encountered no such problems in reading the British Naval Cipher Number 3. As a result, the Admiralty had to guess where the wolf packs might be assembling and attempt to re-route their convoys around them. Unfortunately, all re-routing instructions would also have to go out on the Naval Cipher Number 3 so they could also be read by the B-Dienst. It was clearly a worst case scenario writ large. Under these conditions and until such time as 'Triton' came back on stream, the scope for a disaster was huge. It duly occurred. On 14 March B-Dienst informed Dönitz that two convoys, SC.122 with fifty-one ships and HX.229 with thirty-eight ships, had been re-routed south around the *Raubgraf* group which had been positioned between Greenland and Newfoundland to intercept ONS.169. Responding immediately, he ordered part of the latter group of eight U-boats to give chase and hastily formed another group of eighteen (*Stürmer*) to assist in dealing with SC.122 and the *Dränger* group of eleven, to cope with the inadequately defended HX.229. Over the course of the next four days these groups and a sprinkling of other U-boats played fast and loose with the two convoys and their reinforced escort groups sinking twenty-one ships (140,824 tons) for the loss of only one U-boat and one damaged. It was one of Dönitz's finest hours and a grim reminder for the Allied service chiefs of just how far the Axis Powers were from overall defeat.[29]

Ironically, just when the contrast between the euphoria of those in the U-boat arm and the desolation felt in Admiralty circles over the immediate future of the Battle of the Atlantic was most vivid, the very basis of that respective optimism and pessimism began to change. A number of factors came into play: the Washington Convoy Conference that Admiral King had convened in the first week of March had belatedly ironed out a far more coherent administrative and operational structure for the North Atlantic than had existed hitherto and one that would endure for the rest of the war. Apart from giving the Canadians an enhanced role in the North-West Atlantic at the expense of the Americans, it had widened the responsibility of the British-controlled Western Approaches Command to cover the entire 'mid-Atlantic air gap'. These were sensible, long overdue arrangements that increased efficiency, reduced intra-service confusion and bitterness, and not only improved the Allied ability to safeguard their vital supply lines but also put them into a position to take the fight to the U-boat as never before.[30] They were assisted in this aim by a number of other factors that came together to make it a viable undertaking rather than a pious hope. For a start, springtime and better weather made for fewer equipment failures and easier detection of U-boats; an end to the intelligence blackout of 'Triton' provided the Admiralty with knowledge of where the new wolf packs were being deployed; a marked increase in VLR aircraft (Liberators and Fortresses) meant that the 'mid-Atlantic air gap' was being plugged more effectively than ever before; and far greater aerial support in the Bay of Biscay, where both the 10cm ASV Mark III microwave radar (which effectively countered the 'Metox' receiver sets used by the U-boats) and the 'Leigh Light' became standard issue for two new squadrons of Wellingtons, ensured that the access routes used by U-boats in getting to and from their bases in France and their operational fields in the Atlantic would become far more difficult than ever before.[31]

To be fair, Dönitz suspected that time was not on his side. Allied technology was clearly improving and their detection methods were already making it more difficult to claim the bags of easy kills that his U-boats had been used to in the past. He was also well aware of the danger posed to his fleet by improvements in radar equipment, HF/DF signals detection and ASW weaponry on both enemy aircraft and surface escort groups. He desperately needed counter-measures of his own, but until such time as the new revolutionary U-boat that Professor Walter had designed was developed, Dönitz was left with little alternative other than to make the best of the old workhorses that he had at his disposal. He knew that much needed to be done to combat the menace of the aircraft and better radar detectors and A.A. armament were vital in this respect. Equally, while design improvements had been made with the introduction of FAT (*Federapparat Torpedo*), or pattern running torpedoes, major problems with faulty detonators on all types of torpedo still persisted to undermine the achievements of the U-boat crews and cause maximum frustration to all within the service. While some of these matters were out of his hands, one simple revision in operating procedure could have helped to safeguard his U-boats from Allied HF/DF detection. Until far too late in the war, U-boats made frequent use of radio to stay in touch with one another and provide information to the shore establishment, but by so doing they unwittingly gave the Allies many opportunities for obtaining an accurate fix on their position. It was only after they had suffered many losses in the convoy battles later in the year that steps were taken by the BdU to impose radio silence upon the U-boats and reduce the length of whatever signals were sent by radio to less than thirty seconds. A sensible precaution though it was, it came too late to revive the U-boat cause.[32]

Although Raeder had paid for his enduring loyalty to the heavy surface ships of the Kriegsmarine by being hounded into premature retirement by an irate Führer, Dönitz – after initially preparing a scheme for the decommissioning of these ships – began to think better of it and by 26 February had become disinclined to pay off their crews and send the largest units of the fleet to the breakers' yard as Hitler had sanctioned earlier on 8 February. Dönitz reasoned that such a move would be a blow to the prestige of the Reich and a massive psychological boost and propaganda victory for the Allies. Despite their record in the recent past, the fact that the ships remained a 'fleet-in-being' meant that their enemies would have to continue taking account of them in their operational deliberations and expending considerable efforts to eliminate them. Apart from their magnetic passivity which never failed to attract the attention of Churchill and his service chiefs, Dönitz felt that his capital ships could still contribute on two levels by helping the U-boat arm and the Luftwaffe to seal off the Arctic supply route to the Soviets by attacking the convoys on the Murmansk run, and by threatening to indulge in the occasional sortie out into the North Sea or beyond – a manoeuvre that would drive the Whitehall crowd apoplectic with both angst and rage. By remaining in existence, therefore, the German heavy ships aided the Axis war effort by preventing both the Home Fleet and Bomber Command from redeploying their forces more profitably elsewhere. For Dönitz, the case for the maintenance of the capital ship fleet had become conclusive. Though irritated by its lack of aggressive zeal, Hitler had no wish to give aid to the enemy, so he did not overrule his naval chief and the surface fleet remained intact. It soon proved its value.[33]

In shifting the repaired battleship *Scharnhorst* from Gotenhafen to join the battleship *Tirpitz* and the heavy cruiser *Lützow* in Altenfjorden in late March, Dönitz put the Allies on notice that convoy operations in the Arctic Circle were about to become more intense. Pressed to form new Support Groups from the already hard pressed Home Fleet for the new phase of ASW in the Bay of Biscay, the Admiralty responded to the news of the arrival of the *Scharnhorst* in Norwegian waters by proposing that the supply convoys to Murmansk and Archangel should be suspended during the long daylight hours of spring and summer in the northern latitudes. Churchill accepted the argument and passed it on to Stalin. While it was not music to the ears of the Soviet dictator, particularly at a time when Soviet forces were building on their stunning victory at Stalingrad and finally taking the initiative throughout the Black Sea and along the Caucasus front, he did not issue a caustic note of protest. Churchill was surprised and undoubtedly relieved at the conciliatory tone of his reply. It would not always be so easy to give Stalin bad news.[34]

While the Atlantic had taken most of Dönitz's attention in the first quarter of 1943, the situation in the Mediterranean could not be totally ignored even though it was more in the nature of a holding operation rather than a progressive theatre-changing undertaking. After all, the Allies were in North Africa to stay and there was nothing now that Rommel and the Panzerarmee could do about it. They could delay the inevitable by attacking the Allied supply network by submarine and aircraft, but they couldn't reverse the process as they had been able to do in 1941. Moreover, when these attacks were resorted to in February and March 1943 a low average level of destruction was actually achieved by the Axis forces at an unacceptably high attrition rate. In truth, whatever was thrown at it by the enemy, the British 'Inshore Squadron' largely prevailed, landing 115,137 tons of supplies for the Eighth Army during the month of February alone.[35]

Far more effort was devoted by the Italians to supplying reinforcements for the German and Italian troops that had been forced to retreat from Tripolitania into Tunisia in late January leaving much of their supplies behind them. In order to shore up their position and delay the moment when the Allies could clear North Africa of Axis troops, a series of troop and supply convoys sailed from Sicily to Tunis and Bizerte over the next three months escorted by Italian destroyers, torpedo boats and on occasion by a German submarine-chasing flotilla. All kinds of efforts were made by the Allies from the outset to destroy these convoys, but while a mixture of bombs, mines and torpedoes destroyed forty-nine vessels of various kinds, they were quite unable to put a stop to these sailings.[36] From the Allied perspective, however, once their nemesis, Rommel, had been replaced at the head of the Afrika Korps and had flown out of Sfax for Rome on 9 March, victory was never in doubt. It remained no longer a question of if but purely of when. Even so, it would take another two months to the day for the Allied armies to secure their hard earned victory in Tunisia.[37]

268 *A change in momentum*

Imminent victory in one theatre did not make the Americans rest on their laurels. Much closer to home in the Northern Pacific, their bombardment of Attu in mid-February gave notice to the Japanese that they had their eyes on reconquering the Aleutian chain. Since this operation took place only a couple of days before that of Operation *Cleanslate*, the landing of 9,000 Regimental Combat Team troops on Russell Island approximately 7,000km (4,350 miles) away in the Solomons, the message was clear – the Japanese Empire throughout the Pacific was about to face a sustained challenge from an emboldened United States. While they could not be strong everywhere – and some landings, such as on Russell Island, would be uncontested – the Japanese were equally determined to exact a large price for those territories that had strategic, as distinct from purely egotistical, value for them.[38]

New Guinea was just such an island. Although they had never controlled the whole of it and hadn't been able to use it to invade Australia (even if they had wanted to), the Japanese had established a significant hold over the coastal fringes of the northeast providing an operational base for their activities at Lae and Salamaua, two key ports on the Solomon Sea. Used as entry points to penetrate inland, these towns and those of Gona and Buna further down the east coast had received far more attention from the Japanese once their naval quest for the capital city of Port Moresby had been thwarted at the Battle of the Coral Sea in May 1942. Thereafter, they had switched their attention to trying to capture Port Moresby from the landward side by forcing a route across the rugged Owen Stanley mountain range and further north along the Markham and Bulolo Valleys of the Southern Highlands in the face of heroic opposition from both indigenous tribesmen and doughty Australian infantry resistance. Although both of these efforts had failed to make the offensive breakthrough they had been seeking, the Japanese had come to see that their position on New Guinea was important defensively since it provided a useful shield to protect their military position in the Bismarck Archipelago and prevent Lae and Finschhafen on the Huon Peninsula from being used as forward bases by the Allies for an invasion of New Britain, the largest and most crucial island of the Bismarck chain. For this reason, the Japanese had opted to tie down the Allies for as long as possible in this unforgiving terrain and had resolved that reinforcements should be sent to stiffen their existing troops' hold on what they hoped would become a defensive perimeter in New Guinea and one that would be difficult to dislodge.[39]

Consequently, a matching set of eight transports and destroyers left Rabaul on 28 February with 6,900 troops of the 51st Division bound for Lae. Spotted by an Allied reconnaissance plane early in the morning of 2 March, northeast of the Dampier Strait, the place where the waters of the Bismarck Sea funnel between the west coast of New Britain and the much smaller island of Umboi, the convoy was attacked a couple of hours later by twelve Flying Fortresses with one of the transports being sunk and two others suffering damage. Two of the Japanese destroyers picked up 950 survivors and they were taken immediately to Lae. Next day a swarm of 355 Allied aircraft appeared over the rest of the convoy and in a series of often very low level passes destroyed the rest of the transports and four of the destroyers. What was left of the destroyer force and a couple of Japanese submarines collected 2,734 survivors, but those that weren't scooped up were bombed, strafed and machine-gunned in the water by the fighter-bombers and the seven MTBs that were sent to the scene. Crimes against humanity can never be heroic and shouldn't be condoned even though the exigencies of war will always be advanced by those who seek to rationalise their use. On this occasion, it was grisly and effective work since over 3,200 members of the 51st Division never made it to shore to swell the Japanese numbers on New Guinea. This scale of destruction helped to bring an end to the 'Tokyo Express' supply convoys. Supplies and reinforcements would soon be made exclusively by submarines rather than surface vessels.[40]

As the Japanese geared themselves up to contest the next stage in the fierce struggle to retain their empire throughout Oceania, the Americans continued to dictate the strategy to be employed by the Allies in the Southwest Pacific. At a conference of the Joint Chiefs of Staff held in Washington on 12 March, the general guidelines were set down for what amounted to a dual advance that would be launched later in the year through the islands of New Georgia and Bougainville in the Solomons and a concerted assault to breach Japanese lines in New Guinea. This twin-pronged strategy evolved into Operation *Cartwheel* with victory in both of these places not being an end in itself but a step on the road to recovering Rabaul, the main Japanese naval base in the region on the northeast tip of New Britain.[41]

Before *Cartwheel* began in earnest at the end of June, the Americans had been engaged in trying to cut off all supplies from reaching the Japanese forces in the Aleutians while the British had been mounting a sustained attack on U-boats using the Bay of Biscay. Despite the effort applied to these activities, the end result in both places left something to be desired. Japanese forces remained for a few weeks more on Attu and Kiska after the inconclusive naval engagement in the Komandorski Islands in late March, and the U-boats continued to be frustratingly elusive regardless of RAF Coastal and Bomber Commands' trawling of the Bay of Biscay and the existence of several Allied Support Groups in these waters too.[42] In the more sustained European operation named *Enclose* (20–28 March), twenty-six U-boats out of a total of forty-one crossing the Bay of Biscay were spotted, fifteen were engaged and yet only one was sunk. Things didn't improve in the follow-up operation, *Enclose II* (6–13 April) where, once again, there was only one success, but it was only a matter of time before the link between location and destruction was more firmly established. Dönitz did what he could to make the task harder for Coastal Command by ordering his U-boat captains to go through the area submerged at night time and to surface only in daytime to recharge their boats' batteries. As the RAF estimated that it would take five hours of running on the surface for U-boats to recharge their batteries up to the eighty per cent level, this provided a fair amount of time for Coastal Command and its aggressive leader, Air Marshal Sir John Slessor, to scour the Bay and do some damage when they had found them. By the end of April and the onset of Operation *Derange*, the RAF had seventy-two aircraft carrying out these search and destroy missions over the Biscay access routes and the next and far more successful phase in the U-boat war was underway.[43]

Out in the Central Atlantic, the wolf packs which had operated earlier in the year with some success against a range of convoys in a belt of territory between the Azores and the Canaries found that increasing aerial support for convoy escorts soon restricted their opportunities for creating mayhem. Operations off the coast of Sierra Leone appeared to offer better prospects and Dönitz dispatched some of his Type IX boats to take care of business there while he waited impatiently for his engineers and design technicians to make long overdue improvements to his existing U-boat fleet's current inability to detect enemy aircraft, lessen both the sound and radar image given off by his individual workhorses, and provide them with the means to distort the HF/DF signal detection equipment on board surface escorts. All the while these technological improvements failed to materialise, Dönitz and the U-boat arm were living on borrowed time regardless of whether they had the services of the newly developed *Falke* acoustic torpedo or not.[44]

Further north the picture was even less attractive. Far greater aerial scrutiny of the U-boats in the Bay of Biscay was spilling over into the North Atlantic proper. Some of the wolf packs, such as the *Seeteufel* with fifteen U-boats and the *Seewolf* with nineteen, found themselves south of Iceland battling against Fortress bombers and carrier aircraft as well as more plentiful destroyer escorts. Elsewhere attrition rates among the U-boats began to rise as convoy losses fell.[45] Again the explanation lay in improved intelligence, the existence of stronger air and sea escorts with better means of destruction at their disposal, and poor weather. Notwithstanding the distinctly modest achievements of some of his groups, the fact that so many convoys were underway at this time and that B-Dienst was able to keep track of them meant that there was no need for the commander of U-boats to be totally discouraged. As long as priceless opportunities existed on a daily basis to inflict real harm on the enemy's cause, the wolf packs would continue to be formed in the expectation that enough of these convoys would come unstuck in the face of dogged persistence and skilful handling to make it worth their while. Results soon suggested otherwise.[46] As a case in point, ONS.5, having been battered by the weather and previous U-boat attacks over several days, steamed straight into the path of yet another hastily formed wolf pack (*Fink*) in early May. Just when it seemed that another rout was in the offing, a fortuitous change in the weather finally came to the aid of the Allies. A bank of early evening mist settled over the ships obscuring them from the pack of U-boats, while leaving the seven escorts to employ their Type 271M radar sets to maximum effect. By the following morning (6 May) Dönitz was obliged to count the cost of a horrendous night's work with six of his U-boats being sunk by a variety of methods and a dozen more being damaged, some seriously. He was not used to being on the receiving end of this kind of punishment. Would it prove to be a new sign of the times?[47] Disinclined though he was to making any knee-jerk reactions, Dönitz was to receive confirmation that the heyday of his beloved U-boat fleet had passed as the month of May drew on.

Well before that evidence was to hand, Axis fortunes had taken a series of nasty blows in three other crucial and widely separated theatres of the war. In the Southwest Pacific the man responsible for plotting the attack on Pearl Harbor, Admiral Yamamoto, had been killed when the transport aircraft he had been travelling in was shot down on 18 April before it could land at Buin Airfield on Bougainville, the largest of the Solomon Islands. This had not been an accidental stroke of luck for the Americans but had derived from their ability to read Japanese signals traffic. Knowing of his flight plans in advance, they had assigned sixteen Lightning fighter aircraft from Henderson Field to intercept his plane and that of his chief of staff, Vice-Admiral Ugaki. They did so, shooting down two transport planes and three of Yamamoto's fighter escorts for the loss of one Lightning.[48] Whenever a talismanic figure, such as Yamamoto, dies the loss is bound to be keenly felt by those who have relied upon him in the past to provide inspirational leadership. Nonetheless, it is possible to suggest that the events of the past year, specifically the epic battles in the Coral Sea and at Midway and the loss of Guadalcanal, had dimmed a good deal of the lustre once associated with his name. Regardless of how Yamamoto was viewed by the military leadership in Tokyo, the Allies were just glad to be rid of him.

They had thought the same when Rommel had left Tunisia in early March. His departure had been taken as a sign that the game was almost up for the Axis forces in North Africa. It soon was. In the Mediterranean the last rites of the Tunisian campaign had been observed from late April onwards with a series of crushing attacks by Allied aircraft and destroyers on the Italian supply convoys. Most of the vessels engaged in making these trips from Sicily to Tunis and Bizerte (a mix of destroyers, torpedo boats and transports) never made it beyond Cape Bon and once an Allied naval blockade had been established by a network of destroyers from Malta and Bone on 7 May, any spectre of replenishment from the Italian mainland was at an end.[49]

Feeling both elation and relief, Churchill, his COS and their planning staffs left for Washington to attend the ninth Anglo-American staff conference. Designated *Trident*, the conference opened on 12 May and lasted nearly a fortnight. As one might expect, the strategic blueprint thrashed out at the *Symbol* conference in January was subject to detailed discussion in the light of the latest developments in the war. Churchill led from the front as usual and informed his American hosts that his interpretation of the 'Europe First' commitment was influenced by his genuine belief that the best way to deliver the 'Second Front' against Germany in 1944 was to knock Italy out of the war in 1943. For him, therefore, Operation *Husky* (the invasion of Sicily) should not be an end in itself but the springboard for a major attack on the Italian mainland to exploit what he believed was the soft underbelly of the Axis. His proposals, though eloquently presented, failed to convince the American representatives in the audience. They had seen how dislocative the *Torch* offensive had been both in terms of the diversion of resources from the build up of US forces in the United Kingdom (*Bolero*) and in the time spent on clearing the Axis troops out of North Africa. This experience had illustrated the problems of investing scarce resources in a subordinate theatre of war. For them the prime focus of the war and the grand strategic vision they remained committed to was the launching of a cross-Channel attack on Germany at the earliest opportunity. They were, therefore, very wary about becoming sucked into a full-scale Italian campaign and other Mediterranean-related adventures, such as an Aegean campaign, which might well end up in retarding rather than advancing the cause of the 'Second Front'. After a series of increasingly acrimonious discussions, an eventual compromise strategy was thrashed out that owed much to the influence exerted by General George C. Marshall within the CCOS. This allowed Eisenhower, the Supreme Allied Commander, to do more than merely wrest Sicily from the grasp of the Italians. At this stage, however, it was not known whether the invasion of the mainland would prove to be the springboard that Churchill had envisaged or become an uncomfortable sofa from which all movement was slow and painful. Time would prove that the latter metaphor was far more appropriate than the optimistic notion engendered by the former.[50]

By the time of the *Trident* conference and well before the next stage in the Mediterranean campaign had got underway, the United States had shown its hand in the North Pacific by launching Operation *Landcrab* – the invasion of Attu by the 7th Infantry Division. Little was left to chance. 'Ultra' intelligence windfalls from Japanese signals traffic were disseminated and from these decrypts the Americans knew that Combined Fleet Headquarters was most unwilling to risk using either battleships or aircraft carriers to supplement the defence of their garrisons in the Aleutian chain. Buoyed up by the knowledge that only three enemy submarines were in the area, the Americans gathered a trio of task groups to cover the operation. Rear-Admiral Francis Rockwell at the head of Task Force 51 escorted the first wave of five transports containing 3,000 men from Cold Bay, Alaska to a successful landfall on Attu on 11 May. Although delayed by the prevailing bad weather at its inception, the operation soon made up for lost time and had got 12,000 men ashore by 2 June. Cut off from receiving any reinforcements themselves, the approximately 2,600 Japanese defenders fought bravely and against steadily increasing odds. By the time they had thrown in the towel at the end of the May, over 2,350 of them had been killed – many in a final suicidal attack – for the loss of 549 American troops. A paltry number of Japanese (twenty-three) gave themselves up while the rest were evacuated by what few submarines remained.[51]

On the same day that they had decided that Attu could not be retained (21 May), the Japanese authorities had ruled that their hold on Kiska (where they retained a much larger force variously estimated at roughly 7,000 men) must also be abandoned. If Attu had proved much about the power and supremacy of the United States fighting forces and the fanatical desperation of a waning power in Japan, Kiska was to be an episode that, while not redressing the overall situation, brought a few crumbs of comfort to the military leadership in Tokyo and demonstrated that Washington wasn't quite the omnipotent force it might appear to be on occasion. In a series of evacuations which began on the anniversary of their historic naval success over the Russians at Tsushima (27 May 1905) and were suspended after the loss of three and damage to another three of the thirteen submarines assigned to this task in the first fortnight, the Japanese resumed the withdrawal of what remained of their garrison two months later on 28 July with a force of three light cruisers, twelve destroyers and a tanker.[52] In an extraordinary operation unseen by the Americans and dogged by bad weather, the Japanese pulled off the rest of their 5,183 men on Kiska in a total of fifty-five minutes and returned with them to Paramushiro, the most north-easterly island of the Kuriles. In between these evacuations which had successfully retrieved a total of over 6,000 troops in all, the Americans had expended much effort in battering Kiska and were to continue their shelling and bombing of the abandoned island until 34,426 of their assault force landed on it from an impressive armada of troop transports, LSTs and other vessels on 15 August. Operation *Cottage* showed that 'Ultra' did not yield all of the Japanese secrets. Kiska, or rather the atmospherics 80nm (148km) off the island, were also notable for demonstrating that technology did not always have the answers to everything one encountered at sea. It proved this point by providing a surreal experience for an American task group containing two battleships, three heavy cruisers and several destroyers on 27 July. These warships expended over a thousand shells in a deafening skirmish with what turned out to be radar phantoms rather than Japanese warships in what became known as 'the Battle of the Pips'. On the whole, therefore, Kiska was quite a salutary experience for the US military.[53]

While the Aleutian Islands bore witness to increasing US assertiveness, the other members of the Grand Alliance showed that they too lacked nothing in taking the fight to the enemy. In the far north, for instance, the Soviets had repeatedly staged a series of operational forays against German supply convoys along the Norwegian Polar Coast once the worst of the winter weather had abated. Occasional successes were made by the motley collection of submarines, destroyers, sub-chasers and torpedo cutters engaged in these attacks, but the Germans were not incapacitated by the few losses they sustained and not forced to rethink their convoy strategy. In the Baltic the Soviets had even less success in trying to get some of their submarines through the *Seeigel* mine and net barrage that the Germans and Finns had reinforced in March and April. A series of efforts lasting from May to mid-September were made to breach the barrier, but the Soviets learnt the hard way that instead of submarine attacks on German trade and shipping in the Baltic the long-term answer actually lay in aerial preponderance over these waters and they switched to that type of strategy from early October onwards.[54]

Further south around the Black Sea, the jubilant Soviets had been unable to build quickly on their staggering success at Stalingrad. Any thoughts that the Germans would have been so dispirited by their eclipse in late January that they would not fight to hold on to their hard won positions on the Caucasus front were effectively dispelled over the course of the next few months. As a result, the Soviets spent much of the early part of the year trying to stifle German reinforcements from getting through by sea to their Kuban bridgehead. Mutual attacks continued on supply convoys and port facilities for months without seriously disrupting the other's chain of supply, despite the efforts applied to this task by submarines, destroyers, MTBs, torpedo and patrol cutters, as well as minelayers. Aircraft did feature sporadically but were not a major factor – their presence being called for elsewhere. As the summer months wore on, however, the German position in the Caucasus became increasingly exposed and vulnerable as the Soviets consolidated their overall military position on the Eastern front and then dramatically improved it with decisive success at the massive tank battles of Kursk and Orel in July. Thereafter, the capture of Kharkov in August and the entire Donetz Basin in early September left the Soviets in a wonderful position to exploit the situation, and the Germans with little realistic alternative but to begin a phased withdrawal of their 17th Army from the Kuban bridgehead (*Fall Brunhild*) while they still could.[55]

Well before the Axis was forced into this major evacuation, it had been on the receiving end of further punishment at the hands of nineteen mostly British submarines in the Mediterranean, the southern Adriatic and the Aegean. While their tonnage yield was not comparable to the rich harvest once enjoyed by Dönitz's crews in their 'Happy Time' in the Atlantic, it reflected a larger reality – a growing sense of Allied naval superiority throughout this theatre that could not be denied.[56] This impression was reinforced by a series of heavy air attacks carried out on the Italian naval bases in Sardinia (La Maddalena) and in Sicily (Cagliari) in April and May. Unlike the futility of their repeated bombing campaign against the U-boat bases on the French Atlantic coast, these massed Allied air attacks actually caused some harm to something other than the buildings and infrastructure of the ports and the cities that supported them.[57]

These results encouraged the Allies to pursue the aerial option in preparation for their attack on Pantelleria, the island fortress situated off the northeast coast of Tunisia which had once posed a real military threat to the safety of the Mediterranean convoys and to Malta itself. While no longer cast in that role, the Italian military forces on Pantelleria still needed to be cleared out of the way (Operation *Corkscrew*) before any concerted attempt was made to invade Sicily (Operation *Husky*). As was usual in these matters, the island was subject to severe bombardment before any amphibious operation was mounted. Apart from an opening burst administered on the night of 12–13 May by the light cruiser *Orion*, and five other occasions when a varying combination of light cruisers and destroyers shelled Pantelleria from 31 May to 8 June, Allied aircraft did most of the damage by flying 5,285 sorties over the island and dropping a total of 6,200 bombs on those parts of it that were thought to be of any further military value to the Italians. Once the enemy troops had been softened up by this firestorm, Rear-Admiral Rhoderick McGrigor, on board the Headquarters ship *Largs*, landed the 1st British Division during the night of 10–11 June. Allied Commander-in-Chief General Dwight D. Eisenhower witnessed the uncontested invasion from the bridge of the light cruiser *Aurora* and was on hand a few hours later to see Rear-Admiral Gino Pavesi, the Italian C-in-C, surrender Pantelleria to the Allies without any further loss of blood.[58]

Although the loss of North Africa, Pantelleria and the Pelagiean islands presaged growing problems for the Axis Powers, whether Mussolini's fascists admitted them or not, the Germans were themselves reeling from a series of crushing setbacks to their U-boats in the North Atlantic. After three and a half years of being able largely to dictate the course of the Battle of the Atlantic and almost bring the Allied convoy system to its knees, Dönitz's U-boats were finally and emphatically brought to heel in May 1943. Graphic evidence that the Allied counter-measures referred to earlier in this chapter were working effectively and virtually neutralising his U-boat fleet was shown over a dramatic fifteen-day period (8–23 May) in which a total of seventy-two U-boats were deployed in twelve wolf packs against seven convoys. Despite locating the enemy ships, the U-boats only managed to sink seven out of a total of 276 ships – a paltry loss rate of 2.54%. Even worse from Dönitz's point of view was the success of the Allied Escort and Support Groups in inflicting lasting harm on the U-boats who dared attack either them or the ships under their charge. Fourteen of his U-boat fleet had been sunk and four more had been more than superficially damaged by a mixture of the old methods – bombing, depth charging, gunfire and ramming – and disturbing new ones – the use of 'Hedgehogs' (contact-fused bombs), acoustic homing torpedoes and armour-piercing rockets. This meant he had lost the services either permanently or temporarily of 25% of those vessels that he had assigned to these duties.[59] It was an unflattering equation and one that he could not ignore. Dönitz decided reluctantly on 24 May, therefore, that for the time being he would have to suspend the massed attacks on the convoys in what had once been the highly vulnerable 'mid-Atlantic air gap'. He would return to the fight once he had the vessels, technology and weapons systems necessary to stymie and outwit the Allies once again.[60] It was a judicious move by a shrewd operator. After all, the 'air gap' was being effectively plugged by the Support Groups and covered by various types of VLR or carrier aircraft. Moreover, things were about to become even more fraught for his beloved U-boat arm with the formation on 20 May of the US 10th Fleet under the American Chief of Naval Operations, Admiral Ernest J. King. His brief was to take the fight to the U-boats in the Atlantic by targeting especially their tankers, or *Milchkühe* (milk cows), which allowed them to remain out on operational duty for far longer than they would be able to without getting replenishment and anyone who knew Admiral King didn't doubt for a second that he would do so with both tenacity and purpose.[61]

Dönitz responded to this setback by breaking up his wolf packs and withdrawing many of his U-boats from the waters of the North Atlantic. Obviously this had to be done in a stealthy way since he wished to deny the Allies any sense of immediate victory in the U-boat war. Accordingly, he sent those vessels with sufficient fuel stocks south to attack the US convoy route to Gibraltar and redistributed the rest across the northern routes where they were ordered to patrol independently and use their W/Ts in such a manner that the listening Allies might suspect that the wolf packs were still in business. Such a sleight of hand couldn't last indefinitely and in Admiral Max Horton, at the helm of

Western Approaches Command, the Allies had a cunning opponent for the wily Dönitz. He wouldn't remain ignorant of this ploy for long. Within days the ruse had been discovered by the simple expedient of sending convoys through the areas of supposed wolf pack formations with strong Support and Escort Groups. These convoys not only got through the danger areas unscathed, they were also unable to spot any evidence of U-boats being anywhere in the vicinity. Dönitz's bluff had been called and the successful passage of each convoy across the North Atlantic throughout the summer proved that this once formidable menace had been tamed to a large extent.[62]

Although subdued for the time being, Dönitz had no intention of being perpetually cowed by the Allies and remained adamant that his government must continue to budget for a large rise in new U-boat construction and development. At the end of May he enlisted Hitler's support for bringing all naval armaments under the control of the armaments minister, Albert Speer. He was confident that with Speer on his side he would not lose out to the other arms of the military when it came to steel appropriation. He remained absolutely convinced that once the next generation of larger, faster, quieter, and more deadly U-boats had been built they would help him regain the initiative in the war on trade. His continuing frustration, however, was that Professor Walter's revolutionary new designs for hydrogen peroxide-powered units were beset with engineering problems.[63] Dönitz was advised by Bröking and Schürer, the prestigious firm of German naval builders, that they could modify the planned 1,600-ton Type XVIII U-boat to take diesel engines and power it with a vastly improved battery unit capable of giving the submarine a top speed of up to 19 knots while underwater and an ability to remain in a submerged state for up to sixty hours at a stretch. This was to be the Type XXI for which Dönitz was to hold out great hopes. By the time it was ready for operational duty in the spring of 1945, however, the war would be virtually over.[64]

If Dönitz had hoped that the U-boats' recent travails in the North Atlantic were merely a temporary blip in an otherwise progressive record of achievement, the story that unfolded in both the Central Atlantic and the Bay of Biscay during the summer of 1943 didn't give him much cause for renewed optimism. In the former not only were the large American convoys locating and avoiding the patrol lines of his wolf packs with surprising ease, thanks largely to the HF/DF equipment that their escorts carried on board with them, but Allied aircraft of various types were also making a continual nuisance of themselves by turning defence into attack by finding and harrying his vessels relentlessly. Although the newly installed 2cm (0.79-inch) quadruple gun and 37mm (1.46-inch) rapid fire A.A. gun markedly improved their A.A. armament, the U-boats were soon to be on the receiving end of the new acoustic torpedo known as 'Fido' (otherwise referred to as the 'Mark 24 Mine') carried on both carrier and land-based aircraft. It was a deadly combination which inflicted a heavy toll on the U-boat fleet. In a little over seven weeks (6 July–27 August) the 'Fido' torpedo accounted for five of the sixteen U-boats that were destroyed by aircraft in the waters off the Azores. Since his thirty-two U-boats had only been able to shoot down two aircraft in this area of the Central Atlantic, Dönitz proceeded to cut back on some of his fleet's long-range operations.[65]

There was no better news for him in the Bay of Biscay either. Although he had been able to cope effectively with Bomber Command's mining offensive from April onwards by employing the minesweeping, patrol boat, mine-detonating and submarine-chaser flotillas of Naval Defence Forces West to sweep the channels very thoroughly, Coastal Command's extensive search and destroy missions had proved to be a different matter entirely. Too many U-boats were being spotted and attacked for his liking. Although the flak batteries on the U-boats had improved markedly and individual boats now had the means to shoot down aircraft that were either poised to attack them or were actually in the process of so doing, they stood far more chance of downing a plane if they travelled in groups of between two and five and used their combined armament to direct a heavier wall of fire into the path of the oncoming aircraft. Dönitz wasted little time in effecting this change and providing his boats with better all-round protection, but the loss of his own aircraft only provoked Sir John Slessor, the head of Coastal Command, in mid-June to adopt a new set of counter-measures in the outer Bay northwest of Cape Finisterre (on the Galician coast of Spain). These search areas became known as *Musketry* and *Seaslug*, and each were combed on a thrice daily basis by seven aircraft flying abreast of one another on parallel courses. In this way they were able to monitor the entire access routes with their radar equipment and magnetic anomaly detectors (MAD). Once a group of U-boats were located in this way, the rest of the aircraft on the search trawl of these corridors could be called upon to attack them. It did not take long for Slessor's tactics to begin to work. By the beginning of August nineteen U-boats and an Italian submarine had been sunk and twelve more had been damaged for the loss of sixteen aircraft (ten shot down as a result of U-boat A.A. fire and six by German fighter planes).[66]

Dönitz simply could not ignore the stark nature of these figures. Apart from his conventional craft, he was also losing the services of both his tankers and the special reinforced flak U-boats which he had hoped would be able to more than hold their own against the aircraft sent against them. Once again, Allied success forced him into changing his tactics. Group sailings were disbanded and U-boats were not allowed to leave port until they were equipped with the new '*Hagenuk*' search receiver which had been designed to give his commanders warning of the enemy's use of 10cm radar. In addition, they were assigned new and safer access routes to and from the Atlantic that hugged the Spanish coast and were supported by intensive Luftwaffe sorties flown both within the inner Bay and increasingly with the use of long-range aircraft in the outer waters as well. Disrupting Allied Support Groups became a primary consideration and these were targeted with the new 'Hs 293' glider bomb. This new device, which was carried under the wings of the Dornier 217 K3 bomber, quickly established itself as the weapon of choice against shipping since it was released when beyond the range of A.A. defences and found its own way to the target often with devastating effects. All of these reforms made it far more difficult for Coastal Command to combat with its existing number of aircraft. Although he desperately needed many more planes to improve the effectiveness of his Bay offensive, Slessor was not the first in line to receive these much sought after aircraft from either British or American sources. Neither Air Marshal Portal's Bomber Command nor General Arnold's US Army Air Force (USAAF) were inclined to divert the 160 planes the Admiralty thought were necessary to keep this campaign going in the Bay of Biscay and it would take several weeks and much cajoling to get a fraction of that number in place. By then an opportunity to turn the screw on the U-boats had been missed.[67]

Coinciding with the Bay offensive in mid-June, the Allies began to orchestrate their preparatory moves for the invasion of Sicily (Operation *Husky*) scheduled for the early hours of 10 July. Planning for this massive enterprise which would involve landing 160,000 troops, 600 tanks, 1,800 guns and no less than 14,000 vehicles on Sicilian beaches stretching in a semi-circular fashion from Licata in the southwest to Siracusa in the southeast of the island had been eventful to say the least. Many hours had gone into the planning and much rancour had come out of it too with neither the Americans nor the British particularly satisfied with the end product. An entire recasting of the operational blueprint by General Alexander, Eisenhower's deputy and C-in-C Land Forces, as late as May told its own story. Despite having serious reservations about various aspects of this latest plan, Admiral Cunningham, the C-in-C, Naval Forces, and his subordinate commanders, Bertram Ramsay and Kent Hewitt, could not help but acknowledge that in amphibious operations the Army's will usually prevailed. While it was the Navy's responsibility to offer advice to the other services at all stages of the planning process on matters that bore on its own ability to fulfil the duties assigned to it, once final approval had been given to the operation the time for dissent was over and the Navy's main task became that of a logistic facilitator, ferrying troops to the designated landing sites of the invasion and keeping the beachheads, once established, fully supplied for the duration of the campaign in the teeth of whatever hostile forces were mounted against them. This meant that before an operation of *Husky*'s magnitude could be put together, a large number of vessels of all types, numbering in excess of three thousand, were gathered together for use either directly in the assault phase of the operation or on the supply runs once the main body of troops were ashore.[68]

After Alexander's invasion plan was approved, final arrangements were hastily put in hand and troop convoys set out from Norfolk, Virginia on 16 June as well as the Clyde a few days later to bolster the forces that were already waiting in a swathe of North African ports and on the island of Malta for the signal to go. Apart from the 121 ships in these seven convoys, strong covering forces, spearheaded by two carriers and eight battleships, were moved into position from Gibraltar to Alexandria to assist in launching what was the largest amphibious operation yet undertaken by the Allies. Beginning on 3 July and stretching over the next six days, a total of seventeen convoys and a total of 612 ships of various kinds left the docksides of Alexandria, Algiers, Bizerte, Oran, Port Said, Sfax and Tripoli to rendezvous southeast of Malta before descending on Sicily. Bad weather was not in the plan but it turned up with a vengeance as the morning of 9 July wore on. By the afternoon when the two convoys of landing craft left Malta to join the other fifteen in crossing the 60nm (111km) of the Mediterranean to the open beaches of Sicily, gale force winds from the northwest had turned the sea into a foul, heaving state that threatened to wreak havoc with the invasion force even before the Italians waiting for them onshore could raise a weapon in anger. Although the intensity of the storm lessened before the convoys reached their designated landing sites in the early hours of the morning, it still remained sufficient to lull the Italians into thinking that the Allies would not be foolhardy enough to invade in such weather. Despite making the landings far more difficult than they otherwise may have been, the bad weather and the heavy surf, though complicating and slowing the assault, had not decimated the entire operation as Cunningham feared it might. Landings were made by the Americans in an arc on the exposed southwest coast from Licata to Gela and Scoglitti, where the conditions were at their worst, while the British and Canadian troops were put ashore in five main areas stretching from the west coast of the Pachino Peninsula around Cape Pessaro and up the southeast coast beyond Avola to a position south of the Maddalena Peninsula where they would be within striking distance of the city of Siracusa. Allied submarines, acting as inshore beacons, performed a vital task by guiding the landing craft in to the otherwise unlit beaches.[69]

Once ashore the US 7th Army under Patton and the British Eighth Army under Montgomery did not have everything their own way. Neither Gela in the southwest nor the cities of Augusta and Catania in the southeast fell into their laps with ease, but progress was nonetheless steadily made and by the time that Hewitt and Ramsay's appointments as commanders of the two task forces lapsed on 19 July the invasion was already well advanced. By then they had used the naval forces under their command to support the invasion in numerous ways. Apart from establishing the supply link to land more troops and supplies, they were used in more advanced roles to shell enemy positions in order to assist their ground troops, such as at Gela, Catania and Porto Empedocle, to create diversionary forays as at Favignana and Marsala, or to occupy the ports of Augusta, Pozzallo and Siracusa. While German and Italian air attacks accounted for the loss of a destroyer, a minesweeper and eight transports (54,306 tons), and as MTBs on both sides continued to engage one another in various duels, the threat posed by both U-boats and Italian submarines failed to materialise on the scale anticipated once the invasion began.[70]

By the time that Dönitz had committed another dozen U-boats to Sicilian waters, the capital city of Palermo had fallen to Patton's troops on 22 July and the race was on to reach the port of Messina along the northern coast road before Montgomery and the Eighth Army coming from the south could secure the city. Patton's quest was helped from 27 July by the activities of the two cruisers and six destroyers of Task Force 88. Apart from shelling enemy positions from offshore, they assumed ultimate responsibility for putting a battalion-strength landing team and two regimental combat teams ashore behind enemy lines during the second week of August. By the time of the last of these three sorties (14–15 August), the concept of 'being behind enemy lines' no longer applied since the Germans had already begun to withdraw from Sicily. Over the course of several days the Allies were powerless to prevent the Axis forces from crossing the narrow Straits of Messina by night and regaining the relative security of the Italian mainland. *Fall Lehrgang* proved to be a remarkably successful evacuation, primarily because of the very strong A.A. cover – both batteries and searchlights – that blanketed the Straits at this time and kept the stream of Allied aircraft at bay. Equally as important was the short distance and time it took to cross the open body of water between Sicily and the mainland at its narrowest point, for even the slowest of vessels could make the journey within an hour. By the time *Lehrgang* was over, more than 100,000 German and Italian troops had made it safely across the three mile Straits and had brought 9,832 vehicles, forty-seven tanks, 135 guns, roughly 15,000 tons of supplies and over 2,000 tons of ammunition and fuel with them as they went. On the same day that Kapitän zur See Gustav Freiherr von Liebenstein completed the evacuation and brought organised resistance on the island to an end – 17 August – the city of Messina fell to Patton's forces. Montgomery's troops joined him later the same day. It had taken thirty-eight days to subdue the island and seal the Allied triumph.[71]

During the time that it had taken to seize the island, military leaders on both sides of the Atlantic had been wrestling further with the thorny question of how the Allies could best exploit their success. Their discussions at the *Trident* conference had focused on the issue of the 'Second Front' and had revealed a real fissure in their thinking on this question. In essence, while both the Americans and the British wanted to knock Italy out of the war, it was not known how long that would take or the degree of resistance the Germans might offer if they were drawn into the peninsula in significant numbers in support or lieu of Italian resistance. What the Americans did not want to see happen was a full-scale Allied campaign to wrest the entire mainland from the Axis; one, in other words, that would require a large diversion of the key resources that were being built up for an invasion of Northwest France in 1944. For this reason, Eisenhower, as Supreme Allied Commander, had been promised a maximum of twenty-nine divisions for initial operational involvement on the Italian mainland once *Husky* had delivered Sicily into Allied hands, but he had been warned that he would lose seven of them on 1 November when they were to be transferred to the United Kingdom so that they would not be lost to the cross-Channel attack in the following year. Within days of *Husky* beginning, Eisenhower's own thinking on the 'Second Front' became crystal clear when his chief of staff, Lieutenant-General Frederick Morgan, put a draft plan before the CCOS calling for two invasions of France in the spring of 1944 – *Overlord* in the Normandy region of the northeast and *Anvil* along the Riviera in the south. While *Overlord* would, as it name suggested, remain the main strategic thrust of the Allied campaign, Eisenhower was encouraged by General Marshall to develop a plan for attacking not just the toe (Calabria) and heel (Puglia) of Italy, but the knee (the province of

Campania and principally the city of Naples) as well. What neither Marshall nor Eisenhower had predicted, however, was Mussolini's fall from power less than a fortnight later. They reacted to King Victor Emmanuel III's appointment of Field Marshal Pietro Badoglio as head of the Italian government on 25 July by redoubling their support for maximum pressure to be applied on the mainland in the hope that Badoglio would recognise the frailty of his position and sue for peace.[72]

With this in mind Eisenhower's staff worked out a tripartite scheme to take the southern part of Italy before the Germans could do much to counter these moves. Operation *Baytown* would start proceedings and involve the bulk of the British Eighth Army crossing the Straits of Messina to launch a direct attack on the province of Calabria. This would be followed a few days later by Operation *Avalanche* – the landing of the US 5th Army in the Gulf of Salerno just to the south of Naples. Ambiguity clouded the issue of just how far the Allies should go in Italy once Naples was secured. Rome beckoned, but what then? Obviously, much depended on what would happen to Badoglio's government. With this and other important matters in mind, Churchill and the British COS took themselves off to Quebec to meet Roosevelt and his military advisors for the *Quadrant* conference held in the Citadel on 14–24 August.[73]

While they were there Messina fell, Sicily was secured, and the first hints of an armistice were heard from clandestine Italian sources in neutral Lisbon. It would take three more weeks of furtive negotiations before Eisenhower could announce on 8 September that Italy had surrendered. By then the primacy of *Overlord* and its scheduled start date of 1 May 1944 had been confirmed by the *Quadrant* discussions, Operation *Baytown* was underway in southern Italy, and rising Danish anger at German domination of their country vested itself in civil unrest and industrial anarchy, and spread into the political and military realms with the scuttling of the majority of their fleet.[74]

A day after the *Quadrant* conference was wrapped up came news of the latest success for the Americans in the Solomons campaign with victory in New Georgia. This had been the culmination of a three-month slog that had begun in early May with the laying of mine barrages in Blackett Strait and off the Kula Gulf and the bombardment of the Japanese air bases at Munda and Vila by units of Rear-Admiral Walden Ainsworth's task force TF68.[75] Although the Americans had caught the Japanese by surprise with these raids, they were far too small scale to do more than temporary harm. Supplies still got through by sea and the main airfield at Munda still functioned. Until this was put out of action any invasion of New Georgia, let alone the other islands of the central Solomons, was going to be made much more difficult than it otherwise might have been.[76]

Capturing this air base was to prove to be far harder than the Americans had expected when they landed scouting detachments of the 4th Marine Raider Battalion and two companies of infantry troops near Seghe (Segi) Point on Vangunu Island on 21–22 June as a prelude to a full-scale attack on New Georgia (Operation *Cartwheel*) a week later.[77] Kelly Turner was on hand to land the first battle group of the US 43rd Infantry Division on the island of Rendova in the early hours of 30 June and at other spots on the southern shore of New Georgia in the next few days.[78] Despite mounting air attacks on the invasion fleet and orchestrating a ten-ship bombardment of Rendova on the night of 2–3 July, little was achieved by the Japanese and nothing forestalled the Americans from sending in seven fast transports to put ashore three battalions of the 37th Infantry Division near Bairoko Harbour in the Kula Gulf a couple of nights later (4–5 July).[79] At the same time as they were being landed, the Japanese entered the Kula Gulf with three destroyers in a bid to land 1,200 troops near the town of Vila so that they could strengthen the defences around the key airfield of Munda. Using a 'Long Lance' torpedo they managed to sink the US destroyer *Strong* and indirectly damage another (*Chevalier*). Their success encouraged them to return to the same spot on the following evening with ten destroyers and another 2,800 troops. Standing in their way on this occasion was Ainsworth's TF68 consisting of three light cruisers and four destroyers. Once again the Japanese demonstrated their attacking potential by sinking the *Helena* with three torpedo hits, but suffered the loss of *Niitsuki* to the radar-controlled guns of the light cruiser *Honolulu* and the eventual loss of *Nagatsuki* which was damaged and went aground before being finished off in daylight by a group of dive bombers sent from Henderson Field. Further bombardment efforts to quell the resistance from Munda were thwarted by roughly 100 Japanese aircraft on 9 July, but they were resorted to again during the night of 11–12 July by a much larger bombardment group.[80] On the following night the waters off Kolombangara revealed once again that, at sea at least, the Japanese were able to hold their own against the Americans. Learning of the latest Japanese supply operation with 1,200 troops destined for the Kula Gulf, Ainsworth intercepted the Japanese light cruiser *Jintsu* and eight destroyers with his force of three cruisers and ten destroyers. Without the benefit of radar, the Japanese ships still managed to spot the Allied task force first and start the attack. By the time that the night's action was over, the *Jintsu* had been sunk, Rear-Admiral Shunji Izaki, the C.O., had been killed, but all three Allied cruisers had sustained torpedo damage and one of Ainsworth's destroyers had also been sunk.[81]

While it didn't represent more than a modest blip in Allied fortunes, it did show that the Japanese should not be taken for granted. They underscored that lesson by taking little time to torpedo one of the Australian light cruiser replacements for Ainsworth's task force (*Hobart*) within four days of her setting out from Espiritu Santo on 16 July. Thereafter the fight for Munda was largely left to the other two services to contest with aircraft from Henderson Field sinking three destroyers, a seaplane tender and two submarines, while damaging the heavy cruiser *Kumano* and five destroyers in the days before the airfield at Munda finally fell on 5 August and the Japanese shifted their supply operations further north to the island of Kolombangara.[82] It was there in the Vella Gulf on 6–7 August that six American destroyers gained a measure of revenge for the earlier embarrassment their cruisers had suffered by sinking three of four Japanese destroyers trying to land 900 men and 50 tons of supplies to aid the garrison on the island.[83]

It had taken eight weeks to subdue New Georgia, but fighting continued on some of the outer islands in the archipelago for several weeks more. Admiral Halsey had seen enough. He was certainly not going to invade Kolombangara and be forced into another battle of attrition with General Noburo Sasaki, the mastermind of the Munda resistance campaign. Halsey much preferred the option of avoiding Kolombangara altogether and chose instead to invade the very sparsely defended and poorly armed island of Vella Lavella which lay to the northwest of it. After reconnoitring the island on 12 August, Halsey duly sent an amphibious force of seven fast transports and fourteen landing ships with 4,600 troops escorted by twelve destroyers to Barakoma Beach on the southern shore of Vella Lavella on 15 August and landed them largely without incident.[84]

Halsey's strategic feint had taken the Japanese IGHQ completely by surprise. Admiral Koga had been expecting an invasion of Kolombongara and had been prepared to scupper it if possible, but this new and surprising twist in the fortunes of the war now dictated an entirely different response from the Japanese. Halsey and MacArthur waited to see what that would be.[85]

Notes

1 Farrell, *Basis and making of British grand strategy*, 2, pp.519–50; Hayes, *History of the Joint Chiefs of Staff*, pp.250–303.
2 Bruce Allen Watson, *Exit Rommel: the Tunisian campaign 1942–1943* (Westport, Conn: Praeger, 1999); Bernard Ireland, *The war in the Mediterranean 1940–1943* (London: Arms and Armour, 1993), pp.181–212; Kenneth Macksey, *Crucible of power: the fight for Tunisia 1942–1943* (London: Hutchinson, 1969); Farrell, *Basis and making of British grand strategy*, 1, pp.410–19.
3 Greene and Massignani, *Naval war in the Mediterranean*, p.277; Rohwer, *Chronology*, pp.223–24.
4 Five freighters which were unable to get away from Tripoli were scuttled on 20 January before the port was evacuated by the last of the Italian personnel three days later. Rohwer, *Chronology*, pp.224–25.
5 A combination of Maltese-based submarines, torpedo and dive-bombing aircraft and mines accounted for another thirty-five ships from this convoy traffic by the end of the first week in February. Amongst those destroyed were a U-boat, four destroyers, three torpedo boats, two former French submarines and a corvette. Ibid., p.225; Sadkovich, *Italian Navy in World War II*, pp.316–17; Alan J. Levine, *The war against Rommel's supply lines, 1942–43* (Westport, Conn: Praeger, 1999), pp.115–43.
6 According to Dönitz, on New Year's Day 1943 he had 164 U-boats in the Atlantic, 24 more were stationed in the Mediterranean, 21 were based in the Arctic and 3 were lodged in the Black Sea. Doenitz, *Memoirs*, p.315.
7 Farrell, *Basis and making of British grand strategy*, 2, pp.521–22.
8 A remarkable scientist and a leading figure in Operational Research, Professor Patrick Blackett went on to win the Nobel Prize for Physics in 1948. Peter Hore, *Patrick Blackett: sailor, scientist, and socialist* (London: Routledge, 2002); Milner, *Battle of the Atlantic*, pp.135–55; Gardner, *Decoding history*, pp.115–18.
9 Sebag-Montefiore, *Enigma*, p.243.
10 Each year the weather report codebook was changed by the German authorities. 1942's version which *U559* had been using prior to her sinking at the hands of HMS *Petard* had been issued on 20 January 1942. Ibid., pp.246, 263; Stephen Harper,

284   *A change in momentum*

  Capturing Enigma: how HMS Petard seized the German naval codes (Stroud, Glos: Sutton Publishing, 2000); G.G. Connell, *Fighting destroyer: the story of H.M.S. Petard* (London: William Kimber, 1976), pp.64–71; Rohwer, *Chronology*, p.208.
11 A new book on the fate of the oil convoy suggests an altogether more sinister strategic reason for its demise. See Liam Nolan and John E. Nolan, *Torpedoed: was convoy T.M.1 sacrificed? The facts about the near-total destruction of the first special oil convoy of World War II* (Victoria, BC: Trafford Publishing, 2007); Milner, *Battle of the Atlantic*, pp.136–37; Rohwer, *Chronology*, pp.220–21.
12 In the eastern Caribbean – particularly in the waters off Trinidad – the hunting grounds still offered a U-boat with a little luck on her side the opportunity to wreak some havoc even amongst escorted convoys – a fact exemplified by *U124*'s successful foray in sinking five of the twelve ships of TB.1 on 9 January. In the North Atlantic, however, the appalling weather was such that in the first fortnight of the New Year no U-boat was able to spot a convoy, let alone destroy units of it. Bernard Edwards, *Dönitz and the wolf packs* (London: Arms and Armour, 1996), p.140; Blair, *Hitler's U-boat war: hunted*, pp.158–233; Rohwer, *Chronology*, pp.218–19, 222, 225–28, 230–31.
13 Despite intensive bombing strikes conducted by RAF Bomber Command and the US Eighth Air Force against the naval building yards in Bremen, Emden, Flensburg, Hamburg, Kiel, Wilhelmshaven and Vegesack, the fact remained that during the period from January to March 1943 twenty-six new U-boats were added on average each month to the Kriegsmarine. Doenitz, *Memoirs*, pp.356–57; Rössler, *The U-boat*, pp.231–34, 248–54; Randolph Bradham, *Hitler's U-boat fortresses* (Westport, Conn: Praeger, 2003); Mallmann Showell, *Hitler's U-boat bases*; Rohwer, *Chronology*, pp.226, 228–29, 232, 234–36, 239, 242–43, 246–48, 251, 253, 256, 259, 264–65, 276.
14 Farrell, *Basis and making of British grand strategy*, 2, p.527; Buell, *Master of sea power*, pp.269–81; Hayes, *History of the Joint Chiefs of Staff*, pp.278–303.
15 In January alone twenty-six American submarines on operational duty off Japan and spread very thinly throughout the Central and Southwestern Pacific helped themselves to twenty-two merchant ships (95,152 tons), in addition to two destroyers, a fast transport and three sailing vessels, while torpedoing a further thirteen vessels including a light cruiser, two destroyers and a munitions ship for the loss of only one of their own. Rohwer, *Chronology*, p.223.
16 Boyd and Yoshida, *Japanese submarine force*, pp.105–7.
17 Galen Roger Perras, *Stepping stones to nowhere: the Aleutian Islands, Alaska, and American military strategy, 1867–1945* (Vancouver, BC: UBC Press, 2003), pp.105–10; Brian Garfield, *The thousand-mile war: World War II in Alaska and the Aleutians* (New York: Ballantine Books, 1973), pp.186–90; Dull, *Battle history of IJN*, pp.260–61; Rohwer, *Chronology*, p.225.
18 A New Zealand cruiser, *Achilles*, was bombed and two US patrol torpedo boats were sunk while trying to interrupt the 'Tokyo Express' supply missions. Frank, *Guadalcanal*, pp.540–97; Dull, *Battle history of IJN*, pp.258–60; Rohwer, *Chronology*, pp.223–24.
19 Boyd and Yoshida, *Japanese submarine force*, p.105; Prados, *Combined Fleet decoded*, pp.397–403; Frank, *Guadalcanal*, pp.575–76.
20 Frank, *Guadalcanal*, pp.577–81; Smith, *Emperor's codes*, pp.173–80; Stafford, *Big E*, pp.252–58.
21 Robert Leckie, *Challenge for the Pacific: the bloody six-month Battle of Guadalcanal* (New York: Da Capo Press, 1999); Harry A. Gailey, *The war in the Pacific: from Pearl Harbor to Tokyo Bay* (Novato, Ca: Presidio, 1995), pp.173–207; Frank, *Guadalcanal*, pp.582–97; Rohwer, *Chronology*, p.224.
22 John Erickson, *The road to Berlin. Stalin's war with Germany. Vol.II* (New Haven, Conn: Yale University Press, 1999), p.38; Stephen Walsh, *Stalingrad, 1942–1943: the infernal cauldron* (London: Simon & Schuster, 2000), pp.162–63.
23 *Fuehrer conferences*, pp.306–8; Padfield, *Dönitz*, pp.262–64; Thomas, *German Navy in the Nazi era*, pp.217–18, 225; Bird, 'Erich Raeder', pp.185–209.

24 Although now Oberbefehlshaber der Kriegsmarine (C-in-C of the German Navy), Dönitz retained his post as Befehlshaber der U-boote (Commander of the U-boat arm of the service) and transferred his headquarters to the Hotel am Steinplatz, Charlottenburg, in Berlin. His chief of staff Eberhardt Godt was promoted to Konteradmiral (Rear-Admiral) and appointed Führer der U-boote (chief of the U-boat arm), while Admiral Hans-Georg von Friedeburg retained his role in charge of U-boat personnel which he had overseen since the outbreak of war in 1939. Dönitz and his close operational staff moved in the summer of 1943 to a building codenamed 'Koralle' in Bernau, a small village situated some nineteen miles northeast of Hitler's headquarters. Other staff elements of the OKM (Naval Command) were originally housed in Berlin at Tirpitzufer alongside the Landwehr Canal. When this was bombed in November 1943 they were relocated to new premises in Eberswalde which was known by the codename 'Bismarck'. In early 1945 many of the OKM staff were ordered to retreat first to Varel near Wilhelmshaven and then subsequently to Eutin in Schleswig-Holstein to avoid the encroaching menace of Soviet troops. Dönitz, for his part, felt it incumbent upon him to remain at 'Koralle' in order to be close to Hitler. On 19 April 1945, however, he and his close staff were forced to leave their complex in a hurry to avoid capture as Soviet ground troops moved ever closer to them. After staying in Dönitz's flat for a few days, the staff moved to Plön in Schleswig-Holstein and finally to Flensburg where the Seekriegsleitung (Naval War Staff) was to be found at the end of the European war. Mallmann Showell, *German Navy in World War Two*, pp.63–65; Padfield, *War beneath the sea*, p.308.

25 Milner, *Battle of the Atlantic*, pp.138–40; Edwards, *Dönitz and the wolf packs*, pp.140–50.

26 A fifteenth victim, the rescue ship *Stockport* (1,683 tons) also succumbed in this battle. Although *U529*, *U606* and *U623* were sunk in these exchanges, *U91* was also bombed and *U604* was damaged by depth charges. Milner, *Battle of the Atlantic*, pp.140–43; Beesly, *Very special intelligence*, pp.209–61; Edwards, *Dönitz and the wolf packs*, pp 152–62; Rohwer, *Chronology*, p.232.

27 Padfield, *Dönitz*, pp.267–74.

28 Another straggler (5,754 tons) from *SC.121* was dispatched on 11 March by a member of the *Raubgraf* group that was in the area to locate and attack other convoys. Edwards, *Dönitz and the wolf packs*, pp.163–72; Rohwer, *Chronology*, pp.234–39; Milner, *Battle of the Atlantic*, p.146.

29 Hughes and Costello, *Battle of the Atlantic*, pp.267–72; Martin Middlebrook, *Convoy: the battle for convoys SC.122 and HX.229* (London: Allen Lane, 1976); Padfield, *War beneath the sea*, pp.322–28; Jürgen Rohwer, *The critical convoy battles of March 1943: the battle for HX.229/SC122* (London: Ian Allen, 1977); Rohwer, *Chronology*, pp.238–39.

30 Milner, *North Atlantic run*, pp.231–34.

31 J.H. Greswell, 'Leigh Light Wellingtons of Coastal Command', *The RUSI Journal*, Vol.140, No.3 (June 1995): 55–58; Brown, *Radar history*, pp.338–44; Milner, *Battle of the Atlantic*, pp.142–55; Farrell, *Basis and making of British grand strategy*, 2, pp.568–70.

32 Hughes and Costello, *Battle of the Atlantic*, pp.275–87; Padfield, *Dönitz*, pp.208–12, 230, 243–44, 259, 301–2, 309; Padfield, *War beneath the sea*, pp.44, 58, 66–67, 81–84, 89, 191, 324–25; Syrett, 'The infrastructure of communications', pp.163–64.

33 *Fuehrer conferences*, pp.308–12; Padfield, *Dönitz*, pp.272–74; Thomas, *German Navy in the Nazi era*, pp.227–28.

34 Gilbert, *Churchill, VII*, p.365; Rohwer, *Chronology*, p.240; Farrell, *Basis and making of British grand strategy*, 2, pp.572–73.

35 *Fuehrer conferences*, pp.313–16; Rohwer, *Chronology*, pp.223–26, 230, 236.

36 Greene and Massignani, *Naval war in the Mediterranean*, p.282; Rohwer, *Chronology*, p.231; Sadkovich, *Italian Navy in World War II*, pp.313–28.

37 David Irving, *The trail of the fox: the life of Field-Marshal Erwin Rommel* (London: Weidenfeld & Nicolson, 1977), p.258; Watson, *Exit Rommel*, pp.112–13.

38 Russell Sydnor Crenshaw Jr., *South Pacific destroyer: the battle for the Solomons from Savo Island to Vella Gulf* (Annapolis, Md: NIP, 1998), pp.79–88; Edwin P. Hoyt, *The glory of the Solomons* (New York: Stein & Day, 1983), pp.33–43; Garfield, *Thousand-mile war*, pp.190–92.

39 A sense of just how desperate that struggle was on New Guinea can be seen by referring to sources such as Lida Mayo, *Bloody Buna: the campaign that halted the Japanese invasion of Australia* (Newton Abbot: David & Charles, 1975); Lex McAuley, *To the bitter end: the Japanese defeat at Buna and Gona 1942–43* (Milsons Point, NSW: Arrow, 1993).

40 Controversy continues to reverberate over the disputed figures for Japanese losses of both ships and men in this battle. For a flavour of it see Clayton James, *Years of MacArthur: 1941–1945*, pp.292–303; Hamer, *Bombers versus battleships*, pp.237–46; Dull, *Battle history of the IJN*, pp.268–70; Gill, *Royal Australian Navy 1942–1945*, pp.270–73; John Miller Jr., *CARTWHEEL: the reduction of Rabaul* (Washington, D.C.: Dept. of the Army, 1959), pp.39–41; Rohwer, *Chronology*, pp.235–36; Gailey, *War in the Pacific*, pp.223–24; Timothy D. Gann, *Fifth Air Force light and medium bomber operations during 1942 and 1943: building the doctrine and forces that triumphed in the Battle of the Bismarck Sea and the Wewak raid* (Maxwell Air Force Base, Al.: Air University Press, 1993), pp.3–21; www.pngbd.com/forum/showthread.php?t = 5923 (07/02/2005).

41 There was to be a good deal of 'horse trading' over the next strategic step to be taken in the Pacific with MacArthur pushing his *Elkton* plan for the eventual capture of Rabaul as part of a five-pronged offensive that would first encompass territorial objectives in New Guinea (Lae, Salamaua, Finschhafen and Madeng), New Georgia, New Britain, Bougainville, New Ireland and an eventual attack on Rabaul. In these plans MacArthur's forces were scheduled to conduct the New Guinea and west New Britain operations, while Admiral Nimitz would be asked to set his C-in-C Admiral Halsey on the tasks of seizing New Georgia and Bougainville. Once these objectives had been achieved, both sets of forces would combine to launch a combined offensive against Rabaul. Halsey had argued the case for an early attack on New Georgia followed by that on Bougainville, from where Rabaul, only some 250 miles distant, could be attacked ceaselessly by USAAF bombing forces. Halsey's views, naturally supported by Admiral King, prevailed. Clayton James, *Years of MacArthur:1941–1945*, pp.304–20; Miller, *CARTWHEEL*, pp.9–19; Gailey, *War in the Pacific*, pp.227–28, 230–35; Hayes, *History of the Joint Chiefs of Staff*, pp.303–34.

42 For the inconclusive clash between the heavy cruiser *Salt Lake City*, a light cruiser and four destroyers under the command of Rear-Admiral Charles McMorris and a Japanese supply convoy of two transports escorted by the two heavy cruisers *Maya* and *Nachi*, two light cruisers and four destroyers under Vice-Admiral Boshiro Hosogaya in the Bering Sea, see Dull, *Battle history of IJN*, pp.261–65; John A. Lorelli, *The battle of the Komandorski Islands March 1943* (Annapolis, Md: NIP, 1984); Garfield, *Thousand-mile war*, pp.196–206; Perras, *Stepping stones to nowhere*, pp.123–24; Rohwer, *Chronology*, pp.240–41.

43 Milner, *Battle of the Atlantic*, pp.147–48; Hughes and Costello, *Battle of the Atlantic*, p.287. For a more comprehensive history of RAF Coastal Command operations in the war see John Buckley, *The RAF and trade defence 1919–1945: constant endeavour* (Keele, Staffs: Ryburn Publishing, 1995); Christina J.M. Goulter, *A forgotten offensive: Royal Air Force Coastal Command's anti-shipping campaign, 1940–1945* (London: Frank Cass, 1995); Roy Conyers Nesbit, assisted by Oliver Hoare, *RAF Coastal Command in action 1939–1945* (Stroud, Glos: Sutton in association with the Public Record Office, 1997).

44 A modified electric G7e torpedo, the T-3 *Falke* (Falcon) acoustic torpedo was designed to run a short circle pattern once it had detected the noise of a propeller. It had a speed of 20 knots and a range of roughly 7,200 yards (6.6km). It was thought to be effective against vessels travelling at up to 12 knots. In fact, it was quite disappointing as a weapon and was superseded by a far better version, the T-5 *Zaunkönig* (Wren) which ran directly towards the noise of a propeller and was equipped to tackle ships doing up to 15 knots. Blair, *Hitler's U-boat war: hunted*, pp.171, 315.

45 Rohwer, *Chronology*, pp.239–40, 243–45; David Syrett, *The defeat of the German U-boats: the battle of the Atlantic* (Columbia, SC: University of South Carolina Press, 1994), pp.25–62.
46 Fifty-four U-boats were deployed against four convoys (HX.235, ONS.5, SC.127 and SC.128) over a hectic eleven-day period beginning on 25 April. They sank only thirteen ships (61,958 tons) out of the 169 (a figure not including the escort vessels) on offer in the convoys – a rate of return of 7.83% – and lost nine of their own in doing so. Blair, *Hitler's U-boat war: hunted*, pp.287–94; Rohwer, *Chronology*, pp.246–47.
47 Ibid.; Padfield, *War beneath the sea*, pp.328–31; Hughes and Costello, *Battle of the Atlantic*, pp.277–79; Syrett, *Defeat of the German U-boats*, pp.63–95.
48 Ugaki survived the plane crash. Admiral Mineichi Koga succeeded Yamamoto as Commander-in-Chief, Combined Fleet. Agawa, *Reluctant admiral*, pp.347–68; Goldstein and Dillon (eds), *Fading victory*, pp.330–31, 350–60; Hoyt, *Yamamoto*, pp.244–50; Dull, *Battle history of the IJN*, pp.272–73; Prados, *Combined Fleet decoded*, pp.458–63; Smith, *Emperor's codes*, pp.181–93.
49 Once Tunis and Bizerte had fallen on 9 May, a host of German, Italian and French vessels, numbering seventy-five in all, including four submarines and two destroyers, were sunk in Tunisian ports either in response to a series of air raids or through scuttling. Gill, *Royal Australian Navy 1942–1945*, pp.298–302; Rohwer, *Chronology*, pp.247–48; Sadkovich, *Italian Navy in World War II*, pp.325–28.
50 It was also decided what the main naval focus would be for the USN in the Pacific during the coming year. Apart from ousting the Japanese from the Aleutians, the Americans were anxious to seize both the Marshall and Caroline Islands, the rest of the Solomons group and beyond to the Bismarck Archipelago and those parts of New Guinea that were not currently in Allied hands. Farrell, *Basis and making of British grand strategy*, 2, pp.582–98; Hayes, *History of the Joint Chiefs of Staff*, pp.363–409; Buell, *Master of sea power*, pp.330–39.
51 Casualty figures for the Attu campaign differ amongst the various sources. Perras indicates that the Americans committed more than 15,000 troops to the recapture of the island and sustained 1,148 wounded and had over 2,100 more suffering from exposure, frostbite and trench foot by the end of the gruelling campaign. Prados, *Combined Fleet decoded*, pp.474–78, 480; Garfield, *Thousand-mile war*, pp.221–38; Perras, *Stepping stones to nowhere*, pp.124–35; Rohwer, *Chronology*, p.249.
52 In the first fortnight before the evacuation operation was suspended, 820 men were taken off from Kiska by submarines. Rohwer, *Chronology*, pp.252, 260; Prados, *Combined Fleet decoded*, pp.479–81.
53 Brown, *Radar history*, pp.376–77; Garfield, *Thousand-mile war*, pp.314–37; Perras, *Stepping stones to nowhere*, pp.136–57; Masataka Chihaya, 'The withdrawal from Kiska', in David C. Evans, *The Japanese Navy in World War II: in the words of former Japanese naval officers* (Annapolis, Md: NIP, 1986), pp.245–77; Rohwer, *Chronology*, p.260.
54 Rohwer, *Chronology*, pp.240, 249, 264, 279; Achkasov and Pavlovich, *Soviet naval operations*, pp.204–10, 239–45; Ruge, *Soviets as naval opponents*, pp.33–38, 150–53, 162–67.
55 Achkasov and Pavlovich, *Soviet naval operations*, pp.270–83; Ruge, *Soviets as naval opponents*, pp.94–110; Rohwer, *Chronology*, pp.234, 254, 274; Overy, *Russia's war*, pp.186–222.
56 *Fuehrer conferences*, pp.320–30; Padfield, *Dönitz*, pp.290–97; Rohwer, *Chronology*, pp.244, 249.
57 At La Maddalena, for instance, the heavy cruiser *Trieste* was sunk along with two MAS boats and the heavy cruiser *Gorizia* was badly damaged. Greene and Massignani, *Naval war in the Mediterranean*, pp.282, 286–88.
58 Pantelleria's coastal battery did manage to hit and damage the cruiser, *Penelope*, on 1 June, but received far more punishment from the Allies than she administered to them. Further east towards Malta, the smaller Pelagic island of Lampedusa offered little or no resistance after a night's shelling from four Allied light cruisers and surrendered on 12 June. A solitary destroyer (*Nubian*) was dispatched to the even smaller islands of Linosa and Lampione to gain the same results, which she did on 13 and 14

June respectively. Rohwer, *Chronology*, p.253; Sadkovich, *Italian Navy in World War II*, p.328; Tomblin, *With utmost spirit*, pp.125–31.
59 Dönitz lost his youngest son Peter on 19 May while serving as a watch officer on board *U954*. His Type VIIC boat was sunk by a 'Hedgehog' fired from the British frigate *Jed* and the coast guard cutter *Sennen*. Blair, *Hitler's U-boat wars: hunted*, pp.333, 569.
60 From 1 February to 31 May 1943, RAF Coastal Command enjoyed a very productive period in their fight against the U-boat: 15 Group had sunk thirteen U-boats and damaged three others (one badly); 18 Group had sunk one and damaged two more; 19 Group had sunk four and damaged seven (one seriously); 19 Group had sunk ten and damaged thirteen (one seriously); Iceland's tally was nine sunk and four damaged; and AHQ Gibraltar and Middle East Command's total was eight sunk and one damaged. Norman Franks, *Search, find and kill: the RAF's U-boat successes in World War Two* (London: Grub Street, 1995), pp.7–18, 45–47, 102–19, 187–95, 224–30; Syrett, *Defeat of the German U-boats*, pp.96–144; *Fuehrer conferences*, pp.331–36; Milner, *Battle of the Atlantic*, pp.154–55, 159; Rohwer, *Chronology*, pp.250–51.
61 Hughes and Costello, *Battle of the Atlantic*, pp.287–91; Milner, *Battle of the Atlantic*, pp.159–69; Buell, *Master of sea power*, pp.293–96; Rohwer, *Chronology*, p.252.
62 Syrett, *Defeat of the German U-boats*, pp.145–80; Rohwer, *Chronology*, p.252.
63 Only three prototypes of the 300-ton Type XVII were ever built and tested and the large 1,600-ton Type XVIII had to be dropped eventually although its streamlined hull was used as the basis for the much vaunted Type XXI. Only four of Walter's hydrogen peroxide-powered U-boats (Type XXVI) were being built as the war came to an end. Miller, *U-boats*, pp.60–81.
64 From June 1944 to the war's end in May 1945, 120 of the Type XXI were commissioned, but only two began operational patrols by the time the conflict was over. As Miller suggests, this was perhaps just as well for the Allies as the Type XXI would have been a most formidable weapon in Dönitz's armoury. Ibid., pp.60–69; Hughes and Costello, *Battle of the Atlantic*, pp.283–87; *Fuehrer conferences*, pp.332–36.
65 Milner, *Battle of the Atlantic*, pp.157, 163–64, 167, 171–72; Rohwer, *Chronology*, pp.260–61.
66 Rohwer, *Chronology*, pp.229–30, 256–57.
67 Increasing use of long-range 'Heinkel He 177' aircraft by the Luftwaffe led to a large number of aerial jousts which proved costly to the Allied cause. Glider bombs were used for the first time against Support Groups on 25 August and claimed their first victims in a second attack three days later when a sloop was hit and blown up and a destroyer was struck and badly damaged. Nonetheless, there were some practical limitations to the bomb of choice. It needed a minimum cloud ceiling of 800 metres to be most effective, but the Bay of Biscay's prevailing weather patterns were such as to deny the Luftwaffe bomb aimers these perfect conditions. Ibid., pp.257, 268–69; Hughes and Costello, *Battle of the Atlantic*, pp.287–89; Milner, *Battle of the Atlantic*, pp.169–72; Sönke Neitzel, 'Kriegsmarine and Luftwaffe co-operation in the war against Britain, 1939–45', *War in History*, Vol.10, No.4 (Nov. 2003): 448–63.
68 Viscount Cunningham of Hyndhope, *A sailor's odyssey: the autobiography of Admiral of the Fleet Viscount Cunningham of Hyndhope, K.T., G.C.B., O.M., D.S.O* (London: Hutchinson, 1951), pp.534–56; Gill, *Royal Australian Navy 1942–1945*, pp.304–5.
69 Cunningham, *A sailor's odyssey*, pp.534–56; Greene and Massignani, *Naval war in the Mediterranean*, pp.284–99; *Fuehrer conferences*, pp.343–46; Rohwer, *Chronology*, pp.255–56, 261–62; Tomblin, *With utmost spirit*, pp.147–94.
70 It was just as well because U-boats stationed off the Algerian and Libyan coasts had already sunk seven ships and torpedoed four more from the feeder convoys before the attack on Sicily had actually begun. This kind of return was missing from the operational record of the Italian submarines. Of sixteen submarines which engaged the Allies in torpedo attacks in the early post-invasion period, six were sunk by a mix of submarines, destroyers and MTBs, while one was captured. Even those U-boats that tried to intervene came off second best at this time, losing three of their number

before the end of the month. Rohwer, *Chronology*, p.262; S.W.C. Pack, *Operation Husky* (Newton Abbot, Devon: David & Charles, 1977); Carlo D'Este, *Bitter victory: the battle for Sicily 1943* (New York: E.P.Dutton, 1988); Field Marshal Lord Carver, *The war in Italy 1943–1945: a vital contribution to victory in Europe* (London: Pan Books 2002), pp.10–58; D.J. Haycock, *Eisenhower and the art of warfare: a critical appraisal* (Jefferson, NC: McFarland & Co, 2004), pp.45–53.

71 Rohwer, *Chronology*, pp.263–64, 266–67; Greene and Massignani, *Naval warfare in the Mediterranean*, pp.296–97; Richard L. DiNardo, *Germany and the Axis powers: from coalition to collapse* (Lawrence, Ks: University Press of Kansas, 2005), pp.176–77.

72 Mack Smith, *Mussolini*, pp.267–300; *Fuehrer conferences*, pp.343–63; Gilbert, *Churchill, VII*, pp.452–54, 459.

73 Analysts of the making of Allied Grand Strategy are inclined to see a 'changing of the guard' taking place at *Quadrant* with American views coming to the fore at the expense of the British. This reflected a larger military dynamic – one in which the United States was no longer just an equal member of the Anglo-American wartime partnership but the dominant one. Roosevelt's 'Arsenal of Democracy' had certainly become that and more by August 1943. Farrell, *Basis and making of British grand strategy*, pp.633–60; Hayes, *History of the Joint Chiefs of Staff*, pp.448–71; Mark A. Stoler, *Allies and adversaries: the Joint Chiefs of Staff, the Grand Alliance, and U.S. strategy in World War II* (Chapel Hill, N.C.: The University of North Carolina Press, 2000), pp.119–21, 125, 136.

74 Germany had also faced resistance from the Danish government who had resisted their plans to impose a state of emergency throughout the country in response to growing industrial unrest and acts of sabotage directed against German interests. Rejecting the German demands for the introduction of a series of draconian measures aimed at putting a stop to this escalating civil unrest, the Danish government resigned on 28 August and the Germans moved quickly to impose Martial Law and disarm the Danish Army on the following day. They were too late to prevent the scuttling of nine submarines, five patrol boats, eight assorted minesweepers, four minelayers and a coastal defence ship in the waters off Copenhagen. This act of defiance ordered by Vice-Admiral Aage Vedel in the early hours of 29 August was not appreciated by the German authorities and they sent troops to other naval bases to ensure that the same thing wouldn't happen to the rest of the fleet. There was not much left to save. Richard Petrow, *The bitter years: the invasion and occupation of Denmark and Norway April 1940–May 1945* (New York: W.W. Morrow, 1974), pp.184–95; John Oram Thomas, *The giant-killers: the Danish resistance movement 1940/5* (London: Michael Joseph, 1975), pp.19–23; Christopher Tuck, 'Amphibious operations: the Italian campaign, 1943–45', in Speller (ed.), *Royal Navy and maritime power*, pp.88–107; Rohwer, *Chronology*, pp.266–67, 269–72.

75 A start on weakening resistance on New Georgia had actually begun in March 1943 with the four destroyers of the 'Cactus Striking Force' and three light cruisers and three fleet destroyers of TF68 pummelling the vital airfield at Munda on New Georgia and the subordinate one of Vila on the island of Kolombangara in a vain bid to restrict their use. For sources on the fierce struggle that would unfold on New Georgia see Brian Altobello, *Into the shadows furious: the brutal battle for New Georgia* (Novato, Ca: Presidio, 2000); Eric Hammel, *Munda trail: the New Georgia campaign* (New York: Orion Books, 1989); Rohwer, *Chronology*, pp.237, 249–50, 257–59, 262–63.

76 Gill, *Royal Australian Navy 1942–1945*, pp.288–90.

77 Before *Cartwheel* got off the ground on 29 June, MacArthur's forces had struck elsewhere by putting the 112th Cavalry Regiment ashore on Woodlark Island on 23–24 June and the 158th Infantry Regiment on Kiriwina off the east coast of New Guinea on 28–29 June. Both landings on these Trobriand Islands were uncontested. An airfield was subsequently built on Woodlark. Daniel E. Barbey, *MacArthur's amphibious navy* (Annapolis, Md: United States Naval Institute, 1969), pp.58–68; Gailey, *War in the Pacific*, pp.224–25.

78 While they didn't cause much damage with their air raids, Japanese planes did torpedo the attack transport *McCawley* forcing Turner to abandon his flagship and transfer his flag to the destroyer *Farenholt*. Rohwer, *Chronology*, p.258.
79 Although the bombardment of Rendova was conducted by the light cruiser *Yūbari* and nine destroyers, the effects were minimal. Ibid.
80 Only four destroyers had taken part in the bombardment of 9 July but the subsequent operation was conducted by a group of three cruisers and ten destroyers who pumped 3,204 6-inch (152mm) and 5,470 5-inch (127mm) shells into Munda. Dull, *Battle history of the IJN*, pp.274–76; Hoyt, *Glory of the Solomons*, 91–117; Rohwer, *Chronology*, pp.258–59.
81 HMNZ *Leander* was torpedoed by the *Jintsu* before the Japanese light cruiser was demolished by a fearsome accumulation of shells directed at her by the other two Allied cruisers. Before the action finished, however, both of the US cruisers *Honolulu* and *St. Louis* were torpedoed and the destroyer *Gwin* was sunk by the Japanese destroyers. Altobello, *Into the shadows furious*, pp.172–75; Dull, *Battle history of the IJN*, pp.276–77; Hoyt, *Glory of the Solomons*, pp.131–35; Rohwer, *Chronology*, p.259.
82 Despite the loss of Munda, it took another nineteen days of hard fighting to overcome the stubborn Japanese resistance around the port of Bairoko, lying a mere eight miles north of the airfield. They used this port to evacuate many of the men on New Georgia who had fought so tenaciously to hold Munda and who had done so for so long. Hoyt, *Glory of the Solomons*, pp.137–71; Altobello, *Into the shadows furious*, pp.345–46.
83 Altobello, *Into the shadows furious*, pp.343–44; Harker, *Well done Leander*, pp.295–309.
84 In the hours that followed the landings in the early morning of 15 August, the invasion fleet, their fighter cover and the forces now onshore were subject to a series of three massed attacks by the Japanese who managed to put 219 aircraft aloft to dispute these landings. Apart from roughly sixty casualties at the beachhead, only *Cony*, the flagship of the US III Amphibious Force under Rear-Admiral T.S. Wilkinson and one of his LSTs were damaged by near-misses. Hoyt, *Glory of the Solomons*, pp.173–99; Dull, *Battle history of the IJN*, pp.277–83.
85 Hoyt, *Glory of the Solomons*, pp.176–79.

9 Striking back (September–December 1943)

While the Allies remained stuck in the central Solomons, they were poised to move vigorously forward in the Mediterranean. British and Canadian forces began gearing up for their attack on Calabria (*Baytown*) by using a mix of vessels to batter the coast around Reggio di Calabria and soften up the Italian defences for the invasion to come. In truth, there was little to soften up. Badoglio's representatives were in the final stages of secret armistice negotiations with Eisenhower's command headquarters and Italian soldiers in the area were not spoiling for a fight even on home soil. This much became clear in the early hours of 3 September when the first troops of the British Eighth Army were ferried across the Straits of Messina in masses of landing craft and came ashore between Villa San Giovanni and Reggio di Calabria to the accompaniment of a deafening barrage of fire from shore batteries and the assorted guns of several monitors, cruisers, destroyers and gunboats. It was an impressive artillery fanfare but not much more than that. It didn't quell resistance to the invasion because there really wasn't any. Lacking any military threat to the repeated sailings that took place over the next few days, the Allied sailors involved in the operation quickly dubbed *Baytown*, the 'Messina Straits Regatta'. It proved to be the lull before the storm of Salerno.[1]

While there was no fighting in the toe of Italy, the knee was unlikely to be so accommodating. Scheduled to begin on 9 September, *Avalanche* was always going to be a far sterner test and so it proved. In the days beforehand a total of fifteen convoys and their escorts left a string of North African and Sicilian ports to make their way across the Tyrrhenian Sea. They were formed into one of two attack forces: a northern group of roughly 300 assorted landing craft that would seek to put the British 10th Corps, two British Commando units and a US Ranger Battalion Landing Team ashore on beaches both west and south of the town of Salerno, while a southern group of more than 150 vessels were to land the US 6th Corps on open beaches further south close to the town of Paestum. Both the northern and southern attack forces had escorts containing several cruisers, a monitor and at least seventeen destroyers. Covering all of these ships was a Support Carrier Force commanded by one of Churchill's favourite officers, Rear-Admiral Sir Philip Vian, which was to provide fighter cover over the landing sites during the assault phase while Force H, under Vice-Admiral Sir

Algernon Willis, with two carriers (*Formidable* and *Illustrious*), four battleships (*Nelson*, *Rodney*, *Valiant* and *Warspite*), and twenty destroyers would be on hand to cope with any enemy threat that might come from the sea.[2]

Before nightfall on 8 September when they turned into the Gulf of Salerno, the Allied troops were aware from Eisenhower's announcement that Italy had formally surrendered. Although jubilation was widespread amongst the troops as they plunged towards the shoreline, not all expected *Avalanche* to be the cakewalk that *Baytown* had been. As armistice talks with Badoglio's government moved from the realm of the intriguingly possible into that of the firmly probable, Eisenhower and his team of planners decided to use the opportunity that the surrender of the Italian fleet afforded them to send the 1st British Airborne Division to occupy the erstwhile naval base at Taranto. An improvised and rushed operation at best, *Slapstick* was a little onomatopoeic in nature. Admiral Cunningham, in overall command of naval operations for the Italian invasion, offered the use of the 12th Cruiser Squadron (*Aurora*, *Dido*, *Penelope* and *Sirius*), along with the US light cruiser *Boise* and the fast minelayer *Abdiel*, to take the troops from Bizerte across the Ionian Sea to the heel of Italy on 8 September. While reasonably confident that no trouble was to be expected from the Italian naval authorities, he was only too well aware that the same could not be said of any Germans in the vicinity. For this reason he decided to send Vice-Admiral Sir Arthur Power with the two battleships *Howe* and *King George V*, a destroyer flotilla and a few minesweepers to try to ensure that *Slapstick* passed off without a hitch. Aware from intelligence sources that a couple of German E-boats (fast torpedo boats) had been mining the harbour, Power wisely let his minesweepers enter Taranto first of all in the late afternoon of 9 September.[3] Finding no apparent trace of the enemy, the rest of the 'occupation force' was ushered into the harbour and began disembarking its troops. Just when it seemed that *Slapstick* had been trouble-free, *Abdiel*, the old workhorse of the Mediterranean Fleet, struck a German mine on 10 September and sank with heavy loss of life.[4]

An hour or so before *Slapstick* got underway in the evening of 8 September, arrangements were put in hand to fulfil the terms of the armistice agreement that had been secretly arranged several days earlier by Badoglio's plenipotentiary, General Giuseppe Castellano and Eisenhower's representative, General Bedell Smith.[5] Admiral Carlo Bergamini, flying his flag in the battleship *Roma*, left the naval base at La Spezia accompanied by the two battleships *Italia* (previously named *Littorio*) and *Vittorio Veneto*, three light cruisers and eight destroyers to join up with another three light cruisers and a solitary torpedo boat coming from Genoa. Bergamini was, of course, not wildly happy about this course of events or the uncertain future it presaged for his fleet. Although the Allies had urged Admiral Raffaele de Courten, the Italian C-in-C, to order his fleet to steam south to the Tunisian coast before proceeding to Malta where they were to be formally surrendered to the Allies, he instructed Bergamini to steam first of all to La Maddalena, the naval base on the northern tip of Sardinia, where King Victor Emmanuel III and his government had fled to from Rome. Hitler's suspicions about Badoglio's commitment to the Axis cause had been such that the Germans had already begun implementing a series of counter-measures, codenamed *Achse* and *Schwarz*, even before Eisenhower's confirmation of Badoglio's 'treachery' was broadcast on 8 September. Determined not to let the British get their hands on those units of the Italian fleet in northern Italy if he could help it, Hitler urged the Luftwaffe to do all it could to trace them once they had left port and bomb them out of existence. Once news reached Bergamini that German troops had begun to take over a number of naval bases in the Tyrrhenian Sea – La Maddalena included – he changed course and steamed towards the island of Asinara on the northwest coast of Sardinia. It was too late. Eleven Dornier 217s (Do-217s) from their base at Istres near Marseilles found his fleet west of the Straits of Bonifacio (between Corsica and Sardinia) shortly after 1500 hours on 9 September and using FX 1400 wireless-controlled bombs did their best to ram home the message that reneging on an alliance obligation risked death and destruction. Two direct hits on Bergamini's flagship eliminated *Roma* in a fiery explosion, killing the commander-in-chief and 1,351 of the 1,948 officers and men on board, while other bombs damaged *Italia* as well. Two other destroyers on their way to join the rest of the northern-based fleet were themselves lost to gunfire and mines.[6] Leaving a cruiser, three destroyers and some patrol boats to pick up the survivors and seek refuge in Bone (Annaba) in Algeria and Port Mahon in the Balearics, Admiral Romeo Oliva assumed the role of C-in-C and pressed on for the North African coast with the rest of the fleet. They met a number of Allied warships off the Tunisian coast early in the morning of 10 September and were led into Malta by them the next morning. By that time Admiral Alberto da Zara had already arrived from Taranto with his two battleships *Andrea Doria* and *Caio Duilio*, a pair of light cruisers and a lone destroyer.[7]

While the Regia Marina was in the throes of realigning itself with the Allies, Operation *Avalanche* had begun in the Gulf of Salerno. This was to be no *Baytown* or *Slapstick* adventure. Feldmarschall Albert Kesselring, Oberbefehlshaber Süd (Commander-in-Chief South), made sure of that. Although the initial landings were successful both south of the Sele River and further north around Salerno, the increasing scale of German resistance from 11 September onwards threatened to forestall any major breakout from the beachheads and for several days the final outcome of this amphibious operation lay in the balance.[8] During this decisive phase of the land battle, the Allied fleet played an immensely important contribution in maintaining its logistical supply duties to the troops on shore but also in carrying out a persistent heavy bombardment of the German positions all along the more than twenty-mile coastal front. Their presence offshore helped to keep General Heinrich von Veitinghoff from driving a massive wedge between Lieutenant-General Richard McCreery's British troops in the north and those of Major-General Ernest Dawley's American forces in the southern sector. Although targeted by the Luftwaffe with their new wireless-controlled FX 1400 bombs and Henschel Hs-293 glider bombs, warship losses were kept down by Allied carrier plane sorties, and a defensive screen that consisted of strong A.A.

defences and the erection of barrage balloons. Heavy German counter-attacks continued on 12 September and intensified over the next two days forcing the Americans to retreat and putting the entire operation in jeopardy.[9]

Reinforcements were called for and three cruisers were dispatched to Tripoli to bring these fresh troops to assist in bolstering the Allied numbers. Even so, by 14 September Lieutenant-General Mark Clark, in overall command of the ground troops, was forced to even consider an evacuation of one or both of the army sectors. Such a move could have been disastrous and he was fortunately talked out of it by his subordinate commanders. A real crisis was averted and the Allied lines held out. Again, the naval fire support team, consisting of the monitor *Roberts*, six light cruisers and seven destroyers had borne the brunt of more aerial attacks. It became essential that four of the damaged warships be speedily replaced and more guns brought to bear on the German armoured divisions to blunt the inroads being made by the Panzer tanks in squeezing the beachhead. When things seemed at the worst on 14 September, the arrival of four Allied light cruisers bringing with them troop reinforcements and much needed firepower came not a moment too soon. They helped to maintain the intense bombardment of the German positions and they were assisted in this regard by the arrival on the following day of the two battleships *Valiant* and *Warspite*, who used their guns to rake the German lines to maximum effect at ranges of up to 21,800 yards (19.9km). Veitinghoff recognised that his chance had gone. A combination of Montgomery's Eighth Army coming up from the south, the extra aerial clout summoned by the Allies to exert pressure over the battlefield and the enemy's reinforced naval presence offshore told him that the Allied beachhead was not going to crack. By 16 September the crisis had been largely averted. Even so *Warspite* was still in the thick of things when she was hit and brought to a standstill by one of the new wireless-controlled bombs.[10] In the days thereafter the Allied hold on matters grew as Veitinghoff began to pull back his troops and armour from the Salerno front. *Avalanche* had survived its biggest test and the road to Naples now lay open before the combined Allied forces. When the first units entered the outskirts of the southern Italian city on 1 October they found they had inherited a largely shattered prize. Wreckage on this scale induced by massive Allied bombing and an orgy of German destruction revealed once again the horrendous material costs to those caught up in war.[11]

As the Allied forces readied themselves to leave Sicily for the mainland of Italy at the start of September, another major amphibious operation got underway in the Southwest Pacific. It was time for MacArthur to take the initiative once again in New Guinea. On 1 September the US VII Amphibious Force under the command of Rear-Admiral Daniel Barbey left Milne Bay on the extreme southeast coast with three brigades of Australian troops in a convoy of ninety-seven vessels escorted by nine destroyers. He successfully landed these 8,000 troops in two batches east of the port of Lae during the nights of 3–4 and 5–6 September respectively. Skilful use of radar by the escort's picket destroyer *Reid* and the ability to call on US fighter planes to assist in breaking up incoming Japanese bombing formations, helped to keep losses of landing craft to a bare minimum.¹² An offshore bombardment also helped to soften up the Japanese defences around Lae, a town that had been used hitherto by the Japanese as an important supply base for making a series of attacks on the interior. It finally fell to the Australians on 16 September four days after the port of Salamaua had fallen.¹³ Once the larger port of Lae had been taken, the southern coastal route along the Huon Peninsula to the port of Finschhafen at its eastern extremity lay open. MacArthur knew that a victory on the Huon Peninsula in New Guinea would enable him to build a number of airfields there for use in supporting the invasion of the western end of New Britain and the capture of Cape Gloucester (Operation *Dexterity*) later in the year. Once his troops had established a foothold in New Britain, they could begin their drive towards Rabaul. Apart from its naval facilities, Rabaul was home to four crucial airfields, vast munitions warehouses and a garrison of 100,000 Japanese troops. MacArthur believed that its seizure would provide the key necessary to unlock the entire Bismarck Archipelago.¹⁴

If the Japanese grudgingly gave ground in New Guinea, the same was true of the central Solomons too. Although they had been startled and discomforted by Halsey's island-hopping strategy of late, the Japanese had responded by putting reinforcements ashore on the northern coast of Vella Lavella to build up their slender supply base at Horaniu. It was never going to be sufficient to do anything more than make an eventual victory harder than it otherwise would have been. It was nothing less than a delaying tactic and one which reflected a new defensive mentality adopted by the Japanese IGHQ. Despite the significance MacArthur gave to Rabaul, the Japanese had decided that even this naval base would have to be ultimately sacrificed in favour of falling back on Truk. Nonetheless, the intention was not to give the Americans and their allies any easy victories. After a series of inconclusive naval skirmishes off the coast of Vella Lavella, a final evacuation was ordered from the Japanese garrison on Kolombangara in late September and early October.¹⁵ These men were to be withdrawn so that they could be employed in the defence of Bougainville, the largest island in the Solomons, where the Japanese would be able to muster 35–40,000 troops to slow the progress of the Allied war effort. Rear-Admiral Matsuji Ijuin helped the cause by engineering a remarkable evacuation effort in which more than a hundred assorted landing craft and other small vessels were employed. In a series of evacuations that began on 25 September and lasted for several days, 9,400 men were plucked from the northern shore of Kolombangara despite the early imposition of an Allied destroyer blockade around the island that did much to complicate and imperil the entire operation.¹⁶

Withdrawals were much in vogue in September and October. In the Caucasus region the Germans, anxious to avoid another military disaster, methodically prepared for and then perfectly executed an outstanding evacuation of General Erwin Jaenecke's 17th Army from the Kuban bridgehead while keeping the Red Army and Rear-Admiral Sergei Gorshkov's redoubtable Azov Flotilla at bay throughout. What made *Fall Brunhild* so special was that considerable time and effort went into setting up the defensive positions through which the withdrawal would be effected. In this way, a large body of troops and a literally staggering amount of supplies of all types were spirited away from the advancing Soviet forces by Vizeadmiral Gustav Kieseritzky, the leading German naval commander in the Black Sea, and Kapitän zur See Friedrich Grattenauer, his subordinate in the Caucasus, who took responsibility for organising the evacuation effort. Using a host of assorted ferries, tugs and lighters on repeated trips across the narrow Kerch Strait to the Crimean peninsula, their success can be measured in the sheer numbers of those that they brought to safety in the three-week operation that began on 12 September: 239,669 troops, an additional 16,311 wounded and 27,456 civilians. This would have been dramatic enough but the figures of what else they shifted: 115,477 tons of supplies, 74 tanks, 1,815 guns, 21,230 vehicles, 27,741 horse-driven vehicles, 74,657 horses and 6,255 head of cattle almost defies belief and stands as one of the greatest evacuations of modern times. Overseeing the withdrawal in the Kerch Strait when these sailings were going on were an MTB and a Motor Minesweeper (MMS) flotilla, and a number of gunboats which were there to protect the vessels making these trips from the unwelcome attentions of any Soviet naval forces that threatened to interfere with them. There were many such engagements but the Soviets tasted little or no success in these tussles. As a fitting addendum to *Brunhild*, an operation was mounted by the Germans (*Fall Wiking*) to extricate the evacuation vessels that had performed so successfully across the Kerch Strait. From 8 to 10 October, 240 of these craft were moved in four large convoys from the Kuban bridgehead to the naval base of Sevastopol. Escorted by two MMS flotillas and one submarine-chaser flotilla, with an additional MTB flotilla as cover, these slow moving convoys reached Sevastopol for the loss of only two vessels: an assault boat sunk by a Soviet aircraft and a ferry barge by a submarine. By any yardstick this had been a quite brilliant coda to a bitterly disappointing Caucasus campaign for the Germans and a warning to the Soviets that even after Stalingrad, Kursk and Orel they should not imagine that the Germans would be inclined to roll over and play dead. While military retreats are usually and quite naturally associated with failure, *Brunhild* and *Wiking* can nonetheless be rightly regarded as stirring epics of an almost Wagnerian kind.[17]

A much smaller scale German evacuation also took place from Sardinia beginning almost immediately after *Avalanche* had begun and shortly after Eisenhower's announcement of the Italian armistice. Organised by Kapitän zur See Gustav von Liebenstein, the hero of *Fall Lehrgang* (the evacuation of Sicily), fifteen steamers and more than 120 barges and smaller vessels were used in taking 25,000 troops, 2,300 vehicles and 5,000 tons of supplies across the Straits of Bonifacio to the French island of Corsica. After fashioning an agreement with the Italian garrison on the island, the Germans moved on to the city of Bastia on the northeast coast of the island from where more than 21,000 of their troops and 350 tons of supplies were airlifted to the Italian mainland. Von Liebenstein then assumed responsibility for evacuating the rest of the German troops and supplies on the island by sea to the island of Elba and the town of Livorno on the coast of Tuscany. These sailings were not pleasure trips. Allied air attacks accounted for the loss of five steamers, enemy submarines took out another six ships, including a minelayer and a tanker, and few on board the minelayer *Pommern* appreciated the classic irony of falling victim to a mine.[18]

While retreats were being staged in these months, the ebb and flow of war was seen in the staging of a number of operations that were designed to take the initiative and strike a blow against their adversaries. One of the most daring and heroic occurred on 17 September when three two-man kayak teams each with nine delayed-action magnetic limpet mines weighing a total of forty-five kilograms were released late at night from the motor drifter *Krait* in the waters off Pandjang, an island in the Riau archipelago south of Batam and more than 50km (over 27nm) from their final objective – to sabotage Japanese shipping in the port of Singapore.[19] Over the course of the next ten days they rested up on uninhabited islands during the daylight hours and paddled closer to Singapore under cover of darkness. Major Ivan Lyon, the leader of Operation *Jaywick*, decided that the attack should be made during the night of 26–27 September. One team (Davidson and Falls), finding nothing in Keppel Harbour, attached their limpet mines to three Japanese cargo vessels lying offshore in the Singapore Roads before sculling away noiselessly in the darkness of the night. Another team (Lyon and Huston), unable to penetrate the gloom of the Examination Anchorage, opted to place all nine limpet mines on a 10,000-ton tanker that they came across. Page and Jones in the final kayak targeted the wharves and waters off the oil refinery of Pulau Bukom where two freighters and a rusting cargo ship were on hand. As all three teams sought to put some distance between themselves and the scene of their recent nocturnal activities, they heard the reassuring sound of several explosions coming from the direction of Singapore. All of their mines had worked flawlessly with the result that the damage caused to two of the freighters was sufficient to sink them, the solitary tanker was badly holed and the other four vessels involved in the raid were put out of action for the immediate future. Surveying the damage caused to their shipping understandably infuriated the Japanese military who strove incredibly hard to find the saboteurs over the next few days. Amazingly, perhaps, given the manhunt that was mounted for them, all six of the saboteurs remained free. They did so by only stirring at night. During the day they remained hidden on the countless small islands that form the Riau chain and only as darkness came would they emerge to paddle back towards the rendezvous point off Pulau Pompong – more than 100km from Singapore. When the *Krait* returned from her leisurely meanderings in the waters off Borneo to meet them in the early hours of 2 October only one of the kayak teams (Davidson and Falls) had managed to reach the rendezvous point in time to clamber aboard the motor drifter. A couple of days later the *Krait* returned to pick up the other kayak teams and take all three crews safely to a heroes' reception in Western Australia. Daring though it was, Operation *Jaywick* was in reality more a severe jolt to Japanese pride than a critical blow to their mercantile ambitions in the region. While it would be churlish to devalue the heroism of Major Lyon and his men in carrying out this raid, one wonders whether the benefits of bloodying the nose of the Japanese were really worth it since the human cost to an innocent set of victims in Singapore was far more significant than the commercial losses sustained by the occupying power.[20]

Well before *Jaywick* got underway, the Germans had sent a group of eleven U-boats and a flying boat to patrol Siberian waters in the hope that they could locate a number of Soviet convoys and bring the heavy cruiser *Lützow*, waiting at her base in Altenfjorden, into play. *Fall Wunderland II* belied its name – no Soviet convoys were located, while mining the seas to the east of Novaya Zemlya and the shelling of shore installations, such as the W/T stations at Pravdy and Blagopoluchiya, was unglamorous and unrewarding work.[21] It was galling for Dönitz that the *Lützow* could not be employed in a marauding northern capacity on the Siberian route because his surface fleet remained bottled up in its base in Norway where it remained more of a potential threat than an actual one. He would have also liked to have used his heavy ships to telling effect in the Arctic against the Murmansk convoys, but even that possibility had been forestalled by the Allied decision to suspend these sailings for the duration of the long northern summer. While its 'fleet-in-being' status could be advanced by him to justify their existence, Dönitz wished to show the doubting Hitler that the days of the capital ship had not entirely passed. For this reason, if for no other, a dual exercise in flag-waving was arranged for them (*Fall Sizilien* and *Fall Zitronella*) in early September in which a task force under Oskar Kummetz consisting of the battleships *Tirpitz* and *Scharnhorst* and nine destroyers carried out an attack on the Allied bases on Spitsbergen (Svalbard). While *Scharnhorst* and two of the destroyer flotillas deposited a battalion of the 349th Grenadier Regiment at Grönfjord and Advent Bay, *Tirpitz* steamed on to shell Barentsburg where her 15-inch (381mm) guns wrecked power, fuel and supply sources on the shoreline and took out the coastal batteries and the wireless station before both ships returned to their base in Altenfjorden.[22]

Even before the Admiralty could express its annoyance at this latest adventure by the German surface fleet, its head – the First Sea Lord Admiral Sir Dudley Pound – had fallen desperately ill.[23] Before a replacement (Admiral Sir Andrew Cunningham) was put in place in mid-October, Churchill's imprint on naval operations became unmistakable. One of his enduring fears was that Raeder's old surface fleet would once again play an active part in the war. In his opinion, the guns of the German heavy ships could wreak havoc with even the best Allied warships, so what they would do to convoy traffic hardly bore thinking about. It was precisely for this reason that the Arctic supply convoys had been halted in March for several months.[24] This state of affairs could not continue indefinitely. Stalin was already incensed at what he saw as the deliberate failure on the part of the other Allies to help him in his hour of need. He had not regarded the invasion of Sicily and southern Italy as a true 'Second Front' or one that would do anything to draw off masses of German forces from Soviet territory, so he was highly unlikely to accede to any further requests for the postponement of these supply convoys to Murmansk and Archangel.[25]

In order for these convoys to be resumed, however, Churchill felt it was essential to continue trying to knock out these big ships by whatever means were available to him. His resolve on this question was given added vigour by the attacks on Spitsbergen. Such sorties showed that Dönitz had no intention of merely keeping them out of harm's way at the head of Altenfjorden. Since air raids had been unable to either sink or put them out of action, Churchill deemed it was time to try a new approach. In Operation *Source*, the method used would be by midget submarine. Six of these X-craft were built with the *Tirpitz* and the *Scharnhorst* especially in mind. In essence the plan was for six ordinary patrol submarines to tow each of these X-craft to a point off the northern Norwegian coast where they would be released and from where they could use their own diesel electric power to get them to the berths of the two capital ships in the fjord at Kaa and at Lange for the *Lützow*. Once they had located their chosen target and negotiated their way around the defensive booms and nets protecting each of the ships, they would aim to release their side cargoes underneath them. Each of these side cargoes contained 3,500 tons of Amatex high explosive with a time fuse that would supposedly give the saboteurs up to six hours to escape before the mines would detonate. If they worked as they were supposed to, the results were thought likely to be catastrophic for any ship, including the *Tirpitz*. Although the Admiralty had thought of using them in the spring of 1943, the plan had been deferred to allow their crews more time to practise their skills and for the X-craft to become more seaworthy. Despite the intervening months little had been done to correct the basic faults of the midget submarines which meant that the six in service for *Source* had persistent problems with their periscopes, gyro compasses, depth handling and side cargoes' buoyancy tanks. Any one of these shortcomings would have made life difficult for the officers and crew of the X-craft, but the accumulation of these defects meant that it was not always possible for them to see where they were going, to manoeuvre properly, or to keep their submersible at periscope depth. It would prove to be a deadly combination for some of these very gallant submariners. That anything came of the operation, given these inherent design faults and the fact that the tow lines on several snapped, is quite staggering. Unfortunately for Churchill, two of the X-craft never survived the outward journey (*X-9*, *X-8*), and one suffered a mechanical breakdown (*X-10*) once she had slipped her tow. That left fifty per cent of the force to soldier on. All three of the remaining midget submarines (*X-5*, *X-6* and *X-7*) had been originally assigned to the *Tirpitz* and it was she they sought to destroy on the early morning of 22 September. Each of them appears to have become fouled in the torpedo netting that protected the battleship from conventional submarine attacks and though each one eventually managed to extricate themselves from it they were only able to do so at some cost to their submersible. Although the crew of *X-5* did not survive the mission, it is distinctly possible that they did lay their side cargoes underneath the starboard side of the *Tirpitz* before they were discovered and battered by her armament and the depth-charges dropped by one of the destroyers in the fjord. *X-6* also managed to lay her charges beside 'B' turret on the port bow before she was scuttled and her crew was forced to surrender. This left *X-7* alone to tackle the battleship. She released one of her side cargoes abreast of 'B' turret and her other one under what her crew hoped was 'C' turret. *X-7* initially survived the blasts that rocked *Tirpitz* shortly after 0800 hours, but not for long and neither, alas, did two of her four-man crew. Despite the succession of heavy explosions that took place underneath her, *Tirpitz* – though grievously damaged and taking in 1,430 tons of water – did survive although she would need extensive repairs that would take until the middle of March 1944 to complete. In terms of operational results, it was not all that Churchill would have wanted, but at least it was a start. He would not tire of trying to eliminate the rest of Dönitz's capital ship fleet, but the German Großadmiral was determined to make it as difficult as possible for him to do so. On the day following the attack on *Tirpitz*, *Lützow* was ordered to return to the Baltic and her port of Gotenhafen (Gdynia). Despite being located by aerial reconnaissance on both 26 and 27 September while on passage, the planes of the Fleet Air Arm that were scrambled to bomb her and five accompanying destroyers out of existence never caught a further glimpse of the enemy group and *Lützow* made it into port safely on 1 October. Like *Scharnhorst*, she appeared to be a lucky ship. Would it hold? Churchill hoped not.[26]

Hitler remained distinctly unimpressed by his surface fleet, but he had far bigger issues to distract him at this time. Italy's defection from the Axis in September meant that the entire Mediterranean region was now up for grabs unless Germany could hold what they had. Crucial to this strategic imperative was the fate of Greece. If the Allies gained control in the Aegean they might just persuade the previously reluctant Turks to either enter the war on their side or become benevolently non-belligerent. Even if they jibbed at putting their own men into the field against the Germans, the Turks might be prepared to offer the Allies the use of their bases for operations against the Germans in the Balkans. If that were to happen, the Germans would be fighting on yet another front and something would have to give somewhere. So for Hitler the Aegean had to become an 'Iron Ring' – one that could not be allowed to fall gratuitously into the hands of Churchill. He saw it as key to keeping the lid on Turkey and preventing the Balkans from being turned once again into the tinder-box of Europe. Churchill, who had foreseen this situation but whose plans on the subject had been stifled by official opposition, sensed that there was still scope for a little manoeuvring, and that plans could be improvised by General Henry Wilson using purely British forces to exploit what he saw as a favourable situation on the island of Rhodes and throughout the Dodecanese.[27]

Unfortunately, his desire to profit from the Italian armistice outstripped the means at Wilson's disposal to bring it about. There was little other than light forces available to him and even fewer means of transporting them to the Aegean since the majority of the landing craft in the region were being used for the Italian campaign. Light forces could be moved onto some of the Dodecanese islands, but to capture Rhodes would take more than the willingness of his men to run a few risks on Britain's behalf. This much became clear when existing German units on Rhodes were ordered by Hitler to take over the Italian garrison on the island once news of the Italian armistice had been broadcast. By 11 September the Italians had yielded their garrison and Rhodes had become a

German preserve. Pre-empted by the German action on Rhodes and wishing to give the Italians more reason to resist their erstwhile Axis allies elsewhere, Wilson opted to bring a number of small battle and commando groups from their bases in the Middle East and used a collection of caiques, motor launches and MTBs to land them on Kos, Leros, Samos and Symi, amongst other islands in the Dodecanese chain. His response was matched elsewhere in the Aegean by Konteradmiral Werner Lange, the German naval commander in the region, who began to convoy troops from their bases in Greece to those islands that had previously been controlled by Axis forces, taking off the Italian POWs once control on the island had changed hands. In a bid to prevent this policy from succeeding, the British stepped up their presence in the area with the transfer of six destroyers to Alexandria. It was hoped that they would attack the convoys – which they did – but there weren't sufficient of them to ensure that real disruption took place, let alone force the abandonment of Lange's operation.[28]

In many ways British policy in the Aegean remained in a state of improvisation and suffered because of it. It appeared to rest on too much wishful thinking and lacked a clear vision. After all, hope is not a convincing substitute for a well thought out strategic plan. While no strategic genius, Hitler knew what he wanted to happen in the Aegean and was prepared to put sufficient forces, both air and naval, into ensuring that his will would prevail there. Churchill and Wilson knew what they wanted too, but simply couldn't rouse the Americans into going along with them. Eisenhower was persuaded by the intelligence windfalls he continued to receive from 'Ultra' sources that there was more than a reasonable chance the Germans would continue to make a stand south of Rome. If that was indeed the case (and it proved to be so), Eisenhower was simply not prepared to divert badly needed resources from the Italian theatre to the Aegean in order to recapture Rhodes and expel the Germans back onto the Greek mainland, no matter how appealing that notion might be to the British prime minister.[29] So the unsatisfactory cat and mouse game in the region persisted until 26 September when the Germans launched the first of a series of attacks on Allied held islands in the Aegean. It didn't take the German troops long to make their presence felt. Kos soon fell and in doing so *Fall Eisbär* (Case *Polar Bear*) netted more than 4,500 POWs. This news aggravated Churchill greatly. His agitation at the dichotomy between what could be and what was being achieved in the Aegean grew with the news that the two light cruisers *Penelope* and *Sirius*, along with a couple of destroyers, had wiped out virtually an entire troop convoy consisting of a freighter, six of seven naval ferry barges and a submarine-chaser bound for Kos on 7 October. Admiral Andrew Cunningham felt less 'gung-ho' than his prime minister about what could be done in these waters with the forces at his disposal. In less than a fortnight, he had lost four destroyers and a minelayer sunk, one cruiser was so badly damaged that she would never become operational again and a destroyer needed to be repaired. It was something that he couldn't feel entirely sanguine about since their losses had not been achieved in a winning cause. German control of Rhodes and Kos spelt problems for the British position in the rest of the

Dodecanese group unless their forces were dramatically increased in the Aegean. If Churchill entertained hopes that Marshal Badoglio's formal declaration of war on Nazi Germany on 13 October would help to resolve these issues by making the Allies stronger in the Eastern Mediterranean, he was destined to be grievously disappointed. It wouldn't.[30]

Before those problems were addressed in the most direct manner by the German attack on Leros and Samos in November, however, Whitehall and Washington's attention had been reluctantly drawn back to the North Atlantic with the resumption of the U-boat war on the Allied convoys. This was especially galling as Churchill had made a point of informing the House of Commons on 21 September that no merchant vessel crossing the North Atlantic had been sunk by enemy action for four months.[31] This news, welcomed with considerable satisfaction in parliament, was already out of date. U-boat wolf packs were back in business. Dönitz had returned to the fray knowing he couldn't do anything to prevent the Allies bridging the 'mid-Atlantic air gap' with the use of VLR aircraft, but believing he could provide his U-boat fleet with more effective means of coping with this new situation. He was anxious that his U-boats would henceforth be sent out equipped with the *W.Anz* search receiver to detect Allied use of 10cm radar and an *Aphrodite* radar decoy balloon to confuse those tracking them. He had eight 20mm A.A. guns fitted to ward off the additional threat his boats faced from both land-based and carrier aircraft; and the *Zaunkönig*, or T5 acoustic torpedo, was added to their arsenal of weapons for use against the stronger convoy destroyer escorts they were expected to encounter.[32] After earlier problems, he had become confident that his boats would get through the Bay of Biscay and out into the Atlantic because the deployment of long-range He-177 planes had largely nullified RAF Coastal Command's offensive in these waters – a point proved by the failure of Operation *Percussion* in late August to seal off the new access routes hugging the Spanish coast that the U-boats were using to get to and from their bases on the Atlantic coast of France. Those U-boats that escaped out into the Atlantic at this time would form the nucleus of his new offensive that began in earnest on 20 September and recorded its first success with the torpedoing of a frigate and the sinking of two Liberty ships the day before Churchill stood at the Commons Despatch Box and proclaimed that the U-boat threat had been largely vanquished. It was soon shown to be a little premature but not wholly fictional.[33]

After three days of renewed hostilities against convoys ON.202 and ONS.18 on the eastern side of the North Atlantic, and boosted by exaggerated reports from his submariners of the success of the acoustic torpedo, Dönitz was led to believe that the twenty-two boats of his *Leuthen* group had achieved a real breakthrough in punishing rather than evading the two convoy escort groups. In reality, the actual returns were far more modest.[34] A new group of twenty-one U-boats (*Rossbach*), operating in what was once an authentic 'mid-Atlantic air gap' and then north of it in late September and early October, neither saw the two convoys (ON.203 and ONS.19) it had been formed to destroy nor two others that it was on the lookout for (HX.258 and ON.204). A nil return from this initial phase of the operation suggested that Dönitz's new campaign had stalled, particularly since Allied aircraft and escort ships had managed to sink two of his U-boats and damage four more of them. Ordered to move south of their original position on 6 October, *Rossbach* proceeded to lose another three U-boats and had one damaged while sinking only one Polish destroyer in return. It made sobering reading for all those associated with the U-boat arm. Was this an aberration from the norm or was it the new norm? That question would be answered pretty emphatically over the course of the next two months as various wolf packs were tested and generally found wanting by a combination of Allied aircraft and combative battle-hardened escort groups who attacked them with tenacity, skill and destructive intent. Too many U-boats were being located, harried, bombed, depth-charged or rammed out of existence for Dönitz's liking. Allied convoys were being re-routed away from the wolf packs he had put in place and since the Admiralty had replaced both its Naval Cypher No.3 and No.4 with an improved Naval Cypher No.5 on 10 June, B-Dienst had no longer been able to read Admiralty signals or provide him and the U-boat arm with information about specific convoy routes.[35]

Dönitz had other things on his mind too. Admiral King's 10th Fleet had done a really good job in using 'Ultra' intelligence to target his U-boat tankers and once located to sink them. By the time autumn had arrived they had accounted for seven of these tankers in various parts of the Atlantic. When these were added to the two sunk in the Biscay offensive, the loss of these *Milchkühe* were a serious blow. Without them Dönitz's plan to refuel more of his U-boats at sea so that they could spend a longer time out on operational duty and lessen the aerial threat to them while on passage to and from their home bases was seriously undermined. October brought more of the same. Escort carriers combed the Central Atlantic on the lookout for the tanker fleet and using their aircraft to great effect succeeded in sinking four more *Milchkühe* and three other conventional U-boats in addition to damaging three more.[36] More bad news for the entire U-boat arm came with the arrival on 18 October of the first of the Allied VLR aircraft to be granted base rights by the Portuguese government on the islands of Fayal and Terceira in the Azores. Use of these bases would do much to eliminate what remained of the 'mid-Atlantic air gap' and bring about some redeployment of the wolf packs to other parts of the ocean, since congregating in what was previously an area of Allied weakness would be, in all probability, no longer as profitable as it once was.[37] By early December, therefore, it was possible to say that for the time being at least the Allies had definitely established the upper hand in their dealings with the C-in-C of the Kriegsmarine and the former commandant of the U-boats.[38]

While Dönitz fretted about his loss of control in the North and Central Atlantic, his Japanese allies were confronting a similar overall situation in various parts of the South Pacific. Their well-documented struggles in New Guinea and in what was left to them of the Solomon Islands had continued and intensified throughout the autumn, but a new and worrying development for the leadership in Tokyo were the new initiatives that the Americans had been taking in other parts of the ocean. If their action in the Aleutians had been about restoring pride, what did the Japanese make of the American landings on two of the Ellice Islands (Nukufetau and Nanomea) and on Baker Island in the Gilbert Islands at the end of August, or of the intensive bombing raids carried out against Marcus Island, Tarawa and Wake Island in the following weeks?[39] As none of these actions were necessary for the success of future operations against Bougainville or New Britain, the notion that the Americans may have been devoted to a single overarching strategic plan for the Pacific went out of the window. What these raids had done was to show that the Americans were prepared to mount simultaneous operations across thousands of miles of ocean if they deemed the risks to be worth it. Rueful Japanese military officers could consider that their enemy had learnt a thing or two from studying the moves Yamamoto had made so brilliantly in the early months of the war. Confirmation – if such was needed – of the separate strands of American policy was provided in November with the opening of the invasion of Bougainville in the Solomons and the costly attacks on the islands and atolls of the Gilbert Islands.[40]

Recovering Bougainville from the Japanese was always expected to be a tough assignment for the Americans. Apart from being the largest of the Solomon Islands, it had the most enemy soldiers (roughly 40,000) defending it and was near enough to the regional base of Rabaul in New Britain (approximately 200nm or 370km) to receive regular reinforcements of both troops and supplies, as well as substantial air cover should it be attacked or invaded. For this reason, the USAAF had begun a massive air offensive against Rabaul on 12 October in a bid to try to lessen its influence, wreck its infrastructure and destroy as many planes both on the ground and in the air as possible ahead of an invasion. These massed attacks drew forth a swift Japanese response from Admiral Mineichi Koga, Yamamoto's successor as C-in-C. In a novel twist he decided to transfer the aircraft from six of his carriers (*Hiyo, Jun'yō, Ryūhō, Shokaku, Zuihō* and *Zuikaku*) to the air base at Rabaul (Operation *RO*) in order to supplement the numbers of Japanese planes on New Britain capable of countering the American offensive. It would prove to be a costly error. So many of these planes were lost in the American carrier raids on Rabaul and in the skies over New Britain and Bougainville that Koga was forced to withdraw them and fly them back to Truk (Chuuk) on 12 November.[41]

After failing with two diversionary exercises in the Treasury Archipelago and on the island of Choiseul to delude the Japanese into thinking that Bougainville would not be their next target, the Allies began their invasion proper with the landing of 14,321 Marines and their supplies from a convoy of twelve transports at Cape Torokina in the early hours of 1 November. Escorted by eleven destroyers, four destroyer minesweepers and eight minesweepers, the invasion fleet got ashore on Bougainville without any interference. It wouldn't remain like that for long. While the Americans were still engaged in building up a substantial beachhead at Empress Augusta Bay (known to the Japanese as Gazelle Bay), Admiral Tomoshige Samejima, in command of the 8th Fleet, decided to send the ships he had immediately available at Rabaul to attack the invasion fleet. As a result, the two heavy cruisers *Haguro* and *Myokō*, accompanied by the light cruisers *Agano* and *Sendai* and six destroyers, reached the Empress Augusta Bay during the night of 1–2 November and found the four cruisers and eight destroyers belonging to the American task force TF 39 waiting for them. In a confusing encounter in which collisions featured prominently on both sides and most ships received some damage from shellfire, torpedoes or close encounters with their own kind, the Americans had rather the better of the exchanges, sinking both the *Sendai* and one of the Japanese destroyers and lightly damaging all three of their remaining cruisers. In contrast, only four American destroyers had been hit and of those only one was sufficiently damaged to be put under tow.[42]

Koga felt obliged to make up for the loss and damage from this first incident by sending Vice-Admiral Kurita from Truk to Rabaul on 3 November with a mix of ten cruisers and twelve destroyers. It would again prove to be a costly deployment. Learning from a reconnaissance flight that this fleet had been spotted making its way to Rabaul on 4 November, Rear-Admiral Frederick Sherman, in command of TF 38, prepared a carrier force of forty-five dive and torpedo-bombers and fifty-two fighter planes to attack them. In the wave of attacks that followed their arrival off Rabaul, the Japanese suffered grievous damage to four of their heavy cruisers (*Atago*, *Maya*, *Mogami* and *Takao*), two of their light cruisers (*Agano* and *Noshiro*) and a destroyer in return for downing ten of these carrier aircraft. Viewed from Koga's perspective this was a very poor return, but more damage to his cruisers followed another raid on the port of Rabaul by twenty-seven land-based Liberator bombers shortly afterwards. Needing no further proof that Rabaul was not what it once was, he duly recalled Kurita's cruiser squadrons and most of his destroyers to the safety of Truk. This left Samejima again under pressure for he had to try to establish a supply route for the Japanese troops on Bougainville at a time when Allied aircraft were pounding Rabaul more often than not. Unable to prevent substantial reinforcements being landed off Cape Torokina, Samejima soon found himself confronting a new danger in the guise of Rear-Admiral Alfred Montgomery's Allied task group (TG 50.3) whose three new fast carriers and nine destroyers soon began to take a toll on the 8th Fleet.[43] Truth is often a casualty of war and wishful thinking can just as frequently be used by warriors to turn hope into 'fact'. So it was with the returning Japanese pilots who after engaging in a savage series of battles with US naval and air forces off Bougainville recorded vastly exaggerated claims of destruction in which ten carriers, five battleships, nineteen cruisers, seven destroyers and nine transports had been allegedly put to the sword and twenty-four other vessels had been mythically damaged. In reality, the losers had been the Japanese carrier planes which had suffered a horrendous beating with 121 of the total number of 173 being destroyed (70%). Koga's carrier fleet was for a time something of a misnomer since it didn't have enough aircraft to function as one.[44] Bougainville would remain a drain on Samejima's surface fleet for months to come, but it was seen by the military authorities in Tokyo as an acceptable cost as long as the Japanese forces on the island held up the progress of the Americans in the region.[45]

This was the crux of the problem for the United States military since it was one thing landing and supporting Allied troops on targeted islands, such as on Bougainville, but quite another clearing it of Japanese forces. This would take hard fighting sometimes at very close quarters before the defenders would be vanquished. Bougainville would prove to be no exception to the rule established elsewhere.[46] While they expected to have to fight hard for every bit of ground won in the central Solomons, the severity of the fighting and the casualties sustained on Tarawa and Makin in the Gilbert Islands was a shock to the system. It was also a warning that the island-hopping strategy devised by Admiral Nimitz, in which Allied forces would sweep selectively through the Japanese Mandates (the Marshalls, Carolines and Marianas) to the mainland itself, would take time, resolution, dogged persistence and courage of a very high order before it was likely to succeed. It was not that Nimitz and his subordinates underestimated what was needed to gain victory in the Gilbert Islands (Operation *Galvanic*), it was the sheer brutality and frenzied nature of the contest, the savage hand-to-hand fighting in foxholes and the willingness of servicemen on both sides to give their all that took the breath away. One could have the most meticulous planning, sufficient assault forces, naval hardware and aerial support, but if the enemy was disciplined and passionate enough, well-defended and in a position to direct withering fire on the invading troops as they struggled ashore, the results could be horrendous and they often were.[47]

Nimitz had mobilised two attack force convoys – a northern one (TF 52) from Pearl Harbor containing five transports and a dock ship under the command of Kelly Turner with 6,472 troops from the 27th US Infantry Division and a much larger southern counterpart (TF 53) commanded by Rear-Admiral Harry Hill that was sent from the New Hebrides (Vanuatu) with 18,600 Marines and their supplies in fifteen transports and a dock ship. Apart from their regular destroyer escorts, they were each supported by two powerful task groups that could call on the services of nearly fifty warships in which escort carriers, battleships and heavy cruisers featured prominently. Both attack forces rendezvoused on 17 November southeast of the Gilbert Islands and then moved northwest to the target area. In addition to these northern and southern attack forces, TF 50 which had been divided into four task groups was also in the area providing another eleven carriers, five battleships and twenty-seven other principal warships for the Allied cause. Each of these task groups were assigned to soften up the defences on the islands of Makin, Mili, Nauru and Tarawa on 19 November in preparation for the landing of troops on Makin and Tarawa on the following day. While carrier planes flew repeated sorties over the intended invasion beaches and the rest of the group bombarded the shoreline for several hours at a time, far more damage was done to banana and coconut trees than to the well dug-in defenders. Instead of a mopping-up operation, the invasion of both Makin and Tarawa was anything but straightforward. In both places coral reefs barred the way to shore and the depth of tide was insufficient for the landing craft to float over the submerged obstacles and run up onto the beach. This would mean the infantry troops either transferring to shallower draught vessels or, in the worse case scenario, wading ashore. Further carrier strikes and an offshore bombardment were carried out on 20 November ahead of the first wave of assault forces reaching the coral reefs outside the lagoon in their landing craft. Crucially, however, the interval between the ending of the bombing and shelling offensive and the arrival of the troops outside the lagoon was just sufficient for the Japanese to return to their positions and take full advantage of the exposed assault forces as they struggled ashore.[48] In addition to their troops on the ground, the Japanese also mounted several air attacks from Truk and Kwajalein on the invasion fleet over the next few days, but these efforts were generally sporadic and uninspired with the solitary exception of the torpedoing of the light carrier *Independence* off Tarawa on the first day of the invasion. Nine submarines were also deployed by Takeo Takagi in the Gilberts but in such a thoughtless way that they rarely threatened to do much harm to the invasion fleet. Skilful use of ASW tactics by the Americans managed to sink six of the nine submarines within a week of the invasion, although the *I-175* did manage to sink the escort carrier *Liscombe Bay* with three torpedoes off Makin on 23 November with the loss of 644 lives.[49]

A solitary success such as this was never going to be enough to forestall the Americans. As their forces built up on shore, the sheer weight of numbers began to tell on the heavily outnumbered enemy. After the fiercest struggles, both Makin and Tarawa finally fell on 23 November. In the latter case the major prize had been the airfield at Betio. It took three days to wrest it free from those defending it. Only seventeen Japanese and 129 Koreans were taken prisoner from a force of roughly 4,500. American losses were 1,009 dead and 2,101 wounded. A sombre message had, therefore, been beaten out in the Gilberts: an island-hopping campaign might be able to avoid some trouble spots, but in places deemed crucial to both sides victory was only likely to be won after a long, hard slog and at very high personal cost. Moreover, the Japanese were no fools – it was obvious to them what the American twin-pronged strategy in the Pacific entailed and where they were going to strike next. This allowed them to take steps in advance to hinder the progress of those campaigns and prepare ultimately for battles to come on ground more favourable to them. Whatever happened in Europe, therefore, the Pacific war looked to be a long way from being over in late 1943.[50]

No one who had experienced Kesselring and Veitinghoff's 'welcome' around Salerno, however, could be in much doubt that the same was true of the contest against the rest of the Axis Powers (even though they were now shorn of the Italians and had been pushed back on both the Eastern and Southern Fronts). They demonstrated their capacity to make life difficult for the Allies by taking the initiative in the Aegean. Mindful of the Führer's determination to hold on to Greece, retain Turkey's quiescence and ensure that the Balkans didn't go up in flames once again, the Germans were never going to be content to stop at the recapture of Kos and the consolidation of Rhodes. British garrisons on Leros and Samos, islands within the Dodecanese group, were tempting targets for Axis operations and Whitehall knew that as well as those charged with their defence in Alexandria. In an effort to dissuade the Germans from taking the next step, a limited number of units from the Mediterranean Fleet, the RAF and the USAAF carried out sweeps of the Aegean in an effort to knock out German supply convoy traffic to Kos. If a mix of mainly submarines and destroyers, along with Mitchell and Beaufighter bombers could keep the Germans from accumulating the means to push elsewhere into the Dodecanese, the threat to Leros and Samos might be curtailed. This, at least, was the theory, but it soon became apparent that despite some success in sinking a few transports and steamers their efforts weren't going to be rewarded in starving the Kos garrison of reinforcements.[51] Unable to prevent this traffic from getting through and building up Axis forces on the island, the Allies were forced into playing a similar game. Escorting their own transports to Leros and Samos became the primary focus of British naval operations in the Eastern Mediterranean. Unfortunately for them, these duties were to take a toll on their forces without making Leros and Samos much safer. Committed as they were to the Italian campaign and the continued build up for *Overlord*, the Allies were unwilling to do more on the Aegean front. Churchill might wring his hands in despair, but the best he could hope for in the short term was the maintenance of the status quo.[52]

It increasingly looked like pie in the sky. On 12 November the Germans went over onto the offensive with an invasion of Leros by the Müller infantry battle group (*Fall Leopard*). Churchill received this unwelcome news on the very day he set out for Cairo and the *Sextant* conference with Roosevelt and the Chinese leader, Chiang Kai-shek. Further progress reports over the next few days didn't improve his mood as his fleet destroyers and Hunt Class escort destroyers were unable to locate, let alone destroy, the original German transports or the torpedo boats that brought more troops from Piraeus to Kalymnos. No such detection problems hobbled the performance of the Luftwaffe and the Allied warships were duly discovered and introduced to the glider bomb. *Dulverton* didn't survive the attacks on 13 November and the other eleven units were left to do the best they could in circumstances that were far from ideal. Most resorted to shelling German positions on Leros, but these bombardments failed to prevent the Müller battle group from gaining the ascendancy and forcing the capitulation of the Anglo-Italian garrison on the island three days later. Thereafter, torpedo boats brought in supplies for the victorious Germans and oversaw the occupation of a number of islands lying between Leros and Samos. Samos would obviously be next on the list and after the pounding the town of Tigani received at the hands of the Luftwaffe on 22 November, the 2,500 Italian troops on the island signalled their intention of being ready to quit. They did so once the Germans got ashore at Vathy Bay on the following day. In claiming Samos, the Axis forces had brought their seizure of the Dodecanese to an end. After a string of depressing reverses, they had recovered a little of their pride and had retained control of the 'Iron Ring' that Hitler had demanded. While the Dodecanese campaign didn't undo the damage wrought by the loss of the Caucasus, North Africa or southern Italy, the manner in which the Germans had undertaken their mission and the halting nature of the Allied response had not been lost on the Turkish government in Ankara who could see no good purpose in abandoning its existing position of neutrality in order to enter a war that appeared to have taken on a new lease of life.[53]

German successes were not confined solely to the Aegean either. Small-scale invasions of the Adriatic islands of Krk, Cres and Losinj had taken place on 13 November, mining operations had been resorted to in the Ligurian Sea and along the southern Adriatic littoral, while the Luftwaffe carried out a series of attacks on the port facilities at Bastia, La Maddalena and Naples, and its torpedo and dive bombers became a far deadlier threat to the Allied convoys off the North African coast than anything which the U-boat could muster.[54]

Furthermore, after a campaign renowned for its carnage, the Caucasus offered up yet more evidence in the late autumn of just how relentless the Eastern Front was and how far the Germans were from being finished as a military force. In deteriorating weather in early November, the Soviet front line moved ever closer to Kerch. Despite being forced to give ground initially at Enikale, the Germans led by Kapitänleutnant Helmut Klassmann responded to the Soviet landings at Eltigen by blockading the sea route to their bridgehead with a force of five MTBs, six motorised minesweepers (MMS) and thirty-one naval ferry barges. Over the course of the next month these vessels took part in 355 operations against Rear-Admiral G.N. Kholostyakov's forces as the Soviets tried in various ways to penetrate the blockade and bring supplies and reinforcements to their troops on the ground. Both sides sustained heavy losses in these encounters, but the Soviets were the hardest hit losing over two hundred boats in their frustrated bid to seize Kerch. Their failure on this occasion was due in no small measure to the difficulties they had in circumventing Klassmann's effective blockade. A violent series of bombing raids along with the presence of mines in these waters cut a huge swathe amongst the blockading ships. Patched up as best they could be, his vessels remained on station as the noose around the Soviet bridgehead was gradually tightened from 4 to 11 December. By the time the operation had petered out in mid-December, roughly 10,000 had died and 2,827 Soviet troops had been taken prisoner. Kerch and the Crimea beyond remained elusively beyond the reach of the Red Army for the time being.[55]

Whatever the heroics displayed by Klassmann and his men, the Germans were clearly on the defensive in the Black Sea theatre and the same sense prevailed throughout the Atlantic much to Dönitz's immense frustration. What had once been a rich harvest for his U-boats in the Caribbean and off the West African and Brazilian coasts had shrivelled to modest proportions by the close of 1943. Although individual U-boats could still deliver a fatal blow to any ship sailing independently, their success against all types of convoys had fallen to precipitous lows. Isolated successes rather than killing sprees became the norm. As the rival intelligence services did their best to provide the most complete information for their services to exploit, the Battle of the Atlantic had turned from being an area of acute Allied weakness to one of positive and indisputable strength.[56] Until such time as he had newer and better alternatives to offer them, Dönitz was forced to order his U-boat captains to keep their existing craft submerged for extended periods and to run on the surface only when it was essential to recharge their batteries. While the U-boat arm was forced into a waiting game, the Allies had not had everything their own way either. They had failed to close off the U-boat access routes to the Atlantic through the Bay of Biscay, where the Luftwaffe's presence remained very strong, or to turn it into a 'no-go' area for blockade runners seeking to return home to Axis ports – a point illustrated by their failure to prevent the *Osorno* from being ushered through the Bay by a flotilla of destroyers and torpedo boats over the Christmas period.[57]

Further north in the Channel and the southern part of the North Sea the Germans had resorted throughout the year to a number of MTB and torpedo boat raids on British ports and shipping from Plymouth in the southwest up as far as the Humber estuary on the East Yorkshire coast. Rarely large scale, these aggravating ad hoc sorties showed in their sinking of the Allied light cruiser *Charybdis* and the Hunt class escort destroyer *Limbourne* on 23 October off the northern coast of Brittany, or in the sinking of three freighters off Hastings in early November, that they represented something more than mere nuisance value to the Admiralty.[58] It was not fanciful to suggest that these fast moving craft might be used profitably against the build-up of Allied shipping for *Overlord* that would be taking place all along the southern coast of England in the months leading up to 'D-Day'. As such, their capacity to execute hit-and-run raids in and around the Channel meant that vigilance was required at all times in these waters and that adequate precautions would have to be taken by the British to try to keep these light forces under control.[59]

Although Admiral Sir Bruce Fraser, the C-in-C Home Fleet, could safely delegate these duties to the appropriate naval authorities in the south and east of the country, he was uniquely responsible for the safety of the Arctic supply convoys to Murmansk and Archangel and overcoming the triple threat posed to them by the German surface and U-boat fleets in Norwegian waters and the presence of the Luftwaffe overhead.[60] By the time these convoys had resumed on 1 November after the almost perpetual daylight of the northern summer had given way to the enveloping gloom of winter, Fraser was ready to assert himself.[61] He sensed the nature of the German threat had been substantially diminished not only with the temporary withdrawal from service of both the *Lützow* and the *Tirpitz*, but also as a result of a cut back in the numbers of German bombers on Norwegian bases. After several convoys had safely negotiated their way between the Soviet ports and Loch Ewe without incident, Fraser wondered how much longer the *Scharnhorst* would be content to remain in her fjord while the trade that she had been originally deployed to plunder sailed on unmolested a few nautical miles from her berth. It seemed incongruous that Hitler would allow her to remain idle when these convoys were bringing much needed supplies to his enemy for use against the Wehrmacht on the Eastern Front.[62]

Fraser had read the situation perfectly. Dönitz, frustrated by his U-boats' relative lack of success in the Atlantic and galled by their total inability to do real harm in the Arctic, had reached the conclusion that the time had come to teach the Allies a lesson about complacency and that the *Scharnhorst* would be the instrument to do just that. What Dönitz failed to grasp, however, was that the cryptanalysts of Bletchley Park were able to read even his most important signals issued in the *Offizier* code and provide the Admiralty with vital information – admittedly delayed by up to forty-eight hours – concerning the battleship's readiness to sail.[63] Fraser began receiving this information at the Icelandic port of Akureyri where he had returned after making an uneventful trip to the Kola Inlet ahead of the convoy JW.55A. Something was afoot. Learning that *Scharnhorst* had varied her readiness to sail from three hours to six and then back to three once again over the course of several days (20–22 December), Fraser thought a break out from Altenfjorden might be imminent. If this was so then there was no time to lose because convoy JW.55B (nineteen loaded supply ships) had already set out from Loch Ewe on 20 December and another one, RA.55A (twenty-two empty ships), was due to sail from the Kola Inlet in the opposite direction three days later. Although both convoys had virtually identical escort groups with them – ten destroyers, a minesweeper and two corvettes for JW.55B and an additional corvette for RA.55A – they were unlikely to prevent the *Scharnhorst* and her battle group from exacting a terrible punishment on either of the convoys should they sortie against them. Worse still, if the *Scharnhorst* picked her moment when the two convoys met, the results could be catastrophic since Fraser's distant covering force would be too far away from the convoy routes to prevent the possibility of massive destruction from taking place. It didn't help that JW.55B had been spotted by a German aircraft on the late morning of 22 December, because this was just the type of information that the Germans might use as the trigger for sending the *Scharnhorst* out to intercept it.[64]

Fraser was now in an uncomfortable situation. His ships had to refuel before leaving Akureyri on 23 December, but every hour that passed put JW.55B further in jeopardy if Dönitz decided to strike. While underway in foul weather on 24 December, Fraser received the latest signals intelligence intercepts from the Admiralty indicating that preparations for the departure of the German battle group had been put in hand two days previously and that aerial reconnaissance flights were being arranged for Christmas Eve. Such was his concern at this news that he increased the speed of his own force to 19 knots and took the highly unusual step of breaking radio silence at 1325 hours to order the convoy to reverse course until 1700 hours so as to keep it out of the danger area before night fell. Fraser's concern to preserve the convoy and avoid a tragedy was such that he opted to break radio silence even though his action ought to have alerted the Germans to the possibility that the Allies either had or would shortly have superior forces in the area – a situation that could have led to a cancellation of the *Scharnhorst* operation (*Fall Ostfront*). It didn't, but he was not to know that. Shortly after midnight on Christmas Day, Fraser decided to take RA.55A out of the strategic equation by diverting it far to the north of Bear Island to ensure that it wouldn't be drawn into any surface action that might ensue if the Germans did decide to come out looking for a fight. At the same time he requested that four of its destroyers be sent south to join JW.55B to provide an extra measure of protection for the convoy which was making slower than anticipated progress in rough seas and poor weather. Fraser learnt nothing more from signals intelligence until 0130 hours on Boxing Day when he received a message from the Admiralty that indicated *Ostfront* (known by the British codeword *Epilepsy*) was in the offing.[65] This much was confirmed less than an hour later when he was informed that *Scharnhorst* had probably sailed at 1800 hours on 25 December. It didn't take him long to work out that if the Germans attacked at dawn neither Vice-Admiral Robert Burnett's cruisers (designated Force 1) nor his own ships (Force 2) would be close enough to do anything to prevent it. For this reason, he broke radio silence once more at 0401 hours to alert JW.55B – then some 50nm (93km) south of Bear Island and making some 6–8 knots in heavy seas – to steer a more northerly course and ordered Force 1 (150nm [278km] east of the convoy) to reach the vulnerable convoy by dawn. His own group was still 210nm (389km) southeast of the convoy at 0400 hours and despite making 24 knots in difficult conditions it would take them well into the afternoon to be on hand to provide any assistance to Burnett and the convoy.[66]

Dönitz had sent out five destroyers with *Scharnhorst* on Christmas Day and had instructed Konteradmiral Erich Bey, the commander of the battle group, to do something for the German troops on the Eastern Front by getting in amongst the convoy and sinking as many of these cargo ships as possible. Bey was not wildly enthusiastic about the plan from the outset and his disquiet grew in the teeth of a gale force 8 storm which not only knocked his destroyers about and undermined any chance they might have had of using their guns to any great effect, but also ensured that he would be denied the benefit of any aerial reconnaissance until the weather improved. Bey approached the estimated position of the convoy with his five destroyers fanned out 10nm (18.5km) ahead of him in the *Scharnhorst* – a position that was curiously too far for either them or him to maintain visual contact with one another in the murky conditions that prevailed at this time. To compound matters further and for some inexplicable reason best known to himself, Bey decided to make a turn west-northwest away from his destroyers without informing them, so they continued on a southwest bearing blissfully ignorant that they were now at a dangerous 90° angle from that of their leader. For her part, the battleship, now alone, and after carrying out a number of course changes had contrived either by luck or judgement to get between the convoy and Force 1 – a distance of 50nm (93km) and closing. Her good fortune was not to last. *Scharnhorst* was first picked up on the heavy cruiser *Norfolk*'s radar at 0834 hours on 26 December at 33,000 yards (30km) and Burnett ordered his three cruisers to turn to intercept her. Once she was visible the light cruiser *Belfast* tried to illuminate her with a star shell at 0924 hours. It didn't work. *Norfolk* tried three minutes later and that too failed. *Scharnhorst* altered course immediately to the north and *Norfolk* opened fire at 0930 hours at a range of 9,800 yards (9km) with her 8-inch (203mm) guns hitting the battleship twice, knocking out the top FuMO27 radar in so doing. It was a critical loss that would come back to haunt Bey later in the day. After this blow, *Scharnhorst* increased her speed to 30 knots to get out of range and fired back with her 11-inch (279mm) guns as she swiftly began to put some distance between her and Burnett's cruisers, the best of which were 6 knots slower than the battleship. Burnett didn't help matters by not altering course immediately to pursue the enemy capital ship. He waited several minutes before doing so, but didn't pursue her for long before turning back towards the convoy to ensure that the *Scharnhorst* did not get a second chance to come between Force 1 and JW.55B. A cautious man, Burnett did not endear himself to Fraser by his signal at 1035 hours to the effect that he had lost contact with the enemy battleship. This was about the last thing Fraser had wanted to hear for it might mean any one of three scenarios for the *Scharnhorst*: a swift return to her base; a delayed attack on the convoy; or most calamitously a break out into the North Atlantic.[67]

Knowing that Dönitz wished him to grasp the initiative, Bey opted for the second option. Having eluded the cruisers, he proceeded to alter course to 240° in a bid to loop round and intercept the convoy from the other side. In this way he could carry out the Großadmiral's bidding by carrying out a hit-and-run raid on the convoy while the cruisers were chasing shadows elsewhere. It is a moot point whether he would have adopted this strategy had he been informed in advance that another group of warships (Force 2) including a 'heavy vessel' (*Duke of York*) had been detected by a German B&V 138 reconnaissance aircraft at 1012 hours. Amazingly, he did not become privy to this information as the German authorities in the Lofoten Islands, assuming the radar location report to be faulty, had struck out the reference to a 'heavy vessel' altogether. Bey's options might also have changed had he been able to rely upon his own five destroyers. When he needed them most they were miles away sticking to their original course of 230° and speed of 12 knots. Despite dictating several course and speed changes to them from 1027 hours onwards, Bey never saw his destroyers again. They had neither rejoined the *Scharnhorst* nor intercepted the convoy (even though they passed within a few miles of it at 1300 hours) before they were ordered to return to base at 1420 hours.[68]

Although Burnett had not always been an inspiring figure in the past and has been much criticised for breaking off his pursuit of *Scharnhorst* in the mid-morning, he deserved credit for guessing correctly that Bey would try to attack the convoy and for steering a course that put Force 1 (by now reinforced with the four destroyers that Fraser had sent him from RA.55A), between the battleship and her quarry. Burnett's positioning was such that *Sheffield*'s Type 273 radar picked up the presence of the enemy warship at a distance of some 12nm (22km) at 1210 hours. Burnett altered course to intercept the *Scharnhorst* and nine minutes later at a range of 11,000 yards (10,058m), *Belfast* opened proceedings with a star shell followed by her main guns and those of *Sheffield* and *Norfolk*, and subsequently, when the range closed, by the destroyers as well. In poor light the shelling continued for just over twenty minutes with the *Sheffield* being splintered by near misses and the *Norfolk* struck twice – once on 'X' turret which created a flaming column of fire and another on the deck amidships – resulting in the death of an officer and six ratings, and serious injuries amongst five more of the crew. Whether Bey or *Scharnhorst*'s captain, Fritz Hintze, mistook the tongue of flame from the cruiser for the guns of a battleship or not is unknown, but shortly thereafter the German battleship altered course to the southward and swiftly moved out of torpedo range. Unfortunately for the Germans, the course chosen was just about the worst that they could have made since it drew them towards Fraser and Force 2 fast approaching from the southwest. Burnett's ships kept well to the rear of *Scharnhorst* being quite content to follow her lead as she plunged onwards unknowingly towards the other members of the Home Fleet who were moving to cut her off from regaining the safety of Altenfjorden.[69]

Equipped with Type 273 radar, Fraser's flagship, *Duke of York*, first picked up the enemy battleship at a distance of 45,500 yards (41.6km) at 1617 hours. Force 2 drew ever closer with the *Scharnhorst* unable to detect its presence. After deploying his destroyers on either side of *Duke of York*, Fraser ordered *Belfast*, coming up from the rear of the German warship, and his own battleship to open hostilities with a burst of star shells. They did so at 1647 hours. Once again, those on *Scharnhorst* were taken by surprise but they quickly responded. *Duke of York* brought her ten 14-inch (356mm) guns into play four minutes later and the first of a series of hits were made on Bey's flagship which cumulatively put 'A' turret permanently and 'C' turret temporarily out of action and killed many of the gun crews. Those that had survived were ordered to take shelter, a decision that ensured those who usually operated the 4.1-inch (104mm) guns were not at their posts to use them against the Allied destroyers. *Scharnhorst* swung away to the north at 1655 hours and then east at 30 knots firing as she went in a bid to escape from the trap she found herself in. She was being hit regularly as she increased the distance between herself and Force 2 to 18,000 yards (16.5km) by 1742 hours when the light cruiser *Jamaica* stopped firing, and had increased it further to 21,400 yards (19.6km) by 1824 hours when *Duke of York* was forced to stop firing because her Type 284 gunnery control radar was malfunctioning. Fraser admitted defeat. He hadn't the speed to catch the battleship and, with his radar down, he no longer possessed the accuracy to continue hitting her with salvoes from his 14-inch guns. As such, he signalled Burnett that he was going to return to the convoy. Before he could wheel away in disappointment, however, he learnt from the plotting room that *Scharnhorst* must have undisclosed problems because she had lost speed dramatically (struggling forward for a time at between 8 to 10 knots) and that the gap between them was narrowing rapidly. She had. Her famed luck had run out. One of *Duke of York*'s last shells had struck through the starboard side of the ship wrecking a boiler room and rupturing a steam pipe. Until steam could be raised once again by some emergency repairs, the battleship would be forced to lose two-thirds of her top speed.[70]

Scharnhorst's misfortune was exactly what Fraser's four destroyers had been hoping for. Divided into two groups by his earlier deployment, they now had the chance to carry out a torpedo attack on the German capital ship. *Saumarez* and *Savage* were both northwest and astern of *Scharnhorst* when she began to falter. They stole up unnoticed and at a range of 7,000 yards (6,401m) opened fire with star shells at 1850 hours to both distract and illuminate her while *Scorpion* and

Stord tried to manoeuvre themselves into position to fire their Mark IX 533mm (21-inch) torpedoes at the battleship. This was going to be difficult as *Scharnhorst*, having solved some of her steam problems, was now moving in a southeasterly direction straight towards them at 22 knots. Through the light of the star shells, Bey and Hintze now saw *Scorpion* and *Stord* lying ahead of them and fatally opted to take violent emergency action by hauling the helm over from southeast to southwest. In so doing she presented all four of the Allied destroyers with a far better torpedo target than they otherwise would have had. Even so, the level of accuracy was distinctly ordinary: *Scorpion* fired eight torpedoes from a distance of roughly 2.1 km (2,300 yards) with only one of them striking home just forward of the bridge on the battleship's starboard side, while *Stord* fired her eight from 1.8 km (1,968 yards) without gaining a single hit. Five minutes later *Saumarez* and *Savage* also entered the act. *Saumarez* fired four torpedoes from 1.6 km (1,750 yards) missing with all of them before she was herself struck by a 280mm (11.02-inch) shell lobbed at close range from *Scharnhorst* killing eleven of her crew and injuring another eleven, as well as damaging her starboard engine. *Savage* did far better than all the rest put together. At a distance of 3.2 km (3,500 yards) she fired eight torpedoes and three of them struck home on the port side of the battleship damaging a boiler room and causing severe flooding amongst other things. *Scharnhorst*'s speed slackened once more, recovered, but would never regain the level sufficient to take her away from danger that lurked everywhere. Although she couldn't see them she was effectively surrounded by thirteen Allied warships intent on destroying her. Once *Duke of York* and *Jamaica* had returned to the fray, opening fire from 10,400 yards (9.5 km) at 1901 hours, followed by *Belfast* at 1912 hours from 15,500 yards (17 km), that destruction was virtually assured. Over the course of the next forty-five minutes *Scharnhorst* was systematically destroyed. It began with her being repeatedly hit and set on fire, it grew worse once she could no longer use any of her gun turrets and as she took on more water, listed and became steadily more sluggish. After delivering eighty salvoes, Fraser stopped firing at 1928 hours having ordered both *Belfast* and *Jamaica* to complete the job by sinking the battleship with their torpedoes. Once more most missed (five out of six launched), but the four destroyers from Force 1 took up the slack and claimed seven hits from nineteen Mark IX torpedoes fired at ranges of 1,000–2,800 yards (914–2,560 metres) at a target which was moving at perhaps no more than 3 knots. Once these torpedoes struck home the warship was enveloped in smoke and flames. At 1945 hours a massive explosion was heard and the *Scharnhorst* broke up and sank. None of the Allied warships saw her go down but by the time that *Belfast* and the destroyer *Matchless* came in to attack her again at 1948 hours, she was gone. Only thirty-six sailors survived out of her 1,968 officers and crew. Once he was satisfied that the *Scharnhorst* had been sunk, Fraser ordered his ships to leave the area immediately and rejoin convoy JW.55B before proceeding with it to the Kola Inlet. Such an order consigned many sailors to a watery grave. Officially, Fraser claimed that his decision was dictated by concern about possible U-boats being in the area. Unofficially, the story may be a little different.[71]

Emerging victorious at the Battle of the North Cape definitely cemented Fraser in Churchill's affections and provided the prime minister with his most satisfactory Christmas present, but, in truth, the sinking of the *Scharnhorst* had been very fortuitous. Victory had been achieved despite the fact that some aspects of the Home Fleet's performance had been quite unsatisfactory. To begin with, Fraser's flagship might have fired the critical shot, but the flaws in her main armament had been exposed for all to see. Although her ten 14-inch guns had fired eighty broadside salvoes only 446 shells were sent on their way out of the 800 they were designed to propel. Moreover, torpedo execution by the cruisers and destroyers was patchy even when the battleship was virtually dead in the water. Nonetheless, some elements had been outstanding – foremost of which had been the use of radar – while the importance of competent signalling and vital intelligence windfalls could not be denied. Above all, however, luck had played an enormous part in determining the final outcome of what was, after all, a very uneven contest. For once, and most decisively, it had deserted *Scharnhorst* when she needed it most. From the German perspective, this had not been Dönitz's finest hour. His tactical instructions had mixed robust aggression with defensive caution and would have been sufficient to have confused more adept commanders than Erich Bey. To compound matters, Bey himself committed a number of serious positional and signalling errors during the course of the day, the effect of which was to deprive him of the protection afforded by his five destroyers. This crucial weakness might still have been overcome had Kapitän zur See Rolf Johanneson, the commanding officer of the 4th Destroyer Flotilla, shown any flair or initiative. He didn't and so the battleship was left alone to fend off the thirteen warships of the Home Fleet. That she very nearly made it, despite the odds against her, spoke volumes for the courage, esprit de corps and professionalism of her ship's company and demonstrated some of the renowned engineering and technical accomplishments of German shipbuilding. Ships like the *Scharnhorst* were not easily sunk in surface engagements, but that was scant consolation to those at the Seekriegsleitung who had hoped the capital ship would still have an active role to perform in the war either in decimating Soviet convoy traffic or at the very least in forming a passive, if potent, fleet-in-being. After *Scharnhorst*'s loss, *Tirpitz*'s extensive damage and *Lutzöw*'s removal from the scene, however, either option looked somewhat fanciful.[72]

While Churchill toasted the heroes of North Cape on Boxing Day in the northern hemisphere, General MacArthur was looking for his own post-Christmas cheer south of the equator with the invasion of New Britain (Operation *Backhander*). He had been working up to this attack for several weeks. Destroyers had started shelling Japanese positions near Gasmata on the southern coast of the island at the end of November and an amphibious force of three transports and an LSD (Landing Ship Dock), well protected by ten destroyers and covered by another two cruisers and two destroyers, had actually landed 1,600 troops of the 112th US Cavalry Regimental Combat Team at Arawe on 14 December (Operation *Director*) so that they could reconnoitre the island and prepare the ground for a massed landing later in the month.[73] Although

MacArthur was wedded to an attack on New Britain not all of the US military were as enthusiastic as he was, believing that the island was no longer as vital as it had been when Rabaul had been the main Japanese base in the region and the pivot of their operations in the Solomons and New Guinea. This was no longer the case. After the American carrier planes had done their work in November, Rabaul was now considered to be too vulnerable and Truk (Chuuk) had become the preferred and safer option for the majority of their planes and warships. Even the utterly loyal George Kenney was of the opinion that by devoting so much attention to New Britain, the Americans risked slowing their progress on New Guinea.[74]

MacArthur's voice carried the greater weight, however, and he was not to be denied his attack on Cape Gloucester. Assembling nearly a hundred landing craft and backed by the two heavy cruisers *Australia* and *Shropshire*, and supported by the pair of light cruisers and twenty-two destroyers, 13,000 Marines and their supplies were embarked and set sail on Christmas Day, the first units making landfall at Cape Gloucester on the following day.[75] Although sixty Japanese planes attacked the invasion fleet, they succeeded in sinking only a single destroyer, badly damaging another one and lightly damaging two more and a couple of LSTs. It rather summed up their year. A further depressing note for the Japanese military's intention of holding the so-called 'Bismarck Barrier' was struck by the American submarine *Skate* when she disrupted their plans to deploy the monster battleship *Yamato* in the area by torpedoing the behemoth. *Yamato* survived, but her scheduled deployment did not. If Rabaul and Kavieng were to keep the Americans at bay, they would have to do so without her assistance.[76]

Notes

1 Martin Blumenson, 'Salerno and the fight for Southern Italy', in Basil Liddell Hart (ed.), *History of the Second World War*, pp.287–91, 301; Cunningham, *A sailor's odyssey*, p.559; Rohwer, *Chronology*, pp.269–70; John Strawson, *The Italian campaign* (London: Secker & Warburg, 1987), p.129.
2 Des Hickey and Gus Smith, *Operation Avalanche: the Salerno landings, 1943* (London: Heinemann, 1983); Wragg, *Carrier combat*, pp.128–32; Tomblin, *With utmost spirit*, pp.241–93.
3 E-boats were the shortened form of the English name given by the Allies to an 'Enemy War Motor Boat'. Their actual German name was *Schnellboote* (or fast boat). For action involving E-boats and Allied coastal forces, see Jefferson, *Coastal forces*, pp.62–63, 94, 118, 133, 137, 144–47, 150, 182.
4 Rohwer, *Chronology*, p.272; Cunningham, *A sailor's odyssey*, pp.563–64.
5 Daniel K.R. Crosswell, *The chief of staff: the military career of General Walter Bedell Smith* (Westport, Conn: Greenwood Press, 1991), pp.182–91.
6 Bragadin, *The Italian Navy in World War II*, pp.315–19; Rohwer, *Chronology*, pp.271–72.
7 A battleship, *Guilio Cesare*, the seaplane-carrier *Miraglia*, as well as a destroyer and a torpedo boat made it to Malta from Pola and other Adriatic ports over the course of the next few days. At the same time Allied ports in the Mediterranean became temporary homes for a collection of submarines, torpedo boats, corvettes and other smaller vessels, whereas those ships in Italian harbours that were non-operational were mostly scuttled by their crews before they could be taken over by the Germans. In this way the cruisers, *Bolzano* and *Taranto*, several destroyers and torpedo boats were lost.

318   *Striking back*

Bragadin, *The Italian Navy in World War II*, pp.307–22; Cunningham, *A sailor's odyssey*, pp.564–65; Greene and Massignani, *Naval War in the Mediterranean*, pp.300–309. Rohwer, *Chronology*, pp.271–72; www.regiamarina.it/armistice.htm.

8 While *Avalanche* was getting under way, the Germans implemented *Fall Eiche* (the rescue of Mussolini) on the evening of 9 September. He had been held prisoner of the Carabinieri on the orders of Badoglio's government at a secret location – the Villa Weber near La Maddalena in Sardinia. Once the Germans learned of his whereabouts earlier that day the plan to restore him to power at the head of a puppet administration was set in motion. He was rescued just after midnight on 9–10 September by members of a German parachute regiment. Over the course of the next fortnight *Fall Student* was implemented and on 23 September Mussolini took power at the head of a new fascist regime that was created in those areas of central and northern Italy controlled by the Germans. Elena Agarossi, *A nation collapses: the Italian surrender of September 1943* (Cambridge: CUP, 2000); DiNardo, *Germany and the Axis powers*, pp.177–80; *Fuehrer conferences*, p.363; Mack Smith, *Mussolini*, pp.300–301

9 A light cruiser, *Savannah*, had been hit and put out of action and her sister ship *Philadelphia* had received a near-miss in these attacks. In addition, two hospital ships had also been struck, the *Newfoundland*, sinking with heavy loss of life on the morning of 13 September. Blumenson, 'Salerno and the fight for Southern Italy', pp.287–302; Cunningham, *A sailor's odyssey*, pp.568–70; Rohwer, *Chronology*, p.273.

10 Cunningham, *A sailor's odyssey*, p.570; Hickey and Smith, *Operation Avalanche*, pp.61–282; Rohwer, *Chronology*, p.273.

11 Blumenson, 'Salerno and the fight for Southern Italy', pp.300–302.

12 Barbey, *MacArthur's amphibious navy*, pp.69–87; Gill, *Royal Australian Navy 1942–1945*, pp.326–31.

13 Having participated in the capture of Lae, the 20th Australian Brigade was embarked once more on the ships of the VII Amphibious Force and landed about six miles north of Finschhafen on 22 September. As a measure of the resistance they encountered, it took them until 2 October to capture the town. Clayton James, *Years of MacArthur: 1941–1945*, pp.289–335; Thomas E. Griffith, Jr., *MacArthur's Airman: George C. Kenney and the war in the southwest Pacific* (Lawrence, Ks: University Press of Kansas, 1998), pp.71–96; William Manchester, *American Caesar* (London: Hutchinson, 1979), pp.332–33.

14 Clayton James, *Years of MacArthur: 1941–1945*, pp.289–335; Thomas E.Griffith, Jr., *MacArthur's Airman*, pp.71–96; William Manchester, *American Caesar*, pp.332–33.

15 American progress on clearing Japanese troops from the islands of the New Georgia group, particularly Arundel and Vella Lavella, had been frustratingly slow and far too painstaking for Halsey's liking. Arundel eventually fell on 20 September, but the barge staging base at Horaniu on Vella Lavella had only been seized by the Allies a mere six days before. It would take nearly three more weeks to finally secure Vella Lavella. Hoyt, *Glory of the Solomons*, pp.170–90.

16 At least a third of the smaller vessels were sunk by the destroyers at the cost of roughly 1,000 lives. In the early hours of 6–7 October, 589 men were brought off Vella Lavella by three Japanese destroyers. Six more Japanese destroyers which had formed the covering force for the evacuation had already been confronted by three US destroyers in an action that took place before midnight in these waters. In this engagement both sides lost a destroyer (*Yugumo* and *Chevalier*) and serious damage was caused to the other two US destroyers (*O'Bannon* and *Selfridge*). Hoyt, *Glory of the Solomons*, pp.185–99.

O'Hara, *U.S. Navy against the Axis*, pp.193–206; Rohwer, *Chronology*, p.277.

17 To add to Stalin's frustration, German aircraft in the Crimea, which were always on standby, showed what they could do by sinking the flotilla leader *Kharkov* and two Soviet destroyers (*Besposhchadnyy* and *Sposobnyy*) which were on a sortie in Crimean waters on 5–6 October. Stalin was so incensed by these losses that from this time

onwards he forbade the employment of surface warships from the ranks of destroyer and above on sorties without his permission. Achkasov and Pavlovich, *Soviet naval operations*, pp.275–79; Rohwer, *Chronology*, pp.274, 280–81; Ruge, *Soviets as naval opponents*, pp.110–13.

18 In this way, 6,240 troops, 1,200 POWs and 5,000 tons of supplies were moved by sea. As the Germans withdrew from Corsica, the Allies began shifting Free French troops and a US Commando unit from Algiers to the capital city of Ajaccio on the west coast of the island. In thirteen trips made over the course of the month 7,139 troops were brought to the island in mostly French ships along with 992 tons of supplies, 43 guns and 116 vehicles. Both of the cruisers, five of the eight destroyers and all three of the submarines that made these trips were French. Auphan and Mordal, *French Navy in World War II*, pp.294–97; Rohwer, *Chronology*, p.274.

19 Gill, *Royal Australian Navy 1942–1945*, pp.317–25.

20 *Jaywick* was to have tragic consequences for those POWs and civilian internees on Singapore who were rounded up on 10 October (the 'Double Tenth' incident) by the Japanese *Kempetai* (the security police) and accused of providing intelligence to the enemy saboteurs in this audacious attack. A series of horrendous consequences were meted out to those innocent individuals suspected of involvement in this daring raid. Brian Connell, *Return of the Tiger* (London: Evans Bros., 1965); Ronald McKie, *The heroes* (Sydney: Angus & Robertson, 1967), pp.1–151; Lynette Ramsay Silver, *The heroes of Rimau* (Kuala Lumpur: S. Abdul Majeed, 1992), pp.65–104; Murfett et al., *Between two oceans*, p.268.

21 Because the return on this investment – only six ships sunk for the loss of one U-boat over a period of two months – was so disappointing it made Dönitz wary of releasing more U-boats for operations in the Kara Sea or the vast expanses east of it. Rohwer, *Chronology*, p.265.

22 Although the German occupation was only to last for six weeks before the Allies landed Norwegian troops on 19 October to recover the bases lost on this expedition, the deed had been done and in Dönitz's opinion that was the main thing. His surface fleet had left port and by so doing had caused the Admiralty in London much anxiety. Grove, *Sea battles in close-up*, 2, p.123; Rohwer, *Chronology*, p.271.

23 Pound had fallen ill during the *Quadrant* conference in Quebec. Robin Brodhurst, 'Admiral Sir Dudley Pound (1939–43)', in Murfett (ed.), *First sea lords*, pp.185–200.

24 Gilbert, *Churchill*, VII, p.365.

25 Ibid., pp.515–16.

26 Stephen, *Sea battles in close-up*, pp.123–31; Levy, *The Royal Navy's Home Fleet*, pp.136–37; Paul Kemp, *Underwater warriors* (London: Arms and Armour, 1996), pp.128–57.

27 Gilbert, *Churchill*, VII, pp.312, 362, 373, 388, 400, 440, 445, 448, 453–54, 475, 497, 500–501, 503, 506, 511–13, 520–24, 526, 530, 532, 536, 559, 562–64, 572, 578–80, 598, 619–20; Farrell, *Basis and making of British grand strategy*, 2, pp.583, 620–21, 631, 644, 672–78, 680, 688.

28 One such attack on 23 September ended up with the destroyer, *Eclipse*, sinking a German torpedo boat and a steamer, *Donizetti*, which had at least 1,576 (or perhaps as many as 1,835) Italian POWs on board, the vast majority of whom failed to survive. O'Hara, *German fleet at war*, pp.166–71; Rohwer, *Chronology*, p.273. See also, Lew Lind, *The battle of the wine dark sea: the Aegean campaign 1940–45* (Kenthurst, NSW: Kangaroo Press, 1994), pp.134–68; Jeffrey Holland, *The Aegean mission: Allied operations in the Dodecanese, 1943* (New York: Greenwood Press, 1988); Peter C. Smith and Edwin Walker, *War in the Aegean* (London: Kimber, 1974); Christopher Buckley, *Five ventures: Iraq–Syria–Persia–Madagascar–Dodecanese* (London: HMSO, 1977), pp.211–43.

29 Matthew Jones, *Britain, the United States and the Mediterranean war, 1942–44* (Basingstoke: Macmillan, 1996), p.100.

30 A little of the gloss was taken off *Penelope*'s destruction of the troop convoy when the light cruiser was hit and damaged by bombs on her return from this sortie. Gilbert,

Churchill, VII, pp.520–28; *Fuehrer conferences*, pp.368–69; Lind, *The battle of the wine dark sea*, pp.133–68.
31 Charles Eade (ed.), *The war speeches of the Rt. Hon. Winston S. Churchill, Volume III*, (London: Cassell & Co, 1952), p.7.
32 *Zaunkönig* acoustic torpedoes were more often referred to by the Allies as GNATs – or German Naval Acoustic Torpedoes – rather than by their translated name of Wren.
33 Syrett, *Defeat of the German U-boats*, pp.181–229; Beesly, *Very special intelligence*, pp.261–71; Hughes and Costello, *Battle of the Atlantic*, pp.291–93; Milner, *Battle of the Atlantic*, pp.169–72; Rohwer, *Chronology*, pp.268–69, 275–76.
34 His *Leuthen* group of U-boats had sunk seven ships out of the sixty-five making up the two convoys (10.8%) and three out of their twenty-one escorts (14.3%), while the escorts themselves had got some of their own back by sinking three U-boats (13.6%) and damaging four others (18.2%). Hughes and Costello, *Battle of the Atlantic*, pp.292–93; Milner, *Battle of the Atlantic*, pp.172–76; Rohwer, *Chronology*, pp.275–77.
35 Rohwer, *Chronology*, pp.256, 280–83, 286–90, 292–93. There are plentiful sources on Dönitz's wolf packs. Recent work in this area includes the following: Gordon Williamson, *Wolf pack: the story of the U-boat in World War II* (Oxford: Osprey Publishing, 2005); David Jordan, *Wolf pack: the U-boat war and the Allied counter-attack 1939–1945* (Staplehurst: Spellmount, 2002); Robert C. Stern, *Battle beneath the waves: the U-boat war* (London: Arms and Armour, 1999).
36 Hughes and Costello, *Battle of the Atlantic*, pp.289–91.
37 This development resulted from the signing of the Anglo-Portuguese agreement of 18 August 1943. Three Allied convoys shifted both men and supplies to the Azores in early October (Operation *Alacrity*) in order to establish No.247 Group RAF on the islands. Within a day of arriving, the first of the Fortress bombers to be based in the Azores left on its inaugural operational sortie out into the Central Atlantic on 19 October. Norman Herz, *Operation Alacrity: the Azores and the war in the Atlantic* (Annapolis, Md: NIP, 2004), pp.185, 208; Rohwer, *Chronology*, p.279.
38 Syrett, *Defeat of the German U-boats*, pp.230–58.
39 Rohwer, *Chronology*, pp.267, 269–70, 276, 280.
40 Hoyt, *Glory of the Solomons*, pp.201–311; Gailey, *War in the Pacific*, pp.254–62.
41 Ibid.; David C. Fuquea, 'Bougainville: the amphibious assault enters maturity', *Naval War College Review, Vol.50, No.1* (Winter 1997): 104–21; Dull, *Battle history of IJN*, pp.286–94; Gill, *Royal Australian Navy 1942–1945*, pp.332–34; Rohwer, *Chronology*, p.281–82.
42 Rear-Admiral Sentaro Omori paid for his failure to do better in this action by losing his command. Harry A. Gailey, *Bougainville: the forgotten campaign 1943–1945* (Lexington, Ky: The University Press of Kentucky, 1991), pp.39–92; Dull, *Battle history of IJN*, pp.288–90; Hoyt, *Glory of the Solomons*, pp.240–44; Prados, *Combined Fleet decoded*, pp.509–11; Rohwer, *Chronology*, pp.284–85.
43 *Essex* and *Bunker Hill* were carriers of the new Essex class which was to become the backbone of the US Fast Carrier Fleet from 1943 onwards and would do so much to win the Pacific War. Essex class carriers were essentially heavier and much improved versions of the earlier Yorktown class and carried at least 91 aircraft (36 fighters, 37 dive-bombers and 18 torpedo-bombers). Montgomery's other carrier was *Independence*, a light carrier of the new Independence class. All nine of the light carriers in this class had been converted from the Cleveland class of cruiser as a temporary expedient while the USN awaited the completion of its Essex class. Displacing 14,751 tons at deep load, the Independence class could achieve a top speed of 31.6 knots and carry a complement of 30 aircraft. Gardiner (ed.), *Conway's all the world's fighting ships*, pp.104–5.
44 Dull, *Battle history of IJN*, pp.290–94; Prados, *Combined Fleet decoded*, pp.511–15; Rohwer, *Chronology*, pp.284–85.
45 Eugene Wolfe, 'De-railing the last Tokyo express', *Naval History, Vol.10, No.2* (Mar/Apr. 1996): 34–39; Dull, *Battle history of IJN*, pp.294–95; Rohwer, *Chronology*, pp.288, 290.

46 Gailey, *Bougainville*, pp.93–148; Peter Medcalf, *War in the shadows: Bougainville 1944–45* (Sydney: Collins & Australian War Memorial, 1986).
47 Apart from the range of anecdotal histories about the grim campaign on Tarawa which give a graphic account of what that struggle was like, the following may be consulted profitably: Eric Hammel and John E. Lane, *Bloody Tarawa* (Pacifica, Ca: Pacifica Press, 1999); Robert Sherrod, *Tarawa: the story of a battle* (Fredericksburg, Tx: Admiral Nimitz Foundation, 1999); Derrick Wright, *A hell of a way to die: Tarawa Atoll, 20–23 November 1943* (London: Windrow & Greene, 1997); Bernard Ireland, *Jane's naval history of World War II* (New York: Harper Collins, 1998), pp.148–52; E.B. Potter and Chester W. Nimitz, *The great sea war: the naval action in World War II* (New York: Bramhall House, 1960), pp.320–31.
48 Ibid.; Gailey, *War in the Pacific*, pp.254–62.
49 Boyd and Yoshida, *Japanese submarine force*, pp.124–27.
50 By 19 November Japanese cruisers were beginning to send reinforcements from Truk to a number of bases in the Marshall Islands – Eniwetok, Kwajalein, Maloelap and Mili – that appeared to be the most likely focus of future American attacks through the Central Pacific. A new wave of fast carrier raids took place against Kwajalein on 4 December in which six Japanese transports were sunk and damage was caused to two cruisers (*Isuzu* and *Nagara*) as well as three other ships. In the course of the air raids conducted by a total of 386 planes belonging to six Allied carriers, fifty-five Japanese aircraft were destroyed either in the air or on the ground. Ibid.; Driskill and Casad, *Admiral of the hills*, pp.188–91; Potter, *Nimitz*, pp.247–64; Rohwer, *Chronology*, p.289; Stafford, *Big E*, pp.283–315.
51 O'Hara, *German fleet at war*, pp.171–73.
52 By 7 November Allied surface ships had shifted 2,230 troops and 470 tons of material to the islands, while two British and four Italian submarines had been engaged in moving a further seventeen troops and 288 tons of supplies to the same destinations. In doing so, a mine barrage had contrived to sink two British destroyers and remove the bows of a Greek one, while two cruisers and a destroyer had been hit in air attacks. Gilbert, *Churchill*, VII, pp.536, 559, 562–63, 578–80; Rohwer, *Chronology*, p.281.
53 On Leros, 3,200 British and 5,350 Italian troops surrendered to the Germans. Gilbert, *Churchill*, VII, pp.552–56, 558, 562; Rohwer, *Chronology*, p.287; Holland, *The Aegean mission*, pp.105–17.
54 This point was harrowingly confirmed by the loss of five troop transports, a destroyer and a tanker off Algiers on 6 November and Oran five days later. More than a thousand lives were lost later in the month when a glider bomb sank the British troop transport *Rohna* off the Algerian coast on 26 November. A similar calamity also occurred in the Adriatic with over a thousand casualties resulting from an attack on Bari during the night of 2–3 December when eighty-eight bombers destroyed eighteen transports (71,566 tons) and 38,000 tons of cargo in what became an inferno. Rohwer, *Chronology*, pp.281–82, 286, 288–91.
55 Ibid., p.285; Achkasov and Pavlovich, *Soviet naval operations*, pp.116–24; Ruge, *Soviets as naval opponents*, pp.114–22.
56 British cipher security belatedly improved in the latter half of 1943 and became effectively secure in January 1944 with the introduction of a new edition of the naval code to be used with the stencil subtractor system. B-Dienst could not penetrate the system thereafter despite putting roughly 250 cryptanalysts on the task. Once the Combined Cipher Machine (an adaptation of the American ECM Mk.II and the British Typex cipher machines) became operational with all five Anglo-American armed services and the RCN in April 1944, the Germans were thwarted in their efforts to break the system even though, as Ralph Erskine points out, the CCM was astonishingly insecure. Ralph Erskine, 'The Admiralty and cipher machines during the Second World War: not so stupid after all', *The Journal of Intelligence History*, 2 (Winter 2002): 49–68; White, *Bitter ocean*, pp.231–52.

57 Operation *Stonewall* was one such operation mounted by the Allies using two cruisers in mid-December in an effort to prevent blockade runners from using the Bay of Biscay. For their part, the Germans launched *Fall Bernau* on Christmas Eve in which six destroyers and six torpedo boats from the Gironde Estuary put to sea in a bid to meet and bring the blockade runner, *Osorno*, through the Bay and into port. After beating off a succession of attacks by Allied aircraft, *Osorno* arrived in port on 26 December, only to damage her hull on a submerged wreck. She was forced to beach herself so that her cargo could be saved. In the aftermath of *Fall Trave* (the failed operation to rescue the blockade runner, *Alsterufer*, which was sunk by a Liberator bomber on 27 December), an Allied force of two light cruisers (*Enterprise* and *Glasgow*) caught up with the *Alsterufer*'s intended escort party of six destroyers and five torpedo boats and in an exchange of gunfire managed to sink one of the German destroyers and two of their torpedo boats. O'Hara, *German fleet at war*, pp.195–99; Rohwer, *Chronology*, pp.290, 292–95.

58 O'Hara, *German fleet at war*, pp.182–99.

59 Rohwer, *Chronology*, pp.282–83, 286, 290–91, 294, 297, 301, 303, 306, 308, 311–12, 317–18, 321, 324, 331–32, 336, 338, 340–42. See also Peter C. Smith, *Hold the narrow sea: naval warfare in the English Channel 1939–1945* (Ashbourne, Derby: Moorland Publishing Co., 1984), pp.173–200; Peter Scott, *The battle of the narrow seas: a history of the light coastal forces in the Channel and North Sea, 1939–1945* (London: White Lion, 1974), pp.119–74.

60 John Winton, 'Admiral of the Fleet Lord Fraser of North Cape', in Howarth (ed.), *Men of war*, pp.474–90.

61 It may not have been coincidental that these Arctic convoys had begun in earnest again before the first gathering of the 'Big Three' – Churchill, Roosevelt and Stalin – which was due to take place in Teheran (*Eureka*) at the end of November. *Eureka* would prove to be the most satisfactory and least contentious of the Allied wartime conferences. For a useful discussion of the main strategic points raised in the conference see Farrell, *Basis and making of British grand strategy*, 2, pp.743–64; Gilbert, *Churchill, VII*, pp.570–93; Herbert Feis, *Churchill, Roosevelt, Stalin: the war they waged and the peace they sought* (Princeton, NJ: Princeton University Press, 1967), pp.257–69; Hayes, *History of the Joint Chiefs of Staff*, pp.531–34.

62 Richard Humble, *Fraser of North Cape* (London: Routledge & Kegan Paul, 1983), pp.178–86; Levy, *The Royal Navy's Home Fleet*, pp.138–43; Woodman, *Arctic convoys*, pp.344–54; Stephen, *Sea battles in close-up*, p.198; *Fuehrer conferences*, pp.373–75.

63 Sebag-Montefiore, *Enigma*, pp.293–303.

64 Blair, *Hitler's U-boat war: hunted*, pp.470–72; Rohwer, *Chronology*, pp.292–93.

65 Beesly, *Very special intelligence*, pp.272–89; Humble, *Fraser of North Cape*, pp.187–202.

66 Ibid.; Stephen, *Sea battles in close-up*, pp.198–218; Woodman, *Arctic convoys*, pp.355–75; O'Hara, *German fleet at war*, pp.155–65; Doenitz, *Memoirs*, pp.374–85; Evans, *Great World War II battles*, pp.111–26; Rohwer, *Chronology*, pp.292–93.

67 Ibid.; Padfield, *Dönitz*, pp.337–46.

68 O'Hara, *German fleet at war*, pp.158–60; Stephen, *Sea battles in close-up*, pp.204–5, 207.

69 O'Hara, *German fleet at war*, pp.159–60; Stephen, *Sea battles in close-up*, pp.209–10.

70 Humble, *Fraser of North Cape*, pp.205–12; O'Hara, *German fleet at war*, pp.160–62; Stephen, *Sea battles in close-up*, pp.210–13.

71 Indeed, some might see it as an act of spiteful or justified retribution for the failure of *Scharnhorst* and *Gneisenau* to save the crew of the carrier *Glorious* and her two escort destroyers, *Acasta* and *Ardent*, in April 1940. While the popular modern expression of 'what goes around comes around' may not have been coined at the time, the sentiment that it speaks to would certainly have had echoes in the fate of the *Scharnhorst* in December 1943. Fritz-Otto Busch, *The sinking of the 'Scharnhorst': a factual account from the German viewpoint* (London: Futura Publications, 1974); Humble, *Fraser of North Cape*, pp.212–24; O'Hara, *German fleet at war*, pp.162–65; Stephen, *Sea battles in close-up*

pp.213–16; www.scharnhorst-class.dk/scharnhorst/history.scharnhorstfront.html (accessed 13 Mar. 2005); www.bbc.co.uk/history/war/wwtwo/scharnhorst_print.html (accessed 13 Mar. 2005).
72 As a bitter postscript to *Fall Ostfront* for Dönitz, neither JW.55B, the convoy that the German battle group had been formed to destroy, nor RA.55A, which could easily have fallen victim to it as well, lost any of their ships while on passage to their final destination, Murmansk and Loch Ewe respectively. Stephen, *Sea battles in close-up*, pp.216–17; Woodman, *Arctic convoys*, pp.355–75; Rohwer, *Chronology*, pp.292–93.
73 Barbey, *MacArthur's amphibious navy*, pp.97–108; Gill, *Royal Australian Navy 1942–1945*, pp.334–41.
74 Griffith, *MacArthur's airman*, p.145.
75 Barbey, *MacArthur's amphibious navy*, pp.109–25.
76 Clayton James, *Years of MacArthur: 1941–1945*, pp.341–46, 352; Gill, *Royal Australian Navy 1942–1945*, pp.341–46; Griffith, *MacArthur's airman*, pp.91–146; Edwin P. Hoyt, *MacArthur's navy: the Seventh Fleet and the battle for the Philippines* (New York: Orion Books, 1989), pp.23–29; Rohwer, *Chronology*, p.294.

10 Seizing the initiative (January–August 1944)

The end of 1943 saw the Axis Powers driven firmly onto the defensive against an increasingly confident set of Allies who were making headway in most of the major theatres of the war. Although fears of world domination by Germany and Japan may have been arrested by the events of the past year, defeating both of them in 1944 looked a tall order since both still held on to large swathes of territory beyond their own borders and had proved repeatedly that they could be obdurate opponents even when they were caught in the most hopeless of military positions. Ground gained at their expense was, therefore, unlikely to come cheaply and it looked as though it would take many months to roll back the military juggernaut that had once carried all before it in 1941 and early 1942.

Evidence of the assertion that 1943 signified a distinct change in momentum was illustrated in the New Year with the vast improvement in military muscle given to Sir James Somerville's Eastern Fleet based in Ceylon. Before the reinforcements arrived, Somerville had been forced to rely upon a modest collection of naval hardware, led by his flagship the old battleship *Ramillies*, an American-built escort carrier (*Battler*), a mixed force of eight cruisers, two auxiliary cruisers, eleven destroyers, a total of thirteen corvettes, frigates and sloops, and six submarines.[1] As a fleet it wouldn't disturb Koga or the leading figures within the IJN and it wasn't capable of doing much more than operating a convoy supply service in the Indian Ocean. Churchill and Cunningham, his first sea lord, knew that as well as anyone else but the removal of the Italian Fleet from the strategic equation in the Mediterranean meant that Somerville's forces could now be vigorously supplemented.[2]

Increases in submarine strength in December allowed eleven to be sent to operate against Japanese shipping in the Malacca Strait and off the west coast of Thailand and the arrival in January of Vice-Admiral Sir Arthur Power with the carriers *Illustrious* and *Unicorn*, the battleships *Queen Elizabeth* and *Valiant*, the battle-cruiser *Renown*, two more cruisers and a couple of Dutch destroyers meant that Somerville now possessed a cutting edge to his fleet and one that would be able to take the initiative against the enemy throughout the Indian Ocean in the months to come.[3] Initially the task would be to try to eliminate the German U-boat tankers that were supplying the *Monsun* (Monsoon) group of six U-boats operating out of Penang; tackling likely blockade runners southwest of the Cocos

Islands; and providing additional support for increasing numbers of troop transport convoys that would be running from Kilindini to Colombo as the build up for the invasion of the Arakan coastline of Burma was consolidated. These duties weren't glamorous; they were rarely exciting and often very routine, but they did reflect the changing role of the Navy in the war. Apart from the carriers, the rest of the fleet was now performing more of a supportive and logistical role – crucial in landing or evacuating troops and supplies, clearing the seas of enemy submarines and protecting all forms of mercantile traffic – than one that saw them regularly engaging in set piece encounters with their enemies on the high seas. There would still be such battles but their outcomes were unlikely to determine the fate of the war. Ultimate victory would be won on land and in the air and no longer at sea unless the suppression of the U-boat menace could be reversed.[4]

While he remained utterly loyal to the Führer, Dönitz did not need reminding that the Kriegsmarine found itself in a rather abject situation at the outset of the New Year, being both short in numbers of operational U-boats and virtually defunct as a surface fleet at a time when the Allied military threat to continental Europe was steadily growing. Despite remaining ostensibly confident that the design improvements being incorporated into the new generation of faster, sleeker and more deadly U-boats would ultimately allow them to wrest back the initiative at sea, the sobering fact was that Dönitz possessed only 160+ U-boats in January 1944 which could be relied upon immediately to assist the cause of the Fatherland.[5] Frustrated by construction delays for the Type XXI and Type XXIII U-boats and renewed engineering development problems for the Walter boats, Dönitz was not a man to give up hope easily. Impatient though he was for his new U-boats to become operational, he hoped that the fitting of the new *schnorchel* 'breathing' device on his existing fleet would make the individual U-boats much more difficult to spot from the air and cut down on the number of 'kills' that were being made by both the USAAF and RAF Coastal Command.[6]

Despite the loss of his heavy ships, he was disinclined to go on the defensive everywhere. In line with Hitler's decision to increase the strength of his U-boat fleet in the Arctic, Dönitz urged Kapitän zur See Rudolph Peters, the commanding officer of the U-boat fleet in Norwegian waters, to redouble his efforts to maul the Allied convoys and thereby disrupt the supply chain to Soviet forces in the Polar region. Peters sought to comply with these instructions by ambushing the two convoys that were scheduled to make the journey from Loch Ewe to the Kola Inlet (JW.56A and JW.56B) as well as a returning convoy (RA.56) from Murmansk in late January. Receiving timely information from B-Dienst, a group of ten U-boats (*Isegrim*) waited for the first of these convoys in the Bear Island (Bjørnøya) Passage and launched a series of attacks on the fifteen steamers and thirteen escort vessels of JW.56A on 25–26 January using both their acoustic torpedoes (T5s) and pattern running torpedoes (FAT). During one of these exchanges, the FAT torpedoes struck home sinking three of the steamers (21,530 tons), while a T-5 damaged a destroyer. They had no further success before three Soviet destroyers and five minesweepers joined the convoy later that day and escorted it safely into the Kola Inlet on 28 January. Heartened by this early success, Peters formed a new group, *Werwolf*, to combat the next two convoys JW.56.B and RA.56, but a mixture of resolute defence and a faulty set of coordinates ensured that there would be no repetition of the 20% success rate enjoyed by the *Isegrim* group. Sinking only three supply ships out of a total of sixty-eight on offer in these three convoys (an overall attrition rate of 4.4%) could hardly be trumpeted as a new dawn in the war on trade, particularly as the destruction of the V-class destroyer *Hardy* had been cancelled out by the loss of *U314*.[7]

This conspicuous lack of success against these convoys was reproduced by Dönitz's U-boats in the North Atlantic during the first seven weeks of the year where sixty-eight of them managed only to sink a total of five ships and shoot down a similar number of aircraft while losing twenty of their number to a combination of aggressive hunt and destroy missions by the convoy escorts and a series of intensive aerial operations.[8] Dönitz was far from satisfied with this turn of events since these results were a far cry from what his crews had achieved in the good old days. Apart from the effectiveness of the new A.A. gun, the only other crumb of comfort he could glean was that some of his vessels had escaped the clutches of the enemy by successfully deploying their *Aphrodite* balloons with their anti-radar metal foil. Even so, losing so many U-boats within the first two months of the year, including the first U-boat fitted with the *schnorchel* device (*U264*), represented a very unhealthy statistic for him especially as there was a dearth of real success elsewhere in the Atlantic. Three of his blockade runners had been caught and sunk in the South Atlantic in the first few days of the New Year, and neither the African coast nor that of the Caribbean had yielded the rich harvest of former times. In contrast, Admiral Sir Max Horton, the C-in-C Western Approaches, could feel well pleased with the Allied return.[9]

Moreover, in Norwegian waters the Allies showed both friend and foe alike that their torpedo-bombers were more than a match for anything that the Luftwaffe possessed and their submarines and MTBs could be relied upon to disrupt German convoy traffic more often than not. Cunningham and the Admiralty were also pleased that additional pressure was being put on the Axis in the Mediterranean. Use by the Allies of air bases in southern Italy allowed them to conduct a raid on the Pola (Pula) naval base on the Istrian peninsula in early January which managed to put two more U-boats out of action (one permanently) and indulge in repeated forays against German supply traffic along the Dalmatian coast, which made these sailings a far more hazardous enterprise than ever before. In addition, their new destroyer base at Bari enabled them to shell ports along the Albanian and Adriatic coastlines and make them far less desirable anchorages for Axis mercantile shipping.[10]

Cunningham was much less enamoured with Churchill's pet project – the landings at Anzio and Nettuno – which was orchestrated in late January.[11] Operation *Shingle* was meant to draw off troops from the Gustav defensive line that Kesselring had constructed to remarkably durable effect across the Apennine mountain range with the town of Cassino at its heart and lead to an easier passage for the rest of the Allied armies up through the spine of Italy and into Rome.[12] Such, at least, was the thinking behind the armada of boats that set sail from the Bay of Naples on 21 January with the 1st British Infantry Division and their immediate supplies in the northern attack force commanded by Rear-Admiral Tom Troubridge (150 ships) and with the VI US Corps in the southern attack force (230 vessels) under the American Rear-Admiral F.J. Lowry. Reaching their landing sites early on 22 January, the two landing teams began working and by the end of the first day they had landed some 36,034 troops and 3,069 vehicles ashore. Despite the presence of mines and a series of German air raids over the Allied beachhead that managed to sink nine ships and damage five others, the Allies had landed 68,886 troops, 508 guns and 237 tanks by 29 January. This impressive start was not maintained and it would take four months for these troops to push themselves out of their constricted beachhead and join up with the other Allied armies as they pushed on towards Rome. In the interim period, the Allies would be forced into supplying them by sea from Naples using eight cruisers and several destroyers. It was a task that the Admiralty would have preferred to have been without, particularly since the ever resourceful Dönitz ensured that over a dozen U-boats were on hand to carry out a series of attacks on these supply trains and other Mediterranean convoys. Although some initial success was indeed obtained by them, the stationing in Morocco of a US Catalina squadron fitted with the MAD (Magnetic Anomaly Detector) device in the middle of February threatened to quash even the remotest hint of U-boat resurgence in these waters.[13]

While the Germans flirted with success, the Soviet Baltic Fleet actually tasted it. In a long two-month slog, Admiral Gordei Levchenko used a host of small vessels to bring 44,000 troops, over 200 tanks, 600 guns, 2,400 vehicles, 6,000 horses and 30,000 tons of supplies belonging to the 2nd Assault Army from Leningrad to the forward positions around Oranienburg so that a major push could be made to break through German lines that had surrounded the Soviet second city for two years. This landward offensive began on 14 January supported by the guns of the two battleships *Petropavlovsk* and *Oktyabrskaya Revolyutsiya*; the three cruisers *Kirov*, *Maksim Gorkiy*, and *Tallin*; as well as eight destroyers and four gunboats. A total of 24,000 shells were fired by them at the German front lines over the course of the first week of the campaign.[14]

As the Axis was forced to give ground in northern Russia, so their allies, the Japanese, were subject to similar pressure in the Central Pacific. In preparation for an attack on some of the islands in the Marshall Islands group, Marc Mitscher divided TF 58 into four groups and sent them to shell Eniwetok (Enewetak), Kwajalein, Maloelap, Roi and Wotje over the course of a week from 29 January onwards. Aircraft from all twelve carriers were involved in flying 6,232 sorties against these islands and atolls in a bid to soften up their defences and enable Vice-Admiral Raymond Spruance to orchestrate the landing of over 41,000 troops on Kwajalein and Roi which began on 31 January and lasted until the vast majority of the 8,675 Japanese men on these atolls had been killed eight days later. Divided into two separate forces under Kelly Turner (Kwajalein) and Richard Conolly (Roi), the Americans first bombarded the defenders from offshore and then moved in with overwhelming force to begin taking the low-lying terrain around the lagoon, losing 372 dead and 1,582 wounded in so doing.[15]

While Operation *Flintlock* was being launched in this way, Rear-Admiral Harry Hill took a battalion of the 27th US Infantry on a small number of landing craft to seize Majuro Atoll on 31 January. Unlike Kwajalein it was undefended by the Japanese and it was soon made into a very useful base for the US Navy. Some of Mitscher's carriers began arriving there as early as 2 February. It would serve as the springboard for an aerial assault on the major Japanese naval base of Truk in the Carolines a couple of weeks later. Nine carriers, six battleships, five heavy cruisers, an equal number of light cruisers, as well as thirty-three destroyers left Majuro on 15 February to begin Operation *Hailstone*. Using fleet carriers to launch an initial strike against the 365 Japanese aircraft on Truk and light carriers against enemy shipping both in the port and in the waters off the island, the Americans really caused mayhem throughout 17–18 February. Although a force of seven Japanese torpedo-bombers ('Kates') got through and managed to hit the carrier *Intrepid*, knocking her out of the action, American carrier aircraft did far more damage to the Japanese cause. In a total of 1,250 sorties, 400 tons of bombs were dropped to such effect that by the end of the operation at least two-thirds of the Japanese aircraft had been destroyed along with seventeen assorted warships, and twenty-five other vessels totalling 137,019 tons. In addition, American submarines off Truk managed to sink another light cruiser, *Agano*, the submarine *I-43*, and seven other assorted vessels.[16] *Hailstone* had therefore been an unqualified success and it was followed up by attacks on the islands of Jaluit, Saipan, Tinian and Rota in the Marianas over the course of the next few days. Again damage and destruction went hand-in-hand with the three task groups. While this was going on to the southwest, Operation *Catchpole* began with another invasion of the Marshall group. This time it was Eniwetok's turn. Harry Hill brought ashore 8,000 men of 22nd Marine RCT and two battalions of the 27th US Infantry Division in twenty-seven landing craft, supported once again by an impressive amount of firepower provided by three escort carriers, three battleships, three cruisers and nineteen destroyers. After an initial landing was made on Engebi on 17 February, troops landed on Eniwetok two days later. Once again, the Japanese defenders fought bravely but perished in droves, only sixty-four surviving out of an original force of 3,431. Although it took only four days to smash their resistance, the Americans were shown the extraordinary nature of the enemy confronting them. Death appeared not to faze the Japanese and even if it did there was no visible sign of a dereliction of duty by individuals. Sometimes there would be no alternative but bloody close quarter combat to evict the defenders. It was clear that ground would only be grudgingly given up and at great expense. Securing Eniwetok would cost the lives of 195 US servicemen and end up wounding another 521.[17]

While Nimitz's 'island hopping' strategy was paying off with bouts of tough fighting and accelerated progress through the Central Pacific, MacArthur's alternative route to Japan through the island territories of Southeast Asia was being advanced in smaller, but no less important, strides. As the bulk of his troops moved forward from Cape Gloucester towards Rabaul in New Britain, 2,400 others were landed near Saidor in New Guinea on 2 January (Operation *Dexterity*) with the aim of isolating 12,000 troops from the Japanese 18th Army in the area around Sio and cutting off the possibility of their retreat to the important Japanese-held port of Madang.[18] Once Lieutenant-General Hatazô Adachi had been evacuated by the Japanese submarine *I-177* during the night of 7–8 January, his troops tried to make their way to safety by making for Gali and Madang, but this only brought them within range of the American cruisers and destroyers offshore who tore into them with devastating effect. Clearing New Guinea of enemy troops was always likely to be a lengthy affair, given its size, the nature of its terrain and the considerable pockets of resistance to be encountered there. Despite the fact that Allied warships would be brought in to shell coastal towns and troop concentrations, or land new contingents of infantry forces and fresh supplies, success or otherwise in the struggle to secure New Guinea would rest primarily upon the daily grind of soldiers rather than sailors.[19]

Naval support – both tactical and logistical – for ongoing Army operations was now an established fact of life in the Pacific war with its amphibious role being a vital component of each campaign. Green Island, off the east coast of New Ireland, was the next target to be identified for attention and Rear-Admiral Theodore Wilkinson, in command of III Amphibious Force, landed the 3rd New Zealand Division there from twenty-eight landing craft on 15 February with the customary destroyer escorts in attendance. A further turn of the screw was now administered by several destroyer flotillas who engaged in repeated bombardments of Kavieng, the Japanese base at the northern tip of New Ireland, and Rabaul, the besieged and by now rather bedraggled air and naval base on New Britain. Both would take some time to fall finally to the Allies, but their once prominent role in the Japanese penetration of the Southwest Pacific had already passed. In an effort to apply even more pressure to both of these strongholds of resistance, MacArthur looked to establish a military presence and a new air base on the Admiralty Islands in the Bismarck Archipelago. Three task groups were assigned to the task of landing the first batch of troops in Hyäne Harbour on the islands of Los Negros on 29 February. Although the 1,026 troops of the 5th Cavalry Regiment landed, they were greeted by sturdy resistance from both the Japanese defenders on the main island and those of Hauwei and Norilo as well as the batteries overlooking the northern entrance to Seeadler Harbour. Reinforcements amounting to another 2,410 troops were landed under fire on 2 and 5 March, and it was only after repeated pounding from Rear-Admiral Victor Crutchley's task force of the heavy cruiser *Shropshire*, the two light cruisers *Nashville* and *Phoenix* and four destroyers that MacArthur's new airfield was finally secured on 9 March. Although a fourth convoy of troops and supplies duly arrived three days later it took to the end of the month for all the islands off Seeadler Habour to be cleared of Japanese troops. By then four regimental combat teams of the 4th Marine Division had established a new air and patrol boat base on Emirau in the Bismarck Archipelago; Kavieng had been reduced still further by the guns of Rear-Admiral Charles Griffin's four battleships; and six destroyers under the command of Captain Petersen had been engaged in helping to beat off the attack by 12,000 Japanese infantry troops on the Allied bridgehead near Cape Torokina (Operation *TA*) on Bougainville in which over 45% of the attacking force (5,469) were killed for the loss of 263 American servicemen.[20]

As the Allies made measured progress in the Southwest Pacific, Mitscher's carrier-led task force (TF 58) stepped up the pressure on the Japanese presence in Micronesia by conducting Operation *Desecrate* – a series of bombing raids against the islands of Palau, Woleai and Yap at the end of March. Japanese reconnaissance aircraft located the task force southeast of Truk on 26 March and these reports had prompted Admiral Koga, the Japanese C-in-C, to order his major warships to leave their base in Palau and join the Carrier Fleet and the 2nd Fleet in their new base of Tawi Tawi in the Solo Archipelago. Weathering an attack by Japanese aircraft on the evening of 28 March, all eleven carriers in Mitscher's three task groups mounted attacks on Palau on 30 March and 1 April, splitting their forces on 31 March to conduct raids on both Palau and Yap in which a combination of air mines, bombs and torpedoes accounted for the loss of a fast transport, four submarine-chasers and thirty-one other enemy vessels totalling 129,807 tons. Such rewards did not come light. Twenty-five of TF 58's carrier aircraft were shot down in these raids, but with the submarine *Harder* on hand to rescue twenty-six of the aircrew, losses were not as grievous as they otherwise would have been. Hounded out of Palau, the Japanese Combined Fleet also lost its second successive C-in-C to a plane crash. Koga's death on his way to Mindanao in the Philippines on 31 March led to the appointment of Admiral Soemu Toyoda as his successor on 5 May.[21]

Good news was hard to come by for the Axis Powers at this time. Whether out in the North Atlantic, up in the Arctic or throughout the Mediterranean, the cutting edge of German naval power – the U-boat – was being blunted by an increasingly effective Allied response that used intelligence gained through Enigma decrypts, stronger escort groups and more plentiful aircraft equipped with the latest technology to shield more of their convoys from them while on passage. Worse still for Dönitz, improved convoy protection came with an increasing ability to locate and destroy his U-boats whether they operated in groups or as individual entities. In the place where they had formerly thrived the most – the North Atlantic – the monthly returns were very revealing. From 22 February to 22 March, thirty-six U-boats spreadeagled across the ocean had been able to sink two destroyer escorts, a corvette, a landing ship, and a tanker and shoot down three aircraft, but had suffered ten losses and one damaged U-boat in doing so. If it was a sign of the times it was a depressing one for the U-boat arm and its greatest supporter. Unfortunately for both, the results over the next six weeks were even more dismal. Despite the presence of seventeen U-boats between Newfoundland and the Irish coast only two ships and two more enemy aircraft were dispatched, while eight more U-boats were sunk and another one was damaged. Even if they could be sustained in the short term, losses of this kind made little sense. Dönitz had seen enough; for the time being at least the war against trade had to be considered as being lost on the high seas. He could return to it once his new generation of U-boats had made it off the test beds or when he had more *schnorchel* boats available to him. Meanwhile, he considered that his U-boats might be more profitably used in the coastal waters off the British Isles where there was increasing activity as preparations intensified for a major amphibious operation in the months to come.[22]

Although he saw little choice in pulling back his U-boats from the Atlantic, Dönitz still hoped that they could recapture their past glories in northern Europe. It was a vain hope. In their exploits against four convoys (JW.57/RA.57, JW.58/RA.58) stretching from late February to early April, thirty-one of his U-boats were used in six different groups. Despite locating the various convoys and carrying out many attacks on them, they rarely succeeded in penetrating the escort and support group screens surrounding the 158 ships on offer – a fact exemplified by the sinking of only a solitary freighter and a destroyer escort in addition to the shooting down of a patrolling aircraft in many days of sustained activity. In compiling this modest record, nine U-boats were sunk, another one was badly damaged and six accompanying aircraft were destroyed. Dönitz could be forgiven for wondering how long this nightmare might last.[23]

Something was clearly amiss. Acoustic as well as pattern running torpedoes were not striking home with the regularity that they were designed to achieve. Near-misses were not good enough. Were they the product of design flaws, poor marksmanship by his U-boat commanders, or aggressive hunting methods adopted by the enemy? As with most things, the blame for these lamentable failures could be apportioned all round. Nonetheless, one development was becoming very noticeable, namely, that if contact was made with a U-boat, the escort and support groups locating it would continue their pursuit for hours on end and their pattern of depth-charging and the weapons of destruction at their disposal, such as the 'Hedgehog' and the new 'Squid' mortar, would more often than not finally win the day. For this reason, Dönitz realised that his boats must remain submerged for as long as possible so as to avoid detection. This, of course, was the singular advantage which the new *schnorchel* boats offered. While evading detection was a crucial asset for any submarine, the breathing tube which these new vessels could float to the surface at night time to replenish air supplies was ruled out during daylight hours because it could be spotted by alert and trained observers. Therefore, to preserve oxygen during the day while they remained submerged, the crews of the *schnorchel* boats were forced into spending many silent hours on their bunks. At night, however, the same privations could be eased with U-boat commanders employing the *schnorchel* breathing tube while remaining submerged and using their diesel engines to make headway although, admittedly, at a slower pace than if they were travelling on the surface.[24]

Dönitz's marked lack of achievement in the Arctic was more than matched by the laboriously sterile operations of the Soviet Northern Fleet in attacking

German convoy traffic around the Polar Coast. Allied efforts to strike a more emphatic note in these waters were illustrated by their repeated attempts to finish off the damaged battleship *Tirpitz* which remained in Altenfjorden after the earlier midget-submarine operation of September 1943 had damaged but not sunk her. A sense of frustration grew as the year went on and she remained in existence. Fifteen Soviet bombers tried to destroy her with 1,000 pound (453.6 kilo) bombs on 11–12 February, but only one near-miss resulted from that foray. Although she didn't represent an imminent danger to Allied shipping in her existing condition, once she had been fully repaired, she would present the same old dangers that the *Scharnhorst* and the *Bismarck* had posed before her. 'Ultra' intelligence gleaned through the work of the Bletchley Park cryptanalysts left the Admiralty in no doubt that she had been patched up sufficiently by early April to make her anticipated return journey to a naval base in Germany for a thorough overhaul. An attack was judged vital and Vice-Admiral Sir Henry Moore was asked to launch Operation *Tungsten* at dawn on 3 April spearheaded by fighter aircraft from four escort carriers to deal with enemy planes and strafe the deck and bodywork of the *Tirpitz* if she could be found and pave the way for the forty-one Fairey Barracuda bombers from the fleet carriers *Furious* and *Victorious* to finish her off with an arsenal of armour-piercing, semi-armour-piercing and high-explosive bombs. Despite a partial smokescreen, *Tirpitz* was found by the Corsairs and Hellcats, and strafed accordingly and then the Barracudas managed at least fourteen hits or near-misses, in two waves of attacks. Although the damage caused was very significant – Eric Grove describes the upper decks as being 'reduced to a shambles' – the bombs did not penetrate below the armoured deck. Notwithstanding this failing, the damage done was such as to ensure that the battleship was not going anywhere fast and the trip to Germany was put off once more until the new damage could be repaired.[25]

Despite struggling to eliminate the last of the German capital ships in Norwegian waters, the Allies still enjoyed considerable success in this theatre of operations.[26] Apart from the Arctic convoys that largely defied all that the Luftwaffe and Dönitz's U-boats could throw at them, and the exploits of their own submarine crews in these waters, it was the aircraft of 18 Group Coastal Command that really made a dramatic impact off Norway by waging war on both those conventional and *schnorchel*-fitted U-boats that were endeavouring to use these waters to gain access to the Atlantic. In a series of attacks they launched over a five-month period from late February to late July, they destroyed seventeen U-boats, damaged fifteen others and forced several others to either return to port or interrupt their transit journeys.[27] Disturbing though these figures were for the officers of the Kriegsmarine, the more worrying aspect was that the *schnorchel* boats were being identified and picked off in daylight by vigilant air crew that looked for tell-tale signs of a foaming wake left behind by these vessels. Although the U-boats had exacted some revenge by downing five of the Allied aircraft and badly damaging six others, the cost–benefit analysis was distinctly going against the Axis forces in these northern latitudes as it was elsewhere.[28]

While the Germans languished in the far north, they and their Finnish partners grasped the initiative in the Gulf of Finland with the laying of new mine and net barrages and the renewal of existing barriers to Soviet submarines attempting to make their way out into the Baltic. By 20 May 7,599 new mines and 2,795 barrage protection devices had been laid in these relatively narrow waters.[29] Mining was also resorted to in the Black Sea. Here the tactic was employed to try to slow the speed of the Soviet advance rather than gain the upper hand. It was far too late for that. All across the Caucasian front, the Soviets were on the march – a fact underlined by the fall of Nikolayev (Mykolayiv) on 28 March and the headlong retreat of the German and Romanian forces across the Lower Bug and towards the mouth of the River Dniester and beyond to the border of Romania in the days that followed. Caught up in this maelstrom of activity were those Axis forces that found themselves in the port city of Odessa. Once again, the Germans displayed their talent for organisation by staging an orderly evacuation in which 14,845 troops, 9,300 wounded soldiers and 54,000 tons of supplies were taken off the quays by an assortment of ships, naval ferry barges, tugs and towing vessels that made repeated trips in and out of the port. Hitler's stubborn refusal to accept the impending loss of the Crimea meant that instead of arranging an early withdrawal of the 17th Army from Sevastopol, reinforcements from the 111th Infantry Division and 45,000 tons of supplies were brought in during March to try to stem the tide of war in these parts. It was a foolhardy exploit since they would never be enough even to remotely accomplish that aim. By 10 April, the day that Odessa fell, two major Soviet offensives were already underway – in the north on the Perekop Peninsula and in the east on the Kerch Peninsula – and the Germans were forced to beat a hasty retreat to Sevastopol. This forced them to evacuate another 10,000 troops of the V Army Corps from the eastern front to Balaklava and Sevastopol in a series of naval ferry barges. Once there they joined the beleaguered remnants of Colonel-General Erwin Jaenecke's 17th Army. Still Hitler refused to countenance retreat, though an evacuation of non-essential personnel to the Romanian port city of Constanza was started using destroyers, motor minesweepers, sub-chasers, gunboats, steamers, naval ferry barges, tugs, lighters and miscellaneous light craft, as well as aircraft, from 12 April. By the time that Hitler finally and reluctantly consented to a withdrawal on 8 May, the fate of the Crimea was already sealed and the Soviets had opened their final offensive against Sevastopol. His belated concession spelt doom for over thirty ships and 8,100 troops when they were caught by enemy aircraft on these evacuation runs. By the time the evacuation was called off, roughly 130,000 German and Romanian troops had been taken off the Crimea by naval means and a further 21,457 soldiers had been airlifted from this lost cause. This left approximately 78,000 behind in the shattered city and garrison.[30]

If Axis power was being curtailed up in the Arctic, across broad swathes of the Atlantic and throughout the Black Sea, the Mediterranean represented something different: an ongoing joust that would take some time to resolve. In the Aegean the Germans held the controlling interest; the Adriatic was up for grabs, while both the central and western sectors of the Mediterranean were firmly in Allied hands. Even so, the Germans felt they could still exert some pressure on convoy traffic and disrupt the passage of war supplies to Eisenhower's forces in southern Italy. Thrust and counter-thrust were delivered and parried as the two sides tried to take what advantage they could wherever an opportunity presented itself. While Allied aircraft carried out destructive raids on the naval bases at Toulon and Livorno, the Germans hit back by conducting minelaying operations in the Tyrrhenian Sea; Allied offshore shelling of Curzola (Korčula), Rhodes, and Kos was replied to by many Luftwaffe sorties in the Eastern Mediterranean; both sides attacked enemy convoys with relish but rarely with astounding success – the destruction of an entire convoy of German naval ferry barges off Vado on 27 March by surface craft being an exception.[31]

Of all the seas in Europe, none was busier during the first five months of the year than the English Channel. Here there were almost daily sorties carried out by flotillas of MTBs and other torpedo boats in which the Germans were well to the fore, mining harbours, attacking convoys and exchanging blows with destroyers and corvettes. They assumed a pest-like aggravation and swatting them effectively proved to be impossible. Short of employing air cover over everything that moved by sea – obviously a non-starter given the amount of traffic and RAF Coastal Command's lack of airframes – the MTBs and other fast, light craft that packed a punch could be expected to do some damage in the Allied build up towards D-Day and Operation *Neptune* and they did. Hundreds of mines were sown around the English coast from Cornwall to Lincolnshire with particular emphasis on the Strait of Dover, as well as off Cherbourg and the other Normandy ports. Convoys were always fair game and yielded decent returns given that they were mostly inadequately defended in these coastal waters. While there was to be no Channel version of PQ.17, a resourceful and experienced MTB flotilla, such as the German 5th, commanded by officers of Bernd Klug and Karl Müller's abilities, could destroy several ships at one sitting, and did so on more than one occasion. While on the receiving end of much of this waspish activity, the British employed their own MTB resources in much the same way off the Dutch coast without gaining as much success and from mid-April concentrated on attempting to block German access to the Channel by laying 3,000 mines in these waters. Five groups of RAF Bomber Command were also similarly employed. They dropped 4,000 mines, some of which were acoustic ground mines for low frequencies and some acoustic anchor mines too. This minelaying activity was to reap considerable rewards with approximately 100 German ships coming to grief on these mines in the weeks to come.[32]

Further afield in the Indian Ocean, Admiral Somerville's reinforced Eastern Fleet was now able to make forays into Japanese-held areas in the Dutch East Indies. Beginning in March the warships left Trincomalee and Colombo once a month on operations that took them southeastwards to the Cocos Islands (*Diplomat*), Sumatra (*Cockpit*) and Java (*Transom*).[33] Of the three carrier-based operations, *Diplomat* (21 March–2 April) seemed to be more of a morale-boosting exercise than anything else and an opportunity to get the kinks out of the system;

Cockpit was the most successful in that the attacks launched against Sabang, off the northern tip of Aceh (16–24 April), did result in twenty-four Japanese aircraft and a steamer being destroyed; while *Transom* – the attack on the port and oil refineries of Surabaya (6–27 May) – destroyed much less of its infrastructure and mobile facilities than the returning carrier pilots estimated it had. Twelve enemy planes had been destroyed for the loss of one Allied aircraft, but only one small freighter had been sunk, the port continued to operate as before and the oil kept flowing.[34]

It was just as well it did since oil was vital for the Japanese military machine and the defence of their vast but steadily shrinking empire. After all, one of the great alluring features behind the Japanese concept of *nanshin* (southward advance), and the enduring fascination with the peninsula of Malaya and the Dutch East Indies archipelago throughout the inter-war period, was that military control over these territories would yield vast mineral resources, principally oil, rubber and tin, that Japan did not naturally possess. After the astonishing military successes of December 1941–April 1942, Japan had acquired access to vast seams of resources and it was not about to give these up easily. Without oil, in particular, industrial productivity would fall, fuel stocks would inevitably diminish and the military machine would become starved of its lifeblood. All three services depended upon it to a greater or lesser extent. Without sufficient supplies of it, the warships of the IJN would not have the means to leave port, aircraft would be grounded, tanks and most forms of vehicular transport would become inoperable. For this reason, the Japanese wished to retain their hold over both Malaya and as much of the East Indies as possible. Since the authorities in Tokyo could see what the Allies were intending to do in Southeast Asia, the task they set themselves was to delay this process by as long as possible. Vigorous defence could be expected of those already on the ground, but reinforcements were necessary if the Allies were to be held up for months rather than weeks at a time.[35]

With this in mind, 20,000 troops were embarked at Shanghai on 15 April (Operation *Take-Ichi*) in a convoy of transports to begin the journey to the island of Halmahera in the Molucca (Maluku) Sea to boost the numbers of Japanese troops already on the Vogelkop Peninsula. Halmahera was a natural barrier to Sulawesi (Celebes) and the all-important oil rich island of Borneo to the westward and an obvious stepping stone to Mindanao and the rest of the Philippines to the northwest. Therefore, it made considerable strategic sense to hold it for as long as possible. This plan was very rapidly undermined by two US submarines, *Jack* and *Gurnard*, who helped themselves to four of the transports while the convoy was underway ensuring that nearly half those who strode up the gangways in China never disembarked in the Moluccas.[36]

Japanese concern about American planning for the region was not exaggerated. Within a week of the *Take-Ichi* operation being launched, General MacArthur had embarked on two new amphibious operations along the northern coast of New Guinea which were designed to give his forces access to useful air and naval base facilities: Operation *Reckless* was to make landfall in the Hollandia

(Jayapura) area and Operation *Persecution* targeted the important town of Aitape. These operations were made possible by the quality of the 'Ultra' intelligence that he received in the weeks leading up to these two assaults which indicated that the Japanese were confidently expecting the American troops to land at Hansa Bay to the east of Wewak and had only relatively light forces (estimated at 16,000 troops) in place to defend both Hollandia and Aitape. Armed with this priceless information, MacArthur gained approval from the Joint Chiefs of Staff in March to exploit this situation. Softened up in advance by the aircraft from twelve fleet carriers belonging to Mitscher's TF 58, and closely supported by those from the eight escort carriers of Rear-Admiral Ragsdale's task groups (TG 78.1 and TG 78.2), a total of seventy-seven landing craft successfully disgorged units of the 24th and 41st Infantry Divisions at Aitape, and in both Humboldt Bay and Tanahmerah Bay from 22 to 24 April against little organised opposition.[37] By establishing themselves in Aitape and Hollandia in this way, the Americans had managed to get behind Japanese lines and bring off a pincer move that trapped some 55,000 troops of General Adachi's 18th Army lying to the east of them in the Hansa Bay and Wewak region and west of the advancing Allied troops that were making their way up the coast towards Madang and the Sepik River. It also provided the Allies with the means to move forward at a faster pace – literally a jumping off point – which they could use as a springboard to begin breaking into the East Indian archipelago.[38] They were to use these newly acquired bases for a further push up the coast of New Guinea to the town of Arara (Sarmi) and the small offshore island of Wakde in the middle of the following month. In this operation, 7,000 men of the 163rd Regimental Combat Team (RCT) were put aboard twenty destroyers and twenty-nine landing craft and landed in these two spots on 17 and 18 May respectively. Wakde has an onomatopoeic ring to it and proved to be as uncompromising as the name sounds with the Japanese troops on the island fighting determinedly to hold on to their strategically important airfield. They failed to do so losing 759 of their own number and killing 110 enemy soldiers in the process before control of the airfield was seized by the Americans.[39]

As MacArthur's troops surged forward in New Guinea, Admiral Nimitz switched Japanese attention back to the Central Pacific by using Mitscher's TF 58 to conduct a series of punishing raids on Truk on 29–30 April. Although Mitscher lost thirty-five of his own planes in these raids, the Japanese fared much worse losing ninety-three out of the 104 aircraft that were serviceable on the island. Extensive shelling of the Satawan Islands (30 April) and of Ponape (Pohnpei) in the Carolines at the beginning of May by two other naval task groups only served to reinforce the fact that Micronesia was now something of a broken reed as far as the Japanese were concerned. Admiral Soemu Toyoda, the latest naval C-in-C, didn't need anyone to spell out what this meant for the IJN. Truk had been consigned to the past, Palau was living on borrowed time, and Guam, Saipan, Tinian and the rest of the Marianas were likely targets since the seizure of these islands and their air bases would enable the Americans to strike at the Volcano, Bonin and Ryukyu Islands and beyond to the Japanese mainland.[40]

Toyoda was determined to prevent their loss and put forward a defence plan for the Marianas which was named Operation *A-GO*. This involved moving the regional fleet base to Tawi Tawi in the southern Philippines in mid-May in preparation for the launching of a major and decisive offensive against the Americans once they moved towards Guam. What Toyoda and the *Gunreibu* (Naval General Staff) didn't know for certain was where the Allies would strike next. Carrier attacks on Marcus Island and Wake Island from 19 to 23 May looked like diversionary affairs to them, but the crucial questions of where and when the enemy would go next – to the southwest or the northwest – remained unanswered. Of the two, the Japanese focused far more attention on the strategic triangle formed by linking the western part of New Guinea, the island of Palau and that of Mindanao, believing that this was the more likely target in the short term. It was to be another critical mistake.[41]

Alerted to Japanese dispositions by their ability to read their enemy's signals, the Americans sent several of their submarines to reconnoitre the situation as the still formidable Japanese fleet exercised in the waters off Tawi Tawi. What the Americans discovered was that Jisaburo Ozawa was there with the 1st Mobile Fleet (nine carriers with 450 aircraft, six battleships, eleven heavy and two light cruisers, thirty-nine destroyers and eleven oil tankers), and that Takeo Takagi's 6th Fleet's of thirty-nine submarines had joined him.[42] Given that Kakuji Kakuta's First Air Fleet of roughly 1,000 land-based aircraft and several divisions of troops belonging to Chuichi Nagumo's Central Pacific District Fleet were also on hand, the Americans couldn't fail to sense that the Japanese really meant business and that they must seek to avoid being caught in the trap that Toyoda and the Gunreibu were planning to spring upon them. Convinced that he had discerned the will of the Americans, Toyoda ordered Takagi to deploy his submarine force throughout the Southwest and Central Pacific in such a way as to give early warning of strong US carrier forces coming into the area since this would signal their intention of prosecuting the next instalment of the war. This deployment was not without incident and the losses incurred by the submarine arm would have immediate implications for the Japanese military.[43]

Knowing what one's opponent is planning to do in advance of them being able to orchestrate it is an invaluable tool when it comes to any competitive endeavour; in war it is a matter of life or death. Intelligence gathering provided the Allies with huge advantages that the Japanese simply did not possess and they used them to great effect. Learning where the submarine picket lines were going to be meant that warships and mercantile craft could avoid them. Equally, though, it meant that parties of destroyers could be sent to hunt and destroy them. No group on a single mission in the entire Pacific war was more successful in this respect than the three destroyers *England*, *George* and *Raby*. They began their reign of destruction on 19 May when they found *I-16* on her way to deliver supplies to Buin in the Solomons. A 'Hedgehog' swiftly accounted for her. This was merely a starter. *England* then systematically destroyed five other submarines (*Ro-106*, *Ro-104*, *Ro-116*, *Ro-108* and *Ro-105*) off the coast of New Ireland over the course of the next twelve days using the same methods. In contrast, the US submarines that were sent to keep watch on the Japanese fleet exercises off Tawi Tawi managed to sink three destroyers and three tankers besides torpedoing the carrier *Chitose*.[44]

In an effort to keep the Japanese guessing about their intentions, the Americans arranged a series of simultaneous strikes over large distances. Apart from the carrier attacks on Marcus Island and Wake already referred to, destroyers from the US 5th Fleet also shelled Engebi, Wotje and Mili in the Marshall Islands from 17 to 26 May. At the same time an invasion of Biak was set in motion which did much to confirm the Japanese belief that the Americans were intent on an attack within the 'Great Triangle' of the Southwest Pacific. Biak, a fortified island off the northwest coast of New Guinea, would prove to be a far harder target to conquer than Aitape, Hollandia or Wakde had been. For a start, it was home to 10,000 Japanese troops who were determined to give Major-General Horace Fuller's men of the 41st US Infantry Division a lesson in hard combat. Rear-Admiral William Fechteler was charged with landing the VII Amphibious Force on the southern shore of the island. Bringing 119 landing craft with him, including twenty-five DUKWs – the remarkable amphibious vehicles that became a boon to any beach landing – Fechteler succeeded in getting the first of four assault waves onto the beaches on 27 May.[45]

News of this latest Allied operation seemed to confirm what the *Gunreibu* already thought was likely to happen in the near future, namely, that the Americans would make a major thrust towards Palau in the hope of using it as a forward base for a subsequent invasion of the Philippines. Recognising Biak to be a subordinate aim rather than a major objective requiring the support of the US Pacific Fleet, the Japanese responded to this latest incursion by mounting a modest series of reinforcement efforts from Tawi Tawi and Zamboanga in early June, codenamed *KON*, which not only failed to put any troops ashore, but also lost two destroyers and had another one damaged in the process. A third attempt to do something for their beleaguered troops on Biak was abandoned by the Japanese once news was received in mid-June that the Americans had confounded their predictions by eschewing an attack on Palau in favour of an all-out offensive on the Marianas (Operation *Forager*).[46]

In June 1944 as the Allied and Axis forces on both sides of the world waited expectantly and nervously, in the words of the popular expression 'for the balloon to go up' in both the European and Pacific theatres of war, the vital secret of where and when these attacks would begin was somehow preserved. It is still quite staggering to think that either or both of these operations could have been fatally compromised by anything from a twist of fate – an intercepted communication, or a piece of ill luck – to either a calamitous error on the part of the Allied protagonists, or even an inspired hunch by the Axis defenders. Neither was undermined in any of these ways, so the secret of D-Day remained intact until the early hours of 6 June when the massive invasion was already underway. A similar fate befell their Axis partners a few days later when the American attack on the Marianas caught the Japanese equally by surprise. These were to be defining moments in the history of the Second World War. Both in their own way were to confirm something that was already apparent, namely, that the tide of war – which had already been moving strongly in the Allies' favour – had strengthened still further. Thereafter one did not need to be an unabashed optimist to feel that realistically there would be no way back for the Axis Powers from these catastrophes.[47]

Although D-Day was launched in early June it had been in the planning stage for months. Meticulous planning preceded both the *Neptune* and *Overlord* operations and organisational gifts of a most exemplary kind were needed to turn the most detailed schemes into a set of viable, logistic undertakings. For this most demanding of appointments the Allies turned to the Admiralty's Retired List and one of their heroes of the past – Admiral Sir Bertram Ramsay – the naval officer who had so impressively succeeded in withdrawing the bulk of the British Expeditionary Force from the beaches of Dunkirk in late May and early June 1940 (Operation *Dynamo*). After having taken an active part in both the *Torch* and *Husky* invasions in 1942–43, he had been inexplicably allowed to strike his flag and return ashore to lapse into a well-merited, but still chafing, retirement. Fortunately for the Allied cause it was not to last long. Operation *Neptune*, the naval component of the overall invasion of Northwestern Europe (Operation *Overlord*), demanded special skills and preferably a proven track record of achievement in amphibious operations – no-one possessed more of these special qualities and experience than Ramsay. Once again the striking old adage of 'cometh the hour, cometh the man' came into vogue. In a wonderful riposte to the Board of Admiralty who had earlier chosen to dispense with his services, the Supreme Headquarters Allied Expeditionary Force (SHAEF) now acquired his unique talents. He was invited to become Allied Naval Commander Expeditionary Force (ANCXF) and had submitted his first proposals before he actually returned to the Active Duty List of the Royal Navy in March 1944.[48]

Ramsay's logistical task was formidable in every respect. He had to bring together by far the largest amphibious undertaking ever assembled and then ensure that the troop and supply convoys landed in the designated places on the French coast at the correct time and in the order that the overall plan specified. Thereafter he would be responsible for bringing in reinforcements to the beachhead for as long as they were required. As an indication of the size of this enterprise, the first wave of this armada would involve no less than 2,775 assorted landing vessels carrying 132,715 troops and be escorted and covered by a force of warships that included seven battleships, twenty-four cruisers, two monitors, 135 assorted destroyers, fourteen destroyer escorts, sixty-eight corvettes, sixteen frigates, twenty-four trawlers and a vast number of smaller naval vessels that were employed in ferrying supplies from the larger ships offshore to the actual beachhead. Eric Grove estimates that roughly 7,000 vessels were involved in ensuring *Neptune*'s success over the course of the next three months. This immense armada had been gathering in British ports from the Bristol Channel to the Thames Estuary for weeks on end.[49]

Aware of this Allied build up from reconnaissance flights, intelligence reports and the sterling efforts of B-Dienst in cracking some of the naval code, the

Germans remained in the dark about where it would seek to make landfall once it had crossed the Channel. Feldmarschall Erwin Rommel – the man charged by Hitler with organising the defence of northern France – believed that the Allied invasion would take place somewhere in the coastal zone sandwiched between Flanders in the north and the mouth of the River Somme to the south of the Pas-de-Calais. He reasoned that if the Allied armies could establish themselves there it would reduce the distance to the Ruhr – the industrial heartland of Germany. For his part, Hitler thought that the shortest route across the Strait of Dover was far too obvious and dangerous to be undertaken since the Allies didn't wish to be hurled back into the sea by a massive concentration of German power as they came ashore. He sensed correctly that they might be tempted to land further away on the coast of Normandy and Brittany even if this would involve a seaborne passage of at least 100nm (185km) rather than the 30nm (55.5km) represented by a quick dash across the Channel to the closest point on the French coastline. Rommel ardently refused to subscribe to this view and Hitler, perhaps surprisingly, never insisted on his own strategic ideas becoming the established orthodoxy. In this way the mistaken assumptions became entrenched and led to a fatal complacency that enveloped many members of the German High Command in France. As the days of waiting continued an air of ennui replaced that of excited apprehension. A spell of bad weather added to the gloom and appeared to rule out any imminent threat materialising from across the water. In such conditions where monotony reigned, it is easy to let one's guard down. Nothing illustrated this better than the fact that when D-Day opened not all the divisional commanders were at their posts; even Rommel himself was away from the front on furlough with his family at their home in Herrlingen, a village close to the city of Ulm in the southern German state of Baden Württemberg.[50]

They wouldn't have been so complacent had they had any indication of the surprise Ramsay's team at their battle headquarters at Southwick House near Portsmouth was planning for them. Although the stormy conditions in the Channel had led to Eisenhower postponing the offensive by twenty-four hours to 6 June, the tidal conditions were still judged acceptable for the landings to go ahead as planned on the revised date. According to the detailed plan that Ramsay had drawn up, it was vital that the assault phase should begin quite specifically anywhere from twelve minutes before to ninety minutes after sunrise and between three to four hours before high tide. Some minimal flexibility was built into the plan because the necessary tidal conditions were not exactly the same across the five beaches that had been selected for the landings in the Baie de la Seine (Bay of the Seine). Presented with the five landing sectors: *Utah* (a 5km sector on the southeast coast of the Cotentin Peninsula near La Madeleine), *Omaha* (a 7km sector east of the Pointe de la Percée between Vierville and Colleville), *Gold* (a 9km sector lying roughly 14km away from that of *Omaha* between Arromanches and la Rivière), *Juno* (the adjoining 11km sector stretching eastwards past Courseulles towards Langrune), and *Sword* (another 9km adjoining sector that took in Lion-sur-mer and ended at Ouistreham), Ramsay divided his vessels into two task forces. A Western Naval Task Force was placed under the command of the American naval officer, Rear-Admiral Alan Kirk, who already knew a great deal about difficult amphibious operations from the *Husky* landings on Sicily the year before. He would be responsible for landing men of the 4th US Infantry Division in the *Utah* sector and those of the 1st US Infantry Division on that of *Omaha*. An Eastern Naval Task Force was to be organised under the command of Rear-Admiral Sir Philip Vian – a dashing favourite of Churchill and veteran of many a Mediterranean convoy run. His task was to put the 50th British Infantry Division ashore in the *Gold* sector, the 3rd Canadian Infantry Division on *Juno* and the 3rd British Division in *Sword*. Under each commander would be a force commander responsible for each of the individual beaches.[51] Naturally, each of the convoys designated for the five beaches were provided with a nimble escort screen and were supported by a group of heavier warships with superior firepower.[52] Each of the support forces (A, C, K, E and D) were required to deal with and preferably silence the heavy fixed shore batteries that covered the entire Baie de la Seine during the landings. In this task they were to be helped by massive waves of Allied aircraft which were used to soften up the defences and enable the paratroopers of the 82nd and 101st US Airborne Divisions to land on the southern part of the Cotentin Peninsula around the small villages of Ste Mère-Eglise, Ste Marie-du-Mont, and Vierville, while the British 6th Airborne Division parachuted in to the south and east of the town of Ouistreham.[53]

Assuming his task forces could get the landing craft and the troops to the correct beach, they would need to receive their military supplies and stores onshore with the minimum of delay. Efficiency became the watchword and Ramsay chose his subordinate from the days of Operation *Dynamo*, Rear-Admiral William Tennant, to organise the supply chain. He took responsibility for the establishment of 'Mulberry Harbours' – artificial harbours built of large concrete caissons that were designed to be towed across the Channel and sunk offshore to provide ships with a sheltered anchorage to offload their cargo regardless of how rough the sea conditions were. Admiral Cunningham was inclined to believe they added a 15% improvement to the amount of supplies that were taken ashore.

Tennant was also responsible for the 'Pluto' system in which fuel was piped across the Channel for storage and use at the beachhead by all forms of vehicular transport.[54]

To ensure that each of the convoys had a clear route to the beaches, Ramsay had to arrange for the laying of several thousand mines in protective fields all along the French and Belgian coastlines and for an extensive minesweeping of all access routes to each of the landing sectors. Naturally enough, this latter task couldn't be done until the operation was almost ready to go since it would have otherwise given the game away to the enemy and allowed the Germans time to stiffen their defences in the crucial area. Nonetheless, some preparatory work had to be undertaken several days in advance of *Neptune* being launched. On 31 May ten sonic underwater buoys on delayed fuses for later activation were laid out in the Channel to mark the outer extremity of the German minefield and determine where the minesweepers would commence their work in the hours before the assault phase of the operation began. Ramsay's staff had chosen to sweep five channels south-southeast (SSE) of the Isle of Wight right through the German minefields that had been sown extensively all along the Channel from Cherbourg to Boulogne. Using ten flotillas of fleet minesweepers – two for each channel – the flotillas would remain together until they neared the known minefields and then would be divided so that for each landing beach there would be two swept channels – one designated for fast convoys and the other for slower ones. These swept channels – known as 'The Spout' – would be marked by lighted danbuoys laid by a group of at least four trawlers following in the wake of each of the minesweeping flotillas.[55] Once the ten channels had been swept, the minesweepers were to sweep the sea parallel to the beaches that were going to be used by warships on bombardment duty and other areas offshore that were assigned to the larger transports that couldn't get closer inshore and needed swept anchorages to disembark both troops and supplies to smaller vessels that would take them up to the beaches. In addition to these vitally important preparatory measures, two midget submarines, *X-20* and *X-23*, were charged with marking the beaches for the Eastern Naval Task Force so that the landing craft would deposit their troops at the right site and not on adjoining beaches which were not assigned to them. Each of the X-craft were identified by a large yellow flag and a white ensign and were obliged to surface twenty minutes before H-hour (the time when the first troops went ashore) and begin transmitting on radio and sonar beacons, while shining a flashing light out to sea to attract the incoming convoys. They were also meant to assist the individual landing craft by using a powerful light from an anchored dinghy to show the distance to the beach.[56]

Deferred for twenty-four hours by the onset of bad weather, the landing craft of Operation *Neptune* would make landfall in the early hours of 6 June. They began moving towards the assembly point southeast of the Isle of Wight – 'Area Z' – on 5 June in stormy conditions which made for a queasy passage for all but the hardiest of troops. Once at 'Area Z', dubbed affectionately 'Piccadilly Circus' because so much was going on, the convoys would be sent on down 'The Spout' according to the detailed timetable prepared in advance and marshalled into the appropriate swept channel – fast or slow – that would lead to the landing sector assigned to them. It was a remarkable administrative and logistical coup. Ramsay's team had been brilliant at the time of *Dynamo* in rescuing as many troops as they had from the beaches of Dunkirk four years previously, but the organisational efforts that made both D-Day and the subsequent reinforcement operations such a resounding success may be said to have surpassed even these in terms of scale and effectiveness.[57]

While Allied activity was frantic, German ignorance of what was afoot on 5 June was almost total. Apart from the foul weather which convinced many in authority that an invasion in those conditions was scarcely credible – an attitude shared by the Luftwaffe, resulting in a failure to conduct reconnaissance sorties over the Channel – the means of detection available to the Kriegsmarine was limited. Its surface warning radar system had been badly bombed in the previous week and those that remained operational were jammed in the Normandy vicinity, while those north of the River Seine only picked up those 'decoy' convoys (barrage balloons towed by motor launches) that had been sent to confuse them and make them think that landings were intended at scattered sites in the Pas-de-Calais. As a result, the first sign that the Allies were up to something off the Baie de la Seine was only established at 0230 hours on 6 June off *Utah* beach. Even then confusion reigned and it took another two hours and thirty-five minutes before the shore batteries opened fire on two of the destroyers and the minesweepers that were completing their work so that the landing craft belonging to the *Utah* convoy (Force U) and the bombardment squadron supporting it (Force A) could do theirs. Although the shore batteries soon received a pummelling from the first wave of bomber aircraft, they continued to fire on the ships off *Utah* beach. Since this wasn't going according to the script, Rear-Admiral Deyo advanced the bombardment phase by fourteen minutes and ordered his warships to open fire at 0536 hours. Force C, the fire support group under Rear-Admiral Bryant off *Omaha* beach, had been forced into action six minutes earlier by the shelling of the coastal batteries. These had not had to endure a bombing attack and were firing at his ships and the landing craft of the *Omaha* convoy (Force O) without any restraint at all. Unable to silence them, Force C was obliged to watch helplessly as the German guns wreaked terrible havoc with the American troops as they attempted to come ashore. By the late afternoon over 4,000 men had been killed or injured on *Omaha* alone.

On the three stretches of beaches allocated to the British and Canadian forces – *Gold*, *Juno* and *Sword* – the landings were made without the grave difficulties or the acute losses of men and vessels encountered on *Omaha*. Allied aircraft took out gun emplacements or quietened them down; bombardment of the shoreline defences was fairly accurate; and despite the occasional logistic or navigational foul up, troops, vehicles, equipment and stores got ashore in substantial numbers. Although enemy activity was fairly restricted, a lone attempt in the evening by the 5th Torpedo Boat Flotilla to run amok amongst the landing craft of Force S off *Sword* beach took everyone by surprise, but it didn't do as much damage as the Le Havre-based outfit had hoped it would. Out of a total of fifteen torpedoes fired by the four boats, the Norwegian destroyer *Svenner* was hit amidships by one and broken apart, while the two battleships of the bombardment squadron *Ramillies* and *Warspite* and the headquarters ship *Largs* of Force S had perilous encounters with three others, but their officers and crew survived to tell the tale. By the close of the first day's action a total of 23,250 troops had been landed on *Utah*, 34,250 on *Omaha*, 24,970 on *Gold*, 21,400 on *Juno* and 28,845 on *Sword* making a total of 132,715.[58] According to Eric Grove, 304 assorted landing craft had been destroyed by mines, gunfire, traps or obstacles during the first day of the assault, but once night drew on the Germans brought an offensive component to bear on the convoy traffic that continued to plough its way to the shoreline.[59]

Flotillas of enemy MTBs, torpedo boats and motorised minesweepers were deployed from their bases in the Channel ports of Cherbourg, Le Havre and Boulogne to interdict the well-defended supply trains where and when they could. It was hardly an unexpected response and was bound to achieve some success, but the scale of destruction was largely contained and countered by the durable effectiveness of the Allied escort groups and through a series of aggressive patrols mounted by packs of their destroyers, MTBs and frigates beyond 'The Spout' and the invasion beaches. A series of violent clashes were rapidly joined and broken off as each set of combatants sought to gain a momentary and often elusive advantage over the other. Skirmishing became part of the expected nightly order and an integral feature of the assault phase. Attack was resorted to whenever the opportunity presented itself and the combat toll grew on both sides as did the number of claims and counter-claims of even more damage and destruction.[60] While the flotillas of fast, light surface vessels largely cancelled themselves out, German mines, coastal artillery and air attacks accounted for a light cruiser (*Scylla*), and eight more fleet destroyers before the month was out. Many smaller supply ships succumbed to the same dangers as they closed the shore or sought to retreat from it.[61]

Notwithstanding the inroads made into the invasion forces, far more might have been expected from the thirty-six U-boats which Dönitz had immediately mobilised from their Biscay ports to form the *Landwirt* group in the Channel. In truth, this deployment was ill-starred from the outset. None of the non-*schnorchel* boats could escape detection as they tried to enter the Channel. Ten Allied Support Groups were on the lookout for them as were aircraft from RAF Coastal Command and the three escort carriers *Activity*, *Tracker* and *Vindex*. Five of the U-boats were located and sunk and another five were damaged as they made their way through the Bay of Biscay. Reinforced by several more *schnorchel* boats from Norwegian waters, the Germans persevered and managed to get thirteen into the western part of the Channel within the next few days. Their attempts to begin chipping away at the destroyer escorts, however, were blighted by malfunctioning torpedoes and when they actually got to the convoy routes on 14 June they found themselves the focus of even closer and more vigorous attention from several of the reassigned Support Groups. By the end of June the U-boats that had reached the English Channel had achieved a modest record of success, but this had only been achieved at the cost of fourteen *schnorchel* craft and damage to ten others. Their efforts were hardly going to put a stop to the invasion.[62]

Allied counter-measures also extended to the mounting of a pair of massive air raids on Le Havre and Boulogne on the nights of 14 and 15 June respectively in an effort to strike a blow at the flotillas of light surface craft that were based there. In the first of these raids, 234 aircraft from RAF Bomber Command left the naval base at Le Havre in chaos after attacking the harbour and port facilities with a mixture of 'Tallboy' bombs (each weighing 12,000 pounds) and more conventional bombs. Next evening a repeat dose was administered to Boulogne with 297 more bombers taking part in the mayhem.[63] If such a swarm of aircraft appeared over a port, they could quickly overwhelm the defenders and create real disruption amongst whatever shipping was present. Nonetheless, ports such as Cherbourg, Le Havre, Dieppe and Boulogne revived quickly after a raid and remained a distinct thorn in the Allied side either as bases for attack craft or the site of coastal batteries which – in the case of Cherbourg and Le Havre – were within range of some of the invasion beaches.

Means of offering protection for these ongoing amphibious operations was vital given that over 200 supply vessels were reaching the anchorages of both the Western and Eastern Naval Task Force on a daily basis. William Tennant's two 'Mulberry Harbours' had been erected to serve the needs of both task forces and had markedly helped in this respect until a violent storm that raged for four days from 18 to 22 June destroyed the poorly built 'Mulberry A' and led to several hundred landing craft being driven ashore with destructive venom on *Omaha* beach. This unfavourable combination of massive disruption to landing supplies with great destruction of landing craft rather undermined the case for the 'Mulberries' in some naval eyes. Tennant and Ramsay were not among them. They remained convinced of their worth even though 'Mulberry A' had been poorly sited and improperly erected. After all, the whole point of these artificial constructions was that they were meant to withstand the severest of storms – as 'Mulberry B' did off *Gold* – and not collapse into a sorry heap as 'Mulberry A' had done off *Omaha*. In their eyes at least, egregious human error rather than a critical design flaw had been at the heart of the problem. One of Tennant's other responsibilities had been to oversee the creation of 'Gooseberries' – old warships that were brought close to the shore and sunk as blockships by the breakwater – so that they could provide more shelter and protection on the beaches themselves. In this way the old British target battleship *Centurion* met her inglorious but pragmatic end along with the French battleship *Courbet*, the Dutch light cruiser *Sumatra*, and the Royal Navy's old eastern warhorse, the light cruiser *Durban*, from 7 June onwards. Regardless of whether these external aids to help the disembarkation of troops and supplies worked or not, they were still much inferior to a dockside in a sheltered harbour of a port.[64]

'Mulberry A's unfortunate engineering demise brought the urgent need to acquire such a port back into focus. Both Cherbourg and Le Havre would be major assets once they could be taken, but all the while they remained in German hands their nuisance value would remain very high and their potential for claiming more victims on the invasion routes a factor that could not be lightly dismissed. Extensive attempts to knock out Cherbourg's well-protected artillery defences had not succeeded during the first fortnight after *Overlord* had been launched. Its three batteries of 11-inch (279mm) and twenty sets of 5.9-inch (150mm) guns were still in place when the Kriegsmarine moved the last of their warships out of the port during the night of 23–24 June. Until these guns were finally silenced, however, the Allies couldn't begin to use the port for their own vessels. To accelerate progress in this direction, therefore, two task groups were formed on 25 June under the overall command of Rear-Admiral Morton Deyo with the express purpose of shelling the batteries on either side of the town. He took control of Group I, containing the battleship *Nevada*, four cruisers, six destroyers and a minesweeping flotilla, and moved them into position to concentrate their firepower on the western batteries near Querqueville. Daniel Barbey was put in charge of Group II and given the task of silencing the battery 'Hamburg' south of Cap Levi on the eastern side of Cherbourg with the two battleships *Arkansas* and *Texas*, five destroyers and the obligatory minesweeping flotilla at his disposal. Neither Deyo nor Barbey had things their own way. In orchestrating the heaviest shelling since *Neptune* had begun, the Germans at Querqueville drove off the minesweepers and hit Deyo's light cruiser (*Glasgow*), while 'Hamburg' proved even more lethal in striking three of Barbey's destroyers as well as the bridge of the battleship *Texas*. Despite the pounding these batteries received from hundreds of shells, it is instructive to remember that they weren't finally silenced for another couple of days. Ultimately, Cherbourg would only be safe after Allied troops had captured it on 27 June – but even then much work had to be done to clean up the port and make its waters safe from mines and other obstructions. It would take more than two months of hard work to restore it to a fully operational state once again.[65]

Meanwhile, the Allies were forced into continuing to use the supply methods already well established in the assault sectors and on the beaches themselves. In this way by 2 July the Allies had landed 929,000 troops, 177,000 vehicles and 586,000 tons of supplies from well over 4,000 vessels ranging in size from large landing craft and troop transports to Liberty ships and small coastal shipping vessels.[66] It was a truly formidable supply operation and one that did Ramsay and his team enormous credit. Unlike some of the smaller island-hopping amphibious invasions, the attack on continental Europe was so vast an undertaking that it would need constant replenishment until the war against Nazi Germany was finally over. Protecting these convoyed supplies from German interference on a daily basis for what was likely to be months at a time would remain a taxing and much less glamorous commitment than that conjured up by the initial excitement and enthusiasm of the assault phase. Although the world of convoy was often a tiresome experience, it was still a vital undertaking that contrasted markedly with the tedium of the enterprise.

While the Allies had made a decisive move against Nazi Germany with the launching of Operation *Overlord* on 6 June, the Japanese High Command still awaited the next major American move in the Pacific, uncertain where it would actually fall but confident that once it had begun it would be repelled with devastating force somewhere within the 'Great Triangle'. When one is convinced that something is bound to happen and it doesn't, the concept of inevitability is undermined and the element of surprise takes a greater toll than it might otherwise have done. Japanese conviction that the next American attack would be in the Southwest Pacific had hardened over time and had assumed the official orthodoxy within the *Gunreibu*. When a reconnaissance flight on 10 June revealed that the Majuro atoll used by some of the US carrier groups was empty, Ozawa, in command of the First Mobile Fleet, responded by sending the two largest battleships ever built, *Musashi* and *Yamato*, southwards from Tawi

Tawi towards Biak and the northern coast of New Guinea to see what was going on. Something was obviously afoot, but without any signals or any other intelligence to go on, locating the American fleet was a far from straight forward task. Ozawa knew that only after the American carriers had been spotted could the Japanese activate Operation *A-GO* in a bid to trap them on their push southwestwards. One can imagine the sense of unease in these IJN circles, therefore, when the news that arrived in the Philippines and Japan next day did not put the American carrier force on such a route at all but 1000nm (1,852km) away in the Central Pacific carrying out raids on the islands of Guam, Saipan and Tinian in the Marianas chain.[67]

Caught unawares, both Toyoda and Ozawa wondered what on earth it could possibly mean. Was this merely a softening up before a major strike or was it a classic piece of strategic deception – a diversion to hide a movement elsewhere in a widely divorced theatre of operations? Since neither man knew for certain, they waited for confirmation of whether it was one thing or the other. Further carrier raids on all three islands on 12 and 13 June were sufficient to convince Ozawa at least that the Americans had opted to avoid targets within the 'Great Triangle' at this stage in favour of those in the Marianas. He issued an order to the warships under his command at 1727 hours on 13 June requiring them to prepare themselves for the commencement of Operation *A-GO*. This meant abandoning their deployment in the Philippines and gearing up for a decisive battle to the northeast.[68]

In a savage twist of irony, the Americans had chosen to invade the very same island – Saipan – on which Vice-Admiral Takagi had recently established the Japanese Submarine Sixth Fleet Headquarters. Takagi, like many of his peers, had thought that Palau was likely to be chosen by the Americans as the site for their next major incursion and so he had had no qualms whatsoever in moving to Saipan and using the port of Garapan as the most appropriate base for his own Advance Expeditionary Force. It was another ghastly mistake that would undermine any chance he would have of directing submarine operations in the region. It would end up with him and his staff hiding in the mountains of Saipan awaiting rescue rather than plotting some counter-attack against the shipping involved in *Forager* or the American carrier force that would be pitted against Ozawa's fleet in the Philippine Sea. Unable to be rescued, Takagi decided that it was better to die in combat than to be made a POW and with a final signal to Toyoda on 6 July he charged the American lines in a hopeless *Banzai* attack. While Takagi's fate didn't mirror that of his submarine force, there was a certain symbolism to it. Poorly positioned in any case, the submarines adopted picket lines that could be detected and effectively dealt with by enemy warships that were employing a markedly improved set of ASW techniques developed as the war had progressed. Subject to rather haphazard and uncoordinated sets of orders which did them no favours, the submarines found survival difficult. By the time Saipan fell on 9 July nine of the twenty-one submarines around the Marianas at the time of *Forager* had been sunk and four more would be destroyed before the end of the month.[69]

After the initial softening up of Guam, Saipan and Tinian from 11 June, *Forager* began in earnest three days later with a more sustained bombardment of Saipan. Spruance had given Kelly Turner's TF 52 a solid core of warships amounting to seven battleships, eight escort carriers, eleven cruisers and no less than thirty-seven destroyers to pound the Japanese defences remorselessly from both offshore and overhead throughout 14 June and set the tone for the first assault wave that would come ashore on the following morning. Assisted by these warships, two transport groups brought thirty-four attack and supply transports with two Marine divisions and four LSDs (Landing Ship Docks) onto the beaches of Saipan beginning at 0844 hours on 15 June and these were followed by many more landing craft and other vessels in the following days. In all Turner was responsible for the safety of 551 ships in this operation. It seems extraordinary that he lost none to either submarine or aircraft attacks in the initial and subsequent landings on the island. What seems incomprehensible becomes more readily understandable if one accepts that there was a marked shortfall both in the number of operational aircraft that had survived Mitcher's carrier raids over the Marianas and in trained pilots capable of flying them. Many of the latter had been lost in combat and illness had also hit many of the rest hard as well. As a result, TF 52 succeeded in putting 67,451 troops ashore under the command of General Holland M. Smith and into an uncompromising three-and-a-half-week battle with Lt. General Yoshitsuyu Saito's infantry troops and Vice-Admiral Chuichi Nagumo's naval forces who exploited both the terrain and the gap between the two American forces superbly.[70] It was a measure of the intensity of the action on Saipan that only 1,780 Japanese troops were taken prisoner out of a force of 25,591 – the rest being killed in the campaign that also took the lives of 3,426 American servicemen and injured another 13,099 Marines by the time the island was taken on 9 July. Nagumo committed suicide three days earlier when it was clear that the Japanese were going to be defeated.[71]

Receiving news of the first landings on Saipan, Admiral Toyoda wasted no time in ordering the Combined Fleet to activate Operation *A-GO* and seek the decisive battle with the Americans. Shortly afterwards, at 0900 hours he repeated the signal that his illustrious predecessor, Admiral Togo, had used before the Battle of Tsushima Strait in May 1905: 'The rise and fall of Imperial Japan depends on this one battle. Every man shall do his utmost.'[72] When battle was joined four days later, however, the same dashing success that Togo had achieved against the Russians some thirty-nine years before would not be savoured by Ozawa. In truth, the parallels between the decrepit fleet that Togo faced and the formidable striking force that Ozawa would line up against on 19 June – Marc Mitscher's TF 58 – were utterly misplaced. TF 58 consisted of seven fleet carriers, eight light carriers, seven battleships, eight heavy cruisers, thirteen light cruisers and fifty-nine destroyers. It also possessed twice as many carrier aircraft as that under Ozawa's command (over 900 to the 450 the Japanese carried with them) and in the Hellcat the Americans had a faster, if less manoeuvrable but far better armed and protected, air frame than the 'Zero' it was up against. If that wasn't sufficient an advantage, the American fighter pilots were generally more experienced than their Japanese counterparts, while the skill level of their bomber pilots also exceeded that of their opponents who had lost so many of their first-rate pilots in the war. They were now forced to rely upon those who couldn't really make the most of their demanding Yokusuka Suisei dive-bomber (known by the Allies as a 'Judy') and the Nakajima Tenzan torpedo-bomber (referred to by the Americans as a 'Jill'). Against this concentrated mass of firepower, Ozawa divided his own forces into three main groups. In the Vanguard and under Vice-Admiral Takeo Kurita's command were three light carriers, four battleships, four heavy cruisers and eight destroyers led by the light cruiser *Noshiro*. In the main body of the fleet, Carrier Group A, Ozawa was to be found in his flagship the fleet carrier *Taihō*, with two other carriers (*Shokaku* and *Zuikaku*), veterans of earlier naval battles, in attendance. Rounding out the group were a couple of heavy cruisers and six destroyers led by the light cruiser *Yahagi*. In Carrier Group B Rear-Admiral Takaji Joshima had the two converted carriers *Hiyō* and *Jun'yō*, the old training carrier *Ryūhō*, the battleship *Nagato*, the heavy cruiser *Mogami*, along with seven destroyers. Supporting the entire fleet were a total of six tankers including the *Hayasui*, which was designed as a modern fleet tanker with seaplane carrier potential, and six destroyer escorts formed into two uneven groups. While some of Ozawa's warships, most notably his own flagship, were fine vessels, the aggregate sum of the individual parts was simply not the match of Mitscher's TF 58 either in terms of quantity or quality.[73]

While the Japanese were still capable of doing massive damage with their carrier aircraft, Spruance, the Commander of the 5th Fleet, and Mitscher, his Task Force commander, flying their flags in the *Indianapolis* and the *Lexington* respectively, held the whip hand not least because they were the beneficiaries of a sophisticated and integrated system of fighter control that far exceeded anything their enemy possessed. From the outstandingly effective 'SC' and 'SK' radars that could pick up objects at anything from 60 to 100nm (85 to 111km), height information would be supplied from 'SM' radars, and surface approach radars ('SG' and 'Mk1 Eyeball') could detect low-level attack formations. All of this information was relayed to Combat Information Centers where enemy raids were plotted and the details passed on to a Fighter Direction Officer (FDO) at the heart of the task force and to others who were present in each one of the five task groups of TF 58. This enabled the task force to operate either as a coordinated whole or as a set of independent groups depending upon the situation it faced. Armed with this crucial information, the FDOs could vector in their combat air patrols to intercept the enemy planes many miles away from the American carriers. It was a superbly efficient system built upon technology that rarely let them down and an experienced staff who knew what they were supposed to do and did it repeatedly.[74]

Spruance knew from the submarine reports he had been receiving from 15 June onwards that Ozawa was on the move.[75] Being the cautious man he was and not wanting to be duped by his opposite number, Spruance opted to keep TF 58 positioned west of Tinian so as to ensure that his ships would straddle

Ozawa's path and prevent him from falling upon TF 52 and the troops Turner's ships had disgorged onto Saipan. Although he had received a report from the submarine *Cavalla* just before 0400 hours on the 18th confirming that she had found fifteen vessels of Ozawa's 1st Mobile Fleet some 800nm (1,482km) WSW of Saipan at midnight. Spruance wondered whether it was some kind of decoy force set up to lure him away from the Marianas while the rest of the main fleet, lurking elsewhere, would strike at the denuded invasion fleet. As a result, he didn't approve Mitscher's request that he should immediately set off in hot pursuit of the enemy in the hope of closing the Japanese position before nightfall. Mitscher thought that if his planes found Ozawa they would also find Kurita in close attendance. His plan was typically aggressive and rested on the possibility of launching a carrier attack in the late afternoon or early evening. Neither Spruance nor Lee wished to quit the waters off Saipan for a high speed chase after a dubious quarry and both were far from enthusiastic about engaging in a confrontation in the dark with an enemy who had mastered the tactics of night fighting. Mitscher (known throughout the USN as 'Bald Eagle') and his fellow aviators were grievously disappointed with Spruance's 'safety first' tactics. Spruance opted on this occasion for caution and consolidation over risk. He thought the Japanese were capable of duplicitous action and didn't wish to fall into a trap of their making. Consequently, he waited for further confirmation of where the enemy was before planning his next move.[76]

Mitscher's attacking instincts were by now thoroughly roused and when *Cavalla* radioed in at 0730 hours to say that the Japanese warships she had seen at midnight were by now 700nm (1296km) from Saipan and closing, he returned to plead his case for aggressive action. Mitscher proposed yet again a high speed chase to the southwest to get within a carrier strike of the enemy before nightfall and wished to commit Lee's battle group to a surface action as the night proceeded. Spruance was unconvinced by this strategy and preferred to play a waiting game. He sensed that the various elements of the Japanese fleet would be bound eventually to seek him out and he wanted to be in a strong position to deal with them when they did. As a result, Mitscher's request was turned down once more in favour of preserving a consolidated shield for Turner's amphibious fleet at Saipan and running aerial sweeps to the westward to try to locate the various elements of the Japanese fleet that had come out to contest the invasion of the Marianas. A kind of cat and mouse duel proceeded as both sides stalked the other on 18 June. In the middle of the afternoon Ozawa finally received the first reconnaissance reports specifying the location of Mitscher's carriers. He decided to keep out of range for the time being and surprise them with a massive raid the next day. Although American reconnaissance aircraft were unable to establish the whereabouts of the Japanese fleet, Nimitz sent a signal at 2230 hours reporting that a shore-based DF station had managed to get a fix on the enemy flagship from a signal communication that Ozawa had made to Guam. It put him roughly 350nm (648km) from TF 58 and conformed with *Cavalla*'s report of the estimated course and speed of the Japanese force. Mitscher once again sought to change course, close the Japanese during the rest of the night and seek action at first light on the following day. Spruance once again demurred not knowing whether the Japanese fleet was concentrated or divided, and uneasy about quitting what he saw as his primary responsibility to protect Turner's fleet. So to the maximum frustration of the naval aviators, Spruance decided to wait for corroboration of the DF report. He might have granted Mitscher's wish had he received the report issued at 0115 hours from a USN patrol bomber flying boat indicating a radar fix on Kurita's fleet close to the DF location. This radio signal wasn't picked up and so the waiting continued. At first light on 19 June Mitscher sent off his combat air patrols to locate the enemy carriers and Ozawa opted for a similar response sending forty-three planes airborne at 0600 hours to discover the latest whereabouts of TF 58.[77]

At 0730 hours Ozawa began receiving the information he sought and preparations for the launching of his carrier planes against the three US carrier groups located about 300–380nm (556–704km) away were immediately put in hand. Instead of sending his planes against them in one or two huge waves, however, Ozawa was soon to discover that one of his subordinate commanders, Rear-Admiral Sueo Obayashi, had pre-empted him by unilaterally sending off two 'Kate' pathfinders at 0800 hours followed by a mixed force of seventy planes drawn from his three light carriers *Chitose*, *Chiyoda* and *Zuihō* some twenty-five minutes later.[78] Ozawa's three carriers in Group A (*Shokaku*, *Taihō* and *Zuikaku*) eventually flew off 131 planes at 0856 hours, and Joshima's three carriers in Group B (*Hiyō*, *Jun'yō* and *Ryūhō*) got theirs airborne a little later. In all 374 aircraft were finally committed to the attack on the American carriers. Picked up on radar while still at great distance from TF 58, each of the four waves of attacking planes was successively confronted by a superior force of Hellcats which cut most of them to pieces. Of those that got beyond the US fighter screen to attack the warships beyond it, one registered a bomb hit on the battleship *South Dakota*, a torpedo-bomber actually crashed into the side of the battleship *Indiana* wiping out the plane but not the capital ship, while two others managed near-misses on the carriers *Bunker Hill* and *Wasp* as well as the heavy cruiser *Minneapolis*. This was the extent of their success, however, since most of the planes that had eluded the Hellcats were then subject to withering A.A. fire from the ships. While the Americans lost a total of thirty-one fighter planes in these sorties on 19 June, the Japanese lost 244 carrier planes in the four raids on TF 58, and somewhere between thirty and forty-nine more planes on Guam. Twenty-two other carrier planes would be lost when the US submarines *Albacore* and *Cavalla* entered the act by torpedoing and crippling the carriers *Shokaku* and Ozawa's flagship *Taihō* respectively. Both carriers exploded and sank during the afternoon carrying 2,913 of their officers and crew down with them. Ozawa and his close staff were not among them. They had been transferred in stages to the heavy cruiser *Haguro* once it had become clear that the carrier could no longer function as the nerve centre of the fleet and was, in fact, living on borrowed time. So ended a day in which the art of the counter-attack had decisively prevailed. It would henceforth be known rather irreverently in the annals of the Pacific war as 'The Great Marianas Turkey Shoot'.[79]

Unaware for many hours of the scale of his own losses, Ozawa still remained convinced that his carrier force had inflicted severe damage upon the Americans – a distorted opinion shared by his C-in-C Admiral Toyoda – and both were more than willing to take on the enemy again once their own carriers had been refuelled and the 1st Mobile Fleet had shed its damaged warships and redeployed others for further training. Wishful thinking and staggering overconfidence gripped both men as plans were developed for what they erroneously assumed would be a mopping-up exercise against their battered opponents on 22 June. Mitscher and Spruance had other ideas and were more in tune with objective reality. There was no reason for them to wait for two days to accomplish the next stage of their operation against the Japanese and scouting missions were dispatched early on 20 June to try to discover the location of the wounded foe. It was mid-afternoon before two groups of Ozawa's fleet were spotted more than 200nm (370km) from TF 58. Mitscher was all for tackling the enemy even though at such distance his planes could not afford to dwell over the target but would have to release their pay loads and then head for home immediately in order to have just enough fuel to get back to their carriers. At 1605 hours the enemy's estimated position was revised putting them even further away and at the extreme range of Mitscher's planes. Supported by Spruance, he decided that the risks were worthwhile. His own carriers turned into the wind at 1621 hours and began flying off 226 aircraft shortly thereafter. Once they had cleared the decks, Mitscher turned his ships back to the west and made speed to cut the gap between them and the 1st Mobile Fleet to try to give his pilots a platform to land on when they returned from the attack on Ozawa's warships.[80]

By this time Ozawa had transferred his flag to the *Zuikaku*, and it was on this carrier at 1715 hours that he learnt from one of his own reconnaissance planes that the Americans were in more formidable shape than he had previously supposed. Reckoning that his ships were now vulnerable to a renewed carrier thrust, Ozawa ordered his fleet onto the defensive at 1754 hours and nine minutes later they began picking up a radar trace of a wave of approaching planes. Before the American planes got to the *Zuikaku*, some had fastened upon the oil tankers hitting two so badly that they eventually had to be scuttled and damaging the seaplane carrier *Hayasui* into the bargain. Then it was turn of the denuded Carrier Group A to feel the wrath of the American pilots. Although struck many times by bombs and in a fiery and unstable condition, the *Zuikaku* was saved by her crew's timely damage control efforts. A well directed torpedo could have meant the end for the struggling carrier, but the flight wing had already used theirs with damaging effect against the battleship *Haruna* and the heavy cruiser *Maya* and there were no surplus ones available to finish her off. Another flight wing took on Carrier Group B attacking all three carriers. *Jun'yō*, the flagship of Rear-Admiral Joshima, was bombed twice and received no less than six near-misses, whereas *Ryūhō*, protected to some extent by *Nagato*'s 16-inch (406mm) guns, only received one near-miss. *Hiyō*, however, was not so fortunate receiving two massive torpedo hits that wrecked her hull, stopped her dead in the water and ultimately led to her fiery end a couple of hours later. Other attacks on the warships of Kurita's former Vanguard concentrated on the light carrier *Chiyoda* and the battleship *Haruna*, both of which were hit several times and received several near-misses, but even so they and the heavy cruiser *Maya* somehow avoided the fate of the *Hiyō* – the only ship to sink as a result of this series of attacks. Once again, however, the main Japanese casualties were their carrier aircraft. Another sixty-five were destroyed in the afternoon's attacks, leaving a mere thirty-five for use by Ozawa's entire fleet thereafter. It was manifestly obvious that the 1st Mobile Fleet was in a dire state; three of its nine carriers and over 300 planes and their aircrews had been forfeited without denting the US 5th Fleet at all. There were no crumbs of comfort for the stunned Ozawa and Toyoda as they had to come to terms with the fact that the carrier fleet, as they had known it, had been consigned to history. What was left of it was incapable any longer of prosecuting a forward policy in the Pacific. While the Battle of the Philippine Sea marked the end of an era, it had a sting in the tail for the Americans as well. Apart from the nineteen carrier planes that were lost in combat in these final raids, another eighty perished as they tried to make their way back to TF 58 as the evening of 20 June drew on, either running out of fuel and being forced to land in the sea or crashing on the illuminated decks of the carriers and in some cases attempting to do so on other warships as well. Amazingly, only sixteen pilots and thirty-three air crew lost their lives in these hair-raising exploits. Although both Mitscher and Ozawa were still inclined to press ahead with some of their forces during the night in an effort to continue grappling with the enemy, neither had the final say in the matter. Before midnight on 20 June Toyoda finally ordered what was left of the 1st Mobile Fleet to withdraw from the scene and steam northwestwards to Okinawa putting as many miles as possible between it and TF 58 during the hours of darkness. Spruance's caution returned to stifle Mitscher's plans to take any further initiative. In his eyes, a famous victory had already been won, so why should he jeopardise it by adopting a risky nighttime strategy? By the time dawn appeared and he was finally prepared to leave Kelly Turner's vulnerable transports exposed to external threats in order to pursue Ozawa's forces, the Japanese were forging ahead through the Pacific towards the Ryukyu Islands and out of harm's way. Spruance had missed a golden opportunity to strike an even bigger blow against the IJN than had already been achieved in the Philippine Sea over the course of the last few days. It was a decision he would come to rue for the rest of his life. He had chosen the conservative option. While it was perfectly defensible on the grounds that he had preserved the fleet for the long, arduous slog ahead of it in the Marianas, the overwhelming suspicion is that on this occasion a bolder strategy would have been a better option in a calculated bid to put the wounded enemy to the sword. Once again, it was a question of what might have been rather than what was.[81]

While the Axis Powers were reeling from these two body blows, there was other disquieting news to absorb on the European war front. Allied troops had seized control of Rome late on 4 June – the first of the Axis capitals to fall – and had pressed on towards the northern Apennines in the days thereafter in the hope that their defensive nemesis, Feldmarschall Alfred Kesselring, would be unable to complete his plans for northern Italy before the US 5th Army and the British 8th Army would be upon them. Although substantial progress was made by them with Florence (Firenze) and the River Arno being reached by the end of July, Kesselring still had sufficient time to organise his forces in such a way as to delay the Allies an easy advance up the rest of the peninsula and into the heart of Europe.

Following the fall of Rome, Allied naval units under Rear-Admiral Troubridge began to snipe at various targets in the northern Tyrrhenian Sea and ports along the Ligurian coast. Using shallow draught vessels to circumvent German mine barrages in the waters off Elba on 17 June, the Senegalese riflemen of the French 9th Colonial Division did the rest and had secured the island within two days. Shortly thereafter a small group of Anglo-Italian saboteurs entered the harbour of La Spezia at night and laid charges that finally destroyed the heavy cruiser *Bolzano* which was being repaired at the time. Four days later another Anglo-Italian chariot raid into La Spezia led to the blowing up of *Gorizia*, the last of the Zara class heavy cruisers, the rest of which had perished at Matapan three years before.[82]

June also witnessed a creeping Soviet penetration of both shores of the Gulf of Finland in which all three services were involved. This led to their seizure of the offshore islands of Narvi and Koivisto on 22–23 June. Using fast light forces, such as torpedo cutters, backed up with fire support by older heavy units like the battleship *Oktyabrskaya Revolyutsiya*, the Soviets forced the reluctant but overwhelmed Finns to evacuate both places. Having expelled them, the Soviets had no intention of letting either them or their German friends return. By shoring up the defences of their newly acquired territories and exploiting the tactical weaknesses of their opponents, they were able to repulse a series of enemy Commando raids in the Narva Bay. Furthermore, by attacking Axis shipping wherever it could be found throughout the Gulf and in the Estonian and Finnish harbours they used, the Soviets began to tighten their grip relentlessly on the eastern Baltic despite the presence of thirteen U-boats in the area.[83]

While developments elsewhere were disquieting, the threat posed by the establishment of the Allied armies in Normandy was so grave that the Germans were bound to focus much of their efforts on resisting it. This meant that all along the Channel coast from Normandy to the Dutch border their light forces were engaged in a constant nightly battle against similar units deployed by the Allies.[84] Supply convoys and their destroyer escorts were, of course, fair game for both sides, but neither combatant scored much more than a few isolated successes against this type of protected shipping. As an alternative, the German Kleinkampfverband (Small Battle Unit or K-Verband for short) established originally at Timmersdorfer Strand near Lübeck under Konteradmiral Helmuth Heye came into its own. They began using a force of twenty-six Marder one-man submersibles (slightly larger than the original Neger craft of the same type) from their forward operational base at Villers-sur-Mer in early July to attack the supply traffic off the assault beaches. While they sank and damaged a handful of smaller warships, they sustained such an appalling rate of attrition in doing so that the K-Verband were obliged to leave things up to the Luftwaffe and its new circling torpedo the 'T3d *Dackel*' (*Dachshund*) to try to take a toll of the Allied shipping off the Normandy beaches.[85] Some success was achieved but how much was due to the *Dackel* and how much to mines is difficult to judge. What is known is that in the period between 7 August and 11 September only a hospital ship and a balloon ship were sunk, the transport *Iddesleigh* was beached and eight other vessels, including the seaplane carrier *Albatross* and the old cruiser *Frobisher*, were damaged by underwater explosions with mines being the likely cause for most of these seemingly random hits. Further Marder attacks were made in mid-August, but apart from hitting the old French battleship *Courbet* which had already been sunk as a blockship, and sinking a freighter and a landing craft, the losses of Marder just kept mounting up. Seven out of fourteen committed on 15–16 August never returned and only sixteen came back of forty-two that left Villers-sur-Mer on the following night. A new one-man midget submarine – the Biber – was introduced at the end of the month but as the original operational base slated for their use – Le Havre – was overrun, Korvettenkapitän Hans Bartels moved them to the port of Fécamp. After an inconclusive operation in bad weather on 29–30 August from which they all returned, Bartels was forced to abandon the port and destroy most of the Biber craft too. In so doing, the K-Verband's operations off Normandy came to an inglorious end.[86]

Dönitz hoped that his *schnorchel* U-boats would do much more damage than that achieved by the willing but not wildly successful K-Verband, but by the end of August the record showed that this too was a case of wishful thinking. Although fourteen Allied vessels were sunk in the Channel and four more were torpedoed, the cost was prohibitively high; twenty-four U-boats had been sunk by a combination of mines, destroyer escorts, Search Groups, and accompanying aircraft, and two more had been damaged sufficiently to be forced out of action and into Le Havre and Boulogne for repairs. If ever there was a time for the development of the 'Alberich' U-boats with their Oppanol rubber coating to combat Asdic it was now. *U480*'s trials in August showed that the results were indeed promising, but without this type of masking the *schnorchel* boats were cruelly exposed everywhere they operated. Reduced to being not much more than an irritant in the Channel, they were rendered so ineffective in the Mediterranean that by the middle of September they had been withdrawn from there too.[87]

All things considered, June had been a bad month for the Axis and the rest of the summer didn't improve. In July attention shifted once more to the Pacific with preparations for the invasion of both Guam and Tinian in the Marianas. By now there was no mystery attached to the American plans at all. Several task groups belonging to TF 58 poured thousands of shells onto Guam with impunity from virtually the beginning of July onwards knowing there was little or nothing that the Japanese could do to prevent them from doing so.[88] Tinian had also come under sustained assault from US Army groups on Saipan from 20 June and was also obviously an invasion target. In these fraught days for the military major changes were being made in Japanese government circles in Tokyo. Both General Tōjō Hideki, who had held the portfolios of premier, minister of war and CAGS, and Admiral Shimada Shigetarō, who had been the Navy minister and CNGS for three years, had not survived the disaster in the Philippine Sea. Pressure had mounted on both of them. Shimada, who was highly idiosyncratic and much disliked, was certainly expendable, but Tōjō was a different proposition altogether. Even so, two days after relieving Shimada of his duties, Tōjō was forced to resign as well (19 July). He had been unable to resist the call for a change of government. It was the end of an era. Shimada's position was eventually given to Admiral Oikawa Koshirō, but more authority ended up in the lap of Admiral Toyoda who would eventually assume Oikawa's position as CNGS on 29 May 1945. Toyoda, unlike some of the politicians and members of the Navy ministry, was not inclined to take the peace route. This meant that an element of tension grew perceptibly between those factions who believed the war was already lost and those who were determined to keep it alive. It did nothing to assist the overall Japanese cause and, lacking true consensus, Japanese naval policy continued to stagger forward along the same old path it had taken for the past two years since its progress in the Pacific had been initially stalled by the Battle of the Coral Sea and reversed by that of Midway.[89]

Two days after Tōjō's fall and three days before Harry Hill and TF 52 put 15,614 troops of the 2nd and 4th Marine Divisions ashore on Tinian (24 July), Richard Conolly and TF 53 had brought the III Amphibious Corps ashore at two points on the west coast of Guam. Thirty-two assorted landing craft had been escorted to the area west of Agana, while another thirty disgorged their troops under cover of their destroyer escorts further south near the coastal town of Agat. Some 54,891 troops were landed in these two spots under cover of their twenty-one destroyer escorts and with fire support coming from a host of battleships, cruisers and destroyers. Air support was present in the shape of five escort carriers together with Mitscher's carrier planes from TF 58 who had joined in too. Confronting them were roughly 19,000 Japanese infantry troops who were determined to hold on to Guam whatever the odds facing them. Once again intense fighting took place before the island was wrested from their hold. In the three weeks it took to gain control of much of Guam, the Americans lost 1,435 of their troops dead or missing and had another 5,648 servicemen injured, whereas the Japanese dead amounted to 10,693. Another ninety-eight were captured, but the rest of their forces retreated into the jungle and became guerilla fighters – the last one being finally discovered in 1972 quite oblivious to the fact that the war had been over for twenty-seven years.[90]

Before the V Amphibious Corps landed on Tinian and were pitched into yet another bloodbath in the Central Pacific, James Somerville had taken his reinforced Eastern Fleet out into the Indian Ocean from Trincomalee to carry out yet another raid on an important Japanese air base on the island of Sabang off the northern coast of the Sumatran province of Aceh. Rich in oil, the massive island of Sumatra was desperately important to the Japanese military machine, so anything that the Eastern Fleet could do to disrupt both on and offshore production and its distribution through the narrow Strait of Malacca would be useful for the Allies. One means of doing just that was to try to remove the air cover for the oil industry provided by the Japanese planes based at Sabang. Somerville had tackled the same target with a far smaller squadron just prior to the commencement of Operation *Forager* in June. On that earlier occasion it had been more of a diversionary affair than a full-blooded operation, but Operation *Crimson* was an entirely different affair. Armed with two carriers (*Illustrious* and *Victorious*), four battleships (*Queen Elizabeth, Renown, Richelieu* and *Valiant*), a heavy cruiser (*Cumberland*), six light cruisers and ten destroyers, Somerville had the means to make a mess of the air base and the harbour installations and wreck any vessels found sheltering there. Thirty-four Corsairs were flown off to attack the airfields and destroy or scatter any enemy planes in the vicinity. Once this raid had been completed early on the morning of 25 July, the bombardment group came into its own, saturating the shoreline and the harbour in an effort to knock out the coastal batteries with the following weight of shot: 294 × 15-inch (381mm), 134 × 8-inch (203mm), 324 × 6-inch (152mm), roughly 500 × 5-inch (127mm) and 123 × 4-inch (102mm). If Sabang's defenders managed to survive that onslaught, there was more to come from close quarters. *Tromp* and three destroyers entered the harbour and pumped in another 208 × 6-inch (152mm), 717 × 5-inch (127mm) and 668 × 4-inch (102mm) shells along with eight torpedoes to add to the general destruction on the dockside. Despite the punishment they had received, the stoical Japanese gunners managed to get in some blows of their own: *Tromp* received four hits and two of the destroyers were each hit once. While the two sides traded blows, a Japanese air raid that had been homing in on the Eastern Fleet was broken up with seven of the ten enemy planes being shot down for the loss of two Corsairs. While *Crimson* may have been an emphatic statement by Somerville and the Eastern Fleet, it was merely the beginning of a long running series of operations against Sumatra. Each month from then onwards the Allies would mount a carrier-based operation against the Sumatran oil fields – *Boomerang* and *Banquet* in August; *Light* in September; *Millet* in October; *Outflank* in November and *Robson* in December – while deploying a number of submarines in the busy Strait of Malacca where they could hardly go wrong. Somerville was not at the helm for the other tilts at Japanese power in the region. He struck his flag on 23 August and proceeded to Washington, D.C., to be the Admiralty's voice with the Roosevelt administration and his place at the head of the Eastern Fleet was taken by Admiral Sir Bruce Fraser, whose exploits against the *Scharnhorst* at the North Cape had done his long-term promotion prospects no harm at all.[91]

Although it hadn't taken a genius to work out that the Americans would roll up the other main islands in the Marianas to give them the air bases necessary to strike at the Ryukyu island chain that lay in their path to the Japanese mainland itself, the question of where their amphibious forces might strike next was not so obvious. By the time that the bloody battle for Tinian had been resolved in the Americans' favour on 1 August, they had also occupied three offshore islands further along the New Guinea coast in the Southwest Pacific: Noemfoor on

2 July and those of Amsterdam and Middelburg (Operation *Globe Trotter*) at the end of the month.[92] These acquisitions suggested that the next major amphibious undertaking might be either further westward to the Moluccan islands of Halmahera or Morotai, or to the northwest to Palau which could then be used as a very convenient naval base for an all-out invasion of the Philippines in the months to come. This was where the Japanese hoped to be able to do such damage to the American cause that it would stall their momentum and make them begin to question the cost of continuing the war. This was the basis of their planning for Operation *SHO* (*Victory*) which they were determined to unleash just at the very moment when they judged the Americans would be concentrating upon putting their troops ashore in the Philippines and therefore at their most vulnerable.[93] While it was inconceivable for MacArthur and the Americans to forgo an attack on the Philippines ultimately, Chester Nimitz wanted to keep the Japanese guessing about their immediate plans. For this reason, he continued to orchestrate carrier raids on Palau and the closest islands scattered to its northeast, namely, Ngulu, Ulithi, Sorol, Tais and Yap, but he also sent his task forces to the east to operate against Wake Island in the Central Pacific and much further north to pound the islands of Iwo Jima and Chichi Jima in the Volcano and Bonin Island chains.[94]

While the Japanese agonised about where the Americans would go next, the Germans needed no such clairvoyance since they were simultaneously confronted by advancing Allied armies on several fronts across the European theatre. As the Western armies consolidated their position in Normandy and were poised to break out eastwards towards Paris, the Soviet Red Army had reached the eastern bank of the River Vistula opposite the Polish capital of Warsaw on 1 August. While on the Southern Front the Allied advance up the Italian peninsula had been halted temporarily at the Arno, yet another invasion beckoned in the south of France. Preparations for this latest amphibious undertaking – previously referred to as Operation *Anvil* but subsequently altered to *Dragoon* because the Allies feared that the original codename had been compromised – had been long in the works.[95] After suffering a postponement of several weeks because of the demands and rigours of *Overlord*, eventually the troop and supply convoys along with the attack and support forces that had been gathered together for *Dragoon* began leaving the ports of Brindisi, Malta, Naples, Oran, Palermo and Taranto in stages from 9 to 13 August. Joining them in the Mediterranean as they homed in on the Côte d'Azur were a collection of forty-nine destroyers and destroyer escorts, two corvettes, five sloops and a number of other supporting craft. Bombing raids on Toulon which had been conducted by the USAAF in recent months had rather undermined its effectiveness as a U-boat sanctuary. After a raid by 233 B-24 bombers on 5 July only one of the eight U-boats berthed there remained operational and when the dose was repeated on 6 August four of those previously extensively damaged were destroyed altogether. Before the five task forces assigned to *Dragoon* reached their landing sectors just before dawn on 15 August, 1,300 land-based aircraft had begun their bombing runs all along the coastline between the large naval base of Toulon and the opulent Riviera port of Cannes. As part of the first assault wave 396 troop transport aircraft were scheduled to drop 5,000 parachutists from the 1st Airborne Task Force into the district of Le Muy as dawn broke so that they could take the high ground positions behind Fréjus and Ste. Raphaël and prevent the Germans from securing them and pouring shells on the disembarking troops as they waded ashore on the assault beaches. Although the pathfinders were actually dropped in the wrong place, the rest of the transport pilots found their way to the correct dropping zones and 85% of the force landed as planned and achieved their objectives in thwarting German designs to the extent that by the end of the first day their efforts had helped to make *Dragoon* an outstanding amphibious operation.[96]

While the parachute drops were proceeding, Vice-Admiral Kent Hewitt oversaw the amphibious operation from his headquarters flagship *Catoctin*. Using infantry troops redeployed from the US 5th Army in Italy and a large collection of shipping drawn from several Allied sources that Churchill would have preferred to have used elsewhere in the Eastern Mediterranean, Hewitt's naval commanders brought a large body of American and French troops ashore in four spots along the Riviera coastline.[97] Air support came from the 216 fighter aircraft on board nine escort carriers which were divided into two task groups to cover both the western and eastern landing sites. Rear-Admiral Troubridge, in command of TF 88, also had four light cruisers, thirteen destroyers (including one sporting the family name of *Troubridge*) and six minelayers to protect his carriers. Despite expressing serious reservations about the unnecessary nature of *Dragoon* and the strategic repercussions it might have on the Allied campaign in Italy, the British prime minister was nonetheless on hand in the afternoon of the first day to see the Allied troops going ashore in the south of France in a largely untroubled way.[98] Losses were kept to a minimum with only eight vessels associated with the landing being destroyed – seven by mines and one by a glider bomb – and eighteen landing craft damaged by static beach defences, mines or by gunfire. When one considers that 881 assault craft and 1,370 other smaller boats were involved in the operation the material cost of opening up a second land front in France was remarkably negligible. After the first three full days of the operation a total of 86,575 troops had been landed along with 12,250 vehicles and 46,140 tons of supplies. From then onwards the numbers soared. By 25 September the figures had reached 324,069 troops, 68,419 vehicles and 490,237 tons of supplies.[99]

As the Allies consolidated their position in the south of France with the capture of Cannes, Marseilles and Toulon before the end of the month, the situation in the northwest was also extremely promising for them. After breaking through the German lines near Avranches at the southwest foot of the Cotentin Peninsula at the end of July, the American troops had made swift progress towards the Atlantic ports of Brest, Lorient and St. Nazaire, cutting them off by 13 August – the very day that the city of Nantes on the River Loire was taken. As they advanced overland, the Allies also made some progress at sea sending Support Groups of warships, usually consisting of four or five destroyers with a light cruiser, to penetrate into the Bay of Biscay in an effort to seek and destroy Axis vessels plying out of the Atlantic ports of St. Nazaire and Nantes, and those that could be found further south along the coast past the Ile d'Yeu, Les Sables d'Olonne, La Pallice and La Rochelle, as far as Royan and Le Verdon-sur-Mer on either side of the Gironde estuary and up the river to Pauillac and Bordeaux. While these sweeps didn't net a vast number of enemy vessels, they were at least illustrative of the loss of French coastal waters to the Germans. Air attacks over these and other bases, such as Lorient and Brest, as well as the Channel port of St. Malo, were numerically more successful. Faced with the necessity of evacuating one port after the other, the German forces resorted to scuttling their mercantile vessels. At Nantes, for example, they destroyed six tankers, two freighters and a passenger ship (82,248 tons) and many smaller fry on 10–11 August and blew up eight warships and two more tankers that were either unfinished or non-operational at that time. At Bordeaux in addition to the usual victims, there were three U-boats, a destroyer and twenty-one merchant vessels totalling 70,720 tons.[100]

On the ground the pressure that had been mounting on the German positions around Le Havre had reached the point by 23 August that an evacuation of the port could no longer be delayed. During that night the 15th Patrol Boat Flotilla began to escort twenty-three of the German ships that would be needed elsewhere from Le Havre to Dieppe and onward to Boulogne-sur-Mer. Although small-scale supply missions to Le Havre were still carried out at some cost to itself by the 8th Gun Carrier Flotilla, more vessels would be spirited away from the naval base during the nights of 27–28 August and 29–30 August to Fécamp and on around the Channel coast and through the Strait of Dover to the Dutch border and beyond. By the beginning of September an exposed Le Havre could hardly hold out for much longer and the impetus given by the pounding its defenders received from the battleship *Warspite* and the monitor *Erebus* on 10 September and the 807 tons of bombs dropped by the RAF on the city the very next day certainly helped to convince those sheltering there to do the sensible thing and surrender on 12 September. Paris had already fallen more than a fortnight before (25 August); Lyons and Brussels had been liberated on 3 September; followed by Antwerp and Ghent respectively on the next two days. By the time that the Allied armies met in Burgundy on 11 September, the success of *Neptune/Overlord* and the *Dragoon* operations could not be doubted. Hitler's troops had already lost much of France and Belgium and those that held out in key ports, such as Calais and Dunkirk, were isolated, encircled and given little opportunity to escape.[101]

Notes

1 Rohwer, *Chronology*, p.299.
2 H.P. Willmott, *Grave of a dozen schemes: British naval planning and the war against Japan, 1943–1945* (Annapolis, Md: NIP, 1996), pp.151–85.
3 Another eighteen destroyers would be sent to join the Eastern Fleet in early March 1944. Rohwer, *Chronology*, p, 299.

4 Willmott, *Grave of a dozen schemes*, pp.58–59, 64, 85, 92, 103, 116, 147–48, 166; Rohwer, *Chronology*, pp.299–300; Donald Macintyre, *Fighting admiral: the life and battles of Admiral of the Fleet Sir James Somerville, G.C.B., G.G.E., D.S.O.* (London: Evans Bros., 1961), p.245.
5 Blair, *Hitler's U-boat war: hunted*, pp.478–82; *Fuehrer conferences*, pp.376–83.
6 *Schnorchel* itself was neither new nor invented by Professor Walter. It was first designed by the Dutch Kaptein-luitenant J.Wichers in 1927. It was a pipe device attached to a submarine that could be raised just above the waves while the submarine remained submerged. Its purpose was to draw in fresh air to operate its diesel engines without having to run on the surface of the sea for extended periods. When the Germans took over Den Helder, the main Dutch naval base, in May 1940, they found two submarines which had been fitted with this type of apparatus called a *snuiver*. Four more *snuiver*-equipped submarines escaped to the UK, but neither the Germans nor the British immediately recognised what a boon this gear was for the submarine. Professor Walter was the first to see its potential and by the beginning of 1944 all the main types of U-boat were being fitted with the device. Dan Van der Dat, *The Atlantic campaign: the great struggle at sea 1939–1945* (London: Hodder & Stoughton, 1988), pp.346–48, 351, 369, 373–79; Padfield, *War beneath the sea*, pp.374, 424–31; Mark C. Jones, 'Give credit where credit is due: the Dutch role in the development and deployment of the submarine schnorchel', *The Journal of Military History*, 69, No.4 (Oct. 2005): 987–1012; www.Uboat.net/technical/ schnorchel_fitted.htm (accessed 8 Nov. 2007).
7 To be fair, the Soviets were unable to do any better in their quest to batter the German convoy traffic on the Polar Coast. Despite utilising the air force of the Northern Fleet for reconnaissance duties and deploying a mix of destroyers, patrol cutters and submarines against this shipping over a three-week period, only one ship succumbed. Rohwer, *Chronology*, p.300; Woodman, *Arctic convoys*, pp.376–86.
8 In addition to the two merchantmen (8,891 tons) that they sunk, the U-boats also eliminated a destroyer, a frigate and a sloop. Apart from the high loss rate inflicted upon the wolf packs, four more U-boats were damaged in these exchanges and another (*U972*) went missing before she could join up with *Rügen* wolf pack. Rohwer, *Chronology*, pp.294–95, 298, 304.
9 Ibid., pp.298, 302, 304; Blair, *Hitler's U-boat war: hunted*, pp.486–501.
10 Rohwer, *Chronology*, pp.294–98, 301–2, 304; O'Hara, *German fleet at war*, pp.173–75.
11 Gilbert, *Churchill, VII*, pp.619–20, 623–25, 628, 630–31, 636–37, 640, 650–51, 653, 656.
12 Apart from the works already cited, there are numerous other sources that refer to Operation *Shingle* and the Anzio episode of the Italian campaign. See Eric Linklater, *The campaign in Italy* (London: HMSO, 1977), pp.184–209; Strawson, *Italian campaign*, pp.140–63; Raleigh Trevelyan, *Rome '44: the battle for the Eternal City* (London: Secker & Warburg, 1981); Peter Verney, *Anzio 1944: an unexpected fury* (London: Batsford, 1978).
13 Gilbert, *Churchill, VII*, pp.661–64, 666–68, 678–81, 694–96, 704, 706–7, 710, 721; Hoyt, *Backwater war*, pp.119–25, Rohwer, *Chronology*, pp.301–3; Cunningham, *A sailor's odyssey*, p.595.
14 Achkasov and Pavlovich, *Soviet naval operations*, pp.175–77; Rohwer, *Chronology*, p.300; Ruge, *Soviets as naval opponents*, pp.38–39.
15 These landings involved eighty landing craft, accompanied by seven battleships, six escort carriers, eight cruisers and forty destroyers. Edwin P. Hoyt, *To the Marianas: war in the Central Pacific: 1944* (New York: Van Nostrand Reinhold, 1980), pp.1–63; Philip A. Crowl, *Campaign in the Marianas* (Washington, D.C.: Center of Military History, US Army, 1989), pp.13–15; Dull, *Battle history of the IJN*, pp.298–300; Gailey, *War in the Pacific*, pp.262–65; Rohwer, *Chronology*, pp.303–4.
16 O'Hara, *U.S. Navy against the Axis*, pp.222–26; Rohwer, *Chronology*, pp.306–7.
17 Rear-Admiral Hill's TF.51.11 was supported in Operation *Catchpole* by Rear-Admiral Samuel Ginder's TG 58.4 consisting of an additional three fleet carriers, three

cruisers and eight destroyers. Mark R. Peattie, *Nan'yō: the rise and fall of the Japanese in Micronesia, 1885–1945* (Honolulu: University of Hawaii Press, 1988), pp.265–74; Lin Poyer, Suzanne Falgout and Laurence Marshall Carucci, *The typhoon of war: Micronesian experiences of the Pacific War* (Honolulu: University of Hawaii Press, 2001), pp.118–24; Dull, *Battle history of the IJN*, p.300; Hoyt, *To the Marianas*, pp.64–86; Potter, *Nimitz*, pp.264–78.
18 Barbey, *MacArthur's amphibious navy*, pp.126–32; Rohwer, *Chronology*, p.297.
19 Clayton James, *Years of MacArthur: 1941–1945*, pp.346–48, 375–77; Manchester, *American Caesar*, pp.320, 325, 328, 332–33, 335–38, 340, 369; Rohwer, *Chronology*, p.297.
20 Barbey, *MacArthur's amphibious navy*, pp.144–57; Clayton James, *Years of MacArthur: 1941–1945*, pp.377, 380–91; Gill, *Royal Australian Navy 1942–1945*, pp.365, 372, 374, 377–79; Stephen R. Taafe, *MacArthur's jungle war: the 1944 New Guinea campaign* (Lawrence, Ks: Univ. Press of Kansas, 1998), pp.56–76; Gailey, *Bougainville*, pp.149–68; Rohwer, *Chronology*, pp.306, 309, 313.
21 Prados, *Combined Fleet decoded*, pp.546–50; Rohwer, *Chronology*, pp.313–14.
22 Hughes and Costello, *Battle of the Atlantic*, pp.294–95; Padfield, *War beneath the sea*, pp.375–77; Rohwer, *Chronology*, pp.308–9, 313.
23 Woodman, *Arctic convoys*, pp.383–95; Rohwer, *Chronology*, pp.307–8, 314–15.
24 Submarine crews were not favourably inclined towards the *schnorchel* at the outset because of the problems associated with early versions of them. Less sophisticated versions of the *schnorchel* mast had a tendency to malfunction and not 'breathe' in the way they were designed to do. When the *schnorchel* closed prematurely for any reason the diesel engines, starved of fresh supplies of air, would draw in air from the submerged boat itself. This made life very uncomfortable for the submariners on these boats, causing them to experience sharp earache and in some extreme cases of prolonged deprivation even damage to the ear drum itself. Other design and construction problems were also experienced. For example, it soon became clear that *schnorchel* masts would snap off if the U-boat attempted to go beyond 6 knots per hour in a submerged state and waste disposal became a real problem for those boats that remained submerged for prolonged periods. Life on board the *schnorchel* boats could be said, therefore, to be even more tedious than normal. Hughes and Costello, *Battle of the Atlantic*, pp.294–95; Milner, *Battle of the Atlantic*, pp.183–99; www.Uboat.net/technical/schnorchel_fitted.htm (accessed 8 Nov. 2007).
25 Grove, *Sea battles in close-up, 2*, pp.131–36; Wragg, *Carrier combat*, pp.133–40; Rohwer, *Chronology*, pp.306, 314; Zetterling and Tamelander, *Tirpitz*, pp.265–84.
26 In a seven-week period lasting from early March to late April, a collection of twenty Allied submarines and a solitary midget submarine claimed a variety of victims in Norwegian waters – fourteen ships totalling 58,701 tons and a U-boat (*U974*) – even though they lost *Syrtis* while doing so. Rohwer, *Chronology*, pp.310–11, 315, 317.
27 Franks, *Search, find and kill*, pp.48–70; Hughes and Costello, *Battle of the Atlantic*, p.294; Rohwer, *Chronology*, pp.326, 328, 330.
28 Ibid.
29 Although Achkasov and Pavlovich state that 1,015 mines and 307 anti-minesweeping devices had been cleared from Narva Bay between May and October 1944, the Finns were to lay a total of 13,873 mines and anti-minesweeping devices in the Baltic in the period from March to September 1944. Achkasov and Pavlovich, *Soviet naval operations*, pp.320–26; Rohwer, *Chronology*, pp.311, 318, 329, 337–39, 355, 361, 363; Ruge, *Soviets as naval opponents*, pp.38–40.
30 Achkasov and Pavlovich, *Soviet naval operations*, pp.283–88; *Fuehrer conferences*, pp.385, 387; Rohwer, *Chronology*, pp.315–17, 319–20, 322–23; Ruge, *Soviets as naval opponents*, pp.122–34.
31 A number of French warships, including their cruiser *Marseillaise* and the destroyers *Gerfaut*, *L'Indomptable*, *Le Fantasque*, *Le Malin* and *Le Terrible*, were prominent in the surface action that took place across the Mediterranean in these weeks. As an

exercise in futility, however, sadly nothing could beat the operation of one-man submersible chariots ('*Neger*') against Allied ships that were continuing to bring in supplies to the port of Anzio. Of thirty-seven that began the operation on 20–21 April, fourteen got no further than the sandbanks where they remained marooned, ten were lost on the return leg of the mission and the other thirteen made it back to their mother ship without registering any hits at all. Auphan and Mordal, *French Navy in World War II*, pp.297–98; Rohwer, *Chronology*, pp.297–99, 301–5, 308–12, 315–17, 319–22, 324–25, 327–29.

32 Jefferson, *Coastal forces at war*, pp.147–50; Scott, *Battle of the narrow seas*, pp.176–83; M.J. Whitley, *German coastal forces of World War Two* (London: Arms and Armour, 1992), pp.69–72; Rohwer, *Chronology*, pp.297, 301, 303, 306, 308–12, 317–18, 320–24, 330–36, 338, 340–48; O'Hara, *German fleet at war*, pp.200–207.

33 Wragg, *Carrier combat*, pp.167–73.

34 Somerville returned from the attack on Surabaya to find that Admiral Lord Louis Mountbatten had already established the headquarters of the newly-formed South East Asia Command in the Botanical Gardens at Kandy, Ceylon. Their relationship would prove to be both stormy and complicated in the few months they remained together. As supreme commander, Mountbatten was technically Somerville's boss. This did not go down well with the C-in-C Eastern Fleet who didn't wish to have his freedom of initiative affected in any way and certainly not by a commanding officer who had far less experience of driving ships than Somerville possessed. After being appointed to head the British Admiralty Delegation in Washington, D.C., Somerville finally took his leave of the Eastern Fleet and SEAC in August 1944. Macintyre, *Fighting admiral*, pp.238–54; Rohwer, *Chronology*, pp.313, 319, 323; Willmott, *Grave of a dozen schemes*, pp.64, 161–62, 184; Philip Zeigler, *Mountbatten: the official biography* (London: Collins, 1985), pp.227–40, 255, 267, 285.

35 Peattie, *Nan'yō*, pp.262–65.

36 Clay Blair, Jr., *Silent victory: the U.S. submarine war against Japan* (Philadelphia: J.B. Lippincott, 1975), pp.622–24; Rohwer, *Chronology*, p.319; Taafe, *MacArthur's jungle war*, p.53.

37 A set of vital IJA codebooks were captured in January 1944 by Allied troops at Sio in north-east New Guinea in a position held formerly by the troops of the Japanese 20th Infantry Division. Instead of destroying the codebooks as they were supposed to, the Japanese troops in a rush to escape placed the top secret codebooks in a metal box and dropped it in a swampy bog from where it was fortuitously recovered later by some Australian troops. This providential material was then sent to MacArthur's cryptanalytic division, known as the Central Bureau, in Brisbane. As a direct consequence of this discovery, the Allies were able to read IJA messages without delay during February and March 1944. This 'Ultra' intelligence windfall was incredibly important for MacArthur and raised his stock substantially amongst the Allied hierarchy. Edward J. Drea and Joseph E. Richard, 'New evidence on breaking the Japanese Army codes', *Intelligence and National Security*, Vol.14, No.1 (Spring 1999): 62–83; Barbey, *MacArthur's amphibious navy*, pp.158–84; Clayton James, *The years of MacArthur: 1941–1945*, pp.443–54; Smith, *Emperor's codes*, pp.252–57.

38 Gill, *Royal Australian Navy 1942–1945*, pp.396–409.

39 Edward J. Drea, *MacArthur's ULTRA. Codebreaking and the war against Japan, 1942–1945* (Lawrence, Ks: University Press of Kansas, 1992), pp.94–122; Nathan Prefer, *MacArthur's New Guinea campaign: March–August 1944* (Conshohocken, Pa: Combined Books, 1995), pp.19–103; Barbey, *MacArthur's amphibious navy*, pp.185–204; Clayton James, *Years of MacArthur: 1941–1945*, pp.454–65, 483–86, 490; Griffith, *MacArthur's airman*, pp.154–76; Taafe, *MacArthur's jungle war*, pp.77–103, 119–43; Rohwer, *Chronology*, pp.318–21, 326.

40 Peattie, *Nan'yō*, pp.274–83.

41 Goldstein and Dillon (eds), *Fading victory*, pp.366–75; Rohwer, *Chronology*, p 326.

42 Ozawa's 1st Mobile Fleet consisted of nine carriers (*Chitose, Chiyoda, Hiyo, Jun'yō, Ryūhō, Shokaku, Taihō, Zuihō, Zuikaku*) with 450 aircraft, six battleships (*Fusō, Haruna, Kongō, Musashi, Nagato, Yamato*), eleven heavy (*Atago, Chikuma, Chōkai, Haguro, Kumano, Maya, Mogami, Myokō, Suzuya, Takao, Tone*) and two light cruisers (*Noshiro, Yahagi*), thirty-five destroyers and eleven oil tankers. Rohwer, *Chronology*, p.325.

43 Ibid., pp.325–26, 329, 335–37; Blair, *Silent victory*, pp.620–21, 625–2; Boyd and Yoshida, *Japanese submarine force*, pp.136–40.

44 Blair, *Silent victory*, pp.632–41; Prados, *Combined Fleet decoded*, pp.563–65; John A. Williamson, *Antisubmarine warrior in the Pacific: six subs sunk in twelve days* (Tuscaloosa, Al.: University of Alabama Press, 2005), pp.108–46.

45 Clayton James, *Years of MacArthur: 1941–1945*, pp.457–65; Gill, *Royal Australian Navy 1942–1945*, pp.409–13, 415–36, 441–43; Prefer, *MacArthur's New Guinea campaign*, pp.105–47; Taafe, *MacArthur's jungle war*, pp.144–76; Rohwer, *Chronology*, pp.326–28.

46 Dull, *Battle history of the IJN*, pp.302–3; Goldstein and Dillon (eds), *Fading victory*, pp.376–402.

47 Part of the reason, of course, lay in the Allied counter-measures taken to reduce the effectiveness of the chain of German *Freya, Seetakt* and *Würzburg* radar stations that had been established along the Channel coast. This was achieved by a process of both airborne dipolar interference through the dropping of metal foil strips that distorted the radar beam and noise jamming on the radar wavelengths from seaborne assault vessels which overwhelmed the ground operating stations and proved enormously difficult to filter out. These methods were ably assisted by a process of deception in which operational feints, aided and abetted by electronic measures, were devised to confuse the enemy and reinforce the impression that the landing would be in the Pas de Calais area rather than along the coast of Normandy. Various ruses were dreamt up and implemented both before D-Day and on the day in question. Most worked, if not flawlessly, to such an extent that the secret of where the invasion fleet would land was preserved and must be seen as contributing significantly to the success of Operation *Neptune*. For more information on these issues, see the chapters on both *Bodyguard* and *Fortitude South* in Michael Howard, *Strategic deception in the Second World War* (New York: W.W. Norton, 1995), pp.103–33, 185–200; Craig Bickell, 'Operation *Fortitude South*: an analysis of its influence upon German dispositions and conduct of operations in 1944', *War & Society*, Vol.18, No.1 (May 2000): 91–121; Thaddeus Holt, 'The deceivers', in Robert Cowley (ed.), *No end save victory: perspectives on World War II* (New York: G.P. Putnam's Sons, 2001), pp.385–405; Brown, *Radar history*, pp.386–92.

48 Barnett, *Engage the enemy*, pp.753–809; Robert W. Love, Jr., and John Major, *The year of D-Day: the 1944 diary of Admiral Sir Bertram Ramsay* (Hull: University of Hull Press, 1994); Grove, *Sea battles in close-up, 2*, p.140.

49 Grove, *Sea battles in close-up, 2*, p.141; Warren Tute, John Costello and Terry Hughes, *D Day* (London: Sidgwick & Jackson, 1974), pp.57–65, 71–105; Julian Thompson, *The war at sea: The Royal Navy in the Second World War* (London: Sidgwick & Jackson, 1996), pp.216–30; Adrian R. Lewis, *Omaha beach: a flawed victory* (Chapel Hill, NC: University of North Carolina Press, 2001); Rohwer, *Chronology*, pp.330–31.

50 David Fraser, *Knight's Cross: a life of Field Marshal Erwin Rommel* (London: Harper Collins, 1993), pp.452–85; Samuel W. Mitcham, Jr., *The desert fox in Normandy: Rommel's defense of fortress Europe* (Westport, Conn: Praeger, 1997); Friedrich Ruge, *Rommel in Normandy* (San Rafael, Ca: Presidio Press, 1979), pp.1–169.

51 Under Kirk in the heavy cruiser *Augusta* the troop convoys would be designated either Force U (*Utah*) led by Rear-Admiral D.P. Moon in the headquarters ship *Bayfield*, or Force O (*Omaha*) where the leading role would be assumed by Rear-Admiral J.L. Hall in the headquarters ship *Ancon*. Under Vian in the light cruiser *Scylla*, Commodore C.E. Douglas-Pennant, aboard his headquarters ship *Bulolo*, took command of the landing craft assigned to Force G (*Gold*); Commodore G.N. Oliver

on board the headquarters ship *Hilary* fulfilled a similar function for those of Force J (*Juno*) and Rear-Admiral A.G. Talbot, on the headquarters ship *Largs* did the same for Force S (*Sword*). Stephen W. Roskill, *The war at sea. Vol.III, Part II* (London: HMSO, 1961), pp.5–40; Rohwer, *Chronology*, pp.330–31.

52 Seven destroyers and two corvettes escorted the Force U convoy across the Channel and were supported by Force A under the command of Rear-Admiral M.L. Deyo consisting of the battleship *Nevada*, the monitor *Erebus*, a mixed force of five cruisers (*Black Prince, Enterprise, Hawkins, Quincy* and *Tuscaloosa*), the Dutch gunboat *Soemba*, eight destroyers and two destroyer escorts. Six destroyers, three destroyer escorts and two frigates were selected to escort the O convoy. They were both supported by Force C, under Rear-Admiral C.F. Bryant, which brought together the battleships *Arkansas* and *Texas*, the light cruisers *Georges Leygues, Glasgow* and *Montcalm* and eleven fleet destroyers. Escorting the G, J and S convoys were six destroyers, eight frigates, seventeen corvettes, four sloops and twenty-one trawlers. Supporting the Gold convoy was Captain Longley-Cook with the four cruisers *Ajax, Argonaut, Emerald* and *Orion*, the Dutch gunboat *Flores* and thirteen destroyers (Force K); Juno was entrusted to Rear-Admiral F.H. Dalrymple-Hamilton with the pair of light cruisers *Belfast* and *Diadem* and eleven destroyers (Force E); and Sword was given to Rear-Admiral Patterson with the two battleships *Ramillies* and *Warspite*, the monitor *Roberts*, five cruisers (*Arethusa, Danae, Dragon, Frobisher* and *Mauritius*) and thirteen destroyers (Force D). Rohwer, *Chronology*, pp.330–31.

53 In these attacks 3,467 heavy bombers, 1,645 medium, light and torpedo bombers and 5,409 fighters would take part. Ibid., pp.330–34; Grove, *Sea battles in close-up*, 2, pp.142–52; R.W. Thompson, 'D-Day the great gamble', in Liddell Hart (ed.), *History of the Second World War*, pp.319–38.

54 Grove, *Sea battles in close-up*, 2, pp.144–45; Cunningham, *A sailor's odyssey*, pp.595–96; Guy Hartcup, *Code name Mulberry: the planning, building and operation of the Normandy harbours* (Newton Abbot: David & Charles, 1977).

55 Kirk's Western Naval Task Force was assigned 102 minesweepers and sixteen buoylayers; and 102 minesweepers and twenty-seven buoylayers were provided for Vian's Eastern Naval Task Force. Rohwer, *Chronology*, pp.330–31; Brendan A. Maher, *A passage to Sword Beach: minesweeping in the Royal Navy* (Annapolis, Md: NIP, 1996), pp.108–62.

56 Grove, *Sea battles in close-up*, 2, pp.146–47.

57 Ibid., p.147; Roskill, *War at sea*, III, II, pp.39–73.

58 Adrian R. Lewis, *Omaha Beach: a flawed victory* (Chapel Hill, N.C.: University of North Carolina Press, 2001); Barnett, *Engage the enemy*, pp.810–38; Rohwer, *Chronology*, p.331.

59 Grove, *Sea battles in close-up*, 2, p.150.

60 In the first week alone, the Allies lost a Norwegian destroyer, seven large landing craft, three small freighters, an MTB and a motor gunboat from these jousts alone, while additionally the battleship *Nelson*, two destroyers, a frigate and an LST suffered varying degrees of damage. For their part, the Germans permanently lost two destroyers, six S-boats, an MTB, a sub-chaser, two motor minesweepers, four gun ferries and five patrol boats to a combination of mines, gunfire and bombing attacks and, more crucially, had thirteen S-boats, two MTBs, eight minesweepers and two motor minesweepers damaged and withdrawn from service. Rohwer, *Chronology*, pp.331–32; Whitley, *German coastal forces of World War Two*. pp.72–74.

61 James Foster Tent, *E-boat alert: defending the Normandy invasion fleet* (Shrewsbury: Airlife, 1996), pp.108–45, 183–204; O'Hara, *German fleet at war*, pp.207–19; Rohwer, *Chronology*, pp.331–33.

62 In the second half of June U-boats in the Channel accounted for one escort destroyer, a frigate, a corvette, an LST and five other ships (over 30,000 tons) in addition to shooting down seven aircraft. Rohwer, *Chronology*, pp.333–34; *Fuehrer conferences*, pp.395–404; V.E. Tarrant, *The last year of the Kriegsmarine: May 1944 – May*

1945 (London: Arms and Armour, 1995), pp.46–113; Blair, *Hitler's U-boat war*, pp.570–92.
63 In the raid on Le Havre 221 Lancaster and 13 Mosquito planes of Bomber Command wrecked fifteen S-boats, three torpedo boats, eight patrol boats, two escort vessels, two motorised minesweepers and seven minesweepers, along with many other smaller vessels. In the raid on Boulogne a combination of 155 Lancasters, 130 Halifaxes and 12 Mosquitoes finished off six motorised minesweepers, three of their tenders, three other minesweepers, two gun ferries, a couple of patrol boats, three tugs and several other smaller vessels. Alan Harris Bath, *Tracking the Axis enemy: the triumph of Anglo-American naval intelligence* (Lawrence, Ks: University Press of Kansas, 1998), pp.218–19; Martin Middlebrook and Chris Everitt, *The Bomber Command war diaries: an operational reference book, 1939–1945* (London: Penguin Books, 1990), pp.528–29; Rohwer, *Chronology*, p.335.
64 Grove, *Sea battles in close-up*, 2, p.155; Hartcup, *Code name Mulberry*, pp.123–30.
65 Grove, *Sea battles in close-up*, 2, pp.157–58; Robin Neillands, *The battle of Normandy 1944* (London: Cassell, 2002), pp.136–54.
66 Jürgen Rohwer credits 788 coastal motor boats, 570 Liberty ships, 372, LCIs, 1,442 LCTs, 905 LSTs and 180 troop transports with having been convoyed to the assault area by the end of June 1944. Rohwer, *Chronology*, p.334; John Gorley Bunker, *Liberty ships: the ugly ducklings of World War II* (Annapolis, Md: NIP, 1972), pp.163–72.
67 These surprise attacks destroyed thirty-six Japanese aircraft and broke up a convoy off Saipan in which a torpedo boat, three submarine-chasers and ten other ships of 30,000 tons were sunk. Crowl, *Campaign in the Marianas*, pp.69–70; Grove, *Sea battles in close-up*, 2, p.165; Hoyt, *To the Marianas*, pp.105–9; Rohwer, *Chronology*, p.335.
68 Dull, *Battle history of the IJN*, pp.304–5; Rohwer, *Chronology*, pp.335–37.
69 Boyd and Yoshida, *Japanese submarine force*, pp.140–47.
70 Benis M. Frank, 'Lieutenant-General Holland M. Smith', in Howarth (ed.), *Men of war*, pp.562–86.
71 D. Colt Denfeld, *Hold the Marianas: the Japanese defense of the islands* (Shippensburg, Pa: White Mane, 1997), pp.44–101; Crowl, *Campaign in the Marianas*, pp.33–266; Harry A. Gailey, *'Howlin' Mad vs the Army: conflict in command, Saipan 1944* (Novato, Ca: Presidio, 1986), pp.115–249; Hoyt, *To the Marianas*, pp.116–32, 184–226; Grove, *Sea battles in close-up*, 2, p.165; Rohwer, *Chronology*, pp.335–36; Holland M. Smith and Percy Finch, *Coral and Brass* (Washington, D.C.: Zenger Publishing Co., 1979), pp.156–200.
72 Grove, *Fleet to fleet encounters*, p.115.
73 Dull, *Battle history of the IJN*, pp.303–11; Grove, *Sea battles in close-up*, 2, pp.165–77; Prados, *Combined Fleet decoded*, pp.566–80; Stafford, *Big E*, pp.382–417; William T. Y'Blood, *Red sun setting: the battle of the Philippine Sea* (Annapolis, Md: NIP, 1981), pp.63–93.
74 Grove, *Sea battles in close-up*, 2, pp.165–77; Hamer, *Bombers versus battleships*, pp.247–69.
75 Ozawa's warships had been spotted leaving their base at Tawi Tawi early on 13 June by *Redfin*, one of four US submarines cruising in the area. *Redfin's* report made its way swiftly into the hands of Admiral Spruance, the commander of the 5th Fleet, who could chart the progress of Ozawa's warships through Philippine waters from further submarine reports he received over the next few days. *Flying Fish* spotted Ozawa's carriers passing through the San Bernardino Strait on 15 June, the same day that *Seahorse* located the returning two behemoths *Musashi* and *Yamato* east of Mindanao some miles from the Surigao Strait. *Cavalla* also got into the act by discovering the reunited fleet refuelling from two tanker groups on 16–17 June. This essential information allowed Spruance time to get Mitscher and TF58 into position west of the Marianas to cut off the First Mobile Fleet from disrupting Operation Forager, the ongoing amphibious assault on this island chain. Blair, Jr., *Silent victory*, pp.650–53. Gill, *Royal Australian Navy 1942–45*, pp.453–60.

76 Theodore Taylor, *The magnificient Mitscher* (Annapolis, Md: NIP, 1991), pp.217–23; Buell, *The quiet warrior*, pp.257–80.
77 Ibid.; Grove, *Sea battles in close-up*, 2, pp.177–79; Hamer, *Bombers versus battleships*, pp.247–69.
78 Obayashi committed 45 'Zero' fighter-bombers, eight 'Jill' torpedo-bombers and seventeen 'Zero' fighters to the attack. Grove, *Sea battles in close-up*, 2, p.179.
79 Ibid., pp.177–87; Buell, *The quiet warrior*, pp.273–80; Taylor, *The magnificent Mitscher*, pp.224–29; Prados, *Combined Fleet decoded*, pp.574–75; Smith, *Carrier battles*, pp.233–36; Wragg, *Carrier combat*, pp.158–66; Y'Blood, *Red sun setting*, pp.94–139.
80 Ninety-five Hellcats, fifty-four Avengers, fifty-one Helldivers and twenty-six Dauntless took part in the long-range attack on Ozawa's 1st Mobile Fleet. Grove, *Sea battles in close-up*, 2, pp.187–91.
81 Ibid., pp.191–97; Clark G. Reynolds, *Admiral John H. Towers: the struggle for naval air supremacy* (Annapolis, Md: NIP, 1991), pp.474–77; Buell, *The quiet warrior*, pp.275–80; Dull, *Battle history of the IJN*, pp.303–11; Rohwer, *Chronology*, p.337; Smith, *Carrier battles*, pp.230–41; Spector, *Eagle against the sun*, pp.306–12; Taylor, *Magnificient Mitscher*, pp.230–37; Y'Blood, *Red sun setting*, pp.140–213.
82 Hoyt, *Backwater war*, pp.81–186; Rohwer, *Chronology*, pp.336–37.
83 Achkasov and Pavlovich, *Soviet naval operations*, pp.247, 250–51; Rohwer, *Chronology*, pp.337–38; Ruge, *Soviets as naval opponents*, pp.40–42.
84 Robert Jackson, *Churchill's moat: the Channel war 1939–1945* (Shrewsbury: Airlife, 1995), pp.119–46.
85 By early August no less than 75 Marder and 22 Linsen had been lost in these raids. Kemp, *Underwater warriors*, pp.183–200; Whitley, *German coastal forces*, pp.123–25.
86 Ibid.; O'Hara, *German fleet at war*, pp.220–41; Rohwer, *Chronology*, pp.338, 344.
87 Coated with sheets of Oppanol synthetic rubber, *U480* had been used in the English Channel during the months of August and September 1944 where it sank three victims – a corvette, a minesweeper and the merchantman *Orminster* – and seriously damaged another merchantman *Fort Yale*. *U480* had then been hunted for a total of seven hours but had successfully evaded her attackers. Miller, *U-boats*, pp.110–11; Rohwer, *Chronology*, pp.341–43; David Syrett, 'Communications intelligence and the sinking of the *U-860* April–June 1944', *The Mariner's Mirror*, Vol.85, No.1 (Feb. 1999): 68–75.
88 Jeffrey G. Barlow, 'Admiral Richard L. Conolly', in Stephen Howarth (ed.), *Men of war: Great naval captains of World War II* (New York: St. Martin's Press, 1993), pp.295–312.
89 Arthur J. Marder, Mark Jacobsen and John Horsfield, *Old friends new enemies: the Royal Navy and the Imperial Japanese Navy. Vol.II. The Pacific War, 1942–1945* (Oxford: Clarendon Press, 1990), pp.387–98; Robert J.C. Butow, *Tojo and the coming of the war* (Princeton, NJ: Princeton University Press, 1961), pp.425–44; Rohwer, *Chronology*, p.342.
90 Casualty figures differ, alas, according to the source one consults. Buell, *The quiet warrior*, pp.281–304; Crowl, *Campaign in the Marianas*, pp.269–447; Denfeld, *Hold the Marianas*, pp.102–27, 136–206; Hoyt, *To the Marianas*, pp.227–78; Harry A. Gailey, *The liberation of Guam 21 July–10 August 1944* (Novato, Ca: Presidio, 1988), pp.71–206; Rohwer, *Chronology*, p.344.
91 Somerville's relations with King (COMINCH) in Washington were a lot stormier than even Cunningham's had been. Simpson (ed.), *Cunningham papers, II*, pp.167, 304, 344, 350; Rohwer, *Chronology*, pp.334, 344, 348, 359, 365, 373, 377.
92 Different sources provide differing body counts for the campaign on Tinian. According to Rohwer, *Chronology*, p.344, by the time that the battle for Tinian was over, 6,050 of the Japanese troops had been killed and only 252 had been taken prisoner. American losses were 389 dead and 1816 wounded. Philip Crowl is less specific but suggests that the Japanese lost most of their garrison whose strength exceeded 8,000 men. Crowl, *Campaign in the Marianas*, p.303. For the New Guinea struggles around Noemfoor, see Barbey, *MacArthur's amphibious navy*, pp.205–16; Gill,

Royal Australian Navy 1942–45, pp.413, 424, 441–43, 460; Prefer, *MacArthur's New Guinea campaign*, pp.185–96; Taafe, *MacArthur's jungle war*, pp.177–87.
93 Prados, *Combined Fleet decoded*, pp.585–88, 601, 604–6, 608, 615, 617, 625, 627, 635, 642–43.
94 Driskill and Casad, *Admiral of the hills*, pp.200–208; Potter, *Nimitz*, pp.298–320; Rohwer, *Chronology*, pp.344–45, 347, 354–55.
95 Jones, *Britain, the United States and the Mediterranean war*, pp.138–44, 159–80.
96 William B. Breuer, *Operation Dragoon: the Allied invasion of the South of France* (Shrewsbury: Airlife, 1988); Arthur Layton Funk, *Hidden ally: the French Resistance, Special Operations and the landings in Southern France, 1944* (Westport, Conn: Greenwood Press, 1992), pp.57–108; Rohwer, *Chronology*, pp.342, 348–50; Auphan and Mordal, *French Navy in World War II*, pp.328–40; Gilbert, *Churchill, VII*, pp.830, 873–81, 886, 891, 896, 898–99, 901.
97 TF 86 – codenamed *Sitka* – and its forty-four landing craft brought the 1st Special Force ashore on the island of Levant with covering fire from the battleship *Lorraine*, the heavy cruiser *Augusta*, four light cruisers and four destroyers. TF 84 – codenamed *Alpha* – was decidedly more substantial and had 204 assorted landing vessels which were responsible for bringing the 3rd US Division ashore in the Baie de Cavalaire to the east of Toulon. *Alpha* was given fire support by the old battleship *Ramillies*, the heavy cruiser *Quincy*, five light cruisers and another six destroyers. TF 85 – known as *Delta* – had 229 landing vessels and headed for the Baie de Bugnon with the 45th US Infantry Division. On hand to register fire support if needed were the two battleships *Nevada* and *Texas*, three light cruisers, three large and eight regular destroyers. Rounding off the assault forces was TF 87 – *Camel* – which brought 247 vessels to bear and landed the 36th US Division at the Rade d'Agay with fire support from the battleship *Arkansas*, the heavy cruiser *Tuscaloosa*, five light cruisers and ten destroyers. Rohwer, *Chronology*, pp.349–50.
98 Considerable criticism of Eisenhower's advocacy of *Dragoon* was evident both before the operation began and particularly after the war in Europe was over. Clearly some individuals like Churchill and US General Mark Clark thought that it was a strategic diversion that had incalculable consequences for the Allied cause since it took the pressure off the Germans in Italy and slowed the Allied momentum in this theatre. Instead of reaching the central heart of Europe months earlier than they did, they became bogged down in Italy and were not therefore in a military position to prevent a rapid Soviet penetration of Austria, Czechoslovakia, the eastern part of Germany and Hungary in the latter months of the war. While it is a classic case of counter-factual criticism, it's one that should not be lightly discarded. D.J. Haycock, *Eisenhower and the art of warfare: a critical appraisal* (Jefferson, NC: McFarland & Co., 2004), pp.60–73; Breuer, *Operation Dragoon*, pp.245–49.
99 Rohwer, *Chronology*, p.350; Ministry of Defence, *Invasion of the South of France: Operation 'Dragoon', 15th August, 1944* (London: HMSO, 1994).
100 Rohwer, *Chronology*, pp.347–48.
101 Ibid., pp.352–53; Auphan and Mordal, *French Navy in World War II*, pp.341–50; Scott, *Battle of the narrow seas*, pp.193–213; O'Hara, *German fleet at war*, pp.220–32; Tarrant, *Last year of the Kriegsmarine*, pp.84–113.

11 Tightening the grip (September–December 1944)

As German resistance was being rolled back across much of northwestern Europe, it was being snuffed out entirely in the Black Sea and increasingly in the Baltic as well. In the former a massive air raid by the Soviet Black Sea Fleet on the Romanian naval base of Constanza on 20 August spelt the beginning of the end for the pro-German administration of the Romanian military dictator Marshal Antonescu. Apart from wreaking considerable damage amongst the Axis warships and other light craft that were using the port, it proved to be a lightning rod for wholesale change within the Romanian body politic. Three days later Antonescu was removed from power in a coup d'état and a caretaker government was installed under General Sănătescu that was opposed to continuing the war. Within hours the Red Army had been assisted in crossing the River Dniester by Sergei Gorshkov's Soviet Danube Flotilla. Not unnaturally, both of these moves were interpreted unfavourably by the German military authorities in Romania and promptly led them to evacuate as much of their shipping as possible from the most important southern port of Constanza. Those vessels that were inoperable were scuttled where they rested in the harbour on 24 August. Although the Germans sailed some of their ferry barges up the Danube, the rest of their vessels in Romanian and Bulgarian waters, roughly 200 in number, were scuttled off Varna on 29–30 August as the Soviets, using thirty torpedo cutters and six patrol cutters, prepared to take control of Constanza later that same day. As a fitting *dénouement* for the German campaign in the Black Sea, the last three German U-boats (*U19, U20, U23*) remained reasonably operationally proficient – sinking a Soviet minesweeper and writing off an already damaged freighter – in the waters off Constanza until their fuel began to run out. Finally, left with nowhere to go and rejected by the Turkish government, they scuttled themselves off the northern Turkish port of Ereğli on 11 September – the day before the new Romanian administration and the USSR signed an armistice in Moscow bringing the war between them to an end and preparing the way for the Romanians to switch sides and declare war on their erstwhile allies.[1]

In the Baltic States the Germans found themselves forced to rely upon shelling from the heavy cruiser *Prinz Eugen*, four destroyers and two torpedo boats in the Gulf of Riga on 20 August in a successful bid to restore the access routes to

Army Group North which had formerly been cut off by the Red Army in its surge from Estonia into Latvia. It was merely a temporary solution to an unsolvable problem. Its intractability grew once the Finnish Prime Minister Antti Hackzell announced on 2 September that his government's diplomatic relations with Germany had been terminated and all German troops were to be withdrawn from Finland. A couple of days later the Finns unilaterally stopped fighting the Soviet Union. This forced the Germans to begin evacuating as many of their armed forces, equipment and supplies as possible from a variety of Finnish harbours over the course of the next two-and-a-half weeks.[2] While engaged on these depressing tasks, the Germans tried to get a little of their own back by embarking upon an invasion of the Finnish island of Suursaari on 14 September. Only a delaying operation at best, *Fall Tanne Ost* was quickly undermined by the hostile resistance put up by the Finnish defenders and through a series of punishing attacks by Soviet aircraft which forced the abandonment of the invasion within a few hours of its start. Those troops that survived the amphibious leg of the operation were quickly rounded up and taken into custody to begin life as POWs. Having learnt their lesson, the Germans concentrated thereafter on withdrawing their garrisons from outlying islands in the Gulf of Finland and laying new mine barrages to try to prevent their Soviet pursuers from gaining easy access into the Baltic, while arranging convoys that left Tallinn in Estonia with troops and evacuees for the Baltic islands of Dagö, Moon Island and Ösel. By 23 September, when the last such convoy left port, over 50,000 troops and 85,000 evacuees had made this journey to relative safety. It was, however, only a stop-gap situation since the Soviet armed forces appeared on the scene within a matter of days and began to make inroads into the German positions off the Estonian and Latvian coasts.[3]

German observance that the war was coming much closer to home was seen in the often lacklustre, defensive manner of their Mediterranean campaign in 1944. Whatever U-boats were employed – *schnorchel* or the older conventional type – in conducting mining operations and reconnaissance missions in the Ligurian and Tyrrhenian Seas, their success rate lagged unconvincingly behind that of the Allied submarines throughout the entire reach of the Mediterranean and into the Aegean. By the end of September there were no longer any operational U-boats of either type at any point from the Strait of Gibraltar to the Suez Canal, and Allied success both in the air and on and under the water throughout the entire region could no longer be denied. Aircraft and warships shelled German-held bases, such as Genoa and Rimini, attacked their supply convoys with impunity and disrupted evacuation procedures, while their Commandos had already begun seizing some of the Adriatic islands off the Dalmatian coast, such as Hvar, in mid-July and were poised for much more damage as part of the British Aegean Force that was formed under Rear-Admiral John Mansfield in September to put the Allies back in control of the Aegean islands and to lay claim to the Greek mainland.[4] Composed of seven escort carriers, seven light cruisers and nineteen assorted destroyers, Mansfield's force was a powerful weapon to wield in a region that had always held special significance for the British prime minister. In a five-week tour of duty lasting from 24 September to the end of October, the British Aegean Force fell upon the retreating Germans with alacrity as though making up for lost time and repaying them for the past defeats the Allies had suffered at their hands in this quite spectacularly beautiful region of southeastern Europe. Assisting them in this enterprise were half a dozen Allied submarines which needed little encouragement to get into the act by sinking a variety of enemy vessels caught up in the general withdrawal. Engagements between the Allies and their retreating foes were numerous in these hectic days as the Germans finally pulled back from the port of Piraeus on 12 October. Athens fell a couple of days later. Many of those German ships that were sent north to Salonika (Thessaloniki) for safe keeping in early October were given a torrid time by Mansfield's carrier planes and destroyers and never made it beyond Volos. Those that managed to run the naval gauntlet imposed by the superior forces at his disposal, or evaded the mines that had been sown in these waters by both sides, only prolonged their operational life by a few weeks at most. Once the last of the German troops had left Salonika on 31 October, the remaining seven Axis warships that lay at anchor there were scuttled by their crews. It was a time for Churchill to savour. His Greek adventures in the past had been fraught affairs, but now at last the Aegean had been wrested back from German hands.[5]

Frankly, wherever one looked on the naval side of the war in the early autumn of 1944 the picture for the Grand Alliance appeared to be promising. All across Europe the Germans were in retreat and largely unable to do much more than slow the rate at which their opponents were hounding them from one evacuated port to the other. It was the same general picture across Asia too from a peculiarly quiescent Indian Ocean in which the British were gradually resuming their once customary position of authority to the grim dynamism of the Pacific where the term 'a backwater' had no place and in which the Americans were evidently in the ascendant. Their submarines continued to enjoy a useful harvest of mercantile vessels and warships across the ocean from the Kuriles in the northwest through the mandated island chains in the Central and Southwest Pacific to the area of the Philippines and the waters of the Malayan archipelago. While their continued war on trade helped to deprive the Japanese Empire of much needed supplies, they were unable to inflict the same kind of panic in Axis circles that had been caused by the U-boat campaign in the Atlantic. Useful though they were, these submarines were not going to win the war for the Allies in the Pacific theatre unlike the carriers which represented real striking potential.[6]

Marc Mitscher's carrier group, TF 38, soon underlined what fifteen carriers – well supported and protected by an accompanying force of battleships, cruisers and destroyers – could do for the Allied war effort by conducting a series of punishing raids on the Pacific islands of Iwo Jima, Chichi Jima and Wake in late August and early September, before turning to probe the defences of Palau and assault the airfields on both Mindanao and the Visayan Islands in the Philippines in a sustained burst of action during 6–14 September. In the last three days devoted to destroying the air defences of the central and southern Philippines, the Americans flew 2,400 sorties and eliminated over 200 Japanese aircraft. This was but a prelude to an even more astonishing wave of attacks that swept over the airfields of Luzon and the Visayas on 21–22 and 24 September respectively destroying over 1,000 planes and sinking 150 ships for the loss of a total of seventy-two US aircraft. Such was the intensity of this campaign and its success that Admiral Halsey recommended that instead of invading the islands of Mindanao, Palau, Talaud and Yap which had all been identified in the original operational plan for the autumn of 1944, the resources earmarked for these operations should be conserved instead for the staging of a direct assault on the island of Leyte in the central Philippines in late October. Although unwilling to drop the operation against the Palau chain, Nimitz did see some merit in the proposal to bypass Mindanao in order to have a crack at Leyte. He forwarded this proposal up the chain of command and it was swiftly approved by the Joint Chiefs of Staff at their meeting in Quebec.[7]

Admiral King and General Marshall were in the Canadian province because Churchill, Roosevelt and the Combined Chiefs of Staff (CCOS) had assembled there to settle some outstanding issues about future Allied strategy in the war. Churchill's rather ambivalent offer to put the Royal Navy at the disposal of the Americans in the Pacific was made on the first morning of the *Octagon* Conference on 13 September 1944. Although willingly accepted by President Roosevelt, Admiral King was not wildly enamoured about the proposal, suspecting that the British had an ulterior political motive for becoming involved in the Far East and Oceania. While he was a lone, critical voice in the planning sessions at *Octagon*, King's views reflected an attitude of mind held by others in the Roosevelt administration which harboured similar suspicions about the long-term goals of the British in Southeast Asia and their likely desire to reclaim or even extend their imperial presence in the region. Apart from the avowedly imperialistic distrust he entertained for the British, King was inclined to think that because the Royal Navy had not been designed to fight a war in the Pacific, its warships were barely suitable for such tasks and integrating them into the strategic planning process would complicate the task of his commanders in this theatre of operations. There was some force in these arguments, of course, but, as usual with King, his suspicion of the British was somewhat exaggerated. Moreover, he also saw the Pacific as an American preserve and one in which there was no place for sentiment. His candour did not appeal to Churchill who was gruffly offended by the CNO's general demeanour. Nonetheless, Roosevelt had accepted Churchill's offer and King was left with little option but to take his concerns back to the CCOS in the hope that he would be able to influence the type of warship that the British would provide for Nimitz in the future.[8]

Before then, however, there were two other main targets to invade: Morotai, in the Moluccan island chain, and the islands of Palau, one of the former Japanese military strongholds in the Southwest Pacific, both of which were to be invaded simultaneously on 15 September. That was where the similarities between these two operations ended. Whereas TF 77 oversaw the assault phase on Morotai in which ninety-seven landing craft from the Aitape, Hollandia and

Wakde bases on New Guinea brought 19,960 troops ashore on the first day and another 38,200 subsequently in a very straightforward and uncontested operation, *Stalemate II* – the two-staged landing on the northern island of Peleliu and the southern island of Angaur in the Palau group – was anything but easy.[9] These islands were targeted originally because of the potential menace they held as bases for Japanese air strikes against MacArthur's transport fleet once his invasion of Mindanao in the Philippines began. Recent intelligence suggested to Halsey that their importance had been exaggerated since the Japanese had few planes in the area, little oil and even less shipping and that their danger had been consequently overstated. Nonetheless, Nimitz wanted to secure Ulithi Atoll – the former Japanese naval base situated northeast of both the Palau and Yap Islands – and saw it as a strategic possession that the USN could profitably use for its future operations in the region.[10] In order to ensure that it would become a safe anchorage, however, the air strip on Peleliu had to be taken – or so the theory went. This was why Nimitz was unwilling to bypass the Palau islands. In truth, this was not Nimitz's finest hour as CINCPAC. He was both confusingly unenthusiastic and yet unresponsive to changing the strategic plan at this late stage and so a grim sort of administrative inertia took over, guaranteeing that *Stalemate II* went ahead. It was to be a costly mistake.[11]

Both Peleliu and Anguar were subject to a tremendous artillery bombardment from the Fire Support Group attached to TF 31 on both 13 and 14 September. Peleliu was also bombed and strafed by the planes from a group of escort carriers which flew 382 sorties on the first day of the amphibious assault (15 September) in a bid to prevent Colonel Kunio Nakagawa and his nearly 11,000 troops of the Japanese 14th Division from interfering with the landing. Despite reeling from all this preparatory action before the 1st Marine Division got ashore on Peleliu, the enemy still proved to be extremely resourceful. They made excellent use of the mountainous terrain and were willing to die in vast numbers to prevent yielding the territory easily to the Americans. Overcoming Japanese resistance on Peleliu proved to be a long and costly struggle. It would take until Christmas Day before the last forty-five Japanese troops were finally overrun by a regimental unit of the 81st Infantry Division. On Angaur the American infantry troops found themselves caught up in another frenetic battle for survival against a force of 1,600 troops under Major Ushio Goto. This campaign lasted for five weeks before the Americans eventually prevailed and the Japanese were subdued. Casualty figures for this two-pronged operation are disputed. According to Professor Rohwer, only 301 Japanese were taken prisoner on these two islands, while American losses amounted to at least 1,209 troops dead and 6,585 wounded.[12] Such were the costs of war in the Pacific. By fighting so aggressively and being willing to die in large numbers for Emperor Hirohito as they were, the Japanese were laying down a marker for their compatriots in the rest of the empire and in the home islands as well. Pledged to fight and die for the emperor and to take as many Allied personnel with them as they could, the Japanese hoped that they might make their own defeat too onerous and expensive for American public opinion and the Roosevelt administration to contemplate and become the harbinger of a peace proposal that would enable them to preserve their independence and as much honour and territorial possessions as possible under the circumstances.[13]

A world away from Micronesia in virtually every other respect, the Arctic shared the distinction of being an active theatre of naval operations. In these cold northern waters the Western Allies and the Soviet Union were engaged against the Germans in a remorseless struggle for supremacy around the Polar coast and the Barents Sea. Apart from the Loch Ewe–Murmansk convoys which had now become a continuing source of frustration for the Germans, where once they had afforded rich promise, the Soviets were themselves confronted by the difficulty of laying waste the strongly defended German shipping convoys operating out of the naval base of Kirkenes. Despite possessing the advantages of aerial reconnaissance and having active support from units of fighter and torpedo-bombers, as well as submarines and fast torpedo cutters, these combined arms operations rarely came close to inflicting real harm, let alone major destruction, on this enemy shipping until the Germans finally decided to pull back their troops from the Murmansk front in October 1944.[14] Only then as the XIX Mountain Corps was withdrawn and the Soviet 14th Army, ably assisted by the Northern Fleet under Admiral Arseni Golovko, launched their offensive into the region the Germans had left behind was there any real change in the situation. By the time the 131st Rifle Corps entered the port of Kirkenes on 26 October, the Germans had already left. Although great efforts were made by the Soviet military to attack as many of the evacuation convoys as possible, the sweeping claims about the degree of destruction inflicted upon this shipping made by the submariners and those on the Soviet torpedo cutters and MTBs assigned to the task could not be sustained. Of the twenty assorted vessels that were sunk, twelve succumbed to the waves of air attacks that broke over them. Despite this unwanted attention from enemy forces, the vast majority of the German shipping got away from the Polar coast unscathed taking with them over 40,000 tons of supplies.[15] Once again the Germans had pulled off a successful evacuation under trying conditions. They were learning fast and becoming masters of the art, a distinction undoubtedly helped by the fact that they were getting the most practice at staging this sort of retreat. Before they finally withdrew or were pushed from Russian territory, the Germans had tried to take the fight to the Soviets elsewhere on the Northern Front, but these adventures had enjoyed only mixed success. Their U-boat operations against Soviet mercantile traffic along the Siberian sea route were very much hit-and-miss affairs with greater accent on the latter than the former. Theirs was a lonely and unglamorous quest – but even the potentially more eye-catching spectacles, such as the repeated attempts in September and October by the *schnorchel* U-boats *U315* and *U313* to penetrate the Kola Inlet in order to attack the old battleship *Arkhangelsk*, didn't succeed either.[16]

As the Germans were mulling over their options in the north, the Soviets, with a little help from their Scandinavian neighbours, made up their mind for them in the Baltic. On 27 September the neutral Swedish government announced that its Baltic harbours were no longer open to German shipping of any kind and a couple of days later the Finns led the first three of fifteen Soviet submarines from the Gulf of Finland past the defence posts on Hangö and Abo out into the Baltic beyond where they could begin operating off the Latvian, Lithuanian and Polish coastlines. On 29 September the Soviets reinforced the message that the Germans were unwelcome in these waters by landing troops on Moon Island. A German retreat to Ösel (Hiiumaa) swiftly followed. Dagö was taken next on 3 October and a further withdrawal from Ösel to the Sworbe Peninsula on the island of Saaremaa followed later in the month. In an effort to arrest this breakthrough into the Baltic, the Germans employed their heavy cruisers, *Lützow* and *Prinz Eugen*, three destroyers and four torpedo boats against the new Soviet positions on the coast between Libau (Liepāja) and Memel (Klaipėda) in the second week of the month and then used some of these vessels to bombard the enemy troops on the Sworbe Peninsula on 22–24 October. Few could have doubted that these were merely delaying tactics by the Germans for the war in the Baltic States had moved inexorably against them. Much of Estonia had gone, entry into the Gulf of Riga had been secured and Latvia's 'liberation' was at most only weeks away. As part of these measures, the final attack on the Sworbe Peninsula was made by the Soviet 8th Army on 18 November, with fire support coming from three gunboats and eleven armoured cutters gathered off the east coast. Despite putting up some naval resistance over the next few days, the game was essentially up for the Germans and the arrival of the pocket battleship *Admiral Scheer*, along with a task force of two destroyers and six torpedo boats, was merely designed to slow the advance of the 8th Army and cover the latest evacuation that took place during the night of 23–24 November.[17]

On the road to being beaten in the Baltic States, repulsed in the Arctic, and yielding ground to their enemies on their eastern, southern and western flanks as well, the Germans could not even turn to their *schnorchel* U-boat fleet for salvation. Wherever they were deployed in either the Atlantic or British coastal waters, the results remained stubbornly disappointing to Dönitz. Admittedly, if he had looked hard enough he could have discerned a few crumbs of comfort. Individual boats, such as *U482*, *U300* and *U486*, could on occasion feast well off the amount of shipping that could be found in these waters, and the latest electronic advances, namely, the *Naxos* centimetre search receiver and the *Kurier* automatic radio transmitter, offered exciting possibilities of evading those Allied search groups out trawling for them. Nonetheless, the overall picture was hardly reassuring given the fact that the U-boat arm had lost more of its own vessels in the last six months of 1944 than the number of enemy ships it had been able to sink. It was a troubling statistic for those in Dönitz's circle and underlined the necessity for his new larger *Elektro* U-boats (Type XXI and XXIII) to make their appearance sooner rather than later.[18]

If the day of the submarine appeared to be virtually over in much of the northern hemisphere, the situation in the Indian Ocean suggested that there was still a place for them. A number of the Type IXD-2 U-boats coming from the North Atlantic turned up in various places from June onwards and quickly established a reputation from the Arabian Sea to the Strait of Malacca for elusiveness and predatory behaviour that was redolent of their productive days of the past. It did not take long for the Allies to hit back. While both forces enjoyed success in these waters, they met failure too. None of the British submarines were able to cope with either *Ro-113* and *Ro-115*, the two Japanese submarines that were sent out from Singapore to cruise off the Indian sub-continent in the last quarter of the year, and three of the U-boats deployed to take raw materials from the Dutch East Indies to Norway in October and November never made it beyond the Sunda Strait at the southern tip of the island of Sumatra before coming to grief.[19]

It was a totally different story in the waters off East and Southeast Asia and throughout the Central Pacific. Here the monthly haul of shipping of all types sunk by American submarines must have made Dönitz and Toyoda green with envy. While the vast majority of those destroyed were mercantile craft, a sizeable fleet of two escort carriers, a seaplane carrier, six cruisers, twenty-three destroyers, four submarines, eleven frigates, four corvettes, six sub-chasers, four minesweepers and two gunboats had perished with them.[20] In anticipation of the forthcoming invasion of the Philippines, many of the ninety US submarines operating in the Pacific in October were formed into loosely associated groups in those locations where it was thought there might be a likely upsurge in Japanese naval activity in the coming weeks. While some of the new deployments did not work out and quite a few of the submarines did not achieve any success at all, plenty of others did find much to interest them and a new monthly record of 104 vessels sunk and seventeen damaged suggested that a new 'happy time' was here again but with an ironic twist for this time it would be the Allies who would be celebrating at the expense of the Axis Powers.[21]

Although an objective reading of the situation in the Pacific ought to have meant that there was little to inspire either happiness or confidence in Japanese military circles at this time, the deeply held conviction that the empire was only one victory away from reversing the misfortunes of the recent past drove these passionately nationalistic individuals onward. Despite losing the defensive shield of the Marianas in such an incomparable fashion in mid-June, the Japanese scripted a number of scenarios which they were ready to implement against their American aggressors from 1 August. Four *SHO* (or victory) plans were devised to take account of possible action against Formosa and the Ryūkyūs (*SHO-GO 2*), Honshū (*SHO-GO 3*), Hokkaido and the Kuriles (*SHO-GO 4*), but the premier plan and the one that most in the Japanese military hierarchy expected was *SHO-GO 1* – the counterattack on the US 3rd Fleet under the command of Admiral 'Bull' Halsey which was expected to attack the Philippines.[22] This plan was conceived as a series of swift and punishing lunges against the invasion fleet and its supporting forces involving initially an all-out attack by Japanese aircraft based in the Philippines which was designed to catch the American carrier fleet by surprise. Woven into the scheme was a decoy operation that would bring a lightweight carrier force down from Japan to attract what was left of Halsey's carrier planes, while in the ensuing chaos, the Japanese would seek to use their super-battleships, *Musashi* and *Yamato*, and the rest of the surface battlefleet coming from Brunei Bay and the Pescadores to form two distinct groups in order to exert a classic north–south pincer movement against the vulnerable Allied invasion fleet and its landing craft gathered in Leyte Gulf between the island of Samar in the north and Mindanao in the south. If all went according to plan, the Americans would be routed.[23]

Needless to say, it didn't go according to plan. Part of the bottom fell out of it once Mitscher's TF 38 with its four groups of carriers began to make major headway against the land-based aircraft the Japanese possessed in the Ryūkyūs, on Formosa, and at their base at Aparri on the northern coast of Luzon. In five days of punishing activity from the Double Tenth (10 October) onwards, Mitscher lost ninety-two of his planes in conducting over 4,700 sorties against these targets, but the Japanese Air Fleet which roused itself to making 881 of its own was decimated both on the ground and in the air losing hundreds of aircraft in sorties against the four American carrier task groups. Some did get through and made their presence count. A few of the Japanese planes were wielded as kamikaze weapons, with one crashing onto the deck of the carrier *Franklin* and two others damaging the cruiser *Reno* and the destroyer *Cassin*, while the rest used their torpedoes in a conventional way. This was sufficient to put both the heavy cruiser *Canberra* and the light cruiser *Houston* out of action, even though the rest of the American fleet emerged unscathed. Tokyo heard a quite different story from the euphoric Japanese air crews upon their return to base. In their battle reports they wildly exaggerated their success rates and asserted that they had sunk eleven carriers, two battleships and a cruiser, while damaging a further eight carriers, two more battleships, another cruiser and thirteen other warships from Halsey's forces! If these reports had been accurate, the Japanese would have broken his carrier fleet apart and dramatically stalled the dynamic of American progress in the Pacific war. It was, of course, just the sort of news that those running the naval administration back in Japan were so anxious to hear and it led to much satisfaction that finally deliverance from the immediate American threat had been accorded them. Convinced by the power of wishful thinking, the Japanese Navy Ministry failed to examine these claims carefully even though they were astonishing. Could Halsey's entire carrier force have been disabled in this way? Was it likely? Where was the independent corroboration? Unfortunately, for Toyoda and the rest of his staff, the figures were so far from the truth that when later reconnaissance reports indicated that far from being decimated the US 3rd Fleet remained overwhelmingly active the disappointment felt by these leading individuals in the Gunreibu must have been crushing.[24]

While the Japanese deluded themselves that their hold over the Philippines would endure after the alleged achievements of their air crews off Formosa, the Americans knew what the true picture was and were poised for the next stage in demonstrating it. Waves of land-based long-range aircraft from Biak, Morotai and Sansapor began the process of enlightening the Japanese on the true state of affairs by raiding the airfields on Mindanao on 16–17 October, as planes from Rear-Admiral Thomas Sprague's eighteen escort carriers did the same on Cebu,

Leyte and the northern part of Mindanao. Shortly after Sprague's sprawling escort carrier force, TF 77, appeared off the small island of Suluan at the entrance to Leyte Gulf in the early morning of 17 October, the Gunreibu learnt conclusively that it was business as usual in the Southwest Pacific. If Toyoda and his staff were in need of additional confirmation that something big was afoot it soon came with the start on the same day of a massive wave of air raids and artillery bombardment conducted by Mitscher's TF 38 against the Japanese 1st Air Fleet and the 4th Army Air Fleet and their bases on the large northern island of Luzon. Further raids by Sprague's escort carriers took place on Mindanao and Leyte on the following two days (18–19 October). Although efforts were made by 125 Japanese aircraft to attack and disable both task forces, they failed to penetrate the fighter screen set up around them. By the early morning of 17 October, therefore, Toyoda had come to the belated conclusion that *SHO-GO 1* would have to be launched and so Takeo Kurita's impressive Centre Force was ordered to leave its base in the Lingga Roads (southeast of Singapore) and depart for Brunei Bay to refuel and be prepared for decisive action somewhere in the Philippines. At this point it was still debatable where the Americans would choose to land, but that matter was cleared up in the early hours of 20 October when a tri-service armada involving the 7th US Fleet (commanded by Vice-Admiral Thomas Cassin Kinkaid), the 6th US Army (led by Lieutenant-General Walter Krueger) and George Kenney's 5th USAAF, together with Mitscher's and Sprague's carrier group planes, appeared in, on and above the waters of Leyte Gulf.[25] Sixty-two landing craft from TF 78 brought the men of X Corps ashore in the north of the Gulf and ninety-five landing vessels from TF 79 did the same for XXIV Corps in the south under the watchful gaze of a trio of battleships, six cruisers and twenty-one destroyers assembled to provide fire support along both the northern and southern invasion beaches. Later on in the afternoon of the same day MacArthur also went ashore and using a microphone proclaimed that he – the self-styled 'voice of freedom' – had returned to the Philippines and called upon the Filipino people to rally to him and strike a telling blow against the occupying but retreating Japanese forces.[26] Confronted by the size of the invasion force, the Japanese 16th Infantry Division chose not to contest the landings but retired into the hills to await reinforcements from Luzon that would be landed through the port of Ormoc in the days to come.[27]

Toyoda now strove to bring the various elements that underpinned *SHO-GO 1* together in the hope that a flawless coordinated strategy could be worked out as the requirements of the theoretical plan demanded. One of those essential prerequisites was that the Japanese would have sufficient land-based aircraft to cause real problems for the American carrier forces and prevent them from turning their full attention on any of the Japanese surface fleet. Although they had lost a great number of their cutting edge forces in the air battles of the past few days, Japanese aircraft were still able to mount some attacks on the invasion fleet, torpedoing the light cruiser *Honolulu* during the evening of the first day of the landings and knocking out the heavy cruiser *Australia* when one of its planes crashed onto it on the following day. While planes from Sprague's escort carriers concentrated on attacking Japanese positions on Leyte, some of Mitscher's bombers proceeded to attack the Western Visayas on 21 October as others took turns to refuel. Despite their signals intelligence and their ability to read some of the Japanese codes, the Americans did not know for sure what the Japanese planned to do about the invasion of the Philippines. They were certain that it would prompt a fairly immediate military response from them, but quite what this counterattack would consist of was still open to doubt.[28]

While the Americans puzzled about what the next Japanese move would be, Toyoda readied his various forces on 20 October for the decisive action to come. Setting dawn of 25 October as 'X-Day', he ordered Kurita and Vice-Admiral Shoji Nishimura's forces to leave Brunei Bay on 22 October and instructed the three other components of the plan: the transport unit of Vice-Admiral Naomasa Sakonju from Manila, the 2nd Striking Force of Vice-Admiral Kiyohide Shima from the islands of the Pescadores in the waters off Formosa, and the diversionary force of Jisaburo Ozawa from the Inland Sea to set out on their travels so that they could meet the requirements of the plan. Despite their major setbacks in the recent past, the Japanese were still able to put a formidable naval force together for this latest and most decisive battle with the Americans. Apart from *Musashi* and *Yamato*, the two super-battleships that formed the apex of his designated Centre Force, Kurita could rely upon the substantial battleship *Nagato*, the two fast ex-battlecruisers that had been reclassified as battleships *Haruna* and *Kongō*, ten heavy cruisers, two light cruisers and fifteen destroyers. Shoji Nishimura's warships, which were expected to form the southern part of the pincer movement against the invasion fleet in Leyte Gulf, were much less impressive both in quantitative and qualitative terms than Kurita's Centre Force. Although the southern force contained two battleships (*Fusō* and *Yamashiro*), the heavy cruiser *Mogami* and four destroyers, both of the battleships were relatively old, slow and ponderous. Because their route to Leyte Gulf by way of the Surigao Strait was more direct than that to be taken by Kurita, Nishimura left Brunei Bay seven hours after the cutting edge of *SHO-GO 1* had left port at 0805 hours on 22 October for its longer, more circuitous voyage through the Philippines to Leyte Gulf via the Sibuyan Sea, the San Bernardino Strait and along the east coast of Samar – a distance of some 1400nm (2,593km). Shima's group was meant to join it in the Sulu Sea west of Leyte and bring a further mix of two cruisers and seven destroyers to bear when the southern part of the pincer snapped shut. That at least was the theory, but would it work out in practice? Much hung on theory and speculation at this time. Ozawa's appearance with the 1st Mobile Fleet was a case in point. It was to be a decoy force meant to lure Admiral Halsey's 3rd Fleet away from Leyte to the north and enable Kurita, Nishimura and Shima to execute a brilliant pincer movement trapping and eliminating Vice-Admiral Thomas Kinkaid's 7th Fleet off the invasion beaches in Leyte Gulf. Despite losing so many planes and, even more importantly, experienced pilots in the Pacific campaign, Ozawa could muster more than 100 aircraft for the fleet carrier *Zuikaku* and the light carriers

Chitose, *Chiyoda* and *Zuihō* to use. Along with him, Ozawa brought two old battleships (*Hyūga* and *Ise*) which, despite having been converted into seaplane carriers, were carrying only guns – a battery of over a hundred light A.A. guns and six rocket launchers – and no aircraft for this operation. Their main purpose was to be the initial magnet for Halsey's carrier fleet and then subsequently to defend the rest of Ozawa's carriers with their A.A. armament. Rounding off his force were three light cruisers, eight destroyers and a supply force that brought together a further destroyer, two tankers and six corvettes. Commanding a decoy force with few aircraft at his disposal was no easy undertaking, but if any Japanese naval officer could pull off this risky manoeuvre Ozawa had the fearless qualities to do so.[29]

As part of the plan to shore up resistance on Leyte to assist the 20,000 Japanese troops already there, Naomasa Sakonju was made responsible for bringing in troop reinforcements in the shape of the 30th and 102nd Infantry Divisions to Ormoc, a port on the northwest coast of the island. His force, consisting of the heavy cruiser *Aoba* and the old light cruiser *Kinu*, a destroyer and four fast transports, stayed well clear of the invasion sites in Leyte Gulf, but was still found a few miles south of Cape Calavite off the northeast coast of the island of Mindoro at 0325 hours on 23 October by the US submarine *Bream* which managed to torpedo the *Aoba* before making good her escape.[30] That hadn't been in the script and neither were the activities of two other American submarines, *Dace* and *Darter*, which were to strike with even more telling effect a few hours after *Bream*'s moment of partial success. Cruising off the west coast of the island of Palawan, the two submarines picked up Kurita's Centre Force on their radar screens at 0116 hours on 23 October. They reported the contact to Halsey and closed in on the warships which were intent on conserving fuel and only making about 15 knots during the hours of darkness. Manoeuvring their way into position before dawn broke, the two submarines waited for the Centre Force to pass before *Darter* fired a spread of six torpedoes at Kurita's flagship *Atago* at 980 yards (274m) distance at 0632 hours. Four of them hit home with deadly effect a minute later. *Atago* took on an almost immediate 25° list and sank within twenty minutes. *Darter* was far from finished. She also managed to hit the *Takao* twice two minutes later on her starboard side totally destroying her rudder, carving two sizable holes in her hull, smashing two of her four propellers and flooding three of her boiler rooms. Not surprisingly, she took on a 10° list to starboard. Her day was done. She was forced to limp back to port in Brunei Bay in the company of the two destroyers *Asashimo* and the *Naganami*. Well before arrangements could be carried out to save the *Takao*, however, *Dace* announced her entrance onto the scene by firing four torpedoes at the heavy cruiser *Maya* – all of which hit her port side at 0657 hours and literally blew her apart. She took a few minutes to join her flagship in sinking. Rescued from the wreck of the *Atago* before she foundered, Kurita quickly transferred his flag to the *Yamato* (much to Ugaki's chagrin) and forged on ahead determined that he would fulfil his part of the *SHO-GO 1* plan even if the element of surprise had been lost, which it obviously had been![31]

His opposite number, the ebullient Admiral William 'Bull' Halsey, was an aggressive and attack-orientated commander, but one who was often impatient and prone to occasional injudicious flourishes which other, more subtle, opponents could, on occasion, exploit. In boxing parlance he was not a counter puncher like Spruance was inclined to be, but an old fashioned slugger – a naval equivalent of Jake LaMotta. Anxious to be doing something more decisive than merely being in covering attendance, Halsey had intimated to both Nimitz and MacArthur on 21 October that he would like to take the fight to the enemy forces wherever they might be found. Neither of them supported such a proposal and told him so on 21 October. His duty did not lie in the South China Sea but in the waters off Leyte. Nimitz told him bluntly that a foray through the San Bernardino Strait or Surigao Strait in search of any Japanese warships that might have been sent to disrupt the American invasion would first require the authorisation of CINCPAC.[32]

Denied a more aggressive role, Halsey deployed the carrier groups of TF 38 so that they could continue to hammer the air bases on Luzon and catch the Centre Force if it came towards Leyte Gulf. Two fleet carriers (Mitscher's flagship *Lexington* and *Essex*), accompanied by the two light carriers *Langley* and *Princeton*, the battleships *Massachusetts* and *Washington*, four light cruisers and twelve destroyers (TG 38.3) were placed under the command of Rear-Admiral Frederick ('Ted') Sherman and situated east of the main island of Luzon. Halsey was with Rear-Admiral Gerald Bogan's TG 38.2 east of the San Bernardino Strait with the fleet carriers *Bunker Hill* and *Intrepid*, the light carriers *Cabot* and *Independence*, the battleships *Iowa* and *New Jersey* (Halsey's flagship), four light cruisers and sixteen destroyers. TG 38.4 under Rear-Admiral Ralph Davison was deployed a little further south and on the eastern side of the island of Samar. It consisted of the fleet carriers *Enterprise* and *Franklin*, the light carriers *Belleau Wood* and *San Jacinto*, the battleships *Alabama* and *South Dakota*, the heavy cruisers *Wichita* and *New Orleans* and fifteen destroyers. Some 125nm (231.5km) separated these three task groups along a diagonal north–south axis.[33]

TG 38.1, deprived of two of its four cruisers through bomb and torpedo damage and missing two others on towing and escort duty, had already left Philippine waters at 2030 hours on 22 October under the command of Vice-Admiral John McCain and was proceeding to Ulithi for replenishment and a few days of rest and recuperation for their officers and crew. By sending off McCain with his fleet carriers *Hornet* and *Wasp*, the light carriers *Cowpens* and *Monterey*, and fifteen destroyers, along with the fleet carrier *Hancock* from TG 38.2 as additional cover, Halsey was reducing his aerial power appreciably. He evidently thought the five carriers could be dispensed with for a few days and that in their absence the Japanese were unlikely to pose an acute aerial threat to the rest of his ships on station in Philippine waters. This was not one of the 'Bull's' better decisions. He had allowed McCain to leave Philippine waters even though he was aware from the latest intercepted Japanese signals traffic that an enemy carrier fleet had most probably left the Inland Sea in Japan for an undisclosed location only two days before (20 October). Obviously Halsey was not unduly concerned by this disclosure and had sent TG 38.1 on its way. It would only begin making its return when he learnt that Kurita's Centre Force was in the offing on the morning of 24 October.[34]

While McCain was still well out of the way, Vice-Admiral Takijiro Onishi, in command of the 1st Japanese Air Fleet based on Luzon, managed to get at least 150 aircraft airborne after first light on 24 October with orders to attack the nearest carrier group (Sherman's TG 38.3) and destroy as much of it as possible. Onishi's motives for doing so may have been understandable – he evidently believed that such a raid would assist Kurita's Centre Force by reducing its potential enemies – but his thinking was flawed. His task was to protect Kurita, but he could only do that if his own Air Fleet and Vice-Admiral Shigeru Fukudome's 2nd Air Fleet (much of which had been transferred the previous evening from Formosa to Luzon) remained in existence. Pitching these aircraft against the American fighter planes was not a good way of doing that. Fukudome seems to have felt the same way and had resisted calls from Onishi to commit most of the 450 planes he had sent to Luzon to the attack on TG 38.3. It was just as well he did. In order to preserve as many of his aircraft as possible, Onishi needed to catch the Americans by surprise. It didn't happen. American radar saw to that. Alerted to the incoming wave of enemy attackers by his ships' radar capability, Sherman had sufficient time to scramble his fighter planes to intercept the enemy force at some distance from his carriers. In a series of merciless engagements that lasted well over an hour, the fast and manoeuvrable American Hellcats cut a deep swathe through the three waves of enemy bombers that Onishi had sent off from Luzon. Just when it looked as though the Americans had won a most comprehensive victory, a sole Japanese 'Judy' dive-bomber suddenly emerged out of a bank of low cloud at 0938 hours to put a 550 pound (249.5 kilo) bomb through the deck of the light carrier *Princeton* striking loaded torpedo bombers on the hangar deck and starting a fire and a series of explosions that grew in intensity as the day wore on. Wreathed in smoke and flames, *Princeton* remained afloat even after a massive explosion in the afternoon had finished off the carrier as a going concern and had killed 229 and wounded another 420 officers and men of the light cruiser *Birmingham* which had been alongside in a fire-fighting capacity. Abandoned too late in the day, the carrier was finally sunk by the light cruiser *Reno* after the damage had been done.[35]

What Onishi had tried to do to Sherman's task group, General Kyoji Tominaga attempted to copy with the 4th Army Air Fleet against Kinkaid's 7th Fleet in Leyte Gulf. Sortie after sortie went over the invasion sites on 24 October forcing Thomas Sprague's escort carriers to meet the Japanese aerial challenge directly rather than flying missions in support of Krueger's 6th Army as it consolidated its beachhead on Leyte. Lacking experience but not heroism, Tominaga's aircrews could do little to puncture the invasion fleet and they suffered badly at the hands of Sprague's fighter pilots and from accurate A.A. fire directed at them from the ships they were seeking to attack. By the end of the day Tominaga had lost over sixty of his planes and had little to show for their loss.[36]

Halsey was far more fortunate. He had decided that the time had come to give Kurita's Centre Force a searching examination and had sent scout planes out at dawn on 24 October to try to find its whereabouts. It was not certain at this stage that Kurita was intent on reaching the invasion site and doing battle with the US 3rd Fleet. It was just as conceivable that he might be intent on making for Manila Bay to bring reinforcements for the IJA troops on the ground in southern Luzon. Despite the advantages of signals intelligence, the Americans didn't know for certain where Kurita was headed but the mystery was soon solved when a lone scout plane from the carrier *Intrepid* made radar contact with these enemy ships at 0746 hours on 24 October. It located them a few minutes later and reported the find at 0810 hours as they were passing south of Mindoro and moving eastwards in the direction of the Sibuyan Sea. Such a route meant only one thing to Halsey. Manila was out of the reckoning and Leyte Gulf was the obvious intended destination. This would be reached by going through the San Bernardino Strait. He ordered all his three task groups to close up and signalled McCain to abandon his trip to Ulithi and rejoin the rest of the task groups in the Philippines. It would take a couple of days to do just that since by this stage McCain and his ships were already roughly 600nm (1111km) east of the Philippines. In their absence, Halsey ordered an all out attack on the Centre Force. In all a total of 251 planes flew off from his carriers to the Sibuyan Sea in four waves to attack Kurita's ships. A mix of forty-five Avengers, Hellcats and Helldivers were the first ones to leave the *Cabot* and the *Intrepid* at about 0910 hours and they were followed by another forty-two from the same carriers at 1045 hours. A third wave of sixty-eight planes left the *Essex* and the *Lexington* within minutes of the second wave getting airborne, while a final group of ninety-six planes from the *Cabot, Enterprise, Franklin* and *Intrepid* began their sortie at 1313 hours.[37]

Locating Kurita's fleet at 1026 hours, the first wave of American planes found the enemy ships sailing in a battle formation notable for the fact that they were divided into two quite separate groups some distance apart. Each of these groups operated on the basis of an inner and outer set of concentric circles. Kurita's new flagship, the *Yamato*, lay at the heart of the leading group. She was surrounded by a circle of heavy ships consisting of the super-battleship *Musashi*, the battleship *Nagato*, along with the heavy cruisers *Chōkai, Haguro* and *Myokō* – all of which were spearheaded by the light cruiser *Noshiro*. Each of these ships maintained a distance of 2km from the *Yamato* at all times. Beyond this 'inner' 2km diameter circle was an outer ring of seven destroyers which maintained their positions a further 1.5km away from the inner core. A second group of warships followed some 12km behind the vanguard with the battleship *Kongō* at its heart. She was surrounded by an inner ring of heavy ships – the battleship *Haruna* and the heavy cruisers *Chikuma, Kumano, Suzuya* and *Tone*, with the light cruiser *Yahagi* fulfilling the same role as the *Noshiro* did in the first group. An outer circle of six destroyers completed this rear group. Kurita had devised this battle formation because he felt he needed better cover against the possibility of any heavy air attack launched by the Americans and trusted that the Japanese A.A. potential was as good in practice as it might be judged on paper. It wasn't.[38]

Although confusion reigns to this day about just what happened in these air strikes and who did what to whom, there is sufficient evidence to suggest that the first strike succeeded initially in both torpedoing *Myokō* and knocking her out of the line and even more significantly obtaining both a bomb hit and torpedo strike against *Musashi*, one of the two behemoths in the Centre Force. Each wave thereafter targeted the super-battleship and more bombs and torpedoes struck home with devastating effect over the next few hours. At least thirty-two hits were recorded against her and she received eighteen near-misses before she finally sank at 1935 hours later that same day with the loss of 1,023 officers and crew. All the other battleships, including the *Yamato*, were bombed as well, but none of them received the treatment accorded to the *Musashi*, or were disabled even if they were hit. Four hours before *Musashi* sank, seeing his fleet worn away first by enemy submarines and then by Mitscher's aircraft, Kurita had decided not to tempt fate any longer and to reverse course temporarily so as not to sail in daylight into the narrow confines of the San Bernardino Strait where his remaining warships could be subject to yet another deadly series of attacks. About an hour after Kurita turned round again and resumed his original course, he received an emphatic signal from Toyoda at 1815 hours that made it very clear where the Vice-Admiral's duty lay. Attack was the only option and he was instructed to put his faith in divine assistance.[39] Kurita knew what that meant. His presence in Leyte Gulf was essential regardless of what losses his Centre Force sustained in getting there. Abandoning his concentric circle formation, Kurita gathered his remaining ships into what Ugaki would later describe as a 'compound column' and pressed on towards his original destination.[40]

While the Centre Force had been receiving the unwanted attention of Mitscher's carrier planes during the morning, one of Ozawa's reconnaissance aircraft from the north had finally located Sherman's ships off Luzon some 160nm (296km) southeast of the Japanese carrier force at 1115 hours. Upon receiving this news Ozawa was at last able to begin the risky decoy operation that the Japanese *SHO-GO 1* war plan demanded of him. By sending off seventy-six of his aircraft to attack Sherman's Task Group (TG.38.3) just before midday, Ozawa hoped that his pilots would be able to make a dramatic intervention in the proceedings. It was imperative that the Americans discover Ozawa's presence to the north of them for the decoy ploy to work. If Halsey remained oblivious to their presence, he wouldn't have any incentive to remove his ships from their existing stations. He needed to believe that a major enemy carrier force was coming to contest the invasion of Leyte from the north, but this message was hardly going to be delivered by Ozawa's inexperienced air crew, half of whom were shot down by Sherman's fighter pilots well before they got anywhere near the warships of TG.38.3. Those that weren't shot down flew on to land at Clark Field in Luzon where the Americans suspected they had come from in the first place. Clearly the decoy operation was not working in the way that it was hoped, the bait was not being taken and it looked as if time was running out for *SHO-GO 1*. Something needed to be done, but with only about twenty-five aircraft left to cover his entire fleet Ozawa was forced to order Rear-Admiral Chiaki

Matsuda southwards at 1430 hours with a group of ships including his two partially converted battleship carriers (*Hyūga* and *Ise*) to shell Sherman's group and force the Americans to run reconnaissance checks on what enemy force, if any, lay to the north of them. Ozawa's ploy finally worked. Matsuda's force was detected at 1540 hours and the rest of Ozawa's fleet was found by a Helldiver scout plane an hour later.[41]

Although Ozawa's carrier fleet had now become a known factor, the success or otherwise of *SHO-GO 1* still depended almost entirely upon the aggressive instincts of Admiral Halsey. Not known as 'Bull' for nothing, Halsey was a dominant, hard-charging figure who was used to taking bold, decisive action if the occasion demanded it and he deemed the prize was worth it. While this made him a very attractive figure in some quarters, Halsey was also inclined to be rather impetuous and lacking in finesse. Learning about Ozawa's existence, Halsey was determined not to repeat the mistake made by Spruance at the Battle of the Philippine Sea and allow the Japanese carriers to escape once again. In order to ensure that this didn't happen, he had to convince himself that Kurita's reduced battlefleet, though still numerically impressive, was no longer the threat to American shipping in the area that it had been before it lost both *Musashi* and *Myokō*. Drawing comfort from the haphazard progress it had been making before nightfall, Halsey reached the very dubious conclusion that it might even withdraw from the scene altogether. Furthermore, he was not disposed to worry much about it even if Kurita tried to press home an attack on the invasion fleet gathered in Leyte Gulf since it would have to contend with further Allied air attacks from not only the newly acquired air base at Tacloban on Leyte, but also the three escort carrier groups belonging to Sprague based off Samar and Leyte Gulf. If that was not enough, he would also have to confront the rest of the 7th Fleet which Kinkaid had at his disposal to protect the amphibious invasion fleet in these waters.[42] Under these circumstances, therefore, Halsey felt empowered to take precipitate action. Ignoring any advice to the contrary, he had decided by the early evening to send his entire fleet northwards to hunt down Ozawa's carrier force during the hours of darkness and be ready to annihilate it at first light on 25 October. This was a controversial enough decision in any case, but he compounded it by not leaving behind any heavy ships to guard the San Bernardino Strait and prevent the Centre Force from emerging through it unscathed.[43]

Halsey's brash confidence in American fire power and underestimation of the threat posed by Kurita's Centre Force lacked shrewdness and reeked of impetuosity. If the American air threat could be neutralised in some way – a spell of bad weather to ground the planes or rigorous A.A. defence to down them – the enemy fleet could fall upon Kinkaid's 7th Fleet and do enormous damage to it. Kinkaid would hardly have approved of Halsey's sweeping deployments had he known about them, but when he received a signal from Halsey at 2024 hours to the effect that he was going north to track down Ozawa's carriers with three task groups, he misinterpreted the information assuming that an earlier message that his staff had picked up from Halsey's flagship at 1512 hours still held good. In this earlier message Halsey had informed his 3rd Fleet commanders, as well as his superior officers, Nimitz and King, that he was planning to form a new Task Force (TF 34) under Vice-Admiral Willis Lee, his battle line commander, to fight a surface engagement with the enemy at long range. Halsey indicated that TF 34 would contain his own flagship *New Jersey* and the three other battleships *Alabama*, *Iowa* and *Washington*, two heavy cruisers, three light cruisers, as well as two destroyer divisions. It was obviously intended to deal with Kurita's Centre Force if it attempted to make passage through the San Bernardino Strait. Halsey's message was sent out as a 'Battle Plan' and not as an executive order, but Kinkaid, who shouldn't have received the information in the first place, Nimitz, and King all failed to spot the ambiguity. Indeed there may have been none at all if the situation prevailing at 1512 hours remained, but it didn't. At this stage Halsey had not yet learnt of Ozawa's existence. Once the enemy carrier fleet had been spotted, however, his pugnacious impetuosity proved impossible to thwart. Unfortunately, what neither Kinkaid nor his staff knew was that Halsey had given a verbal update on the TBS (Talk Between Ships) network to Bogan and Davison, the two task group commanders that would be affected by the formation of TF 34, at 1710 hours to the effect that TF 34 would only be formed by him alone at a later stage should Kurita's Centre Force pass through the San Bernardino Strait and opt to do battle with the invasion fleet in Leyte Gulf. Quite how this was to be done was not spelt out by Halsey at this or any other stage. As he continued to mull over the possibilities open to him, he presumptuously decided that forming TF 34 and placing it on guard off the San Bernardino Strait would not be in his interests since it would need a carrier group assigned to it in order to defend itself against any threat from land-based enemy planes sent to attack it. Since McCain's TG 38.1 wouldn't be back in time, providing TF 34 with carrier planes would ensure that Halsey could only take two carrier groups north with him to engage Ozawa's fleet. Concluding that this may not have given him a decisive balance of advantage over the enemy carriers, he opted to forgo the possible deployment of the now mythical TF 34 but failed to spell out this information explicitly to Kinkaid, let alone King or Nimitz who were sent copies of the following signal at 2024 hours: 'Enemy force [Kurita's Centre Force] Sibuyan Sea 1925 position 12° 45′N 122°40′E course 120 speed 12 knots. Strike reports indicate enemy heavily damaged. Am proceeding north with three groups to attack enemy carrier force at dawn.'[44] While admittedly Halsey was not to know that Kinkaid's staff had intercepted his earlier message (1512 hours) about the possible formation of Task Force 34, he didn't seem to think that the wording of his latest signal was in the least bit ambiguous – which, alas, it was.

Unfortunately there was no other direct radio communication between Halsey and Kinkaid to clear up this misunderstanding because MacArthur, as COMSOWESPAC, had forbidden such contact between his 7th Fleet and Halsey's 3rd Fleet which reported to Nimitz (CINCPAC).[45] This wholly contrived and frankly absurd situation meant that if Kinkaid wished to send any messages to Halsey he would be forced to send them in code to the radio station on Manus Island who would retransmit them on the so-called Fox schedule to all ships of the US Pacific Fleet according to priority and the order in which they had arrived at the receiving station. In an on-going series of battles, such as Leyte Gulf, with action taking place in various theatres simultaneously, the radio operators at Manus were besieged by tons of messages most of which were listed as urgent. Consequently a considerable delay in passing on these coded messages was experienced. This appalling lack of direct communication between the 3rd and 7th Fleet insisted upon by MacArthur was indicative of the problems that arose out of the dual strategic approach adopted by the Americans in the Pacific campaign. In a situation in which Halsey reported directly to Nimitz and Kinkaid to MacArthur, but direct communication between the respective fleet commanders was forbidden, could the left hand really know what the right was doing? In a joint operation such as this one in the Philippines where both strategic approaches and forces were involved, the degree of communication between them was vital or should have been. Instead Halsey went his own way believing that Kinkaid would have no difficulty in filling the void which his three task groups would leave behind. Lacking the direct radio contact that would have cleared up any ambiguity between them, Kinkaid was left to make a series of critical assumptions as to what strategic arrangements had been made in the wider theatre and how they might impinge upon his own forces. Regrettably, his assumptions lacked validity and his actions were blatantly injudicious. Believing that Halsey must have left a strong support force behind to bar the way should Kurita seek to break through the San Bernardino Strait and set course for the northern entrance of Leyte Gulf, Kinkaid failed to keep the former under aerial surveillance as Halsey himself had expected he would have done. It was a classic misunderstanding and one that should have been catastrophically punished by Kurita on 25 October.[46]

What might appear inexplicable at first sight becomes a little less so when one remembers that Kinkaid was already well aware from reconnaissance reports that Nishimura and Shima's forces were approaching in two distinct groups from the south, so he was naturally focused on dealing with them before they could get into Leyte Gulf. Although he had delegated the task of dealing with both these sets of warships to Rear-Admiral Jesse Oldendorf who had been in charge of the Fire Support Group when the landings had taken place on the southern shore of Leyte Gulf a few days before, Kinkaid's attention was firmly fixed on the two-pronged southern threat to his forces. While it doesn't excuse his lack of vigilance in the north, it does perhaps make it a little more understandable. Fortunately, Oldendorf had responded to his new responsibilities with *élan*. He decided that he could throttle both of these groups as they entered the narrow Surigao Strait immediately to the south of the island of Leyte during the night of 24–25 October. His job was made somewhat easier for him by the mutual antipathy existing between the two Japanese commanders he would be facing – Shoji Nishimura and Kiyohide Shima – neither of whom were prepared to do anything to liaise with one another and so the planned coordination of their two forces that was supposed to be effected by a rendezvous between them in the Sulu Sea never happened. As a result, the desired southern claw of the tactical pincer movement that was supposed to be made with Kurita's Centre Force coming down from the north to slam shut on the enemy ships in between them became instantly fractured. Nishimura never sought to repair it. Whether it would have made any material difference in the end even if they had joined up is debatable, but the opportunity for working as a cohesive unit was never seized upon. Nishimura seems the more culpable in this regard. Although he had made flag rank and devotedly did his duty, his career had been somewhat disappointing and littered with less than stellar results. Shima, on the other hand, had gained preferment largely through a series of less than taxing staff jobs ashore. Nishimura's contempt for him and his alleged penchant for intrigue and scheming was well known in IJN circles. More galling still for Nishimura was the fact that Shima was the more senior admiral. Whether Nishimura sensed that the man he so evidently distrusted might, in theory, have attempted to assume tactical command of the combined force once they had joined up is unknown. If he thought there was a risk that this might happen it could explain his subsequent attitude. Whatever dark and sinister thoughts he may have entertained about Shima, it is clear that he was a man nursing great personal sadness at this time. His only and beloved son, Teiji, of whom much had been expected, had been killed while serving as a naval pilot in the Philippines. While this may not have made him suicidal, it almost certainly was sufficient for him not to care any longer about his personal safety. His latest mission would be his last.[47]

Things began to go wrong for both Nishimura and Shima early on 24 October. At 0800 hours Shima's 2nd Striking Force had been discovered in the waters off Panay and attacked by some of the returning carrier planes from the *Franklin*. These attacks managed to sink the destroyer *Wakaba*, but within minutes of this initial discovery came news of yet another. At 0820 hours Nishimura's Southern Force had also been detected much further south while it was still in the Sulu Sea. Gathering together a force of twenty-six fighter planes and dive bombers from the *Enterprise*, an attack was pressed home at 0905 hours when Nishimura's warships were some 215nm (398km) from the Surigao Strait which it would have to pass through en route to Leyte Gulf. These attacks caused some light damage to the battleship *Fusō* and five fatalities and six casualties aboard the destroyer *Shigure*, but both vessels survived the encounter and were able to plough on with no discernible reduction in speed. At this rate of progress the Southern Force would reach the narrow confines of the Surigao Strait later that same evening. These sightings were made known to Kinkaid and he passed on the information to Oldendorf at 1443 hours with the order to prevent the enemy from reaching Leyte Gulf. As the hours went by no further reports came in from Mitscher's carrier planes about the location of Nishimura's warships and so Kinkaid sent two of his own Catalina patrol planes to search for them but, again, to no avail. In the interim period Oldendorf busied himself with a plan to ambush the Southern Force should it enter the Surigao Strait. In this objective he was aided by the natural features of a waterway that was essentially a funnel carved between rocky cliffs: 30nm (55.6km) in length, it tapered down from 25nm (46.3km) wide at its northern mouth to 12nm (22.2km) across at its most southerly point. It was perfect ambush country since the cliffs prevented Japanese radar from detecting what lay in store for them. Instructing Rear-Admiral George Weyler to deploy his six battleships some 1,000 yards (914m) apart as a patrol line across the northern mouth of the Strait to block off access from it, Kinkaid gave him a screen of six destroyers to assist him in this. At the same time he began deploying his eight cruisers in two flanking groups ahead of the capital ships. Oldendorf took his place in the heavy cruiser *Louisville* on the left flank, operating some 4nm (7.4km) ahead of the battleships and to the north of the islands of Hibuson and Dinagat, with the heavy cruisers *Minneapolis* and *Portland* and the light cruisers *Columbia* and *Denver* accompanying him. At the same time he asked Rear-Admiral Berkey to form a right flank roughly 5nm (9.3km) from the battle line and situated close to the eastern shore of Leyte with the heavy cruiser *Shropshire* and the two light cruisers *Boise* and *Phoenix*. In addition he deployed nine of his remaining twenty destroyers along the left flank stringing them out in three groups of three, and assigned the rest to Berkey on the right flank with a group of three acting as a picket patrol between Leyte and Hibuson and the remaining eight spread out on a north–south axis close to the shore of Leyte. Completing the deployment he had thirty-nine patrol boats dispersed in thirteen groups of three spread across the southern approaches to the Surigao Strait and within the Strait itself to report on the progress of the enemy force and cause as much disruption to the oncoming forces as possible.[48]

Nishimura had little trouble in discerning the grave danger posed by this confined body of water, but he had no alternative other than to attempt to traverse it. It was essential he did this at night using the darkness to prevent his force being attacked by carrier planes that he knew were waiting for him in the Leyte Gulf area once he had emerged from the Surigao Strait. A scout plane from the cruiser *Mogami* had already confirmed the presence of a formidable enemy force lying in these waters, but regardless of the fact that his own force was dwarfed by the Americans, Nishimura didn't demur. He staunchly believed in the Bushido code and was prepared to do his duty to the emperor and the nation he loved. He signalled Kurita at 2230 hours that he planned to enter Leyte Gulf at 0400 hours (25 October) while the night still held sway and action against enemy surface forces could be conducted in the dark to increase the element of surprise. Kurita responded by approving of Nishimura's plan of action while revealing that his own Centre Force would not be able to reach Leyte Gulf before 1100 hours. His reply scotched any hope there might have been for a coordinated attack on the USN by both the northern and southern claws of the Japanese pincer. If this seriously inconvenienced Nishimura it does not seem to have shown. Once he had been given the green light by Kurita, he drove on relentlessly without waiting for Shima's group of ships to join him even though the latter was only 40nm (74km) behind his own at midnight. This underlines the cussedness of Nishimura and the limitations of the ad hoc operational arrangements that had been cobbled together belatedly as *SHO-GO 1* evolved in the last few days before it was set in motion. Although it is impossible to prove it, Nishimura's controversial decision to ignore his old adversary and press on alone may not have contributed much, if anything, to the scale of defeat he experienced in the next few hours. As it was, Oldendorf retained all the advantages and had deployed his forces with great skill. In essence, there was little that Nishimura and Shima could do to alter these factors even if they had been together.[49]

Although skirmishing started at 2254 hours with the first torpedo attacks by two groups of US patrol boats that were furthest west in the gap between the islands of Camiguan and Bohol in the Mindanao Sea, little was achieved by these and the other overmatched PT craft in the approaches to the Strait to hinder Nishimura's progress. Using their lights, star shells and guns to good effect, the Japanese force had little trouble swatting away these attacks and entering the Surigao Strait just after 0130 hours. More attacks followed, but after thirty out of the thirty-nine PT boats had engaged the Southern Force the disconcerting fact was that they had little or nothing to show for it apart from the damage sustained by ten of them. Despite their lack of a true cutting edge (only one of these vessels *PT-137* caused any real material damage during the night's engagements and that was in torpedoing one of Shima's light cruisers, *Abukama*, at 0325 hours), the primary value of the PT boats actually came in notifying Oldendorf of the existence of the enemy force even though their reports on its size and composition were often faulty. If the patrol boats didn't achieve the aims that he may have invested in them, his destroyer force more than made up for the disappointment. They confronted Nishimura's ships at around 0300 hours after the Japanese had already assumed battle formation. This took the form of the four destroyers *Asagumo, Michishio, Shigure* and *Yamagumo* steaming abreast of each other. They were followed in single file formation by Nishimura's flagship *Yamashiro*, the old battleship *Fuso* and the heavy cruiser *Mogami*. Over the course of the next eighty minutes they were assailed by torpedo attacks coming from the destroyers on both the western and eastern sides of the Strait and subsequently from the northwest and northeast directions too. Executing their attacks brilliantly, the destroyer captains soon saw some reward for their efforts. *Fuso* was the first to be hit at 0309 hours and three of the destroyers soon followed. *Asagumo* had her bows blown off, *Michishio* was stopped dead in her tracks, and *Yamagumo*, after taking several hits, blew up in spectacular fashion at 0319 hours. *Yamashiro* was the next to be torpedoed and more attacks followed on the damaged *Fusō* and *Michishio* with the former breaking in two and the latter sinking before 0400 hours. No matter what Nishimura tried to do there was no escape. *Yamashiro* was hit by another swathe of torpedoes and soon was being peppered by shells from the two banks of cruisers positioned on her northwest and northeast wings ahead of her and from five of the six battleships lying some 3.5nm (6.5km) adrift of them.[50] A vast weight of shot was turned on the remaining Japanese warships with 3,100 rounds coming from the cruisers alone and 285 armour-piercing shells from the capital ships. It was too much for Nishimura's flagship to resist and she sank with her commanding officer aboard at 0419 hours. Ten minutes before she did so Oldendorf had ordered a ceasefire. It wasn't quite the end of the story, however, as the *Mogami*, which had been shelled and badly damaged, turned away to the south to escape certain destruction only to collide sickeningly with Shima's flagship *Nachi* at 0430 hours. It took only ten minutes for the two ships to extricate themselves from one another, but the effects of the collision were such as to reduce *Nachi*'s speed to a maximum of 20 knots and bring any idea that Shima may have had for a rescue mission to an abrupt end.[51]

As Shima's force wheeled away to avoid any further trouble, he reported the news of Nishimura's defeat and the loss of the southern pincer to Kurita and Toyoda. It must have made doleful reading for both of them. *SHO-GO 1* was in danger of falling apart at the seams. In the end, only the destroyer *Shigure* escaped unharmed from Nishimura's Southern Force. Those vessels that were damaged but not sunk at the time (*Asagumo* and *Mogami*) failed to see much of the new day before they eventually succumbed to a mixture of surface and aerial threats and one of Shima's destroyers (*Abukama*) only lasted for another day before she too was eclipsed by American aircraft. Of Oldendorf's forces only the destroyer *Albert W. Grant* had been damaged, and that heavily by shells from both Japanese and American sources. She wasn't lost thanks to the prompt action of her damage control parties, but it had been a very close run thing.[52]

If things went the way of the Americans in the south they were about to go badly awry in the north. Despite being detected by American planes from TG 38.2's light carrier *Independence* before midnight, Kurita had taken his Centre Force into the narrow, lit and unguarded San Bernardino Strait at 2320 hours on 24 October. He had begun emerging from it into the Philippine Sea some seventy-five minutes later. Thereafter his ships rounded the northern coast of Samar before heading south towards Leyte Gulf untroubled by any American interference. This quite extraordinary lapse on behalf of the Americans arose directly from the ongoing miscommunication between Halsey and Kinkaid and the failings of both commanding officers to exercise due caution. Despite learning of Kurita's whereabouts and his obvious intention of entering the San Bernardino Strait before midnight, Halsey still hadn't seen fit to form TF 34 at this stage even though there were officers on his team who evidently thought he should have. Gerald Bogan, the commander of TG 38.2, Captain Arleigh Burke, Mitscher's chief of staff, and Commander James Flatley, the operations officer, all believed that TF 34 ought to have been formed and sent back to deal with Kurita's Centre Force, but their views neither swayed Mitscher, who deferred to Halsey in these matters, nor were repeated directly to the sleeping C-in-C. Whether he rated Kurita's fleet or not, Halsey should have ensured that the sightings made by the *Independence* were passed on to Kinkaid – not to have done so for whatever reason lay somewhere between being mistaken at best and a dereliction of duty at worst. What defence there was for this curious inaction lay in Halsey's obvious belief that relaying the information to Kinkaid wouldn't tell him anything he didn't already know. There is some defence to this argument since Kinkaid had the use of five 'Black Cat' Catalina flying boats that were based in Hinunangan Bay in southern Leyte. Halsey was not to know that only three of these got aloft during the night of 24–25 October and only one flew over the San Bernardino Strait about an hour before Kurita reached it and saw nothing untoward to report. Without the 'Black Cats' performing up to scratch, Kinkaid had nothing else that could have mounted regular surveillance sorties over the approaches to the San Bernardino Strait after nightfall on 24 October. Despite having eighteen escort carriers with him, none of these planes were equipped to fly during the hours of darkness. Notwithstanding the likelihood that the 'Black Cats' would have alerted the 7th Fleet to Kurita's presence in the area, Halsey should have passed on the sighting information to Kinkaid with the minimum of delay. If he had done so, Kinkaid would at least have known what his 'jeep' carriers were up against and could have worked out a rough estimate of Kurita's estimated time of arrival off Leyte Gulf. One can hardly imagine Kinkaid not following up with a reply seeking reconfirmation of TF 34's existence and its intention of taking on the battered Japanese Centre Force at long distance as it came through the San Bernardino Strait and before it could even begin to do damage to any of his task units off Samar, let alone the invasion fleet in Leyte Gulf. But that is counterfactual history – the 'what might have been if' syndrome. In reality, Halsey didn't send on the message and so Kinkaid remained in the dark about Kurita's uncontested passage through the San Bernardino Strait. Convinced that Halsey's 'Battle Plan' signal at 1512 hours would have been put into effect by this stage, Kinkaid saw no reason to challenge the wording of Halsey's message of 2024 hours reporting his intention of taking three task groups to attack and hopefully rout Ozawa's carrier fleet. It seems incredible to think that he didn't seek some reassurance on this matter, but the fact remains he didn't. His first message to Halsey thereafter was sent via Manus Island at 0412 hours on 25 October reporting on the surface action that was taking place in the Surigao Strait involving elements of the 7th Fleet against Nishimura's forces. Tied to that disclosure was the question that should have been posed a long time before, namely, was TF 34 in place and guarding the San Bernardino Strait? Halsey didn't even receive the signal until 0648 hours, but by the time he replied at 0705 hours disclosing that TF 34 was with him in pursuit of Ozawa's carrier fleet and not where the 7th Fleet commander had supposed it was, the menace of Kurita's Centre Force had become all too apparent to Kinkaid and the officers and men under his command.[53]

A few minutes before Kurita's warships were detected on radar or actually seen from the air, Japanese language transmissions were first heard at 0637 hours by a radio operator within the Combat Information Center (CIC) aboard the Casablanca class escort carrier *Fanshaw Bay*, the 8,188 ton flagship of Rear-Admiral Clifton 'Ziggy' Sprague's task unit TU 77.4.3 which was on patrol off the southeastern coast of Samar. Known by its call sign 'Taffy 3', Sprague's task unit consisted of five other escort or 'jeep' carriers of the same Casablanca-class, three Fletcher-class fleet destroyers of 2,325 tons and four 1,430-ton WGT-class destroyer escorts.[54] 'Taffy 3' formed the most northerly of three similar units belonging to Rear-Admiral Thomas ('Tommy') Sprague's Task Group TG 77.4

which had been deployed roughly 40nm (74km) apart from one another in a north–southeast diagonal tier to provide protection for the invasion fleet in Leyte Gulf.[55] Further south and lying off the northeastern entrance to Leyte Gulf was 'Taffy 2' (TU 77.4.2) under Rear-Admiral Felix Stump, containing another six 'jeep' carriers, three destroyers and five destroyer escorts. An equivalent contingent of vessels belonging to 'Tommy' Sprague's 'Taffy 1' (77.4.1) brought up the rear of the task group and was positioned to the northeast of Mindanao where it could cover the southeastern entrance to Leyte Gulf. Within ten minutes of overhearing the Japanese radio conversation, the men of *Fanshaw Bay*'s CIC were to be made painfully aware that a substantial enemy force had somehow suddenly materialised off Samar and was bearing down upon them. Once 'Ziggy' Sprague received word from his CIC at 0647 hours that one of his pilots from the 'jeep' carrier *St. Lo* had seen four Japanese battleships, seven cruisers and eleven destroyers 20nm (37km) north-northwest of 'Taffy 3' and closing at 30 knots, he called immediately for visual reconfirmation of this quite astonishing development. Once it had been obtained he immediately ordered his ships to turn to the east into the wind so that they could fly off their aircraft and he broadcast an uncoded radio message over the TBS system at 0701 hours informing the other members of Kinkaid's 7th Fleet of the imminent danger that awaited them from the north. Sprague's ships stood in mortal danger, but unless something extraordinary took place their immediate state of peril would ultimately be faced by other members of Kinkaid's 7th Fleet further south. Sprague was not exaggerating the nature of the crisis. Although eighteen 'jeep' carriers formed the spine of TG 77.4, they were far smaller, slower (rarely if ever able to exceed 18 knots even in calm conditions) and more defensively vulnerable than fleet carriers; they carried fewer aircraft, had less offensive weapons and were essentially designed for amphibious support duties rather than battling it out with Kurita's Centre Force. What kind of shield would they be for the invasion fleet in Leyte Gulf without Oldendorf's battle group to support them? It didn't bear thinking about.[56]

Although he was not to know it, Kurita had not only managed to take 'Ziggy' Sprague's modest collection of warships completely by surprise, he stood poised to destroy Kinkaid's entire 7th Fleet. If he had suspected such a thing it might have made up for the depressing news he had received from Shima at 0530 hours to the effect that Nishimura's Southern Force had been wiped out and the anticipated southern jaw of the pincer would not be functioning any longer, let alone snapping shut on its intended American foes. Ironically, by the time his radar gave notice of enemy aircraft in the area at 0623 hours, he may have needed all the help he could get. If Eric Grove and Evan Thomas are correct, Kurita may have been suffering from dengue fever – an illness which in its acutest form carries the threat of death.[57] High fever, intense pain and total lassitude are hardly the ideal symptoms that a naval commander needs to be coping with on the eve of an important battle, so if Kurita had dengue fever there is little doubt that he ought to have been in the sick bay and should have had no business remaining in command of the Centre Force. If he was ill, he ought to have yielded his command to his deputy, Vice-Admiral Matome Ugaki, who had been in command of the *Yamato* before Kurita had made his unscheduled arrival on board the battleship on the previous afternoon. Ugaki was a very able naval officer in his own right and someone in whom the revered Admiral Yamamoto had reposed considerable trust since he had chosen him as his chief of staff. Whether Kurita had the same confidence in him, however, is debatable. Even if he did, his pride would not allow him to pass over command to Ugaki. If Kurita did have dengue, it was a colossal mistake for him not to have yielded command in this way and one which would have significant consequences for both sides before the Battle of Leyte Gulf was over. It was obvious that Kurita needed to be sharp and decisive, intuitive and resourceful in the hours that lay ahead; but instead he displayed little or none of these virtues, so a plausible case can be made out for suggesting that the enervating effects of this illness and a significant lack of sleep may have taken their toll on him and at the very least impaired his judgement. If he wasn't suffering from dengue, his actions over the course of the morning of 25 October are far more inexplicable and illogical.[58]

Whatever his physical state, Kurita knew from his radar plot that enemy planes were in the area – a fact confirmed with his own eyes some twenty minutes later when he saw an Avenger torpedo bomber making a lone and unsuccessful run at one of his heavy cruisers. Almost immediately thereafter reports began to come in from other members of the Centre Force to the effect that a substantial enemy fleet, including a number of carriers, lay about 20nm (37km) to the southeast of them. Owing to the curvature of the earth the maximum range at which the Japanese would be able to see the masts of any enemy ship on the horizon from the highest spotting point of any of their surface vessels was 21.5–25.6km even in the best optical conditions. These were not entirely met early on the morning of 25 October as a few occasional patches of squally weather were present in the area to spoil the view and further restrict the ability of onlookers to discern correctly what it was they were straining to see in the distance. Without getting a spotting plane aloft, the visibility factor was always going to be problematic for the Japanese. When they attempted to clarify the situation with a reconnaissance flight, the float plane they dispatched was swiftly engaged, holed and driven off by the Avenger torpedo bomber that was still in the area. It would not feature again that day. As the distance between Kurita's Centre Force and 'Taffy 3' closed and visual contact began to be hazily established, the Japanese were guilty of confusing the identity of 'Ziggy' Sprague's six escort carriers for a group of fleet carriers. Since Kurita had expected to find some of Halsey's 3rd Fleet waiting for him at the San Bernardino Strait, the misidentification of these vessels did not seem wildly out of place. Despite the fact that a battle was imminent and an attack by carrier planes upon his Centre Force was virtually guaranteed, Kurita, for some reason best known to himself, continued to keep his warships divided in cruise formation – three columns to port and three to starboard – rather than redeploying them into a conventional battle line. Had he done so he would have concentrated his A.A. defence fire, enabled his leading destroyers to launch a disruptive torpedo attack, while providing his big guns with the opportunity of concentrating their fire on a few key targets amongst the enemy fleet. By opting for a general attack as distinct from a coordinated engagement, however, he virtually ensured that Japanese gunfire would become more random and, as Thomas Cutler memorably commented later, both 'chaotic and wasteful'.[59]

Notwithstanding these odd preparatory moves on Kurita's behalf, his flagship *Yamato* opened fire at 0659 hours at the enemy fleet that lay before her. Little came of these early salvoes other than to confirm the Japanese presence to 'Taffy 3'and the other astonished members of Kinkaid's 7th Fleet. But as the range and the accuracy of the Japanese fire increased, it looked as though it could only be a matter of time before the 'jeep' carriers of 'Taffy 3' would be blown out of the water. To try to prevent this from occurring 'Ziggy' Sprague did everything he could to confuse his attacker while beating a hasty retreat from the scene. Once his carriers had flown off their planes with whatever munitions they could store aboard them, he ordered his ships to change course for a run to the southwest, with the destroyers laying a dense smokescreen while they were doing so to obscure their whereabouts and the rest of 'Taffy 3' from the prying eyes and heavy guns of the oncoming enemy fleet. Thereafter his own planes and some of those belonging to 'Taffy 2' began to make their presence felt by persistently attacking the Centre Force. Just to add to the degree of chaos, the three fleet destroyers dodged in and out of their own smokescreen – as well as a fortuitous rain squall – to launch a daring series of torpedo and shelling raids against the leading units of Kurita's fleet, often at considerable cost to themselves. If that wasn't sufficient, three of Sprague's four destroyer escorts also got into the act by bringing whatever gunfire they had to bear on their much more august opponents as the battle off Samar wore on. Harried constantly and unable to settle, the massive advantage of Japanese power was to some extent neutralised by these aggressive antics on the part of the Americans. Apart from the behemoth *Yamato*, the battleship *Kongō* and a number of Kurita's heavy cruisers were forced into taking violent evasive action to avoid being hit by whatever projectile could be dispatched in their direction. For the most part they at least avoided trouble; the heavy cruiser *Kumano* was not so fortunate. She became the first major casualty of the action at 0727 hours when her bow was blown off by the force of several torpedoes dispatched in her direction by *Johnston* and she was forced to retire in the direction of the San Bernardino Strait. By punching way above their weight in this manner, the members of 'Taffy 3', therefore, managed to convince Kurita and his staff that they were confronted by several fleet carriers, a pack of cruisers and several fleet destroyers rather than the far more vulnerable assembly of vessels that barred their way into Leyte Gulf!.[60]

In the end, however, this kind of spirited persistence couldn't last forever as the range between the two forces fell, visibility improved, and the weight and accuracy of shot ensured that the Japanese offensive would finally take its toll. It had been a long time in coming but a start on clearing the American force out of its way was made at 0830 hours when *Hoel* was struck by *Tone* and then systematically pummelled into destruction some twenty-five minutes later, exactly two hours after Kurita's flagship had opened fire on the enemy. *Gambier Bay*'s fiery demise followed shortly thereafter at 0907, while *Samuel B. Roberts* somehow defied the laws of physics and stayed afloat until 1005, and *Johnston* eventually disappeared at 1010 hours after a truly memorable performance from both her captain and crew. Typical of the entire task unit, the heroic defiance exhibited by this fleet destroyer has often been extolled by naval historians and with good reason considering she was the first of Sprague's warships to be hit at 0725 hours and the last to succumb 165 minutes later. Of the rest of this extraordinary cast, *Dennis*, *Fanshaw Bay*, *Heermann* and *Kalinin Bay* had all been hit (sometimes repeatedly), while the 'jeep' carriers *Kitkun Bay*, *St. Lo* and *White Plains* had come perilously close to sharing a similar fate on several occasions. Only the two destroyer escorts *John C. Butler* and *Raymond* had avoided a dose of the same treatment, but with ammunition stocks low or exhausted on all of Sprague's ships, the immediate future looked bleak and survival extremely unlikely for all of those who remained afloat.[61]

Nonetheless, while 'Taffy 3' was beginning to be picked off by the Japanese onslaught, some of their carrier planes, reinforced with others from Stump's 'Taffy 2' and armed with more appropriate weapons than those used in the initial attacks earlier in the morning, homed in to attack the enemy fleet at 0842. Kurita's heavy cruisers found themselves the object of much of this attention: *Chikuma* was hit and lost her rudder to a torpedo, *Chōkai* had her engines (and ultimately herself) bombed out of existence, while *Haguro* and *Tone* had also been bombed or strafed but had survived these attacks with minimal casualties and negligible loss of momentum. At this point as he received damage reports on his own ships and exaggerated claims of enemy destruction from his officers, Kurita decided to take stock of the situation and at 0911 hours ordered what remained of the Centre Force to curtail their pursuit of Sprague's carriers and gather instead around his flagship, the *Yamato*, and the battleship *Nagato* which were required to turn north and away from Leyte Gulf. Kurita's extraordinary decision not to continue his drive to the south at a point when the enemy were probably no more than 10,000 yards (9.14km) away from *Haguro* and *Tone* has been the subject of incredulity to most observers – friend and foe alike – virtually from that moment onward. For whatever reasons – mental and physical exhaustion, mistaken assumptions, innate conservatism, a lack of bold leadership, or any combination thereof – Kurita issued the order that was to end the battle of Samar. Decades later historians still continue to seek a definitive explanation for the seemingly inexplicable. What does seem clear is that Kurita had become alarmed that his ships were low on both fuel and A.A. ammunition – which they were – and that with more air attacks expected as the morning continued a consolidation of the Centre Force to provide his battleships with greater protection made a great deal of tactical sense – which indeed it did. Nonetheless, he made two major blunders: one, he became erroneously convinced that his heavy cruisers were not gaining on 'Taffy 3' (which they were) and two, after turning his ships away from Leyte Gulf, he spent an inordinate amount of time (two hours) in gathering them together again.[62]

Well before 'Ziggy' Sprague's ships had been given their unlikely reprieve by Kurita, the 'jeep' carriers of 'Taffy 1' had found themselves confronting a new type of aerial terrorism brought about by Japanese 'special attack' kamikaze ('divine wind') units whose pilots were intent on becoming suicide bombers at the expense of all forms of enemy shipping. It now became a question of who would eliminate the other first: the target or the predator? Ships that faced up to the new menace were left with the challenge of either knocking the kamikaze out of the sky or being on a time bomb which could go up at any time, for if any kamikaze plane got past the ship's defences it could wreak a terrible vengeance on whatever naval vessel they managed to strike.[63] A clue as to what was possible was shown well before midday on 25 October. Attacks by five 'Zeke' fighter aircraft flown from their base at Davao on Mindanao resulted in hits being made on the 'jeep' carriers *Santee* and *Suwanee* and near misses against the *Petrof Bay* and *Sangamon* at about 0740 hours. Despite the damage and the casualties caused by these kamikaze units, the 'jeep' carriers (or 'baby flattops') survived their first brush with this new aerial menace. Not all would be so fortunate. 'Taffy 3' found this out later in the morning when two further waves of Japanese aircraft – five kamikaze and fifteen 'Judy' dive bombers – sent out by Vice-Admiral Onishi from Luzon found 'Ziggy' Sprague's small and vulnerable carriers between 1050 and 1110 hours. *Kalinin Bay* and *Kitkun Bay* were both hit, the *White Plains* received a near-miss and the flagship *Fanshaw Bay* escaped unharmed. This was not to be the fate of *St. Lo* which took a devastating hit on her flight deck by one of the kamikaze from Mabalacat airfield, and immediately became engulfed in smoke and flames and – racked by a series of spectacular explosions that tore her apart – she sank within thirty minutes. It was a graphic and ominous warning to the Americans of what was about to occur with increasing frequency in the months to come.[64]

While the *St. Lo* was going through her agonising death throes well to the south of him and just before Kurita decided to renew his attack on Leyte Gulf at 1120 hours, another air raid broke over the heavy cruiser *Suzuya* leaving her either torpedoed or bombed and in a serious state of decline. Further attacks within the next hour mainly by the carrier aircraft of 'Taffy 2' didn't wreck any more of his ships, but they – and an unconfirmed signal locating an enemy task force to the north of him – seem to have finally tipped the balance and convinced Kurita that he was caught between elements of Halsey's 3rd Fleet and that its vengeance was about to break over the remaining core of his Centre Force if he continued on his southward expedition. At 1236 hours, therefore, he gave the order to abandon the Leyte Gulf option and turn once again to the north. Forty minutes later the first of the planes sent at extreme range from McCain's TG 38.1 reached his ships, but apart from an unexploded bomb that hit the *Tone* no material damage was done to them. Despite this lack of success, their presence may have provided Kurita with some kind of *ex post facto* justification for his controversial decision not to plough on into Leyte Gulf. Working out why he disobeyed Toyoda's orders and abandoned the attack on the American invasion fleet has mystified historians for more than six decades. Was he convinced that a trap was being set for him in Leyte Gulf now that Nishimura had been routed and Shima had withdrawn from the Surigao Strait? Did he invent the sighting of a fleet to the north? Was he opting to chase after Halsey in a belated bid to help Ozawa? Was he merely putting himself into a position to retire from the scene by making for the San Bernardino Strait while he still could and save both the fleet and the lives of the men under his command? Who knows for certain? Kurita's own testimony was contradictory. According to Seiichiro Tokoi – a classmate from his hometown of Mito – Kurita was unwilling to sacrifice the lives of so many Japanese officers and men in what was described as 'a futile gesture of nobility'.[65] Whatever the reason for his decision, the effect had been to throw Kinkaid's 7th Fleet a remarkable lifeline that few could have expected.[66]

While Kurita and Kinkaid's forces were slugging it out off the coast of Samar, most of Halsey's 3rd Fleet were forging north at high speed in an effort to get at Ozawa's carrier force which had been formed at 0600 hours on 25 October into two carrier groups separated from one another by a distance of 8km. By first light on 25 October Halsey was off the northern coast of Luzon and within striking range of his quarry. He and Mitscher had agreed at 0230 hours about forming TF 34 – a task force of six battleships, a mixed force of seven cruisers and eighteen destroyers – under the command of Willis Lee and it was deployed 10nm (18.5km) ahead of his carriers to shell what would be left of the enemy once Mitscher's aircraft had finished dealing with them. As dawn broke the carriers began to ready their planes for the coming engagement. In all, six waves of planes – 326 dive and torpedo bombers, along with 201 fighters – were committed to the series of attacks that lasted throughout the morning and well into the afternoon. In the first wave that lasted from 0813 to 0859 hours the large fleet destroyer *Akitsuki* was bombed and sunk; the light cruiser *Tama* was torpedoed and dropped out of the formation; and four of the six carriers had been hit: *Chitose* so badly that she sank at 0937, and *Zuikaku* to the extent that she developed a 6° list and a sharp reduction in speed. Ozawa was finally prevailed upon to transfer his flag from the fleet carrier to the light cruiser *Ōyodo*, which he did rather reluctantly at 1100 hours. By the time he did so the light carrier *Chiyoda* had been badly damaged in the second wave of air attacks that had been launched at about 1000 hours. She was abandoned to her fate once a third wave of air attacks began at 1310 hours. This new assault concentrated first on *Zuikaku* and after she became a floating corpse, the light carrier *Zuihō*. Both were unable to resist for long – the former flagship sank at 1414 hours and the light carrier did the same at 1526. *Chiyoda* was finally dispatched by 15 minutes of gunfire from the heavy cruisers *New Orleans* and *Wichita* and the light cruisers *Mobile* and *Santa Fé*, and sank at 1650 hours. More attacks followed as dusk came on with the hybrid battleship-carriers *Hyūga* and *Ise* somehow managing to escape after surviving many near misses (thirty-four in *Hyuga*'s case alone). There were to be two more victims of Ozawa's Northern Force: the fleet destroyer *Hatsutsuki* was caught and sunk at 2059 hours by the cruisers which had finally put *Chiyoda* out of her misery four hours before, while the damaged light cruiser *Tama* was the last of the warships of this diversionary magnet to succumb and the only one to be sunk by a US submarine, in this case *Jallao*, shortly before 2300 hours.[67]

As Mitscher's carrier planes were conducting their first raid of the day on Ozawa's forces to the north of Cape Engaño, Halsey began to receive the first in a series of increasingly fraught messages from Kinkaid indicating that all was not well 400nm (740.8km) to the southeast of him where a strong force of enemy warships had suddenly materialised off Samar and was firing upon the 'jeep' carriers of 'Taffy 3' from a distance of only 15nm (28km) away. Stressing that his own battleships were running low on ammunition, Kinkaid urged Halsey to release Willis Lee's battle group (TF 34) immediately and send it south towards Leyte Gulf at all speed. A mixture of agitation and panic was discernible in the tone and content of Kinkaid's signals as the unequal battle between Kurita's heavy ships and 'Ziggy' Sprague's relatively fragile task unit was joined. These strident and unwelcome pleas for help induced a measure of stupefied bemusement and growing exasperation in their recipient who believed he stood on the verge of wiping out the entire Japanese carrier fleet and didn't wish to be distracted from executing this career-defining task by having to deal with an unexpected emergency far to the south. Nonetheless, Halsey had to respond in some way. He couldn't just ignore what was taking place off Samar or reject Kinkaid's calls for air strikes as though these were matters of little consequence. It was obvious that the 7th Fleet needed help, so Halsey ordered McCain, who was already on his way back from his abortive trip to Ulithi with TG.38.1, to provide it and duly informed Kinkaid that he had done so. It is clear at this stage that the 'Bull' was disinclined to defer his date with destiny. Far from going anywhere near Leyte Gulf, therefore, TF 34 would continue to track north at high speed in a bid to finish off the rump of Ozawa's Northern Fleet once Mitscher's carrier planes had dealt with the threat of the Japanese carriers. In Halsey's mind at least this mission still took precedence over anything going on elsewhere.[68]

Unfortunately for Halsey, not everyone in the command loop shared this opinion. At the headquarters of the Pacific Fleet in Hawaii, Chester Nimitz had grown more uneasy about the critical situation that was unfolding in Philippine waters as the morning had worn on and Kinkaid's desperation had increased. A deafening silence on Halsey's part hadn't help to reassure him that all would be well. After previously resisting the temptation to contact his old friend, Nimitz was finally persuaded by his assistant chief of staff Captain Bernard Austin to intervene directly by asking Halsey where TF 34 was. Austin passed on the agreed message to the yeoman of signals who, sensing a note of anxiety in his voice, decided to give it additional emphasis by repeating the first two words of what was originally intended to be a simple and straightforward question. A further ominous twist was given to the revised message by the ensign who eventually transmitted it. In order to enhance the security of their codes, all outgoing signals were given additional words or phrases (known as 'padding') at both the start and the end of a specific message. In theory these additional words should bear no possible relation to the core, or indeed the context, of the true message itself and were to be discarded by the signal staff who received it before the bare message, shorn of its 'padding', was finally passed on to its intended recipient. It was a routine requirement and one made very straightforward because the start of the 'core' message was immediately preceded by a double letter in the text and the end of it was followed by yet another double letter. In this case the ensign who encoded the signal followed customary practice by beginning it with a random phrase – he chose 'TURKEY TROTS TO WATER' – and added the double consonant 'QQ' to mark it off from the real message that was to follow. Using the yeoman's revised message, the ensign encoded the text of the following message which now read: 'WHERE IS RPT WHERE IS TASK FORCE 34.' After adding the double consonant 'RR,' the ensign then finished off the signal by using the three words 'THE WORLD WONDERS' as 'padding' before relaying the entire message to Halsey at 0944 hours with copies to Admiral King in Washington and Kinkaid in Leyte Gulf. Far from appearing to be meaningless padding, however, the three words formed a curious phrase that seemed more than tangentially relevant to the message which preceded it. Under these circumstances, therefore, the signals staff aboard Halsey's flagship, *New Jersey*, didn't know whether to discard the three words or not, even though they appeared after the second double consonant. In the end, it was decided to give Halsey the following version: 'WHERE IS RPT WHERE IS TASK FORCE 34 RR THE WORLD WONDERS.'[69] Halsey who normally didn't get to see any 'padding' ignored the designator RR and assumed that the final three words that followed it were designed to be a critical comment on his operational deployment of TF 34. Astonished that Nimitz could have sent him such a message in the first place and incensed that he had shared it with both King and Kinkaid, Halsey's legendary anger was instantly volcanic. Once he had been informed that the phrase he had initially found so offensive was almost certainly 'padding' and not a source of humiliation, Halsey calmed down somewhat. Nonetheless, it remained obvious to him that Nimitz may well have been unimpressed that TF 34 was well to the north of Cape Engano chasing Ozawa's Northern Fleet when it might have been better deployed off Samar protecting Kinkaid's vulnerable 7th Fleet from Kurita's Centre Force.[70]

While not ordered to abandon his northern advance, Halsey sensed that his freedom to manoeuvre had suddenly become much more limited than it had been before CINCPAC's intervention. Even so he didn't immediately change his plans. As a result, the three carrier task groups belonging to Sherman, Bogan and Davison, along with Lee's TF 34, continued on their northern course in pursuit of Ozawa. It was only after receiving heartening news from Mitscher at 1030 hours confirming that his planes had begun their destruction of Ozawa's carriers that Halsey began to take active steps to assist Kinkaid's forces well to the south. At 1055 he ordered Lee to detach the heavy cruisers *New Orleans* and *Wichita*, the light cruisers *Mobile* and *Santa Fé* and ten destroyers from TF 34 and allow them to continue forging north as a Light Surface Striking Force under the command of Rear-Admiral Laurence DuBose. This new group would be put at

Mitscher's disposal so that they could finish off whatever enemy shipping was left over after the two carrier groups belonging to Sherman (TG.38.3) and Davison (TG.38.4) had taken their toll of Ozawa's Northern Force. So after leading the chase to catch Ozawa for over eight hours and having closed to within 42nm (78km) of their quarry, Lee, Halsey and a somewhat denuded TF 34 abandoned the quest and turned away at 1115 hours taking their six battleships, three light cruisers and their eight remaining destroyers with them and set course for Leyte Gulf. They were to be accompanied down the east coast of Luzon by Bogan's carrier task group (TG.38.2) which was detached from Mitscher's command in order to provide TF 34 with air fighter cover against any land-based aerial threat the Japanese might have formed against it. Bogan's dive and torpedo bombers would also vastly improve TF 34's striking potential should it confront Kurita's Centre Force at any stage on its rescue mission.[71]

Halsey duly went south but without any great enthusiasm. As a result, TF 34 continued to make sedate rather than rousing progress during the early part of its return journey. An injection of pace and urgency was only belatedly introduced by him in the late afternoon after more than two-and-a-half hours had been spent on transferring fuel from his four slowest battleships to his eight destroyers. At 1701 hours, learning that Kurita was no longer threatening any part of the 7th Fleet, hadn't entered Leyte Gulf and appeared to have retired north, Halsey formed a new task group (TG. 34.5) in which his two fastest battleships, *Iowa* and *New Jersey*, accompanied by the three light cruisers and all eight destroyers from Lee's TF 34, were dispatched ahead of the slower battleships in an effort to reach the San Bernardino Strait before the Centre Force could use it to withdraw back into the Sibuyan Sea and away from the Philippines. In keeping with the sense of listless ennui that pervaded the day for Halsey, the deployment was made far too late for TG.34.5 to do the job it was assigned to do. Kurita's warships entered the San Bernardino Strait at 2140 hours having survived a series of long-range attacks by McCain's aircraft during the afternoon and a number of sorties from Sprague's 'jeep' carriers, but they had not been required to repel a single attack from any of Bogan's carrier planes which were in range the longer the afternoon wore on and as the distance between the two sets of forces narrowed. Why Halsey didn't request such an air strike remains a mystery. It may have been merely precautionary, or perhaps he truly believed that McCain's aircraft would be sufficient to do the trick against an enemy fleet he hadn't rated after its toils in the Sibuyan Sea on the previous day. Whatever the explanation, Halsey had seen fit to radio Nimitz at 2126 hours (fourteen minutes before Kurita reached the San Bernardino Strait) claiming an emphatic victory for the 3rd and 7th Fleets over the enemy – which indeed it was. But it may not be churlish to suggest that the margin of this victory could have been even greater but for some of Halsey's questionable operational deployments in the previous twenty-four hours.[72]

Despite the slightly premature nature of Halsey's verdict on the Battle of Leyte Gulf, there were still 'mopping up' operations to conduct even if major fleet actions were now a thing of the past. TG.34.5 moving at 28 knots was still

40nm (74km) from the entrance to the San Bernardino Strait at midnight. All but one of Kurita's warships had long since departed the area except for the destroyer *Nowake* which, in rescuing survivors from the day's action, had become detached from the rest of the Centre Force much as *Hatsutsuki* had been from Ozawa's Northern Force and with notably similar fateful results. In her case, *Nowake* was brought under fire by the light cruisers and summarily sunk by the destroyers *Miller* and *Owen* at 0135 hours. It was a small reward for such a long trek and the abandonment of the chase to catch and eliminate Ozawa who retreated to his base in the Inland Sea with the hybrids *Hyūga* and *Ise*, his flagship the light cruiser *Ōyodo* and five destroyers. Kurita could also count himself fortunate. Having escaped the clutches of Halsey's battleships, his Centre Force received further attacks as it proceeded through the Sibuyan Sea on 26 October. McCain and Bogan's carrier planes, as well as some B-24s from their bases on Biak and Morotai, did sink his light cruiser *Noshiro*, but he still had the *Yamato* and three other battleships, two heavy cruisers, a light cruiser and a number of destroyers to take back with him to Brunei Bay. While they didn't wreck more of the Centre Force, American air groups were able to sink three vessels from Sakonju's transport unit – the light cruiser *Kinu* and the destroyers *Uranami* and *Hayashimo* – and put an end to Shima's damaged light cruiser, *Abukama*, off the coast of Panay. Although the Battle of Leyte Gulf had been a crushing victory for the United States, it could have been so much more. It could have effectively finished off the Imperial Japanese Navy as a going concern. It didn't. Toyoda still had some warships capable of mounting selective attacks on the Allies and at the very least possessed a decent sized fleet-in-being.[73]

Although *SHO-GO 1* had failed and the Japanese naval threat to the invasion fleet in Leyte Gulf had disappeared, TF 38 (under the command of McCain from the end of October when Mitscher and many of his staff returned to Pearl Harbor) was still needed to support the 200,000 troops of Krieger's 6th Army on the island of Leyte itself. Increasing Japanese resistance – bolstered by a series of reinforcement convoys to Ormoc in November that added approximately 45,000 men to the original 20,000 infantry troops on Leyte – and monsoon rain did their best to hold up the Americans, preventing them from establishing a series of effective air strips for use in attacking the entrenched enemy, so both the fleet and escort carriers were pressed into service to support the infantry in its struggle to subdue Lieutenant-General Sosaku Suzuki's XXXV Army. Over the course of the next month the Americans tried hard to staunch the flow of Japanese troops getting to Ormoc. As each contingent landed Krieger's problems multiplied. What MacArthur had wanted was a swift and conclusive victory so that he could use Leyte for the next major prong of his attack on the Philippines – recovering the island of Luzon. November proved difficult in this respect. Worse still the longer the campaign on Leyte lasted, the more replenishment operations had to be orchestrated by Kinkaid.[74]

Unfortunately, that too had knock-on effects as the more American shipping there was in the anchorages in the Gulf the more magnetic appeal they had for the new weapon of choice used by the Japanese – the kamikaze. Deadly and unpredictable, these suicide missions flown from bases on Cebu and Luzon were difficult to defend against and presented a new and unnerving phenomenon for those caught up in their raids. Although some were shot down before they could deliberately crash into a ship, their ability to hurt the US Navy was soon shown in the statistics for the month from 27 October onwards when they badly damaged three of the American fleet carriers, *Franklin*, *Intrepid* and *Lexington*; two of their light carriers, *Belleau Wood* and *Cabot*; and slightly damaged the fleet carriers *Essex* and *Hancock*, the battleships *Colorado* and *Maryland*, as well as the light cruisers *Denver*, *Montpelier* and *St. Louis*.[75] This was a far greater toll than anything hitherto seen from or exacted by the Japanese surface, carrier or air fleets in the past. These were worrying statistics for Nimitz and his staff, his subordinate commanders and their officers and men. It was impossible to ignore the spectacle of a pilot intent on committing suicide for his emperor and nation at the expense of as many of the enemy as possible.[76]

This kind of fanatical commitment made it essential that the Americans strain every sinew to smash the land-based Japanese air fleet in the Philippines first of all and knock out the dedicated kamikaze bases wherever they could be found. Since the air base at Tacloban on Leyte was incapable of handling a large number of aircraft, McCain's carrier planes were engaged more often than not in attacking all forms of enemy activity in the Philippines. They too had a good month. For the loss of fifty-one of their own aircraft, they destroyed roughly 500 of their enemy, in addition to sinking a significant number of warships and merchant vessels found in these waters.[77] Despite the slow but remorseless campaign on Leyte by Krieger's 6th Army, the degree of Japanese resistance on the island encouraged Suzuki's superiors. MacArthur's springboard to Luzon had turned into a soggy bed and General Yamashita urged the commander of the XXXV Army to try to regain the initiative on Leyte by recapturing the air bases from the US invaders with a little help from General Kyoji Tominaga's Commando troops in late November and early December. These efforts didn't amount to much in concrete terms even though they led to more intense naval skirmishing in the waters of Ormoc Bay in which both sides sustained casualties.[78] Although the air strip at Burauen was taken by Japanese paratroopers on 5 December, it was only a nominal prize and they didn't hold it for long before they were wiped out. Indeed once the 77th US Infantry Division was landed south of Ormoc during the night of 6–7 December by forty-nine landing craft and a group of minesweepers, the American grip on Leyte tightened ever more. While this latest setback didn't stop the Japanese from trying to bring in reinforcements by sea, their repeated efforts were largely thwarted by US aircraft from their base at Tacloban. A fast transport and seven transports were sunk by them on 7–8 December, but another 3,000 Japanese troops and some amphibious tanks left Manila in a convoy of transports and LSTs escorted by three destroyers and a couple of sub-chasers for Ormoc Bay on 9 December. After suffering attacks by US Army aircraft en route, the Japanese landed what remained of their troops and tanks late at night on 11–12 December, but in the hours that followed lost the services of the destroyer transport *Yuzuki* (destroyed by aircraft), the destroyer *Uzuki* to two torpedoes from the US patrol boats *PT-490* and *PT-492*, and an LST to the destroyer *Coghlan*.[79] This would be the last attempt to assist Suzuki. Unable to get any reinforcements, Suzuki and what remained of his 15,000 troops were driven out of the Ormoc Valley and into the unprepossessing terrain that became their home thereafter. For all practical purposes, however, the campaign was now virtually over and MacArthur decreed that it was so on Christmas Day.[80] Kamikaze activity had been largely transferred to the western Visayas by that time, but not before another set of pilots had forfeited their lives in attacking a range of Allied vessels in the sea off Leyte.[81]

While the Americans were caught up in advancing their cause in the Philippines during the late autumn, their Western Allies were endeavouring to put the Japanese under some pressure in the Indian Ocean. Monthly sorties arranged for the Eastern Fleet designed to either disrupt oil production in the onshore Sumatran fields, attack enemy airfields, or carry out reconnaissance flights for future planning and operational purposes continued in a methodical, but hardly intensive, fashion. Well meaning though they were, these operations were hardly going to take a back-breaking toll on the Japanese. Operation *Millet* – the attack on the Nicobar Islands – was a somewhat typical example. Launched a few days prior to the invasion of Leyte, it was supposed to be a diversionary operation that would leave the Japanese uncertain about where their enemy was going to strike next, complicate their planning and perhaps lead to a division of their strategic resources. It did none of these things. Mounted by three task groups from Trincomalee under the guidance of Vice-Admiral Power, carrier attacks and sustained shelling of the Nicobars took place on 17–19 October. By then the American designs on the Philippines were so obvious that *Millet* received only scant attention from the Japanese. As a result, the Eastern Fleet retired back to Ceylon, its mission only partly accomplished.[82] Much the same could be said in the following month for the appropriately named Operation *Outflank* – the attack on Pangkalan Brandan in northwest Sumatra – which was aborted in mid-November because of the monsoon weather and diverted to Belawan Deli and its oil installations further south in the island.[83]

By the time Rear-Admiral Philip Vian had brought his task force back to Trincomalee on 23 November, the Eastern Fleet was no more. As a result of the agreement forged at the Octagon Conference in mid-September when Churchill's offer of using the Royal Navy in the Pacific theatre had been rather grudgingly accepted by Admiral King on behalf of the USN, the British naval presence east of Suez had been reorganised into two quite distinct fleets. Sir Arthur Power was assigned to take charge of the more antiquated British East Indies Fleet (BEIF) formed with the battleship *Queen Elizabeth*, the battlecruiser *Renown*, a mixed bag of eight cruisers and twenty-four destroyers. Admiral Sir Bruce Fraser took command of the far more prestigious and powerful British Pacific Fleet (BPF), which was spearheaded by the four carriers *Indefatigable*, *Indomitable*, *Illustrious* and *Victorious*, and supported by the battleships *Howe* and *King George V*, seven light cruisers and three flotillas of destroyers.[84] This division merely reinforced the impression already gained that the Indian Ocean had become, temporarily at least, something of a backwater in naval terms, a large expanse of water that could nonetheless be effectively policed by a modest fleet of warships with active help from more than a dozen submarines in those areas, such as the narrow Strait of Malacca or off the western coast of the Malayan archipelago, where they could cruise at will and do the most damage. It also suggested that with the naval war against Germany winding down, the British could at last offer some help to their American allies in the one ocean – the Pacific – where there was still much fighting to be done.[85]

Notwithstanding the progress being made in the war, Churchill himself may have been a little too expansive for his own good at Chateau Frontenac in Quebec. His understanding of a role for the Royal Navy in the Pacific was not intended to pre-empt his undoubted commitment to recapturing Sumatra (Operation *Culverin*) as a precursor to a reconquest of Malaya and Singapore (Operation *Zipper*) and undoing some of the grave damage that had been caused to the British Empire by the inability of its armed forces to prevent General Yamashita and the IJA from rampaging through their colonial territories and defeating them so convincingly in the first two months of the Pacific War. Not for the first time had Churchill been hoisted on his own petard. From *Octagon* onwards, the British prime minister wasn't really in control of the strategic destiny of even former British territory in the Far East. Once the BPF was formed and subordinated to Nimitz's command, his yearning for *Culverin* would have to be tempered by patience. Other targets had precedence over Sumatra, Malaya and Singapore since their recapture wouldn't bring about the downfall of the Japanese Empire or force it to sue for peace. A more direct assault was needed to secure that objective. Churchill would have to wait in line until mopping up operations became the order of the day. These wouldn't necessarily be held soon.[86]

Regardless of its subordinate position in the grand scheme of things, the waters of the Indian Ocean still washed the shores of some of the islands, such as Sumatra and Java, that provided Japan with a significant amount of its vital oil supplies. Left without any carrier planes, Power's fleet was not the best equipped to try to reduce the Japanese air cover in this region, even though its guns could be used either to shell enemy positions along coastal routes, or in a fire supporting capacity to assist Allied troop incursions, such as on the Arakan Front in Burma in mid-December.[87] While in theory the BEIF had the wherewithal to shell the on-shore refineries, destroy storage tanks and rolling stock, as well as batter port and communication facilities to disrupt the flow of oil getting back to the Japanese forces where it was vitally needed, Fraser's carriers remained the capital ship of choice for this type of operation. Operation *Robson*, launched by Vian's task force against Belawan Deli on 17 December, was a case in point.[88]

Whether the BPF was ever going to be anything more than a mere token force in the Pacific on behalf of the British would ultimately depend upon the progress of the war that was being waged in Europe. All the while Germany was still in the war in a belligerent capacity, 'Europe First' would remain the key strategic doctrine underpinning the Allied war effort. Pearl Harbor hadn't shifted it in 1941–42 and neither would the battle for the Philippines in late 1944 or early 1945. In a naval sense, at least, the war against Dönitz's Kriegsmarine was being won. German naval bases were being targeted and bombed as never before. Massive air strikes had been conducted against Bremerhaven, Emden, Gotenhafen, Hamburg, Kiel, Stettin and Wilhelmshaven since the beginning of the year and German shipping routes in the Baltic, Kattegat, North Sea and Skagerrak had been mined relentlessly by the RAF from June onwards. In a total of 1,900 sorties, the RAF had laid 7,863 air mines and caused a large amount of damage and destruction amongst the vessels plying these waters. Although the RAF lost thirty-six aircraft on these missions, its air mining offensive managed to sink 124 ships totalling 74,545 tons and damage sixty-six more (100,915 tons).[89]

Air support for the Royal Navy which had been such a vital ingredient in winning the Battle of the Atlantic in 1943, and much else besides ever since, was demonstrated repeatedly in the North Sea in the latter months of 1944 when ports along the west and south coast of Norway, such as Aalesund, Bergen, Egersund and Kristiansand, along with the German convoy traffic using them, were being targeted with great intensity and purpose by RAF Bomber Command as well as by carrier aircraft, cruisers, destroyers and submarines from the Home Fleet.[90] Further south off the Belgian and Dutch coasts German shipping convoys often found themselves confronted not only by the aerial menace of the Beaufighters but also by the surface threat posed by flotillas of MTBs that were now beginning to assert themselves after living in the shadow of their Axis rivals for so long. As the Allies began to exert a growing stranglehold throughout the English Channel and southern North Sea after the success of Operation *Overlord*, the Germans found themselves being squeezed out of these coastal waters entirely. Attempts to stage an occasional dramatic coup against the enemy surface presence by using patrol boats or other craft seldom worked any longer, as thirty-six Linsen (explosive motor boats) from the River Scheldt discovered to their cost off the Belgian coast on 5–6 October. Pushed from one naval base to the next by the success of the Allied ground troops, the Germans soon found themselves facing the loss of Antwerp, the important Belgian inland port served by the River Scheldt and defended by the coastal batteries housed on the Dutch island of Walcheren in its estuary. It had proved to be a graveyard for British troops in the Napoleonic past, and it would do so again in early November. Twenty-six landing craft were lost in getting the Commandos ashore on 1 November and despite heavy shelling from the battleship *Warspite* and the monitors *Erebus* and *Roberts* it took a week to shift the German garrison on this occasion. Operation *Infatuate*, though costly, was vital in opening the route to Antwerp and allowing the Allies to begin using it for their own convoy traffic three weeks later.[91]

Four days after the German 70th Infantry Division surrendered on Walcheren, Bomber Command launched its latest bid to finish off the German battleship *Tirpitz*. Unlike previous operations – and many had been mounted throughout the year – Operation *Cathechism* was finally successful. A combination of bad weather, poor marksmanship, stout design, excellent use of smokescreens, technical malfunctions and more than a solitary slice of good fortune had managed to keep both the Royal Navy and the RAF at bay in the past. Sir Henry Moore and the carrier planes of the Home Fleet had failed to make a lasting impression on the resilient German battleship despite mounting several operations throughout the spring and summer in a bid to finish her off. *Planet* (24–25 April), *Brawn* (15 May), *Tiger Claw* (28 May) and *Mascot* (17 July) had all been conspicuous failures with only a near-miss on the last occasion to show for the time and expense devoted to the task. By departing for a two-day exercise into the Arctic Ocean accompanied by five destroyers on 31 July, *Tirpitz* had flaunted her survival instincts and demonstrated her capacity to endure whatever the British could throw at her. This calculated insult infuriated the British authorities even more and caused them to redouble their efforts to put an end to her existence. Four more operational sorties were undertaken on 20, 22, 24 and 29 August respectively (*Goodwood I–IV*), involving 247 carrier aircraft – eleven being lost on 22 August to a combination of A.A. defence and fighter protection. In the third of these raids over Kaafjorden, however, *Tirpitz* was finally hit by two bombs, but the failure of at least one of them to explode prevented catastrophic damage being done to the battleship. Had the bomb which cut through *Tirpitz*'s armour and settled in the No.4 electrical switchboard room exploded, there might have been no need for the RAF to mount another attack, but it didn't and so the struggle to sink her continued.[92]

Where the Fleet Air Arm had failed, Bomber Command was determined to succeed and on 15 September twenty-seven Lancaster bombers took off from the Soviet Naval Air Force base at Yagodnik near Archangel with the intention of finding and eliminating *Tirpitz* in the steadfastness of her Norwegian fjord (Operation *Paravane*). Twenty-one of them carried 'Tallboy' bombs of 12,000 pounds (5,443 kilos) which not even a Bismarck class battleship was likely to withstand. Although forewarned by her radar of an incoming strike, *Tirpitz* made smoke and filled the sky with A.A. fire and time fused shells against the Allied bombers. Despite the impenetrable gloom that settled over the fjord as a result of the smokescreen, one of these 'Tallboy' bombs managed to find the quarry striking her about fifty feet (15.2m) from the forward stem of the ship. Such was its impact that it drove through the deck and the rest of the battleship exiting through the bow and exploding beneath her keel, mangling the entire bow section in the process and causing extensive flooding over an area of 120 sq. feet (37m^2). Once a thorough damage assessment was undertaken after the raid it became clear that it would take at least nine months to repair *Tirpitz*. Dönitz and the Seekriegsleitung were faced with the decision of what to do about her in the immediate future. Frustrated by her record of incapacity, they decreed that the *Tirpitz*'s days of roaming the high seas as a capital ship were over. Although they opted to put an end to her active career on 23 September, they still found a limited role for her to play as a floating battery further south in Norwegian waters at Lyngenfjorden where she would be anchored on the southern shore of Haakøy island close to Tromsø. *Tirpitz* limped to her final resting place at 10 knots during the night of 15 October. Although Dönitz had reduced her status and mobility, Churchill and his COS still found her an irresistible target. Once discovered in her new abode, she soon encountered the next phase of Bomber Command's operational sorties against her. By moving her southward, Dönitz had unwittingly aided the enemy for her new location brought her within range of the long-range Lancasters based at Lossiemouth in Scotland. They were now detailed to find her and put her out of her misery. Operation *Obviate* – the first attack on her sheltered anchorage on 29 October by No 9 and No 617 Squadrons – only resulted in a near-miss as poor weather once again intruded. *Tirpitz* had survived yet another close call, despite the fact that a near-miss on this occasion had been enough to damage her port rudder and make her effectively immobile. It was left up to the Lossiemouth-based Lancasters to try once again on the morning of 12 November. This time Bomber Command, having failed with temporal names like *Brawn* and *Mascot,* perhaps invoked higher authority by naming the latest attack Operation *Cathechism.* Coincidental though it may have been on this occasion, the Lancasters had good weather over the target area and a clear line of sight to the battleship. There was no smokescreen, no enemy fighter defence from Bardafoss, and little A.A. resistance to prevent the bomb aimers from hitting the pride of the retired Raeder's old-style Kriegsmarine with several 5.4 tonne bombs. Once she had been hit *Tirpitz* took on an immediate list to port of 15–20° which worsened in the coming minutes to 70°. Ablaze after a hit on the magazine of her port side 150mm turret, *Tirpitz* suffered a massive internal explosion once those flames reached the 'C' turret magazine. In blowing the entire gunhouse into the air and carrying it 12 metres (39 feet) from its original position, the battleship's already impaired stability was dealt a mortal blow and she immediately rolled over to port and capsized settling on the bottom of the fjord at an angle of 135° at 0950 hours. It had taken only eleven minutes after the bombing had commenced for *Tirpitz* to be finally routed. Although 888 crew members managed to survive her swift and brutal end – eighty-two of whom were rescued through a hole cut in the upturned hull of the ship – a total of over 900 officers and crew perished on board the German battleship. Her loss abruptly extinguished the era of the Axis battleship and provided yet another cause for Allied satisfaction in late 1944.[93]

There was, in truth, much to celebrate. In the Arctic Circle the Murmansk convoys continued to resist all the efforts made by various dedicated U-boat wolf packs to interfere with them. As each convoy passed through or around his U-boats, Dönitz found himself singularly bereft of an effective tool to strike at the Allied cause.[94] It was obvious that until his new craft appeared, he would remain powerless to do anything to arrest the momentum of the war. His confidence in the new *Elektro* boats and their ability to turn the war on its head remained unflagging. More than any of the other leading service members of Hitler's entourage, Dönitz kept faith with his Führer and in the mistaken belief that it was still not too late to change the course of history. There is more than a shred of evidence to suggest that despite the extraordinary spell which Hitler seems to have cast over him (an intense loyalty and confidence bordering on infatuation), Dönitz hadn't taken leave of all of his senses as there was initial evidence to suggest that his new generation of U-boats would prove to be so much better than anything that stalked the oceans at the end of 1944. Just when he needed them most, however, the larger 1,621-ton ocean-going Type XXI and the much smaller 234-ton coastal Type XXIII boats continued to suffer delays in their production which were not helped by increasing Allied bombing raids that targeted those bases and shipyards where they were being readied for operational duty. Dönitz's continuing and growing frustration that he was being denied the very tools of victory can only be imagined. Whether he was plunged into gloom by the thought that regardless of their qualities they might come on stream too late to have any real effect on the progress of the war is unrecorded in his diary or in the recorded minutes of the conferences he had with Hitler. Even if Dönitz didn't let this fear take hold of his emotions, the Allies were very concerned that his new U-boats would pose a real threat to their shipping once more and strove by every means at their disposal to delay their introduction into the war for as long as possible.[95] Marc Milner probably best summed it up by devoting the final chapter in his book *Battle of the Atlantic* to this theme, entitling the short summary 'The Crisis That Never Was'.[96] While Milner is correct to point out that the crisis didn't materialise, it makes a wonderful catalyst for that classic piece of wishful thinking – the 'if only' syndrome!

Toyoda and the Japanese High Command could also relate to this old adage. Had Kurita been well and not hobbled by dengue fever (or acute tiredness) as one may suspect he was, and had he not mistaken Sprague's escort carriers for fleet carriers and pushed on into Leyte Gulf, the Japanese might have been celebrating a brilliant, dashing victory rather than a pulsating defeat. Instead the news from the Pacific was that the Americans were extending their invasion of the Philippines to Mindoro in the northwestern Visayan Islands. Despite a damaging kamikaze attack on the light cruiser *Nashville*, the flagship of Rear-Admiral Arthur Struble, on 13 December, which left his command staff in disarray, TG 78.3 ploughed on with its 112 assorted landing craft and got the men of both the 503rd Parachute Regiment and the 19th RCT of the 24th Division successfully ashore on 15 December.[97] They were helped in this enterprise by the carriers of TF 38 which had set out from Ulithi on 11 December in order to make a constant stream of attacks over Luzon in the hope of destroying as many Japanese aircraft as possible. It was a sensible strategy. If the Japanese Air Fleet was worrying about its own survival, its aircraft could hardly be influencing events on the beaches or bridgehead of Mindoro. It had plenty to worry about. McCain's three task groups, containing some thirteen carriers, eight battleships, thirteen cruisers and fifty-six destroyers, had the potential to wield enormous destructive power when applied to any target. They meant business over hostile territory in Luzon. Their fighter planes flew a total of 1,427 sorties and 244 of their bombers delivered their payloads over the island's airfields used by the enemy. Despite possessing the initial advantages of surprise and waves of fresh planes and aircrew, the constant attacks proved to be very wearing for McCain's men. Losses were quite high. A total of sixty-five carrier planes never returned to operational duty: twenty-seven of them being lost in combat and as many as thirty-eight through a series of accidents. Although they destroyed roughly 170 Japanese planes, the kill loss ratio of 2.61 was lower than normal. These figures were somewhat mitigated by the sinking of four steamers and a landing ship as well, but the whirlwind of destruction that the carrier pilots had been used to achieving in the recent past was not matched on this occasion.[98] Was this an augury of what was to come as the Allies moved ever closer to the Japanese mainland? Would the forthcoming battle for Luzon become another Guadalcanal? If one was the slightest bit superstitious the omens for that attack may have looked a lot bleaker once McCain's force was struck by a typhoon on 18 December. Apart from the loss of 146 aircraft and three destroyers, TF 38 had four light carriers and an equal number of 'jeep' carriers damaged by the storm, as well as the light cruiser *Miami*, seven destroyers, three destroyer escorts, a tanker and a tug. Although bad enough, the fact that the typhoon didn't cut an even larger swathe through these warships may have given the more optimistically inclined hope for the future. Luzon lay in the near future. Of more immediate concern for the Allies over the Christmas festivities were the persistent and destructive kamikaze attacks on those engaged in landing new batches of troops on Mindoro – an unwelcome gift in every way – and other conventional air raids that managed to sink three transports and a tanker in Philippine waters immediately after Christmas. It convinced both Nimitz and MacArthur that more had to be done to knock out Japanese aircraft wherever they could be found. Halsey's 3rd Fleet was duly assigned the task of doing just that in the New Year.[99] Of the languid Japanese naval threat at the end of the year the best that could be said of it was that it remained a muted fleet-in-being and one that had given up on contesting matters in the Philippines. What on earth would Yamamoto have made of it all?

Notes

1 Achkasov and Pavlovich, *Soviet naval operations*, p.287; Rohwer, *Chronology*, pp.351–53; Ruge, *Soviets as naval opponents*, pp.133–34.
2 In this time they withdrew 4,049 active troops, 3,336 wounded personnel, over 300 evacuees, 746 vehicles and 42,144 tons of Wehrmacht property. Only slightly over two-thirds of the latter ever got back into German hands again. Worse still from their standpoint, another 110,000 tons of this war material had to be destroyed because there was no time to ship it away. Rohwer, *Chronology*, pp.351, 355.
3 Ibid., pp.356–57, 359; Ruge, *Soviets as naval opponents*, pp.40–51.
4 As an example of the type of action that took place in the Ligurian Sea at this time, see the vivid account of the interception by the US destroyer *Gleaves* of a German minelaying operation off the coast of Imperia on the Italian Riviera on 2 October 1944 in O'Hara, *German fleet at war*, pp.241–45.
5 Rohwer, *Chronology*, pp.359–60; Gilbert, *Churchill, VII*, p.1054; O'Hara, *German fleet at war*, pp.175–81, Lind, *Battle of the wine dark sea*, pp.165–68; Tarrant, *Last year of the Kriegsmarine*, pp.117–25.

6 Rohwer, *Chronology*, pp.354–55.
7 According to the original operational timetable, CINCPAC forces under Halsey were due to attack Peleliu and Angaur in the Palaus in the middle of September, while MacArthur's SOWESPAC forces would invade Morotai. CINCPAC forces would then take Yap and Ulithi on 5 October before MacArthur's forces would occupy the Talaud Islands (halfway between Morotai and southern Mindanao) before attacking southern Mindanao in mid-November. An invasion of Leyte was originally scheduled to begin on 20 December. When Nimitz's proposal reached Admirals Leahy and King and Generals Marshall and Arnold they hurriedly withdrew from a banquet they were attending and conferred for a few minutes before reaching a unanimous decision to support the revised plan for an attack to be launched on Leyte on 20 October 1944. E.B. Potter, *Bull Halsey* (Annapolis, Md: NIP, 1985), pp.272–79; Taylor, *Magnificent Mitscher*, pp.245–52; Rohwer, *Chronology*, p.354.
8 Michael Coles, 'Ernest King and the British Pacific Fleet: the conference at Quebec, 1944 ('Octagon')', *The Journal of Military History*, Vol.65, No.1 (2001):105–29; Nicholas Evan Sarantakes, 'One last crusade: the British Pacific Fleet and its impact on the Anglo-American alliance', *The English Historical Review*, Vol.CXXI, No.491 (2006): 429–66; Bath, *Tracking the Axis enemy*, pp.199–204; Hayes, *History of the Joint Chiefs of Staff*, pp.625–44; Gilbert, *Churchill, VII*, pp.954–70; Potter, *Nimitz*, pp.323–24; Winton, *Cunningham*, pp.355–60.
9 TF.75 consisting of two heavy and three light cruisers and ten destroyers provided cover for the Morotai operation and TG.77.1 with six escort carriers and eight destroyers providing the necessary air support. Barbey, *MacArthur's amphibious navy*, pp.217–28; Gill, *Royal Australian Navy 1942–1945*, pp.478–87; Clayton James, *Years of MacArthur: 1941–1945*, pp.486–90; Rohwer, *Chronology*, pp.358–59.
10 A light cruiser, *Denver*, flanked by a couple of destroyers, reached the waters of the lagoon at Ulithi without incident on 22 September and these vessels were on hand next day as men of the 323rd RCT of the 81st Infantry Division landed on the atoll and took control of this sheltered anchorage without having to endure any of the dour combat that typified the conquest of both Peleliu and Angaur. As a measure of how important it was to become to the Allied war effort, in March 1945 617 ships were anchored in the lagoon. Rohwer, *Chronology*, p.359; Costello, *Pacific war*, pp.495–98, 539, 561–62; Ross, *Peleliu*, pp.348–50.
11 Clayton James, *Years of MacArthur: 1941–1945*, pp.491–92; Potter, *Nimitz*, pp.321–25; Eric Larabee, *Commander in Chief Franklin Delano Roosevelt, his lieutenants, and their war* (Annapolis, Md: NIP, 2004), p.400; Allan R. Millett, *Semper Fidelis: the history of the United States Marine Corps* (New York: The Free Press, 1991), pp.419–23.
12 Rohwer, *Chronology*, pp.358–59. For sources on the intense struggle for Peleliu, see Harry A. Gailey, *Peleliu: 1944* (Annapolis, Md: Nautical & Aviation Publishing, 1983); James H. Hallas, *The devil's anvil: the assault on Peleliu* (Westport, Conn: Praeger, 1994); Bill D. Ross, *Peleliu: tragic triumph. The untold story of the Pacific war's forgotten battle* (New York: Random House, 1991); Derrick Wright, *To the far side of hell: the battle for Peleliu, 1944* (Ramsbury, Wilts: The Crowood Press, 2002).
13 Most of the Japanese 14th Infantry Division, under the command of Lieutenant-General Inoue, was confined to the largest of the islands in the Palau chain – Babelthuap – for the duration of the war. Here was the value of the island-hopping campaign. One didn't need to take every island – some and their defenders could be allowed to remain cut off from the rest of the Japanese military machine and 'wither on the vine'. Robert Ross Smith, *The approach to the Philippines* (Washington, D.C.: Department of the Army, 1953), pp.450–578; Larabee, *Commander in Chief*, pp.339–42.
14 Achkasov and Pavlovich, *Soviet naval operations*, pp.210–19; Rohwer, *Chronology*, pp.351, 357, 359; Ruge, *Soviets as naval opponents*, pp.176–82.
15 Rohwer, *Chronology*, pp.364–65; Aubrey Mansergh (ed.), *With the Red Fleet: the war memoirs of the late Admiral Arseni G. Golovko* (London: Putnam, 1965), pp.203–24.

412   *Tightening the grip*

16 *Arkhangelsk* formerly belonged to the British and was known as *Royal Sovereign*. She was protected by the net barrages in the inner basin of the Kola Inlet which neither U-boat could penetrate successfully. Rohwer, *Chronology*, pp.348, 350, 357–58, 368.

17 On this occasion, naval ferry barges took off 4,694 German troops from their increasingly exposed position on the Sworbe Peninsula. Ibid., pp.361–63, 373–74; Achkasov and Pavlovich, *Soviet naval operations*, pp.251–52; O'Hara, *German fleet at war*, pp.256–58; Ruge, *Soviets as naval opponents*, pp.44–51.

18 These new craft would be substantially faster than any U-boat Dönitz possessed hitherto as their diesel-electric engines would run off triple the battery capacity of the existing models in operation. Rohwer, *Chronology*, pp.353, 360–61, 373, 378–79, 381; Roger Sarty, 'The limits of Ultra: the *schnorkel* U-boat offensive against North America, November 1944–January 1945', *Intelligence and National Security*, Vol.12, No.2 (April 1997): 44–68; Tarrant, *Last year of the Kriegsmarine*, pp.22–27.

19 German U-boat successes amounted to the destruction of sixteen ships (98,453 tons) in these waters over a three-month period (June–September). In response, nine Allied submarines cruising in and around the Malayan archipelago in September alone dispatched twenty-one vessels – admittedly mostly sailing vessels and small craft, but with a U-boat and four merchant ships thrown in for good measure. October's results were even better for the British. They managed to sink sixty-seven vessels – again mostly small craft, but with a U-boat and a Japanese minesweeper as part of the overall bounty. Rohwer, *Chronology*, pp.327, 334, 339, 343, 348, 354–55, 363, 365, 371–72, 377.

20 Monthly figures for submarine kills in the Pacific were as follows: seventy-two vessels in January, forty-three in February, thirty-two in March, fifty-four in April, seventy-nine in May, seventy-eight in June, seventy-nine in July, ninety-two in August and fifty-six in September making a grand total of 584. Ibid., pp.296–97, 305, 309–10, 315–16, 321–22, 329, 339–40, 345–46, 355.

21 Among those warships sunk in October were a seaplane carrier, four cruisers, a solitary destroyer and two corvettes. Among the vessels that were torpedoed but which survived to fight another day were a seaplane carrier, a heavy cruiser, three destroyers and three corvettes. Ibid., pp.362–63.

22 Halsey and Spruance alternated in command of the US Pacific Fleet which changed its designation to reflect this situation. When Halsey was in command it became the 3rd Fleet and when he went ashore to rest and prepare for the next campaign and was relieved by Spruance it became the 5th Fleet and vice versa.

23 Dull, *Battle history of the IJN*, pp.313–31; Boyd and Yoshida, *Japanese submarine force*, pp.150–51; Gill, *Royal Australian Navy 1942–1945*, pp.500–40; Griffith, Jr., *MacArthur's airman*, pp.177–80, 186–206; Prados, *Combined Fleet decoded*, pp.585–88, 601, 604–6, 608.

24 H.P. Willmott, *The battle of Leyte Gulf: the last fleet action* (Bloomington and Indianapolis, Indiana University Press, 2005), pp.23–57; Rohwer, *Chronology*, pp.363–64; Blair, *Silent victory*, pp.758–66; Boyd and Yoshida, *Japanese submarine force*, pp.151–52; Stanley L. Falk, 'Battle of Leyte', in Liddell Hart (ed.), *History of the Second World War*, pp.361–64; Prados, *Combined Fleet decoded*, pp.615–87; Goldstein and Dillon (eds.), *Fading victory*, pp.447–525; Grove, *Sea battles in close-up*, 2, pp.198–220.

25 It was planned that Kinkaid should assume temporary control of Kenney's air fleet until 25 October when the command would change with the capture of the Tacloban and Dulag air bases. Kenney moved ashore from the *Nashville* with MacArthur on 25 October but was in no position to direct air operations over Leyte because the airfields were not ready to receive his land-based planes. Tacloban received its first squadron of planes two days later, but six weeks after the invasion began Kenney still had only 200 aircraft on Leyte. As a result, Halsey's carrier planes were forced to remain in the area until late November. Blame for the shortcomings of US air support in the Philippines was heaped on Kenney, somewhat deservedly, for underestimating the extent of the problem in advance. He resented the incessant demands made upon

him and so relations between the Army Air Force and the USN became very fraught in the autumn of 1944. Griffith, Jr, *MacArthur's airman*, pp.177–206, 240–41; George C. Kenney, *General Kenney reports: a personal history of the Pacific War* (Washington, D.C: Office of Air Force History, United States Air Force, 1987), pp.445–90.

26 Barbey, *MacArthur's amphibious navy*, pp.229–76; Clayton James, *Years of MacArthur: 1941–1945*, pp.542–60; Rohwer, *Chronology*, pp.366–67; Potter, *Nimitz*, p.330.
27 Kenneth I. Friedman, *Afternoon of the rising sun: the battle of the Leyte Gulf* (Novoto, Cal: Presidio, 2001), pp.25–59; Falk, 'Battle of Leyte', pp.364–71; Hamer, *Bombers versus battleships*, pp.270–91. There are many other books on the Battle of Leyte Gulf that may be consulted profitably. See, for example, Thomas J. Cutler, *The battle of Leyte Gulf, 23–26 October,1944* (New York: HarperCollins, 1994); Adrian Stewart, *The battle of Leyte Gulf* (London: Robert Hale, 1979); Evan Thomas, *Sea of thunder: four commanders and the last great naval campaign, 1941–1945* (New York: Simon & Schuster, 2006); Milan Vego, *The battle for Leyte 1944: Allied and Japanese plans, preparations, and execution* (Annapolis, Md: NIP, 2006); O'Hara, *U.S. Navy against the Axis*, pp.239–78.
28 Cutler, *The Battle of Leyte Gulf*, pp.86–88; Smith, *Emperor's codes*, p.227; Vego, *The battle for Leyte 1944*; Willmott, *The battle of Leyte Gulf*, p.92.
29 Thomas, *Sea of thunder*, pp.143–45; Dull, *Battle history of the IJN*, pp.314–15; Patrick Degan, *Flattop fighting in World War II*, pp.199–218; Barbey, *MacArthur's amphibious navy*, 1969, pp.229–76; Grove, *Sea battles in close-up*, pp.198–201; Stanley Falk, 'Battle of Leyte', in Liddell Hart (ed.), *History of the Second World War*, pp.361–64; Rohwer, *Chronology*, p.462.
30 Cutler, *The battle of Leyte Gulf*, p.144; Willmott, *The battle of Leyte Gulf*, pp.100–101.
31 *Darter* did not survive these operations in the dangerous waters of the Palawan Passage. She tore open her keel on a coral reef of the Bombay Shoal a few minutes after midnight on 25 October in a forlorn attempt to get into position to sink the *Takao* on her return journey to Brunei Bay. Despite being a total write off she didn't sink even after various attempts had been made to destroy her. Eventually *Nautilus* finished her off on 31 October almost a week after she went aground on the reef. Friedman, *Afternoon of the rising sun*, pp.79–101; Willmott, *The battle for Leyte Gulf*, pp.101–5.
32 Potter, *Nimitz*, pp.330–31; Wukovits, *Admiral 'Bull' Halsey*, pp.176–209.
33 Potter, *Bull Halsey*, pp.286–90; Blair, *Silent victory*, pp.749–58; Grove, *Sea battles in close-up*, 2, pp.201–5; Stafford, *Big E*, pp.458–74.
34 Friedman, *Afternoon of the rising sun*, pp.157–59; Willmott, *The battle of Leyte Gulf*, 92–95, 105, 107.
35 Edwin P. Hoyt, *The death of the Princeton* (New York: Avon Books, 1972); Friedman, *Afternoon of the rising sun*, pp.102–8; Falk, 'Battle of Leyte', p.365; Grove, *Sea battles in close-up*, 2, p.205; Hamer, *Bombers versus battleships*, p.275.
36 Stewart, *Battle of Leyte Gulf*, pp.45–66; Wragg, *Carrier combat*, pp.176–87.
37 Willmott, *Battle of Leyte Gulf*, pp.106–15; Rohwer, *Chronology*, p.367; Falk, 'Battle of Leyte', pp.365–66.
38 Ibid.; Friedman, *Afternoon of the rising sun*, pp.121–22.
39 O'Hara, *U.S. Navy against the Axis*, pp.259–60.
40 Goldstein and Dillon (eds.), *Fading victory*, pp.489–92; Dull, *Battle history of the IJN*, pp.316–19; Grove, *Sea battles in close-up*, 2, p.207; Rohwer, *Chronology*, p.367.
41 Ibid.; Cutler, *The battle of Leyte Gulf*, pp.155–57; Hamer, *Bombers versus battleships*, p.278.
42 Gerald E. Wheeler, 'Admiral Thomas C. Kinkaid', in Howarth (ed.), *Men of war*, pp.331–48.
43 Potter, *Bull Halsey*, pp.293–97.
44 Ibid.; Willmott, *Battle of Leyte Gulf*, pp.120–29; Friedman, *Afternoon of the rising sun*, pp.173–83.
45 This peculiar situation arose as a result of the fudged command structure for the Pacific campaign which the Joint Chiefs had never satisfactorily resolved. Although

MacArthur and Nimitz were responsible for operations in their own sectors, sometimes action in these supposedly distinct theatres overlapped or threatened to do so. There had been problems over the Solomons campaign but these had been resolved by enlarging Nimitz's area of responsibility to include Guadalcanal at MacArthur's expense. In the subsequent *Cartwheel* and *Forager* operations Halsey, who commanded the Fifth Fleet under Nimitz, had been loaned to MacArthur to provide sufficient carrier cover for these amphibious operations. This remained the case for the invasion of the Philippines. While relations between MacArthur and Nimitz were little better than cordial, those between the General and Halsey were excellent. They liked one another from the outset and there was a mutual respect between them that didn't seem to diminish over the months they worked together. Clayton James, *Years of MacArthur: 1941–1945*, pp.223, 242, 315–16, 322–23, 339–40, 387–90, 393–402, 522–42, 564–65; Wukovits, *Admiral 'Bull' Halsey*, pp.97, 136, 144–45, 166, 202, 205.

46 Carl Solberg, *Decision and dissent: with Halsey at Leyte Gulf* (Annapolis, Md: NIP, 1995), pp.114–73; James M. Merrill, *A sailor's admiral: a biography of William F. Halsey* (New York: Thomas Y. Crowell, 1976), pp.148–76; Gerald E. Wheeler, *Kinkaid of the Seventh Fleet: a biography of Admiral Thomas C. Kinkaid, U.S. Navy* (Annapolis, Md: NIP, 1996), pp.389–406.

47 Friedman, *Afternoon of the rising sun*, pp.39–41, 43–44, 57–58, 146–49, 191–99, 204–6, 209–10; 237–44; Willmott, *Battle of Leyte Gulf*, pp.55–57, 85, 87–90, 95–97, 104, 106, 110, 134, 136, 138–42, 144–47, 149–54, 253.

48 Friedman, *Afternoon of the rising sun*, pp.190–204; O'Hara, *U.S. Navy against the Axis*, pp.244–59; Willmott, *Battle of Leyte Gulf*, pp.138–45.

49 Friedman, *Afternoon of the rising sun*, pp.194–95, 204–5; Willmott, *Battle of Leyte Gulf*, pp.138–40.

50 Of the six battleships that were strung across the mouth of the Strait, only those fitted with the most up-to-date Mark VIII fire-control radar, namely, *California*, *Tennessee* and *West Virginia*, were the most actively involved. They opened fire earlier than the *Maryland* and *Mississippi* whose Mark III radar struggled to pick out the enemy in the first place and was responsible for a rather fitful commitment on their part. Even so, both did more than the *Pennsylvania* which contributed nothing at all to the engagement. Willmott, *Battle of Leyte Gulf*, pp.148–49.

51 Friedman, *Afternoon of the rising sun*, pp.205–49; Willmott, *Battle of Leyte Gulf*, pp.136–55;

52 Dull, *Battle history of the IJN*, pp.319–22; Falk, 'Battle of Leyte', p.366; Grove, *Sea battles in close-up*, 2, pp.207–12; Goldstein and Dillon (eds), *Fading victory*, pp.497–99.

53 Cutler, *The battle of Leyte Gulf*, pp.208–16, Friedman, *Afternoon of the rising sun*, pp.346–50; Potter, *Bull Halsey*, pp.293–301; Willmott, *Battle of Leyte Gulf*, pp.121–32, 159–60.

54 O'Hara sets out the deep load displacement of these American warships in the following way: the six 'jeep' carriers (*Fanshaw Bay*, *Gambier Bay*, *Kalinin Bay*, *Kitkun Bay*, *St. Lo* and *White Plains*) at 10,902 tons each; the three destroyers (*Hoel*, *Johnston* and *Heermann*) at 2,924 tons each; and the four destroyer escorts (*Dennis*, *John C. Butler*, *Raymond* and *Samuel B. Roberts*) at 1,811 tons. O'Hara, *U.S. Navy against the Axis*, pp.259–72; Thomas, *Sea of thunder*, pp.267–68.

55 Sprague is hardly a common name and to have two such naval officers with the same name but not related to one another fighting in the same battle is rather confusing. In his biography of 'Ziggy' Sprague, John Wukovits indicates that 'Taffy 3' was approximately 130nm (240.8km) distant from 'Taffy 1' by sunrise on 25 October. John F. Wukovits, *Devotion to duty: a biography of Admiral Clinton A.F. Sprague* (Annapolis, Md: NIP, 1995), p.146.

56 Cutler, *The battle of Leyte Gulf*, pp.219–27; Willmott, *Battle of Leyte Gulf*, pp.159–67; Rohwer, *Chronology*, pp.366–67.

57 Dengue fever comes in various forms. All are associated with high fevers, but the haemorrhagic fever is the most virulent kind. Patients with haemorrhagic fever usually suffer from some form of internal bleeding and 'bone-breaking' pain. A mosquito-borne

virus rather than a parasitic infection, such as malaria, it can be lethal on occasion. Even if Kurita had dengue, but not the haemorrhagic kind, he would still have been running a high fever and (most probably) feeling distinctly unwell.

58 Grove, *Sea battles in close-up*, 2, pp.198, 207; Thomas, *Sea of thunder*, p.192; Evan Thomas, 'Understanding Kurita's mysterious retreat', *Naval History*, Vol.18, No.5 (Oct. 2004): 22–26.
59 Cutler, *The battle of Leyte Gulf*, p.236.
60 Thomas, *Sea of thunder*, pp.261–82, 285–94.
61 Dull, *Battle history of the IJN*, pp.322–27; Goldstein and Dillon (eds), *Fading victory*, pp.492–99; Falk, 'Battle of Leyte', pp.366–67; Grove, *Sea battles in close-up*, 2, pp.212–17.
62 Willmott, *Battle of Leyte Gulf*, pp.178–92; Thomas, *Sea of thunder*, p.289.
63 There are numerous sources available on the kamikaze. Amongst those that have stood the test of time and scrutiny are Rikihei Inoguchi and Tadashi Nakajima with Roger Pineau, *The divine wind* (Westport, Conn: Greenwood Press, 1978); Denis Warner and Peggy Warner with Sadao Seno, *The sacred warriors: Japan's suicide legions* (New York: Van Nostrand Reinhold, 1982); and Edwin P. Hoyt, *The kamikazes* (New York: Arbor House, 1983). Two more recent studies worthy of consulting are Raymond Lamont-Brown, *Kamikaze: Japan's suicide samurai* (London: Arms and Armour, 2002); Albert Axell and Hideaki Kase, *Kamikaze: Japan's suicide gods* (London: Longman, 2002).
64 M.G. Sheftall, *Blossoms in the wind: human legacies of the kamikaze* (New York: NAL Caliber, 2005), pp.3–11; Cutler, *The battle of Leyte Gulf*, pp.266–73; Dull, *Battle history of the IJN*, pp.330–31; Falk, 'Battle of Leyte', pp.367–70; Grove, *Sea battles in close-up*, 2, pp.217–19; Wragg, *Carrier combat*, pp.188–98.
65 Thomas, *Sea of thunder*, pp.307–11, 351–53.
66 Willmott, *Battle of Leyte Gulf*, pp.206–13.
67 Ibid., pp.158–59, 177–78, 198–202; Dull, *Battle history of the IJN*, pp.327–30; Grove, *Sea battles in close-up*, 2, pp.217–19; E.B. Potter, *Admiral Arleigh Burke* (New York: Random House, 1990), pp.192–217.
68 O'Hara, *U.S. Navy against the Axis*, pp.272–76; Thomas, *Sea of thunder*, pp.295–302.
69 Potter, *Nimitz*, pp.335–40; Willmott, *Battle of Leyte Gulf*, p.193; Spector, *Eagle against the sun*, pp.417–44.
70 Potter, *Bull Halsey*, pp.303–5; Thomas, *Sea of thunder*, pp.295–302; Willmott, *Battle of Leyte Gulf*, pp.193–97
71 Ibid.
72 O'Hara, *U.S. Navy against the Axis*, pp.276–78; Thomas, *Sea of thunder*, pp.314–16; Willmott, *Battle of Leyte Gulf*, pp.213–16.
73 Potter, *Bull Halsey*, pp.303–7; Wheeler, *Kinkaid of the Seventh Fleet*, pp.395–406; Goldstein and Dillon (eds), *Fading victory*, pp.499–502; Cutler, *The Battle of Leyte Gulf*, pp.283–97; Friedman, *Afternoon of the rising sun*, pp.385–91; Stewart, *Battle of Leyte Gulf*, pp.205–14.
74 O'Hara, *U.S. Navy against the Axis*, pp.279–81.
75 Of the smaller vessels, in addition to sinking the destroyer *Abner Read*, the sub-chaser *SC-744* and an escort vessel, kamikazes were responsible for damaging seven fleet destroyers, an equal number of transports and a couple of repair ships. Rohwer, *Chronology*, pp.369–70.
76 Driskill and Casad, *Admiral of the hills*, pp.207–8, 211–12; Hoyt, *The kamikazes*, pp.98–125; Lamont-Brown, *Kamikaze*, pp.64–77; Potter, *Nimitz*, pp.346–47.
77 Apart from sinking the heavy cruiser *Nachi*, the three light cruisers *Kiso*, *Kumano* and *Yasoshima*, ten destroyers, seven submarines, a minesweeper, two sub-chasers, two *Kaiten*, nine transports, fourteen steamers, two freighters, two patrol boats, a tanker, an auxiliary minelayer and three landing ships all succumbed, while another light cruiser (*Isuzu*), three destroyers, two frigates, two corvettes, two transports and five more steamers were damaged by kamikazes. Rohwer, *Chronology*, pp.369–70.

416   *Tightening the grip*

78 In a clash on 3 December, the Japanese lost the destroyer escort *Kuwa* to gunfire from two Sumner class super-destroyers (each of which displaced 3,218 displacement tons at full load) *Cooper* and *Allen M. Sumner*, the flagship of Commander John Zahm and his Destroyer Division 120. In the confusion of the action just after midnight, the Japanese got their own back when a torpedo probably fired from the other destroyer escort *Take* hit and sank *Cooper* in thirty seconds. O'Hara, *U.S. Navy against the Axis*, pp.281–85.

79 Ibid., pp.285–87; Rohwer, *Chronology*, p.376.

80 By the time the Leyte operation was finally over, it had cost the lives of roughly 5,000 American servicemen and had wounded another 14,000. Barbey, *MacArthur's amphibious navy*, pp.281–84; Falk, 'Battle of Leyte', pp.370–71; Clayton James, *Years of Mac Arthur: 1941–1945*, pp.566–610; William L. Griggs, *Preludes to victory: the battle of Ormoc Bay in WWII* (Somerville, N.J.: W.L. Griggs, 1997), pp.125–210.

81 According to Hattori Syohgo, the Japanese Army Air Forces flew a total of 338 kamikaze missions in the Philippines and lost 240 of these aircraft and a total of 277 airmen. In December alone some of these missions sank two destroyers (*Mahan* and *Reid*), a troop transport, three landing vessels and a tender and had badly damaged the light cruiser *Nashville*, hit but not sunk the 'jeep' carrier *Marcus Island* and no less than twelve fleet destroyers and a number of landing craft, freighters and other smaller vessels. Hattori Syohgo, 'Kamikaze: Japan's glorious failure', *Air Power History*, Vol.43, No.1 (Spring 1996): 14–27; Hoyt, *The kamikazes*, pp.138–45; Lamont-Brown, *Kamikaze*, pp.70–77; Rohwer, *Chronology*, pp.374–76, 378, 380.

82 Rohwer, *Chronology*, p.365.

83 Ibid., p.373.

84 *Cumberland*, *Kenya*, *London*, *Newcastle*, *Nigeria*, *Phoebe*, *Tromp* and *Suffolk* were the cruisers assigned to the BEIF, while *Achilles*, *Argonaut*, *Black Prince*, *Ceylon*, *Gambia*, *Newfoundland* and *Swiftsure* were the light cruisers that were to see action with the BPF. John Winton, *The forgotten fleet* (London: Michael Joseph, 1969), pp.48–67. Ministry of Defence, *War with Japan. Vol.VI* (London: HMSO, 1995), pp.251–52.

85 Jon Robb-Webb, '"Light two lanterns, the British are coming by sea": Royal Navy participation in the Pacific 1944–45', in Kennedy (ed.), *British naval strategy east of Suez*, pp.128–53; Winton, *The forgotten fleet*, pp.32–47; Rohwer, *Chronology*, p.374.

86 Marder, Jacobsen and Horsfield, *Old friends, II*, pp.344–49.

87 Gill, *Royal Australian Navy 1942–1945*, pp.558–74.

88 Rohwer, *Chronology*, p.377; Peter C. Smith, *Task Force 57: the British Pacific Fleet 1944–1945* (London: Kimber, 1969), pp.72–81; Willmott, *Grave of a dozen schemes*, pp.136–37, 165–67, 178; Winton, *Forgotten fleet*, pp.70–74; Hobbs, *The British Pacific Fleet*, pp.63–65.

89 Martin Middlebrook and Chris Everitt, *The Bomber Command diaries: an operational reference book: 1939–1945* (London: Penguin Books, 1985), pp.462–64, 466, 476, 479–80, 485–86, 500–502, 533, 547–48, 550–52, 568–69, 573, 575, 577–78, 583–84, 586, 590, 592, 594, 598, 601–3, 606, 612, 625, 630, 635, 638.

90 O'Hara, *German fleet at war*, pp.248–52.

91 Tarrant, *Last year of the Kriegsmarine*, pp.155–81; Tent, *E-boat alert*, pp.205–33; Rohwer, *Chronology*, pp.363, 370, 372, 375, 379.

92 Gerhard Koop and Klaus-Peter Schmolke, *Battleships of the Bismarck class* (London: Greenhill Books, 1998), pp.63–67; Rohwer, *Chronology*, pp.306, 311, 314, 320, 322, 343, 345, 350–52.

93 John Asmussen, 'Operation Catechism: 12 November 1944', at www.bismarck-class. dk/tirpitz/history/tiropertungsten.html (accessed 1 April 2006); Evans, *Great World War II battles*, pp.127–33; *Fuehrer conferences*, pp.388–89; Gilbert, *Churchill, VII*, p.1060; Grove, *Sea battles in close-up, 2*, pp.136–39; Hamer, *Bombers versus battleships*, pp.292–306; Koop and Schmolke, *Battleships*, pp.65–67; Levy, *The Royal Navy's Home Fleet*, pp.143–50; Rohwer, *Chronology*, pp.314, 320, 322, 343, 345, 350–52, 358, 368, 370; Tarrant, *Last year of the Kriegsmarine*, pp.126–44; Zetterling and Tamelander, *Tirpitz*, pp.296–317.

94 Woodman, *Arctic convoys*, pp.405–16; Rohwer, *Chronology*, pp.358, 368, 370, 375, 380.
95 *Fuehrer conferences*, pp.413–87; Hughes and Costello, *Battle of the Atlantic*, pp.294, 296–302; Tarrant, *Last year of the Kriegsmarine*, pp.182–92.
96 Milner, *Battle of the Atlantic*, pp.231–36.
97 Barbey, *MacArthur's amphibious navy*, pp.285–88; Rohwer, *Chronology*, p.378; Spector, *Eagle against the sun*, pp.515, 517–18.
98 Rohwer, *Chronology*, p.377.
99 Clayton James, *Years of MacArthur: 1941–1945*, pp.607–10; Driskill and Casad, *Admiral of the hills*, pp.211–13; Prados, *Combined Fleet decoded*, pp.694–97; Rohwer, *Chronology*, pp.377–78, 380.

12 Stranglehold (1945)

While naval power had contributed mightily to the rolling up of the Japanese Empire in the Pacific from the Battle of the Coral Sea onwards, it had been much less influential in dictating the progress of the war in the littoral states of the Indian Ocean. This was about to change in January 1945 with the success of the third Arakan offensive. A start was made with Operation *Lightning* on 2 January when Rear-Admiral Bernard Martin left Chittagong with TF 64, part of Vice-Admiral Sir Arthur Power's British East Indies Fleet (BEIF), to put 1,000 Commandos ashore on the Akyab Peninsula so that they could capture the port city of Akyab (Sittwe) from which Japanese troops had already withdrawn. Securing Akyab would provide the Allies fighting in northern Burma with a very useful port for the landing of both additional troop reinforcements and supplies – a point underlined by the landing shortly thereafter of the Indian 74th Brigade.[1] A few days later TF 64 was again on hand to land more Commando units further south near Myebon on Hunter Bay (Operation *Passport*). These were small-scale affairs and mere precursors for Operation *Matador* which put the British 4th and Indian 71st Brigades ashore from eighty-four landing craft on the northern coast of Ramree Island off the Arakan coast on 16 January. Martin, with his flag in the Australian destroyer *Napier*, was assisted in this enterprise by the presence of a fire support group, containing the battleship *Queen Elizabeth*, which pounded the landing sites ahead of the invasion and by an air wing provided by the escort carrier *Ameer* which soon proved its worth by repelling an attack on the invasion fleet by eighteen Japanese aircraft bent on its destruction. Another incremental incursion followed on 26 January with the landing further south on Cheduba Island (Operation *Sankey*) of 500 Marines and an even smaller contingent found their way to the island of Sagu Kyun on 30 January (Operation *Pendant*).[2]

Power's BEIF may have been sufficient for mopping up what was left of Japanese resistance on the Burmese coast, but it was not sufficient to take issue with the real centres of enemy power concentrated around the oil industry in the Indian Ocean and the South China Sea. For these the four carriers *Illustrious*, *Indefatigable*, *Indomitable* and *Victorious* of the British Pacific Fleet (BPF) were required not only to cope with the threat posed by the Japanese land-based aircraft, but also to deal effectively with onshore refineries that were situated, for example, in the hinterland of Sumatra, so far removed from the coast that they were not accessible to even the guns of the largest battleships. If the BPF was going to be representative of its name, however, it would need to move much closer to the Pacific than Trincomalee. So on 16 January Admiral Fraser steamed eastwards away from the Ceylonese naval base with the battleship *King George V*, all four carriers (listed above), three light cruisers and nine destroyers in order to get much closer to the scene of the action. Also known as TF 63, the BPF would collect the light cruiser *Ceylon*, a couple of destroyers and four oil tankers en route to Sumatra before making a couple of successful attacks on the oil refineries of Pladjoe (Plaju) and Soengi Gerong near Palembang in late January (Operation *Meridian* I and II). In this operation Vian's carrier planes destroyed 132 Japanese planes for the loss of forty-one of his own aircraft – more of which succumbed to crash landings rather than enemy action. Air frames could be replaced, but experienced air crew were always at a premium and in this respect the Japanese war effort was doubly hit, losing far more planes and pilots than the Allies did in the Pacific and failing to replace either with the same urgency and dispatch.[3]

Although efforts to disrupt the enemy's oil supplies in Southeast Asia were obviously extremely important, the dominant theme in the Pacific campaign in January 1945 was one of invasion. Having secured Leyte and Mindoro, the Allies next looked to make landfall in the Lingayen Gulf well to the north of Manila on the island of Luzon.[4] This would be no easy feat for the invasion fleet to accomplish particularly in view of the fact that Vice-Admiral Takijiro Onishi's 1st Air Fleet had its kamikaze pilots operating out of both Cebu and Luzon, so getting to the invasion beaches would be difficult enough without even putting the men ashore. Nevertheless, a start had to be made and on 2 January preparations got underway when the sixty-eight minesweepers and a small escort group belonging to TG 77.6 left Leyte for the passage through the Surigao Strait, the Sulu Sea and Mindoro Strait, before forging out into the South China Sea on a northern track towards the Lingayen Gulf. A two-tiered Fire Support Group, commanded by Vice-Admiral Jesse Oldendorf, bristling with six battleships, five heavy cruisers, a light cruiser and nineteen destroyers, set off on the following day. It was accompanied to the invasion beaches of San Fabian and Lingayen by a dozen 'jeep' carriers, twenty-one destroyers and a group of ten fast transports carrying several underwater demolition teams. All of these vessels put to sea to clear the way for the amphibious invasion fleet, known as the San Fabian Attack Force (TF 78), to leave Leyte on 4 January under Vice-Admiral Daniel Barbey on the headquarters ship *Blue Ridge* to put I Corps ashore a few days later.[5] On 5 January the Lingayen Attack Force (TF 79) set out under the command of Vice-Admiral Theodore Wilkinson on the headquarters ship *Mount Olympus*. The XIV Corps were put aboard eighty-three assorted landing craft and given six destroyers and three destroyer escorts in one task group (TG 79.1), while ninety-six landing vessels and thirteen fleet destroyers along with three destroyer escorts made up TG 79.2. Wilkinson, like Barbey, could rely upon air cover provided by two 'jeep' carriers to try to ward off attacks by kamikaze units primed for the purpose of attacking the invasion force as it steamed towards Luzon.[6] Disappointed at failing to interrupt the San Fabian Attack Force in the Sulu Sea on 5 January, three midget subs turned their attention to the headquarters group belonging to Admiral Kinkaid and General MacArthur (TG 77.1) narrowly missing the light cruiser *Boise* as they did so. A total of thirty-five kamikazes based at Mabalacat airfield in Luzon took off aiming to do better. They targeted the Fire Support Group (TG 77.2) and the Carrier Group (TG 77.4) and achieved some success hitting an escort carrier (*Manila Bay*) and two heavy cruisers (*Louisville* and *Australia*) amongst others and achieving near misses on another 'jeep' carrier and two destroyers. These attacks left fifty-four servicemen dead and 168 injured. As the ships of TG 77.2 reached Lingayen Gulf on 6 January to begin their shelling of the shoreline around the assault sectors, a fresh wave of twenty-nine kamikazes and fifteen fighter escorts swept in to try to pummel the Allies. Their success can be measured in the sinking of the minesweeper *Long* and the damage caused to the battleships *California* and *New Mexico*, the already battered heavy cruisers *Australia* and *Louisville*, as well as adding new victims in the form of a light cruiser (*Columbia*), three destroyers and two more minesweepers. Even their near-misses counted as the heavy cruiser *Minneapolis* and three more destroyers found to their cost. By the time the day's attacks were over another 156 servicemen lay dead and 452 had been injured.[7] It might have been even more costly had the escort carriers not been in attendance to launch well over a hundred sorties to try to break up these attacks. Kamikazes had to be shot down either by accurate A.A. fire or by fighter planes. It was virtually impossible for ships to outmanoeuvre them – they did not have sufficient time or distance to do so. It did not take ships' crews long to appreciate the fact that kamikazes were more accurate than bomber or torpedo-aircraft and so they could not be safely left to their own devices for fear that the victim of their attentions would be made to pay the most terrible price. For the Allies it soon became a stark case of an 'us or them' mentality. If they did not destroy 'them' the committed kamikaze pilots were certainly capable of making them rue the day they didn't. What this new and terrifying form of warfare did was to strike fear into the heart of many onlookers who were caught up in situations that they could often do little about. It was suicide bombing by any other name and about as random. More death and destruction followed over the next couple of days with 100 more servicemen dying and 120 being injured with further hits being registered on the two escort carriers *Kadashan Bay* and *Kitkun Bay*, the much struck *Australia*, a minesweeper, transport and a landing craft. It was sobering to remember that as yet no amphibious landing had been made even though the cost of getting the troops to the point of delivery had already been high in both personal and material terms. While the individual kamikaze pilot represented a new aspect of engagement, the last of the old surface action in the Pacific was played out between four Allied destroyers and the Japanese escort destroyer *Hinoki*, during the night of 7–8 January after the latter had emerged from Manila Bay. She had tried such a manoeuvre a couple of days before but had been driven back as her accompanying destroyer, *Momi*, had been picked off by the Allies. Now it was *Hinoki*'s turn to be hunted down and sunk late at night by four US destroyers in what was the last surface action of the Pacific campaign.[8]

Ironically, after a tough passage to Luzon the actual landing in Lingayen Gulf – Operation *Mike I* – went ahead on 9 January in a fairly uncontested way. On the first day alone, 70,000 troops were landed as the Japanese troops previously defending the coastline had been redeployed in the Zambales Mountains before the invasion started. What resistance there was to the two landings came from a mixture of kamikazes and explosive boats. Nine of the former appeared over Oldendorf's Fire Support Group on 9 January and three made their mark in striking the battleship *Mississippi* and the cruisers *Australia* and *Columbia* (yet again), while some of the others caused damage to the destroyer escort *Hodges* by achieving near-misses on her. During the night it was the turn of seventy explosive boats to make their appearance. Sent out from San Juan with high hopes of disabling a number of significant warships, the boats failed to live up to the hopes of those who sent them on their way, only sinking two landing craft and damaging a transport and three LSTs in the process. Despite not cutting a greater swathe amongst the invasion fleet than they did, the Japanese still managed to kill another 114 servicemen and injure another 377 in the first twenty-four hours of the operation. Further attacks were mounted on 11 January in response to the massed landing by Amphibious Group 3 of both armoured and infantry troops from 108 landing craft in the same location. Kamikaze attacks over the course of the next couple of days left another six victims, including the 'jeep' carrier *Salamaua*, damaged but afloat off Lingayen, while four Liberty ships and a further LST suffered a similar fate off Bataan. In all, another 194 died in these attacks and 218 were injured, but the landings were successful. Unlike fighter or bomber planes, kamikaze units never expected to return to base and so once committed to a raid it often meant a solo one-way mission which would end in a crash one way or the other. Without an inexhaustible supply of both men and machines, the more kamikaze raids there were the quicker the stock of airframes and pilots who were willing to die for the cause was depleted. By 14 January that situation had been reached off Luzon with the result that four new supply convoys made their way to the shoreline over the next fortnight without any interference from Takejiro Onishi's 1st Naval Air Fleet. By the time the escort carriers were withdrawn on 17 January – their job done with Krueger's 6th Army onshore no longer in need of their help – Rear-Admiral Calvin Durgin's planes had flown a total of 6,152 sorties and had only lost two aircraft in these operations. It was a quite spectacular return and one which almost certainly saved many Allied lives and ships in the process.[9]

After the successful penetration of Lingayen Gulf, other landings were swiftly put in train for other areas on the western side of Luzon. On 29 January in Operation *Mike VII*, fifty-seven transports and landing craft dropped 30,000 infantry troops near to Zambales north of Subic Bay and the next day a detachment of infantry troops were taken by a few fast transports to Gamble Island in Subic Bay itself. Before the day was out Subic Bay was in American hands and so was the town of Olongapo. Both landings were achieved with the minimum of fuss and at the cost of torpedo damage to only one fast transport, *Cavalier* – the work of the Japanese submarine *Ro-46*. Up to this point the performance of the Japanese submarine fleet had been immensely disappointing. It would fail to win many plaudits in these waters in future.[10] Operation *Mike VI* saw Amphibious Group 8 use another forty-seven landing craft to put the 11th Airborne Division ashore near Nasugbu on the coast southwest of Manila on 31 January. Despite entering the outskirts of the Philippine capital on 4 February, the American troops didn't have everything their own way.[11] Manila didn't fall immediately and MacArthur could not begin to use the natural harbour that Manila Bay provided until the Japanese defenders on Bataan had been quelled. On the same day (13 February) that a number of American MTBs re-entered Manila Bay for the first time in three years and a group of their minesweepers began the task of clearing the approaches of mines and other debris, the light cruisers *Boise* and *Phoenix* and four destroyers began their initial shelling of the gaunt island fortress of Corregidor off the southern tip of the Bataan Peninsula. They repeated the dose on the following day. Although Corregidor did not possess the same strategic significance in early 1945 that MacArthur had accorded it at the time of the earlier Japanese conquest of Luzon in 1941–42, it still retained a psychological value for the COMSOWESPAC. He wanted to wrest control of it once again and thus make good his promise given three years before that he would return. MacArthur determined that both Bataan and Corregidor would fall and so on 15 February 1945 a start was made to achieve both goals. Three years to the day since General Yamashita had accepted the surrender of Singapore from Lieutenant-General Arthur Percival, the sixty-two landing craft of Amphibious Group 9 used the North Channel to bring two Regimental Combat Teams ashore on the extreme southern shore of the Bataan Peninsula. On the following day paratroopers surprised the defenders of the fortress by dropping onto a hill called Topside – the highest point on Corregidor – and the one place from which all access routes to the entire island and every one of its beaches could be surveyed. Despite their successful parachute drop, the Americans struggled to subdue their opponents and a battalion of combat troops were brought to the island later in the day to assist in securing the fortress which they did only ten days later.[12]

Elsewhere in the Pacific the New Year had opened on a positive note for the Allies. Their submarines continued to plunder Japanese shipping from the Kuriles to the Dutch East Indies sinking on average a vessel a day throughout January at a cost to their enemy of 89,300 tons of merchant shipping but with a handful of their warships thrown in too for good measure. Their surface vessels were also active early in the month in the Volcano Islands, where a task group of three heavy cruisers and six destroyers had bombarded Iwo Jima and further north in the Bonin Islands, where Haha Jima and Chichi Jima were given similar treatment by the same warships under Rear-Admiral Allen Smith's command. Of these islands, Iwo Jima, which already possessed two important air bases and with a third under construction, was by far the most important. Located a mere three hours' flying time away from Tokyo, this molar-shaped island couldn't be ignored or by-passed. Appreciating this fact from early on, Nimitz had been planning its demise for well over a year and had arranged for a ferocious bombing assault of the 8 square mile (20.7sq.km) island by waves of B-24s and B-25s. These intensive strikes had begun on 8 December and would last for a total of seventy-two days – the longest and heaviest series of bombing raids of the entire Pacific war. Thousands of bombs were dropped in these raids and others mounted by B-29s. In addition, the coastal defences of Iwo Jima were shelled vigorously by Smith's task group several times in the run up to the invasion. Despite the accumulation of firepower expended upon them, the Japanese defences were not blown apart. Showing enormous resourcefulness which the Vietcong would copy twenty years later, the Japanese burrowed beneath the terrain to carve out underground caverns and a maze of tunnels radiating in every direction in which the outnumbered defenders could live and operate from. Using guerrilla tactics and the features of the terrain to their best advantage, these infantrymen would have many unpleasant surprises in store for the Marines who were to be landed relatively close to the imposing slopes of Mount Suribachi on 19 February. For three days prior to the landing, Rear-Admiral Bertram Rodgers' strong force of six battleships, four heavy cruisers, a light cruiser and sixteen destroyers (TF 54) pummelled Iwo Jima from offshore in a sustained bombardment designed to knock out what was left of the large coastal batteries on the southeast coast of the island and leave the Marine Corps with the task of mopping up the rest of what the planners hoped would by now be a bedraggled enemy.[13]

Underestimating the enemy's resistance is a classic mistake to make. It is clear that regardless of the lessons of recent history, the Americans did just that. They had put their faith in a quantitative assault believing that if sufficient bombs and shells rained down on the exposed Japanese positions even the extraordinary courage and bravery shown by their enemy in other battles would not be sufficient to enable them to survive the onslaught, let alone hit back and cause the invading troops too many problems. Nothing could have been further from the truth. Iwo Jima would go down in history as arguably the toughest and bloodiest battle in the 168-year history of the Marine Corps.

A clue to the real state of play was given by the Japanese soldiers manning the coastal batteries on 16 February. After receiving a day's bombardment from the heavy ships of TF 54 along with 158 sorties flown by the planes of ten escort carriers, the Japanese gun crews revealed their durability rather than fragility on the following day by getting a confirmed hit on the battleship *Tennessee* and no less than six more on the heavy cruiser *Pensacola*. Warming to their task they recorded another hit on the destroyer *Leutze* and struck all twelve of the landing craft used for support purposes, ruining nine of them and causing 170 casualties in the process. Calvin Durgin's carrier planes flew 226 sorties on 17 February and another 228 on the following day using both conventional and napalm bombs and losing three planes while doing so. As the aerial assault continued from both carrier and land-based planes, other task groups of minesweepers and underwater demolition teams of frogmen were also on hand to assist in clearing obstructions from the path of the assault force. Although their work had attracted the attention of the Japanese batteries, they had still managed stoically to finish the tasks assigned to them of preparing the way for the Marines to hit the beach on the morning of 19 February.[14]

Operation *Detachment* – the invasion of Iwo Jima – began deceptively well. Under the overall command of the experienced Kelly Turner, TF 51 geared up to bring Lieutenant-General Holland Smith and his V Amphibious Corps ashore in no less than 495 ships. Rodgers with TF 54, reinforced by the two battleships *North Carolina* and *Washington*, the heavy cruiser *Indianapolis*, a pair of light cruisers and ten destroyers loaned from TF 58, engaged in another bombardment of the shoreline and the coastal batteries before the two task groups came ashore in two places on the southeast coast: the 4th Marine Division in fifty-four landing craft just to the east of the first airfield and the 5th Marine Division in fifty-seven more further south in what Don Yoder has described as the 'neck of the island' to the north and east of Mount Suribachi which dominates the southern tip of Iwo Jima.[15] Although the Marines encountered only light resistance as they clambered ashore they soon faced an extraordinary backlash from a defensive force pledged to take ten American lives for each one of their own. From their hidden positions dotted all around the assault area, the Japanese defenders, led by Lieutenant-General Tadamichi Kuribayashi, poured artillery and mortar shells and small arms fire onto the now exposed US Marines, the leading members of whom were now several hundred metres from the shoreline. Ground from now on could only be gained through adversity. Planes from the fleet carriers of Mitscher's TF 58 and Durgin's escort carrier group did what they could to provide support for the Marines by flying 606 sorties on the first day of the invasion alone during which they dropped 274 tons of bombs, over 100 napalm bombs and fired 2,254 rockets at what they hoped were Japanese positions. In conditions that Dante might have found depressingly familiar, 30,000 American troops came ashore on the first day of the invasion. Progress thereafter was painfully slow. It took four days for a Marine detachment to clear the enemy off the slopes of Mount Suribachi and be able to plant an American flag on the summit of the peak – a graphic, iconic image captured in one of the most famous photographs of this or any other war.[16]

Frustratingly for the Japanese High Command the possibility of mounting an effective naval response from beyond Iwo Jima was outside their scope at this stage of the war. Other than employing the kamikaze units, the IJN could not go much beyond using their submarine cruisers to deploy *kaiten* torpedoes against the invasion fleet. These had been used against American bases in the Pacific in January (Operation *Kongō*) without being wildly successful and their use at Iwo Jima proved once again that they were an extremely inefficient weapon and only employable when virtually all hope was lost.[17] Kamikaze units were a symbol of desperation too, but they were frighteningly more effective. Conspicuous by their absence on the first couple of days of the invasion, a group of thirty-two such aircraft made an appearance on 21 February and proved just what an uncompromising weapon they had become by sinking the escort carrier *Bismarck Sea* and damaging the fleet carrier *Saratoga*, the light carrier *Langley*, the 'jeep' carrier *Lunga Point*, a transport and two LSTs, causing the death of 341 American servicemen and injuring another 192.[18]

Left largely to their own devices, the Japanese proved that Mount Suribachi did not equal Iwo Jima, so the taking of the peak by the Americans didn't lead to the immediate folding of Kuribayashi's 109th Infantry Division's resistance. Such was the bitter fighting that occurred as the Marines forged inland and then struggled to seize the northern part of the island that the 3rd Division, which had been held in reserve for just such an eventuality, had to enter the fray on 25 February and assist in carving a way through the impassioned lines of the enemy. It took until 4 March for the first of the American B-29s to land on the captured airstrips of Iwo Jima and twelve days more until the Marines could relax. Even then the few remaining Japanese were not finished as a *Banzai* charge by 300 of them on 26 March proved. In the end only 1,083 out of 20,703 Japanese troops survived the fighting on Iwo Jima to become POWs. For their part, the Marines lost 5,931 dead or missing and had another 22,099 wounded. In addition US Navy personnel lost a total of 982 killed, while 1,652 were wounded in this most uncompromising fight for a relatively small rocky island. If the Allies could sustain this scale of losses on Iwo Jima, what on earth were they likely to lose when they came to invading the Ryukyu Islands, let alone the Japanese mainland?[19]

This was a matter of great concern to the Allied leadership in both Washington and London as could be seen by their earnest discussions with Stalin at the Allied conference (codename *Argonaut*) held at Yalta in the Crimea from 4 to 11 February about a future Soviet entry into the Pacific War three months after the conflict with Germany had come to an end. If the Soviets could be relied upon to share the military burden in this way once Germany had been defeated, the horrendous military cost of invading Japan and subduing its people might be made a little less daunting.[20] In the meanwhile, however, the Anglo-American members of the Grand Alliance were required to embark upon the next major test lying before them, namely, invading the formidable island of Okinawa. Before they did so, however, there was still much to do in picking off those islands in the Philippine chain that remained in the possession of the Japanese. A start was made at the end of February with the invasion of Palawan (Operation *Victor III*), a long, narrow island lying between the islands of Borneo and Mindoro with its western coast washed by the South China Sea and its eastern shore by the Sulu Sea. On 28 February, 8,000 troops of the 41st Infantry Division were brought ashore by Rear-Admiral William Fechteler's Amphibious Group 8 using seventy-two landing craft duly supported by the three light cruisers, nine destroyers, a minesweeping force and land-based air support. Palawan received its first supply convoy consisting of nineteen LSTs the very next day and would soon become a base for two PTB (patrol torpedo boat) squadrons.[21] Next up was a landing near Zamboanga, the port at the extreme southwestern tip of Mindanao, on 10 March (Operation *Victor IV*). It was a larger enterprise involving 102 landing craft of various kinds duly supported by a mixed force of light cruisers, destroyers, escorts and minesweepers. Over the course of the next month, units of these forces would land on the Basilan Islands (16 March), the former Japanese fleet base of Tawi Tawi (2 April) and on Jolo (9 April) in the Sulu Archipelago. Further attacks were mounted on the south coast of Panay (*Victor I*) where 14,000 troops of the 40th Infantry Division were landed by fifty-seven landing craft on 22 March and another 14,000 troops were deposited on Cebu (*Victor II*) by sixty-one landing craft four days later. Of the two islands, Cebu had proved to be a real thorn in the side of the American forces over the past few months as it had been home to a squadron of Onishi's 1st Air Fleet and a forward base for one of its kamikaze wings. April saw the American grip on the southern and central Philippines tighten with additional invasions of the islands of Bohol, Masbate, Los Negros and Sulu and a two-stage landing in the Moro Gulf in western Mindanao (*Victor V*). By then they had also seized control of the San Bernardino Strait by landing men on the shores of both southern Luzon and northwest Samar, as well as the offshore islands of Biri, Capul and Dalupiri.[22]

Although the eventual loss of Luzon was prefigured in this mopping up of the rest of the Philippines, the Japanese military, inspired by the traditional *Bushido* warrior code with its utterly uncompromising *Samurai* principles of loyalty, justice and honour and marked by an aversion to surrendering, meant that even when facing certain defeat death was preferable to a life of captivity. In other words, the Allies might be able to bring overwhelming force to bear in order to defeat the obdurate Japanese, but they would need to dig deep in order to do so and be able to accept a high attrition rate at the same time.[23] While the various *Victor* operations succeeded in their stated intention of clawing back the main islands of the Philippine archipelago to the south of Luzon, the Allies steeled themselves for much harder campaigns in future. They also pondered the conundrum of whether there was some way of avoiding the fanatical resistance they had already observed in the Southwest and Central Pacific. While Roosevelt and Churchill hoped that the atomic physicists working at Los Alamos might succeed in producing a massively destructive bomb that could actually work in practice, they couldn't rely on it being ready in time to prevent thousands of their own servicemen losing their lives in trying to invade and conquer the islands of Kyūshū, Shikoku, Honshū or Hokkaidō of the Japanese homeland. If there was no way of securing an easy series of victories over the Japanese military, a way had to be found to bring the reality of the war home to the emperor, his advisors, the ruling government elite and the general public. One way of bringing some psychological pressure to bear was to follow the example set by the Doolittle Raid in 1942 and begin bombing Tokyo as well as some of the other main industrial and military centres. A start had been made in mid-February when the fighters and bombers of TF 58's fifteen carriers had flown a total of 2,761 sorties in an effort to attack aircraft factories in Tokyo and shipping and port facilities at Yokohama. Bad weather had rather diluted the effects of this raid and reduced its potency, but even so eighty-eight planes had been lost in making these attacks and that in itself was a cause for concern. It wasn't sufficient to stop follow-up raids, but it made the Allies a little more hesitant about what targets they should set themselves.[24]

On 14 March TF 58 set out once again from Ulithi with sixteen carriers, eight battleships, two battlecruisers, fifteen cruisers and sixty-three destroyers. Once in place early on the morning of 18 March, the carriers flew off their planes to attack the airfields on Kyūshū – home to Matome Ugaki's 5th Air Fleet and a host of kamikaze planes, forty-eight of which had been sent off to find the US carrier fleet. Thirty of them found Mitscher's carriers but enjoyed little success in pressing home their attacks on them. Although *Intrepid* survived a fiery near-miss and minimal damage was done to both *Enterprise* and *Yorktown*, none of the three were put out of action.[25] Next day the American planes attacked Kure and the other naval bases built around the Inland Sea. While Mitscher's planes found and bombed six Japanese carriers (*Amagi*, *Hoshō*, *Ryuho*, *Ikoma*, *Kaiyo* and *Katsuragi*), the battleships *Haruna*, *Hyūga* and *Yamato*, the heavy cruiser *Tone*, the light cruiser *Ōyodo* and three submarines *I-205*, *I-400* and *Ro-67*, the results were nothing like as severe as had been hoped. Once again, the debt this raid left was soon repaid with interest. Ugaki's bombers got through the fighter cover over the carrier fleet to hit the *Franklin* twice, causing massive damage from a fire and explosions resulting in 724 of her servicemen being killed and another 265 being injured. *Wasp* was also hunted down, bombed once and set on fire. Although the flames were quickly extinguished, 101 of her crew had perished in the attack and 269 more had been injured. Thirty-nine kamikazes tried to add to the chaos but only managed to get a solitary hit on the *Enterprise*, while the *Essex* managed to damage herself inadvertently through her own A.A. fire. There was little cause for celebration in American circles that evening. Further kamikaze attacks took place on succeeding days without hitting any of the carriers, although a destroyer and a submarine were not so fortunate. On 21 March Ugaki sent a mix of bombers, fighters and kamikazes to attack TF 58 once more. This time the Americans were waiting for them and it was just as well they were for the eighteen bombers brought two new suicide weapons with them – *ohka* (cherry blossom) manned rocket torpedoes and *Baka* piloted bombs. Before the Japanese twin-engine bombers had released their *ohka* payloads, 150 US fighters cut through their ranks and downed seventeen of them together with ten kamikazes and twelve escort fighters before they could do any damage. It didn't make up for those who had perished and been injured on the *Franklin* and the *Wasp*, but at least it prevented the Japanese from capitalising on the situation. As the Allies comforted themselves with the thought that ultimate victory over the Japanese in the Pacific was no longer a far-fetched concept, it was still more of a medium to long-term goal than a short-term objective.[26]

Success in rolling back the over-extended Imperial Empire from Southeast Asia was not, however, confined to the waters of the Pacific. In the Indian Ocean the IJN no longer featured. Their military was being pushed back relentlessly in Burma with bridgeheads being established across the River Irrawaddy both north and south of Mandalay by mid-February and the supply route to and from China – the Burma Road – having been re-opened for business by 27 January. What naval activity there was in this theatre was mostly, if not exclusively, generated by the Allies. While for the most part this meant the British East Indies Fleet, Indian vessels were also employed in bringing additional troops to bear on the Burmese front. In this way the sloops *Jumna* and *Narbada* oversaw the landing of 6,635 Commandos and other units on the banks of the Myebon River on 22–23 February. Nonetheless, the BEIF was the usual naval catalyst for Allied action in the early months of 1945. Apart from maintaining a lively presence in and around the Andaman Islands, where its ships took turns to raid Japanese coastal shipping and shell the infrastructure of Port Blair on a monthly basis, the BEIF also conducted reconnaissance surveys of the Isthmus of Kra, Sumatra, Penang and other ports on the Malayan coast as far south as Port Dickson (Operation *Stacey*) in late February and early March, and indulged itself in raids on oil installations on Sumatra (Operation *Sunfish*) in mid-April. This type of activity could be planned in these days without too many safety concerns as the last of the German U-boats sent out to East Asia had returned to Germany in the early months of 1945.[27]

Back in Europe Dönitz at long last had the means to prosecute another phase of the U-boat war. His new Type XXI and XXIII U-boats were now in full production and becoming operational on a monthly basis. Appreciating this fact, the Admiralty's Operational Intelligence Centre had alerted the First Sea Lord Sir Andrew Cunningham in October 1944 to the idea that a renewal of the U-boat threat was merely weeks away from being realised. In fact, the figures of growing U-boat successes in British inland waters as well as those out into the Atlantic during the last quarter of 1944 suggested that the underwater menace had already been revived. Things were expected to get much worse once Dönitz could get his hands on large numbers of his new U-boats and Cunningham was warned in January 1945 that his German opposite number would have more operational U-boats at his disposal in March 1945 than he had enjoyed at the height of their last success exactly two years before when the Allies suffered crippling losses at sea. These figures seemed to be borne out by the addition of thirty-one U-boats to the fleet in December 1944 – twenty-one of which were the new Type XXI. Fortunately for the first sea lord, numbers in the end didn't mean everything.[28]

In the Arctic, increasing U-boat activity was discernible in the U-boats marshalled against Allied convoys of all kinds. 'Ultra' intelligence kept these missions from being turned into grim disaster areas, but even so German U-boat deployment off the Kola Inlet and in the Bear Island Passage, along with squadrons of Ju-88s still based in northern Norway, remained more of an actual threat to the Arctic convoy route than that posed by any surface ships as the corvette *Denbigh Castle* (from convoy JW.64), the Liberty ship *Horace Gray* and the Norwegian tanker *Norfjell* (from local Soviet convoy BK.3) all found out to their cost on 13–14 February.[29] While the escorts generally prevented mayhem from breaking out once a convoy was formed, RA.64 had barely got out of the Kola Inlet en route for the Clyde when it was set upon by the *Rasmus* wolf pack. Within hours of helping to eliminate *U425* with a volley of depth charges, the sloop *Lark* was repaid for her handiwork by being put out of action by a T-5 torpedo fired by *U968*, which went on to do the same to the freighter *Thomas Scott*. *U711* also got into the act by destroying the corvette *Bluebell* with another T-5. After such an inglorious start, RA.64 and its remaining thirty-two ships then sailed into one of the worst spells of weather the North Sea could conjure up. A series of violent and prolonged storms scattered the convoy and gave the escorts a horrendous job of reforming it at sea. They had accomplished most of that task by 20 February, but one of the stragglers, *Henry Bacon*, another Liberty ship, never returned to the fold. It was finally found and torpedoed out of existence by forty Ju-88s three days later – becoming the last ship to be sunk by German aircraft in the Second World War. There were four more victims of U-boat attacks in the entrance to the Kola Inlet on the next convoy run too (JW.65), but the feared convoy battles of the past only materialised once more at the end of April and were then overtaken by other more climactic events.[30]

This in many ways was to become a template for the entire U-boat campaign in 1945: it promised so much more than it actually ended up in providing. This was true in other theatres as well. Many attacks were made in British coastal waters, for example, but all too often, for Dönitz's liking, a U-boat's initial success merely attracted forces bent upon her destruction. Count Matuschka, of *U482* and his fellow captains, Kuhlmann of *U1172*, Loos of *U248*, Nollmann of *U1199* and von Holleben of *U1051*, all found that out to their cost in January 1945. Some like Meyer in *U1055*, who sank four ships in the Irish Sea and Dobratz in *U1232*, who sank five off Halifax, just managed to keep their pursuers at bay, but, generally speaking, the days of the easy kills were long gone. As long as sufficient Support Groups were in existence, the problem posed by the U-boats could be contained. Cunningham's concern was that with only eighteen of the minimum number of twenty-three Support Groups operable at the end of 1944, the U-boats might still be able to re-assert themselves and fall upon their prey with undiminished vigour. Cunningham's pessimism may have been understandable but it was also quite exaggerated. If the waters around the British Isles and throughout the North Atlantic were a guide, the situation seemed to be that piecemeal destruction was still possible but massive carnage was now unlikely. Indeed in a six-week period from 26 January, twenty-one ships, ranging from small tugs to freighters and two corvettes, were sunk but so were sixteen of their U-boat attackers. As fourteen of the sixteen U-boats had been dispatched without any involvement of supporting aircraft whatsoever, it was clear that the Allies were not as bereft as the first sea lord had intimated that they were. This impression gained ground in March and early April as more inroads were made into Dönitz's fleet. Scattered from the Pentland Firth down into the Irish Sea and throughout the Channel and North Sea, his U-boats were able to penetrate Allied convoy traffic to sink eleven ships, but lost eighteen of their own craft in doing so. It was a depressing statistic for the grand admiral and his staff in the OKM to absorb not least because the 'Type XXIII' boats weren't proving to be anything like as lethal as had been hoped. Dönitz's utter frustration was obvious. This was not what was supposed to happen. It was an inversion of the rules of the game which he had done so much to create in the first place. By the beginning of April, however, the master tactician was confronted by the glum fact that he had run out of time and that the war at sea was not going to be won by either the new or the old generation of U-boats, a fact duly confirmed by another limp performance of these vessels in the last month of the European war. Once again, more U-boats than Allied ships would be destroyed in British coastal waters (seventeen to eight) and in the Atlantic they would fare no better. Even with the new 'Type IX-C' U-boats in place, on even the busiest of routes only six Allied vessels were sunk and three more were torpedoed, but these isolated successes came at the cost of nine more U-boats.[31]

A far more depressing exercise in futility was set by the courageous men of the K-Verband in the northern reaches of the English Channel, especially in Belgian and Dutch coastal waters, during the early months of the year. Operational losses were so high amongst the ranks of the one-man midget submarine (*Biber*) and the one-man human torpedo (*Molch*) that Dönitz referred to the operators of these underwater vessels as *Opferkämpfer* (suicide fighters). A far healthier return was experienced by the two-man crews of the new Type XXVIIB U-boat (popularly known as the *Seehund*). Operating in the same waters as the other members of the K-Verband did, the *Seehunde* enjoyed far more success – sinking nine ships and damaging another nine – at less cost – losing only thirty-five of their number in making a total of 142 sorties before the war came to an end. Frustratingly for Dönitz and the Kriegsmarine, these vessels came on stream six months too late to be of any real material value to the German cause. It might not have been the same story had they been operationally deployed in sufficient numbers in the waters off Normandy in June 1944 where their presence could have caused significant problems for the Allied invasion fleet.[32]

Deprived of any sort of new cutting-edge, Dönitz and the OKM had been powerless to arrest the course of the naval war in the early months of 1945. Their MTBs and S-boat flotillas continued to mine British waters and sortie against Allied convoys in the North Sea, achieving some successes in so doing, but apart from a few skirmishes the toll from these activities and those of the explosive *Linsen* boats was never going to be large enough to make Washington or London sit up and take much notice of them. They were capable of ensnaring some victims – and they did – but they were, in truth, little more than a nuisance to the Admiralty's coastal authorities and not a grave threat to the Allied war machine. It was much the same for the Mediterranean where the German naval presence was even weaker. A desultory spot of mining in the Ligurian Sea in March seemed to say it all, particularly as they couldn't get to use either the damaged Italian battleship *Conte di Cavour* or the unfinished battleship *Impero* before both were sunk in a bombing raid on Trieste harbour on 17 February.[33]

Much closer to home in the Baltic, the writing had been on the wall for Dönitz and the Kriegsmarine from mid-January onwards when the Soviets had opened their three-front drive on East Prussia from Pultusk in the south and Gumbinnen (Gusev) and Tilsit (Sovetsk) in the north. This move had prompted the Germans to evacuate their XXVIII Corps from Memel (Klaipėda) across the ice to the Kurische Nehrung over a four-day period (24–28 January) and to withdraw the injured, sick and refugees by boat from Memel before either Soviet submarines or the men of the 1st Baltic Front from Tilsit could prevent them from doing so. Unless the Soviets were stopped in their tracks, all hope for Germany would be lost. Staring defeat in the face, the Germans responded by organising a series of counter-attacks in an effort to restore land communications between Königsberg (Kaliningrad) and its port of Pillau (Baltiysk). Dönitz was obliged to support these efforts from offshore and did so by deploying the heavy cruisers *Admiral Scheer*, *Lützow* and *Prinz Eugen*, a couple of gun carriers, together with a handful of destroyers and torpedo boats to provide as much artillery bombardment as possible against the advancing Soviet troops around Königsberg. It was never going to be anything more than a mere delaying tactic, but it was vital if the Germans were to succeed in organising a massive evacuation from the Baltic States and East Prussia to the western ports of Germany. Generaladmiral Oskar Kummetz and the Marineoberkommando Ost/Ostsee (German Naval High Command East) were given overall responsibility for planning and delivering what was to become the largest evacuation exercise ever attempted. Faced with the enormity of this problem, Kummetz and his team needed to utilise as many ships of a decent size as they could lay their hands on. This vital task was entrusted to Konteradmiral Conrad Engelhardt, the Wehrmacht's naval transport commander and he became responsible for procuring the evacuation vessels. Fourteen large passenger ships, a dozen of which were over 13,000 tons, twenty-two freighters of over 5,000 tons, unknown numbers of smaller vessels, as well as auxiliary warships and escort vessels were all pressed into service over the course of the next few months as the scale of the military crisis became increasingly more evident as time went by. Organising convoys was difficult enough at the best of times, but under real pressure from an advancing army the logistical complexities became even more horrendous than normal. In order for their scheduling system to work efficiently, Kummetz and Engelhardt needed more than organisational discipline and great stoicism. They also needed a monumental slice of luck – not least because the Soviet submarine fleet had every intention of disrupting the evacuation as and when it could. Lacking the cutting-edge of a suitable number of destroyers and other anti-submarine vessels until the latter half of February, the Germans were left with making the best of the flotillas of minesweepers, patrol boats, submarine chasers, heavy and light gunboats, gun ferry barges, naval fishing cutters, naval ferry barges, converted trawlers and many small fishery vessels that were available to them in Baltic waters.[34]

A start was made to the evacuation on 25 January when three passenger ships sailed from Pillau with the first batch of 7,100 refugees. Within three days some 62,000 people had been moved westwards away from the Red Army, but merely boarding the boats that ranged alongside the dockyards was no guarantee that safety was assured. Apart from the Soviet submarines that initially concentrated on the sea route from Courland, and their larger boats which congregated in the area of the Stolpe Bank and off the Danish island of Bornholm, the greatest threat to these evacuees came from the RAF dropping a total of 3,220 air mines in the western Baltic and as far east as the Pomeranian coast in the first three months of 1945. These mines were to reap a rich harvest of shipping victims.[35] In all some 137,764 tons of German shipping was sunk and 71,224 tons was damaged in this mining blitz. Although the mines were completely undiscriminating – taking out hospital ships as well as transports, destroyers and minesweepers – it could have been much worse had the Soviet Air Force been actively involved. Instead they were largely deployed on land operations and so Kummetz and Engelhardt were given an extended opportunity to continue evacuating large numbers of Germans from the dwindling Eastern Front. Each of the large passenger ships involved in these operations could take 5–9,000 passengers on board and the freighters could hold up to 5,000 at a time. It was crucial, therefore, that these ships should be pressed into making as many return journeys as possible to extricate the largest number of evacuees from the Baltic States. Unfortunately, not all of these ships could be escorted to and fro and occasionally a passenger vessel or a freighter sailing independently was discovered by a submarine and sunk with impunity. In this way the third largest passenger ship used in the evacuation operation, *Wilhelm Gustloff*, a liner of 25,484 tons with 10,582 people on board, was sunk off the Polish coast on 30 January by *S-13* with the loss of over 9,330 victims making it the largest maritime disaster of all time. *S-13*, loitering with intent off the Stolpe Bank, also managed to evade two escorts in order to sink the tenth largest passenger ship *General Steuben* on 10 February with the loss of another 3,608 lives.[36]

Complications set in with the Soviet advance on Eastern Pomerania in late February since some of the ships and naval ferry barges as well as the Gun Carrier Flotilla being used in the East Prussian and Courland evacuations were now needed off the Pomeranian coast to take more refugees from the port of Kolberg (Kolobrzeg), or to support the heavy cruiser *Admiral Scheer*, three destroyers and a torpedo boat in defending the bridgehead at Wollin (Wolin). Desperate measures resulted in another 75,000 refugees, soldiers and wounded being withdrawn from this front by 18 March. They had not even finished this tricky assignment when the Germans were forced to respond to yet another setback – this time the opening of a Soviet drive from Marienwerder (Kwidzyn) to Gotenhafen (Gdynia) and Danzig (Gdańsk). Once again, naval firepower was needed to keep the Soviet 2nd White Russian Front from breaking through before refugees could be evacuated. On 10 March the heavy cruiser *Prinz Eugen* was pressed into service and five days later the obsolete battleship *Schlesien* along with three heavy auxiliary gunboats and a gunnery training vessel also battered the Soviet positions from offshore. After *Schlesien* ran out of shells, the heavy cruiser *Lützow* and two destroyers replaced her on 23 March and the light cruiser *Leipzig* was added to the bombardment force. Evacuations of refugees began from the naval base at Gotenhafen and the ports of Danzig and Hela (Hel) as the Red Army moved ever closer to the Gulf of Danzig, but on this occasion two divisions of the Soviet Naval Air Force were also involved in carrying out over 2,000 sorties against the operation. In an effort to neutralise the torpedo-bombers over these ports, Kummetz ordered a group of destroyers, torpedo boats and other warships to stand by and provide an effective curtain of A.A. fire to cover the transports as they took on their passengers and left port with them. Although Soviet aircraft still managed to sink five transports, two minesweepers and a submarine-chaser, many German ships were still able to enter and leave these three ports unscathed. Soviet mine barrages did claim a couple of torpedo boats and a U-boat (*U367*) and their submarines did sink a freighter, a patrol boat and a tug while on passage, but the vast majority of craft laden with refugees made safe landfall in other German ports further to the west. A day before Gotenhafen fell on 28 March the battleship *Gneisenau* – a constant and frustrating nemesis of the Allies throughout the war – made an undistinguished exit when she was finally sunk as a blockship. At that late stage this sacrificial act served very little useful purpose. Once Danzig was captured on 30 March, Hela became the operational centre for the evacuation. It became a kind of halfway house for refugees from those ports around the Gulf that hadn't been occupied by Soviet troops and a total of 264,887 evacuees found their way to the port in a multitude of small boats and naval ferry barges in April alone. Adding to the armada of vessels making for Hela were retreating troops and other refugees from collapsed fronts, such as the Oxhöfter Kämpe bridgehead and Engelhardt's passenger ships which by now had plenty of practice at being used as evacuation transports. Such was the scale of the operation that by 10 April 157,270 wounded servicemen had left Hela for the west. Increasingly, however, the casualties of this evacuation would grow as Soviet air and sea forces devoted more time and resources to attacking this traffic.[37]

There could be no more reliable barometer of the deteriorating state of the war than the fact that instead of taking their home waters for granted, Dönitz and the OKM were forced to pay such attention to the Baltic in these early months of 1945. Whatever grand plans and high hopes the grand admiral and his staff may have entertained for the New Year were dashed soon afterwards by the stunning realisation that these schemes and aspirations actually counted for nothing. They were losing ground to the Allied armies on both the Western and Eastern Fronts, so no matter what their U-boats, MTBs and other patrol craft might have been able to do in the Arctic, Atlantic, the Channel and the North Sea the reality was that they couldn't do anything to delay the inevitable – the war was already lost beyond recall. By the beginning of April the Western Allies had captured Bonn and Köln, Koblenz and Mainz and had even encircled the *Ruhrgebiet* – the industrial heartland of Hitler's Reich. Their aircraft were by now dropping massive bomb loads on all the major German ports and naval bases and causing massive damage to port facilities and naval vessels caught sheltering in them.[38] In one day alone (30 March), B-17s and B-24s of the USAAF dropped 2,019 tons of bombs on Bremen and Wilhelmshaven, while 469 aircraft drawn from units of the RCAF and RAF Bomber Command attacked the Hamburg shipyards on 30–31 March. In so doing they put an end to the light cruiser *Köln*, nineteen U-boats, an S-boat, a couple of minesweepers and eight other vessels. A few nights later (3–4 April) the same treatment was accorded to

Kiel with some 2,200 tons of bombs being dropped on the port and six U-boats, five assorted minesweepers, a mine transport, a tanker and two large passenger ships (one of which had been converted into a hospital ship) paying for the privilege. Dönitz was powerless to prevent it from happening and so the sorry tale continued. Six more U-boats were sunk by aircraft from RAF Bomber Command at Hamburg during the night of 8–9 April and three more were caught and destroyed in the Kattegat during the hours of daylight by RAF Coastal Command over the same two days. Encouraged by its previous success, Bomber Command sent even more aircraft to attack Kiel during the night of 9–10 April; 2,634 tons of bombs rained down on the naval base destroying three more U-boats and five other vessels as well as sinking the storied pocket battleship *Admiral Scheer* and badly damaging the heavy cruiser *Admiral Hipper* and the light cruiser *Emden*. A few days later (16 April) Lancaster bombers of RAF Bomber Command dealt another heavy blow to the old German surface fleet by discovering the heavy cruiser *Lützow* at her berth south of Swinemünde and achieved a near-miss that caused her to go aground in the Kaiserfahrt. It was not quite the end for her but that wasn't far off.[39]

By the beginning of April the Baltic was the only area where the Kriegsmarine could make a real contribution to the war. It couldn't win it any longer, but it could do something to rescue its comrades in arms and other German citizens from falling into the hands of the dreaded Soviet enemy. All around the eastern shoreline of the Baltic from Courland in the north to East Prussia in the south the various campaigns were beginning to show very similar responses. Soviet attacks were held for a time and possibly even beaten off (as had been the usual case in Courland) but eventually the incessant pressure told and a breakthrough was made. Amazingly in these extraordinarily dramatic circumstances, the logistical exercise that was the evacuation operation continued in unabated fashion from Windau (Ventspils) and Libau (Liepāja) in Latvia south to Pillau. Disruptions and delays in the schedule of sailings became more pronounced as the war closed in on the German forces. Once a renewed drive on Königsberg began on 6 April, for example, the situation at Pillau became increasingly critical. Within three days the city was surrounded and on 10 April its defenders capitulated. Faced with a swelling refugee population and the necessity of trying to get as many people away from the port as possible before it fell, German ships kept on returning for another fortnight before the town and its harbour were finally abandoned to the Soviets on 25 April. By that time, however, 451,000 refugees and 141,000 wounded servicemen had been evacuated from this ice-free port in the four months that the operation had lasted. It was a quite staggering achievement and reflected the pivotal role Pillau had played in the entire evacuation operation. As the escape routes through that port and others around the Gulf of Danzig were being choked off, however, the Germans had been forced to rely upon the facilities at Hela to keep the process going. These went into overdrive as the port became besieged with refugees from the region of the Lower Vistula. As they did so, the Soviets immediately responded by increasing their aircraft sorties over the port. In the process five transports, two supply ships and a hospital ship were lost along with a handful of other craft. Notwithstanding these losses, Hela performed with distinction. In the month of April alone as many as 387,000 evacuees left the port for the west. These sailings were chillingly tense affairs with the ships hounded by air and sea attacks and with survival never guaranteed. Nonetheless, the alternative – of not attempting to run the Allied gauntlet and accepting captivity at the hands of the Soviets – was unthinkable. For every ship that was sunk on passage from Hela, many more somehow managed to get through with their precious human cargo. There was little time to waste and the Germans herded the refugees aboard with admirable and startling efficiency. In so doing they set a record of embarking 28,000 passengers in a single day (21 April) and ran it close a week later when a mere seven steamers collected a further 24,000. They were the lucky ones. Many more who tried to leave in the last days of the war were nothing like as fortunate.[40]

On the day that the Soviets completed their encirclement of Berlin (25 April), Dönitz and the OKM were forced into beginning a policy of destruction and deprivation. Principal units of their Kriegsmarine were not going to be allowed to fall into the hands of the hated communists and so those ships that couldn't be moved and were most in danger of being seized by the Red Army – such as the uncompleted aircraft carrier *Graf Zeppelin* – were blown up in Stettin (Szczecin) along with four steamers and other smaller vessels. *Schlesien* and *Lützow* were the next to go. *Schlesien*, after being gravely damaged by a British air ground mine as she attempted to make her way into the Griefswalder Bodden on 2 May, was towed back to Swinemünde and beached as the *Lützow* had been just over a fortnight before. They shared the same fate again when both were blown up on 4 May. It signified that Swinemünde was finished as a German base. Elsewhere the story of self-destruction was much the same. Before the Italian port of Genoa was yielded during the night of 24–25 April, German troops busied themselves in either scuttling in the harbour or blowing up in the building yards a total of two U-boats, six destroyers, ten corvettes, six torpedo boats, three patrol boats and thirty-one motor minesweepers. They did the same at the ports of Imperia and Oneglia where another destroyer and three more torpedo boats were scuttled. In the Adriatic, the collapse of German resistance at Venice and Trieste (29–30 April) led to the rest of their torpedo boats going the same way.[41]

In Germany itself the news of Hitler's suicide in the Chancellery bunker in Berlin (30 April) thrust Dönitz into a new role as leader of a beaten power. It was not one that he would have chosen for himself. It was not the leadership that he found irksome but the manner of it. Defeat was not something which could be anything other than deeply unsatisfactory for a competitive individual such as him. Although he could do nothing to stave off total and unmitigated defeat, he was also disinclined to 'throw in the towel' before he had to. Before any formal surrender could be negotiated, let alone a ceasefire inaugurated, therefore, he saw to it that the Germans still had much work to do. Not all of it was self-destructive. For example, he was not against his U-boats indulging themselves in a few last minute forays against the Allies before the war could be formally wound up.[42] In the Arctic, for example, fourteen of his U-boats were stationed off the Kola Inlet waiting for convoy RA.66 to emerge from Murmansk. When it did leave port for the Clyde on 29 April, it had with it twenty-seven merchant vessels and an even larger mixed escort force. Here was an opportunity to sign off in some style and the U-boats that were in place went about their task with grim determination. There was to be much skirmishing over the next three days with the frigate *Goodall* and two U-boats (*U286* and *U307*) being sunk and other vessels being missed or depth-charged, but the end result was that the escort vessels had prevented the U-boats from getting through the outer screen to the merchant ships beyond. Dönitz's submariners wouldn't get another chance to strike at this or any other convoy before peace was proclaimed.[43] That didn't stop about sixty of them in the Baltic from opting to try to get to Norway. In making this journey they found themselves, as did many other surface vessels, confronted by swarms of RAF bombers seeking to destroy them. In a four day blitz (2–6 May) a mixture of Beaufighters, Liberators, Mosquitoes and Typhoons did just that. Seventeen of the U-boats, eleven steamers, three minesweepers, a gunboat and an MTB, along with other minor vessels, were set upon anywhere from the Baltic to the Kattegat and didn't survive the experience.[44] Lt. Frömsdorf of *U853* didn't have his eyes on Norway at all. He was cruising off Rhode Island when the war in the West was coming to an end and in sinking the freighter *Black Point* off Block Island on 5 May he recorded the last successful U-boat attack in American waters. He didn't survive for long. On the following day he too was killed when *U853* was sunk by a destroyer escort and a frigate working in tandem. Frömsdorf was not even posthumously accorded the accolade of being the last U-boat captain to sink an enemy vessel. That distinction went to Lt. Klusmeier in *U2336* when he sank the two freighters *Avondale Park* and *Sneland* off the Firth of Forth in Scotland in the late evening of 7 May.[45]

Action on the high seas, or even in coastal waters, was not, however, the prerogative of the majority of the U-boat fleet. Those submariners in German ports from Wilhelmshaven and Bremerhaven in the west to Lübeck and Warnemünde in the east, for instance, were left with the defiant, if doleful, task of scuttling their own craft. In the first three days of May as many as 135 U-boats perished in this way. Even more extraordinary scenes greeted the British XII Corps as they occupied the city of Hamburg on 3 May when as many as nineteen floating docks, fifty-nine large and medium-size ships and roughly 600 smaller vessels littering the harbour were scuttled or blown up by German forces within the port. The next day (4 May) when the U-boat captains in the area heard about the signing of the surrender document applicable to German forces in Denmark, Holland and northwest Germany, they put the coded operation *Regenbogen* (*Rainbow*) into practice scuttling eighty-three U-boats in fourteen different locations stretching from the Danish port of Aarhus in the Kattegat southeast to Lübeck in the Baltic and west to the outer Weser in the North Sea.[46]

While this was going on in the North Sea and the Belts around Denmark, every kind of ship from naval barges, freighters and transports to destroyers, torpedo boats and much smaller vessels were making their way either to or from

Hela in the Baltic with the last of the refugees and troops to be moved from the east to relative safety in the west. By the time the German unconditional surrender came into force on 8 May some 1,420,000 refugees had made their way by sea to the west from the Pomeranian coast and the ports around the Gulf of Danzig in the period from 25 January to the end of the war. In addition, at least another 600,000 had also been evacuated over much smaller distances within the Gulf of Danzig itself. It had been a quite phenomenal achievement. It took raw courage to keep going back into the dangerous maelstrom that swirled around the eastern half of the Baltic. It ended characteristically with the last two convoys containing sixty-one small naval vessels leaving Windau and four convoys of sixty-five similar craft escaping from Libau on 8 May with a total of 25,700 troops and other refugees on board. Of these only a few of the smallest and slowest ships, containing roughly 300 men, were caught by the Soviets on the following day – the rest made it through safely to the west.[47]

There was a heroic quality to the German performance in the Baltic which was not matched to the same extent elsewhere. In the Bay of Biscay the German bases in the Gironde estuary had been bombed senseless for two days (14–16 April) by the USAAF and then shelled repeatedly by a French force of ten warships commanded by Vice-Admiral Joseph Rue before the defenders of Royan (Gironde-Nord) were confronted with a land attack by the 10th French Division and the 66th US Division. Operation *Vénérable* proved far too much for them to handle and they capitulated on 20 April. Nine days later it was the turn of the German garrison on the Île d'Oléron to feel the weight of another Rue-inspired attack (Operation *Jupiter*) in which the heavy cruiser *Duquesne*, three destroyers and other light forces landed purely French forces to reclaim the Gironde for France. They did so within two days.[48] Those other German bases on the Atlantic coast of France – La Rochelle, Lorient and St. Nazaire – that had done so much to facilitate Dönitz's U-boat campaign and had seen plenty of garlanded homecomings for some of the greatest submarine aces of all time had nothing dramatic to offer on 9 May. They merely surrendered. It was to be a fate shared by the German defenders on those islands in the Eastern Mediterranean and Aegean that had caused so much grief to the Allies earlier in the war – Crete, Kos, Leros, Milos and Rhodes.[49]

On the same day (9 May) Captain Herbert Williams, with the light cruisers *Birmingham* and *Dido* and four destroyers, entered the Danish harbour of Copenhagen to receive the surrender of the German heavy cruiser *Prinz Eugen* and the light cruiser *Nürnberg*. On 13 May Oslo became the first of the Norwegian ports to receive an Allied naval delegation. In Rear-Admiral James Ritchie's party was Crown Prince Olaf of Norway. There was more than a certain symbolism in the fact that Ritchie entered the capital in the *Devonshire*, the very same heavy cruiser that Vice-Admiral Sir John Cunningham had used to spirit the Norwegian royal family away from the west coast of their nation in the spring of 1940. Over the course of the next three days Allied warships entered the bases of Kristiansand/South and Stavanger (14 May), Bergen (15 May), and Trondheim and Tromsö (16 May) to join a mixed assembly of sixty-seven

U-boats in a most unlikely set of gatherings.[50] Twenty of these U-boats were passed over to the Allies as war booty, while the rest were sunk by the British in an area west of the Hebrides in an operation (*Deadlight*) lasting from 25 November 1945 to 7 January 1946. Fifteen other U-boats that had been performing in the Arctic were transferred to Loch Eriboll on the north coast of Scotland on 19 May and they too would be sunk in the same operation later in the year.[51]

An air of anti-climax had been hanging over the German naval bases on the North Sea – Bremerhaven, Brunsbuttel, Cuxhaven, Emden and Wilhelmshaven – for a couple of years. Their importance had been tied to Raeder's surface fleet, so once Hitler had decided that the capital ship fleet was surplus to requirements, much of the old vibrancy and prestige had left these ports. After the surrender document relating to German forces in northwest Germany, Denmark and Holland had been signed on 4 May, the ports were taken over by Allied troops over the next few days. On the Channel coast, the German garrison in Dunkirk, not covered by this agreement, initially chose defiance over diplomacy but eventually surrendered on 11 May. In doing so the German troops maintained a tradition of indecision and lateness that the Allies had capitalised upon five years before at the time of Operation *Dynamo*.[52]

As the war in Europe ground to a halt, half a world away in the Pacific the deadly campaign showed no sign of imminent fatigue, still less of total collapse. While Allied armies were crossing the Rhine and the Moselle in March, Admiral Spruance and the US 5th Fleet were preparing themselves for their biggest test yet – the invasion of Okinawa.

Few in the know deluded themselves about what might be in store for them, but whether even they could have visualised the sheer scale of the Japanese response and the related horrors of such a bloodbath may be doubtful. Okinawa was in every way a far more formidable test that Iwo Jima had been. For a start it was considerably larger – at roughly 500 square miles (1,295sq. km) – but it was also more mountainous, had far more Japanese defenders pledged to defend it and possessed five airfields. Worse still from the Allied perspective, planes from another 120 air bases in the region could also reach it since the island lies only 340nm (630km) from the southern tip of Kyūshū. Because it was closer to the Japanese mainland than Formosa (Taiwan), Admiral Nimitz thought Okinawa would be a better forward base for an invasion of Japan than the Chinese island would prove to be. For these reasons, therefore, it couldn't be safely ignored and left to wither on the vine as some of the other Japanese island settlements had been.[53]

Operation *Iceberg* – the attack on Okinawa – was always likely to bring forth fanatical resistance on the part of the Japanese and it did. In the week leading up to the first wave of troops going ashore on 1 April (Easter Sunday), the carrier aircraft from Mitscher's TF 58 made a series of attacks on Okinawa and the islands of the northern Ryukyus and cleared the waters off Kyūshū of enemy craft. For once the Americans didn't have to operate alone. Their British allies entered the Pacific theatre with the appropriately named British Pacific Fleet (BPF). Designated as TF 57, the BPF, consisting of the four fleet carriers

Indefatigable, Indomitable, Illustrious and *Victorious*, the battleships *Howe* and *King George V*, five light cruisers and eleven destroyers, left Ulithi on 23 March under the command of Vice-Admiral Sir Bernard Rawlings to carry out a series of carrier raids on airfields in the southern Ryukyus.[54] These were designed to eliminate the planes stationed there and destroy the runways and infrastructure so that these bases couldn't be used by the Japanese in contesting the landings on Okinawa once they had begun. Supporting both TF 57 and TF 58 in this preparatory phase before *Iceberg* began in earnest were two other task forces, TF 52 under Rear-Admiral William Blandy and TF 54 under Rear-Admiral Morton Deyo. They were there initially to take up the slack when the other task forces were being replenished.[55]

A day before the ships of the Fire Support Group opened their bombardment of Okinawa on 26 March, the Underwater Demolition Teams (UDTs) had already been put ashore to begin their hazardous task of clearing the landing beaches of any major underwater obstructions. As they did so, the Japanese Imperial General Headquarters (IGHQ) implemented its defensive plan for Okinawa and southern Japan (Operation *TEN-GO*). The first signs of just what an uncompromising response this would be were shown at dawn on 25 March when a wave of twenty-five kamikaze planes appeared over the transport squadron that was taking the troops of the 77th Infantry Division to land on the small island of Kerama Retto off the southwest coast of Okinawa. In the attacks that followed a destroyer, a minelayer and two transports were hit and damaged and twenty-two of the kamikaze planes were lost. Another eleven kamikazes returned to take on the Fire Support Group on the following evening and obtained hits on another seven warships including the battleship *Nevada*. Fifteen more swept in on 27 March damaging a minelayer and a minesweeper. Conventional air raids added to the confusion and the damage toll; an attack by explosive boats on the sixty-six landing craft of the Western Islands Attack Group off Kerama Retto was foiled, but existing mines delivered some surprises of their own most noticeably to the minesweeper *Skylark* which ran over one and was sunk by it. On 30 March, four more kamikaze planes homed in on Deyo's force and one of them got through to smash into Spruance's flagship, the heavy cruiser *Indianapolis*. Although Spruance was unhurt in the attack and swiftly transferred his flag to the battleship *New Mexico*, a point had been proved that in this type of attack there really was no hiding place once the action started – anyone could get hit. It might be planned or it could be random and arbitrary; either way it was disquieting. More kamikaze planes appeared on the eve of the landing (31 March) and once again casualties occurred: on this occasion a minelayer, a fast transport and two LSTs were hit but not sunk.[56]

On the unfortunately named April Fools' Day, the vastly experienced and rather tempestuous Kelly Turner oversaw the process of landing the men of the 10th US Army on Okinawa. He was not a man to be trifled with and there was no better or more experienced amphibious commander for such an operation. Regardless of the name of the day, Turner was not one of life's victims. In the armada of 1,213 vessels he had assembled for this invasion were 603 landing craft that were assigned to either the Northern Attack Force of Rear-Admiral Lawrence Reifsnider or the Southern Attack Force of Rear-Admiral John Hall. They brought Lieutenant-General Simon Buckner and the first batch of his 451,866 troops to the assault beaches early in the morning and began landing them against light opposition. Relative quiescence on shore would last for only a few days before the men of the Japanese 32nd Army who had deliberately retired into the mountains would use the terrain to draw in and then strike at the forward troops of the enemy. While the assault troops encountered few difficulties in getting ashore, covered as they were by a variety of carrier aircraft and the guns of Deyo's Fire Support Group, the ships offshore were not to enjoy even a period of calm before the storm broke over them. On the first day of the invasion the Japanese hit back with a combination of dive and high-level bombing raids which caused some damage to a destroyer, a minesweeper and a transport and then in the evening brought in the suicide squad of kamikazes and *ohka* manned rocket torpedoes to rough up the landing and support fleets. In these latter attacks, the British carrier *Indomitable* and a destroyer belonging to TF 57, the battleship *West Virginia* from TF 54, two transports and a landing craft were all hit and several more vessels were damaged by more conventional means. Six more transports were hit by kamikazes on the following evening – one so badly that it had to be scuttled two days later. On 3 April another wave of kamikaze attacks hit an LST and later in failing light the 'jeep' carrier *Wake Island*, along with a destroyer, a destroyer escort, a minesweeper and another landing craft. Although foul weather prevented any kamikaze activity on 4 April, the storms proved very much a mixed blessing as the waves that crashed in on shore took a heavy toll on the LSTs exposed on the beaches. The next day (5 April) the battleship *Nevada*, having already survived one kamikaze collision in the preparatory phase of the operation on 26 March, found herself targeted and struck again – this time five shells from a coastal battery rained down upon her as she loosed off her guns against the Japanese positions on shore.[57]

All of this, of course, proved to be a mere prelude to what was to come from the Japanese in the following weeks. Turner, sensing that the enemy would spare no efforts to bury the American offensive on Okinawa, knew his landing fleet needed as much notice as possible of what was in the offing and consequently established a line of sixteen radar picket destroyers around the island. Matome Ugaki, in command of the 3rd, 5th and 10th Air Fleets operating out of Kyūshū, was just as adamant about putting them out of action and devoted *Kikusui 1* – the first of what would become ten massed kamikaze raids – to doing just that. On 6 April, 198 kamikazes set off from Kyūshū and lost ninety of their number to a mixture of Allied fighter cover and A.A. defence before they could press home their attack. Even so there were more than enough left to inflict a series of punishing hits upon the invasion fleet and its supporting cast of hundreds.[58] It was a salutary message that had been delivered. Self-preservation was not written into the script of these kamikaze pilots. Although forty-one returned to base, it was hardly a heroic homecoming for them. On the next day, 179 kamikazes drawn from the ranks of both Army and Navy units returned to Okinawa and penetrated the fighter cover to record severe hits on the battleship *Maryland* and the picket destroyer *Bennett*. Crashes on the fleet carrier *Hancock* and a destroyer escort achieved medium level damage and a destroyer and a minesweeper were hit but sustained only slight damage.[59]

Desperate times call for desperate measures and the Japanese penchant for using shock tactics against the invasion force was exemplified in a final operational sortie for the giant battleship *Yamato*. Vice-Admiral Seiichi Ito was given command of what was always likely to be a suicide mission – one designed to take out as many of the Allied fleet as he could train his guns on before being overwhelmed by sheer force of numbers. On 6 April, Ito left the naval base at Tokuyama on the *Yamato* accompanied by a light cruiser and eight destroyers. His task force was spotted by a B-29 reconnaissance plane shortly thereafter and twice more after emerging from the Bungo-suido (Bungo Channel) by two American submarines. Further sightings were made by flying boats and reconnaissance planes from two carrier groups belonging to TF 58 situated south of Amami Ōshima as Ito's force steamed southwest of Kyūshū towards Okinawa. At 1000 hours 280 aircraft set off from TG 58.1 and TG 58.3 to attack the oncoming ships. They succeeded in sinking the light cruiser *Yahagi* and one of the destroyers *Hamakaze* and in torpedoing and getting two bomb hits upon the centrepiece of Ito's force the *Yamato*. Wounded, but not mortally so, the superbattleship ploughed on and Mitscher was forced to send off another 106 aircraft to finish off the task force in the mid-afternoon. This time three more destroyers perished (*Asashimo*, *Isokaze* and *Kasumi*) and the *Yamato*, after being torpedoed nine more times and receiving three bomb hits, sank too with the loss of all 2,498 officers and crew on board. All four remaining destroyers limped home. Ito's sortie had been an expensive exercise of waste and futility. It had cost the lives of 3,665 sailors and had destroyed six perfectly good warships including the largest remaining capital ship ever built. If ever an operation was misguided this was it. Kamikaze and *ohka* pilots at least set out with an opportunity of securing a glorious and fiery end to their lives, but it is difficult to see how those on board the *Yamato* and the other warships accompanying her on this one-way trip to oblivion were given even the briefest glimmer of such a chance. Apart from the ten US carrier aircraft that were lost in these two sets of attacks, the Allied invasion fleet was not affected by this extravagant and hopeless manoeuvre.[60]

A change of premier – the eighty-year old Admiral Baron Suzuki Kantarō replacing Lieutenant-General Koiso Kuniaki on 7 April – did nothing to change the fortunes of the Japanese military. After failing with their surface fleet and losing all four of their submarines deployed in Operation *TEN-GO* by 9 April, the Japanese returned to using explosive boats and *kaiten* torpedoes for their surface and underwater threats and kamikaze and *ohka* planes for their more penetrative aerial blows. Over the course of the next few days (11–14 April) more than 280 kamikazes and sixteen *ohka* planes came in to do battle with the invasion fleet and while they failed to sink more than two picket ships, sufficient numbers of them got under and through the fighter cover and evaded the A.A. fire to register hits on no less than four battleships (*Idaho*, *Missouri*, *New York* and *Tennessee*), the fleet carriers *Enterprise* and *Essex* and another twenty-five assorted warships.[61] It was to become a familiar pattern that would last for the next two months and result in the sinking of thirty-six US vessels and 368 suffering some degree of damage in the mixed attacks that were orchestrated against the invasion fleet in the period before the spirited resistance on Okinawa finally ended on 22 June after the suicide of Lieutenant-General Mitsuru Ushijima, the Japanese commander on the island, and his Chief of Staff, Lieutenant-General Isamu Cho.[62]

While the Japanese were attacking the invasion fleet, the American and British task forces tried their level best to thwart these efforts. Mitscher's TF 58 not only provided essential fighter cover for the on-going supply operations and as a shield against the suicide missions hatched by both Ugaki and the Army, but also used his resources to strafe and bomb Japanese positions on the island and conduct punishing raids on the kamikaze bases and airfields used by the *ohka* planes on Kyūshū. For his part, Vian (Mitscher's counterpart on TF 57) concentrated on keeping the southern Ryukyu Islands of Sakishima Shotō as quiet as possible and neutralising the threat posed by Japanese aircraft on Formosa. Without either of them being in place the Okinawa operation would have become a prolonged nightmare for the Allies. Sufficient damage was done by the kamikaze in any case, but *Iceberg* couldn't have been a stand-alone amphibious operation without on-going carrier support.[63]

Barely a week after Spruance and Mitscher had handed over their commands to Halsey and McCain with the 5th Fleet being renamed the 3rd Fleet and all the task forces being renumbered to reflect that fact, TF 38 was to encounter another serious test from which it did not escape unscathed. This time it was neither triggered by the enemy nor was it man-made. Nature entered the picture in the shape of a tropical storm that had formed in the Western Pacific and had begun pushing towards the central Ryukyus. Weather conditions had been deteriorating for more than twenty-four hours before the eye of the storm struck Okinawa. Supply operations had been cancelled on 4 June as those elements of the invasion fleet that couldn't get out of the way battened themselves down to await and ride out the worst of the weather. A typhoon struck with immense ferocity on 5 June smashing into TG 38.1 and leaving Rear-Admiral 'Jocko' Clark's task group much the worse for wear. By the time the typhoon had carved its way through his warships, the four carriers *Belleau Wood*, *Bennington*, *Hornet* and *San Jacinto*, his three battleships *Alabama*, *Indiana* and *Massachusetts*, the three heavy cruisers *Baltimore*, *Pittsburgh* (minus thirty metres of her bows wrenched off by the whirlwind) and *Quincy*, three light cruisers and eleven destroyers had all suffered extensive damage and were in need of substantial overhaul. Defiantly, TG 38.1 soldiered on for a few days with a number of replacements and was able to carry out a handful of other sorties against Okinawa and a napalm-bombing run over one of its offshore islands before retiring to lick its wounds in Leyte on 13 June three months after Spruance and TF 58 had originally set out from Ulithi to begin operations off Japan.[64]

Just over a week later the final massed bi-service kamikaze raid – *Kikusui 10* – launched by forty-five Army and Navy pilots after the ritual suicide of both

Ushijima and Cho on 21 June brought the fierce eighty-three day struggle for control of Okinawa to an end on an eerie and unrewarding note. It had been a punishing campaign and had cost the lives of roughly 172,000 Japanese soldiers and civilians and seen the destruction of 7,830 of their aircraft. On the American side the US Army suffered a total of 7,613 dead and missing, including Simon Buckner, the highest-ranking US Army casualty of the entire war, and had 31,807 listed as wounded, while the US Navy had lost 4,907 of its servicemen dead and missing in the waters off Okinawa and had another 4,824 wounded.[65] A set of dispassionate statistical returns can hardly reveal the true horror of the battle for Okinawa. What this ordeal must have done to the nerves and blood pressure of those involved – even tangentially – in this campaign can be easily imagined. Nonetheless, since Okinawa was only an offshore island, the difficulties and the cost of invading Kyūshū or the other main Japanese home islands (Operation *Olympic*) were bound to be far worse in every way and hardly bore thinking about.[66]

Planning for such an eventuality with a target date of 1 November 1945 had been going on for months, but few outside the Joint Planning Staff (JPS) embraced the idea with any great conviction. One thing was certain, however: if *Olympic* was to go ahead as planned General Marshall was determined that the existing command structure in the Pacific would have to be altered to give overall responsibility for Army operations to MacArthur since the bulk of any campaign against Kyūshū was going to have to take place on land rather than at sea. After much heated discussion and contrariness (a common feature of Ernie King's approach to life), an agreed formula was devised on 3 April by which MacArthur was designated CINCAFPAC (Commander-in-Chief, US Army Forces, Pacific) and charged with responsibility for all land campaigns and Nimitz, as CINCPAC, was given responsibility for all operations at sea. While Nimitz's position was little changed by this JCS directive, MacArthur's future role in the war against Japan was set to grow considerably. Jurisdictional problems between the two commanders and their sets of forces would also grow, but the acid test that might arise over complex amphibious operations in support of *Olympic* was fortunately not tested in time of war.[67]

While the BPF had been engaged in neutralising the southern Ryukyus, units of the other part of the former Eastern Fleet, the BEIF, had been involved in helping to put pressure on those corners of the far flung Japanese military empire that were creaking most at this time. Burma was one such place. Losing ground on several fronts, the Japanese looked intensely vulnerable. A plan was therefore hatched by the Allies to strike a further blow against their self-esteem by seizing the capital Rangoon (Operation *Dracula*). Given command of Assault Force W, Rear-Admiral B.C.S. Martin organised the amphibious operation that took six convoys, composed of a headquarters ship and 162 landing craft, escorted by six Indian sloops and twenty-two minesweepers from the Burmese ports of Akyab and Kyaukpyu (Ramree Island) to make landfall close to Rangoon on 1 May. Martin had the four escort carriers *Emperor*, *Hunter*, *Khedive* and *Stalker* and sixteen other warships with him to cover what turned out to be an uncontested landing. Japanese troops had already left the city and its environs and the 26th Indian Division walked into the capital unopposed on 3 May.[68]

Elsewhere in the Indian Ocean other elements of the BEIF attacked the Japanese forces holed up in the Andaman and Nicobar Islands (Operation *Bishop*). Neither of these islands was deemed important enough to invade. They could be regularly shelled and shipping convoys between the two and Sumatra and/or the Southeast Asian mainland could be put to the sword, but the reality was that whatever occurred in these island chains was not going to affect the outcome of the war against Japan.[69] It was very apparent that the Japanese had reached the same conclusion themselves because they sent the heavy cruiser *Haguro* and the destroyer *Kamikaze* out from Singapore on 10 May to evacuate their troops from both the Andamans and the Nicobars. Spotted initially by submarines in the Strait of Malacca, the enemy warships immediately attracted the attention of the BEIF in Trincomalee. Operating as TF 61 under the command of Vice-Admiral H.T.C. 'Hookey' Walker, the Allied force sought to intercept the two enemy warships in the Eleven Degree Channel just south of Port Blair in the Andamans. Forced to play cat and mouse with the enemy ships which were aware of their presence in the area, Walker deployed some of his ships in the area between the island of Great Nicobar and the tip of Aceh on the vast island of Sumatra. It fell to Captain Manley Power and his five destroyers to confront the Japanese warships during the night of 15–16 May southwest of the island of Penang in the Strait of Malacca. Power deployed his flotilla in such a way as to catch his elusive prey in a pincer movement that finally succeeded in overwhelming the *Haguro* after one of his destroyers (*Saumarez*) had taken three body blows from the cruiser. Power's ruse may have claimed the principal prize but the destroyer *Kamikaze* escaped from the trap and returned to Singapore with only modest damage.[70] Further attempts on behalf of the Japanese to evacuate their troops from Port Blair to the port of Mergui in Burma over the course of the next month were consistently foiled by the maintenance of an Allied interception patrol in these waters consisting of a light cruiser – either the *Phoebe* or the *Ceylon* – and half a dozen Indian sloops. Meanwhile, Japanese frustration at their predicament in this part of Southeast Asia grew as efforts to run supplies between the Nicobars and the island of Sabang off Aceh were often nipped in the bud by Allied destroyer sorties from Trincomalee. Other signs of the Allies picking off the declining shipping resources of the Japanese in the region rested with their submarines which managed to sink more sub-chasers in June than ordinary merchant vessels. On 8 June the British submarine *Trenchant* achieved the best result of the month anywhere in the Pacific by sinking the heavy cruiser *Ashigara* in the Bangka Strait after hitting her with five of eight torpedoes and missing the lucky *Kamikaze* with three others.[71]

On the same day that the opening moves of Operation *Dracula* began (27 April), another series of attacks orchestrated by General MacArthur's planning staff and approved rather unenthusiastically by the Joint Chiefs were underway against the island of Tarakan off the northeast coast of Borneo (Operation *Oboe I*).[72] Borneo remained a prize possession of the Japanese. Its vast oilfields and refineries had been one of the vital sources of the Japanese military's energy needs during the war and one that they would be most loath to yield. As usual the preparatory phase was dominated by a sustained bombardment of the coastal defences in the landing sector. On this occasion it was led by the three light cruisers *Boise*, *Hobart* and *Phoenix* and supported by six destroyers. They shelled the assault area south of the main port for three days before a battalion was landed on the small offshore island of Sadan on 30 April to test the resolve of the Japanese defenders. On the following day Rear-Admiral Forrest Royal brought his Amphibious Group 6 into play, landing some 18,000 men of the 26th Australian Brigade on Tarakan from forty-nine landing craft which were escorted into the assault area by a mix of destroyers, escorts, frigates and patrol torpedo boats. Although the landing was successful, a combination of mines and coastal shelling managed to cause some casualties amongst the support group sinking a minesweeper and damaging three others as well as a destroyer in the early days of the invasion. Resistance on Tarakan was not expected to be inconsequential and so it proved. It lasted seven weeks and only came to a formal end on the very day that similar resistance ended on Okinawa (22 June).[73]

While news of the attacks on Borneo and Burma was being digested by the Japanese, more evidence that the noose was being applied to their imperial outposts came with the landings in the Philippines on Los Negros in the Visayan Islands (29 April) and around Santa Cruz in the Gulf of Davao on the southern coast of Mindanao (3–4 May), followed a few days later by those in Macajalar Bay on the northern coast of the island (10 May). This was followed by the loss of the Japanese 18th Army's position on the Wewak Peninsula in New Guinea on 23 May, after some typical bludgeoning from offshore orchestrated by the light cruisers *Hobart* and *Newfoundland* and a couple of Australian destroyers a fortnight before and the landing of over 600 men in Dove Bay to the east of Wewak on 11 May.[74]

On the large islands in the region, such as Borneo, New Guinea and Sumatra, beaten forces could retreat into the vast hinterland so progress was often measured in small incremental steps rather than in giant strides. Next on General MacArthur's target agenda was the oil facility and naval base in Brunei Bay (Operation *Oboe VI*). Several days of minesweeping and bombardment were a necessary prelude to the assault phase of the operation which began when the men of the Australian 9th Infantry Division were brought ashore in the first of 126 landing craft belonging to Amphibious Group 6 on 10 June.[75] MacArthur was on hand to see these 29,361 troops go ashore on the island of Labuan and at points around Brunei Bay. Ten days later Forrest Royal and his group shifted a Battalion Landing Team along the coast to Lutong in Sarawak so as to put them in place for an attack on the oilfields of Miri which they had taken by 25 June. MacArthur was soon witnessing a far trickier assignment – the subduing of opposition and the landing of the Australian 7th Infantry Division in the oil-rich area of Balikpapan several hundred miles south of Tarakan on the east coast of Borneo (Operation *Oboe II*). There was much to do before any of the landing craft could go safely ashore on 1 July.[76] Apart from the anchor and magnetic mines that had been sown out in the waters off Balikpapan and which would require extensive sweeping in the fortnight before the amphibious operation began, underwater obstructions had to be cleared by the demolition teams of frogmen. What had become by now an obligatory bombardment phase – in this case no less than 38,052 rounds of 3–8 inch (76–203 mm) shells from the cruisers and destroyers of three entire task groups – had to be mounted before Rear-Admiral Albert Noble was given approval to bring his 117 landing craft and 33,446 troops ashore. In addition to the normal destroyer escort, Noble was supported by the planes of the 5th and 13th USAAF and for the first three days by an escort carrier group as well, so that Japanese torpedo-bombers based at the airfield at Sepinggan would not become a factor in the invasion. In the event, the airfield was seized on 3 July and the oilfields a day later on American Independence Day.[77]

By then the US 6th Army had already reached Aparri on the north coast of Luzon (27 June) bringing to an end organised Japanese resistance on the island. As the campaign on Mindanao had already ground to a halt on 18 June, the Americans could effectively say that the ground war in the Philippines was over. Although there were still thousands of enemy troops scattered throughout the archipelago and sporadic acts of guerilla warfare continued to erupt from time to time, in essence the Japanese military had been beaten there – a situation that probably had been unavoidable from the time of the naval reverse in Leyte Gulf. Another former scene of triumph for the Japanese – Malaya – was also now fast becoming the latest hostage to fortune. This was the place where a shattering blow had been administered to the aura and confidence of the British Commonwealth in December 1941–February 1942. Churchill, for one, looked forward eagerly to the redemption that a reconquest of both Peninsular Malaya and the colonial island of Singapore would bring to the 'mother country' lying 8,222nm (15,227km) away. It was a campaign that was necessary to rebuild some respect and integrity in Britain's ability to govern and protect its peoples. Before Operation *Zipper* could begin, however, the Andaman Sea and the Strait of Malacca had to be thoroughly swept for mines. A start was made in early July when three flotillas of minesweepers cleared 167 mines off the northwest coast of Malaya and from the waters around the Nicobars (Operation *Collie*). More minesweeping was undertaken off the island of Phuket on the west coast of Siam (Thailand) later in the month in an operation covered by warships from the BEIF. Planes from the escort carriers *Ameer* and *Empress* carried out raids on the Isthmus of Kra and the battleship *Nelson*, the heavy cruiser *Sussex* and four destroyers bombarded the shore line drawing the first kamikaze raids in the Andaman Sea upon them at the cost of a minesweeper being sunk and the *Ameer* being damaged.[78]

After Okinawa had been taken and with the rolling up of the Japanese empire in Southeast Asia progressing satisfactorily, the Americans decided to bring the war home to the Japanese people by carrying out a mix of attacks – massive carrier raids on air bases around Tokyo and the naval facilities at Yokohama; the bombardment by surface warships of principally iron and steel works on the main island of Honshū and in southern Hokkaido; and bombing sorties on shipping found in the Tsugaru Strait between these two northern islands. In a series of attacks that began on 10 July and spread over eight days featuring no less than fifteen carriers, eight battleships, fifteen cruisers and fifty-five destroyers belonging to Admiral Halsey's TF 38 and supported by three carriers, a battleship, six cruisers and fifteen destroyers from the BPF for the latter part of the operation on 16–18 July, extensive damage was done. Forty-seven naval craft of various kinds were sunk, the battleship *Nagato* was made inoperable, while the two new carriers *Amagi* and *Katsuragi*, the battleship *Haruna* and forty-five other vessels were damaged. In addition, well over 5,000 rounds of 5–16 inch (127–406 mm) shells rained down on industrial targets on the home islands.[79]

This operation was followed by one led by Vice-Admiral Jesse Oldendorf at the head of TF 95 in which the principal focus was on shipping in the East China Sea, the Yangtze River estuary and the Yellow Sea. It lasted nearly a month (16 July–12 August) and was one of Oldendorf's least successful and more frustrating ventures. He lost a destroyer sunk, another two damaged (one of them grievously) and the battleship *Pennsylvania* torpedoed, for little positive gain. It was not often that Japanese submarine operations became anything other than a by-word for frustration, but in what turned out to be their last sortie with *kaiten* torpedoes they at last showed what they might have been able to have contributed to the war effort had they been used properly in the past: *I-53* armed with two *kaiten* sunk the destroyer escort *Underhill* and *I-58* damaged the destroyer *Lowry* on the night of 27–28 July. A couple of nights later *I-58* struck again – this time with conventional torpedoes – hitting the US heavy cruiser *Indianapolis* twice and sinking her. Unbeknown to Lt-Cdr. Mochitsura Hashimoto, his victim had already brought parts of the atomic bomb from San Francisco to Tinian and was on her way back to Leyte when he found her running alone east of Luzon and sent a salvo of six torpedoes in her direction. Only 316 out of the total number of 1,199 officers and crew survived the sinking. *I-58* continued to use her *kaiten* to attack convoys but further success narrowly eluded her on both 10 and 12 August.[80]

Although most of the naval action in the Pacific had been concentrated in the central and southwest regions in 1945, American task groups – usually consisting of a cruiser division and a flotilla of destroyers – had continued to make their presence felt further north by indulging in a series of periodic visits to the Kuriles where they would spend usually a couple of days shelling enemy positions around Paramushiro and Matsuwa without attempting any amphibious operations. One suspects these sorties were designed to be a monthly reminder to the Japanese military that the Americans possessed the strategic and logistical reach necessary to tackle all parts of the empire and that the physical damage wrought by these raids was if anything rather secondary in importance to the psychological blows they were administering to the defenders. An invasion could wait, their turn would come. When it did come, however, it was to be far sooner (18 August) and from a completely different source (the Soviet Union) than might have been expected.[81]

Allied action elsewhere in the Pacific before the first of the atomic bombs was dropped on Hiroshima on 6 August took in action against islands, such as Truk and Wake, which had been robbed of their former prominence. By mid-1945 the Japanese defenders on both of these former bases were left as isolated pockets of resistance and ones that remained utterly bereft of making any impact on a war that had passed them by. The Allies resorted to a combination of carrier raids and offshore shelling of both of these islands for much the same reasons as those advanced against the Kuriles – it reminded the Japanese of how much their stock had fallen and who now held the ascendancy in this ocean.[82]

An illustration of just how dominant the Americans had become in this vast theatre was vividly shown on 21–22 July when a US task group of fifteen tankers, five transports and four freighters carried out the replenishment of both TF 38 and units of the British TF 37 whilst they remained on station providing them with roughly 60,000 tons of oil, 6,369 tons of ammunition, 1,635 tons of supplies, ninety-nine aircraft and 412 reservists, in what became the largest supply operation of the entire war at sea. This impressive logistical exercise was arranged primarily to keep the two fleets operational and in a position to launch a further series of attacks on Japan in the next few days. On 24 July, for instance, their carrier aircraft conducted 1,747 sorties along the shoreline of the Inland Sea attacking major naval bases such as Kobe and Kure. In these raids a significant amount of damage was done to the infrastructure of the ports and the warships that were caught at anchor in these harbours. By the time that the last Allied planes had wheeled away and headed back towards their carriers, the bases were littered with the wrecks of the fleet carrier *Amagi*, the three battleships *Haruna*, *Hyūga* and *Ise*, the heavy cruiser *Aoba*, the light cruiser *Ōyodo*, and the training cruiser *Iwate*, along with over 22,000 tons of merchant vessels and auxiliary ships which had either been sunk directly or had become so badly holed and waterlogged that they had ended up by slithering to the harbour floor. In addition, bombs had struck a trio of carriers (*Hōshō*, *Katsuragi* and *Ryūhō*), the escort carrier *Kaiyo*, the light cruiser *Kitakami*, a destroyer, three escort destroyers, two corvettes, a target ship and a landing craft. These raids demonstrated most graphically that there was no longer any hiding place for naval vessels in Japan. Further raids on 28 and 30 July reinforced that impression by finishing off the heavy cruiser *Tone*, the training cruiser *Izumo*, as well as the escort destroyer *Nashi*, the large, but uncompleted, submarine *I-404* and eight other assorted ships, while badly damaging ten other warships including a submarine, a frigate and five corvettes.[83] Apart from deploying carrier planes to assist their Allies in the bombing of Japanese naval targets, the British also sent their battleship *King George V* and three destroyers to join forces with Rear-Admiral John Shafroth's task group (TG 34.8) for a night's bombardment of aircraft and other military-related factories situated close to Hamamatsu in the southern part of Honshū (29–30 July).[84]

At the same time they were also planning another surprise for the Japanese in Singaporean waters. Two midget submarines, *XE 1* and *XE 3*, were towed by the submarines *Spark* and *Stygian* into position off the island. They then left their mother ships and entered Keppel Harbour alone on 30 July with the intention of destroying the two Japanese heavy cruisers *Myokō* and *Takao* stationed there with explosive charges. They achieved only 50% of their objective with *Takao* being holed and sunk, while *Myokō* escaped unharmed.[85]

Despite the success of their aerial forays into Japanese waters, the Allied leaders, both military and political, were not lulled into thinking that the invasion of the main islands would be anything less than a long and bloody affair. For this reason great diplomatic efforts were being made to try to persuade the Soviet Union to join in the war against Japan. Some encouragement had been afforded them on 5 April when the USSR had formally notified the Japanese government that it was giving the obligatory one-year's notice of terminating the neutrality treaty between the two countries that had been in place for four years. Even so this didn't mean that Stalin was willing to become an active partner in the Pacific War immediately. He would take a watching brief and wait upon developments before deciding whether to engage his forces in the Pacific War or not.[86] Whatever the Western Allies thought about his cynical detachment and it wasn't much, judged from Stalin's own perspective what value was there in engaging in yet another dour and costly military campaign if he could afford to wait and join in the struggle at a later date when victory over Japan might be closer to being realised? Although this announcement had triggered a political crisis in Japan and had led to the ousting of Prime Minister General Kuniaki Koiso, the reluctance of the USSR to become actively involved in the war had appealed neither to the new Truman administration in Washington nor to the old Churchill administration in London – both of which were united in believing that this attitude didn't augur well for the post-war period or improve the prospects for an early collapse of the Suzuki administration.[87]

Fortunately for them something else did – the atomic bomb. After several years of trying, a team of brilliant Allied scientists and engineers working on a top-secret development programme at the Los Alamos laboratories in the desert of New Mexico finally managed to produce a weapon of potentially astonishing power. On 6 August 1945 a USAAF B-29 bomber nicknamed 'Enola Gay' and piloted by Colonel Paul Tibbets of the 509th Composite Group dropped the first of these bombs on the southern city of Hiroshima on the main island of Honshū. Marked by its signature mushroom cloud, the bomb unhappily named 'Little Boy', exploded at 0815 hours roughly 1,740 feet (530.3 metres) above the Shima Surgical Hospital near the Aioi Bridge in the city centre with a burst temperature estimated as exceeding one million degrees Celsius. It had a destructive toll that was simply unprecedented in scope and intensity. Hiroshima as a city was ravaged: 92,167 of its citizens were killed and another 37,425 were injured by just one weapon. Eighty per cent of its buildings were either razed to the ground or were so damaged by the terrible force of the explosion that they became uninhabitable.[88] Hiroshima became an eerie city – one that had been reduced in an instant from a recognisable urban community to an incinerated wasteland of misery and radioactive fall out. Brilliant physics had brought about an epochal moment in the history of civilisation – the possibility of man possessing the means of mass destruction on a hitherto unimaginable scale. Here was the most savage of ironies – a supreme positive being turned into a crushing negative. What was an academic achievement of enormous sophistication had become the most awesome and deadliest weapon ever devised and built. While some people undoubtedly saw the dropping of the atomic bomb as an appropriate 'pay back' time for Pearl Harbor, the Allied leadership viewed it as a vivid demonstration that would provide them with the means of saving the lives of vast numbers of their own servicemen who would otherwise have to pay the ultimate price for invading and conquering Japan. If the Japanese leadership was wavering about what to do after the catastrophe over Hiroshima, the Allies helped to remove the mental, emotional and nationalistic log jam by dropping another atomic bomb – known inappropriately as 'Fat Man' – on the city of Nagasaki in southwest Kyūshū at 1058 hours on 9 August. This one, equivalent to 20,000 tonnes of TNT, exploded some 500 feet (152 metres) away from the Mitsubishi Steel and Armament Works and set off a wave of destruction that wrecked an area of 1.45 sq. miles (375.55 hectares) and killed at least 40,000 inhabitants of the city and injured approximately another 60,000.[89]

Stalin needed no further persuasion. Japan would be beaten – that much was clear – and more likely sooner rather than later. If he wanted to share in the spoils of its defeat – which he did – it was evident that he would have to join the other Allies and declare war on Japan before it caved in. Not waiting for a further demonstration of the destructive potential of the atomic bomb, Stalin issued the orders that led to the Soviet Union's declaration of war on Japan on 8 August, just hours before 'Fat Man' took its dreadful toll of Nagasaki. Initially Soviet action against Japanese naval and maritime targets was confined to aerial assaults of enemy controlled ports in North Korea, such as Chongjin, Najin, Unggi and Wonsan, sinking four minor warships and sixteen merchant vessels over the course of several days' raids. These attacks were followed by several amphibious landings along the northeast coast of North Korea in which small groups of advance troops usually numbering hundreds rather than thousands were put ashore by a mixture of frigates, minesweepers, torpedo cutters, patrol boats and other landing craft to await the arrival of ground troops of the 25th Army that were pouring over the Russian border (Operation *August Storm*).[90]

As the Allies waited to see what the Japanese government would do in the aftermath of the Hiroshima and Nagasaki bombings, the British joined the Americans in sending a carrier task force north to carry out further attacks against airfields and railways in both Honshū and Hokkaido and against all forms of shipping spotted in these waters. Apart from the infrastructural damage done in these raids, 505 enemy aircraft were destroyed on the ground and eighteen more were shot down in the air, while fourteen naval and mercantile ships were sunk and eleven more suffered extensive damage. By 15 August uncertainty about what the Japanese might do was dispelled when Emperor Hirohito went on radio at midday to address his subjects for the first time ever. His message was stark. Japan would not continue the war. His words, crafted deliberately in an ambiguous register, failed to acknowledge that his nation had been defeated by the Allies but tacitly accepted that the war should no longer be prosecuted and called upon his armed forces to stop fighting. 'Despite the best that has been done by everyone ... the war situation has developed not necessarily to Japan's advantage, while the general trends of the world have all turned against her interest.'[91] Few of the Japanese people had ever heard their emperor speak before. Many listened in stunned disbelief: the war was over.[92] Despite the official avowal of the end of the campaign, further carrier attacks were mounted on the Tokyo municipality on 15 August before an order was received from Admiral Nimitz to suspend the bombing offensive. In a signal gesture of despair, the last of the kamikaze units in the Tokyo area, including Vice-Admiral Matome Ugaki, the Commander of the 5th Air Fleet, took to the skies for one final suicidal flourish. It would change nothing as far as the war was concerned, but in dying they removed themselves from watching the humiliating spectacle of a military and national defeat taking place in their own homeland.[93]

Before the Allies arrived in Japan to sign the instrument of surrender, there was much work to be done elsewhere. Soviet landings were swiftly made in southern Sakhalin where the men of the North Pacific Flotilla encountered initial opposition from the Japanese 88th Division and in the northern Kuriles where the Naval Defence Sector Petropavlovsk found the Japanese 91st Division anything but accommodating victims. Nonetheless, whatever flurries of resistance there had been were cleared away in a few days as the Japanese defenders followed the orders of their emperor and surrendered without indulging in a final massed *banzai* attack against the enemy. By 3 September Soviet penetration in the Kuriles had gone beyond Paramushiro, Matsuwa and Urup and had reached the southern islands of Kunajiri, Shikotan and Taraku.[94]

By this time the Japanese forces in China had also surrendered (19 August) setting off the struggle for control of the country between the Nationalist (Kuomintang) troops under Generalissimo Chiang Kai-shek (Jiang Jieshi) and the Communist (Peoples' Liberation Army) forces led by Mao Tse-tung (Mao Zedong).[95] After General Yasugi Okamura, the C-in-C of the Japanese China Area Army, had signed the instrument of surrender in Nanking on 9 September, the acrimonious dispute between the two sets of Chinese forces grew ever more divisive as the weeks passed and culminated on 21 September in Chiang asking the Americans for military support. In the end no fewer than 53,000 US Marines were drafted into the region of northern China to accept the surrender of 50,000 Japanese troops in Tientsin (Tianjin) on 6 October and another 10,000 in Tsingtao (Qingdao) four days later. Soviet involvement in the Chinese imbroglio complicated the process markedly by favouring Mao's troops over those of Chiang's. As relations between the PLA and the KMT worsened, both sides in the simmering dispute resorted to military action to further their own political ends. As a result, a furious four-year civil war ensued that ended with the defeat of the KMT and the founding of the People's Republic of China on 1 October 1949.[96]

While the victors squabbled amongst themselves in China, their Anglo-American allies busied themselves in bringing hostilities to an end in Japan, throughout the Pacific and Southeast Asia. Minesweeping activities were resorted to in these waters prior to the landing of troops and the staging of the formal grand surrender ceremonies in both Japan and Singapore in September.[97] Before the Japanese Foreign Minister Mamoru Shigemitsu and the Chief of the Army General Staff Yoshijiro Umezu accepted defeat on behalf of the Japanese nation and signed the instrument of unconditional surrender in the presence of General MacArthur, Chester Nimitz, Sir Bruce Fraser and the rest of the Allied party on board the battleship *Missouri* in Sagami Bay (off the naval base at Yokosuka and Yokohama, the port for Tokyo) on 2 September, other isolated acts of surrender were made by military representatives of Japanese garrisons on Atoll Mili in the Marshall Islands (22 August), on Morotai and Halmahera in what had once been the Dutch East Indies (27 August), and on Marcus Island (30 August). Thereafter, signatures were appended to surrender documents by Vice-Admiral Sueto Hirose on board the heavy cruiser *London* at Sabang on 31 August for the Japanese forces in Sumatra and by Rear-Admiral Jisaku Uozumi on board the battleship *Nelson* for those in the Penang area on 2 September. Lieutenant-General Sadao Inoue did the same for the Palau Islands on the same day and General Tomoyuki Yamashita followed suit by signing the document for the Philippines at Baguio on 3 September.[98]

On the same day that MacArthur witnessed the formal defeat of Japan and spoke eloquently on radio about the ending of a great tragedy (2 September), three minesweeping flotillas cleared the Straits of Malacca and Sir Arthur Power, the C-in-C of the BEIF, brought the first Allied warships back into Singaporean waters for over forty-two months. A couple of days later more ships and Allied troops arrived to witness the formal surrender on board the heavy cruiser *Sussex* by Lieutenant-General Seishiro Itagaki and Vice-Admiral Shigeru Fukudome of all Japanese forces in Singapore and Johor. Although Allied troops had gone ashore in Singapore after that ceremony had been completed on 4 September, the larger show of reclaiming the entire Malayan peninsula on behalf of the former colonial power still had to go on. Admiral Lord Louis Mountbatten, the Supreme Allied Commander, South East Asia Command (SACSEA), did not need any encouragement from London to orchestrate this rather contrived act of politico-military theatre.[99] Despite the logistical and organisational problems associated with it, Operation *Zipper* was duly launched five days later on 9 September. In what became a three-day propaganda spectacle launched against an inactive foe, over 100,000 troops of the 23rd and 25th Indian Divisions were put ashore between Port Swettenham (Pelabuhan Kelang) and Port Dickson on the west coast of the peninsula covered by a force that contained two battleships, six escort carriers, four light cruisers and a Spitfire transport.[100] Apart from giving the British media plenty of film and photographic opportunities, *Zipper* was designed to demonstrate to the local inhabitants that the colonial authorities hadn't forgotten them and had returned to liberate them from the yoke of Japanese oppression. Frankly, if the British thought that such an orchestrated enterprise was going to make up for the disasters of December 1941–February 1942, when they had been shown up in the most dramatic fashion, they were to be gravely disappointed. *Zipper* achieved a hollow victory since one could not help but sense that those left bereft earlier in the decade had reached the conclusion that their 'freedom' had actually come about more as a result of the work of a group of atomic scientists than from anything the British military had been able to do to rescue them.[101]

Operation *Blacklist* (the American occupation of Japan) had a far greater symbolic and material effect than *Zipper* was destined to have. Launched in early September, it too was stage-managed, but the principal difference was that it brought the Japanese people into contact with a conquering invader in their own homeland. It was unprecedented in this respect. Malaya and Singapore had not suffered from anything like the atomic devastation endured by the citizens of Hiroshima and Nagasaki. Furthermore, unlike the British who were returning to their colonial possessions, the Americans had no previous sovereign claims on Japan. A new page in the history of Japan was being written. Japanese subordination to a foreign power had become a reality. Adherence to the military precepts of *nanshin* (southward expansion), which had been executed with such daring panache by Admiral Isoroku Yamamoto at the outset of the Pacific war in 1941–42, had unintentionally led to a chilling, nationalistic *dénouement* three years later. Japan had been wrecked as a military power – such was the astonishing legacy of the attack on Pearl Harbor.[102]

World War I had been dubbed 'the war to end all wars' and hadn't been. Few would make the same claim for the Second World War and with good reason.

Notes

1 Willmott, *Grave of a dozen schemes*, pp.167–68; Winton, *Forgotten fleet*, pp.177–79.
2 Rohwer, *Chronology*, pp.382–83, 387; Willmott, *Grave of a dozen schemes*, pp.168–69; Winton, *Forgotten fleet*, pp.180–88.
3 Rohwer, *Chronology*, pp.387–88; Smith, *Task Force 57*, pp.84–101; Winton, *Forgotten fleet*, pp.77–101.
4 Gill, *Royal Australian Navy 1942–1945*, pp.575–93.
5 Barbey commanded an invasion fleet of eighty-five landing craft, nine destroyers and two destroyer escorts in one task group (TG 78.1) and had another seventy-six landing craft, seven destroyers and four more destroyer escorts under Rear-Admiral Fechteler in TG 78.2. Barbey, *MacArthur's amphibious navy*, pp.288–300; Rohwer, *Chronology*, p.383.
6 Some initial success was achieved by kamikazes on 4 January with such severe damage to the escort carrier *Ommaney Bay* that she became a floating wreck and had to be sunk by the destroyer *Burns*. Another 'jeep' carrier *Lunga Point* received a near-miss, but a freighter was not so lucky. She was hit by a kamikaze and broke up in the most violent way damaging an oiler and a minelayer in the process. Rohwer, *Chronology*, p.383.
7 Warner and Warner, *Sacred warriors*, pp.151–58; Holt, *Kamikazes*, pp.153–58; Rohwer, *Chronology*, pp.383–84.
8 Griffith, *MacArthur's airman*, pp.207–19; Hoyt, *Kamikazes*, pp.163–65; O'Hara, *U.S. Navy against the Axis*, pp.288–92; Rohwer, *Chronology*, pp.383–84.
9 Rohwer, *Chronology*, p.385; Spector, *Eagle against the sun*, pp.518–20; John Toland, *The rising sun: the decline and fall of the Japanese empire 1936–1945* (London: Cassell, 2003), pp.629–31.

10 Boyd and Yoshida, *Japanese submarine force*, pp.166–90.
11 Barbey, *MacArthur's amphibious navy*, pp.301–3.
12 Ibid.; pp.304–9; Clayton James, *Years of MacArthur: 1941–1945*, pp.613, 615–16, 619–20, 625, 628, 632, 648–53; Rohwer, *Chronology*, p.389; Spector, *Eagle against the sun*, pp.518–26.
13 Driskill and Casad, *Admiral of the hills*, pp.216–17; Potter, *Nimitz*, pp.358–64, 367–68; Rohwer, *Chronology*, pp.377, 384, 388–89, 393; Spector, *Eagle against the sun*, pp.494–503; Toland, *Rising sun*, pp.639–69.
14 Robert S. Burrell, 'Breaking the cycle of Iwo Jima mythology: a strategic study of Operation Detachment', *The Journal of Military History*, Vol.68, No.4 (Oct.2004):1143–86; Rohwer, *Chronology*, p.394.
15 Don Yoder, 'The fight for Iwo Jima', in Liddell Hart (ed.), *History of the Second World War*, pp.392–98.
16 Gerald Astor, *The greatest war: Americans in combat 1941–1945* (Novato, Ca: Presidio, 1999), pp.835–44; Parker Bishop Albee, Jr., and Keller Cushing Freeman, *Shadow of Suribachi: raising the flags on Iwo Jima* (Westport, Conn: Praeger, 1995); George C. Dyer, *The amphibians came to conquer: the story of Admiral Richmond Kelly Turner, Vol.II.* (Washington, D.C: U.S. Government Printing Office, 1972), pp.969–1051; Alan R. Millett, *Semper Fidelis*, pp.426–32; Williamson Murray and Allan R. Millett, *A war to be won: fighting the Second World War* (Cambridge, Mass: The Belknap Press of Harvard University Press, 2000), pp.510–13; Rohwer, *Chronology*, pp.393–95; Richard Wheeler, *Iwo* (New York: Lippincott & Crowell, 1980); Derrick Wright, *The Battle for Iwo Jima 1945*, (Stroud, Glos: Sutton Publishing, 2003).
17 Boyd and Yoshida, *Japanese submarine force*, pp.170–72.
18 Hoyt, *Kamikazes*, pp.195–96, 199, 201, 203, 205, 211, 217, 220–24, 250, 263, 277, 288; Rohwer, *Chronology*, pp.394–95; Warner and Warner, *Sacred warriors*, pp.171–74.
19 Not surprisingly, perhaps, different casualty figures are cited by the main sources on the struggle for Iwo Jima. Those cited in this text are drawn from Richard B. Frank, *Downfall: the end of the Imperial Japanese Empire* (New York: Random House, 1999), pp.60–61. They differ in several respects from those quoted by Rohwer, *Chronology*, p.395. While the total of both Japanese and Marines killed remains the same, the number of surviving Japanese is larger (1,083 as opposed to 216) and if Frank is to be believed the total of Marines wounded is substantially higher (22,099 as distinct from 17,272). John Toland's figures are distinctly different, see *Rising sun*, p.669.
20 Peter Lowe, 'The war against Japan and Allied relations', in Ann Lane and Howard Temperley (eds), *The rise and fall of the Grand Alliance, 1941–45* (Basingstoke: Macmillan, 1995), pp.190–206; Hayes, *History of the Joint Chiefs of Staff*, pp.653–85.
21 Barbey, *MacArthur's amphibious navy*, pp.310–14.
22 Rohwer, *Chronology*, pp.395–96, 398–99, 401, 403–4, 409–12; Spector, *Eagle against the sun*, pp.526–27.
23 Clive Sinclaire, *Samurai: the weapons and spirit of the Japanese warrior* (Guildford, Conn: The Lyons Press, 2004), pp.8–25.
24 Frank, *Downfall*, pp.3–19; Rohwer, *Chronology*, pp.393, 395.
25 USS *Yorktown* (CV10), an Essex-class fleet carrier, was formerly named *Bon Homme Richard* and was renamed in September 1942 in honour of the USS *Yorktown* (CV5) which was sunk by the Japanese submarine *I-168* at the Battle of Midway on 7 June 1942. Gardiner (ed.), *Conway's all the world's fighting ships*, pp.102–4.
26 Hoyt, *Kamikazes*, pp.215–51; Rohwer, *Chronology*, pp.399–400, 402; Goldstein and Dillon (eds.), *Fading victory*, pp.552–60.
27 Rohwer, *Chronology*, pp.384, 392, 394–95, 399, 401, 403, 408; Willmott, *Grave of a dozen schemes*, pp.170–73; Winton, *Forgotten fleet*, pp.212–13.
28 Milner, *Battle of the Atlantic*, pp.217–20; Hughes and Costello, *Battle of the Atlantic*, p.300.

29 Surface action in these waters, such as the convoy action off Egersund on 11–12 January and a further joust with the enemy off Bergen on 28 January, left neither side contented with the results. See O'Hara, *German fleet in war*, pp.252–56.
30 Woodman, *Arctic convoys*, pp.421–35; Rohwer, *Chronology*, pp.392–94, 399.
31 *Fuehrer conferences*, pp.421–22, 425–26, 428–29, 431–34, 436–37, 443, 445–48, 450–51, 454–55, 457, 459–60, 462–64, 467–70, 476, 480, 483, 489; Rohwer, *Chronology*, pp.384, 390–91, 396–97, 406; Tarrant, *Last year of the Kriegsmarine*, pp.182–207.
32 Kemp, *Underwater warriors*, pp.202–14; Paterson, *Weapons of desperation*, pp.112–73; 185–222; Rohwer, *Chronology*, pp.382, 388, 392, 397, 405–6.
33 Bryan Cooper, *The E-boat threat* (London: Macdonald & Jane's, 1976), pp.120–25; Levy, *The Royal Navy's Home Fleet*, pp.150–51; O'Hara, *German fleet at war*, pp.245–47; Rohwer, *Chronology*, pp.386, 388, 394, 401, 407, 409, 411.
34 Rohwer, *Chronology*, pp.387, 389; Achkasov and Pavlovich, *Soviet naval operations*, pp.252–54; C.W. Koburger, *Naval warfare in the Baltic, 1939–1945: war in a narrow sea* (Westport, Conn: Praeger, 1994), pp.87–103; Ruge, *Soviets as naval opponents*, pp.51–62.
35 Eighteen ships were sunk and eight more were damaged in January alone; another twenty-three ships of all kinds succumbed in February with thirteen more being damaged; and twenty-six capsized and were lost in March, with another eleven suffering damage. Rohwer, *Chronology*, pp.389–90.
36 Ibid.; Koburger, *Naval warfare in the Baltic*, pp.92–94.
37 Rohwer, *Chronology*, pp.395, 398.
38 In bombing raids on Hamburg, Kiel and Swinemünde on 11–12 March, for example, two U-boats, three minesweepers, six motor minesweepers, twenty naval fishing cutters, a small tanker, ten merchant vessels, a passenger ship, a patrol craft and a tug were all destroyed. Rohwer, *Chronology*, p.399; Tarrant, *Last year of the Kriegsmarine*, pp.185–89.
39 *Fuehrer conferences*, pp.481–82; Middlebrook and Everitt, *Bomber Command diaries*, pp.692–96; Rohwer, *Chronology*, pp.404–5, 408–9.
40 Rohwer, *Chronology*, pp.407–8, 410.
41 All the vessels at the port of Swinemünde that could move independently – including an auxiliary cruiser, four destroyers, a couple of torpedo boats and the A.A. ship *Hummel* with 35,000 people on board – were sent on their way to exile in Copenhagen. Ibid., pp.410–12.
42 Blair, *Hitler's U-boat war: hunted*, pp.694–700.
43 Rohwer, *Chronology*, p.412; Woodman, *Arctic convoys*, pp.437–38.
44 Rohwer, *Chronology*, p.414.
45 Ibid., pp.416–17; Van der Dat, *Atlantic campaign*, pp.381–82.
46 Rohwer, *Chronology*, pp.413–14, 415–16; Tarrant, *Last year of the Kriegsmarine*, p.227–28.
47 Rohwer, *Chronology*, pp.414, 417.
48 Ibid., pp.409, 412; Auphan and Mordal, *French Navy in World War II*, pp.348–54.
49 Lind, *Battle of the wine dark sea*, p.168; Rohwer, *Chronology*, p.417.
50 There were thirty of these craft in Bergen alone, a further seventeen in Kristiansand/South, nine in Stavanger, eleven in Trondheim and eleven more in Horten, the base closest to Oslo. Rohwer, *Chronology*, p.418.
51 Ibid.; www.u-boot-greywolf.de/udeadlight (accessed 15 Oct.2005), pp.1–9.
52 Allied naval vessels reached the main German naval ports only after information pinpointing the precise location of the mine barrages that had been erected in the Kattegat and the Skagerrak had been received by the Home Fleet in the Firth of Forth on 14 May. Rohwer, *Chronology*, pp.416–17.
53 Sources on the battle for Okinawa are many and varied. Amongst the best are Gerald Astor, *Operation Iceberg: the invasion and conquest of Okinawa in World War II – an oral history* (New York: Donald I. Fine, 1995), pp.1–20; George Feifer, *Tennozan: the battle for Okinawa and the atomic bomb* (New York: Ticknor & Fields, 1992), pp.xi-128; Simon Foster, *Okinawa 1945* (London: Arms and Armour, 1996); T.M. Huber,

Okinawa 1945 (Havertown, Pa: Casemate, 2004); Prados, *Combined Fleet decoded*, pp.702, 706–19; Spector, *Eagle against the sun*, pp.532–40; Goldstein and Dillon (eds.), *Fading victory*, pp.560, 562, 564, 567–68, 570–71, 573–74, 576–78, 581–82, 585–88, 590–93, 596, 598, 600, 603, 605, 607–8, 610, 613–14, 616–17, 619, 621–24, 626, 628–37, 639–41, 644, 647–48, 650, 652, 658, 661–64, 666, 670.

54 Gill, *Royal Australian Navy 1942–1945*, pp.604–15.

55 Blandy's task force (TF.52) brought together seventeen escort carriers, ten destroyers and nineteen destroyer escorts and an impressive collection of minesweepers and minelayers in a number of other groups. In overall command of the entire operation, Admiral Spruance was to be found on board his flagship the heavy cruiser *Indianapolis* as part of Deyo's Fire Support Group (TF.54) surrounded by ten battleships, nine other cruisers, twenty-four destroyers, eight destroyer escorts and fifty-three support landing craft equipped with rocket throwers. Rohwer, *Chronology*, p.403.

56 Hamer, *Bombers versus battleships*, pp.307–25; Hoyt, *Kamikazes*, pp.252–60; Winton, *Forgotten fleet*, pp.102–67; Rohwer, *Chronology*, pp.402–3; Smith, *Task Force 57*, pp.114–20; Wragg, *Carrier combat*, pp.199–209.

57 Hoyt, *Kamikazes*, pp.260–66; Rohwer, *Chronology*, p.404; Smith, *Task Force 57*, pp.121–28.

58 *Kikusui* (Floating Chrysanthemum) 1 was responsible for sinking two of the picket destroyers (*Bush* and *Colhoun*), a destroyer-minesweeper, two ammunition transports and an LST, and so badly damaging three more destroyers and a destroyer escort that they were effectively written off. In addition, another destroyer and two minesweepers were so extensively damaged that they were put out of action for the entire war. Three more destroyers and an escort suffered medium-level damage, while the fleet carriers *Illustrious* and *San Jacinto*, thirteen other warships and a landing craft received lighter damage. Rohwer, *Chronology*, p.407; Harker, *HMNZS Achilles*, pp.216–27.

59 Feifer, *Tennozan*, pp.195–229; Rohwer, *Chronology*, p.407

60 It is evident that not all subscribe to this view. Russell Spurr describes the episode as one of 'hopeless heroism' and claims that the Japanese traditionally admire this trait and even more so because of the sheer scale of the losses involved in the sinking of the superbattleship. Russell Spurr, *A glorious way to die: the kamikaze mission of the battleship Yamato, April 1945* (London: Sidgwick & Jackson, 1982); Yoshia Mitsuru, *Requiem for battleship Yamato* (London: Constable, 1999); Astor, *Operation Iceberg*, pp.181–88; Dull, *Battle history of IJN*, pp.333–35; Hoyt, *Kamikazes*, pp.276–80; Prados, *Combined Fleet decoded*, pp.710–15; Rohwer, *Chronology*, p.407; Taylor, *Magnificent Mitscher*, pp.281–85; Goldstein and Dillon (eds.), *Fading victory*, pp.567, 572, 574–76, 579, 586, 595.

61 Harker, *HMNZS Achilles*, pp.228–33; Rohwer, *Chronology*, p.408; Stafford, *Big E*, pp.534–38.

62 There was also an enforced change at the top of the US administration with the sudden death of President Roosevelt on 12 April. He was succeeded in office by his vice president, the Missouran Harry S. Truman. Feifer, *Tennozan*, pp.506–8; Gailey, *War in the Pacific*, pp.426–46; Rohwer, *Chronology*, pp.407–12, 414–15, 418–21.

63 It is interesting to note that in relative terms, as Professor Willmott points out, the BPF suffered heavier losses than the US Pacific Fleet did from December 1944 to August 1945. In the first phase of its Okinawan involvement lasting from 26 March to 20 April, the BPF lost a third of its complement of carrier aircraft. During its second phase from 4 to 22 May, it lost another 42% of its original aircraft numbers and 79% of its Corsair establishment. Willmott indicates that in twenty-four carrier strike days of the forty-six it spent on station, the BPF lost a total of 81% of the aircraft with which it had begun Operation *Iceberg*. Willmott describes the BPF as the equivalent of a weak US carrier task group, but indicates that the equivalence lies more in quantitative rather than qualitative terms. He does concede, however, that although the BPF was not as experienced in carrier-led operations as the Americans

and did suffer problems in servicing their aircraft, it was still better to have it assisting the Allied cause in the Pacific rather than being elsewhere. Willmott, *Grave of a dozen schemes*, pp.137–41; Rohwer, *Chronology*, pp.407–10, 412, 414–15, 418–19; Smith, *Task Force 57*, pp.130–56; Winton, *Forgotten fleet*, pp.102–67.

64 Clark G. Reynolds, *On the warpath in the Pacific: Admiral Jocko Clark and the fast carriers* (Annapolis, Md: NIP, 2005), pp.420–28; Potter, *Bull Halsey*, pp.336–40; Rohwer, *Chronology*, pp.418–19; Wukovits, *Admiral 'Bull' Halsey*, pp.215–21.

65 Statistical tallies of dead and wounded differ substantially according to the source one uses. Those figures cited in the text come from Rohwer, *Chronology*, p.421. He indicates that approximately 130,000 Japanese military lost their lives, whereas Astor, *Operation Iceberg*, p.439, puts the figure at 110,071. Rohwer suggests 10,755 became POWs as opposed to 7,401 according to Astor. The sources concur on the number of US military losses as being 12,520 and those American servicemen wounded in the struggle for the island (36,631), but Astor's numbers for civilian casualties are much higher ranging from 75,000 to 140,000 as against the 42,000 listed by Rohwer. Both agree on the number of US ships lost in the campaign (36) and damaged (368) and the number of US aircraft lost (763), but Rohwer suggests that 7,830 Japanese aircraft were lost as opposed to 7,700 listed by Astor. Gailey, *War in the Pacific*, p.445, settles on 110,000 Japanese military losses, 7,400 POWs and more than 80,000 Japanese civilian deaths. He accepts the same figure as the other two do for US military deaths and lists the US wounded as 36,931.

66 Edward J. Drea, 'Previews of hell', in Cowley (ed.), *No end save victory*, pp.658–70.

67 Command responsibilities for the Pacific were rounded out when General Carl A. Spaatz was appointed by the JCS in early July as Commander of the US Army Strategic Air Force (USASTAF). While he would be independent of both MacArthur and Nimitz, he was nonetheless required to cooperate with both of them. Hayes, *History of the Joint Chiefs of Staff*, pp.686–95; Clayton James, *Years of MacArthur: 1941–1945*, pp.722–30.

68 Winton, *Forgotten fleet*, pp.195–99

69 Ibid., pp.215–18; Rohwer, *Chronology*, p.412.

70 John Winton, *Sink the Haguro!: the last destroyer action of the Second World War* (London: Seeley, Service & Co., 1979); Rohwer, *Chronology*, p.417.

71 Winton, *Forgotten fleet*, pp.258–62; Rohwer, *Chronology*, pp.418–19.

72 Hayes, *History of the Joint Chiefs of Staff*, pp.695–97; Clayton James, *Years of MacArthur: 1941–1945*, pp.714–17; Gill, *Royal Australian Navy 1942–45*, pp.616–24.

73 Edwin P. Hoyt, *MacArthur's navy: the Seventh Fleet and the battle for the Philippines* (New York: Orion Books, 1989), pp.195–98; Barbey, *MacArthur's amphibious navy*, p.315; Clayton James, *Years of MacArthur: 1941–1945*, pp.751–63; Rohwer, *Chronology*, pp.412, 420–23.

74 Progress in New Guinea was rarely rapid and Lt-Gen. Hatazo Adachi and the 18th Army were still four months from surrendering. Rohwer, *Chronology*, pp.412, 417; Gill, *Royal Australian Navy 1942–1945*, pp.625, 627–33.

75 Barbey, *MacArthur's amphibious navy*, p.315.

76 Gill, *Royal Australian Navy 1942–1945*, pp.646–58.

77 Barbey, *MacArthur's amphibious navy* pp.316–20; Clayton James, *Years of MacArthur: 1941–1945*, pp.753–54, 756, 759, 761–62; Rohwer, *Chronology*, pp.420–22.

78 Rohwer, *Chronology*, pp.421, 423–24; Winton, *Forgotten fleet*, pp.233–35.

79 Hobbs, *The British Pacific Fleet*, pp.252–93; Robb-Webb, '"Light two lanterns"', in Kennedy (ed.), *British naval strategy east of Suez*, pp.128–53; Rohwer, *Chronology*, pp.421–22.

80 Ibid., pp.423–24; Edwin P. Hoyt, *Closing the circle: war in the Pacific: 1945* (New York: Van Nostrand Reinhold, 1982), pp.27–133; Dan Kurzman, *Fatal voyage: the sinking of the USS Indianapolis* (New York: Broadway Books, 2001); Doug Stanton, *In harm's way: the sinking of the USS Indianapolis and the extraordinary story of its survivors* (New York: Henry Holt, 2001); Winton, *Forgotten fleet*, pp.308–47.

81 Rohwer, *Chronology*, pp.384, 393–94, 400, 418, 420–24, 427–28.
82 Ibid., pp.420–21, 424; Smith, *Task Force 57*, pp.157–68.
83 Rohwer, *Chronology*, pp.424–25; Richard B. Frank, *Downfall: the end of the Imperial Japanese Empire* (New York: Random House, 1999), pp.157–58.
84 Smith, *Task Force 57*, pp.169–87; Winton, *Forgotten fleet*, pp.316–32.
85 Rohwer, *Chronology*, p.424; Winton, *Forgotten fleet*, pp.266–68.
86 Hayes, *History of the Joint Chiefs of Staff*, pp.713–21.
87 Thomas B. Allen and Norman Polmar, *Code-name Downfall: the secret plan to invade Japan and why Truman dropped the bomb* (New York: Simon & Schuster, 1995); John Paton Davies, Jr., *Dragon by the tail: American, British, Japanese and Russian encounters with China and one another* (New York: W.W.Norton, 1972), pp.399–408; Frank, *Downfall*, pp.90–96, 101–2, 107, 109–15, 227, 233–38; Martin Gilbert, *Winston S. Churchill. Vol.VIII. 'Never despair' 1945–1965* (Boston: Houghton Mifflin, 1988), pp.6–7, 13–14, 20, 24, 26, 32, 45, 60–104, 119, 154, 167, 191–92, 194–95; David McCullough, *Truman* (New York: Simon & Schuster, 1992), pp.370, 374–76, 378–84, 390–92, 395–96, 398–99, 443, 450, 460, 463–64, 476, 486, 488–89, 516–17, 544, 546; David Elstein, 'Decision', in Liddell Hart (ed.), *History of the Second World War*, pp.435–39.
88 Despite all the scholarly research that has been carried out on the immediate aftermath and the longer term consequences of the dropping of the atomic bombs on Hiroshima and Nagasaki, the exact casualty figures will probably never be known. Although Rohwer provides specific casualty figures for Hiroshima and these have been used by me in the main body of the text, they are at best only a reasonable guide but they cannot be regarded as being absolutely authentic or totally reliable. In his book on the end of the Imperial Japanese Empire, Richard Frank addresses this issue and provides a range of estimates that have been published in four different official reports that were held from 1946 to 1966 on the bombings of both cities. These claim that the numbers who died at Hiroshima were in the range 66,000–80,000 while those at Nagasaki were in the range 23,753–45,000. Those injured as a result of the two blasts were given as 69,000–151,000 at Hiroshima and 25,000–60,000 at Nagasaki. Frank, *Downfall*, pp.252–68, 283–87.
89 A huge body of work has been devoted to the emotive subject of the dropping of the atomic bombs on Hiroshima and Nagasaki in August 1945. As of 21 November 2007 there were no less than 9,670,000 websites on the subject of the first two atomic bombs and a further 1,860,000 entries on the casualties caused by those two bombs. This is quite separate from the truly immense and ever growing body of printed works on aspects of the atomic bomb and its legacy. Selecting a few volumes amongst such an immense literary output is, therefore, little more than a random and highly subjective offering but, even so, each of the following works has something to recommend: Kai Bird and Lawrence Lifschultz (eds.), *Hiroshima's shadow* (Stony Creek, Conn: The Pamphleteers Press, 1998); Herbert Feis, *The atomic bomb and the end of World War II* (Princeton, N.J: Princeton University Press, 1966); Lawrence Freedman and Saki Dockrill, 'Hiroshima: a strategy of shock', in Saki Dockrill (ed.), *From Pearl Harbor to Hiroshima: the Second World War in Asia and the Pacific, 1941–45* (Basingstoke: Macmillan, 1994), pp.191–212; Tim Maga, *America attacks Japan: the invasion that never was* (Lexington, Ky: The University Press of Kentucky, 2002); Bess, *Choices under fire*, pp.198–253. For more specific and sadly more harrowing, details on the bombs themselves, see Louis Allen, 'The nuclear raids: August 1945 Hiroshima and Nagasaki' in Liddell Hart (ed.), *History of the Second World War*, pp.439–46; Walter L. Hixson, *The American experience in World War II. Vol.7: the atomic bomb in history and memory* (New York: Routledge, 2003); Frank Barnaby, 'The Effects of the atomic bombings of Hiroshima and Nagasaki', in Douglas Holdstock and Frank Barnaby, (eds), *Hiroshima and Nagasaki: retrospect and prospect* (London: Frank Cass, 1995), pp.1–9; Donald M. Goldstein, Katherine V. Dillon, and J. Michael

Wenger, *Rain of ruin: a photographic history of Hiroshima and Nagasaki* (Washington, D.C: Brassey's, 1995), pp.xi–116; Rohwer, *Chronology*, p.426.
90 Bruce Cumings, *The origins of the Korean War: liberation and the emergence of separate regimes 1945–1947* (Princeton, NJ: Princeton University Press, 1981), pp.384–90; Frank, *Downfall*, pp.273–83, 322–26; Mark S. Gallicchio, *American East Asian policy and the fall of the Japanese empire, 1945* (Ann Arbor, MI: University Microfilms International, 1986), pp.95–96, 102–3, 117–21, 139–40, 147–53, 160–65, 174–82, 191, 195–200, 205–6, 230–35, 252–90, 303–4; Rohwer, *Chronology*, pp.426–27; Charles M. Dobbs, *The United States and East Asia since 1945* (Lewiston, NY: The Edwin Mellen Press, 1990), pp.27–32.
91 Herbert P. Bix, *Hirohito and the making of modern Japan* (London: Duckworth, 2001), pp.526–28; Frank, *Downfall*, p.320; Goldstein et al., *Rain of ruin*, pp.117–24.
92 Ibid.
93 Goldstein and Dillon (eds.), *Fading victory*, pp.623–24, 658–66; Thomas, *Sea of thunder*, pp.339–40.
94 David Rees, *Soviet seizure of the Kuriles* (New York: Praeger, 1985), pp.69–84; Rohwer, *Chronology*, p.428.
95 Political reverberations began immediately. First blood went to the PLA who seized the city of Kalgan (Zhangjiakou) on the following day (20 August) and the northeastern ports of Chefoo (Yantai) and Wei-hai-wei (Weihai) four days later. Marshal Chiang's fury was not appeased by the KMT's occupation of the Yangtse port of Nanking (Nanjing) only hours later on 25 August. According to him, Mao had been disrespectful and treacherous and would have to be put in his place. It was inconceivable to Chiang that he might lose the peace to Mao's Communists after being on the winning side in the war against Japan. For his part, Mao sought to ensure that Chiang would taste defeat. So the scene was set for another fierce military campaign once the Japanese had been removed from the strategic equation. Philip S. Jowett, *The Chinese Army 1937–49: World War II and civil war* (Oxford: Osprey, 2005); Rohwer, *Chronology*, p.428.
96 Odd Arne Westad, *Cold War and revolution: Soviet–American rivalry and the origins of the Chinese Civil War, 1944–1946* (New York: Columbia University Press, 1993), pp.49–55, 77–97; Davies, *Dragon by the tail*, pp.408–12; Rohwer, *Chronology*, pp.431–32.
97 Clayton James, *Years of MacArthur: 1941–1945*, pp.788–92; Driskill and Casad, *Admiral of the hills*, pp.226–29; Frank, *Downfall*, p.330; Peter Dennis, *Troubled days of peace: Mountbatten and South East Asia Command 1945–46* (Manchester: Manchester University Press, 1987), pp.1–2; John W. Dower, *Embracing defeat: Japan in the wake of World War II* (New York: W.W. Norton, 1999), pp.34–45; Goldstein et al., *Rain of ruin*, pp.125–46.
98 Further surrenders were arranged on Truk and in the central Carolines and by commanding officers of garrisons on the Bonin Islands, Jaluit, Ulithi, Wake and Yap over the course of the next couple of days. Substantial forces left in Borneo, Formosa, Hong Kong, Korea and New Guinea, together with those scattered throughout the island chains of the Bismarck Archipelago, the Dutch East Indies, New Ireland, the Ryukyus, Solomons and the Wewak Islands, in addition to those on individual islands, such as Maloelap, Nauru, Ponape, Woleai and Wotje, had all capitulated by 19 September. Other outlying outposts of the Japanese empire, such as the Andaman Islands and the island of Timor, surrendered later on 26 September and 3 October respectively. Rohwer, *Chronology*, pp.428–31; Gill, *Royal Australian Navy 1942–1945*, pp.676–701; Pfennigwerth, *Missing pieces*, pp.140–44.
99 Mountbatten's responsibilities increased after the Japanese gave notice of their decision to end the war on 15 August. After discussing the matter at their conference at Potsdam, the Allies merged MacArthur's South West Pacific Area with that of Mountbatten's South East Asia Command. This meant that Mountbatten, as Supreme Allied Commander, South-East Asia Command (SACSEA), was now

responsible for the liberation of the East Indies and the southern part of Indo-China below the 16° North parallel, in addition to his existing duties overseeing similar military and repatriation operations in Burma, Malaya, Siam, Singapore and Sumatra. Dennis, *Mountbatten and South East Asia Command*, pp.5–23.
100 Rohwer, *Chronology*, p.429; Clayton James, *Years of MacArthur: 1941–1945*, p.791.
101 Another major ceremony took place on the steps of City Hall in Singapore on 12 September when Mountbatten in his capacity as SACSEA presided over the signing by Lt-Gen. Seishiro Itagaki and Lt-Gen.Takazo Numata (the chief of staff to the indisposed Field Marshal Count Terauchi) of the formal document surrendering all Japanese forces in Southeast Asia. Dennis, *Mountbatten and South East Asia Command*, p.1; Winton, *Forgotten fleet*, pp.348–85.
102 Goldstein, *et al.*, *Rain of ruin*, pp.147–65; Rohwer, *Chronology*, p.430.

Conclusion: Rising to the challenge of fighting the war at sea

Despite the march of scientific and engineering progress in the first half of the twentieth century and the sophisticated applications that some of these advances brought to the navies of the world from 1919 onwards, raw power alone was rarely sufficient to determine the success or failure of any encounter at sea in the years leading up to 1945. As we have seen in this study, a host of other factors both technical and personal as well as geophysical and unfathomable often had a role to play in determining the eventual outcome of these clashes.

Emerging from a costly attritional war that had demonstrated just how unpredictable armed conflict can be, all of the leading naval powers found themselves paying a substantial price for peace in the tumultuous years that followed the armistice of November 1918.[1] While the scarcely vanquished Central Powers succumbed for some time to the draconian clauses of the Peace Settlement, the jaded victors could hardly strike a triumphalist note since most were grappling with massive economic problems that would take years to overcome. Apart from the likely knock-on effects of curtailed military expenditure for most of the Allied and Associated Powers, an even starker predicament was in store for their naval delegates who found themselves most effectively ambushed by Charles Evans Hughes at the Washington Conference in November 1921.

Forced to accept a far more comprehensive system of disarmament than they had ever contemplated, the naval establishments were obliged to begin a major reconstruction programme of their own – decommissioning surplus stocks of warships and cutting back on a range of different research and development programmes (including rigorous testing of equipment) because of the shortfall in public expenditure. While disarmament was not all bad, as the British discovered in removing a host of obsolescent vessels from Admiralty inventories, it wasn't destined to last. As the international politico-economic climate worsened in the wake of the Great Depression and international aggression again resurfaced on the world's stage, the attraction of disarmament waned and the lure of re-armament became unmistakable.[2]

Nonetheless, money remained tight in these years and the naval establishments, juggling their budgets and knowing that they hadn't the funds to be strong everywhere, opted in the first instance to improve the design and construction of their principal classes of warship. Among the more remarkable transitions of this period was the evolution of the aircraft carrier from being a primitive surface platform in the 1920s to a formidable fighting unit by the end of the 1930s and one that was destined to replace the battleship at the top of the capital ship pecking order during the Pacific War. Unfortunately, the rate of progress in other technical fields, such as ASW, remained spotty, inconsistent and deficient in places.[3] Improvements would come with time, but that was a commodity that couldn't be bought by those European naval powers that were pitched into war by their political leaders in September 1939.

Once Raeder's grandiose hopes for a massive fleet presence by the mid-1940s were sabotaged by the attack on Poland and the resumption of war with the Allies, the Kriegsmarine was left with little alternative other than to embark once again on a war on trade against their enemies.[4] Leading the way in this unrelenting fight to the death was the U-boat – the stalking predator of the 1914–18 conflict – which the Treaty of Versailles had forbidden Germany to possess thereafter. This embargo hadn't deterred the resourceful Germans from establishing a clandestine submarine bureau in Holland in the early 1920s which not only designed and built a number of vessels for other countries in these years, but also drew up a host of plans for new models that could be put into production once Germany had been given the green light officially to re-arm.[5] Shortly after Hitler had established himself in power, submarine construction in German shipyards began once again but in secret. That charade was dispensed with in March 1935 and received controversial British approval in the Anglo-German Naval Agreement of June 1935. Although the coastal Type II and ocean-going Type VII U-boats were swiftly adopted in the mid-1930s and the Type VIIC and IXC became standard issue for the Atlantic patrols during the early years of the war, Dönitz waited years for a new generation U-boat that could perform with the underwater speed and endurance promised by Professor Hellmuth Walter in 1936. He was still waiting for a safe, hydrogen-peroxide (*Ingolin*) powered breakthrough when the war came to an end in 1945.[6] Thwarted on this revolutionary front, he and the Kriegsmarine had been forced to settle for an engineering compromise – the *schnorchel*-equipped *elektroboote* – which in the shape of the long-range, ocean-going Type XXI and the coastal Type XXIII could well have advanced the cause of the U-boat arm had they come on stream in sufficient numbers earlier in the campaign, but were often uncomfortable and potentially hazardous to operate when they first made their appearance in 1944–45.[7]

Dönitz's problems didn't end there. While he always wanted more and better U-boats at his disposal, he and his crews needed a far more reliable weapon than the deeply flawed Mark G7a and G7e torpedoes with which they were expected to wage war on the enemy in the early years of the war. Many of the persistent failures associated with these models – guidance system problems, inadequate depth-keeping, defective pistols and faulty detonators – resulted from using inferior equipment that had been inadequately tested in the inter-war period. It would take two to three years to overcome most of these problems, but in the meantime well over 30% of these torpedoes would fail either to reach their assigned target or to explode upon impact even if they did.[8] It takes very little imagination to wonder what further chaos and catastrophe could have been inflicted upon the Allied war effort – already reeling from the impact of the war on trade – had the Germans possessed a truly reliable weapon in the 1939–42 period.[9]

Fortunately, the Allies had learnt from their galling experiences in the Great War and remembered that the most effective way of countering the U-boat threat lay in convoying ships between ports. A convoy system across the North Atlantic was swiftly established after the outbreak of war and repaid the Allies handsomely thereafter.[10] Once again, convoy proved to be a stunning success. If one excludes the Arctic and Caribbean routes, out of 88,286 ships under convoy from 1939–45 only 1,180 were lost in transit – a rate of 1.34%. Even on the troubled Russian route 105 ships were lost from 1,583 that sailed in convoy – a loss percentage of only 6.63.[11] It is all the more surprising, therefore, that the Americans didn't institute a systematic convoy system throughout the Americas and the Caribbean earlier than they did. Had they imposed a through convoy system along their own coastlines as quickly as possible after their abrupt entry into the war in December 1941, they would have denied Dönitz's U-boat crews many easy spoils in these unprotected waters. As it was, however, a 'happy time' for the Axis meant considerable grief for the Allies.[12] It was to be a lesson painfully learnt in British and Irish coastal waters too.

According to the Trade Division of the Admiralty, 4,786 merchant ships over 100 GRT belonging to the Allied and Neutral Powers were lost in the Second World War. Of this figure, no fewer than 2,775 succumbed to submarine attack.[13] Despite their own problems, U-boats were undoubtedly aided in their mastery of mercantile shipping in the 1939–42 period through the Allied failure to close the mid-Atlantic 'air gap' with VLR or carrier group aircraft and by the B-Dienst's ability to read the British Naval Cypher and discover priceless information, such as the course coordinates and anticipated speed of their potential victims.[14] Although the professionalism of Dönitz's crews may have contrasted sharply with that of their Italian allies, the grim toll reaped on merchant shipping in the first three years of war arose in part from the dire state of Allied ASW which in some particulars was the same as those in place at the end of the Great War. Asdic was a case in point. Its powers of detection had not markedly improved in the inter-war years. Its inability to detect a surfaced target – a real drawback in the dark – remained unsolved and its difficulty in penetrating seas with substantial thermal layers, such as those in the Arctic Ocean and in the estuary of the St. Lawrence River, often meant that a U-boat could remain hidden in these waters even when those hunting it were at relatively close quarters. To make matters worse, even when Asdic could detect a submerged vessel it had a frustrating tendency to lose contact with the target the closer the Asdic-equipped warship came to it.[15]

Overcoming these very considerable shortcomings would take months of inspired effort, quality laboratory research and extensive testing. While this was taking place, the U-boat continued to reign supreme. Its fortunes started to plummet only when the Allies began using radically different methods of detection, such as 10-cm radar, radio direction finding (RDF) and magnetic anomaly detection (MAD) against their submersible foes.[16] Success in these rather exotic and sophisticated fields was supported by more mundane practices, such as aerial reconnaissance and by the installation of a beguilingly simple gadget known as the 'Leigh Light' which vastly enhanced the striking potential of the Wellingtons of Coastal Command. Therefore, as in other theatres, aircraft proved to be a key component in changing the dynamic of the war at sea. In closing what had previously been a mid-Atlantic 'air gap', VLR aircraft and escort carrier support groups did much to seal the fate of the U-boat.[17] There would be no way back from this unenviable position unless and until Dönitz and his crews had a revolutionary type of submersible that could provide them with the means of prosecuting the war effectively once again.[18]

If anyone had doubted the value of radar in modern warfare, the performance of 'Chain Home' at the time of the Battle of Britain would have convinced all but the most sceptical that it would have a crucial role to play at sea in the months and years to come.[19] Once the scientists and engineers had developed scaled down radar sets that could be deployed in aircraft and ships of all types, advances could be made in detecting both aerial and surface threats as well as vastly improving a ship's gunnery effectiveness.[20] Although Cunningham had reason to be grateful for radar at the Battle of Matapan, as did Fraser at the North Cape, it didn't always work flawlessly as Lütjens discovered to his cost on board the *Bismarck* in May 1941.[21] Close proximity to land could also undermine its overall reliability as the Americans found out at Savo Island in August 1942 and Nishimura experienced in the Surigao Strait in October 1944, but even so the manifold advantages that radar offered to those using it on a daily basis far exceeded its well documented limitations.[22]

While radar became an essential asset for the Allied Powers in their global struggle with their formidable enemies, they were unwittingly assisted in their mission by mistakes made by their adversaries. One of the most telling of these errors lay in the indiscriminate and widespread use of VHF wireless transmissions by U-boat radio operators. Radio chatter of an almost incessant kind lasted until deep into the war and provided their enemies with the means of accurately identifying a U-boat's position through the use of RDF. German confidence that seaborne detection of these signals was impossible proved to be misplaced – a situation borne out by the fact that the British had first begun using their HF/DF ('Huff-Duff') system as early as 1941 – a device that improved as the war proceeded and its operators became more skilled in its use.[23] Other aids to identification and location of radio transmissions came in the form of RE (Range Estimation) and RFP (Radio Finger Printing) which could be used to detect the unique 'waveform signatures' of particular transmitters, capture them on an oscilloscope, photograph them, and provide a key to their likely whereabouts.[24]

Quite apart from airborne radar, the American scientific community developed a complex but viable system of MAD that was in place by the summer of 1943. It worked by measuring disturbances in the earth's magnetic field caused by a metal hull moving through water. Sets for measuring these changes were installed aboard reconnaissance aircraft and especially in Catalina flying boats (the so-called 'Mad Cats'). They were another feature of why the Allies were able to identify and take the fight to enemy submersibles in the latter years of the war. Even so, the degree of success exhibited by MAD equipment depended upon both distance from the submarine target and its cruising depth – the further away and deeper the submarine was, the less likely the MAD set was to detect it.[25]

Once a submarine was detected, however, the hunter still had to have the means of destroying his quarry. At the outset of hostilities, this essentially came down to the ubiquitous depth charge (a hydrostatic pressure fuse designed to explode at the estimated depth of a target) since neither of the other possibilities – the throw ahead mortar system (abandoned due to shortage of funds in 1934) and the RAF's anti-submarine bomb (a hazardous contraption) – could be immediately exploited.[26] It took several years to develop and improve mortars, such as the 'Hedgehog', the 'Squid' and the 'Shark', to produce the airborne-launched 'Retro-bomb', and the Mark 24 Mine known as 'Fido'. By 1943–44 these devices had supplemented the traditional depth-charge and improved upon its destructive capacity. Even the depth-charge packed a greater explosive punch the longer the war proceeded with the use of Torpex and a shallower depth-setting increasing its overall lethality.[27]

For their part, in order to prevent being detected either by acoustic or visual means, the submarine fleets had to employ a range of counter-measures to either thwart the penetrative gaze of radar and the sono-buoy or reduce the amount of time the individual U-boats spent on the surface to make it far more difficult for reconnaissance planes to discover their whereabouts. Unfortunately for the Germans none of the main radar warning receivers they developed (*Borkum, Metox, Naxos, Tunis* and *Wanze*) operated flawlessly against aircraft; their own active radar sets (*Gema, Hohentwiel* and *Lessing*) though effective went into service tardily; what radar and sonar decoys (*Aphrodite* and *Thetis* for the former and *Bold, Sieglinde* and *Siegmund* for the latter) they produced failed to achieve any lasting success; and the anti-sonar synthetic rubber Oppanol coating they used on the hulls of the U-boats to disguise their acoustic signature (known by the codename *Alberich*) had major adhesive problems that restricted its application.[28] In addition, it was soon discovered that the use of a *schnorchel* air induction tube, which enabled submarines to run their air-breathing diesel engines and recharge their batteries while still submerged, was not quite all that it seemed at the outset. Quite apart from the health risks (specifically, oxygen-deprivation) that the early non-fully automated models posed for the U-boat crews, a *schnorchel* boat could also be detected even if its mast was coated with the camouflage anti-radar coating of synthetic rubber and iron oxide powder (*Tarnmatte*).[29]

Defeating the war on trade and repelling the submarine was not exclusively a Western hemispheric concern, it also had a Pacific dimension. In this theatre the roles were dramatically reversed with the Axis on the receiving end as the Americans conducted an increasingly effective campaign against enemy shipping in Japanese home waters and throughout those in their newly acquired empire as well. This particular *guerre de course* was to net 8.1 million tons of Japanese merchant vessels during the war with submarines accounting for 4.9 million tons or 60.5% of that figure. These attacks contributed to a significant weakening of Japanese industrial strength with imports of sixteen essential commodities (raw materials and mineral wealth) down from 20 million tons in 1941 to half that figure in 1944. It became even worse in the first six months of 1945.[30] A systematic convoy system would have almost certainly helped to preserve some of this vital trade, but it was only haphazardly resorted to on some routes and rarely if ever on others. A mix of institutional culture and overconfidence on the part of the IJN seems to have worked against the adoption of convoy. In this respect at least it seemed as if the Japanese had learnt none of the lessons of the First World War, let alone those of the Second.[31]

Strangely, the Japanese submarine fleet with unquestionably the best torpedo amongst the active combatants – the Type 93 or 'Long Lance', and the even faster, longer range Type 95 – didn't make as big a mark on the Pacific campaign as they ought to have done. Unlike both their Axis brethren and Allied enemies, who were stymied by equipment failures and technological glitches in the use of their torpedoes, the Japanese submarine commanders possessed the means to do real harm to the Allied cause with the weapons at their disposal.[32] Ironically, they were largely prevented from doing so by their own senior officers ashore who tinkered endlessly with their operational assignments and often either ended up putting them in harm's way or deploying them in locations where they were almost totally irrelevant.[33]

Another method of pinpointing the whereabouts of enemy surface and submersible shipping was through the dissemination of signals intelligence (SIGINT) by the outstanding team of cryptanalysts hastily assembled for the task on both sides of the Atlantic after the outbreak of war. Their critical breakthroughs in reading enemy signals traffic have illuminated this study. As we have seen, Axis enciphering systems began by being far more sophisticated than those used by the British in particular, but even the most bewilderingly complex codes could fall victim to the dynamic interplay between man and the machine. Ironically, some codes were too complex and unwieldy for everyday use, such as the secure Japanese *KO* naval cipher, while others were undermined by a combination of hubris on the part of the military intelligence hierarchy and a rash of simple errors committed by those entrusted with encrypting the material and dispatching it to their naval units.[34] Mistakes were made on both sides. Allied personnel made sufficient mistakes in handling 'Ultra' material during the war that the German authorities ought to have been alerted to the fact that their codes were being read by the enemy. John Winton provides a useful chapter on how this priceless asset was nearly lost in his book *Ultra at sea*. A mixture of luck and conceit seems to have combined to blinker the German intelligence services from recognising what was afoot and to preserve the 'Ultra' secret when enough diverse evidence existed to suggest that something other than mere coincidence or good fortune was assisting the Allies in waging the naval war against them.[35]

Quite how the war in Europe and the Pacific would have proceeded for the Allies without the benefit of this 'Ultra' intelligence is disputable. W.J.R. Gardner in his controversial study – *Decoding history* – suggests that the world and particularly the military historians within it have gone overboard in ascribing too much importance to the use of this intelligence and that its application was not as vital as it may appear to be on a *prima facie* basis. While Gardner's thesis in demystifying SIGINT's contribution to the war is immensely provocative and not entirely spurious, one senses a degree of revisionism for the sake of it in his conclusions.[36] Apart from anything else, they fail to do sufficient justice to the role of 'Ultra' as an operational tool on a daily basis. While 'Ultra' did not always lead to a correct assessment of a situation by the staff of operational intelligence or result in the most appropriate response on the part of the Allied naval establishments, the receipt of timely information must have saved countless lives that would have otherwise been lost in the unremitting war at sea. At the very least it shortened the odds on survival and offered those acquiring this intelligence the opportunity of becoming proactive rather than merely reactive.[37]

Brilliant though the Allied cryptanalysts were on both sides of the Atlantic in developing ever more sophisticated machines to examine the changing pattern of enemy codes and decipher the messages enshrouded in these endless streams of letters, major advances in breaking the code came from attacking the weakest end of the security chain – the interface of man and machine. An untested but inspired hunch by Harry Hinsley about the intelligence vulnerability of weather ships, trawlers and supply ships used by the Germans in the North Atlantic and the likelihood that their seizure might lead to an intelligence windfall proved to be the case.[38] Capturing this type of target and boarding sinking U-boats to retrieve as much information about enemy codes as possible from the inner bowels of the ship also definitely aided the codebreaking process by providing operating manuals, tables of classified information and even vital parts of the Enigma machine itself for use by the staff at Bletchley Park. Despite the fact that every German captain was made to understand it was their duty to destroy this incriminating material if there was ever any danger of their vessel being captured by the enemy, not all did. Some indeed tried to scuttle their own craft, but the procedure did not go smoothly or took too long, while others gave way to a heightened sense of self-preservation which dictated a retreat from the scene by both officers and crew before the top secret information had been destroyed.[39] Although the leading figures within the OKM questioned their experts in naval communications about whether the Enigma Naval code had been compromised by any of these mishaps or the loss of the U-boat *U13* (31 May 1940), let alone the suspicious destruction of their supply ships *Atlantis* (22 November 1941), *Python* (30 November 1941) and *Brake* (12 March 1944), they were assured that it was unlikely that a security breach had occurred. Lulled by the B-Dienst's recurrent ability to read the British Naval Cypher No.3 from February 1942 onwards and the fact that this cipher showed no enhanced security features during the Battle of the Atlantic, Raeder and Dönitz were assured that all was well: Enigma was doing its complicated job brilliantly.[40]

468 *Conclusion*

Another element in denying Dönitz victory in the war on trade was the degree to which the Allies could replace those vessels lost to U-boat destruction. Leading the drive to innovate and mass produce ships of every conceivable kind were the American shipyards. Situated well beyond the reach of enemy bombing missions, they could draw upon the unrivalled industrial capacity of the US economy to make good the shortfall in mercantile and naval craft. This enabled them to pour money and resources into the fields of new construction, design modification, and hardware improvements to existing types of vessels in an effort to ensure that their surface and underwater fleets could make the most of their opportunities once they were at sea. In American yards the accent was on improving high-pressure boiler systems to give their sophisticated warships far greater endurance, much stronger armour protection both at the deck level and around their underwater belt for safety purposes, and the provision of far greater A.A. firepower to try to quell the aerial menace. All of these welcome additions came at the cost of vastly increasing the weight of the individual ships to which they were applied. In many cases American ships were rugged, overweight, top-heavy and, with a reduced freeboard, notoriously bad sea-keepers. But while they were uncomfortable to live on, they performed their duties admirably and were less prone to foundering even under the most extreme forms of duress than older vessels of the same general classification. Once they geared up for the war and began using a modification of the factory assembly line system that Henry Ford had used with such telling effect in the automobile industry, the American shipbuilding yards from the state of Washington to that of Maine began to produce a seemingly endless supply of vessels from the most basic Liberty ships and amphibious landing craft to 'jeep' carriers, cruisers, destroyers and submarines. It makes Hitler's gratuitous decision to go to war with the US in the wake of the attack on Pearl Harbor even more absurd than ever.[41]

By the time these new craft entered service, the primacy of the battleship had been replaced by that of the aircraft carrier. In the new war at sea the latest cutting edge was no longer being supplied by ships with the largest guns but by waves of fighter and bomber aircraft that in combination could inflict grave harm on the enemy at great distances and vastly extend the strategic reach of all the combatants who possessed them. In their various types from fleet to 'jeep' carrier, they provided the means to fulfil a wide range of indispensable tasks from aerial reconnaissance and ASW, to a slew of striking and defensive combat roles.[42] Once war had broken out in Europe it soon became apparent that carriers offered the most efficient power projection platform available to any commander-in-chief. If any doubt remained on this score after Taranto, Pearl Harbor must have dispelled it. Thereafter the fleet engagements in the Coral Sea and at Midway in 1942 reconfirmed that impression and their strategic use in the island-hopping campaign adopted by Nimitz through the Central Pacific in the last two years of the war provided the final exclamation point if such was needed.[43] For all their merits, however, carriers, like all warships, were vulnerable. Individual U-boats managed to sink *Courageous, Ark Royal, Audacity* and *Eagle*; two battleships got the better of *Glorious*; and carrier-based dive bombers eliminated *Hermes* in the first three years of the European war. In the Pacific theatre dive and torpedo bombers from both sides represented the gravest threat to the life of the carriers and demonstrated this perfectly by inflicting the initial combustible damage that helped to send fifteen of the twenty-three that eventually succumbed to the bottom of the ocean. Despite their vulnerability, however, carriers also proved to be hardy beasts that could take a great deal of punishment, be patched up and come back for more as this study has shown.[44]

While the battleship no longer stood at the apex of the capital ship fleet, they still had an uncanny allure about them. Although they had lost a good deal of their former sheen, they remained a potential threat and one that their enemies took great pains to wipe out. Churchill was always wary of German battleships and insisted that great efforts be made by the Royal Navy to eliminate them. British concern for the battleship lingered longer than that in other capitals. In Berlin Hitler had little good to say for them and even in Tokyo where the IJN had built the largest warships ever seen to this point, Yamamoto and his advisers had revised their opinion of the Yamato class of super-battleships by completing *Shinano*, the third one of the class, and converting her into an aircraft carrier and cancelling No.111, the fourth and final behemoth, and dismantling her in the building dock at Kure.[45] Those that survived to complete their trials and go into service made little impact while they were operationally afloat. *Musashi* was clinically destroyed by carrier aircraft in the Battle of the Sibuyan Sea on 24 October 1944 and her sister ship, *Yamato*, came to a wasteful and anti-climactic end on 7 April 1945.[46]

Notwithstanding the deficiencies exhibited by the battleship, however, the rest of the surface fleet still performed a vitally important series of roles from protecting convoys and troop transports to resupplying besieged forts and bases; from repelling enemy submarine and surface threats to providing the amphibious means of supporting invasions and organising evacuations. Much of this work was often exhausting and repetitive even though it remained perilous since the men of the surface fleet and those of the merchant marine consistently put themselves in harm's way. No other agency could assume the burden of the surface fleets in providing the means for states to continue prosecuting the war, but since much of what they did was rarely glamorous and awe-inspiring, these vessels and those who sailed in them rarely attracted headlines. Little wonder then that they have often remained the unsung heroes of this global conflict.[47]

This was hardly the fate of the air crews who enjoyed a much higher profile than their service colleagues at sea. Paradoxically enough, however, the advance of air power which could, on occasion, bring about dramatic and sometimes critically decisive interventions in so many different theatres of war, was not always able to provide a ready solution to a persistent problem. Aerial bombing of naval targets in ports or naval bases proved to be far more difficult than one would have imagined it would be. A vivid demonstration of the inadequacy of such bombing operations was readily at hand. To the gall of Churchill and the British service chiefs, the *Gneisenau* and *Scharnhorst* had defiantly survived the numerous air raids that had been mounted against them while they remained holed up at Brest throughout 1941 and at the outset of 1942 and the nature of the problem had not really been solved by either the Royal Navy or the RAF by the time the Fleet Air Arm and Bomber Command were prompted by the British authorities to eliminate *Tirpitz* in the fastness of her Norwegian fjord in 1944. Although *Tirpitz* eventually succumbed in November 1944 to a raid by a squadron of VLR Lancasters, she had survived a host of attempts before she finally did so.[48]

A failure in the bombing of static targets was not solely confined to the Allies, of course, as those who had to endure the punishing aerial assault by the Axis Powers on Malta could testify. Regardless of its location in the Central Mediterranean and its proximity to the Italian mainland, Malta somehow lingered on as an Allied redoubt when logic dictated that it could not survive in the face of such overwhelming odds. It did so to the continuing bewilderment and sardonic fury of the German Führer whose lack of respect for the Italian military grew apace as its inability to get the job done on land (North Africa, Yugoslavia and Greece), at sea (securing the Mediterranean for the Axis and preventing the Allies from running convoys between Gibraltar, Malta and Alexandria) and in the air (Malta, Tobruk and elsewhere within the Mediterranean theatre) was manifestly demonstrated as 1941–42 proceeded.[49]

Aerial attacks against moving targets ought in theory to have been far more difficult to orchestrate successfully, but the chilling demonstration given by Japanese land-based dive and torpedo-bombers against the *Prince of Wales* and *Repulse* in the South China Sea on 10 December 1941 suggested otherwise. What was needed above all was to gain information about the exact position of the moving target and it didn't really matter whether this was gleaned by reconnaissance flights or through the decryption of enemy signals traffic as long as it was accurate. Once this had been obtained the Japanese raid off Kuantan had proved that it was feasible to overwhelm even the most powerful of warships – a point that Billy Mitchell and other pioneers of air power had been making for two decades. If this emphatic performance didn't prove to the naval establishment that the era of the capital ship was over it was difficult to know what further proof was necessary to convince the sceptics. In this case, after all, two capital ships had been caught out in the open sea without any sort of air cover and both had been routinely dispatched by a brilliantly coordinated series of bombing runs orchestrated by enemy pilots whose eyesight and general competence had been disparaged beforehand by leading members of the Western armed services who ought to have known better. Despite the grave shock to the system administered by the Japanese at Pearl Harbor and in the South China Sea, not everybody would be convinced that the capital ship was no longer the queen on the chessboard. Diehard 'Black Shoe' admirals of the 'Gun Club' who had served in the post-*Dreadnought* era might comfort themselves with the thought that the loss of the *Prince of Wales* and *Repulse* was a tragically unique event brought about by a constellation of factors that was unlikely to be repeated in future. Holding to such an opinion, however, more or less implied that the capital ship required aerial protection to enable it to perform and survive in a hostile world. If this was indeed the case, even posing the question about the ability of *Force Z* to withstand such an attack if it had had an appropriate level of air cover undermined the case for the primacy of the capital ship.

But if air power was now in the ascendant it was not always so stunningly effective. Bomber Command, Coastal Command and the Fleet Air Arm all found this out to their cost in February 1942 when over six hundred of their aircraft took to the skies and yet failed to detect, let alone cope with, the impertinent Channel Dash of the three heavy ships *Gneisenau, Scharnhorst* and *Prinz Eugen*, and a group of assorted other light craft. Given that the most important of these vessels were in exclusively Anglo-French coastal waters for the first half of their journey back to Germany (*Fall Cerberus*), the inability to counter this operation was breathtaking. While it may have shown utter incompetence on the part of the existing British air defence system, as Barnett forcefully asserted it did, it proved beyond all reasonable doubt that scouring the sea to find enemy vessels was hardly a guarantee of success even in relatively confined areas.[50] Actually, it was far from being automatic even when the aircraft undertaking the search were equipped with the best ASV radar sets available and regardless of how methodical the planes were in sweeping the grid pattern assigned to them. While reconnaissance was definitely made easier by the introduction of better and more sophisticated radar and sonar equipment, if these sets malfunctioned for any reason the odds against detection rose fairly steeply. Reconnaissance in sufficient depth was in any case rarely possible particularly in mid-ocean or in those locations which were hundreds of miles distant from bases on land or on carriers. In these situations, therefore, without the additional aid of intelligence windfalls the hunters were far from assured of securing their prey.[51]

Whenever enemy vessels were discovered by whatever means available to the enemy, air power could on occasion be absolutely decisive, such as at Midway and in the Battle of the Philippine Sea, or devastating in conjunction with a functioning submarine fleet as convoys PQ.17 and PQ.18 found out to their cost in the Arctic Ocean in the summer and autumn of 1942 respectively. While air power was not invincible in every situation, it proved to be the crucial key to Malta's survival and indeed to that of Guadalcanal later in 1942. In both of these situations, the retention of an air base from which fighter aircraft could be launched to break up incoming enemy air raids was absolutely imperative as neither island could have resisted indefinitely otherwise. In the case of the former, the fact that the Italian submarine fleet didn't try more consistently to deal with Force H's fortnightly forays to the waters off the Balearic Islands where its carriers would fly off Hurricanes and Spitfires to supplement the air defence of Malta is remarkable for its lack of gumption. In the case of Guadalcanal, the Marine Corps performed heroically in absorbing the heavy aerial and offshore bombardment of the air base (both of which, in truth, left an awful lot to be desired) while continuing to beat off determined thrusts against Henderson Field mounted by the Japanese troops on the ground. It was just as well they did.

Vital though it was and decisive though it could be, air power alone remained an insufficient resource to guarantee the survival of a base under siege, such as

Odessa, Sevastopol and Tobruk. Replenishment by sea was critical if both the civilians and the troops defending them were to survive for as long as possible. This remained the most effective means of bringing in large quantities of stores and men and that is why great efforts were devoted by all the powers to logistics and the means of establishing a regular supply train to assist their forces at the war front whether they were hemmed in on the defensive or pushing on from their beachhead and taking the fight to the enemy. Often undertaken at night with speed and stealth to outwit the enemy's defences, these were invariably hazardous missions that could have ended in tragedy. Once again, however, the accent is on what might have been since the vast majority didn't end up battered and sunk but somehow managed to get the job done in spite of all the potential dangers. Although little short of remarkable, one is entitled to ask why were these missions so successful? It was hardly ignorance on the part of the enemy who knew what was happening but seemed powerless to do much about preventing it from taking place. In some cases the enemy's resources were stretched too thin to mount an effective naval blockade of a port or a stretch of coastline, in others a mixture of shocking incompetence on the part of one side and inspired derring-do on behalf of the other may have had something to do with it.[52]

Maintaining secrecy about one's intentions in war is obviously crucial and could be the vital difference between winning and losing a single battle, a series of engagements or even the entire war itself. If it is evident that a planned event is about to happen or has become 'inevitable' (surely one of the most overworked terms used in the modern world), the ability to preserve that secret becomes all the more difficult. At this point the need to confuse, mislead or delude the enemy becomes of paramount importance. Without sowing doubt into the mind of the enemy's strategists, the combatant that is about to make an operational sortie, let alone unleash a massive amphibious invasion, would face in all probability a tortuous struggle against a well-prepared defender. If the Germans knew in advance on which day and on what stretch of French coastline the Allies would choose to invade the continent of Europe in June 1944, the D-Day offensive might even have been repulsed with untold casualties. Operation *Neptune* might have ended up in a massive soggy defeat for the Allies and an astonishingly recuperative victory for the beleaguered Axis. Without engaging endlessly in counter-factual history, the 'what-might-have-been' syndrome, the point is that *Neptune* was successful in putting the troops and their supplies ashore because it was not just a brilliantly planned, logistically sound and efficiently executed amphibious operation but because it carried with it the key element of surprise. This resulted in part from a finely planned campaign of disinformation – Operation *Bodyguard* – that had been instrumental in confirming the prejudices of Rommel and his generals that the cross-Channel invasion would come ashore in the Pas de Calais rather than along the beaches of Normandy.[53] Eisenhower had also been assisted to some extent by the fact that there were two or three coastal areas of northwestern France that could have been used for *Neptune/Overlord*. This had helped to ensure that the German defences were stretched over several hundred kilometres rather than concentrated in one specific area even though admittedly the heart of their defensive positions and the bulk of their forces were assigned to the Pas de Calais. Nonetheless, the fact that the Germans did not receive unimpeachable intelligence on the exact location of the Allied invasion still amazes one over sixty years later. 'Careless talk costs lives' was an advertising slogan used by the Allies in the war; rarely, if ever, could this expression have been more faithfully observed than in the weeks and months preceding D-Day. Despite all the speculation that the Allied servicemen and women indulged in at this time, most could only hazard a guess at where landfall would be made. Very few actually knew. This was not the case with thousands of staff officers, however, who had to be intimately involved in the detailed planning of *Overlord*. Yet with a few isolated exceptions the veil of secrecy cast over the whole mission was not penetrated by German spies and Rommel and his staff became none the wiser as the days passed and the invasion came closer.[54]

Coincidentally at the very same time in the Pacific the Japanese were expecting the Americans to strike somewhere at their extended empire in the near future, but had convinced themselves it would be within 'the Great Triangle' rather than hundreds of miles away against the Marianas in the Central Pacific. While it is true that the Japanese had been encouraged to think along these lines by action taken within the region by the US military, they had needed little prompting to continue supporting their preconceived view on American policy in the Southwest Pacific. Caught by surprise by the American move against Saipan, the *A-GO* plan began on a distracted note and never really recovered from that point onwards.[55] In such military situations where the element of surprise has been used profitably against an enemy combatant, it becomes imperative for the power that has been thrust onto the defensive to show some spontaneity in discarding its mistaken assumptions and irrelevant plans in favour of adopting a more flexible response. Ideally it ought to possess a contingency plan to which it can revert with the minimum of delay or disruption, but if that proves to be impossible it should have the flair, initiative and self confidence to 'think out of the box' in trying to come to terms with its new unfamiliar situation. Not all the combatants were adept at doing this.

Military spontaneity, in particular, did not come easily to the Japanese IGHQ. Both of the services were guilty of forming sets of plans that often proved to be unnecessarily elaborate and too complicated for their own good. Yamamoto, the architect of the attack on Pearl Harbor, was notorious for 'gilding the lily' in this way. Supremely self-confident and buoyed by the breathtaking nature of his successes, he became a law unto himself. An inveterate gambler used to winning, his philosophy was often to unsettle opponents at cards by attacking them relentlessly. This was reflected to some extent in his early war planning. He lived up to his promise to Prince Konoye that he would 'run wild considerably for the first six months or a year', but the sheer scale of his successes in the early months of the war may have burnished his ego to such an extent that his arrogance became a weakness.[56] Simplicity wasn't sufficient. Victory would come about from outwitting his enemies at every turn. His obsessive example was followed by others in the military hierarchy not nearly as gifted as he was. This often resulted in too much being expected of Japanese forces. As a result, objectives were sought that either weren't immediately necessary (Port Moresby) or where the necessary ingredient of bamboozlement – daring feints to confuse the enemy or benefit from their preoccupation elsewhere – actually did more to divide Japanese forces than those of the Americans the IJN wished to put to the sword (Coral Sea and Midway).[57] A mixture of too many objectives and too much rigidity often conspired to undermine the outstanding qualities of the plans that were made and increase the likelihood that things would go wrong when they were implemented. When this planning template was abandoned in favour of adopting a more flexible approach, as occurred in *SHO-GO 1*, the last minute revisions that were grafted on to the original plan spoke more for adhocracy than they did for coherence.[58]

If the Japanese were especially guilty of over-elaboration in their planning, they could also be faulted for perhaps over-extending themselves in some of their territorial conquests. While this study has confined itself to naval-related matters, there is little doubt that the lure of the Indian sub-continent was to prove too magnetic for the Japanese to resist, even though this attraction was to have serious consequences drawing them into a torrid campaign in Burma – awful for everyone involved – and a constant running sore to the IJA. If the Japanese can, therefore, be accused of overstretch in the Indian Ocean littoral, the Allies were not immune from bad strategic planning too. Churchill's decision to aid Greece in March 1941 (Operation *Lustre*) immediately comes to mind as does the Americans' insistence upon invading the south of France (Operation *Dragoon*) in August 1944. On both occasions, these controversial deployments seriously undermined on-going and arguably potentially more decisive campaigns elsewhere (North Africa and Italy respectively).[59]

Sometimes, alas, gratuitous planning mistakes were made that led to calamitous results. Of these the Dieppe Raid of August 1942 remains a classic example. Hindsight notwithstanding, it is difficult not to see the Mountbatten-inspired Operation *Jubilee* as being anything other than a wholly excessive adventure of dubious strategic value. There is certainly a case for saying that it ought never to have got off the drawing board, let alone been approved at the highest levels and put into action. At Dieppe, 38.9% of those operationally engaged paid for these errors and became casualties. Did it teach the Allies anything new about amphibious operations? Mountbatten and his supporters would argue it did and the operational lessons learnt were successfully implemented in June 1944. Even so one is left with the nagging doubt that *Jubilee* wasn't ultimately worth the costs involved. After all, what it proved beyond all reasonable doubt was that these operations shouldn't be launched where the enemy was expecting them. It was a powerful but obvious lesson to learn and one that could and perhaps should have been avoided.[60]

Although Nimitz can't be accused of making the same type of haughty strategic error in the Gilberts in November 1943 as Mountbatten did at Dieppe fifteen months before, the grisly experience of Operation *Galvanic*, and in particular the invasions of Makin and Tarawa, demonstrated that amphibious landings could go wrong very easily if one worked too much on wishful thinking and the bludgeoning instruments of military power and didn't take sufficient notice of either the existence of geophysical constraints, such as coral reefs, or the subtleties employed by those seeking defensive cover. Aerial bombing and offshore bombardments rarely softened up troops that were well dug in and in the case of the Gilberts far more damage was done to the groves of banana and coconut trees on the islands than to the Japanese forces they were supposedly targeting. This much became starkly clear when the Japanese defenders, having melted away into the jungle to escape both the aerial strafing and the battleship broadsides, returned in sufficient time to rake the exposed Allied assault troops with withering fire as they finally came ashore.[61] In the end it wasn't enough to prevent the Allies from getting ashore in sufficient numbers to secure the Gilberts; but what *Galvanic* underlined graphically was that while raw power might win ultimately against the Japanese in an island-hopping campaign it would only do so at great personal cost to the Americans and their companions in arms.[62]

Galvanic had also revealed that even detailed planning was not foolproof. Mistakes were made both in the technical details and the over-confident assumptions that suffused the plan. Should this surprise anyone? Mistakes are a common feature of life itself. War is not immune from them – indeed it could be said that the very nature of increasing agitation and tension brought about by conflict may actually help them to proliferate. In such situations some issues can be easily ignored or overlooked when the pressure is on and attention is divided. This was certainly true of the Japanese whose failure to replace their experienced air crew became an enduring feature of the Pacific War. Too often their best and most able pilots were sacrificed needlessly. Aircraft were relatively cheap to replace, but flair and skill were another thing altogether. Ultimately the loss of their most gifted pilots would hurt the Japanese cause since as the war proceeded younger, less able, but still highly motivated, air crew could not always get the best out of their demanding aircraft. In these situations their zeal and perseverance were not enough to offset the Allied possession of radar equipment which could betray their presence at great distance and enable superior American fighter aircraft to be vectored in to deal with them. Although the 'Great Marianas Turkey Shoot' demonstrated this trend most emphatically, experienced pilots were always missed.[63] This much was made manifest two years before at the time of Midway when the Japanese had to do without both their carriers *Shokaku* and *Zuikaku* after the Coral Sea engagement. Whether the presence of an extra carrier with a full complement of planes and the flamboyant pilots who flew them would have made a crucial difference at Midway is arguable. It is certainly the stuff of a debate that is explored in the fascinating realm of counter-factual history – the linkage of 'What if?' to 'What might have been' – and a scenario that may be pursued profitably by officers in the war gaming laboratories of the military academies. For our purposes it is sufficient to say that the presence of the *Zuikaku* may have contributed an extra dimension to the Japanese cause that was missing at the time of this debilitating battle.[64]

Whatever the individual services may have thought of the other arms of the military – and it was often not much – the nature of conflict strung out across the globe and the sheer distances and numbers involved dictated that combined arms operations would have to be resorted to increasingly by all the major powers involved in the war at sea. It was an open question as to whether the institutional differences and historic rifts that had grown up between the services could be laid aside so that these type of operations might function effectively. A willingness on all sides to work together was naturally the basic requirement; but it was far from certain that a spirit of compromise (which it usually entails) would prove to be a very satisfactory formula for strategic and operational war planning. One need look no further than the contorted decision-making of the JCS in settling the command arrangements between MacArthur and Nimitz in the Pacific theatre to see that the spirit of compromise was alive and kicking in World War II. A decidedly contrived arrangement, given the wariness of King for MacArthur and the latter's deep disdain of the USN, it says something for both Halsey and Nimitz that the Pacific campaign was as successful as it was.[65]

Combined arms operations were not always blessed with such success. Poor planning and hamfisted execution, such as that experienced by the Allies in the Norwegian campaign, did nothing to inspire confidence in them. For every success achieved by combined arms operations, such as those performed in the Mediterranean during the 1940–42 period, there were always instances of failure in the same theatre, such as the Greek and Aegean misadventures, to allow the inter-service wounds to fester. Consequently, maintaining control of what they saw as their own prerogatives became all too often the key determinant in the way that each of the services responded to calls for cooperation. If it wasn't the RAF and the Royal Navy clashing over the strategic choice of what could be spared, as distinct from what was needed, in fighting the Battle of the Atlantic – a disagreement that played into Dönitz's hands for far longer than it ought to have done – it was the Marine Corps and the US Army at loggerheads over most things and particularly over the invasion of the Marianas where relations plumbed to new depths of animosity. Although the Marine Corps and the US Navy had a far healthier relationship, the question of command responsibilities led to a running confrontation between Holland M. 'Howling Mad' Smith and the equally abrasive Kelly Turner, commander of the V Amphibious Force, that lasted from the Gilberts campaign to beyond that of the Marshalls. Problems between the services, however, were not solely confined to the Allies. None of the major military powers were immune from inter-service jealousy and rancour – it more or less came with the territory. What was essential was finding a way to work together effectively. Success in this field in the end rested not so much on institutional seals of approval but more on the individual willingness of the leading officers of one service to cooperate with those of another in the best interests of all. It took a new mind set that those who were resistant to change could not easily adopt. Combined arms operability as the norm, therefore, still remained a long way off.[66]

While the type of misunderstandings that arose between the services in both the planning and execution phases of combined arms operations were hardly unexpected, neither were the grave issues that dogged the practical implementation of joint operations in which the military forces of one power would either agree, or be forced, to cooperate with those of one of its allies.[67] Coalition warfare, therefore, brought both the concept and practical realisation of joint operability in its wake. It proved at times to be something of a mixed blessing for both sides in the war. At the grand strategic level, joint operations were not always a zero-sum game as German–Finnish relations proved during the war. Their willingness to work together in laying and reinforcing a chain of very dense mine barrages and submarine nets in the Gulf of Finland made life vastly more complicated and dangerous for the Soviet Navy in trying to negotiate these waters and effectively kept them from reaching the Baltic in large numbers until after the Finns had withdrawn from the war in September 1944.[68] Nonetheless, one didn't need to peer too closely to see the other side of the coin emerge in the quixotic and much less productive relationship established between the members of the Rome–Berlin Axis. Hitler was repeatedly let down by his Axis partner whose truculent and limitless egotism often vastly exceeded his capacity to achieve the ends he set itself. Forced to pick up the pieces left by the inadequacy of Mussolini's forces, Hitler's military plans had to undergo costly adjustment in order to rescue the Italians from a pit of their own making.[69] An acute lack of respect for the Italian military in all of its forms was commonplace amongst the German military even before Mussolini's extravagances in the Balkans and Greece in the autumn of 1940 had reinforced the feeling that the Italian services were profoundly unreliable. Dönitz shared that sentiment when it came to the submarines of the Regia Marina. While conceding that they might be good nautical designers, he sensed that the Italians lacked the physical and mental toughness that his submariners possessed and their largely disappointing results in sinking Allied shipping seemed to prove the point – or at least they did to him. While he took those boats that were given to him (rather grudgingly it has to be admitted), his efforts to integrate them with his own U-boats lacked conviction. Instead he was prone to keeping them largely out of harm's way where, of course, their results didn't improve or make him re-evaluate their net worth to the Axis cause.[70] If this wasn't bad enough, a perceived failure on the part of Iachino's surface fleet to make a truly meaningful contribution to the North African campaign, along with the failure of the RAI to snuff out Maltese resistance, ensured that neither Hitler nor Rommel put much faith in joint operations or coalition warfare.[71]

One of the most positive features on the Allied side was the heroic way in which the countries of the Commonwealth rallied to assist the British in prosecuting the war against the Axis nations.[72] While units of the RAN and RNZN were intimately and productively involved with the Royal Navy in a number of naval theatres throughout the war, the stupendous role performed by the Australian forces under MacArthur's command in the Southwest Pacific showed that joint operability could work really effectively on occasion where there was a common will to do so.⁷³ For its part, in the Battle of the Atlantic, the RCN proved to be absolutely crucial to the eventual Allied success in defeating the German war on trade. As Marc Milner acknowledges, the Canadians entered the war with only six destroyers, five minesweepers and a total of 1,800 officers and men of all ranks. It ended the war less than six years later having expanded its warship strength by roughly fifty-fold and its personnel to 96,000 all ranks, becoming in doing so the third largest Allied Navy and the one that became primarily responsible for the close escort of the main North Atlantic trade convoys. In addition, its experiences in repelling the U-boat threat in the Atlantic made it an increasingly fine partner in ASW operations in European waters later in the war.⁷⁴

Joint operations were not always so rewarding. In Southeast Asia, for example, ABDACOM's scrambled response to the Japanese attack within the region did little to inspire confidence in the concept and instances, such as the failure to establish a signal code common to all the members of the mixed command, which came back to haunt the Allies off Bawean Island in February 1942, demonstrated that there was still much to learn before joint operability could be successfully applied in all theatres and against all opponents.⁷⁵ Worse still, the lopsided ideological divide in the Grand Alliance helped to create a far more stressful, disputatious and controversial operational environment for its members than was desirable. Few imagined that the sudden emergence of the Anglo-Soviet coalition in the summer of 1941 and the Grand Alliance six months later was little other than a testimony to pragmatism and the sharing of a common enemy. Goodwill between these powers proved difficult to build up and easy to erode; mutual mistrust was never far from the surface, and criticism – whether deserved or unfair – swirled around the fate of the Arctic convoys and erupted over the entire question of the 'Second Front'. Sadly, support on both sides seemed grudging and yet Soviet participation in these convoy operations proved quite steadfast.⁷⁶

While the Grand Alliance encountered practical problems in employing joint operations, the nature of the Anglo-American partnership both before and after Pearl Harbor proved that its virtues were still considerable. Even so, one need only look at the struggles that attended the planning of joint operations when the CCOS came together to underline Sir Ronald Lindsay's earlier wistful admission that Anglo-American relations were foolproof and only in danger when attempts were made to improve them.⁷⁷ Compromise isn't something that any service relishes and yet an ability to fashion something less than what one wants but more than others would initially provide becomes a virtual certainty in such discussions and the more so the greater the number of service chiefs there are sitting around the table deciding these things. Already bad enough if the other services come from the same nation, the potential problem areas often grow apace once other powers and their politicians are involved. Michael Simpson and Brian Farrell, amongst others, have shown how fraught these sessions could be as obstinacy and belligerency, jealousy and distrust combined to take hold of the debate as the service ministers of both sides pushed their service agendas in vigorous ways and sought to win their negotiating duels with their opposite numbers. Although anger and resentment was never far from the surface whenever victory or defeat was at hand, it helped if a sense of mutual respect was formed between the members of the CCOS. In this respect, at least, the longer the war continued the warmer relations became between the abrasive Ernest King and the equally combative and dynamic Andrew Cunningham, who proved to be more of a match for the volatile COMINCH than the older, more quiescent, and desk-bound Dudley Pound had been. Anglo-American naval cooperation benefited from their frank dialogue and the trust that came to be forged between them.[78]

Fortunately, Roosevelt's support for the cause of the democracies had been seen long before the US actually became a formal ally of Churchill's government in December 1941. In establishing the cash-and-carry provisions, arranging the destroyer for bases deal and agreeing to the Lend-Lease arrangements, all of which were fashioned in the early years of the European war, the US demonstrated its commitment to becoming the 'arsenal of democracy' that its president had eloquently spoken about in one of his famous fireside chats to the American public on 29 December 1940. Intimately involved from the outset with mounting a system of neutrality patrols that sought to keep the war from American shores, the USN wasted little time in demonstrating where its sympathies lay in the war at sea. As the months passed, the Roosevelt administration shed the fiction of neutrality and assumed the contradictory role of active non-belligerency against the Axis forces. Increasingly thereafter, it became more inclined to use attack as the best method of defence against Dönitz's U-boat fleet and Roosevelt's 'shoot on sight' order against all Axis warships after the *Greer* incident in early September 1941 was accurately depicted as yet another step along the road to full-scale involvement in the war. Once the US had been propelled into war by the Japanese attack on Pearl Harbor, the nature of its involvement became crucial for the Allied cause. Its seminal decision to adopt a 'Germany First' strategy remains arguably, therefore, the most compellingly positive feature of Coalition Warfare from the Allied perspective. After all, from this unselfish undertaking so much else flowed. Although differences between the Allies were almost bound to arise in prosecuting this overarching strategy, the tone was set by the most powerful nation in the world and in the end its will prevailed.[79]

Attacking the United States was always going to incur great risk since it was inconceivable that the Americans would not strike back with unrestrained fervour against any Power that had the temerity to open hostilities with it. Japan's military leadership, imbued with an astonishing degree of resolution and self-reliance, was prepared to take that chance. Pearl Harbor was brilliantly and audaciously conceived by Yamamoto and if the USN's carrier fleet had been in port on the morning in question the attack might have been even more of a shock to the American system than it was. In essence, if all went according to Yamamoto's plan, the waves of attacks on Pearl Harbor would have caused havoc to the Pacific Fleet and to its main naval base while affording the Japanese time to consolidate their gains both in Southeast Asia and throughout the Pacific

480 *Conclusion*

at the expense of the Western Powers and their colonial empires. But a single day of infamy would hardly remove the spectre of American industrial and military power from re-entering the Pacific theatre at some point in the foreseeable future. Yamamoto's coup, therefore, could only be a temporary one. It wouldn't destroy the American potential or desire to strike back at Japan. Indeed quite the opposite. Nothing would galvanise American society more than the attack on Pearl Harbor. This was an act of war and the American republic, its government and people, would hardly be anaesthetised by it. Such was their anger that revenge rather than accommodation was their natural response. Their pride had been savagely hurt by these sneak attacks and they would not shirk their responsibility to respond to this act of wanton aggression. Yamamoto and the Japanese high command, therefore, took a daring step by attacking the US. They may have done so in response to an escalating series of anti-Japanese measures and to pre-empt whatever else the Roosevelt administration and congress may have had in store for them, but the rash decision to risk doing battle with the world's most powerful nation is still breathtaking in the extreme. Some might even say that the fate of the Japanese military government and its Axis partners was sealed by this single act – Churchill certainly believed so – and he and others who share this view could point not unreasonably to the fact that the action on 7 December 1941 did not go according to plan. Instead of removing an active American presence from the Pacific and eliminating their capacity to project power through the use of both their carrier and capital ship fleets, the carriers went untouched, the vast oil stores weren't decimated and the infrastructure of the naval base wasn't totally reduced to rubble. Admittedly, Battleship Row was a mess, but it could have been even worse. While the personal casualty toll was high at over 3,500, this figure could have been dwarfed if Yamamoto had had his way and the carrier fleet had been in port on 7 December and not out on manoeuvres. In many ways, therefore, Pearl Harbor wasn't the glittering success that Yamamoto had been hoping for. Instead his plan became a bold, desperate gamble which did not pay off in quite the way that was intended. It shocked; it dismayed; it appalled; it exposed complacency and defensive deficiencies; and it carried a high personal cost; but this one single humiliating act didn't drive the US presence from the Pacific and it did unite the American people with a collective sense of purpose which had been previously lacking. On most grounds, therefore, this daring coup by the IJN may be seen to be at best a logistical rather than strategic success and at worst a reckless act that would eventually prove to be Imperial Japan's undoing.[80]

Logistical success on a grand scale requires organisational acumen of a very high order; one in which the ability to think logically, rationally and systematically about the schematic processes needed at every stage is marked. While Yamamoto possessed some of these qualities to a fine degree he was still more of a grand strategist than an administrative plotter per se. Exponents of a 'purer' form of logistics did not share the almost cult status of the acclaimed Japanese hero. Naval officers, such as Konrad Engelhardt, Sergei Gorshkov, Friedrich Grattenauer, Matsuji Ijuin, Gustav Kieseritzky, Oskar Kummetz, Gustav Freiherr von Liebenstein and Bertram Ramsay were hardly household names at the time they first came to prominence during the war as highly skilled and brilliantly successful organisers of mass evacuations. Despite the fact that every one of them conducted forced withdrawals under the most intense enemy pressure, few of these figures – apart from Gorshkov and Ramsay – were acknowledged by the world's media either at the time or subsequently as being masters of the art. They deserve a better and more enduring legacy.[81] Part of the problem surely stems from the nature of the task – evacuations are rarely considered to be anything other than a depressing acknowledgement of a military reverse. Indeed it was exceedingly rare for a power to celebrate the evacuation of its forces as a miracle of deliverance as the British did at the time of Dunkirk in May–June 1940. Operation *Dynamo* may have made Ramsay's name late in his career, but after working profitably on both the *Torch* and *Husky* invasions he had been eased off the active list and shifted onto the retirement rolls by the Admiralty. Much to his profound regret, he had become one of those administrative victims of age. Despite the fact that his physical and mental powers remained largely undiminished, his active participation in war seemed over. Fortunately his remarkable talents were not allowed to go to waste for long, however, before SHAEF invited him to put his gardening exploits aside and take responsibility for orchestrating the naval side of D-Day (Operation *Neptune*). It was just as well they did because what was needed was someone with the expertise to draw up a detailed plan for what was to become nothing less than the largest amphibious operation in history. This was not the time to experiment. One required the best and most skilful logistician in the field and by this time and regardless of his age Ramsay was simply the best of the best.[82] He proved this by fashioning his greatest logistical achievement to date – the administrative manual upon which *Neptune* was based. Reunited with his resourceful assistant Rear-Admiral William G. Tennant, Ramsay saved his best for last. *Neptune* became a stupendous success. No finer epitaph could be raised for the architect of the Allies' greatest logistical operation.[83]

Setting hundreds or thousands of troops ashore in often hostile territory became a marked feature of the Allied war effort from the autumn of 1942 onwards as the struggle began to recover territory lost in the early phases of the European and Pacific campaigns. While not all invasions were smoothly accomplished and some landings proved exceptionally hazardous and very costly in human terms, the fact remained that most of the amphibious assault operations were successfully orchestrated with minimal casualties. This is a tribute to a dedicated and able group of men like Daniel Barbey, Henry Kent Hewitt, Alan Kirk and Kelly Turner who, despite their considerably different temperaments, all became skilled masters of the art. Apart from the accent on detailed planning that such an enterprise demanded, the officer placed in charge of an invasion fleet needed courage, dogged determination and a knack for dealing with the unexpected. After all, much could go wrong with an invasion from a sudden deterioration in the weather, poor visibility, and the running of heavy seas off the invasion beaches, to any number of equipment breakdowns which could seriously disrupt the landing, or the failure of deception, and shortfalls in OPINTEL (operational intelligence) which could leave the invading troops at the mercy of an enemy that was expecting them. In heavily contested landings, the problems were accentuated by the presence of enemy aircraft and artillery so that being aboard a headquarters ship off an assault beach was not without its dangers and could hardly be described as a sinecurial appointment.[84]

It has been noted before that naval warfare is multi-dimensional. Power isn't everything; individual battles at sea and larger campaigns within regions can be won or at least profoundly influenced by individuals with special gifts to impart to the task in hand. Much has been said of Dönitz in this study and while some may think his role has been exaggerated, it is difficult not to see him as a formidable foe. Quite apart from his orchestration of the wolf pack attacks, he had provided the impetus for the development of the U-boat tanker (*Milchküh*) and remained a ceaseless champion of improving the U-boat so that it could retain its edge in the war on trade. It needed individuals with special gifts to combat as wily a figure as Dönitz and in Max Horton and Ernest J. King the Allies finally found their men. Abrasive and opinionated though they undoubtedly were, they were also shrewd, experienced men of judgement and incisive enough to use their initiative in ways that might not have been obvious to less leaden footed naval officers. While the popular expression of 'better late than never' is apt, the delay in making these appointments still rankles as does the Allies' slow and measured response to dealing with the main issues raised by the Battle of the Atlantic. Horton and King were to provide the impetus for a far more decisive and intuitive approach and one that was to leave Dönitz scrambling for an effective response. He was still looking for one at the end of the war.[85]

It was not as though he lacked initiative; but sometimes a fertile imagination and a proactive temperament were not sufficient in themselves to get the job done. One also needed the means to use these personal intuitive gifts in productive ways. On shore naval strategists like Nimitz, King and Dönitz were fortunate in usually having some time to reflect and ruminate before plotting their next moves. Those at sea charged with the tactical responsibility of making the strategy devised by others' work rarely got much lag time to pause and examine the rapidly unfolding situation they were in before making their next move.[86] In fast moving crises it helped if the commanding officer remained unfazed by the chaos and din of war. Raymond A. Spruance demonstrated this art perfectly at Midway. Calm, methodical and uncharismatic, he was the antithesis of the dashing mercurial figure of military fiction. Yet it was Spruance who was the real hero of Midway. After all, his inspired hunches led to the eclipse of all four Japanese carriers belonging to Vice-Admiral Nagumo's strike force on 4 June 1942, while his other less prescient and potentially more reckless decisions went unpunished.[87]

Unlike Spruance at Midway, little luck featured in Jesse Oldendorf's triumph at the Battle of the Surigao Strait. It's true that he had more time at his disposal than the so-called 'quiet warrior', but his tactical initiative in choosing to deploy his Fire Support Group across the narrow Strait in the way he did and the success of his destroyers' brilliantly executed torpedo attacks in destroying Nishimura's Southern Force on the night of 24–25 October 1944 wrecked the southern jaw of the Japanese pincer and undermined a crucial part of the Japanese plan to attack and destroy the US invasion fleet at Leyte Gulf.[88]

Andrew Browne Cunningham (ABC) was another naval officer who was rarely averse to taking the initiative and the fight to the enemy. Taranto and Matapan sealed his reputation as a fighting admiral and made him far more at home on the water than in panelled rooms ashore. It was no simple coincidence that the naval officers under ABC's command in the Mediterranean Fleet were mostly quick-witted rather than dull plodders, more inclined to demonstrate a little dash and verve than innate conservatism. But even the James Somervilles and Philip Vians of this world could only get their ships and men to perform as an effective coordinated unit with sufficient training. What they did with this practice when they were being tested in real battle rather than in simulated conditions was, of course, the key.

When things don't go according to plan, however, the necessity for individuals to use their initiative becomes of paramount importance. Osborne on the *Hotspur* at Narvik showed just what a spot of unconventional engineering could do to overcome boiler problems, while the unsung heroes that formed damage control parties on vessels of all types in the war often performed minor miracles with improvised articles to keep their ships operational under the most extreme conditions. Even when things do go according to plan it still requires another type of initiative to make the most of it. This much was shown by Lieutenant Sir Marshall Warmington in the Lofoten Islands in March 1941 when he pressed his reluctant captain to allow him to board the German armed trawler *Krebs* after a fierce artillery duel had left the enemy ship and her crew in great distress. Whether Warmington would have been able to find either the Enigma cipher disks or the settings for the Home Waters network had one of *Somali*'s shells not struck the wheelhouse earlier killing the trawler's captain instantaneously is debatable, but that deadly shot was to enable him to seize a precious intelligence windfall that was of inestimable value to the cryptanalysts of Bletchley Park and Allied shipping around the coastal areas of the British Isles and the North Sea in the weeks to come.[89]

Sometimes in the 'fog of war' even some experienced officers lost the plot entirely, whereas others responded with conviction and panache to a sudden and unexpected emergency. For whatever reason – natural aptitude or superior training – some officers demonstrated better ship-handling skills than others. A number of examples stand out in this respect: Tennant off Kuantan before the *Repulse* finally succumbed on 10 December 1941; Vian at the Second Battle of Sirte (22 March 1942); Crace in dodging anything but 'friendly-fire' from USAAF B-26s at the time of the Coral Sea (7 May 1942); Sherbrooke and his destroyer flotilla in carrying out a series of simulated torpedo attacks on the heavy cruiser *Admiral Hipper* on New Year's Eve 1942. While Tennant, Vian, Crace and Sherbrooke all lived to tell the tale, many others who took the initiative and displayed great courage under fire were not so fortunate. Commander

Charles Glasfurd, the captain of the destroyer *Acasta*, was one of those who were forced to pay the ultimate sacrifice for doing his duty in a heroic way. Unable to outrun the vastly more powerful *Gneisenau* and *Scharnhorst* on 8 June 1940 and with no means of protection from the weight of shot coming in his direction, Glasfurd opted to go down fighting by attacking the *Scharnhorst*. He died in the attempt, but not before he had succeeded in torpedoing the German battleship, forcing an abandonment of her search for the vulnerable Allied troop convoys which were making their way slowly back from Norway at the time.[90] A similar type of heroic defiance was shown by the officers and crew of Clifton Sprague's small force of three destroyers and four destroyer escorts off Samar on 25 October 1944 when they attacked Kurita's Centre Force with such venom that the Japanese admiral and his staff were convinced that they were confronted by a pack of cruisers and fleet destroyers. These attacks delayed the enemy and helped save the escort carrier fleet in Leyte Gulf, but at the cost of many of those, like Commander Ernest Evans of USS *Johnston*, who had orchestrated these attacks in the first place.[91]

Courage came in innumerable forms during the war at sea. Even so, it's difficult not to see submariners as a special breed of seamen. They not only had to put up with being cloistered for much of the time in a claustrophobic environment, but had to possess the steady nerves to cope with the perils inherent in their profession. Submarine aces, like Fluckey, Kretschmer, Lüth, O'Kane, Prien, Tomkinson and Wanklyn fully deserved the accolades they gained. Their skill at stealthily manoeuvring their boats into position to attack and then extricating themselves from the scene once those attacks had been pressed home became legendary. While these moments of exhilaration existed, boredom and danger became a daily staple as the war proceeded and the enemy's ASW detection methods improved exponentially and attacks became more systematic and lasted longer. Survival was never guaranteed.[92] This was certainly true of service in the K-Verband or their equivalents whose missions were often hazardous in the extreme and made the more so because of the unreliable craft that undertook them. While it took a special form of courage to straddle human torpedoes or clamber on board the *Maiali* chariots or the X craft submersibles, it also required enormous stoicism, skill and daring on the part of all those in both submarines and surface vessels who continued to run relief supplies on hotly contested routes to beleaguered fortresses, naval bases and continental or island beachheads in each of the naval theatres. One form of courage is not necessarily greater than the other – and should not be measured in the success of the act or whether the person is working alone or with others – but the linking factor is that all displays of courage reveal one consistent theme, namely, the quite extraordinary lengths that some human beings will go to in order to get a specific job done even under the most trying and dangerous of conditions.[93]

For example, extraordinary feats of human endurance were performed consistently by both sides on the Eastern Front throughout the 1941–45 conflict. Sevastopol once again became a by-word for heroic defiance and the Kerch, Taman and Kuban peninsulas violent witnesses to the cut and thrust of war.

Here the fleets were expected to perform any number of crucial amphibious roles from disgorging troops and supplies at invasion sites to embarking them at overcrowded and shrinking bridgeheads around the Black Sea often under the most intense aerial bombardment. Needless to say, fleet commanders were also expected to continue denying the waters around these sites to the enemy by employing whatever blockading methods could be devised at short notice. It was in situations such as these calling for considerable ingenuity and tenacity of purpose that Sergei Gorshkov and Helmut Klassmann rose to prominence on either side of the Great Patriotic War.[94]

While these acts of bravery are legion in warfare, not everybody performs heroically or does what is expected of them in emergencies. It is a curious fact of life that despite the rigorous training and strict discipline that the services instill in their officers and men, some of these individuals will still behave unpredictably at times. Behavioural unpredictability is a factor that makes the human being the ultimate variable in warfare as in civilian life. One may have the most elaborate and brilliant plans and the most intensive training and preparation, but there is no guarantee that at the critical time all of these positive aspects will not be undermined by someone or a group of people failing, for whatever reason, to do what they are required to do. Sometimes even the most predictable of people act in unexpected ways. What was Tom Phillips doing wasting a couple of hours he couldn't afford off the coast of Kuantan on the morning of 10 December 1941 when Force Z ought to have been making for Singapore at all speed and then why did he compound the error by not radioing for fighter protection when his ships were spotted by a Japanese reconnaissance plane off the coast of Pahang? Why did Kummetz seem almost obsessed with wiping out the minesweeper *Bramble* during *Fall Regenbogen* on 31 December 1942 when it posed little threat to the operation or the cruisers involved in it and merely wasted time that would have been better spent on searching for convoy JW.51B? Why did Bey decide to part company with his destroyers at the North Cape on 26 December 1943 and steam off in another direction altogether without informing them either at the time or subsequently? All of these peculiar decisions ended up by being costly and in some cases fatal mistakes.[95]

Sometimes the ultimate variable strikes in the shape of decision-making that actually shows a total disregard for established orders. Fritz-Julius Lemp, the captain of the U-boat *U30*, for example, demonstrated this to perfection within hours of the war between Germany and the Western Allies breaking out on 3 September 1939. He did so by ignoring the existing rules of engagement and torpedoing the Atlantic liner *Athenia* off the northwest coast of Ireland. Whether it was an adrenalin-fuelled case of mistaken identity, as Lemp later claimed, or an instinctive piece of glory-hunting that caused him to attack and sink the *Athenia*, the sad fact is that more than a hundred passengers (including many women and children) paid with their lives for his single act of disobedience.[96]

Overconfidence may also have a role to play in cases where orders are ignored or interpreted in a lax manner. Hans Langsdorff has been accused of disregarding the Seekreigsleitung's instructions to avoid engaging enemy warships with his pocket battleship the *Admiral Graf Spee* and use purely 'hit-and-run' tactics on his commerce raiding foray in the South Atlantic in the autumn of 1939. Critics of Langsdorff from the outset have indicated that the Battle of the River Plate could have been avoided had he not flouted his orders and that the price of his disobedience was a double blow for the Kriegsmarine: the loss of one of their fine *Panzerschiff* and a boost in morale for the Royal Navy. While he certainly tempted fate for too long, the charge of active disobedience may be more difficult to sustain than has hitherto been the case.[97]

Gunichi Mikawa's reputation could have been made in August 1942 had he exploited his unexpected success in destroying four US heavy cruisers at Savo Island to go on to bring carnage to bear on Kelly Turner's undefended transport fleet off Guadalcanal and Tulagi. Contrary to his orders to do just that, Mikawa opted to quit the scene while he was still ahead. Preferring caution over adventure, he chose not to waste any more time scouring the waters for other trophies but to remove his ships under cover of darkness to ensure that they would not be caught by Fletcher's carrier planes once dawn broke on the following day.[98] Mikawa's aversion to risk and Inouye's tepid performance at the Coral Sea may not have played well with Yamamoto's attacking instincts, but they were far from alone in adopting a conservative approach when it came to the safety of their fleet.

Angelo Iachino was no gambler either and, conscious of being without any effective ship-borne radar until late in 1942, he wasn't prepared to risk his ships in any night action if he could avoid it. While his prudence sufficed to give the Italians the sense of victory in the Gulf of Sirte on 17–18 December 1941, it didn't always endear him to the leading members of the RMI ashore who felt he lacked the brio necessary to make the most of his opportunities. Erich Raeder also had cause to regret appointing Kapitän zur See Rudolf Stange to take command of the heavy cruiser *Lützow* for *Fall Regenbogen* in December 1942. Stange's inept performance at sea helped to convince Hitler that the surface fleet had become a worthless anachronism – a fact that directly contributed to Dr. Raeder's early retirement as Oberbefehlshaber der Kriegsmarine. A 'safety first' policy on the part of these commanding officers may not have imperiled their warships, but it had also done little either to seize the initiative in the war at sea or help to elevate each of these figures into some kind of iconic status in the eyes of their nation.[99]

Despite gambling and succeeding at Midway, Raymond Spruance chose to rein in that attacking zeal during the Battle of the Philippine Sea, rejecting Marc Mitscher's suggestion that he be allowed to steam after the enemy fleet on 18 June and send in the battle group to engage it that night with the carrier aircraft to follow up with a series of attacks on the following morning. Spruance rejected the suggestion preferring to consolidate his Task Force in the waters off Saipan where it was meant to protect the landing forces. It was a controversial decision and one that the naval aviators (the 'brown shoes') under his command bitterly resented. Although the Japanese carrier aircraft were to suffer horrendously at the hands of Mitscher's pilots subsequently, Spruance's defensive caution reasserted itself throughout the next few days in rejecting several of the Bald Eagle's plans for attacking what was left of the Japanese fleet. In the end, it was difficult to resist the temptation of concluding that he had let the enemy 'off the hook'.[100] It was a decision that Spruance and others came to regret. It certainly proved to be a big factor in 'Bull' Halsey's charging run after Ozawa's phantom fleet at Leyte Gulf in the following October. Halsey didn't want the Japanese to escape again as they had done on Spruance's watch. While there may be faint echoes here of Beatty after Jutland, there is still much wisdom in holding what you have and preferring to keep risks to a minimum. Foresight, after all, is an elusive gift. One suspects that even those who may claim to have it don't possess it all of the time. Moreover, who can claim to be infallible?[101]

Other decisions can come back to haunt those making them. While Admiral Iachino may not have displayed much verve, he was a man of integrity and deeply concerned about the welfare of his officers and men. He was unlikely, therefore, to expose them to undue risk if he could help it. Ironically, his humanitarianism was to do just that when he ordered the two heavy cruisers *Fiume* and *Zara* and the four destroyers of the 1st Division to go back to help the officers and crew of the stricken heavy cruiser *Pola* off Cape Matapan on the evening of 28 March 1941. This was not Angelo Iachino's finest hour. His assumptions were a mess and so were most of this detachment of warships later that same night off the southern Greek coast as they steamed straight into the steely embrace of Cunningham's Force A and were largely destroyed for their pains. Over 2,300 Italian sailors perished in this action and of those that survived more than 960 were forced to become POWs as a result of Iachino's miscalculations. It was such a significant reverse that Gianni Rocca, in his book *Fucilate gli Ammiragli* (*Shoot the Admirals*), has described Matapan as the naval version of Caporetto. This may smack a little of journalistic licence, but there is little doubt that an even worse defeat for the Italians was narrowly avoided in the hours after the 1st Division had been largely destroyed. If Cunningham had not dictated an ambiguously worded signal that ended up in confusing Pridham-Wippell and led to him calling off his light cruisers from pursuing Iachino's flagship, the damaged *Vittorio Veneto*, the battleship may not have been able to make good her escape.[102]

A blunder that didn't cost any lives at the time but could have had incalculable consequences in the future was made by the captain of the auxiliary ocean boarding vessel *Marsdale* only a few weeks later. After rescuing top secret Enigma codebooks from what appeared to be the doomed German supply ship *Gedania* on 4 June, the captain of the *Marsdale* decided to patch up the ship and take her in tow as a prize back to port in Scotland. Why the Germans didn't make more of her capture and the security implications for their Naval Enigma enciphering system when they learnt of it is still surprising, but the price of hubris is often very high. Had they reacted with far greater concern than they did and introduced a series of extra features to preserve the secrecy of their communications, it is no exaggeration to say that the effects would have been felt instantly and to Allied disadvantage in all the theatres in which German ships were operating.[103]

Pride and, one suspects, the saving of face also caused Vice-Admiral Takeo Kurita to commit a major blunder before his ships got even close to fulfilling the *SHO-GO* plans at Leyte Gulf in October 1944. If he was suffering from dengue fever, as Eric Grove and Evan Thomas suggest he was, Kurita ought to have yielded overall command to Vice-Admiral Matome Ugaki on board the super-battleship *Yamato*, but he didn't. Even if he hadn't succumbed to dengue, we know he refused to retire to his quarters and went without sleep for at least a couple of days. Sleep deprivation doesn't usually sharpen the intellect and didn't in his case. After his flagship *Atago* had been torpedoed and the super-battleship *Musashi* had been bombed out of existence, Kurita's tentativeness and general vacillation became quite marked. Nevertheless, once he had recommitted himself to the task of driving on rather than retiring from the scene, Kurita may have hoped for better luck, but tangling with the waspish destroyers of Clifton Sprague's 'Taffy 3' seems to have unsettled him still further and may have contributed to his most perplexing decision of all, namely, to withdraw from the scene when his path to Leyte Gulf and a host of vulnerable Allied shipping lay open a mere 10,000 yards (4.9nm) away. One is left to speculate whether this curious decision would have been made if he had been healthy and well rested or if Ugaki had been running affairs off Samar rather than himself. Somehow it appears unlikely. Kurita never satisfactorily explained the rationale for his withdrawal before he could finish the job he had been set by Admiral Toyoda. Evan Thomas, however, believes that the real reason emerged long after the war when Kurita admitted to an old friend of his that he wasn't prepared to sacrifice the lives of thousands of Japanese sailors on what he thought would ultimately prove to be a suicide mission.[104]

In war, as in life, individuals are bound to make mistakes. Even so, some errors are more excusable than others. Those born of strategic or tactical misjudgements fall into the former category, even though they may waste precious material resources, while the latter should be reserved for really crass mistakes or those that cannot be condoned. Frank J. Fletcher's decision to send his carrier planes to Tulagi on 4 May 1942 when the Japanese invasion had already been carried out ended up in wasting scarce resources for little or no purpose and could easily have resulted in exposing his carrier planes – or the *Yorktown* part of his fleet – to the unwanted attentions of Takeo Takagi's carrier strike force had it been in the vicinity. Fletcher's move was a little rash, didn't do anything to scupper the Japanese hold over Tulagi and could have had an important effect on the Battle of the Coral Sea, but one can still understand his motives for preferring action to caution. It would be difficult to be as sanguine about his controversial decision to withdraw from the waters off Guadalcanal in the early evening of 8 August 1942 while the transports were still unloading the supplies for the Marines who had gone ashore. It was just fortuitous that Mikawa and his 8th Fleet didn't push on into the transport anchorage in the Lunga Roads after their stunning victory at Savo Island in the early hours of the following morning; otherwise Turner's undefended transports would have almost certainly been decimated.[105]

Mineichi Koga – a poor man's Yamamoto – was not immune from making the wrong decisions. He did it quite frequently. His classic misjudgement came in transferring the planes from six of his carriers to shore up the Japanese base at Rabaul in November 1943. Operation *RO* was designed to retain Rabaul as the most important Japanese naval and air base in the region and one from where support could be lent to their comrades on the vital island of Bougainville and on other islands in the neighbouring archipelagos. Koga's deployment proved costly as many of the carrier planes were destroyed in massive American air raids conducted by George Kenney's 5th and 13th Air Forces within hours of arriving in New Britain and those that weren't had to be flown out of danger to Truk within a few days.[106]

These mistakes were at least understandable. Others arose from rank errors of judgement that are difficult to condone. Both Richardson's squalid opportunism in the aftermath of the *Laconia* incident in September 1942 and Dönitz's equally corrosive reaction to the bombing of *U156* show a wanton disregard for humanitarian virtues and are illustrative of this culpability. They were far from alone in exercising the wrong option. It's a basic requirement that commanding officers exercise a duty of care to those sailing with them, but some failed to live up to that privilege in the most spectacular ways imaginable. Infamous in this regard was the eccentric and possibly deranged Guy D'Oyly-Hughes who, when returning from Norway to Scapa with the carrier *Glorious* and her two escorting destroyers *Acasta* and *Ardent* in June 1940, behaved with such extreme recklessness that he imperilled all who sailed with him. By failing to post any kind of reconnaissance and running his carrier in a very relaxed mode, D'Oyly-Hughes ignored the most basic of precautions and left his group highly vulnerable to any aerial or surface attack mounted by the enemy. Acting on intercepted signals intelligence, the *Scharnhorst* and *Gneisenau* took advantage of these mistakes by interdicting and sinking the trio of British warships in the late afternoon of 8 June. Taken completely by surprise, D'Oyly-Hughes didn't survive the ordeal but neither, alas, did over 1,500 men who paid the ultimate sacrifice for his bizarrely irresponsible behaviour.[107]

D'Oyly-Hughes may have been certifiable, but that wasn't an excuse that could be said of Howard Bode who, despite being left temporarily in charge of the Southern Covering Force, retired to his cabin on the *Chicago* and failed to exercise either the requisite amount of vigilance or any kind of leadership at Savo Island on the night of 8–9 August 1942. A mixture of exhaustion, complacency, inadequate communications, and the failure of the surveillance patrols and their radar sets to detect the enemy allowed Mikawa's 8th fleet to come down 'The Slot' to rout the US heavy cruisers that lay unsuspectingly in their path. While Bode committed suicide, the charge of complacency was also levelled at both Crutchley and Kelly Turner and not without some justification. Whichever way one looked at it, the rout at Savo had resulted from a serious underestimation of the IJN's attacking instincts by the mixed Allied naval force.[108]

Some lessons are not learnt all that well. A failure to ensure a proper system of aerial surveillance was something that Halsey and Kinkaid were to be accused of at Leyte Gulf more than two years later. Kinkaid's cardinal error lay in assuming that Halsey's carrier aircraft had been carrying out a systematic reconnaissance patrol over the Sibuyan Sea and the San Bernardino Strait to ensure that the 'Bull' knew where Kurita was. He compounded this initial error by misinterpreting an intercepted communication from Halsey that was never intended for him and confidently imagined that Lee's mythical TF.34 had been hived off and left behind to deal with the Centre Force should it recommence its run through the San Bernardino Strait. Worse still, what independent surveillance he had mounted before midnight had not revealed any trace of either the Centre Force or Halsey's total disappearance off Samar by the evening of 24 October. Thereafter, despite being unable to corroborate any of his mistaken assumptions by visual means, he was unperturbed believing that the protective shield offered by the mythical TF 34 was in place to the north of his own fleet. Such was his misplaced confidence on this matter that he chose only belatedly to signal Halsey asking for confirmation of Lee's location at 0412. By the time he had received the 'Bull's' reply, he knew that much was amiss. In truth, his mistakes should have had catastrophic consequences for the US 7th Fleet on the morning of 25 October 1944 had the Japanese Centre Force bludgeoned its way into Leyte Gulf and taken issue with the invasion force it would have found there.[109]

Halsey's errors were also manifold, springing largely from grossly mistaken assumptions about Kurita's plans and Kinkaid's decision-making, both of which proved to be dangerously wide of the mark. His decision to chase off after Ozawa's decoy force in a bid to finish off the Japanese carrier fleet once and for all was a typical hard charging and impetuous move on the part of the 'Bull' and one that could so easily have backfired on him had Kurita made the most of the gilt-edged opportunity presented to him. Being duped by an enemy is always possible if the move is brilliantly executed, as Ozawa's was, and designed to appeal to a bold but intemperate naval commander, such as Halsey, prone to the grand gesture and 'flying by the seat of his pants'. Apart from issuing his famous telegraphic query about the location of TF 34, a signal which Halsey misinterpreted as a rebuke and finally arrested his run to the north, Nimitz did not choose to take serious career-threatening issue with his naval subordinate. On the one hand, this was generous of him since both Halsey and Kinkaid had ironically been saved from the consequences of their own incompetence and extravagance at Leyte Gulf by the failure of their principal adversary to grasp the initiative fully when it came his way. On the other, Nimitz didn't need reminding that although both Halsey and Kinkaid had made the most serious mistakes at Leyte, some of the confusion between them was not entirely of their own making. After all, Halsey continued to report directly to Nimitz and Kinkaid to MacArthur and coordination between the two supreme commanders charged with the twin-pronged Pacific campaign left much to be desired. Moreover, disciplining Halsey directly may have had a serious effect on morale and so the 'Bull' was allowed to see out the war in an active capacity even though his promotion to fleet admiral was held back until the end of 1945.[110]

Kurita was not alone in failing spectacularly to make the most of his opportunities, his compatriot Chuichi Nagumo was also tarred with the same brush. Apart from spurning the chance of following up his carrier planes' first strike at Pearl Harbor on 7 December 1941 with another air raid designed to target the oil installations and port facilities at the naval base, he committed another egregious blunder during the raid on Ceylon in early April 1942. On this latter occasion, he might have discovered Somerville's Eastern Fleet had he devoted a little effort, rather than none at all, to even the most rudimentary of reconnaissance duties. He didn't and most of Somerville's force lived to fight another day. That at least didn't end up in costing him any ships. At Midway he was not to be so fortunate. His failure to mount sufficient aerial reconnaissance left him acutely vulnerable once the enemy carriers that he didn't think were in the offing suddenly appeared on the scene. Thereafter, his general indecisiveness and lack of spontaneity when things didn't go according to plan combined to cost him and the IJN dearly.[111]

Somerville, who had inadvertently been spared during Nagumo's Easter raid into the Indian Ocean in April 1942, was hardly a stranger to negligence. He had demonstrated this undesirable trait when he was obliged to take action against the French fleet at Mers-el-Kebir in early July 1940. His heart wasn't in Operation *Catapult* and it showed when his faulty naval dispositions allowed the battleship *Strasbourg* and five destroyers to escape from under his very nose. He had also not been at his best in coping with the Ceylon raid. Once again, his decision-making was flawed, irresponsible and costly. Somerville clearly mishandled both of these tasks and either one could have led to him losing his command.[112] He made mistakes, but at least he was a man of action. His First Sea Lord hadn't been for many years and it showed. Dudley Pound's decision to scatter convoy PQ.17 in July 1942 has invariably been held up as a panic-stricken move dictated by an intelligence blackout and a genuine belief on his part that the wolf packs and bomber planes already attacking the convoy would soon be supplemented by an even greater menace – Raeder's heavy ships. While this interpretation has stood the test of time, it also says something about Pound's lack of real confidence in convoy. He clearly took the view that to stick together when the *Tirpitz* was in the offing would be an invitation to wipe out the entire convoy that the Germans would accept with alacrity. His decision to withdraw the destroyer escorts and scatter PQ.17 is only explicable if he thought that convoy wouldn't work in such an emergency and that going it alone represented a better chance of survival for some of the ships. It was a disastrous error with tragic consequences and one that could easily have cost him his job. Perhaps it ought to have done so.[113]

A serious lack of communication between two fleets while engaged on the same operation is a recipe for misunderstanding, a lack of cohesion and muddled coordination at sea. This was precisely what beset the forces of Shoji Nishimura and Kiyohide Shima as they each made their own way towards Leyte Gulf from Borneo and the Inland Sea respectively. A personal history of jealousy and spite had left Nishimura and Shima loathing one another, so using them on the same operation where communication between the two was vital made no sense at all. Instead of liaising, the two commanders did the minimum possible to keep the other informed of his progress en route to the Philippines. Ahead of his rival, Nishimura did not wait to allow Shima to rendezvous with him before entering the Surigao Strait and quickly paid the price for his culpable intolerance at the hands of Jesse Oldendorf's intelligently deployed mixed force of warships which succeeded in cutting the first half of the Southern Force to pieces. Nishimura certainly played into Oldendorf's hands, but he appears to have done so with almost suicidal intent. Heartbroken by the loss of his only son, he embraced his dangerous mission with fatalistic relish. As a member of the 'old school' in the IJN, he was determined to do his duty to his emperor. It is equally evident that he didn't expect to return from Leyte Gulf and probably didn't wish to.[114]

Sometimes it is not a lack of communication that poses a problem both ashore and at sea, it is miscommunication. Mention has already been made of ABC's sloppily worded signal to Pridham-Wippell at the time of Matapan, but ambiguity is one thing and can be addressed by a further query or a request for an explanation; misreporting reconnaissance information and the over-exaggeration of operational successes are quite another. During the Second World War the latter problems beset all the services even if by far the most spectacular emanated from returning euphoric air crews. Ships that were incorrectly identified by those on reconnaissance missions were likely to be reported as heavier, more ominous, vessels than they actually were. In their operational debriefings, air crews would, on occasion, give estimates of the damage caused by their bombing raids to enemy infrastructure and shipping, or the number of planes destroyed in aerial combat by fighter aircraft that, at times, ranged from the wildly optimistic to the most craven forms of wishful thinking. Italian estimates of damage done to the convoy *Halberd* in September 1941, and those reports issued by US Army pilots about the damage inflicted upon Tanaka's invasion fleet while still far away from Midway on 3 June 1942, at least passed the initial credibility test before being rejected as little more than baseless, unsubstantiated rumours. Some claims were so outrageous, however, that it is difficult to imagine anyone other than the most fanatical supporter believing them even on a *prima facie* basis. In this area, alas, the Japanese pilots developed something of an unenviable monopoly. Not content with their carrier-based compatriots claiming the destruction of ten carriers, five battleships, nineteen cruisers, seven destroyers and nine transports amongst other damaging hits on the American invasion fleet around Bougainville on 12–13 November 1943, the men of the 1st and 2nd Air Fleets arguably outdid even these colossal fantasies eleven months later in the lead up to *SHO-GO 1* in mid-October 1944. On this latter occasion 'Bull' Halsey's 3rd Fleet was supposed to have lost eleven carriers, two battleships, and a cruiser and had another eight carriers, two battleships, a cruiser and thirteen other warships incapacitated in some way. Despite the enormity of these claims, the Japanese military, both in the Pacific and back at home, appear to have been uplifted by these fictional stories of destruction, seeing in them some kind of remarkable deliverance from the American scourge. Amazingly, even once the shroud of hyper-optimism created by these astounding yarns had been punctured by reality, the morale of the Japanese did not appear to be badly affected. On the contrary, they continued to believe that decisive victory was only one campaign away.[115]

Confidence is a wonderfully positive and motivating quality to possess at any time, but if that feeling of self-assuredness spills over into arrogance and the underestimation of one's opponents it leaves all those basking in complacency vulnerable to any number of unwelcome surprises. Japanese euphoria, as we have seen, influenced the planning and yet cost them dearly in the Coral Sea engagement; and hubris born of an exaggerated belief in the secrecy of their encrypted communications was a failing shared by all the Axis Powers throughout the war. Underestimating one's opponents in any competition, let alone in the conduct of war, is a serious flaw and usually stems from insufferable arrogance. By haughtily dismissing the resourcefulness and intellectual capacity of their Occidental foes, the Japanese played initially into the hands of Joe Rochefort and his inspirational team at Station HYPO and subsequently into the much expanded American intelligence community assembled under the Joint Intelligence Center, Pacific Ocean Area (JICPOA).[116] For their part, the Allies didn't give the Japanese sufficient credit for their overall ability to make war and were often surprised by their opponent's technical mastery, individual skill, tactical awareness and astonishing esprit de corps – a bond that virtually ensured all battles between them would be brutal and unyielding.[117]

This latter quality ensured that the Allied island-hopping campaign became a tortuous procession in which massive effort and much blood would be spilled on both sides before the Americans would gain their objective and be able to move on to their next grisly assignment. Previously unfamiliar names of islands like Attu, Betio, Guadalcanal, Iwo Jima, Peleliu, Tarawa, Saipan and Okinawa would become commonly associated with valorous deeds, stubborn resistance and extraordinary sacrifices on the part of both sides.[118] In these intense campaigns, the Allies noted that all ranks of the Japanese military appeared to be strongly influenced by the Bushido code and a belief that personal honour would be best served in fighting and dying in combat for the Imperial cause rather than in tamely consenting to be captured as a POW. What else could they conclude after witnessing a series of hopeless *banzai* attacks in the face of overwhelming odds? Death appeared to be the preferred option.[119]

It certainly was for those pilots who signed up for the kamikaze missions in the last months of the war. Their role was that of the suicide bomber: intent on causing mayhem by choosing targets for destruction in an often random and unpredictable way and being willing to die in the inferno they caused. They introduced a new nerve-wracking dimension to the Pacific War causing disquiet among those on Allied warships in the theatre who got to witness first hand just what lengths these young men would go to in pressing home their attacks and how little they could do to stop them. Good ship-handling and ferocious A.A. defence was not always enough to guarantee survival. Sometimes the fickle hand of fate seemed to be involved too.[120]

War is a brutal business and has always been so. Unfortunately, atrocities were committed by both sides in the conflict at sea. Unrestricted submarine warfare took its toll of innocent women and children as well as civilian males; shipwrecked servicemen were often deliberately left to their fate in the oceans of the world and others on occasion were intentionally wiped out to ensure they wouldn't be able to survive to swell the numbers of the enemy afloat or ashore. Naturally enough, there is no glory associated with these acts of butchery. War is gruesome enough without the callousness that it can so readily inspire and for which a stout defence can be swiftly mounted by those who believe anything goes in a fight to the finish.

War is not always predictable and it does appear to have an imponderable side to it. For good or ill, luck is one of those elements that appears to be linked to the ordeal of war and is something which cannot be easily explained away. What deep analysis may be drawn from a chance encounter, a fortuitous discovery, a stray shot, or a sudden or prolonged bout of bad weather that turns out to have profound consequences? By the same token while Tom Phillips contributed to his own downfall by dwelling for too long off Kuantan on the morning of 10 December 1941, Force Z was still only eventually spotted by a lone reconnaissance aircraft while on its final homeward leg and running short of fuel. Would the two British capital ships have survived for a little longer with crisper decision-making and a little more luck? Maybe, but luck was in desperately short supply for the fledgling Eastern Fleet. Even before it could leave home waters it had lost the services of the carrier *Indomitable* after she had gone aground in the West Indies and been put out of action. This was a bad blow and could be said to have compromised Phillips's task from the very outset.[121]

While neither the carrier *Ark Royal* nor the battlecruiser *Hood* could claim to be as lucky a ship as the *Gneisenau* and the *Scharnhorst* and proved that by not surviving beyond 1941, they might have both gone down in the first month of the war if luck had been against them. In a U-boat hunting group off the west coast of Scotland on 14 September 1939 the *Ark Royal* was spared when two torpedoes from *U39* which were on course for her both prematurely exploded. Only a few days later bombs from a group of Ju-88s and He-111s landed near the carrier and actually struck the *Hood* but rebounded off her without exploding.[122] One may talk about equipment deficiencies, as we have done earlier, but not all torpedoes malfunctioned in this way and not all bombs failed to explode on impact, so a measure of luck has to be involved in these situations too. This luck would not always be present and in her fiery end at the hands of the *Bismarck* in May 1941 it deserted the *Hood* totally. This is not to diminish the role played in her demise by the accuracy of the German gun crews or by her own design flaws, inadequate protection and dangerous operational habits, but in order to benefit from these factors a certain amount of luck was required as well.[123]

Over the course of time some individuals began to get a reputation for being lucky or unlucky. Was it just coincidental that some commanding officers emerged from even the tightest spots with their record intact? One did not need to be overly superstitious to regard sailing with such an individual as a bonus by all of those on board his ship. William G. Tennant, who survived the sinking of the *Repulse*, was one such figure as was Robert Burnett who flew his flag in the light cruiser *Belfast* at the North Cape. Some figures could even survive various misfortunes and still be regarded as 'unlucky' – as was the case with Rear-Admiral Stuart Bonham-Carter whose experiences on ill-fated cruisers at the hands of the Germans led his ratings to describe their lifejackets as 'Bonhams' in expectation that they were likely to be used in the sea at some stage while the rear-admiral remained in command![124] Luck, therefore, is often inexplicable. When it strays into the realm of ill-health, however, cause and effect are often well-known but it is the random nature of why it strikes the person it does that becomes the issue. Therefore, Kurita may well have had good cause to curse his luck if he had been bitten by a dengue-infected mosquito before he even got the chance to cross swords with his American enemies in the Philippines in October 1944.[125]

Whether one makes one's own luck or not is a moot point, but it is clear that sometimes questionable decision-making goes unpunished for some individuals whereas others don't get away with even a dubious order. If Spruance was considered to be lucky at Midway when his bold stoicism paid off and his carriers' vulnerability was not exposed, what can be said of the fact that Burnett's series of misjudgements on Boxing Day 1943 didn't end up in allowing the *Scharnhorst* to destroy convoy JW.55B, as had been the German plan, or to escape the clutches of the Allied task forces that had been deployed to catch and finish her off? Luck, fate, or whatever one may call it certainly smiled on the British at North Cape. Bruce Fraser knew this only too well. He went from despair at missing out on the *Scharnhorst*'s destruction to joy as one of the last shells that the *Duke of York* fired in the German battleship's direction at very long range actually managed to hit home, driving its way through the starboard side of the ship, cutting her power and speed and setting up her eventual destruction. Maybe it was a lucky strike, but even so the crucial hit could not have been made without professional skill of a high order.

No captain, however 'lucky' he was meant to be, could control the weather even if he was able to use it to cloak his activities and assist in preserving the safety of his ship and men from imminent danger. In countless actions across all the naval theatres sudden squalls were known to transform a situation at sea hampering a predator or helping a fugitive and evening up the hunt between them. Sherbrooke's destroyers had reason to be grateful for these inclement conditions at the time of *Fall Regenbogen* in late December 1942 when the German heavy ships were hunting vainly for them and 'Ziggy' Sprague's 'Taffy 3' were relieved to find a convenient rain squall in which to hide for a time from Kurita's Centre Force off Samar on 25 October 1944. Moreover, a mixture of either fog or low cloud and poor visibility often prevented aircraft of all types from carrying out effective reconnaissance and ASW operations, while blunting their fighting ability and making their bombing runs even more of a lottery than they tended to be in good weather conditions. In some regions bad weather was a known quantity and often expected. Bouts of severely foul weather in the upper reaches of the North Sea, for instance, composed of gale force winds, mountainous seas and freezing temperatures would disrupt even the best controlled convoys, forcing ships to fall out of line, sail independently and pose a threat (natural or otherwise) to their very existence. Although storms could play havoc with convoy, persistent bad weather did manage to come to the aid of the remaining ships of PQ.18 by hiding them from their adversaries; otherwise the carnage already experienced by this convoy might well have continued. So awful were the conditions on occasion that ships could founder in the roughest weather without any additional destructive help from enemy aircraft or submarines. Typhoons in the Pacific were a case in point. These could batter a fleet with such force that even if the ships were in a reasonably sheltered location they could still emerge much the worse for wear as the Americans found out twice in 1945.

Accidents happen in war and the leading naval powers were not immune from lethal incidents of 'friendly fire' in which a vessel was attacked and in some cases sunk or damaged by a member of her own side. Most of these incidents involved air crew not recognising their own ships and submarines, but in a few cases, admittedly, ships, especially when caught up in a mêlée, were known to have fired upon friendly forces too.

Some of the most notorious examples of friendly fire in the naval war were the bombing of the destroyer *Leberecht Maass* by He-111 aircraft off Borkum on 22 February 1940; the loss of three members of the British 1st Minesweeping Flotilla at the hands of RAF Typhoon fighter bombers off the Normandy coast on 27 August 1944; and the sinking of the French minelaying submarine *La Perle* by Swordfish aircraft belonging to two Allied merchant carriers (MAC ships) in the Atlantic on 8 July 1944. *U333* managed to make this undesirable list by sinking the German blockade runner *Spreewald* on 31 January 1942 and *U43* did the same to *Doggerbank* on 3 March 1943. Identification was on the whole better, as one might expect, between surface ships of the same side but mistakes could still be made as the German destroyer *Friedrich Eckholdt* proved by almost certainly assuming that the British light cruiser *Sheffield* was actually the *Admiral Hipper* when they met briefly at the Battle of the Barents Sea on 31 December 1942. She paid mightily for her mistake with her own loss only minutes later. Sometimes confusion took place when a battle was being conducted in poor weather. Lousy conditions have been known to lead to bouts of trigger-happiness on the part of some ships' companies. This helps to explain why the British F class destroyer *Fury* attacked its E class counterpart *Eclipse* without even going through any identification procedures during a testing Arctic run shepherding convoy PQ.13 to Murmansk in March 1942. At other times the very nature of night fighting in a crowded operational area would be sufficient to sow confusion and doubt in the minds of those intimately engaged in the combat. This was the case on 28 May 1940 when the minesweeper *Lydd* and the destroyer *Grafton* mistook the drifter *Comfort* for a German S-boat and began shelling her at short range before the minesweeper rammed the innocent drifter with such force as to cut her in half. Occasionally the hectic nature of a wolfpack pursuit would bring

U-boats into such close confines with one another that unfortunate incidents could occur as they did when *U221* rammed and sank *U254* on 8 December 1942 as both were gearing up to carry out an assault on convoy HX.217. This had definitely not been in the script, but in these roiling circumstances it was the proverbial accident waiting to happen. Furthermore, it wasn't an isolated event either. *U254*'s fate was shared a few months later by both *U439* and *U659*. These two Type VIIC boats were in the midst of convoy skirmishing off Cape Finisterre during the night of 3–4 May 1943 when they collided in such a grievous way that neither could survive the impact and both sank unceremoniously.[126]

There were already enough ways to lose in naval warfare without having to absorb any self-inflicted blows, but these were in the offing for some. At least two U-boats are thought to have been sunk by their own T5 torpedoes in the later stages of the war. It was a tragic fate that those on board the British Fiji class light cruiser *Trinidad* could empathise with as one of their own torpedoes malfunctioned, went off track and homed in on the mother ship blasting a large hole in her port side and a smaller, but still significant, hole in her starboard wing for good measure. After being patched up in the Kola Inlet, *Trinidad* was on her return to the British Isles some six weeks later on 14 May when she was bombed and received near-misses to such an extent that her starboard patch gave way, she took on a large amount of water and being unable to cope she had to be finally abandoned. *Schnellboot S.26* didn't even manage to get a second chance. Her own errant torpedo returned home and blew her out of the water in the Black Sea on 5 September 1942. USS *Tang*'s deadly self-destruction took place in the Formosa Straits on 25 October 1944 after carrying out an extremely successful patrol – her fifth – but the Balao class submarine's last Mark 18 electric torpedo proved to be her undoing. It failed to run true, turning and homing in on the American submarine which had fired it in the first place. There were still other ways in which losses to friendly fire could be sustained. Straying into minefields sown by one's own side occurred too. Arguably the worst example of this type of accident happened on 5 July 1942 when nineteen ships of convoy QP.13 returning from the Soviet Union in foul weather and seeking navigational aid along the north coast of Iceland mistook an iceberg for the North Cape and blundered into an Allied mine barrage that took a heavy toll of the shipping, sinking the minesweeper escort *Niger*, along with five other ships from the convoy, and damaging a sixth one into the bargain.[127]

Historians are taught to be wary of using cliché-ridden phrases in their work and yet it is easy to see why they are resorted to since there is a ghastly truism that surrounds the fickleness of fate and the tantalising margins that separate victory and defeat in war. A would-be triumph can just as easily and swiftly turn into a galling defeat if some factors that would have secured the former are inexplicably missing at the vital moment. This conclusion has outlined a range of these substantive as well as elusive, highly idiosyncratic, and often ephemeral qualities whose existence or critical lack thereof contributed to the winning or losing of small-scale skirmishes as well as decisively affecting the outcome of larger battles and entire theatre campaigns. It is with this volatility in mind that any discussion of what constitutes a 'turning point' in this six-year conflict needs to be addressed. Although not quite a cliché, the ubiquity associated with such a retrospective concept is something which historians often wrestle with when reviewing the linear dimension of time. Those that opt for a single 'turning point' can be very persuasive (Churchill over Pearl Harbor for example) and yet one shouldn't forget that history isn't a precise, finite science and that definitive prescriptions about it – even when confidently expressed by experts in the field – need not be regarded as constituting the final word on the subject. One thing to bear in mind is that the lasting significance of a single triumph or a crushing defeat may not always be obvious at the time and even if it was – such as at Midway – the result of one epic battle need not prefigure the rest of the war. It is clear that the Japanese had chances after Midway to hurt the American war effort in a serious way and seriously disrupt its momentum. In the waters off Guadalcanal and the Philippines, in particular, the Japanese were at times perilously close to exacting substantial revenge for their defeats elsewhere. If some of these clashes had turned out a little differently and several missed opportunities had been seized, the war could easily have been prolonged and made far more fraught than it already was. In looking back at their campaigns, therefore, the Japanese could be forgiven for sensing that Trevelyan's assessment of the 1848 revolutions as a 'turning point at which history failed to turn' was apposite to their own experiences in the Pacific almost a century later. What I hope this study has shown above all is that little in life is inevitable and that the concept of a sole 'turning point' in such a multi-faceted war looks to be a singularly inappropriate piece of retrospective analysis and one that has limited forensic value.

In summing up this study, there is abundant evidence to suggest that fighting the war at sea from 1939–45 was an immensely challenging business often waged in the most taxing of environments. Success – whether in individual forays or large campaign operations – was never something that any power could take for granted since the unpredictable and the imponderable were elements that could combine to thwart even the best laid plans and offset the advantages of power and domination that one side possessed over the other. While the Second World War may not be quite the exemplar of the Revolution in Military Affairs that the Great War had been, there is little doubt that the legacy of the earlier conflict did much to affect the way in which states were able to project their military power two decades later. Some of these seminal developments, such as the strategic use of air power (both land and carrier-based), the exponential growth in amphibious warfare, combined arms operations and joint operations, the role of the *blitzkrieg* offensive, the struggle to subdue the submarine, and the acclaimed benefits of both radar and signals intelligence – all of which could be said to have profoundly affected military effectiveness at sea – have already been touched on in this conclusion. Even so, a revolutionary development that was not spawned by the 1914–18 war – the atomic bomb – had unarguably the greatest impact of them all. Whether or not it was immoral and unnecessary to drop the two bombs on Hiroshima and Nagasaki will always remain a touchstone of individual consciousness. Those who loathe war in all of its forms and despair of the untold tragedies inflicted by it will rarely, if ever, be appeased by the argument that it may well have hastened the end of the Pacific War and saved countless thousand lives. While this is not the place to continue that debate, there is little doubt that the destructive magnitude of those two bombs did usher in a new era in international relations and leave the military establishments across the world wondering what lay in store for them.

Notes

1. D. MacGregor, 'The use, misuse and non use of history: the Royal Navy and the operational lessons of the First World War', *Journal of Military History*, Vol.56, No.4 (1992): 603–15.
2. For a lucid, scholarly and vivid account of international history for the period 1919–33, see Steiner, *The lights that failed*.
3. Willem Hackmann, *Seek and strike: sonar, anti-submarine warfare and the Royal Navy 1914–54* (London: HMSO, 1984), pp.97–231; Malcolm Llewellyn-Jones, *The Royal Navy and anti-submarine warfare, 1917–49* (London: Routledge, 2006), pp.8–24.
4. Sönke Neitzel, 'The deployment of the U-boats', and Werner Rahn, 'The campaign: the German perspective', both in Stephen Howarth and Derek Law (eds), *The Battle of the Atlantic 1939–1945: the 50th anniversary international naval conference* (London: Greenhill Books, 1994), pp.276–301, 538–53.
5. Eberhard Rössler, 'U-boat development and building', in ibid., pp.118–37; Gardiner (ed.), *Conway's all the world's fighting ships*, pp.239–40; Miller, *U-boats*, pp.16–17.
6. Efforts to provide hydrogen peroxide as a safe means of propulsion were never really resolved even in the post-war years. See W.J.R. Gardner, 'Anti-submarine warfare', in Richard Harding (ed.), *The Royal Navy, 1930–2000: innovation and defence* (London: Frank Cass, 2005), pp.117–34 (especially note 2); Doenitz, *Memoirs*, p.128.
7. Gardner (ed.), *Conway's all the world's fighting ships*, pp.240, 244; Miller, *U-boats*, pp.60–72.
8. These figures don't take into account torpedo misses caused as a result of operational firing errors or enemy-avoidance measures. Anthony Newpower, *Iron men and tin fish: the race to build a better torpedo during World War II* (Westport, Conn: Praeger Security International, 2006), pp.33–54; Edwyn Gray, *The devil's choice: Robert Whitehead and the history of the torpedo* (Annapolis, Md: NIP, 1991), pp.222–26; Miller, *U-boats*, pp.86–97; Doenitz, *Memoirs*, pp.84–99, 270–71, 418–19.
9. Greater sophistication in torpedo control and warhead reliability was expected to come with the introduction of the T5 *Zaunkönig* (Wren) acoustic torpedo in August 1943. Its hydrophones, placed in the nose of the acoustic torpedo, were meant to pick up the noise signature of a potential target's propellers. While it could run at 24.5 knots for 5.75km, it could only detect moving targets that were making 10–18 knots – anything going at a lower or higher speed eluded the idiosyncratic hydrophonic search capability of the *Zaunkönig*. Allied acoustic countermeasures took the form of using a mechanical noise maker known as a 'foxer' which was a contraption towed 200 yards (183m) behind escorting vessels consisting of two parallel steel pipes which would continually strike one another and generate a high frequency sound that dwarfed the noise of the propellers and would attract the attention of the T5's hydrophones instead. While the British tended to tow two sets of 'foxers' set 100 yards (91m) apart, the USN's version, the FXR, was towed on its own some 500 yards (457m) astern of the escorting vessel and the RCN produced another single noise maker, the CAT, which was lighter than the British version and could be towed even faster. Partly as a result of these countermeasures, the T5 was not the success that Doenitz had initially envisaged. It is thought that roughly 640 T5s were fired at

targets but only 25 A/S vessels and 20 merchant ships were sunk by them – a success rate of only 7.03%. Hackmann., *Seek and strike*, pp.303–23; Miller, *U-boats*, p.89.
10 Whatever the merits of the principle of convoy were, much depended for its effectiveness upon the vessels that formed the escort. For a sense of what those duties involved, see Peter Coy, *The echo of a fighting flower: the story of HMS Narcissus and B3 Ocean Escort Group in WWII* (Upton upon Severn, Worcs: Square One Publications, 1997); Peter Gretton, *Convoy escort commander* (London: Cassell, 1964); Milner, *North Atlantic run*; Frank B. Walker, *Corvettes – little ships for big men* (Budgewoi, NSW: Kingfisher Press, 1995); Michael G. Walling, *Bloodstained sea: the U.S. Coast Guard in the Battle of the Atlantic, 1941–1944* (Camden, Maine: International Marine/McGraw-Hill, 2004).
11 See the cumulative convoy statistics for WWII compiled by Hague, *Allied convoy system*, pp.107–8, 116–19, 123–25 and reproduced in Appendix A.
12 *Fall Paukenschlag* did not show the upper echelons of the USN in a good light as Michael Gannon reveals in absorbing detail in his book on the crisis entitled *Operation Drumbeat*. For a far more sympathetic treatment of the logistical problem and the paucity of escort vessels, see Robert W. Love, Jr., 'The U.S. Navy and Operation Roll of Drums, 1942', in Timothy J. Runyan and Jan M. Copes, *To die gallantly: the Battle of the Atlantic* (Boulder, Col: Westview Press, 1994), pp.95–120. Whichever way one looked at it, however, the German U-boats enjoyed a very profitable period of dominance and destruction. See Doenitz, *Memoirs*, pp.195–224.
13 Hague, *Allied convoy system*, p.108.
14 Efforts to use Catapult Aircraft Merchant Ships (CAM ships) and Fighter Catapult Ships (FCS) to try to offset the use by the Germans of the Focke Wulf FW 200 aircraft in the North Atlantic in the 1940–43 period achieved only fairly modest results. Out of 170 round trips made by 35 CAM ships only eight aircraft were ever catapulted into the air. Of the handful of aircraft launched for which there could be no on-board recovery, seven were thought to have destroyed enemy aircraft – a 'kill' rate of 87.5%. Of the four FCS that made it beyond their trials, ten fighter aircraft were launched. One claimed to have destroyed an FW 200 and two others were thought to have damaged the same type of enemy aircraft. Merchant Aircraft Carriers – known as MAC ships – were altogether more productive in the 1943–45 period. They were converted from bulk grain carriers and oil tankers and had flight decks so their aircraft could return to land on the MAC ship after their sorties. MAC ships made a total of 323 round trips; their aircraft flew 4,177 sorties and destroyed or irreparably damaged 114 enemy aircraft for the loss of eight of their own aircrew. Ibid., pp.77–88.; David Wragg, *The Fleet Air Arm handbook 1939–1945* (Stroud, Glos: Sutton Publishing, 2001), pp.32–35, 71, 84, 100, 109, 178.
15 At distances of roughly 100–200 yards (91–183m) from the contact the sound transmission would consistently overshoot the target and fail to register an echo. Hague, *Allied convoy system*, p.62; Padfield, *War beneath the sea*, pp.23–24; Terraine, *Business in great waters*, pp.30, 177–78, 245, 250, 264, 278, 280, 439–40, 657; www.uboat.net/allies/technical/asdic.htm (accessed 5 March 2008).
16 Success with the 10 centimetre radar set was first achieved on 16 November 1941 with the detection and destruction of *U433* by the corvette *Marigold*. Ship-borne radar had claimed its first U-boat victim when the destroyer *Vanoc*, equipped with a fixed antennae Type 286M, detected and then rammed and sank *U100* on 17 March 1941. *Vetch's* success on 14 April 1942 became notable for the range (7km) at which her radar set (Type 271) detected *U252*. HF/DF had established its first operational success against *U587* just over a fortnight before on 27 March 1942. Howse, *Radar at sea*, pp.72, 79–80, 99, 115–16, 277; D.G. Kiely, *Naval electronic warfare* (London: Brassey's Defence Publishers, 1988), pp.5–11; Lovell, *Echoes of war*, p.53; Rohwer, *Chronology*, pp.113, 155, 159.
17 Paradoxically enough, the 'Leigh Light', though much less sophisticated than these other technological advances, took what seemed to be an inordinate time to become

operational. Whether this resulted from a systemic quirk in the system, bureaucratic inertia or sheer bloodymindedness, the delay frustrated those who were engaged in ASW operations in the North Atlantic and the Bay of Biscay. Once in service as a piece of standard issue equipment, however, the 'Leigh Light' proved to be a very effective aid in taking the fight to the U-boats. They didn't have it all their own way, however, as 111 Wellingtons equipped with 'Leigh Lights' were lost between 3 June 1942 and the end of the war. Norman L. Franks, *Dark sky, deep water: first hand reflections on the anti-U-boat war in WWII* (London: Grub Street, 1997), pp.1–12; Greswell, 'Leigh Light Wellingtons of Coastal Command', pp.55–58; Gardner, 'Anti-submarine warfare', pp.123–28.
18. Convoy's success was predicated upon the performance of its escort vessels. Their role was vital in shepherding the merchant vessels and troop carriers across the Atlantic or in any contested stretch of sea. See David K. Brown, 'Atlantic escorts 1939–45', in Howarth and Law (eds), *The Battle of the Atlantic 1939–1945*, pp.452–75.
19. Colin Dobinson, *Building radar: forging Britain's early-warning chain, 1935–1945* (London: Methuen, 2006); David Zimmerman, *Britain's shield: radar and the defeat of the Luftwaffe* (Stroud: Sutton, 2001); Brown, *A radar history of World War II*, pp.45–46, 53, 97, 110–13.
20. Howse, *Radar at sea*, pp.73, 97, 102–7, 117–18, 122, 135–38, 153, 163, 176, 178, 181–85, 188, 205–6, 209, 222–26, 229–30, 232, 234, 242–43, 247–48, 254–55, 304–5.
21. Brown, *A radar history of World War II*, pp.124–27; Howse, *Radar at sea*, pp.43–45, 75–76, 90–98, 187–90.
22. Johnson, *The Pacific campaign in World War II*, pp.177–96; Willmott, *Battle of Leyte Gulf*, pp.141–42, 145, 148, 151–53, 158; B.W. Lythall, 'Basic science and research for naval radar, 1935–45', in Kingsley (ed.), *Development of radar equipments for the Royal Navy*, pp.67–93.
23. HF/DF was ultimately capable of detecting VHF signals of even the shortest duration and accurately establishing their bearing to within a degree. A skilled HF/DF operator was able to distinguish between a ground wave signal, i.e. one within 30nm (55.6km), or a longer-range transmission that was bounced off the ionosphere. Armed with this information and the strength of the signal, a vessel equipped with a HF/DF set could home in on the errant U-boat and mount a surprise attack upon it. Hague, *Allied convoy system*, p.83; Williams, *Secret weapon*, pp.75–99, 184–240; Jürgen Rohwer, 'The wireless war', in Howarth and Law (eds), *The Battle of the Atlantic 1939–1945*, pp..408–17.
24. Material on RE and RFP can be gauged by consulting Wilford, 'Watching the North Pacific', pp.131–64.
25. MAD was also developed by the Japanese and given the name *Jikitanchiki*. It failed to be as effective as it might have been against US submarines largely because of the prevailing shortages of both aircraft and fuel. Padfield, *War beaneth the sea*, pp.400–402, 447–48; Terraine, *Business in great waters*, pp.661–62.
26. It soon became clear that the A/S bomb posed as many dangers to the air crew operating it as it did for the submarine it was targeted to destroy. Several aircraft were lost because their own A/S bomb exploded before it could be released or because the bomb ricocheted off the surface of the sea and struck the dive bomber that had released it. Two Skua aircraft from the British carrier *Ark Royal* were blown up in this way when mounting an attack on *U30* on 14 September 1939. It was finally abandoned in 1941 and replaced with a modified depth-charge that eventually became more effective once a new bomb sight improved the aim of RAF Coastal Command's bombing crews and scientists from Operational Research had determined that the new version of the A/S bomb could be given a much shallower depth setting. Hague, *Allied convoy system*, p.62; Alfred Price, *Aircraft versus submarine in two World Wars* (Barnsley: Pen & Sword, 2004), pp.34–35, 39–40, 62–64, 85–86, 91–93, 127, 157. For an excellent account of the weaponry available to the leading

naval powers in the 1939–45 period, see John Campbell, *Naval weapons of World War II* (Annapolis, Md: NIP, 2002).

27 Ireland, *Jane's naval history*, pp.76–91; Price, *Aircraft versus submarine*, pp.62–64, 100–104.

28 Miller, *U-boats*, pp.108–12; Axel Niestlé, 'German technical and electronic development', in Howarth and Law (eds), *The Battle of the Atlantic 1939–1945*, pp.430–51.

29 Despite claiming that *Tammatte* could absorb 90% of the waves emitted by the Allied airborne Mark III radar sets, *schnorchel* boats could be let down on occasion by the wake left by their mast on the surface of the sea or by a telltale cloud of diesel exhaust fumes that revealed their presence to the eyes of a trained aerial observer hunting for them. Miller, *U-boats*, p.111, 122–24.

30 Figures for these key imports between January and June 1945 were 2.7 million tons. For example, imports of pig iron fell precipitously by 89%; pulp by 90%, raw cotton and wool by 91%, fats and oils by 92%, iron ore by 95%, soda and cement by 96%, lumber by 98%, fodder by 99% and not even a gram of either sugar or raw rubber was landed. Michel Thomas Poirier, 'Results of the American Pacific Submarine campaign of World War II' (30 Dec.1999) (accessed through www.navy.mil/navy-data/cno/n87/history/pac-campaign.html on 14 Feb.2008); Ireland, *Jane's Naval history*, pp.102–11.

31 Steven Trent Smith, *Wolf pack: the American submarine strategy that helped defeat Japan* (Hoboken, NJ: John Wiley & Sons, 2003); Marder, Jacobsen and Horsfield, *Old friends new enemies, II*, pp.206–12, 250–53, 371–88, 559–65; Davis and Engerman, *Naval blockades*, pp.321–82.

32 Despite *I-19*'s legendary performance east of San Cristobel on 15 September 1942, in which three of his Type 95s wrecked the fleet carrier *Wasp* at a distance of 914 metres and two others put the battleship *North Carolina* and the destroyer *O'Brien* out of action a further 6nm (11.1km) away, the feat remained an eloquent footnote in the history of what might have been for the Japanese submarine arm. Once again, therefore, one senses that the Allies had dodged a metaphorical bullet from the Axis Powers even though its submarines did eliminate another fleet carrier *Yorktown* and the two escort carriers *Liscombe Bay* and *Block Island* during the Pacific campaign. This meant that they achieved the same number of carrier casualties (four) as their American opponents who eliminated *Shokaku*, *Taihō*, *Shinano* and *Unryū* in a six-month period from 19 June to 19 December 1944. Blair, *Silent victory*, pp.279–81, 302; Gardner (ed.), *Conway's all the world's fighting ships*, pp.181–84; Newpower, *Iron men and tin fish*, pp.37–38, 113–15, 117–23, 125–26, 128–30, 156. Japanese destroyers also demonstrated the true potentialities of the Type 93 'Long Lance' torpedo in the gallant torpedo actions they undertook in the Pacific campaign and were particularly dangerous and skilled in night fighting. See Allyn D. Nevitt's online discussion of their merits and that of the torpedoes they wielded at www.combinedfleet.com/lancers.htm (accessed 15 Feb. 2008).

33 Boyd and Yoshida, *Japanese submarine force*, pp.53–107,120–27, 133–90.

34 In a very fluid situation, such as an on-going confrontation at sea, tactical instructions and other vital information need to be passed on and understood by the recipients with the minimum of fuss and delay. If the code is too complex to use in such a swift fashion, it is unlikely to remain in service for long. Its singular advantage – the utmost security it provides – would not be sufficient in itself to ensure its retention if it took too long to relay and decipher messages drawn up in it. There is something profoundly odd and slightly ludicrous about a situation in which codes can be too complex for their own good, such that the very secrecy all powers seek for their communications is actually compromised by the need to cater to a series of routine administrative operations. By taking signalling shortcuts in relaying their encoded messages, operators could provide at the very least an identifiable 'fingerprint' to enemy cryptanalysts. Those who were less than circumspect might provide other clues as well. Wilford, 'Watching the North Pacific', pp.131–64.

35 Beesly, *Very special intelligence*, pp.93–107; John Winton, *Ultra at sea: how breaking the Nazi code affected Allied naval strategy during World War II* (New York: William Morrow, 1988), pp.181–96.

36 Gardner, *Decoding history*, pp.217–18. Gardner is not alone. Although Harry Hinsley believed that the use of 'Ultra' shortened the war against Germany by up to two years and Chester Nimitz thought that the superior intelligence he received was worth the equivalent of an additional fleet, Jeffrey Richelson thinks that this estimate is wildly exaggerated and that it is impossible to be so specific about its actual contribution. James Bamford, *The puzzle palace* (New York: Penguin, 1983), p.66; F.H. Hinsley, 'The influence of ULTRA in the Second World War', *Intelligencer, Vol.14, No. 2* (2004): 103–13; Jeffrey Richelson, *A century of spies: intelligence in the twentieth century* (New York: OUP, 1995), pp.173–96; Bath, *Tracking the Axis enemy*, pp.106–8; John Ferris, 'Ralph Bennett and the study of Ultra', *Intelligence and National Security, Vol.6 No.2* (1991): 473–86.

37 It wasn't just the receipt of timely intelligence but the interpretation of that information that was key as Admiral Somerville and his Eastern Fleet found out to their cost in early April 1942. See John Winton, *Ultra in the Pacific: how breaking Japanese codes and ciphers affected naval operations against Japan* (London: Leo Cooper, 1993), pp.23–31. For a wider dimension, see Christopher Ford and David Rosenberg, *The admirals' advantage: U.S. Navy operational intelligence in World War II and the Cold War* (Annapolis, Md: NIP, 2005), pp.1–29; Jurgen Röhwer, 'The wireless war', in Howarth and Law (eds), *Battle of the Atlantic*, pp.408–17.

38 Professor Sir F.H. (Harry) Hinsley would subsequently carve out a significant academic career for himself as the doyen of those historians writing about the British Intelligence scene. He was the lead author in the HMSO series *British Intelligence in the Second World War* and wrote extensively about the subject in the post-war world. He subsequently became Master of St. John's College and Vice-Chancellor of Cambridge University.

39 It is abundantly clear that the Allies gleaned invaluable information from the vessels they boarded: the trawlers *Polares* (26 April 1940), *Krebs* (4 March 1941), *Geier* (26 December 1941), *Föhn* (27 December 1941) and *Donner* (27 December 1941); the weather ships *München* (7 May 1941) and *Lauenburg* (28 June 1941); the supply ship *Gedania* (4 June 1941); and the U-boats *U33* (12 February 1940), *U110* (9 May 1941), *U570* (27 August 1941), *U559* (30 October 1942), *U205* (17 February 1943) and *U505* (4 June 1944).

40 Although the British changed their Naval Cypher No.2 to No.4 on 1 January 1942, the Naval Cypher No.3 remained the means by which the Royal Navy and its Allies, the USN and the RCN, communicated with one another in the Atlantic. Winton, *Ultra at sea*, pp.103,105, 110; Beesly, *Very special intelligence*, pp.59–60, 99–100; Sebag-Montefiore, *Enigma*, pp.248, 357–62, 365; Rohwer, *Chronology*, p.131. As far as the making rather than breaking of codes is concerned, John Ferris and Ralph Erskine, amongst others, have done much to reveal the state of British cryptography before and during the war. See John Ferris, 'The British 'Enigma:' Britain, signals security and cipher machines, 1906–46', *Defence Analysis, Vol.3, No.2* (1987): 153–63; Ralph Erskine, 'Naval Enigma: a missing link', *International Journal of Intelligence and Counterintelligence, Vol.3* (1989): 493–508, and 'The Admiralty and cipher machines during the Second World War: not so stupid after all', *The Journal of Intelligence History, Vol.2, No.2* (2002): 49–68.

41 Output from the shipyards of Henry J. Kaiser and those of Bethlehem Steel alone during World War II amounted to more than 2,600 vessels. Poolman, *The winning edge*, pp.172–74; Gary E. Weir, 'A truly Allied undertaking: the progeny of Britain's Empire Liberty 1931–43', in Howarth and Law (eds), *The Battle of the Atlantic 1939–1945*, pp.101–17; Robert J. Winklareth, *Naval shipbuilders of the world: from the age of sail to the present day* (London: Chatham Publishing, 2000), pp.130–209; Edward M.

MacCutcheon, 'World War II development and expansion', in Randolph W. King (ed.), *Naval engineering and American seapower* (Baltimore, Md: The Nautical & Aviation Co. of America, 1989), pp.207–55. For a flavour of the role performed by these mass produced vessels in the naval war, see Sherod Cooper, *Liberty ship: the voyages of John W. Brown 1942–1946* (Annapolis, Md: NIP, 1997).

42 David Hobbs, 'Ship-borne air anti-submarine warfare', in Howarth and Law (eds), *The Battle of the Atlantic 1939–1945*, pp.388–407; Robbins, *The aircraft carrier story*, pp.67–108, 130–65, 178–214, 217–84.

43 Chester G. Hearn, *Carriers in combat: the air war at sea* (Westport, Conn: Praeger Security Int., 2005); Smith, *Carrier battles*; A.J. Smithers, *Taranto 1940: prelude to Pearl Harbor* (Annapolis, Md: NIP, 1995); Wragg, *Carrier combat*.

44 Nonetheless, Japanese aircraft inflicted massive and irreparable damage upon *Lexington*, *Hornet* and *Princeton*, while American aircraft did the same to *Soryu*, *Kaga*, *Akagi*, *Hiryu*, *Shōhō*, *Ryūjō*, *Shokaku*, *Taihō*, *Hiyo*, *Chitose*, *Chiyoda*, *Zuihō*, *Zuikaku* and *Amagi*.

45 *Shinano* was sunk by the submarine *Archer-Fish* on 29 November 1944 en route to Kure. Joseph F. Enright with James W. Ryan, *Shinano! The sinking of Japan's secret supership* (London: The Bodley Head, 1987); Mark P. Parillo, 'The Imperial Japanese Navy in World War II', in James J. Sadkovich (ed.), *Reevaluating major naval combatants of World War II* (Westport, Conn: Greenwood Press, 1990), pp.61–77; Stephen Howarth, *Morning glory: a history of the Imperial Japanese Navy* (London: Hamish Hamilton, 1983), pp.192, 211, 217–19, 223, 245–46, 248, 271, 285, 293, 295, 298, 307–8, 318, 333, 342, 345–48, 351, 361–62, 383–84.

46 Akira Yoshimura, *Battleship Musashi: the making and sinking of the world's biggest battleship* (Tokyo: Kodansha International, 1999); Mitsuru Yoshida, 'The sinking of the *Yamato*', in Evans (ed.), *The Japanese Navy in World War II*, pp.474–98; Gardiner (ed.), *Conway's all the world's fighting ships*, p.178.

47 Peter Elphick, *Life line: the Merchant Navy at war 1939–1945* (London: Chatham Publishing, 1999). See also two books by Bernard Edwards, *The Merchant Navy goes to war* (London: Robert Hale, 1990) and *The quiet heroes: British merchant seamen at war* (Barnsley, Yorks: Leo Cooper, 2003).

48 Buckley, *The RAF and trade defence*, pp.187, 189, 192, 195–96, 199–201; Denis Richards, *The hardest victory: RAF Bomber Command in the Second World War* (London: Hodder & Stoughton, 1995), pp.59, 78, 80–82, 93–94, 101–5, 116, 124, 155, 162–63, 179, 181, 228, 239, 244–45, 251–53, 285, 322–23.

49 *Fuehrer conferences*, pp.169–73, 180–81, 185–86, 190, 219, 243–44, 266–67, 277–79, 285, 288, 292, 298–301, 314–16, 320–30, 343–63; Kershaw, *Hitler: nemesis*, pp.360–69, 538, 542–43, 546, 549, 588.

50 Barnett, *Engage the enemy*, pp.450–55. See also the online section on 'Operation "Cerberus" (11–13 February 1942)' by John Asmussen at www.scharnhorst-class.dk/scharnhorst/history/scharncerberus.html (accessed 10 Mar.2008).

51 Christina J.M. Goulter, *A forgotten offensive: Royal Air Force Coastal Command's anti-shipping campaign, 1940–1945* (London: Frank Cass, 1995); Henry Probert, 'Allied land-based anti-submarine warfare', in Howarth and Law (eds), *The Battle of the Atlantic 1939–1945*, pp.371–87.

52 Geoffrey Till, 'Naval blockade and economic warfare in the European War, 1939–45', in Bruce A. Elleman and S.C.M. Paine (eds), *Naval blockades and seapower: strategies and counter-strategies, 1805–2005* (Abingdon, Oxon: Routledge, 2006), pp.117–30.

53 Michael Dewar, *The art of deception in warfare* (Newton Abbot: David & Charles, 1989), pp.69–77; Alfred Price, *Instruments of darkness: the history of electronic warfare 1939–1945* (London: Greenhill Books, 2005), pp.211–19; David Glantz, *Soviet military deception in the Second World War* (London: Frank Cass, 1989); Jock Haswell, *The intelligence and deception of the D-Day landings* (London: B.T.Batsford, 1979); Roger Hesketh, *Fortitude: the D-Day deception campaign* (London: St. Ermin's Press, 1999); Howard, *Strategic deception in the Second World War*, pp.103–200.

54 Undoubtedly the highest ranking casualty of careless talking was Major General Henry Miller, the 53-year-old chief supply officer of the US 9th Air Force, who at a cocktail party held in Claridge's Hotel in London on 18 April 1944 discussed the supply difficulties he was experiencing in the build up to *Overlord* and was quoted as saying that matters would improve after D-Day and that he was willing to take bets on the offensive starting before 15 June. When this indiscretion was reported to his West Point classmate General Eisenhower, Miller was swiftly demoted to colonel and sent back to the United States where he took an early unscheduled retirement. Carlo D'Este, *Eisenhower: a soldier's life* (New York: Henry Holt, 2002), p.487; Forrest C. Pogue, *The supreme command* (Washington, D.C.: Department of the Army, 1954), pp.163–64.

55 Crowl, *Campaign in the Marianas*, pp.56–78; Moore, *Spies for Nimitz*, pp.99–116; Prados, *Combined fleet decoded*, pp.545–63.

56 Morison, *Rising sun in the Pacific*, p.46.

57 Yamamoto was a gambler and an accomplished one too. He enjoyed duping opponents amidst the cut and thrust of games, such as bridge, go, poker and shoji, where he could apply his quick intelligence and the competitive and aggressive spirit that was a hallmark of this gifted naval officer. Hiroyuki Agawa, *The reluctant admiral: Yamamoto and the Imperial Navy* (Tokyo: Kodansha International, 1979), pp.8, 24, 41, 49–50, 54, 75, 83–85, 269; Edwin P. Hoyt, *Yamamoto: the man who planned Pearl Harbor* (New York: McGraw Hill, 1990), pp.35, 41, 44, 49, 55–56, 58, 85, 116, 157.

58 Prados, *Combined fleet decoded*, pp.585–88; 601, 604–6, 608, 615, 617, 621, 625, 627, 635, 642–43; Thomas, *Sea of thunder*, pp.142, 145, 148, 169, 177–78, 189, 210–11, 331.

59 Haycock, *Eisenhower and the art of warfare*, pp.60–73; Ronald Lewin, *Churchill as warlord* (London: B.T. Batsford, 1974), pp.65–67, 69, 229–30, 233, 236–38, 250–51; R.W. Thompson, *Generalissimo Churchill* (London: Hodder & Stoughton, 1973), pp.105–25.

60 Campbell, *Dieppe revisited*; Farrell, *Basis and making of British grand strategy*, pp.327–29; Villa, *Unauthorized action*. For an alternative view see Will Fowler, *The commandos at Dieppe: rehearsal for D-Day* (London: HarperCollins, 2002); Kenneth Macksey, *Commando strike: the story of amphibious raiding in World War II* (London: Leo Cooper, 1985), pp.122–33; Zeigler, *Mountbatten*, pp.185–97, 200, 204, 207, 523, 657–58.

61 Drez, *Twenty-five yards of war*, pp.84–110; Ireland, *Jane's naval history of World War II*, pp.148–52, 163–64.

62 This lesson was not thoroughly learnt by the Americans. Pre-invasion blitzes carried out both by surface warships and by aircraft didn't soften up the enemy's defences as much as the US planners had hoped. This could be seen most graphically in the invasion of Iwo Jima (Operation *Detachment*).in February 1945. Joseph H. Alexander, *Storm landings: epic amphibious battles in the Central Pacific* (Annapolis, Md: NIP, 1997), pp.19, 21, 26–27, 40–50, 52–61, 126–34, 136–39, 141–48, 199, 201–2, 205; Robert S. Burrell, 'Breaking the cycle of Iwo Jima mythology: a strategic study of Operation Detachment', *Journal of Military History*, Vol.68, No.4 (2004): 1143–86; John A. Lorelli, *To foreign shores: U.S. amphibious operations in World War II* (Annapolis, Md: NIP, 1995), pp.1, 4–6, 57–58, 96, 164–73, 175–81, 186, 191, 193–95, 197, 199, 201, 218, 227–28, 244, 246, 256, 266, 269, 279–89, 291–93, 295–97, 299–300, 311–14.

63 Smith, *Carrier battles*, pp.233–36; Wragg, *Carrier combat*, pp.158–66.

64 Her sister ship *Shokaku* was in no position to fight any battle for several months after the Battle of the Coral Sea.

65 Clayton James, *Years of MacArthur, II*, pp.168–69, 183–93, 212, 226–29, 348, 357–61, 387–91, 397–402, 503–4, 531, 538, 588, 603–7, 630–31, 727, 731–34, 757, 870; Potter, *Nimitz*, pp.221, 238, 242, 245–46, 279–82, 287, 289–91, 312, 315–19, 321, 323, 325–28, 330–32, 335, 343, 346–47, 351, 353, 361, 378–80.

66 Millett, *Semper fidelis*, pp.319–441; Horst Boog, 'Luftwaffe support of the German Navy', in Howarth and Law (eds), *The Battle of the Atlantic 1939–1945*, pp.302–22.

67 Paul Kennedy, 'Military coalitions and coalition warfare over the past century', in Keith Neilson and Roy A. Prete (eds), *Coalition warfare: an uneasy accord* (Waterloo, Ont: Wilfrid Laurier University Press, 1983), pp.3–15.
68 Earl F. Ziemke, *The German northern theater of operations 1940–1945* (Washington, DC: Department of the Army, 1959), pp.113–21, 132–36.
69 F. W. Deakin, *The brutal friendship: Mussolini, Hitler and the fall of Italian fascism* (New York: Harper & Row, 1962); V. Issraeljan and L. Kutakov, *Diplomacy of aggression: Berlin–Rome–Tokyo axis, its rise and fall* (Moscow: Progress Publishers, 1970), pp.95–112, 192–202, 261–62, 268–77, 305–25; Arthur Stam, *The diplomacy of the 'new order': the foreign policy of Japan, Germany and Italy: 1931–1945* (Soesterberg, Netherlands: Uitgeverij Aspekt, 2003), pp.60–106.
70 Alberto Santoni, 'The Italian submarine campaign', in Howarth and Law (eds), *The Battle of the Atlantic 1939–1945*, pp.323–44.
71 This lack of appreciation for one's ally wasn't entirely one way. See James J. Sadkovich, 'German military incompetence through Italian eyes', in Jeremy Black (ed.), *The Second World War, Vol.VII. Alliance politics and grand strategy* (Aldershot, Hants; Ashgate, 2007), pp.1–24.
72 Alastair Cooper, 'The effect of World War II on RAN–RN relations'; Eric Grove, 'The Royal Australian Navy in the Mediterranean in World War II'; and David Brown, 'The forgotten bases: the Royal Navies in the Pacific, 1945', in Stevens (ed.), *The Royal Australian Navy in World War II*, pp.44–52, 66–78, 100–110.
73 G. Hermon Gill, *Royal Australian Navy 1942–1945* (Sydney: Collins in association with the Australian War Memorial, 1985), passim; Ian Cowman, 'Forging an alliance? The American naval commitment to the south Pacific, 1940–42'; Bruce Loxton, 'Savo in retrospect', and David Stevens, 'South-West Pacific sea frontiers: seapower in the Australian context', in Stevens (ed.), *The Royal Australian Navy in World War II*, pp.31–43, 79–86, 87–99. For a perspective on the New Zealand contribution to the war, see I.C. McGibbon, *Blue-water rationale: the naval defence of New Zealand 1914–1942* (Wellington, NZ: Government Printer, 1981), pp.343–79; Howard, *The Navy in New Zealand*, pp.44–106; Matthew Wright, *Blue water Kiwis: New Zealand's naval story* (Auckland, NZ: Reed, 2001).
74 Marc Milner, 'Squaring some of the corners: the Royal Canadian Navy and the pattern of the Atlantic war', in Runyan and Copes (eds), *To die gallantly*, pp.121–36; Michael Hadley, *U-boats against Canada: German submarines in Canadian waters* (Kingston and Montreal: McGill-Queen's University Press, 1985); Robert C. Fisher, 'We'll get our own: Canada and the oil shipping crisis of 1942', *The Northern Mariner, Vol.3 No.2* (1993): 33–40; Milner, *North Atlantic run*.
75 Willmott, *Empires in the balance*, pp.349–50; Grove, *Sea battles in close-up, II*, pp.75–97; Spector, *Eagle against the sun*, pp.123–41; Rohwer, *Chronology*, pp.147–48.
76 Simon Berthon and Joanna Potts, *Warlords: the heart of conflict 1939–1945* (London: Politico's Publishing, 2005); Robin Edmonds, *The big three: Churchill, Roosevelt and Stalin in peace and war* (New York: W.W. Norton, 1991); Herbert Feis, *Churchill Roosevelt Stalin: the war they waged and the peace they sought* (Princeton, NJ: Princeton University Press, 1970).
77 Lindsay to Foreign Office, 22 Mar. 1937, No.247, A2378/38/45, FO 371/20651; Kevin Smith, *Conflict over convoys: Anglo-American logistics diplomacy in the Second World War* (New York: Cambridge University Press, 1996); Steve Weiss, *Allies in conflict: Anglo-American strategic negotiations, 1938–44* (Basingstoke, Hants: Macmillan, 1996); Philip Lundeberg, 'Allied co-operation', in Howarth and Law (eds), *The Battle of the Atlantic 1939–1945*, pp.345–70.
78 Thomas B. Buell, *Master of seapower: a biography of Fleet Admiral Ernest J. King* (Boston: Little, Brown, 1980), pp.144–45, 162–72, 206, 274, 290–92, 339, 391, 426–27, 432, 471, 506; Farrell, *Basis and making of British grand strategy*, 2 vols, passim; Simpson (ed.), *Cunningham papers, II*, pp.3–6, 13–15, 26–29, 31–35, 74–75, 78, 152, 156–58, 160–65,

167, 169–73, 208–10, 212, 299–302, 304, 309, 312–13, 319–20, 326, 331, 341, 344, 346, 350, 360, 380, 400; King and Whitehill, *Fleet Admiral King*, pp.409, 426, 461, 500, 646.

79 John S. Eisenhower, *Allies: Pearl Harbor to D-Day* (Cambridge, Mass: Da Capo Press, 1982); Kimball, *Forged in war*; W.J.R. Gardner, 'An Allied perspective', in Howarth and Law (eds), *The Battle of the Atlantic 1939–1945*, pp.516–37.

80 Hitler and Mussolini's gratuitous declarations of war against the US in the immediate aftermath of Pearl Harbor were yet another colossal mistake by the Axis Powers that would come back to haunt them ultimately. Kershaw, *Hitler: nemesis*, pp.442–48, 486–87, 490; Mack Smith, *Mussolini*, p.273.

81 There is an astonishing dearth of published sources on the master logisticians of the war. It is an area that could be profitably filled by a general study of the art and its leading exponents.

82 Love and Major (eds), *The year of D-Day*; Gardner, 'Admiral Sir Bertram Ramsay', in Howarth (ed.), *Men of war*, pp.349–62..

83 Tennant, whose fine ship-handling skills could not save the ill-fated HMS *Repulse* on 10 December 1941, was specifically responsible for overseeing the use of mulberry harbours and gooseberry blockships to provide temporary sheltered docking offshore and the establishment of the cross-Channel Pluto oil pipeline. Michael Harrison, *Mulberry: the return in triumph* (London: W.H. Allen, 1965), pp.44, 220–21, 260–61, 270, 273–75; Hartcup, *Code name Mulberry*, pp.15, 25, 58, 73–76, 86, 111–12, 118, 123, 126, 128, 134, 137–38.

84 Alexander, *Storm landings*, pp.1–4, 11, 14–15, 34, 38–39, 47, 50, 57, 67, 88–93, 128, 134, 139–41, 150, 153–58, 161,165–66, 174–78, 188; Lorelli, *To foreign shores*, pp.20–21, 34, 37, 43–48, 52–57, 66–68, 70, 75–76, 82–83, 94, 96–98, 100–3, 105–6, 108, 112, 114–17, 119–23, 125, 127, 132, 135–38, 142–45, 148–56, 158, 174–75, 178–81, 183–84, 186, 192–95, 197–203, 205–7, 209–14, 217–18, 221, 226–27, 231–37, 241, 243–45, 247, 251–52, 254–56, 258–62, 270–71, 273, 275, 280–82, 284, 288, 291, 299–300, 302, 304–5, 308; William L. McGee, *The amphibians are coming! Emergence of the 'gator navy and its revolutionary landing craft* (Santa Barbara, Ca: BMC Publications, 2000), pp.8, 10–11, 14, 17, 20, 31, 82, 94, 115, 134, 162–63, 183, 223, 237. Information on one of the top American logisticians in the Pacific, Commodore Nick Carter, can be found in Worrall R. Carter, *Beans, bullets, and black oil: the story of fleet logistics afloat in the Pacific during World War II* (Newport, RI: Naval War College Press, 1953).

85 Ladislas Farago, *The tenth fleet* (New York: I. Obolensky, 1962); Buell, *Master of sea power*, pp.283–99; Michael Gannon, *Black May: the epic story of the Allies' defeat of the German U-boats in May 1943* (New York: HarperCollins, 1998), pp.74–75, 79, 83–86, 105–7, 109, 113–14, 121, 128–29, 133, 175, 217, 236–39, 256, 344, 362, 394; Blair, *Hitler's U-boat war: hunted*, pp.87, 92, 103–4, 120, 122, 149, 152, 160, 177, 239, 241–43, 248, 290, 293, 308–10, 321–23, 357, 376, 410, 474, 476–77, 498, 527, 537, 544–45, 553–54, 656, 660, 662, 672, 683; Padfield, *War beneath the sea*, pp.16, 75, 79, 133, 149, 194–98, 203, 205, 211–12, 218, 222–24, 227, 245–46, 252, 273, 281, 305, 309–12, 318–20, 327–28, 351, 358, 364, 367, 410, 436–37, 478.

86 On some occasions, however, the extra time wasn't always put to good use. Sometimes the degree of detailed planning could hinder spontaneity. Nimitz's stubborn unwillingness to change the plans that had been made for the invasion of Peleliu was a costly example of that inflexibility coming to the fore. Alexander, *Storm landings*, pp.104–19, 122–25; Lorelli, *To foreign shores*, pp.5, 256, 262–69, 271, 300, 309.

87 Spruance replaced Halsey when the latter was hospitalised just prior to the Battle of Midway. He was almost the complete opposite of Halsey, being somewhat taciturn and aloof in temperament and laconic in speech. Worse still he was not seen as having any particular fondness for naval aviation. Spruance was regarded as a 'black shoe' member of the 'Gun Club' on Nimitz's staff – those traditionalists who

preferred battleships to carriers. It is easy, therefore, to imagine the unflattering response of Halsey's staff when the news broke about who was to command TF16 in their beloved 'Bull's' absence. Bess, *Choices under fire*, pp.136–65; Buell, *The quiet warrior*, pp.129–44; Schom, *The eagle and the rising sun*, pp.282–96, 391–92, 405–6.

88 Friedman, *Afternoon of the rising sun*, pp.167, 177, 190–249; Howard Sauer, *The last big-gun naval battle: the Battle of Surigao Strait* (Palo Alto, Ca: Glencannon Press, 1999), pp.101–26.

89 Sebag-Montefiore, *Enigma*, pp.132–36.

90 It shouldn't be forgotten that heroism both began as well as ended the belated and ill-starred Norwegian adventure. Gerard Broadmead Roope and the crew of the destroyer *Glowworm* in ramming the heavy cruiser *Admiral Hipper* on 8 April set a courageous tone that Charles Glasfurd would emulate in the *dénouement* of that campaign. Roope was awarded the VC posthumously for his action against the *Hipper*. Levy, *The Royal Navy's Home Fleet*, pp.54, 173 n.27.

91 Sadly, many of those who died did so after being in the sea for up to two days after their vessels were sunk. Regrettably, more than 898 men were lost and 913 were injured as a result of the Japanese attacks on the American ships. Thomas, *Sea of thunder*, pp.248–50, 261–67, 269–70, 272–82, 288, 290–94, 311–12, 316–18, 320–22, 353–55; www.bosamar.com/usforces/casualty.html (accessed on 15 Feb.2006).

92 Padfield, *War beneath the sea*, pp.14, 16, 55–58, 61–64, 67, 81, 90–98, 100, 102, 106, 109–16, 120–21, 132–38, 140–41, 148, 163, 167–70, 177–78, 225–27, 260, 271, 288, 301–5, 339–44, 346, 352–53, 357, 369–71, 399–400, 403–5, 414, 431–32, 442–43, 449, 471, 478; Eugene B. Fluckey, *Thunder below! The USS Barb revolutionizes submarine warfare in World War II* (Urbana: Ill: University of Illinois Press, 1992); William Tuohy, *The bravest man: the story of Richard O'Kane and U.S. submariners in the Pacific War* (Stroud, Glos: Sutton Publishing, 2002).

93 In addition to the sources already listed that aptly demonstrate the courageous spirit of those who fought the war at sea, one may also profitably consult C.D. Bekker, *K-men: the story of the German frogmen and midget submarines* (Maidstone, Kent: George Mann, 1973); Donald L. Miller, *D-days in the Pacific* (New York: Simon & Schuster, 2005); William Tuohy, *The bravest man*.

94 Achkasov and Pavlovich, *Soviet naval operations*, pp.116–24; Ruge, *Soviets as naval opponents*, pp.114–22; Rohwer, *Chronology*, pp.102, 129, 193, 218, 274, 280, 285, 319, 352.

95 O'Hara, *German fleet at war*, pp.146–47; Stephen, *Sea battles in close-up*, pp.108–9, 203–5; David Ian Hall, 'Looking skyward from below the waves: Admiral Tom Phillips and the loss of the *Prince of Wales* and the *Repulse*', in Kennedy (ed.), *British naval strategy east of Suez*, pp.118–27.

96 Blair, *Hitler's U-boat war: hunters*, pp.57, 64, 66–69, 75, 79, 93, 423; Geoffrey Jones, *U-boat aces* (Bristol, Glos: Cerberus Publishing, 2004), pp.10, 13, 32.

97 Grove, *Price of disobedience*; Joseph Gilbey, *Langsdorff of the Graf Spee: prince of honor* (Hillsburgh, Ont: Joseph Gilbey Books, 1999).

98 Toshikazu Ohmae, 'The Battle of Savo Island', in David C. Evans (ed.), *The Japanese Navy in World War II: in the words of former Japanese naval officers* (Annapolis, Md: NIP, 1986), pp.212–44; Regan, *In bitter tempest*, pp.195–211.

99 Iachino was unable to exploit some of the most promising situations in the Mediterranean because he lacked ship-borne radar, naptha, accurate intelligence, sufficient escorts and consistent air support. To make matters worse, he also seemed fated to experience bouts of poor weather at critical junctures which either hid the enemy or impaired operations. His frustration was as marked as was his ill luck. Iachino may not have cut a dashing figure, but he was a solid individual who may well have deserved a better fate than he actually received. He was eventually replaced by Carlo Bergamini in early April 1943. James J. Sadkovich, 'The Italian Navy in World War II: 1940–43', in Sadkovich (ed.), *Reevaluating major naval combatants*, pp.129–54.

100 His enemies had a field day, Vice Admiral John Towers principal among them. Towers loathed the 'black shoe' admiral and in his capacity as advisor on naval aviation to Nimitz suggested to all and sundry that Spruance be sacked for incompetence. Reynolds, *Admiral John H. Towers*, pp.474–77; Buell, *The quiet warrior*, pp.257–80.

101 Taylor, *The magnificent Mitscher*, pp.217–40; Thomas, *Sea of thunder*, pp.121–25, 140, 145, 149, 175–76, 218–21, 229, 255; Wukovits, 'Admiral Raymond A. Spruance', in Howarth (ed.), *Men of war*, pp.158–76.

102 Marc De Angelis, 'Operation "Gaudo" and the Battle of Matapan: March 27–29, 1941', at www.regiamarina.net/battles/matapan/matapan_us.htm (accessed 15 March 2006).

103 Sebag-Montefiore, *Enigma*, pp.179–80, 189–90, 359–60.

104 Thomas, *Sea of thunder*, pp.349–53.

105 Turner utterly denounced Fletcher's withdrawal and left no one in any doubt that he saw it as an act of desertion. John Towers agreed with him and went on record as saying 'He ran away!' Dyer, *The amphibians came to conquer*, *I*, pp.355–402; Reynolds, *Admiral John H. Towers*, p.399; Johnson, *The Pacific campaign in World War II*, pp.160–96; Schom, *The eagle and the rising sun*, pp.327–46; Spector, *Eagle against the sun*, pp.191–96.

106 Spector, *Eagle against the sun*, pp.159, 242–43; Griffith, Jr., *MacArthur's airman*, pp.122–53, Kenney, *General Kenney reports*, pp.312–27.

107 John Winton, *Carrier 'Glorious': the life and death of an aircraft carrier* (London: Cassell Military, 1999).

108 Warner and Warner, *Disaster in the Pacific*, pp.98–259; Johnson, *The Pacific campaign in World War II*, pp.177–96; Loxton with Coulthard-Clark, *The shame of Savo*, pp.134–270; Brown, *A radar history of World War II*, pp.250–52.

109 Solberg, *Decision and dissent*, pp.68, 79–80, 82, 84, 96–97, 100, 114, 119, 128, 133–35, 139–40, 146, 150–55, 163, 170–73; Wheeler, *Kinkaid of the Seventh Fleet*, pp.386–406; Vego, *The battle for Leyte 1944*; Willmott, *Battle of Leyte Gulf*, pp.121, 124–31, 142, 154, 157–60, 172–78, 192–96, 202, 211, 225, 242, 244–47, 329–30.

110 Buell, *Master of sea power*, pp.474–79; King and Whitehill, *Fleet Admiral King*, pp.577–80; Merrill, *A sailor's admiral*, pp.146–77, 184–85, 209–10, 251; Potter, *Nimitz*, pp.331–45, 349–52.

111 Mitsuo Fuchida, 'The air attack on Pearl Harbor' and Toshikazu Ohmae, 'Japanese operations in the Indian Ocean', in Evans (ed.), *The Japanese Navy in World War II*, pp.39–70, 105–18; Kiyoshi Ikeda, 'Vice Admiral Chuichi Nagumo', in Howarth (ed.), *Men of war*, pp.263–77.

112 Tute, *The deadly stroke*, pp.112–205; Macintyre, *The fighting admiral*, pp.55–69,185–99.

113 Farrell, 'Admiral Sir Dudley Pound', in Harrison (ed.), *Oxford dictionary of national biography*, Vol.45, pp.54–58; Peter Kemp, 'Admiral of the Fleet Sir Dudley Pound', in Howarth (ed.), *Men of war*, pp.17–41.

114 Spector, *Eagle against the sun*, pp.417–44; Friedman, *Afternoon of the rising sun*, pp.43–44, 57–58, 68, 146, 148, 191–98, 204–14, 222, 224–25, 228, 233–48, 385–86, 388–89; Stephen, *Sea battles in close-up*, 2, p.208; Thomas, *Sea of thunder*, pp.238–41, 251, 309.

115 Rohwer, *Chronology*, pp.285, 364; Goldstein and Dillon (eds), *Fading victory*, pp.472–77.

116 Rochefort's undeserved fall from grace at the hands of jealous rivals within the American intelligence community at a time when there was still much work to be done to crack the most complicated Japanese codes is chronicled in a number of books. See Moore, *Spies for Nimitz*, pp.4, 7–8, 12, 229–43; Prados, *Combined fleet decoded*, pp.67, 72, 77, 174–75, 283–84, 301–2, 552–54, 597, 603, 729–31; Johnson, *The Pacific campaign in World War II*, pp.86–88, 128, 166, 174–75, 219; Lewin, *The American magic*, pp.137–40. Notwithstanding these sources, John Winton's *Ultra in the Pacific* and Michael Smith's *The emperor's codes* arguably remain the best works in English on the breaking of those codes. Rochefort's singular contribution to

American cryptanalysis was belatedly recognised by the US government when he was awarded the DSM posthumously by President Reagan. D.M. Showers, 'ULTRA: the Navy's COMINT weapon in the Pacific', *American Intelligence Journal*, Vol.15, No.1 (1994): 49–53.

117 As late as June 1939 the Chiefs of Staff and the Admiralty were still working on their arbitrary assessment of the IJN being only 80% as efficient as the Royal Navy. See COS 931 ' Situation in the Far East', 24 June 1939, DP(P)61, para.10, Cab a quoted in Murfett, *Fool-proof relations*, p.76. Unfortunately, the Americans were inclined to be dismissive about the Japanese capacity to wage war. Kelly Turner had seen enough of the Japanese fighting potential by Guadalcanal to criticise this complacent attitude. See Frank, *Guadalcanal*, p.123.

118 Japanese initiative in digging an extensive warren of tunnels and underground caverns for the movement and storage of supplies and men on Iwo Jima would be copied by the Vietcong years later in the war against the US.

119 Operation *Landcrab*, the invasion of Attu that lasted from 4 May to 2 June 1943, may have been a small campaign in itself but the percentage of losses suffered by the IJA was extraordinary even by its own standards. Although virtually all figures for this campaign are in dispute, it does seem that at least 2,351 Japanese were buried by the Americans and an undisclosed number, perhaps several hundred more, received the same treatment from their Japanese compatriots. Only twenty-three Japanese troops remained alive by the end of the fighting to become POWs. Peleliu was hardly a household name before an unremitting struggle for control of the airfield on the small coral island in the Palau group left more than 10,600 Japanese dead, but much worse was to come once the fighting reached the Marianas with over 23,000 dying on Saipan alone. It was a bitter foretaste of what would unfold in the horrendous 82-day campaign that was fought on Okinawa during the spring and early summer of 1945. Miller, *D-Days in the Pacific*, pp.161–82, 134, 146–48, 151–58, 245, 257, 305, 308–11; Robert J. Mitchell (ed.), *The capture of Attu: a World War II battle as told by the men who fought there* (Lincoln, Neb: University of Nebraska Press, 2000), pp.1–23; Perras, *Stepping stones to nowhere*, pp.113, 121–22, 124–33, 136.

120 The vast majority of kamikaze pilots were young adults. Vice-Admiral Ugaki ended his life in a forlorn kamikaze raid preferring to die rather than be a witness to an American occupation of Japan. Rikihei Inoguchi and Tadashi Nakajima, The Kamikaze attack corps', and Toshiyuki Yokoi, 'Kamikazes in the Okinawa campaign', in Evans (ed.), *The Japanese Navy in World War II*, pp.415–52; 453–73; Thomas, *Sea of thunder*, pp.330–41, 355.

121 Middlebrook and Mahoney, *The sinking of the Prince of Wales and Repulse*, pp.167, 283–314.

122 Barnett, *Engage the enemy*, pp.69–70; Blair, *Hitler's U-boat war: hunters*, pp.84–88; Hoyt, *The life and death of HMS Hood*, pp.40–41; Rohwer, *Chronology*, pp.3, 5.

123 Rhys-Jones, *The loss of the Bismarck*, pp.111–22, 221–25.

124 Stephen, *Sea battles in close-up*, p.180.

125 Thomas, *Sea of thunder*, p.192; Grove, *Sea battles in close-up*, 2, p.198.

126 Kemp, *Friend or foe*, pp.40–46, 54, 112–16, 130–33, 144–46.

127 Ibid., pp.151–57, 160–61.

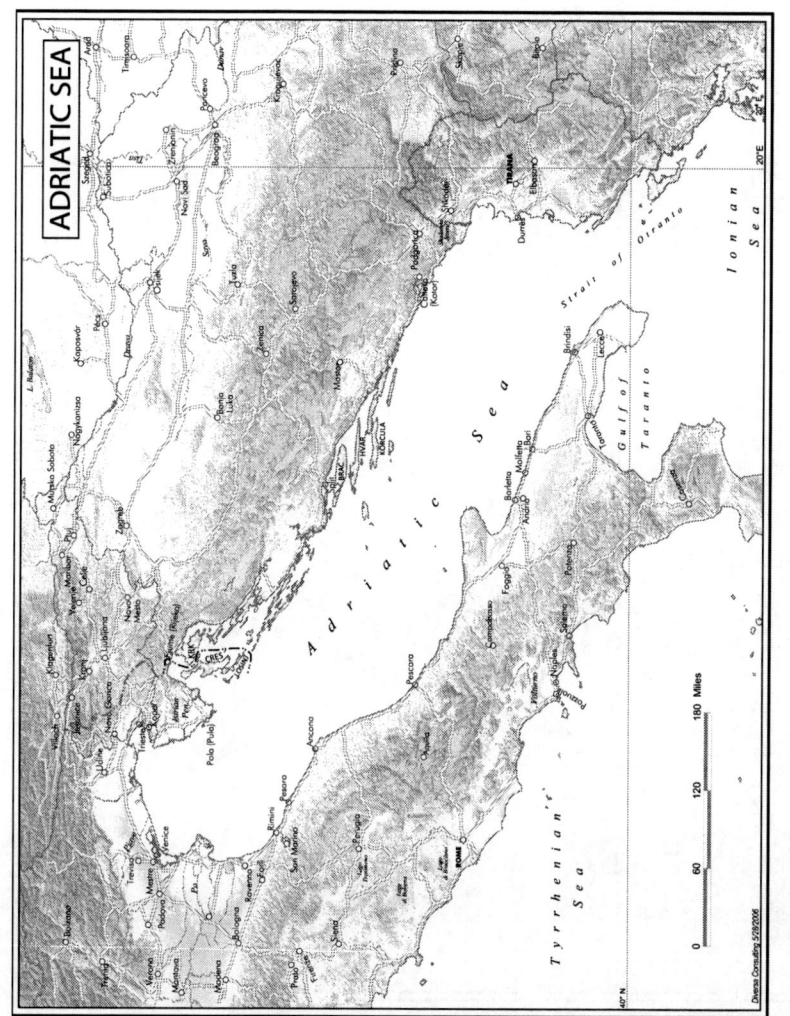

Map 1 Adriatic Sea

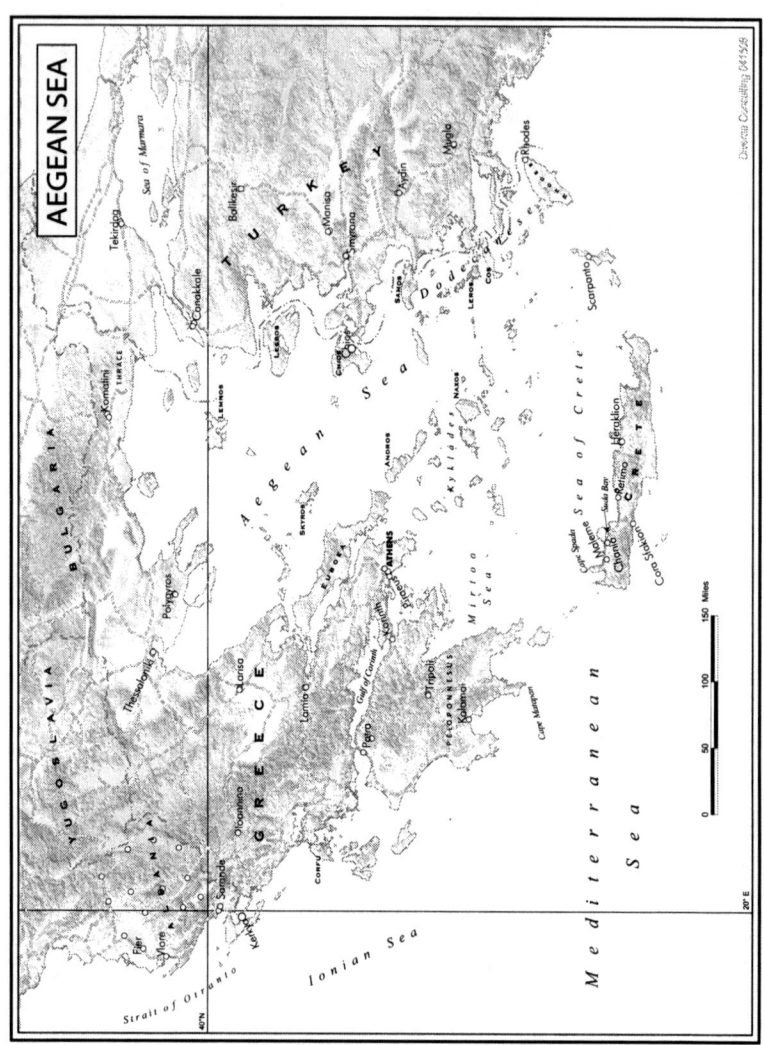

Map 2 Aegean Sea

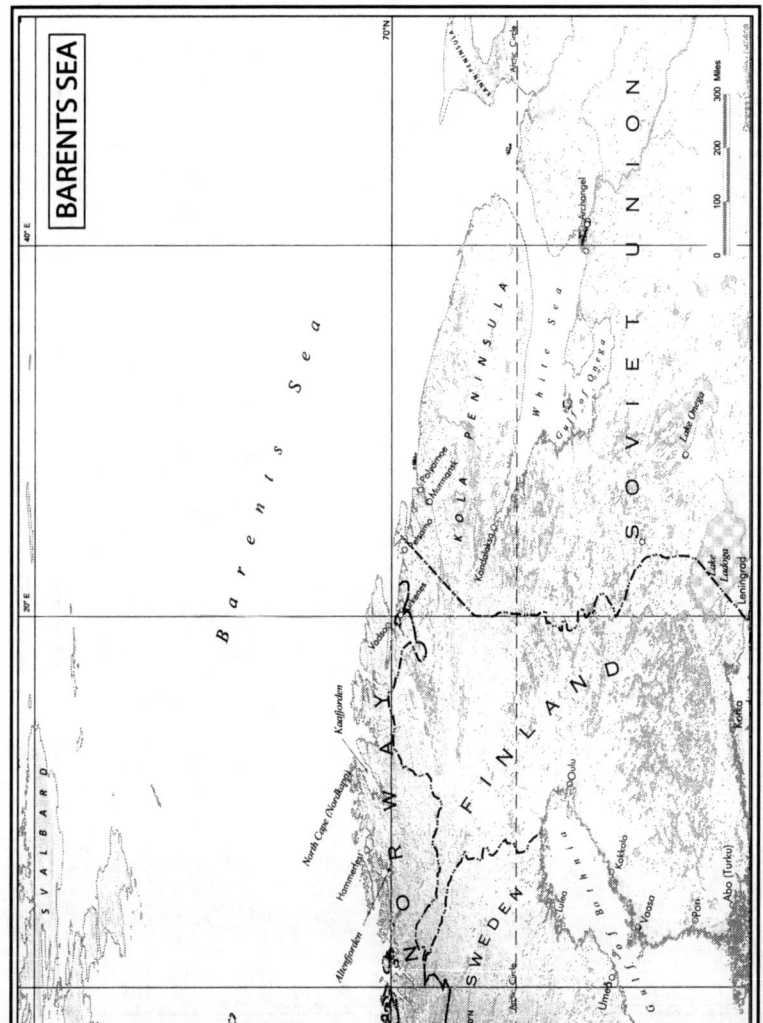

Map 3 Barents Sea

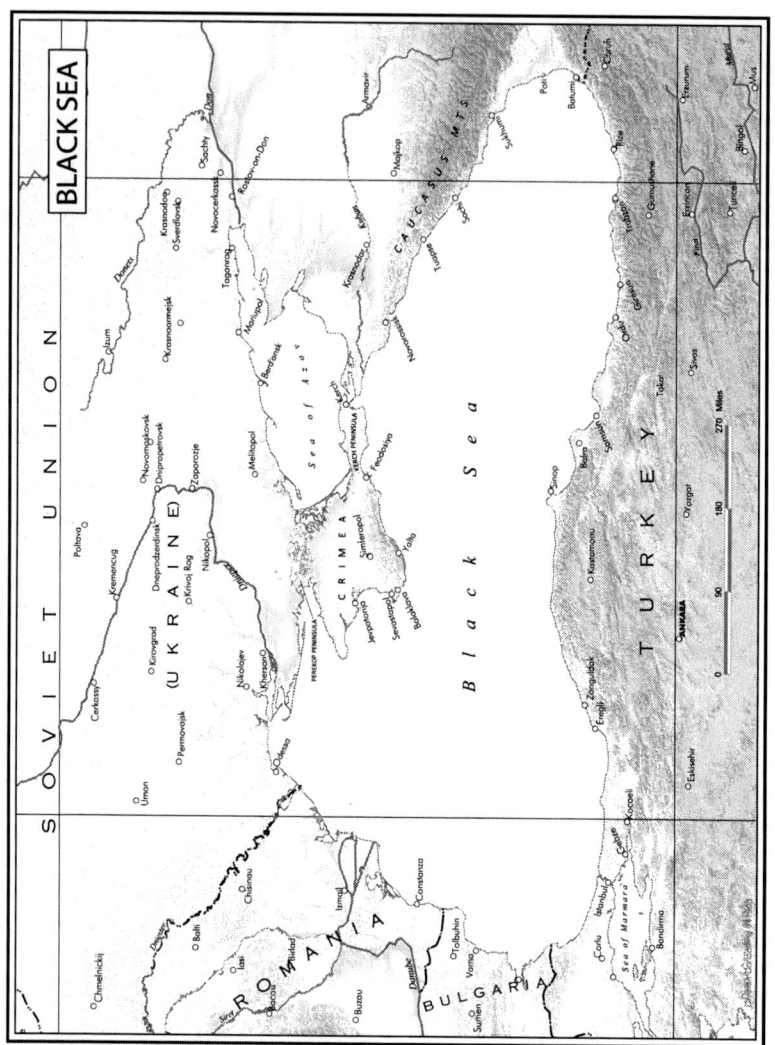

Map 4 Black Sea

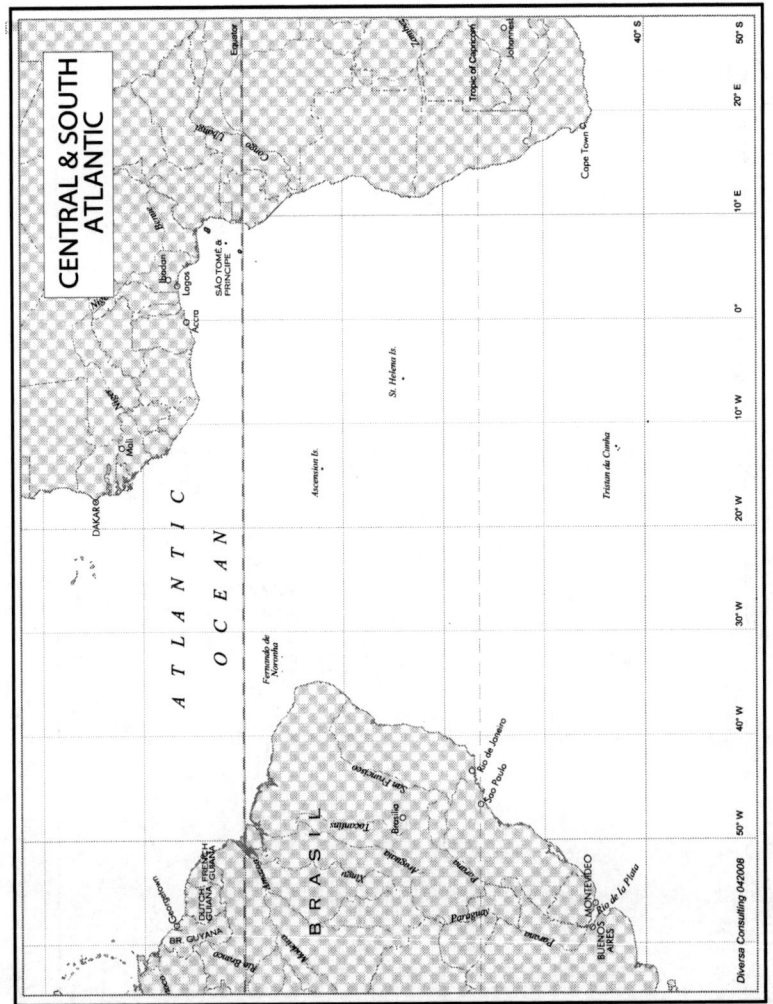

Map 5 Central and South America

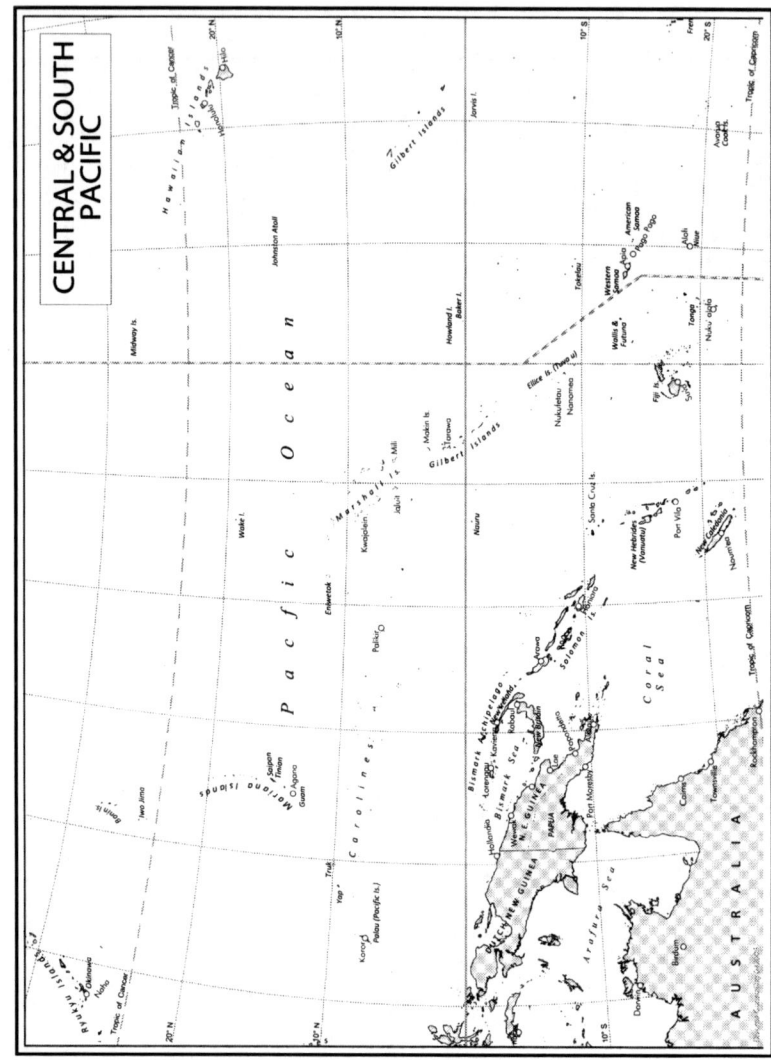

Map 6 Central and South Pacific

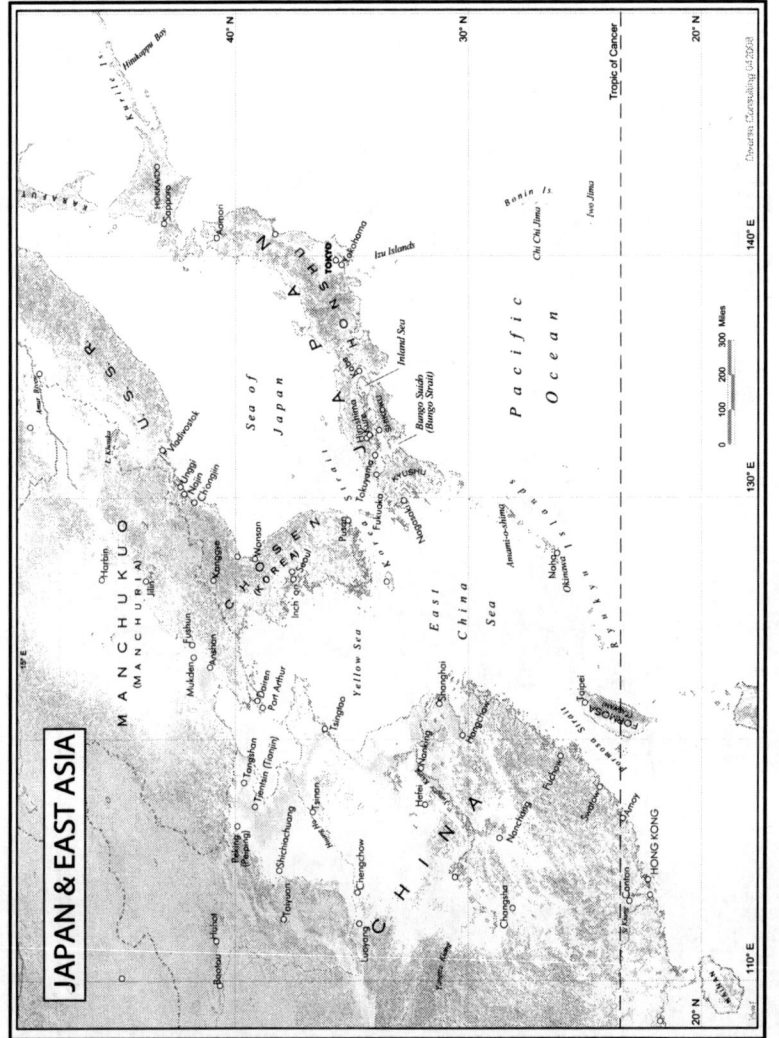

Map 7 Japan and the Ryukyu Islands

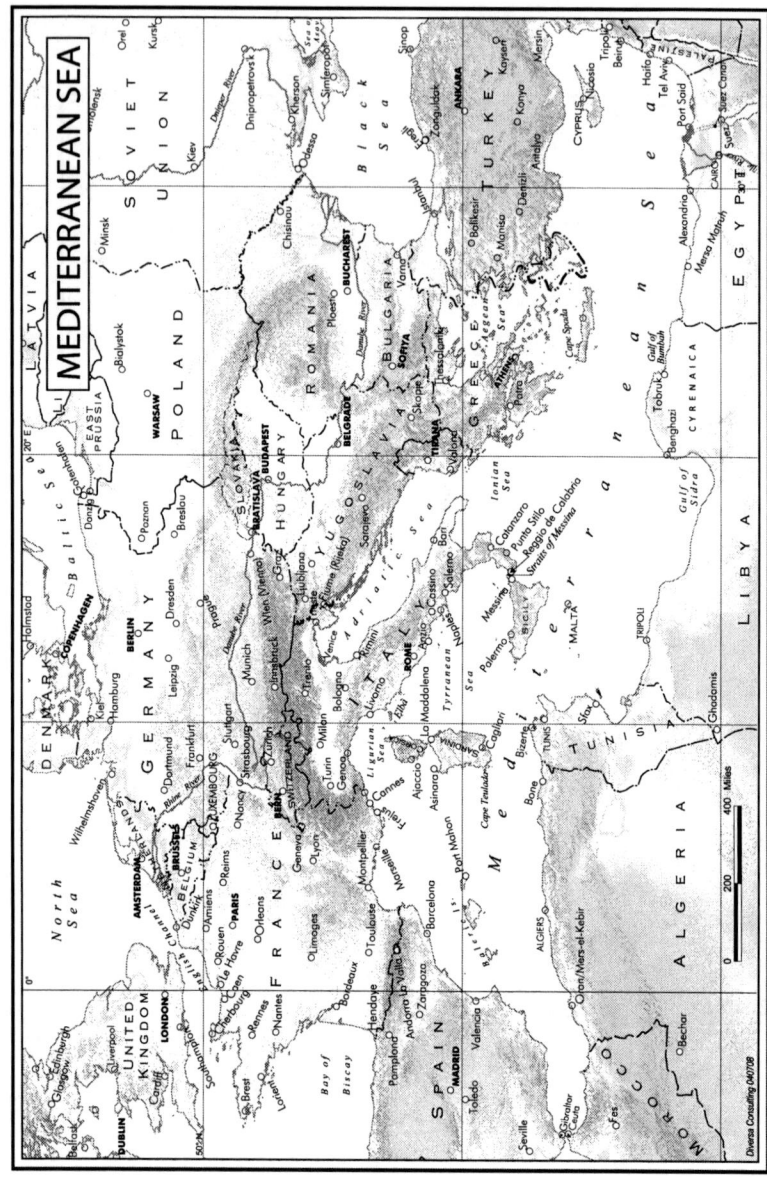

Map 8 Mediterranean

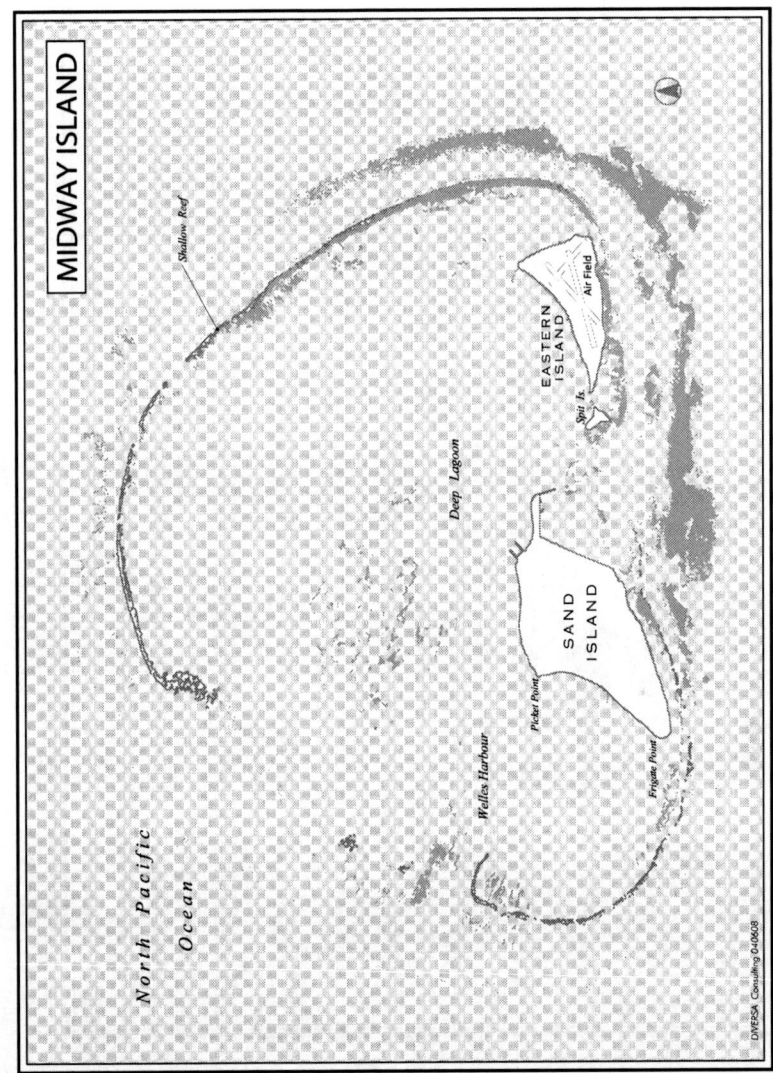

Map 9 Midway Island

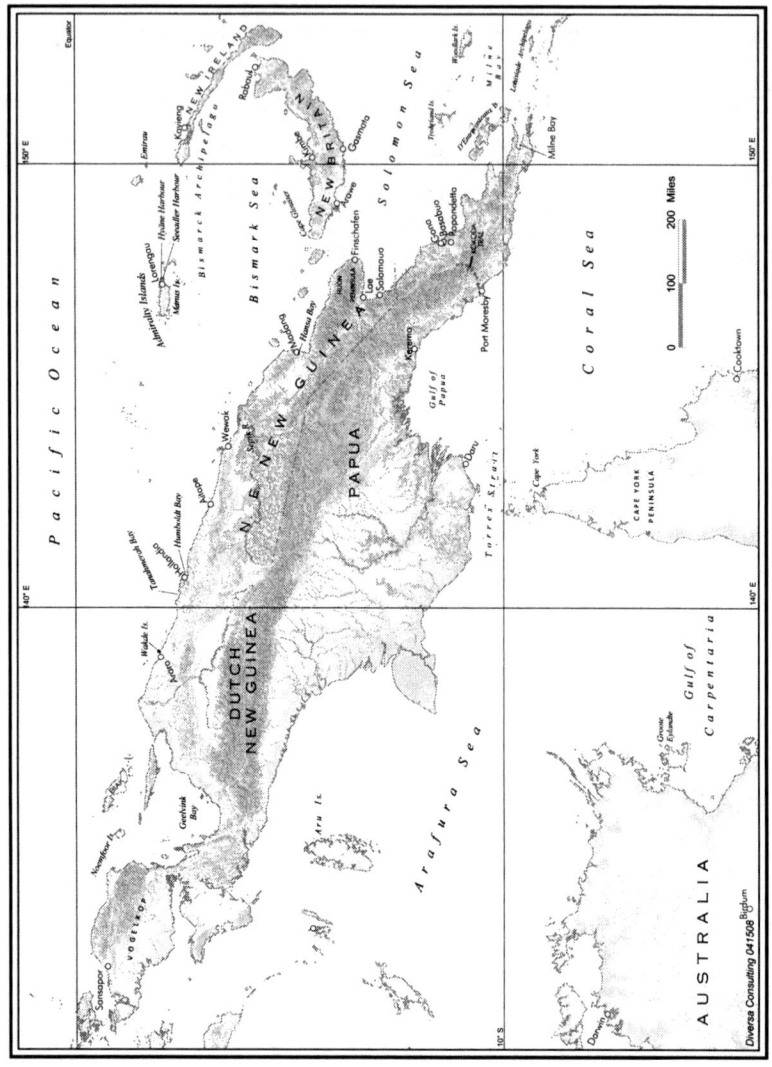

Map 10 New Guinea

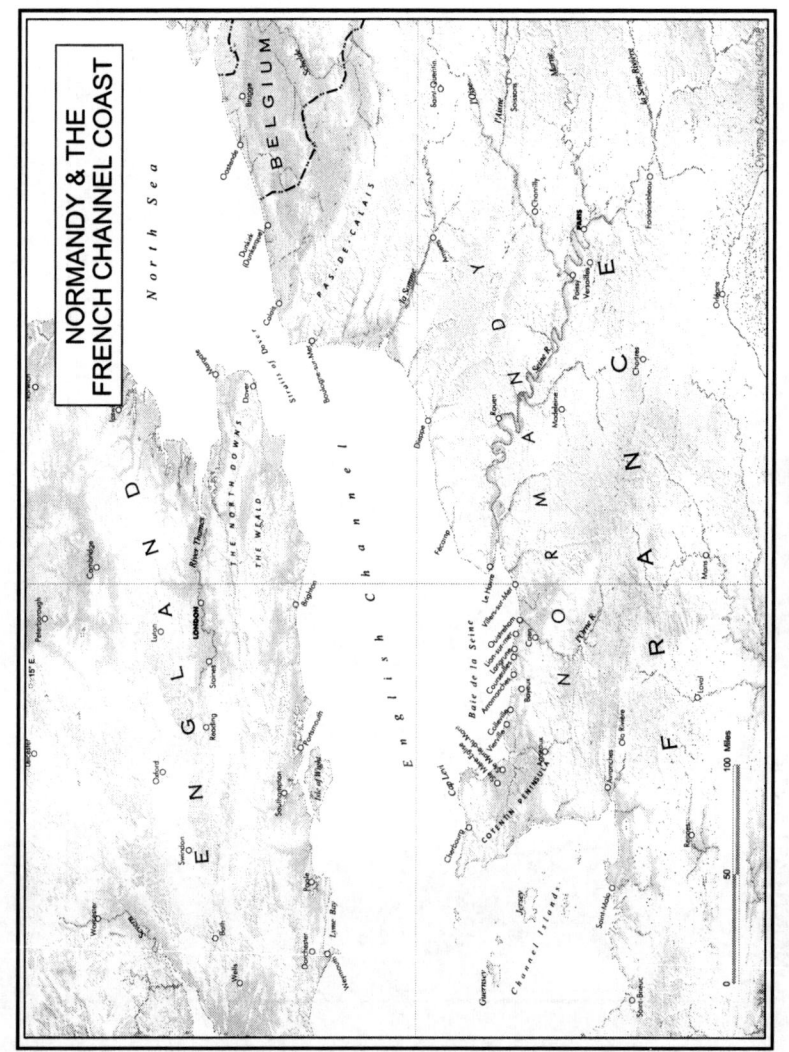

Map 11 Normandy and the French Channel coast to the Belgian border

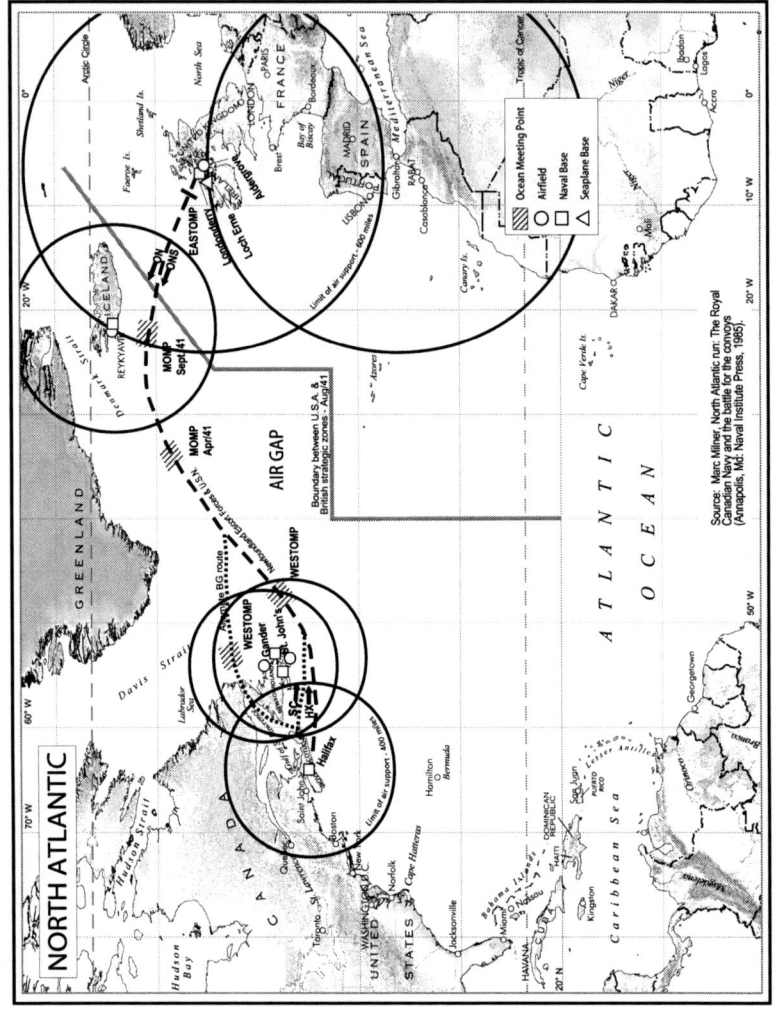

Map 12 North Atlantic

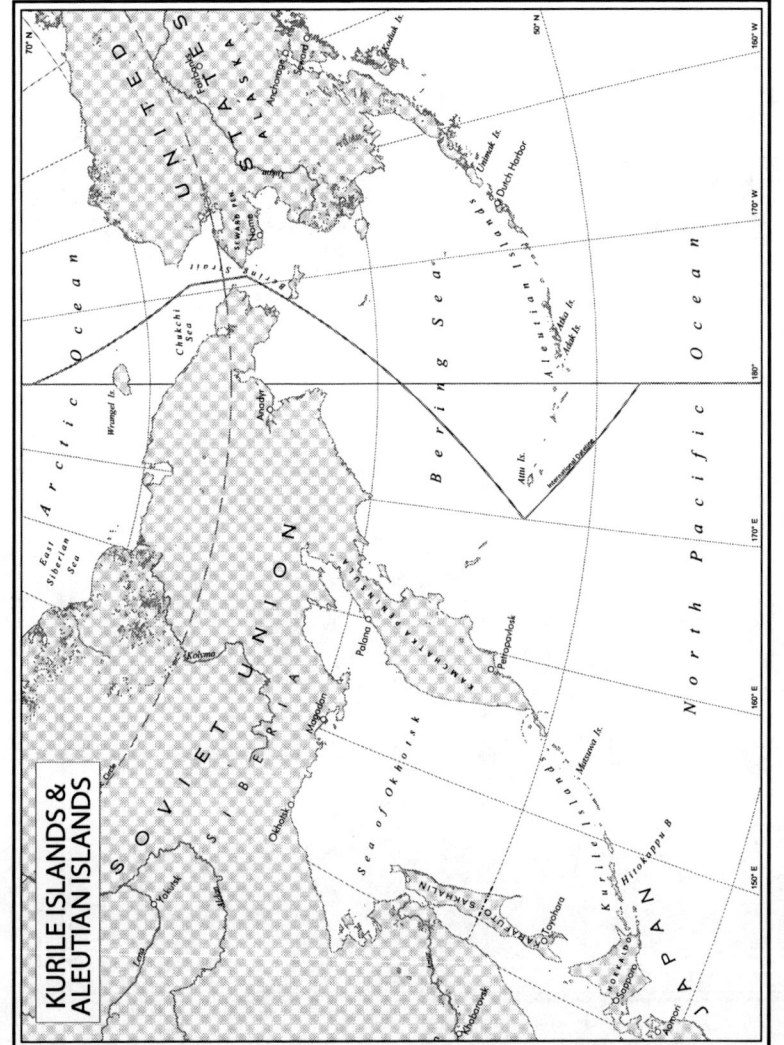

Map 13 North Pacific

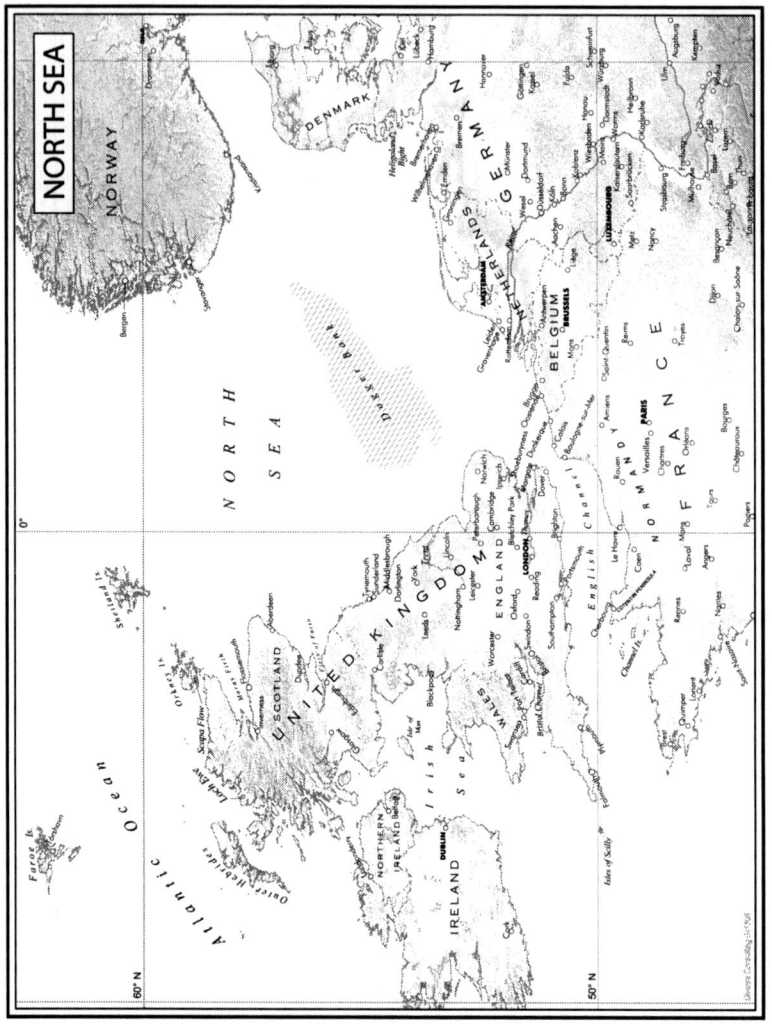

Map 14 North Sea

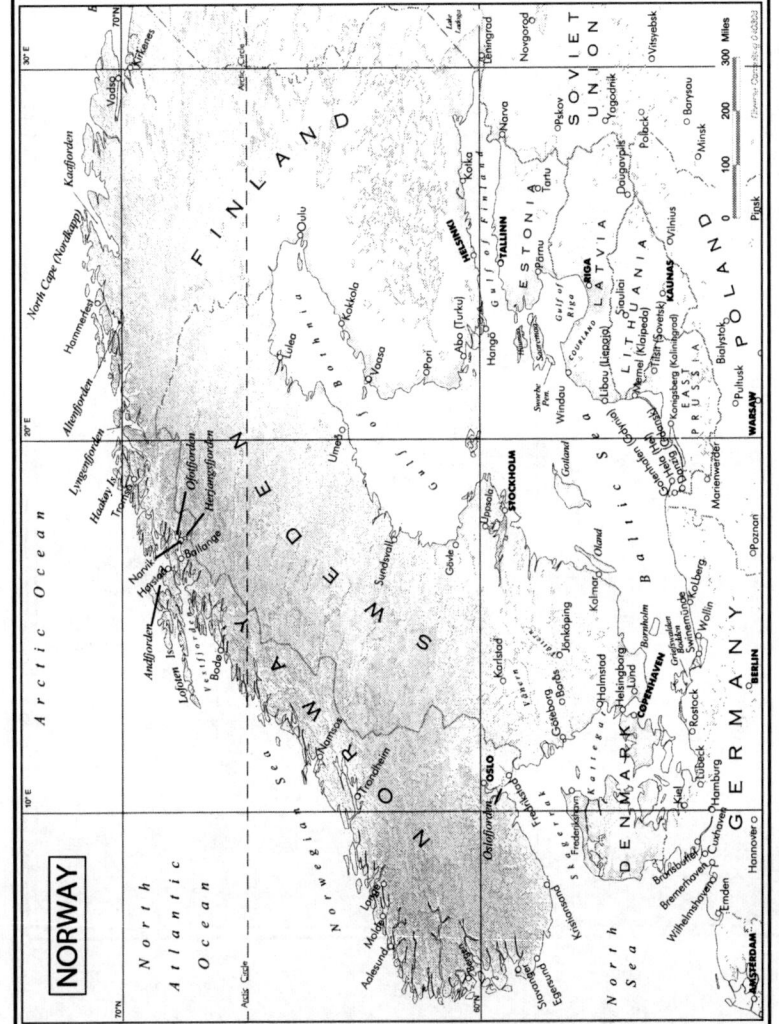

Map 15 Norway

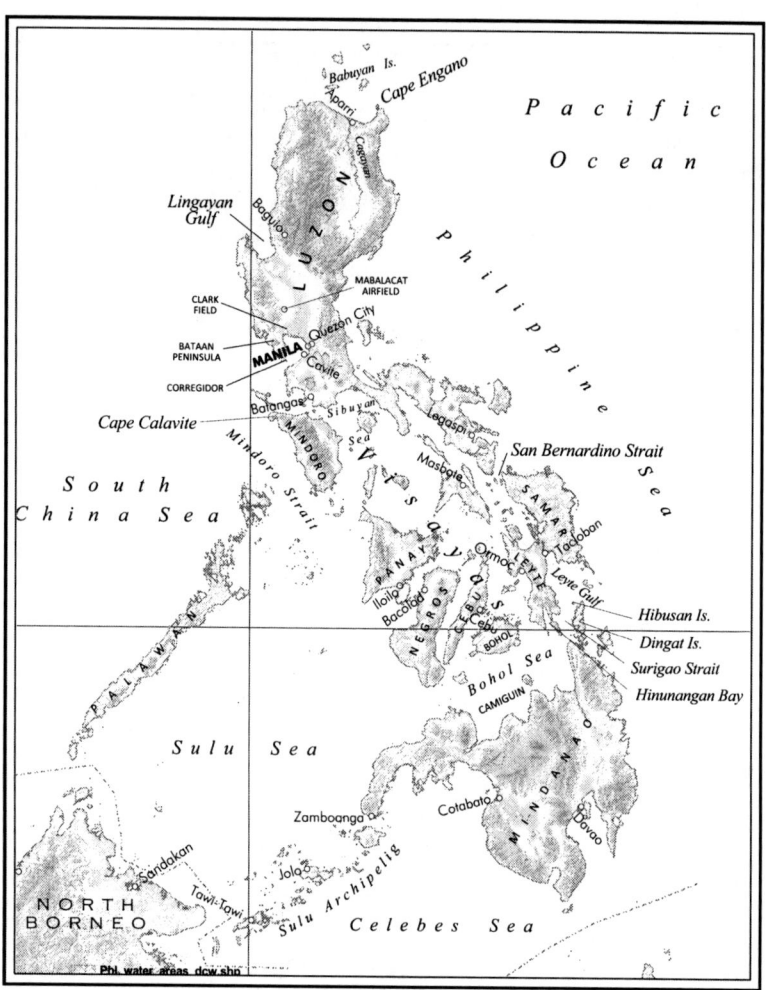

Map 16 Philippines

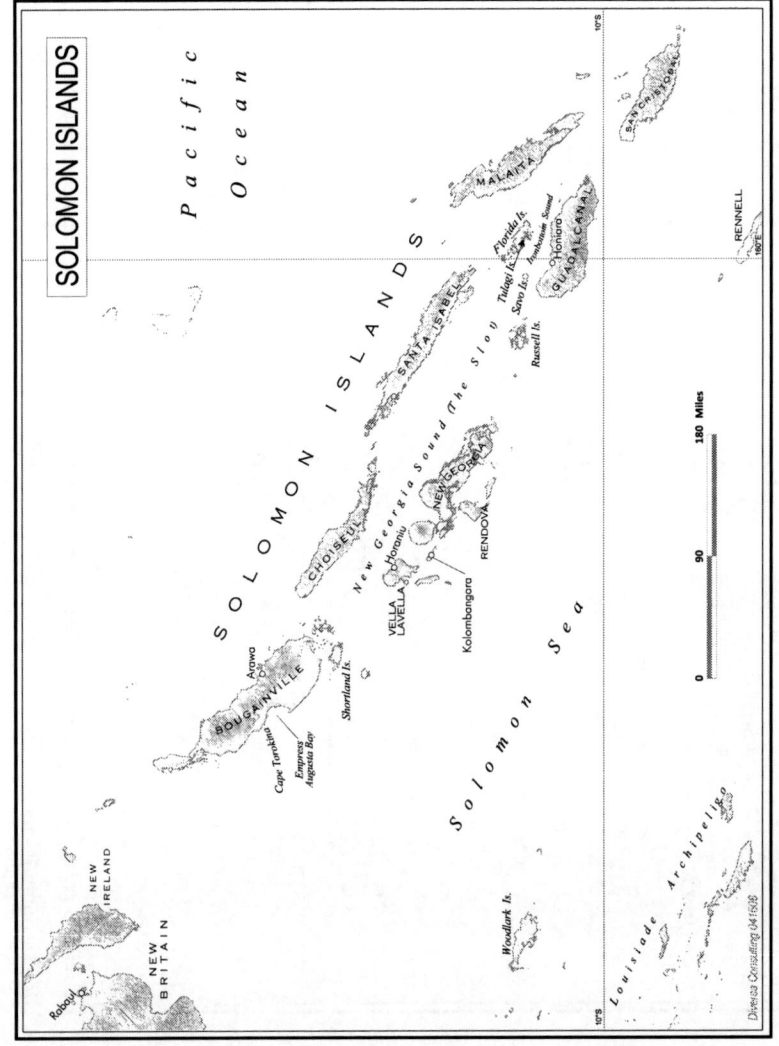

Map 17 Solomon Islands

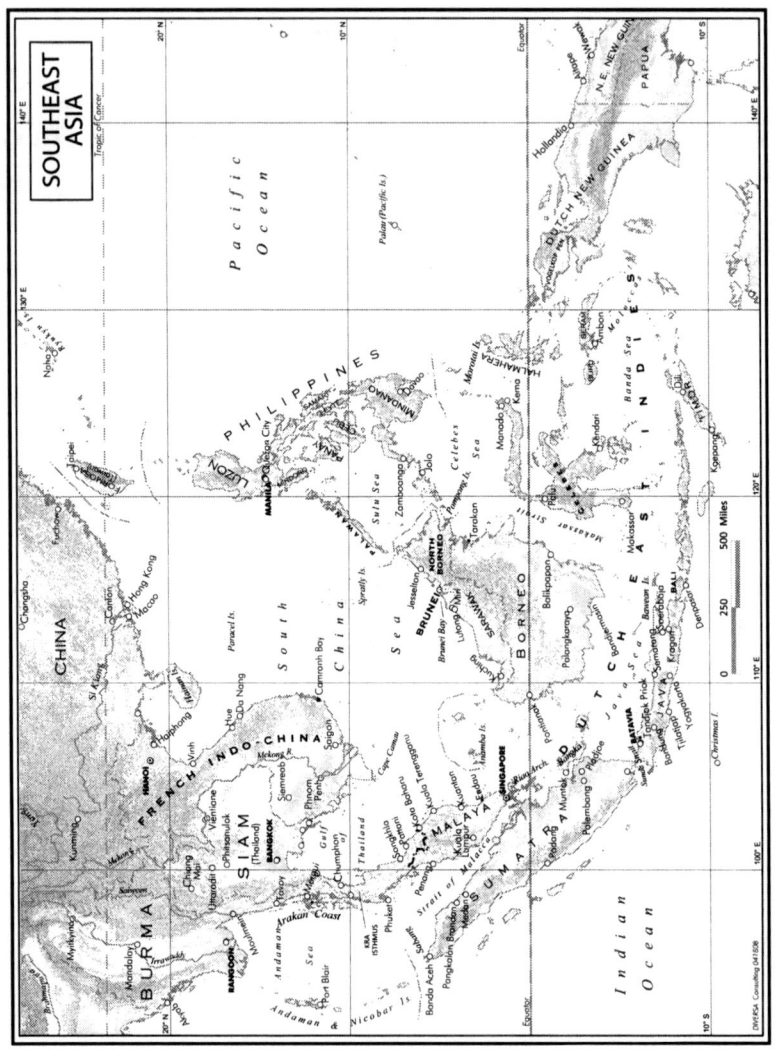

Map 18 South Pacific

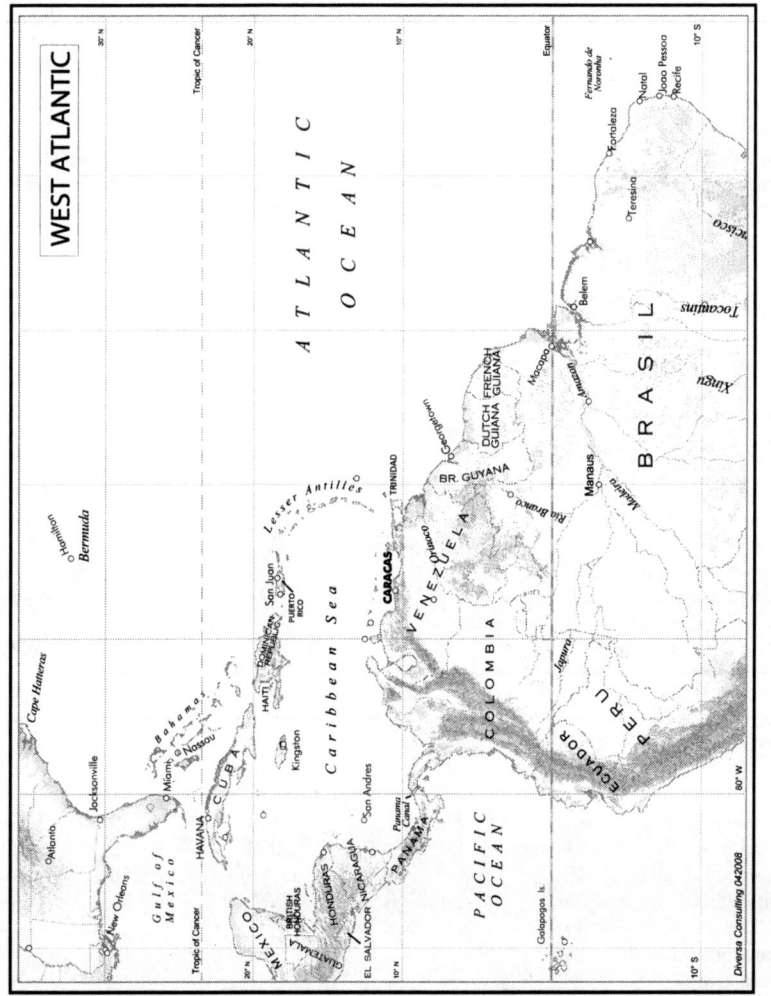

Map 19 West Atlantic

Appendix I: Allied convoy statistics

Table 1

Allied Convoy Statistics

Route	Numbers of convoys	Convoy code	Number of ships in convoy	Ships lost	% of ships lost
1939					
Halifax–UK	22	HX	431	3	0.70%
Gibraltar–UK	14	HG/XK	473	3	0.63%
Outward bound UK-US/Canada	120	OA/OB	2,516 (OA/OB+OG)	8	0.32%
Outward bound to Gibraltar	11	OG			
Sierra Leone–UK	21	SL	302	2	0.66%
Total:	**188**		**3,722**	**16**	**0.43%**
1940					
Halifax–UK	91	HX	3,424	94	2.75%
Sydney, Cape Breton/UK	16	SC	508	46	9.10%
Gibraltar–UK	61	HG	1,718	11	0.64%
Sierra Leone–UK	69	SL	1,502	22	1.46%
Outward bound UK–US/Canada	367	OA/OB	9,055	118	1.30%
Outward bound UK–Gibraltar	58	OG	2,197	9	0.41%
Total:	**662**		**18,404**	**300**	**1.63%**
1941					
Halifax–UK	70	HX	3,050	46	1.5%
Sydney, Cape Breton–UK	44	SC	1,740	70	4.0%
Sierra Leone–UK	45	SL	1,150	60	.2%
Outward bound UK–US/Canada	84 / 49	OBON	3,038 / 1,994	122 / 10	4.0% / 5.0%
Gibraltar–UK	28	HG/XK	570	31	5.4%
UK–Gibraltar	30	OG/KX	1,004	55	5.5%
Outward bound south (Sierra Leone)	14	OS	505	11	2.2%
Total:	**364**		**13,051**	**405**	**3.10%**
1942					
Halifax–UK	54	HX	1,811	17	0.94%
Sydney, Cape Breton/UK	52	SC	1,903	52	2.73%
Outward bound UK–US/Canada	106	ON	3,523	104	2.95%

Table 1 (continued)

Allied Convoy Statistics

Route	Numbers of convoys	Convoy code	Number of ships in convoy	Ships lost	% of ships lost
Sierra Leone–UK	38	SL/MKS	1,216	24	1.97%
UK–Sierra Leone	34	OS/KMS	1,379	27	1.96%
Gibraltar–UK	14	HG/XK	233	5	2.15%
UK–Gib	12	OG/KX	256	12	4.69%
UK–Med (fast)	5	KMF	112	1	0.89%
USA–Gib	2	UGS	85	0	0.00%
USA–Gib	3	UGF	59	0	0.00%
Oran–USA (fast)	3	GUF	58	0	0.00%
Total	**323**		**10,635**	**242**	**2.28%**
1943					
Halifax–UK	53	HX	2,958	41	1.39%
Sydney, Cape Breton/UK	37	SC	1,661	38	2.29%
Outward bound North	61	ON	3,012	43	1.43%
Outward bound North (slow)	24	ONS	898	19	2.12%
Sierra Leone–UK	33	SL/MKS	1,409	14	0.99%
UK–Sierra Leone	29	OS/KMS	1,545	29	1.88%
UK–Med (fast)	19	KMF	216	0	0.00%
USA–Med	27	UGS	1,603	8	0.50%
USA–Med	9	UGF	177	0	0.00%
Med–USA (slow)	28	GUS	1,231	0	0.00%
Med–USA (fast)	7	GUF	130	0	0.00%
Total	**327**		**14,840**	**192**	**1.29%**
1944					
Halifax–UK	55	HX	4,085	2	0.05%
Outward bound North	57	ON	4,023	4	0.10%
Outward bound North (slow)	13	ONS	488	0	0.00%
Sydney, Cape Breton/UK	14	SC	601	3	0.50%
Sierra Leone (SL)–UK	39	SL/MKS	1,555	2	0.13%
UK–SL	39	OS/KMS	1,351	4	0.30%
UK–Med (fast)	15	KMF	191	0	0.00%
Med–UK (fast)	16	MKF	163	0	0.00%
US–Gib (Med)	39	UGS	2,747	0	0.00%
US–Gib (Med)	10	UGF	120	0	0.00%
Med (Gib)–USA (fast)	9	GUF	124	0	0.00%
Med (Gib)–USA (slow)	38	GUS	2,352	0	0.00%
Total	**344**		**17,800**	**15**	**0.08%**

Appendix I

Table 1 (continued)

Allied Convoy Statistics

Route	Numbers of convoys	Convoy code	Number of ships in convoy	Ships lost	% of ships lost
1945 (January–June)					
Halifax/UK	32	HX	1,985	3	0.15%
Sydney, Cape Breton/UK	14	SC	393	2	0.51%
Outward bound North	34	ON	2,312	1	0.04%
Outward bound North (slow)	14	ONS	387	0	0.00%
US–Gib (Med)	32	UGS	1,443	0	0.00%
US–Gib (Med)	4	UGF	15	0	0.00%
Med (Gib)–USA	31	GUS	1,383	0	0.00%
Med (Gib)–USA	24	GUF	342	0	0.00%
Sierra Leone/ Gibraltar/UK	31	SL/MKS	733	0	0.00%
	3	HG/XK	12	0	0.00%
	31	OS/KMS	599	4	0.67%
	1	OG/KX	6	0	0.00%
	9	MKF	115	0	0.00%
	9	KMF	109	0	0.00%
Total	**269**		**9,834**	**10**	**0.10%**

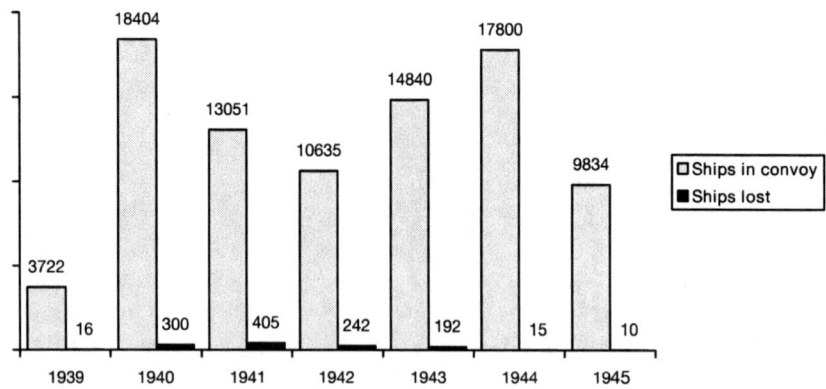

Table 2

	Convoy statistics 1939–1945 cumulative figures		
Year	Number of ships in convoys	Ships lost	% of ships lost
1939	3,722	16	0.43%
1940	18,404	300	1.63%
1941	13,051	405	3.10%
1942	10,635	242	2.28%
1943	14,840	192	1.29%
1944	17,800	15	0.08%
1945	9,834	10	0.10%
1939–1945	**88,286**	**1,180**	**1.34%**

Additional statistics

Note on the Arctic convoys (PQ and JW/QP and RA) from 1941–45

42 convoys and 1 unescorted independent operation were undertaken to North Russia (PQ and JW) involving 848 ships with 65 being lost – a loss rate of 7.66%.

36 convoys and 1 unescorted independent operation went in the opposite direction involving 735 ships with 40 being lost – a loss rate of 5.44%.

Overall, therefore, out of a total of 1,583 ships plying these hazardous routes, 105 were lost. This amounts to a loss rate of 6.63%.

Additional information on the Icelandic convoys (UR/RU) from 1941–45

167 convoys went from Loch Ewe or Belfast to Reykjavik in these years (UR) taking 1,033 ships with them. Of these only 8 were lost – a loss rate of 0.77%.

166 convoys set out in the opposite direction (RU) with 1,008 ships. Only 3 were lost – a loss rate of 0.30%.

Overall, therefore, a total of 2,041 ships were convoyed between these destinations with only 11 being lost en route – a loss rate of 0.54%.

Note on CU/UC tanker series from 1943–45

74 convoys made the crossing from Curacao/New York to the UK in these years (CU) shepherding 2,255 tankers across the Atlantic. Only 3 were lost – a loss rate of 0.13%.

103 convoys went in the opposite direction in these years. Again only 3 were lost (one of which was a straggler). Once more the loss rate was 0.13%.

Appendix II

Units of measurement: Conversion equivalents

Metric

1 mm (1/1000m)	=	0.03937 inch
1 cm (m)	=	0.39370 inch
1m	=	1.0936143 yards
1km (1,000m)	=	0.62137 mile

Imperial

1 inch	=	25.3999 millimetres (mm)
1 foot (12 inches)	=	0.30480 metre (m)
1 yard (3 feet)	=	0.914399 metre
1 mile (1,760 yards)	=	1.60934 kilometres (km)
1 nautical mile (6,076 feet)	=	1.852 km

Glossary

ACG Specialised Command Ships which were used as Headquarters Ships on amphibious operations by the Allies in the 1943–45 period

Adler Tag Opening day of the Luftwaffe offensive against the UK on 8 August 1940–the start of the 'Battle of Britain'

Afrika Korps German armoured defence force engaged in Libya under the command of Field Marshal Erwin Rommel in 1941–42

Aft The after part of a ship – the furthest from the bow

Alberich Rubber coating for U-boat hulls to deaden the metallic ping that would otherwise be picked up by enemy radar

Amidships Midway between the bow and the stern of a vessel

Amrum U-boat wolfpack named after a small German island in the North Sea

Anti-Comintern Pact A diplomatic and ideological agreement directed against the Soviet Union forged originally between Germany and Japan in November 1936 and acceded to by Italy in November 1937

Anti U-Boat Committee Allied committee that met for the first time in the autumn of 1942 and whose responsibility it was to come up with plans for dealing with the U-boat menace

Aphrodite German radar decoy balloon with anti-radar metal foil used by U-boats to confuse Allied detection methods

Arcadia Allied meeting to discuss grand strategy at Washington, D.C. in December 1941–January 1942

Argonaut Allied conference at Yalta in February 1945

Asdic A British name for the use of high frequency sound waves to detect underwater objects such as U-boats and other submersible craft. This method was known by the Americans as sonar

Astern Rear quarter of a vessel

Auxiliary Cruiser A warship that had been converted from a merchant vessel and given considerable armaments, but which retained its disguise so that it appeared as an innocent trading vessel. It was designed to wage war on all unsuspecting mercantile traffic

Avenger US carrier-based torpedo-bomber

B-17 US high-level bomber also known as a Flying Fortress

B-24 US heavy bomber also known as a Liberator

B-25 US medium-range bomber also known as a Mitchell
B-26 US torpedo-bomber also known as a Marauder
B-29 US heavy bomber also known as a Superfortress
B-Dienst Beobachtungs-Dienst or German centre for naval signals intelligence
Banburismus A highly complex procedure worked out by Alan Turing at Bletchley Park to narrow down the possibilities of which specific wheel orders might have been in place on the Enigma cipher machine at a certain time when a coded message was being sent out by the Germans
Banzai A battle cry often accompanying a headlong and reckless charge towards enemy lines by Japanese troops
Battlecruiser A slightly smaller size of warship to that of the battleship with less armour, a slightly higher maximum speed, and a longer cruising range
Battleship Heavy armoured warship with an array of the largest guns
Beaufighter An Allied long-range, multi-engine, fast night-fighter which was mass produced by the Bristol Aeroplane Company and was so effective in its role that it came to be referred to by the Japanese as 'The Whispering Death'
Betty American name for Mitsubishi G4M Japanese medium-bomber
BETASOM Italian Submarine Command
Bigram A combination of two letters
Bletchley Park British Headquarters in Buckinghamshire for the breaking of enemy codes and ciphers
Blitz All-out bombing offensive waged by the Luftwaffe against major British industrial cities and ports in the midlands and south of England
Blitzkrieg 'Lightning war' – a massive military offensive against an enemy state or formation in which all three services are utilised in an unrestrained way in order to secure a swift and overwhelming victory, e.g. the attack by Germany on Poland on 1 September 1939
Bombe Electro-mechanical machine devised by Alan Turing and Gordon Welchman which, when programmed with the information derived from a 'Crib', could begin to work out the daily Enigma settings
Bow The front end of a vessel
Brewster Buffalo Old, lumbering American fighter planes used by the Allies in the Far East
BX Designated letters for the first of the feeder convoys from New York to Halifax, Nova Scotia which began on 19 May 1942
C3 Planned Axis invasion of Malta in the spring of 1942
Caiques Small fishing vessels
Catalina Perhaps the most famous of all the flying boats in operational use during the war
Chariot A two-man human submersible shaped like a torpedo that was used by frogmen to penetrate harbour defences and mine enemy shipping
Cipher An encryption system that worked on a letter-for-letter basis as distinct from a word-for-word basis

Code An encryption system that gives all words, phrases, numbers and even punctuation marks either a multi-digit number or a string of letters that are listed in a code book. Operatives must use this code book if they are to send and receive messages correctly

Commandos Battalion strength unit of the Royal Marines trained for tough amphibious operations

Convoy A number of merchant ships grouped together in an agreed formation and escorted along the course of their journey through potentially hostile waters by a range of naval vessels, assisted as the war proceeded by aircraft for reconnaissance and search and destroy missions

Corsair Carrier-based fighter-bomber

Crib A piece of guessed plain language text that exactly matched a corresponding piece of cipher text – essential for operating in conjunction with a 'Bombe'

Crossing the T A tactical masterstroke gained in a fleet operation if one line of ships (Fleet A) can be deployed in such a way as to cross on a horizontal plane when an enemy formation (Fleet B) is in line ahead mode (or tantamount to a vertical axis in relation to Fleet A). By staging such a tactical coup the ships of Fleet A will theoretically be able to fire a sustained broadside at Fleet B whose own capability to respond will be circumscribed by its line ahead formation, thereby ensuring that the ships in the line could not bring their main armament to bear on Fleet A

Cruiser A warship designed for long-range trade protection duties

D Less complex code used by the Japanese naval authorities after they had experienced difficulties handling the much more complex *KO* code

Dan buoy A buoy with a light stave and flag that is used as a temporary mark especially in minesweeping

Dauntless American dive-bomber

Degaussing A means of reducing the magnetic field of a vessel to make it less susceptible to magnetic mines

Depth Charge Anti-submarine warfare explosive dropped or catapulted from ships in a bid to destroy them or force them to the surface. They were colloquially referred to as an 'Ashcan'

Desant Small-scale amphibious landing operations designed to have a tactical impact such as those at Termoli from 3 to 6 October 1943

Desert Rats Members of the British Eighth Army pitched against Rommel's Panzerarmee in Libya and Tunisia in 1941–42

Destroyer A high-speed, medium size warship that was designed to support amphibious forces and offer escort protection for convoy traffic

Devastator US carrier-based torpedo-bomber manufactured by Douglas and also known as a TBD

DH 98 British twin-engine, fast fighter-bomber also known as a Mosquito

Diktat A German word for a dictated order. Appalled at their country's treatment at the hands of the Allies in 1919, German nationalists applied it to the terms of the peace settlement at Versailles

DO 217 German heavy bomber/night fighter with a range of 1,300 miles (2,100 km) with a full bomb load

Dolphin Name used by the codebreakers at Bletchley Park for the German *Heimisch* Enigma code

Double Tenth Incident A round-up by the Kempetai on the tenth day of the tenth month 10 October 1943 of those POWs and civilian internees who were accused of helping the Allied saboteurs to carry out attacks on Japanese shipping in Singapore harbour 26–27 September 1943

DUKW Amphibious all-wheel-drive-vehicle with a dual rear axle mainly used for transporting supplies from ships lying offshore to storage dumps upon the beach or slightly further inshore

E-boat An English term for an enemy MTB

Elektro A more powerful U-boat, such as the Type XXI, that had treble the battery capacity of conventional U-boats in a steamlined hull allowing the U-boat to reach speeds underwater of up to 15 knots

Enigma German cipher machine used for the encrypting of secret messages

Enola Gay Name of the USAAF B-29 bomber piloted by Colonel Paul Tibbetts that dropped the first atomic bomb on Hiroshima, Japan on 6 August 1945

Eureka Allied meeting in Teheran in November–December 1943

F4F Grumman Wildcat – US carrier-based fighter-bomber

F4U-4 Vought Corsair – US carrier-based fighter-bomber which was over-engineered making it difficult to handle and maintain and much less popular than the Wildcat

F6F Grumman Hellcat – the leading US shipboard fighter aircraft in the Pacific theatre during 1944–45

Fall German word for Case or operation

FAT *Federapparat* – German search pattern running torpedo

Feldmarschall German term for Field Marshal

Fido Air-launched acoustic homing torpedo also known as the 'Mark-24 Mine'

Fireside Chat A weekly radio broadcast given by President Roosevelt during the Second World War

Flak German word for A.A. gun (*Fliegerabwehrkanonen*)

Fleet Air Arm Airborne arm of Royal Navy warships from 1937 onwards

Fliegerkorps German Air Corps

Flottenchef Fleet Commander

Flying boat A single-hull aircraft that is able to take off and land on water

Flying Squadron A small but fast and powerful unit of warships that could be sent to Singapore in an emergency instead of the Main Fleet (see Force G)

Flying Fortresses US B-17 bombers manufactured by Boeing Aircraft Corporation

Force G Deployment of small capital ship force ('flying squadron') to Singapore in October 1941 (renamed Force Z after its arrival in Southeast Asian waters in December 1941)

Force H Western half of the British Mediterranean Fleet based on Gibraltar

Force Z Formerly known as Force G and commanded by acting Admiral T.S.V. Phillips. It was destroyed off Kuantan by Japanese aircraft on the morning of 10 December 1941

Free French Supporters and forces loyal to General Charles de Gaulle and steadfastly opposed to the collaborationist Vichy regime of Marshal Pétain

Fregattenkapitän Captain (Junior)

Freighter A vessel carrying freight (cargo)

Freya German radar equipment installed along the French coastline in 1941

Führer Leader

Galvanic US invasion of the Gilbert Islands in November 1943

Geschwader Largest of the German Air Groups (It normally contained ninety aircraft in three to four air wings, or *Gruppen*, which were further sub-divided into three or four *Staffeln* – literally relay teams – or squadrons)

Gold A 9km stretch of beach between Arromanches and la Rivière which was used by the Allies as one of their five landing sectors in Normandy on 6 June 1944

glückliche Zeit 'Happy Time' – the most successful period of U-boat domination

Gooseberry Old warships that were brought close to the shore of the Normandy invasion beaches and sunk as blockships by the breakwater so that they could provide more shelter and protection for the Allied forces on the beaches themselves

Great Triangle A Japanese operational planning zone in the Southwest Pacific drawn in the shape of a triangle hauled on its side and bounded by the island of Mindanao in the southern Philippines, Palau in the western Carolines and the extreme western sector of New Guinea. It was in this area that the Japanese Gunreibu confidently expected the US armed forces would strike next against their Imperial interests in the early summer of 1944

Großadmiral Grand Admiral – equivalent in rank to Admiral of the Fleet in the Royal Navy

Gunreibu Japanese Naval General Staff

He 177 A German long-range strategic bomber that proved to be much less effective than some of the other Heinkel planes that took to the skies in World War II

H-hour When operational hostilities begin. For example, the time on D-Day when the first Allied assault wave was planned to reach the first of the five beaches at Normandy.

Hagenuk German search receiver which was fitted to U-boats from mid-summer 1943 and was designed to identify the use of Allied 10cm radar equipment

Headquarters Ship A vessel with an extensive communications facility that can help to coordinate a complex amphibious operation. A LSH (L) was often used in this capacity, e.g. *Bulolo*, *Hilary* and *Largs*, at the time of the D-Day landings in Normandy. Such was the demand for specialised command ships that a specific class for this purpose (ACGs) was commissioned in the 1943–45 period

Heavy Cruiser A warship whose guns did not exceed 8 inches (203mm)

Hedgehog An Allied mortar for use against submarines

Heimische Gewässer Enigma code for all German ships in home waters – often shortened to *Heimisch* in the 1939–41 period

Hellcat Main US carrier fighter plane for the last two years of the Pacific War. Also known as the Grumman F6F

Helldiver US carrier-based dive-bomber

Henschel Hs 293 A potentially devastating glider bomb that was carried under the wings of a Dornier 217 K3 aircraft and was designed to become the weapon of choice against Allied shipping

Huff-Duff HF/DF or High Frequency Direction-Finding; a method of determining the position of an enemy ship by monitoring its radio signal calls

Hunt Class A class of British escort destroyer of four types, capable of 27 knots

HX Fast convoy from WESTOMP to EASTOMP

Hydra Another name used by the Germans for the *Heimisch* code in 1942

Il Duce Italian word for undisputed leader – a term much beloved by Mussolini who applied it to himself

Ingolin Another name for the hydrogen peroxide fuel used in both experimental submarines and torpedoes

Iron Ring Name given to the territories of the Aegean, the Balkans and the Middle East which Hitler believed must be retained by the Germans lest the Turks yield their neutrality in favour of supporting the Allies

Island-hopping Strategy devised by and associated with Admiral Nimitz for making a swift advance across the Central Pacific towards the Japanese homeland. Not every island in a group needed to be captured as long as the main Japanese air and naval bases were put out of action.

Jake Allied codename for the Aichi E13A Japanese Navy single-engine reconnaissance seaplane

Jill Allied codename for Nakajima B6N Japanese torpedo-bomber

JN-25 Japanese Naval Operational Code

Ju-87 A feared German dive-bomber, also known as a *Stuka*, which was designed and built by the Junkers aircraft company

Ju-88 German medium range bomber that was modified to become more of a fighter than a dive-bomber

Judy Name given by the Americans to the Yokosuka D4Y Suisei Japanese dive-bomber

Juno An 11km sector of beach from Courseulles in the direction of Langrune that was used as one of the five D-Day landing zones in Normandy on 6 June 1944

Kaigunshō Japanese Navy Ministry

Kaiserliche Marine Imperial Navy – name used for the German Navy between 1871 and 1919

Kaiten Japanese manned torpedo

Kamikaze Japanese aerial suicide missions against Allied shipping in 1944–45
Kapitänleutnant Lieutenant-Commander
Kapitän zur See Captain
Kate US name for Nakajima B5N2 Japanese torpedo-bomber
KE Japanese evacuation operation from Guadalcanal in February 1943
Kempetai Feared Japanese security police (equivalent to the Gestapo) known for their ruthless and sadistic methods of torturing those who fell into their hands
Kikusui Japanese term for 'Floating Chrysanthemum' – an expression used for a series of ten Kamikaze operations in April 1945 at the time of the Allied invasion of Okinawa
KN Designated letters for convoys from Key West, Florida to Hampton Roads, Virginia beginning on 15 May 1942
KO Highly complex code used for communication between Japanese flag officers and for communication at the highest levels between Admiral Yamamoto of the Combined Fleet and Admiral Nagano, the Chief of the Naval General Staff, in Tokyo
Konteradmiral Rear-Admiral
Korvettenkapitän Commander
Kriegsmarine Name for the German Navy from 1935 to 1945
Kurier German automatic radio transmitter fitted on board the latest *schnorchel* U-boats in 1944
K-Verband Kleinkampfverband or small battle unit
Leigh Light A powerful searchlight fitted to Allied aircraft in a bid to illuminate U-boats running on the surface and assist in their ultimate destruction
Lehrgeschwade*r* Air Trainer Group
Lend-Lease US policy initiative to get around the restrictions of its neutrality legislation which became law on 11 March 1941
Liberator US heavy bomber manufactured by Consolidated and also known as a B-24
Liberty Ships Basic Allied vessels made in large numbers in the US to offset freight losses on the Atlantic trade route
Light Cruiser Shortened form of light armoured cruiser. A warship whose guns did not exceed 6.1 inches (155mm)
Linsen Explosive boats used by the Germans to attack Allied shipping in the invasion area of Normandy after D-Day
Long Lance A Japanese Type-93 torpedo. It was almost thirty feet in length (9 metres). It had a diameter of two feet and was tipped with a half-ton explosive warhead. It could reach astounding speeds of up to 49 knots because the more than three-ton torpedo was driven by a 500-h.p. engine that used liquid hydrogen peroxide rather than compressed air for its propulsion and was effective at any distance of up to 22 miles. Because it ran without a telltale wake, the Long Lance was very difficult to spot in the water as it homed in on its target

Luftwaffe   German air Force

Madcats   Catalina flying-boats that were equipped with Magnetic Anomaly detection (MAD) for ASW

MAGIC   Intelligence gained by the U.S. in the decoding of Japanese cryptosystems – the American equivalent of the results gained from the British penetration of the German codes (ULTRA)

Maiali   Translated as 'hog', it was the Italian nickname for *Siluro Lento Corso* (SLC) or slow, human submersibles. Essentially an underwater chariot which took a two-man crew, it was designed to operate in ports or harbours against shipping that were at anchor. Each *Maiali* would have a number of limpet mines that the crew members were to fix against stationary targets.

Main Fleet   Expression used in the 1920s and 1930s that meant, in effect, a substantial proportion of the principal units drawn from the Royal Navy's Home and Mediterranean Fleets that would be needed for deployment in the Far East upon the outbreak of war with Japan

Marauder   US medium torpedo-bomber manufactured by Martin and also known as a B-26

Marines   Sea-going soldier corps of the US Department of the Navy used especially for rigorous combat assignments

Metox   German R-600A electronic radar receiver which replaced the larger 'Biscay Cross' on U-boats and was able to give warning of Allied aircraft equipped with ASV on 1.5 metre band. Unfortunately, many of these devices also released radiation which meant that Allied tracking devices could detect its use and target the U-boats accordingly

Milchkühe   'Milk cows' – U-boat supply tankers

Mitchell   US medium bomber manufactured by North American Aviation and also known as a B-25

Mosquito   British twin-engine, fast fighter-bomber also known as a DH 98 and manufactured by the De Havilland Aircraft Company

MTB   Motor Torpedo Boat – these were in effect fast patrol boats with an armament that included torpedoes

Mulberry Harbours   Artificial harbours made of large concrete caissons which could be towed across the Channel and then sunk offshore to provide a sheltered anchorage for the amphibious fleet at the time of the Normandy landings

Nanshin   Southward advance

Nanshin-ron   Southward advance school of thought

Naval Cipher Number 3   Cipher used by the Admiralty for ships on the Atlantic convoy run

Naxos   U-boat radar receiver that was used to give warning of impending Allied aircraft using ASV on 10 centimetre band

Neger   A type of one-man submersible chariot

Nell   American name for G3M Japanese medium-range attack bomber superseded by the G4M medium-bomber ('Betty')

NK Designated letters for convoys from Hampton Roads, Virginia to Key West, Florida beginning on 14 May 1942

Northern Patrol An Allied cruiser patrol established between the Faeroes and Iceland at the outset of the war which was designed to interdict merchant shipping linked to Germany and carry out a search of that trade for contraband goods

Oberleutnant zur See Lieutenant (Senior)

Octagon Allied meeting between Churchill, Roosevelt and their staffs at Chateau Frontenac in Quebec (mid-September 1944) at which British naval involvement in the Pacific War was discussed and accepted (if reluctantly by Admiral King)

Offizier Most secure and complex Enigma code that was used for the relaying of very important messages between the OKM and the Kriegsmarine

Ohka Japanese manned rocket torpedoes also known by the translated name of 'cherry blossom'

Omaha A 7km sector of beach between Colleville and Vierville used by the Allies as one of the five Normandy beaches to be used on D-Day. It proved to be the most costly to subdue. More than 4,000 US troops were killed or injured on this sector alone by the close of the first day of the D-Day landings on 6 June 1944

ON Fast Allied convoys from EASTOMP to WESTOMP

ONS Slow Allied convoys from EASTOMP to WESTOMP

Op-20-G US Navy cryptographic section in Washington, D.C.

Overlord Allied invasion of northern France on 6 June 1944

Panzerarmee Rommel's armoured divisions in North Africa (1941–42)

Panzerschiff Pocket battleship

Paukenschlag Translated as 'drumbeat' – the codeword for the U-boat operation against shipping off the east coast of the USA in early 1942

Pluto A system in which fuel oil was piped across the Channel to the beachhead in Normandy for storage and use by all forms of Allied vehicular transport

Pocket battleship Also known as a *Panzerschiff*. Germany had three of these warships at the outset of hostilities in 1939 (*Admiral Graf Spee*, *Admiral Scheer* and *Deutschland*). These were warships whose guns did not exceed 11 inches (280mm). After the loss of the *Graf Spee* in December 1939, the two remaining ships of this class were reclassified in February 1940 as heavy cruisers and the name of the *Deutschland* was changed to *Lützow*

Port The area to the left side of the bows when one is on board a vessel and facing her bows

Prize Regulations Rules on the capturing and retention of vessels in wartime.

Purple Japanese Type B cryptograph

Q-ship A warship disguised as a merchant vessel for the purposes of attracting the attention of an unsuspecting enemy submarine and drawing her close enough so that she could be destroyed by the hidden guns of the Q-ship. President Roosevelt was keen to use these decoy ships in 1942

Quadrant Allied conference held at the Citadel in Quebec in August 1943

Rs Often dubbed the four Rs – the four battleships of the Royal Sovereign class that remained in commission after the sinking of the *Royal Oak* on 14 October 1939. Churchill was to describe them unflatteringly as the four coffins because of their obsolescence

Radar 'Radio Direction and Range' – US Navy term which became universally adopted replacing the old British term R.D.F. (Radio Direction Finding)

Red Banner Fleet Soviet Baltic Fleet

Reichsmarine Name given to the German Navy between 1920 and 1925 (Reich is translated as empire)

Riviera Codename for the meeting between Churchill and Roosevelt in Argentia Bay, Newfoundland from 9–12 August 1941

RO A less complex Japanese naval code that handled a significant amount of signals traffic and was broken by the US codebreakers

Roto-bomb ASV bomb that was fired backwards from a MAD-equipped plane

Rudeltaktik Coordinated tactics used by a group of U-boats (wolf pack) against enemy shipping

S79 Italian Savoia torpedo-bomber

Salvo A group of shots fired simultaneously, even though technically it refers to a group of shots that are spread over different ranges in a bid to find the correct range for a target

SB2C Curtiss Helldiver – US carrier-based dive bomber

SC Slow Allied convoys from WESTOMP to EASTOMP

Schnellboot *S-Boot* literally a fast boat and another name for an MTB

Schnorchel A device that when fitted to a U-boat allowed it to take in air for its diesel engines through a tube while it remained submerged. Sometimes spelt in English as *Snorkel* or even *Schnorkel*

Schuyts A small Dutch sloop

Seaslug One of RAF Coastal Command's operational search areas for U-boats in the Bay of Biscay from June 1943

Second Front An expression used by the Allies between 1942 and 1944 to denote an invasion of continental Europe in such strength as to draw off a large body of German troops from the Eastern Front

Seekriegsleitung Naval War Staff (successor to Allgemeines Marineamt – General Naval Office from October to November 1939)

Seelöwe *Sealion* was the operational codename for the aborted invasion of the UK

Seetakt A German surface-search radar that first entered service on board the *Admiral Graf Spee* in 1938

Sextant Allied meeting between Churchill, Chiang Kai-shek and Roosevelt in Cairo in November 1943

SG American surface approach radar

Shark Another name for the 'Triton' Enigma code that was used for messages to and from Atlantic-based U-boats. This code caused real problems for the Bletchley Park codebreakers because the Germans had added an extra wheel and reflector to their cipher machine making the enhanced code immensely difficult to solve.

Shō Literally translated as 'victory' – the name of several Japanese operational plans for the coming decisive battle in 1944

Show the flag Public relations exercise in which a warship or a larger grouping of such vessels would visit a foreign port

SIGINT Signals Intelligence

Singapore Strategy British strategic plan devised in the 1920s to deploy the Main Fleet (see above) to Singapore in the event of war with Japan

SK American 1.5m shipboard radar set that was effective at locating enemy aircraft at ranges of up to 161km

Snowflake A pyrotechnical means of illuminating an area at sea after nightfall

Sonar An American name for sound navigation and ranging – the detection of underwater objects by sound waves (also known as Asdic)

Sperrbrecher Literally a 'barrier breaker' – a vessel such as an auxiliary minesweeper

Squid ASV mortar that proved to be very effective from 1944 onwards in the North Atlantic

Starboard Opposite to port side – the area to the right of the bows when one is on board a vessel and facing her bows

Steamer Usually derogatory name for old, steam-powered vessels that were assigned to carrying freight (cargo)

Stern Rear-end of a vessel

Straddle When shots straddle a target they describe a salvo of shells that have the correct range and narrowly miss a target

Stuka A term referring to more than one type of German dive-bomber, even though it became most particularly associated with the Ju-87 in the early phase of the war. *Stuka* is short for *Sturzkampfflugzeug*

Superfortress US heavy bomber manufactured by Boeing and also known as a B-29

Supermarina Italian Naval Staff

Support Groups A number of warships including an escort carrier that were organised as an operational unit to support other forces, such as convoy escort groups. Owing to their reliance upon aircraft and sophisticated radar these became very effective ASW units

Sword A 9km sector of beach that encompassed Lion-sur-mer and Ouistreham in Normandy which was to be used as one of the five open beaches in the D-Day assault on 6 June 1944

Symbol Codename for Allied meeting at Casablanca in January 1943

T3d German electric-powered torpedo – also known as a *Dackel* (*Dachshund*) – that had a very long range of 57km at the slow speed of 9 knots and was intended for use in harbours or bays

T5 German electric powered acoustic torpedo – also known as a *Zaunkönig* (Wren) or GNAT – which had a range of 5.7km and a speed of 24 knots and was intended for use against convoy escorts

Taishō   A brief period of democratic rule in Japan lasting from 1912 to 1926

Tallboy   A massive bomb weighing 12,030 pounds designed by Barnes Wallis to be dropped from high altitude and reach the speed of sound and explode with great venom upon impact

TBF-1   Grumman Avenger – US carrier-based torpedo bomber

The Spout   A passage route through the extensive German minefield off the coast of Normandy that had been swept by Allied minesweepers, one channel of which was used by fast and the other by slow Allied transports on D-Day and the early days of the *Neptune/Overlord* amphibious operation in June 1944

Tokyo Express   Japanese supply runs from Rabaul and Shortland to Guadalcanal in the autumn of 1942

Torpedo Boats   Light craft used for carrying torpedoes to attack larger warships

Tramp Steamer   An old merchant vessel without any fixed route, timetable, or cargo.

Trident   Allied meeting at Washington (May 1943)

Triton   Also known by the Bletchley Park codebreakers as 'Shark' – this was an improved Enigma code for use by Atlantic-based U-boats only. It was much more difficult to read because the Germans had added a new wheel and reflector to their cipher machine

Typex   British cipher machine – the equivalent of the German Enigma

Typhoon   British fast ground attack aircraft built and developed by the Hawker Siddeley Aircraft Company

ULTRA   Intelligence gained from the breaking of German Enigma codes

Unterseeboot   U-boat

Utah   A 5km stretch of beach on the southeast coast of the Cotentin Peninsula near La Madaleine which was used as one of the five landing sectors of the D-Day offensive on 6 June 1944

Val   US name for Aichi D3A2 Japanese dive-bomber

Vichy   The spa town in France that was the base for Marshal Pétain's collaborationist regime after the fall of France in June 1940. Hence the term Vichy French meant those forces supporting the veteran 'hero of Verdun'

Vizeadmiral   Vice-Admiral

W.Anz   German U-boat search receiver for detecting Allied use of 10cm radar

Weather Ship   German ocean-going vessel equipped to make meteorological observations and report on enemy movements at sea

Wehrmacht   German Armed Forces

Westerplatte   Peninsula located in the Danzig (Gdansk) harbour channel in an estuary of the so-called Dead Vistula which was fortified by the Poles and stoutly defended by them in the early days of the war

Wildcat   US carrier-based fighter plane

Wolf pack   Colloquial name for a group of U-boats that worked together to attack a victim on the high seas

Würzburg   German paraboloid radar set that worked on wavelengths of roughly 53cm

X craft   Allied midget submarines

X-Day   First day of Japanese counter-attack in the Battle of Leyte Gulf (25 October 1944)

Z Plan   German projected naval construction programme covering the years 1939–45 which was suspended once WWII began

Zaunkönig   Wren – a German acoustic homing torpedo

Zeke   US name for Mitsubishi A6M2 Zero-sen fighter aircraft also known as the Zero

Select Bibliography

Abbreviations:

AL	-	Alabama
Berks	-	Berkshire
Ca	-	California
Col	-	Colorado
Conn	-	Connecticut
CUP	-	Cambridge University Press
D.C.	-	District of Columbia
Glos	-	Gloucestershire
Hants	-	Hampshire
HMSO	-	Her Majesty's Stationery Office
Ill	-	Illinois
Ind	-	Indiana
Ks	-	Kansas
Ky	-	Kentucky
Mass	-	Massachusetts
Md	-	Maryland
Mi	-	Michigan
Mn	-	Minnesota
NAL	-	New American Library
N.C.	-	North Carolina
NIP	-	Naval Institute Press
N.J.	-	New Jersey
NSW	-	New South Wales
NY	-	New York
N.Z.	-	New Zealand
Ok	-	Oklahoma
ODNB	-	*Oxford Dictionary of National Biography*
Ont	-	Ontario
OUP	-	Oxford University Press
Oxon	-	Oxfordshire
Pa	-	Pennsylvania
S.C.	-	South Carolina
Tx	-	Texas
US	-	United States
Wilts	-	Wiltshire

Select bibliography 549

Patrick Abbazia. *Mr. Roosevelt's Navy: the private war of the U.S. Atlantic Fleet, 1939–1942*. Annapolis, Md: NIP, 1975.

V.I. Achkasov and N.B. Pavlovich. *Soviet naval operations in the Great Patriotic War 1941–1945*. Annapolis, Md: NIP, 1981.

Jack Adams. *The doomed expedition: the Norwegian campaign of 1940*. London: Leo Cooper, 1989.

John A. Adams. *If Mahan ran the great Pacific War: an analysis of World War II naval strategy*. Bloomington, Ind: Indiana University Press, 2008.

Anthony Adamthwaite. 'French military intelligence and the coming of war 1935–39', in Christopher Andrew and Jeremy Noakes (eds), *Intelligence and international relations 1900–1945*. Exeter: Exeter University Publications, 1987.

Admiralty: Historical Section. *The Royal Navy and the Mediterranean convoys: a naval staff history*. London: Routledge, 2007.

Elena Agarossi. *A nation collapses: the Italian surrender of September 1943*. Cambridge: CUP, 2000.

Hiroyuki Agawa. *The reluctant admiral: Yamamoto and the imperial navy*. Tokyo: Kodansha International, 1979.

Parker Bishop Albee, Jr., and Keller Cushing Freeman. *Shadow of Suribachi: raising the flags on Iwo Jima*. Westport, Conn: Praeger, 1995.

Richard J. Aldrich. *Intelligence and the war against Japan: Britain, America and the politics of secret service*. Cambridge: CUP, 2000.

——. *The key to the south: Britain, the United States, and Thailand during the approach of the Pacific War, 1929–1942*. Oxford: OUP, 1993.

Joseph H. Alexander. *Storm landings: epic amphibious battles in the Central Pacific*. Annapolis, Md: NIP, and Shrewsbury: Airlife, 1997.

——. *Utmost savagery: the three days of Tarawa*. Annapolis, Md: NIP, 1995.

Jim Allaway. *Hero of the Upholder: the story of Lieutenant Commander M.D. Wanklyn VC, DSO**. Shrewsbury: Airlife, 1991.

Louis Allen. 'The nuclear raids: August 1945 Hiroshima and Nagasaki', in Basil Liddell Hart (ed.), *History of the Second World War*. London: Phoebus, 1980.

Thomas B. Allen and Norman Polmar. *Code-name Downfall: the secret plan to invade Japan – and why Truman dropped the bomb*. New York: Simon & Schuster, 1995.

Brian Altobello. *Into the shadows furious: the brutal battle for New Georgia*. Novato, Ca: Presidio, 2000.

Charles R. Anderson. *Day of lightning, years of scorn: Walter C. Short and the attack on Pearl Harbor*. Annapolis, Md: NIP, 2005.

Christopher Andrew. *For the president's eyes only: secret intelligence and the American presidency from Washington to Bush*. New York: HarperCollins, 1995.

——. *Her Majesty's secret service: the making of the British intelligence community*. New York: Viking, 1986.

Christopher Andrew and David Dilks (eds). *The missing dimension: government and intelligence communities in the twentieth century*. Basingstoke: Macmillan, 1985.

Marc de Angelis. 'Operation "Gaudo" and the Battle of Matapan', Accessed from www.regiamarina.net/battles/matapan/part2_us.htm (15 March 2006).

Greg Annussek. *Hitler's raid to save Mussolini: the most infamous commando operation of World War II*. Cambridge, Mass: Da Capo Press, 2005.

Walter Ansel. *Hitler and the middle sea*. Durham, N.C.: Duke University Press, 1972.

Peter D. Antill. *Crete 1941: Germany's lightning airborne assault*. Oxford: Osprey, 2005.

Sadao Asada. 'From Washington to London: the Imperial Japanese Navy and the politics of naval limitation, 1921–30', in Eric Goldstein and John Maurer (eds), *The Washington Conference, 1921–22: naval rivalry, East Asian stability and the road to Pearl Harbor*. London: Frank Cass, 1994.

Gunnar Åselius. *The rise and fall of the Soviet Navy in the Baltic, 1921–1941*. London: Frank Cass, 2005.
John Asmussen. 'Operation Catechism: 12 November 1944', at www.bismarck-class.dk/tirpitz/history/tiropertungsten.html (accessed 1 April 2006).
——. 'Operation Cerberus (11–13 February 1942)' at www.scharnhorst-class.dk/scharnhorst/history/scharncerberus.html (accessed 10 Mar. 2008).
Gerald Astor. *Operation Iceberg: the invasion and conquest of Okinawa in World War II – an oral history*. New York: Donald I. Fine, 1995.
——. *The greatest war: Americans in combat 1941–1945*. Novato, Ca: Presidio, 1999.
Ronald Atkin. *Dieppe 1942: the Jubilee disaster*. London: Macmillan, 1980.
Paul Auphan and Jacques Mordal. *The French Navy in World War II*. Westport, Conn: Greenwood Press, 1976.
Douglas Austin. *Malta and British strategic policy, 1925–43*. London: Frank Cass, 2004.
Albert Axell and Hideaki Kase. *Kamikaze: Japan's suicide gods*. London: Longman, 2002.
Jean-Pierre Azema. *1940, l'année terrible*. Paris: Seuil, 1990.
George W. Baer. *One hundred years of sea power: the US Navy, 1890–1990*. Stanford, Ca: Stanford University Press, 1994.
Thomas A. Bailey and Paul B. Ryan. *Hitler vs Roosevelt: the undeclared naval war*. New York: The Free Press, 1979.
Clive Baker and Greg Knight. *Milne Bay 1942: the story of 'Milne-Force'*. Fourth Edition. Loftus, NSW: Australian Military History Publications, 2000.
Joseph Balkoski. *Utah beach*. Mechanicsburg, Pa: Stackpole Books, 2005.
Iain Ballantyne. *Killing the Bismarck: destroying the pride of Hitler's fleet*. Barnsley: Pen & Sword Maritime, 2010.
James Bamford. *The puzzle palace*. New York: Penguin, 1983.
Arthur Banks. *Wings of the dawning: the battle for the Indian Ocean 1939–1945*. Malvern Wells, Worcs: Images Publishing, 1996.
Laurie Barber and Ken Henshall. *The last war of empires: Japan and the Pacific War 1941–1945*. Auckland, N.Z.: David Bateman, 1999.
Daniel E. Barbey. *MacArthur's amphibious navy*. Annapolis, Md: United States NIP, 1969.
Jeffrey G. Barlow. 'Admiral Richard L. Conolly', in Stephen Howarth (ed.), *Men of war: great naval captains of World War II*. New York: St. Martin's Press, 1993.
J. Valerio Barghese. *Sea devils: Italian Navy commanders in World War II*. Annapolis, Md: NIP, 1995.
Frank Barnaby. 'The effects of the atomic bombings of Hiroshima and Nagasaki', in Douglas Holdstock and Frank Barnaby, (eds), *Hiroshima and Nagasaki: retrospect and prospect*. London: Frank Cass, 1995.
Correlli Barnett. *Engage the enemy more closely: the Royal Navy in the Second World War*. London: W.W. Norton, 1991.
Merrill L. Bartlett (ed.). *Assault from the sea*. Annapolis, Md: NIP, 1983.
William H. Bartsch. 'Operation *Dovetail*: bungled Guadalcanal rehearsal, July 1942', *The Journal of Military History*, Vol.66, No.2 (2002): 443–76.
Alan Harris Bath. *Tracking the Axis enemy: the triumph of Anglo-American naval intelligence*. Lawrence, Ks: University Press of Kansas, 1998.
W.G. Beasley. *The rise of modern Japan: political, economic and social change since 1850*. London: Weidenfeld & Nicolson, 1995.
Allan Beckman. 'Taranto: catalyst of the Pearl Harbor attack', *Military Review*, Vol.LXXI, No.11 (Nov.1991): 73–78.
Patrick Beesly. 'Convoy PQ 17: a study of intelligence and decision-making', in Michael I. Handel (ed.), *Intelligence and military operations*. London: Frank Cass, 1990.

——. *Room 40: British naval intelligence 1914–18*. London: Hamish Hamilton, 1982.
——. *Very special intelligence: the story of the Admiralty's Operational Intelligence Centre, 1939–1945*. London: Sphere, 1980.
Antony Beevor. *The battle for Spain: The Spanish Civil War 1936–1939*. London: Weidenfeld & Nicolson, 2006.
——. *Crete: the battle and the resistance*. London: John Murray, 1991.
Edward Behr. *Hirohito: behind the myth*. New York: Vintage Books, 1990.
C.D. Bekker. *K-men: the story of the German frogmen and midget submarines*. Maidstone, Kent: George Mann, 1973.
Christopher M. Bell. 'The "Singapore strategy" and the deterrence of Japan: Winston Churchill, the Admiralty and the dispatch of Force Z', *The English Historical Review*, Vol. CXVI, No. 467 (2001): 604–34.
——. *The Royal Navy, seapower and strategy between the wars*. Stanford, Ca: Stanford University Press, 2000.
James H. and William M. Belote. *Titans of the seas: the development and operations of Japanese and American carrier task forces during World War II*. New York: Harper & Row, 1975.
Tito Benady. *The Royal Navy at Gibraltar*. Grendon, Northants: Gibraltar Books, 1993.
Geoffrey Bennett. *Naval battles of World War II*. London: Batsford, 1975.
Ralph Bennett. *Ultra and Mediterranean strategy*. New York: William Morrow, 1989.
David J. Bercuson and Holger H. Herwig, *Bismarck: the story behind the destruction of the pride of Hitler's navy*. London: Pimlico, 2003.
Meredith W. Berg. 'Protecting national interests by treaty: the second London Naval Conference, 1934–36', in B.J.C. McKercher (ed.), *Arms limitation and disarmament: restraints in war, 1899–1939*. Westport, Conn: Preager, 1992.
David Bergamini. *Japan's imperial conspiracy: how Emperor Hirohito led Japan into war against the West*. London: Heinemann, 1971.
Eric M. Bergerud. *Fire in the sky: the air war in the South Pacific*. Boulder, Col: Westview Press, 2000.
Marc D. Bernstein. 'He predicted Leyte Gulf', *Naval History*, Vol.15, No.5 (2001): 26–29.
Simon Berthon and Joanna Potts. *Warlords: the heart of conflict 1939–1945*. London: Politico's Publishing, 2005.
Michael Bess. *Choices under fire: moral dimensions of World War II*. New York: Alfred A. Knopf, 2006.
Antony Best. *British intelligence and the Japanese challenge in Asia, 1914–1941*. Basingstoke: Palgrave Macmillan, 2002.
——. '"This probably over-valued military power": British intelligence and Whitehall's perception of Japan, 1939–41', *Intelligence and National Security*, Vol.12, No.3 (July 1997): 67–94.
——. *Britain, Japan and Pearl Harbor: avoiding war in East Asia, 1936–41*. London: Routledge, 1995.
Richard K. Betts and Thomas G. Mahnken. *Paradoxes of strategic intelligence: essays in honor of Michael I. Handel*. London: Frank Cass, 2003.
Kenneth M. Beyer. *Q-ships versus U-boats: America's secret project*. Annapolis, Md: NIP, 1999.
Alan Beyerchen. 'From radio to radar: interwar military adaptation to technological change in Germany, the United Kingdom, and the United States', in Williamson Murray and Alan R. Millett (eds), *Military innovation in the interwar period*. Cambridge: CUP, 1998.
Hugh Bicheno. *Midway*. London: Cassell Military, 2001.
Craig Bickell. 'Operation *Fortitude South*: an analysis of its influence upon German dispositions and conduct of operations in 1944', *War & Society*, Vol.18, No.1 (2000): 91–121.

Kai Bird and Lawrence Lifschultz (eds). *Hiroshima's shadow*. Stony Creek, Conn: The Pamphleteers Press, 1998.

Keith W. Bird. *Erich Raeder: Admiral of the Third Reich*. Annapolis, Md: NIP, 2006.

——. 'Grand Admiral Erich Raeder', in Stephen Howarth (ed.), *Men of war: great naval captains of World War II*. New York: St. Martin's Press, 1993.

Herbert P. Bix. *Hirohito and the making of modern Japan*. London: Duckworth, 2001.

Jeremy Black (ed.). *The Second World War*. 7 vols. Aldershot, Hants: Ashgate, 2007.

Clay Blair, Jr. *Hitler's U-boat war*. 2 vols. New York: Random House, 1996 and 1998.

——. *Silent victory: the U.S. submarine war against Japan*. Philadelphia: J.B. Lippincott, 1975.

Joel Blatt. 'France and the Washington Conference', in Eric Goldstein and John Maurer (eds), *The Washington Conference: naval rivalry, East Asian stability and the road to Pearl Harbor*. London: Frank Cass, 1994.

Michael Bloch. *Ribbentrop*. London: Bantam Books, 1992.

Martin Blumenson. 'Salerno and the fight for Southern Italy', in Basil Liddell Hart (ed.), *History of the Second World War*. London: Phoebus, 1980.

Philip Bobbitt. *The shield of Achilles: war, peace and the course of history*. New York: Knopf, 2002.

Horst Boog. 'Luftwaffe support of the German Navy', in Stephen Howarth and Derek Law (eds), *The Battle of the Atlantic 1939–1945: the 50th anniversary international naval conference*. London: Greenhill Books, 1994.

Fred Borch and Daniel Martinez. *Kimmel, Short, and Pearl Habor: the final report revealed*. Annapolis, Md: NIP, 2005.

Dorothy Borg and Shumpei Okamoto (eds). *Pearl Harbor as history: Japanese–American relations 1931–1941*. New York: Columbia University Press, 1973.

Roman Bose. *Secrets of the battlebox: the history and role of Britain's Command HQ in the Malayan campaign*. Singapore: Marshall Cavendish Editions, 2005.

Carl Boyd and Akihiko Yoshida. *The Japanese submarine force and World War II*. Annapolis, Md: NIP, 1996.

Randolph Bradham. *Hitler's U-boat fortresses*. Westport, Conn: Praeger, 2003.

Marc Antonio Bragadin. *The Italian Navy in World War II*. Annapolis, Md: US NIP, 1957.

William B. Breuer. *Operation Dragoon: the Allied invasion of the south of France*. Shrewsbury: Airlife, 1988.

Robin Brodhurst. *Churchill's anchor: Admiral of the Fleet Sir Dudley Pound, O.M., G.C.B., G.C.V.O.* Barnsley: Leo Cooper, 2000.

——. 'Admiral Sir Dudley Pound (1939–43)', in Malcolm H. Murfett (ed.), *The First Sea Lords*. Westport, Conn: Praeger, 1995.

John Brooks. *Dreadnought gunnery and the Battle of Jutland: the question of fire control*. Abingdon, Oxon: Routledge, 2006.

Captain Jack Broome. *Convoy is to scatter*. London: William Kimber, 1972.

David Brown. *Road to Oran: Anglo-French naval relations, September 1939–July 1940*. London: Frank Cass, 2004.

——. 'The forgotten bases: the Royal Navies in the Pacific, 1945', in David Stevens (ed.), *The Royal Australian Navy in World War II*. St. Leonards, NSW: Allen & Unwin, 1996.

——. 'Norway 1940: the balance of interference', in Patrick Salmon (ed.), *Britain and Norway in the Second World War*. London: HMSO, 1995.

——. 'Admiral John Godfrey', in Stephen Howarth (ed.), *Men of war: great naval captains of World War II*. New York: St. Martin's Press, 1993.

——. 'Admiral of the Fleet Sir James Somerville', in Stephen Howarth (ed.), *Men of war: great naval captains of World War II*. New York: St. Martin's Press, 1993.

——. *Warship losses of World War Two*. London: Arms and Armour, 1990.

———. *Carrier operations in World War II*. [2 Vols]. London: Ian Allen, 1974.
David K. Brown. 'Atlantic escorts 1939–45', in Stephen Howarth and Derek Law (eds), *The Battle of the Atlantic 1939–1945: the 50th anniversary international naval conference*. London: Greenhill Books, 1994.
Louis Brown. *A radar history of World War II: technical and military imperatives*. Bristol: Institute of Physics Publishing, 1999.
Colin J. Bruce. *Invaders: Britain and American experience of seaborne landings, 1939–1945*. Annapolis, Md: NIP, 1999.
George Bruce. *Second Front now!* London: MacDonald & Jane's, 1979.
Peter Brune. *The spell broken: exploding the myth of Japanese invincibility*. London: Allen & Unwin, 1997.
Christopher Buckley. *Five ventures: Iraq–Syria–Persia–Madagascar–Dodecanese*. London: HMSO, 1977.
John Buckley. *The RAF and trade defence 1919–1945: constant endeavour*. Keele, Staffs: Ryburn Publishing, 1995.
Thomas H. Buckley. 'The Icarus factor: the American pursuit of myth in naval arms control, 1921–36', in Eric Goldstein and John Maurer (eds), *The Washington Conference: naval rivalry, East Asian stability and the road to Pearl Harbor*. London: Frank Cass, 1994.
Stephen Budiansky. *Battle of wits: the complete story of codebreaking in World War II*. New York: The Free Press, 2000.
Thomas B. Buell. *Master of seapower: a biography of Admiral Ernest J. King*. Boston: Little, Brown & Co., 1980.
———. *The quiet warrior: a biography of Admiral Raymond A. Spruance*. Boston: Little, Brown & Co., 1974.
Alan Bullock. *Hitler: a study in tyranny*. Harmondsworth, Middlesex: Penguin Books, 1971.
John Gorley Bunker. *Liberty ships: the ugly ducklings of World War II*. Annapolis, Md: NIP, 1972.
H. James Burgwyn. *Italian foreign policy in the interwar period 1918–1940*. Westport, Conn. Praeger, 1997.
Burl Burlingame. *Advance force Pearl Harbor*. Annapolis, Md: NIP, 1992.
Roger Burlingame. *General Billy Mitchell: champion of air defense*. Westport, Conn: Greenwood Press, 1978.
Robert S. Burrell. 'Breaking the cycle of Iwo Jima mythology: a strategic study of Operation *Detachment*', *The Journal of Military History, Vol.68, No.4* (Oct.2004): 1143–86.
Fritz-Otto Busch. *The sinking of the 'Scharnhorst': a factual account from the German viewpoint*. London: Futura Publications, 1974.
Robert J.C. Butow. *Tojo and the coming of the war*. Princeton, NJ: Princeton University Press, 1961.
James Cable. *The Royal Navy and the siege of Bilbao*. Cambridge: CUP, 1979.
John Campbell. *Naval weapons of World War II*. Annapolis, Md: NIP, 2002.
———. *Dieppe revisited: a documentary investigation*. London: Frank Cass, 1993.
David Cannadine (ed.) *Blood, toil, tears and sweat*. London: Cassell, 1997.
Elliot Carlson. *Joe Rochefort's war*. Annapolis, Md: NIP, 2011.
Worrall R. Carter. *Beans, bullets, and black oil*. Washington, D.C: Government Printing Office, 1953.
Field Marshal Lord Carver. *The war in Italy 1943–1945: a vital contribution to victory in Europe*. London: Pan Books, 2002.
Christopher Catherwood. *The Balkans in World War II: Britain's Balkan dilemma*. Basingstoke: Palgrave Macmillan, 2003.
J.W.M. Chapman. 'Japanese intelligence, 1918–45: a suitable case for treatment', in Christopher Andrew and Jeremy Noakes (eds), *Intelligence and international relations*. Exeter: Exeter University Publications, 1987.

———. 'No final solution: a survey of cryptanalytical capabilities of German military agencies, 1926–35', *Intelligence and National Security*, Vol.1 No.1 (1986):13–47.
Lord Chatfield. *It might happen again. Vol. 2, The navy and defence*. London: Heinemann, 1947.
Roger Chesneau. *Hood: life and death of a battlecruiser*. London: Cassell, 2002.
Winston S. Churchill. *The Second World War, Vol. III. The Grand Alliance*. London: Penguin Books, 1985.
Adam R.A. Claasen. 'Germany's expeditionary operation: the invasion of Norway, 1940', in Peter Dennis and Jeffrey Grey (eds), *Battles near and far: a century of operational deployment*. Canberra: Army History Unit, Department of Defence, 2005.
———. *Hitler's northern war: the Luftwaffe's ill-fated campaign, 1940–1945*. Lawrence, Ks: University Press of Kansas, 2001.
Alan Clark. *The Russian German conflict 1942–45*. New York: Quill Publishing, 1965.
Patricia Clavin. *The great depression in Europe, 1929–1939*. New York: St. Martin's Press, 2000.
Tim Clayton and Phil Craig. *The end of the beginning: from the siege of Malta to the Allied victory at El Alamein*. New York: Free Press, 2003.
J.F. Coales. 'The origins and development of radar in the Royal Navy, 1935–45, with particular reference to decimetric gunnery equipments', in F.A. Kingsley (ed.), *The development of radar equipments for the Royal Navy, 1935–45*. Basingstoke, Hants: Macmillan, 1995.
C.A. Cochrane. 'Development of naval warning and tactical radar operating in the 10-cm band, 1940–45', in F.A. Kingsley (ed.), *The development of radar equipments for the Royal Navy, 1935–45*. Basingstoke, Hants: Macmillan, 1995.
Warren Cohen. 'American leaders and East Asia, 1931–38', in Akira Iriye and Warren Cohen (eds), *American, Chinese, and Japanese perspectives on wartime Asia 1931–1949*. Wilmington, Del: SR Books, 1990.
Michael Coles. 'Ernest King and the British Pacific Fleet: the conference at Quebec, 1944 ('Octagon')', *The Journal of Military History*, Vol.65, No.1 (2001): 105–29.
———. 'The Channel dash', in Robert Cowley (ed.), *No end save victory: perspectives on World War II*. New York: G.P. Putnam's Sons, 2001.
Paolo E. Coletta. 'Admiral Richmond K. Turner', in Stephen Howarth (ed.), *Men of war: great naval captains of World War II*. New York: St. Martin's Press, 1993.
———'Daniel E. Barbey: amphibious warfare expert', in William M. Leahy (ed.), *We shall return! MacArthur's commanders and the defeat of Japan*. Lexington, Ky: The University Press of Kentucky, 1988.
———. *The American naval heritage*. 3rd Edition. Lanham, Md: University Press of America, 1987.
Basil Collier. *The war in the Far East 1941–1945: a military history*. New York, William Morrow, 1969.
Charles Cook. *The battle of Cape Esperance: encounter at Guadalcanal*. Annapolis, Md: NIP, 1992.
James J. Cooke. *Billy Mitchell*. Boulder, Col: Lynne Rienner, 2002.
Jack D. Coombe. *Derailing the Tokyo Express: the naval battles for the Solomon Islands that sealed Japan's fate*. Harrisburg, Pa: Stackpole Books, 1991.
Brian Connell. *Return of the Tiger*. London: Evans Bros., 1965.
G.G. Connell. *Fighting destroyer: the story of H.M.S. Petard*. London: William Kimber, 1976.
John Connell. 'Wavell's 30,000', in Sir Basil Liddell Hart (ed.), *History of the Second World War*. London: Phoebus Publishing, 1980.
Alastair Cooper. 'The effect of World War II on RAN-RN relations', in David Stevens (ed.), *The Royal Australian Navy in World War II*. St. Leonards, NSW: Allen & Unwin, 1996.
Bryan Cooper. *The E-boat threat*. London: Macdonald & Jane's, 1976.
Sherod Cooper. *Liberty ship: the voyages of John W. Brown 1942–1946*. Annapolis, Md: NIP, 1997.

Alvin D.Coox. 'Needless fear: the compromise of U.S. plans to invade Japan in 1945', *The Journal of Military History*, Vol.64, No.2 (2000): 411–37.

James S. Corum. 'The Spanish Civil War: lessons learned and not learned by the Great Powers', in Jeremy Black (ed.), *The Second World War, Vol. VI*. Aldershot, Hants: Ashgate, 2007.

John Costello. *The Pacific War*. London: Collins, 1981.

Ian Cowman. *Dominion or decline: Anglo-American naval relations in the Pacific, 1937–1941*. Oxford: Berg, 1996.

——. 'Forging an alliance? The American naval commitment to the South Pacific, 1940–42', in David Stevens (ed.), *The Royal Australian Navy in World War II*. St. Leonards, NSW: Allen & Unwin, 1996.

Peter Coy. *The echo of a fighting flower: the story of HMS Narcissus and B3 Ocean Escort Group in WWII*. Upton upon Severn, Worcs: Square One Publications, 1997.

Russell Sydnor Crenshaw, Jr. *South Pacific destroyer: the battle for the Solomons from Savo Island to Vella Gulf*. Annapolis, Md: NIP, 1998.

Robert J. Cressman. *The official chronology of the US Navy in World War II*. Annapolis, Md: NIP, 2000.

Robert F. Cross. *Shepherds of the sea: destroyer escorts in World War II*. Annapolis, Md: NIP, 2010.

Daniel K.R. Crosswell. *Beetle: the life of General Walter Bedell Smith*. Lexington, Ky: University Press of Kentucky, 2010.

——. *The chief of staff: the military career of General Walter Bedell Smith*. Westport, Conn: Greenwood Press, 1991.

Philip A. Crowl. *Campaign in the Marianas*. Washington, D.C: Center of Military History, US Army, 1989.

Brian Cull with Don Minterne. *Hurricanes over Tobruk: the pivotal role of the Hurricane in the defence of Tobruk, January–June 1941*. London: Grub Street, 1999.

Bruce Cumings. *The origins of the Korean War: liberation and the emergence of separate regimes 1945–1947*. Princeton, NJ: Princeton University Press, 1981.

Anthony J. Cumming. *The Royal Navy and the battle of Britain*. Annapolis, Md: NIP, 2010.

Viscount Cunningham. *A sailor's odyssey: the autobiography of Admiral of the Fleet Viscount Cunningham of Hyndhope, K.T., G.C.B., O.M., D.S.O*. London: Hutchinson, 1951.

Thomas J. Cutler. *The battle of Leyte Gulf, 23–26 October,1944*. New York: HarperCollins, 1994.

Cristiano D'Adamo. 'The Conference of Merano: 13–14 February 1941', at www.regiamarina.net/battles/matapan/part2_us.htm.

Robert Dallek. *Franklin D. Roosevelt and American foreign policy, 1932–1945*. Oxford: OUP, 1995.

Josephus Daniels. *The Wilson Era, Vol. I: Years of peace 1910–1917*. Chapel Hill, N.C: University of North Carolina Press, 1946.

Raymond Dannreuther. *Somerville's Force H: the Royal Navy's Gibraltar-based fleet, June 1940 to March 1942*. London: Aurum, 2006.

Kev Darling. *US carrier war*. Barnsley: Pen & Sword Aviation, 2011.

Joel R. Davidson. *The unsinkable fleet: the politics of U.S. Navy expansion in World War II*. Annapolis, Md: NIP, 1996.

John Paton Davies, Jr. *Dragon by the tail: American, British, Japanese and Russian encounters with China and one another*. New York: W.W.Norton, 1972.

Pete Davies. *The devil's flu*. New York: Owl Books, 2000.

Burke Davis. *The Billy Mitchell affair*. New York: Random House, 1967.

Lance E. Davis and Stanley L. Engerman. *Naval blockades in peace and war: an economic history since 1750*. Cambridge: CUP, 2006.

F. W. Deakin. *The brutal friendship: Mussolini, Hitler and the fall of Italian fascism*. New York: Harper & Row, 1962.

Patrick Degan. *Flattop fighting in World War II: the battles between American and Japanese aircraft carriers.* Jefferson, N.C.: McFarland & Co, 2003.

Douglas E. Delaney. 'Churchill and the Mediterranean strategy: December 1941 to January 1943.' *Defence Studies*, Vol.2, No.3 (Autumn 2002):1–26.

D. Colt Denfeld. *Hold the Marianas: the Japanese defense of the islands.* Shippensburg, Pa: White Mane, 1997.

Peter J. Dennis. *Troubled days of peace: Mountbatten and South East Asia Command 1945–46.* Manchester: Manchester University Press, 1987.

—— 'The unknown and the unknowable: the loss of HMAS *Sydney*', in Malcolm H. Murfett (ed.), *The imponderables of war* (forthcoming 2009).

Peter J. Dennis and Jeffrey Grey (eds). *Battles near and far: a century of operational deployment.* Canberra: Army History Unit, Department of Defence, 2005.

Carlo D'Este. *Eisenhower: a soldier's life.* New York: Henry Holt, 2002.

——. *World War II in the Mediterranean: 1942–1945.* Chapel Hill, N.C.: Algonquin Books of Chapel Hill, 1990.

——. *Bitter victory: the battle for Sicily 1943.* New York: E.P. Dutton, 1988.

Cipher A. Devours (ed.). *Selections from cryptologia: history, people and technology.* Boston: Artech House, 1998.

Michael Dewar. *The art of deception in warfare.* Newton Abbot: David & Charles, 1989.

Captain Peter Dickens. *Narvik: battles in the fjords.* London: Ian Allan, 1974.

Roger Dingman. *Power in the Pacific: the origins of naval arms limitation.* Chicago: University of Chicago Press, 1976.

Richard L. DiNardo. *Germany and the Axis powers: from coalition to collapse.* Lawrence, Ks: University Press of Kansas, 2005.

Roger Dingman. *Deciphering the rising sun.* Annapolis, Md: NIP, 2009.

Charles M. Dobbs. *The United States and East Asia since 1945.* Lewiston, NY: The Edwin Mellen Press, 1990.

Colin Dobinson. *Building radar: forging Britain's early-warning chain, 1935–1945.* London: Methuen, 2006.

Christopher Dobson, John Miller and Ronald Payne. *The cruellest night: Germany's Dunkirk and the sinking of the Wilhelm Gustloff.* London: Hodder and Stoughton, 1979.

Saki Dockrill (ed.). *From Pearl Harbor to Hiroshima: the Second World War in Asia and the Pacific, 1941–45.* New York: St. Martin's Press, 1994.

Justus D. Doenecke. *Storm on the horizon: the challenge to American intervention, 1939–1941.* Lanham, MD: Rowman & Littlefield Publishers, 2000.

Karl Doenitz. *Memoirs: ten years and twenty days.* New York: Da Capo Press, 1997.

Max Domarus (ed.). *Hitler speeches and proclamations 1932–1945. Vol. Two 1935–1938.* Wouconda, Ill: Bolchazy-Carducci Publishers, 1992.

James G. Dorrian. *Storming St. Nazaire: the gripping story of the dock-busting raid March 1942.* London: Leo Cooper, 1998.

W.A.B. Douglas, Roger Sarty and Michael Whitby. *No higher purpose: the official history of the Royal Canadian Navy in the Second World War, 1939–1943. Vol.II, Part 1.* St. Catherines, Ont: Vanwell Publishing, 2002.

John W. Dower. *Embracing defeat: Japan in the wake of World War II.* New York: W.W. Norton, 1999.

Edward J. Drea. 'Previews of hell', in Robert Cowley (ed.), *No end save victory: perspectives on World War II.* New York: Penguin Putnam, 2001.

——. 'Preview of hell: intelligence, the bomb, and the invasion of Japan', *American Intelligence Journal*, Vol.16, No.1 (Spring 1995): 51–57.

———. 'Audacious but hardly reckless', *Army*, Vol.44, No.4 (April 1994): 51–55.
———. *MacArthur's ULTRA. Codebreaking and the war against Japan, 1942–1945*. Lawrence, Ks: University Press of Kansas, 1992.
———. 'Reading each other's mail: Japanese communication intelligence 1920–41', *The Journal of Military History*, Vol. 55 No. 2. (1991): 185–205.
Edward J. Drea and Joseph E. Richard. 'New evidence on breaking the Japanese Army codes', *Intelligence and National Security*, Vol.14, No.1 (Spring 1999): 62–83.
Ronald J. Drez. *Twenty-five yards of war: the extraordinary courage of ordinary men in World War II*. New York: Hyperion, 2001.
Frank A. Driskill and Dede W. Casad. *Admiral of the hills: Chester W. Nimitz*. Austin, Tx: Eakin Press, 1983.
James P. Duffy. *The sinking of the Laconia and the U-boat war*. Santa Barbara, Ca: ABC Clio, 2009.
Paul S. Dull. *A battle history of the Imperial Japanese Navy (1941–1945)*. Annapolis, Md: NIP, 1979.
R. Blake Dunnavent. *Brown water warfare: the U.S. Navy in riverine warfare and the emergence of a tactical doctrine, 1775–1970*. Gainesville, Fla: University Press of Florida, 2003.
David Dutton. *Anthony Eden: a life and reputation*. London: Arnold, 1997.
George C. Dyer. *The amphibians came to conquer: the story of Admiral Richmond Kelly Turner*. 2 vols. Washington, D.C: U.S. Government Printing Office, 1972.
Charles Eade (ed.). *The war speeches of the Rt. Hon. Winston S. Churchill, Volume III*. London: Cassell & Co, 1952.
Stuart Eadon (ed.). *Kamikaze: the divine wind*. London: Crécy, 1995.
Robin Edmonds. *The big three: Churchill, Roosevelt and Stalin in peace and war*. New York: W.W. Norton, 1991.
Bernard Edwards. *The twilight of the U-boats*. Annapolis, Md: NIP, 2004.
———. *The quiet heroes: British merchant seamen at war*. Barnsley: Leo Cooper, 2003.
———. *The road to Russia: Arctic convoys 1942*. Barnsley: Leo Cooper, 2002.
———. *Beware raiders! German surface raiders in the Second World War*. Barnsley: Leo Cooper, 2001.
———. *Dönitz and the wolf packs*. London: Arms and Armour, 1996
———. *The Merchant Navy goes to war*. London: Robert Hale, 1990.
John S. Eisenhower. *Allies: Pearl Harbor to D-Day*. Cambridge, Mass: Da Capo Press, 1982.
Bruce A. Elleman and S. C. M. Paine (eds.). *Naval Coalition Warfare: from the Napoleonic War to Operation Iraqi Freedom*. Abingdon, Oxon: Routledge, 2008.
Peter Elphick. *Life line: the Merchant Navy at war 1939–1945*. London: Chatham Publishing, 1999.
———. *Far Eastern file: the intelligence war in the Far East 1930–1945*. London: Hodder & Stoughton, 1997.
David Elstein. 'Decision', in Basil Liddell Hart (ed.), *History of the Second World War*. London: Phoebus, 1980.
Eloise Engle and Lauri Paananen. *The winter war: the Russo-Finnish conflict, 1939–40*. Boulder, Col: Westview Press, 1985.
Joseph F. Enright with James W. Ryan. *Shinano! The sinking of Japan's secret supership*. London: The Bodley Head, 1987.
Marc Epstein. 'The historians and the Geneva naval conference', in B.J.C. McKercher (ed.), *Arms limitation and disarmament*. Westport, Conn: Praeger, 1992.
John Erickson. *The road to Berlin. Stalin's war with Germany.Vol.II*. New Haven, Conn: Yale University Press, 1999.
———. *The Soviet high command: a military-political history 1918–1941*. Boulder, Col: Westview Press, 1984.
Ralph Erskine. 'The Admiralty and cipher machines during the Second World War: not so stupid after all', *The Journal of Intelligence History*, Vol.2, No.2 (2002): 49–68.

———. 'Naval Enigma: a missing link', *International Journal of Intelligence and Counterintelligence*, Vol.3 (1989): 493–508.

A.S. Evans. *Destroyer down: an account of H.M. destroyer losses 1939–1945*. Barnsley: Pen & Sword Maritime, 2010.

Mark Llewellyn Evans. *Great World War II battles in the Arctic*. Westport, Conn: Greenwood Press, 1999.

Martin Marix Evans. *Invasion! Operation Sealion 1940*. Harlow: Pearson Longman, 2004.

David C. Evans and Mark R. Peattie. *Kaigun: strategy, tactics, and technology in the Imperial Japanese Navy, 1887–1941*. Annapolis, Md: NIP, 1997.

Stanley L. Falk. 'Douglas MacArthur and the war against Japan', in William M. Leahy (ed.). *We shall return! MacArthur's commanders and the defeat of Japan*. Lexington, Ky: The University of Kentucky, 1988.

———. 'Battle of Leyte', in Basil Liddell Hart (ed.), *History of the Second World War*. London: Phoebus, 1980.

Francis Douglas Fane and Don Moore. *The naked warriors: the story of the U.S. Navy's frogmen*. Annapolis, Md: NIP, 1995.

Richard W. Fanning. 'The Coolidge conference of 1927: disarmament in disarray', in B.J.C. McKercher (ed.), *Arms limitation and disarmament: restraints on war, 1899–1939*. Westport, Conn: Praeger, 1992.

Ladislas Farago. *The tenth fleet*. New York: I. Obolensky, 1962.

Brian P. Farrell. *The defence and fall of Singapore 1940–1942*. Stroud, Glos: Tempus, 2005.

———. 'Layton, Sir Geoffrey', in Brian Harrison (ed.), *Oxford dictionary of national biography (ODNB), Vol.32*. Oxford: OUP, 2004.

———. 'Pound, Admiral Sir Dudley', in Brian Harrison (ed.). *ODNB, Vol.45*. Oxford: OUP, 2004.

———. 'Ramsay, Sir Bertram Home', in Brian Harrison (ed.), *ODNB. Vol.45*. Oxford: OUP, 2004.

———. *The basis and making of British grand strategy, 1940–43: was there a plan?* [2 Vols.] Lewiston N.Y.: The Edward Mellen Press, 1998.

George Feifer. *Tennozan: the battle for Okinawa and the atomic bomb*. New York: Ticknor & Fields, 1992.

Herbert Feis. *Churchill, Roosevelt, Stalin: the war they waged and the peace they sought*. Princeton, NJ: Princeton University Press, 1967.

———. *The atomic bomb and the end of World War II*. Princeton, N.J: Princeton University Press, 1966.

Niall Ferguson. *The war of the world: history's age of hatred*. London: Allen Lane, 2006.

———. *The pity of war*. London: Allen Lane, The Penguin Press, 1998.

Robert H. Ferrell. *Peace in their time: the origins of the Kellogg–Briand Pact*. New York: Norton, 1969.

John.R. Ferris. 'Intelligence and diplomatic signalling during crises: the British experiences of 1877–78, 1922 and 1938', in Len Scott and R. Gerald Hughes, *Intelligence, crises and security: prospects and retrospects*. Abingdon, Oxon: Routledge, 2008.

———. *Intelligence and strategy: selected essays*. London: Routledge, 2005.

———. 'The British "enigma": Britain, signals security and cipher machines, 1906–53', in John Robert Ferris, *Intelligence and strategy: selected essays*. London: Routledge, 2005.

———. 'Far too dangerous a gamble? Britain, intelligence and policy during the Chanak crisis, September–October 1922', *Diplomacy and Statecraft, Vol. 14, No. 3* (2003): 139–84.

———. '"FORTITUDE" in context: the evolution of British military deception in two world wars, 1914–45', in Richard K. Betts and Thomas G. Mahnken (eds), *Paradoxes of strategic intelligence: essays in honor of Michael I. Handel*. London: Frank Cass, 2003.

——. 'The road to Bletchley Park: the British experience with signals intelligence, 1892–1945', *Intelligence and National Security*, Vol. 17, No.1 (2002): 53–84.
——. '"It is our business in the Navy to command the seas": the last decade of British maritime supremacy, 1919–29', in Greg Kennedy and Keith Neilson (eds), *Far-flung lines: essays on imperial defence in honour of Donald Mackenzie Schurman*. London: Frank Cass, 1996.
——. 'Ralph Bennett and the study of Ultra', *Intelligence and National Security*, Vol.6, No.2 (1991): 473–86.
——. 'From Broadway House to Bletchley Park: the diary of Captain Malcolm Kennedy, 1936–46', *Intelligence and National Security*, Vol.4, No.3 (1989): 421–50.
——. *Men, money and diplomacy. The evolution of British strategic policy, 1919–26*. Basingstoke, Hants: Macmillan, 1989.
——. 'The British "Enigma": Britain, signals security and cipher machines, 1906–46', *Defence Analysis*, Vol.3, No.2 (1987): 153–63.
——. 'Treasury control, the ten year rule and British service policies, 1919–24', *Historical Journal* Vol.30 (1987): 359–83.
——. 'Whitehall's black chamber: British cryptology and the Government Code and Cypher School, 1919–29', *Intelligence and National Security*, Vol. 2, No. 1 (1987): 54–91.
Andrew Field. *Royal Navy strategy in the Far East 1919–1939: planning for war against Japan*. London: Frank Cass, 2004.
Klaus P. Fischer. *Nazi Germany: a new history*. New York: Continuum 1995.
Robert C. Fisher. 'We'll get our own: Canada and the oil shipping crisis of 1942', *The Northern Mariner*, Vol.3 No.2 (1993): 33–40.
Peter Fleming. *Operation Sea Lion: Hitler's plot to invade England*. London: Tauris Parke Paperbacks, 2011.
Eugene B. Fluckey. *Thunder below! The USS Barb revolutionizes submarine warfare in World War II*. Urbana: Ill: University of Illinois Press, 1992.
Christopher Ford and David Rosenberg. *The admirals' advantage: U.S. Navy operational intelligence in World War II and the Cold War*. Annapolis, Md: NIP, 2005.
Simon Foster. *Okinawa 1945*. London: Arms and Armour, 1996.
Will Fowler. *The commandos at Dieppe: rehearsal for D-Day*. London: HarperCollins, 2002.
Timothy Long Francis. *Poseidon's tribute: maritime vulnerability, industrial mobilization and the Allied defeat of the U-boats, 1939–1945*. Ann Arbor, Mi: UMI Dissertation Services, 2003.
Benis M. Frank, 'Lieutenant-General Holland M. Smith', in Stephen Howarth (ed.), *Men of war: great naval captains of World War II*. New York: St. Martin's Press, 1993.
Richard B. Frank. *Downfall: the end of the Imperial Japanese Empire*. New York: Random House, 1999.
——. 'Guadalacanal: the pivotal campaign', *Naval Institute Proceedings*, Vol.118, No.8 (1992): 75–77.
——. *Guadalcanal*. New York: Random House, 1990.
Wolfgang Frank. *The sea wolves: the story of Germany's U-boats at war*. Maidstone, Kent: George Mann, 1973.
Norman L. Franks. *Dark sky, deep water: first hand reflections on the anti-U-boat war in WWII*. London: Grub Street, 1997.
——. *Search, find and kill: the RAF's U-boat successes in World War Two*. London: Grub Street, 1995.
Norman Franks and Eric Zimmerman. *U-boat versus aircraft: the dramatic story behind U-boat claims in gun action with aircraft in World War II*. London: Grub Street, 1998.
David Fraser. *Knight's Cross: a life of Field Marshal Erwin Rommel*. London: Harper Collins, 1993.

Lawrence Freedman and Saki Dockrill, 'Hiroshima: a strategy of shock', in Saki Dockrill (ed.), *From Pearl Harbor to Hiroshima: the Second World War in Asia and the Pacific, 1941–45*. Basingstoke: Macmillan, 1994.

Maurice Freedman. *Unravelling Enigma: winning the code war at Station X*. London: Leo Cooper, 2000.

Kenneth I. Friedman. *Afternoon of the rising sun: the battle of the Leyte Gulf*. Novoto, Ca: Presidio, 2001.

Norman Friedman. *British destroyers and frigates: the Second World War and after*. London: Chatham Publishing, 2006.

——. *U.S. destroyers: an illustrated design history*. Annapolis, Md: NIP, 2004.

——. *U.S. cruisers: an illustrated design history*. London: Arms and Armour Press, 1985.

Mitsuo Fuchida. 'The air attack on Pearl Harbor', in David C. Evans (ed.), *The Japanese Navy in World War II: in the words of former Japanese naval officers*. Annapolis, Md: NIP, 1986.

Mitsuo Fuchida and Masatake Okumiya. *Midway: the battle that doomed Japan: the Japanese Navy's story*. Annapolis, Md: NIP, 1992.

Fuehrer conferences on naval affairs 1939–1945. London: Chatham Publishing, 2005.

Mary Fulbrook. *History of Germany 1918–2000; the divided nation*. Oxford: Blackwell, 2002.

Arthur Layton Funk. *Hidden ally: the French Resistance, Special Operations and the landings in southern France, 1944*. Westport, Conn: Greenwood Press, 1992.

David C. Fuquea. 'Bougainville: the amphibious assault enters maturity', *Naval War College Review, Vol.50, No.1* (1997): 104–21.

Paul Fussell. *The Great War and modern memory*. Oxford: OUP, 2000.

Harry A. Gailey. *The war in the Pacific*. Novato, Ca: Presidio Press, 1995.

——. *Bougainville: the forgotten campaign 1943–1945*. Lexington, Ky: The University Press of Kentucky, 1991.

——. *The liberation of Guam 21 July–10 August 1944*. Novato, Ca: Presidio, 1988.

——. *'Howlin' Mad vs the Army: conflict in command, Saipan 1944*. Novato, Ca: Presidio, 1986.

——. *Peleliu: 1944*. Annapolis, Md: Nautical & Aviation Publishing, 1983.

J.K. Galbraith. *The great crash, 1929*. Boston: Houghton Mifflin, 1972.

Mark S. Gallicchio. *American East Asian policy and the fall of the Japanese empire, 1945*. Ann Arbor, MI: University Microfilms International, 1986.

Bruce Gamble. *Fortress Rabaul: the battle for the Southwest Pacific, January 1942–April 1943*. Minneapolis, Mn: Zenith Press, 2010.

Timothy D. Gann. *Fifth Air Force light and medium bomber operations during 1942 and 1943: building the doctrine and forces that triumphed in the Battle of the Bismarck Sea and the Wewak raid*. Maxwell Air Force Base, Al: Air University Press, 1993.

Michael Gannon. *Pearl Harbor betrayed: the true story of a man and a nation under attack*. New York: Henry Holt, 2001.

——. *Black May: the epic story of the Allies' defeat of the German U-boats in May 1943*. New York: HarperCollins, 1998.

——. *Operation Drumbeat: the dramatic true story of Germany's first U-boat attacks along the American coast in World War II*. New York: HarperPerennial, 1991.

Robert Gannon. *Hellions of the deep: the development of American torpedoes in World War II*. University Park, Penn: The Pennsylvania State University Press, 1996.

Robert Gardiner, (ed.). *Conway's all the world's fighting ships 1922–1946*. London: Conway Maritime Press, 1980.

W.J.R. Gardner. 'Anti-submarine warfare', in Richard Harding (ed.), *The Royal Navy, 1930–2000: innovation and defence*. London: Frank Cass, 2005.

——(ed.). *The evacuation from Dunkirk: 'Operation Dynamo'*. London: Frank Cass, 2000.

——. *Decoding history: the battle of the Atlantic and Ultra*. Basingstoke: Macmillan, 1999.

——. 'An Allied perspective', in Stephen Howarth and Derek Law (eds), *The Battle of the Atlantic 1939–1945: the 50th anniversary international naval conference*. London: Greenhill Books, 1994.
——. 'Admiral Sir Bertram Ramsay', in Stephen Howarth (ed.), *Men of war: great naval captains of World War II*. New York: St. Martin's Press. 1993.
Brian Garfield. *The thousand-mile war: World War II in Alaska and the Aleutians*. New York: Ballantine Books, 1973.
Richard Garrett. *Scharnhorst and Gneisenau: the elusive sisters*. Newton Abbot, Devon: David & Charles, 1978.
William H. Garzke, Jr. and Robert O. Dulin, Jr. *Battleships: United States battleships, 1935–1992*. Annapolis, Md: NIP, 1995.
Norman Gelb. *Desperate venture: the story of Operation Torch, the Allied invasion of North Africa*. New York: W.W. Morrow, 1992.
Norman H. Gibbs. 'The naval conferences of the inter war years: a study of Anglo-American relations', *Naval War College Review, 30* (1977): 50–63.
——. *Grand strategy. Vol I: Rearmament policy*. London: HMSO, 1976.
Adrian Gilbert. *Germany's lightning war*. London: David & Charles, 2000.
Alton Keith Gilbert, *A leader born: the life of Admiral John Sidney McCain, Pacific carrier commander*. Drexel Hill, Pa: Casemate, 2006.
Martin Gilbert. *A history of the twentieth century. Volume one: 1900–1933*. New York: William Morrow & Co., 1997.
——. (ed.). *The Churchill war papers. Vol. I: At the Admiralty. September 1939–May 1940*. London: Heinemann, 1993.
——. (ed.). *The Churchill war papers. Vol. II: Never surrender. May 1940–December 1940*. New York: W.W. Norton & Co., 1995.
——. (ed.). *Winston S. Churchill. Vol. VIII. 'Never despair 1945–1965'*. Boston: Houghton Mifflin, 1988.
——. (ed.). *Winston S. Churchill. Vol. VII. 'Road to victory 1941–1945'*. Boston: Houghton Mifflin, 1986.
Joseph Gilbey. *Langsdorff of the Graf Spee: prince of honor*. Hillsburgh, Ont: Joseph Gilbey Books, 1999.
G. Hermon Gill. *Royal Australian Navy 1939–1942*. Sydney: Collins in association with the Australian War Memorial, 1985.
——. *Royal Australian Navy 1942–1945*. Sydney: Collins in association with the Australian War Memorial, 1985.
David Glantz. *Soviet operational and tactical combat in Manchuria, 1945: 'August Storm'*. London: Frank Cass, 2003.
——. *Soviet military deception in the Second World War*. London: Frank Cass, 1989.
Carroll V. Glines. *Attack on Yamamoto*. Atglen, Pa: Schiffer Publishing, 1993.
——. *The Doolittle raid: America's daring first strike against Japan*. West Chester, Pa: Schiffer Military History, 1991.
Donald M. Goldstein and Katherine V. Dillon (eds). *The Pacific War papers: Japanese documents of World War II*. Washington, D.C.: Potomac Books, 2004.
——(eds). *Fading victory: the diary of Admiral Matome Ugaki 1941–1945*. Pittsburgh, Pa: University of Pittsburgh Press, 1991.
Donald M. Goldstein, Katherine V. Dillon and J. Michael Wenger. *Rain of ruin: a photographic history of Hiroshima and Nagasaki*. Washington, D.C: Brassey's, 1995.
Ian Gooderson. *A hard way to make a war*. London: Conway, 2008.
——. 'Shoestring strategy: the British campaign in the Aegean, 1943.' *The Journal of Strategic Studies, Vol.25, No.3* (2002): 1–36.

G.A.H. Gordon. *British seapower and procurement between the wars: a reappraisal of rearmament.* Basingstoke: Macmillan Press in association with King's College, London, 1988.

Walter Görlitz. *History of the German General Staff 1657–1945.* New York: Praeger, 1954.

Sergei G. Gorshkov. *Red star rising at sea.* Annapolis, Md: NIP, 1974.

Christina J.M. Goulter. *A forgotten offensive: Royal Air Force Coastal Command's anti-shipping campaign, 1940–1945.* London: Frank Cass, 1995.

James W. Grace. *The naval battle of Guadalcanal: night action 13 November 1942.* Annapolis, Md: NIP, 1999.

Norman A. Graebner. 'Hoover, Roosevelt, and the Japanese', in Dorothy Borg and Shumpei Okamoto (eds), *Pearl Harbor as history: Japanese–American relations 1931–1941.* New York: Columbia University Press, 1973.

Michael B. Graham. *Mantle of heroism: Tarawa and the struggle for the Gilberts, November 1943.* Novato, Ca: Presidio Press, 1993.

Edwyn Gray. *Hitler's battleships.* Annapolis, Md: NIP, 1999.

——. *The devil's choice: Robert Whitehead and the history of the torpedo.* Annapolis, Md: NIP, 1991.

——. *A damned un-English weapon: the story of British submarine warfare 1914–18.* London: Seeley, Service & Co., 1971.

Jack Greene. *The Midway campaign, December 7, 1941–June 6 1942.* Conshohocken, Pa: Combined Books, 1995.

Jack Greene and Alessandro Massignani. *The naval war in the Mediterranean 1940–1943.* London: Chatham Publishing, 1998.

——. *Rommel's North Africa campaign: September1940–November1942.* Conshohocken, Pa: Combined Books, 1994.

J.A.S. Grenville. *The Collins history of the world in the twentieth century.* London: HarperCollins, 1994.

J.H. Greswell. 'Leigh Light Wellingtons of Coastal Command', *The RUSI Journal, Vol.140, No.3* (1995): 55–58.

Peter Gretton. 'The Nyon Conference – the naval aspect', *The English Historical Review, Vol. 90, No. 354* (1975): 103–12.

——. *Convoy escort commander.* London: Cassell, 1964.

Thomas E. Griffith, Jr. *MacArthur's airman: General George C. Kenney and the war in the Southwest Pacific.* Lawrence, Ks: University Press of Kansas, 1998.

William L. Griggs. *Preludes to victory: the battle of Ormoc Bay in WWII.* Somerville, N.J.: W.L. Griggs, 1997.

Erich Gröner. *German warships 1815–1945. Vol. One: major surface vessels.* Annapolis, Md: NIP, 1990.

Eric Grove. *The Royal Navy since 1815: a new short history.* Basingstoke, Hants: Palgrave Macmillan, 2005.

——. *Price of disobedience: the battle of the River Plate reconsidered.* Stroud, Glos: Sutton, 2000.

——. 'The Royal Australian Navy in the Mediterranean in World War II', in David Stevens (ed.), *The Royal Australian Navy in World War II.* St. Leonards, NSW: Allen & Unwin, 1996.

——. 'A service vindicated, 1939–46', in J.R. Hill (ed.), *The Oxford illustrated history of the Royal Navy.* Oxford: OUP, 1995.

——. *Sea battles in close-up: World War 2. Volume two.* Shepperton, Surrey: Ian Allan, 1993.

——. *Fleet to fleet encounters.* London: Arms and Armour, 1991.

Philip D. Grove. *Midway.* London: Brassey's, 2004.

Major-General Sir Francis de Guingand. 'Alamein: the tide turns', in Basil Liddell Hart (ed.), *History of the Second World War.* London: Phoebus, 1980.

Michael Gunton. *Dive! Dive! Dive! Submarines at war.* London: Constable, 2003.

Geirr H. Haarr. *The battle for Norway: April–June 1940.* Barnsley: Seaforth, 2010.
——. *The German invasion of Norway: April 1940.* Barnsley: Seaforth, 2009.
Willem Hackmann. *Seek and strike: sonar, anti-submarine warfare and the Royal Navy 1914–54.* London: HMSO, 1984.
Michael Hadley. *U-boats against Canada: German submarines in Canadian waters.* Kingston and Montreal: McGill-Queen's University Press, 1985.
Arnold Hague. *The Allied convoy system 1939–1945: its organization, defence and operation.* Annapolis, Md: NIP, 2000.
Peter Haining. *Where the eagle landed: the mystery of the German invasion of Britain, 1940.* London: Robson Books, 2004.
Christopher Hall. *Britain, America and arms control, 1921–37.* New York: St. Martin's Press, 1987.
David Ian Hall. 'Looking skyward from below the waves: Admiral Tom Phillips and the loss of the *Prince of Wales* and the *Repulse*', in Greg Kennedy (ed.), *British naval strategy east of Suez, 1900–2000: influences and actions.* London: Frank Cass, 2000.
James H. Hallas. *The devil's anvil: the assault on Peleliu.* Westport, Conn: Praeger, 1994.
Paul G. Halpern. *A naval history of World War I.* Annapolis, Md: NIP, 1994.
David Hamer. *Bombers versus battleships.* Annapolis, Md: NIP, 1998.
C.I. Hamilton. 'The character and organization of the Admiralty Operational Intelligence Centre during the Second World War.' *War in History*, Vol.7, No.3 (2000): 295–324.
John Hamilton. *War at sea 1939–1945.* Poole, Dorset: Blandford Press, 1986.
Eric Hammel. *Carrier clash: the invasion of Guadalcanal and the Battle of the Eastern Solomons: August 1942.* Pacifica, Ca: Pacifica Press, 1997.
——. *Guadalcanal: starvation island.* Pacifica, Ca: Pacifica Press, 1995.
——. *Munda Trail: the New Georgia campaign.* New York: Orion Books, 1989.
——. *Guadalcanal: the carrier battles.* New York: Crown Publishers, 1987.
Eric Hammel and John E. Lane. *Bloody Tarawa.* Pacifica, Ca: Pacifica Press, 1999.
Michael I. Handel (ed.). *Intelligence and military operations.* London: Frank Cass, 1990.
Victor Davis Hanson. *Courage and culture: landmark battles in the rise of Western power.* New York: Anchor, 2002.
Richard Harding (ed.). *The Royal Navy, 1930–2000.* London: Frank Cass, 2005.
Jack S. Harker. *Well done Leander.* Auckland, NZ: Collins, 1971.
Stephen Harper. *Capturing Enigma: how HMS Petard seized the German naval codes.* Stroud, Glos: Sutton Publishing, 2000.
Michael Harrison. *Mulberry: the return in triumph.* London: W.H. Allen, 1965.
Guy Hartcup. *Code name Mulberry: the planning, building and operation of the Normandy harbours.* Newton Abbot: David & Charles, 1977.
Jock Haswell. *The intelligence and deception of the D-Day landings.* London: B.T. Batsford, 1979.
Hattori Syohgo. 'Kamikaze: Japan's glorious failure.' *Air Power History*, Vol.43, No.1 (1996): 14–27.
D.J. Haycock. *Eisenhower and the art of warfare: a critical appraisal.* Jefferson, NC: McFarland & Co, 2004.
Grace Person Hayes. *The history of the Joint Chiefs of Staff in World War II: the war against Japan.* Annapolis, Md: N.I.P., 1982.
Chester G. Hearn. *Carriers in combat: the air war at sea.* Westport, Conn: Praeger Security International, 2005.
T.A. Heathcote. *The British admirals of the fleet 1734–1995.* Barnsley: Leo Cooper, 2002.
Waldo Heinrichs. *Threshold of war: Franklin D. Roosevelt and American entry into World War II.* Oxford: OUP, 1988.

Jan G. Heitmann. 'The front line: convoy HG76 – the offence', in Stephen Howarth and Derek Law (eds), *The Battle of the Atlantic 1939–1945: the 50th anniversary international naval conference*. London: Greenhill Books, 1994.

David Henry. 'British submarine policy, 1918–39', in Bryan Ranft (ed.), *Technical change and British naval policy 1860–1939*. London: Hodder & Stoughton, 1977.

Peter J. Henshaw. 'The British Chiefs of Staff Committee and the preparation of the Dieppe raid, March–August 1942: did Mountbatten really evade the committee's authority?' *War in History*, Vol.1, No.2 (1994): 197–214.

Holger H. Herwig, 'Innovation ignored: the submarine problem – Germany, Britain, and the United States, 1919–39', in Williamson Murray and Allan R. Millett (eds), *Military innovation in the interwar period*. Cambridge: CUP, 1998.

———. 'The failure of German sea power, 1914–45: Mahan, Tirpitz and Raeder reconsidered', *The International History Review*, Vol. X, No. 1 (1988): 68–105.

———. *'Luxury' fleet: the Imperial German Navy 1888–1918*. London: George Allen & Unwin, 1980.

Norman Herz. *Operation Alacrity: the Azores and the war in the Atlantic*. Annapolis, Md: NIP, 2004.

Bodo Herzog. 'Admiral Otto Kretschmer', in Stephen Howarth (ed.), *Men of war: great naval captains of World War II*. New York: St. Martin's Press, 1993.

Roger Hesketh. *Fortitude: the D-Day deception campaign*. London: St. Ermin's Press, 1999.

Geoff Hewitt. *Hitler's armada: the Royal Navy and the defences of Great Britain April–October 1940*. Barnsley: Pen & Sword Maritime, 2008.

Christopher Hibbert. 'Operation Dynamo', in Basil Liddell Hart (ed.), *History of the Second World War*. London: Phoebus, 1980.

Des Hickey and Gus Smith. *Operation Avalanche: the Salerno landings, 1943*. London: Heinemann, 1983.

Trumbull Higgins. *Winston Churchill and the Second Front, 1940–1943*. Westport, Conn: Greenwood Press, 1974.

F.H. Hinsley. 'The influence of ULTRA in the Second World War', *Intelligencer*, Vol.14, No.2 (2004): 103–13.

F.H. Hinsley and Alan Stripp (eds). *Codebreakers: the inside story of Bletchley Park*. Oxford: OUP, 1993.

F.H. Hinsley, E.E. Thomas, C.F.G. Ransom and R.C. Knight (eds). *British intelligence in the Second World War. Vol.One: Its influence on strategy and operations*. London: HMSO, 1979.

——— *British intelligence in the Second World War: its influence on strategy and operations. Vol.2*. London: HMSO, 1981.

Walter L. Hixson. *The American experience in World War II. Vol.7: the atomic bomb in history and memory*. New York: Routledge, 2003.

David Hobbs. *The British Pacific Fleet: the Royal Navy's most powerful strike force*. Barnsley: Seaforth, 2011.

———. 'Ship-borne air anti-submarine warfare', in Stephen Howarth and Derek Law (eds), *The Battle of the Atlantic 1939–1945: the 50th anniversary international naval conference*. London: Greenhill Books, 1994.

A.A. Hoehling. *The Lexington goes down: a fighting carrier's last hours in the Coral Sea*. Mechanicsburg, Pa: Stackpole Books, 1993.

James Holland. *Fortress Malta: an island under siege 1940–1943*. New York: Miramax, 2003.

Jeffrey Holland. *The Aegean mission: Allied operations in the Dodecanese, 1943*. New York: Greenwood Press, 1988.

W.J. Holmes. *Double-edged secrets: U.S. naval intelligence operations in the Pacific during World War II*. Annapolis, Md: NIP, 1979.

Thaddeus Holt. *The deceivers: allied military deception in the Second World War.* London: Phoenix, 2005.
——. 'The deceivers', in Robert Cowley (ed.), *No end save victory: perspectives on World War II.* New York: G.P. Putnam's Sons, 2001.
Thomas Hone, Norman Friedman and Mark D. Mandeles. *American and British aircraft carrier development, 1919–1941.* Annapolis, Md: NIP, 1999.
Trent Hone. '"Give them hell!": the US Navy's night combat doctrine and the campaign for Guadalcanal', *War in History*, Vol.13, No.2 (2006): 171–99.
Peter Hore. *Patrick Blackett: sailor, scientist, and socialist.* London: Routledge, 2002.
James D. Hornfischer. *The last stand of the tin can sailors: the extraordinary World War II story of the U.S. Navy's finest hour.* New York: Bantam, 2004.
Chihiro Hosoya. 'The role of Japan's foreign ministry and its embassy in Washington, 1940–41', in Dorothy Borg and Shumpei Okamoto (eds), *Pearl Harbor as history: Japanese–American relations 1931–1941.* New York: Columbia University Press, 1973.
Richard Hough. *Naval battles of the twentieth century.* London: Constable, 1999.
——. *The longest battle: the war at sea 1939–45.* London: Weidenfeld & Nicolson, 1986.
——. *The great war at sea 1914–1918.* Oxford: OUP, 1983.
Michael Howard. *The Mediterranean strategy in the Second World War.* New York: Frederick A. Praeger, 1968.
——. *Strategic deception in the Second World War.* New York: W.W. Norton, 1995.
Grant Howard. *The Navy in New Zealand: an illustrated history.* London: Janes, 1981.
Stephen Howarth. *To shining sea: a history of the United States Navy 1775–1998.* Norman, Ok: University of Oklahoma Press, 1999.
——. 'Admiral of the Fleet Isoroku Yamamoto', in Stephen Howarth (ed.), *Men of war: great naval captains of World War II.* New York: St. Martin's Press, 1993.
——. 'Admiral of the Fleet Sir Philip Vian', in Stephen Howarth (ed.), *Men of war: great naval captains of World War II.* New York: St. Martin's Press, 1993.
—— 'Admiral of the Fleet Isoroku Yamamoto,' in Howarth (ed.), *Men of war: great naval captains of World War II.* New York: St. Martin's Press, 1993., pp.108–28.
——. *Morning glory: a history of the Imperial Japanese Navy.* London: Hamish Hamilton, 1983.
Ivor Howcroft. 'From beachhead to bridgehead: the Royal Navy's role in the amphibious assault across the Rhine, Spring 1945', *The Mariner's Mirror*, Vol.85, No.3 (1999): 308–19.
Vernon W. Howland. 'The loss of HMS *Glorious*: an analysis of the action', www.warship.org/no11994.htm.
Derek Howse. *Radar at sea: the Royal Navy in World War 2.* Basingstoke: Macmillan, 1993.
Gerald Howson. *Arms for Spain: the untold story of the Spanish Civil War.* London: John Murray, 1998.
Edwin P. Hoyt. *Backwater war: the Allied campaign in Italy, 1943–1945.* Westport, Conn: Praeger, 2002.
——. *Tojo against the world.* Lanham, Md: Scarborough House, 1993.
——. *Yamamoto: the man who planned Pearl Harbor.* New York: McGraw Hill, 1990.
——. *MacArthur's navy: the Seventh Fleet and the battle for the Philippines.* New York: Orion Books, 1989.
——. *The glory of the Solomons.* New York: Stein & Day, 1983.
——. *The Kamikazes.* New York: Arbor House, 1983.
——. *Closing the circle: war in the Pacific: 1945.* New York: Van Nostrand Reinhold, 1982.
——. *Guadalcanal.* New York: Stein & Day, 1982.
——. *To the Marianas: war in the central Pacific: 1944.* New York: Van Nostrand Reinhold, 1980.

——. *The life and death of HMS Hood.* London: Barker, 1977.
——. *Leyte Gulf: the death of the Princeton.* New York: Avon Books, 1972.
——. *The death of the Princeton.* New York: Avon Books, 1972.
Immanuel C.Y. Hsü. *The rise of modern China.* 5th Edition. New York: OUP, 1995.
Claude Huan. 'The French Navy in World War II', in James J. Sadkovich (ed.), *Reevaluating major naval combatants of World War II.* Westport, Conn: Greenwood Press, 1990.
T.M. Huber. *Okinawa 1945.* Havertown, Pa: Casemate, 2004.
Terry Hughes and John Costello. *The battle of the Atlantic.* New York: The Dial Press/John Wade, 1977.
Richard Humble. *Fraser of North Cape: the life of Admiral of the Fleet Lord Fraser, 1888–1981.* London: Routledge & Kegan Paul, 1983.
Barry Hunt and Donald Schurman. 'Prelude to Dieppe: thoughts on Combined Operations policy in the "raiding period" 1940–42', in Gerald Jordan (ed.), *Naval warfare in the twentieth century.* London: Croom Helm, 1977.
Kevin Don Hutchinson. *World War II in the North Pacific.* Westport, Conn: Greenwood Press, 1994.
Kiyoshi Ikeda. 'Vice Admiral Chuichi Nagumo', in Stephen Howarth (ed.), *Men of war: great naval captains of World War II.* New York: St. Martin's Press, 1993.
——. 'Vice Admiral Jisaburo Ozawa', in Stephen Howarth (ed.), *Men of war: great naval captains of World War II.* New York: St. Martin's Press, 1993.
Rikihei Inoguchi and Tadashi Nakajima. 'The Kamikaze attack corps', in David C. Evans (ed.), *The Japanese Navy in World War II: in the words of former Japanese naval officers.* Annapolis, Md: NIP, 1986.
Rikihei Inoguchi and Tadashi Nakajima with Roger Pineau. *The divine wind.* Westport, Conn: Greenwood Press, 1978.
Bernard Ireland. *Jane's naval history of World War II.* New York: Harper Collins, 1998.
——. *The war in the Mediterranean 1940–1943.* London: Arms and Armour, 1993.
Akira Iriye. *The origins of the Second World War in Asia and the Pacific.* London: Longman, 1987.
David Irving. *The trail of the fox: the life of Field-Marshal Erwin Rommel.* London: Weidenfeld & Nicolson, 1977.
Dallas Woodbury Isom. *Midway inquest: why the Japanese lost the battle of Midway.* Bloomington, Ind: Indiana University Press, 2007.
——. 'The battle of Midway: why the Japanese lost', *Naval War College Review, Vol.53, No.3* (Summer 2000): 60–100.
V. Issraeljan and L. Kutakov. *Diplomacy of aggression: Berlin–Rome–Tokyo axis, its rise and fall.* Moscow: Progress Publishers, 1970.
David Jablonsky. *War by land, sea and air: Dwight Eisenhower and the concept of unified command.* New Haven, Conn: Yale University Press, 2010.
Robert Jackson. *Kriegsmarine: the illustrated history of the German Navy in World War II.* London: Aurum, 2001.
——. *The Royal Navy in World War II.* Shrewsbury: Airlife, 1997.
——. *Churchill's moat: the Channel war 1939–1945.* Shrewsbury: Airlife, 1995.
Alf R. Jacobsen. *Scharnhorst.* Stroud: Sutton, 2003.
Philip H. Jacobsen. 'Radio silence and radio deception: secrecy insurance for the Pearl Harbor strike force', *Intelligence and National Security, Vol.19, No.4* (2004): 695–718.
Jon Jacobson. *Locarno diplomacy: Germany and the West, 1925–1929.* Princeton, NJ: Princeton University Press, 1972.
D. Clayton James. *The years of MacArthur. Vol.II, 1941–1945.* Boston: Houghton Mifflin, 1975.
T.C.G. James (ed.). *The Battle of Britain.* London: Frank Cass, 2000.

William Jameson. *Ark Royal: the life of an aircraft carrier at war 1939–41*. Penzance: Periscope Publishing, 2004.
H. Paul Jeffers. *Billy Mitchell: the life, times and battles of America's prophet of air power*. St. Paul, Mn: Zenith Press, 2005.
David Jefferson. *Coastal forces at war: Royal Navy 'little ships' in World War 2*. Sparkford, Somerset: Patrick Stephens, 1996.
E.H. Jenkins. *A history of the French Navy*. London: MacDonald & Jane's, 1973.
L. Johnman and H. Murphy. '"The first fleet victory since Trafalgar": the battle of Cape Matapan and signals intelligence, March 1941', *The Mariner's Mirror*, Vol.91, No.3 (2005): 436–53.
William Bruce Johnson. *The Pacific campaign in World War II*. London: Routledge, 2006.
Geoffrey Jones. *U-boat aces*. Bristol, Glos: Cerberus, 2004.
——. *Defeat of the wolf packs*. London: William Kimber, 1986.
Mark C. Jones. 'Give credit where credit is due: the Dutch role in the development and deployment of the submarine schnorchel', *The Journal of Military History*, 69, 4 (Oct.2005): 987–1012.
Matthew Jones. *Britain, the United States and the Mediterranean War, 1942–44*. Basingstoke: Macmillan, 1996.
R.V. Jones. *The wizard war*. New York: Coward, McCann & Geoghegan, 1978.
David Jordan. *Wolfpack: the U-boat war and the Allied counter-attack 1939–1945*. Staplehurst, Kent: Spellmount, 2002.
Gerald Jordan (ed.). *Naval warfare in the twentieth century, 1900–1945: essays in honour of Arthur Marder*. London: Croom Helm, 1977.
John Jordan. *Warships after Washington: the development of the five major fleets 1922–1930*. Annapolis, Md: NIP, 2011.
Philip S. Jowett. *The Chinese Army 1937–49: World War II and civil war*. Oxford: Osprey, 2005.
Donald Kagan and Frederick W. Kagan. *While America sleeps: self delusion, military weakness, and the threat to peace today*. New York: St. Martin's Press, 2000.
David Kahn. *Seizing the Enigma: the race to break the German U-boat codes 1939–1943*. Annapolis, Md: NIP, 2012.
——. *The codebreakers: the comprehensive history of secret communication from ancient times to the internet*. New York: Scribner, 1996.
Philip Kaplan and Jack Currie. *Wolfpack: U-boats at war 1939–1945*. Annapolis, Md: NIP, 1997.
J.E. Kaufmann and H.W. Kaufmann. *Fortress France: the Maginot Line and French defenses in World War II*. Westport, Conn: Praeger Security International, 2006.
John Keegan. *Battle at sea: from man of war to submarine*. London: Pimlico, 1993.
——. *Intelligence in war: knowledge of the enemy from Napoleon to Al-Qaeda*. London: Hutchinson, 2003.
Keesing's contemporary archives, 1937.
Gaylord T.M. Kelshall. *The U-boat war in the Caribbean*. Annapolis, Md: NIP, 1994.
Paul Kemp. *U-boats destroyed: German submarine losses in the World Wars*. Annapolis, Md: NIP, 1997.
——. *Underwater warriors*. London: Arms and Armour, 1996.
——. *Friend or foe: friendly fire at sea 1939–1945*. London: Leo Cooper, 1995.
——. *Convoy! Drama in Arctic waters*. London: Arms and Armour, 1993.
——. *Convoy protection: the defence of seaborne trade*. London: Arms and Armour, 1993.
Peter Kemp. 'Admiral of the Fleet Sir Dudley Pound', in Stephen Howarth (ed.), *Men of war: great naval captains of World War II*. New York: St. Martin's Press, 1993.
——. *Decision at sea: the convoy escorts*. New York: Elsevier-Dutton, 1978.

——. *The escape of the Scharnhorst and Gneisenau*. London: Ian Allen, 1975.
Greg Kennedy. 'The Royal Navy and imperial defence, 1919–56', in Greg Kennedy (ed.), *Imperial defence: the old world order 1856–1956*. Abingdon, Oxon: Routledge, 2008.
——. 'Sea denial, interdiction and diplomacy: the Royal Navy and the role of Malta, 1939–43', in Ian Speller (ed.), *The Royal Navy and maritime power in the twentieth century*. London: Frank Cass, 2005.
——. 'What worth the Americans? The British strategic foreign policy-making elite's view of American maritime power in the Far East, 1933–41', in Greg Kennedy (ed.), *British naval strategy east of Suez 1900–2000*. London, Routledge, 2005.
——. *Anglo-American strategic relations and the Far East, 1933–1939*. London: Frank Cass, 2002.
——. 'The 1930 London Naval Conference and Anglo-American maritime strength, 1927–30', in B.J.C. McKercher (ed.), *Arms limitation and disarmament: restraints on war*. Westport, Conn: Praeger, 1992.
Paul Kennedy. *The rise and fall of British naval mastery*. London: Penguin Books, 2004.
——. "British 'net assessment' and the coming of the Second World War", in Williamson Murray and Allan R. Millett (eds). *Calculations: net assessment and the coming of World War II*. New York: Free Press, 1992, pp.19–59.
——. *The rise and fall of the great powers*. New York: Vintage Books, 1989.
——. 'Military coalitions and coalition warfare over the past century', in Keith Neilson and Roy A. Prete (eds), *Coalition warfare: an uneasy accord*. Waterloo, Ont: Wilfrid Laurier University Press, 1983.
——. *The realities behind diplomacy: background influences on British external policy, 1865–1980*. London: George Allen & Unwin, 1981.
George C. Kenney. *General Kenney reports: a personal history of the Pacific War*. Washington, D.C: Office of Air Force History, United States Air Force, 1987.
Alvin Kernan. *The unknown Battle of Midway: the destruction of the American torpedo squadrons*. New Haven, Conn: Yale University Press, 2005.
Ian Kershaw. *Hitler 1936–1945: nemesis*. New York: W.W. Norton, 2000.
——. *Hitler 1889–1936: hubris*. London: Allen Lane, The Penguin Press, 1998.
Jean Kessler. 'U-boat bases in the Bay of Biscay', in Stephen Howarth and Derek Law (eds), *The Battle of the Atlantic 1939–1945: the 50th anniversary international naval conference*. London: Greenhill Books, 1994.
Michael Kettle. *Churchill and the Archangel fiasco: November 1918–July 1919*. London: Routledge, 1992.
D.G. Kiely. *Naval electronic warfare*. London: Brassey's Defence Publishers, 1988.
Warren F. Kimball. *Forged in war: Roosevelt, Churchill, and the Second World War*. New York: William Morrow & Co, 1997.
——(ed.). *Churchill & Roosevelt: the complete correspondence*. 3 vols. Princeton, N.J.: Princeton University Press, 1984.
Ernest J. King and Walter Muir Whitehill. *Fleet Admiral King: a naval record*. New York: W.W. Norton & Co., 1952.
F.A. Kingsley, (ed.). *The applications of radar and other electronic systems in the Royal Navy in World War 2*. Basingstoke: Macmillan, 1995.
——. *The development of radar equipments for the Royal Navy 1935–45*. Basingstoke: Macmillan, 1995.
Robert P. Kissel. 'PQ-17: convoy or bait?' *Command*, Vol.31 (1994): 84–91.
Carolyn J. Kitching. *Britain and the problem of international disarmament 1919–1934*. London: Routledge, 1999.

Charles W. Koburger, Jr. *Naval warfare in the Baltic, 1939–1945: war in a narrow sea*. Westport, Conn: Praeger, 1994.
——. *Naval warfare in the Eastern Mediterranean 1940–1945*. Westport, Conn: Praeger, 1993.
——. *The Cyrano fleet: France and its navy, 1940–1942*. Westport, Conn: Praeger, 1989.
Keichiro Komatsu. *Origins of the Pacific War and the importance of 'Magic'*. Richmond, Surrey: Japan Library, 1999.
Angus Konstam. *The battle of North Cape: the death ride of the Scharnhorst, 1943*. Barnsley: Pen & Sword Maritime, 2009.
Gerhard Koop and Klaus-Peter Schmolke. *Battleships of the Bismarck class*. London: Greenhill Books, 1998.
Ken Kotani. 'Could Japan read Allied signal traffic? Japanese codebreaking and the advance into French Indo-China, September 1940', *Intelligence and National Security, Vol. 20, No. 2* (2005): 304–20.
Wlayslaw Kozaczuk and Jerzy Straszak. *Enigma: how the Poles broke the Nazi code*. New York: Hippocrene Books, 2004.
John T. Kuehn. *Agents of innovation: the General Board and the design of the fleet that defeated the Japanese Navy*. Annapolis, Md: NIP, 2008.
Dan Kurzman. *Fatal voyage: the sinking of the USS Indianapolis*. New York: Broadway Books. 2001.
Eric Lacroix and Linton Wells, II. *Japanese cruisers of the Pacific War*. Annapolis, Md: NIP, 1997.
J.D. Ladd. *Assault from the sea*. Vancouver: David & Charles, 1976.
John Laffin. *Raiders: Great Exploits of the Second World War*. Stroud, Glos: Sutton Publishing, 1999.
Margaret Lamb and Nicholas Tarling. *From Versailles to Pearl Harbor: the origins of the Second world war in Europe and Asia*. Basingstoke: Palgrave, 2001.
Richard Lamb. *The drift to war 1922–1939*. London: W.H. Allen, 1989.
Andrew Lambert. 'Seapower 1939–40: Churchill and the strategic origins of the battle of the Atlantic', *The Journal of Strategic Studies, Vol.17, No.1* (1994): 86–108.
Raymond Lamont-Brown. *Kamikaze: Japan's suicide samurai*. London: Arms and Armour, 2002.
Ann Lane and Howard Temperley (eds). *The rise and fall of the Grand Alliance, 1941–45*. Basingstoke: Macmillan, 1995.
Eric Larabee. *Commander in Chief Franklin Delano Roosevelt, his lieutenants, and their war*. Annapolis, Md: NIP, 2004.
Joseph P. Lash. *Roosevelt and Churchill 1939–1941: the partnership that saved the west*. London: André Deutsch, 1977.
Sheila Lawlor. *Churchill and the politics of war, 1940–1941*. Cambridge: CUP, 1995.
Edwin T. Layton with Roger Pineau and John Costello. *'And I was there': Pearl Harbor and Midway – breaking the secrets*. New York: William Morrow, 1985.
Malcolm A. Le Compte. 'Radar and the air battles of Midway', *Naval History, Vol.6, No.2* (1992): 28–32.
William M. Leahy (ed.). *We shall return! MacArthur's commanders and the defeat of Japan*. Lexington, Ky: The University Press of Kentucky, 1988.
Robert Leckie. *Challenge for the Pacific: the bloody six-month Battle of Guadalcanal*. New York: Da Capo Press, 1999.
Alan J. Levine. *The war against Rommel's supply lines, 1942–43*. Westport, Conn: Praeger, 1999.
Ariel Levite. *Intelligence and strategic surprises*. New York: Columbia University Press, 1987.
James P. Levy. 'Race for the decisive weapon: British, American, and Japanese carrier fleets, 1942–43', *Naval War College Review, Vol.58, No.1* (2005): 138–50.
——. *The Royal Navy's Home Fleet in World War II*. Basingstoke: Palgrave Macmillan, 2003.
——. 'Lost leader: Admiral of the Fleet Sir Charles Forbes and the Second World War', *The Mariner's Mirror, Vol.88, No.2* (2002): 186–95.

——. 'The inglorious end of the *Glorious*: the release of the findings of the Board of Enquiry into the loss of HMS *Glorious*', *The Mariner's Mirror*, Vol.86, No.3 (2000): 302–9.
Ronald Lewin. *The American Magic: codes, ciphers and the defeat of Japan*. New York: Farrar Straus Giroux, 1982.
——. *Ultra goes to war: the secret story*. London: Hutchinson, 1978.
——. *Churchill as warlord*. London: B.T.Batsford, 1974.
Adrian R. Lewis. *Omaha beach: a flawed victory*. Chapel Hill, NC: University of North Carolina Press, 2001.
Sir Basil Liddell Hart. 'Operation Torch', in Basil Liddell Hart (ed.), *History of the Second World War*. London: Phoebus, 1980.
Lew Lind. *The battle of the wine dark sea: the Aegean campaign 1940–45*. Kenthurst, NSW: Kangaroo Press, 1994.
Eric Linklater. *The campaign in Italy*. London: HMSO, 1977.
Stanford E. Linzey. *God was at Midway: the sinking of the USS Yorktown (CV-5) and the battles of the Coral Sea and Midway*. San Diego, Ca: Black Forest Press, 1999.
Malcolm Llewellyn-Jones. *The Royal Navy and anti-submarine warfare, 1917–49*. London: Routledge, 2006.
Walter Lord. *Incredible victory*. Short Hills, N.J.: Burford Books, 1997.
John A. Lorelli. *To foreign shores: U.S. amphibious operations in World War II*. Annapolis, Md: NIP, 1995.
——. *The battle of the Komandorski Islands March 1943*. Annapolis, Md: NIP, 1984.
Robert W. Love, Jr. 'The U.S. Navy and Operation *Roll of Drums*, 1942', in Timothy J. Runyan and Jan M. Copes, *To die gallantly: the Battle of the Atlantic*. Boulder, Col: Westview Press, 1994.
——. 'Fleet Admiral Ernest J. King', in Stephen Howarth (ed.), *Men of war: great naval captains of World War II*. New York: St. Martin's Press, 1993.
——. *History of the U.S. Navy 1775–1941*. 2 Vols. Harrisburg, Pa: Stackpole Books, 1992.
——(ed.) *The Chiefs of Naval Operations*. Annapolis, Md: NIP, 1980.
Robert W. Love, Jr. and John Major. *The year of D-Day: the 1944 diary of Admiral Sir Bertram Ramsay*. Hull: University of Hull Press, 1994.
Bernard Lovell. *Echoes of war: the story of H2S radar*. Bristol: Adam Hilger, 1991.
Peter Lowe. 'The war against Japan and Allied relations', in Ann Lane and Howard Temperley (eds), *The rise and fall of the Grand Alliance, 1941–45*. Basingstoke: Macmillan, 1995.
——. *Great Britain and the origins of the Pacific War: a study of British policy in East Asia 1937–1941*. Oxford: Clarendon Press, 1977.
Bruce Loxton. 'Savo in retrospect', in David Stevens (ed.), *The Royal Australian Navy in World War II*. St. Leonards, NSW: Allen & Unwin, 1996.
Bruce Loxton with Chris Coulthard-Clark. *The shame of Savo*. Annapolis, Md: NIP, 1994.
Laddie Lucas. *Malta: the thorn in Rommel's side*. London: Stanley Paul, 1992.
C.E. Lucas-Phillips. *Cockleshell heroes*. London: Pan Books, 1956.
Philip Lundeberg. 'Allied co-operation', in Stephen Howarth and Derek Law (eds), *The Battle of the Atlantic 1939–1945: the 50th anniversary international naval conference*. London: Greenhill Books, 1994.
John B. Lundstrom. *Black shoe carrier admiral: Frank Jack Fletcher at Coral Sea, Midway, and Guadalcanal*. Annapolis, Md: NIP, 2006.
——. *The first team: Pacific naval air combat from Pearl Harbor to Midway*. Annapolis, Md: NIP, 2005.
——. 'Frank Jack Fletcher got a bum rap: Part One', *Naval History*, Vol.6, No.2 (1992): 22–27.
——. 'Frank Jack Fletcher got a bum rap: Part Two Guadalcanal', *Naval History*, Vol.6, No.3 (1992): 22–28.

——. *The first South Pacific campaign: Pacific Fleet strategy, December 1941 – June 1942*. Annapolis, Md: NIP, 1976.

B.W. Lythall. 'Basic science and research for naval radar, 1935–45', in Fred A. Kingsley (ed.), *The development of radar equipments for the Royal Navy 1935–45*. Basingstoke: Macmillan, 1995.

Edward M. MacCutcheon. 'World War II development and expansion', in Randolph W. King (ed.), *Naval engineering and American seapower*. Baltimore, Md: The Nautical & Aviation Co. of America, 1989.

Callum MacDonald. *The lost battle: Crete 1941*. London: Macmillan, 1993.

D. MacGregor. 'The use, misuse and non use of history: the Royal Navy and the operational lessons of the First World War', *The Journal of Military History*, Vol.56, No.4 (1992): 603–15.

Donald Macintyre. *Fighting admiral: the life and battles of Admiral of the Fleet Sir James Somerville, G.C.B., G.G.E., D.S.O.* London: Evans Bros., 1961.

Denis Mack Smith. *Mussolini*. London: Phoenix Giants, 1994.

Kenneth Macksey. *Commando strike: the story of amphibious raiding in World War II*. London: Secker & Warburg, 1985.

——. *Crucible of power: the fight for Tunisia 1942–1943*. London: Hutchinson, 1969.

Victor Madeira. '"Because I don't trust him, we are friends": signals intelligence and the reluctant Anglo-Soviet embrace, 1919–24', *Intelligence and National Security*, Vol. 19, No. 1 (2004): 29–51.

Tim Maga. *America attacks Japan: the invasion that never was*. Lexington, Ky: The University Press of Kentucky, 2002.

Brendan A. Maher. *A passage to Sword beach: minesweeping in the Royal Navy*. Annapolis, Md: NIP, 1996.

Joseph A. Maiolo. *Cry havoc: the arms race and the Second World War, 1931–41*. London: John Murray, 2010.

——. *The Royal Navy and Nazi Germany, 1933–39: a study in appeasement and the origins of the Second World War*. New York: St. Martin's Press, 1998.

John Major. 'The navy plans for war, 1937–41', in Kenneth Hagan (ed.), *In peace and war: interpretation of American naval history, 1775–1978*. Westport, Conn: Greenwood Press, 1978.

Robert Mallett. *The Italian Navy and fascist expansionism, 1935–1940*. London: Frank Cass, 1998.

Jak P. Mallmann Showell. *Hitler's U-boat bases*. Stroud, Glos: Sutton, 2002.

——. *Enigma U-boats: breaking the code*. Shepperton, Surrey: Ian Allen Publishing, 2000.

——. *The German Navy in World War Two: a reference guide to the Kriegsmarine, 1935–1945*. London: Arms and Armour Press, 1979.

William Manchester. *American Caesar*. London: Hutchinson, 1979.

Chris Mann and Christer Jorgensen. *Hitler's Arctic War: The German campaign in Norway, Finland and the USSR 1940–1945*. New York: St. Martin's Press, 2003.

Aubrey Mansergh (ed.). *With the Red Fleet: the war memoirs of the late Admiral Arseni G. Golovko*. London: Putnam, 1965.

Arthur J. Marder. *Operation Menace: the Dakar expedition and the Dudley North affair*. London: OUP, 1976.

——. *From the Dardanelles to Oran: studies of the Royal Navy in war and peace 1915–1940*. London: OUP, 1974.

Arthur J. Marder, Mark Jacobsen and John Horsfield. *Old friends new enemies: the Royal Navy and the Imperial Japanese Navy. Vol.II. The Pacific War, 1942–1945*. Oxford: Clarendon Press, 1990.

Sally Marks. *The ebbing of European ascendancy. An international history of the world, 1914–1945*. Oxford: OUP, 2002.

——. *The illusion of peace: international relations in Europe, 1918–1933.* New York: St. Martin's Press, 1976.
Francis Mason. *Battle over Britain: a history of the German air assaults on Great Britain, 1917–18 and July–December 1940, and of the development of Britain's air defences between the wars.* London: McWhirter Twins Ltd., 1969.
Robert K. Massie. *Castles of steel: Britain, Germany, and the winning of the great war at sea.* New York: Random House, 2003.
Yoshihisa Tak Matsusaka. *The making of Japanese Manchuria, 1904–1932.* Cambridge, Mass: Harvard University Press, 2001.
Masataka Chihaya. 'The withdrawal from Kiska', in David C. Evans (ed.), *The Japanese Navy in World War II: in the words of former Japanese naval officers.* Annapolis, Md: NIP, 1986.
S. May. 'Strangling Rommel: British submarine commanders in the Mediterranean, June 1940 to September 1943', *The Mariner's Mirror,* Vol.88, No.4 (2002): 456–68.
Evan Mawdsley. *The Russian Civil War.* Boston, Mass: Allen & Unwin, 1987.
Lida Mayo. *Bloody Buna: the campaign that halted the Japanese invasion of Australia.* Newton Abbot: David & Charles, 1975.
Lex McAuley. *MacArthur's Eagles: the U.S. air war over New Guinea, 1943–1944.* Annapolis, Md: NIP, 2005.
——. *To the bitter end: the Japanese defeat at Buna and Gona 1942–43.* Milsons Point, NSW: Arrow, 1993.
David McCullough. *Truman.* New York: Simon & Schuster, 1992.
William L. McGee. *The Solomons campaigns 1942–1943. From Guadalcanal to Bougainville.* Santa Barbara, Ca: BMC Publications, 2002.
——. *The amphibians are coming! Emergence of the 'gator navy and its revolutionary landing craft.* Santa Barbara, Ca: BMC Publications, 2000.
I.C. McGibbon. *Blue-water rationale: the naval defence of New Zealand 1914–1942.* Wellington, NZ: Government Printer, 1981.
Donald McIntyre. *Fighting admiral: the life of Admiral of the Fleet Sir James Somerville, G.C.B., G.B.E., D.S.O.* London: Evan Bros. 1961.
B.J.C. McKercher. 'The politics of naval arms limitation in Britain in the 1920s', in Erik Goldstein and John Maurer (eds), *The Washington Conference, 1921–22: naval rivalry, East Asian stability and the road to Pearl Harbor.* London: Frank Cass, 1994.
——. 'Of horns and teeth: the Preparatory Commission and the World Disarmament Conference, 1926–34', in B.J.C. McKercher (ed.), *Arms limitation and disarmament.* Westport, Conn: Praeger, 1992.
Ronald McKie. *The heroes.* Sydney: Angus & Robertson, 1967.
Donald McLachlan. *Room 39: naval intelligence in action 1939–45.* London: Weidenfeld & Nicolson, 1968.
David Mearns and Rob White. *Hood and Bismarck.* London: Channel 4 Books, 2001.
Peter Medcalf. *War in the shadows: Bougainville 1944–45.* Sydney: Collins & Australian War Memorial, 1986.
Charles L. Mee Jr. *The end of order, Versailles 1919.* New York: Dutton, 1980.
Philip S. Meilinger. 'Between the devil and the deep blue sea: the Fleet Air Arm before the Second World War.' *The RUSI Journal,* Vol.144, No.5 (1999): 73–78.
Jürg Meister. *Soviet warships of the Second World War.* New York: Arco, 1977.
James A. Merrill. 'Fleet Admiral William F. Halsey Jr.', in Stephen Howarth (ed.), *Men of war: great naval captains of World War II.* New York: St. Martin's Press, 1993.
James M. Merrill. *A sailor's admiral: a biography of William F. Halsey.* New York: Thomas Y. Crowell, 1976.

Martin Middlebrook. *Convoy: the battle for convoys SC.122 and HX.229*. London: Allen Lane, 1976.
Martin Middlebrook and Chris Everitt. *The Bomber Command diaries: an operational reference book: 1939–1945*. London: Penguin Books, 1990.
Martin Middlebrook and P. Mahoney. *The sinking of the Prince of Wales and the Repulse*. Barnsley: Leo Cooper, 2004.
George Reid Millar. *The Bruneval Raid: stealing Hitler's radar*. London: Cassell's Military Paperbacks, 2002.
David Miller, *U-boats: history, development and equipment 1914–1945*. London: Conway Maritime Press, 2000
Donald L. Miller. *D-days in the Pacific*. New York: Simon & Schuster, 2005.
Edward S. Miller. *War plan ORANGE*. Annapolis, Md: NIP, 1991.
John Miller, Jr. *CARTWHEEL: the reduction of Rabaul*. Washington, D.C: Dept. of the Army, 1959.
Nathan Miller. *War at sea*. New York: Scribner, 1965.
Thomas G. Miller, Jr. *The Cactus Air Force: the story of the handful of fliers who saved Guadalcanal*. New York: Harper & Row, 1969.
Allan R. Millett. *Semper fidelis: the history of the United States Marine Corps*. New York: The Free Press, 1991.
Marc Milner. *Battle of the Atlantic*. Stroud, Glos: Tempus, 2003.
——. 'Squaring some of the corners: the Royal Canadian Navy and the pattern of the Atlantic war', in Timothy J. Runyan and Jan M. Copes (eds), *To die gallantly: the battle of the Atlantic*. Boulder, Col: Westview Press, 1994.
——. *The U-boat hunters: the Royal Canadian Navy and the offensive against Germany's submarines*. Annapolis, Md: NIP, 1994.
——. *North Atlantic run: the Royal Canadian Navy and the battle for the convoys*. Annapolis, Md: NIP, 1986.
Ministry of Defence. *War with Japan: Vols.I–VI*. London: HMSO, 1995.
——. *Invasion of the south of France: Operation 'Dragoon', 15th August, 1944*. London: HMSO, 1994.
Samuel W. Mitcham, Jr. *The desert fox in Normandy: Rommel's defense of fortress Europe*. Westport, Conn: Praeger, 1997.
Donald W. Mitchell. *A history of Russian and Soviet sea power*. London: André Deutsch, 1974.
Robert J. Mitchell (ed.). *The capture of Attu: a World War II battle as told by the men who fought there*. Lincoln, Neb: University of Nebraska Press, 2000.
Yoshida Mitsuru. *Requiem for battleship Yamato*. London: Constable, 1999.
Jeffrey M. Moore. *Spies for Nimitz*. Annapolis, Md: NIP, 2004.
Joseph Moretz. *The Royal Navy and the capital ship in the interwar period: an operational perspective*. London: Frank Cass, 2002.
Kenneth O. Morgan. *Consensus and disunity: the Lloyd George coalition government, 1918–1922*. Oxford: Clarendon Press, 1979.
Samuel Eliot Morison. *History of United States Naval Operations in World War II Vols. I-XIV*. Boston: Little, Brown & Co., 1964–68.
——. *The two-ocean war: a short history of the United States Navy in the Second World War*. Boston: Little, Brown & Co, 1963.
James Morley (ed.). *Deterrent diplomacy: Japan, Germany, and the USSR 1935–1940*. New York: Columbia University Press, 1976.
August Karl Muggenthaler. *German raiders of World War II*. Englewood Cliffs, N.J.: Prentice-Hall, Inc., 1977.

Timothy P. Mulligan. '*Bismarck*: not ready for action', *Naval History*, Vol.15, No.1 (2001): 20–26.

Malcolm H. Murfett. 'Backhouse, Sir Roger Roland', in Brian Harrison (ed.), *ODNB*, Vol.3. Oxford: OUP, 2004.

———. 'Cunningham, Sir John Henry Dacres', in Brian Harrison (ed.). *ODNB*. Vol.14. Oxford: OUP, 2004.

———. 'Phillips, Sir Tom Spencer Vaughan', in Brian Harrison (ed.), *ODNB*, Vol.44. Oxford; OUP, 2004.

———. 'Reflections on an enduring theme: the "Singapore strategy" at sixty', in Brian Farrell and Sandy Hunter (eds), *Sixty years on: the fall of Singapore revisited*. Singapore: Eastern Universities Press, 2002.

——— 'Living in the past: a critical re-examination of the Singapore naval strategy, 1918–41', *War & Society*, vol. 11, no. 1 (1993): 73–103.

———. 'Look back in anger: The Western Powers and the Washington Conference of 1921–22', in B.J.C. McKercher (ed.), *Arms limitation and disarmament: restraints in war, 1899–1939*. Westport, Conn: Praeger, 1992.

———. '"Are we ready?" The development of American and British naval strategy, 1922–39', in John B. Hattendorf and Robert S. Jordan (eds), *Maritime strategy and the balance of power: Britain and America in the twentieth century*. Basingstoke, Hants: Macmillan, 1989.

———. *Fool-proof relations: the search for Anglo-American naval cooperation during the Chamberlain years 1937–1940*. Singapore: Singapore University Press, 1984.

——— (ed.). *Imponderable but not inevitable: warfare in the 20th century*. Santa Barbara, Cal: ABC Clio-Praeger S.I., 2010.

———, John N. Miksic, Brian P. Farrell and Chiang Ming Shun. *Between Two Oceans: A Military History of Singapore from 1275 to 1971*. 2nd Edition. Singapore: Marshall Cavendish, 2011.

Williamson Murray. *Strategy for defeat. The Luftwaffe 1933–1945*. Maxwell Air Force Base, Al: Air University Press, 1983.

Williamson Murray and Allan R. Millett. *A war to be won: fighting the Second World War*. Cambridge, Mass: The Belknap Press of Harvard University Press, 2000.

———. *Calculations: net assessment and the coming of World War II*. New York: Free Press, 1992.

Peter V. Nash. *Development of mobile logistics support in Anglo-American naval policy, 1900–1953*. Gainesville, Fl: University of Florida Press, 2009.

James Lord Neidpath. *The Singapore naval base and the defence of Britain's eastern empire, 1919–1941*. Oxford: Clarendon Press, 1981.

Robin Neillands. *The Dieppe raid: the story of the disastrous 1942 expedition*. London: Aurum Press, 2006.

———. *The battle of Normandy 1944*. London: Cassell, 2002.

Keith Neilson. 'The Royal Navy, Japan and British strategic foreign policy 1932–1934,' *Journal of Military History*, vol. 75, no. 2 (April 2011): 505–31.

———. '"Unbroken thread": Japan, maritime power and British imperial defence, 1920–32', in Greg Kennedy (ed.), *British naval strategy east of Suez 1900–2000*. Abingdon, Oxon: Frank Cass, 2005.

———. 'The Defence Requirements Sub-Committee, British strategic foreign policy, Neville Chamberlain and the path to appeasement', *English Historical Review*, Vol.118, No.477 (2003): 651–84.

Sönke Neitzel. 'Kriegsmarine and Luftwaffe co-operation in the war against Britain, 1939–45', *War in History*, Vol.10, No.4 (Nov. 2003): 448–63.

——. 'The deployment of the U-boats', in Stephen Howarth and Derek Law (eds), *The Battle of the Atlantic 1939–1945: the 50th anniversary international naval conference*. London: Greenhill Books, 1994.

Craig Nelson. *The first heroes: the extraordinary story of the Doolittle Raid – America's first World War II victory*. London: Viking, 2002.

Curtis L. Nelson. *Hunters in the shallows: a history of the PT boat*. Washington, D.C: Brassey's, 1998.

Roy Conyers Nesbit, assisted by Oliver Hoare. *RAF Coastal Command in action 1939–1945*. Stroud, Glos: Sutton in association with the Public Record Office, 1997.

Anthony Newpower. *Iron men and tin fish: the race to build a better torpedo during World War II*. Westport, Conn: Praeger Security International, 2006.

Arthur Nicholson. *Hostages to fortune: Winston Churchill and the loss of the Prince of Wales and Repulse*. Stroud, Glos: Sutton Publishing, 2005.

Axel Niestlé. 'German technical and electronic development', in Stephen Howarth and Derek Law (eds), *The Battle of the Atlantic 1939–1945: the 50th anniversary international naval conference*. London: Greenhill Books, 1994.

Ian H. Nish. *Japan's struggle with internationalism: Japan, China and the League of Nations, 1931–33*. London: K. Paul International, 1993.

Tajima Nobuo. 'The Berlin–Tokyo Axis reconsidered: from the Anti-Comintern Pact to the plot to assassinate Stalin', in Christian W. Spang and Rolf-Harald Wippich (eds.), *Japanese–German relations, 1895–1945: war, diplomacy and public opinion*. Abingdon: Oxon: Routledge, 2006.

Liam Nolan and John E. Nolan. *Torpedoed: was convoy T.M.1 sacrificed? The facts about the near-total destruction of the first special oil convoy of World War II*. Victoria, BC: Trafford Publishing, 2007.

Andrew Norman. *HMS Hood: Pride of the Royal Navy*. Staplehurst, Kent: Spellmount, 2002.

Phillips Payson O'Brien. 'Politics, arms control and US naval development in the inter-war period', in Phillips Payson O'Brien (ed.). *Technology and naval combat in the twentieth century and beyond*. London: Frank Cass, 2001.

Raymond O'Connor (ed.). *The Japanese Navy in World War II*. Annapolis, Md: NIP, 1969.

Ed Offley. *Turning the tide*. New York: Basic Books, 2011.

Vincent P. O'Hara. *The German fleet at war, 1939–1945*. Annapolis, Md: NIP, 2011.

——. *Struggle for the middle sea: the great navies at war in the Mediterranean Theater, 1940–1945*. Annapolis, Md: NIP, 2009.

——. *The U.S. Navy against the Axis: surface combat, 1941–1945*. Annapolis, Md: NIP, 2007.

——. 'The Duisburg [sic] (Beta) Convoy Battle: November 9th, 1941'. Accessed through www.regiamarina.net/engagements/duisburg/duisburg_us.htm.

Vincent P. O'Hara, W. David Dickson and Richard Worth. *On seas contested: the seven great navies of the Second World War*. Annapolis, Md: NIP, 2010.

Toshikazu Ohmae. 'Japanese operations in the Indian Ocean', in David C. Evans (ed.), *The Japanese Navy in World War II: in the words of former Japanese naval officers*. Annapolis, Md: NIP, 1986.

——. 'The Battle of Savo Island', in David C. Evans (ed.), *The Japanese Navy in World War II: in the words of former Japanese naval officers*. Annapolis, Md: NIP, 1986.

Wesley Olson. *Bitter victory: the death of HMAS Sydney*. Annapolis, Md: NIP, 2000.

Eric W. Osborne. *Destroyers: an illustrated history of their impact*. Santa Barbara, Ca: ABC-Clio, 2005.

Richard Overy. *Russia's war*. London: Allen Lane, 1997.

Eloise Paananen. *The winter war: the Russo-Finnish conflict 1939–40.* Boulder, Col: Westview Press, 1985.
S.W.C. Pack. *Operation Husky.* Newton Abbot, Devon: David & Charles, 1977.
——. *The battle of Matapan.* New York: Macmillan, 1961.
Peter Padfield. *Maritime dominion and the triumph of the free world.* London: John Murray, 2009.
——. *War beneath the sea: submarine conflict during World War II.* New York: John Wiley, 1996.
——. 'Grand Admiral Karl Dönitz', in Stephen Howarth (ed.), *Men of war: great naval captains of World War II.* New York: St. Martin's Press, 1993.
——. *Dönitz: the last führer.* London: Victor Gollancz, 1984.
Mark P. Parillo. 'The Imperial Japanese Navy in World War II', in James J. Sadkovich (ed.), *Reevaluating major naval combatants of World War II.* Westport, Conn: Greenwood Press, 1990.
R.A.C. Parker. *Chamberlain and appeasement: British policy and the coming of the Second World War.* New York: St. Martin's Press, 1993.
Oscar Parkes (ed.). *Janes's fighting ships 1933.* London: Sampson Low, Marston & Co., 1933.
——. *Jane's fighting ships 1931.* London: Sampson Low, Marston & Co., 1931.
Oscar Parkes and Francis McMurtrie (eds). *Jane's fighting ships 1929.* London: Sampson Low, Marston & Co., 1929.
——. *Jane's fighting ships 1927.* London: Sampson, Low, Marston & Co, 1927.
Jonathan Parshall and Anthony Tully. *Shattered sword: the untold story of the battle of Midway.* Washington, DC: Potomac Books, 2005.
Jonathan P. Parshall, David B. Dickson and Anthony Tull. 'Doctrine matters: why the Japanese lost at Midway', *Naval War College Review, Vol.54, No.2* (2001): 140–51.
Lawrence Paterson. *Black flag: the surrender of Germany's U-boat forces 1945.* Barnsley: Seaforth, 2009.
——. *Dönitz's last gamble: the inshore U-boat campaign 1944–45.* Barnsley: Seaforth, 2008.
——. *Weapons of desperation: German frogmen and midget submarines of World War II.* London: Chatham Publishing, 2006.
——. *Second U-boat flotilla.* London: Leo Cooper, 2003.
——. *The first U-boat flotilla.* London: Leo Cooper, 2002.
Frank Pearce. *Running the gauntlet: the battles for the Barents Sea.* London: Fontana, 1989.
Michael Pearson. *Red sky in the morning: the battle of the Barents Sea, 31 December 1942.* Shrewsbury: Airlife, 2002.
Mark R. Peattie. *Sunburst: the rise of Japanese naval air power, 1909–1941.* Annapolis, Md: NIP, 2001.
——. *Nan'yō: the rise and fall of the Japanese in Micronesia, 1885–1945.* Honolulu: University of Hawaii Press, 1988.
George Peden. *British rearmament and the Treasury: 1932–1939.* Edinburgh: Scottish Academic Press, 1979.
Léonce Peillard. *U-boats to the rescue: the Laconia incident.* London: Coronet, 1976.
Galen Roger Perras. *Stepping stones to nowhere: the Aleutian Islands, Alaska, and American military strategy, 1867–1945.* Vancouver, BC: UBC Press, 2003.
Michael Alfred Peszke. *Poland's Navy 1918–1945.* New York: Hippocrene Books, 1999.
Richard Petrow. *The bitter years: the invasion and occupation of Denmark and Norway, April 1940–May 1945.* New York: W.W. Morrow, 1974.
Ian Pfennigwerth. *Missing pieces: the intelligence jigsaw and RAN operations from 1939–71.* Canberra: RAN, 2008.
Tobias R. Philbin III. *The lure of Neptune: German–Soviet naval collaboration and ambitions, 1919–1941.* Columbia, S.C.: University of South Carolina Press, 1994.
Roger Pineau. 'Captain Joseph John Rochefort', in Stephen Howarth (ed.), *Men of war: great naval captains of World War II.* New York: St. Martin's Press, 1993.

Charlotte and Denis Plimmer. *A matter of expediency: the jettison of Admiral Sir Dudley North*. London: Quartet Books, 1978.
Forrest C. Pogue. *The supreme command*. Washington, D.C.: Department of the Army, 1954.
Michel Thomas Poirier. 'Results of the American Pacific Submarine Campaign of World War II'. (30 Dec. 1999). (Accessed through www.navy.mil/navydata/cno/n87/history/pac-campaign.html on 14 Feb. 2008.)
Norman Polmar. *Aircraft carriers: a graphic history of carrier aviation and its influence on world events*. Garden City, NY: Doubleday & Co, 1969.
Kenneth Poolman. *The winning edge: naval technology in action, 1939–1945*. Annapolis, Md: NIP, 1997.
——. *The sea hunters: escort carriers v. U-boats, 1941–1945*. London: Arms and Armour, 1982.
——. *Scourge of the Atlantic: Focke-Wulf Condor*. London: Macdonald & Jane's, 1978.
Dudley Pope. *73 north: the Battle of the Barents Sea*. London: Secker & Warburg, 1988.
Gaines Post, Jr. *Dilemmas of appeasement: British deterrence and defense, 1934–1937*. Ithaca, NY: Cornell University Press, 1993.
E.B. Potter. 'Fleet Admiral Chester William Nimitz', in Stephen Howarth (ed.), *Men of war: great naval captains of World War II*. New York: St. Martin's Press, 1993.
——. *Admiral Arleigh Burke*. New York: Random House, 1990.
——. *Bull Halsey*. Annapolis, Md: NIP, 1985.
——. *Nimitz*. Annapolis, Md: NIP, 1976.
E.B. Potter and Chester W. Nimitz. *The great sea war: the naval action in World War II*. New York: Bramhall House, 1960.
John Deane Potter. *Fiasco: the break-out of the German battleships*. London: Heinemann, 1970.
Ronald E. Powaski. *Lightning war: blitzkrieg in the west, 1940*. Hoboken, N.J.: John Wiley, 2003.
Michael Powell. *Last voyage of the Graf Spee*. London: White Lion, 1976.
Lin Poyer, Suzanne Falgout and Laurence Marshall Carucci. *The typhoon of war: Micronesian experiences of the Pacific War*. Honolulu: University of Hawaii Press, 2001.
John Prados. *Combined fleet decoded: the secret history of American intelligence and the Japanese Navy in World War II*. New York: Random House, 1995.
Gordon W. Prange. *At dawn we slept*. New York: McGraw Hill, 1981.
Gordon W. Prange, Donald M. Goldstein and Katherine V. Dillon. *Miracle at Midway*. New York: McGraw-Hill, 1982.
Lawrence R. Pratt. *East of Malta, west of Suez*. Cambridge: CUP, 1975.
Nathan Prefer. *MacArthur's New Guinea campaign: March–August 1944*. Conshohocken, Pa: Combined Books, 1995.
Anthony Preston. *Cruisers: an illustrated history 1880–1980*. London: Arms and Armour Press, 1980.
Paul Preston. *The politics of revenge: fascism and the military in twentieth-century Spain*. London: Routledge, 1995.
Alfred Price. *Instruments of darkness: the history of electronic warfare, 1939–1945*. London: Greenhill Books, 2005.
——. *Aircraft versus submarine in two world wars*. Barnsley: Pen & Sword Aviation, 2004.
Henry Probert. 'Allied land-based anti-submarine warfare', in Stephen Howarth and Derek Law (eds), *The Battle of the Atlantic 1939–1945: the 50th anniversary international naval conference*. London: Greenhill Books, 1994.
Glyn Prysor. *Citizen sailors: the Royal Navy in the Second World War*. London: Viking, 2011.
Philip Pugh. *The cost of seapower: the influence of money on naval affairs from 1815 to the present day*. London: Conway Maritime Press, 1986.

Erich Raeder. *My life*. Annapolis, Md: US NIP, 1960.

Werner Rahn. 'The campaign: the German perspective', in Stephen Howarth and Derek Law (eds), *The Battle of the Atlantic 1939–1945: the 50th anniversary international naval conference*. London: Greenhill Books, 1994.

Alan Raven and John Roberts. *British cruisers of World War Two*. Annapolis, Md: NIP, 1980.

——. *British battleships of World War Two: the development and technical history of the Royal Navy's battleships and battlecruisers from 1911 to 1946*. London: Arms and Armour Press, 1976.

John Ray. *The night blitz 1940–1941*. London: Arms and Armour, 1996.

——. *The battle of Britain: new perspectives behind the scenes of the great air war*. London: Arms and Armour, 1994.

Anthony Read and David Fisher. *The deadly embrace: Hitler, Stalin and the Nazi–Soviet Pact 1939–1941*. London: Michael Joseph, 1988.

Jeff Reardon, 'Breaking the U.S. Navy's "gun club" mentality in the South Pacific,' *Journal of Military History*, vol. 75, no. 2 (April 2011): 533–64.

David Rees. *Soviet seizure of the Kuriles*. New York: Praeger, 1985.

Stephen D. Regan. *In bitter tempest: the biography of Admiral Frank Jack Fletcher*. Ames, Iowa: Iowa State University Press, 1994.

Clark G. Reynolds. *On the warpath in the Pacific: Admiral Jocko Clark and the fast carriers*. Annapolis, Md: NIP, 2005.

——. 'Admiral Marc A. Mitscher', in Stephen Howarth (ed.), *Men of war: great naval captains of World War II*. New York: St. Martin's Press, 1993.

——. *Admiral John H. Towers: the struggle for naval air supremacy*. Annapolis, Md: NIP, 1991.

Graham Rhys-Jones. *The loss of the Bismarck: an avoidable disaster*. Annapolis, Md: NIP, 1999.

Brooks Richards. *Secret flotillas: the clandestine sea lines to France & French North Africa 1940–1944*. London: HMSO, 1996.

Denis Richards. *Hardest victory: RAF Bomber Command in the Second World War*. New York: W.W. Norton, 1995.

Jeffrey Richelson. *A century of spies: intelligence in the twentieth century*. New York: OUP, 1995.

Jon Robb-Webb. '"Light two lanterns, the British are coming by sea": Royal Navy participation in the Pacific 1944–45', in Greg Kennedy (ed.), *British naval strategy east of Suez 1900–2000*. London, Routledge, 2005.

——. 'Sea control in narrow waters: the battles of Taranto and Matapan', in Ian Speller (ed.), *The Royal Navy and maritime power in the twentieth century*. London: Frank Cass, 2005.

Gary Robbins. *The aircraft carrier story 1908–1945*. London: Cassell & Co, 2001.

Andrew Roberts. *The storm of war: a new history of the Second World War*. New York: Harper Perennial, 2012.

Geoffrey Roberts. 'The alliance that failed: Moscow and the Triple Alliance negotiations, 1939', in Jeremy Black (ed.), *The Second World War: Vol. VI, Causes and background*. Aldershot, Hants: Ashgate, 2007.

——. *The Soviet Union and the origins of the Second World War: Russo-German relations and the road to war, 1933–1941*. Basingstoke, Hants: Macmillan, 1995.

Derek Robinson. *Invasion, 1940: the truth about the battle of Britain and what stopped Hitler*. London: Constable, 2005.

Nicholas A.M. Rodger (ed.). *Naval power in the twentieth century*. London: Macmillan, 1996.

Anthony Rogers. *Churchill's folly: Leros and the Aegean*. London: Cassell, 2003.

Jürgen Rohwer. *Chronology of the war at sea 1939–1945: The naval history of World War Two*. London: Chatham Publishing, 2005.

——. *War at sea 1939–1945*. Annapolis, Md: NIP, 1996.

——. 'The wireless war', in Stephen Howarth and Derek Law (eds), *The Battle of the Atlantic 1939–1945: the 50th anniversary international naval conference*. London: Greenhill Books, 1994.
——. *The critical convoy battles of March 1943: the battle for HX.229/SC122*. London: Ian Allen, 1977.
Jürgen Rohwer and Mikhail S. Monakov. *Stalin's ocean-going fleet: Soviet naval strategy and shipbuilding programmes 1935–1953*. London: Frank Cass, 2001.
Lisle A. Rose. *Power at sea. Vol. 2*. Columbia, Mo: University of Missouri Press, 2007.
——. *The ship that held the line: the USS Hornet and the first year of the Pacific War*. Annapolis, Md: NIP, 1995.
Philip T. Rosen. 'The treaty navy, 1919–37', in Kenneth J. Hagan (ed.), *In peace and war: interpretation of American naval history, 1775–1978*. Westport, Conn: Greenwood Press, 1978.
Stephen W. Roskill. *Naval policy between the wars*. 2 vols. London: Collins, 1968 and 1977.
——. *The war at sea 1939–1945. Vol. I*. London: HMSO, 1954.
——. *The war at sea. Vol. III, Part 2*. London: HMSO, 1961.
Bill D. Ross. *Peleliu: tragic triumph. The untold story of the Pacific war's forgotten battle*. New York: Random House, 1991.
Alexander B. Rossino. *Hitler strikes Poland: blitzkrieg, ideological atrocity*. Lawrence, Ks: University Press of Kansas, 2003.
Eberhard Rössler. 'U-boat development and building', in Stephen Howarth and Derek Law (eds), *The Battle of the Atlantic 1939–1945: the 50th anniversary international naval conference*. London: Greenhill Books, 1994.
—— *The U-boat: the evolution and technical history of German submarines*. London: Arms and Armour Press, 1981.
Frank B. Rowlett. *The story of Magic: memoirs of an American cryptologic pioneer*. Laguna Hills, Ca: Aegean Park Press, 1998.
Friedrich Ruge. *Rommel in Normandy*. San Rafael, Ca: Presidio Press, 1979.
——. *The Soviets as naval opponents 1941–1945*. Cambridge: Patrick Stephens, 1979.
——. *Der Seekrieg: the German Navy's story 1939–1945*. Annapolis, Md: U.S. NIP, 1957.
James J. Sadkovich. 'German military incompetence through Italian eyes', in Jeremy Black (ed.), *The Second World War. Vol.VII*. Aldershot, Hants: Ashgate, 2007.
——. 'Re-evaluating who won the Italo-British naval conflict, 1940–42', in Jeremy Black (ed.), *The Second World War, Vol. I*. Aldershot, Hants: Ashgate, 2007.
——. 'The Italo-Greek War in context: Italian priorities and Axis diplomacy', in Jeremy Black (ed.), *The Second World War. Vol.I*. Aldershot, Hants: Ashgate, 2007.
——. *The Italian Navy in World War II*. Westport, Conn: Greenwood Press, 1994.
—— 'The Italian Navy in World War II: 1940–43', in James J. Sadkovich (ed.), *Reevaluating major naval combatants of World War II*. Westport, Conn: Greenwood Press, 1990.
John Sadler. *Operation Mercury: the fall of Crete 1941*. Barnsley: Pen & Sword Military, 2007.
A.B. Sainsbury. 'The front line: convoy HG76 – the defence', in Stephen Howarth and Derek Law (eds). *The Battle of the Atlantic 1939–1945: the 50th anniversary international naval conference*. London: Greenhill Books, 1994.
Henry Sakaida. *The siege of Rabaul*. St.Paul, Mn: Phalanx, 1996.
Reynolds M. Salerno. 'Italy's pirate submarine campaign of 1937', in Gregory C. Kennedy and Keith Neilson (eds), *Incidents and international relations: people, power, and personalities*. Westport, Conn: Praeger, 2002.
——. *Vital crossroads: Mediterranean origins of the Second World War, 1935–1940*. Ithaca, NY: Cornell University Press, 2002.

———. 'Multilateral strategy and diplomacy: the Anglo-German Naval Agreement and the Mediterranean crisis, 1935–36', *Journal of Strategic Studies, Vol. 17, No. 2* (1994): 39–78.
Michael Salewski, 'The submarine war: a historical essay', in Lothar-Günther Buchheim. *U-boat war*. New York: Alfred A. Knopf, 1978: unpaginated.
Patrick Salmon (ed.). *Britain and Norway in the Second World War*. London: HMSO, 1995.
Alberto Santoni. 'The Italian submarine campaign', in Stephen Howarth and Derek Law (eds), *The Battle of the Atlantic 1939–1945: the 50th anniversary international naval conference*. London: Greenhill Books, 1994.
Nicholas Evan Sarantakes. 'One last crusade: the British Pacific Fleet and its impact on the Anglo-American Alliance', *The English Historical Review, Vol.CXXI, No.491* (2006): 429–66.
Roger Sarty. 'The limits of Ultra: the schnorkel U-boat offensive against North America, November 1944–January 1945', *Intelligence and National Security, Vol.12, No.2* (1997): 44–68.
———. *The maritime defence of Canada*. Toronto: Canadian Institute of Strategic Studies, 1996.
Howard Sauer. *The last big-gun naval battle: the Battle of Surigao Strait*. Palo Alto, Ca: Glencannon Press, 1999.
Paul Schmalenbach. *German raiders: a history of auxiliary cruisers of the German Navy 1895–1945*. Cambridge: Patrick Stephens, 1977.
K. Schmider. 'The Mediterranean in 1941: crossroads of lost opportunities', *War and Society. Vol.15, No.2* (1997): 19–41.
B.B. Schofield. *The Arctic convoys*. London: Macdonald & Jane's, 1977.
Alan Schom. *The eagle and the rising sun: the Japanese–American war 1941–1943*. New York: W.W. Norton, 2004.
Peter Scott. *The battle of the narrow seas: a history of the light coastal forces in the Channel and North Sea, 1939–1945*. London: White Lion, 1974.
David Sears. *At war with the wind*. New York: Citadel Press, 2008.
Hugh Sebag-Montefiore. *Enigma: the battle for the code*. London: Phoenix, 2001.
Adrian Seligman. *War in the islands: undercover operations in the Aegean 1942–4*. Stroud: Alan Sutton, 1996.
W.R. Sendall. 'Lost opportunities of amphibious warfare in World War Two', in Merrill L. Bartlett (ed.), *Assault from the sea*. Annapolis, Md: NIP, 1983.
Alan Sharp. *The Versailles settlement: peacemaking in Paris 1919*. Basingstoke, Macmillan, 1991.
J.S. Shayler. 'Royal Navy metric warning radar, 1935–45', in F.A. Kingsley (ed.), *The development of radar equipments for the Royal Navy, 1935–45*. Basingstoke, Hants: Macmillan, 1995.
M.G. Sheftall. *Blossoms in the wind: human legacies of the kamikaze*. New York: NAL Caliber, 2005.
Robert Sherrod. *Tarawa: the story of a battle*. Fredericksburg, Tx: Admiral Nimitz Foundation, 1999.
William L. Shirer. *The collapse of the Third Republic: an inquiry into the fall of France in 1940*. London: William Heinemann/Secker & Warburg, 1970.
Christopher Shores and Brian Cull with Nicola Malizia. *Malta: the Spitfire year 1942*. London: Grub Street, 1991.
———. *Malta: the Hurricane years 1940–41*. London: Grub Street, 1987.
Jak P. Mallmann Showell. *German naval code breakers*. Annapolis, Md: NIP, 2003.
———. *Hitler's U-boat bases*. Stroud, Glos: Sutton, 2002.
———. *U-boat warfare: the evolution of the wolf pack*. Annapolis, Md: NIP, 2002.
———. *Enigma U-boats: breaking the code*. Shepperton, Surrey, Ian Allen Publishing, 2000.
———. *U-boat command and the battle of the Atlantic*. London: Conway Maritime Press, 1989.
———. *The German Navy in World War Two: a reference guide to the Kriegsmarine, 1935–1945*. London: Arms and Armour Press, 1979.

D.M. Showers. 'ULTRA: the Navy's COMINT weapon in the Pacific', *American Intelligence Journal*, Vol.15, No.1 (1994): 49–53.
Lynette Ramsay Silver. *The heroes of Rimau*. Kuala Lumpur: S. Abdul Majeed, 1992.
G.W.G. Simpson. *Periscope view*. London: Macmillan, 1972.
Michael Simpson (ed.). *Anglo-American relations 1919–1939*. Farnham: Ashgate for Navy Records Society, 2010.
——— (ed.). *The Cunningham papers. Vol.II: the triumph of Allied sea power 1942–1946*. Aldershot: Ashgate for the Navy Records Society, 2006.
———*A life of Admiral of the Fleet Andrew Cunningham: a twentieth-century naval leader*. London: Frank Cass, 2004.
———(ed.). *The Cunningham papers. Vol. I: the Mediterranean Fleet, 1939–1942*. Aldershot: Ashgate for the Navy Records Society, 1999.
Tony Simpson. *Operation Mercury: the battle for Crete, 1941*. London: Hodder & Stoughton. 1981.
Clive Sinclaire. *Samurai: the weapons and spirit of the Japanese warrior*. Guildford, Conn: The Lyons Press, 2004.
Tim Slessor. 'The tragedy of HMS *Glorious*', *The RUSI Journal*, Vol.144, No.1 (1999): 68–74.
Kevin Smith. *Conflict over convoys: Anglo-American logistics diplomacy in the Second World War*. Cambridge: CUP, 1996.
Douglas V. Smith. *Carrier battles: command decision in harm's way*. Annapolis, MD: NIP, 2006.
Holland M. Smith and Percy Finch. *Coral and brass*. Washington, D.C.: Zenger Publishing Co., 1979.
Michael Smith. *The emperor's codes: Bletchley Park and the breaking of Japan's secret ciphers*. London: Bantam, 2007.
———. *Station X: the codebreakers of Bletchley Park*. London: Channel 4 Books, 1998.
Peter C. Smith. *Pedestal: the Malta convoy of August 1942*. London: Crécy Books, 1994.
———. *Massacre at Tobruk: the story of Operation Agreement*. London: William Kimber, 1987.
———. *Hold the narrow sea: naval warfare in the English Channel 1939–1945*. Ashbourne, Derby: Moorland Publishing Co., 1984.
———. *Arctic victory; the story of convoy PQ18*. London: William Kimber, 1975.
———. *Task Force 57: the British Pacific Fleet 1944–1945*. London: Kimber, 1969.
Peter C. Smith and Edwin Walker. *War in the Aegean*. London: Kimber, 1974.
Robert Ross Smith. *The approach to the Philippines*. Washington, D.C.: Department of the Army, 1953.
Steven Trent Smith. *Wolf pack: the American submarine strategy that helped defeat Japan*. Hoboken, NJ: John Wiley & Sons, 2003.
A.J. Smithers. *Taranto 1940: prelude to Pearl Harbor*. Annapolis, Md: NIP, 1995.
Gerard S. Snyder. *The Royal Oak disaster*. London: Kimber, 1976.
Carl Solberg. *Decision and dissent: with Halsey at Leyte Gulf*. Annapolis, Md: NIP, 1995.
Lawrence Sondhaus. *Navies of Europe: 1815–2002*. London: Longman, 2002.
Ronald H. Spector. *At war at sea: sailors and naval combat in the twentieth century*. New York: Viking Penguin, 2001.
———. *Eagle against the sun: the American war with Japan*. New York: The Free Press, 1985.
Ian Speller, (ed.). *The Royal Navy and maritime power in the twentieth century*. London: Frank Cass, 2005.
Tony Spooner. *Supreme gallantry: Malta's role in the Allied victory, 1939–1945*. London: John Murray, 1996.
Russell Spurr. *A glorious way to die: the kamikaze mission of the battleship Yamato, April 1945*. London: Sidgwick & Jackson, 1982.
Edward P. Stafford. *The big E: the story of the USS Enterprise*. Annapolis, Md: NIP, 2002.

Arthur Stam. *The diplomacy of the new order: the foreign policy of Japan, Germany and Italy: 1931–1945.* Soesterberg, Netherlands: Uitgeverij Aspekt, 2003.

Doug Stanton. *In harm's way: the sinking of the USS Indianapolis and the extraordinary story of its survivors.* New York: Henry Holt, 2001.

Zara Steiner. *The lights that failed: European international history, 1919–1933.* Oxford: OUP, 2005.

———. 'The war, the peace and the international state system', in Jay Winter, Geoffrey Parker and Mary R. Habeck (eds), *The Great War and the twentieth century.* New Haven, Conn: Yale University Press, 2000.

Robert B. Steinnert. *Day of deceit: the truth about FDR and Pearl Harbor.* London: Constable, 2000.

Jean Stengers. 'Enigma, the French, the Poles and the British, 1931–40', in Christopher Andrew and David Dilks (eds), *The missing dimension.* Basingstoke: Macmillan, 1985.

Martin Stephen. *The price of pity: poetry, history and myth in the Great War.* London: Leo Cooper, 1996.

———. *The fighting admirals.* Annapolis, Md: NIP, 1991.

———.*Sea battles in close-up: World War 2.* London: Ian Allen, 1988.

Robert C. Stern. *Fire from the sky.* Barnsley: Seaforth, 2010.

———. *Battle beneath the waves: the U-boat war.* London: Arms and Armour, 1999.

Donald P. Steury. 'The character of the German naval offensive: October 1940–June 1941', in Timothy J. Runyan and Jan M. Copes (eds), *To die gallantly: the battle of the Atlantic.* Boulder, Col: Westview Press, 1994.

David Stevens. 'South-West Pacific sea frontiers: seapower in the Australian context', in David Stevens (ed.), *The Royal Australian Navy in World War II.* St. Leonards, NSW: Allen & Unwin, 1996.

Adrian Stewart. *Guadalcanal: World War II's fiercest naval campaign.* London: William Kimber, 1985.

———. *The battle of Leyte Gulf.* London: Robert Hale, 1979.

Mark A. Stoler. *Allies and adversaries: the Joint Chiefs of Staff, the Grand Alliance, and U.S. strategy in World War II.* Chapel Hill, N.C.: University of North Carolina Press, 2000.

———. 'The "Pacific-first" alternative in American World War II strategy', *The International History Review*, Vol.11, No.3 (1980): 432–52.

———. *The politics of the Second Front: American military planning and diplomacy in coalition warfare, 1941–1943.* Westport, Conn: Greenwood Press, 1977.

John Strawson. *The Italian campaign.* London: Secker & Warburg, 1987.

Brian R. Sullivan. 'Italian naval power and the Washington Disarmament Conference of 1921–22', in Erik Goldstein and John Maurer (eds), *The Washington Conference, 1921–22: naval rivalry, East Asian stability and the road to Pearl Harbor.* London: Frank Cass, 1994.

———. 'A fleet in being: the rise and fall of Italian sea power, 1861–1943', *The International History Review*, Vol. X, No. 1 (Feb.1988): 106–24.

Jon Tetsuro Sumida. 'British naval procurement and technological change 1919–39', in Phillips P. O'Brien (ed.), *Technology and naval combat in the twentieth century and beyond.* London: Frank Cass, 2002.

———. '"The best laid plans": the development of British battle-fleet tactics, 1919–42', *International History Review* Vol.XIV, No.4 (1992): 681–700.

Jack Sweetman (ed.). *The great admirals: command at sea, 1587–1945.* Annapolis, Md: NIP, 1997.

Craig L. Symonds. *Decision at sea: five naval battles that shaped American history.* Oxford: OUP, 2005.

Hattori Syohgo. 'Kamaikaze: Japan's glorious failure', *Air Power History*, Vol.43, No.1 (1996): 14–27.

David Syrett. 'The battle for convoy OG 69, 20–29 July 1941', *The Mariner's Mirror*, Vol.89, No.1 (2003): 71–81.

——. 'The infrastructure of communications intelligence: the Allied D/F network and the battle of the Atlantic', *Intelligence and National Security*, Vol.17, No.3 (2002): 163–72.
——(ed.). *Battle of the Atlantic and signals intelligence: U-boat tracking pages 1941–47*. Aldershot, Hants: Ashgate, 2002.
——. 'Communications intelligence and the battle for convoy OG 71, 15–23 August 1941', *The Journal of Strategic Studies*, Vol.24, No.3 (2001): 86–106.
——. 'Communications intelligence and the sinking of the *U-860* April–June 1944', *The Mariner's Mirror*, Vol.85, No.1 (1999): 68–75.
——. *The battle of the Atlantic and signals intelligence: U-boat situations and trends, 1941–1945*. Aldershot, Hants: Ashgate, 1998.
——. *The defeat of the German U-boats: the battle of the Atlantic*. Columbia, S.C.: University of South Carolina Press, 1994.
Stephen R. Taafe. *MacArthur's jungle war: the 1944 New Guinea campaign*. Lawrence, Ks: University Press of Kansas, 1998.
Nicholas Tarling. *A sudden rampage: the Japanese occupation of Southeast Asia 1941–1945*. London: Hurst, 2001.
V.E. Tarrant. *The last year of the Kriegsmarine: May 1944–May 1945*. London: Arms and Armour, 1995.
——. *The U-boat offensive 1914–1945*. London: Arms and Armour, 1989.
Bruce Taylor. *Battlecruiser HMS Hood: an illustrated biography, 1916–1941*. London: Chatham, 2005.
Theodore Taylor. *The magnificient Mitscher*. Annapolis, Md: NIP, 1991.
——. *Battle in the Arctic seas: the story of convoy PQ17*. New York: Thomas Crowell, 1976.
Brian Tennyson and Roger Sarty. *Guardian of the Gulf: Sydney, Cape Breton and the Atlantic wars*. Toronto: University of Toronto Press, 2000.
James Foster Tent. *E-boat alert: defending the Normandy invasion fleet*. Shrewsbury: Airlife, 1996.
John Terraine. *Business in great waters: the U-boat wars 1916–1945*. London: Leo Cooper, 1989.
——. *The right of the line: the Royal Air Force in the European War 1939–45*. London: Hodder & Stoughton, 1985.
Charles S. Thomas. *The German Navy in the Nazi era*. London: Unwin Hyman, 1990.
Evan Thomas. *Sea of thunder: four commanders and the last great naval campaign, 1941–1945*. New York: Simon & Schuster, 2006.
——. 'Understanding Kurita's "mysterious retreat."', *Naval History*, Vol.18, No.5 (2004): 22–26.
Hugh Thomas. *The Spanish Civil War*. New York: Harper & Row, 1961.
John Oram Thomas. *The giant-killers: the Danish resistance movement 1940/5*. London: Michael Joseph, 1975.
Martin Thomas. *Britain, France and appeasement: Anglo-French relations in the Popular Front era*. Oxford: Berg, 1996.
R.T. Thomas. *Britain and Vichy: the dilemma of Anglo-French relations 1940–42*. London: Macmillan, 1979.
Julian Thompson. *The war at sea: the Royal Navy in the Second World War*. London: Sidgwick & Jackson, 1996.
R.W. Thompson. 'D-Day the great gamble', in Basil Liddell Hart (ed.), *History of the Second World War*. London: Phoebus. 1980.
——. *Generalissimo Churchill*. London: Hodder & Stoughton, 1973.
Peter Thompson and Robert Macklin. *Kill the Tiger: Operation Rimau and the battle for Southeast Asia*. Meath, Ireland: Maverick House, 2007.

Christopher Thorne. *The limits of foreign policy: the West, the League, and the Far Eastern crisis of 1931–33*. New York: Putnam, 1973.

D.R. Thorpe. *Eden: the life and times of Anthony Eden*. London: Chatto & Windus, 2003.

Geoffrey Till. 'Naval blockade and economic warfare in the European War, 1939–45', in Bruce A. Elleman and S.C.M. Paine, (eds), *Naval blockades and seapower: strategies and counter-strategies, 1805–2005*. Abingdon, Oxon: Routledge, 2006.

——. 'Adopting the aircraft carrier: the British, American and Japanese case studies', in Williamson Murray and Allan R. Millett (eds). *Military innovation in the interwar period*. Cambridge: CUP, 1998.

——. 'Retrenchment, rethinking, revival, 1919–39', in J.R. Hill (ed.), *The Oxford illustrated history of the Royal Navy*. Oxford, OUP, 1995.

——. *Air power and the Royal Navy 1914–1945: a historical survey*. London: Macdonald & Jane's, 1979.

——. 'Air power and the battleship in the 1920s', in Ranft (ed.), *Technical change and British naval policy 1860–1939*. London: Hodder & Stoughton, 1977.

Barrett Tillman. *Clash of the carriers: the true story of the Marianas Turkey Shoot of World War II*. New York: NAL Caliber, 2005.

H.M. Tillotson. *Finland at peace and war 1918–1993*. Norwich: Michael Russell, 1993.

John Toland. *The rising sun: the decline and fall of the Japanese Empire 1936–1945*. New York: The Modern Library, 2003.

Kemp Tolley. *Yangtze patrol: the US Navy in China*. Annapolis, Md: NIP, 1971.

Barbara Brooks Tomblin. *With utmost spirit: Allied naval operations in the Mediterranean 1942–1945*. Lexington, Ky: The University Press of Kentucky, 2004.

Arnold J. Toynbee (ed.). *Survey of international affairs 1936*. London: OUP, 1937.

——. *Survey of international affairs 1926*. London: OUP, 1928.

Nicholas Tracy (ed.). *The collective naval defence of the empire, 1900–1940*. Aldershot: Ashgate for the Navy Records Society, 1997.

——. *Attack on maritime trade*. Basingstoke: Macmillan, 1991.

Ian Trenowden. *Stealthily by night: the COPPists: clandestine beach reconnaissance and operations in World War II*. London: Crécy Books, 1995.

Raleigh Trevelyan. *Rome '44: the battle for the eternal city*. London: Secker & Warburg, 1981.

Christopher Tuck. 'Amphibious operations: the Italian campaign, 1943–45', in Ian Speller (ed.), *The Royal Navy and maritime power in the twentieth century*. London: Frank Cass, 2005.

Anthony Tucker-Jones. *Operation Dragoon: the liberation of Southern France 1944*. Barnsley: Pen & Sword Military, 2009.

Thaddeus V. Tuleja. 'Admiral H. Kent Hewitt', in Stephen Howarth (ed.), *Men of war: great naval captains of World War II*. New York: St. Martin's Press, 1993.

Anthony Tully. *Battle of Surigao Strait*. Bloomington, Ind: Indiana University Press, 2009.

William Tuohy. *The bravest man: the story of Richard O'Kane and U.S. submariners in the Pacific War*. Stroud, Glos: Sutton Publishing, 2002.

Warren Tute. *The reluctant enemies: the story of the last war between Britain and France 1940–42*. London: Collins, 1990.

——. *The deadly stroke*. London: Collins, 1973.

Warren Tute, John Costello and Terry Hughes. *D Day*. London: Sidgwick & Jackson, 1974.

Walt Unsworth. *Everest*. London: Allen Lane, 1981.

Gregory J.W. Urwin. *Facing fearful odds: the siege of Wake Island*. Lincoln, Neb: University of Nebraska Press, 1997.

Jonathan G. Uttley. *The grand scuttle: the sinking of the German fleet at Scapa Flow in 1919*. Edinburgh: Birlinn, 2007.

——. 'Günther Prien', in Stephen Howarth (ed.), *Men of war: great naval captains of World War II*. New York: St. Martin's Press, 1993.
——. *Going to war with Japan 1937–1941*. Knoxville, Tenn: The University of Tennessee Press, 1985.
Carl Van Dyke. *The Soviet invasion of Finland, 1939–40*. London: Frank Cass, 1997.
F.C. Van Oosten. *The battle of the Java Sea*. Annapolis, Md: NIP, 1976.
Dan Van der Vat. *The grand scuttle: the sinking of the German fleet at Scapa Flow in 1919*. Edinburgh: Birlinn, 2007.
——. 'Günther Prien', in Stephen Howarth (ed.), *Men of war: great naval captains of World War II*. New York: St. Martin's Press, 1993.
——. *The Atlantic campaign: the great struggle at sea 1939–1945*. London: Hodder & Stoughton, 1988.
Jordan Vause. *Wolf: U-boat commanders in World War II*. Shrewsbury: Airlife, 1997.
Milan Vego. 'On major naval operations', *Naval War College Review*, Vol. 60, No. 2 (2007): 94–126.
——. *The battle for Leyte 1944: Allied and Japanese plans, preparations, and execution*. Annapolis, Md: NIP, 2006.
Peter Verney. *Anzio 1944: an unexpected fury*. London: Batsford, 1978.
Anthony Verrier. *Assassination in Algiers: Churchill, Roosevelt, de Gaulle and the murder of Admiral Darlan*. London: Macmillan, 1990.
Sir Philip Vian. *Action this day; a war memoir*. London. Frederick Muller, 1960.
George Victor. *The Pearl Harbor myth*. Washington, D.C.: Potomac Books, 2007.
Brian L. Villa. *Unauthorized action: Mountbatten and the Dieppe Raid*. Toronto: OUP, 1989.
Frank B. Walker. *Corvettes – little ships for big men*. Budgewoi, NSW: Kingfisher Press, 1995.
Douglas Waller. *A Question of loyalty: Gen. Billy Mitchell and the court martial that gripped the nation*. New York: Harper Collins, 2004.
Michael G. Walling. *Bloodstained sea: the U.S. Coast Guard in the Battle of the Atlantic, 1941–1944*. Camden, Maine: International Marine/McGraw-Hill, 2004.
Stephen Walsh. *Stalingrad, 1942–1943: the infernal cauldron*. London: Simon & Schuster, 2000.
Wesley K. Wark. 'Beyond intelligence: the study of British strategy and the Norway campaign, 1940', in Michael G. Fry (ed.), *Power, personalities and policies: essays in honour of Donald Cameron Watt*. London: Frank Cass, 1992.
Denis Warner and Peggy Warner with Sadao Seno. *Disaster in the Pacific: new light on the Battle of Savo Island*. Annapolis, Md: NIP, 1992.
——. *The sacred warriors: Japan's suicide legions*. New York: Van Nostrand Reinhold, 1982.
Edward Warner. 'Douhet, Mitchell, Seversky: theories of air warfare', in Edward M. Earle (ed.), and with the collaboration of Gordon A. Craig and Felix Gilbert, *Makers of modern strategy: military thought from Machiavelli to Hitler*. Princeton, NJ: Princeton University Press, 1971.
Bruce Allen Watson. *Exit Rommel: the Tunisian campaign 1942–1943*. Westport, Conn: Praeger, 1999.
D.C. Watt, Frank Spencer and Neville Brown. *A history of the world in the twentieth century*. London: Hodder and Stoughton, 1967.
Anthony J. Watts. *The Royal Navy: an illustrated history*. London: Arms and Armour, 1994.
A.J. Watts and B.G. Gordon. *The Imperial Japanese Navy*. London: MacDonald, 1971.
H.J. Weaver. *Nightmare at Scapa Flow: the truth about the sinking of H.M.S. Royal Oak*. Peppard Common, Oxon: Crescelles, 1980.
Gary E. Weir. 'A truly Allied undertaking: the progeny of Britain's Empire Liberty 1931–43', in Stephen Howarth and Derek Law (eds), *The Battle of the Atlantic 1939–1945: the 50th anniversary international naval conference*. London: Greenhill Books, 1994.

Steve Weiss. *Allies in conflict: Anglo-American strategic negotiations, 1938–44*. Basingstoke, Hants: Macmillan, 1996.

Alexander Werth. *Russia at war*. New York: Carroll & Graf Publishers, 1964.

Odd Arne Westad. *Cold War and revolution: Soviet–American rivalry and the origins of the Chinese Civil War, 1944–1946*. New York: Columbia University Press, 1993.

J.N. Westwood. *Russian naval construction 1905–45*. Basingstoke: Macmillan, 1994.

Gerald E. Wheeler. *Kinkaid of the Seventh Fleet: a biography of Admiral Thomas C. Kinkaid, U.S. Navy*. Annapolis, Md: NIP, 1996.

——. 'Admiral Thomas C. Kinkaid', in Stephen Howarth (ed.), *Men of war: great naval captains of World War II*. New York: St. Martin's Press, 1993.

——. 'Thomas C. Kinkaid: MacArthur's master of naval warfare', in William M. Leahy (ed.), *We shall return! MacArthur's commanders and the defeat of Japan*. Lexington, Ky: The University Press of Kentucky, 1988.

——. *Admiral William Veazie Pratt, U.S. Navy*. Washington, D.C.: Department of the Navy, 1974.

Richard Wheeler. *Iwo*. New York: Lippincott & Crowell, 1980.

David Fairbank White. *Bitter ocean: the battle of the Atlantic 1939–1945*. New York: Simon & Schuster, 2006.

M.J. Whitley. *German coastal forces of World War II*. London: Arms and Armour, 1992.

——. *German capital ships of World War Two*. London: Arms and Armour, 1989.

——. *German cruisers of World War Two*. Annapolis, Md: NIP, 1987.

Richard Wiggan. *Hunt the Altmark*. London: Robert Hale, 1982.

Thomas Wildenberg. 'Midway: sheer luck or better doctrine', *Naval War College Review*, Vol. 58, No. 1 (2005): 138–50.

——. *Destined for glory*. Annapolis, Md: NIP, 1998.

Timothy Wilford. 'Watching the North Pacific: British and Commonwealth intelligence before Pearl Harbor.' *Intelligence and National Security*, Vol.17, No.4 (2002): 131–64.

John Williams. *The guns of Dakar: September 1940*. London: Heinemann, 1976.

Kathleen Broome Williams. *Secret weapon: U.S. high-frequency direction finding in the battle of the Atlantic*. Annapolis, Md: NIP, 1996.

Gordon Williamson. *Wolf pack: the story of the U-boat in World War II*. Oxford: Osprey Publishing, 2005.

——. *U-boat bases and bunkers 1941–45*. Oxford: Osprey, 2003.

John A. Williamson. *Antisubmarine warrior in the Pacific: six subs sunk in twelve days*. Tuscaloosa, Al: University of Alabama Press, 2005.

H.P. Willmott. *The last century of sea power*. Vol. 2. Bloomington, Ind: Indiana University Press, 2010.

——. *The battle of Leyte Gulf: the last fleet action*. Bloomington and Indianapolis, Ind: Indiana University Press, 2005.

——. *The war with Japan: the period of balance. May 1942–October 1943*. Wilmington, Del: SR Books, 2002.

——. *The Second World War in the east*. London: Cassell, 1999.

——. *Grave of a dozen schemes: British naval planning and the war against Japan, 1943–1945*. Annapolis, Md: NIP, 1996.

——. 'Operation Jupiter and possible landings in Norway', in Patrick Salmon (ed.), *Britain and Norway in the Second World War*. London: HMSO, 1995.

——. *The barrier and the javelin: Japanese and Allied Pacific strategies February to June 1942*. Annapolis, Md: NIP, 1983.

——. *Empires in the balance: Japanese and allied Pacific strategies to April 1942*. Annapolis, Md: NIP, 1982.

H.P. Willmott, with Haruo Tohmatsu and W. Spencer Johnson. *Pearl Harbor*. London: Cassell, 2001.
Chester Wilmot. *Tobruk 1941*. Ringwood, Vic: Penguin Books, 1993.
David Wilson. *The decisive factor: 75 and 76 Squadrons – Port Moresby and Milne Bay 1942*. Melbourne, Vic: Banner Books, 1991.
Michael Wilson. *A submariner's war: the Indian Ocean 1939–45*. Stroud, Glos: Tempus, 2000.
——. 'Admiral Sir Max Horton', in Stephen Howarth (ed.), *Men of war: great naval captains of World War II*. New York: St. Martin's Press, 1993.
John Wingate. *The fighting tenth: the tenth submarine flotilla and the siege of Malta*. London: Leo Cooper, 1991.
Robert J. Winklareth. *Naval shipbuilders of the world: from the age of sail to the present day*. London: Chatham Publishing, 2000.
W.G. Winslow. *The ghost that died at Sunda Strait*. Annapolis, Md: NIP, 1984.
F.W. Winterbotham. *The Ultra secret*. London: Weidenfeld and Nicolson, 1975.
John Winton. *Carrier 'Glorious': the life and death of an aircraft carrier*. London: Cassell Military, 1999.
——. *Cunningham*. London: John Murray, 1998.
——. 'Admiral of the Fleet Lord Fraser of North Cape', in Stephen Howarth (ed.), *Men of war: great naval captains of World War II*. New York: St. Martin's Press, 1993.
——. *Ultra in the Pacific: how breaking Japanese codes and ciphers affected naval operations against Japan 1941–45*. London: Leo Cooper, 1993.
——. *ULTRA at sea: how breaking the Nazi code affected Allied naval strategy during World War II*. New York: William Morrow, 1988.
——. *Sink the Haguro!: The last destroyer action of the Second World War*. London: Seeley, Service & Co., 1979.
——. *The forgotten fleet: the British Navy in the Pacific 1944–1945*. New York: Coward-McCann, 1969.
Richard Woodman. *The real cruel sea: the Merchant Navy in the Battle of the Atlantic, 1939–1943*. London: John Murray, 2004.
——. *Malta convoys 1940–1943*. London: John Murray, 2003.
——. *The Arctic convoys 1941–1945*. London: John Murray, 1994.
Eugene Wolfe. 'Derailing the last Tokyo express', *Naval History*, Vol.10, No.2 (1996): 34–39.
David Wragg. *The Pacific naval war 1941–1945*. Barnsley: Pen & Sword Maritime, 2011.
——. *Plan Z: the Nazi bid for naval dominance*. Barnsley: Pen & Sword Maritime, 2008.
——. *Second World War carrier campaigns*. Barnsley: Pen & Sword, 2004.
——. *Swordfish: the story of the Taranto raid*. London: Weidenfeld & Nicolson, 2003.
——. *The Fleet Air Arm handbook 1939–1945*. Stroud, Glos: Sutton, 2001.
——. *Carrier combat*. Stroud, Glos: Sutton Publishing, 1997.
Derrick Wright. *The Battle for Iwo Jima 1945*. Stroud, Glos: Sutton Publishing, 2003.
——. *To the far side of hell: the battle for Peleliu, 1944*. Ramsbury, Wilts: The Crowood Press, 2002.
——. *A hell of a way to die: Tarawa Atoll 20–23 November 1943*. London: Windrow & Greene, 1997.
Matthew Wright. *Blue water Kiwis: New Zealand's naval story*. Auckland, NZ: Reed, 2001.
John F. Wukovits. *Admiral 'Bull' Halsey*. New York: Palgrave Macmillan, 2010.
——. *Pacific Alamo: the battle for Wake Island*. New York: New American Library, 2003.
——. *Devotion to duty: a biography of Admiral Clinton A.F. Sprague*. Annapolis, Md: NIP, 1995.
——. 'Admiral Raymond A. Spruance', in Stephen Howarth (ed.), *Men of war: great naval captains of World War II*. New York: St. Martin's Press, 1993.
Kenneth G. Wynn. *U-boat operations of the Second World War*. London: Chatham, 1997.
William T. Y'Blood. *The little giants: U.S. escort carriers against Japan*. Annapolis, Md: NIP, 1987.

588   Select bibliography

——. *Hunter killer: U.S. escort carriers in the battle of the Atlantic*. Annapolis, Md: NIP, 1983.

——. *Red sun setting: the battle of the Philippine Sea*. Annapolis, Md: NIP, 1981.

Don Yoder. 'The fight for Iwo Jima', in Basil Liddell Hart (ed.), *History of the Second World War*. London: Phoebus, 1980.

Toshiyuki Yokoi. 'Kamikazes in the Okinawa campaign', in David C. Evans (ed.), *The Japanese Navy in World War II: in the words of former Japanese naval officers*. Annapolis, Md: NIP, 1986.

Mitsuru Yoshida. *Requiem for battleship Yamato*. Annapolis, Md: NIP, 1999.

——. 'The sinking of the Yamato', in David C. Evans (ed.), *The Japanese Navy in World War II: in the words of former Japanese naval officers*. Annapolis, Md. NIP, 1986.

Akira Yoshimura. *Battleship Musashi: the making and sinking of the world's biggest battleship*. Tokyo: Kodansha International, 1999.

Christopher D. Yung. *Gators of Neptune: naval amphibious planning for the Normandy invasion*. Annapolis, Md: NIP, 2006.

Peter Zarrow. *China in war and revolution, 1895–1949*. London: Routledge, 2005.

Philip Zeigler. *Mountbatten: the official biography*. London: Collins, 1985.

Niklas Zetterling and Michael Tamelander. *Bismarck: the final days of Germany's greatest battleship*. Drexel Hill, Pa: Casemate, 2009.

—— *Tirpitz: the life and death of Germany's last super battleship*. Newbury: Casemate, 2009.

Earl F. Ziemke. *The German northern theater of operations 1940–1945*. Washington, DC: Department of the Army, 1959.

Alan D. Zimm. *Attack on Pearl Harbor: strategy, combat, myths, deceptions*. Newbury: Casemate, 2011.

David Zimmerman. *Britain's shield: radar and the defeat of the Luftwaffe*. Stroud: Sutton, 2001.

Although sources obtained off the Internet are infinitely variable in quality, I have found the following helpful in supplementing existing published sources of information.

www.bbc.co.uk/history/war/wwtwo/scharnhorst_print.html
www.bletchleypark.org.uk
www.bosamar.com/usforces/casualty.html
www.combinedfleet.com/lancers.htm
www.cr.nps.gov/nr/travel/wwIIbayarea/ric.htm
www.hmsfalcon.com/Wanhsien/Wangxian.htm
www.ibiblio.org/hyperwar/USA/USA-C-Luzon
www.navweaps.com/Weapons/WNBR_Radar.htm
www.navy.mil.nz/mzn/article
www.pngbd.com/forum/showthread.php?t = 5923
www.rathbonemuseum.com/GB/FAA/GPCWilliams.html
www.regiamarina.it/armistice.htm
www.regiamarina.net/battles/matapan/casualties/missing_us.asp
www.regiamarina.net/battles/matapan/part1_us.htm
www.regiamarina.net/battles/matapan/part2_us.htm
www.regiamarina.net/battles/matapan/part3_us.htm
www.regiamarina.net/battles/matapan/part4_us.htm
www.regiamarina.net/battles/matapan/part5_us.htm
www.regiamarina.net/engagements/duisburg/duisburg_us.htm

www.scharnhorst-class.dk/scharnhorst/history.scharnhorstfront.html
www.thehistorynet.com/wwii/bldeathconvoypg17/index1.html
www.uboat.net/allies/technical/asdic.htm
www.uboat.net/ops/wolfpacks/names.htm
www.Uboat.net/technical/schnorchel_fitted.htm
www.u-boot-greywolf.de/udeadlight.html
www.vectorsite.net/ttwiz_01.html.
www.warship.org/no11994.htm.

Index

A.A. (anti-aircraft) fire 173n.69, 180, 188–89, 192–3, 218n.82, 276–7, 280, 293–4, 302, 326, 351, 380, 382–3, 385, 394, 396, 407–8, 420, 427, 433, 440–1, 468, 493
Aalesund 406
Aarhus 436
Abbéville 77
ABC-1 staff talks (1941) 117
ABDACOM (American, British, Dutch and Australian Command) 146, 148, 150, 169n.31, 170ns.40–1, 478
ABDAFLOAT 149–50
Abdiel 124, 292
Abe, Vice-Admiral Hiroshi 232–3, 248–9
Abo 375
Abukama 390–1, 402
Abyssinia 20–22, 29
Acasta 81–2, 95n.62, 322n.71, 484, 489
Aceh 335, 356, 444
Achates 245
Achilles 56, 58–9, 64n.41, 284n.18, 416n.84
Achkasov, Vasiliy 218n.87, 362n.29
Activity 344
Adachi, Lt.Gen. Hatazō 329, 336, 457n.74
Adak 184–5, 215n.36
Addu Atoll 161–2
Aden 86, 88
Adler Tag 98n.93
Admiral Graf Spee 34, 42n.58, 54–61, 64n.41, 66, 68, 486
Admiral Hipper 34, 44n.81, 70–1, 80–2, 91, 101–2, 197, 199, 244–6, 434, 483, 496, 508n.90
Admiral Scheer 34, 42n.58, 65n.47, 91, 102, 126n.10, 183, 197, 199, 211–12, 375, 431–2, 434

Admiralty 1, 9, 33, 35, 36n.8, 89, 95n.57, 198, 200, 339, 357, 430, 463; Arctic convoys 197–8, 200, 225–6, 243, 267; codes and cyphers 109, 111, 116, 171n.56, 196–7, 259, 264, 303, 311–12; concern about enemy 'heavy' ships 54, 101–2, 112–13, 298–9, 332; disarmament issues 3–4, 10–11, 18, 38n.20, 461; Dunkirk evacuation 78–9; fall of France 83–5; Indian Ocean 160, 163; Mediterranean 20, 104, 163, 201, 229, 239, 326–7; Norway 70–5, 93n.26, 96n, 62; rearmament 12–13, 27–8, 31; Southeast Asia 126, 139, 149; war against U-boats 2, 50, 52, 54, 63n.15, 67, 87, 90, 109, 154, 196, 240, 265, 278, 428, 463
Admiralty Islands 329
Adriatic Sea 99n.101, 126n.13, 128n.36, 274, 309, 317n.7, 321n.54, 326, 333, 370, 435
Ady, Lt. Howard 188
Aegean Sea 83, 103, 107–8, 116, 126n.13, 272, 274, 300–2, 307–9, 333, 370–1, 437, 476
Afrika Korps (Panzerarmee Afrika) 103, 107, 123, 201, 234–5, 242, 252n.13, 267
Agana 356
Agano 305, 328
Agat 356
Agnew, Vice-Admiral Sir William 123–4, 143–4, 169n.20
Ainsworth, Rear-Admiral Walden 281–2
Air Ministry 9, 102
aircraft carriers: British deployment against IJN 160–3, 324–5, 334–5, 357, 404–5, 418–19, 440, 443, 446–8, 450, 452, 456n.63, 494; deployed by British

Index 591

against Axis shipping 52–3, 56, 64n.40, 81–2, 84–6, 88, 90, 95n.63, 96n.67, 98n.91, 100, 104–6, 112, 115, 119–20, 122, 124, 126, 127n.19, 133n.113, 141, 146, 167, 169n.16, 217ns.70, 79, 227–8, 252n.11, 278, 291–2, 370–1, 406–7, 500n.14; IJN and USN deployment in Pacific of *see under individual ship's names and engagements*; IJN deployment in SE Asia 148–50; pre-war construction and deployment of 4, 8, 10–12, 14, 18–19, 22, 28, 31, 33–4, 35n.5, 37n.15, 43n.78, 46n.110, 462; USN deployment in European theatre 131n.70, 236, 253n.35, 254n.37, 303, 359–60
aircraft *see individual types*
Aitape 336, 338, 372
Ajaccio 319n.18
Ajax 38n.20, 56, 58–9, 64n.41, 115, 365n.52
Akagi 12, 19, 184, 188–9, 191–2, 194
Akebono Maru 188
Akigumo 253n.30
Akitsuki 398
Akizuki 232
Akureyri 311
Akyab (Sittwe) 418, 443
Alabama 9, 381, 386, 442
Alanbrooke, Field Marshal Viscount 253n.33
Alaska 41n.48, 272
Albacore 5A (carrier biplane) 105, 127n.25, 351
Albania 31, 90–1, 102–3, 326
Albatross 355
'Alberich' U-boats 355, 465; *see also* Oppanol
Albrecht, Conrad 24
Alcira 26
Aldersdale 200
Alesund 93n.16, 406
Aleutian Islands 184–7, 196, 205, 215n.36, 261, 268–9, 272–3, 287n.50, 304
Alexander, Field Marshal Earl 278
Alexandria 83, 85–6, 96n.67, 104–5, 108, 114–16, 122–5, 129n.53, 142–4, 146, 157, 159–60, 173n.71, 201, 214n.22, 229, 278, 301, 308, 470
'Alfa' (RMI code) 104
Alfieri, Vittorio 106
Algérie 254n.46
Algiers 96n.73, 227, 235–7, 241, 254ns.38–9, 47, 278, 319n.18, 321n.54

Allen M. Sumner 416n.75
Almeria 25
Alster 75
Alsterufer 322n.57
Altenfjorden (Altafjorden) 197, 242, 244, 247, 267, 298–9, 311, 314, 332
Altmark 68–9
Amagi 427, 447–8, 504n.44
Amami-Ōshima 441
Amazon 174n.88
Ambon 148, 170n.35
Ambra 241
Amchitka 261
Ameer 418, 446
Amsterdam 358
Anamba Islands (Kepulauan Anambas) 139, 151
Ancon 364n.51
Andalsnes 76–7
Andaman Islands 162, 444, 459n.98
Andaman Sea 160–1, 428, 444, 446, 459n.98
Anderson 253n.30
Angaur 373, 411ns.7, 10
Anglo-American relations 4–5, 9–10, 13, 22, 27, 140–1, 164, 235, 238, 264, 271, 289n.73, 321n.56, 425, 451, 478–9
Anglo-German Naval Agreement (1935) 19–20, 24, 31, 44n.81, 462
Anglo-Indian 170n.42
Anglo-Japanese Alliance (1902); abrogation (1922) 4, 5
Ankara 143
Anschluss 29
Anson 46n.106
Anti-Comintern Pact (1936) 23, 29, 32, 45n.93, 50
anti-foreignism 8; *see also* xenophobia
anti-submarine bomb (A/S bomb) 465, 501n.26
anti-submarine warfare (ASW) 2, 10, 87, 196, 266–7, 307, 347, 462–5, 468, 478, 484, 495, 500n.17, 501n.26
Anti U-boat Warfare Committee 239–40, 259
Antonescu, Marshal Ion 369
Antwerp 89, 360, 406
Anzio 326, 361n.12, 363n.31
Aoba 41n.51, 218n.89, 220n.101, 231, 380, 448
Aparri 377, 446
Aphrodite (radar decoy balloon). 302, 326, 465
appeasement policy 25, 27, 29–31, 49, 51

Arakan (Burma) 325, 405, 418
Arara (Sarmi) 219n.90, 336
Arashi 191
Arawe 316
Arcadia conference (1941) 140
Archangel 121, 154, 164, 183, 200, 225, 243, 267, 298, 310, 407
Archer-Fish 504n.45
Arctic 56, 69, 120–1, 141, 155, 164, 183, 200, 212, 226, 241–3, 259, 267, 283n.6, 298, 310, 325, 330–1, 333, 374–5, 407–8, 428, 433, 438, 463
Arctic convoys 121, 132n.99, 154–5, 157, 164, 196–200, 211–12, 225, 229, 242–4, 266–7, 298, 310, 322n.61, 332, 408, 428, 435, 463, 471, 478, 496, 533
Ardent 81–2.95n.62, 322n.71, 489
Arendal 93n.18
Arethusa 41n.50, 84, 365n.52
Argentia Bay 120, 125
Argo Fire Control System 1
Argonaut (Allied conference, Yalta 1945) 365n.52, 416n.84, 425
Argus 133n.113, 236
Arillo, Lt. Mario 241
Arizona 136
Ark Royal 18, 33, 52–3, 64n.40, 84–5, 88–9, 98n.91, 112–3, 124, 127n.19, 133n.113, 468, 494, 501n.26
Arkansas 346, 365n.52, 368n.97
Arkhangelsk 374, 412n.16
armed raiders 52, 91, 99n.105, 101–2, 116
Arno, River 354, 358
Arnold, General Henry H. 'Hap' 278, 411n.7
Arundel 318n.15
Asagumo 151, 171n.49, 390–1
Asashimo 380, 441
asdic 52, 63n.19, 355, 463
Ashigara 152, 444
Asinara 123, 293
Assab 117
Astor, Gerald 455n.53, 457n.65
Astoria 193, 207, 219n.92
Atago 148, 218n.89, 249–50, 305, 364n.42, 380, 488
Athenia 50, 62n.6, 485
Athens 108, 371
Atlanta 41n.48, 185, 219n.92, 248
Atlantic, battle of the 66, 77, 100, 154, 265, 275, 309, 406, 409, 467, 476, 478, 482; *see also* convoys; U-boats; wolf packs

Atlantic Charter 121
Atlantic Fleet (USN) 117, 120
Atlantis 467
Attendolo, Muzio 241, 252n.14
Attu 184–5, 196, 215n.36, 268–9, 272, 287n.51, 493, 510n.119
Auboyneau, Capitaine Philippe 85
Aubretia 111
Auckland 131n.77
Audacity 141, 169n.16, 468
Augusta (Sicily) 120, 254n.35, 279, 364n.51, 368n.97
Aurora 123, 144, 254n.37, 274, 292
Austin, Vice-Admiral Bernard 399
Australia 85, 98n.91, 130n.74, 135, 138, 150, 153, 171n.53, 176, 179, 205, 219n.92, 268, 297, 317, 378, 420–1; military contribution 112, 130n.74, 146, 148, 150, 176, 204–5, 207, 211, 282, 294–5, 318n.13, 363n.37, 418, 445, 477; naval contribution *see under ships' names*
Australian 20th Infantry Brigade 318n.13
Australian 26th Infantry Brigade 445
Australian 7th Infantry Division 445
Australian 9th Infantry Division 445
Austria 5, 19, 29, 368n.98
auxiliary cruisers 96n.68, 116, 129n.55, 130n.74, 219n.89, 221n.117, 324
Avenger (US torpedo bomber) 215n.33, 225, 236, 254n.41, 367n.80, 383, 394
Aviemore 62n.11
Avola (Sicily) 279
Avondale Park 436
Avranches 359
Ayanami 250
Azores 260, 270, 276, 303, 320n.37
Azov Flotilla 141, 203, 295

B&V 138 (German reconnaissance aircraft) 313
Babelthuap 411n.13
Badoglio, Field Marshal Pietro 281, 291–3, 302, 318n.8
Baguio 452
Bahamas 87, 166
Baie de la Seine 340–1, 343
Bairoko Harbour 282, 290n.82
Baka (piloted bombs) 427
Baker-Cresswell, Captain Joe 111
Baku 243
Balaklava 333
Baldomir, Alfredo 60
Baldwin, Stanley 8, 18, 24

Baleares 26
Balearic Islands 119, 146, 201, 227–8, 235, 237, 252n.11, 253n.17, 293, 471
Bali 150, 152, 170n.48
Balikpapan 147–8, 151, 445–6
Baltic Fleet 55, 121–2, 327, 369; *see also* Red Banner Fleet, USSR
Baltic Sea 34, 38n.29, 49–50, 56, 112, 116, 118, 120–2, 131n.85, 157, 204, 241, 273, 300, 333, 354, 362n.29, 369–70, 374–5, 406, 430–4, 436–7, 477
Baltic States 32, 369, 375, 431–2
Baltimore 41n.48, 442
Bangka Strait 149–50, 444
Banzai attacks 347, 425, 451, 493
Barbey, Vice-Admiral Daniel 294, 346, 419, 453n.5, 481
Barbiano, Albercio da 142
Barcelona 26
Bardia 124, 131n.77, 133n.113
Bardufoss 81
Barents Sea 56, 120, 211, 242, 247, 374, 496; battle of 244–7, 496
Barham 64n.43, 89, 98n.91, 115, 124, 133n.113
Bari 321n.54, 326
Barnett, Correlli 34, 47n.130, 70, 89, 91n.1, 94n.43, 95n.53, 97n.85, 106, 134n.115, 156, 160, 471
Barracuda (British dive/torpedo-bomber) 332
Bartels, Korvettenkapitän Hans 355
Basilan Islands 426
Basque Republic 25
Bastia 296, 309
Bataan 138, 421–2
Batavia (Jakarta) 148–9, 151–3
battlecruisers, shortcomings of 2, 12, 21, 112–13, 140
Battler 324
Battleship Row 136–7, 480
battleships (capital ships), construction and effectiveness of 2, 9, 12, 21, 28–34, 37n.15, 37n.20, 46n.107, 46n.111, 54, 91, 96n.68, 101–2, 121, 126n.9, 140, 155–8, 160, 196, 211, 351, 368n.97, 379, 384, 388–90, 407–8, 462, 468–9
Batumi 203, 241
Bawean 151, 478
Bay of Bengal 160–1, 163
Bay of Biscay 33, 63n.15, 163, 265, 267, 269–70, 276–8, 288n.67, 302, 310, 322n.57, 344, 360, 437, 500n.17
Bayfield 364n.51

Bayonne 96n.69
Bear Island (Bjørnøya) 311–12, 325, 428
Béarn 33
Beaufighter (Allied long-range, night-fighter) 308, 406, 436
Bedell Smith, General Walter 292
Bedouin 93n.23, 119
Beirut 116–17
Belawan Deli 404–5
Belfast 312–15, 365n.52, 495
Belgium 7, 77, 156, 341, 360, 406, 430
Bell, Captain Frederick S. 58–9
Belleau Wood 381, 403, 442
Benghazi 126n.13, 142–4, 214n.22
Bennett 441
Bennington 442
Beobachtungs-Dienst (B-Dienst) 52, 57, 63n.17, 75, 112, 154, 171n.56, 197, 259, 264–5, 303, 321n.56, 325, 339, 463, 467
Berbera 86
Bergamini, Admiral Carlo 292–3, 508n.99
Bergen 70, 93n.18, 406, 437, 455ns.29, 50
Berkey, Rear-Admiral Russell 389
Berlin 25, 30, 32, 48n.135, 104, 160, 263, 285n.24, 435, 469
Bermuda 87, 117, 131n.70, 166
Bernd von Arnim 71, 73, 94n.31
Berwick 71
Besposhchadnyy 318n.17
Best, Lt. Richard 192
Beta supply convoy 123–4, 133n.111
Betasom (Italian Submarine Command) 98n.87
Betio 307, 493
Betty (Japanese medium bomber) 43n.77, 140
Bévéziers 89, 167
Bey, Konteradmiral Erich 74–5, 312–6, 485
Biak 338, 347, 377, 402
Biber (one-man midget submarine) 355, 430
Bickford, Lt.Com. Edward 61
Bilbao 25
Biri 426
Birmingham 99n.107, 382, 437
Bisciani, Capitano Ugo 124
Bismarck 29, 112–13, 116, 130n.61, 332, 464, 494
Bismarck Archipelago 147, 176, 204, 268, 287n.50, 295, 317, 329–30, 459n.98

Bismarck class 29, 407
Bismarck Sea 424
Bizerte 34, 117, 238–9, 258, 267, 271, 278, 287n.49, 292
Black Point 436
Black Prince 365n.52, 416n.84
Black Sea Fleet (USSR) 202
'black shoe' admirals (USN) 470–1, 507n.87, 509n.10
Blackett, Professor Patrick M.S. 259, 283n.8
Blackett Strait 281
Blair, Jr., Clay 63n.16, 97n.85, 172ns.57, 59, 237, 239, 260
Blandy, Rear-Admiral William 439, 456n.55
Bletchley Park 52, 87, 93n.20, 104, 109–10, 114, 116, 119, 122, 129n.47, 132n.93, 141, 155, 157, 172n.60, 196–8, 259–60, 264, 311, 332, 467, 483
'Blitz', The (1940) 99n.107
Block Island 436, 502n.32
blockade runners 92n.8, 116, 130n.73, 310, 322n.57, 324, 326
Blucher 34, 44n.81, 70, 72
Blue 207
Blue Ridge 419
Bluebell 429
Bode, Captain Howard 220n.106, 489
Bodø 71, 93n.16
Bogan, Rear-Admiral Gerald 381, 386, 391, 400–2
Bohol 390, 426
Boise 231, 292, 389, 420, 422, 445
Bolzano 252n.14, 317n.7, 354
Bomber Command *see* RAF Bomber Command
Bon Homme, Richard 454n.25
Bone (Annaba) 271, 293
Bonham-Carter, Rear-Admiral Stuart 495
Bonin Islands 336, 358, 422, 459n.98
Bordeaux 98ns.86–7, 360
Borneo 140, 147, 151–2, 297, 335, 425, 444–5, 459n.98, 491
Bornholm 431
Boston 167
Bougainville 167, 249, 269, 271, 286n.41, 295, 304–6, 330, 489, 492
Boulogne 77–8, 342, 344–5, 355, 366n.63
Bragadin, Commander Marc Antonio 127ns.31–2
Brake 467
Bramble 245–6, 485

Brazil 56, 240, 309
Bream 380
Breconshire 143, 159
Bremen 284n.13, 433
Bremerhaven 406, 436, 438
Bremse 120
Brest 33, 96ns.68–9, 101–2, 126n.12, 155–7, 261, 359–60, 470
Bretagne 33, 84
Brett, Lt.General George 219n.95
Brewster Buffalo (fighter plane) 140, 168n.11, 215n.33, 216n.39
Briand, Aristide 7
Brindisi 104, 358
Bristol Beaufort (torpedo bomber) 116
Britain, battle of (1940) 87, 89, 98ns.93–4, 464
British 6th Airborne Division 341
British Eighth Army 107, 123–5, 144, 234–5, 237, 258, 267, 279, 281, 291, 294, 354
British Tenth Army 90
British 4th Brigade 418
British 29th Infantry Brigade 211
British 1st Infantry Division 274, 327
British 3rd Infantry Division 341
British 50th Infantry Division 341
British Admiralty Delegation (Washington) 159, 357, 363n.34
British Aegean Force 370–1
British East Indies Fleet (BEIF) 404–5, 416n.84, 418, 428, 443–4, 446, 452
British Expeditionary Force (BEF) 50, 77, 96n.69, 339
British Pacific Fleet (BPF) 404–5, 416n.84, 418–9, 438, 443, 447, 456n.63
British Somaliland 86
British XII Corps 436
Brittany 97n.82, 310, 340
Brivonesi, Admiral Bruno 124, 133n.111
Broadway 111
Broke 254n.39
Bröking and Schürer 276
Brooklyn 40n.45, 41n.48, 254
Broome, Captain Jack 199
'brown shoe' admirals (USN) 486–7, 509n.10
Brunei Bay 377–80, 402, 413n.31, 445
Bruneval 173n.69
Brunsbuttel 157, 438
Brussels 360
Bryant, Rear-Admiral C.F. 343, 365n.52
Buckner, Lt. General Simon 440, 443

Buenos Aires 56, 60
Buin 271, 337
Bulgaria 5, 103, 145, 241, 369
Bulldog 111
Bulolo 236, 364n.51
Bumbah, Gulf of 86
Buna 204, 251, 268
Bunker Hill 320n.43, 351, 381
Burauen 403
Burgundy 360
Burke, Admiral Arleigh 391
Burma 153, 173n.83, 257, 325, 405, 418, 427, 443–5, 460n.99, 474
Burma Road 427
Burnett, Vice-Admiral Robert 247, 312–14, 495
Burns 453n.6
Burrough, Rear-Admiral Harold 236, 254n.38
Bush 456n.58
Bushido warrior code 389, 426, 493

Cabot 381, 383, 403
'Cactus Air Force' 221n.110
'Cactus Striking Force' 262, 289n.75
Cadiz 23
Cagliari 274
Cairo 33
Calabria 86, 280–1, 291
Calais 78, 360; *see also* Pas-de-Calais
Calcutta 33
California 136, 414n.50, 420
Callaghan, Rear-Admiral Daniel 248–9
Calobre 247
Campania 281
Campioni, Admiral Inigo 86, 90–1, 103
Camranh Bay 125, 140, 148–9
Canada 55, 97n.83, 117, 166, 171n.55, 530; *see also under provinces*
Canadian 1st Infantry Division 96n.69, 279
Canadian 2nd Infantry Division 212–13
Canadian 3rd Infantry Division 341, 343
Canary Islands 23, 270
Canberra 41n.49, 207, 377
Cannes 359
Cape Bon 142, 169n.20, 227, 271
Cape Breton 62n.12, 530–2
Cape Calavite 380
Cape Camao 135
Cape Engano 399–400
Cape Esperance 230–1, 250, 262–3
Cape Finisterre 277, 497
Cape Gloucester 295, 317, 329

Cape Hatteras 51, 154
Cape Matapan 106–7, 487; *see also* Matapan, battle of Cape
Cape Pessaro 279
Cape Spada 86
Cape Teulada 90
Cape Torokina 304–5, 330
Cape Town 56
capital ship(s) 1, 3–4, 9–11, 14, 19, 21–2, 27–9, 31, 33, 35n.5, 37n.20, 52–3, 65n.47, 68, 70, 86, 102, 136, 138–40, 156, 196, 198–9, 211, 241, 248, 260, 263, 266, 298–300, 316, 332, 405, 407, 438, 441, 462, 469–71, 480, 494
Cappellini 226
Capul 426
Carducci, Giosue 106
Caribbean 51, 87, 131n.70, 154, 166, 223, 284n.12, 309, 326, 463
Caribbean Patrol (USN) 131n.79
Caroline Islands 287n.50, 306, 328, 336, 459n.98
carriers *see* aircraft carriers
Cartagena 26
Carter, Commodore Nick 507n.84
Casablanca 34, 88, 96n.68, 236, 257–61, 264
Casablanca class 392
'cash-and-carry' provisions 55, 479
Cassin 377
Cassino 326
Castellano, General Giuseppe 292
Catalina flying boats 136, 161, 186–8, 199, 213n.1, 215n.33, 233, 327, 388, 391–2, 465
Catania (Sicily) 279
catapult aircraft merchant ships (CAM) 500n.14
Catoctin 359
Cattaneo, Vice-Admiral Carlo 105–6
Caucasus 141, 203, 263, 267, 273–4, 295–6, 308–9
Cavagnari, Admiral Domenico 90
Cavalier 422
Cavalla 350–1, 366n.75
Cayley, Lt.Cdr. R.D. (Dick) 133n.106
Cebu 164, 377, 403, 419, 426
Celebes (Sulawesi) 147–9, 335
Central Atlantic 91, 117, 131n.70, 132n.91, 223, 260, 264, 270, 276–7, 303, 320n.37
Central Atlantic Neutrality Patrol 117, 131n.70
Central Powers 5–6, 461

Centurion 345
Cesare, Giulio 143, 317n.7
Ceylon 138, 153, 160–3, 324, 363n.34, 404, 416n.84, 419, 444, 491
'Chain Home' (British radar stations) 98n.93, 464
Chamberlain, Austen 7
Chamberlain, Neville (British Prime Minister 1937–40) 25, 27, 29–30, 32, 49–50, 69, 80
Chanak crisis (1922) 7, 39n.31
Channel see English Channel
'Channel Dash' 156–7, 173n.69, 471
Channel Islands 96n.69
Chapelle, Fernand Bonnier de la 254n.47
'chariots' (Allied two-man submersibles) 258
Charybdis 310
Chase, Lt. William 188
Cheduba Island 418
Chefoo (Yantai) 459n.95
Cherbourg 50, 96n.69, 334, 342, 344–6
Chevalier 282, 318n.16
Chevalier Paul 131n.76
Chiang Kai-shek (Jiang Jieshi) 8, 261, 308, 451, 459n.95
Chicago 179, 207, 219n.92, 220n.106, 263, 489
Chichi Jima 358, 371, 422
Chiefs of Staff (COS) 29–30, 69, 76, 83, 115, 222n.120, 239, 242–3, 259, 271, 281, 408, 510n.117
Chikuma 184, 218n.89, 232–3, 364n.42, 383, 396
China 4, 7–8, 15, 18, 27, 165, 257, 261, 335, 427, 438, 447, 451, 459n.95
China Force 149
Chitose 209, 218n.89, 338, 351, 364n.42, 380, 398, 504n.44
Chiyoda 185, 218n.89, 351, 353, 364n.42, 380, 398, 504n.44
Cho, Lt.-General Isamu 442–3
Choiseul 207, 304
Chōkai 148, 218n.89, 220ns.101, 105, 232, 249, 364n.42, 383, 396
Chongjin 450
Christiansen, Kapitänleutnant Georg Stuhr 218n.83
Churchill, Winston: as first lord 52–5, 66, 68–72, 76; as prime minister 80, 92n.12, 95n.64, 98n.96, 113, 115, 138, 173n.69, 222n.120, 235, 239, 253n.33, 298, 316; relations with Roosevelt 117, 120–1, 125, 140–1, 230, 240, 257, 271–2, 281, 308, 322n.61, 479; relations with Stalin 242–3, 267, 322n.61; relations with the French 83–4, 88–9, 236; the war in the Mediterranean theatre 86, 103, 115, 123, 291, 300–2, 308, 326, 359, 368n.98, 371, 474; the war with Japan 140, 324, 372, 404–5, 426, 446, 449; threat posed by German surface fleet 52, 54, 101, 113, 266, 298–300, 408, 469
Ciliax, Vizeadmiral Otto 157
Clan Campbell 159
Clark Field (Luzon) 138, 384
Clark, Admiral J.J.'Jocko' 442
Clark, General Mark 294, 368n.98
Cleveland 254n.35
Cleveland class 40n.45, 41n.48, 320n.43
Clyde 83, 99n.107, 278, 428, 436
Coastal Command see RAF Coastal Command
Cobalto 228
Cocos Islands 324, 334
Colbert 254n.46
Colhoun 456n.58
Collective Security 7, 15, 39n.34
Collins, Vice-Admiral John A. 149
Colombo 107, 149, 153, 161–3, 170n.40, 211, 325, 334
Colorado 186, 219n.92, 403
Columbia 389, 420–1
Combat Information Centers 349, 392–3
Combined Arms Operations 92n.12, 476
Combined Chiefs of Staff (CCOS) 164, 242–3, 272, 280, 372, 478–9
Combined Operations Command 92n.12, 173n.69, 222n.120
Comfort 496
Commandante Teste 33, 84, 96n.73
Commandos see Royal Marines Commandos
Condor Legion 44n.90
Conolly, Rear-Admiral Richard 328, 356
Constanza 118, 333, 369
Conte di Cavour 99n.101, 430
'Continuation War' (Finland vs USSR) 203
Convoy (number) AG.9 104; BK.3 428; Force G (Gold) 364n.51, 365n.52; Force J (Juno) 365ns.51–2; Force O (Omaha) 364n.51, 365n.52; Force S (Sword) 365ns.51–2; Force U (Utah) 364n.51, 365n.52; GA.9 104; H 254n.45; HG.53 101; HG.76 141, 169n.16; HX.112 109; HX.217 497;

HX.229 265; HX.235 287n.46;
HX.258 302; HX.79 90; M.41 142–3;
M.42 143; MF.5 157; MW.10 158–9,
173n.71; OB.293 108; OB.318 110;
OB.4 62n.11; ON.127 224; ON.166
264; ON.202 302; ON.203 302;
ON.204 302; ONS.154 255n.50;
ONS.169 265; ONS.18 302; ONS.19
302; ONS.5 270, 287n.46; SC.100
251n.3; SC.118 264; SC.121 264,
285n.28; SC.122 265; SC.127 287n.46;
SC.128 287n.46; SC.7 90; SLS.64 101;
TB.1 284n.12; TM1 260, 284n.11
Convoy: Arctic 154–5, 164, 196–200,
218n.77, 225–6, 242–7, 255n.64, 267,
298, 310–16, 322n.61, 325–6, 374,
408, 428–9, 436, 471, 478; routes 51,
62ns.12–13, 126n.8, 128n.42, 166–7,
171n.55, 223, 463; support for
principle 2, 36n.8, 51–2, 63n.15, 67–8,
88, 102, 141, 154, 166, 223, 259, 265,
463, 466, 491, 496, 500n.10; Tobruk
111, 125, 173n.71
Convoys: Allied 61, 62ns.11, 46; 86,
90–1, 101, 104, 108–9, 112, 125,
126ns.6, 8; 128n.42; 129n.53; 141,
149, 158–9, 169n.16; 172n.61; 201–2,
224, 227–9, 238–9, 255n.50; 260,
264–5, 275–6, 284ns.11–12; 287n.46;
302, 309, 320n.34; 323n.72; 331, 343,
346, 361n.7; 366n.66; 370, 374, 425–6,
429, 463, 500n.11; 531–3; Axis 107–8,
114, 119, 122–4, 142–4, 146, 204,
206, 238, 254n.45, 258, 267–9, 271,
273, 283n.5, 296, 319n.30, 334,
366n.67, 406, 437; troop 50, 76, 80,
82, 89, 121–2, 133n.103, 135–6,
142–4, 152, 204, 206–7, 230–1, 268–9,
278–9, 291, 294, 301, 304, 306, 329,
335, 339, 358, 364n.51, 365n.52, 402,
426, 443
Cony 290n.84
Coolidge, President Calvin 9
Cooper 416n.78
Copenhagen 93n.18, 289n.74, 437,
455n.41
Cora Sfakion (Sphakia) 115
Coral Sea, battle of 165, 167, 176, 178–
82, 185–6, 196, 204–5, 213n.8,
214ns.13–16, 220n.104, 268, 271, 356,
418, 468, 474–5, 483, 486, 488, 493,
505n.64
Corinthian 226
Cork and Orrery, Admiral Lord 76

Cornwall 41n.49, 129n.55, 162
Corregidor 422
Corsair (US fighter-bomber) 332, 357,
456n.63
Corsica 293, 296, 319n.18
Cossack 68, 94n.39
Costello, John 66, 171n.49, 224
Côte d'Azur 358
Cotentin peninsula 340–1, 359
Courageous 12, 33, 52, 468
Courbet 33, 345, 355
Courland 431–2, 434
Courten, Admiral Raffaele de 292
Coventry 99n.107, 115, 229
Cowpens 381
Crace, Rear-Admiral John 178–9, 483
Cres 308
Crete 86, 104–5, 108, 114–15, 127n.20,
130ns.66, 71, 214n.22, 437
Crimea 121, 131n.85, 142, 145, 163, 183,
202–3, 241, 296, 309, 318n.17, 333,
425
Crowl, Philip 367n.92
cruisers: construction types and
effectiveness 4, 10–11, 14, 18, 22, 31,
40n.45, 41ns.47–51, 43n.75, 44n.81,
50–1, 86, 116, 130n.74, 320n.43;
operational deployment *see under
individual ship names*
Crutchley, Admiral Sir Victor 207–8,
219n.92, 220n.106, 329, 489
cryptanalysis 3, 510n.116
cryptanalysts 52, 87, 93n.20, 109–11,
119, 122, 132n.93, 141, 155, 177, 184,
196, 259–60, 262, 311, 321n.56, 332,
466–7, 483, 502n.34
Cumberland. 56, 59, 64n.40, 98n.91,
217n.70, 357, 416n.84
Cunningham (Admiral) Sir Andrew
Browne: as C-in-C Mediterranean
Fleet 83, 85–6, 90–1, 95n.64, 96n.67,
100, 103–8, 114–19, 122, 124,
133n.114, 134n.115, 144, 146, 157–60,
464, 483, 487, 492; as C-in-C Naval
Forces for Italian invasion 278–9, 292;
as first sea lord 298, 301, 324, 326,
341, 428–9, 479
Cunningham, Admiral Sir John 82, 88,
98n.91, 437
Curzola (Korčula) 334
Cutler, Thomas 395
Cuxhaven 438
Cyrenaica 107, 144, 201, 234–5
Czechoslovakia 30–1, 368n.98

598 *Index*

D-Day (6 June 1944) 310, 334, 338–40, 342, 364n.47, 473, 481, 505n.54
Dace 380
Dackel (German T3d circling torpedo) 355
Dagabur 228
Dagö 370, 375
Dakar 85, 88–9, 96n.68, 97n.77
Daladier, Edouard (French prime minister 1938–40) 30
Dallek, Robert 120
Dalrymple-Hamilton, Admiral Frederick H. 365n.52
Dalupiri 426
Damascus 116
Dampier Strait 268
Dan Helder 361n.6
Danae 365n.52
Dandolo 252n.11
Danube 118, 369
Danzig (Gdańsk) 432–4, 437
Darlan, Admiral Jean-François 34, 84, 236, 239, 254n.47
Darter 380, 413n.31
Dauntless (US dive bomber) 18, 179–80, 189, 191–3, 215n.33, 367n.80
Davao 138, 148, 397, 445
Davis, Captain G.B. 250
Davison, Rear-Admiral Ralph 381, 386, 400–1
Dawley, Major-General Ernest 293
De Gaulle, Charles (leader of Free French) 88–9, 238
De Ruyter 152, 170n.48
Defence Requirements sub-committee (DRC) 27
Defender 131n.77
Delbos, Yvon 25–6
Delphin (wolf pack) 260
Denbigh Castle 428
dengue fever. 393–4, 409, 414n.57, 488, 495
Denmark 63n.23, 69, 71–2, 217n.77, 289n.74, 436, 438
Denmark Strait 101, 217n.77
Dennis 396, 414n.54
D'Entrecasteaux 167
Denver 389, 403, 411n.10
Derrymore 170n.42
destroyer escorts 2, 41n.46, 159, 173n.71, 198–9
'destroyer for bases deal' (1940) 87–8, 117, 479
destroyers: construction and role of 10–11, 14, 22, 25–6, 41n.46, 51, 87–8, 94ns.29, 31, 183; deployment by other forces 105–7, 151–3; IJN deployment 250, 262–3, 268–9, 282, 318n.16, 416n.78, 420–1; Kreigsmarine deployment 25, 73–5, 83, 91n.3, 244–7, 316; RN deployment 71–5, 78–9, 81–3, 108–12, 115, 142, 158–9, 183, 214n.22, 229, 245–6, 308, 314–15, 344, 357, 444; USN deployment 279–80, 283, 289n.75, 295, 304–5, 316–17, 318n.16, 329–30, 337, 348, 356, 395–6, 402, 416n.78, 420–1, 484
Deutschland 12, 25, 34, 42n.56, 58, 54, 56, 72
Devastator (US torpedo bomber) 180, 191
Devonshire 71, 82, 85, 98n.91, 113, 437
Deyo, Rear-Admiral Morton 343, 345–6, 365n.52, 439–40, 456n.55
Diadem 365n.52
Dido 41n.50, 115, 292, 437
Diego Suarez 221n.117
Dieppe 92n.12, 212–13, 222n.120, 223, 345, 360, 474
Diether von Roeder 73
Dikson Island 212
Dinagat 389
direction finding 97n.83, 113, 119, 130n.61, 166, 351, 464; *see also* Huff-Duff, HF/DF
direction finding (D/F) stations 97n.83, 350
disarmament (naval) 3, 9–10, 13–14, 16–17, 31, 214n.27, 461
Disarmament Conference (1932–34) 16–17, 35n.5
Dniester, River 333, 369
Dobratz, Kapitän Kurt 429
Dodecanese 300–2, 307–8
Doggerbank 496
Dollfuss, Engelburt 19
Don, River 202
Donetz basin 274
Dönitz, Grossadmiral Karl: attitude towards surface fleet 266–7, 298–9, 310–13, 316, 319n.22, 323n.72, 407–8, 431; career advancement 54, 64n.27, 263, 285n.24, 435; confronts loss of the war 430–1, 433–36; disdainful of Italian forces 87, 111, 227, 463, 477; favours use of Milche Kuhe 303, 482; frustrated with inadequate equipment 53, 77, 270, 429, 499n.9; relations with Hitler 48n.135, 260, 298, 325, 408–9;

relations with Raeder 48n.135, 50, 155; relations with U-boat crews 50, 62n.7, 269, 288n.59, 309–10, 429, 463; seeks improved U-boats 237, 265–6, 276, 288n.64, 325, 375, 409, 412n.18, 428–30, 462, 464; U-boat war on trade 34, 48n.133, 50, 61, 65n.44, 87, 90, 97ns.82, 85, 100, 119, 154, 166, 169n.16, 196, 223–4, 226–7, 237, 255ns.54–5, 259–60, 264–5, 270, 275–7, 279, 283n.6, 302–3, 319n.21, 325–7, 330–1, 355, 428, 437, 467–8, 482, 489; use of wolf packs 52, 132n.91, 239–40, 255n.50, 260, 264–5, 302, 320n.35, 344
Donizetti 319n.28
Donner 141, 503n.39
'Doolittle raid' 165, 176, 426
Doorman, Rear-Admiral Karel 149–52, 170n.48
Doria, Andrea 143, 293
Doric Star 56
Dornier 217 K3 (German heavy bomber) 277, 293
Dorsetshire 41n.49, 64n.40, 113, 161–2
Douglas-Pennant, Rear-Admiral C.E. 364n.51
Dover, Strait of 33, 50, 53, 63n.24, 77, 155–7, 334, 340, 360
Dowding, Commodore John 197, 199–200
D'Oyly-Hughes, Captain Guy 81–2, 95n.63, 489
D'Oyly Lyon, Vice-Admiral Sir George 157
Dragon 365n.52
Dränger (wolf pack) 265
DRC Fleet 31
Dreyer tables 1
Dröbak Narrows 72
DuBose, Rear-Admiral Laurence 400
Duilio, Caio 99n.101, 143, 293
Duke of York 46n.106, 217n.70, 313–15, 495
DUKW (amphibious vehicle) 338
Dulverton 308
Duncan 231
Dunkerque 12, 19, 33, 43n.79, 84–5, 254n.46
Dunkirk 33, 78–9, 95n.51, 108, 138, 156, 212, 262, 339, 342, 360, 438, 481
Duohet, Giulio: advocate for air power 9, 35n.5
Dupleix 254n.46
Duquesne 97n.76, 437

Durban 345
Durgin, Rear-Admiral Calvin 421, 423–4
Dutch East Indies 138, 146–8, 150, 153, 334–5, 376, 422, 452, 459n.98
Dutch Harbour 184, 186, 215n.36

E-boats (enemy war motor boat; Allied name for S-boats) 156, 317n.3
Eagle 12, 227–8, 252n.11, 468
East Anglian 18th Infantry Division 174
East China Sea 447
East Prussia 430–2, 434
Eastern Fleet 135, 138, 140, 148, 160–1, 163, 167, 211, 324, 334, 356–7, 360n.3, 363n.34, 404, 443, 491, 494, 503n.37
Eastern Force 147, 151–2
Eastern Solomons, battle of 209, 221n.113
EASTOMP (Eastern ocean meeting point) 166, 171n.55
Eclipse 172n.61, 319n.28, 496
Eden, Anthony xiv, 24–7
Edinburgh 41n.50, 174n.88
Egersund 93n.18, 406, 455n.29
Egypt 90, 103, 107–8, 144, 173n.71, 252n.13
Eisbär (wolf pack) 240
Eisenhower, General Dwight D. 272, 274, 280–1, 291–3, 296, 301, 334, 340, 368n.98, 472, 505n.54
Eisteufel (wolf pack) 197
El Alamein 234–5, 237, 252n.13, 258
Elba 296, 354
Elbe 130n.73, 157
Electra 139, 151, 171n.49
elektro submersibles 375, 408–9, 412n.18, 462; *see also* Type XXI U-boats; Type XXIII U-boats)
Elkton (plan for the capture of Rabaul) 286n.41
Ellice Islands 304
Eltigen 309
Emden 284n.13, 406, 434, 438
Emerald 365n.52
Emirau 330
Emo 252n.11
Emperor 443
Empire Haven 226
Empire Song 129n.53
Empire Star 170n.42
Empress 446
Empress Augusta Bay, battle of 304–5
Encounter 151–2
Endau 148–9

Endymion 26
Engebi 328, 338
Engelhardt, Konteradmiral Conrad 431–3, 480
England 337
English Channel 33, 50, 75, 77–9, 83, 87, 89, 96n.69, 155–7, 212–13, 260, 272, 280, 310, 334, 340–4, 354–5, 360, 364n.47, 365ns.52, 62, 367n.87, 406, 429–30, 433, 438, 472
Enigma cypher machine and codes 52, 109–11, 119, 141, 155, 157, 197, 259, 330, 467, 483, 487
Enikale 309
Eniwetok (Enewetak) 321n.50, 327–8,
'Enola Gay' 449
Enterprise 18, 84, 136, 185, 188, 191–3, 207, 209, 212, 215n.31, 219n.92, 233–4, 249, 322n.57, 365n.52, 381, 383, 388, 427, 442
Erebus 360, 365n.52, 406
Ereğli 369
Erich Giese 64n.43, 73–5, 94n.31
Erich Koellner 73–5, 94n.31
Eridge 173n.71
Erskine, Ralph 321n.56, 503n.40
escort ('jeep') carriers 218n.89, 253n.35, 254n.37, 303, 306, 328, 332, 336, 344, 348, 356, 359, 361n.15, 370, 373, 376–9, 382, 392–7, 399, 401–2, 409–10, 411n.9, 414n.54, 416n.81, 419–21, 423, 425, 440, 443, 446, 452, 453n.6, 456n.55, 468, 502n.32
Eskimo 93n.23, 94n.39
Esmonde, Eugene, Lt-Com. 172n.65
Espiritu Santu 177, 221n.113
Essex 46n.110, 320n.43, 381, 383, 403, 427, 442
Essex class (aircraft carriers) 18–19, 320n.43, 454n.25
Esteva, Admiral Jean Pierre 34
Estonia 120, 133n.103, 354, 370, 375
Eugenio di Savoia 252n.14
Eureka (Allied conference, Teheran 1943) 322n.61
'Europe first' 257–8, 261, 271, 406; *see also* 'Germany first' strategy
Euryalus 158
Evans, Commander Ernest 484
Evertsen 153
Exeter 41n.49, 56–9, 61, 64ns.39, 41, 151–2
Exmouth 67
Express 139

Faeroes 50, 80
Falke (T-3 German acoustic torpedo) 270, 286n.44
Falkenhorst, General Nikolaus von 69
Falkland Islands 56, 59
Fall Achse 293
Fall Barbarossa 114, 117–18, 242
Fall Bernau 322n.57
Fall Blücher 203
Fall Brunhild 274, 295–6
Fall Cerberus 156–7, 471
Fall Eiche 318n.8
Fall Eisbär 301
Fall Eisstoss 174n.85
Fall Gelb 77
Fall Götz von Berlichingen 174n.85
Fall Herkules (C3) 252n.13
Fall Juno 80–2
Fall Lehrgang 280, 296
Fall Leopard 308
Fall Lila 238–9
Fall Merkur 114–15
Fall Nordmark 68
Fall Ostfront 311–12, 323n.72
Fall Paukenschlag 154, 500n.12
Fall Regenbogen 244–7, 485–6, 495
Fall Rheinübung 112
Fall Rösselsprung 197–9
Fall Schwarz 293
Fall Seelöwe 75, 89
Fall Sizilien 298
Fall Student 318n.8
Fall Tanne Ost 370
Fall Trave 322n.57
Fall Weiss 49
Fall Weserübung 69, 72, 75–6, 92n.15
Fall Wiking 296
Fall Wikinger 68
Fall Wunderland 211
Fall Wunderland II 298
Fall Zitronella 298
Fanshaw Bay 392–3, 396–7, 414n.54
Far Eastern Combined Bureau 170n.40
Farenholt 231, 290n.78
Farrell, Brian 140, 253n.32, 478
Fascist Grand Council 19
'Fat Man' 450
Faulkner 251n.7
Favignana (Sicily) 279
Fécamp 355, 360
Fechteler, Rear-Admiral William 338, 425, 453n.5
Federapparat torpedo (FAT) 266, 325
Feodosiya 142

Ferris, John 37n.14, 63n.17, 503n.40
'Fido' (air-launched, Allied acoustic homing torpedo) 224, 465
fighter catapult ships (FCS) 500n.14
Fiji 41n.50, 89, 204, 206
Fink (wolf pack) 270
Finland 32, 122, 203, 242, 370
Finschhafen 268, 286n.41, 295, 318n.13
Firth of Forth 436, 455n.52
Fiume 106, 487
Five Power Naval Limitation Agreement (Washington conference, 1921–22) 3
Flatley, Vice-Admiral James 391
Fleet Air Arm 9, 53, 76, 131n.76, 300, 407, 470–1
'fleet-in-being' 2, 138, 155, 157, 161, 199, 266, 298, 316, 402, 410
Flensburg 284n.13, 285n.24
Fletcher, Admiral Frank J. 177–80, 185–6, 188, 193, 208, 213n.7, 215n.31, 219n.92, 220n.104, 221n.114, 248, 486, 488, 509n.105
Fliegercorps X 92n.7, 105
Florence (Firenze) 354
Flores 365n.52
Fluckey, Cdr. Eugene B. 484
Flying Fish 366n.75
Flying Fortress (B-17) 186–7, 189, 195, 215n.33, 221n.113, 268, 433
Foch 254n.46
Föhn 141, 503n.39
Forbes, Admiral Sir Charles 71–2, 80, 93ns.23, 26, 94n.37, 95n.64
Force 1 312–13, 315
Force 2 312–14
Force A 104–6, 161–2, 343, 365n.52, 487
Force B 104–5, 142–3, 158, 161–2
Force C 343, 365n.52
Force D 365n.52
Force E 365n.52
Force G 56–60, 64n.40, 126, 135, 364n.51
Force H 84–5, 88, 119, 127n.19, 133n.113, 146, 201, 235–6, 252n.11, 291, 471
Force I 197–8
Force II 197
Force J 365n.51
Force K 108, 123–4, 133n.113, 143–4, 169n.29, 258, 365n.52
Force O 236, 343, 364n.51
Force Q 254n.45
Force R 245–6
Force S 343, 365n.51
Force U 343, 364n.51, 365n.52
Force Z 139–40, 471, 485, 494
Ford, Henry 468
Foresight 174n.88
Forester 174n.88
Formidable 46n.108, 100, 104, 107, 115, 126n.3, 292
Formosa (Taiwan) 376–7, 379, 382, 438, 442, 459n.98, 497
Fort Yale 367n.87
Fortune 129n.53
Fougueux 96n.68
Four Power Treaty (Washington conference 1921–22) 5
foxers (Allied acoustic counter measures against torpedoes) 499n.9
France 6–7, 14–15, 17, 19–23, 26, 31–2, 51, 85; *see also* Vichy French
Franco, General Francisco 23, 26, 31, 83, 90
Frank, Richard 209, 454n.19, 458n.88
Franklin 377, 381, 383, 388, 403, 427
Fraser, Admiral Lord (Bruce) 310–16, 357, 404–5, 419, 452, 464, 495
Fredenhall, Major-General Lloyd 236
Free French forces 88–9, 100, 238, 254n.47, 319n.18
French 9th Colonial Division 354
French 10th Division 437
French Army 79, 354, 359, 437
French Navy 2–3, 7–8, 12, 14, 19, 21, 25, 29, 33, 78, 83–5, 96n.68, 96n.71, 96n.73, 362n.31, 437, 491; *see also* Vichy French
French riviera 280, 359, 410n.4
Freya (German radar) 364n.47
Friedeburg, Admiral Hans-Georg von 285n.24
Friedman, Norman 10, 40n.45, 41n.46
Friedrich Eckholdt 244–7, 496
Frobisher 355, 365n.52
Frömsdorf, Oberleutnant Helmut 436
Frondeur 96n.68
Fubuki 153, 231
Fubuki class (Japanese destroyers) 11
Fujita, Rear-Admiral Ruitaro 185
Fukudome, Vice-Admiral Shigeru 382, 452
Fuller, Major-General Horace 338
FuMO27 (German radar) 312
Furious 12, 33, 72, 93n.26, 120, 227–8, 253n.17, 332
Furutaka 41n.51, 180, 218n.89, 220n.101, 231

Fury 496
Fusō 218n.89, 364n.42, 379, 388, 390
FW 200 Condor (reconnaissance planes) 100–1, 111, 126n.4, 164, 169n.16, 500n.14

G7a (German compressed air torpedo) 77, 462
G7e (German electric torpedo) 77, 286n.44, 462
Gailey, Harry A. 457n.65
Gaisma 118, 131n.84
Galatea 142–3, 169n.21
Gambia 416n.84
Gambier Bay 396, 414n.54
Gannon, Michael 500n.12
Garapan 347
Gardner, W.J.R. 467, 503n.36
Gasmata 316
Gaudo 104–5, 127n.20
Gazala 252n.13
Gedania 130n.73, 487, 503n.39
Geier 141, 503n.39
Gela (Sicily) 279
Gelendzhik 203
General Board (USN) 11, 28
General Steuben 432
Geneva 10, 13, 16–17
Genoa 127n.19, 292, 370, 435
Gensoul, Admiral Marcel 84, 97n.74
'Gentlemen's Agreement' (1937) 24
Georg Thiele 73, 94n.31
George 337
Georges Leygues 365n.52
Gerfaut 362n.31
German Sixth Army 263
German Eleventh Army 145, 183, 202
German Seventeenth Army 274, 295, 333
German Eighteenth Army 79
German V Army Corps 203, 333
German Army Group North 174n.85, 370
German XXVIII Corps 430
German 8th Gun Carrier Flotilla 360
German High Seas Fleet 5
German 22nd Infantry Division 308
German 46th Infantry Division 142, 203
German 70th Infantry Division 406
German 111th Infantry Division 333
German XIX Mountain Corps 374
German 15th Patrol Boat Flotilla 360
German radar (active sets and decoys) 302, 326, 465; warning receivers 196, 265, 302, 375, 465; *see under individual types*

German 5th Torpedo Boat Flotilla 334, 343
'Germany first' 230, 479
Germany: aftermath of World War I 5–7, 42n.58, 462; inter-war period 17, 20, 23, 29–31, 44n.90; involvement in World War II 49–50, 69, 77, 80, 100, 137, 237, 242, 257, 260, 263, 271–2, 289n.74, 300, 302, 324, 346, 368n.98, 370, 405, 425, 431, 435–6, 438, 503n.36
Ghent 360
Ghormley, Vice-Admiral Robert 207, 256n.74
Giada 228
Gibraltar 21, 61, 83–4, 88–9, 96n.67, 97n.83, 98n.92, 119, 122–4, 126n.6, 126n.8, 127n.19, 129n.53, 133n.113, 142, 144, 146, 157, 160, 169n.16, 174n.96, 201, 228, 235, 237, 252n.11, 260, 275, 278, 288n.60, 370, 470, 530–32
Gilbert Islands 304, 306–7, 474–6
Ginder, Rear-Admiral Samuel 361n.17
Gioberti, Vincenzo 106
Gironde estuary 322n.57, 360, 437
Giussano class (light cruisers) 11
Glasfurd, Commander Charles 484, 508n.90
Glasgow 99n.107, 322n.57, 346, 365n.52
Glauco 132n.91
Gleaves 410n.4
glider bomb *see* under 'Hs 293'
Glorious 12, 81–2, 95ns.62–3, 322n.71, 468, 489
Gloster Gladiator (British biplane fighter aircraft) 81
Gloucester 41n.50
Glowworm 71–2, 508n.90
Gneisenau 19, 34, 43n.79, 55, 68, 70, 80–3, 91, 101–2, 155, 157, 322n.71, 433, 469, 471, 484, 489, 494
Godfroy, Admiral René 85
Godt, Konteradmiral Eberhard 62n.6, 285n.24
Goeben (wolf pack) 123
Gold (Normandy landing sector) 340–1, 343, 345, 364n.51, 365n.52
Golovko, Vice-Admiral Arseni 131n.85, 374
Goodall 436
Goodenough Island 211
'Gooseberries' (blockships) 345, 507n.83
Göring, Hermann 44n.88, 66, 95n.51

Gorizia 241, 252n.14, 287n.57, 354
Gorshkov, Admiral Sergei 141, 203, 295, 369, 480–1, 485
Gotenhafen (Gdynia) 112, 157, 267, 300, 406, 432–3
Goto, Major Ushio 373
Gotō, Rear-Admiral Aritomo 178–9, 231
Government Code and Cypher School (GC&CS) 52, 63n.17, 87, 93n.20
Graf Zeppelin 435
Grafton 496
Grant, Albert W. 391
Grattenauer, Kapitän zur See Friedrich 296, 480
Great Depression 1, 13, 461
'Great Marianas Turkey Shoot' 351, 475
'Great Triangle' 338, 346–7, 473
Greece 6, 31, 90, 103–4, 107–8, 113–14, 300–1, 307, 321n.52, 370–1, 470, 474, 476–7, 487
Green Island 329
Greene, Jack 127n.31
Greenland 34, 111, 117, 131n.81, 166, 265
Greer 125, 479
Greif 93n.22
Grenville 66
Griffin, Rear-Admiral Charles 330
Grove, Eric 72, 75, 171n.49, 176, 332, 339, 343, 393, 488
Guadalajara 24
Guadalcanal 178, 204–11, 219ns.90, 94, 220ns.99, 104, 220n.109, 221n.110, 230–2, 234, 248–51, 261–3, 271, 410, 414n.45, 471, 486, 488, 493, 498, 510n.117
Guam 41n.48, 140, 147, 185, 336–7, 347–8, 350–1, 355–6
'guerre de course' 466; *see also* 'war on trade'
Guinea 23, 255n.54
Guissano, Amberto di 142
Gulf of Danzig 432, 434, 437
Gulf of Finland 56, 118, 120, 122, 203, 218n.88, 242, 333, 354, 370, 375, 477
Gulf of Mexico 154, 223
Gumbinnen (Gusev) 430
gunboats, used by the powers against China 7–8
gunnery 1, 38n.20, 46ns.107, 111, 57–9, 73–4, 112, 124, 156, 158, 167, 173n.73, 192, 196, 229, 231, 235, 245–7, 250, 282, 291, 294, 298, 312–14, 316, 327, 330, 343, 345, 352, 357, 390, 395, 405, 419, 432, 440–1, 464, 468; *see also under individual naval engagements*
Gunreibu (Japanese naval general staff) 337–8, 346, 377–8
Gurnard 335
Gwin 249, 290n.81

Hácha, Emil 30
Hackzell, Antii 370
'Hagenuk' (radar search receiver) 277
Hagikaze 216n.53
Haguro 151–2, 180, 218n.89, 305, 351, 364n.42, 383, 396, 444
Haha Jima 422
Halifax (British heavy bomber) 366n.63
Halifax (Nova Scotia) 51, 61, 167, 171n.55, 429, 530–2
Hall, Jr., Rear-Admiral John L. 364n.51, 440
Halmahera 335, 358, 452
Halsey, Admiral William 'Bull' 185, 216n.60, 249–50, 256n.74, 283, 286n.41, 295, 318n.15, 372–3, 376–7, 379–81, 383–7, 391–2, 394, 397–402, 410, 411n.7, 412ns.22, 25, 414n.45, 442, 447, 476, 487, 489–90, 492, 507n.87
Hamakaze 441
'Hamburg' (gun battery) 346
Hamburg 226, 284n.13, 406, 433–4, 436, 455n.38
Hammann 194
Hampton Roads (Virginia) 167
Hancock 381, 403, 441
Hangö 122, 133n.104, 375
Hannover 141, 92n.8
Hans Lüdemann 71, 73
'happy time' ('glückliche Zeit') 87, 97n.82, 240, 274, 376, 463
Hara, Rear-Admiral Chuichi 178–81, 209
Harden, Lt. James 226–7
Harder 330
Harding, President Warren Gamaliel 4, 6, 9
Hardy (H class destroyer-leader) 74–5
Hardy (V class destroyer) 326
Harstad 76, 80, 82
Hart, Admiral Thomas 135, 149
Hartenstein, Kapitänleutnant Werner 226–7
Haruna 148, 184, 218n.89, 231, 352–3, 364n.42, 379, 383, 427, 447–8

Harwood, Commodore Henry 56–60, 64n.40
Hashimoto, Lt-Cdr. Mochitsura 447
Hashirajima Bay 184–5
Hastings 310
Hatsutsuki 398, 402
Hatsuyuki 231
Hauwei 329
Havock 25, 73–4, 158
Hawaii 136–8, 184–5, 204, 399
Hawkins 365n.52
Hawkins class 12, 365
Hayashimo 402
Hayasui 349, 352
Hebrides 89, 438
Hector 162
'Hedgehog' (mortar) 87, 224, 275, 288n.59, 331, 337, 465
Heermann 396, 414n.54
Heimisch Gewässer (home waters) naval Enigma 110, 141, 155, 172n.60, 259
Heinkel He 111 (German medium bomber) 53, 68, 92n.7, 198, 252n.15, 494, 496
Heinkel He 177 (German long-range bomber) 288n.67, 302
Hela (Hel) 432–5, 437
Helena 248, 282
Helfrich, Vice-Admiral Conrad 150–3
Heligoland Bight 34, 61, 65n.47
Hellcat (US fighter aircraft) 332, 348, 351, 367n.80, 382–3
Helldiver (US dive-bomber) 367n.80, 383, 385
Henderson airfield (Guadalcanal) 206, 209, 221n.110, 230–2, 234, 248–51, 271, 282, 471
Henry Bacon 429
Heraklion (Iraklion) 114, 214n.22
Herjangsfjorden 73
Hermann Künne 73
Hermes 33, 85, 161–2, 469
Hermione 201
Herrlingen 340
Hewitt, Vice-Admiral H. Kent 236, 253n.35, 278–9, 359, 481
Heye, Konteradmiral Helmuth 354
Heythrop 173n.71
HF/DF ('huff-duff') 166, 175n.98, 255n.50, 266, 270, 276, 464, 500n.16, 501n.23
Hibuson 389
Hiei 218n.89, 232, 248
Hilary 365n.51

Hill, Vice-Admiral Harry 306, 328, 356, 361n.17
Hindenburg, Feldmarschall Paul von 14, 16
Hinoki 420–1
Hinsley, Professor Harry 70, 110, 119, 467, 503ns.36, 38
Hintze, Kapitän zur See Fritz 314–15
Hipper *see* Admiral Hipper
Hirohito, Emperor 373, 450–1
Hirose, Vice-Admiral Sueto 147, 452
Hiroshima 448–50, 453, 458ns.88–9, 498
Hiryū 19, 148, 184, 188–9, 191, 193–4
Hitler, Adolf: attitude to capital ships 155–7, 244, 247, 260, 266, 298, 300, 310, 438, 469, 486; launches attack on Poland 1, 49, 51; planned invasion of UK 75, 89, 98n.95, 212; pre-war plans for military & territorial expansion 19, 22, 29–32; relations with Dönitz 48n.135, 263, 276, 285n.24, 408–9; relations with Franco 83, 90; relations with Kriegsmarine 44n.81, 60–1, 83, 103, 263; relations with Mussolini 29–30, 32, 119, 477; relations with Roosevelt 31, 138; relations with Stalin 25, 32, 56; rise to power 7, 13–14, 16; support for U-boat war 50, 53–4, 64n.27, 65n.44, 225, 260, 325, 462; war leader and military strategist 69, 78, 87, 89, 92n.15, 95n.51, 102, 107, 118, 126n.13, 238, 252n.13, 263, 293, 300–1, 308, 333, 340, 468, 477, 507n.80
Hiyō 218n.89, 253n.26, 304, 349, 351–3, 364n.42, 504n.44
Hoare-Laval Pact (1935) 21
Hobart 219n.92, 282, 445
Hodges 421
Hoel 395, 414n.54
Hokkaido 184, 376, 426, 447, 450
Holland 63n.23, 156, 334, 354, 360, 361n.6, 406, 430, 436, 438, 462
Holland, Vice-Admiral Lancelot 112
Hollandia (Jayapura) 219n.90, 335–6, 338, 372
Holleben, Oberleutnant Heinrich von 429
Hollyhock 162
Home Fleet 33, 35, 53–5, 70–2, 75–6, 93n.26, 95n.64, 101, 112, 266–7, 310, 314, 316, 406–7, 455n.52
Hong Kong 140, 148, 459n.98
Honolulu 219n.92, 282, 290n.81, 378

Honshū 181, 376, 426, 447–50
Hood 12, 28, 33, 53, 84, 112–13, 494
Horace Gray 428
Horai Maru 153
Horaniu 295, 318n.15
Horii, General Tomitaro 204, 206
Horn of Africa 20, 103; *see also* Abyssinia, Somaliland
Hornet 18, 46n.110, 165, 185, 188, 191, 193, 210, 215n.31, 216n.48, 219n.92, 221n.115, 231, 233, 253n.30, 381, 442, 504n.44
Horten 455n.50
Horton, Admiral Sir Max 62n.9, 71, 93n.22, 240, 275–6, 326, 482
Hōshō 12, 185, 427, 448
Hosogaya, Vice-Admiral Boshiro 185, 286n.42
Hostile 73–4, 93n.23, 94n.27
Hotspur 74, 94n.39, 483
House of Commons 98n.96, 302
Houston 151–3, 170n.41, 377
Howe 46n.106, 292, 404, 439
'Hs 293' (glider bomb) 277, 288n.67, 293, 308, 321n.54, 359
Hughes 234
Hughes, Charles Evans 3–4, 37n.20, 461
Hughes, Terry 66, 224
Hughes-Hallett, Vice-Admiral Sir (Cecil) Charles 94n.37
Humber 33, 66, 99n.107, 310
Hummel 455n.41
Hungary 103, 368n.98
Hunt class (destroyer escorts) 41n.46, 159, 169n.16, 173n.71, 229, 308, 310
Hunter (escort carrier) 443
Hunter (H class destroyer) 74–5
Huon peninsula 219n.90, 268, 295
Hurricanes (British fighter planes) 81, 119, 121, 129n.53, 133n.113, 162, 173n.76, 225, 471
Hvar 370
Hyäne Harbour 329
HYPO (later FRUPac) 184, 493
Hyūga 380, 385, 398, 402, 427, 448

I-1 262
I-4 253n.24
I-5 253n.24
I-11 210
I-16 221n.117, 337
I-19 210–11, 502n.32
I-20 221n.117
I-21 234
I-22 253n.24
I-26 210
I-31 210
I-43 328
I-53 447
I-55 170n.42
I-58 447
I-65 139
I-168 194, 454n.25
I-175 307
I-177 329
I-205 427
I-400 427
I-404 448
Iachino, Admiral Angelo 91, 103–6, 122–3, 127n.32, 143, 158–9, 202, 477, 486–7, 508n.99
Ibiza 25
Iceland 35, 50, 55, 80, 92n.8, 110–11, 117, 119, 121, 125, 154, 197, 199, 225, 243, 270, 288n.60, 311, 497, 533
Idaho 219n.92, 441
Iddesleigh 355
IGHQ (Japan) 183, 204, 251, 261–2, 283, 295, 439, 473
Ijuin, Rear-Admiral Matsuji 295, 480
Ikoma 427
Il Duce 24, 90, 212; *see also* Mussolini
Île d'Oléron 437
Ile d'Yeu 360
Illustrious 28, 46n.108, 90, 100, 292, 324, 357, 404, 418, 439, 456n.58
Imperia 410n.4, 435
Imperial Japanese Army (IJA) 14–15, 27, 150, 178, 204–5, 219n.90, 232, 250, 261–3, 272, 295, 304–5, 307, 318n.15, 327–30, 335–6, 338, 348, 356, 363n.37, 367n.92, 373, 378, 380, 383, 402–5, 411n.13, 422–6, 438, 440, 442–6, 451–2, 454n.19, 457n.65, 460n.101, 474, 493, 510n.119
Imperial Japanese government 4–5, 14–15, 17, 22–3, 27, 121, 125, 177, 251, 261–2, 356, 441, 449–50, 452
Imperial Japanese Navy (IJN) 3–4, 7–8, 11–12, 14, 17–19, 21–2, 27, 29, 40n.45, 41n.51, 43n.77, 46n.111, 135–6, 161–3, 167, 176–82, 184–7, 195–6, 204–5, 207–8, 218n.89, 230–4, 248–50, 261–3, 268–9, 273, 282, 286n.42, 295, 304, 317, 318n.16, 321n.50, 324, 335–8, 347–8, 350–3, 377–9, 384, 387–99, 402–4, 410, 416n.78, 420, 422, 42
Impero 29, 46n.114, 430

Impulsive 252n.7
Indefatigable 404, 418, 439
Independence 307, 320n.43, 381, 391
Independence class 320n.43
India 153, 161–3, 259, 376, 474
Indian Army Units 149, 418, 444, 452
Indian 71st Brigade 418
Indian 74th Brigade 418
Indian 11th Infantry Division 149
Indian 23rd Infantry Division 452
Indian 25th Infantry Division 452
Indian 26th Infantry Division 444
Indian Ocean 56, 83, 102, 129n.55, 130n.74, 149, 152, 161, 163, 167, 170n.40, 176, 211, 324, 334, 356, 371, 375, 404–5, 418, 427, 444, 474, 491
Indiana 9, 351, 442
Indianapolis 187, 219n.92, 349, 412n.24, 424, 439, 447, 456n.55
Indomitable 28, 126, 227–8, 404, 418, 439–40, 494
Inland Sea 184–5, 209, 379, 381, 402, 427, 448, 491
Inoue, Lt.General Sadao 411n.13, 452
Inouye, Vice-Admiral Shigeyoshi 177, 179, 182, 486
'Inshore Squadron' (RN) 267
inter-service rivalry 476–7
Intrepid 328, 381, 383, 403, 427
Ionian Sea 292
Iowa 381, 386, 401
Ireland 52, 101, 166, 485
Iride 25
Irish Sea 429
Iron Bottom Sound 249
'Iron Ring' (Hitler's plan for the Aegean) 300, 307–8
Irrawaddy 427
Isaac Sweers 142
Ise 380, 385, 398, 402, 448
Isegrim (wolf pack) 325–6
'island-hopping' strategy 295, 306–7, 328, 346, 411n.13, 468, 475, 493
Isle of Wight 342
Isokaze 216n.53, 441
Isthmus of Kra 136, 428, 446
Isuzu 249, 321n.50, 415n.77
Itagaki, Lt-Gen.Seishiro 452
Italia (previously Littorio) 292
Italian Navy 3, 11, 14, 83, 86, 96n.66, 104, 218n.80; *see also* Regia Marina Italiana
Italy 14, 19–21, 23–6, 29, 31–2, 45n.90, 86, 90, 100, 102–3, 107, 117, 126n.13, 127n.19, 138, 146, 212, 234, 241, 252n.13, 258, 260, 267, 271, 293, 296, 298, 300, 318n.8, 410n.4, 430, 435, 470, 477; Allied invasion 272, 274, 279–81, 283n.4, 291–4, 296, 326–7, 334, 354, 359, 368n.98, 474; contribution by RAI 119, 123, 128n.36, 202, 218n.82, 228–9, 252n.15
Ito, Vice-Admiral Seiichi 441
Iwate 448
Iwo Jima 358, 371, 422–5, 438, 454n.19, 493, 505n.62, 510n.118
Izaki, Rear-Admiral Shunji 282
Izumo 448

Jack 335
Jackal 214n.22
Jaenecke, General Erwin 295, 333
Jaguar 156
'Jake' (Japanese long-range reconnaissance plane) 189–90
Jallao 399
Jaluit 328, 459n.98
Jamaica 51, 97n.83, 126, 245–7, 254n.37, 314–15
Jan Mayen Island 119, 197
Japan 4, 14–15, 32, 50, 90, 100, 120, 165, 284n.15, 325, 329, 335, 381, 405, 425–6, 438–9, 442–4, 448–53, 466, 480; attack on Pearl Harbor 136–7, 145, 479; campaigns in the Pacific *see under individual battles*; complex military plans 176–7, 183–4, 190, 209, 214n.23, 232, 376–7, 473–74; invasion of Southeast Asia 135–6, 138–41, 146–53, 160, 164, 170n.35, 170n.48, 173n.83, 478; *see also* Japanese IGHQ
Japanese Eighteenth Army 329, 336, 445, 457n.74
Japanese Twenty-Fifth Army 140, 150, 450
Japanese Thirty-Second Army 440
Japanese Thirty-Fifth Army 402–3
Japanese 1st Army Air Fleet 337, 378, 382, 419, 421, 426, 492
Japanese 2nd Army Air Fleet 377, 382, 492
Japanese 3rd Army Air Fleet 440
Japanese 4th Army Air Fleet 378, 382
Japanese 5th Army Air Fleet 427, 440, 451
Japanese 10th Army Air Fleet 440
Japanese Army Air Force 337, 377–8, 382, 416n.81, 419, 421, 426, 440, 492

Japanese Carrier Striking Force 178–80, 182
Japanese Centre Force 378–86, 388–9, 391–7, 400–2, 484, 490, 495
Japanese codes and ciphers 177, 184, 466
Japanese Combined Fleet 177, 209, 232–3, 272, 287n.48, 330, 348
Japanese Sixth Fleet 337, 347
Japanese IGHQ (Imperial General Headquarters) 177, 183, 204, 251, 261–2, 283, 295, 439, 473
Japanese 14th Infantry Division 373, 411n.13
Japanese 16th Infantry Division 378
Japanese 18th Infantry Division 174n.83
Japanese 20th Infantry Division 363n.37
Japanese 38th Infantry Division 232, 249
Japanese 51st Infantry Division 268–9
Japanese 88th Infantry Division 451
Japanese 91st Infantry Division 451
Japanese 109th Infantry Division 425
Japanese 3rd Kure Special Landing Force 177
Japanese First Mobile Fleet 337, 346, 350, 352–3, 364n.42, 366n.75, 367n.80, 379
Japanese 1st Mobile Striking Force (Kidō Butai) 161–2, 192, 214n.27, 217n.62, 233
Japanese 22nd Naval Air Flotilla 140
Japanese 23rd Naval Air Flotilla 147–8
Japanese 2nd Striking Force 379, 388
Java 149–53, 170n.40, 170n.48, 334, 405
Java Sea, battle of 151–3
Jean Bart 19, 33, 96n.68, 236
Jed 288n.59
Jellicoe, Earl 137, 250
Jersey 64n.43
Jervis 144
Jikitanchiki (Japanese MAD) 501n.25
'Jill' (Japanese torpedo-bomber) 349, 367n.78
Jintsu 209, 218n.89, 282, 290n.81
JN25 (D) code 177, 184
Johanneson, Kapitän zur See Rolf 316
John C. Butler 396, 414n.54
Johnston 395–6, 484
Johor, Strait of 9, 135
Joint Chiefs of Staff (JCS) 205, 269, 336, 372, 413n.45, 443–4, 457n.67, 476
Joint Intelligence Center, Pacific Ocean Area (JICPOA) 493
Joint Operations 477–8
Joint Planning Staff (JPS) 443
Jolo 426
Jomard Passage 178–9

Joshima, Rear-Admiral Takaji 349, 351–2
Jössingfjorden 68
'Judy' (Japanese dive-bomber) 349, 382, 397
Juminda mine barrage 120, 122, 133n.103
Jumna 428
Juneau 248
Junkers Ju-87 (German dive-bomber; 'Stuka') 18, 100, 146, 202, 228, 252n.15, 258
Junkers Ju-88 (German multi-role bomber) 53, 183, 202, 214n.22, 252n.15, 428–9, 494
Juno (Normandy landing sector) 340–1, 343, 365ns.51–2
Jun'yō 184, 187, 218n.89, 233, 304, 349, 351–2, 364n.42
Jupiter: Churchill's planned invasion of Norway 242–3; RN destroyer 151–2; US collier 11
JW.51A 243
JW.51B 243–4, 247, 255n.64, 485
JW.55A 311
JW.55B 311–13, 315, 323n.72, 495
JW.56A 325
JW.56B 325–6
JW.57 331
JW.58 331
JW.64 428
JW.65 429

K-XVIII 147
Kaafjorden 407
Kadashan Bay 420
Kaga 12, 19, 184, 188–9, 191–2, 216n.53, 504n.44
Kaiser, Henry J. 503n.41
Kaiten (manned torpedoes) 415n.77, 424, 441, 447
Kaiyo 427, 448
Kako 218n.89, 220ns.101, 105
Kakuta, Rear-Admiral Kakuji 184–7, 194, 337
Kalinin Bay 396–7, 414n.54
Kalymnos 308
Kamerun 23
Kamikaze ('Divine Wind') aerial suicide assaults 377, 397, 402–4, 409–10, 415ns.63, 75, 416n.81, 419–21, 424, 426–7, 439–42, 444, 446, 451, 453n.6, 493, 510n.120
Kamimbo Bay 262
Kandahar 144
Kara Sea 211, 319n.21

Karlsruhe 93n.22
Kasumi 441
'Kate' (Japanese torpedo bomber) 18, 137, 179–81, 188–9, 192–3, 214n.13, 328, 351
Katsuragi 427, 447–8
Kattegat 71, 75, 406, 434, 436, 455n.52
Kavieng 147, 220n.105, 317, 329–30
Keith 79
Kellogg-Briand Pact (1928) 13, 15
Kelvin 115
Kemal, Mustapha (Kemal Ataturk) 7
Kendari 147, 149
Kenney, General George C. 219n.95, 317, 378, 412n.25, 489
Kent 41ns.48–9
Kenya 416n.84
Keppel Harbour (Singapore) 297, 449
Kerama Retto 439
Kerch peninsula 141, 183, 296, 309, 333, 484
Kerch Strait 296
Kershaw, Ian 95n.51
Kesselring, Feldmarschall Albert 252n.13, 293, 307, 326, 354
Key West (Florida) 167
Keyes, Sir Roger 53
Kharkov 274, 318n.17
Khedive 443
Kholostyakov, Rear-Admiral G.N. 309
Khota Bharu 136, 138–9
Khrushchev, Nikita 160
Kidō Butai *see* Japanese 1st Mobile Striking Force
Kiel 34, 68, 80, 82, 102, 116, 157, 284n.13, 406, 434, 455n.38
Kieseritzky, Vizeadmiral Gustav 296, 480
Kikusui 1–10 (Massed Japanese air raids on Allied shipping at Okinawa) 440, 456n.58
Kiliindini 163, 170n.40, 325
Kimmel, Admiral Husband E. 145
Kinashi, Cdr.Takahazu 210–11
King George V 28, 37n.20, 46ns.106–7, 112–13, 173n.78, 174n.88, 292, 404, 419, 439, 448
King Victor Emmanuel III 281, 292
King, Admiral Ernest J. 145, 164, 169n.27, 205–6, 221n.114, 261, 265, 275, 286n.41, 303, 367n.91, 372, 386, 400, 404, 411n.7, 443, 476, 479, 482
Kingston (Jamaica) 51, 126, 158
Kinkaid, Admiral Thomas C. 233, 378–9, 382, 385–8, 391–3, 395, 398–400, 402, 412n.25, 420, 489–90

Kinloch, Commander D.C. 245–6
Kinryu Maru 209, 221n.113
Kinu 152, 380, 402
Kinugasa 180, 218n.89, 220ns.101, 105, 231–2, 249
Kipling 214n.22
Kirishima 184, 190, 218n.89, 232, 248–50
Kirk, Admiral Alan G. 341, 364n.51, 365n.55, 481
Kirkenes 120, 374
Kirov 174n.85, 327
Kiska 184–5, 196, 215n.36, 269, 272–3, 287n.52
Kitakami 448
Kitkun Bay 396–7, 414n.54, 420
Kiwi 262
Klassmann, Kapitänleutnant Helmut 309, 485
Kleinkampfverband (K-Verband) 354–5, 430, 484
Klüber, Admiral Otto 247
Klug, Korvettenkapitän Bernd 334
Klusmeier, Kapitänleutnant Emil 436
Knappen (wolf pack) 264
Knox, Dilly 104
KO (complex Japanese naval cipher) 177, 466
Kobe 165, 448
Koga, Admiral Mineichi 283, 287n.48, 304–5, 324, 330, 489
Koiso, Lt.-General Kuniaki 441, 449
Kokoda Trail 204, 206
Kola Inlet 120, 225, 243, 311, 315, 325–6, 374, 412n.16, 428–9, 436, 497
Kolberg (Kolobrzeg) 432
Köln 433
Kolombangara 282–3, 289n.75, 295
Komandorski Islands 269
Komatsu, Vice-Admiral Teruhisa 210
Kondo, Vice-Admiral Nobutake 185, 194, 209, 231–2, 249–50
Kongō 46n.111, 148, 218n.89, 231, 364n.42, 379, 383, 395
Königsberg (Kaliningrad) 431, 434
Konoye, Prince Fumimaro 125, 473
'Koralle' (Dönitz's HQ in Bernau) 285n.24
Kortenaer 151–2
Kos 301, 307–8, 334, 437
Krait 297
Krasnyy Kavkaz 146
Krebs 110, 483, 503n.39
Kretschmer, Fregattenkapitän Otto 97n.85, 109

Kriegsmarine (German Navy 1935–45) 19, 24, 31, 33–4, 44n.81, 49, 51, 75, 103, 124, 154, 263, 284n.13, 325, 332, 343, 345, 406, 430, 434–5, 462, 486
Kristiansand 72, 93n.18, 437, 455n.50
Krk 309
Kronstadt 39n.29, 122, 133n.104
Kuantan 139, 148, 470, 483, 485, 494
Kuban peninsula 273–4, 295–6, 484
Kubo, Rear-Admiral Kyuji 147
Kuhlmann, Oberleutnant Jürgen 429
Kula Gulf 281–2
Kumano 148, 195, 218n.89, 282, 364n.42, 383, 395, 415n.77
Kummetz, Generaladmiral Oskar 197, 244–7, 298, 431–3, 480, 485
Kunajiri 451
Kuomintang (KMT) 8, 451, 459n.95
Kure 148, 181, 427, 448, 469, 504n.45
Kure Special Landing Force 177, 211
Kuribayashi, Lt.Gen. Tadamichi 424–5
Kurier (radio transmitter) 375
Kuriles 273, 371, 376, 422, 447–8, 451
Kurische Nehrung 431
Kurita, Vice-Admiral Takeo 185, 195, 231, 305, 349–51, 353, 378–80, 382–9, 391–402, 409, 415n.57, 484, 488, 490–1, 495
Kursk 274, 296
Kuwa 416n.78
Kuznetsov, Admiral Nikolai G. 118
Kwajalein 307, 321n.50, 327–8
Kyūshū 426, 438, 440–1, 443, 450

La Maddalena 123, 241, 274, 279, 287n.57, 292–3, 309, 318n.8
La Pallice 261, 360
La Perle 496
La Rochelle 360, 437
La Spezia 99n.101, 127n.19, 241, 292, 354
Laborde, Admiral Jean de 238–9
Labuan 445
Laconia 226–7, 489
Lae 219n.90, 268, 286n.41, 294–5, 318n.13
Lampedusa 287n.58
Lampione 287n.58
Lancaster (British long-range, heavy bomber) 366n.63, 407–8, 434, 470
Lance 123
Landwirt (wolf pack) 344
Lange, Konteradmiral Werner 301
Langley (CV1) 11, 152

Langley (CVL27) 381, 425
Langsdorff, Hans 54–61, 485–6
Lansdowne 211
Largs 236, 274, 343, 365n.51
Lark 429
Latvia 120, 370, 375, 434
Lauenburg 119, 503n.39
Lavansaari 242
Layman, Commander Herbert 74
Layton, Admiral Sir Geoffrey 148–9
Lazaretto Creek (Malta) 163
Le Fantasque 362n.31
Le Havre 89, 96n.69, 156, 173n.69, 343–5, 355, 360, 366n.63
Le Malin 362n.31
Le Muy 359
Le Terrible 362n.31
Le Verdon-sur-Mer 360
Leach, Captain John 140
League of Nations 6–7, 15–17, 20–1, 29, 39n.34
Leander (HMNZ) 290n.81
Leander class 41ns.50–1, 43n.75
Lebanon 116
lebensraum (living space) 30, 32
Leberecht Maass 68, 92n.7, 496
Lee, Vice-Admiral Willis 233, 249–50, 350, 386, 398–401, 490
Legion 142, 159
'Leigh light' 87, 265, 464, 500n.17
Leipzig 25, 61, 432
Lemp, Kapitänleutnant Fritz-Julius 50, 62n.6, 97n.85, 110–11, 129n.49, 485
Lend-Lease 117, 479
Leningrad 44n.81, 56, 122, 163, 174n.85, 327
Leros 301–2, 307–8, 321n.53, 437
Leuthen (wolf pack) 302, 320n.34
Leutze 423
Levchenko, Admiral Gordei 327
Lever, Mavis 104
Lexington 11, 136, 177–82, 214ns.14–16, 349, 381, 383, 403, 504n.44
Leyte 372, 402–4, 411n.7, 416n.80, 419, 442, 447
Leyte Gulf, battle of 377–402, 409, 412n.25, 446, 483–4, 487–8, 490–2
Libau (Liepāja) 375, 434, 437
Libeccio 99n.101, 124
Liberator (VLR heavy bomber; B-24) 226, 240, 265, 305, 322n.57, 358, 402, 423, 433, 436
liberty ships 224, 302, 346, 366n.66, 421, 468

610 Index

Libreville (Gabon) 88
Libya 102–3, 124, 142–4, 252n.13, 258, 288n.70
Licata (Sicily) 279
Liebenstein, Kapitän zur See Gustav Freiherr von 280, 296, 481
'light blue' (Luftwaffe code) 104
Limbourne 310
L'Indomptable 362n.31
Lindsay, Sir Ronald 478
Lingayen Gulf 419–21
Lingga roads 378
Linosa 287n.58
Linsen (explosive torpedo boats) 367n.85, 430
Liscombe Bay 307, 502n.32
List, Feldmarschall Wilhelm 108
Lithuania 375
'Little Boy' 449
Littorio 19, 29, 46n.114, 99n.101, 143, 158–9, 173n.73, 202, 218n.80, 241, 292
Lively 123, 158, 214n.22
Liverpool 62n.13, 99n.107, 128n.42, 240
Livorno 127n.19, 296, 334
Lloyd George, David 6–7
Locarno agreement (1925) 7, 16, 22
Loch Eriboll 438
Loch Ewe 243, 310–11, 323n.72, 325, 374, 533
Lockwood, Vice-Admiral Charles 186–7
Lofoten Islands 74–6, 80, 109, 141, 313, 483
Lohs (wolf pack) 251n.3
London 6, 9–10, 14, 29, 32, 41n.49, 49, 51, 69, 85, 99n.107, 101, 108, 115, 118, 125, 138, 141, 145, 159, 235, 244, 319n.22, 416n.84, 425, 430, 449, 452, 505n.54
London class 41n.49
London Naval Treaty: (1930) 11, 14, 17–19, 21, 40n.45; (1936) 22, 28–9, 44n.81
Long 420
'Long Lance' (Japanese torpedo) 151, 282, 466, 502n.32
Longley-Cook, Captain Eric 365n.52
Loos, Oberleutnant Johann-Friedrich 429
Lorient 48n.135, 97ns.82, 85, 109, 261, 359–60, 437
Lorraine 33, 97n.76, 368n.97
Los Alamos (New Mexico) 426, 449
Los Negros (Admiralty Islands) 329
Los Negros (Visayas) 426, 445
Losinj 309

Louisiade Archipelago 176–7, 179
Louisville 187, 219n.92, 389, 420
Love, Jr., Robert W. 500n.12
Lowry, Vice-Admiral F.J. 327, 447
Lübeck 354, 436
Luftwaffe 44n.88, 53, 76–8, 89, 94n.43, 95n.51, 98n.93, 102, 104, 107–8, 114–18, 121–22, 133n.103, 146, 156, 174n.85, 197–8, 200, 202–3, 217n.64, 225, 242, 252n.15, 266, 277, 288n.67, 293, 308–10, 326, 332, 334, 342, 355
Lundstrom, John B. 220n.104
Lunga Point 208, 220n.106, 230–2, 248, 253n.24, 425, 453n.6, 488
Lüth, Komm.Wolfgang 484
Lütjens, Admiral Günther 83, 112–13, 130n.61, 464
Lutong 445
Lützow (formerly Deutschland) 56, 70, 72, 93n.22, 116, 183, 197–8, 244, 246–7, 267, 298–300, 310, 316, 375, 431–2, 434–5, 486
Lützow (renamed Petropavlovsk) 44n.81
Luzon 138, 372, 377–8, 381–4, 397–8, 401–3, 409–10, 419–22, 426, 446–7
Lydd 496
Lyon, Major Ivan 297
Lyons 360
Lytton Commission 15–16

M-95 218n.88
Mabalacat airfield 397, 420
MacArthur, General Douglas 153, 164, 171n.53, 205–6, 219n.95, 283, 286n.41, 289n.77, 294–5, 316–17, 328–9, 335–6, 358, 363n.37, 373, 378, 381, 386–7, 402–4, 410, 411n.7, 412n.25, 414n.45, 420, 422, 443–5, 452, 457n.67, 459n.99, 476–7, 490
MacDonald, James Ramsay 9, 13–14, 16
Mack, Captain Philip 108
Mackesy, Major General P.J. 76
Madagascar 167, 211
Madang 329, 336
Madrid 24, 31
'Magic' (decrypted Japanese signals) 125
Maginot line 14, 19
Magnetic Anomaly Detection (MAD) 223–4, 277, 327, 464–5, 501n.25
Mahan, Alfred Thayer 140, 416n.81
Maiali chariots (slow, human torpedoes) 123, 144, 484
Majorca 25
Majuro Atoll 328, 346

Makassar 149, 170n.41
Makigumo 194, 253n.30
Makin 306–7, 474
Maksim Gorkiy 174n.85, 327
Malacca, Strait of 162, 324, 357, 376, 405, 444, 446, 452
Malaya 9, 32, 127n.19, 135, 138, 140, 148, 161, 335, 371, 405, 412n.19, 428, 446, 452–53, 459n.99
Malcolm 254n.39
Maleme 114
Mallory, George 183
Maloelap 321n.50, 327, 459n.98
Malta 21, 83, 91, 96n.67, 97n.83, 100, 103, 107, 118–19, 122–3, 129n.53, 131n.88, 132n.89, 133n.113, 143–4, 146, 157, 159–60, 163, 169n.29, 173n.76, 173n.78, 174n.84, 201–2, 217n.79, 227–30, 235, 238, 252n.11, 252n.13, 253n.17, 258, 271, 274, 278–9, 287n.58, 292–3, 317n.7, 358, 470–1
Manado 147
Manchester 228
Manchuria (renamed Manchukuo by the Japanese) 15, 17, 20, 27
Manila 135, 138, 379, 383, 403, 419–20, 422
Manila Bay 420
Mansfield, Rear-Admiral John 370–1
Manus Island 219n.90, 387, 392
Manvantara 170n.42
Mao Zedong (Mao Tse-tung) 451, 459n.95
Maori 142
Marblehead 170n.41
Marcus Island 304, 337–8, 416n.81, 452
Marder (one-man submersibles) 354–5, 367n.85
Mariana Islands 185, 306, 328, 336–8, 347–8, 350–1, 353, 355, 357, 366n.75, 376, 473, 475–6, 510n.119
Marienwerder (Kwidzyn) 432
Marigold 174n.96, 500n.16
Marineoberkommando Ost/Ostsee (German Naval High Command East) 431
Marineoberkommando West see Naval Group West
Mark 24 mine see 'Fido'
Marsala (Sicily) 279
Marschall, Admiral Wilhelm 68, 80–3
Marsdale 487
Marseillaise 362n.31
Marseilles 293, 359

Marshall Islands 287n.50, 306, 321n.50, 327–8, 338, 452, 476
Marshall, General George C. 205, 272, 280–1, 372, 411n.7, 443
Martin, Rear-Admiral Bernard 418, 443
Marumo, Rear-Admiral Kuninori 179
Maryland 136, 186, 219n.92, 403, 414n.50, 441
MAS (Italian fast motor torpedo boats) 107, 228, 287n.57
Masbate 426
Massachusetts 253n.35, 381, 442
Massawa 107
Massignani, Alessandro 127n.31
Matapan, battle of Cape 105–7, 127ns.31–2, 143, 218n.80, 354, 464, 483, 487, 492
Matchless 214n.21, 315
Matochkin Strait 200
Matsuda, Rear-Admiral Chiaki 385
Matsuwa 447, 451
Matuschka, Kapitänleutnant Graf von Hartmut 429
'Mauriceforce' 76–7
Mauritius 365n.52
Max Schultz 68, 92n.7
May Fourth movement (1919) 8
Maya 148, 184, 218n.89, 232, 249, 286n.42, 305, 352–3, 364n.42, 380
McCain, Vice-Admiral John 381–3, 386, 397, 399, 401–3, 409–10, 442
McCawley 290n.78
McCreery, General Sir Richard 293
McGrigor, Admiral Sir Rhoderick 274
McMorris, Rear-Admiral Charles 286n.42
Mediterranean Fleet 7, 20–21, 85–6, 90, 100, 103–4, 106–8, 114–15, 119, 122, 125, 126n.3, 129n.53, 133n.113, 144, 158, 160, 183, 201, 238, 292, 308, 483
Mediterranean Sea 11, 21, 23–4, 26, 29, 33–4, 83, 85–6, 88, 90–1, 99n.101, 102–4, 107, 111, 113–15, 117–19, 122–4, 129n.53, 131n.88, 133n.106, 133n.113, 142–4, 146, 157, 159–60, 163, 165, 183, 201–2, 227, 229–30, 234–8, 252n.13, 254n.42, 258, 267, 271–2, 274, 279, 283n.6, 291, 300, 302, 308, 317n.7, 324, 326–7, 330, 333
Memel (Klaipėda) 375, 430–1
merchant aircraft carriers (MAC) 496, 500n.14
Mergui 160, 444
Mersa Matruh 117

Mers-el-Kebir 33, 84–5, 236, 491
Merula 170n.42
Messina 104, 142, 158, 241, 279–81, 291
'Messina Straits Regatta' 291
metox (radar search receiver) 196, 265, 465
Meyer, Oberleutnant Rudolf 429
Miami 410
Michishio 171n.48, 390
Micronesia 181, 330, 336, 374
'mid-Atlantic air gap' 51, 166, 223, 240, 259–60, 264–5, 275, 302–3, 463–4
Midway 165, 176, 213n.1
Midway, battle of 165, 176, 181–96, 204–6, 215ns.28, 31–33, 216ns.38–40, 48, 52–3, 60, 217ns.61–2, 230, 271, 356, 454n.25, 468, 471, 474–5, 482, 486, 491–2, 495, 498, 507n.87
Mikawa, Vice-Admiral Gunichi 207–9, 220ns.101, 105–6, 232, 249, 486, 488–9
Mikuma 148, 195
'Milchkühe' (U-boat tankers) 166, 275, 277, 303, 324, 482
Mili atoll 306, 321n.50, 338, 452
Miller, Major-General Henry 402, 505n.54
Milne Bay 211, 294
Milner, Marc 129n.52, 154, 259, 409, 478
Milos 437
Mindanao 138, 164, 330, 335, 337, 366n.75, 371–3, 377–8, 390, 393, 397, 411n.7, 425–6, 445–6
Mindoro 380, 383, 409–10, 419, 425
mines and minelaying: Aegean 321n.52, 371; Baltic 49, 118, 120, 122, 133n.103, 203–4, 218n.88, 242, 273, 333, 362n.29, 370, 432–3, 435; effectiveness of 91n.1, 126n.3, 132ns.95, 101, 144, 151–2, 204, 277, 297–8, 477; English Channel 50, 53, 63n.24, 66, 99n.107, 334, 346, 355, 365n.60, 430; Mediterranean 90, 127n.19, 146, 159, 230, 238, 258, 267, 292–3, 309, 327, 334, 354, 359, 410n.41; North Sea 50, 53, 61, 66, 69–70, 91n.3, 99n.107, 156–7, 217n.77, 406, 455n.52, 497; Pacific 281, 330, 422, 439, 445–6, 452
minesweepers, role and importance 38n.29, 170n.35, 200, 242, 251n.6, 254n.38, 292, 296, 304, 309, 325, 333, 342–44, 346, 365n.55, 403, 419, 422–3, 443, 446, 450, 456n.55

Minneapolis 219n.92, 250, 351, 389, 420
Minsk 122
Miraglia, Giuseppe (formerly Citta de Messina) 317n.7
Miri 445
Misima Island 179
Mississippi 219n.92, 414n.50, 421
Missouri 441, 452
Mitchell (US medium-range bomber also known as a B-25) 165, 308, 423
Mitchell, William ('Billy') L. 9, 470
Mitscher, Admiral Marc A. 216n.48, 219n.92, 327–8, 330, 336, 348–53, 356, 366n.75, 371, 377–9, 381, 384, 388, 391, 398–402, 424, 427, 438, 441–2, 486
Moa 262
Mobile 398, 400
Mogador 84
Mogami 41n.51, 43n.75, 148, 195, 305, 349, 364n.42, 379, 389–91
Molch (one-man human torpedo) 430
Molde 77
Molotov 121
Molucca (Maluku) 148, 335, 358, 372
Momi 420
MOMP (mid-ocean meeting point) 171n.55
Monsun (wolf pack) 324
Montcalm 365n.52
Montecuccoli, Raimondo 252n.14
Monterey 381
Montevideo 57, 59–50
Montgomery, Field Marshal Viscount 234–5, 237–8, 253n.32, 258, 279–80, 294
Montgomery, Rear-Admiral Alfred 305, 320n.43
Montpelier 403
Moon Island 370, 375
Moon, Rear-Admiral Don Pardee 343, 364n.51, 365n.52
Moore, Admiral Sir Henry 332, 407
Morgan, General Frederick 280
Moro Gulf 426
Morocco 98n.92, 236–7, 260, 327
Morotai 358, 372, 377, 402, 411ns.7, 9, 452
mortars *see* 'Hedgehog'; 'Squid'
Mosquito (British multi-purpose bomber) 366n.63, 436
motor torpedo boats (MTBs): deployment of 79, 128n.36, 131n.84, 156, 201–2, 218n.81, 229, 250, 258, 269, 274, 279,

288n.70, 296, 301, 309–10, 326, 334, 344, 365n.60, 374, 406, 422, 430, 433
Mount Olympus 419
Mount Suribachi 423–5
Mountbatten, Admiral Lord Louis (later Earl) 173n.69, 222n.120, 363n.34, 452, 459n.99, 460n.101, 474
Mukden incident (1931) 15, 26
'Mulberry Harbours' 341, 345, 507n.83
Müller, Generalleutnant Friedrich Wilhelm 308
Müller, Kapitänleutnant Karl 334
München 110, 119, 503n.39
Munda 251, 262, 281–3, 289n.75, 290ns.80, 82
Munich settlement (1938) 30–1, 46n.117, 49
Murmansk 121, 131n.85, 154, 164, 172n.61, 183, 214n.21, 225, 243, 255n.64, 266–7, 298, 310, 323n.72, 325, 374, 408, 436, 496
Murray, Vice-Admiral George 233
Musashi 19, 29, 218n.89, 346, 364n.42, 366n.75, 377, 379, 383–5, 469, 488
Musketry (Biscay search areas) 277
Mussolini, Benito 11, 14, 19–21, 23–5, 29–32, 83, 86, 90, 123–4, 138, 252n.13, 281, 318n.8, 477, 507n.80
Mustin 253n.30
Mutsu 185, 218n.89
Mutsuki 209, 221n.113
Myebon 418, 428
Myōkō 41n.51, 152, 180, 218n.89, 232, 305, 364n.42, 383–5, 449

Nachi 151–2, 185, 218n.89, 286n.42, 391, 415n.77
Naganami 380
Nagano, Admiral Osami 177
Nagara 184, 216n.52, 219n.89, 248, 321n.50
Nagasaki 450, 453, 458ns.88–9, 498
Nagato 185, 218n.89, 349, 352, 364n.42, 379, 383, 396, 447
Nagatsuki 282
Nagoya 165
Nagumo, Vice-Admiral Chuichi 135, 137, 161–2, 168n.6, 173n.83, 184, 188–95, 209, 214n.27, 216n.52, 231–3, 337, 348, 482, 491
Najin 450
Nakagawa, Colonel Kunio 373
Namsos 76–7
Nanking 27, 451, 459n.95

Nanshin (southward advance) 138, 335, 453
Nantes 96n.69, 359–60
Napier 418
Naples 99n.101, 104, 123, 241, 281, 294, 309, 327, 358
Narbada 428
Narva Bay 354, 362n.29
Narvik 69–77, 80, 183, 198, 212, 242, 483
Nashi 448
Nashville 219n.92, 329, 409, 412n.25, 416n.81
Nasugbu 422
Nauru 306, 459n.98
Nautilus 190–1, 413n.31
naval cyphers (RN) 154, 171n.56, 259, 303, 321n.56, 463, 467, 503n.40
Naval Group West (Marineoberkommando West) 74–5, 113
Naval Intelligence Division (Admiralty) 109
Naxos 375, 465
Nazi Party (National Socialist German Workers Party) 13, 16–17, 30
Nazi-Soviet Pact (1939) 32, 56, 83, 118
Nebojša 128n.36
Neches 148
Neger (German one-man submersibles) 354, 363n.31
'Nell' (Japanese torpedo bomber) 43n.77, 140
Nelson 33, 37n.20, 46n.107, 123, 228, 292, 365n.60, 446, 452
Nelson class 12, 28
Neosho 178–9
Neptune 64n.40, 144
Nestor 110
Nettuno 326
Neutrality Act (US) 55, 125
neutrality patrols 51, 479
Nevada 136, 346, 365n.52, 368n.97, 439–40
New Britain 145, 147, 205, 268–9, 286n.41, 295, 304, 316–17, 329, 489
New Georgia 207, 251, 262, 269, 281–3, 286n.41, 289n.75, 290n.82, 318n.15
New Guinea 148, 153, 176, 204–6, 211, 219ns.90, 95, 251, 268–9, 286ns.39, 41, 287n.50, 289n.77, 294–5, 303, 317, 329, 335–8, 347, 357, 363n.37, 367n.92, 373, 445, 457n.74, 459n.98
New Hebrides (Vanuatu) 306
New Ireland 147, 205, 286n.41, 329, 337, 459n.98

New Jersey 381, 386, 400–1
New Mexico 219n.92, 420, 439
New Orleans 41n.48, 219n.92, 250, 381, 398, 400
'New Standard of Naval Strength' 20, 27, 31
New York 253n.35, 441
New Zealand 3rd Division 329
New Zealand Star 129n.53
Newcastle 99n.107, 416n.84
Newfoundland 87, 91, 101, 120, 125, 154, 265, 318n.9, 330, 416n.84, 445
Newport, Christopher 198
Nezamozhnik 163
Ngulu 358
Nicobar Islands 404, 444, 446
Nicosia 131n.76
Niger 497
Nigeria 217n.70, 416n.84
Niitsuki 282
Nikolayev 121, 333
Nimitz, Admiral Chester W. 145, 164, 177, 182, 184–7, 205–6, 216n.60, 219n.94, 221n.114, 286n.41, 306, 328, 336, 350, 358, 372–3, 381, 386–7, 399–401, 403, 405, 410, 411n.7, 414n.45, 423, 438, 443, 451–2, 457n.67, 468, 474, 476, 482, 490, 503n.36, 507ns.86–7, 509n.100
Nine Power Treaty (Washington Conference 1921–22) 5
Nishimura, Rear-Admiral Shoji 249, 379, 387–93, 398, 464, 483, 491–2
Nishimura, Teiji 388
No.111 (Yamato class superbattleship) 469
Noble, Rear-Admiral Albert 446
Noemfoor 357, 367n.92
Nollmann, Kapitänleutnant Rolf 429
Nomura, Admiral Kichisaburo 125
Non-Intervention Committee 23–5
Norfjell 428
Norfolk 33, 41n.49, 113, 312–13
Norfolk (Virginia) 278
Norilo 329
Normandy 213, 280, 334, 340, 343, 354–5, 358, 364n.47, 430, 472, 496
North Africa 21, 102–3, 107–8, 118, 126n.13, 131n.88, 142, 145–6, 160, 229, 234–5, 237–8, 242, 252n.13, 258, 260, 267, 271, 275, 278, 291, 293, 308–9, 470, 474, 477
North Atlantic 34, 48n.139, 50, 55, 67, 70, 80, 88–9, 91, 92n.8, 100–2, 110, 113, 116–17, 119, 126n.6, 132n.91, 154, 166, 171ns.54, 56, 223, 237, 239, 255n.49, 265, 270, 275–6, 284n.12, 302, 313, 326, 330, 375, 429, 463, 467, 478, 500ns.14, 17
North Carolina 28, 46n.111, 211, 219n.92, 424, 502n.32
North Channel 101, 422
North Korea 450
North Sea 20, 24, 33–4, 50, 53, 55, 61, 67–8, 70–1, 80, 83, 91, 92n.6, 101, 104, 116, 155–6, 241–2, 266, 310, 406, 429–30, 433, 436, 438, 483, 496
North, Admiral Sir Dudley 88–9
Northampton 40n.45, 41n.48, 219n.92, 250
Northern Expedition (1926) 8
Northern Fleet (USSR) 131n.85, 331, 361n.7, 374
Northern Patrol 55, 62n.9
Norway 35, 69, 71–7, 80, 92n.8, 116, 155, 157, 196–7, 242, 244, 289n.74, 298, 332, 376, 406, 428, 436–7, 484, 489
Noshiro 305, 349, 364n.42, 383, 402
Noumea 207, 230–1
Novaya Zemlya 200, 298
Novorossisk 163, 202–3
Nowake 402
NP.1 (troop convoy) 76
Nubian 115, 287n.58
Numata, Lt-Gen. Takazo 460n.101
Nürnberg 61, 437
Nyon Conference (1937) 26

Oahu 135–7, 168n.4, 184–6
O'Bannon 248, 318n.16
Obayashi, Rear-Admiral Sueo 351, 367n.78
Obdurate 245–7
Obedient 245–6
Oberkommando der Marine (OKM) 31, 53, 61, 68–9, 116, 119, 285n.24, 429–30, 433, 435, 467
Oberkommando der Wehrmacht (OKW) 66, 89
O'Brien 211, 502n.32
Ochakov 121
Octagon (Allied military conference, Quebec 1944) 372, 404–5, 411n.8
Odessa 121, 333, 472
Offizier (German code) 311
Ofotfjorden 73, 94n.27
Oglala 136

O'Hara, Vincent P. 256n.66, 414n.54
Ohka (manned rocket torpedoes) 427, 440–2
Ohno, Captain Takeji 185
Oikawa, Admiral Koshirō 356
Oil, importance to war effort 21, 114, 117, 120, 137, 140, 147, 150, 255n.64, 335, 356–7, 373, 404–5, 418–19, 428, 444–6, 480, 491, 502n.30, 507n.83
Okamura, General Yasugi 451
O'Kane, Cdr. Richard 484
Okinawa 353, 425, 438–43, 445–6, 455n.53, 456n.63, 493, 510n.119
Oklahoma 136
Oktyabrskaya Revolutsiya 174n.85, 327, 354
Oktyabrskiy, Vice Admiral F.S. 131n.76, 202
Olaf, Crown Prince (Norway) 437
Oldendorf, Vice-Admiral Jesse 387–91, 393, 419, 421, 447, 482, 492
Oliva, Admiral Romeo 293
Oliver, Admiral Sir Geoffrey N. 364n.51
Olongapo 421
Olson, Wesley 99n.105
Omaha (Normandy landing sector) 10, 41n.48, 340–1, 343, 345, 364n.51
Omaha class 10, 41n.48
Ommaney Bay 453n.6
Omori, Rear-Admiral Sentaro 185, 232, 320n.42
Oneglia 435
Onishi, Vice-Admiral Takijiro 382, 397, 419, 421, 426
Onslow 244–5, 251n.7
Operation A-GO 337, 347–8
Operation Agreement 229–30
Operation AL 184–6
Operation Alacrity 320n.37
Operation Alphabet 80
Operation Anklet 141
Operation Archery 141
Operation Ariel 96n.69
Operation August Storm 450
Operation Avalance 281, 291–4, 296, 318n.8
Operation Backhander 316
Operation Banquet 357
Operation Baritone 229
Operation Baytown 281, 291–3
Operation Bishop 444
Operation Biting 173n.69
Operation Blacklist 453
Operation Bodyguard 364n.47, 472

Operation Bolero 224, 260, 271
Operation Boomerang 357
Operation Brawn 407–8
Operation C3 (Fall Herkules) 252n.13
Operation Cartwheel 269, 281, 289n.77, 414n.45
Operation Catapult 84–5, 97n.77, 491
Operation Catchpole 328, 361n.17
Operation Cathechism 407–8
Operation Chronometer 117
Operation Claymore 109
Operation Cleanslate 268
Operation Cockpit 334–5
Operation Collar 90
Operation Collie 446
Operation Corkscrew 274
Operation Cottage 273
Operation Crimson 357
Operation Crusader 124
Operation Culverin 405
Operation Cycle 96n.69
Operation Deadlight 438
Operation Demon 108
Operation Derange 269
Operation Desecrate 330
Operation Detachment 424, 505n.62
Operation Dexterity 295, 329
Operation Diplomat 334
Operation Director 316
Operation Dracula 443–4
Operation Dragoon (formerly Anvil) 358–60, 368n.98, 474
Operation Dynamo 78–80, 95n.51, 339, 341–2, 438, 481
Operation EB 110
Operation EC 119
Operation Enclose 269
Operation Enclose II 269
Operation Epilepsy 312
Operation Flintlock 328
Operation Forager 338, 347–8, 357, 366n.75, 414n.45
Operation Fortitude South 364n.47
Operation Galvanic 306–7, 474–5
Operation Globe Trotter 358
Operation Goodwood I-IV 407
Operation Grasp 84
Operation Hailstone 328
Operation Halberd 122–3, 492
Operation Hammer 76
Operation Harpoon 201–2
Operation Hats 86
Operation Husky 271, 274, 278, 280, 289n.70, 339, 341, 481

616 *Index*

Operation Iceberg 438–43, 456n.63, 457n.65
Operation Infatuate 406
Operation Insect 252n.11
Operation Ironclad 167
Operation Jane 211
Operation Jaywick 297–8, 319n.20
Operation Jubilee 212, 222n.120, 229, 474
Operation Judgment 90
Operation Jupiter 437
Operation KA 209
Operation KE 263
Operation KON 338
Operation Kongō 424
Operation Landcrab 272, 510n.119
Operation Light 357
Operation Lightning 418
Operation Lustre 103, 474
Operation Mascot 407–8
Operation Matador 418
Operation Maurice 76–7
Operation Menace 89, 98n.91
Operation Meridian 419
Operation MI 181, 183–5, 187–8, 195
Operation Mike I 421
Operation Mike VI 422
Operation Mike VII 421
Operation Millet 357, 404
Operation MO 176–7, 182–3
Operation Neptune 334, 339, 341–2, 346, 360, 364n.47, 472, 481
Operation Oboe I 444
Operation Oboe II 445
Operation Oboe VI 445
Operation Obviate 408
Operation Olympic 443
Operation Outflank 357, 404
Operation Overlord 280–1, 308, 310, 339, 345–6, 358, 360, 406, 472–3, 505n.54
Operation Paravane 407
Operation Passport 418
Operation Pedestal 227–9
Operation Pekin 62n.2
Operation Pendant 418
Operation Percussion 302
Operation Perpetual 133n.113
Operation Persecution 336
Operation Pestilence 205
Operation Pinpoint 252n.11
Operation Planet 407
Operation Primrose 111
Operation Railway 132n.89

Operation Reckless 335
Operation Riviera 120–1
Operation RO 304, 489
Operation Robson 357, 405
Operation Rocket 132n.89
Operation Rupert 76
Operation Rutter 222n.120
Operation Sankey 418
Operation Shingle 326, 361n.12
Operation SHO 358, 376
Operation SHO-GO 1, 376–80, 384–5, 389–91, 402, 474, 488, 492; *see also* Leyte Gulf, battle of
Operation Sickle 76
Operation Slapstick 292–3
Operation Source 299
Operation Splice 132n.89
Operation Stacey 428
Operation Stalemate II 373
Operation Stone Age 238
Operation Stonewall 322n.57
Operation Stream 211
Operation Sunfish 428
Operation TA 330
Operation Take-Ichi 335
Operation TEN-GO 439, 441
Operation Tiger 129n.53
Operation Tiger Claw 407
Operation Torch 234–9, 242, 254n.42, 258, 260, 271, 339, 481
Operation Tracer 132n.89
Operation Transom 334–5
Operation Tungsten 332
Operation Vénérable 437
Operation Victor III 425
Operation Victor IV 425
Operation Vigorous 201–2
Operation Watchtower 205–6, 230
Operation Wilfred 70–1
Operation Zipper 405, 446, 452–3
Operational Intelligence Centre (OIC) 64n.28, 70, 109, 116, 259–60, 428, 467
Operational Research 283n.8, 501n.26
OPINTEL (Operational Intelligence) 467, 482, 503n.37
Oppanol (rubber coating) 355, 367n.87, 465
Oran 33–4, 84, 96n.73, 138, 236–7, 254n.39, 278, 321n.54, 358, 531
Oranienburg 327
Ordzhonikidze 121
Orel 274, 296
Orion 115, 274, 365n.52
Orione 142

Orkney Islands 3, 33, 62n.9, 93n.19, 95n.63
Orminster 367n.87
Ormoc 378, 380, 402–4
Orwell 245
Orzel 49, 62n.2, 72, 93n.22
Osborne, Engineer Officer Johnny, (HMS Hotspur) 74, 483
Osel (Hiiumaa) 370, 375
Oslo 70, 72, 437, 455n.50
Osorno 310, 322n.57
Ostende 77
Ostfriesland 9
Ostmark (wolf pack) 264
Otario 252n.11
Ottawa 224
Ouistreham 340–1
Owen 402
Owen Stanley Range 204, 268
Oxhöfter Kämpe 433
Ōyodo 398, 402, 427, 448
Ozawa, Vice-Admiral Jisaburo 149, 161–2, 173n.83, 337, 346–53, 364n.42, 366n.75, 379–80, 384–6, 392, 398–402, 487, 490

P-39 159
P551/Jastrzab 174n.88
Pachino peninsula (Sicily) 279
Pacific Fleet (US) 136–7, 184, 205, 207, 338, 387, 399, 456n.63, 479
Pacific Fleet (USSR) 131n.85
Pacific theatre 28, 46n.110, 120, 135–7, 140–1, 145–8, 183–4, 187, 196, 204–6, 218n.89, 230, 251, 257, 261, 268, 287n.50, 304, 307, 329, 337–8, 346, 351, 353, 355–6, 371–3, 376–7, 379, 387, 404–5, 409, 412ns.20, 22, 413n.45, 418–25, 427, 438, 443–4, 448–9, 452–3, 457n.67, 462, 465–6, 469, 473, 475–6, 480–1, 490, 492–3
Pacific, Central 176, 185–7, 195, 220n.104, 284n.15, 321n.50, 327–8, 336–7, 347, 356, 358, 371, 376, 426, 468, 473
Pacific, North 268, 272, 447, 451
Pacific, SW 141, 147, 153, 164–5, 176–7, 183, 204–7, 211, 219n.94, 230, 234, 248–9, 251, 261, 269, 271, 284n.15, 286n.41, 294, 303, 329–30, 337–8, 346, 357, 371–2, 378, 426, 452, 459n.99, 473, 477
Pacific, Western 4, 8, 27, 442
Pact of Steel (1939) 31

Padfield, Peter 62ns.5–6, 63n.19
Paestum 291
Palau 148, 330, 336–8, 347, 358, 371–3, 411ns.7, 13, 452, 510n.119
Palawan 380, 413n.31, 425
Palembang 149–50, 419
Palermo 258, 279, 358
Palliser, Admiral Sir Arthur F. 139
Palomares 200
Pampas 159
Pan-American Security Zone 55, 154
Panay 164, 388, 402, 426
Pandjang 297
Pandora 96n.73
Pantelleria 274–5, 287n.58
Panzerschiff (pocket battleship) 12, 486
Papua 204–5, 211; *see also* New Guinea
Paramushiro 273, 447, 451
Paris 6, 33, 48n.135, 358, 360
Parizhskaya Kommuna 121
Parona, Rear-Admiral Angelo 98n.87
Parshall, Jonathan 184, 192, 213n.1, 216ns.38, 53, 217n.62
Parthian 131n.76
Pas-de-Calais 340, 343, 364n.47, 472–3
Patani 136, 148
patrol boats 218n.88, 262, 293, 389–390, 404, 406, 431, 450
Patterson, Rear-Admiral Wilfred 207, 365n.52
Patton, General George C. 236, 279–80
Pauillac 360
Paulus Potter 200
Paulus, Feldmarschall Friedrich 263
Pavesi, Rear-Admiral Gino 274
Pavlovich, Nikolai 218n.87, 362n.29
Pearl Harbor 4, 18, 117, 135–7, 145, 148, 153, 164–5, 167n.4, 176–7, 182, 184–7, 193, 195, 205, 209–10, 271, 306, 402, 406, 450, 453, 468, 470, 473, 478–80, 491, 498, 507n.80
Peary 170n.46
Pegaso 165
Pegasus 12
Pelagie 275, 287n.58
Peleliu 373, 411ns.7, 10, 12, 493, 507n.86, 510n.119
Peloponnesus 108
Penang 324, 428, 444, 452
Penelope 71, 94n.39, 123, 144, 287n.58, 292, 301, 319n.30
Pennsylvania 136, 219n.92, 414n.50, 447
Pensacola 40n.45, 41n.48, 219n.92, 250, 423

Pentland Firth 93n.19, 429
Peoples Liberation Army (PLA) 451, 459n.95
Percival, Lt.Gen. Arthur E. 422
Perekop 121
Perekop Isthmus 121, 333
Perkins 179
Pernambuco 34
Perras, Galen Roger 287n.51
Perseus 142
Perth 41n.50, 151–3, 171n.49
Pescadores 148, 377, 379
Pétain, Marshal Philippe 83–4, 238
Petard 283n.10
Peters, Kapitän zur See Rudolph 325–6
Petersen, Captain Wallis F. 330
Petrof Bay 397
Petropavlovsk: battleship 39n.29; cruiser (formerly Lützow) 44n.81, 174n.85, 327
Petsamo 120
Pfeil (wolf pack) 251n.3, 264
Phelps 181
Philadelphia 254n.35, 318n.9
Philippine Sea, battle of 348–53, 356, 385, 471, 486
Philippines 138, 140, 148, 153, 171n.53, 205, 330, 335, 337–8, 347, 358, 371–73, 376–9, 383, 387–8, 401–4, 406, 409–10, 412n.25, 414n.45, 416n.81, 426, 445–6, 452, 492, 495, 498
Phillips, Vice-Admiral Sir Tom 83, 135, 138–40, 485, 494
Phoebe 416n.84, 444
Phoenix 329, 389, 422, 445
Phuket 160, 446
Piet Hein 170n.48
Pillau (Baltiysk) 431, 434
Pips, battle of the 273
Piraeus 104, 308, 371
Pittsburgh 442
Pladjoe (Plaju) 150, 419
Platino 252n.11
'Pluto' (cross-Channel fuel system) 341
Plymouth 84, 310
pocket battleship (Panzerschiff) 12, 25, 34, 54–60, 65n.47, 72, 93n.22, 102, 197, 211, 244, 375, 434, 486
Point Luck 185–6
Pola (Pula) 105–6, 127n.25, 317n.7, 326, 487
Poland 1, 6, 31–2, 34–5, 49, 51, 358, 375, 432, 462; military forces 49, 62n.2, 71–2, 96n.69, 174n.88, 226, 303

Polar coast 164, 242, 273, 325, 332, 361n.7, 374
Polares 503n.39
'Polish corridor' 30–1, 49
Pollen, Arthur Hungerford 1
Pomerania 432, 437
Pommern 297
Ponape (Pohnpei) 336, 459n.98
Pope 152
Port Blair 160, 428, 444
Port Darwin 135, 150
Port Dickson 428, 452
Port Moresby 176–9, 182–3, 204, 268, 474
Port Said 260, 278
Port Stanley 56, 59
Port Swettenham (Pelabuhan Kelang) 452
Portal, Marshal of the RAF Viscount 278
Porter 234
Portland 41n.48, 219n.92, 234, 248, 389
Porto Empedocle (Sicily) 279
Portsmouth 50, 84, 340
Potsdam 459n.99
Pound, Admiral Sir Dudley 49, 71–2, 76, 79, 83, 88, 113, 123, 198–200, 298, 319n.23, 479, 491
Power, Admiral Sir Arthur 292, 324, 404–5, 418, 452
Power, Vice-Admiral Manley 444
Powers, Lt. John 180
Pozallo (Sicily) 279
Pozarica 200
PQ.13 155, 496
PQ.15 164
PQ.16 197
PQ.17 155, 197–200, 217n.77, 225, 229, 244, 334, 471, 491
PQ.18 155, 225–6, 251n.6, 471, 496
Pratt, Captain Veazie 14
Preussen 12
Pridham-Wippell, Admiral Sir Henry 104, 106, 108, 487, 492
Prien, Korvettenkapitän Günther 54, 64n.27, 77, 108–9, 484
Prieto, Indalecio 25
Primauguet 236
Prince of Wales 46n.106, 112–13, 120, 126, 139–40, 148, 470
Princeton 381–2, 504n.44
Prinz Eugen 34, 44n.81, 112–13, 155, 157, 183, 369, 375, 431–2, 437, 471
Prize Regulations 62n.7, 65n.44
Proteus 96n.73
Provence 33, 84, 254n.46

Prunella 80
PT-137 390
PT-490 404
PT-492 404
Puglia 280
Pulau Bukom 297
Pulau Pompong 297
Pultusk 430
Punjabi 93n.23, 94n.39, 174n.88
Punta Stilo, battle of 86
Purple (Japanese diplomatic code) 177
Python 467

QP.11 164
QP.13 197, 217n.77, 497
QP.14 225
QP.15 243
Q-ships 80, 95n.57
Quadrant (Allied military staff conference, Quebec 1943) 281, 289n.73, 319n.23
Quebec 281, 289n.73, 319n.23, 372, 405
Queen Elizabeth: battleship 28, 31, 115, 144, 324, 357, 404, 418; ocean liner 224
Queen Mary 224
Querqueville 346
Quincy 207, 219n.92, 365n.52, 368n.97, 442

RA.55A 311, 313, 323n.72
RA.56 325–6
RA.57 331
RA.58 331
RA.64 428–9
RA.66 436
Rabaul 147, 177, 179, 182, 204–5, 207, 230, 248, 251, 262, 268–9, 286n.41, 295, 304–5, 317, 329, 489
Raby 337
Radar: British 98n.93, 105–6, 108–9, 112, 124, 166, 174n.96, 223, 312–14, 316, 464–5; effectiveness of 2, 53, 87, 98n.93, 112, 128n.44, 156, 173n.69, 174n.96, 218n.80, 240, 264–6, 270, 273, 282, 316, 352, 389, 471, 486, 500n.16, 502n.29, 508n.99; German 53, 57–8, 81, 196, 277, 302, 312, 326, 343, 364n.47, 407; IJN 352, 389, 394; Red Navy 118; USN 180, 186, 188, 193, 207, 220n.102, 223–4, 231, 250, 265, 294, 349, 351, 380, 382–3, 392, 414n.50, 440, 464–5, 475, 489
Radio 2, 44n.90, 49, 63n.17, 82, 113, 135, 139, 158, 184, 189, 226, 264, 266, 311–12, 342, 350–51, 375, 386–87, 392–93, 401, 450, 452, 464, 485; *see also* direction finding; 'huff-duff'
Radio Finger Printing (RFP) 97n.83, 464, 501n.24
Raeder, Grossadmiral Dr. Erich 30–1, 34, 48n.135, 50–2, 54, 60, 65n.44, 69, 83, 112, 155–7, 198–9, 246, 252n.13, 263, 266, 462, 467, 486
RAF Bomber Command 65n.47, 157, 240, 261, 266, 269, 277–8, 284n.13, 334, 344, 366n.63, 406–8, 433–4, 470–1
RAF Coastal Command 35, 48n.139, 116, 240, 269, 277, 286n.43, 288n.60, 302, 325, 332, 334, 344, 434, 464, 471, 501n.26
Ragsdale, Rear-Admiral Van 336
Ralph Talbot 207
Ramillies 32–3, 221n.117, 324, 343, 365n.52, 368n.97
Ramree Island (Kyaukpyu) 418, 443
Ramsay, Vice-Admiral Sir Bertram, evacuation from Dunkirk 77–79, 157, 278–9, 339–42, 345–6, 481
Range Estimation (RE) 97n.83, 464, 501n.24
Ranger 12, 28, 131n.70, 236, 253n.35
Rangoon 160, 174n.83, 443
Rasmus (wolf pack) 428
Raubgraf (wolf pack) 265, 285n.28
Rauenfels 74
Rawalpindi 55
Rawlings, Vice-Admiral Sir Bernard 439
Raymond 396, 414n.54
Re-2001 (Italian fighter-bomber) 228, 252n.15
Read, Abner 415n.75
rearmament 18–19, 22, 28–33, 43ns.74–5, 43n.79, 44n.81
Red Army (USSR) 6, 38n.29, 56, 118, 121, 241–3, 263, 295, 309, 358, 369–70, 431–2, 435
Red Banner Fleet (USSR) 56, 118, 131n.85, 163, 327, 369
Red Navy 118, 131n.85, 145, 163, 451; *see also* Soviet Union *and under individual fleets and ships*
Red Sea 83, 88, 96n.67, 107, 116–17
Redfin 366n.75
Regenbogen (Rainbow) 436
Reggio di Calabria 291
Regia Aeronautica Italiana (RAI) 119, 123, 228–9, 477

620   Index

Regia Marina Italiana (Royal Italian Navy) 3, 11, 14, 19, 25, 29, 46n.114, 63n.16, 83, 86, 88, 90, 96n.66, 99n.101, 103–7, 117–18, 122–4, 127ns.31, 32, 142–4, 146, 158–9, 165, 173n.73, 218ns.80–1, 227–30, 238, 241, 252ns.11, 14, 254n.45, 258, 271, 274, 287n.49, 288n.70, 292–3, 317n.7, 321n.52, 354, 471, 477, 486–7, 492, 508n.99; Axis submarine cooperation 87, 98n.86, 101, 111, 159, 223, 237, 463
Reichsmarine (Imperial German Navy) 5–6, 44n.81
Reichstag (German parliament) 13, 16–17, 31
Reid 294, 416n.81
Reifsnider, Rear-Admiral Lawrence 440
Rendova 282, 290n.79
Rennell Island 231, 262–3
Reno 377, 382
Renown 12, 31, 33, 64n.40, 71, 112, 127n.19, 324, 357, 404
Republican military forces (Spain) 23–6
Republican Party (US) 6, 16
Repulse 12, 33, 71, 112, 126, 135, 139–40, 470, 483, 495, 507n.83
Resolution 32–3, 84, 89, 98n.91
'Retro-bomb' 224, 465
Revenge 32–3
Revolution in Military Affairs (RMA) 498
Reykjavik 197, 243, 533
Rhineland crisis (1936) 22–23
Rhodes 91, 300–1, 307, 334, 437
Riau (Kepulauan Riau) 149, 297
Ribbentrop, Joachim von 32
Riccardi, Admiral Arturo 90, 103
Richard Beitzen 244, 246–7
Richardson, III, Capt. Robert 226–7, 489
Richelieu 19, 33, 85–6, 96n.68, 357
Richelson, Jeffrey 503n.36
Riga, Gulf of 120, 122, 369, 375
Rigault de Genouilly 96n.73
Rimini 370
Rio de Janeiro 72
Ritchie, Rear-Admiral James 437
River Plate 57, 59–60, 64ns.40–1, 486
RO (Japanese cipher) 177
Ro-46 422
Ro-67 427
Ro-104 337
Ro-105 337
Ro-106 337
Ro-108 337
Ro-113 376
Ro-115 376
Ro-116 337
Roberts 254n.38, 294, 365n.52, 406
Rocca, Gianni 105, 487
Rochefort, Commander Joseph 184, 493, 509n.116
Rochester Castle 228
Rockwell, Rear-Admiral Francis 272
Rodgers, Rear-Admiral Bertram 423–4
Rodney 33, 37n.20, 53, 71, 112–13, 228, 292
Rohna 321n.54
Rohwer, Jürgen 47n.130, 62n.5, 127n.31, 171n.49, 217n.61, 366n.66, 367n.92, 373, 454n.19, 457n.65, 458n.88
Roi 327–8
Roma 29, 46n.114, 241, 292–3
Romania 31, 103, 114, 118, 132n.101, 145, 202–3, 241, 333, 369
Rome 21, 107, 267, 281, 292, 301, 327, 353–4
Rome–Berlin axis (1936) 23, 25, 241, 477
Rommel, Feldmarschall Erwin 107–8, 123, 125, 145–6, 160, 234–5, 237, 252n.13, 253n.32, 258, 267, 271, 340, 472–3, 477
Room 40 (Admiralty) 2
Roope, VC., Lt.Com. Gerard 71, 508n.90
Roosevelt, President Franklin Delano 16–17, 27, 31, 55, 87, 117, 120, 125, 137–8, 141, 145, 153, 205, 230, 240, 257, 281, 289n.73, 308, 322n.61, 372, 426, 456n.62, 479
Rossbach (wolf pack) 302–3
Rosyth 33, 62n.2, 71
Rota 328
Royal Australian Navy (RAN) 41ns.49–50, 64n.40, 85, 98n.91, 110, 112, 130n.74, 131n.77, 139, 146, 151–3, 162, 170n.46, 171n.49, 179, 207, 219n.92, 282, 317, 329, 377–8, 389, 418, 420–1, 445, 477
Royal Canadian Air Force (RCAF) 433
Royal Canadian Navy (RCN) 154, 171ns.54–5, 259, 265, 321n.56, 478, 499n.9, 503n.40
Royal Marines Commandos 109, 163, 167, 173n.69, 212–13, 229, 291, 301, 370, 406, 418, 428
Royal Navy 2–4, 9, 11, 14, 17, 19, 24–5, 28–31, 33–4, 40n.45, 41n.46, 50, 52, 54, 66, 75, 82, 84, 88, 97n.83, 102,

106, 109, 111, 130n.71, 171n.56, 201, 212, 339, 345, 372, 404–7, 469–70, 476–77, 486, 503n.40, 510n.117; *see also under individual ships' names and engagements*
Royal Netherlands Navy 142, 146–7, 149–51, 153, 170n.48, 324, 345, 361n.6, 365n.52
Royal New Zealand Navy (RNZN) 56, 58–9, 64n.41, 284n.18, 290n.81, 416n.84, 477
Royal Oak 32–3, 54, 63n.26
Royal Sovereign 28, 32–3, 412n.16
Royal, Rear-Admiral Forrest 445
Royan (Gironde-Nord) 360, 437
Rudd, Kevin 130n.74
Rudeltaktik 52, 90, 154
Rue, Vice-Admiral Joseph 437
Rügen (wolf pack) 361n.8
Ruhr 7, 340, 433
Rundstedt, Generalfeldmarschall Gerd von 95n.51
Russell Island 268
Russia 6, 38n.29, 56, 120, 155, 242, 327, 374, 432, 450, 463, 533; *see also* Soviet Union
Russian Civil War 6, 38n.29
Ryūhō 304, 349, 351–2, 364n.42, 448
Ryūjō 12, 148–50, 152, 161, 170n.42, 184, 187, 209, 218n.89, 504n.44
Ryukyu Islands 336, 353, 357, 425, 438–9, 442–3, 459n.98

S-13 432
S-26 (S-boat) 497
S-27 (S-boat) 218n.85
S-59 (S-boat) 131n.84
S-60 (S-boat) 131n.84
S38 (USN submarine) 207
S44 (USN submarine) 220n.105
Saalwächter, Admiral Alfred 74, 113
Saaremaa 375
Sabang 335, 356–7, 444, 452
Sables d'Olonne, Les 360
Sadkovich, James 127ns.31–2, 173n.73
Sagami Bay 452
Sagona 144
Sagu Kyun 418
Saidor 329
Saipan 185, 328, 336, 347–50, 355, 366n.67, 473, 486, 493, 510n.119
Saito, Lt.Gen.Yoshitsuyu 348
Sakhalin 451
Sakishima Shotō 442

Sakonju, Vice-Admiral Naomasa 379–80, 402
Sakura Maru 153
Salamaua 219n.90, 268, 286n.41, 295, 421
Salerno 281, 291–4, 307
Salmann, Otto 97n.85
Salmon 61
Salonika (Thessaloniki) 371
Salt Lake City 219n.92, 231, 286n.42
Samar 377, 379, 381, 385, 391–3, 395–6, 398–400, 426, 484, 488, 490, 495
Samejima, Admiral Tomoshige 304–5
Samoa 204
Samos 301–2, 307–8
Samuel B. Roberts 396, 414n.54
San Bernardino Strait 366n.75, 379, 381, 383–7, 391–2, 394–5, 398, 401–2, 426, 490
San Cristobal 210, 219n.94
San Diego 117, 186, 205, 219n.92
San Fabian 419–20
San Francisco 186, 219n.92, 233, 248, 447
San Jacinto 381, 442, 456n.58
San Juan 219n.92, 234, 421
Sănătescu, General Constantin 369
Sangamon 397
Sanhaikwan 27
Sansapor 377
Santa Cruz (Mindanao) 445
Santa Cruz, battle of 233–4
Santa Cruz Islands 205, 210, 230
Santa Fé 398
Santa Isabel 177, 207, 221n.113
Santee 397
Saratoga 11, 148, 170n.36, 186, 207, 209–10, 219n.92, 425
Sardinia 90, 123, 241, 274, 292–3, 296, 318n.8
Sarmi *see* Arara
Sasaki, General Noburo 283
Sasebo Special Landing Forces 211
Satawan Islands 336
Saumarez 314–15, 444
Savage 314–15
Savannah 254n.35, 318n.9
Savo Island 208, 220n.105, 248, 464, 486, 488–9
Savoia S-79 (Italian torpedo-bomber) 202, 218n.82, 252n.15
S-boats (Schnellboote) 93n.19, 118, 131n.84, 218n.85, 220n.105, 297, 365n.60, 366n.63

SC-744 415n.75
Scapa Flow (Orkney Islands) 5, 33, 54, 71, 76, 80, 82, 95n.63, 108, 110, 121, 154, 489
Scarpanto (Karpathos) 114
Scharnhorst 19, 34, 43n.79, 55, 68, 70, 80–3, 91, 101–2, 155–7, 267, 298–300, 310–16, 322n.71, 332, 357, 469, 471, 484, 489, 494–5
Scheldt 156, 406
Schepke, Kapitänleutnant Joachim 109
Schiff 33 Pinguin 129n.55
Schiff 41 Kormoran 130n.74
Schlagetot (wolf pack) 237
Schlesien 34, 70, 432, 435
Schleswig-Holstein 34, 70
Schmitt, Anton 73
Schniewind, Admiral Otto 197–9
Schnorchel (air induction tube for U-boats) 325–6, 331–2, 344, 355, 361n.6, 362n.24, 370, 374–5, 462, 465, 502n.29
Schulze, Otto 24
Scirè 144
Sclater, Lt.-Com. C.E.L. 246
Scoglitti (Sicily) 279
Scorpion 314–15
Scott, Rear-Admiral Norman 231–2, 248–9
Scylla 344, 364n.51
Seahorse 366n.75
Sealion 93n.22
Seaslug (Biscay search area) 277
Seawolf 93n.22
Sebag-Montefiore, Hugh 111, 259
'Second Front' 213, 242, 257, 271–2, 280, 298, 478
Seeadler Harbour 329
Seehund (Type XXVIIB U-boat) 430
Seeigel (mine and net barrage) 218n.88, 273
Seekriegsleitung (German naval war staff) 24, 34, 285n.24, 316, 407
Seeräuber (wolf pack) 169n.16
Seetakt (German radar) 57, 81, 364n.47
Seeteufel (wolf pack) 270
Seewolf (wolf pack) 270
Seghe Point (Vangunu Island) 281
Seine, River 343
Seirstad 170n.42
Selfridge 318n.16
Sendai 41n.51, 152, 218n.89, 305
Sennen 288n.59
Sepinggan 446

Sevastopol 121, 131n.85, 141–2, 145, 163, 183, 202, 296, 333, 472, 484
Sèvres, Treaty of (1920) 5
Sextant (Allied conference in Cairo, 1943) 308
Seydlitz 44n.81
Sfax 108, 267, 278
SHAEF (Supreme Headquarters Allied Expeditionary Force) 339, 481
Shafroth, Rear-Admiral John 448
Shanghai 15, 27, 140, 335
Sheffield 53, 113, 127n.19, 245–7, 313, 496
Sherbrooke, VC, Capt. Robert 244–5, 256n.67, 483, 495
Sherman, Vice-Admiral Frederick 305, 381–2, 384–5, 400–1
Shetland Islands 71, 93n.19
Shigemitsu, Mamoru 452
Shigure 388, 390–1
Shikari 79
Shikoku 426
Shikotan 451
Shima, Vice-Admiral Kiyohide 379, 387–91, 393, 398, 402, 491–2
Shimada, Admiral Shigetarō 356
Shinano 469, 502n.32, 504n.45
Shōhō 177–9, 504n.44
Shōkaku 19, 43n.78, 177–81, 209, 214ns.13–14, 218n.89, 233, 304, 349, 351, 364n.42, 475, 502n.32, 504n.44, 505n.64
Shortland 219n.90, 230, 232, 251
Shropshire 64n.40, 317, 329, 389
Siam *see* Thailand
Sibir 133n.103
Sibuyan Sea 379, 383–4, 386, 401–2, 469, 490; battle of 383–4, 469
Sicily 102, 105, 234–5, 238, 257–8, 267, 271–2, 274, 278–81, 288n.70, 294, 296, 298, 341
'Sickleforce' 76–7
Sierra Leone 61, 62n.13, 97n.83, 126ns.6, 8, 270, 530–2
Signals Intelligence (SIGINT) 52, 67, 75, 80, 87, 93n.20, 104–5, 108, 110–11, 119, 122, 125, 140, 157, 170n.40, 177, 186–7, 197, 235, 262, 266, 271–2, 303, 311–12, 337, 347, 379, 381, 383, 464, 466–7, 470, 489, 498, 501n.23, 503n.40
Sikh 142, 229
Silny 174n.85
Simpson, Michael 105–6, 134n.115, 169n.29, 478

Simpson, Rear-Admiral G.W.G. 'Shrimp' 122, 133n.106, 142, 146
Sims 178–9
'Singapore Strategy' 27, 126
Singapore, naval base of (Sembawang) 4, 8, 9, 27, 97n.83, 126, 135–6, 138–40, 148–50, 161, 170n.40, 173n.83, 297–8, 319n.20, 376, 378, 405, 422, 444, 446, 448, 452–3, 459n.99, 460n.101, 485
Sino-Japanese War (1937–45) 26
Sio 329, 363n.37
Siracusa 124, 278–9
Sirius 292, 301
Sirte (Sidra), battles of 143, 159, 483
Sirte (Sidra), Gulf of 143, 159, 483, 486
Skagerrak 71, 406, 455n.52
Skate 317
Skjeldfjorden 74–5
Skylark 439
Slessor, Marshal of the RAF Sir John 269, 277–8
sloops 8, 33–4, 89, 98n.91, 112, 117, 133n.114, 149, 169n.16, 237, 239, 254n.38, 324, 358, 365n.52, 428, 443–4
'Slot, The' 207, 249, 489
Smith 234
Smith, Rear-Admiral Allen 422–3
Smith, Lt. Harry 221n.114
Smith, General Holland M ('Howling Mad') 348, 424, 476
Smith, Michael 509n.116
Smyrna, fire of (1922) 7
Snapper 93n.22
Sneland 436
Snuiver (submarine breathing apparatus) 361n.6
Soemba 365n.52
Soeng Gerong 419
Sokrushitelny 243
Solomon Islands 176–8, 183, 204–6, 209–11, 219n.90, 230–1, 248, 262–3, 268–9, 271, 281, 287n.50, 291, 295, 303–4, 306, 317, 337, 414n.45, 459n.98
Somali 110, 483
Someri (Sommers Island) 203, 218n.87
Somerville, Admiral Sir James 84–6, 90, 97n.74, 119, 127n.19, 160–3, 324, 334, 356–7, 363n.34, 367n.91, 483, 491, 503n.37
Songkhla 136, 139–40, 148
Sorol 358
Soryu 18, 148, 504n.44
Souffleur 131n.76

South Atlantic 34, 55–7, 91, 129n.55, 226, 240, 326, 486
South China Sea 140, 148, 381, 418–19, 425, 470
South Dakota 234, 249–50, 351, 381
South East Asia Command (SEAC) 363n.34
South Greenland Patrol 131n.81
South Pacific 164, 176, 183, 205–6, 211, 219n.94, 230, 234, 248–9, 256n.74, 303
South Pacific Amphibious Force 206–7
Southampton 41n.50, 50, 99n.107, 100
Southern Highlands (New Guinea) 268
Southwold 159
Sovetskaya Ukraina 121
Soviet Eighth Army 375
Soviet Fourteenth Army 374
Soviet Forty-Seventh Army 203
Soviet 2nd Assault Army 327
Soviet 1st Baltic Front 431
Soviet Red Army 241
Soviet X Rifle Corps 121
Soviet 131st Rifle Corps 374
Soviet 157th Rifle Division 121
Soviet Union (USSR) 32, 49–50, 69, 100, 107, 114, 117, 154–5, 196, 213, 225, 242, 266–7, 298, 310, 316, 325, 368n.98, 370, 425, 447, 449–50, 478, 497; military forces 6, 29, 51, 55–6, 118, 120–2, 132n.101, 141–2, 145, 163, 183, 197–200, 202–3, 218n.85, 225, 241–3, 252n.8, 267, 273–4, 285n.24, 296, 309, 318n.17, 327, 331–3, 354, 358, 361n.7, 369–70, 374–5, 428, 430–5, 437, 450–1, 477
Soviet 2nd White Russian Front 432
Sovyetskiy Soyuz 29
Spaatz, General Carl A. 457n.67
Spain 23–5, 27, 29, 34, 48n.133, 277, 302
Spanish Civil War (1936–39) 23–4, 26
Spark 448
Spearfish 53, 93n.22
Spector, Ronald 150, 169n.31
Speer, Albert 276
Sperrle, Feldmarschall Hugo 156
Spitfire (British fighter plane) 146, 173n.76, 201, 227–9, 235, 252n.11, 452, 471
Spitsbergen (Svalbard) 298–9
Sposobnyy 318n.17
'Spout, The' (swept channels off Normandy coast) 342, 344

Sprague, Rear-Admiral Clifton 'Ziggy' 392–7, 399, 409, 414n.55, 484, 488, 495
Sprague, Rear-Admiral Thomas 377–9, 382, 385, 392–3, 401
Spreewald 496
Spruance, Admiral Raymond A. 185–6, 188, 190, 193–5, 215n.31, 216n.60, 327, 348–53, 366n.75, 381, 385, 412n.22, 438–9, 442, 456n.55, 482, 486–7, 495, 507n.87, 509n.100
Spurr, Russell 456n.60
'Squid' mortar 331, 465
St. Didier 131n.76
St. Germain, Treaty of (1920) 5
St. Helena 56
St. Jean-de-Luz 96n.69
St. Lawrence estuary 240, 463
St. Lo 393, 396–7, 414n.54
St. Louis 219n.92, 290n.81, 403
St. Malo 96n.69, 360
St. Nazaire 33, 48n.135, 96ns.68–9, 163, 174n.84, 261, 359–60, 437
St. Valéry-en-Caux 96n.69
Stadlandet 93n.16
Stalin, Marshal Josef 25, 32, 56, 242–3, 267, 298, 318n.17, 425, 449–50
Stalingrad 241, 263, 267, 273, 296
Stalker 443
Stange, Kapitän zur See Rudolf 244, 246–7, 486–7
Stanley 169n.16
Stark, Admiral Harold R. 169n.27
Stavanger 70, 437, 455n.50
Stephen, Martin 64n.39, 106, 176, 256n.66
Sterlet 93n.22
Stettin (Szczecin) 406, 435
Stewart 171n.48
Stockport 285n.26
Stokes, Commander G.H. 142–3, 169n.20
Stolpe Bank 431–2
Stord 315
Stork 166
Straits of Bonifacio 293, 296
Strasbourg 12, 19, 33, 84–5, 254n.46, 491
Streonshahl 57
Stresa front (1935) 20
Stresemann, Gustav 7, 14
Strong 282
Struble, Rear-Admiral Arthur 409
Stump, Rear-Admiral Felix 393, 396
Sturgeon 61
Stürmer (wolf pack) 265

Stygian 448
Subador 170n.42
Subic Bay 421
Submarine 10th Flotilla (RN) 107, 142, 163
submarines, British 8, 33, 61, 71, 83, 93n.22, 96n.67, 96n.73, 107–8, 117, 122, 142, 144, 146, 161, 163, 169n.29, 230, 235, 258, 274, 283n.5, 324, 376, 412n.19, 444; construction programmes 14, 22; controversial role and effectiveness 2, 19–20, 26, 34, 36n.10, 37n.15, 48n.139, 50, 67, 166, 172n.59, 201, 210, 227, 230, 236–7, 241–2, 254n.42, 255n.49, 279, 299, 307, 331, 347, 361n.6, 362n.24, 362n.26, 370, 375, 405, 412n.20, 422, 463, 465–6, 471, 494, 498; detection of *see* ASW; French 33–4, 71, 89, 97n.76, 236, 319n.18; German 34, 54, 63n.16, 66, 111, 118, 154, 196, 239, 276, 370, 462; (*see also* U-boats); Italian 25, 29, 63n.16, 83, 86–8, 98ns.86–7, 101, 103, 146, 158, 218n.81, 223, 227–8, 237, 279, 288n.70, 471, 477; Japanese 14, 135–6, 148, 163, 184, 186, 209–11, 218n.89, 221n.117, 230–1, 250, 261, 269, 272–3, 287n.52, 307, 337, 347, 376, 422, 447, 466; Polish 49, 62n.2, 71–2, 93n.22; Soviet 29, 121, 199, 202, 204, 218n.88, 241–2, 273–4, 375, 431; Spanish 23, 25; US 136, 177, 186, 250, 261, 284n.15, 328, 337–8, 371, 376; Yugoslav 128n.36
Suda Bay 104, 114, 128n.36
Sudetenland 30
Suez Canal 21, 83, 88, 116, 119, 126n.3, 144, 370, 404
Suffolk 416n.84
Sulawesi (Celebes) 147, 335
Sulu Archipelago 426
Sulu Sea 379, 388, 419–20, 425–6
Suluan 378
Sumatra 149, 334, 345, 356–7, 376, 404–5, 419, 428, 444–5, 452, 460n.99
Sunda Strait 149, 152–3, 376
Sunfish 93n.22
Superfortress (US heavy bomber; B-29) 423, 425, 441, 449
Supermarina (Italian naval operational command) 90, 103–5, 107, 122–3, 142–3, 227, 252n.14
Support Groups (escort carrier-led units) 207, 267, 269, 275, 277, 288n.67, 331, 344, 359, 429, 464

Supreme War Council (UK) 70
Surabaya (Soerbaya) 149, 151, 170n.41, 335, 363n.34
Surigao Strait 366n.75, 379, 381, 387–92, 398, 419, 464, 482, 492; battle of 387–92
Sussex 446, 452
Suursaari 133n.103, 203, 218n.88, 370
Suwanee 397
Suzuki, Admiral Baron Kantarō 441, 449
Suzuki, Lt.Gen. Sosaku 402–4
Suzuya 148, 218n.89, 233, 249, 364n.42, 383, 397
Svenner 343
Sverdlov 121
Swan 170n.46
Swatow (Shan-t'ou) 27
Sweden 49, 62n.2, 69, 77, 374
Swiftsure 416n.84
Swinemünde 434–5, 455ns.38, 41
Sworbe peninsula 375, 412n.17
Sword (Normandy landing sector) 340–1, 343, 365ns.51–2
Swordfish (torpedo bomber) 85, 90, 113, 156, 172n.65, 496
Sydney (Cape Breton) 62n.12, 130n.74, 171n.55, 530–2
Symbol (Allied military staff conference in 1943) 257–8, 260–1, 264, 271
Symi 301
Syohgo, Hattori 416n.81
Syria 116–17
Syrtis 362n.26

T13 156
Tacloban 385, 403, 412n.25
Taihō 349, 351, 364n.42, 502n.32, 504n.44
Tairoa 56
Tais 358
Takagi, Rear-Admiral Takeo 151–2, 178–80, 182, 307, 337, 347, 488
Takama, Rear-Admiral Tamotsu 232–3
Takanami 250
Takao 41n.51, 148, 184, 218n.89, 249, 305, 364n.42, 380, 413n.31, 449
Takasu, Vice-Admiral Shira 185, 194
Take 416n.78
Talador 159
Talaud Islands 372, 411n.7
Talbot, Rear-Admiral A.G. 365n.51
'Tallboy' (massive bomb) 344, 407
Tallin 44n.81, 327
Tallinn 120, 122, 133n.103, 370

Tama 219n.89, 398
Taman peninsula 202–3, 484
Tambor 195
Tanaka, Rear-Admiral Raizo 185–8, 209, 232, 249–51, 492
Tananarive 211
Tang (Balao class submarine) 497
tankers: Allied 172n.59; German 93n.19, 116, 130n.73
Tarakan 147, 444–5
Taraku 451
Taranto 90, 99n.101, 104–5, 128n.33, 142–3, 158, 292–3, 317n.7, 358, 468, 483
Tarawa 304, 306–7, 321n.47, 474, 493
Tarnmatte (anti-radar coating) 465, 502n.29
Task Force TF 1 205, 219n.92
Task Force TF 8 205, 219n.92
Task Force TF 11 148, 178, 205, 219n.92
Task Force TF 14 148
Task Force TF 16 205, 215n.31, 219n.92, 508n.87
Task Force TF 17 178–80, 205, 219n.92, 233
Task Force TF 18 205, 210, 219n.92
Task Force TF 31 373
Task Force TF 34 386, 391–2, 398–401, 490
Task Force TF 37 448
Task Force TF 38 305, 371, 377–8, 381, 402, 409–10, 442, 447–8
Task Force TF 39 305
Task Force TF 44 178, 205, 219n.92
Task Force TF 50 306
Task Force TF 51 272, 424
Task Force TF 51.11 361n.17
Task Force TF 52 306, 348, 350, 356, 439, 456n.55
Task Force TF 53 306, 356
Task Force TF 54 423–4, 439–40, 456n.55
Task Force TF 57 438–40, 442
Task Force TF 58 327, 330, 336, 348–53, 355–6, 366n.75, 424, 426–7, 438–9, 441–2
Task Force TF 61 233, 441
Task Force TF 62 206–7
Task Force TF 63 419
Task Force TF 64 231–3, 249, 418
Task Force TF 67 250
Task Force TF 68 281–2, 289n.75
Task Force TF 75 411n.9
Task Force TF 77 372, 378

Task Force TF 78 378, 419
Task Force TF 79 378, 419
Task Force TF 84 (Alpha) 368n.97
Task Force TF 85 (Delta) 368n.97
Task Force TF 86 (Sitka) 368n.97
Task Force TF 87 (Camel) 368n.97
Task Force TF 88 279, 359
Task Force TF 95 447
Task Group TG 7.3 131n.79
Task Group TG 34.5 401
Task Group TG 34.8 448
Task Group TG 38.1 381–2, 386, 397, 399, 442
Task Group TG 38.2 381, 391, 401
Task Group TG 38.3 381–2, 384, 401
Task Group TG 38.4 381, 401
Task Group TG 50.3 305
Task Group TG 58.1 441
Task Group TG 58.3 441
Task Group TG 58.4 361
Task Group TG 62.1 206
Task Group TG 67.4 248–9
Task Group TG 77.1 411n.9, 420
Task Group TG 77.2 420
Task Group TG 77.4 377–9, 382, 385, 392–7, 399, 401, 420
Task Group TG 77.6 419
Task Group TG 78.1 336, 453n.5
Task Group TG 78.2 336, 453n.5
Task Group TG 78.3 409
Task Group TG 79.1 419
Task Group TG 79.2 419
Tassafaronga 231–2, 250
Tatsuta 179, 219n.89
Tawi Tawi 330, 337–8, 366n.75, 426
TBS (Talk Between Ships) 386, 393
Teheran 322n.61
Tenedos 139, 162
Tennant, Admiral William 78, 135, 140, 341, 345, 481, 483, 495, 507n.83
Tennessee 136, 219n.92, 414n.50, 423, 441
Tenryū 179, 219n.89, 220n.101, 249
ten-year naval building 'holiday' 37n.20
Ten-Year No-War Rule (1919) 11, 16
Terauchi, Field Marshal Count 460n.101
Terre Neuve 85
Texas 253n.35, 346, 368n.97
Thailand (Siam) 135–6, 138–40, 160, 324, 446, 460n.99
Thames 66, 91n.1, 99n.107, 339
Thanet 149
Theobald, Rear-Admiral Robert 187, 215n.36, 219n.92

Theodor Riedel 244
Thomas Scott 429
Thomas, Evan 393, 488
Tibbets, Colonel Paul 449
Tientsin (Tianjin) 451
Tilsit (Sovetsk) 430–1
Timor 150, 459n.98
Tinian 328, 336, 347–9, 355–7, 367n.92, 447
Tipani 308
Tirpitz 29, 197–9, 267, 298–300, 310, 316, 332, 407–8, 470, 491
Tjilatjap 152–3
Tobruk 86, 107, 111–12, 117–18, 122–5, 126n.13, 131n.88, 134n.115, 145, 163, 173n.71, 201, 229, 252n.13, 470, 472
Togo, Admiral Heihachiro 348
Tōjō, General Hideki 125, 165, 251, 262, 356
Tokoi, Seiichiro 398
Tokuyama 441
Tokyo 5, 15, 120, 125, 165, 196, 204, 251, 261–2, 271–2, 303, 305, 335, 356, 377, 422, 426, 446, 451–2, 469
'Tokyo Express' 230, 262, 269, 284n.18
Toland, John 454n.19
Tominaga, General Kyoji 382, 403
Tomkinson, Lt.-Cdr. Edward 133n.106, 484
Tomonaga, Lt. Jōichi 188–9
Tone 41n.51, 148, 184, 189, 209, 218n.89, 233, 364n.42, 383, 395–7, 427, 448
torpedo boats, deployment of 33–4, 66, 83, 88, 93n.19, 118, 128n.36, 146, 156, 197, 199, 258, 267, 271, 284n.18, 292, 308, 310, 317n.7, 322n.57, 334, 344, 369, 375, 431, 433, 436, 445, 455n.41
torpedo, deficiencies 53, 73, 77, 94n.45, 147, 172n.61, 180, 191, 218n.85, 266, 315–16, 331, 344, 462, 466, 494, 497
Torpex (secondary explosive) 465
Toulon 33–4, 85, 117, 238–9, 334, 358–9, 368n.97
Tovey, Admiral Sir John 95n.64, 101, 112–13, 198, 217n.70
Tower, Admiral John 509ns.100, 105
Toyoda, Admiral Soemu 330, 336–7, 347–8, 352–3, 356, 376–9, 384, 391, 397, 402, 409, 488
Tracker 344
Treasury (UK) 27, 31
Treasury Islands 304
Trenchant 444

Trenchard, Sir Hugh (Chief of the Air Staff 1919–30) 9
Trento 11, 99n.101, 105, 124, 202
Trevelyan, G.M. 263, 498
Triad 93n.22
Trianon, Treaty of, (1920) 5
Tributs, Vice-Admiral V.F. 131n.85
Trident (Anglo-American staff conference in 1943) 271–2, 280
Trident 93n.22
Trieste 11, 124, 241, 252n.14, 287n.57, 430, 435
Trincomalee 161–2, 334, 356, 404, 419, 444
Trinidad 155, 172n.61, 214n.21, 223, 240, 260, 284n.12, 497
Tripartite Pact (1940) 90, 138
Tripoli 108, 122–4, 144, 146, 258, 267, 278, 283n.4, 294
'Triton' (Improved version of German Naval Enigma; 'Shark') 93n.22, 259–60, 264–5
Trobriand Islands 289n.77
Tromp 170n.48
Tromsö 82, 437
Trondheim 70, 76, 81–2, 93n.18, 157, 197, 242, 437, 455n.50
Troubridge, Rear-Admiral Thomas 236, 254n.37, 327, 354, 359
Truant 93n.22
Truk (Chuuk) 147, 181, 195, 209–10, 231, 253n.26, 295, 304–5, 307, 317, 321n.50, 328, 330, 336, 448, 459n.98, 489
Truman, President Harry S. 449, 456n.62
Tsingtao (Qingdao) 451
Tsugaru Strait 447
Tuapse 163, 241
Tulagi 177–8, 205, 207–8, 213n.7, 219ns.90, 94, 230, 262, 486, 488
Tully, Anthony *see* Parshall
Tunis 238, 258, 267, 271, 287n.49
Tunisia 227, 235, 237–9, 241, 257–8, 267, 271, 274, 287n.49, 292–3
Turing, Alan 110–11, 119, 132n.93
Turkey 5–7, 300, 307, 309, 369
Turner, Admiral Richmond Kelly 206–9, 219n.98, 220n.104, 231, 248–9, 281–2, 290n.78, 306, 327, 348, 350–1, 353, 424, 439–40, 476, 481, 486, 488–9, 509n.105, 510n.117
Tuscaloosa 131n.79, 254n.35, 365n.52, 368n.97
Tyne 66, 91n.3, 99n.107
Type 284 gunnery control radar 314

Type 95 (Japanese torpedo) 210, 466, 502n.32
Type 271 microwave radiation set 109, 128n.44, 166, 270, 500n.16
Type 273 radar 313–14
Type 286M radar 108, 128n.44, 500n.16
Type II (coastal U-boats) 462
Type VII (ocean-going U-boats) 462, 497
Type IX (ocean-going U-boats) 462
Type IX-C U-boats 430, 462
Type IXD-2 U-boat (long-range, submarine cruisers) 375
Type XXVIIB U-boat 430
Type XXI Elektro (long-range) U-boats 276, 288ns.63–4, 325, 375, 409, 428, 462
Type XXIII Elektro (coastal) U-boats 325, 409, 428–9, 462
Typex cipher machines 63n.17, 171n.56, 321n.56
Typhoon (British fighter-bombers) 436, 496
typhoons (acute weather systems) 410, 442, 496
Tyrrhenian Sea 291, 293, 334, 354, 370

U13 467
U15 67
U19 369
U20 369
U23 369
U29 52
U30 50, 62n.6, 64n.43, 97n.85, 485, 501n.26
U31 62n.11
U33 503n.39
U36 61
U39 52, 494
U43 496
U47 54, 94n.95, 108
U52 97n.85
U73 228
U81 120, 124
U88 200, 251n.7
U91 285n.26
U99 97n.85, 109
U100 109, 500n.16
U110 110–11, 129n.49, 503n.39
U124 284n.12
U155 254n.41
U156 226–7, 489
U175 251n.1
U205 201, 503n.39
U221 497

U248 429
U252 166
U254 497
U255 197, 200
U264 326
U286 436
U300 375
U307 436
U313 374
U314 326
U315 374
U331 124, 133n.113
U333 496
U334 197, 200
U354 244
U367 433
U408 197
U425 428
U433 174n.96
U439 497
U456 197, 200
U457 200, 252n.7
U459 166
U480 355, 367n.87
U482 375, 429
U486 375
U505 503n.39
U506 226
U507 226
U512 251n.1
U514 251n.1, 260
U515 251n.1
U516 251n.1
U529 285n.26
U556 132n.91
U557 142
U559 260, 283n.10, 503n.39
U570 503n.39
U587 166, 500n.16
U589 251n.7
U604 285n.26
U606 285n.26
U623 285n.26
U651 132n.91
U652 120, 173n.71
U659 497
U703 200
U711 429
U751 141
U853 436
U954 288n.59
U968 429
U972 361n.8
U974 362n.26

U1051 429
U1055 429
U1172 429
U1199 429
U1232 429
U2336 436
Uarsciek 228
U-boat tankers *see* Milchekühe
U-boats, in Arctic 120, 154–5, 164, 197–200, 225, 283n.6, 298, 319n.21, 325–6, 331–2, 374, 408, 428–9, 435–6; in Baltic 354, 455n.38; bases 48n.135, 97n.82, 261, 437; in Bay of Biscay 269–70, 277–8, 310, 344; in Black Sea 118, 283n.6, 369; in Central Atlantic 132n.91, 223, 240, 251n.1, 255n.54, 260, 264, 276–7; in Indian Ocean 324–5, 375–6, 412n.19, 428; in Mediterranean 123–4, 144, 146, 158, 218n.81, 227, 237, 258, 279, 283ns.5–6, 288n.70, 326–7, 358, 370; in North American waters 55, 154, 172n.58, 436, 500n.12; in North Atlantic 34, 67, 87, 100–1, 119, 132n.91, 223, 239–40, 260, 264, 270, 275–6, 283n.6, 284n.12, 287n.46, 302–3, 326, 330–1, 361n.8; in North Sea 34, 67, 92n.6, 93n.19
U-boats, in Norwegian waters 73, 76–7, 93n.19, 325, 362n.26, 437–8; operating in British waters 48ns.133–4, 53, 61, 63n.24, 67, 78–9, 169n.16, 344, 365n.62, 428–30, 433–4, 436; role and effectiveness of 2, 30–1, 34, 48n.133, 51–4, 62n.7, 67, 87, 90–1, 97n.85, 100, 109, 112, 154, 166, 196, 223–5, 258, 260, 265–6, 270, 275–7, 283n.6, 284n.13, 288ns.60, 63–4, 302–3, 325, 330, 355, 361n.6, 362n.24, 375, 409, 412n.18, 428–30, 433–38, 462–5, 467–8, 477, 482 (*see also* wolf packs); in South Atlantic 226–7, 240; in Spanish waters 48n.133, 302; in West Atlantic 166, 223, 240, 251n.1, 284n.12, 309
Ugaki, Vice-Admiral Matome 271, 287n.48, 380, 384, 394, 427, 440, 442, 451, 488, 510n.120
Ukraine 121
Ulan (wolf pack) 154
Ulithi Atoll 358, 373, 381, 383, 399, 409, 411ns.7, 10, 427, 439, 442, 459n.98
'Ultra' 70, 93n.20, 104, 114, 116, 119, 122–3, 132n.92, 142, 157, 164, 196, 272–3, 301, 303, 332, 336, 363n.37, 428, 466–7, 503n.36

Umboi 268
Umbra 202
Umezu, General Yoshijiro 452
Underhill 447
Underwater Demolition Teams (UDT) 439
Unequal Treaties 7
Unggi 450
Unicorn 324
United Kingdom (UK) 4–5, 8, 11, 17, 20–1, 27, 31, 50, 61, 62n.2, 62n.12, 65n.44, 75, 87, 92n.12, 97n.83, 101, 126n.8, 169n.16, 264, 271, 280, 361n.6, 530–33
United States 16–17, 51, 100, 102, 120, 125, 138, 154, 165, 167, 167n.4, 224, 268, 272, 289n.73, 306, 402, 479, 505n.54
United States Army 9, 164, 171n.56, 187, 205, 221n.110, 278–79, 281, 294, 306, 329, 354–5, 359, 378, 382, 402–3, 412n.25, 421, 439, 443, 446, 476, 492
United States Army Air Force (USAAF) 179, 226, 278, 286n.41, 304, 308, 325, 358, 378, 412n.25, 433, 437, 446, 449, 483
United States Navy (USN) 3–4, 9–11, 14, 17, 41n.48, 51, 55, 131n.70, 145, 164, 169n.16, 170n.36, 171ns.55–6, 184, 205, 236, 253n.30, 287n.50, 320n.43, 350–1, 373, 389, 404, 412n.25, 476, 479, 499n.9, 500n.12, 503n.40
unrestricted submarine warfare 50, 494
Unryū 502n.32
Unshaken 199
Uozumi, Rear-Admiral Jisaku 452
Upholder 124, 133n.106, 165
Upright 142
Uranami 402
Urge 133n.106, 142
Uruguay 56–7, 59–60, 92n.8
Urup 451
US 5th Air Force 378, 446, 489
US Eighth Air Force 284n.13
US 13th Air Force 378, 446, 489
US 11th Airborne Division 422
US 82nd Airborne Division 341
US 101st Airborne Division 341
US 1st Airborne Task Force 359
US III Amphibious Force 290n.84, 329, 356
US V Amphibious Force 356, 424, 476
US VII Amphibious Force 294, 318n.13, 338

US Amphibious Group 3 421
US Amphibious Group 6 445
US Amphibious Group 8 422, 425
US Amphibious Group 9 422
US Fifth Army 281, 354, 359
US Sixth Army 378, 382, 402–3, 421, 446
US Tenth Army 439
US Seventh Army 279
US Army Strategic Air Force (USASTAF) 457n.67
US 5th Cavalry Regiment 329
US 112th Cavalry Regiment 289n.77, 316
US Coast Guard 131n.81
US I Corps 419
US VI Corps 327
US X Corps 378
US XIV Corps 419
US XXIV Corps 378
US Third Fleet 376–7, 379, 383, 386, 394, 397–8, 410, 412n.22, 442, 492
US Fifth Fleet 338, 349, 353, 366n.75, 412n.22, 438, 442
US Seventh Fleet 378–9, 382, 385–7, 392–3, 395, 398–401, 490
US Tenth Fleet 275, 303
US Houses of Congress 6, 27, 117, 125, 131n.80, 137, 480
US 1st Infantry Division 236, 341
US 3rd Infantry Division 368n.97
US 7th Infantry Division 272
US 24th Infantry Division 336, 409
US 27th Infantry Division 306, 328
US 36th Infantry Division 368n.97
US 37th Infantry Division 282
US 40th Infantry Division 426
US 41st Infantry Division 336, 338, 425
US 43rd Infantry Division 282
US 45th Infantry Division 368n.97
US 66th Infantry Division 437
US 77th Infantry Division 403, 439
US 81st Infantry Division 373, 411n.10
US 158th Infantry Regiment 289n.77
US Marine Corps 207, 209–10, 220n.109, 221n.110, 232, 248, 281, 304, 306, 317, 328–9, 348, 356, 373, 423–5, 451, 454n.19, 471, 476, 488
US 1st Marine Division 207, 317, 373
US 2nd Marine Division 306, 348, 356
US 3rd Marine Division 304, 425
US 4th Marine Division 329, 348, 356, 424
US 5th Marine Division 424

US 4th Marine Raider Battalion 281
US 22nd Marine RCT 328
US 163rd Regimental Combat Team 336
Ushijima, Lt.-General Mitsuru 442–3
Utah (Normandy landing sector) 340–1, 343, 364n.51
Utah (US target ship) 136
Utmost 133n.106
Uzuki 404

V209 61
V1302 156
Vado 334
'Val' (Japanese dive bomber) 18, 137, 179–81, 193, 214n.13
Valetta 100, 124, 159
Valiant 31, 71, 84, 115, 144, 292, 294, 324, 357
Valona 91
Vampire 139, 162
Vanoc 109, 500n.16
Varna 369
Vathy Bay 308
Vedel, Vice-Admiral Aage 289n.74
Vegesack 284n.13
Veitinghoff, General Heinrich von 293–4, 307
Vella Gulf 282
Vella Lavella 283, 295, 318ns.15–16
Venice 435
Verity 109
Versailles Conference and Treaty (1919) 5–6, 12–13, 17, 22, 30, 42n.58, 462
Very Long Range (VLR) aircraft 51, 240, 259, 265, 275, 302–3, 463–4, 470
Vestfjorden 71, 74–5, 93n.16, 94n.39
Vetch 166, 500n.16
Vian, Admiral Sir Philip 68–9, 143–4, 158–9, 173n.74, 291, 341, 364n.51, 365n.55, 404–5, 419, 442, 483
Vichy French 83–5, 88–9, 97n.77, 98n.92, 116–17, 167, 211, 221n.118, 226–7, 236–9, 242, 254ns.39, 46
Victorious 46n.108, 112, 120, 217n.70, 227–8, 332, 357, 404, 418, 439
Vigo 68, 92n.8
Vigors, Flt.Lt. Tim 168n.11
Vila 262, 281–2, 289n.75
Villa San Giovanni 291
Villers-sur-Mer 354–5
Vincennes 207, 219n.92
Vindex 344
Vindicator (US dive-bomber) 189, 215n.33

Vindictive 12
Visayan Islands 371–2, 379, 404, 409, 445
Vistula, River 32, 358, 434
Vittorio Veneto 19, 29, 46n.114, 104–6, 142, 241, 292, 487
Vladimirskiy, Vice-Admiral I.A. 241
Vogelkop peninsula 335
Volcano Islands 336, 358, 422
Volos 371
Vorwärts (wolf pack) 224

W.Anz (radar search receiver; Wanze) 302
Wakaba 388
Wakde 336, 338, 373
Wake Island 140, 148, 170n.36, 220n.104, 304, 337–8, 358, 371, 440, 448, 459n.98
Walcheren 406
Waldron, Lt.-Cdr. John C. 216n.48
Walker, Vice-Admiral H.T.C. 'Hookey' 109, 444
Wall Street crash (1929) 1, 13
Walter, Professor Helmuth 225, 266, 276, 288n.63, 325, 361n.6, 462
Wangoni 92n.8
Wanhsien incident (1926) 8
Wanklyn, VC, Lt.Cdr. David 133n.106, 165, 484
'war on trade' 50, 53, 67, 90, 100, 112, 276, 326, 371, 462–3, 468, 478, 482; see also guerre de course
Warburton-Lee, VC, Captain Bernard 72–4, 94n.27
warlordism 8
Warmington, Lt.Com.Sir Marshall 110, 483
Warsaw 30, 358
Warspite 75, 93n.26, 100, 105, 115, 292, 294, 343, 360, 365n.52, 406
Washington 28, 174n.88, 217n.70, 231, 233, 249–50, 381, 386, 424
Washington, DC 4, 10, 87, 117, 125, 140–1, 145, 159, 171n.53, 200, 235, 269, 271, 302, 357, 363n.34, 367n.91, 400, 425, 430, 449
Washington Conference (1921–22) 3–5, 8, 10, 28, 36n.10, 214n.27, 461
Washington Convoy Conference (1943) 265
Washington treaty system 10–11, 13, 18–19, 21, 37n.20
Wasp 28, 46n.110, 207, 210, 219n.92, 221n.115, 351, 381, 427, 502n.32
Waterhen 131n.77

Watson-Watt, Sir Robert 175n.98
Wavell, Field Marshal Archibald 108, 115, 146, 148–9
weather observation ships 116, 130n.73, 467, 503n.39
Wehrmacht (German Army) 22, 78, 263, 310, 410n.2, 431
Wei-hai-wei (Weihai) 459n.95
Wellington (British medium bomber) 123, 265, 464, 501n.17
Welshman 235
Werwolf (wolf pack) 326
Weser Estuary 436
West (wolf pack) 132n.91
West Africa 23, 62n.13, 88, 97n.77, 223, 226–7, 239, 255n.54, 309
West Virginia 136, 414n.50, 440
Western Approaches 33, 164, 240, 265, 276, 326
Western Force 148–9, 152
Westmark (wolf pack) 264
WESTOMP (western ocean meeting point) 166, 171n.55
'Westwall' (wolfpack) 53, 63n.23, 237
Wewak 336, 445, 459n.98
Weyler, Rear-Admiral George 389
White Plains 396–7, 414n.54
White Sea 121, 131n.85, 200, 211, 242
Whitworth, Admiral Sir Jock 70–1, 75, 80
Wichers, Kaptein-luitenant Jan 361n.6
Wichita 40n.45, 41n.48, 131n.70, 253n.35, 381, 398, 400
Wildcat (US fighter planes) 180, 188, 191, 216n.39
Wilhelm Gustloff 432
Wilhelm Heidkamp 73
Wilhelmshaven 34, 48n.135, 55, 74–5, 104, 157, 284n.13, 285n.24, 406, 433, 436, 438
Wilk 49, 62n.2
Wilkinson, Rear-Admiral Theodore 290n.84, 329, 419
Williams, Sub-Lt. G.P.C. 127n.25
Williams, Captain Herbert 437
Willis, Admiral Sir Algernon 85, 161–2, 292
Willmott, H.P. 136, 153, 160–1, 168n.6, 171ns.48–9, 456n.63
Wilson, General Henry 300–1
Wilson, President Woodrow 6
Windau (Ventspils) 434, 437
Winston Salem 200
Winter War 56, 203
Winton, John 104, 466, 509n.116

Wireless 246, 464; controlled bombs 293–94; interception units (Y), 170n.40; WT (Wireless Telegraphy) 34, 63n.15, 298
Witte de With 151, 171n.49
Woleai 330, 459n.98
wolf packs 52, 67, 132n.91, 175n.98, 251n.3, 254n.48, 255ns.50, 54, 264–5, 270, 302, 320n.34; *see also under U-boat group names*
Wolfgang Zenker 73–5, 94n.31
Wollin (Wolin) 432
Wolverine 109, 228
Wonsan 450
Woodford 25
Woodlark Island 289n.77
World War I 1–2, 5, 7, 20, 27, 35n.4, 88, 250, 463, 466, 498
Wotje 327, 338, 459n.98
Wright, Rear-Admiral Carleton (Bosco) 250
Wukovits, John 414n.55
Würzburg (German radar) 364n.47
Würzburg radar facility (Bruneval) 173n.69

X-5 299
X-6 299
X-7 299–300
X-20 342
X-23 342
X-craft (RN) 299–300, 342, 484
XE 1 448
XE 3 448
xenophobia 8, 15

Yagodnik 407
Yahagi 349, 364n.42, 383, 441
Yalta 241, 425
Yamaguchi, Rear-Admiral Tamon 190
Yamagumo 390
Yamamoto, Admiral Isoroku 18, 43n.77, 165, 176–7, 182–7, 190, 194–6, 204, 207–9, 214n.27, 244, 251, 271, 287n.48, 304, 394, 410, 453, 469, 473, 479–80, 486, 489, 505n.57
Yamashiro 218n.89, 379, 390
Yamashita, General Tomoyuki 140, 150, 185, 403, 405, 422, 452
Yamato 19, 29, 46n.111, 185, 218n.89, 317, 346, 364n.42, 366n.75, 377, 379–80, 383–4, 394–6, 402, 427, 441, 456n.60, 469, 488
Yangtze river 8, 27, 447

Yap 330, 358, 372–3, 411n.7, 459n.98
Yellow Sea 447
Yoder, Don 424
Yokohama 165, 426, 446, 452
Yokosuka 452
Yokota, Captain Minoru 210
York 41n.49, 71
Yorktown (CV5) 18, 177–82, 185, 188, 191–5, 214n.14, 215ns.31–2, 427, 454n.25, 488, 502n.32
Yorktown (CV10) 454n.25
Yorktown class 28, 46n.110, 320n.43
Yūbari 41n.51, 218n.89, 220n.101, 290n.79
Yugoslavia 103.107, 113, 128n.36, 470
Yūgumo 318n.16
Yumashev, Vice-Admiral T.S. 131n.85
Yūnagi 220n.101
Yuru 152, 232
Yūzuki 403

Z29 244
Z30 244
Z31 244
Zagreb 128n.36
Zambales 421
Zamboanga 338, 425
Zara, Admiral Alberto da 293
Zara 106, 487
Zara class 105–6, 354
Zaunkönig (German T-5 acoustic torpedo) 286n.44, 302, 320n.32, 325, 429, 499n.9
'Zeke' (Japanese fighter aircraft) 18, 214n.13, 397
'Zero' (Japanese carrier fighter) 18, 188–94, 348, 367n.78
Ziel Plan (target plan) 30–1
Zuihō 185, 218n.89, 233, 304, 351, 364n.42, 380, 398, 504n.44
Zuikaku 19, 177–82, 209, 214n.13, 218n.89, 304, 349, 351–2, 364n.42, 379, 398, 475, 504n.44
Zulu 229